P9-CDG-147

Human Development

THIRD EDITION

Human Development

THIRD EDITION

James W. Vander Zanden

Ohio State University

Alfred A. Knopf
New York

Dedication
For Brad and Nels

This is a Borzoi Book Published by Alfred A. Knopf, Inc.

Third Edition

9876543

Library of Congress Cataloging in Publication Data

Vander Zanden, James Wilfrid.
Human development.

Bibliography: p.
Includes index.
1. Developmental psychology. I. Title.
BF713.V36 1985 155 84-21308
ISBN 0-394-33621-6

Manufactured in the United States of America

Cover photo: Ed Lettau/Photo Researchers.

Chapter opening photos: *Ch. 1*: Richard Frieman/Photo Researchers; *Ch. 2*: Randolf Falk/Jeroboam; *Ch. 3*: Lennart Nilsson, from *Behold Man*, Little Brown, 1974; *Ch. 4*: Joel Gordon; *Ch. 5*: Suzanne Arms/Jeroboam; *Ch. 6*: Evan Johnson/Jeroboam; *Ch. 7*: Richard Frieman/Photo Researchers; *Ch. 8*: Richard Frieman/Photo Researchers; *Ch. 9*: Sharon L. Fox/The Picture Cube; *Ch. 10*: Andanson/Sygma; *Ch. 11*: Randolph Falk/Jeroboam; *Ch. 12*: Peter Simon/Stock, Boston; *Ch. 13*: Jean-Claude Lejeune; *Ch. 14*: Bob Kalman/The Image Works; *Ch. 15*: Chris Brown/Stock, Boston; *Ch. 16*: Jean-Claude Lejeune/Stock, Boston; *Ch. 17*: Elizabeth Crews; *Ch. 18*: Ray Ellis/Photo Researchers; *Ch. 19*: Frank Siteman/Stock, Boston; *Ch. 20*: Candace Freeland/Picture Group; *Ch. 21*: Alan Carey/The Image Works

Preface

In their prefaces to textbooks, many authors tell us how onerous they found the writing experience. Moreover, they often thank their families for enduring considerable neglect during the process. Such themes fit well with our society's work ethic and the notion that one must somehow sacrifice in order to achieve success. However, I cannot say that either I or my family suffered by virtue of my doing this book. Indeed, quite the contrary, I enjoyed the work immensely and my family benefited from the insights we all gained over the years from the project. I count myself fortunate that society has allowed me to earn a livelihood doing those things—teaching and writing—that I derive considerable pleasure and satisfaction from doing. Moreover, while other parents had to be miles away working at an office or in a factory, I was at home working in a comfortable family environment. Being a parent and writing a book on human development somehow merged, producing a most rewarding life-style.

As I noted in the preface to the first edition, there was also an important personal reason for my undertaking the writing of *Human Development.* Ten years earlier my wife had become ill and subsequently died. Our youngest son was then an infant, and his older brother was a toddler. So except for teaching part-time at Ohio State University, I "dropped out" of academic life for about five years and functioned more or less as a full-time parent. In view of these facts, it was no accident that I wrote this particular book. As a single parent, I have been directly concerned with many matters discussed in the text. And, as a man now in his early fifties, I've been dealing with the issues involved in the mid-life transition.

Thus seeing this textbook through its various editions has been a highly personal experience; it has involved my own search for answers. Indeed, I owe a personal debt to the field of human development. I have found it of profound help in my own life and in rearing my sons. Perhaps students who read this textbook may likewise find answers to questions they have about their own lives. It is my earnest desire that, through courses in human development and developmental psychology, people may move toward Abraham Maslow's ideal and become self-actualized men and women.

ORGANIZATION

The text takes a life-span approach to human development, an orientation that finds expression in its organization. Part One (Chapters 1–3) provides an overview and sets the stage for the later chapters. Chapter 1 outlines the developmental perspective, examines basic concepts, and discusses research methods. Chapter 2 considers five major developmental theories: psychoanalytic, behavioral, humanistic, cognitive, and ethological. Chapter 3 explores the biological foundations of development, treating reproduction, genetics, and the dynamic interplay between heredity and environment.

The remainder of the book is organized by age periods. Part Two (Chapters 4–5) focuses on the prenatal and neonatal periods. Chapter 4 examines the prenatal development and the birth process. A full chapter, Chapter 5, is devoted to the newborn. Part Three (Chapters 6–8) is allocated to infancy: Chapter 6 to the development of basic competencies; Chapter 7 to cognitive and language development; and Chapter 8 to psychosocial development.

Parts Four through Nine continue chronologically, covering early childhood, later childhood, adolescence, early adulthood, middle adulthood, and later adulthood, respectively. In the case of each age period, the first chapter of the part typically considers physical and cognitive development, and the second chapter of the part examines psychosocial development. Finally, Chapter 21 considers the dying process and death.

MULTIDISCIPLINARY APPROACH

As with earlier editions of *Human Development*, my approach in this third edition is multidisciplinary. I include contributions from biology, psychology, sociology, and anthropology. In taking this path, I have asked myself not, "Is this paper from this or that discipline?" but, "Does this paper provide authoritative and insightful data?" In other words, I went to those sources, regardless of discipline, that I thought contained the best information on a given topic. Additionally, I rigorously combed the literature and pursued leads that would allow me to craft a text with the latest state-of-the-art information on human development. The solid research foundations of the book are reflected in the lengthy bibliography found at the back of the text.

ISSUES AND APPLICATIONS

A course in human development does more than provide students with a body of scientific findings. It can benefit them by supplying information and skills that are directly applicable to their daily lives. Accordingly, the textual material and boxed inserts are designed to assist students in the constructive analysis of their circumstances and in the cultivation of attack strategies for problem solving. Issues examined in the boxed inserts include: genetic engineering (Chapter 3), childbirth at home (Chapter 4), malnutrition (Chapter 6), child abuse and neglect (Chapter 8), IQ and race (Chapter 9), the psychology of sex differences (Chapter 9), television and violence (Chapter 10), incest (Chapter 10), amphetamine treatment of hyperactive children (Chapter 12), flying back to the family nest (Chapter 15), theories of homosexuality (Chapter 16), battered women (Chapter 18), and autopsies (Chapter 21).

A large number of boxes also have direct applications, including the following: tips for observing children (Chapter 1), the treatment of infertility (Chapter 3), genetic counseling and testing (Chapter 3), soothing the neonate (Chapter 5), helping children with their fears (Chapter 9), selecting a nursery school (Chapter 10), "Big Guy's school" (Chapter 12), obesity (Chapter 13), anorexia nervosa and bulimia (Chapter 13), helping adolescents build positive self-concepts (Chapter 13), warning signals of suicide intention among adolescents (Chapter 14), postpartum blues (Chapter 16), job burnout (Chapter 18), strategies for managing old age (Chapter 19), caring for family members with Alzheimer's disease (Chapter 19), retirement (Chapter 20), home care for the elderly (Chapter 20), and selecting a nursing home (Chapter 20).

In sum, although courses in human development cannot offer students magical recipes or formulas for living, they can provide them with an informational base and an orientation to problem solving that can prove immeasurably helpful.

NEW TO THE THIRD EDITION

I have made a number of changes in this third edition of *Human Development*. Indeed, over one-third of the material in this edition is new. The first five chapters in the second edition have been condensed to three chapters. This change freed space that then could be allocated to the adult years. Over the past decade, much new, imaginative, and exciting research has been conducted on adulthood. As a result, enough *solid* material now exists to expand the treatment of adulthood to seven chapters, one-third of the entire textbook. Further, this material is now arranged in three broad divisions: early adulthood, middle adulthood, and later adulthood.

This edition has also allowed me to treat in more detail the somewhat different experiences of men and women as they cross the adult years. Too often textbooks blur the distinctions as if there is only one adult experience. However, *Human Development* examines the varying experiences of men and women with regard to differences in health problems, divorce, single parenting, phases in adult development, career patterns, and responses to aging.

Another new feature of this edition is its completely revised design. The larger, more open format contains over 200 new photographs and figures, many in four-color, to enhance the book's visual and pedagogical appeal for students.

In preparing this new edition, my editors pointed out to me that many developmental textbooks no longer pay special attention to the newborn or accord the subject a chapter of its own. Fortunately, they agreed not to follow this procedure. Newborns are something special—both scientifically and humanly. Finally, I have also provided more applications throughout and dealt with a larger number of contemporary issues.

PEDAGOGICAL AIDS

In choosing which pedagogical aids to include, I decided to use those that provide the most guidance to the student with the least clutter. Thus each chapter opens with an outline of its major headings, which allows students to review the material to be covered at a glance. Chapters conclude with a numbered summary, which recapitulates the central points and allows students to review what they have read in a systematic manner, and with a list of key terms and their definitions, which provides students with a convenient vehicle to look up and review key concepts. New terminology has been treated in a somewhat unusual manner. So as not to intimidate students with an almost dictionarylike list of words to be memorized, all new terms have been separated into two categories. The terms most essential to an understanding of human development are set in **boldface** type and are defined as they are presented in the text and also in the list of key terms at the end of each chapter. Other, less critical terms, which students should be exposed to and may want to learn to expand their vocabularies, are *italicized* and defined in the text. The boldfaced terms are also listed separately in the Key Term Index at the end of the book.

ACKNOWLEDGMENTS

One never writes a textbook by oneself. There are those countless individuals who over the generations have contributed to the knowledge we now have concerning human development. Moreover, there are those instructors who prepared critical reviews of the manuscript at various stages. They appraised the clarity of expression, technical accuracy, and completeness of coverage. Their comments proved invaluable to me, and needless to say, I am most grateful to them for their assistance. They include:

- Jerry Aldridge, Samford University
- Norma Bernstein-Tarrow, California State University at Long Beach
- James Blackburn, University of Wisconsin–Milwaukee
- Sandra E. Candy-Gibbs, University of Kentucky
- Beverly Eubank, Lansing Community College
- Richard Fabes, Arizona State University
- Barbara Follosco, Los Angeles Valley College
- Pauline Gillette, North Virginia Community College
- Lois Lane, Western Kentucky University
- Doug Muller, New Mexico State University
- Martin Murphy, University of Akron
- Gary Ritchy, University of New Mexico

- Bea Stern, Los Angeles Valley College
- Robert Stowe, Central Connecticut State University
- Paul Susen, Mt. Wachusett Community College
- Sheldon Weinstock, Community College of Baltimore
- Charles West, University of Illinois at Champaign-Urbana

I have also had the opportunity to work with a number of very fine, able, and wonderful people at Random House/Alfred A. Knopf in preparing this and the previous editions of *Human Development.* Indeed, I have developed very warm feelings for them and greatly appreciate their help. I was delighted when Laurel Miller was assigned to the book as project editor. Sandra Scarr and I had found her an unusually competent and resourceful person in preparing the Fourth Edition of *Understanding Psychology,* traits she evidenced in abundance once again. Additionally, a number of splendid people, including Kathy Bendo (photo manager), Mira Schachne (photo editor), and Nancy Sugihara (text designer), joined with Laurel in fashioning the beautiful new design of this edition. Rochelle Diogenes (developmental editor) coordinated reviews and was responsible for the supplementary materials, tasks that consume much time and vision and make for a sound and rounded package. Elizabeth Thompson (editorial assistant) periodically came to my rescue when I needed someone skilled in working out details. Stacey Alexander (production supervisor) carefully oversaw the production process. And, finally, my thanks go to Mary Falcon (sponsoring editor), who in the course of this and a number of other books has become a good and valued friend. Once more she has proven herself a diligent partner in these endeavors, affording sound advice, zeal, and boundless energy. This text, then, is the collective product of the efforts of a great many people.

James W. Vander Zanden
Columbus, Ohio

Contents

Part One

The Study of Human Development

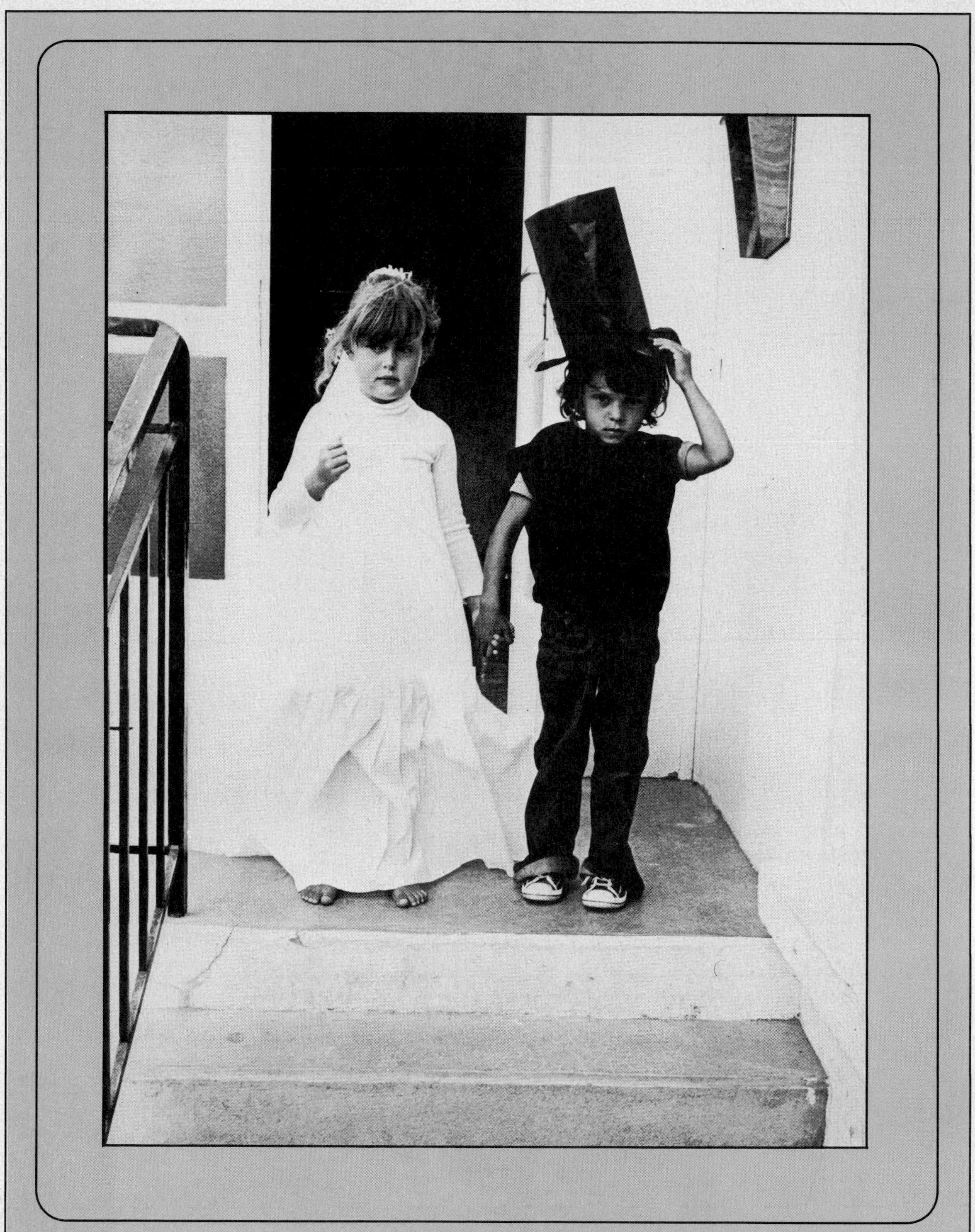

1

Introduction

A sign posted in a Western cowboy bar says: "I ain't what I ought to be, I ain't what I'm going to be, but I ain't what I was." This thought captures the sentiment that lies behind much contemporary interest in the study of human development. It is hoped that with knowledge, we will be able to lead fuller, richer, and more fruitful lives. Knowledge offers us the opportunity to improve the human condition by helping us to achieve self-identity, freedom, and self-fulfillment.

The motto in the bar directs our attention to still another fact—that to live is to *change*. Indeed, life is never static but always in flux. In nature there are not any fixed entities, only transition and transformation. According to modern physics, the objects you normally see and feel consist of nothing more than patterns of energy that are forever moving and altering (Foote, 1978; Sears, Zemansky, and Young, 1982). From electrons to galaxies, from amoebas to humans, from families to societies, every phenomenon exists in a state of continual "becoming." Hence, when you were conceived, you were smaller than the period at the end of this sentence. Over the span of sixty, seventy, eighty, or even ninety years all of us undergo dramatic changes as we pass from the embryonic and fetal stages through infancy, childhood, adolescence, adulthood, and old age. We start small, grow up, and grow old, just as countless generations

Continuity

Human development is a process of continual change across the entire life span. It finds expression in physical, intellectual, personality, and social development. Yet even so, we remain in some respects the same, providing life with a measure of continuity.

Alan Carey/The Image Works

of our forebears have done. Change occurs across many dimensions—the biological, the psychological, and the social. Life-span perspectives of human development focus upon long-term sequences and patterns of change in human behavior (Labouvie, 1982).

Contradictory as it may appear, life also entails *continuity.* At age seventy, we are in many ways the same persons that we were at five or twenty-five. Many aspects of our biological organism, our gender roles, and our thought processes carry across different life periods. Indeed, features of life that are relatively lasting and uninterrupted give us a sense of identity and stability over time. As a consequence of such continuities, most of us do not experience ourselves as just so many disjointed bits and pieces but rather as wholes—larger independent entities that possess a basic oneness. Accordingly, much of the change in our lives is not accidental or haphazard.

All of what we have been saying adds up to the following statement: *Human development over the life span is a process of becoming something different while remaining in some respects the same.* Perhaps what is uniquely human is that we remain in an unending state of development. Life is always an unfinished business, and death is its only cessation (Montagu, 1981).

DEVELOPMENT

Life is never a material, a substance to be molded. If you want to know, life is the principle of self-renewal, it is constantly renewing and remaking and changing and transfiguring itself.

—BORIS PASTERNAK
Doctor Zhivago

Scientists refer to the elements of change and constancy over the life span as **development.** Development is defined as the orderly and sequential changes that occur with the passage of time as an organism moves from conception to death. It includes those processes that are biologically programmed within the organism. It also includes those processes by which the organism is changed or transformed through interaction with the environment (Bronfenbrenner, 1977; Lerner and Busch-Rossnagel, 1981; Eichorn et al., 1982).

The Major Concerns of Science

The most incomprehensible thing about the world is that it is comprehensible.

—ALBERT EINSTEIN

Social and behavioral scientists who study human development focus on four major issues. First, they undertake to *describe* the changes that typically occur across the human life span. When, for instance, does the child generally begin to speak? What is the nature of this speech? Does speech alter with time? In what sequence does the average child link sounds together to form words or sentences?

Second, scientists seek to *explain* these changes—to specify the determinants of developmental change. What behaviors, for instance, underlie the child's first use of words? What part does biological "pretuning" or "prewiring" play in the process? What is the role of learning in language acquisition? Can the process be accelerated? What factors produce language and learning difficulties?

Third, scientists are interested in the *prediction* of developmental changes. Phenylketonuria (or PKU) is a case in point (Scriver and Clow, 1980*a*, 1980*b*). In this inherited disorder, which occurs in about 1 out of every 12,000 live births, the child lacks an enzyme needed to metabolize phenylalanine (an amino acid found in protein foods). The result is the buildup of substances that are toxic to the central nervous system. PKU commonly produces mental retardation. In severe cases, children are impaired in the development of language and may never learn to speak at all. Chemical tests now routinely administered in most states can detect the presence of phenylpyruvic acid in the urine of infants with PKU. Thus, scientists today can predict the likely course of these babies' development.

Fourth, by gaining knowledge, scientists can often intervene in the course of events so as to *control* them. For example, in one form of PKU it has been found that if infants are put on a low-phenylalanine diet after birth, intellectual impairment can often be minimized or prevented. During the past decade, PKU specialists recommended that PKU children stay on their special diets until they were five or six years of age. But recently PKU clinics in the United States and Europe have reported cases of preteen children who discontinued the diet and are showing pronounced drops in intelligence. As a result, some specialists are urging that PKU children stay on their diets until the matter is clarified. Simultaneously, a number of other scientists have been experimenting with enzyme reactors, which, when administered to PKU children, will remove blood phenylalanine from their systems (Ambrus et al., 1978). In other areas as well, scientists are increasingly looking for ways in which knowledge about human development can assist with real life problems and real life institutions.

But even as scientists strive for knowledge and control, they must continually remind themselves of the dangers described by the eminent physicist J. Robert Oppenheimer (1955): "The acquisition of knowledge opens up the terrifying prospects of controlling what people do and how they feel." Chapter 1 returns to this matter later, in connection with ethical standards in scientific research.

Life-Span Development: A Multidisciplinary Field

Life-span development has traditionally been the primary province of psychologists. Most commonly the field is called *developmental psychology* or, if focused primarily on children, *child development* or *child psychology.* Psychology itself is often defined as the scientific study of behavior and mental processes. Thus, developmental psychology is that branch of psychology that deals with how individuals change with time while remaining in some respects the same. Child psychology is that branch of psychology that studies the development of children.

Yet over the past two decades the field of life-span development has become multidisciplinary. It now encompasses not only psychology but biology, sociology, and anthropology. Indeed, we should avoid the tendency to view the various academic disciplines as somehow separated into "watertight" compartments. At best, academic disciplines are only loosely defined. The borderlines are so vague that researchers give little thought to whether or not they are "invading" another discipline's field of study. Such overlap encourages a freshness of approach and functions as a stimulus in advancing the frontiers of knowledge. Researchers increasingly welcome aid and collaboration from any qualified person, whether that person is in the same discipline or not.

In the chapters that follow, we will draw from numerous disciplines as we examine the various aspects of human development. We will consider **physical development**—those changes that take place in a person's body, including changes in weight and height; in the brain, heart, and other organ structures and processes; and in skeletal, muscular, and neurological features that affect motor skills. We will focus on **cognitive development**—those changes that occur in mental activity, including sensation, perception, memory, thought, reasoning, and language. And we will delve into **psychosocial development**—those changes that concern an individual's personality, emotions, and relationships with others. Yet while examining these specific aspects of development, we will not want to lose sight of the unitary nature of the individual human. Indeed, scientists are increasingly aware that what happens on any one level of analysis depends largely on what happens on all others (Lerner and Spanier, 1978*a*, 1978*b*).

The Components of Development

Development meets us at every turn. Infants are born. The jacket that fitted two-year-old Mike in the spring is outgrown by winter. At puberty, youth exhibit a marked spurt in size and acquire various secondary sexual characteristics. Individuals commonly leave their parents' homes and set out on careers, establish families of their own, see their own children leave home, retire, and so on. The concepts of *growth, maturation,* and *learning* are important to our understanding of these processes.

One of the most noticeable features of early development is the *increase in size* that occurs with changing age, which is commonly termed **growth.** Growth takes place through metabolic processes (Tanner and Taylor, 1971: 9):

> The inanimate object [for instance, such crystals as icicles, stalactites, and stalagmites] grows from the outside, by simple accretion. It merely adds onto its surface more and more of the material of which it is composed. The living organism, on the other hand, grows by metabolism, from within. It takes in all kinds of substances, breaks them down into their chemical components to provide energy and then reassembles them into new materials. Living things, no matter what their specific natures, have to work to grow.

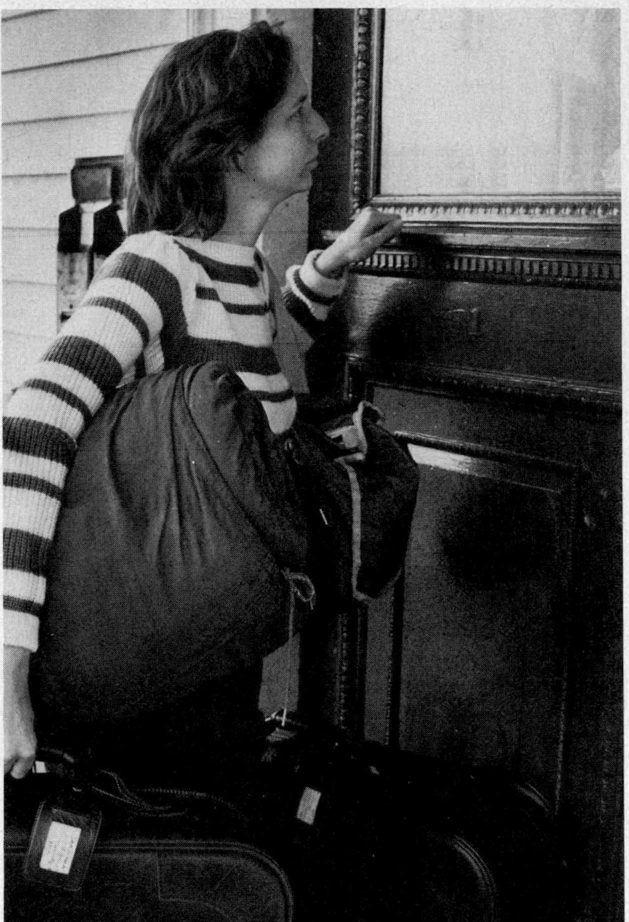

Development Is Unending
To live is to change. Within American life, youth customarily leave their parental homes and set out on careers with college often a way station for many of them.
David Schaefer/The Picture Cube

Most organisms get larger as they become older. For some, including human beings, growth levels off as they approach sexual maturity. Others—many plant and fish forms—continue the growth process until they die.

Maturation is another aspect of development. It concerns the more or less automatic unfolding of biological potential in a set, irreversible sequence. Both growth and maturation entail biological change. But whereas growth refers to the increase in an individual's cells and tissue, maturation concerns the development of his or her organs and limbs to the point where they become functional. In other words, maturation reflects the unfolding of genetically prescribed, or "preprogrammed," patterns of behavior. Such changes are relatively independent of environmental events, so long as environmental conditions remain normal. As we will see in Chapter 6, an infant's motor development after birth—grasping, sitting, crawling, standing, and walking—follows a regular sequence. Similarly, at about ten to fourteen years of age puberty brings many changes, including ovulation in women and the production of live sperm in men, providing the potential for reproduction.

Learning is still another component of development. It is the more or less permanent modification in behavior that results from the individual's experience in the environment. Learning occurs across the entire life span—in the family, among peers, at school, on the job, and in many other spheres as well. It differs from maturation in that maturation typically occurs without any specific experience or practice. Learning, however, depends on both growth and maturation, which underlie an organism's *readiness* for certain kinds of activity, physical and mental. It is clearly a critical capability, for it allows an organism to adapt to changing environmental conditions. Hence, it provides the important element of flexibility in behavior.

As we will emphasize in Chapter 3, it is important that the biological forces of growth and maturation not be counterposed to the environmental forces of learning. Too often the *nature–nurture controversy* is presented as a dichotomy—nature *or* nurture. Clearly, such a view is unacceptable. Carried to its logical conclusion, this dichotomy would define biologically inborn behavior as that which appears in the absence of environment and learned behavior as that which does not require an organism.

Rather, it is the *interaction* between heredity and environment that gives an organism its unique characteristics. We find that as we interact with the world about—as we act upon, transform, and modify it—we in turn are shaped and altered by the consequences of our own actions. *We literally change ourselves through acting*. For instance, as we pass through life our biological organism is altered by dietary practices, alcoholic and drug intake, smoking habits, illness, exposure to x-rays and radiation, and so on. Further, as many of us enter school, finish school, seek a job, marry, settle on a career, have children, become grandparents, and retire, we arrive at new self-conceptions and identities. In these and many other ways we are engaged in a lifetime process in which we are forged and shaped as we interact with our environment. In brief, development occurs at all periods—the embryonic, infancy, childhood, adolescence, adulthood, and old age (see the boxed insert in the right column).

SHAKESPEARE'S SEVEN STAGES OF LIFE

The infant mewling and puking . . .
the whining schoolboy . . .
the lover, sighing like a furnace . . .
a soldier, full of strange oaths . . .
the justice, in fair round belly . . .
the sixth age shifts . . .
with spectacles on nose . . .
his shrunk shank . . .
voice turning again toward childish treble . . .
second childishness . . .
sans teeth, sans eyes, sans taste, sans everything.

—WILLIAM SHAKESPEARE
As You Like It, Act 2, Scene 7

Continuity and Discontinuity in Development

Psychologists generally agree that development entails orderly sequences of change that depend on growth and maturation as individuals interact with their environment. But in examining developmental sequences, some psychologists focus on their *continuity* while others emphasize their *discontinuity*. The former view development as producing smooth, gradual, and incremental change. The latter depict development as a series of steps with clear-cut, even abrupt, changes occurring from one phase to the next.

The two different models of development can be clarified by considering two analogies. The continuous model of development is analogous to the growth of a leaf. After a leaf sprouts from a seed, it grows by simply becoming larger. The change is gradual and uninterrupted. Psychologists who emphasize the part that learning plays in behavior tend to take this point of view. They see the learning process as lacking sharp developmental states between infancy and adulthood. Learning is cumulative, building on itself.

The discontinuous model of development is analogous to the developmental changes that occur in a butterfly. Once a caterpillar hatches from an egg, it feeds on vegetation. After a time it fastens itself to a twig and spins a cocoon within which the pupa develops. One day the pupal covering splits open and the butterfly emerges. Psychologists who adopt the discontinuous model see human development as similar to the process of insect metamorphosis. Each individual is seen as passing through a set sequence of stages in which change constitutes a difference of kind rather than merely of degree. Each stage is characterized by a distinct and unique state in ego formation, identity, or thought. The theories of Sigmund Freud, Erik Erikson, and Jean Piaget that we will examine in the next chapter are of this sort.

Continuity and Discontinuity
Both continuity and discontinuity characterize the human experience. This fact finds striking expression in the similarities and dissimilarities we note among different generations of a family reunion.
Barbara Alper/Stock, Boston

How we view development depends in part on our vantage point. To return to our analogies, when we first observe a caterpillar and then a butterfly we are struck by the dramatic qualitative change. But when we observe the developmental changes that occur within the cocoon, we have a different impression. We see that butterflylike characteristics are gradually acquired, and consequently, we are more likely to describe the process as continuous (Lewis and Starr, 1979). On the other hand, if we look at a seed and then a tree, we are impressed by the magnitude of the change that has occurred.

Increasingly, psychologists are less inclined to divide themselves into sharply opposed camps on the issue of continuity and discontinuity in development. (The same holds true for the debate concerning stability of behavior, discussed in the boxed insert on pages 10–11.) They too recognize that much depends on one's vantage point and hence see both continuities and discontinuities across the life span. Many psychologists have combined the search for a common sequential order from conception to death with a concern for differences in the way that individuals negotiate and experience the various stages (Davison et al., 1980; Runyan, 1980). The approach to adult development taken by Daniel J. Levinson and his associates at Yale University reflects this latter orientation (see Chapters 15–20).

DISSECTING THE LIFE SPAN: CULTURAL AND HISTORICAL PERSPECTIVES

In one way or another, all societies must deal with the life cycle. Nature inescapably confronts us with a biological cycle. The cycle begins with conception and continues through old age and ultimately death. Upon this organic age grid, societies weave varying social arrangements. Childhood may be foreshortened or prolonged. Adolescence may be glossed over or magnified by elaborate puberty rituals. And adulthood and old age may be defined in widely differing terms and with contrasting values. Hence all societies divide biological time into socially relevant units: "Lifetime becomes translated into social time, and chronological age into social age" (Neugarten and Hagestad, 1976: 35). Although birth, puberty, and death are biological facts of life, it is society that gives each its distinctive meaning and assigns its social consequences.

Society and the Individual

All societies employ age as a central reference point for distinguishing among their members. (Figure 1.1 portrays the age distribution of the American population.) Furthermore, all use age for **ascription**. People are assigned roles independently of their unique abilities or qualities. Like sex, age is a master status. Age governs entry to many other statuses and makes its own distinct imprint on them. Within the United States, for instance, age operates *directly* as a criterion for driving a car (age sixteen in some states and seventeen in others), voting (age eighteen), becoming president (age thirty-five), and receiving Social Se-

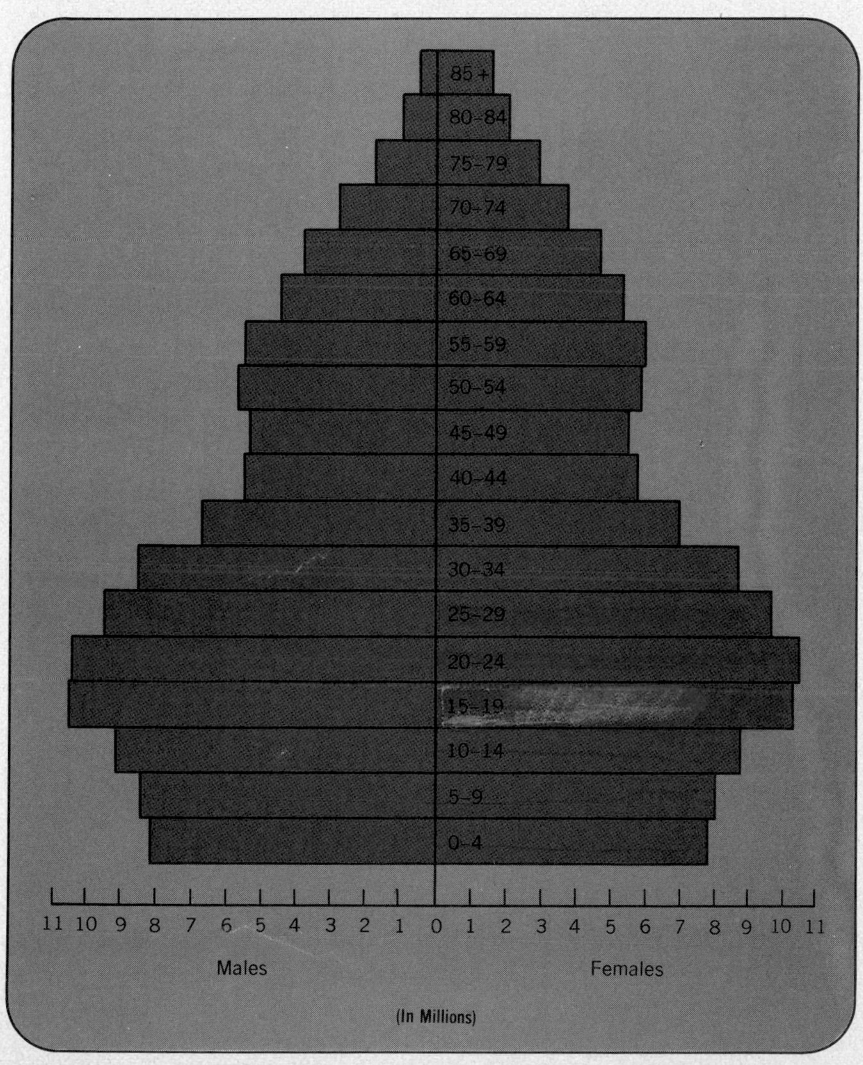

Figure 1.1 U.S. Population by Age, 1980 Census

The figure represents a population pyramid, often referred to as the "tree of ages." Age groupings are placed in order on a vertical scale, with the youngest age group located at the bottom and the oldest age group at the top of the diagram. On the horizontal axis are plotted the number of people in each age group, with the sum corresponding to the male segment placed to the left of the central dividing line and that representing the female segment placed to the right of it. The pyramid itself represents the entire group.

SOURCE: Census Bureau.

STABILITY OF BEHAVIOR

The childhood shows the man as morning shows the day.

—JOHN MILTON
Paradise Regained

Closely related to the continuity–discontinuity debate is the controversy surrounding the stability of behavior (Brim and Kagan, 1980). Are individual differences stable over time? How valid is the old maxim "As the twig is bent the tree's inclined"? Does later experience substantially alter an individual's personality, or is one's individuality stubbornly resistant to modification?

We will be returning to these questions again and again in the chapters that follow. Therefore, it would be well to keep in mind the observations of Jean Macfarlane, who for many years was a researcher at the Institute of Human Development at the University of California, Berkeley. In the late 1920s and the early 1930s the institute had undertaken a series of studies with infants and young children. For more than thirty years the institute's researchers followed up the youngsters as they matured and made their way into adulthood. On the basis of her experiences with the project, Macfarlane (1964) has observed that simply because individuals have certain personality characteristics in childhood is no guarantee that they will have those same characteristics in adulthood. She reports that almost 50 percent of the Berkeley sample became more stable and effective adults than had been predicted, 20 percent of the sample became less so, and slightly less than one-third matured as predicted.

Macfarlane (1964: 121–122) writes that she was continually surprised to see how the children turned out:

> Many of the most oustandingly mature adults in our entire group, many who are well integrated, highly competent, and/or creative, who are clear about their values, who are understanding and accepting of self and others, are recruited from those who were confronted with very difficult situations and whose characteristic responses during childhood and adolescence seemed to us to compound their problems. . . . Our theoretical expectations were also rudely jarred by the adult status of a number of our subjects who early had had easy and confidence-inducing lives. As children and adolescents, they were free of severe strains, showed high abilities and/or talents, excelled at academic work and were the adulated images of success. Included among these were boy athlete leaders and good-looking, socially skillful girls. One sees among them at age 30 a high proportion of brittle, discontented, and puzzled adults whose high potentialities have not been actualized.

Macfarlane (1963) asked herself why so many of the psychologists' predictions had been wrong. One factor seems to have been that the Berkeley researchers overweighted the troublesome and unhealthy aspects and underweighted elements that induced maturity. For instance, two of the children spent much of their time in defiance of regulations. Although they had high IQs, both received only marginal or failing grades. They spent a good deal of their school life "in the principal's office," and each was finally expelled from school. Yet both turned out to be wise, steady, understanding parents and productive members of the community. Another marginal grade-getter who was a social isolate and a self-centered, unhappy boy became manager of a large construction firm. He indicated that his major job satisfaction was "feeding graded doses of increased responsibility and difficulty in assigned jobs to the work staff and watching them grow in confidence as their competencies increase." Another—a large, awkward, shy, periodically depressed girl with mediocre grades—went on to secure an advanced degree, to teach in

curity retirement benefits (age sixty-two). Age also operates *indirectly* as a criterion for certain roles through its linkage with other factors. For example, age linked with reproductive capacity limits entry into the parental role; age linked with twelve years of elementary and secondary school usually limits entry into college (Riley, Johnson, and Foner, 1972; Hogan, 1981).

Because age is a master status, most changes in role over a person's life span are accompanied by a change in chronological age—entering school, completing school, getting one's first job, marrying, having children, being promoted at work, seeing one's youngest child married, becoming a grandparent, retiring, and so on. Age is a critical dimension by which individuals locate themselves within society and in turn are lo-

Youthful Mischief

The psychologist Jean Macfarlane suggests that many youth go through a troubled period yet become capable parents and productive members of the community. Even experiences that initially seem destructive may induce maturity in that they compel young people to come to terms with themselves and accept responsibility for their behavior.

Adolahe/Southern Light

college, to marry and raise children, and to live a zestful, happy life.

Macfarlane says that no one becomes mature without living through the difficulties associated with maturing experiences. Even experiences that earlier seemed highly traumatic and destructive often turned out to be maturity-inducing. These experiences compelled the individuals to come to terms with themselves. They had to decide what they wanted to do with their lives.

On the basis of his reading of various long-term studies, Jerome Kagan (1979: 21) identifies a principle that he terms "growth toward health":

> The child tries to grow toward adaptation, if the environment will permit him. The mistaken assumption made by the early investigators was that a node of pathology in infancy was like a blemish and, like Lady Macbeth's bloody hands, could not be wiped clean. The data do not support that pessimistic view. Dispositions that are maladaptive or pathological can be outgrown, while adaptive characteristics are more likely to be retained.

Yet we must evaluate Kagan's statement cautiously. For it is also true that the more severe the adverse conditions, and the longer they persist, the less likely children are to overcome them through environmental improvement.

Nor should we overlook the fact that, despite change and transformation across the life span, there is a measure of coherence to personality development as well (Rubin, 1981). For instance, Jack Block (1980, 1981*a*, 1981*b*) has carefully examined the data gathered through the years by the Berkeley researchers. He finds that on the vast majority of the ninety rating scales employed, a statistically significant correlation exists between subjects' ratings when they were in junior high school and when they were in their forties. Individuals who were self-defeating in junior high were also self-defeating adults; those who were cheerful or moody then were cheerful or moody in midlife. In sum, human life is characterized by both stability and change.

cated by others. Accordingly, age functions as a reference point that allows people to orient themselves in terms of *what* and *where* they are within various social networks—the family, the school, the church, and the world of work. Age is one ingredient that provides people with the answer to the question "Who am I?" In brief, it helps people establish their identities.

Viewed from this perspective, all societies are divided into **age grades** (also termed *age strata*)—social layers that are based on time periods in life. Age grades organize people in society in much the same way that the earth's crust is organized by stratified geological layers. Age grading has certain similarities to class stratification. Both involve the differentiation and ranking of people as superior or inferior, higher or lower. But unlike movement up or down the class ladder, the mobility of individuals through the age grades is not dependent on motivational and recruitment factors. In large measure mobility from one age grade to the next is biologically determined and accordingly irreversible (Riley, Johnson, and Foner, 1972; Kimmel, 1980).

People's behavior within various age grades is regulated by social norms or expectations that specify what constitutes appropriate and inappropriate behavior for individuals at various periods in the life span. In some cases, an informal consensus provides the standards by which people judge one another's behavior. Hence the notion that you ought to "act your age" pervades many spheres of life. Within the United States, for instance, it is thought that a child of six is "too young" to baby-sit for other youngsters. By the same token, a man of sixty is thought to be "too old" to dance the latest steps in a discotheque. In other cases, laws set floors and ceilings in various institutional spheres: for instance, there are laws regarding marriage without parental consent, entry into the labor force, and eligibility for Social Security and Medicare benefits (Neugarten, 1982*a*, 1982*b*). We need only think of such terms as "childish," "juvenile," "youth culture," "adolescence," "senior citizen," and "the generation gap" to be aware of the potency of age in determining expectations about behavior in our own society. Indeed, we even find apartment buildings exclusively for a particular age group, such as young singles, and cities designed for a particular age group, such as retired people.

Housing for Young Singles
One way in which people organize themselves is by age groups. Some housing complexes are made up of individuals of similar age groups who share compatible life styles.
Rose Skytta/Jeroboam

Historical Conceptions of the Life Span

In the United States we commonly think of the life span in terms of infancy, childhood, adolescence, adulthood, and old age. Yet the French historian Philippe Ariès (1962) says that in the Middle Ages the concept of childhood as we know it today was unheard of. Children were regarded as small adults. Child rearing meant little more than allowing children to participate in adult affairs.

The world we think proper for children—the world of fairy tales, games, toys, and books—is of comparatively recent origin. J. H. Plumb (1972) observes that our words for young males—"boy," *"garçon," "Knabe"*—were until the seventeenth century used to mean a male in an independent position: a man of thirty, forty, or fifty. No special word existed for a young male between the ages of seven and sixteen. The word "child" expressed kinship, not an age stage. The arts and documents of the medieval world portray adults and children mingling together, wearing the same clothes, and engaging in many of the same activities. Only around the year 1600 did a new concept of childhood emerge (see the boxed insert on page 13).

David Bakan (1972) argues that the notion of adolescence is even more recent, dating from the nineteenth and early twentieth centuries in America. Compulsory school legislation, child labor laws, and special legal procedures for "juveniles" made a social

CHILDHOOD: INNOCENCE LOST?

Nowadays we often hear that childhood has changed and that the change is for the worse. For instance, in a recent popular book on children, *Children Without Childhood*, Marie Winn (1983) argues that today's children lack the innocence that once was associated with childhood. Winn says that school-age youngsters are more aware, not just of sex and violence, but also of injustice, cruelty, corruption, war, and human frailty. Whereas once parents struggled to keep their children innocent—in a "carefree" golden age—they now expose them early to adult experience. Although parents may be well intentioned, Winn worries that "new-era child rearing"—in which parents enlist the child as an equal partner—is turning out to be a disaster. She insists that children do not prosper when they are treated as adults. Rather, children require an appreciable shielding from life if they are to accomplish the important tasks of learning and exploration that have traditionally been associated with childhood.

In a similar vein, Neil Postman (1982) complains that the very notion of childhood is based on secrets from which children are excluded but that society no longer withholds any secrets. Television opens all of life—sex, violence, death, illness, money, and disillusionment—to children. Such practices, he contends, deprive children of childhood, at least as it was understood in past generations.

Observers of the American scene find other sources of concern. Some express alarm that middle-class parents are pushing their children to learn at ever earlier ages. Pressure for high achievement often begins in infancy. On the basis of findings of developmental psychologists, parents are coming to recognize that babies are hardly the lumps of protoplasm that they were once held to be but brainy little creatures with an immense capacity for learning. The new danger is that parents then come to stress performance rather than feeling. At times working parents attempt to overcompensate for the hours that they are not at home by scheduling a good many high-pressure, "quality-time" activities (for instance, flashing reading and math cards, providing educational toys, and teaching gymnastic and swimming skills). The intrusion of this rat-race mentality into early childhood may not be a good thing (Langway, 1983).

Yet contemporary debates regarding parenting typically overlook the fact that in years gone by, childhood was anything but a golden age. Lloyd deMause (1974: 1), an authority on psychohistory, writes:

> The history of childhood is a nightmare from which we have only recently begun to awaken. The further back in history one goes, the lower the level of child care, and the more likely children are to be killed, abandoned, beaten, terrorized, and sexually abused.

Prior to modern times, a child's life was uniformly bleak. Until the eighteenth century a very large proportion of all children were what we would today call "battered children." In the seventeenth century the wife of John Milton, the author of *Paradise Lost*, complained that she hated to hear the cries of his nephews as he beat them. Beethoven whipped his pupils with a knitting needle and at times bit them. Even royal children were not exempt from the rod. During his childhood Louis XIII (a seventeenth-century French monarch) was regularly beaten. When he was only seventeen months old the young dauphin knew enough not to cry when his father threatened him with a whip (deMause, 1974).

Not until the nineteenth century, according to deMause, did the notion develop that children need continuous guidance and training in order to become civilized. Severe beating and other forms of abuse gave way to more indirect methods of manipulation and guilt arousal—what deMause terms the "socializing mode." More recently, he suggests, a "helping mode" has begun to gain support. This approach involves the proposition that children know what they need better than parents do. It defines the role of parents primarily as one of empathizing with children and helping them fulfill their expanding needs.

fact out of adolescence. And Kenneth Keniston (1970) suggests that our society appears now to recognize a new stage between adolescence and adulthood: youth—men and women of college and graduate school age. Recent developments—rising prosperity, the prolongation of education, and the enormously high educational demands of a postindustrial society—have lengthened the transition to adulthood.

The notion of "old age" likewise has undergone

Child Labor

Until the 1920s, children were employed as workers in many factories and mines. It was not uncommon for them to work twelve and even fourteen hours six days a week. These boys worked in a Virginia textile mill.

Library of Congress

change in the Western world. Literary evidence indicates that during the Renaissance, men were already considered "old" in their forties. Further, as Bernice L. Neugarten (1982*a*, 1982*b*) points out, it appears that another division is currently emerging, one between "young-old" and "old-old." Young-old signifies a postretirement period in which there is physical vigor, new leisure time, and new opportunities for community service and self-fulfillment. Thus the divisions that societies make in the cycle of life reflect social definitions to a great extent. And these definitions often vary from one historical period to another.

Cultural Variability

The part that social definitions play in dividing up the life cycle is highlighted when one compares the cultural practices of different societies. For instance, a fourteen-year-old girl may be expected to be a junior-high-school student in one culture, a mother of two children in another; a forty-five-year-old man might be at the peak of a business career, still moving up in a political career, or retired from a career in major league baseball—or dead and worshiped as an ancestor in some other society. Indeed, some peoples extend their age strata to include two additional age periods: the unborn and the deceased. The Australian aborigines think of the unborn as the spirits of departed ancestors. These spirits restlessly seek to enter the womb of a passing woman and be reborn as a human child (Murdock, 1934). Similarly, the Hindus regard the unborn as the spirits of persons or animals who lived in former incarnations (Davis, 1949).

Among some peoples the dead are considered continuing members of the community. The anthropologist Ralph Linton (1936: 121–122) found that when a Tanala of Madagascar died, the person was viewed as merely surrendering one set of rights and duties for another:

> Thus a Tanala clan has two sections which are equally real to its members, the living and the dead. In spite of rather half-hearted attempts by the living to explain to the dead that they are dead and to discourage their return, they remain an integral part of the clan. They must be informed of all important events, invited to all clan ceremonies, and remembered at every meal. In return they allow themselves to be consulted, take an active and helpful interest in the affairs of the community, and act as highly efficient guardians of the group's mores [rules].

Societies also show considerable variation in the behavior patterns associated with given age positions. Take old age (Simmons, 1945; Amoss and Harrell, 1981). In many rural societies, such as imperial China, the elders have enjoyed a prominent, prestigious, and authoritative position (Lang, 1946).

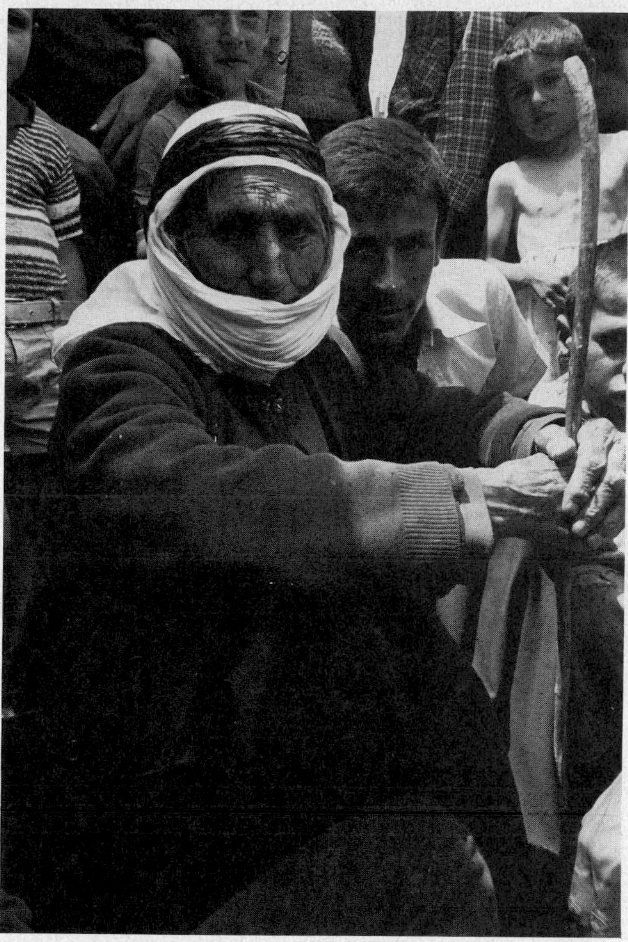

Cultural Variability
Throughout the world, different cultures provide people with somewhat different definitions as to the behavior that is and is not appropriate for the members of different age groups.
Christopher K. Walter/The Picture Cube

Among the agricultural Palaung of North Burma, long life was considered a great privilege that befell those who had lived virtuously in a previous incarnation. People showed their respect by taking great care not to step on the shadow of an older person. And young women sought to appear older than their actual age, since women acquired honor and privilege in proportion to their years (Milne, 1924).

In sharp contrast, the elderly in our society today have a more restricted functional position and considerably less prestige. Our favored age grade is youth. Americans commonly define adulthood as a period of responsibility. In contrast, the youth subculture is portrayed as irresponsible and carefree, dominated by the theme of "having a good time." In short, each culture shapes the processes of development in its own image, defining the stages it recognizes as significant.

THE NATURE OF DEVELOPMENTAL RESEARCH

To him who devotes his life to science, nothing can give more happiness than increasing the number of his discoveries, but his cup of joy is full when the results of his studies immediately find practical application.

—LOUIS PASTEUR

The study of human development is important. It can contribute in a very practical way to human needs. Take the area of mental health. By identifying the "toxic agents" deriving from both environmental and hereditary factors, we may be able to evolve procedures that counteract their harmful effects. Such procedures may be *corrective,* aimed at modifying disturbed or "problematic" behavior. They may be *preventive,* aimed at controlling or hindering the development of problem behavior. Or they may be *optimizing,* aimed at promoting choice, self-fulfillment, and human enrichment (Montada and Filipp, 1976).

Similarly, the field of education can benefit from developmental research. The current state of education, with its strongly antagonistic positions and its rapid, fadlike shifts from one procedure to another, shows a clear need for solid research data on fundamental processes. A better understanding of development could also contribute to a theory of human behavior. Let us consider a number of the more prominent research methods that scientists commonly employ for the study of human development.

The Longitudinal Method

The **longitudinal method** is a research approach in which scientists study the same individuals at different points in their lives. These individuals can thus be compared with themselves at regular intervals between birth and death, and the changes that occur over time in their behavior and characteristics can be noted. The method allows researchers to plot individual growth curves in such areas as language, motor, and cognitive development. It provides a means for discovering which childhood behaviors are marked for future use and which will be lost along the way. And it offers insight into the routes by which people turn out similarly or differently in adulthood (Macfarlane, 1971; Schaie and Hertzog, 1982).

Birth to Maturity, a classic study by Jerome Kagan and Howard A. Moss (1962), is one of the best examples of a longitudinal study. It was carried out at the Fels Research Institute in Yellow Springs, Ohio. The researchers based their work on longitudinal data concerning the personality development of seventy-one subjects. At regular intervals from birth through the mid-teens, children were interviewed, observed, and tested. They were interviewed again in young adulthood.

Probably the most dramatic and consistent finding of the study was that many characteristics of the adult personality begin to take form in early childhood. This was especially true for the period from six to ten years of age and true to a lesser degree for the period from three to six. Thus, children who tended to withdraw passively from stress usually showed reasonably similar tendencies when they became adults. The same held true for children who were highly dependent on family-type relationships, who emphasized intellectual mastery, who experienced considerable anxiety in social settings, who affirmed unique gender identities, and who stressed the sexual components of life.

Moreover, this continuity was strongly influenced by traditional standards of masculinity and femininity. Passive girls were more likely to become passive adults than were passive boys. Boys who were aggressive in childhood were likely to be hot-tempered and quick to retaliate when they were men. In contrast, it was difficult to predict adult aggressive behavior for women from their childhood behavior. In other words, the behaviors that were consistent with society's sex-role standards remained more stable across the years than behaviors that were inconsistent with such standards.

Although the longitudinal method allows us to study development over time, the approach does have a number of disadvantages. One major problem is sample shrinkage. Subjects drop out because they become ill or die, because they move away, or simply because they become "fed up." Those who remain tend to come from the most cooperative and stable families. This biases the sample. Moreover, it is impossible to test every child at every scheduled testing on every test item. Children get sick or go on vacation. They become upset, so that part of the test must be omitted. They refuse to comply on some items. And they and their parents occasionally forget appointments (Bayley, 1965*a*).

Another problem is that the span of years covered by longitudinal research inevitably includes unusual social or economic events. These factors often distort growth curves and analyses (Bayley, 1965*a*: 189):

> War, depression, changing cultures, and technological advances all make considerable impacts. What are the differential effects on two-year-olds of depression-caused worries and insecurities, of TV or no TV, of the shifting climate of the baby-experts' advice from strict-diet, let-him-cry, no-pampering schedules to permissive, cuddling, "enriching" loving care?

Longitudinal studies also require a great deal of money and time. And on long-term studies the inevitable turnover in staff impairs research continuity. Finally, there is the problem of "finding out tomorrow what are the relevant variables one should have taken into account yesterday" (Meyers, 1966: 14). Once the project is set in motion, it is difficult to alter in the light of newer techniques and theories. When innovations are introduced, it is impossible to recapture data using the new or revised methods with the subjects at their earlier ages (Bühler, Keith-Spiegel, and Thomas, 1973).

The Cross-Sectional Method

The hallmark of the longitudinal method is its undertaking successive measurements of the *same* individuals. In contrast, the **cross-sectional method** investigates development by simultaneously comparing *different* groups of persons varying in age (see Figure 1.2). Table 1.1 summarizes the advantages and disadvantages of each approach.

Mildred C. Templin (1957) provides us with a good illustration of a cross-sectional study. She investigated language development by selecting sixty children at a number of age levels—3, 3½, 4, 4½, 5, 6, 7, and 8. Her procedure provided norms, or standards, for various measures of language development: vocabulary, speech sound articulation, sound discrimination, and grammar. This technique has the advantage of saving a great deal of time. The researcher need not wait many years until all the subjects reach a given age for retesting. And the researcher does not have to relocate the same subjects.

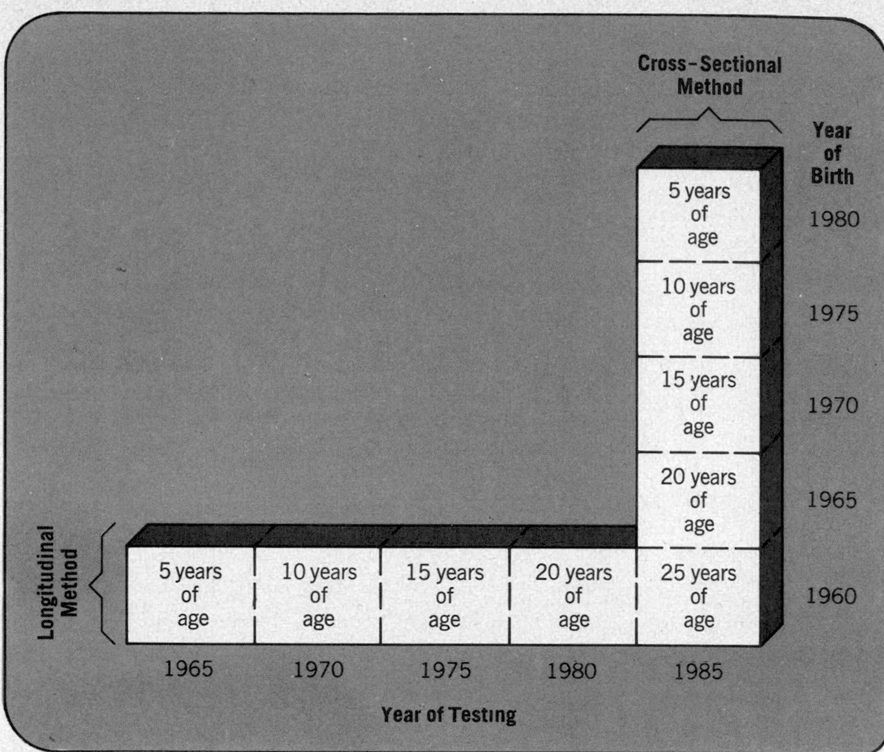

Figure 1.2 Longitudinal and Cross-Sectional Methods

Longitudinal studies are like case histories; they retest the *same* individuals over a period of years. Cross-sectional studies use the "snapshot" approach; they test different individuals of different ages and compare their performances.

Table 1.1 Longitudinal Versus Cross-Sectional Methods

Longitudinal Method	Cross-Sectional Method
Advantages	*Advantages*
Assesses continuity between early childhood and adult behaviors.	Saves a great deal of time.
Avoids problems associated with sample nonequivalence.	Costs less money than longitudinal studies.
Can portray growth increments and patterns.	Demands no continuity or long-term cooperation among research workers.
Permits the formulation of cause-and-effect statements with more certainty than other research designs.	Does not require that data be "frozen" over long periods until subjects reach the desired age for retesting.
Disadvantages	*Disadvantages*
Takes considerable time and money.	Does not indicate the direction of change taking place within the sample groups.
Jeopardizes previous expenditures of time and money if research funds give out.	Lumps together children of the same chronological age but different maturational age. Such averaging may conceal changes like those associated with the growth spurt at puberty.
Requires periodic readjustments associated with staff turnover.	Comparability of the groups being studied is always uncertain.
Sample becomes progressively biased because of subject dropouts.	Neglects the continuity of development as it occurs in a single individual.
Researchers must continually relocate the same subjects for retesting.	
Cannot control the environment of the subjects between testing periods.	
Locks researchers into an earlier research design and theory.	

Cross-sectional research requires careful sampling procedures to make the successive age levels of different subjects reasonably comparable (Ausubel and Sullivan, 1970; Glenn, 1981). In fact, uncertainty regarding comparability is the main weakness of cross-sectional studies. We can never be sure that the reported age-related differences between subjects are not the product of other differences between the groups. For instance, the groups may differ in social environment, intelligence, or diet. Thus the comparability of the groups can only be assumed—and, as a number of developmental psychologists have demonstrated, this assumption is frequently invalid (Schaie, 1965, 1967; Baltes, 1968; Palmore, 1978).

To use a metaphor, the aging process is like riding an escalator (Riley, Johnson, and Foner, 1972: 524):

> Imagine an escalator rising through the several floors (which bound the age strata) of a building. All entrants to the building move directly onto the bottom of this

Generational Effects

Critics of the cross-sectional approach point out that individuals who constitute a generation or cohort share certain common experiences by virtue of coming of age at a given point in time. These experiences frequently derive from decisive economic, social, political, or military events that take place during a particular period of history. A case in point are those youth who passed through the nation's colleges and high schools during the late 1960s and early 1970s. Many participated in student power, Black Power, and peace movements in which they encountered police violence. In cross-sectional research, age differences tend to be confounded by such generational or cohort effects. In brief, successive age levels of different subjects may not be truly comparable by virture of their substantially different experiences.

United Press International

escalator (are born), ride steadily upward (grow older), and exit from the building once they reach the top (die). On the way up, the riders can view the scenes on each of the several floors.

Proponents of the cross-sectional method assume that at successive points in time the riders on the escalator are always *alike* and view essentially the *same* scenes. Critics of the cross-sectional method dispute this. They say that the riders entering the escalator *vary* from one time to the next and view *different* scenes (for instance, women's clothing may have replaced the linen department on the third floor). According to the critics, individuals are not truly comparable from one time period to another.

These problems are highlighted by cross-sectional studies of intelligence. Such studies rather consistently show that average scores on intelligence tests begin to decline around twenty years of age and continue to drop throughout adulthood. But as psychologists Paul B. Baltes and K. Warner Schaie (1974, 1976) have pointed out, cross-sectional studies do not make allowance for *generational* (also termed *cohort*) *differences* in performance on intelligence tests.

Each successive generation of Americans has received more schooling than the preceding generation. Consequently, the overall performance of each generation of Americans on intelligence tests improves. Improvement caused by increasing education creates the illusion that intelligence declines with chronological age (see Chapter 20).

Robert Kastenbaum shows how comparisons among people of different age groups can lead to faulty conclusions:

> Occasionally I have the opportunity to chat with elderly people who live in the communities near by Cushing Hospital. I cannot help but observe that many of these people speak with an Italian accent. I also chat with young adults who live in these same communities. They do *not* speak with an Italian accent. As a student of human behavior and development I am interested in this discrepancy. I indulge in some deep thinking and come up with the following conclusion: as people grow older they develop Italian accents. This must surely be one of the prime manifestations of aging on the psychological level. (Quoted by Botwinick, 1978: 364)

A number of researchers have proposed research designs that link a cross-sectional approach with a modified form of the longitudinal method (Bell, 1953, 1954; Schaie, 1965). Richard Q. Bell, for instance, outlines a "convergence approach." He undertakes a series of shorter-term longitudinal studies that employ overlapping age ranges. One group is tested at ages three, four, and five; another group at five, six, and seven; and still another group at seven, eight, and nine. The method provides "checkpoints" to compare different subjects at the same age. This procedure overcomes some of the difficulties with the cross-sectional method.

The Case Study Method

A special type of longitudinal study focuses on a single individual rather than a group of subjects. It is called the **case study method.** Its aim is the same as that of other longitudinal approaches—the accumulation of developmental information. An early form of the case study method was the "baby biography." Over the past two centuries, a small number of parents have kept detailed observational diaries of their children's behavior. Charles Darwin, for example, wrote a biographical account of his infant son.

A good deal of the early work of Jean Piaget, an influential Swiss developmental psychologist, was based on the case study approach. Piaget (1952*a*) carefully observed the behavior of his own three children: Lucienne, Laurent, and Jacqueline. He would sit by the crib and record his observations of the child's behavior. Or Piaget would watch the child's eye movements and attempt to determine the direction of the child's gaze (Ginsburg and Opper, 1969).

Case studies have also had a prominent place in the clinical treatment of maladjusted and emotionally disturbed individuals. Sigmund Freud and his followers have stressed the part that early experience plays in mental illness. According to this view, the task of the therapist is to help patients reconstruct their own histories. In the process, patients are thought to resolve their inner conflicts. More recently the clinical approach has been extended to the study of healthy individuals. The humanistic psychologists Abraham Maslow (1967, 1970) and Carl Rogers (1970) take this approach.

However, the case study method has a number of drawbacks. Data secured from only one individual are of questionable value. We hear, for instance, that delinquent Freddie came from a "broken home." But a good many children from broken homes never become delinquent. And a considerable share of America's delinquent children come from intact homes. In brief, the case study approach affords little basis for *systematically* comparing people. Further, the observations are frequently biased. In baby biographies, the parents' emotional involvement with the child often colors their presentation.

The Experimental Method

> *I have made a ceaseless effort not to ridicule, not to bewail, nor to scorn human actions, but to understand them.*
>
> —SPINOZA

The **experimental method** is one of the most rigorously objective techniques available to science. An experiment is a study in which the investigator manipulates one or more variables and measures the resulting changes in the other variables. Experiments are "questions put to nature." They offer the most effective technique for establishing a cause-and-effect relationship. This is a relationship in which a particular characteristic or occurrence (X) is one of the factors that determines another characteristic or occurrence (Y). Scientists design an experimental study so that it is possible to infer whether X does or does not enter into the determination of Y. To say that X "causes" Y is simply to indicate that whenever X occurs, Y is likely to follow at some later time (Selltiz, Wrightsman, and Cook, 1976).

In an experiment, researchers try to find out whether a relationship exists between two variables (X and Y). First, they systematically vary the first variable (X). Second, they observe the effects of such variation upon the second variable (Y). X, the factor that is manipulated in an experiment, is the **independent variable.** It is independent of what the subject or subjects do. The independent variable is assumed to be the causal factor in the relationship being studied. We call the factor that is affected—that occurs or changes as a result of such manipulation—the **dependent variable.** The dependent variable is usually some measure of the subjects' behavior. For instance, students may talk noisily when the teacher is out of the room but become quiet when the teacher enters. The change in the level of classroom noise—the dependent variable—is then said to be caused by the teacher's presence—the independent variable (Sanders, 1974).

Let us examine these variables in an actual experiment. Richard H. Walters, Marion Leat, and Louis Mezei (1963) wanted to know whether children who see another child being punished for breaking a rule will themselves become less likely to break that rule. In the experiment, nursery-school boys were individually brought to a room containing a number of attractive toys and told not to play with them.

The independent variable was a movie shown to each boy in which another child (a *model*) violated a similar rule. One group of boys saw a version of the movie in which the child was *punished* by his mother for playing with the forbidden toys. A second group of boys saw another version of the movie in which the child was *rewarded* by his mother for the same behavior. Finally, a third group of boys was *not* shown a movie. Such a group is called a **control group.** The control group is identical to the other groups (called **experimental groups)** except for the fact that the researcher does not introduce change into it. The control group provides a neutral standard against which the changes in the experimental groups can be measured.

In the case of the control group, the experimenter brought the child to a specially equipped room. Here the child's behavior could be observed without the child's knowing it through a one-way mirror from the adjoining room. The experimenter told the child (Walters, Leat, and Mezei, 1963: 237)

> In a little while I am going to play a game with you, but I have forgotten something and must go and get it. You can sit on this chair while you wait for me. Now these toys belong to some other children and have been especially arranged for them. So you better not touch them. But you can look at the book (i.e., the dictionary) while you're waiting for me, if you like.

The child was then left alone for fifteen minutes. When the experimenter returned, she played briefly with the child. She then took him back to his classroom.

The children in the experimental groups were told while being taken to the room that they were going to see a movie. In the room, a male assistant was introduced to the child. He also ran the movie projector. Each child was given the same instructions by the experimenter as the children in the control group. After showing the movie, the male assistant said (238):

> You remember that Miss Leat had to go and get something. She will be back to see you later. You'd better wait for her here. I'm going to shut the door to make sure nobody will bother you while you are here.

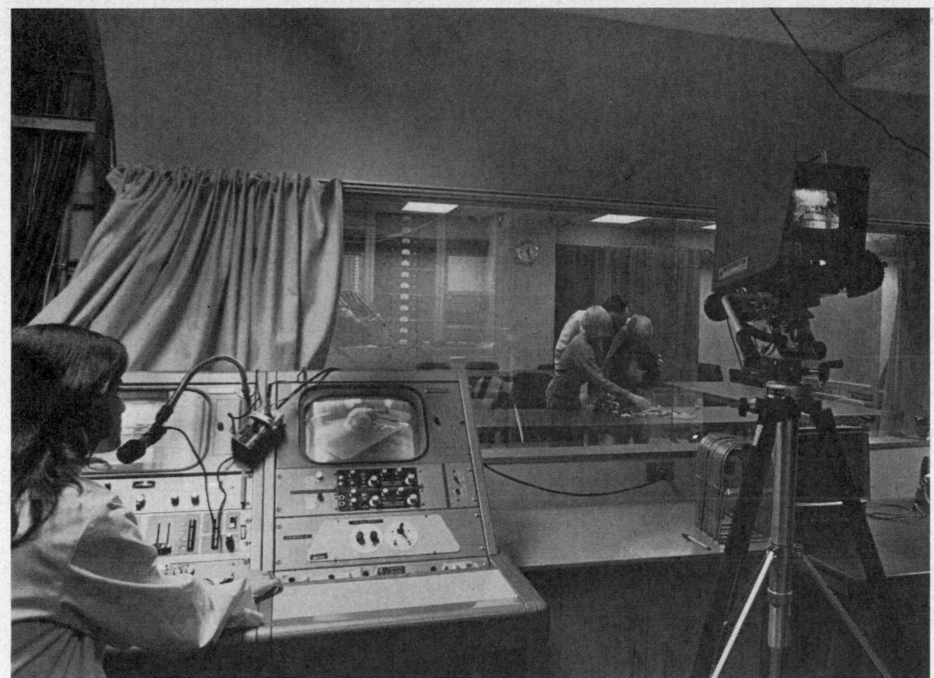

A Small-Group Laboratory

Many college campuses provide researchers with special facilities for observing subjects. For example, this small-group laboratory at Ohio State University consists of two rooms that are separated by a one-way mirror. Researchers in the control room can observe subjects in the experimental room without themselves being observed (and thus interfering with the spontaneous behavior of the subjects). In the top photograph an observer is watching from the control room. Viewed from the experimental room shown in the bottom photograph, the observer's window is a mirror. The Ohio State small-group laboratory also contains television-like equipment so that in neighboring rooms, individual subjects can view on a television screen the behavior which takes place in the experimental room. This allows subjects to observe and interpret behavior without influencing one another's perceptions and interpretations of it. Moreover, the equipment at Ohio State permits researchers to videotape behavior, so that they can replay the tapes later and study the behavior more closely.

Patrick Reddy

In the study, the dependent variable was the speed and frequency with which the boys broke the rule against playing with the toys after the adult left the room. The experiment revealed that boys who had watched the child being rewarded for breaking the rule broke it themselves more quickly and more often than did the boys in the other two groups. In contrast, the group that had seen the model being punished

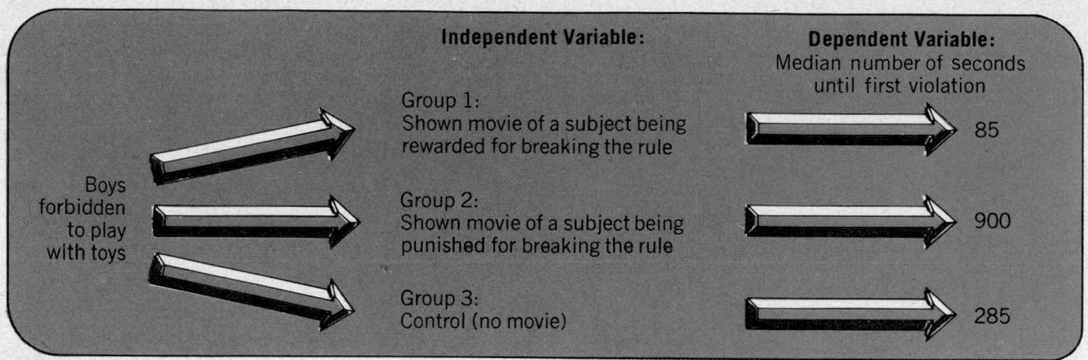

Figure 1.3 The Influence of Filmed Social Models on Young Boys' Resistance to Temptation
In the experiment undertaken by Richard H. Walters and his associates, groups 1 and 2 were experimental groups and group 3 was the control group. The independent variable was introduced in the first two groups but not in the third group.

SOURCE: Adapted from data in R. H. Walters, M. Leat, and L. Mezei, "Inhibition and Disinhibition of Responses Through Empathetic Learning," *Canadian Journal of Psychology*, Vol. 17 (1963), pp. 235–243.

was more unwilling than any of the other groups to break the rule. The performance of the control group fell between the other two groups (see Figure 1.3). The researchers concluded that children who watch the behavior of another person tend to behave in the same way. This evidence supports the social learning theory of the psychologist Albert Bandura (see Chapter 2).

The Social Survey Method

Researchers are often interested in studying the incidence of behavior in a large population: say, to discover the prevalence of certain child-rearing practices, the extent of premarital sexual relations, the frequency of drug use among teenagers, the impact of a mental health advertising campaign, and so on. In this approach, data are collected in numerical form by using various quantitative methods—procedures that entail enumeration and measurement.

Prominent among quantitative methods is the **survey.** Survey data are gathered in two basic ways. In the first, people are interviewed by a researcher who reads them questions from a prepared questionnaire. In the second, individuals receive a questionnaire in the mail, fill it out, and return it by mail.

Both mass interviewing and the mass mailing of questionnaires are exceedingly expensive. Further, questioning millions of people is simply impractical. Accordingly scientists have evolved various techniques for using small samples of people to arrive at broad generalizations about the larger population. Public opinion organizations (including Gallup, CBS, NBC, and Louis Harris) employ small samples of approximately 1,500 representative people to tap the opinions of 200 million Americans with only a small margin of error.

The principle behind polling is simple. Consider a jar filled with 100,000 green and yellow marbles. You do not need to count all the marbles to find out what proportion are green, what yellow. A sample of 1,000 will allow you to estimate the ratio with great confidence, within a small margin of error, so long as each marble has an equal chance of being counted. Doctors proceed on the same assumption when they test our blood. Rather than removing all of it for testing, they take a small sample.

The social survey method has its limitations. It cannot be used with infants, and it has only limited use with preschool children. Further, individuals are often deeply involved with the data they are reporting. Hence they may withhold or distort information if they feel that their self-esteem is threatened. Or they may simply be unable to provide certain types of information because of lack of insight.

The Naturalistic Observation Method

In **naturalistic observation,** researchers intensively watch and record behavior as it occurs. However, they are careful not to disturb or affect the events under investigation. By this method they can secure more

The Social Survey

The social survey is a particularly valuable tool for gaining information from people regarding aspects of their behavior that is not directly accessible to observation. Here a researcher is interviewing Native Americans on the Pine Ridge Indian Reservation in South Dakota.

Owen Franken/Stock, Boston

detail and greater depth of insight than by using the social survey (Willems and Alexander, 1982). But for the same amount of time and money, fewer people can be directly observed than interviewed. Thus naturalistic observation affords less range in the types of people it can study than the social survey does.

An advantage of naturalistic observation is that it is independent of the subject's ability or willingness to report on given matters. Many people lack sufficient self-insight to tell the researcher about certain aspects of their behavior. Or because their behavior is illegal, taboo, or deviant, they may be reluctant to talk about it. The following account of an interview with a mother about her child-rearing practices is a good example (Maccoby and Maccoby, 1954: 484):

> During the interview she held her small son on her lap. The child began to play with his genitals. The mother, without looking directly at the child, moved his hand away and held it securely for a while. . . . [Later] in the interview the mother was asked what she ordinarily did when the child played with himself. She replied that he never did this—he is a very "good" boy. She was evidently unconscious of what had transpired in the very presence of the interviewer.

Naturalistic observation can provide a rich source of ideas for future study. But it is not a particularly strong technique for testing hypotheses. The researcher lacks control over the behavior of the subjects being observed. Further, no independent variable is "manipulated." Consequently, the theorizing associated with naturalistic observation tends to be highly speculative. Still another problem with this method is that the observer's presence may alter the behavior he or she is observing. The knowledge that we are being observed tends to distort our behavior—the so-called *guinea pig effect* (also termed the *Hawthorne effect*). To minimize this problem, some researchers conceal their identity as observers. But this poses ethical problems.

In spite of these shortcomings there is a decided advantage to observing behavior as it takes place spontaneously within its natural context. Indeed, some researchers argue that artificially planned situations do not do justice to the rich, genuine, and dynamic quality of human life. They insist that rigid interviews, questionnaires, tests, and experiments distort and destroy the natural stream of people's behavior (Wright, 1960; Barker, 1963). Rather than compelling the subject to enter the experimenter's world, as other methods do, naturalistic observation requires the experimenter to enter the subject's world.

A number of researchers have introduced modifications in observational techniques in order to provide greater scientific rigor (Lytton, 1971; Altmann, 1973). One of these involves **time sampling.** The researcher counts the number of times an individual

Naturalistic Observation
Much can be learned about human behavior by observing people in their natural habitats. The researcher attempts to capture the full richness and flavor of the human experience as it spontaneously occurs, not as it develops under experimental manipulation.
Patrick Reddy

exhibits quarreling, aggression, cooperation, or some other behavior over a systematically spaced interval of time. When studying children, some researchers record the action every five seconds (Moustakas, Sigel, and Schalock, 1956). Other researchers do not want to lose the sequential flow of events. Consequently, they focus on a class of behaviors, such as fighting on a playground, and record the time that is consumed by each episode (Lambert, 1960; Baumrind, 1967; Caldwell, 1969). This is termed **event sampling.** Still other researchers use precoded behavior categories (Lytton, 1971). They determine beforehand what behaviors they will observe. They then record a behavior by code symbols (see the boxed insert on page 25).

The Cross-Cultural Method

No animal lives under more diverse conditions than man, and no species exhibits more behavioral variation from one population to another.

—ROBERT A. LEVINE

Scientists are interested in establishing which theories hold for all societies, which for only certain types of

TIPS FOR OBSERVING CHILDREN

One of the best ways to learn about children is to observe them. To provide access to the full drama, color, and richness of the world of children, many instructors have their students watch children in the laboratory or in the field. Here are a number of tips that may prove helpful for the observation of children:

- The minimal aids you will need for observation generally include paper, pen, a timepiece, and a writing board.
- Record the date, the time interval, the location, the situation, and the age and sex of the subject or subjects.
- Most observations take place in nursery-school settings. Add diversity to your report by observing children in parks, streets, stores, vacant lots, homes, and swimming pools.
- Have the purpose of your research firmly in mind. You should explicitly define and limit in advance the range of situations and behaviors you will observe. Will you watch the entire playground, giving a running account of events? Will you concentrate upon one or two individuals? Will you record the activities of an entire group? Or will you focus only on certain types of behavior, such as aggression?
- Describe both the behavior and the social context in which it occurs. Include not only what a child says and does but also what others say and do to the child. Report spoken words, cries, screams, startle responses, jumping, running away, and related behaviors.
- Describe the relevant *body language*—the nonverbal communication of meaning through physical movements and gestures. This includes smiles, frowns, scowls, menacing gestures, twisting, and other acts that illuminate the intensity and effect of behavior.
- Do not substitute interpretations that generalize *about* behavior for descriptions *of* behavior.
- Make notes in improvised shorthand. *Immediately after* an observation session, transcribe and enlarge the report in full. The longer the interval between the full recording of observations and the events themselves, the less accurate, the less detailed, and the more biased your report will be.
- Make inferences regarding the motivations and feelings of the children as their behavior occurs.
- Limit your periods of observation to half an hour. This is about as long as a researcher can remain alert enough to perceive and remember the multitude of simultaneous and sequential occurrences.
- At times children will notice you observing them. If they ask what you are doing, be truthful. Explain it openly and frankly. According to Wright and Barker (1950), children under the age of nine generally display little self-consciousness when being observed. Further, most people—children and adults alike—usually adjust to an observer's presence.
- Keep in mind that one of the greatest sources of unreliability in observation is the researcher's selective perceptions influenced by his or her own needs and values. For example, observers who sharply disapprove of aggressive behaviors tend to overrecord these behaviors. Remember at all times that objectivity is your goal.
- Use time sampling for some observations. Time your field notes at intervals of one minute or even thirty seconds. You may wish to tally the children's behavior in terms of helping, resistance, submission, giving, and other responses.
- Use event sampling—behavioral sequences or episodes—for some observations. Helen Dawe's 1934 study of the quarrels of preschool children provides a good model. Dawe made "running notes" on prepared forms that gave space for recording (a) the name, age, and sex of every subject, (b) the duration of the quarrel, (c) what the children were doing at the onset of the quarrel, (d) the reason for the quarrel, (e) the role of each subject, (f) specific motor and verbal behavior, (g) the outcome, and (h) the aftereffects. The advantage of event sampling is that it allows you to structure the field of observation into natural units of behavior.

societies, and which for only a particular society. The **cross-cultural method** is well suited to this purpose. Researchers compare data from two or more societies. Cultures, rather than individuals, are the unit of analysis. The largest number of societies studied in this manner is about one thousand. However, most researchers limit themselves to a smaller sample, generally several adjacent societies in a similar cultural area. They may focus upon a single aspect, such as toilet training or puberty rites, or a wide variety of behaviors and customs (Marsh, 1967; Driver, 1973).

A considerable number of cross-cultural studies have employed data from the Human Relations Area Files at Yale University (Murdock et al., 1971). These files, which are now available on microfilm to other universities, contain verbatim reports from anthropologists, colonial officials, missionaries, explorers, travelers, and others. Information on some four hundred societies is filed by code numbers and indexed by nearly eight hundred subject categories.

For example, if we were interested in infant care, we would look in the Human Relations Area Files under category 854 (Murdock et al., 1971: 136):

> 854 INFANT CARE—care of routine bodily needs, cleaning; dealing with excreta; clothing and swaddling; provisions for sleep (e.g., cradles, cribs); playing with infants (e.g., fondling, dandling, rocking, crooning); emotional care (e.g., distracting techniques, methods of soothing, guarding against emotional upsets); watching and tending; special dangers ascribed to period of infancy; protection from real and supernatural dangers; hygienic and therapeutic measures; methods of holding and carrying infants (e.g., on back, astride hip); distribution of care among members of the family; institutionalized care (e.g., nurseries); etc.

Or if we wished to study adulthood, we would look under category 885 (Murdock et al., 1971: 143):

> 885 ADULTHOOD—conception of the prime of life; cultural definition of adult status; differential status and activities of adult males and females prior to and subsequent to marriage; concepts of the ideal man and the ideal woman; etc.

Studies dealing with grandparenthood provide a good example of cross-cultural research. According to the anthropologist A. R. Radcliffe-Brown (1940), tensions between parents and children tend to draw grandparent and grandchild together. To test this hypothesis, a number of researchers have examined cross-cultural data (Nadel, 1951; Apple, 1956). They have found close and warm relationships between children and their grandparents *only* in cultures where grandparents do not serve as disciplinarians. Where grandparents have a disciplinary role, easy, friendly, playful relations between grandparents and grandchildren are absent.

Like other research approaches, the cross-cultural method has limitations (Marsh, 1967; Cohen, 1968; Munroe and Munroe, 1975). First, the quality of the data varies from casual, unprofessional accounts by explorers and missionaries to the most sophisticated field work by trained anthropologists. Second, data for some research problems are lacking for many cultures. Third, the data tend to focus on the typical

Cross-Cultural Research

By comparing data from two or more societies, scientists are able to generalize about human development under varying cultural circumstances. One aspect of development that has interested scientists over the past decade is the part the father plays in rearing children. Here a Balinese father of Indonesia relaxes with his family.

Ken Heyman

behaviors and practices of a people but seldom provide information on individual differences among them. Nonetheless, as George Peter Murdock (1957: 251), a distinguished anthropologist, has written, cross-cultural research demonstrates that it is "unsafe" for the scientist "to generalize his knowledge of Euro-American societies, however profound, to mankind in general."

ETHICAL STANDARDS FOR HUMAN DEVELOPMENT RESEARCH

> *Hurt not others in ways that you yourself would find hurtful.*
>
> —*A Buddhist Scripture*

Research on humans is essential for medical and scientific progress. Human development research can help parents, teachers, social workers, government officials, and many others to make more informed decisions regarding various practices and policies. However, most scientists and lay people recognize that before any new drug or procedure can be approved for use in human beings, it must be tested first on individuals under appropriate experimental controls (Frankel, 1978). Clearly, such experimentation must be undertaken with proper safeguards. More than four decades ago, the horrors of medical experiments carried out by German physicians working in Nazi concentration camps dramatized the need for a code of ethics in research.

In the past fifteen years or so, a number of studies have sparked controversy within American scientific circles. In an experiment under the auspices of the U.S. Public Health Service, a group of southern blacks went forty years without treatment for syphilis. A family-planning clinic in San Antonio randomly gave placebos (fake pills) to applicants for birth-control pills, and this practice resulted in several unwanted pregnancies. Investigators seeking a cure for hepatitis intentionally injected the disease virus into hundreds of mentally retarded children at Willowbrook State School in New York (Frankel, 1978). And in an experiment by Stanley Milgram (1974), subjects were ordered to give other people electric shocks that the subjects believed were strong enough to injure or kill.

The issues posed by such research have led the American Psychological Association to formulate a series of research guidelines. The preamble states (1982: 5):

> The decision to undertake research should rest upon a considered judgment by the individual psychologist about how best to contribute to psychological science and to human welfare. Having made the decision to conduct research, the psychologist considers alternative directions in which research energies and resources might be invested. On the basis of this consideration, the psychologist carries out the investigation with respect and concern for the dignity and welfare of the people who participate and with cognizance of federal and state regulations and professional standards governing the conduct of research with human participants.

Research with children has aroused particular concern, so that the Society for Research in Child Development has also issued a set of guidelines (1972). It notes:

> Children as research subjects present ethical problems for the investigator different from those presented by adult subjects. Not only are children often viewed as more vulnerable to stress but, having less knowledge and experience, they are less able to evaluate what participation in research may mean. Consent of the parent for the study of his child, moreover, must be obtained in addition to the child's consent.

Both sets of guidelines stipulate that subjects should not be compelled to participate in an experiment, and that they should have the freedom to discontinue participation if they wish. Research on children raises particularly complex and sensitive issues, since the legal and moral legitimacy of experimentation of human beings evolves fundamentally from the consent of the subject (Cooke, 1982). However, the capacity of children to give informed consent is limited, and at very early ages impossible (Frankel, 1978). Even so, research suggests that in many cases children over nine years of age are able to make sensible decisions about whether or not to take part in research (Fields, 1981). While parents and legal guardians are empowered to decide whether or not minors under their control will be used as research subjects, children should not be viewed simply as pawns that can be manipulated at will by their elders. Finally, both organizations state that the experimenter must assume responsibility for detecting and correcting any undesirable results that may follow from an individual's participation in the research.

(a)

(b)

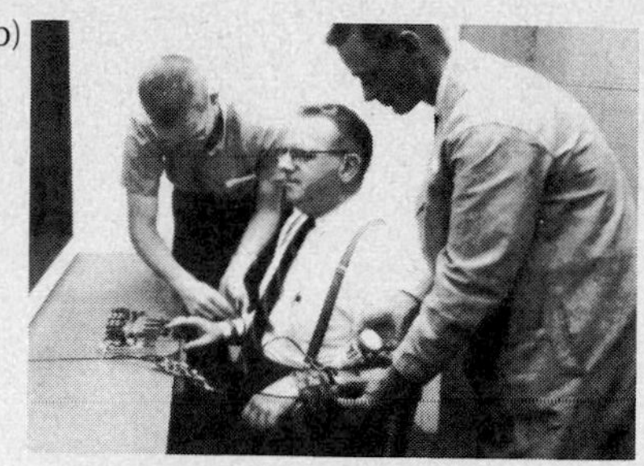

(c)

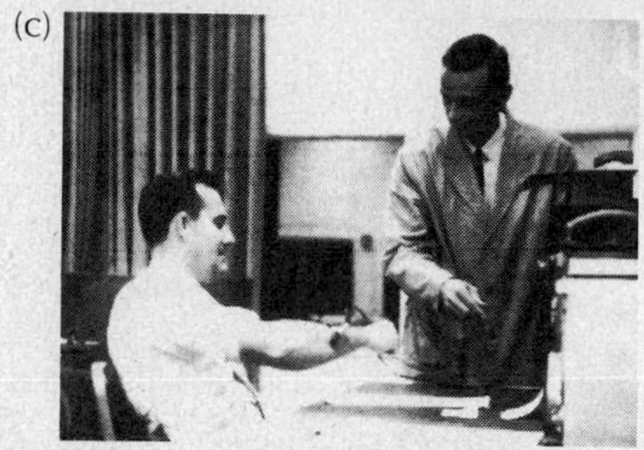

(d)

(e)

Stanley Milgram's Experiment on Obedience
The sequence of photo shows: (*a*) The fake shock generator used by the teacher; (*b*) the learner being connected to the shock apparatus; (*c*) Milgram explaining the procedure to the teacher; (*d*) a subject refusing to shock the learner any further and angrily rising in protest; and (*e*) Milgram explains the truth about the experiment.

In sum, individuals who undertake research assume major responsibilities. Scientists must of course proceed in a rigorous and disciplined way, approaching their data from as objective a perspective as is humanly possible. They must not turn their backs on facts or distort facts simply because they find that the facts are leading them to conclusions they may find distasteful. But over and above this traditional obligation, they have a responsibility for the welfare of their subjects.

SUMMARY

1. Human life involves both change and continuity.
2. The field of human development has four major concerns: (a) to identify and describe the changes that occur across the human life span, (b) to explain these changes, (c) to predict occurrences in human development, and (d) to intervene in the course of events in order to control them.
3. Human development has increasingly become an interdisciplinary and multidisciplinary field, encompassing psychology, sociology, anthropology, and biology.
4. The concepts of growth, maturation, and learning are important to our understanding of human development. It is important that we not counterpose the biological forces of growth and maturation to the environmental forces of learning. It is the interaction between heredity and environment that gives an organism its unique characteristics.
5. In examining developmental sequences, some psychologists focus on continuity while others emphasize discontinuity. However, psychologists are increasingly aware that the human life

span is characterized by both continuity and discontinuity.

6. All societies must deal in one fashion or another with the life cycle. They divide this cycle into strata that reflect social definitions. Such definitions often vary from one historical period to another and from one culture to another.

7. The longitudinal method for studying human development allows the researcher to study the same individuals at regular intervals between birth and death. It provides a means for discovering which childhood behaviors are long-lasting and which will be dropped along the way.

8. Whereas the longitudinal method undertakes successive measurements on the *same* individuals, the cross-sectional method compares different groups of people of different ages at the same time.

9. The case study method is used in baby biographies and in clinical approaches involving maladjusted children and adults.

10. The experimental method is one of the most rigorously objective techniques available to science. It offers the most effective technique for establishing cause-and-effect relationships.

11. The social survey method employs questionnaires and interviews for determining the prevalence of given attitudes and behaviors within a population.

12. Naturalistic observation enables a researcher to study people independently of their ability or willingness to report on themselves. The techniques of naturalistic observation range from reports on the most casual uncontrolled experiences to videotape records taken in a laboratory setting.

13. The cross-cultural method allows scientists to specify which theories in human development hold true for all societies, which for only certain types of societies, and which for only a particular society.

14. Having made the decision to conduct research, a scientist must carry out an investigation with respect for the people who participate and with concern for their dignity and welfare.

KEY TERMS

age grades Social layers that are based upon time periods in life. Age strata order people in society in much the fashion that the earth's crust is ordered by stratified geological layers.

ascription The assignment of roles to individuals independently of their unique abilities or qualities.

case study method A special type of longitudinal study that focuses on a single individual rather than a group of subjects.

cognitive development Those changes that occur in mental activity, including sensation, perception, memory, thought, reasoning, and language.

control group That group in an experiment that is identical to the other groups except for the fact that the researcher does not introduce change into it. It provides a neutral standard against which the changes in the experimental group can be measured.

cross-cultural method A technique that involves the comparison of data from two or more societies, so that cultures, rather than individuals, are the unit of analysis.

cross-sectional method A research approach that investigates development by comparing different groups of individuals varying in age.

dependent variable The factor that is affected in an experimental setting; that which occurs or changes as a result of manipulation.

development The orderly and sequential changes that occur with the passage of time as an organism moves from conception to death. Development includes both hereditary and environmental forces and the interaction between them.

event sampling An observational technique in which the researcher focuses upon a class of behaviors and records the time that is consumed by a given episode.

experimental group That group in an experiment in which the independent variable is introduced.

experimental method A study in which the investigator manipulates one or more variables and measures the resulting changes in the other variables.

growth The increase in size that occurs with changing age.

independent variable The factor that is manipulated in an experimental setting; the causal factor or determining condition in the relationship being studied.

learning The more or less permanent modification of behavior that results from the individual's experience in the environment.

longitudinal method A research approach that investigates development by studying the same individuals at different points in their lives.

maturation The more or less automatic unfolding of biological potential in a set, irreversible sequence.

naturalistic observation A research approach that entails intensive watching and recording of behavior as it occurs; the researcher does not disturb or affect the events under investigation.

physical development Those changes that take place in a person's body, including changes in weight and height, in the brain, heart, and other organ structures and processes; and in skeletal, muscular, and neurological features that affect motor skills.

psychosocial development Those changes that concern an individual's personality, emotions, and relationships with others.

survey A procedure for gathering data in which people are interviewed by reading them questions from a prepared questionnaire, or people receive a questionnaire in the mail, fill it out, and return it.

time sampling An observational technique in which the researcher counts the number of times that a given behavior is exhibited by a subject in a constant, systematically spaced interval of time.

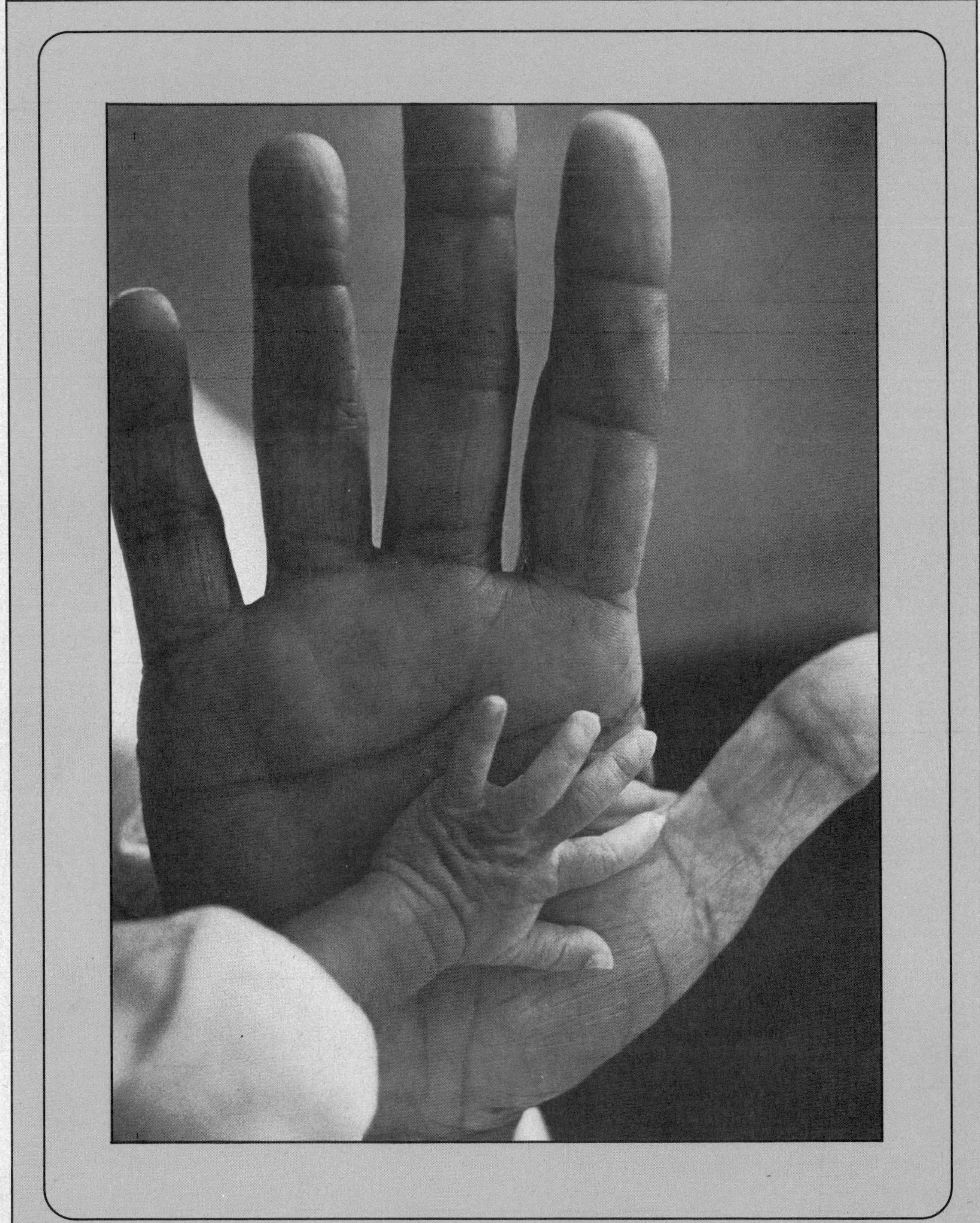

2

Developmental Theories

Nothing is so practical as a good theory.

—KURT LEWIN

A good many Americans hold theory in low regard, some even in contempt. The word excites an image of detached, ivory tower irrelevance. Yet, broadly defined, theory is employed by us *all* in our daily lives. For example, every parent has a theory about how children develop. Often such a theory is in the form of proverbs or popular maxims—"Spare the rod and spoil the child," "Just give them security and a lot of love," "You got to toughen kids up so they can face the rough road of life," and "Spanking children gives rise to neurosis."

In truth, good theory is power. It is a net that we weave to catch the world of observation and describe, explain, predict, and influence it. The best definition may be that **theory** is a *tool.* It is "a way of binding together a multitude of facts so that one may comprehend them all at once" (G. A. Kelly, 1955: 18). The value of the knowledge yielded by the application of theory lies in the control it provides us over our experience. Theory is for the sake of doing. It serves as a guide to action.

More specifically, a theory performs a number of functions (Shaw and Costanzo, 1982). First, it allows us to organize our observations and to deal meaningfully with information that would otherwise be chaotic and useless. Second, it allows us to see relationships among facts and uncover implications that would not otherwise be evident in isolated pieces of data. Third, it stimulates inquiry as we search for knowledge about many different, and often puzzling, aspects of behavior. These various functions will become clear as we examine five major types of theory that provide a foundation for the many components of human development.

PSYCHOANALYTIC THEORY

It is unlikely that the history of psychology—or for that matter, a history of the twentieth century—could be written without discussing the contributions of Sigmund Freud. Both supporters and critics of his theory of personality regard it as a revolutionary milestone in the history of human thought. Indeed, Freud's approach has gained such phenomenal popularity—even though it is superficially or inaccurately understood by much of the general public—that many students in beginning psychology courses equate psychoanalysis with psychology. His notions about how behavior is motivated have been embedded in the work done by a multitude of philosophers, social scientists, and mental health practitioners. And characters in countless plays and novels have been built on Freud's views of people (Greenberg and Fisher, 1978). Central to **psychoanalytic theory** is the view that personality is fashioned progressively as the individual passes through various stages: oral, anal, phallic, latency, and genital. Let us turn, then, to a consideration of psychoanalytic theory.

Sigmund Freud: Psychosexual Stages of Development

Freud was born in 1856 in a small town in what is now Czechoslovakia, but he lived most of his life in Vienna. He became a physician and initially distinguished himself through his research on the human nervous system. Early in his career, Freud used hypnosis in treating patients with nervous disorders. But he soon became disenchanted with this method. He began experimenting with the free association of ideas and with dream analysis, work that culminated in his famous psychoanalytic approach. Freud continued to work in Vienna until 1938, when the Nazis invaded Austria. Freud, a Jew, escaped to England. He died in London a year later of cancer, with which he had first been stricken in 1923.

Freud stressed the part that unconscious motivation—stemming from impulses buried below the level of awareness—plays in our behavior. According to Freud, human behavior arises out of the struggle that takes place between societal prohibitions and the instinctual drives associated with sex and aggression. As a consequence of being forbidden and punished, many instinctual impulses are driven out of our awareness early in life. Nonetheless, they still affect our behavior. They find new expression in slips of the tongue, dreams, bizarre symptoms of mental disorder, religion, art, literature, and myth. For Freud, the early years of childhood assume critical importance. He believed that what happens to an individual later in

Sigmund Freud

Although Freud reached the pinnacle of his fame in the period between 1919 and his death in 1939, he formulated most of the essentials of his psychoanalytic theory in the decade between 1893 and 1903.

Culver Pictures

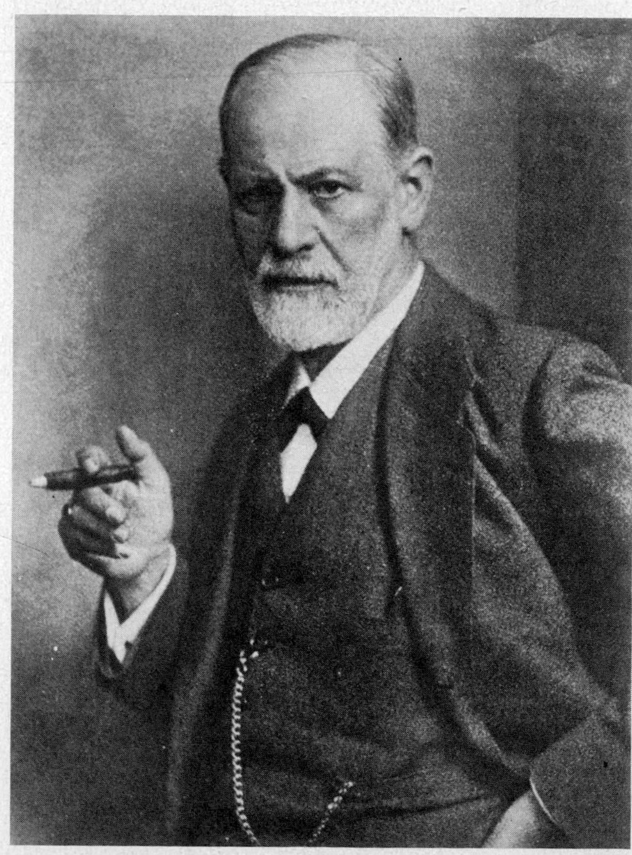

life is merely a ripple on the surface of a personality structure that is fashioned during the child's first six years.

Freud said that all human beings pass through a series of **psychosexual stages.** Each stage is dominated by the development of sensitivity in a particular erogenous or pleasure-giving zone of the body. Further, each stage poses for individuals a unique conflict that they must resolve before they pass on to the next stage. Should individuals be unsuccessful in resolving the conflict, the resulting frustration becomes chronic and remains a central feature of their psychological makeup. Alternatively, individuals may become so addicted to the pleasures of a given stage that they are unwilling to move on to later stages (Liebert, Poulos, and Marmor, 1977). As a result of either frustration or overindulgence, individuals experience **fixation** at a particular stage of development. Fixation is the tendency to stay at a particular stage: the individual is troubled by the conflict characteristic of the stage and seeks to reduce tension by means of the behavior characteristic of that stage.

The characteristics of Freud's key three psychosexual stages of development—the *oral, anal,* and *phallic* stages—are described in detail in Table 2.1. He also identified two later stages, the *latency* period and the *genital* period. He considered these stages less important to the development of the basic personality structure than the stages from birth to age seven. The latency period corresponds to the elementary-school years. During this phase, Freud thought children suppress most of their sexual feelings and become interested in games and sports. Boys associate with boys; girls with girls. Sexual reawakening occurs at puberty, launching the genital period. In this stage the equilibrium of the latency period is upset. Young people begin experiencing romantic infatuations and emotional upheavals.

For years Freud's ideas dominated much clinical therapy. To many people Freud seemed to open an entirely new psychological world. His identification of key ego defense mechanisms (see the boxed insert on page 37) proved particularly insightful and valuable for psychotherapy, and his emphasis on environment, not biology or heredity, as the primary factor in mental health and illness, was particularly hopeful. In fact, people were so fascinated with the novelty of Freud's insights that few questioned their truth (Greenberg and Fisher, 1978; Stannard, 1980). Nonetheless, scientists have come to recognize that Freudian theory is difficult to evaluate. It makes few predictions that can be tested by accepted scientific procedures. Unconscious motivation is, by definition, not in the conscious mind. Consequently, scientists lack the means to observe and study it objectively.

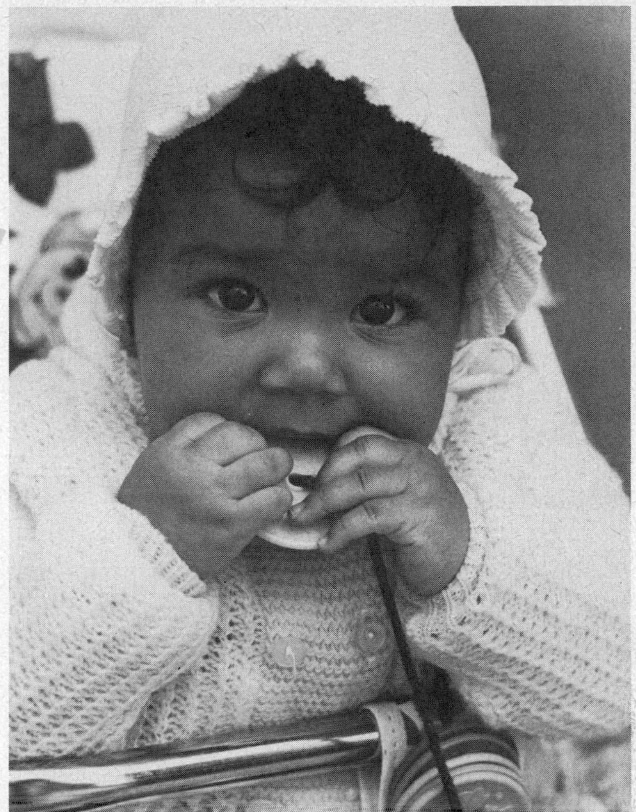

The Oral Stage of Psychosexual Development
For Freud, the oral stage of infancy is a particularly critical period in personality formation. In this stage infants derive considerable satisfaction from mouthing various objects.
Patrick Reddy

Freud constructed his developmental stages almost entirely on the basis of inferences from adult patients. Although stressing the importance of the early years, Freud worked with children only rarely (however, child psychoanalysts, such as his daughter Anna, did apply his theories to the treatment of children). And Freud failed to give adequate consideration to the adolescent and adult periods of the life cycle. Finally, since his patients were suffering from emotional difficulties, critics charge that Freudian theory is a poor guide to healthy personalities.

Over the past two decades, interest in the duration

Table 2.1 Freud's Key Psychosexual Stages

Characteristic	Oral	Anal	Phallic
Time period	Birth to approximately eighteen months	Approximately eighteen months to three years	Approximately the third to seventh year
Pleasurable body zones	Mouth, lips, and tongue	Anus, rectum, and bladder	The genitals
Most pleasurable activity	Sucking during the early phase; biting during the later phase	In the early phase, expelling feces and urine; in the later phase, retaining feces and urine	Masturbation
Sources of conflict	Terminating breast feeding	Toilet training	In boys, the Oedipal complex: boys feel sexual love for the mother and hostile rivalry toward the father, leading them to fear punishment through castration by the father. In girls, the Electra complex: girls feel sexual love for the father and hostile rivalry toward the mother, leading them to conclude that they have been castrated (since they lack the penis). Their sense of castration gives girls a feeling of inferiority that finds expression in "penis envy."
Common problems associated with fixation	An immature, dependent personality with overwhelming and insatiable demands for mothering; a verbally abusive and demanding personality; or a personality characterized by excessive "oral" behaviors, such as alcoholism, smoking, compulsive eating, and nail biting.	A hostile, defiant personality that has difficulty relating to people in positions of authority; a superconformist personality characterized by preoccupation with rules, regulations, rigid routines, compulsive neatness, and orderliness; or a stingy, miserly personality.	Sexual problems in adulthood—impotence or frigidity; homosexuality; inability to handle competitive relationships.
Social relationships	Infants cannot differentiate between self and nonself. Consequently, they are self-centered and preoccupied with their own needs.	Since parents interfere with elimination pleasures, the child develops ambivalent attitudes toward the parents. As children resolve the conflict between their needs for parental love and for instinctual gratification, they evolve lifelong attitudes toward cleanliness, orderliness, punctuality, submissiveness, and defiance.	A successful resolution of phallic conflict leads the child to identify with the parent of the same sex. In this fashion the child achieves a sense of masculinity or femininity and gives up the incestuous desire for the parent of the opposite sex.

EGO DEFENSE MECHANISMS

According to Freudian theory, *ego defense mechanisms* are activated when an individual confronts serious anxiety and emotional conflict. These mechanisms are mental devices by which people protect and insulate themselves from psychic pain. Freud believed that all people employ such devices. They become pathological only when they continually serve to distort reality and impair effective functioning. Among the most common defense mechanisms are the following:

- *Repression.* In repression, an unacceptable or threatening thought or impulse is driven from conscious awareness. When children have been taught that aggression and masturbation are "bad," they may repress knowledge of their own involvement in such practices. By repression they avoid conscious feelings of anxiety and guilt.
- *Projection.* People using the mechanism of projection attribute to someone else their own impulses or acts that are too painful to acknowledge. Thus angry children who have learned that rage is socially unacceptable often project their aggression onto a playmate and justify their own behavior as "self-defense": "He started it."
- *Displacement.* When hostilities are removed from the source of frustration and discharged upon another person (a scapegoat), displacement takes place. Children frustrated by a parent or a teacher usually cannot strike back. It would be too dangerous. Instead, they "take out" their pent-up hostility on a weak or defenseless victim—for instance, a pet or a younger child.
- *Denial.* At times people protect themselves from unpleasant reality by simply not perceiving it. They refuse to acknowledge its existence. A child with a hostile mother may deny that she is hostile and rejecting. Instead, the child insists that the mother is a kind, loving person. The device of denial spares people the emotional pain that would follow from recognizing the truth.
- *Sublimation.* In sublimation, unacceptable behavior is repressed and reemerges in a socially acceptable manner. According to some psychoanalytic psychologists, a coin collector is sublimating a desire to retain feces, a boxing fan is sublimating aggression, and an artist is sublimating sexual energies.
- *Regression.* Individuals who are under stress may invoke behavior that was characteristic of an earlier stage of development. An illustration is the six-year-old child who regresses to thumb-sucking or bed-wetting when confronted with a new baby in the home.
- *Rationalization.* People rationalize by finding a convincing reason for doing something that would otherwise be viewed as unacceptable. Take the teenage girl who wants to break off with her boyfriend but feels guilty about it because "he's been good to me." She can go ahead and make the break, however, if she can justify it through rationalization: "He'd be better off if he could get to know some other girls."
- *Reaction formation.* In reaction formation, people protect themselves against recognizing aspects of their personalities that they would find unacceptable by developing the *opposite* behavior. A case in point is the crusader against pornographic movies who watches them in the name of denouncing them. He thus camouflages his own illicit sexual impulses. Shakespeare's oft-quoted line "The lady doth protest too much, methinks" fits the concept of reaction formation.

of nursing, severity of weaning, age of toilet training, and other psychoanalytic variables has gradually waned (Kagan, 1979). Moreover, the expected cures from psychoanalysis have proven elusive. By the early 1970s, a new generation of American psychiatrists was turning to psychobiology, considering defects of nature, not nurture, to be the primary factor in mental illness. They claimed that neurochemical factors, not childhood traumas, best explained mental illness, and hence they looked to genes, not bad parenting, as the chief means by which it is transmitted from one generation to another (Reich, 1981).

This recent shift in emphasis away from Freudian thought in no way detracts from the revolutionary significance of Freud's work. Perhaps more than anything else Freud deserves considerable credit for directing attention to the importance of social experience in human development.

Erik Erikson: Psychosocial Stages of Development

Among Freud's major contributions was the stimulus his work gave to other theorists and researchers. One of the most talented and imaginative of these is Erik Erikson (1963, 1968*b*). A neo-Freudian psychoanalyst of Danish extraction, Erikson came to the United States in 1933. While acknowledging Freud's genius and monumental contributions, Erikson moved away from the fatalism implicit in Freudian theory, challenging Freud's notion that the personality is primarily established during the first five to six years of life. Erikson said that the personality continues to develop over the entire life cycle. His is a more optimistic view that emphasizes success, greatness, and the flowering of the human potential (Roazen, 1976).

Erikson's chief concern is with psycho*social* development. In contrast, Freud focused chiefly on psycho*sexual* development. Erikson has formulated eight major stages of development, described in Table 2.2. Each stage poses a unique developmental task and simultaneously confronts individuals with a crisis that they must struggle through. As employed by Erikson (1968*a*: 286), a crisis is not "a threat of catastrophe but a turning point, a crucial period of increased vulnerability and heightened potential."

According to Erikson (1959, 1980), individuals develop a "healthy personality" by mastering "life's outer and inner dangers." Development follows the **epigenetic principle**—"anything that grows has a ground plan, and . . . out of this ground plan the parts arise, each having its time of special ascendancy, until all parts have arisen to form a functioning whole" (1968*b*: 92). Hence, according to Erikson, each part of the personality has a particular time in the life span when it must develop if it is going to develop at all. Should a capacity not be developed on schedule, the rest of development is unfavorably altered. The individual is then hindered in dealing effectively with reality.

As shown in Table 2.2, the individual is confronted in each of Erikson's eight stages with a major crisis that must be successfully resolved if healthy development is to occur. The interaction that takes place between an individual and society during each stage can change the course of personality in either a positive or a negative direction. Let us briefly consider Erikson's stages of psychosocial development.

Erik H. Erikson

Although Erik H. Erikson did not publish his first book until 1950, when he was forty-eight years old, he then became a leading figure in the psychoanalytic study of human growth and development. His writings over the past three decades have drawn upon field work with the Oglala Sioux of South Dakota and the salmon-fishing Yurok of northern California, and the clinical treatment of disturbed children and adolescents. Erikson has also written biographies of Martin Luther and Mohandas Gandhi.

Courtesy of W. W. Norton and Company, Inc.

- *Trust versus mistrust* (birth to one year). Basic to Erikson's concept of development is the element of trust. Human life is a social endeavor. It involves linkages and interactions among people. Whether children come to trust or mistrust themselves and other people depends on their early experiences. Infants whose needs are met and who are cuddled, fondled, and shown genuine affection evolve a sense of the world as a safe and dependable place. In contrast, when child care is chaotic, unpredictable, and rejecting, children approach the world with fear and suspicion. These basic attitudes are not resolved in a once-

Table 2.2 Erikson's Eight Stages of Development

Developmental Stage	Psychosocial Crisis	Predominant Social Setting	Favorable Outcome
1. Infancy	Basic trust vs. mistrust	Family	The child develops trust in itself, its parents, and the world.
2. Early childhood	Autonomy vs. shame, doubt	Family	The child develops a sense of self-control without loss of self-esteem.
3. Fourth to fifth year	Initiative vs. guilt	Family	The child learns to acquire direction and purpose in activities.
4. Sixth year to onset of puberty	Industry vs. inferiority	Neighborhood; school	The child acquires a sense of mastery and competence.
5. Adolescence	Identity vs. role confusion	Peer groups and outgroups	The individual develops an *ego identity*—a coherent sense of self.
6. Young adulthood	Intimacy vs. isolation	Partners in friendship and sex	The individual develops the capacity to work toward a specific career and to involve himself or herself in an extended intimate relationship.
7. Adulthood	Generativity vs. stagnation	New family; work	The individual becomes concerned with others beyond the immediate family, with future generations, and with society.
8. Old age	Integrity vs. despair	Retirement and impending death	The individual acquires a sense of satisfaction in looking back upon his or her life.

and-for-all fashion. They arise again at each successive level of development (Elkind, 1970).

- *Autonomy versus shame and doubt* (two to three years). As children begin to crawl, walk, climb, and explore, a new conflict confronts them: whether or not to assert their wills. When parents are patient, cooperative, and encouraging, children acquire a sense of independence and competence. In contrast, when children are not allowed such freedom and are overprotected, they develop an excessive sense of shame and doubt.
- *Initiative versus guilt* (four to five years). During this stage the repertoire of motor and mental abilities that are open to children greatly expands. Parents who give their children freedom in running, sliding, bike riding, skating, and roughhousing are allowing them to develop initiative. Parents who curtail this freedom are giving children a sense of themselves as nuisances and inept intruders in an adult world. Rather than actively and confidently shaping their own behaviors, such children become passive recipients of whatever the environment brings.

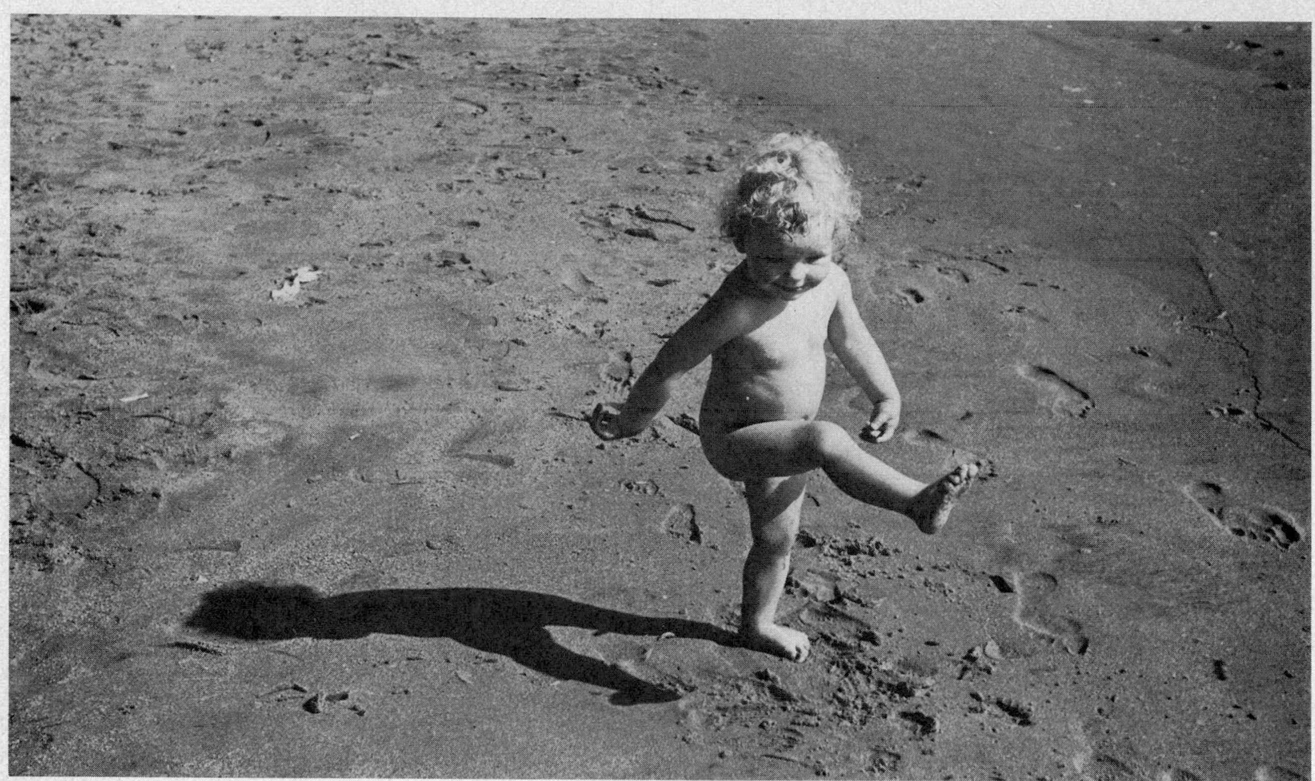

Autonomy Versus Shame and Doubt
Erikson suggests that as children begin to walk and climb, they gain a sense of independence and competence. When children are not permitted the freedom to explore, they become inhibited and develop a sense of shame and doubt.
Jean-Claude Lejeune

- *Industry versus inferiority* (six to eleven years). During the elementary-school years a child becomes concerned with how things work and how they are made. As children move into the world of school, they gain a sense of industry by winning recognition for their achievements. But they may instead acquire a sense of inadequacy and inferiority. Parents and teachers who support, reward, and praise children are encouraging industry. Those who rebuff, deride, or ignore children's efforts are strengthening feelings of inferiority.

- *Identity versus role confusion* (twelve to eighteen years). As children enter adolescence, they confront a "physiological revolution." Simultaneously they must answer the question "Who am I?" They try on many new roles as they grope with romantic involvement, vocational choice, and adult statuses. In the process they must develop an integrated and coherent sense of self. When the adolescent fails to develop a "centered" identity, he or she becomes trapped in either role confusion or a "negative identity." The identities and roles of "delinquent" and "speed freak" are illustrations of this.

- *Intimacy versus isolation* (young adulthood). As Erikson views intimacy, it is the capacity to reach out and make contact with other people—to fuse one's own identity with that of others. Intimacy finds expression in deep friendships. Central to intimacy is the ability to share with and care about another person without fear of losing oneself in the process (Elkind, 1970). Close involvement, however, may also result in rejection. Consequently, some individuals opt for relationships of a shallow sort. Their lives are characterized by withdrawal and isolation.

- *Generativity versus stagnation* (middle adulthood). By generativity, Erikson means a reaching out beyond one's own immediate concerns to embrace the welfare of society and of future generations. Generativity entails selflessness. In contrast, stagnation is a condition in which individuals are preoccupied with their material possessions or physical well-being. Scrooge in Dickens's *A Christmas Carol,* a self-centered, embittered individual, exemplifies stagnation (Elkind, 1970).
- *Integrity versus despair* (old age). As individuals approach the end of life, they tend to take stock of the years that have gone before. Some feel a sense of satisfaction with their accomplishments. Others experience despair—"the feeling that the time is now short, too short for the attempt to start another life and to try out alternate roads to integrity" (Erikson, 1963: 269).

Erikson's work provides a welcome balance to traditional Freudian theory. Although not neglecting the powerful effects of childhood experience, Erikson draws our attention to the continual process of personality development that takes place *throughout* the life span. He offers a more optimistic view than does Freud. Whereas Freud was primarily concerned with pathological outcomes, Erikson holds open the prospect of healthy and positive resolutions of our identity crises.

BEHAVIORAL THEORY

Psychoanalytic theory focuses on those mental and emotional processes that shape the human personality. The data it uses come largely from the self-observations provided by *introspection.* **Behavioral theory** stands in sharp contrast to this approach. As its name suggests, behavioral theory is concerned with the behavior of people—what they actually do and say. Behavioral psychologists believe that if psychology is to be a science, its data must be directly observable and measurable.

Behaviorists are especially interested in how people *learn* to behave in particular ways, and hence the approach is also termed *learning theory.* They deem learning to be a process whereby individuals, as a result of their experience, establish an association or linkage between two events. For example, you very likely have formed an association between a hot stove and a painful, burning sensation, between reading your textbook and passing a course, and between sulking and upsetting your friends. The process by which this occurs is called **conditioning.**

Few psychologists have contributed more to behavioral theory than has B. F. Skinner. During the 1950s and 1960s no American psychologist enjoyed greater prominence or commanded greater influence than did Skinner. Over the past forty years students enrolled in college psychology courses have become familiar with Skinner's famous experimental chamber, which is used for many studies of animal behavior. The apparatus, commonly called a Skinner box, provides a soundproof enclosure that isolates the subject—a pigeon, rat, or mouse—from stray stimuli. When the subject pecks a key or presses a lever in an accidental or exploratory manner, a pellet of food is released. Sooner or later the animal reactivates the food-delivery mechanism in the course of random activity. As the process is repeated over time, the animal reaches the point where it pecks the key or presses the lever so as to receive the reward.

Throughout his career Skinner has been especially concerned with the control of behavior. Like other behaviorists, Skinner attempts to divide behavior into units called **responses** and the environment into units called **stimuli.** His experimental work with pigeons illustrates his approach. He carefully watches a hungry pigeon strut about. When the bird makes a slight clockwise turn, Skinner instantly rewards it with a food pellet—a stimulus. Again the bird struts about, and when it makes another clockwise turn, Skinner repeats the procedure. Skinner finds that he can get a pigeon to make a full circle in two to three minutes. This was the response he was aiming at.

Next Skinner rewards the bird only when it moves in the opposite direction. Then he waits until it makes a clockwise circle followed by a counterclockwise circle. In ten to fifteen minutes Skinner is able to condition the pigeon to do a perfect figure eight. Among other things, Skinner has taught pigeons to dance with each other and to play Ping-Pong

The process whereby one event strengthens the probability of another event's occurring is termed **reinforcement.** Skinner maintains that much of life is structured by arranging reinforcing consequences, or "payoffs." Businesses reward appropriate work behavior by their employees with wages. A man dating a woman whom he likes tries to ensure that she will

B. F. Skinner

As a strict behaviorist, B. F. Skinner has not been concerned with what goes on inside the organism. Instead he stresses the part that learning processes play in an organism's acquisition of given behaviors.

Ken Heyman

go out with him again by reinforcing her with a "good time." And a doctor must make certain that a patient feels benefited by an office visit in order to induce the patient to return for further treatment. But reinforcement may also result in maladaptive behavior, including learned helplessness (see the boxed insert on page 43).

Many of the principles of learning have found a

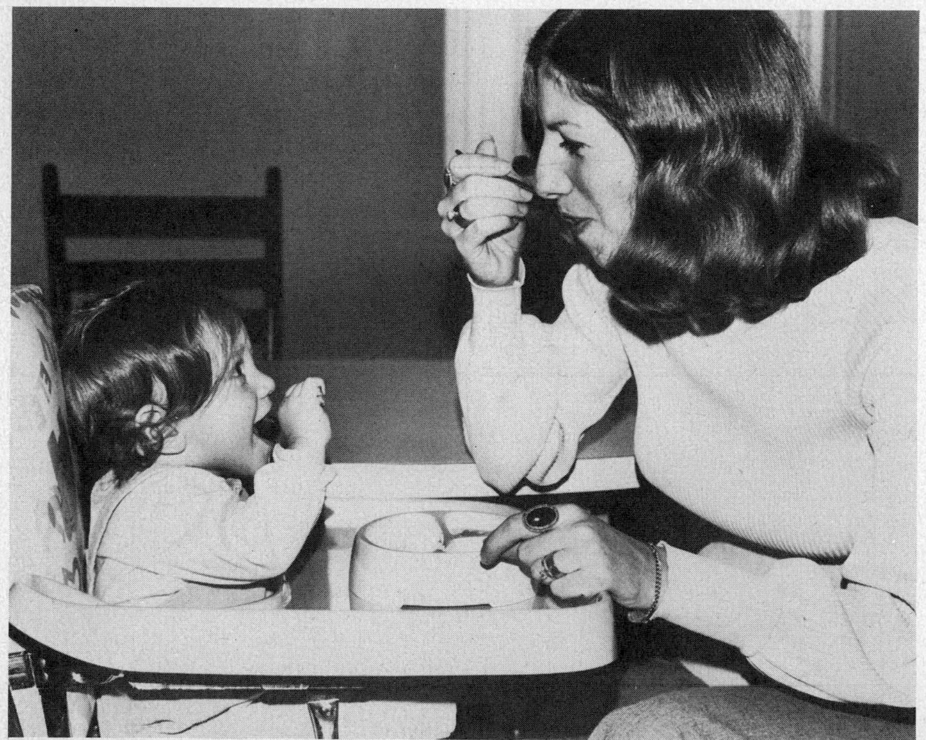

Reciprocal Reinforcement

Much of human interaction is characterized by reciprocal reinforcement. Here the mother and infant are each reinforcing the other. The infant's behavior is reinforced by food and her mother's attention. The mother's behavior is reinforced by her child's smiles and coos.

Patrick Reddy

LEARNED HELPLESSNESS

Life requires that organisms adjust themselves to their environmental circumstances. Toward this end, they commonly learn various coping mechanisms. Yet research conducted over the past ten years by Martin E. P. Seligman and his colleagues (Seligman, 1975, 1978; Abramson, Seligman, and Teasdale, 1978) reveals that some organisms acquire a learned helplessness that impairs their adaptation. **Learned helplessness** refers to a generalized expectancy that events are independent of one's own responses. Consequently, individuals characterized by learned helplessness believe that their coping behaviors are futile.

Seligman stumbled upon learned helplessness while experimenting with dogs that he had traumatically shocked to test a learning theory (Overmier and Seligman, 1967; Seligman and Maier, 1967). In the experiment, Seligman and his colleagues had strapped the dogs in a harness and given them electric shocks. Later, they placed the dogs in a two-compartment shuttlebox where the dogs were expected to learn that they could escape shock by jumping across the barrier separating the compartments.

Dogs that had not previously been exposed to shock had little difficulty learning the exercise. But not so with the dogs that had experienced shock under inescapable conditions (the harness). They would initially run about the compartment and howl. Very soon, however, they would settle down and passively endure the shock. Seligman concluded that the experience in the harness had taught the dogs that their responses were of no consequence, hence they simply gave up. For obvious reasons, Seligman's research has been severely criticized as involving cruelty to animals.

Donald Hiroto (1974) undertook a modified version of the experiment with a sample of college students. He assigned the students to one of three groups. The first group heard loud noise that they could terminate by pushing a button four times. The second group heard the noise but had no way to avoid it. The third group, a control group, did not receive any noise. In the next phase of the experiment, all groups were tested with a "noise box." The subjects could turn off the sound merely by moving a lever from one side of the box to the other. Although the first and third groups quickly learned to shut the noise off, the second group typically listened passively to the noise. Apparently they had learned that they were helpless.

Seligman noted that the behaviors that characterize learned helplessness in many ways parallel the symptoms of depressive disorders. Many depressed individuals are characterized by a seeming paralysis of will, a feeling that their responses are inadequate or doomed to failure. Critics have pointed out that there are many varieties of psychological depression, each of which is characterized by somewhat different symptoms (Depue and Monroe, 1978). Seligman (1978) has agreed with some of these criticisms and has since limited his interpretation to a smaller subclass of depressive disorders.

Mastery-Oriented Students

Mastery-oriented children confront difficulty by searching for new solutions to their problems. Schools can assist children in cultivating mastery attitudes, as this Head Start teacher is doing with a four-year-old.
Elizabeth Crews

Carol S. Dweck and her associates (Dweck, 1975; Diener and Dweck, 1980; Goetz and Dweck, 1980) find that many schoolchildren who give up when they confront failure in academic settings are also victims of learned helplessness. A belief that their learning outcomes are uncontrollable leads the children to become apathetic. They do tend to ponder the cause of their lack of success, but since they attribute their failure to factors beyond their control, they spend little time searching for ways to overcome failure. In contrast, mastery-oriented pupils confront failure by looking for new solutions to their problems. Further, "helpless" students tend to attribute their failure to inadequate ability rather than to inadequate effort. When these children are taught to attribute their failure to lack of motivation, rather than lack of ability, they show striking improvements in their coping responses.

use in what recently has come to be called **behavior modification.** The approach applies the results of learning theory and experimental psychology to the problem of altering maladaptive behavior. According to behaviorists, pathological behavior is acquired just as normal behavior is acquired—through the process of learning. They claim that the simplest technique for eliminating an unwanted behavior is usually to stop reinforcing it. But behavior modification may also entail more deliberate intervention in the form of reward or punishment. This procedure is being used effectively for a variety of purposes (Wolpe, 1973, 1981; Kalish, 1981). It has helped people overcome fear of high places, of taking tests, of sexual inadequacy, of closed-in spaces, and of speaking before an audience.

HUMANISTIC THEORY

To be what we are, and to become what we are capable of becoming, is the only end of life.

—ROBERT LOUIS STEVENSON

In the past thirty years or so a "third-force" psychology has arisen in reaction to the two earlier and established traditions of psychoanalysis and behaviorism. Commonly termed **humanistic psychology,** it stresses the uniqueness of the human condition. Human beings, it maintains, are different from all other organisms in that they actively intervene in the course of events to control their destinies and shape the world around them. Humanistic psychologists, such as Abraham Maslow (1968, 1970) and Carl R. Rogers (1970), share a common concern with maximizing the human potential for self-direction and freedom of choice. As such they take a **holistic approach,** one that views the human condition in its totality and each person as more than a collection of physical, social, and psychological components.

Third-force psychologists criticize psychoanalytic approaches for portraying people as locked by unconscious instincts and irrational forces into a lifetime that is programmed by childhood events. And they disagree with behaviorist theories that depict people as robots who are mechanically programmed by the conditioning force of external stimuli. Humanistic psychologists argue that both psychoanalysts and behaviorists are mistaken in characterizing people as *passive* beings who are acted upon by forces outside their control. In contrast, Maslow and Rogers portray people as capable of *actively* fashioning their personalities and lives with deliberation and insight.

Psychoanalytic psychologists are primarily concerned with the unconscious, whereas behaviorist psychologists label the study of consciousness as "mysticism." Humanistic psychologists, however, place human *consciousness* at the center of the human drama. They insist that it is consciousness—the ability to use symbols and to think in abstract terms—that differentiates human beings from other animals.

One of the key concepts advanced by Maslow is the **hierarchy of needs,** depicted in Figure 2.1. Maslow felt that human beings have certain basic needs that they must meet before they can go on to fulfill other needs. At the bottom of Maslow's pyramid are fundamental requirements to satisfy physiological needs (including food, water, and sex) and safety needs. Next Maslow identified a set of psychological needs centering on belongingness (love) needs and esteem needs. Finally, at the top of the pyramid, he placed the need to realize one's unique potential to the fullest, what he termed **self-actualization.**

To Maslow, such people as Abraham Lincoln, Albert Einstein, Walt Whitman, Jane Addams, and Eleanor Roosevelt are good examples of self-actualizers. From their lives he constructed what he believed to be a composite picture of self-actualized persons (1970):

- They have a firm perception of reality.
- They accept themselves, others, and the world for what they are.
- They evidence considerable spontaneity in thought and behavior.
- They are problem-centered rather than self-centered.
- They have an air of detachment and a need for privacy.
- They are autonomous and independent.
- They resist mechanical and stereotyped social behaviors, although they are not deliberately and flamboyantly unconventional.
- They are sympathetic to the condition of other human beings and seek to promote the common welfare.

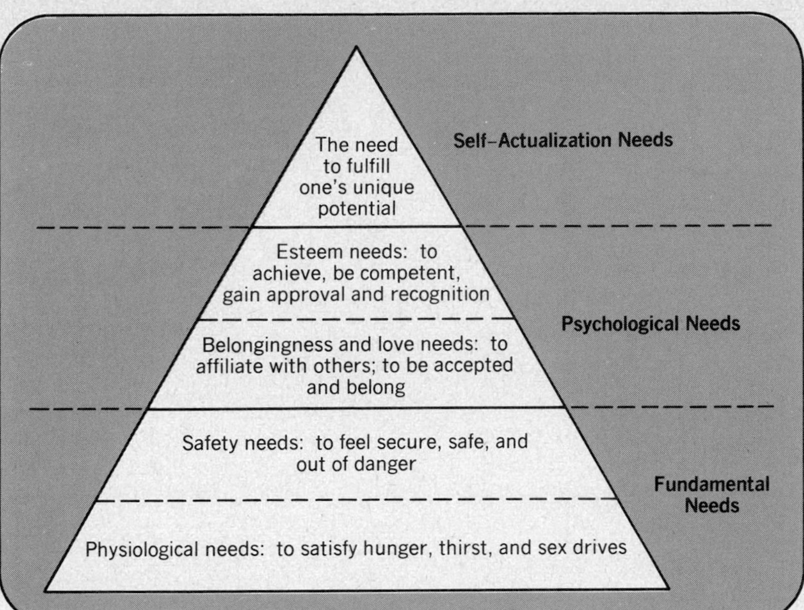

Figure 2.1 Maslow's Hierarchy of Human Needs

According to the humanistic psychologist Abraham Maslow, fundamental needs must be satisfied before an individual is free to progress to psychological needs, and these in turn must be met before the person can realize self-actualization needs.

- They establish deep and meaningful relationships with a few people rather than superficial bonds with a great many people.
- They have a democratic world perspective.
- They transcend their environment rather than merely cope with it.
- They have a considerable fund of creativeness.
- They are susceptible to **peak experiences** marked by rapturous feelings of excitement, insight, and happiness.

Maslow and other humanistic psychologists believe that scientific inquiry should be directed toward helping people achieve freedom, hope, self-fulfillment, and strong self-identities. Maslow (1955: 2) was frank about his goals, for he placed himself in a "tradition that considers the humanistic task of psychology to be that of constructing a scientific system of values to help men live the good life." As such, humanistic psychology is less a research-oriented approach for studying human development than a program of ideals about what psychology should study. Although much skepticism prevails among "hard-headed" and "tough-minded" researchers toward humanistic psychology, it is a young, vital, and growing approach.

Over the past decade or so, humanistic psychology has had a substantial impact on educational thinking and practice. A basic humanistic principle of learning is that information will be acquired and used by students only to the degree to which they have discovered the personal meaning of the information. Don E. Hamachek (1977: 156) points out:

> Humanistic approaches to teaching and learning keep in mind that students bring their total selves to class. They bring heads that think and feel. They bring values that help them to selectively filter what they see and hear, and they bring attitudinal sets and learning styles that render each student unique and different from all the rest. Humanistic teachers do not only *start out* with the idea that students are different, but they recognize that students may still be different at the *end* of an academic experience.

Humanists favor student-centered education, an approach that found expression in the open classroom movement of the 1970s. They believe that students should play an active role in making decisions about what is to be learned and when it is to be studied. Viewed from this perspective, students should select their own directions, formulate their own problems, discover their own learning resources, and live with the consequences of their choices. Humanists conceive of teachers chiefly as facilitators. For instance, Carl R. Rogers (1977) questions whether anyone can

Open Classrooms

Humanistic educators favor approaches to learning that stress individual differences and the informal structuring of the schooling process—like the open classroom.

Bohdan Hrynewych/Stock, Boston

"teach" anyone else anything worthwhile; he says that *real* learning is self-initiated. Humanist teachers regard themselves as flexible resources to be used by students and as providers of a wide range of learning materials.

COGNITIVE THEORY

Like humanistic theory, **cognitive theory** takes issue with a number of behaviorist tenets. In its early formulations, behaviorism regarded human life as if it were a "black box": its proponents viewed input or stimuli as entering the "box" at one end and coming out the other end as output or responses. But over the past twenty years psychologists have become increasingly interested in what goes on inside the "box." They term these internal factors **cognition**—the process of knowing. Cognition encompasses such phenomena as sensation, perception, imagery, retention, recall, problem solving, reasoning, and thinking. More specifically, it entails how organisms receive raw sensory information and transform, elaborate, store, recover, and use this information (Neisser, 1967). The initial impetus to the study of cognition in the United States came from the work of a Swiss developmental psychologist, Jean Piaget (1896–1980).

Jean Piaget: Cognitive Stages in Development

Intelligence is an adaptation. . . . Life is a continuous creation of increasingly complex forms and a progressive balancing of these forms with the environment.

—JEAN PIAGET
The Origins of Intelligence in Children, 1952

Like Freud, Piaget has come to be recognized as a giant of twentieth-century psychology. Anyone who studies Freud and Piaget will never again see children in quite the same way. Whereas Freud was primarily concerned with *personality development,* Piaget concentrated on changes that occur in the child's *mode of thought.* Central to Piaget's work are the **cognitive stages in development**—sequential periods in the growth or maturing of an individual's ability to think—to gain knowledge and awareness of one's self and the environment.

Jean Piaget
Jean Piaget (pictured in 1968) contributed much to our understanding of cognitive development in children. It has been said that Freud discovered the unconscious and Piaget discovered the conscious.
Yves de Braine/Black Star

Adjustment as Process. When Piaget began to work with children in the early 1920s, little was known about the process by which thinking develops. To the extent that they considered the matter at all, most psychologists assumed that children reason in essentially the same way as adults. Piaget soon challenged this view. He insisted that the thought of infants and children is not a miniature version of adult thought. It is qualitatively distinctive and unique. As children "grow up," the form of their thought changes. Consequently, when children say that the sun follows them about when they go for a walk or that dreams come through the window, they are not being illogical. Rather, they are operating from a different mental framework than adults do.

Piaget depicted children as engaged in a continual interaction with their environment. They act upon, transform, and modify the world in which they live. In turn they are shaped and altered by the consequences of their own actions. New experiences interact with an existing structure or mode of thought, thereby altering this structure and making it more adequate. This modified structure in turn influences the person's new perceptions. These new perceptions are then incorporated into a more complex structure. In this fashion, experience modifies structure and structure modifies experience. Hence Piaget viewed the individual and the environment as engaged in continuing interaction. This leads to new perceptions of the world and new organizations of knowledge (Cross, 1976).

Basically, Piaget saw development as adaptation. Beginning with the simple reflexes they have at birth, children gradually modify their repertoire of behaviors to meet environmental demands. By interacting with their environment during play and other activities, children construct a series of schemes—concepts or models—for coping with their world. **Schemes** is the term Piaget used for cognitive structures that peo-

The Piagetian Processes of Assimilation and Accommodation

In Piaget's view, this baby first tries to obtain the toy by using a familiar grasping scheme (assimilation) and then alters it with new knowledge (accommodation) to get the toy through the bars.

George S. Zimbel/Monkmeyer Press

ple evolve for dealing with specific kinds of situations in their environment. Thus, as portrayed by Piaget, children's thoughts reflect not so much the bits of information that they acquire but the scheme or mental framework by which they interpret information from the environment.

As Piaget viewed adaptation, it involves two processes: assimilation and accommodation. **Assimilation** is the process of taking in new information and interpreting it in such a manner that the information conforms to a currently held model of the world. Piaget said that children typically stretch a scheme as far as possible to fit new observations. But life periodically confronts them with the inescapable fact that some of their observations simply do not fit their current schemes. Then disequilibrium or imbalance occurs. As a result children are compelled to reorganize their view of the world in accordance with new experience. In effect, they are required to invent increasingly better schemes or theories about the world as they grow up. **Accommodation** is the process of changing a scheme to make it a better match to the world of reality. Assimilation, then, is the fitting of new experiences to old ones; accommodation is the fitting of old experiences to new ones.

The result of balance between the processes of assimilation and accommodation is **equilibrium.** When equilibrium exists, assimilation again occurs in terms of the new model that the child arrived at through accommodation. Thus, as viewed by Piaget, cognitive development is marked by alternating states of equilibrium and disequilibrium. Each stage consists of particular sets of schemes that are in a relative stage of equilibrium at some point in a child's development.

In studying this process, Piaget and other researchers asked children whether or not they ever had a bad dream. One four-year-old said that she had dreamed about a giant and explained, "Yes, I was scared, my tummy was shaking and I cried and told my mommy about the giant." When asked, "Was it a real giant or was it just pretend?" she responded, "It was really there but it left when I woke up. I saw its footprint on the floor" (Kohlberg and Gilligan, 1971: 1057).

According to Piaget, this child's response is not to be dismissed as the product of wild imagination. Viewed from the perspective of her current scheme, the happenings in dreams are real. As the child matures, she will have new experiences that will cause her to question the scheme. She may observe, for instance, that a "footprint" is not in fact on the floor. This assimilation of new information will result in disequilibrium. Through accommodation, she will then change her scheme to make it a better fit with reality. She will recognize that dreams are not real events. She will then formulate a new scheme that will establish a new equilibrium. In this new scheme, a child her age will typically depict dreams as imaginary happenings. She will still believe, however, that her dreams can be seen by other people.

The process of accommodation continues through additional steps of the same sort. Soon after realizing that dreams are not real, the child comes to recognize that they cannot be seen by others. In the next step the child conceives of dreams as internal, but nevertheless material, events. Finally, somewhere between six and eight years of age, the child becomes aware that dreams are thoughts that take place within her mind.

Characteristics of Piaget's Cognitive Stages. Piaget distinguished four stages in the development of cognition or intelligence (these stages will be treated in greater detail in later chapters). Although teaching and experience can speed up or slow down development, he believed that neither can change the basic order of the stages (Piaget, 1970).

- *Sensorimotor stage* (birth to two years). During this period, infants are busy discovering the relationships between sensations and motor behavior. They learn, for instance, that their hands are part of themselves, whereas a ball is not. They learn how far they need to reach in order to grasp a ball. Perhaps the main feature of this stage is the child's mastery of the *principle of object permanence.* Piaget observed that when a baby of four or five months is playing with a ball and the ball rolls out of sight behind another toy, the child does not look for it even though it remains within reach. Piaget contended that this is because infants do not realize that objects have an independent existence. This explains a baby's delight in playing peek-a-boo. Around the age of eight months, the child grasps the fact of object constancy and will search for toys that disappear from view (Elkind, 1968*b*). Hence, during the sensorimotor stage, infants become able to distinguish between various objects and experiences and to generalize about them. This ability lays the groundwork for later intellectual and emotional development.
- *Preoperational stage* (two to seven years). A key part of the preoperational stage is the child's developing capacity to employ *symbols,* particularly language. Symbols enable people to deal with things in another time and place. Because of symbols, children are no longer limited to the stimuli that are immediately present here and now. Children use symbols to portray the external world internally—for instance, to talk about a ball and form a mental image of it. They do not have this capacity earlier. In the sensorimotor stage, children "know" about a ball in that they can roll it, throw it, or grasp it, but they cannot conceive of a ball as an entity apart from these activities. Now they learn the word "ball" and use it more or less appropriately to refer to round objects (Gardner, 1979).

  Egocentrism is another characteristic of the preoperational stage. By this term Piaget does not mean that the child is self-serving or selfish. Rather, children four and five years of age consider their own point of view to be the only possible one. They are not yet capable of putting themselves in another's place. They are unaware that the other person has a point of view. A five-year-old who is asked why it snows will answer by saying, "So children can play in it."
- *Stage of concrete operations* (seven to eleven years). This is the beginning of rational activity in children. They come to master various logical operations, including arithmetic, class and set relationships, measurement, and conceptions of hierarchical structures. Probably the aspect of this stage that has been most thoroughly investigated is the child's growing ability to "conserve" mass, weight, number, length, area, and volume. Before this stage, for instance, children do not appreciate that a ball of clay can change to a sausage shape and still remain the same in amount.

  Further, before the stage of concrete operations, children cannot understand that when water is poured out of a full glass into a wider glass that the water fills only halfway, the amount of water remains unchanged. Instead, children "concentrate" on only one aspect of reality at a time. They see that the second glass is half empty and conclude that there is less water in it. In the stage of concrete operations, children come to understand that the quantity of water remains the same (see Figure 2.2). Piaget refers to this ability as the *conservation of quantity.* This ability is usually achieved between six and eight years of age.
- *Stage of formal operations* (eleven years and older). In stage three, the child's thought remained fixed upon the visible evidence and concrete properties of objects and events. Now children acquire a greater ability to deal with abstractions. The ad-

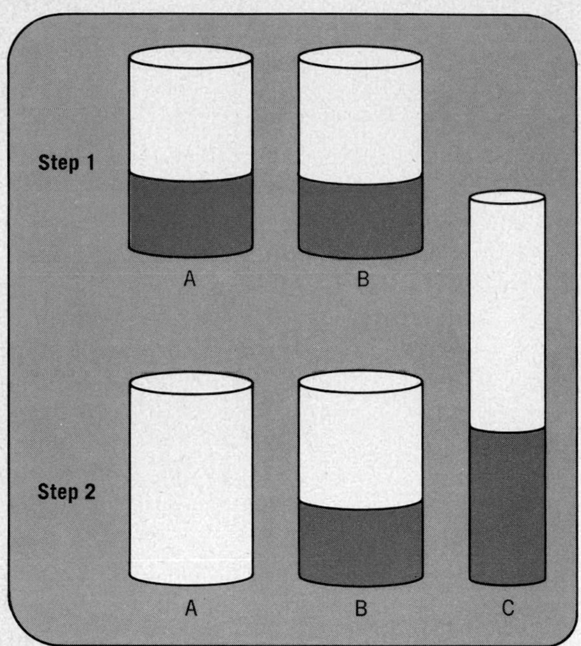

Figure 2.2 The Conservation of Quantity

If a child of about five or six is shown two identical glasses, A and B, which are equally full of liquid, the child will acknowledge that the glasses have the "same to drink." If the liquid from glass A is poured into the taller and narrower glass C, the liquid reaches a higher level. The child is then asked whether there is the same amount to drink in the two differently shaped glasses B and C. Most children younger than six respond that C, the tall, narrow glass, has more liquid. Since the preoperational children "center" on height and ignore width, they cannot deal with this transformation. In the next stage, that of concrete operations, the child comes to recognize that the amount of liquid is the same, regardless of differences in the shapes of the containers. Piaget referred to this ability as "the conservation of quantity," an ability that is usually achieved between six and eight years of age.

olescent can engage in hypothetical reasoning based on logic. When younger children are confronted with the problem, "If coal is white, snow is ______," they insist that coal is black. Adolescents, however, respond that snow is black (Elkind, 1968*a*). In other words, the adolescent acquires the capacity for adult thinking.

In the stage of formal operations, young people become capable of abstract thought with respect to a ball. In addition to anticipating what will happen to a ball under various conditions, they now can discuss it in scientific terms and test hypotheses concerning it. They can explain why it is that a billiard ball shot against a surface at one angle will rebound at a particular complementary angle. And they can discuss Newtonian principles about the behavior of spherical objects (Gardner, 1979).

Appraisal of Piaget's Work. Piaget's discoveries were largely ignored by American scientists until about 1960. Today, however, the study of cognitive factors in development is of central interest to American psychologists. For the most part, psychologists credit Piaget with drawing their attention to the possibility that an unsuspected order may underlie some aspects of children's intellectual development (Egan, 1980). Nonetheless, a number of early American followers of Piaget have become disenchanted with the Piagetian model. One of these is John H. Flavell (1978, 1982). Flavell believes that human cognitive growth is too varied in developmental mechanisms, routes, and rates to be accurately portrayed by an inflexible stage theory.

More particularly, Piaget underestimated the operational thinking capabilities of children from two to seven years of age (Brainerd, 1978, 1979). Apparently, their capabilities depend on the nature or content of the task presented to them, for by altering the components of a cognitive task, it is often possible to elicit from them concrete operational thought and, at times, even formal operational thought. We must therefore conclude that much thinking is specific to the task at hand and that a good many operational capabilities seem to be *available* to five- and six-year-old youngsters. Further, research on other cultures has revealed both striking similarities and marked differences in the performance of children on various cognitive tasks. Certain aspects of cognitive development among children in these cultures seem to conflict with particular assumptions of Piagetian theory (Ashton, 1975; Dasen, 1977).

Yet it is important to recognize that we would not know as much as we do about children's intellectual

Table 2.3 Developmental Stages of Freud, Erikson, and Piaget

Age Period	Freud	Erikson	Piaget
Birth to 18 months	Oral stage	Trust vs. mistrust	Sensorimotor stage (birth to two years)
18 months to year 3	Anal stage	Autonomy vs. shame and doubt	Preoperational stage (symbolic)
Years 3 to 7	Phallic stage	Initiative vs. guilt	Preoperational stage (intuition, representational)
Years 7 to 12	Latency stage	Industry vs. inferiority	Stage of concrete operations
Years 12 to 18	Genital stage	Identity vs. role confusion	Stage of formal thought
Young adulthood		Intimacy vs. isolation	
Middle adulthood		Generativity vs. stagnation	
Old age		Integrity vs. despair	

development without the monumental contributions of Piaget. In fact, Piaget's greatest contribution may not have been his theory. His emphasis on the active nature of the child has had a powerful impact on psychological theory and research. And his work directed psychologists to a whole set of fascinating tasks and questions. Although Piaget's explanations may in some instances be wrong, his work got psychologists interested enough to do the research necessary for better understanding children's cognitive development.

Table 2.3 summarizes the developmental stages of Freud, Erikson, and Piaget.

Cognitive Learning

Piaget's work gave a major impetus to cognitive psychology. Increasingly, psychologists are directing their attention to the part played by inner, mental activity in human behavior. They are finding, for instance, that mental schemes—variously termed "scripts" or "frames"—function as selective mechanisms that influence the information that individuals attend to, how they structure it, how much importance they attach to it, and what they then do with it (Markus, 1977; Vander Zanden, 1984). They are also finding that learning consists of much more than merely bringing two events together (Rescorla, 1967). Individuals are not simply acted upon by external stimuli. They actively evaluate different stimuli and devise their actions accordingly.

Classic behaviorist theory also fails to explain many changes in our behavior that result from interaction with people in a social context. Indeed, if we learned solely by direct experience—by the reward or punishment of our actions—most of us would not survive to adulthood. If, for example, we depended on direct experience to learn how to cross the street, most of us would already be traffic fatalities. Similarly, it is doubtful that we could develop skill in playing baseball, driving a car, solving mathematical problems, carrying out chemistry experiments, cooking meals, or even brushing our teeth if we were restricted to learning through direct reinforcement. We can avoid tedious, costly, trial-and-error experimentation by imitating the behavior of socially competent models. By watching other people, we learn new responses without first having had the opportunity to make the responses ourselves. This process is termed **cognitive learning.** (It is also termed *observational learning, social learning,* and *modeling.*) The approach is represented in the work of theorists such as Albert Bandura (1971*a*, 1971*b*, 1973, 1977), Walter Mischel (1971, 1973), and Ted L. Rosenthal and Barry J. Zimmerman (1978).

Cognitive learning theorists say that our capacity to use symbols affords us a powerful means for comprehending and dealing with our environment. Verbal and imagined symbols allow us to represent events, to analyze our conscious experience, to communicate with others, to plan, to create, to imagine, and to engage in foresightful action. Symbols are the foun-

Cognitive Learning
Through instruction we can learn a good many behaviors, such as how to cross a street safely. If we had to learn this behavior through trial-and-error procedures, most of us would be traffic fatalities.
Alan Carey/The Image Works

dation of reflective thought and enable us to solve problems without first having to enact all the various solutions (Bandura, 1977). Indeed, stimuli and reinforcements are said to exert little impact on our behavior unless they are first represented mentally by us (Rosenthal and Zimmerman, 1978).

Cognitive learning theorists also assign a central role to self-regulatory processes. They insist that we are neither mechanically buffeted about by external influences nor irrationally driven by preprogrammed internal forces. Instead, they depict us as selecting, organizing, and transforming the stimuli that impinge on us. Through mental or cognitive processes, we come to exercise a measure of control over our own behavior. Cognitive learning theorists agree with the behaviorists that direct experience makes a substantial contribution to human learning. But they stress that observational learning, especially as mediated by human thought, plays an equally important part (Bandura, 1977; Rosenthal and Zimmerman, 1978).

ETHOLOGICAL THEORY

Between 1915 and 1965 behavioral theory dominated psychology, leading psychologists to view human behavior primarily in terms of learned responses to incoming stimuli. Behavioral theory focused on environmental influences. Recently, however, interest has grown in the work of a group of European psychologists and zoologists who term their discipline **ethology**—the study of the behavior patterns of organisms from a biological point of view. Notable ethologists include Konrad Lorenz, Nikolaas Tinbergen, and Karl von Frisch.

Natural Selection and Releasing Stimuli

Ethologists rely heavily on the evolutionary theory of Charles Darwin. According to Darwin, evolution consists of a number of basic processes known as **natural selection.** Natural selection comes about because individuals of a species differ from one another. Those individuals who are best adapted to their environment stand a better chance of surviving and reproducing than do individuals who are not so well adapted. Hence later generations resemble their better-adapted ancestors. Thus, over the course of many generations a species changes. In sum, evolution operates to promote the environmental adaptation of organisms.

Ethologists say that evolution applies not only to anatomy and physiology but also to predispositions for certain types of behavior. Organisms are said to be *genetically prepared* for some responses. For instance, as will be discussed in Chapter 8, ethologists hold that human babies are biologically preadapted with behavior systems like crying, smiles, and coos that elicit caring by adults. Similarly, babies' being "cute"—with large heads, small bodies, and distinctive facial features—induce others to want to pick them up and cuddle them. These behaviors and features are termed by ethologists **releasing stimuli.** They function as especially potent activators of parenting.

A number of psychologists, among whom John Bowlby (1969) is perhaps the most prominent, compare the development of strong bonds of attachment between human caretakers and their offspring to the process of **imprinting** encountered among some bird and animal species. Lorenz (1935), the Nobel Prize–winning ethologist, has shown that there is a short period of time early in the lives of goslings and ducklings in which they begin slavishly to follow the first moving object that they see—their mother, a human being, a rubber ball, or whatever. Once this imprinting has occurred, it is irreversible. The object becomes "mother" to the birds, so that thereafter they prefer it to all others and in fact will follow no other. Researchers also report that geese and other domestic birds that form attachments to human beings display subsequent difficulties and sexual inadequacies in relating to birds of their own species (geese, for instance, may make courtship gestures to people).

Konrad Lorenz

Here young ducklings follow the eminent Austrian ethologist rather than their mother. Since he was the first moving object that they saw during the critical imprinting period, they came to prefer him to all other objects.

Thomas McAvoy/Time-Life Picture Agency, © Time, Inc.

Imprinting (Lorenz uses his native German word "*Prägung,*" which literally means "stamping in") is different from other forms of learning in at least two ways. First, imprinting can take place only during a relatively short period of time, termed a **critical period.** (For example, the peak period for the imprinting effect among domestic chickens occurs about seventeen hours after hatching and declines rapidly thereafter.) Second, as already mentioned, imprinting is irreversible; it is highly resistant to change, so that the behavior appears to be innate.

Sensitive Periods

Some developmental psychologists have applied ethological notions to human development. However, many prefer the term **sensitive period** to "critical period," for it implies greater flexibility in the time dimension and greater reversibility in the later structure (Oyama, 1979). According to this concept, during certain times of life particular kinds of experience are believed to affect the development of an organism more than they do at other times (Colombo, 1982).

As discussed in the section on Freud, the notion of sensitive periods occupies a central position in psychoanalytic thought. It was Freud's view that infancy is the crucial period in molding an individual's personality. It was the basis of his famous aphorism "No adult neurosis without an infantile neurosis." Burton L. White (1975), a psychologist at Harvard University, takes a somewhat similar view. He argues that the first two or three years of life are especially important. According to White, the quality of the mothering that a child receives is crucial: "The mother is right on the hook, just where Freud put her" (quoted by Pines, 1971: 97). Further, White (1975: 4) writes, "To some extent, I do believe that it is all over by three."

Theorists who adhere to the view of sensitive periods generally insist that it is almost impossible to make up a deficit in a person's development at some later period. T. G. R. Bower (1974: vii–viii), an authority on perceptual development in infancy, observes:

> I believe that infancy is the critical period in cognitive development—the period when the greatest gains and the greatest losses can occur. Further, the gains and losses that occur here become harder to offset with increasing age.

However, most life-span developmentalists reject the idea that the first five years of a child's life are all-important. Surveying the available evidence, Ann M. Clarke and A. D. B. Clarke (1976: 272) found little research data supporting the notion that either infancy or early childhood constitutes a sensitive period:

> The whole of development is important, not merely the early years. There is as yet no indication that a given stage is clearly more formative than others; in the long-term all may be important.

And (268):

> *It appears that there is virtually no psychosocial adversity to which some children have not been subjected, yet later recovered,* granted a radical change of circumstances. [Italics in original]

More recent research also suggests that the long-term effects of short, traumatic incidents are generally negligible in young children (Douglas, Ross, and Simpson, 1968; Werner and Smith, 1982; Thomas and Chess 1984). And Jerome Kagan comes to a somewhat similar conclusion on the basis of studies that he and his associates conducted in Guatemala (see the boxed insert on page 55). Life apparently offers many individuals a healing capacity, so that they arrive at adulthood without substantial psychological maladjustment. Thus, while all authorities agree that development is influenced by the child's early experiences, considerable debate rages over just how important these experiences are. Chapter 8 returns to the matter of critical periods of considering attachment, sensory deprivation, and maternal deprivation in early childhood.

THEORETICAL CONTROVERSY

> *A clash of doctrines is not a disaster—it is an opportunity.*
>
> —ALFRED NORTH WHITEHEAD

We have considered five major types of theory dealing with human development. Psychoanalytic theories draw our attention to the importance of early experience in the fashioning of personality and to the role of unconscious motivation. Behavioral theories emphasize the part that learning plays in prompting people to act in the ways that they do. Humanistic theories remind us that individuals are capable of intervening in the course of life's events to influence and shape their own beings. Cognitive theories highlight the importance of various mental capabilities and problem-solving skills that arm human beings with a powerful adaptive and coping potential. And ethological theories allow us to bring into focus various biological patterns that predispose and prepare human beings for particular kinds of behavior.

Each theory has its proponents and its critics. Yet the theories are not mutually exclusive. We need not accept one and reject the others. As we pointed out at the beginning of the chapter, theories are simply tools—mental constructs that allow us to visualize (that is, to describe and analyze) something. Any theory limits the viewer's experience, presenting a tunnel perspective. But a good theory also extends the horizon of what is seen, functioning like a pair of binoculars. It provides rules of inference through which new relationships can be discovered and suggestions as to how the scope of a theory can be expanded (Reese and Overton, 1970).

Further, different tasks call for different theories. For instance, behavioral theory helps us to understand why American children typically learn English and Russian children learn Russian. At the same time, ethological theory directs our attention to ways in which the human organism is neurally prewired for certain activities. Hence, in interaction with an appropriate environment, young children typically find that their acquisition of language comes rather "naturally"—a type of *easy learning.* Simultaneously, psychoanalytic theory alerts us to personality differences and to differing child-rearing practices that influence a child's learning to talk. Cognitive theory encourages

JEROME KAGAN ON THE EARLY YEARS

Most Americans—both psychologists and the general public—believe that early experience etches an indelible mark upon the mind. A long intellectual tradition in Western culture has portrayed the adult as locked in a core personality fashioned before the age of six. It is thus hardly surprising that a good many American parents experience considerable anxiety and guilt over the adequacy of their child rearing.

Jerome Kagan, a Harvard University developmental psychologist, challenges the prevailing belief. Since 1971 he and his associates have done research among children in Guatemala. This work has led Kagan to conclude that children are considerably more resilient than we think (Kagan and Klein, 1973; Levitas, 1976).

Among the children Kagan studied is a group in San Marcos, an isolated Indian village on Lake Atitlán. During the first year of life, these infants spend most of their time in the small, dark interiors of windowless huts. Their mothers are busy with domestic chores and rarely speak to their babies or play with them. Since the Indians believe that the outside sun, air, and dust are harmful, children are rarely permitted to crawl on the hut floors or to venture beyond the doorway.

Judged by American standards, the infants appear to be severely retarded. They seem undernourished, listless, apathetic, fearful, dour, and extraordinarily quiet. Indeed, to Kagan the children have a ghostlike quality. Both observations and tests suggest that they are three to twelve months behind American children in acquiring various psychological and cognitive skills. These skills range from the simple ability to pay attention all the way up to the development of meaningful speech.

Nonetheless, Kagan finds that by age eleven the children show no traces of their early "retardation." On tests of perceptual inference, perceptual analysis, recall, and recognition, they perform in a manner comparable to American middle-class children. According to Kagan, they begin to overcome their early retardation when they become mobile at around fifteen months. They leave the dark huts and begin to play with other children, and in the ensuing years they experience challenges that demand and foster intellectual growth and development.

Kagan suggests that a child's experiences can slow down or speed up the emergence of basic abilities by several months or even years. But, he argues, nature will win out in the end. Thus Kagan reaches the highly controversial conclusion that children are biologically preprogrammed with basic mental competencies—an inherent blueprint that equips them with the essentials for perceptual and intellectual functioning. The content of this functioning changes from culture to culture (Kagan and Klein, 1973: 960):

> The San Marcos child knows much less than the American about planes, computers, cars, and the many hundreds of other phenomena that are familar to the Western youngster, and he is a little slower in developing some of the basic cognitive competencies of our species. But neither appreciation of these events nor the earlier cognitive maturation is necessary for a successful journey to adulthood in San Marcos. The American child knows far less about how to make canoes, rope, tortillas, or how to burn an old milpa in preparation for June planting. Each knows what is necessary, each assimilates the cognitive conflicts that are presented to him, and each seems to have the potential to display more talent than his environment demands of him.

Kagan (1973) also points to the findings of Freda Rebelsky, a developmental psychologist who spent several years in eastern Holland, where a stable, middle-class, nuclear family arrangement prevails. She reported that in one region it is a local custom to isolate a child for the first ten months. Children are placed in a room outside the house and tightly bound with no mobiles or toys and minimal human interaction. Like the Guatemalan children, these Dutch children emerge at one year "retarded," but at five years of age they are fully recovered.

Kagan says that his research has implications for America's educational problems. He suggests that the poor test performance of economically impoverished and minority-group children should not be taken as evidence of permanent or irreversible defects in intellectual ability. Although various competencies may lag behind those of middle-class children, Kagan concludes that they eventually appear in lower-class children by age ten or eleven. To class children arbitrarily at age seven as competent or incompetent makes as much sense, Kagan insists, as classifying children as reproductively fertile or sterile depending on whether they have reached physiological puberty by age thirteen.

Easy Learning

When children are exposed to an appropriate environment, they typically acquire language skills with little difficulty. Here a Guatemalan child is engaged in an expressive and voluble conversation.

Nicholas Sapieha/Stock, Boston

us to consider the stages of development and the mental processes that are involved in the acquisition of language. Finally, humanistic theory reminds us that individuals are not passive beings mechanically buffeted about by environmental and biological forces but are themselves creative beings who actively pursue language competence.

Some psychologists attempt to classify developmental theories in terms of two basic categories: a mechanistic world view and an organismic world view (see Table 2.4). The **mechanistic model** represents the universe as a machine composed of elementary particles in motion. All phenomena, no matter how complex, are viewed as ultimately reducible to these fundamental units and their relationships. Each human being is regarded as a physical object, a kind of elaborate machine. Like other parts of the universal machine, the organism is inherently at rest. It is inherently passive, and only responds when an external power source is applied. This is *the reactive organism model.* In keeping with this world view, human development is portrayed as a gradual, uninterrupted, chainlike sequence of events. Indeed, it is questionable if it can be said that a machine "develops." It only changes by some external agent adding, subtracting, or altering the machine's parts (Sameroff and Cavanagh, 1979). Behavioral learning theories fall within the mechanistic tradition.

The **organismic model** focuses not on elementary particles but on the whole. It is the distinctive interrelation between the lower-level components that is seen as imparting to the whole characteristics not found in the components alone. Hence the whole differs in kind from its parts. The human being is seen as an organized configuration. The organism is inherently active. It is the source of its own acts rather than being activated by external forces. This is *the active organism model.* Viewed from this perspective, human development is characterized by discrete, steplike levels or states. Human beings are portrayed as developing by constantly restructuring themselves. The new structures that will be formed are determined by the interaction between the environment and the organism. The stage theories of Freud, Erikson, and Piaget, cognitive learning theory, humanistic theory, and some ethological theories fall within the organismic tradition.

Proponents of mechanistic and of organismic models practice their trades in somewhat different worlds. Even so, in recognition of the many strands associated

Table 2.4 Mechanistic and Organismic Paradigms

Characteristic	Mechanistic Paradigm	Organismic Paradigm
Metaphor	The machine	The organism
Focus	The parts	The whole
Source of motivation	Intrinsically passive	Intrinsically active
Nature of development	Gradual, uninterrupted adding, subtracting, or altering of parts (continuity)	Discrete, steplike levels or states (discontinuity)

with development, most psychologists prefer an **eclectic approach.** This perspective allows them to select and choose from the various theories and models those aspects that provide the best fit for the descriptive and analytical task at hand.

SUMMARY

1. Theory is a tool that allows us to organize a large array of facts so that we can understand them. To understand how nature works is to gain the prospect of securing some control over our destiny.
2. Sigmund Freud postulated that all human beings pass through a series of psychosexual stages: oral, anal, phallic, latency, and genital. Each stage poses a unique conflict that the individual must resolve before passing on to the next stage.
3. Critics complain that Freudian theory is difficult to evaluate because it makes few predictions that can be tested by accepted scientific procedures. Nonetheless, Freud's work is generally regarded as a revolutionary milestone in the history of human thought.
4. Erik Erikson, a theorist in the psychoanalytic tradition, identifies eight psychosocial stages, each of which confronts the individual with a major conflict that must be successfully resolved if healthy development is to occur. Erikson's theory draws our attention to the continual process of personality development that takes place throughout a person's life span.
5. Behavioral theory stands in sharp contrast to psychoanalytic theory. Its proponents believe that if psychology is to be a science it must not rely on introspection but must look to data that are directly observable and measurable.
6. Behaviorists are especially interested in how people learn to behave in particular ways. They deem learning to be a process whereby individuals, as a result of their experience, establish an association or linkage between two events, a process called conditioning. Behaviorists like B. F. Skinner divide the environment into units termed stimuli and the behavior elicited by stimuli into units termed responses.
7. Humanistic psychology—also called "third-force" psychology—has arisen in reaction to psychoanalysis and behaviorism. It maintains that human beings are different from all other organisms in that they actively intervene in the course of events to control their destinies and to shape the world around them. Its proponents seek to maximize the human potential for self-direction and freedom of choice.
8. Jean Piaget has come to be recognized as a giant of twentieth-century psychology. For Piaget the critical question in the study of growing children is how they adjust to the world they live in. Scheme, assimilation, accommodation, and equilibrium are key concepts in Piagetian theory. They find expression in four stages of cognitive development: the sensorimotor stage, the preoperational stage, the stage of concrete operations, and the stage of formal operations.
9. Cognitive learning theorists say that our capacity to use symbols affords us a powerful means for comprehending and dealing with our environment. Verbal and imagined symbols allow us to represent events; to analyze

our conscious experience; to communicate with others; to plan, to create, to imagine; and to engage in foresightful action.

10. Ethological theory studies the behavior patterns of organisms from a biological point of view. Its proponents rely heavily on the evolutionary theory of Charles Darwin. Ethologists say that evolution applies not only to anatomy and physiology but also to predispositions for certain types of behavior. Organisms are said to be genetically prepared for some responses.
11. Each of the five major types of theory we considered has its proponents and critics. Yet the theories are not mutually exclusive; we need not accept one and reject the others. Different tasks simply call for different theories. Thus, most psychologists prefer an eclectic approach to development.

KEY TERMS

accommodation A central concept in Piagetian theory; the process, in cognitive development, of changing a scheme (mental model) to achieve a better match to the world of reality.

assimilation A central concept in Piagetian theory; the process, in cognitive development, of taking in new information and interpreting it in such a manner that the information conforms to a currently held scheme (mental model) of the world.

behavior modification An approach that applies the results of learning theory and experimental psychology to the problem of altering maladaptive behavior.

behavioral theory An approach that is concerned with the behavior of people—what they say and do. Its proponents say that if psychology is to be a science, its data must be directly observable and measurable.

cognition The process of knowing; our reception of raw sensory information and our transformation, elaboration, storage, recovery, and use of this information.

cognitive learning Our learning new responses without first having had the opportunity to make the responses ourselves. It is accomplished by watching other people.

cognitive stages in development Sequential periods in the growth or maturing of an individual's ability to engage in thinking (to gain knowledge and awareness of oneself and one's environment).

cognitive theory The approach to mental activity that stresses the part that sensation, perception, imagery, retention, recall, problem solving, reasoning, and thinking play in behavior.

conditioning The process whereby individuals, as a result of their experience, establish an association or linkage between two events.

critical period A certain time in life when specific experiences affect the development of an organism more than they do at other times.

eclectic approach A perspective that allows scientists to select and choose from various theories those aspects that provide the best fit for the descriptive and analytical task at hand.

epigenetic principle The notion that each aspect of development must develop at a particular time in the life span if it is going to develop at all. Should the capacity not be developed on schedule, the rest of development is unfavorably altered.

equilibrium A central concept in Piagetian theory; a state of balance between the processes of assimilation and accommodation.

ethology The study of the behavior patterns of organisms from a biological point of view.

fixation A central concept in Freudian theory; the tendency to experience throughout life tension and its reduction by means of behavior that had great significance during an earlier period of life.

hierarchy of needs Maslow's concept that human beings have certain basic needs that must be met before they can go on to fulfill other needs. The result is a "pyramid of needs."

holistic approach A perspective that views the human condition in its totality and each person as more than a collection of physical, social, and psychological components.

humanistic psychology A psychological school of thought that stresses the uniqueness of the human condition. It maintains that human beings, unlike other organisms, actively intervene in the course of events to control their destinies and shape the world around them.

imprinting A process of attachment that occurs only during a relatively short period of time and is so resistant to change that the behavior appears to be innate.

learned helplessness A generalized expectancy that events are independent of one's own responses.

mechanistic model The world view that represents the universe as a machine composed of elementary particles in motion. It portrays human development as a gradual, uninterrupted, chainlike sequence of events and the organism as a reactive being.

natural selection The process of evolution described by Charles Darwin. Individuals who are best adapted to their environment stand a better chance of surviving and reproducing than do individuals without these characteristics.

organismic model The world view that represents the universe as a whole made up of interactive parts. It is the distinctive interrelation between the lower-level components that is seen as imparting to the whole characteristics not found in the components alone. It portrays the organism as an active being.

peak experience A rapturous feeling of excitement, insight, and happiness experienced by self-actualized individuals; a notion advanced by Abraham Maslow.

psychoanalytic theory The view advanced by Sigmund Freud that personality is fashioned in progressive steps, or stages, as an individual passes through the oral, anal, phallic, latency, and genital periods. Unconscious motivation—stemming from impulses buried below the level of awareness—are believed to play a powerful part in such development.

psychosexual stages A series of steps or periods, postulated by Sigmund Freud, through which all individuals pass and that are dominated by the development of sensitivity in a particular erogenous zone of the body. The stages are the oral, anal, phallic, latency, and genital periods.

reinforcement The process whereby one event strengthens the probability of another event's occurring.

releasing stimulus An environmental event that functions to activate innately preprogrammed behavior.

response A unit into which behavior is divided; a concept employed by behaviorists.

scheme A central concept of Piagetian theory; a cognitive structure that people evolve for dealing with specific kinds of situations in their environment.

self-actualization A notion advanced by Abraham Maslow that each individual has a basic need to develop his or her potential to the fullest.

sensitive period A certain time in life when particular kinds of experience affect the development of an organism somewhat more than they do at other times.

stimulus A unit into which the environment is divided; a concept employed by behaviorists.

theory A tool; "a way of binding together a multitude of facts so that one may comprehend them all at once" (Kelly, 1955: 18).

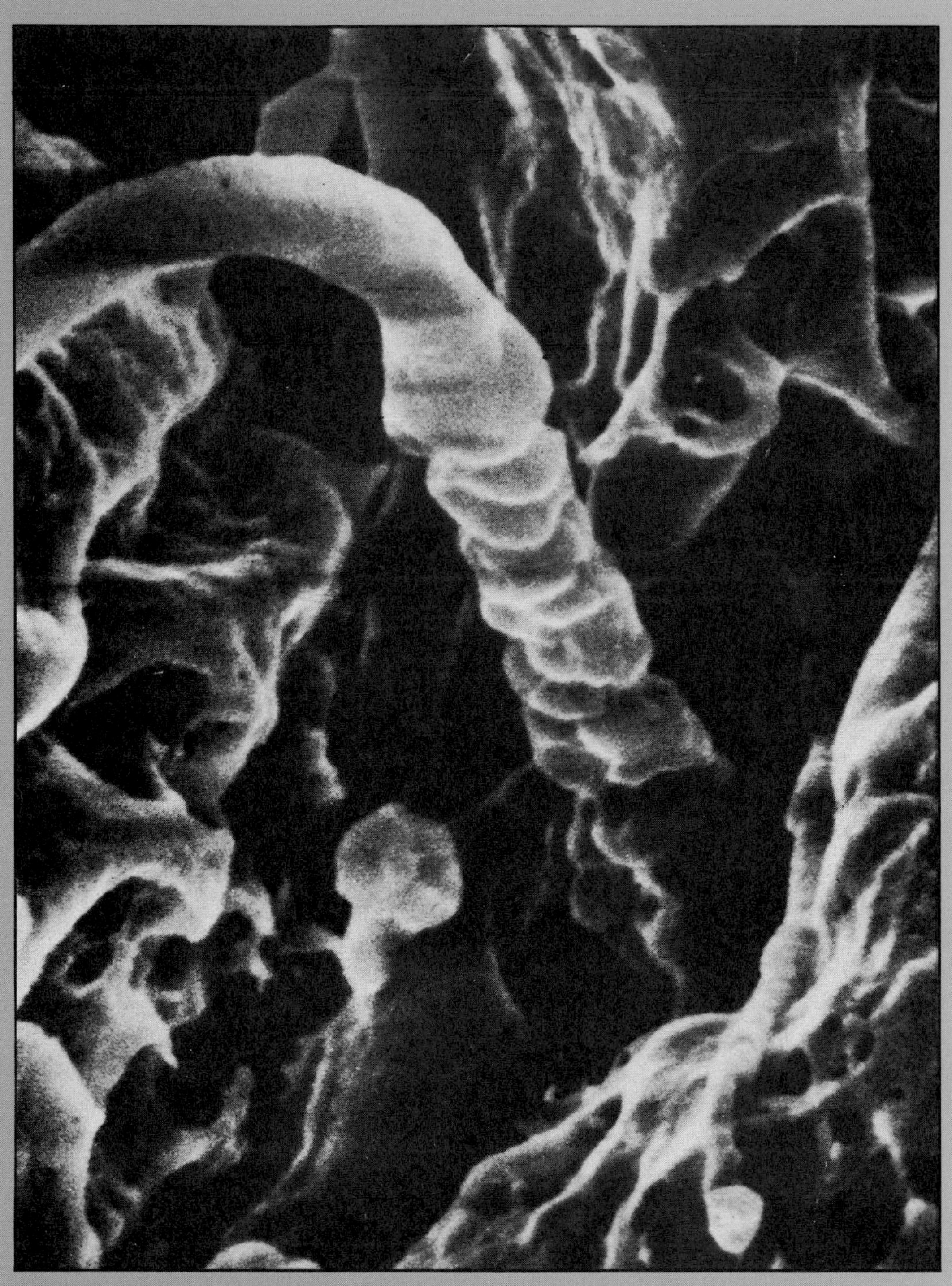

3

Biological Foundations

Today scientists and engineers are building computerized robots that promise to surpass humans in some capabilities. Such machines can assimilate and retrieve vast quantities of information. And they can perform a good many tasks more efficiently and precisely than can human hands. Some can move about and even mimic the human voice. Yet robots do not "know" anything, nor do they appreciate the significance of anything. They do what they are told and no more. Nor do robots display emotions, feel love, or experience loneliness. In sum, human beings have unique and distinctive properties. To understand these properties, we must begin with a consideration of our biological foundations.

REPRODUCTION

Life goes on and on. Like all other living things, human beings are capable of producing new individuals and thus ensuring the survival of the species. **Reproduction** is the term that biologists use for the process by which organisms create more organisms of their own kind. Like Samuel Butler, who said that a chicken is just an egg's way of making another egg, biologists recognize reproduction as the most important result of all life processes.

Reproductive Systems

Two kinds of sex cells, or *gametes,* are involved in human reproduction: the male gamete, or *sperm,* and the female gamete, which is called the *ovum* (egg). A male sperm fuses with a female ovum to form a *zygote* (fertilized egg). A sperm cell is minute. It consists of an oval head, a whiplike tail, and a connecting middle piece, or collar. It moves by lashing its tail. A normal adult man's testes may produce as many as 300 million or more mature sperm each day.

Ova, on the other hand, are not self-propelled. They contain yolk, the stored food substance that sustains the baby early in its development. During the embryonic period, the developing ovaries of females produce more than 400,000 immature ova. Later, during a woman's fertile years between puberty and menopause, one ovum matures and is released each month. Hence only some 400 to 500 of the immature ova ultimately reach maturity. The rest degenerate and are absorbed by the body.

The primary male reproductive organs are a pair of testes lying in a pouchlike structure, the *scrotum.* The scrotum is an outpocket of the abdominal cavity (see Figure 3.1). The testes produce sperm and the male sex hormones, called *androgens.* (The principal hormones are testosterone and androsterone.) The androgens are responsible for producing masculine secondary sexual characteristics, including facial and body hair.

Sperm are produced in winding tubules within each testis. They are then emptied into the *epididymis,* a long, slender, twisted tube, where they are stored. During sexual intercourse the sperm pass from the

Figure 3.1 The Male Reproductive System
This cross section of the male pelvic region shows the organs of reproduction.

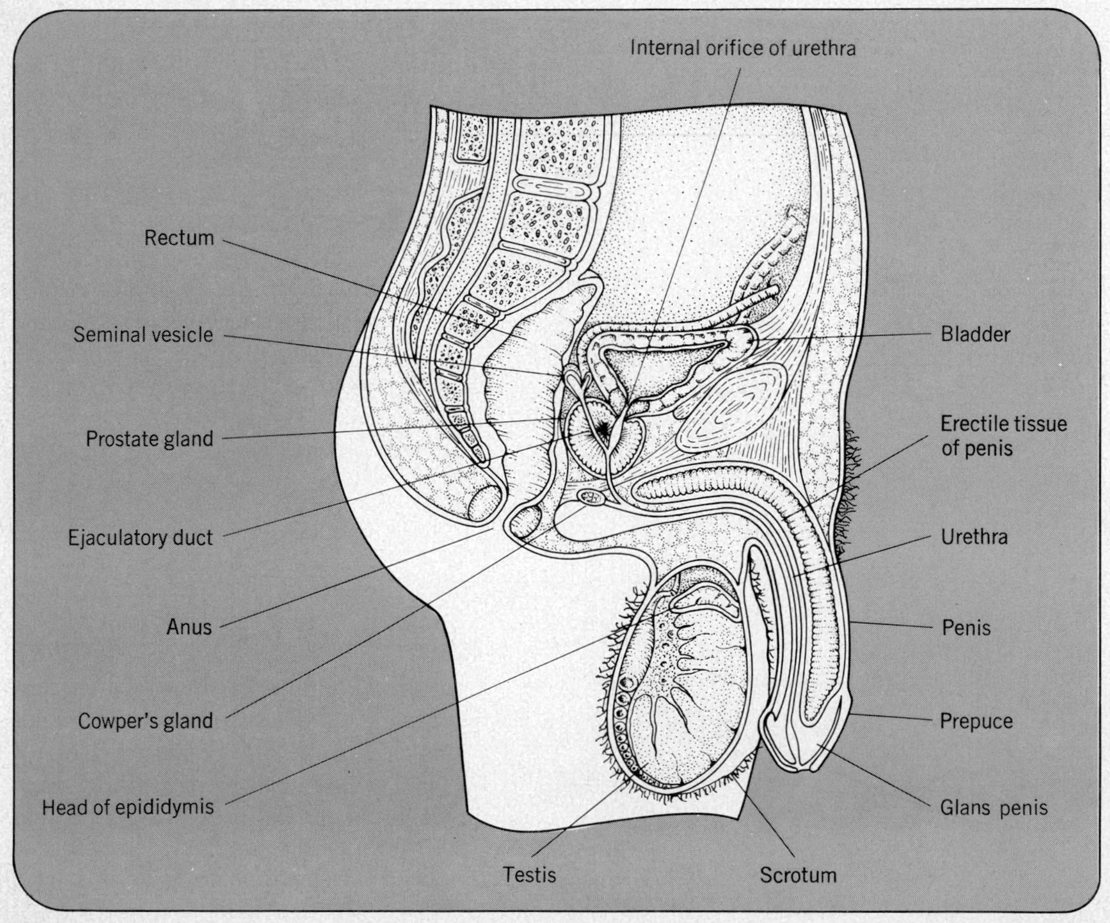

epididymis along muscular ducts into the *urethra*. On the way they are mixed with secretions from the *seminal vesicles* and the *prostate gland*. The mixture of the sperm and secretions is termed *semen*. The urethra—a tube that also connects with the bladder—is surrounded by the external reproductive organ, the *penis*.

The primary female reproductive organs are a pair of ovaries—almond-shaped structures that lie in the pelvis (see Figure 3.2). The ovaries produce mature ova and the female sex hormones, *estrogen* and *progesterone*. These hormones are responsible for the development of female secondary characteristics, including the breasts (mammary glands).

When an ovum is expelled from one of the ovaries, it passes into the abdominal cavity where it is drawn in a siphonlike action into an *oviduct* (Fallopian tube). Each ovary is paired with one oviduct, and it is in the oviduct that fertilization occurs if sperm are present. The oviduct is lined with tiny, hairlike projections, *cilia*, that propel the ovum along its course.

The oviducts are connected with the *uterus*, a hollow, thick-walled, muscular organ that houses the developing embryo. The narrow lower end of the uterus, called the *cervix*, projects into the vagina. The *vagina* is a muscular passageway that is capable of considerable dilation. The penis is inserted into the vagina during sexual intercourse, and the infant passes through the vagina at birth. Surrounding the external opening of the vagina are the external genitalia, collectively termed the *vulva*. The vulva contains the fleshy folds, known as the *labia*, and the *clitoris* (a small erectile structure comparable in some ways to the penis).

Figure 3.2 The Female Reproductive System

A cross section of the female pelvic region, with the organs of reproduction.

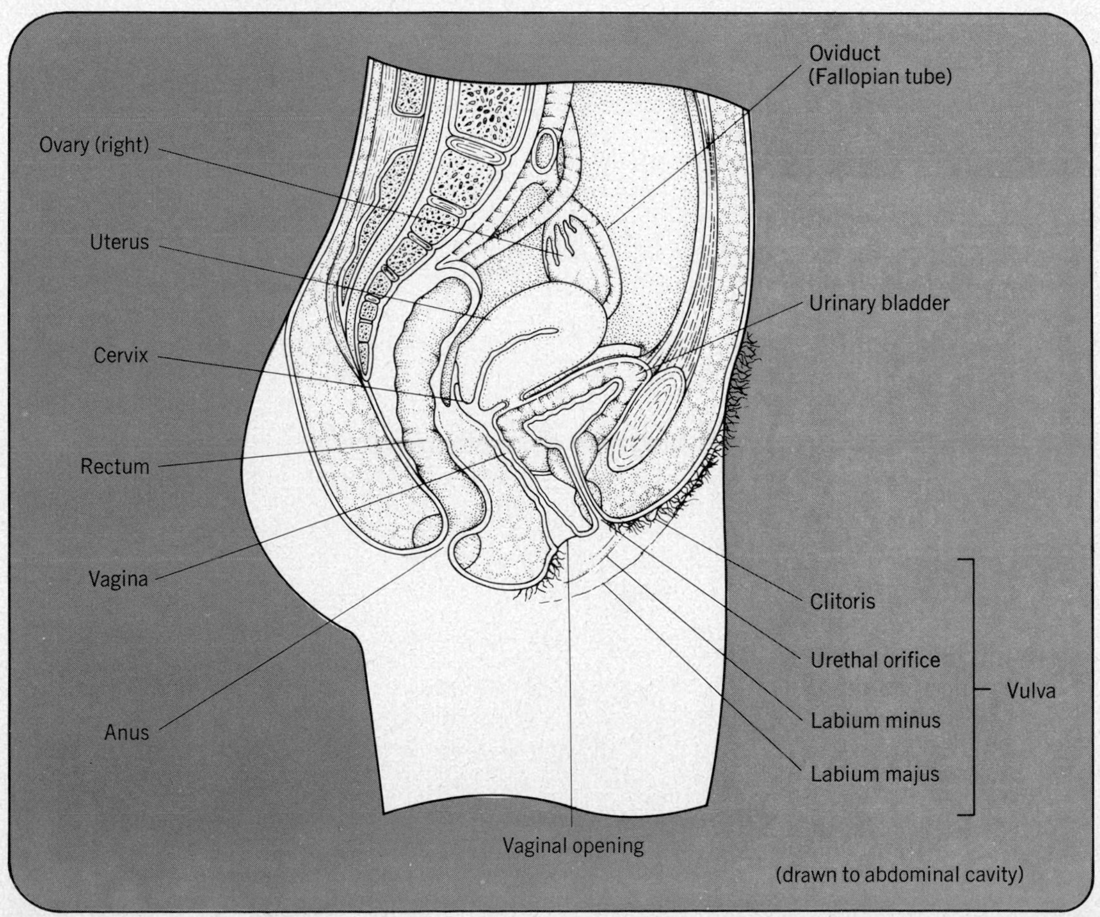

Fertilization

A mature ovum, or egg cell, is produced about every twenty-eight days. (However, variations among women in the length of the ovarian cycle are common and normal.) Toward the middle of each monthly cycle, one ovum usually reaches maturity and passes into one of the oviducts. During the previous fourteen days, the ovum matured in a *follicle* (also termed a *Graafian follicle*). Initially a follicle consists of a single layer of cells, but as it grows, the cells proliferate, producing a fluid-filled sac that surrounds the primitive ovum.

An ovary is composed of many follicles, but normally only one undergoes full development in each twenty-eight-day ovarian cycle. Most women seem to alternate between ovaries from one month to another. If more than one ovum matures and is released, the woman may conceive multiple nonidentical siblings (fraternal twins). Through the influence of hormones secreted by the pituitary gland, the follicle ruptures and the ovum is discharged. This discharge of the ovum is called *ovulation*. The life span of a mature ovum is short. If unfertilized, the ovum begins to degenerate after twenty-four hours.

Fertilization—the union of a sperm and an ovum—usually takes place in the upper end of the oviduct (see the chapter opening photograph). At the time of sexual intercourse, a man customarily introduces 100 to 500 million sperm into the woman's vagina. Sperm ascend the cervical canal and enter the uterus and oviducts. The process of sperm locomotion is assisted by the female system. Sperm have a high mortality rate within the female tract. The obstetrician Alan F. Guttmacher (1973: 35) writes:

> The one sperm that achieves its destiny has won against gigantic odds, several hundred million to one. The baby it engenders has a far greater mathematical chance of becoming president than the sperm had of fathering a baby.

Even then, however, the newly fertilized egg is extremely vulnerable. For one reason or another, about one-third of all zygotes die shortly after fertilization. (For a discussion of infertility and its treatment, see the boxed insert on pages 69–70.)

When the follicle ruptures, releasing its ovum, it undergoes rapid change. Still a part of the ovary, it transforms itself into the *corpus luteum*, a small growth recognizable by its golden pigment. The corpus luteum secretes progesterone (a female hormone), which enters the bloodstream and causes the mucous lining along the inner wall of the uterus to prepare itself for the implantation of the zygote. If conception and implantation do not occur, the corpus luteum degenerates and eventually disappears. If pregnancy occurs, the corpus luteum continues to develop and produces progesterone until the placenta takes over the same function. The corpus luteum then becomes superfluous and disappears.

If pregnancy fails to take place, the decreasing levels of ovarian hormones (estrogen and progesterone) lead to *menstruation* about fourteen days after ovulation. Since the thickened outer layers of tissue lining the uterus are not needed for the support of the zygote, they deteriorate. The body sheds them over a three- to seven-day period, when the debris from the wall of the uterus, a small amount of blood, and other fluids are discharged from the vagina. Before the end of a menstrual flow, the pituitary gland secretes hormones into the bloodstream that direct one of the ovarian follicles to begin rapid growth. As a consequence, the cycle starts anew. Should pregnancy occur, a different process is initiated; it will be described in Chapter 4.

GENETICS

All of us begin life as a single fertilized cell. Fertilization is the major event determining our biological inheritance. The zygote contains all the hereditary material that bridges the generations. Precisely blueprinted in this original cell are the 200 billion or so cells that we possess nine months later at birth. The scientific study of biological inheritance is termed **genetics.**

Chromosomes

Around the turn of the twentieth century, the study of cellular tissue with microscopes led to the discovery of chromosomes. **Chromosomes** are long, threadlike bodies that contain the hereditary materials found in the nuclei of all cells. Chromosomes are normally invisible under ordinary light microscopes. During cell division, however, they coil into thicker bodies

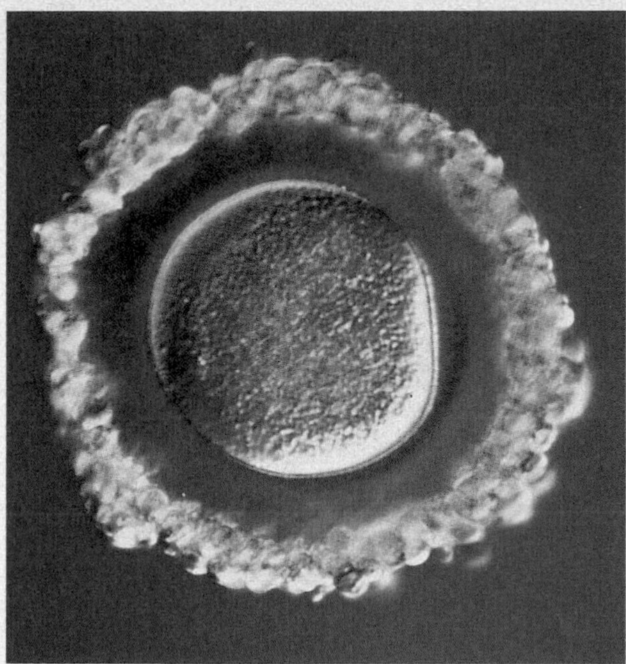

The Ovum

The egg cell is the largest human cell. Other cells are only one-tenth the size of the ovum, which is between 0.1 and 0.2 millimeter in diameter. A protective membrane surrounds the egg cell. A number of yolk granules can be seen in the cytoplasm.

Lennart Nilsson, from *Behold Man*, Little Brown, 1974

and can be seen more easily, particularly if a cell is killed and stained with dyes.

Upon fertilization, the twenty-three chromosomes of the ovum are combined with the twenty-three chromosomes of the sperm, bringing the total number of chromosomes to forty-six, or twenty-three pairs (see Figure 3.3). In the formation of most of the cells of the body (somatic cells), a cell division termed *mitosis* occurs. Each single chromosome splits lengthwise to form a new pair. Through this process, a cell divides into two daughter cells identical with the original one (see Chapter 4).

In reproduction, a new individual arises from the fusion of two cells, an ovum and a sperm; therefore the distribution of the chromosomes cannot occur in the usual manner. **Meiosis** solves this problem. Meiosis involves two cell divisions, during which the chromosome number is halved.

Suppose, for example, that a gamete had one pair of chromosomes. When a sperm and an ovum fused at the time of fertilization, the resulting zygote would have two pairs of chromosomes—a double dose. In the next generation the already doubled number would double again, making four pairs. Since the number would double in each generation, cells would soon contain an astronomical amount of hereditary material. Even the addition of one chromosome to

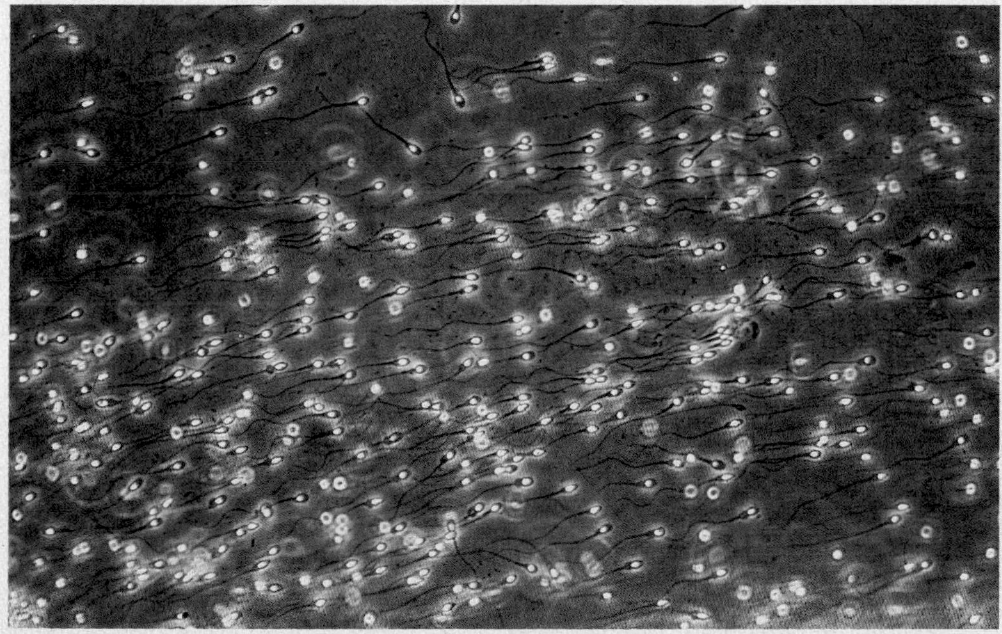

Sperm

Sperm are unusually small cells with very little cytoplasm. Once sperm are ejaculated with semen into the female reproductive tract, they make their way through the cervical canal and then ascend the uterus and oviducts. Of the millions of sperm entering the vagina, only a few thousand complete the journey, and only one succeeds in penetrating the ovum.

Lennart Nilsson, from *Behold Man*, Little Brown, 1974

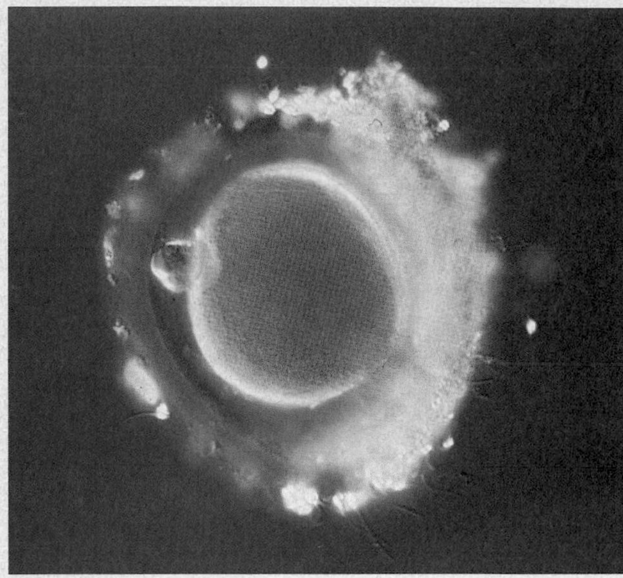

The First Cell Division

After the sperm and ovum fuse, uniting the chromosomes of the father and the mother, the zygote begins a series of cell divisions. The genes in the new cells are identical to those in the fertilized cell. By the time the fertilized egg reaches the uterus, it has become transformed into a solid cluster of cells. The photo shows the first cell division.

Lennart Nilsson, from *Behold Man,* Little Brown, 1974

the standard forty-six can lead to disaster, a topic considered later in the chapter.

To prevent this from occurring and to maintain a constant number of chromosomes, the total number of chromosomes are reduced by half when gametes are formed. As a consequence, each gamete receives only one chromosome from each pair in every parental cell. This is half the usual number, allowing each parent to contribute half the total number of chromosomes. Thus upon fertilization, the full number of chromosomes (and pairs) is restored (see Figure 3.4).

Genes

So far, this chapter has spoken of chromosomes as if they were the ultimate hereditary units. But actually each chromosome contains a number of smaller units that divide it into regions called **genes.** If a chromosome is like a book in a library, then a gene is like a page in the book. In turn, genes are made up of numerous molecules called **deoxyribonucleic acid,** or **DNA.** DNA is the active substance of genes and thus governs the heredity of all life. It stores inherited information that serves as a "recipe" or "blueprint" telling cells how to manufacture vital protein substances (including enzymes, hormones, antibodies,

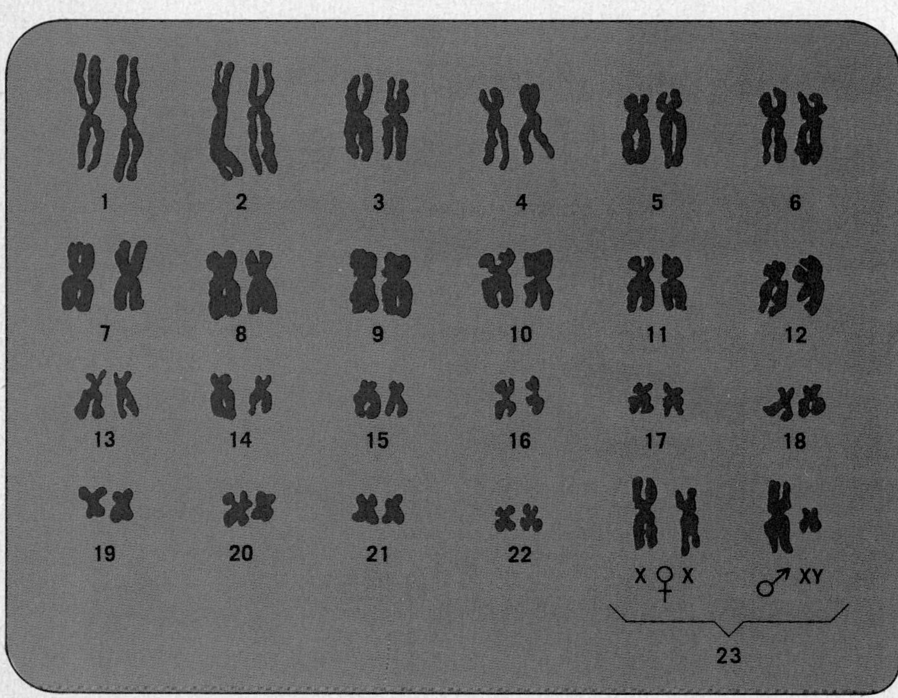

Figure 3.3 Human Chromosomes

Every cell nucleus contains twenty-three types of chromosomes—two of each type. Each parent provides one member of the pair. Chromosomes differ in size and shape. For convenience in talking about them, scientists arrange the twenty-three pairs in descending order by size, and number them accordingly. The members of each chromosome pair look alike, with the exception of the twenty-third pair in males. As the drawing shows, the twenty-third chromosome is the sex-determining chromosome. An XX combination of chromosomes in this pair produces a female; an XY combination, a male.

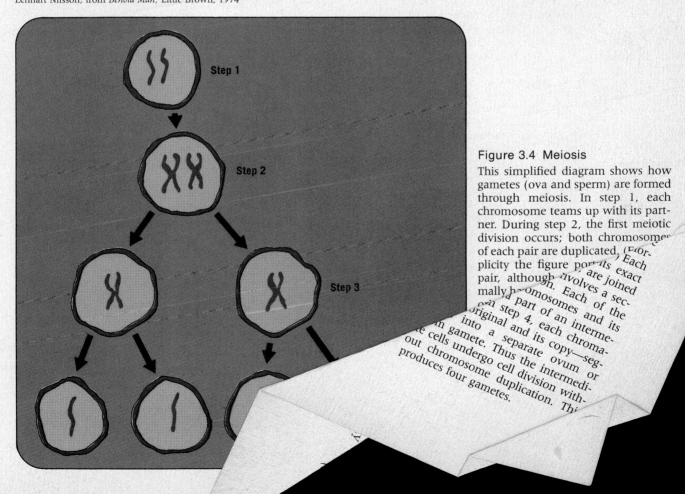

The Process of Cell Division

The series of photos shows a cell dividing. At the far left, the nucleus has already divided into two new nuclei. Next, the newly forming cells bubble and wriggle in freeing themselves from one another. Finally, they achieve complete separation.

Lennart Nilsson, from *Behold Man*, Little Brown, 1974

Figure 3.4 Meiosis

This simplified diagram shows how gametes (ova and sperm) are formed through meiosis. In step 1, each chromosome teams up with its partner. During step 2, the first meiotic division occurs; both chromosomes of each pair are duplicated. (For ... plicity the figure por... its ... Each pair, although ... are joined ... exact mally ... involves a sec... n. Each of the ... omosomes and its ... a part of an interme- ... step 4, each chroma- ... original and its copy—seg- ... into a separate ovum or ... n gamete. Thus the intermedi- ... e cells undergo cell division with- out chromosome duplication. Thi... produces four gametes.

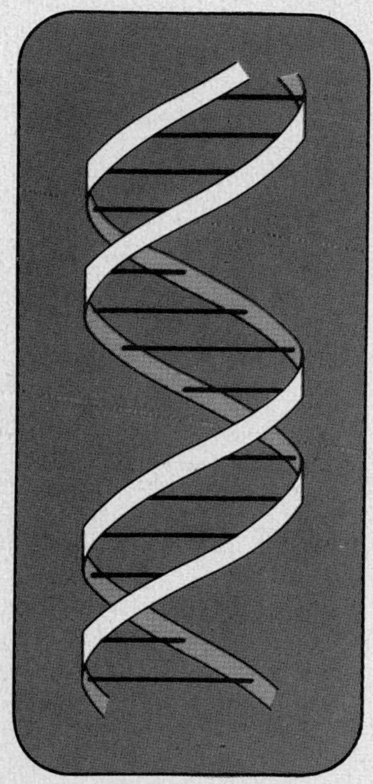

Figure 3.5 A Model of the DNA Molecule

The double-chained structure of a DNA molecule is coiled in a helix. During cell division, the two chains pull apart, or "unzip." Each half is now free to assemble a new complementary half.

and structural proteins). This code of life is carried in a large molecule shaped like a double helix or twisted rope ladder (see Figure 3.5). The boxed insert on page 71 summarizes a number of recent developments in the field of genetic engineering.

The discoveries of Gregor Johann Mendel (1822–[illegible]84), an Austrian monk, laid the foundations for [illegible]dern understanding of genes and for the sci-[illegible]etics. By crossing varieties of peas in his [illegible] garden, Mendel was able to formu-[illegible]nciples of heredity. He published [illegible] for various reasons his work [illegible]900. In that year three [illegible]tly in the Nether-[illegible]d their own ex-[illegible]ions similar [illegible]knowl-[illegible]nd

Central to Mendelian theory is the notion that independent units (which Mendel called *factors*) determine inherited characteristics. As noted earlier, today we call these units genes. Mendel's conclusion regarding hereditary factors was based on his observation that characteristics commonly appear in two alternative forms. He noted, for instance, that his pea plants were characterized by either red *or* white flowers, tall *or* dwarf stems, green *or* yellow pods, smooth *or* wrinkled seeds, and so on.

Mendel reasoned that the genes that control a single hereditary characteristic must exist in pairs. Advances in microbiology and genetics have confirmed Mendel's hunch. Genes occur in pairs, one on a maternal chromosome and the other on the *homologous*, or corresponding, paternal chromosome. The two genes in a pair are said to occupy a certain *locus*, or position, on each of the homologous chromosomes. For instance, scientists have recently been able to produce an image of the gene that directs production of hemoglobin, the substance that carries oxygen in the blood. This has allowed them to detect certain debilitating and sometimes fatal forms of anemia, caused by an inadequate supply of hemoglobin. With a normal gene, the image shows a row of fuzzy-looking black bands. But if one or more bands is missing, part or all of the genetic instruction is missing, a condition associated with two types of anemia (alpha-thalassemia and beta-delta-thalassemia).

We apply the term **allele** to each member of a pair of genes. An allele is a gene at a given locus on a chromosome. Alleles are different forms of the same gene. There can be only two different alleles per person for any characteristic, one from each parent (one on the maternal chromosome and one on the paternal chromosome).

Dominance

Mendel demonstrated that in a cross between pea varieties, one allele—the **dominant character**—completely masks or hides the other allele—the **recessive character.** Mendel used letters of the alphabet as symbols for genes. A capital letter (for example, *A*) signified the dominant allele and a lower-case letter (in this instance, *a*) the recessive allele. Say that we wanted to talk about the alleles responsible for the color of a plant's flowers. We could use *A* as a symbol for red (the dominant allele) and *a* for white (the recessive allele). Then we would refer to a pure-

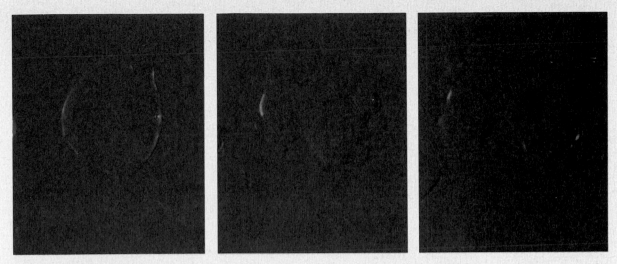

The Process of Cell Division

The series of photos shows a cell dividing. At the far left, the nucleus has already divided into two new nuclei. Next, the newly forming cells bubble and wriggle in freeing themselves from one another. Finally, they achieve complete separation.

Lennart Nilsson, from *Behold Man*, Little Brown, 1974

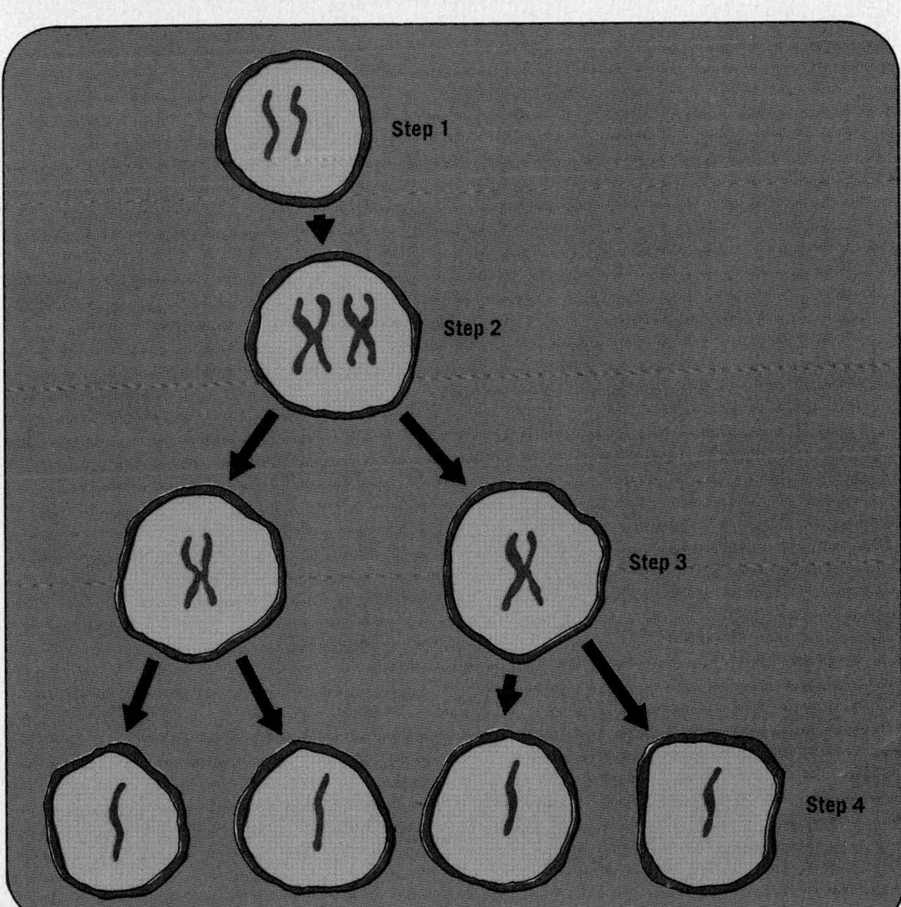

Figure 3.4 Meiosis

This simplified diagram shows how gametes (ova and sperm) are formed through meiosis. In step 1, each chromosome teams up with its partner. During step 2, the first meiotic division occurs; both chromosomes of each pair are duplicated. (For simplicity the figure portrays only one pair, although human beings normally have twenty-three pairs.) Each original chromosome and its exact copy, termed a *chromatid*, are joined at the center. Step 3 involves a second meiotic division. Each of the two original chromosomes and its copy become a part of an intermediary cell. In step 4, each chromatid—the original and its copy—segregates into a separate ovum or sperm gamete. Thus the intermediate cells undergo cell division without chromosome duplication. This produces four gametes.

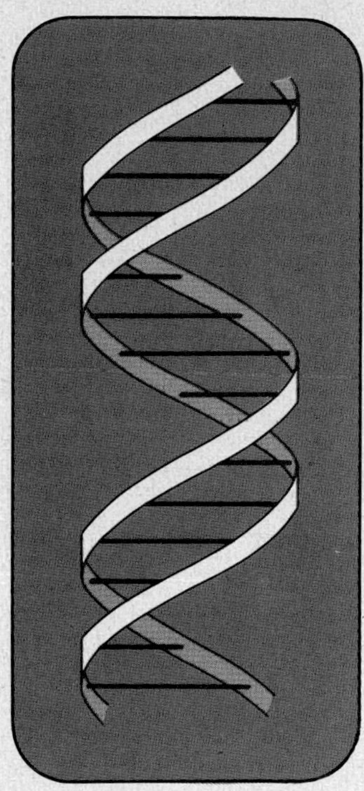

Figure 3.5 A Model of the DNA Molecule

The double-chained structure of a DNA molecule is coiled in a helix. During cell division, the two chains pull apart, or "unzip." Each half is now free to assemble a new complementary half.

and structural proteins). This code of life is carried in a large molecule shaped like a double helix or twisted rope ladder (see Figure 3.5). The boxed insert on page 71 summarizes a number of recent developments in the field of genetic engineering.

The discoveries of Gregor Johann Mendel (1822–1884), an Austrian monk, laid the foundations for our modern understanding of genes and for the science of genetics. By crossing varieties of peas in his small monastery garden, Mendel was able to formulate the cardinal principles of heredity. He published his results in 1866, but for various reasons his work was largely ignored until 1900. In that year three researchers working independently in the Netherlands, Austria, and Germany reported their own experiments, in which they reached conclusions similar to those of Mendel. To their credit, each acknowledged that in searching the literature he had found that Mendel had discovered the principles of heredity thirty-four years before.

Central to Mendelian theory is the notion that independent units (which Mendel called *factors*) determine inherited characteristics. As noted earlier, today we call these units genes. Mendel's conclusion regarding hereditary factors was based on his observation that characteristics commonly appear in two alternative forms. He noted, for instance, that his pea plants were characterized by either red *or* white flowers, tall *or* dwarf stems, green *or* yellow pods, smooth *or* wrinkled seeds, and so on.

Mendel reasoned that the genes that control a single hereditary characteristic must exist in pairs. Advances in microbiology and genetics have confirmed Mendel's hunch. Genes occur in pairs, one on a maternal chromosome and the other on the *homologous*, or corresponding, paternal chromosome. The two genes in a pair are said to occupy a certain *locus*, or position, on each of the homologous chromosomes. For instance, scientists have recently been able to produce an image of the gene that directs production of hemoglobin, the substance that carries oxygen in the blood. This has allowed them to detect certain debilitating and sometimes fatal forms of anemia, caused by an inadequate supply of hemoglobin. With a normal gene, the image shows a row of fuzzy-looking black bands. But if one or more bands is missing, part or all of the genetic instruction is missing, a condition associated with two types of anemia (alpha-thalassemia and beta-delta-thalassemia).

We apply the term **allele** to each member of a pair of genes. An allele is a gene at a given locus on a chromosome. Alleles are different forms of the same gene. There can be only two different alleles per person for any characteristic, one from each parent (one on the maternal chromosome and one on the paternal chromosome).

Dominance

Mendel demonstrated that in a cross between pea varieties, one allele—the **dominant character**—completely masks or hides the other allele—the **recessive character.** Mendel used letters of the alphabet as symbols for genes. A capital letter (for example, *A*) signified the dominant allele and a lower-case letter (in this instance, *a*) the recessive allele. Say that we wanted to talk about the alleles responsible for the color of a plant's flowers. We could use *A* as a symbol for red (the dominant allele) and *a* for white (the recessive allele). Then we would refer to a pure-

THE TREATMENT OF INFERTILITY

Although in recent years the media spotlight has focused on the birth-control and abortion controversies, many couples are confronted with an opposite problem, namely, how to conceive the children they desire. **Infertility** is the term employed by the medical profession to refer to a condition in which a couple fails to achieve pregnancy after one year of having engaged in sexual relations with normal frequency (about three or four times a week) and without contraception. As more and more Americans are marrying at later ages and postponing their childbearing years until the thirties, they are increasing the chances that they will experience fertility problems. Some researchers report a sharp drop in a woman's fertility after the age of thirty (DeCherney and Berkowitz, 1982).

Infertility is a problem that causes a good many couples profound anguish. They view parenthood as an integral part of their development as adults. Indeed, they see parenthood as a credential of adulthood. Consequently, the prospect that they may be sterile confronts them with a sense of helplessness at losing control over their life plans. And many feel that their bodies are damaged or otherwise defective. Women speak of feeling "hollow" or "empty"; men speak of feeling like castrates or say that they only "shoot blanks." And some are troubled by their place in the flow of generations (Mazor, 1979). Associated feelings of rage, depression, self-doubt, guilt, and blame can have devastating consequences for the marital relationship (Brozan, 1982; Bouton, 1982).

Little solid statistical information exists on the incidence of infertility. The American Medical Association estimates that about 15 percent of all married couples are unable to have children and that another 10 percent have fewer children than they wish (Kolata, 1977). Medical specialists view infertility as a "couple problem," a combination of the fertility difficulties of the two individual members. In many cases, neither partner is fully fertile. With another partner, "infertility" may not have arisen, since one "superfertile" member can often compensate for the "subfertility" of the other. More than half of all couples with fertility problems can now be helped to achieve pregnancy. Significantly, however, more than half of all couples diagnosed as infertile conceive either after receiving no treatment or after terminating all treatment (Collins et al., 1983).

The First Test-Tube Baby
The photo shows Louise Brown, the first "test-tube baby," as a healthy one-year-old youngster appearing on the Phil Donahue show.
AP/Wide World Photos

About 40 percent of the time, the male is found to be the primary source of the infertility problem. Medical authorities have differed on how many sperm are required for fertility. The American Fertility Society places the number at over 20 million sperm per milliliter of semen (a normal ejaculation consists of three to five milliliters of semen). However, Dr. Keith D. Smith of the University of Texas Medical School says that he has encountered cases of fertility below 10 million sperm per milliliter (Bronson, 1977*b*). Male infertility may also be related to the quality of the sperm, which may be characterized by poor motility (rate of spontaneous movement) or unsatisfactory morphology (for instance, a large proportion of the sperm may be abnormally shaped or contain defective chromosomes). Exposure to environmental toxins and to industrial chemicals like lead and cadmium in the workplace can contribute to these conditions. Another problem can be traced to tubal blockage, which in some cases can be corrected by microsurgery (surgery per-

(*continued*)

The Treatment of Infertility (continued)

formed using a microscope that magnifies the surgical field four to twenty-five times). Still another rather common cause of infertility is *varicocele,* enlarged or varicose veins in the scrotum (a condition often correctable by surgically tying off the affected veins). Occasionally, some simple factor may be responsible—for example, infrequent intercourse (which is often associated with excessive use of alcohol or some other drug) may be the cause.

About 20 percent of female fertility problems are associated with "hormonal failure." As a result the ovaries do not produce and release ova. A variety of drugs and synthetic hormones are now available for the treatment of this condition. Probably the most common cause of female infertility has to do with congenital or infectious problems (such as gonorrhea) that account for malformation or malfunction of the oviducts. In some cases these conditions can be corrected by microsurgery (or occasionally by the methods employed to diagnose tubal problems, such as passing carbon dioxide into the tubes or inserting dye for x-rays). The poorest candidates for successful microsurgery are women who have incurred severe tubal damage from gonorrhea. Many infertile women have *endometriosis,* a condition in which the growth of uterine tissue in the abdominal cavity impairs the reproductive tract (mild conditions are treatable by drug therapy but more severe cases usually require surgery). Finally, some problems may be traced to the environment of the vagina and the cervix, where sperm are deposited by the penis. These problems may involve anatomic difficulties (such as retroversion of the uterus) or the production of sperm antibodies by the female.

The 1978 birth in England of Louise Brown, the first "test-tube baby," opened another form of fertility treatment for problems associated with tubal blockage in the female. Within four years some 450 additional women had been impregnated by this technique. In truth, the procedure is mislabeled, since the growth and development of the fetus do not occur in a test tube but in the uterus. The technique is a method of combining laboratory conception with subsequent natural embryonic and fetal development. The procedure, termed *in vitro* (meaning "in glass") *fertilization,* involves surgically obtaining a ripe ovum from a patient's ovary. The woman's husband donates a sperm sample. The sperm and ovum are then placed in a medium that facilitates their union. About twelve hours later, the embryo is transferred to a different solution, one that supports embryonic development (it has been found that the medium most suited to fertilization is not, as a rule, good for the developmental stage). Between two and four days later, the developing embryo is inserted in the woman's uterus, where, if all goes well, the embryo implants itself.

Considerable controversy surrounds the procedure of in vitro fertilization. Even more controversial is childbearing by proxy, which goes far beyond the use of in vitro fertilization in the treatment of oviduct infertility. In cases where the husband is infertile, some couples have turned to artificial insemination by an anonymous donor. Where the wife cannot conceive, a few couples have resorted to surrogate mothers who are artificially inseminated with the husband's semen, carry the child for nine months, and then give birth. Even more recently, a number of couples have had children by means of embryo transfer. In this procedure, a donor is artificially inseminated with sperm from an infertile woman's husband. After five days, the tiny embryo is washed out of the donor's uterus and transferred into the wife's womb, where it develops until birth.

These new procedures have raised a host of ethical and legal questions, including "Whose baby is it?" And there is always concern that the surrogate mother may suffer psychological damage from the experience (there is also the matter of how this childbearing by proxy affects the parent-child relationship and early parent-child bonding). Further, if in vitro fertilization is used to conquer sterility today, will it be used to achieve positive eugenics tomorrow? For instance, in the selection of ova and sperm, which qualities are to be screened out, which qualities are to be fostered, and who is to decide these questions? Coupled with these concerns is the specter of "baby farms," in which babies are mass-produced artificially to serve the state, along the lines described by Aldous Huxley in his novel *Brave New World.* Thus, a good many issues have been raised by the considerable strides science has taken in opening new vistas for the treatment of infertility.

GENETIC ENGINEERING

What not too long ago was the stuff of science fiction is today becoming the reality of genetic engineering. In the past decade scientists have learned how to splice strands of genetic material and thus to reshuffle hereditary information. A variety of techniques are currently available for gene splicing. One method rests on the discovery that certain enzymes act like fine chemical scalpels for precisely splitting apart DNA molecules. Because split DNA fragments have "sticky ends," two fragments adhere to each other when they touch. Thus researchers can take DNA from one organism—for instance, human beings, plants, insects, bacteria, or viruses—and join it with DNA from another. They can then place the new DNA material into a living cell, where it will multiply and produce limitless new generations of cells. The foreign DNA can drastically change the characteristics of its host cell. Because distinct organisms that under natural conditions do not exchange genes can now do so, a great many novel genetic combinations are possible.

Another recently introduced method entails the use of "the gene machine." This relatively cheap, desk-top device allows technicians to synthesize fragments of any gene automatically by typing its genetic code onto a keyboard. The synthetic version of a natural gene can then be spliced into the DNA of a living cell. Indeed, the machine also permits scientists to "invent" genes and insert them into bacteria to see what happens (Rensberger, 1981).

By employing techniques such as these, scientists have compelled bacteria to manufacture human proteins. Bacteria are simple organisms that do little more than manufacture proteins and reproduce. By placing bits of human DNA or synthetic DNA into bacterial DNA, bacteria have been programmed to make human insulin, human growth hormone, and interferon. The underlying hope is that these substances can be manufactured cheaply and in quantity to administer to human beings who require them for medical purposes. Some molecular biologists also envisage a day when human gene therapy will be possible. People with hereditary diseases would then be given engineered genes to cure them. Further, some scientists have suggested that they may be able to breed bacteria that will eat up polluting oil spills and that plants can be developed that will increase food production by built-in mechanisms that convert nitrogen in the air directly into fertilizer.

However, many people fear that genetic engineering is a biological atomic bomb. These critics say that even if science should succeed in producing oil-eating bacteria, what will prevent the bacteria from also seeking out and devouring oil in automobiles, machinery, and heating equipment? And what will we do if new varieties of food crops, equipped with their own built-in fertilizer factories, become so tough and prolific that they wipe out other vegetation? Even more alarming, will genetic engineers inadvertently create new disease-causing organisms that will be impossible to control with our present antibiotics and medical procedures? One can stop splitting atoms or stop using aerosols, but one cannot recall a new form of life, including so-called "doomsday bugs."

The National Institutes of Health (NIH) has issued guidelines for the recombinant DNA research done under its auspices. But for the hordes of private genetic-engineering companies springing up all over the world, the guidelines are strictly voluntary. In any event, recent years have witnessed the rush of venture capitalists into the biotechnology market, an area many see as the most promising and profitable new technology since computers.

bred red-flowered pea as *AA*, since this pea is characterized by a pair of two dominant alleles—one allele from each parental unit. And we would call a purebred white-flowered pea *aa*, since the pea is characterized by a pair of two recessive alleles.

In one of his experiments Mendel transferred the pollen of purebred red-flowered peas (*AA*) to plants of white-flowered peas (*aa*). This resulted in first-generation offspring that were all red-flowered, since the red-flowered allele is dominant. The offspring secured one allele from each parent, resulting in an *Aa* pair of alleles. In this manner Mendel demonstrated the distinction between the **genotype,** the genetic makeup of an organism, and the **phenotype,** the observable characteristics of the organism. (Among human beings the phenotype includes physical, physiological, and behavioral traits.)

A genotype that contains two red-flowered genes, or two white-flowered genes, is termed **homozygous,** or "pure" for that trait. A genotype that con-

Table 3.1 Some Dominant and Recessive Human Genetic Characteristics

Dominant	Recessive
Skin pigmentation	Albinism
Curly hair	Straight hair
Brown eyes	Blue or hazel eyes
Near- or farsightedness	Normal vision
Glaucoma	Normal
Normal color vision	Color blindness
Normal hearing	Congenital deafness
Free earlobes	Attached earlobes
Normal metabolism	Phenylketonuria
Polydactylism (extra fingers and toes)	Normal number of digits
Dark hair	Light or red hair
Hereditary cataract	Normal vision
Long eyelashes	Short eyelashes
Broad lips	Thin lips
Ichthyosis (scaly skin)	Normal skin
Achondroplasia (dwarfism)	Normal
Huntington's chorea	Normal

tains one red-flowered gene and one white-flowered gene is termed **heterozygous,** or "hybrid." Recessive genes produce their effect on the phenotype only when they are homozygous. A dominant gene produces its effect on the phenotype whether it is homozygous or heterozygous.

Human beings also possess dominant and recessive genes, some of which are listed in Table 3.1. Albinos (people who have milky white skin and colorless hair) are a case in point. Albinism is a relatively rare condition caused by a recessive gene that results in the failure of melanin (a dark pigment) to form in

An Albino Child

Albinism is a relatively rare condition associated with two recessive genes. The body fails to manufacture melanin, a dark pigment, and hence people with albinism have milky white skin and colorless hair.

Peeter Vilms/Jeroboam

the body. Both parents of an albino are generally normal in phenotype, but in genotype they are heterozygous (*Aa*). Accordingly, both parents carry the albino gene *a*. The genetic combinations that can occur in their offspring are *AA*, *Aa*, and *aa*. Only the *aa* genotype leds to albinism.

Mendel's Principles

Mendel demonstrated that the characteristic that is hidden or masked in the first generation (the recessive allele) is not lost, since it reappears among some members of the second hybrid generation. He reasoned that characteristics do not blend with or contaminate one another but preserve their original integrity as they pass unchanged in succeeding generations from child to grandchild. This is termed the **principle of segregation.**

For example, when Mendel crossed the red-flowered first-generation hybrid plants with each other, about three-fourths had red flowers (*AA* or *Aa*) and one-fourth had white flowers (*aa*). Of the red-flowered plants, about two-thirds were hybrids (*Aa*) and one-third were purebreds (*AA*). All the white-flowered plants, however, were purebreds (*aa*) (see Figure 3.6).

The principle of segregation is highlighted among human beings in cases of genetic disease. Dominant, single-gene defects can be transmitted by one affected parent. For each of the more than 1,000 such disorders so far identified, each pregnancy entails a 50 percent risk of transmitting the defect if one parent is affected, and a 75 percent risk if both parents carry the gene (see Figure 3.7).

Huntington's chorea is probably the best known of the genetic disorders. It is caused by a single *autosomal* (non–sex-linked) dominant gene. The disorder results in the degeneration of the nervous system, mental deterioration, and the uncontrolled twitching of the limbs. It generally appears when patients are in their thirties and forties (see Figure 3.8). There is no known cure, and the disease is fatal. Woody Guthrie, a talented folk singer, was a victim of Huntington's chorea (Klein, 1980). His son Arlo, who is also a popular

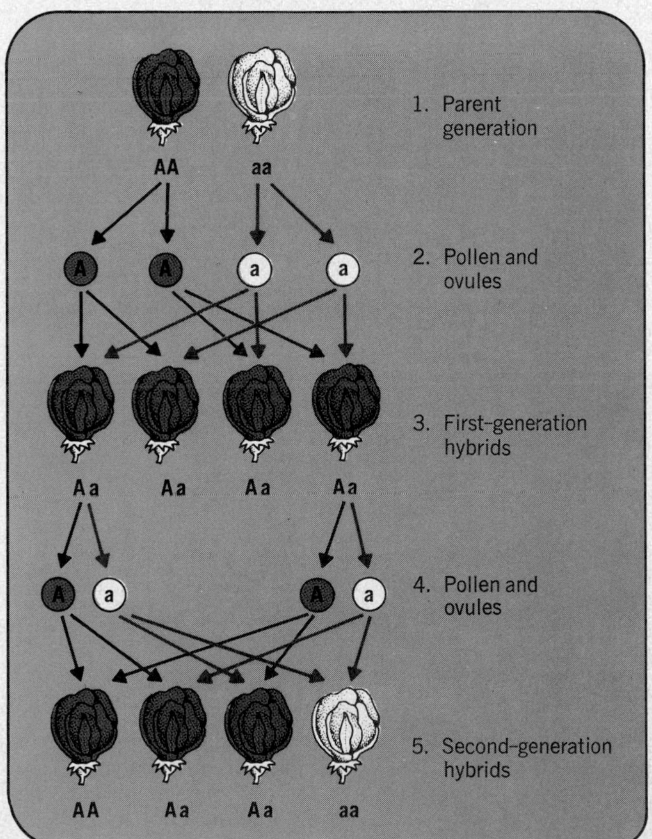

Figure 3.6 Mendelian Principle of Segregation

In step 1, a purebred red-flowered pea plant and a purebred white-flowered pea plant are crossed by transferring pollen from the flower of one plant to that of the other. As step 2 shows, the pollen and ovule grains (gametes) contain one allele for flower color—red (shown here in color) being the dominant allele and white the recessive allele. In step 3 all offspring of the first generation of hybrids have one dominant and one recessive allele, but the dominant trait masks the recessive trait. In step 4, self-fertilization of the first-generation hybrids produces all combinations of alleles. (For the sake of simplicity the gametes for only two of the four first-generation hybrids are shown here.) In step 5, the second generation, three-fourths of the flowers are red, one-fourth white.

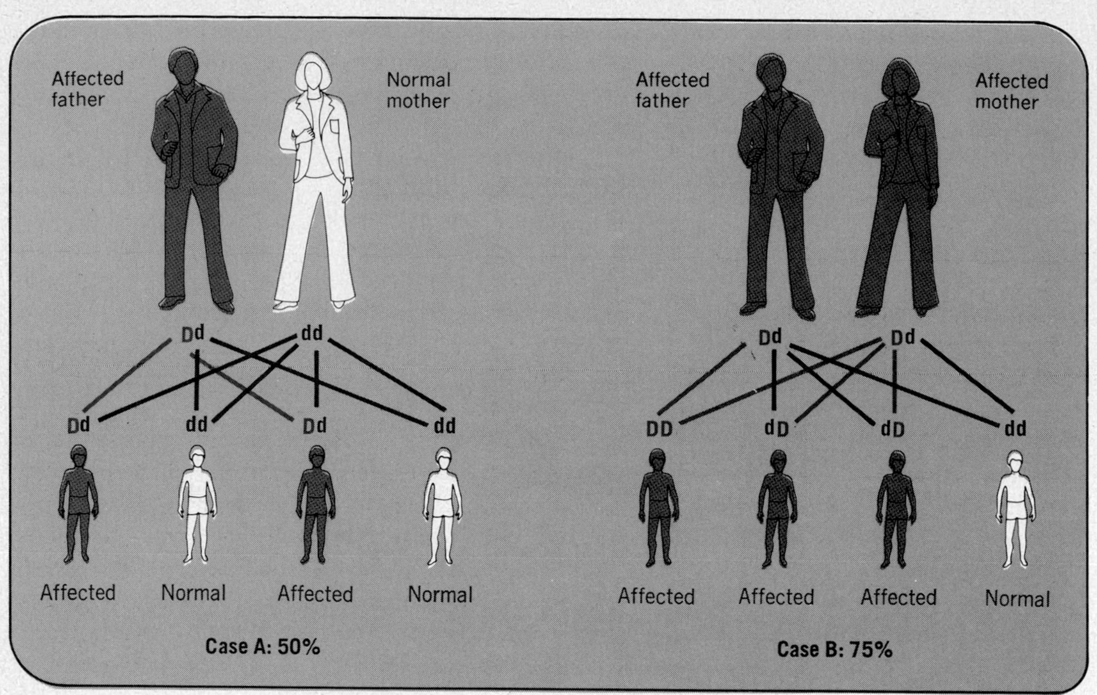

Figure 3.7 The Transmission of Dominant Single-Gene Defects

Case A: One affected parent has a single faulty gene (*D*), which dominates its normal counterpart. Each child's chance of inheriting either the *D* or *d* allele from the affected parent is 50 percent.
Case B: Both affected parents have a single faulty gene (*D*), which dominates its normal counterpart. Each child's chance of inheriting a *D* allele from one of the parents is 75 percent.

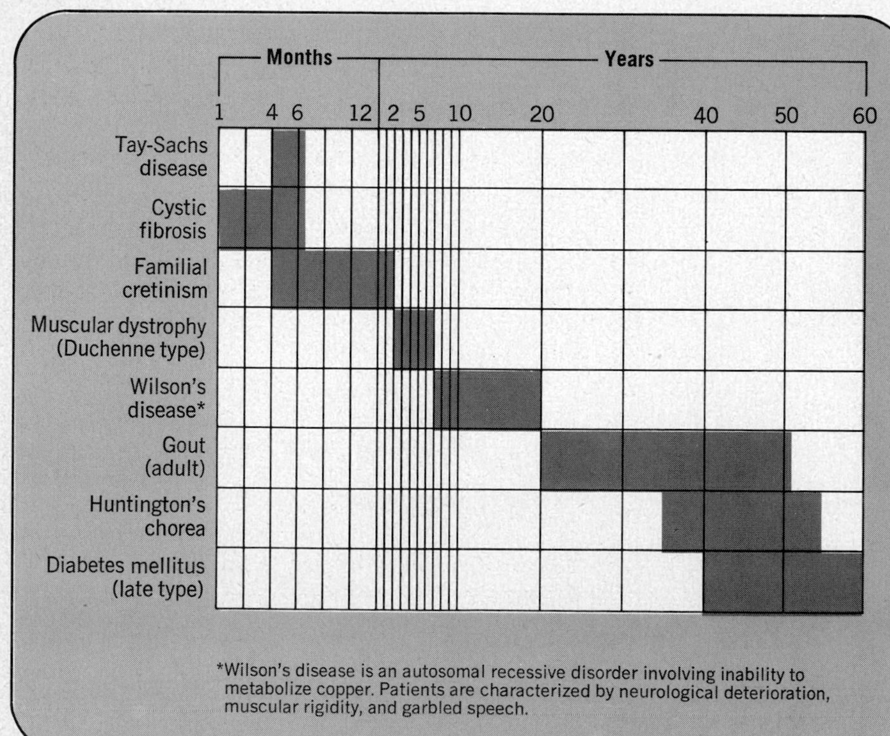

Figure 3.8 Eight Genetic Diseases: Age Range at Onset

In many disorders, a genetic disease shows up during the first year of life. But in others, the symptoms do not become apparent until much later. Huntington's chorea is an example of a late-onset disorder.

singer, songwriter, and movie actor, has a fifty-fifty chance of having inherited the disease (Arlo's mother's genotype is normal). Two of Guthrie's other children have already come down with the disease. Joseph's disease is another disorder caused by an autosomal dominant gene (see the boxed insert on page 76).

Defects caused by recessive genes will occur in the next generation only if the recessive gene is received from each parent. If both parents are carriers of the gene, there is a 25 percent chance in each pregnancy of producing an affected child (see Figure 3.9). Today there are more than 800 recognized recessive single-gene disorders, and the list grows yearly as others are identified. *Tay-Sachs disease,* associated with an enzyme defect, is one. It is a degenerative neurological disorder that leads to death, and it occurs primarily in the children of Ashkenazic Jews whose parents came from eastern Europe. It is estimated that one in thirty Jews with Ashkenazic ancestry carries the gene for the disease.

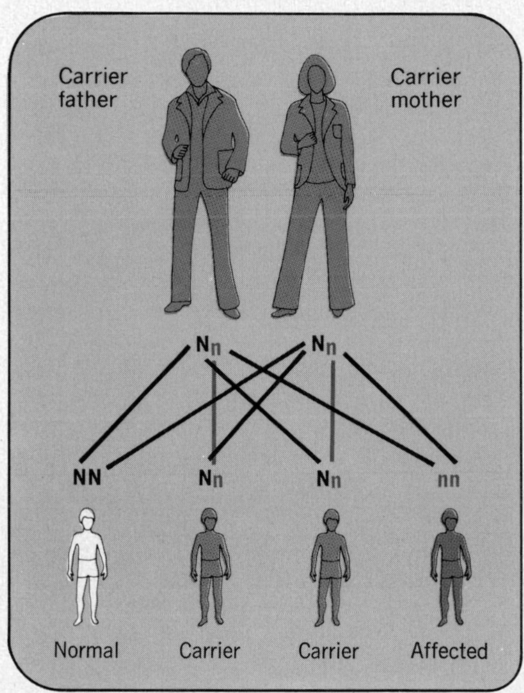

Figure 3.9 Transmission of Recessive Single-Gene Defects

Both parents, usually themselves unaffected by the faulty gene, carry a normal gene (*N*) that dominates its faulty recessive counterpart (*n*). The odds for each child are (1) a 25 percent chance of being *NN,* normal: inheriting two *N*s and accordingly being free of the faulty recessive gene; (2) a 50 percent chance of being *Nn* and therefore a carrier like both parents; and (3) a 25 percent risk of being *nn,* affected: inheriting a "double dose" of *n* genes, which may cause a serious genetic disease.

In the course of his pea experiments, Mendel also found that the distribution of one genetic trait is not affected by the distribution of another genetic trait. He observed, for instance, that the shape of a pod of a pea plant is independent of the color of its flower and the length of its stem. This led Mendel to formulate his second principle: the **principle of independent assortment.** It states that every characteristic is inherited independently of every other characteristic. Thus the genetic composition of an organism is an expression of statistical probability that is based on the laws of chance.* In other words, the combination of traits (the phenotype) that characterizes an organism is a function of the random recombining of given gene pairs.

Determination of Sex

Of the forty-six chromosomes (totaling twenty-three pairs) that each human being normally possesses, twenty-two pairs are similar in size and shape in both men and women. These are termed **autosomes.** The twenty-third pair, the **sex chromosomes,** are similar in females but dissimilar in males. Women have two X chromosomes (XX); men, an X and a Y chromosome (XY). The Y chromosome is somewhat smaller and has considerably fewer genes than the X chromosome.

Among human beings the sex of the offspring is determined by the male. Since women are XX, all their ova carry the X chromosome. But since males are XY, some of their sperm contain X chromosomes and some Y chromosomes. If a sperm with an X chromosome fertilizes the ovum, the offspring will be a female; if a sperm with a Y chromosome, a male. In sum, mothers give one of their X chromosomes to each child, but fathers give a Y chromosome to their sons and an X chromosome to their daughters.

Linked Characteristics

It is now known that Mendel's principle of independent assortment applies only to genes that are transmitted in different "linkage groups." In other words,

* The law of probability states that the chance of two or more independent events occurring together is the product of the chances of their separate occurrences.

TRACKING DOWN A GENETIC DEFECT: JOSEPH'S DISEASE

Antone Joseph was a nineteenth-century Portuguese seaman from the Azores, a group of islands off the Spanish coast (Kiester, 1976; Nylan, 1976; Rosenberg, 1981). About 1855, when his whaling vessel docked in San Francisco, he jumped ship and settled in California. His life was soon marred by a degenerative disease, from which he died at the age of forty-five.

Antone Joseph had six children. He lived long enough to see three of them afflicted by the same disorder. Of all his children, only his eldest daughter, Mary Joseph Rogers, had children—fourteen of them. Nine of these children also contracted the disorder, and six passed it on to some of their descendants.

Usually the first symptoms of Joseph's disease, as the disorder has come to be called, begin around age twenty-five and become more severe with the passage of time, resulting in death after thirteen to fifteen years. Initially the victims begin to stumble or lurch, and as the disorder progresses they need a cane, a walker, and then a wheelchair. Their eyes lose the ability to "track," their speech thickens and slurs, and their facial muscles quiver. In time, patients lose control of their bladder and bowels and have difficulty chewing and swallowing food. Intelligence, however, tends to remain intact to the end. Death commonly results from pneumonia or some other complication.

The disease had long been viewed by the descendants of Antone Joseph as a stigma and even a "curse." Through the years doctors had variously diagnosed individual family members as suffering from congenital syphilis or multiple sclerosis. The mysterious malady seemed to act in a capricious manner, striking down some in the family while ignoring others. Embarrassed and frightened, the family had long been reluctant to talk about the scourge even among themselves.

In 1973 one descendant of Antone Joseph, Rose Marie Silva, mustered her courage and decided to do something about the baffling disease that plagued her family. Her father and her favorite brother had both died from it at the age of thirty-nine. She contacted the National Genetics Foundation, a nationwide organization that has a network of fifty-two genetic counseling and treatment centers. With the assistance of specialists associated with the foundation, Mrs. Silva tracked down dozens of far-flung and long-lost relatives. On the basis of the resulting detailed family pedigree and old medical records, geneticists discovered that Joseph's disease is a disorder of protein metabolism associated with an autosomal dominant gene. The predicted 50 percent occurrence of the genetic defect has been confirmed in the offspring of affected parents. Originally, the gene could either have been inherited by Antone Joseph or have arisen through spontaneous mutation.

One weekend in September 1975, more than 80 of the 125 known living descendants of Antone Joseph gathered at the Children's Hospital in Oakland, California, to learn more about this new evidence regarding their family's scourge. Ten of them already showed the staggering gait and thickened speech typical of the disease. Before the family "reunion" ended, three additional relatives were found to be in the early stages of the disorder, and twenty-six more learned that they were "at risk." Others, however, had the burden of fear lifted when they discovered that they and their descendants did not carry the gene. The identification of Joseph's disease and its mode of transmission is a first step in the scientific endeavor to find some effective treatment and perhaps an eventual cure for this degenerative malady.

genes are inherited independently only if they are on different chromosomes. If they are linked so that they appear on the same chromosome, the genes tend to be inherited together.

Fortunately, as George and Muriel Beadle point out (1966: 68), Mendel did not encounter the effects of linked genes in his experiments:

> Knowing nothing about chromosomes or genes, let alone the phenomenon of linkage, Mendel might well have decided that his hypothesis was wrong—and very possibly he would have quit. He was spared this fate because, out of all the possible traits in peas which he might have picked for study, he happened to choose seven traits *each of which is controlled from a different chromosome.* (The probability of anyone's making such a happy choice, in random picks, is only about 1 in 163!) . . . Because of Mendel's good luck in this matter, linkage did not confuse his results; and each trait *did* segregate independently.

A good example of linked genes is seen in sex-linked traits. The X chromosome, for instance, contains many genes that are not directly related to the sexual traits of the individual. Hemophilia, a hereditary defect that interferes with the normal clotting of blood, is a sex-linked characteristic carried by the X chromosome. There are about 150 other known sex-linked disorders, including red-green color blindness, a type of muscular dystrophy, certain forms of night blindness, Hunter's disease (a severe form of mental retardation), and juvenile glaucoma (hardening of the eyeballs).

The vast majority of sex-linked genetic defects occur in men, since men have only one X chromosome (see Figure 3.10). In women the harmful action of a gene on one X chromosome is usually suppressed by a dominant gene on the other chromosome.* Thus, although they are themselves unaffected by a sex-linked disorder, women can be carriers of it. A man is affected if he receives from his mother an X chromosome bearing the genetic defect. A man cannot receive the abnormal gene from his father. Males transmit an X chromosome only to their daughters, never to their sons, who always receive a father's Y chromosome.

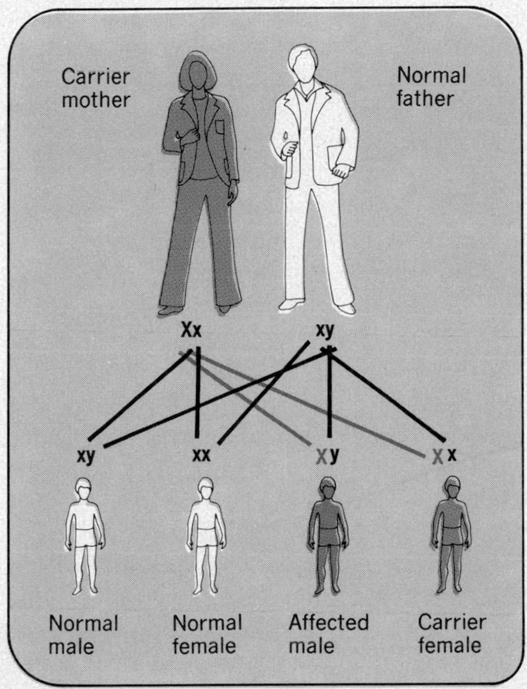

Figure 3.10 Transmission of Sex-Linked Genetic Defects

In most sex-linked genetic disorders, the female sex chromosome of an unaffected mother (a woman who does not herself show the disorder) carries one faulty gene (X) and one normal gene (x). The father carries a normal x and y chromosome. The statistical odds for each male child are (1) a 50 percent risk of inheriting the faulty X chromosome and hence the disorder and (2) a 50 percent chance of inheriting normal x and y chromosomes. For each female child, the statistical odds are (1) a 50 percent risk of inheriting one faulty X chromosome and hence becoming a carrier like her mother and (2) a 50 percent chance of inheriting no faulty gene.

Chromosomal Abnormalities

The normal number of chromosomes in human beings is forty-six, or twenty-three pairs. A number of disorders are associated with the presence of too few or too many chromosomes. For example, *Down's syndrome* (no longer referred to as Mongolism, because of the unfortunate racial connotations of the term) is a disorder that occurs in 1 out of every 600 live births. Down's syndrome is caused by an extra chromosome, which gives the infant a total of forty-seven chromosomes rather than the normal forty-six. (Three chromosomes of type 21 occur in the individual's cells, a condition called *trisomy 21*.) The extra chromosome is responsible for such characteristics as upward-slanted eyes, a short squat nose, a protruding underlip, underdeveloped genitals, broad stubby hands, deep tongue tissue, a short neck, neuromotor disabilities, and serious mental retardation.

Although the children affected by this disorder vary widely in temperament, many are affectionate, cheerful, and good-natured. They readily imitate other people, and they show a fondness for music. Children with Down's syndrome have a higher incidence of congenital disorders and greater susceptibility to infectious disease than normal children. Consequently, most used to die before the age of ten. With the development of antibiotics, however, the life expectancy of children with Down's syndrome has increased about fourfold.

The risk of giving birth to a child with Down's syndrome increases with the woman's age. Before age

* A woman can inherit such a disorder only if the X chromosome she receives from her mother and the X chromosome she receives from her father both bear a gene for a given disease. This rarely happens.

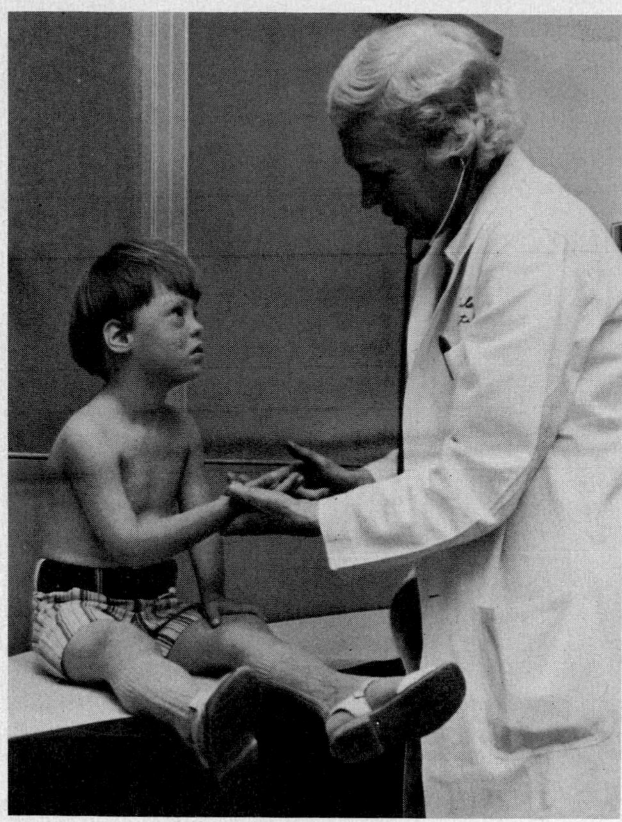

A Child with Down's Syndrome

This child probably has an extra chromosome number 21. As a result, he has characteristic developmental abnormalities.

March of Dimes

thirty the risk is 1 in every 1,000 pregnancies; at age forty it is 1 in 100; and at age forty-five it is 1 in 45. This drastic increase in the incidence of Down's syndrome with advancing maternal age suggests that an environmental factor that has not yet been identified may contribute to the chromosomal defect.

A number of other disorders are linked to sex chromosome abnormalities. Normal men have an X and a Y chromosome (XY). Normal women have two X chromosomes (XX). But in *Klinefelter's syndrome,* males have two X chromosomes and one Y chromosome (XXY). Such individuals possess undeveloped testes and commonly develop into tall, thin men with enlarged breasts. They are sterile and may show some mental impairment (Rubin et al., 1981; Pennington et al., 1982).

In *Turner's syndrome,* women, instead of having two X chromosomes, have only one (XO). These women are usually short in stature, with "webbed" necks, broad chests, and low-set ears. Although they have female sex organs, at puberty they fail to develop secondary sexual characteristics (they do not have ovaries and hence are deficient in female hormones). In some cases they are also mentally impaired.

In the past fifteen years another sex chromosome abnormality, XYY, has attracted considerable attention. Early studies suggested that such men tend to be superaggressive and violent because of the extra Y, or male, chromosome. More recent research reveals that XYY men are no more likely to commit violent crimes than XY men. (The boxed insert on pages 80–81 discusses how various of these conditions can be detected in the unborn child by new testing procedures.)

HEREDITY-ENVIRONMENT INTERACTIONS

The way a question is asked limits and disposes the ways in which any answer to it —right or wrong—may be given.

—SUSANNE K. LANGER
Philosophy in a New Key

To what extent is human behavior the product of biology, based on the unfolding of genetic characteristics that are present at birth? To what extent is human behavior determined by events in the external environment? And to what extent is it shaped by the interaction of hereditary and environmental components? These issues have concerned thinkers through the ages. Time and again the nature-nurture controversy has been officially pronounced dead because it seems to have been answered for all time. Yet in one fashion or another, each generation resurrects it, threshes it out once more, and then presumes to set it to permanent rest.

Some of the difficulties in the nature-nurture controversy stem from the fact that investigators often operate from different assumptions. Various schools ask different questions and hence come up with different answers. The manner in which we phrase our questions structures the alternatives by which the questions are answered.

Scientists began by asking *which* factor, heredity or environment, is responsible for a given trait, such as a mental disorder or a person's level of intelligence.

Later they sought to establish *how much* of the observed differences among people are due to differences in heredity and *how much* to differences in environment. And recently some scientists have insisted that a more fruitful question is *how* specific hereditary and environmental factors *interact* to influence various characteristics (Anastasi, 1958; Weisfeld, 1982). Each of these questions leads to its own theories, interpretations, and methods of inquiry.

The "Which" Question

Most students can recall debating in a class or a bull session the question "Which is more important, heredity or environment?" Yet most scientists today reject this formulation. They believe that phrasing the issue in terms of heredity *versus* environment has caused the scientific community, and society at large, untold difficulties. The "either-or" statement creates a hopeless dichotomy. Counterposing heredity to environment is similar in some respects to debating whether sodium or chlorine is more important in ordinary table salt. The point is that we would not have salt without both sodium and chlorine.

Every person is a joint product of heredity and environment. Broadly defined, **heredity** involves the biological transmission of traits from parents to their offspring through genes. **Environment** entails all the external factors that affect the organism. None of the characteristics that a human being displays could occur in the absence of either an appropriate heredity or an appropriate environment.

The "How Much" Question

As scientists came to recognize the inappropriateness of the "which" question, some of them reformulated the issue. Granted that both heredity and environment are essential for the emergence of any characteristic, they said, *how much* of each is required to produce a given trait? For example, they asked, "Does a person's level of intelligence depend on 80 percent heredity and 20 percent environment, 30 percent heredity and 70 percent environment, or some other ratio?" And they asked, "What are the respective contributions made by heredity and environment to the occurrence of a given mental disorder?"

Family Resemblance Studies. Scientists have traditionally sought answers to the "how much" question by measuring the resemblance among family members with respect to a particular trait. Botanists use similar procedures to discover the separate contributions that heredity and environment make in the plant world. They approach the problem by taking cuttings from a single plant and then replanting the parts in different environments: one at sea level, another at an intermediate elevation, and still another in the alpine zone of a mountain range. Each part develops into a new plant under different environmental conditions. Since the parts of each plant have

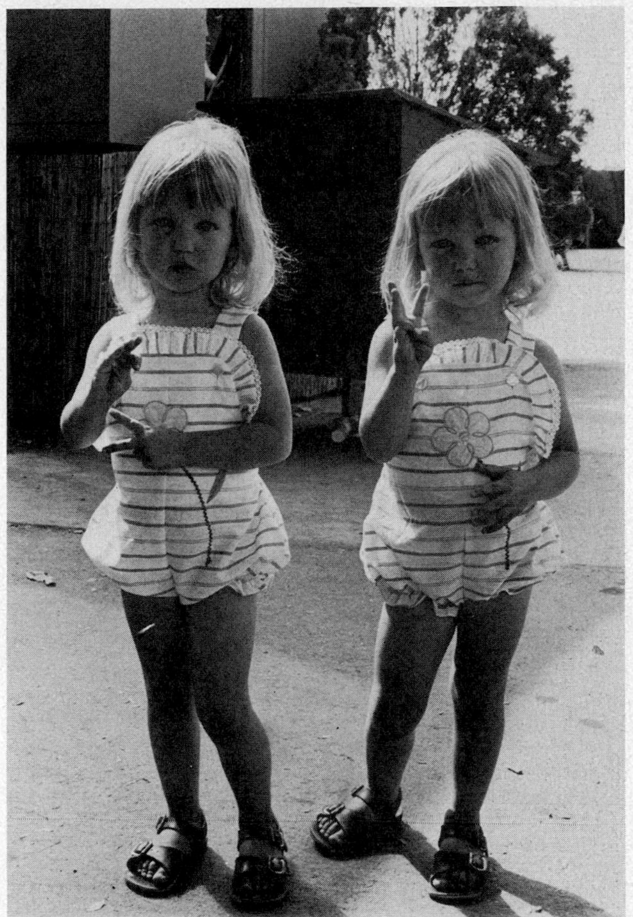

Identical Twins

Since identical twins develop from a single fertilized egg, they share an identical genetic inheritance. Researchers studying the relative contributions that heredity and environment make in shaping a given trait or behavior have concentrated on identical twins. A major difficulty with these studies, however, is that the environments of identical twins are often astonishingly similar. Many of them even spend their childhood wearing identical clothing.

Barbara Klutinis/Jeroboam

GENETIC COUNSELING AND TESTING

Within recent years techniques have been developed to identify many genetic and chromosomal problems before an infant's birth. A variety of tests are now available to parents with strong histories of genetic disease and to couples who, for whatever reason, wish to determine whether the fetus is normal. **Amniocentesis** is one commonly used procedure. In amniocentesis a physician inserts a long, hollow needle through a woman's abdomen into the uterus, drawing out a small amount of the amniotic fluid that surrounds the fetus (see Figure 3.11). The amniotic fluid contains cells of the unborn child, which are then grown in a laboratory culture and analyzed for the presence of various genetic abnormalities. Genetic and chromosomal defects, including those associated with Down's syndrome and about seventy other inherited biochemical disorders, can be detected in this manner. The test can be carried out as early as fourteen weeks after conception, but most physicians prefer to wait until the fetus is eighteen to twenty weeks old. The procedure is not without risk, since amniocentesis poses about a 1 percent risk of causing miscarriage.

Some doctors now utilize amniocentesis as a routine procedure for women who become pregnant after the age of thirty-five. The reason is that although women over thirty-five have only 10 percent of the babies born in the United States, they have half of those born with Down's syndrome. It is also often used in cases where a parent is known to carry abnormal chromosomes or where a previous pregnancy was associated with a chromosome abnormality.

More recently, researchers have devised a means of ultrasound scanning, termed **ultrasonography,** that allows physicians to trace the size and shape of a fetus and determine malformations. The procedure, which uses the principles of sonar devised by the navy, bounces sound waves off the fetus. The result is a picture that is safer than that afforded by x-rays. A number of physicians have found that parental viewing of the fetus by means of ultrasonography affords the additional advantage of accelerating parental bonding with the child (Fletcher and Evans, 1983). Still another procedure, *fetoscopy,* allows a physician to examine the fetus directly through a lens after inserting a very narrow tube into the uterus (a blood sample or skin biopsy can also be taken from the fetus). However, this procedure carries a higher risk than amniocentesis does.

Another new method is **chorionic villus biopsy.** The chorionic villi are hairlike projections of the membrane that surround the embryo during early pregnancy (see Chapter 4). The physician, guided by ultrasound, inserts a thin catheter through the vagina and cervix and, employing suction, removes a small plug of villous tissue. Although the chorion is not an anatomical part of the embryo itself, it is embryonic rather than maternal in origin. The cells can then be tested and the results known within days, even hours. By contrast, amniocentesis cannot be performed until later in a pregnancy and its results are not known for about two weeks. Chorionic villus biopsy allows for an early test that then can be checked later in the pregnancy by amniocentesis.

The University of California Medical Center in San Francisco recently reported on the results of 3,000 prenatal diagnoses done by amniocentesis at its facilities. More than 2,400 of the women were tested because they were over thirty-five years old. The other women were tested because the genetic history of one or both of the partners raised the possibility of a defective fetus. The tests uncovered 113 abnormal fetuses, all but 7 of which were aborted at the parents' request. Of the 3,000 women tested, the amniocentesis was in error in 14 cases, but only 6 of these errors were such as to constitute incorrect guidance in the decision whether to abort or continue pregnancy: 4 of the errors entailed failure to detect a defective fetus; 2 of them, abortion of unaffected fetuses.

In practice, the test results are negative in more than 96 percent of amniocentesis cases. Since most of the women who undergo amniocentesis are in categories of high risk for producing defective children, the procedure has afforded these families many months of relief from anxiety. Some medical authorities point out that prenatal diagnosis also makes childbearing more

identical heredities, any observed *differences* in vigor, size, leaves, stems, and roots are directly traceable to differences in environment (Dobzhansky, 1962). This is not to say that environment is more important than heredity. Even when genetic factors are held constant, they still contribute to the plant's characteristics.

Such deliberate experimentation is not possible with humans. Nonetheless, nature occasionally pro-

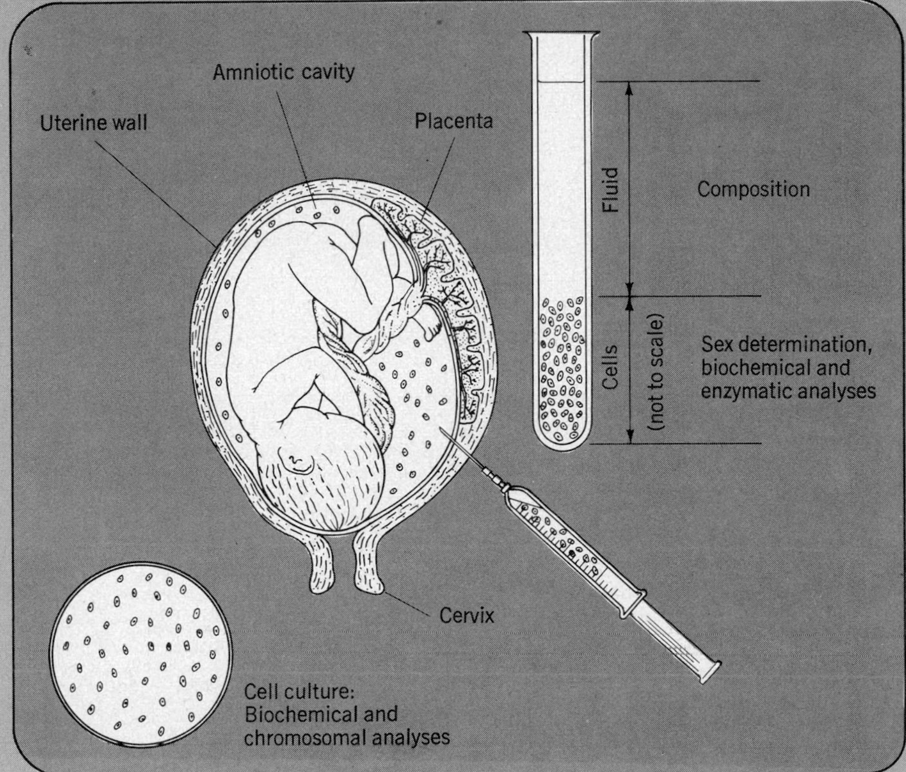

Figure 3.11 Amniocentesis

Amniocentesis is a procedure for detecting hereditary defects in the fetus. A sterile needle is inserted into the amniotic cavity, and a small amount of fluid is withdrawn. This sample is centrifuged to separate fetal cells from the fluid. The cells are then grown in a laboratory culture and analyzed for chromosomal and genetic abnormalities.

SOURCE: Eric T. Pengelley, *Sex and Human Life* (Reading, Mass.: Addison-Wesley Publishing Company, 1978). Figure 10.6, p. 176. © 1978 by Addison-Wesley. Reprinted with permission.

feasible for people who might otherwise be afraid to have children. It has also been employed to detect life-threatening conditions and to treat the fetus while still in the uterus (Henig, 1982). Many investigators expect that the field of fetal medicine will burgeon in the years ahead. Further, the earlier a genetic problem is identified, the greater the possibility that it might someday be corrected by some sort of treatment while the infant is still in the uterus. For instance, medical scientists hope in the future to transplant a healthy gene directly into the afflicted fetus, thus altering the infant's genetic blueprint. The aim is to treat disease by editing a "sick gene" out of the infant's hereditary code.

But procedures like amniocentesis and chorionic villus biopsy have also produced anguish and sorrow. Parents who learn that they are carriers of genetic diseases often feel ashamed and guilty, mortified to be stigmatized as genetic defectives (Restak, 1975; Chedd, 1981). They are also faced with the difficult decision of whether or not they should proceed with an abortion if the test results indicate the presence of a defective fetus. No wonder that lasting psychological problems can develop in parents who learn that the child they are expecting is abnormal. Among the problems are severe guilt reactions, depression, termination of sexual relations, marital discord, and divorce (Brody, 1976). Clearly, parents need psychological counseling in conjunction with genetic counseling.

vides us with the makings of a natural experiment. From time to time a fertilized egg, by some accident, gets split into two parts early in development. Each part grows into separate and complete individuals, termed **identical** or **monozygotic twins.** Genetically, each is essentially a carbon copy of the other.

Identical twins are usually reared together by their natural parents. But in some rare cases they are sep-

IDENTICAL TWIN RESEARCH

We typically marvel when we encounter identical twins because they have a mystique about them—two individuals possessing similar heredities. Not surprisingly, reports on identical twins have the makings of drama, something the popular media have hardly lost sight of. In recent years the University of Minnesota twin research of Thomas J. Bouchard, Jr., has commanded particular interest (Holden, 1980*a*, 1980*b*; Farber, 1981). Resemblances in interests, habits, and likes between identical twins reared apart have been labeled "astounding," "uncanny," "provocative," and "astonishing."

Indeed, some of the twins studied by Bouchard fit these descriptions. Take the case of Oskar Stöhr and Jack Yufe, two forty-seven-year-old brothers brought together by the Minnesota researchers. Separated at six months of age when their parents divorced, Stöhr lived with his mother in Eastern Europe while Yufe was reared in the Caribbean by his father. Stöhr was brought up as a Catholic and later was involved in the Hitler Youth Movement. Yufe was raised as a Jew, joined an Israeli kibbutz in his youth, and served in the Israeli navy.

Despite their different backgrounds, the twins reveal striking similarities in their behavior:

- When they first met at the airport, both sported mustaches and two-pocket shirts with epaulets and each carried wire-rimmed glasses with him.
- Both men like spicy foods and sweet liqueurs.
- Both flush the toilet before using it.
- Both store rubber bands on their wrists.
- Both read magazines from back to front.
- Both find it humorous to sneeze in a crowd of strangers.
- Both are absentminded and both fall asleep in front of the television.
- Both dip buttered toast in their coffee.
- Both have similar personality profiles as measured by the Minnesota Multiphasic Personality Inventory.
- Both reveal a similar tempo in the way they do tasks, ask similar kinds of questions, and exhibit similar personal mannerisms.
- Both excel at sports and have difficulty with math.

The Minnesota researchers have studied some thirty pairs of identical twins who were reared apart. They find that on many psychological and ability tests twins score even more closely than would be expected of the same person taking the same test a second time. And their brain-wave tracings differ no more than would tracings of the same person taken at different times. Hence, in large measure it seems that the twins are identically "wired." Nonetheless, twins differ from each other. For example, one twin is likely to be more confident, aggressive, or outgoing than the other.

It is easy, however, to overestimate the impact of genetic factors. For one thing, by virtue of their common heredities, identical twins are filtering their environmental experiences through similar perceptual and mental screens. And since their temperaments are so similar, they tend to seek out similar kinds of envi-

arated at an early age and adopted by different families. The study of identical twins reared under different environmental conditions is the closest approach possible to the experiments with plant cuttings (see the boxed insert above).

In contrast with identical twins, **fraternal** or **dizygotic twins** come from two eggs fertilized by two different spermatozoa. They are simply siblings who happen to be born at the same time. Important evidence can be obtained from comparing the average differences in the characteristics of identical and fraternal twins—for instance, their performance on intelligence tests. Moreover, comparisons can be made between identical twins reared *apart* and fraternal twins reared *together.* Many scientists believe that such comparisons reveal valuable information about the relative contributions that heredity and environment make to a particular trait or behavior.

Another means for assessing family resemblances is by studying children who were adopted at birth and reared by foster parents. It is possible to compare some characteristic of the adopted children, such as IQ score or the presence of a particular mental disorder, with that of their biological parents and their

Identical Twins: Jack Yufe and Oskar Stöhr

The two brothers who, despite being separated at an early age and living in quite different environments, show remarkable resemblances at age forty-seven. Jack is at the left; Oskar at the right.

Courtesy, Thomas J. Bouchard, Department of Psychology, University of Minnesota

ronment. For instance, sociable children are more likely than less sociable children to search out opportunities in which to interact with others. And thus sociable children draw out from other people social interaction while less sociable children tend to be overlooked and ignored by others.

Further, similarities between identical twins are admittedly quite captivating. Yet their similar physical appearances may accentuate in an observer's mind their overall similarities. Consequently, comparable studies of the similarities and differences between pairs of age-matched strangers are also required—indeed, when paired college students are brought together to discover any resemblances, many similarities in the conduct of their everyday lives are evident (Rose, 1982). And there are also cohort effects in interests, attitudes, and education for twins born at the same time. Thus individuals born in 1890 have quite different experiences from individuals born in 1950. Although studies of twins have been viewed with suspicion in some quarters because they long have been used to prove a genetic point of view, they nonetheless are an invaluable source of data for studying behavioral similarities and differences among human beings.

foster parents. In this fashion, researchers attempt to weigh the relative influences of the genetic factor and the home environment.

As Jerome Kagan (1979) points out, over the past decade the scientific community has been taking a more tolerant attitude toward heredity's contribution to individual variation. Interest in hereditary aspects of behavior had been subdued for nearly half a century by both behaviorism and psychoanalytic theory. The renewed interest in biological factors is partly due to exciting new discoveries in microbiology and genetics and partly to the failure of social scientists to document a consistently strong relationship between measures of environmental experience and behavioral outcome.

A good illustration of the shift toward an increased emphasis on predisposing biological factors is found in genetic studies of such diverse behavior as shyness, stuttering, alcoholism, dyslexia, and juvenile violence (Plomin, DeFries, and McClearn, 1980; Pines, 1982*b*). Take the field of juvenile violence. In recent decades most behavioral scientists have favored psychological and sociological explanations for the violent offenses of delinquent youth. More recently, a group of Yale researchers have challenged this thesis (Adams, 1979). They have found that violent offenders, when compared with nonviolent delinquents, more often show such psychiatric symptoms as paranoia, hallucinations, and delusions, and such neurological symptoms as abnormal electroencephalograms and blackout spells.

A significant proportion of the violent youth had suffered head injuries early in life. The researchers have also found more psychotic and neurological symptoms in the parents of violent offenders than in those of nonviolent delinquents. This suggests to the Yale group that a genetic factor might be implicated in juvenile violence. It is important to stress that the Yale researchers do not say that violent behavior is inherited. Instead, they suggest that *some* children may inherit a vulnerability to stress that can flare into violence if ignited by something in the environment.

Studies of Schizophrenics. Studies dealing with schizophrenia provide a good illustration of scientific efforts to answer the "how much" type of question through family resemblance studies. **Schizophrenia** is a form of severe mental illness. It is commonly characterized by one or more symptoms such as hallucinations, disordered and illogical thinking, inappropriate emotional responses, personality deterioration, bizarre behavior, and gradual withdrawal from reality (American Psychiatric Association, 1980; Grove, 1982). The National Institute of Mental Health (1980) estimates that about 2 million Americans—some 1 percent of the population—can be classified as schizophrenics. Individuals diagnosed as schizophrenics account for an estimated 50 percent of the resident patients in mental hospitals.

Some theoretical explanations of schizophrenia emphasize heredity, some environment. Theorists who accentuate heredity (hereditarians) commonly look to genetic factors that disrupt normal metabolic functioning. Theorists who concentrate on environment (environmentalists) look to factors that are associated with childhood emotional trauma. In studying these alternatives, researchers compare the **concordance rates** for identical and fraternal twins. Generally they begin by screening individuals who have been admitted to mental hospitals, identifying those who have a twin, and finding out whether the twin has also been diagnosed as schizophrenic. If the disorder occurs in both members of the twin pair, it is concordant; if not, discordant. Hence a 60 percent concordance rate means that in six out of every ten twin pairs, both twins have been diagnosed as schizophrenic. During the past forty years, a number of studies have been undertaken in the United States and Europe investigating the concordance rates of schizophrenia for identical and for fraternal twins (Kendler, 1983). Overall, the concordance rate for identical twins is about 60 percent, while that for fraternal twins is about 15 percent.

Another approach designed to separate genetic inheritance from environmental influence entails the study of foster children. Since 1963 the National Institute of Mental Health (NIMH) has sponsored continuing research with a sample of 216 adopted children whose current average age is thirty-three and who are thus still at substantial risk (Kety et al., 1978; Wender, 1979; Kety, 1983; Lowing, Mirsky, and Pereira, 1983). So far, this study shows that about 20 percent of the children born to schizophrenic parents but adopted by nonschizophrenic parents have developed schizophrenia or schizoid symptoms. Among those born to nonschizophrenic parents but adopted by schizophrenic parents, only 5 percent have developed schizophrenia or schizoid symptoms. In a comparison group of nonadoptees, 24 percent of those born to and raised by schizophrenic parents showed signs of the disorder.

This NIMH research points to the conclusion that schizophrenia runs along biological family lines rather than adoptive family lines. As such it provides support for the view that a strong genetic component is associated with schizophrenia (Shields, 1976). This statement should not be taken to mean that somehow a gene clicks on and a person exhibits schizophrenic symptoms. The only thing a gene can do is instruct a cell to make a protein substance. Genetic factors are believed to contribute to various forms of mental illness through genes that code for proteins regulating brain functions, especially the **neurotransmitters** (Wender and Klein, 1981). Neurotransmitters are chemical substances that convey information across the synaptic gaps between the nerve cells that make up the brain and nervous system. In the case of schizophrenia, a prominent hypothesis holds that the neurotransmitter dopamine is excessively active in the brains of its victims (Bunney, 1978; Snyder, 1981; Sternberg et al., 1982). Additionally, some schizophrenics appear to be deficient in another brain enzyme, monoamine oxidase, or MAO (Potkin et al., 1978; Wyatt, Potkin, and Murphy, 1979). It should

SUPERCHILDREN: THRIVING AGAINST INCREDIBLE ODDS

Clinical psychologists and psychiatrists have traditionally focused on the maladjusted and mentally ill. Now a few of them have begun to study the opposite end of the spectrum—children who thrive despite enormous difficulties. Termed by some "superchildren" or "invulnerables," they are the offspring of schizophrenics or are children who are abused, extremely poor, or otherwise at risk. E. James Anthony, a psychiatrist who works with the children of psychotic parents, observes:

> They deal with life with an excellence and an adaptive capacity that don't seem to come from anywhere, as if they had carved out these qualities by themselves. We think, here's this awful home; here are these awful parents; here's this awful upbringing, and, we expect, here is the awful result. But, instead, here's a really remarkable child. (Quoted by Pines, 1979*a*: 53)

A disease ecologist, Jacques May, provides us with an analogy regarding vulnerability and risk (Solnit and Provence, 1979). Imagine that we have three dolls, one made of glass, one of plastic, and one of steel. We hit each doll with a hammer. The first doll shatters into hundreds of pieces, the plastic doll is dented, while the steel doll gives off a fine metallic sound. The steel doll represents the "superchildren." In the middle range between the two extremes, the plastic doll resembles children who suffer some damage from their adverse circumstances but who manage to function for the most part adequately. The glass doll represents those children who are severely disturbed or subject to recurrent psychotic episodes.

"Superchildren" tend to share a number of characteristics (Pines, 1979*a*). First, they are quite at ease with people while simultaneously making others feel comfortable with them. Second, they are adept at extracting support and encouragement from teachers, relatives, baby-sitters, and other adults who compensate for their parents' inadequacies. Third, they actively tackle their environment and have a sense of their own power and competence. Fourth, they minimize their emotional involvement with a sick parent and acquire a high degree of independence early in life. And, fifth, they are an achieving group who generally show a good deal of creativity and originality.

One thing above all stands out. "Superchildren" need challenges to become invulnerables. Low-risk conditions do not compel children to mobilize their resources and do not provide the real life circumstances by which children test, hone, and refine their adaptive capabilities.

"Superchildren" remind us of Greek mythology. When Achilles' mother, Thetis, learned of the fatal destiny awaiting her son, she tried to immunize him against his fate by plunging him into the protective waters of the river Styx. In so doing, Thetis rendered all of Achilles, except for the heel by which she held him, invulnerable to harm. Later, when Achilles was nine, a seer prophesied that he would conquer Troy but that he would die in the process. His resourceful mother disguised Achilles as a girl, but Odysseus discovered the deception, and Achilles was inducted into military service. Achilles died at Troy when his vulnerable heel was pierced by an arrow. By contrast, Hercules triumphed over nearly impossible dangers by virtue of his own efforts, while his mother looked on, always confident that he would succeed.

Like Hercules, "superchildren" have not been overprotected from risk. They seem to gain both in confidence and in competence from their encounters with difficulty. Immunity that is self-generated is apparently more complete and longlasting. In real life, however, there does appear to be a limit to the number and severity of concurrent stresses that even the most resilient children can handle and master. All of this suggests that we still have a good deal to learn about vulnerability and risk in childhood and at what developmental periods and with what outside resources intervention might be most effective.

be stressed, however, that the NIMH study also gives evidence of an environmental component, since the incidence of schizophrenia in the adopted children runs lower than it does among biological family members living together (Lidz et al., 1981). And some children thrive despite incredible odds (see the boxed insert above).

The "How" Question

A number of scientists, such as the psychologist Anne Anastasi (1958), believe that the task of science is to discover *how* hereditary and environmental factors work together to produce behavior. They argue that the "how much" question, like the "which" question,

Adoption Research

Research has found that most of the IQ gap between blacks and whites is closed among black children who are adopted as infants by white middle-class parents.

Steve Hansen/Stock, Boston

is unproductive. The "how much" question assumes that nature and nurture are related to each other in such a way that the contribution of the one is *added* to the contribution of the other to produce a particular behavior.

Anastasi, among others (Wohlwill, 1973; Lerner, 1976, 1978; Weisfeld, 1982), disputes this view. She argues that as applied to human life, neither heredity nor environment exists separately. They are always intertwined, continually interacting. Consequently, Anastasi says, it is a hopeless task to identify "which" of the two factors produces a particular behavior or to determine "how much" each contributes (see Figure 3.12). However, Anastasi recognizes that the role played by hereditary factors is more central in some aspects of development than in others. She thus sets forth the notion of the **continuum of indirectness.** At one end of the continuum are the contributions of heredity that are most direct, such as physical characteristics like eye color and chromosomal disorders like Down's syndrome. At the other end of the continuum are the contributions of heredity that are quite indirect, such as the social stereotypes that the members of a given society attach to various categories of skin color and hair texture.

An analogy may prove helpful in understanding the notion of "interaction" that is so central to Anastasi's position. Consider ordinary table salt. At room temperature, sodium is a soft, solid substance that reacts violently with water and hence would produce devastating effects if we were to place it in our mouths. Likewise, chlorine is a toxic greenish-yellow gas that, if inhaled, would irritate our lungs and make us choke. But when sodium and chlorine are brought together, they combine to form sodium chloride, a white crystalline substance that is an essential human nutrient.

Sodium chloride differs *qualitatively* in its characteristics from either sodium or chlorine. It is the molecular *interaction* between the two elements that gives the compound its unique character. Hence sodium chloride is not a mechanical mixture of sodium and chlorine that we can place in some sort of sieve in order to separate one from the other physically. And by the same token, it is a fruitless task to undertake an assessment of "how much" each element "adds" to the compound. "Which" and "how much" questions, therefore, are relatively meaningless when examining the relationship between the compound sodium chloride and the two elements sodium and chlorine.

Medawar (1977: 14) notes another reason why it may not be possible to attach exact percentages to the contributions of heredity and environment. Since heredity and environment interact in a relationship of varying dependence, what appears to be a hereditary

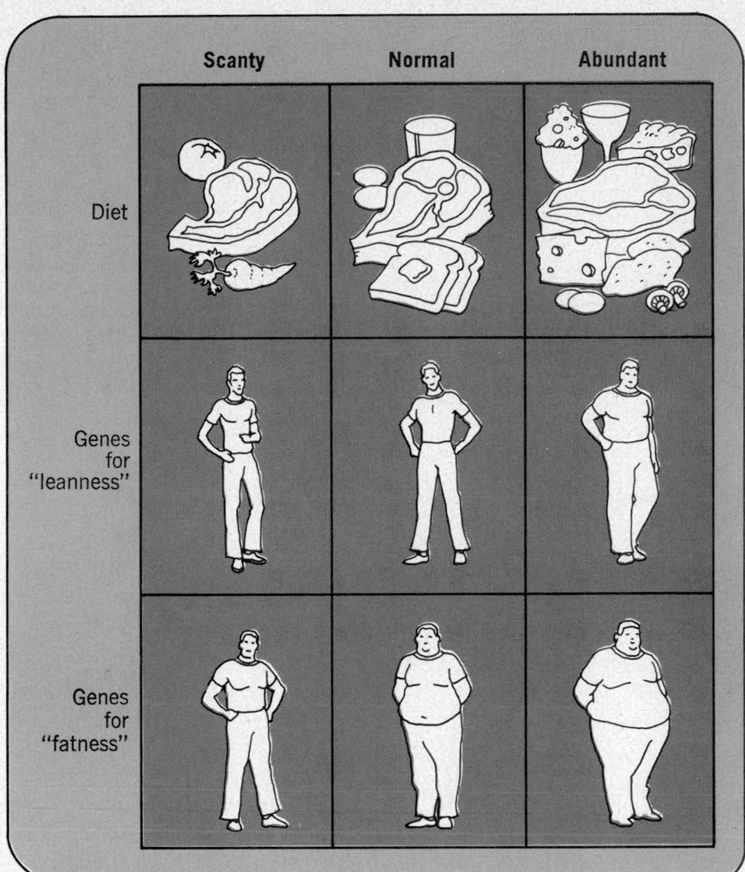

Figure 3.12 Gene-Environment Interaction

A person who has a gene for "fatness" may actually weigh less than one with a gene for "leanness," if the former lives on a scanty and the latter on an overabundant diet.

SOURCE: T. Dobzhansky, *Mankind Evolving* (New Haven: Yale University Press, 1962), Figure 2, p. 45. © 1962 by Yale University Press. Reprinted with permission.

contribution in one context can be seen as an environmental contribution in another. An example is provided by phenylketonuria (PKU), a severe form of mental retardation that was discussed in Chapter 1. PKU results from the inability of the body to metabolize phenylalanine, a common ingredient of our diet. The disorder is transmitted genetically according to straightforward Mendelian rules (Scriver and Clow, 1980*a*, 1980*b*). But if a child who has inherited a susceptibility to the disease is given a diet free of phenylalanine, there is no buildup of toxic materials and the child's development is essentially normal. Hence under the circumstances of a phenylalanine-free diet, PKU can be viewed as entirely environmental in origin. This is due to the fact that PKU shows up in the presence of phenylalanine but not in its absence.

Ethical and practical considerations do not allow scientists to manipulate genetic and environmental variables in experiments with humans. But research with animals has furnished many insights into the process by which hereditary and environmental factors dynamically interact to shape the course of development. For example, neurobiologists have investigated how nerve cells interact with visual stimulation to produce vision in rabbits, cats, and monkeys. In one type of study researchers sew one eye of a kitten shut shortly after it is born. Several months later they reopen the eye and find that the cat cannot see with it. This is because the absence of stimulation affects the way visual stimuli are processed in the kitten's brain. Only a small fraction of the nerve cells in the kitten's visual cortex within the brain respond with electrical signs when researchers shine light on the deprived eye. In contrast, nearly all these cells respond when light is shone on the normal eye. Thus early visual experience interacts with genetic endowment to produce sight (Kolata, 1975; Smith et al., 1978). Similarly, researchers in a number of laboratories have demonstrated that significant differences are produced in several aspects of brain biochemistry and brain anatomy when rats are reared

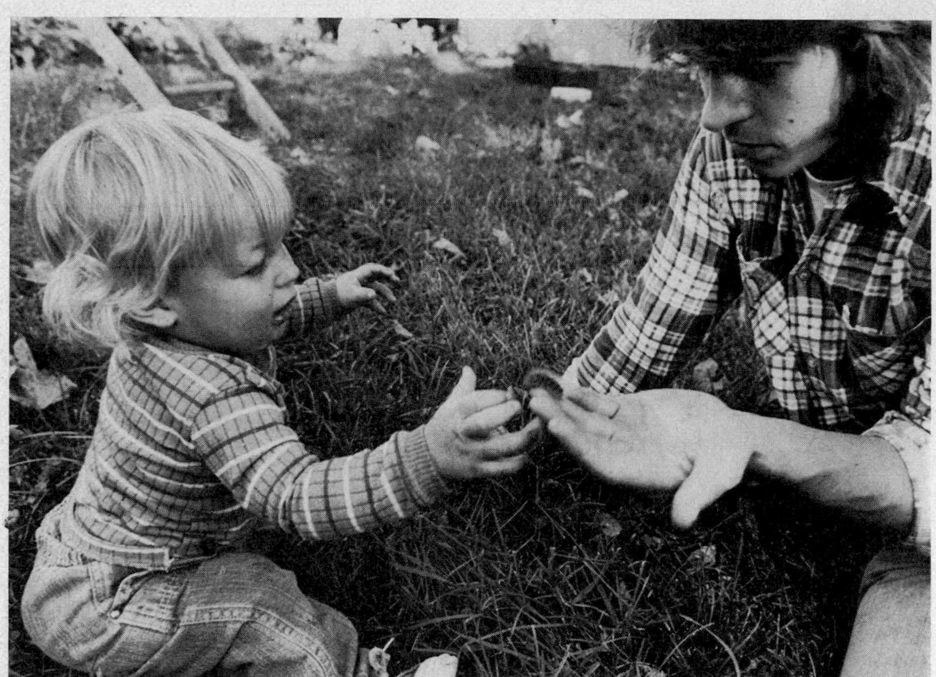

Promoting Learning

Parents who spend time with their children, interact with them, show interest in their experiences, and cultivate their knowledge and skills foster competent and creative youngsters. Parents are not only biological but also social and cultural links between the hundreds of generations that have gone before and the hundreds yet to come. Thus hereditary and environmental factors interact to fashion the generations of humanity.

Patrick Reddy

under differing environmental conditions (Rosenzweig and Bennett, 1978).

Psychologists Harold D. Grotevant, Sandra Scarr, and Richard A. Weinberg (1977*a*, 1977*b*, 1978) have shown how hereditary and environmental factors interact in career selection. They compared the interests of parents with those of their teenage children in two groups: 109 adoptive families and 114 biologically related families. For the most part, both groups of families were similar in education and income. The children and parents were rated on such things as whether they leaned toward pursuits that are artistic, scientific, rugged, enterprising, or social.

The researchers found considerable similarity between parents and children in biologically related families. But in the adoptive families the similarities were no greater than if the subjects had been selected randomly from the general population. This should not be taken to mean that we inherit genes for being a doctor, an auto mechanic, or a teacher. Rather, genetic factors broadly influence our styles of interacting and coping with the world, such as emotionality, sociability, and activity level. In this way genes seemingly predispose us to be more attracted to certain activities and occupations than to others.

SUMMARY

1. Like all other living things, human beings are capable of producing new individuals of their own kind and thus ensuring the survival of the species. This process is termed "reproduction." Two kinds of cells are involved in human reproduction: the male gamete, or sperm, and the female gamete, or ovum. A male sperm fuses with a female ovum to form a zygote (fertilized egg).

2. A mature ovum is produced about every twenty-eight days. Toward the middle of each monthly ovarian cycle, an ovum usually reaches maturity and passes into one of the oviducts. If sperm are present, fertilization takes place in the upper end of the oviduct. Secretions of progesterone from the corpus luteum prepare the uterus for implantation of the zygote. If pregnancy does not occur, the thickened outer layers of uterine tissue are shed. This process, called "menstruation," generally occurs fourteen days after ovulation.

3. Upon fertilization, the twenty-three chromosomes of the ovum are combined with the twenty-three chromosomes of the sperm, bringing the total number of chromosomes to forty-six, or twenty-three pairs. In reproduction, a new individual arises from the fusion of two cells, an ovum and a sperm; therefore the distribution of the chromosomes cannot occur in the usual manner. Instead, a process called "meiosis" takes place. Meiosis involves two cell divisions, during which the chromosome number is halved.
4. Central to Mendelian theory is the notion that genes determine inherited characteristics.
5. Mendel demonstrated that in a cross between purebred pea varieties, one allele—the dominant character—completely masks, or hides, the other allele—the recessive character. This allowed Mendel to distinguish between an organism's genotype and phenotype.
6. Mendel pointed out that characteristics do not blend with or contaminate one another but preserve their original integrity as they pass unchanged in succeeding generations from child to grandchild. He called this the "principle of segregation." In the course of his pea experiments, Mendel also noted that the distribution of one genetic trait is unaffected by the distribution of other genetic traits. He called this the *principle of independent assortment.*
7. Of the forty-six chromosomes normally possessed by human beings, twenty-two pairs are similar in size and shape in both men and women. These are called the *autosomes.* The twenty-third pair, the sex chromosomes, are similar in females but dissimilar in males. Women have two X chromosomes (XX); men have an X and a Y chromosome (XY).
8. It is now known that Mendel's principle of independent assortment applies only to genes that are transmitted in different "linkage groups." If genes are linked so that they appear on the same chromosome, they tend to be inherited together. This is the source of sex-linked genetic defects.
9. Some of the difficulties that surround the nature-nurture controversy stem from the fact that investigators often operate from different models or basic assumptions. The manner in which we phrase our questions structures the alternatives by which the questions are answered.
10. Scientists began by asking *which* factor, heredity or environment, is responsible for the fashioning of a given trait. Most scientists have come to recognize that a great many problems arise from inserting the word "versus" between the words "heredity" and "environment." It serves to separate and oppose two components that, in the context in which they are generally discussed, are neither separable nor opposable.
11. When scientists came to recognize the inappropriateness of the "which" question, some of them took a somewhat different approach. They sought to establish *how much* of the observed differences among people are due to heredity and *how much* to differences in environment. Scientists have traditionally sought answers to the "how much" question through studies that measure resemblances among family members with respect to given traits. Studies dealing with schizophrenia provide a good example of this approach.
12. Recently a number of scientists have argued that the "how much" question, like the "which" question, leads to no productive end. They have insisted that a more fruitful approach is to be found in the question of *how* specific hereditary and environmental factors work together to influence various characteristics.

KEY TERMS

allele One of two or more alternative forms of a gene.

amniocentesis A medical procedure that allows a physician to test for fetal defects by analyzing cells contained in the amniotic fluid.

autosomes The twenty-two pairs of chromosomes that are similar in size and shape in both men and women.

chorionic villus biopsy A medical procedure that allows a physician to test for embryonic defects by analyzing cells contained in the chorionic villus.

chromosome A long, threadlike body that contains the hereditary materials found in the nuclei of all cells.

concordance rate The extent to which two distributions are similar.

continuum of indirectness The view that heredity plays a more central role in some aspect of development than in others. At one end of the continuum the contributions of heredity are quite direct; at the other end, quite indirect.

deoxyribonucleic acid (DNA) The molecules comprising genes; the active substance of genes that serves as a "recipe" or "blueprint" telling cells how to manufacture vital protein substances.

dominant character An allele that completely masks or hides another allele in the phenotypic expression of a genetic characteristic.

environment All the external factors that affect an organism.

fertilization The union of a sperm and an ovum.

fraternal (dizygotic) twins Siblings who are born at the same time and who come from two separate eggs.

gene A unit of a chromosome.

genetics The scientific study of biological inheritance.

genotype The genetic makeup of an organism.

heredity The biological transmission of traits from parents of offspring through genes.

heterozygous A genotype that contains dissimilar alleles within a gene pair.

homozygous A genotype that contains identical alleles within a gene pair.

identical (monozygotic) twins Siblings who are born when a fertilized egg gets split into two parts early in development. Each part grows into separate and complete individuals who in most respects are genetically carbon copies of each other.

infertility A condition in which a couple fails to achieve pregnancy after one year of having engaged in sexual relations with normal frequency and without contraception.

meiosis Two cell divisions, during which the chromosome number is halved.

neurotransmitter A chemical substance that conveys information across the synaptic gaps between the nerve cells that make up the brain and nervous system.

phenotype The observable characteristics of an organism. In human beings the phenotype includes physical, physiological, and behavioral traits.

principle of independent assortment Mendel's law stating that every characteristic is inherited independently of every other characteristic.

principle of segregation Mendel's law stating that characteristics do not blend with or contaminate one another but preserve their original integrity as they pass unchanged in succeeding generations.

recessive character An allele that is completely masked or hidden by another allele in the phenotypic expression of a genetic characteristic.

reproduction The process by which organisms produce more organisms of their own kind.

schizophrenia A severe form of mental illness characterized by one or more symptoms such as hallucinations, distorted and illogical thinking, inappropriate emotional responses, personality deterioration, bizarre behavior, and gradual withdrawal from reality.

sex chromosomes The pair of chromosomes that are similar in women (XX) and dissimilar in men (XY).

ultrasonography A procedure employing ultrasounds that allows physicians to trace the size and shape of a fetus and determine malformations.

Part Two

The Prenatal and Neonatal Periods

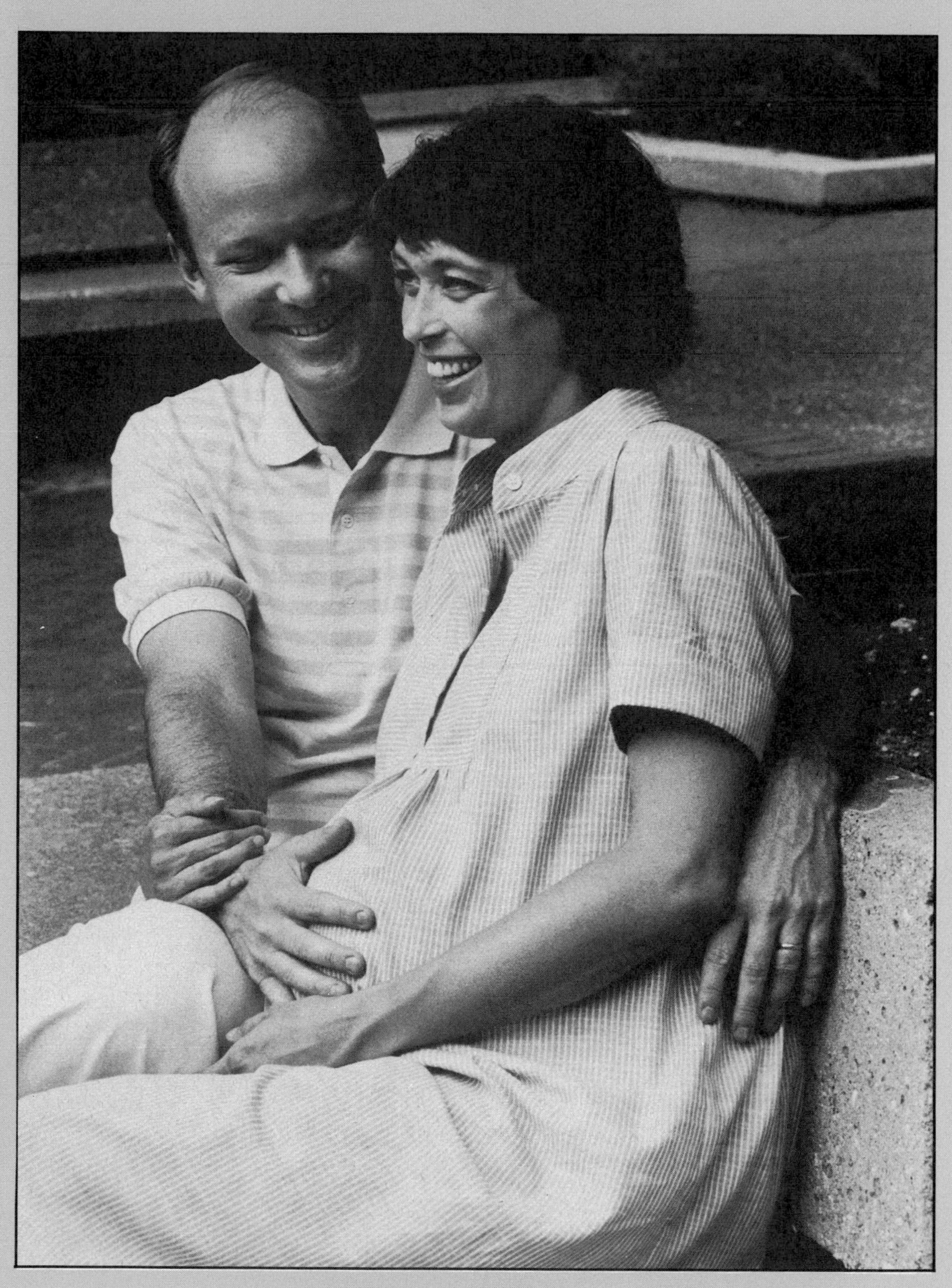

4

Prenatal Development and Birth

One hundred and fifty years ago the English critic and poet Samuel Taylor Coleridge wrote: "The history of man for the nine months preceding his birth would, probably, be far more interesting, and contain events of greater moment, than all the three score and ten years that follow it." Only in recent years have scientists developed the skill to study these nine crucial months, and they have found that Coleridge was quite right.

Between conception and birth, the human being grows from a single cell, barely visible to the naked eye, to a mass of about seven pounds containing some 200 billion cells. Of this period Ashley Montagu, a well-known physical anthropologist, writes (1964: 20–21):

> Never again in his life, in so brief a period will this human being grow so rapidly or so much, or develop in so many directions, as he does between conception and birth. . . . During this critical period, the development of the human body exhibits the most perfect timing and the most elaborate correlations that we ever display in our entire lives. The building and launching of a satellite, involving thousands of people and hundreds of electronic devices, is not nearly so complex an operation as the building and launching of a human being.

This chapter will describe the remarkable and important period of prenatal development and the process of birth.

STAGES OF PRENATAL DEVELOPMENT

The **prenatal period** is the time elapsing between conception and birth. It normally averages about 266 days, or 280 days from the last menstrual period. Embryologists divide prenatal development into three stages. The first, the **germinal period,** extends from conception to the end of the second week; the second, the **embryonic period,** from the end of the second week to the end of the eighth week; and the third, the **fetal period,** from the end of the eighth week until birth.

The Germinal Period

The germinal period is characterized by (1) the growth of the zygote and (2) the establishment of a linkage between the zygote and the support system of the mother. After fertilization, the zygote begins a four-day journey down the oviduct (see Figure 4.1). It is moved along by the action of the cilia and the active contraction of the muscular walls of the oviduct. Within a few hours of fertilization, growth begins with the initiation of **mitosis** (see Figure 4.2). In mitosis the zygote divides, forming two cells identical in makeup to the first cell. In turn each of these cells divides, making four cells. The four cells then divide into eight, eight into sixteen, sixteen into thirty-two, and so on.

The early cell divisions in development are called *cleavage.* Cleavage occurs very slowly. It takes about twenty-four hours for the first cleavage and ten to twelve hours for each subsequent cleavage. These cell divisions soon convert the zygote into a hollow ball of cells termed a **blastocyst.**

For two or three days the blastocyst is free within the uterine cavity. When it is about six to seven days old and composed of some one hundred cells, the blastocyst makes contact with the *endometrium,* the wall of the uterus. The endometrium in turn becomes vascular, glandular, and thick. The blastocyst "digests" its way into the endometrium through the action of enzymes and gradually becomes completely buried in it. As a result, the embryo develops within the wall of the uterus and not in its cavity. This invasion of the uterus by the blastocyst creates a small pool of maternal blood. During the germinal period, the organism derives its nourishment from the eroded tissue and maternal blood that flow through spaces in the outer layer of cells of the blastocyst.

By the eleventh day the blastocyst has completely buried itself in the wall of the uterus. At this stage in development the organism is about the size of a pinhead. As of yet, the mother is seldom aware of any symptoms of pregnancy.

At about the time that the blastocyst starts the implantation process, it begins separating into two layers (see Figure 4.3). The outer layer of cells, called the

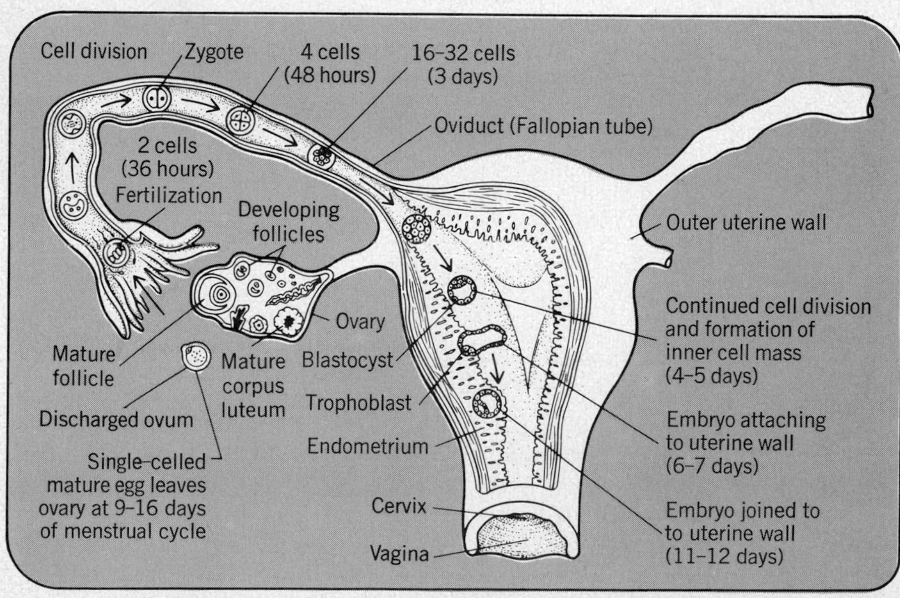

Figure 4.1 Early Human Development: The Course of the Ovum and Embryo
The drawing depicts the female reproductive system, the fertilization of the ovum, and the early growth of the embryo.

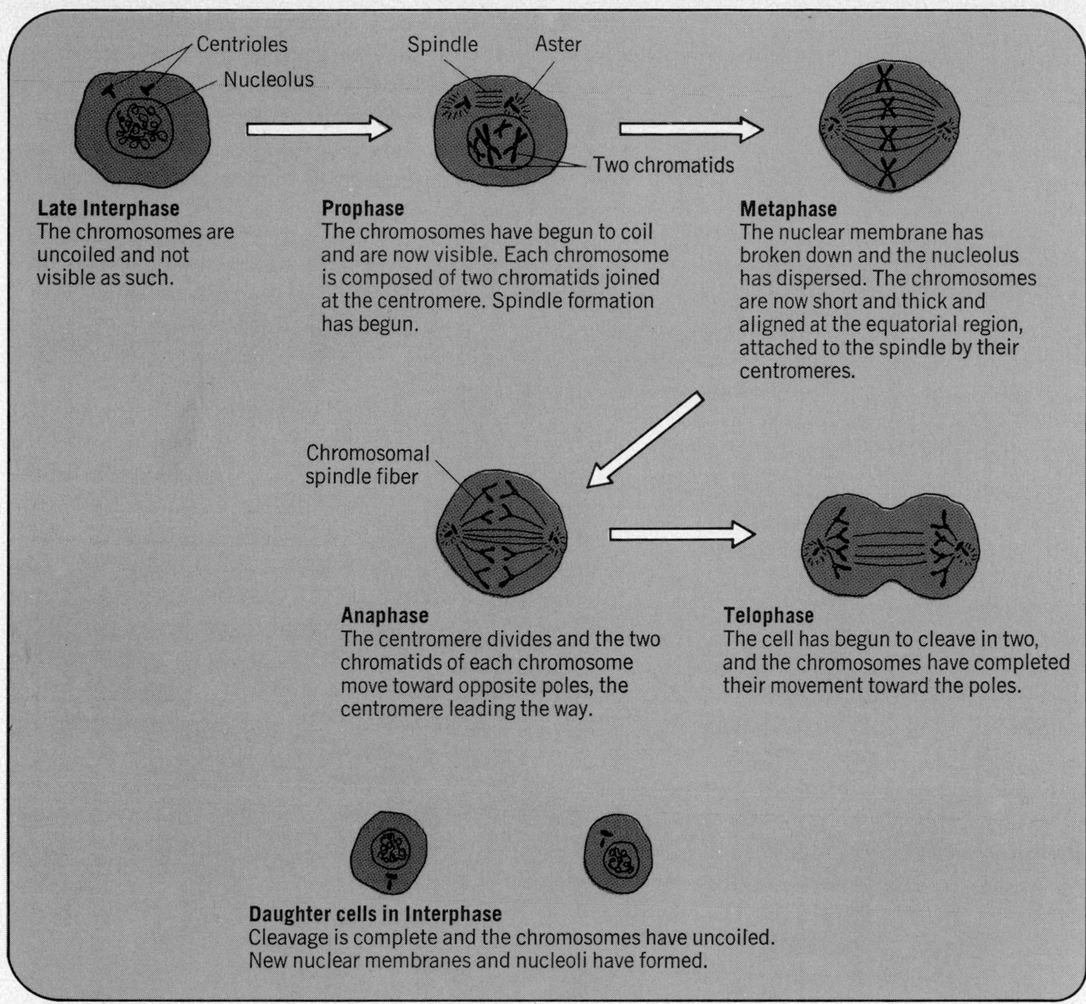

Figure 4.2 Stages in Mitosis

In mitosis the nucleus of a cell divides into two nuclei, each of which has the same kind and number of chromosomes. Through this process two new cells are formed. For descriptive purposes, it is convenient to subdivide mitosis into the four stages shown here: the prophase, metaphase, anaphase, and telephase. The interphase is the resting period during which the chromosomes are in an uncoiled condition and hence difficult to see, but it is in the interphase that each chromosome is duplicated in the seclusion of the nucleus.

SOURCE John B. Jenkins: *Genetics*, Copyright © 1975 by Houghton Mifflin Company. Used with permission.

trophoblast, is responsible for embedding the embryo in the uterine wall. The inner surface of the trophoblast becomes the nonmaternal portions of the placenta, the *amnion* and *chorion.* The amnion forms a closed sac around the embryo. It is filled with a watery amniotic fluid to keep the embryo moist and protect it against shock or adhesions. The chorion is a membrane that surrounds the amnion and links the embryo to the placenta. The internal disc or cluster of cells that compose the blastocyst, termed the *inner cell mass,* produces the embryo. The amnion, chorion, embryo, and related tissues are depicted in Figure 4.4 as they appear in increasingly differentiated and advanced stages of development.

Toward the end of the second week, the embryonic portion of the inner cell mass begins to separate into

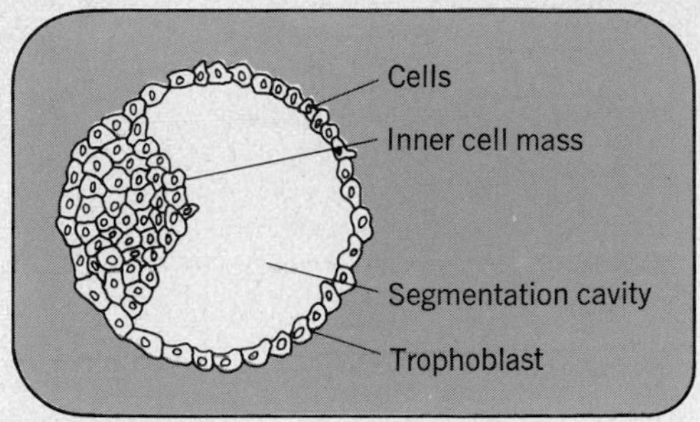

Figure 4.3 Schematic Cross Section of the Blastocyst at About Seven Days

Cleavage of the zygote produces a small ball of cells within which appears a fluid-filled cavity: the *segmentation cavity.* The blastocyst differentiates into two layers. The outer layer, the *trophoblast,* gives rise to the nonmaternal portion of the placenta; the internal cluster of cells, the *inner cell mass,* becomes the embryo. When the blastocyst is about six or seven days old, it begins implanting itself in the uterine wall.

three layers: the *ectoderm* (the outer layer), which is the source of future cells forming the nervous system, the sensory organs, the skin, and the lower part of the rectum; the *mesoderm* (the middle layer), which gives rise to the skeletal, muscular, and circulatory systems and the kidneys; and the *endoderm* (the inner layer), which develops into the digestive tract (including the liver, the pancreas, and the gall bladder), the respiratory system, the bladder, and portions of the reproductive organs.

The Embryonic Period

The embryonic period lasts from the end of the second week to the eighth week. It spans that period of pregnancy from the time the blastocyst completely implants itself in the uterine wall to the time the developing organism becomes a recognizable human fetus. This period is characterized by (1) rapid growth, (2) the establishment of a placental relationship with the mother, (3) the early structural appearance of all the chief organs, and (4) the development, in form at least, of a recognizable human body (see Figure 4.5).

The embryo becomes attached to the wall of the uterus by means of the *placenta* (Beaconsfield, Birdwood, and Beaconsfield, 1980). The placenta forms

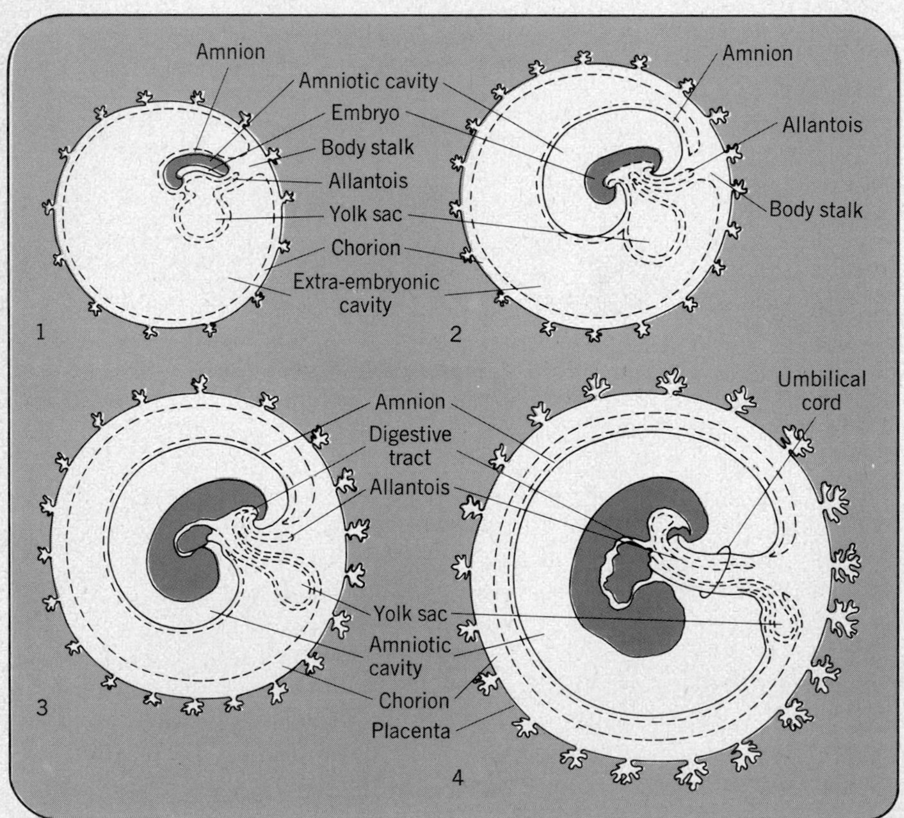

Figure 4.4 Human Embryonic Development: The Early Stages

The figure shows the successive stages in the early development of the human embryo. The primary embryonic membranes are the *amnion* and the *chorion.* The amniotic cavity provides a fluid environment that cushions the embryo. The chorion is the embryonic part of the placenta. From the chorion develop *villi,* small capillaries that extend into the maternal portion of the placenta. The embryo is joined to the placenta by the umbilical cord. The solid lines represent layers of ectoderm; the dashed lines, mesoderm; and the dotted lines, endoderm.

SOURCE: Claude A. Villee, *Biology,* 7th ed. (Philadelphia: W. B. Saunders Company, 1977), Figure 27–15, p. 627. Copyright © 1977 by W. B. Saunders Company. Reprinted by permission of Holt, Rinehart and Winston, CBS College Publishing.

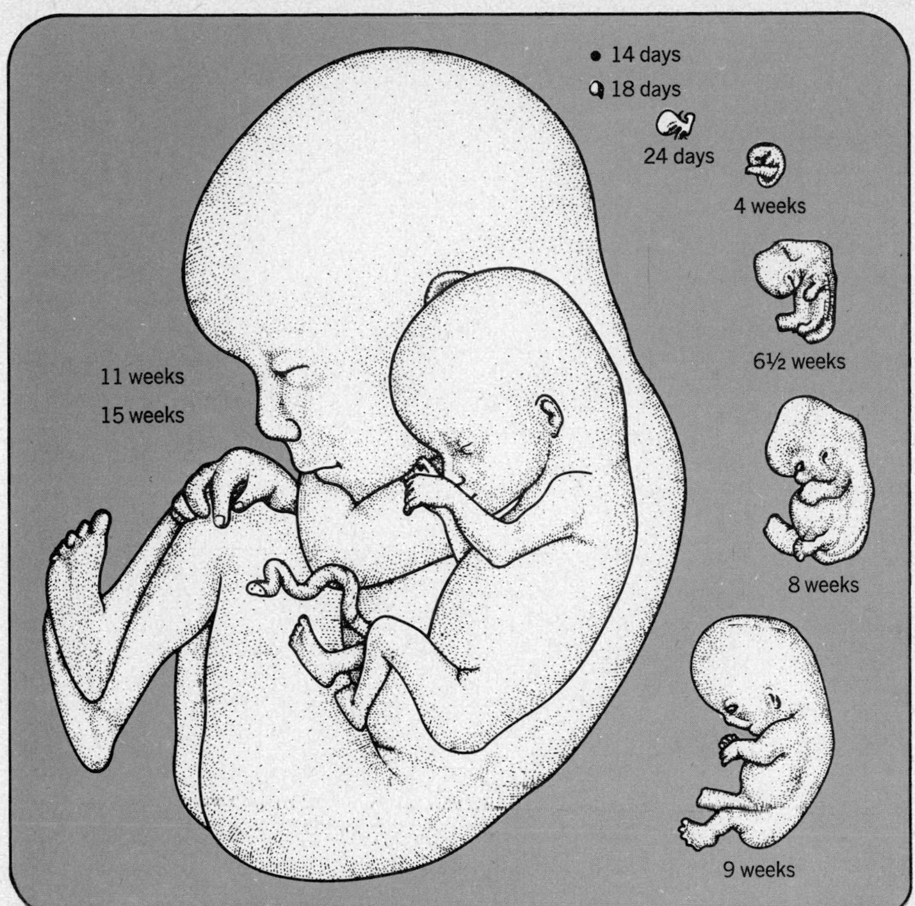

Figure 4.5 Human Embryonic Development: Fourteen Days to Fifteen Weeks

These drawings are *life-size*, showing development of human embryos between fourteen days and fifteen weeks.

SOURCE: Leslie B. Arey, *Developmental Anatomy*, rev. 7th ed. (Philadelphia: W. B. Saunders Company, 1974), Figure 80, p. 101. Reprinted by permission.

from uterine tissue and the trophoblast of the blastocyst. It functions as an exchange terminal that permits the entry of food materials, oxygen, and hormones and the exit of carbon dioxide and metabolic wastes. It is a partially permeable membrane that does not permit the passage of blood cells between the two organisms. This feature provides a safeguard against the mingling of the blood of the mother with that of the embryo. Were the mother's and embryo's blood to intermix, the mother's body would reject the embryo as foreign material.

The transfer between the placenta and the embryo occurs across a web of fingerlike projections—*villi*—that extend into blood spaces in the maternal uterus. The villi begin developing during the second week, growing outward from the chorion. When the placenta is fully developed at about the seventh month of pregnancy, it is shaped like a pancake or disc that is 1 inch thick and 7 inches in diameter. From the beginning, the embryo is linked to the placenta by the *umbilical cord,* a conduit carrying two arteries and one vein. This connecting structure, or lifeline, is attached to the middle of the fetal abdomen.

Development starts with the brain and head areas and then works its way down the body—termed **cephalocaudal development** (see Figure 4.6). In this manner, nature ensures an adequate nervous system for the proper functioning of other systems. During the early part of the third week, the developing embryo begins to take the shape of a pear, the broad, knobby end of which becomes the head. The cells in the central portion of the embryo also thicken and form a slight ridge that is referred to as the *primitive streak.* The primitive streak divides the developing embryo into right and left halves and eventually becomes the spinal cord. The tissues grow in opposite directions away from the axis of the primitive streak, a process termed **proximodistal development.**

By the twenty-eighth day, the head region takes up roughly one-third of the embryo's length (see Figure

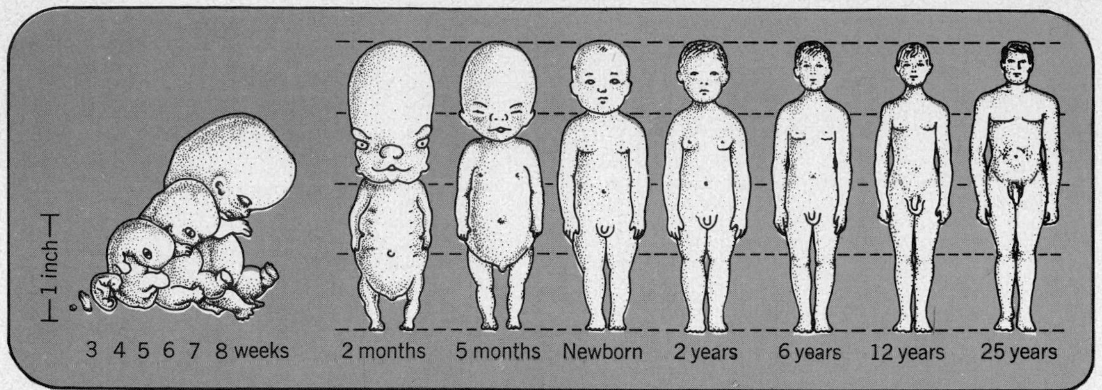

Figure 4.6 Changes in the Form and Proportion of the Human Body

The drawing depicts the growth of a male's body during the embryonic, fetal, and postnatal stages. Note the developmental changes in the size of the head and limbs in relation to the size of the body.

SOURCE: Roberts Rugh and Landrum B. Shettles, *From Conception to Birth: The Drama of Life's Beginnings* (New York: Harper & Row, 1971), p. 37, copyright © 1971 by Roberts Rugh and Landrum B. Shettles, reprinted by permission; and W. J. Robbins et al., *Growth* (New Haven: Yale University Press, 1928), p. 118, reprinted by permission.

4.7). Also about this time, a brain and a primitive spinal cord become evident. As development progresses during the second month, the head elevates, the neck emerges, and rudiments of the nose, eyes, mouth, and tongue appear. Another critical system—the circulatory system—also develops early. By the end of the third week the heart tube has already begun to beat in a halting manner.

Within four weeks of conception, the embryo is about ⅕ inch long—nearly 10,000 times larger than the fertilized egg. About this time, the mother usually becomes suspicious that she is pregnant. Her menstrual period is generally two weeks overdue. She may feel a heaviness, fullness, and tingling in her breasts; simultaneously, the nipples and surrounding areolas may enlarge and darken. Also at this time, about one-half to two-thirds of all pregnant women experience a morning queasiness or nauseous feeling. The condition, popularly called "morning sickness," persists for several weeks or months.

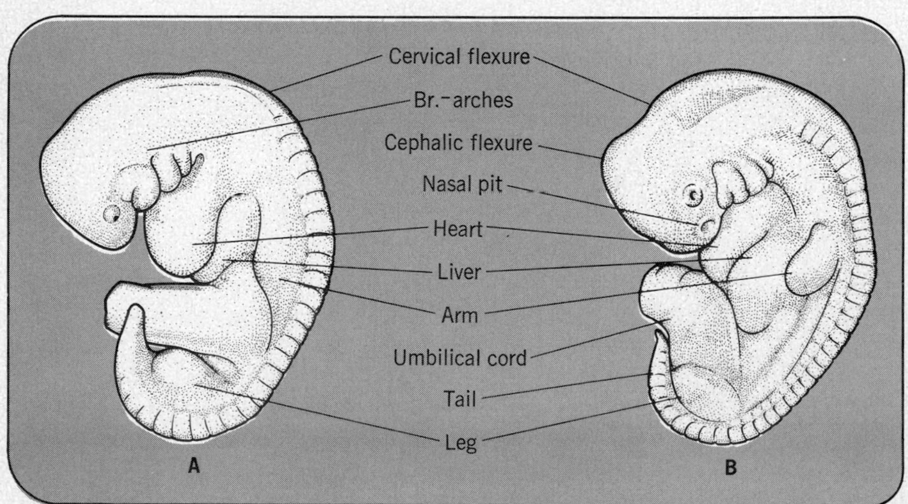

Figure 4.7 Human Embryos of Four and Five Weeks

The embryos are shown from the left side. The size of embryo A is five millimeters (the drawing is magnified 12 times). The size of embryo B is eight millimeters (magnified 7.5 times).

SOURCE: Leslie B. Arey, *Developmental Anatomy,* rev. 7th ed. (Philadelphia: W. B. Saunders Company, 1974), Figure 77, p. 98. Reprinted by permission.

The Fetal Period

The final stage in prenatal life—the fetal period—begins with the ninth week and ends with birth. During this time the major organ systems continue to develop and the organs assume their specialized functions (Arey, 1974). By the end of the eighth week, the organism definitely resembles a human being. It is complete with face, arms, legs, fingers, toes, basic trunk and head muscles, and internal organs. The fetus now builds on this basic form (see the boxed insert on page 100).

Development during the fetal period is less dramatic than that during the embryonic period. Even so, significant changes occur. By the tenth week the fetal face acquires a truly human appearance (see Figure 4.8). During the third month the fetus develops the skeletal and neurological structures that lay the foundation for spontaneous movements of the arms, legs, and fingers. By the fourth month stimulation of the infant's body surfaces activates a variety of reflex responses. About the beginning of the fifth month, the mother generally begins to feel the spontaneous movements of the fetus (called *quickening,* a sensation like a moving butterfly in the abdominal region). Also during the fifth month a fine, downy, woolly fuzz (*lanugo hair*) comes to cover the fetal body.

At six months the eyebrows and lashes are well

Figure 4.8 Development of the Human Face

Between four and a half and ten weeks, the fetal face acquires a truly human appearance. However, even by the tenth week the eyes are still far apart, the ears are not fully elevated, the nostrils are only somewhat closer together, and the mouth is open.

SOURCE: Roberts Rugh and Landrum B. Shettles, *From Conception to Birth: The Drama of Life's Beginnings* (New York: Harper & Row, 1971), pp. 48–49. Copyright © 1971 by Roberts Rugh and Landrum B. Shettles. Reprinted by permission.

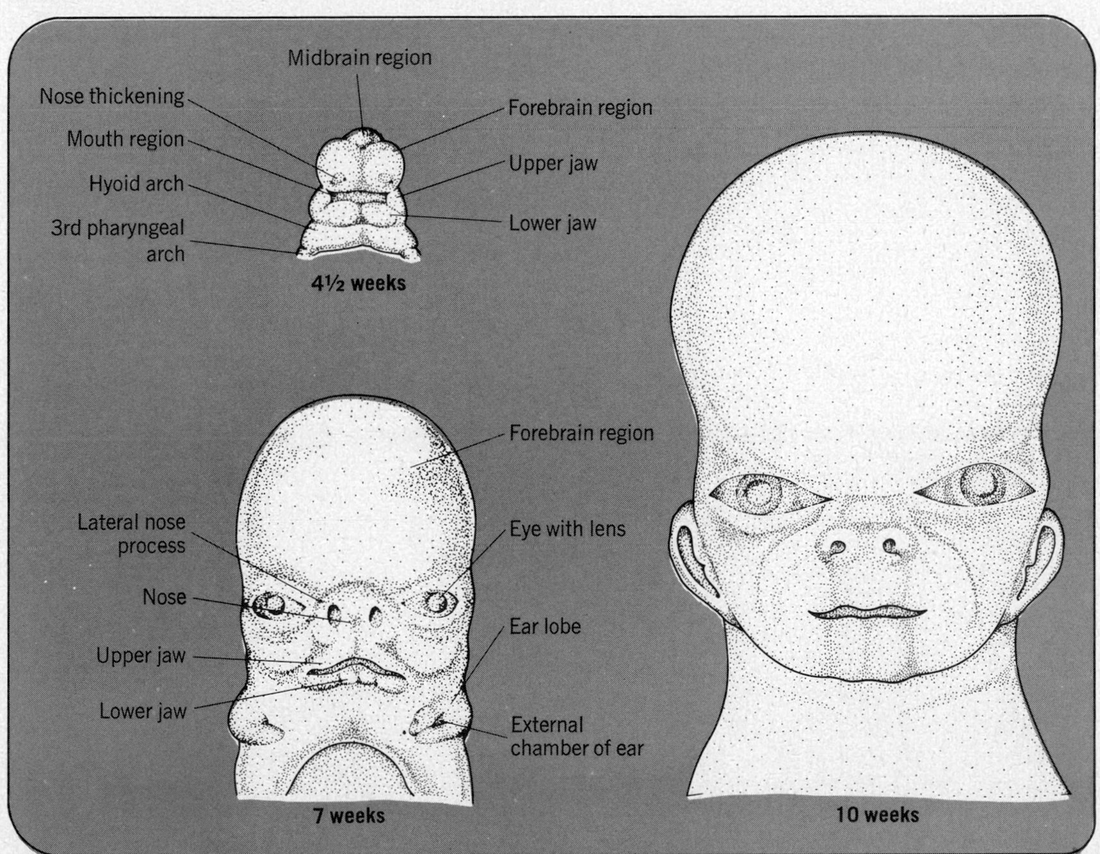

HIGHLIGHTS OF PRENATAL DEVELOPMENT

First Month

- Fertilization occurs.
- Blastocyst implants itself in the lining of the uterus.
- The blastocyst differentiates into the trophoblast and the inner cell mass.
- The inner cell mass differentiates into three layers: the ectoderm, the mesoderm, and the endoderm.
- Nervous and circulatory systems begin to develop.

Second Month

- The head develops rapidly, at first accounting for about half of the embryo's size.
- The face and neck begin to form.
- The eyes rapidly begin converging toward the center of the face.
- Mouth and jaws form and become well differentiated.
- Major organs of the digestive system become differentiated.
- Buds for the limbs form and grow.
- The circulatory system between the embryo and the placenta is completed, and heartbeats begin.

Third Month

- The digestive organs begin functioning.
- Centers of ossification (bone formation) appear.
- Buds for all temporary teeth form.
- Sex organs develop rapidly, especially in males.
- Arms, legs, and fingers make spontaneous movements.

Fourth Month

- The face acquires a human appearance.
- The lower parts of the body show rapid growth, with the body outgrowing the head.
- Reflex movement becomes brisker.
- Most bones are distinctly indicated throughout the body.
- In males, the testes are in position for later descent into the scrotum; in females, the uterus and vagina are recognizable.

Fifth Month

- Lanugo hair (a fine, woolly fuzz) covers the whole body.
- Vernix (a waxy coating) collects.
- The nose and ears begin ossification.
- Fingernails and toenails begin to appear.

Sixth Month

- Eyebrows and lashes are well defined.
- The body is lean, but strikingly human in its head and body proportions.
- The cerebral cortex becomes layered.
- The eyes are completely formed.

Seventh Month

- If born, the fetus is capable of living outside the uterus.
- The fetus looks like a dried-up, aged person with red, wrinkled skin.
- The cerebral fissures and convolutions develop rapidly.

Eighth and Ninth Months

- Subcutaneous fat is deposited for later use.
- The fingernails reach beyond the fingertips.
- A good deal of the lanugo hair is shed.
- Initial myelination of the brain takes place. (Myelin is a fatty substance that forms a sheath around the axons of nerve cells.)
- The activity of the chief organs is stepped up.
- Vernix is present over the entire body.

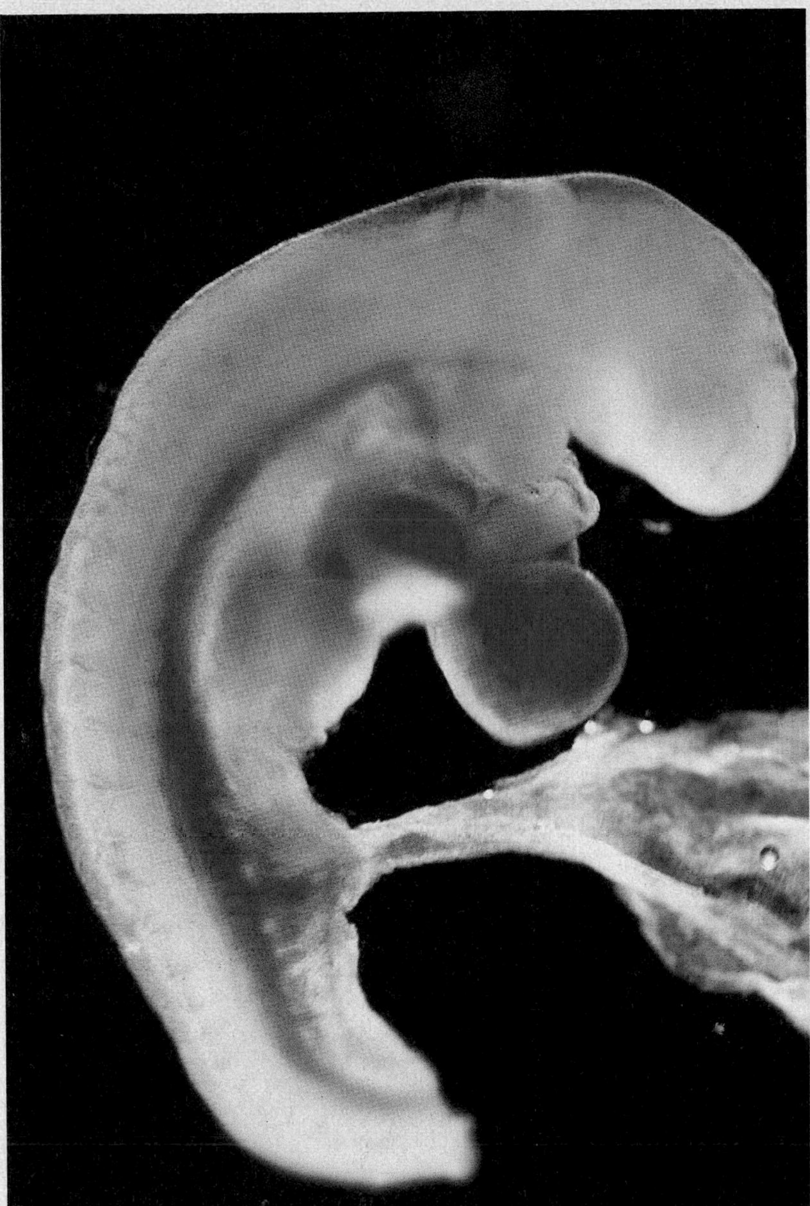

The Embryo

The photo depicts an embryo at thirty days. It is as yet only 1/5th of an inch in size. A large vessel leads from the trunk to the yolk sac. Along the back, horizontal segments that gradually decrease in size toward the bottom or tail can also be seen. The heart is forming at the fourth segment from the top.
Lennart Nilsson, from *A Child Is Born,* Dell, 1966

defined; the body is lean but strikingly human in its proportions; the skin is wrinkled. At seven months the fetus (now weighing about 2½ pounds and measuring about 15 inches in length) gives the appearance of a dried-up, aged person, with red, wrinkled skin covered by a waxy coating (*vernix*); it is now a viable organism and able to cry weakly. At eight months fat is being deposited around the body, the fetus gains an additional 2 pounds, and the infant increases its neuromuscular activity.

At nine months the dull redness of the skin fades to pink, the limbs become rounded, and the fingernails and toenails are well formed. At full term (thirty-eight weeks) the body is plump; the skin has lost most of its lanugo hair, although the body is still covered with vernix; and all the organs necessary to carry on independent life are functioning. The fetus is now ready for birth.

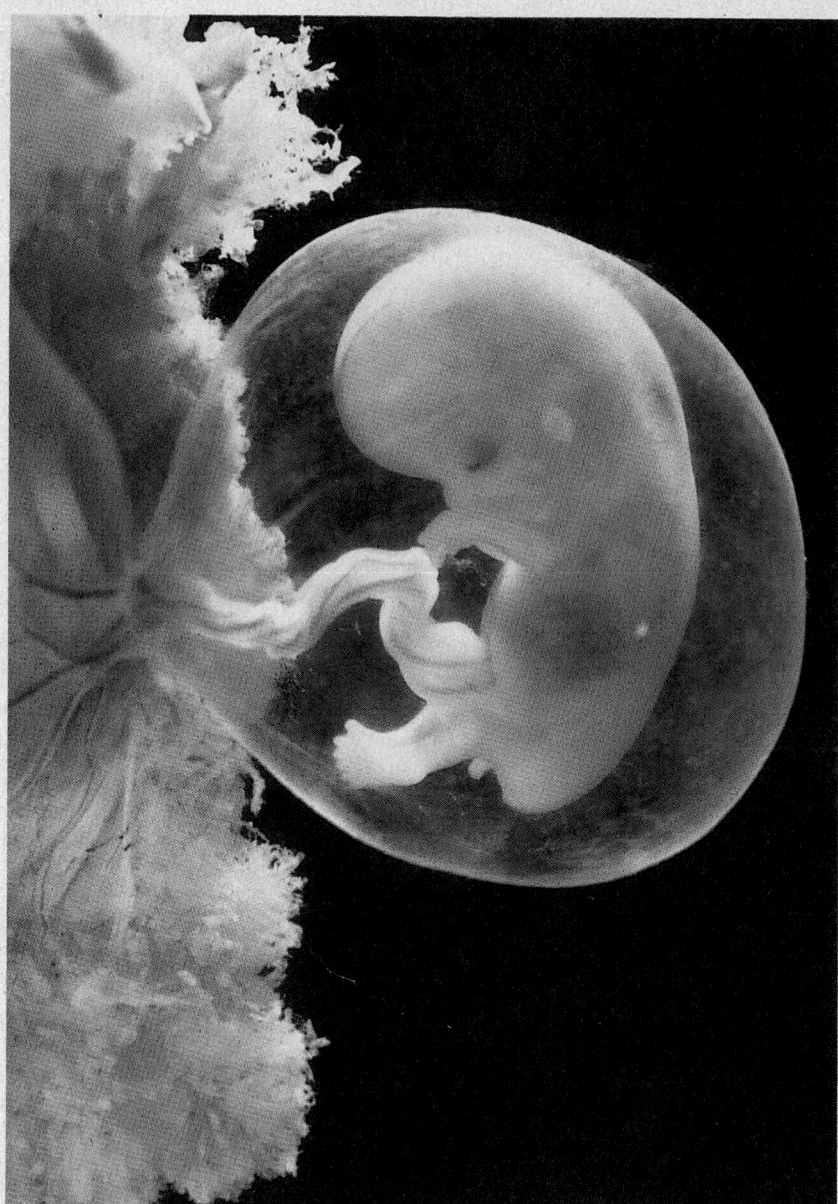

The Fetus at the Ninth Week

At the beginning of the fetal period—about the ninth week—the developing child has already acquired recognizable human features. The face, hands, and feet are forming in a distinctly human fashion.

Lennart Nilsson, from *A Child Is Born*, Dell, 1966

PRENATAL ENVIRONMENTAL INFLUENCES

To most of us, the concept of environment refers to a human being's surroundings *after* birth. In truth, of course, environmental influences are operating from the moment of conception. The fertilized ovum undertakes a hazardous week-long journey down the Fallopian tube and around the uterus, encountering throughout a highly variable and chemically active medium. We generally think of the uterus as providing a sheltered, warm, and protected environment for prenatal development. But even after it has implanted itself in the uterus, the embryo is vulnerable to maternal disease, malnutrition, and biochemical malfunctioning.

Most pregnancies end with the birth of normal,

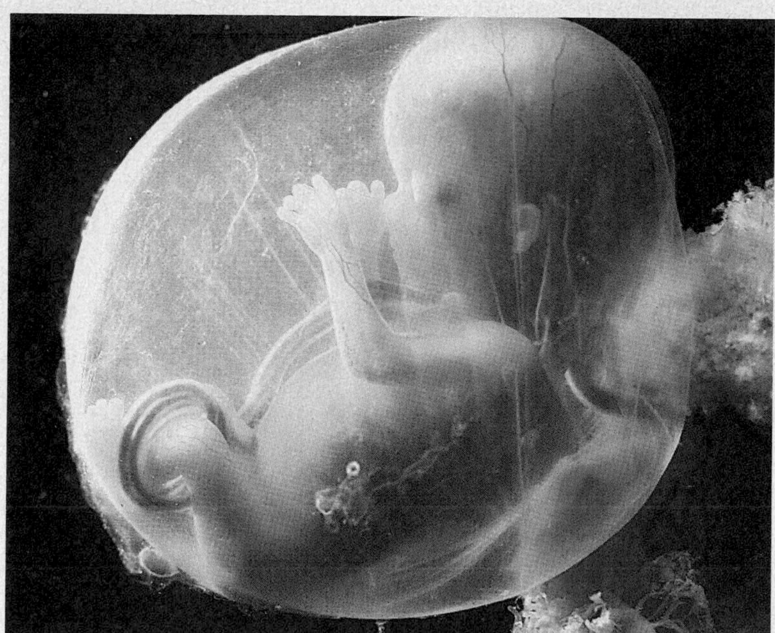

The Fetus at Three Months

At three months the fetus is a little more than three inches long and weighs nearly an ounce. Its head is disproportionally large and appears increasingly like that of a human. By now the external ears and eyelids have formed. The umbilical cord increases in size to accommodate the growing organism. The fetus is developing the skeletal and neurological structures that provide the foundation for moving in its capsule, where it floats weightlessly much in the manner of an astronaut in space.

Lennart Nilsson, from *Behold Man,* Little Brown, 1974

The Fetus at Four Months

At four months the fetus is more than six inches long and weighs about seven ounces. All the organs have formed. The fetus now increases in size, readying itself for birth in five more months. In about a month the mother will begin to feel the fetus's spontaneous movements.

Lennart Nilsson, from *Behold Man,* Little Brown, 1974

healthy babies. Nonetheless, an estimated 10 to 15 percent of all conceptions result in spontaneous abortions or stillbirths. About a quarter of these are the product of chromosomal and gene abnormalities (Mueller, 1983). The remainder result from problems associated with prenatal environment. Another 6 to 7 percent—totaling 250,000 babies each year in the United States—are born with birth defects. Some of these arise from environmental factors (Burnham, 1976; Stechler and Halton, 1982). Scientists term any agent that contributes to birth defects a **teratogen** (derived from the Greek word "tera," meaning monster). The field of study concerned with birth defects is called **teratology.**

Drugs and Other Chemical Agents

The thalidomide tragedy in the early 1960s awakened the medical profession and the public alike to the potential dangers of drugs for pregnant women. Thousands of German, English, and Canadian women who had taken thalidomide (a tranquilizer) during the embryonic stage of pregnancy gave birth to infants with malformed limbs. It is now clear that many drugs and chemical agents cross the placental barrier and affect the embryonic and fetal systems (Heinonen, Slone, and Shapiro, 1977; Spielberg, 1982). Quinine (used in the treatment of malaria) can cause congenital deafness. Barbiturates (sedating drugs) may affect the oxygen supply to the fetus and result in brain damage. Antihistamines may increase the mother's susceptibility to spontaneous abortion. And even aspirin and a number of antibiotics have been tentatively linked in several cases to heart, hearing, and other problems (Bowes et al., 1970; Stuart et al., 1982).

The incidence of drug usage among pregnant women is staggering. One study (Nora et al., 1967) reveals that expectant mothers take an average of three different drugs during the first three months of pregnancy—the period when the embryo is most vulnerable. During the course of their pregnancies, 65 percent of the women took analgesics (including aspirin and related compounds), 42 percent antibiotics, 27 percent appetite suppressants, and 21 percent tranquilizers. According to current medical opinion, pregnant women should not take drugs except when they have conditions that seriously threaten their health, and then *only* under the supervision of a physician. Some authorities even advise against extra vitamins unless they are prescribed by a physician. Likewise, miscellaneous reports of increased rates of spontaneous abortion and birth defects among coffee drinkers prompted the Federal Food and Drug Administration (FDA) to recommend in 1980 that women stop or reduce their consumption of coffee, tea, and cola drinks during pregnancy.

Smoking and Pregnancy

The growing incidence of smoking among women over the past two decades has posed a health hazard not only to themselves but to their unborn infants. Chronic smokers are more likely than nonsmokers to give birth to premature infants and to experience more complications in their pregnancies.

Larry Mulvehill/Photo Researchers

Smoking. Most medical authorities classify the nicotine found in tobacco as a drug. When an expectant mother smokes, her bloodstream absorbs nicotine. The nicotine is then transmitted through the placenta to the embryo. Chronic smokers are twice as likely to give birth to premature infants as nonsmokers are (Peterson, Morese, and Kaltreider, 1965; Himmelberger, Brown, and Cohen, 1978). This is a serious hazard because the mortality rate for premature infants is higher than that for full-term infants. Further, major congenital abnormalities are more prevalent among the infants of women who smoke (Evans, Newcombe, and Campbell, 1979). And smoking by mothers-to-be increases the risk of sudden infant death syndrome ("crib death") among their babies by 52 percent. Recent research even suggests that the risk of miscarriage and infant death varies with how much and how long a woman smoked *before* pregnancy.

Marijuana. Over the past two decades, the use of marijuana has become widespread among young people. Its implications for embryonic development are not yet well documented. However, a report on marijuana issued by the Institute of Medicine of the National Academy of Science (Relman, 1982) concludes that marijuana suppresses the production of male hormones, decreases the size and weight of the prostate and the testes, and inhibits sperm production. It may also interfere with ovulation in women. THC (the primary psychoactive ingredient of marijuana) crosses the placental barrier, and hence there is the potential for harm to the fetus. However, contrary to some earlier studies, the report concludes that neither cannabis nor THC causes chromosome breaks.

Hard Drugs. Heroin, methadone, and cocaine have been shown to be capable of producing a wide range of birth deformities (Kalter and Warkany, 1983*b*). Moreover, infants whose mothers are addicted to morphine and heroin show withdrawal syndromes consisting of hyperactivity, trembling, shrill crying, and vomiting. The infants also display greater irritability and restlessness and have more sleep and feeding disturbances than do their nonaddicted counterparts. Additionally, the behavioral and psychological difficulties appear to persist throughout early and middle childhood (Householder et al., 1982).

Alcohol. In recent years considerable research has been devoted to the effects of alcohol on the fetus (Rosett and Sander, 1979; Abel, 1980). The National Institute of Alcohol Abuse and Alcoholism, a division of the Department of Health and Human Services, warns pregnant women that two drinks of hard liquor a day can cause fetal defects. The risk rate is about 10 percent if the mother drinks from 2 to 4 ounces of hard liquor a day. The rate approaches 74 percent for heavy drinkers. Some of the defects associated with the *fetal alcohol syndrome* are growth retardation, congenital eye and ear problems, heart defects, extra digits, and disturbed sleep patterns (Streissguth et al., 1980). In 1980 the Food and Drug Administration warned pregnant women and women considering pregnancy not to drink any alcoholic beverages because to do so may endanger the health of their unborn children.

Oral Contraceptives. Exposure to female sex hormones has also been linked to birth defects. An estimated 10 percent of pregnant women in the United States use oral contraceptives early in their pregnancies. The birth defects involve the heart, limbs, anus, esophagus, vertebral column, or central nervous system (Nora and Nora, 1973, 1975). One research group examined data on 50,282 pregnancies within the United States (Heinonen et al., 1977). Of the children born to 49,240 women who did not receive hormones, 385 had congenital heart defects—a rate of 7.8 per 1,000. In contrast, 19 children born to 1,042 women who took hormones had serious heart abnormalities—a rate of 18.2 per 1,000.

Toxins in the Environment. Expectant women often encounter potentially toxic agents in their everyday lives, including hair spray, cosmetics, insecticides, cleaning solutions, food preservatives, and polluted air and water. The specific risk associated with these agents remains to be determined. It is known, however, that contact with chemical defoliants should be avoided. The National Cancer Institute has linked chemical sprays used to destroy jungle and forest areas in Vietnam with a substantial increase in the number of malformed Vietnamese infants. In 1979 the federal Environmental Protection Agency ordered an emergency ban on herbicides containing dioxin (including 2, 4, 5-T and Silvex). The federal agency took action because of "significant evidence" linking the spraying of dioxin herbicides with an "alarming" rate of miscarriages among women in Oregon.

Toxins in the Workplace. In recent years, medical authorities have become increasingly concerned over the hazards to the reproductive process that are found in the places where people work (Kalter and Warkany, 1983*a*). Studies reveal, for instance, that continuous exposure to a variety of gaseous anesthetic agents used in hospital settings is associated with an increased number of spontaneous abortions among women workers *and* among the wives of exposed male workers. The children of these people also have a higher incidence of congenital malformations. A California study disclosed that 29.7 percent of pregnant nurses working in operating rooms had spontaneous miscarriages. The figure was only 8.8 percent among pregnant general-duty nurses (Bronson, 1977*a*).

It should not be forgotten that sperm are no less susceptible to damage from environmental causes than are ova. This fact has often been overlooked since the reproductive systems of women—not men—are most often studied. Nonetheless, a number of studies are suggestive of the link that exists between male exposure to chemical agents and reproduction. A survey of oral surgeons and dentists who were exposed to anesthetic gas for three hours or more per week revealed that their wives had a 78 percent higher incidence of spontaneous abortions than did the wives of other such practitioners (Bronson, 1977*a*). Another study shows that the wives of workers who came into contact with vinyl chloride at tire and rubber plants had twice as many miscarriages and stillbirths as the wives of workers who did not handle the material (Burnham, 1976). And a study by the National Institute of Occupational Safety and Health found that the sperm counts of male chemical workers at a Kentucky plant who were exposed to toluenediamine (TDA) and dinitrotoluene (DNT) were only one-third as high as levels in workers who never were exposed to the agents.

Maternal Infectious and Noninfectious Diseases

Under some circumstances, infections that cause illness in the mother can harm the fetus (Kalter and Warkany, 1983*a*). When the mother is directly infected, viruses, bacteria, or malarial parasites may cross the placenta and infect the child. In other cases, the fetus may be indirectly affected by a high fever in the mother or by toxins produced by bacteria in the mother's body. The exact time in the fetus's development at which an infection occurs in the mother has an important bearing. As described earlier, the infant's organs and structures emerge according to a fixed sequence and timetable. Each organ and structure has a critical period during which it is most vulnerable to damaging influences.

Rubella and Other Infectious Agents. If the mother contracts rubella (German measles) in the first three months of pregnancy, there is a substantial risk of blindness, deafness, brain damage, and heart disease in the offspring. In 10 to 20 percent of the pregnancies complicated by rubella, spontaneous abortion or stillbirth ensues. However, should the mother contract the disease in the last three months of pregnancy, there is usually no major damage. Fortunately a preventive vaccine is now available for rubella. However, a woman must be inoculated at least three months before the beginning of pregnancy. Various other viral, bacterial, and protozoan agents are suspected either of being transmitted to the fetus or of otherwise interfering with normal development. These include influenza, poliomyelitis, malaria, typhoid, typhus, mumps, smallpox, scarlet fever, and gonorrhea.

Syphilis. In recent years the incidence of syphilis in the United States has reached epidemic proportions, posing a particularly menacing health problem. Should syphilitic mothers not receive treatment with antibiotics, about 25 percent of the fetuses will be aborted or stillborn; many will arrive prematurely; and 30 percent will die shortly after birth (Rugh and Shettles, 1971). In some cases the effects of the syphilis spirochete are not immediately apparent at birth. Instead the disease takes a gradual toll in a deterioration of thought, speech, and motor abilities before the child finally dies. More than three-fourths of known syphilitic pregnant women do not show clinical evidence of the disease. Consequently, the Wasserman test for syphilis should be administered to all pregnant women.

Genital Herpes. Also of growing concern is the increasing incidence of genital herpes infection. Public health authorities report that the incidence of herpes infections among newborns has been rising sharply (Lyons, 1983*a*). Moreover, infants delivered through an infected birth canal have a much higher mortality rate. About 33 percent of infected babies will die; another 25 percent will suffer permanent brain damage. Consequently, some obstetricians advise delivery by Caesarean section to prevent infection of the newborn should the mother have the disease. Pregnant women with genital herpes also have a considerably higher risk of miscarriage.

Diabetes. Maternal diabetes is another common cause of defects and survival problems for the prenatal infant (Pedersen, 1977; Miller, 1981). This is a metabolic disease characterized by a deficiency in insulin and an excess of sugar in the blood and urine. If medical measures are not taken to control the mother's diet and to administer insulin artificially, there is a 50 percent probability that the fetus will be aborted or stillborn. Deformities, such as unformed spines, misplaced hearts, and extra ear skin, run as high as one in four. When pregnant women have diabetes, the fetal pancreas is required to adjust to the higher-than-normal sugar level of the diabetic mother by producing increased amounts of insulin itself. This contributes to abnormal growth of the fetus's pancreas, which in some cases becomes twenty times its normal size. At birth such babies look fat and puffy, and they are about 20 percent overweight (Rugh and Shettles, 1971). Babies of diabetic mothers often have respiratory problems for a day or so after birth.

Maternal Sensitization: The Rh Factor

The Rh factor is a condition that under some circumstances produces a serious and often fatal form of anemia and jaundice in the fetus or newborn—a disorder termed *erythroblastosis fetalis.* About 85 percent of all whites have the Rh factor; they are called Rh-positive. About 15 percent do not have it; they are Rh-negative. Among blacks only about 7 percent are Rh-negative, and among Orientals the figure is less than 1 percent. Rh-positive blood and Rh-negative blood are incompatible. Each blood factor is transmitted genetically in accordance with Mendelian rules (Rh-positive is dominant).

For the most part the maternal and fetal blood supplies are separated by the placenta. On occasion, however, a capillary in the placenta ruptures. This results in the mixing of a small amount of maternal and fetal blood. Likewise, some admixture usually occurs during the "afterbirth," when the placenta separates from the uterine wall.

An incompatibility results between the mother's and the infant's blood when an Rh-negative mother has a baby with Rh-positive blood. Under these conditions, which occur in about 1 of every 200 pregnancies among whites, the mother's body produces antibodies that cross the placenta and attack the baby's blood cells. This does not usually cause a problem in a woman's first pregnancy. As yet she lacks sufficient contact with her baby's Rh-positive blood to develop a high level of sensitivity. But successive pregnancies with Rh-positive fetuses may raise the antibodies in the mother's blood to a critical level, creating difficulties for the baby.

Erythroblastosis fetalis can now be prevented if an Rh-negative mother is given anti-Rh antibodies (termed *Rhogam*) shortly after the birth of her first child. This neutralizes any Rh-positive blood cells that may enter her circulatory system. As a result the woman does not produce Rh-positive antibodies, and permanent immunity does not result.

If an Rh-negative mother has already been sensitized to Rh-positive blood by several pregnancies in the absence of Rhogam therapy, her infant can be given an interuterine transfusion. The procedure involves guiding an amniocentesis needle by means of a fluoroscope through the uterus to the lower abdominal region of the fetus. The fetal abdominal cavity is punctured, and the baby is given the transfusion of Rh-negative nonimmunized blood of the group O blood type. The procedure frequently needs to be repeated at fourteen-day intervals.

Maternal Nutrition

The unborn infant's nourishment comes from the maternal bloodstream through the placenta. Consequently, nutritional deficiencies in the mother, particularly severe ones, are reflected in fetal development (Zamenhof and Van Marthens, 1978). Considerable evidence suggests that there is more risk of miscarriage or premature birth for the infants of poorly nourished mothers than for infants of well-nourished mothers. Babies of poorly nourished mothers are also more likely to be underweight at birth, to die in infancy, or to suffer rickets, physical and neural defects, low vitality, and certain forms of mental retardation

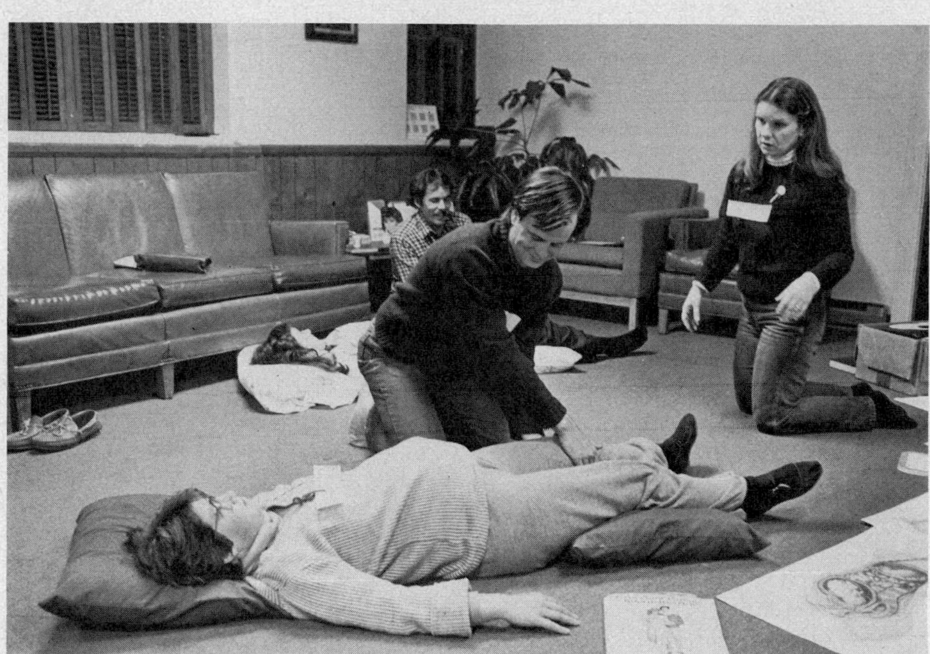

Prenatal Classes

The photo depicts a Lamaze class that prepares a couple for joint participation in labor and delivery. Such classes not only assist couples in dealing with their anxieties regarding childbirth but also provide instruction on proper techniques of exercise and on good nutritional practice.

Bohdan Hrynewych/Southern Light

(Burke et al., 1943; Pasamanick and Knobloch, 1966). These afflictions occur most frequently in American Indian, black, Chicano, and Puerto Rican children, whose mothers are more likely to be undernourished than the mothers of American whites (White House Conference on Children, 1970).

Poor maternal nutrition—associated with war, famine, poverty, and poor dietary practice—has long-term insidious effects on brain growth and intelligence. A seriously deprived fetus may have 15 to 20 percent fewer brain cells than a normal fetus (Brown, 1966; Parekh et al., 1970; Winick et al., 1973). Several studies carried out in the United States correlate birth weight and later measured intelligence (Harper and Wiener, 1965; Caputo and Mandell, 1970; Broman, Nichols, and Kennedy, 1975). Significantly, of all the factors modifying birth weight, maternal nutrition is generally acknowledged to be the most important (Platt and Stewart, 1971). The effects of fetal malnutrition are often compounded by the way the infants deal with others and make use of their environment (Greenberg, 1981*a*; Zeskind and Ramey, 1981). Their lack of energy, reduced responsiveness, and greater social withdrawal seem to stunt their emotional and intellectual growth. In contrast, more active and involved youngsters tend to elicit greater interest, attention, and interaction over time from their mothers and other caretakers.

One of the major studies revealing a link between birth weight and later intelligence is the extensive follow-up from birth to adolescence of a large sample of premature and normal births in Baltimore (Wiener et al., 1965; Wiener, 1968). At regular intervals, researchers administered intelligence tests to the children and examined their school achievement records. At three to five years of age, the low-weight babies had a mean IQ of 94.4, compared with 100.6 for the normal-weight babies. The intellectual deficit of the low-birth-weight children persisted at twelve to thirteen years of age, the point at which the study was terminated.

A Dutch study, however, suggests that no relationship exists between maternal undernourishment and later mental abilities (Stein et al., 1972). During the winter and spring of 1944–1945 there was a severe food shortage in the western Netherlands resulting from the German occupation. In this period, infant birth weights declined by an average of 8 to 9 percent. Nineteen years later investigators compared the intelligence test scores of men born in the famine area with the scores of men born in Dutch nonfamine areas. No significant difference was found. The reason is not entirely clear. It may be that the Dutch women's previous years of good nutrition provided a nutritional reserve on which the developing fetal brain could draw.

Maternal Stress

The effect of maternal emotions on the unborn infant has long been a subject of folklore. Most of us are well aware that being frightened by a snake, a mouse, a bat, or some other creature will not cause a pregnant woman to give birth to a child with a distinctive personality or birthmark. Likewise, most of us view the claims of some primal therapists that their patients are able to recall experiences in the uterus as far-fetched. Medical science does suggest, however, that severe, prolonged anxiety in an expectant mother can have an effect on her child (Stott and Latchford, 1976; Spezzano, 1981). Of course, no direct neural linkage exists between the mother and the fetus. Rather, Lester W. Sontag (1944), long an important figure in the field of child development at the Fels Research Institute, describes the effects of maternal stress on the fetus as "blood-borne" anxieties. When the mother is anxious or under stress, various hormones such as epinephrine (adrenaline) and acetylcholine are released into her bloodstream. These hormones can pass through the placenta and enter the blood of the fetus. Should a pregnant woman feel that she is experiencing prolonged and unusual stress, it might be advisable for her to consult a physician, a trained therapist, or someone in the clergy.

Pregnancy
Environmental influences come to bear upon the developing fetus in many ways. Even the mother's attitude toward her pregnancy, and the emotional joy or stress that she experiences, can affect the fetal environment.
Patrick Reddy

Sontag (1966) has studied pregnant women undergoing stress. During periods when mothers are disturbed, fetal body movements increase several hundred percent. The increased activity normally persists for several hours, even when the maternal disturbance is of short duration. When the stress continues for several weeks, the fetal activity is greatly increased for the entire period. Sontag and his associates (Sontag, Reynolds, and Torbet, 1944) have also found that prolonged emotional stress is associated with low birth weight, infant hyperactivity, and postnatal adjustment difficulties (feeding problems, irritability, and digestive disturbances). Moreover, mothers who are under considerable emotional stress are more likely than other mothers to experience complications during both pregnancy and labor (Davids, Holden, and Gray, 1963; McDonald, 1968; Ferreira, 1969; Stott, 1973.)

However, we must qualify any conclusions about "blood-borne" anxieties. Mothers who are under stress during pregnancy may also continue to be anxious and disturbed after they have given birth. Infant distress may partly reflect a tense mother-child relationship following birth (Stechler and Halton, 1982). In some cases, other factors may be responsible. For instance, genetic factors cannot be excluded.

Pregnancy inevitably brings changes in some of a woman's social roles. She may welcome certain of these roles as a source of ego satisfaction. In some cultures pregnancy enables a woman to prove her biological adequacy, to avoid the reproach of sterility, and to achieve equality with other women (Ausubel and Sullivan, 1970). Nonetheless, even for the woman who anticipates motherhood with enthusiasm, pregnancy does produce some tensions and stress. (See Chapter 16.) Indeed, some stress and anxiety are an inescapable feature of expectant motherhood. In moderate amounts, such stress probably has no harmful effect on the fetus.

Maternal Age

On the whole, younger women have fewer difficulties in pregnancy and labor than do older women. Until relatively recently, medical practitioners believed that teenage pregnancy is more risky to both mother and baby than pregnancy for women in their twenties. More recent studies suggest that this is not the case (Kasun, 1978; Rebenkoff, 1979). Indeed, the younger women may actually have an easier time during pregnancy and delivery, provided they receive adequate prenatal care. However, women who have their first child before they are nineteen years of age feel much less effective in controlling their lives than do those women who have a first child later on (McLaughlin and Micklin, 1983).

Women over thirty-five run progressively greater risks of complications during pregnancy and delivery: risks involving maternal mortality, miscarriage, twinning, and developmental irregularities in their offspring. Also, as noted in Chapter 3, the incidence of Down's syndrome increases drastically with advancing maternal age. In summary, all factors considered, a woman's reproductive and hormonal systems appear to operate at their optimal functional level when she is between seventeen and thirty.

BIRTH

Birth is the transition between dependent existence in the uterus and life as a separate organism. In less than a day, a radical change occurs. The fetus is catapulted from its warm, fluid, sheltered environment into the larger world. The infant is compelled to depend exclusively on its own biological systems. Birth, then, is a bridge between two stages of life.

The Birth Process

A few weeks before birth, the head of the infant generally turns downward. This ensures that it will be born head first. The uterus simultaneously sinks downward and forward. These changes are termed *lightening*. They "lighten" the mother's discomfort, and she now breathes more easily, since the pressure on her diaphragm and lungs is reduced (see Figure 4.9). About the same time, the mother may begin experiencing mild "tuning up" contractions (*Braxton-Hicks contractions*), which are a prelude to the more vigorous contractions of labor.

The birth process consists of three stages: labor,

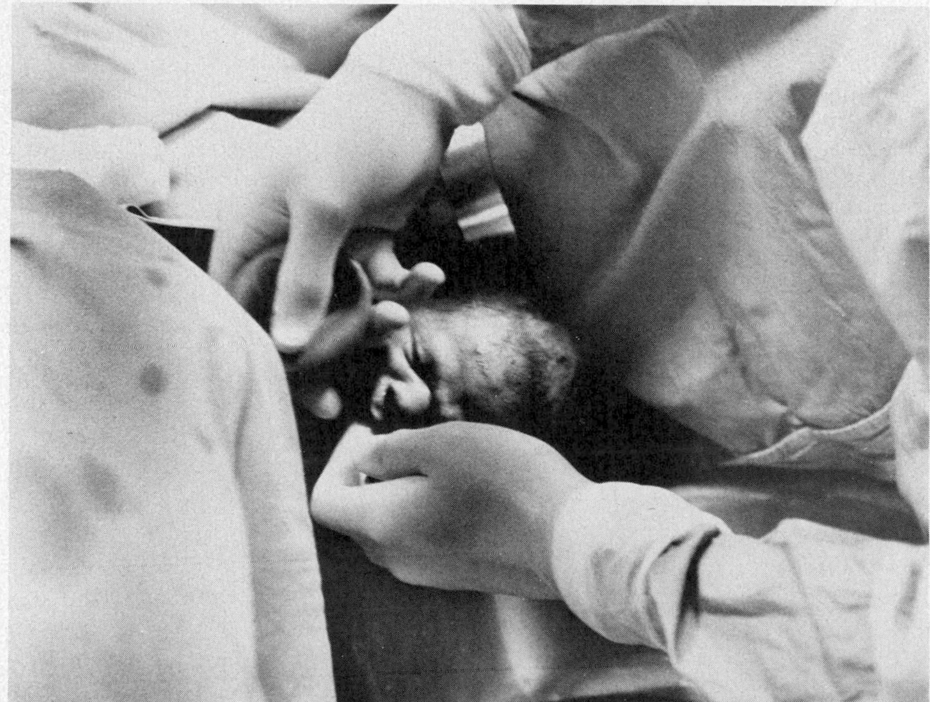

Birth

The baby's head has emerged from the birth canal, although the remainder of the body has yet to appear. The doctor is suctioning mucus from the baby's throat with a hand-operated suctioning device.

Patrick Reddy

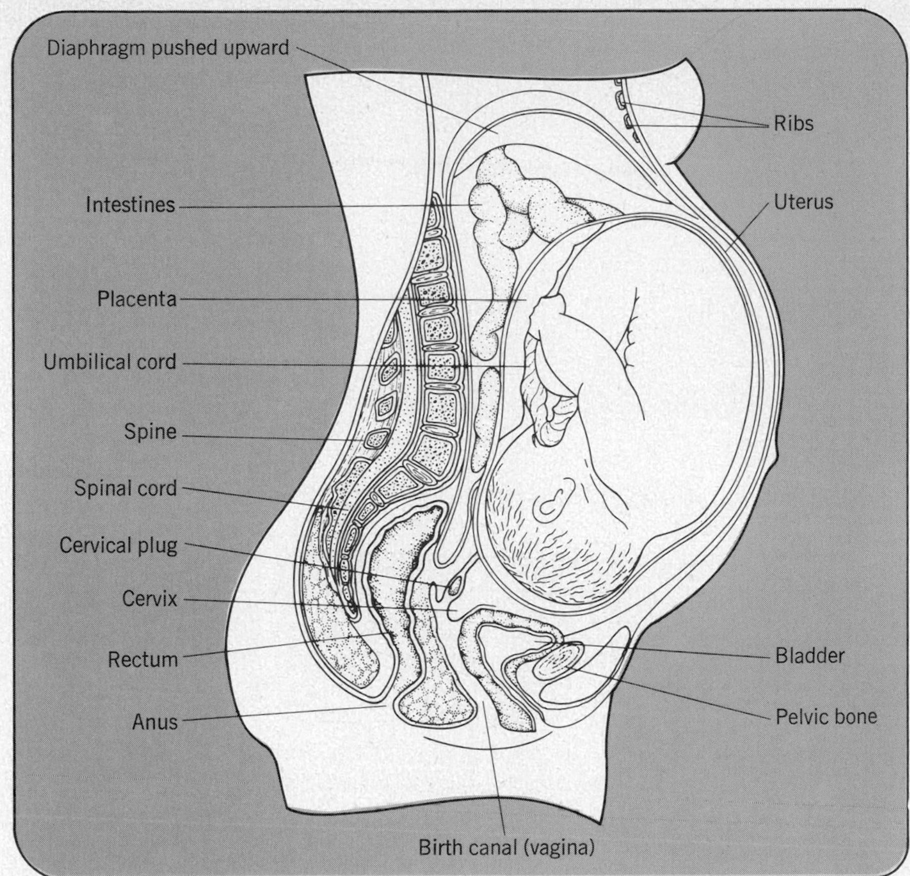

Figure 4.9 The Position of the Fetus About One Month Before Birth
In the month before birth, the head of the fetus usually turns downward and the fetus drops slightly (called *lightening*).

SOURCE: Roberts Rugh and Landrum B. Shettles, *From Conception to Birth: The Drama of Life's Beginnings* (New York: Harper & Row, 1971), p. 81. Copyright © 1971 by Roberts Rugh and Landrum B. Shettles. Reprinted by permission.

delivery, and afterbirth. During **labor,** the strong muscle fibers of the uterus rhythmically contract, pushing the infant downward toward the birth canal (the *vagina*). Simultaneously, the muscular tissue that forms the thick lower opening of the uterus (the *cervix*) relaxes, becoming both shortened and widened, thus permitting the infant's passage (see Figure 4.10).

Labor averages about 14 hours for women having their first babies. Women who have already had at least one baby average about 8 hours. Initially the uterine contractions are spaced about 15 to 20 minutes apart and last for about 25 seconds. As the intervals shorten to 3 to 5 minutes, the contractions become stronger and last for about 45 seconds. Either at the beginning of labor or sometime during it, the amniotic sac that surrounds and cushions the fetus ruptures (commonly termed the "bursting of the water bag"). This releases the amniotic fluid, which then flows as a clear liquid from the vagina.

Delivery begins once the infant's head passes through the cervix (the neck of the uterus), and ends when the baby has completed its passage through the birth canal. The stage generally requires 20 to 80 minutes. During delivery, contractions last for 60 to 65 seconds and come at 2- and 3-minute intervals. The mother aids each contraction by "bearing down" (pushing) with her abdominal muscles. *Crowning* occurs when the widest diameter of the baby's head is at the mother's *vulva* (the outer entrance to the vagina). Once the head has passed through the birth canal, the rest of the body quickly follows (see Figure 4.10).

After the baby's birth, the uterus commonly stops its contractions for about 5 minutes. The contractions then resume and the placenta separates from the uterus. The placenta is forced into the vagina and is finally totally expelled. This process, termed the **afterbirth,** lasts for about 20 minutes.

The normalcy of the baby's condition at birth is usually appraised in terms of the **Apgar Scoring System,** a method developed by Virginia Apgar (1953). The infant is assessed 1 minute and again 5 minutes after birth on the basis of five conditions: heart rate, respiratory effort, muscle tone, reflex irri-

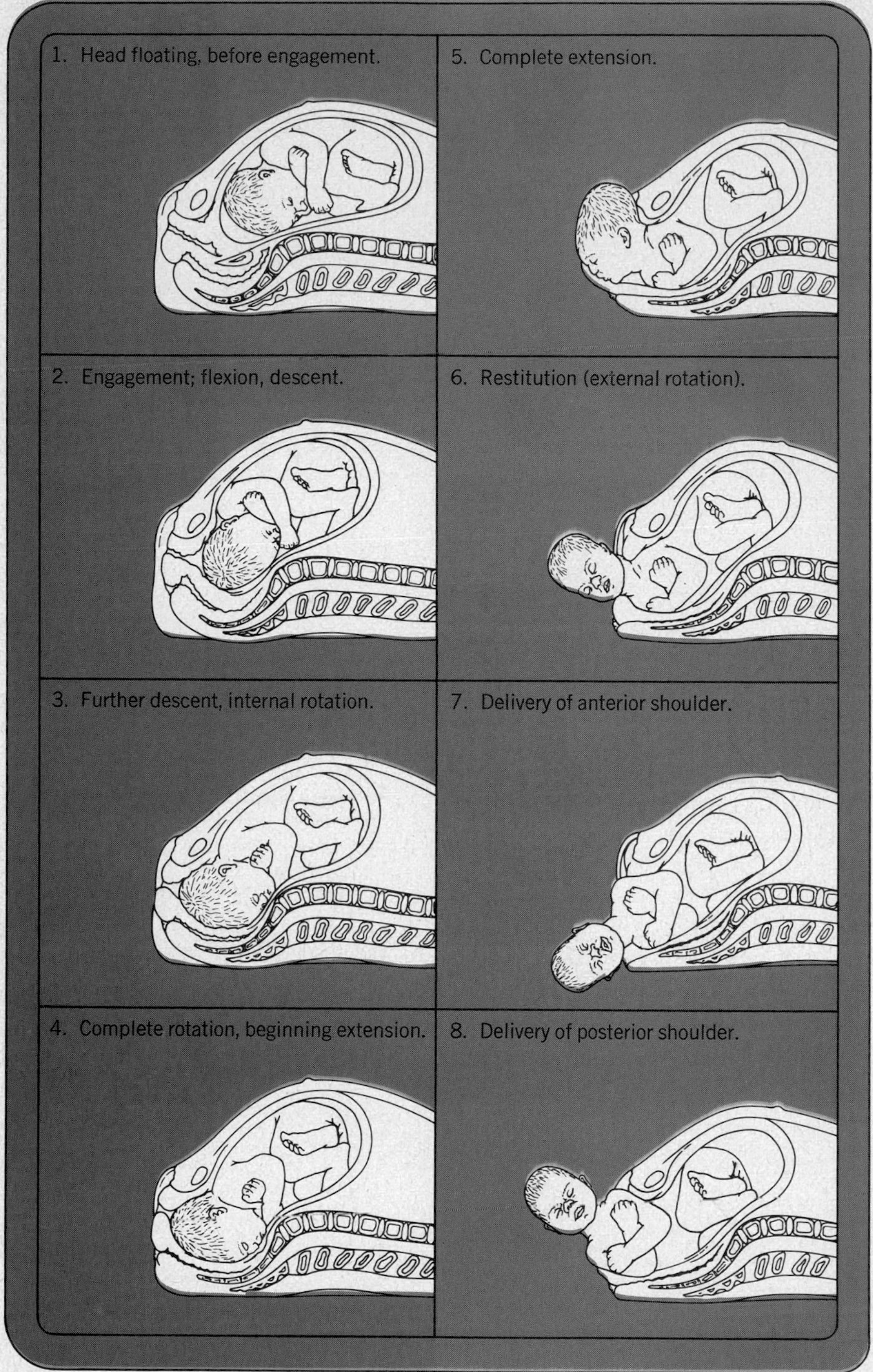

Figure 4.10 Normal Birth

The principal movements in the mechanism of labor and delivery.

SOURCE: Jack A. Pritchard and Paul C. MacDonald, *Williams Obstetrics,* 15th ed. (New York: Appleton-Century-Crofts, 1976), Figure 6, p. 320. Reprinted by permission.

tability (the infant's response to a catheter placed in its nostril), and body color. Each of the conditions is rated 0, 1, or 2 (see Table 4.1). The ratings of the five conditions are then summed (the highest possible score is 10). At 60 seconds after birth, about 6 percent of all infants receive scores of 0 to 2, 24 percent scores of 3 to 7, and 70 percent scores of 8 to 10. A score of less than 5 indicates the need for prompt diagnosis and treatment. Infants with the lowest Apgar scores have the highest mortality rate.

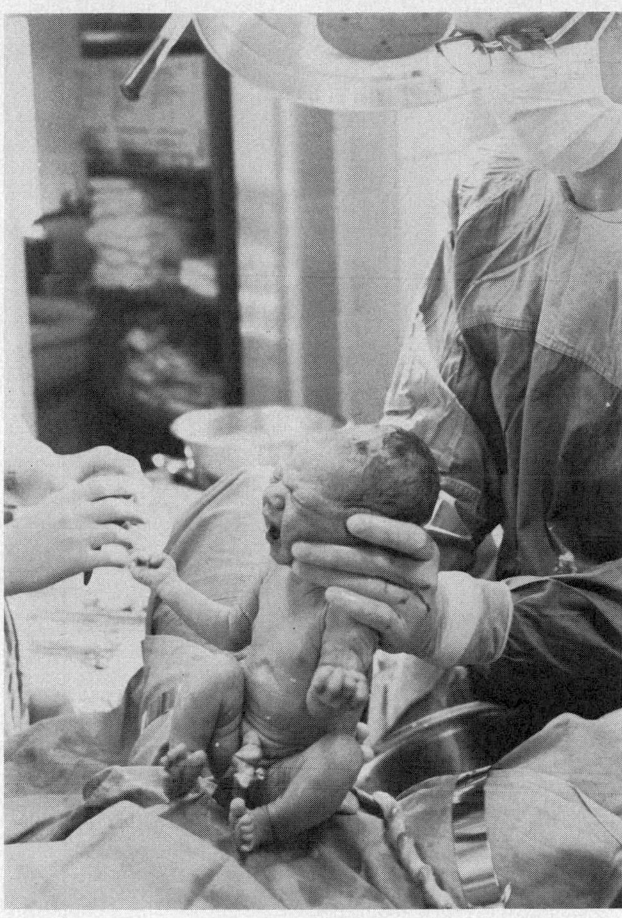

A Newborn

Moments after birth, the infant has been placed on the mother's abdomen. The umbilical cord has been cut and tied. Note the umbilical cord to the right of the baby's left leg. It is still attached to the placenta, which has yet to be expelled in the afterbirth. Also note the "molding" of the infant's head from passing through the birth canal. Molding is possible because of the softness of the bones and the loose connection they have with one another at the sutures of the skull. Accordingly, the head offers a narrow cylinder to the birth canal instead of a round ball. In a matter of days the head will again assume a normal shape.

Patrick Reddy

Natural Childbirth

Natural childbirth refers to a variety of approaches that stress the preparation of the mother and the father for childbirth and their active involvement in the process. Overall, the term has come to mean an awake, aware, and undrugged mother-to-be. In the 1940s the English obstetrician Grantly Dick-Read (1944) began popularizing the view that pain in childbirth could be greatly reduced if women understood the birth process and learned to relax properly. Childbirth, Dick-Read argued, is essentially a normal and natural process. Anxiety and tension, however, prevent the rhythmic cooperation of the muscles in contraction and interfere with relaxation. All of this contributes to the tearing of tissue and the intensifying of pain. Unfortunately, the cultural attitudes and practices in Western societies instill fear and anxiety in the mother. Legends and old wives' tales depict childbirth as a barbaric occurrence that produces agonizing pain.

Dick-Read undertook to train prospective mothers to relax, to breathe correctly, to understand their anatomy and the process of labor, and to develop muscular control of their labor through special exercises. He emphasized the role of calm and supportive attendants who act as sources of confidence and security throughout labor. He believed that anesthesia should be available to women. However, he said it should not be imposed on them or routinely administered. In Dick-Read's view, childbirth needed to be presented as an emotionally satisfying experience. And he undertook to train the father as an active participant in both prenatal preparation and delivery. Fortunately, medical authorities are increasingly coming to conclude that no mother should ever labor and deliver alone (Sosa, Kennell, and Klaus, 1980). Evidence suggests that women who have a friendly companion with them during childbirth experience faster, simpler deliveries; have fewer complications; and are more affectionate toward their babies. Having a friend or relative stay with a woman during delivery may be a simple way to reduce delivery problems, especially for low-income, single, and teenage mothers.

During the 1930s and 1940s, Soviet doctors also began the search for more humane approaches to childbirth. They undertook to apply Pavlov's theories of the conditioned reflex to delivery practices. Like Dick-Read, they concluded that society conditioned women to be tense and fearful during labor. They reasoned that if pain was a response conditioned by society, it could be replaced by a different, more positive response. Accordingly they evolved the *psychoprophylactic method.* Women were encouraged to concentrate on the manner in which they breathed when a contraction occurred.

In 1951 Fernand Lamaze (1958), a French obstetrician, visited maternity clinics in the Soviet Union. When he returned to France, he introduced the fundamentals of the psychoprophylactic method to the

Table 4.1 The Apgar Scoring System

Rating	Heart Rate	Respiratory Effort	Muscle Tone	Reflex Irritability	Body Color
0	Absent	Absent	Limp	Absent	Pale or blue
1	Below 100	Slow, irregular	Fair flexion	Grimace	Body pink, blue extremities
2	100–140	Good respiration accompanied by crying	Active motion	Cough or sneeze	Pink all over

SOURCE: Adapted from Virginia Apgar, "A Proposal for a New Method of Evaluation of the Newborn Infant," *Anesthesia and Analgesia*, Vol. 32 (1953), pp. 260–267.

maternity hospital he directed. Even more than Dick-Read, Lamaze emphasized the active participation of the mother in every phase of labor. He developed a precise and controlled breathing drill in which women in labor respond to a series of verbal cues by panting, pushing, and blowing. The Lamaze method has proved popular among those American physicians and prospective parents who prefer natural childbirth.

Natural childbirth offers a number of advantages. First, childbirth education classes can do much to relieve the mother's anxiety and fear. Second, many wives and husbands find their joint participation in labor and delivery a joyous, rewarding occasion—indeed, what many couples describe as a "peak" experience. Third, the mother takes no medication or is given it only sparingly in the final phase of delivery. Some studies show that infants whose mothers received medication tend to perform less well on standard behavioral tests at one month to one year of age than do infants whose mothers were not medicated during labor (Aleksandrowicz and Aleksandrowicz, 1974; Goldstein, Caputo, and Taub, 1976; Brackbill, 1979; Murray et al., 1981; Lester, Als, and Brazelton, 1982). Other studies show no discernible long-term effects of drugs administered to the mother during the birth process (Muller et al., 1971; Yang et al., 1976; Horowitz et al., 1977; Kolata, 1979). Since consid-

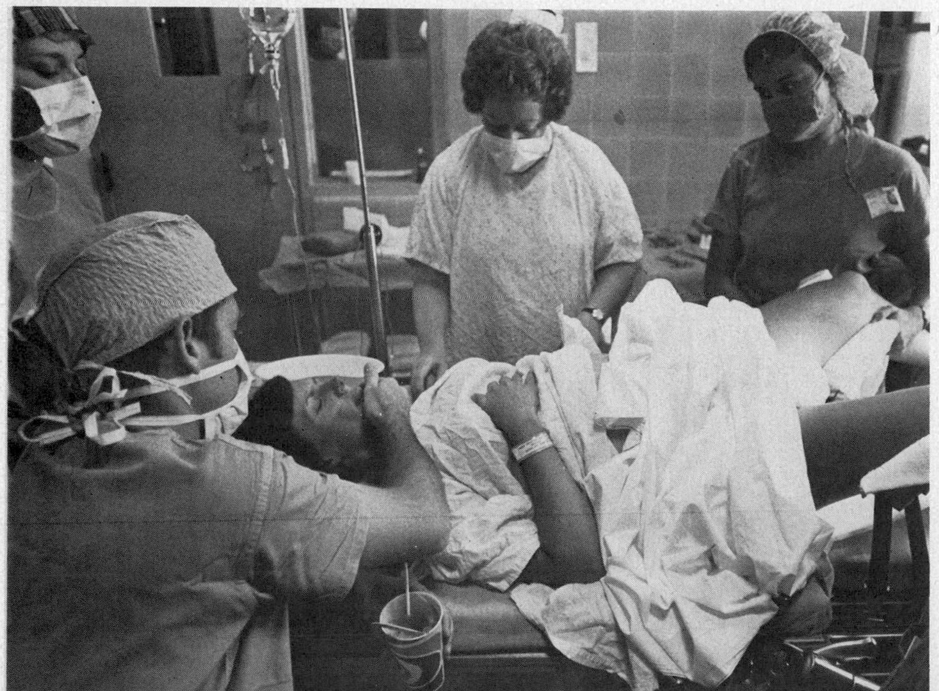

Natural Childbirth

This woman is undergoing an unmedicated delivery employing the Lamaze procedure. The husband is cupping his hand over his wife's mouth to assist her breathing during a contraction and to prevent hyperventilation. The cup at the husband's elbow contains ice chips. The ice chips provide moisture for the woman's mouth, which tends to dry out as a result of the controlled breathing.

Patrick Reddy

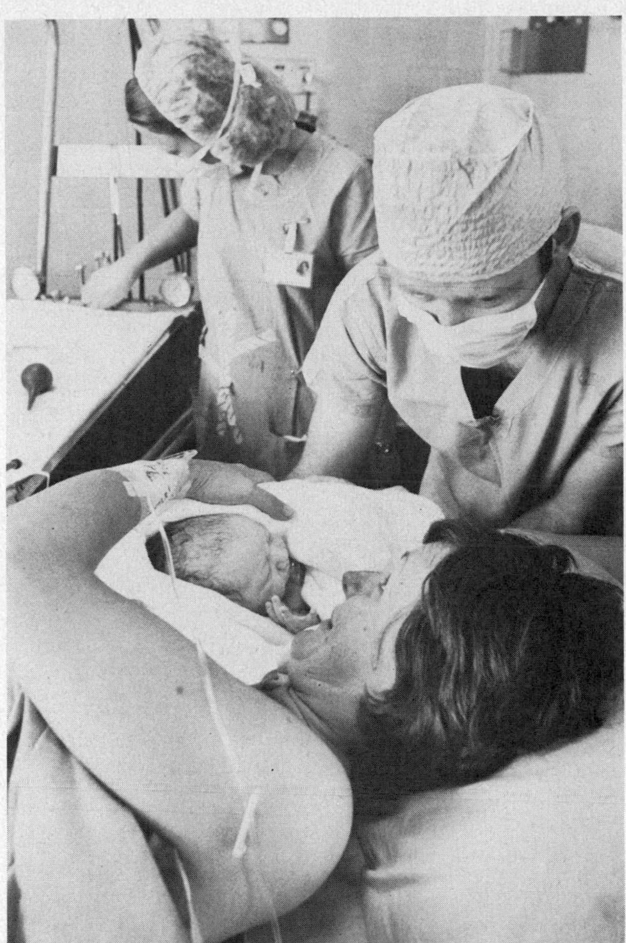

Birth: A Peak Experience

Many couples report that their joint participation in labor and delivery provides an emotionally satisfying and meaningful experience. The tube attached to the mother's wrist is a precaution taken by many obstetricians in the event that she requires an emergency injection of medication or blood transfusion. Some couples object to such procedures and to the surgical masks, charging that they interfere with the "human" qualities of the birth experience. It is considerations of this sort that have given impetus to the childbirth-at-home and midwife movement.

Patrick Reddy

erable controversy exists as to the possible harmful effects that analgesic and sedative medication may have upon the infant, safe obstetric practice seems to suggest caution in the administration of these drugs.

Although natural childbirth clearly offers advantages for many couples, it is important to stress that it is more suitable for some couples and some births than others. In some cases the pain becomes so severe that wise and humane practice calls for medication. And both proponents and critics of natural childbirth agree that women who are psychologically or physically unprepared for it (and considerable preparation is required) should not consider themselves inadequate or irresponsible if they resort to conventional practice.

Parent-Infant Bonding

One of the advantages claimed for natural childbirth is that it facilitates an emotional bonding between parents and their child. Marshall H. Klaus and John H. Kennell (1976), pediatricians at the School of Medicine, Case Western Reserve University, say that closeness between parent and child in the first minutes of life may have a lasting effect. They term this process **parent-infant bonding.** Goats provide an extreme example of this type of attachment. If a mother goat is separated from her kid immediately after birth for over an hour, she will refuse to accept and nurse it, butting and kicking it away. But if the mother and kid are together for just the first five minutes after birth and then separated for an hour, the mother will immediately recognize and accept her kid when it is brought to her. Klaus and Kennell assert that human parents and their offspring undergo a somewhat similar, although less intense, experience.

Although recognizing that most parents sooner or later become attached to their children, Klaus and Kennell say that some women have difficulty forming this attachment. This is particularly so for mothers whose infants are premature, malformed, or initially unwanted. Moreover, follow-up studies by Klaus and Kennell undertaken one month after birth reveal that women who had early contact with their babies are more affectionate mothers than are women lacking early contact. They fondle their children more, try to soothe them more often, and engage in more eye-to-eye contact. Even at two years of age, noticeable differences still exist. The mothers are more likely to speak to their children with a greater number of words and questions and with fewer commands than do other mothers. These dimensions of the mothers' speech seem to be related to their children's superior verbal performance and competence at age five.

Klaus and Kennell report a variety of interlocking features between mother and infant in the first hours of life. Babies appear to move in rhythm with their mothers' voices (see Chapter 5). Further, the cry of the newborn causes an increase in blood flow to the mother's breasts, which stimulates milk production. And the infant's contact with the breast activates the

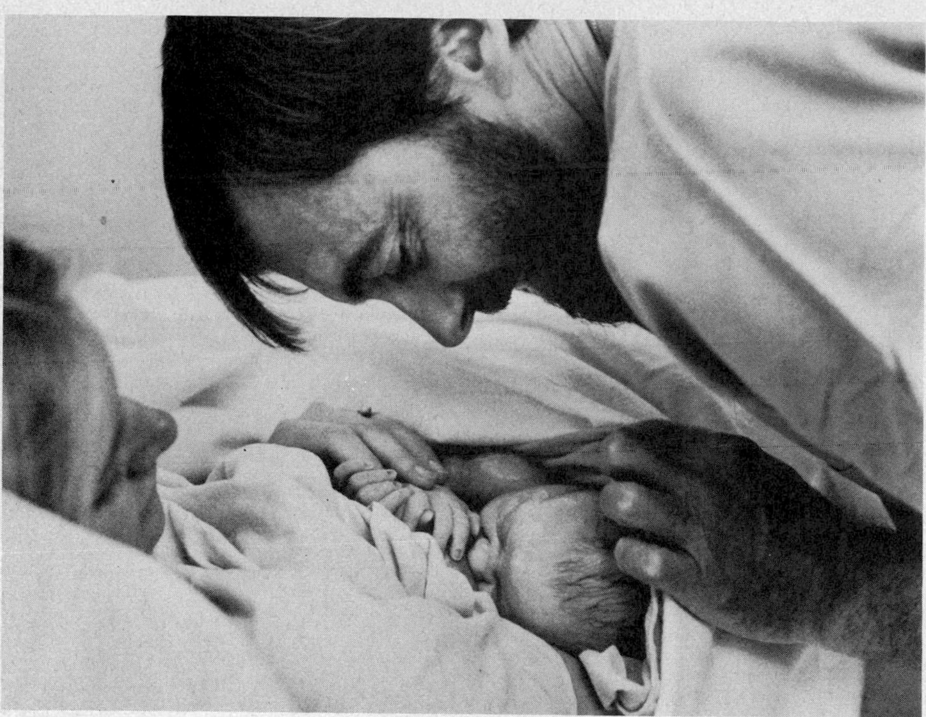

Benefits of Father Participation in the Birth Process

By participating in the birth process, fathers can experience the emotional rewards and joys associated with the birth of their children. Additionally, claim the pediatricians Marshall H. Klaus and John H. Kennell, the practice promotes bonding between a father and his child.

Suzanne Arms/Jeroboam

release of a hormone that hastens the mother's uterine contractions, a process that reduces bleeding in the reproductive tract.

Evidence is also suggestive that fathers can become attached to their infants in the early period following delivery if they are allowed contact with them. Within the United States, fathers have tended to avoid caretaking involvement with their newborns. (For a discussion of father involvement in some other cultures, see the boxed insert on page 117.) Klaus and Kennell speculate that this pattern may be related to practices that have barred fathers from early contact with their children. Overall, the Case Western Reserve researchers say that even the relatively short separation period enforced by traditional hospital procedures can have harmful effects on parent-child relations.

Although attracting considerable interest, the position advanced by Klaus and Kennell remains highly controversial. For instance, Michael Lamb (1982) has reviewed the research on early parent-child physical contact and finds only weak evidence for temporary effects and no evidence for lasting effects. He does not deny that parents may find early contact with their infant to be emotionally satisfying. But he stresses that mothers who have Caesarean deliveries or parents who adopt children should not conclude that they have missed out on something fundamental for a healthy child-parent relationship. In any event, a growing body of research suggests that parents who do not have contact with their infant immediately after delivery typically develop an equally strong attachment to the youngster as do parents who do have such contact (Svejda, Campos, and Emde, 1980; Grossmann, Thane, and Grossman, 1981). It should be noted that Klaus and Kennell have now also modified and softened their original stand (Brody, 1983*a*).

Birthing Rooms and Family-Centered Hospital Care

As a former farmer, if I had separated animal babies from their mothers as soon as they were born, put the babies in a box with a glass window and let the mother only look through the window at them for two or three days, I would have been arrested for cruelty to animals. Yet this is what hospital "routines" do to humans.

—ROBERT A. BRADLEY, M.D.

With smaller families and more childbirth classes, many young couples are seeking out a doctor and a hospital that view uncomplicated pregnancies as a normal process rather than as an illness. And they are rebelling against regimented and impersonal hospital

FATHERHOOD IN CROSS-CULTURAL PERSPECTIVE

The weak link in the family group is the bond between the child and the father. No necessary tie and no easy means of identification exist between the two. Margaret Mead (1949), a leading anthropologist, asserted that human societies have invented the concept of fatherhood as a response to this fact. Bronislaw Malinowski (1964), also a distinguished anthropologist, made the same point. He observed that societies everywhere provide for fatherhood, if only by social definition—the *principle of legitimacy*. The principle of legitimacy is the rule that "no child should be brought into the world without a man—and one man at that—assuming the role of sociological father, that is, guardian and protector, the male link between the child and the rest of the community" (Malinowski, 1964: 13).

The Tallensi, a people of the African Sudan, furnish a good example of the principle of legitimacy (Fortes, 1949). If a Tallensi woman is married, any child she bears is the property of, and a member of, her husband's family (descent group). Should the woman be impregnated by a man other than her husband, it causes no problem. The child is easily absorbed into a legal relationship. The genitor (the agent of conception) does not experience fatherly feelings toward the child. The pater (the woman's husband) does feel all the emotions associated with fatherhood, even though he knows he is not the genitor. And the pater receives all the credit customarily given a father among the Tallensi. The child suffers no stigma, nor is it deprived of any legal rights. However, everything is different for a child born of an unwed mother. In this case the principle of legitimacy is violated, so that the child is stigmatized as an inferior and enjoys fewer legal rights.

Since the tie between the father and the child is less immediately visible than that between the mother and the child, some societies have evolved birth rituals that serve to emphasize and highlight the relationship (Paige and Paige, 1973). The *couvade* is the most widespread birth custom involving men. It usually consists of various dietary and occupational observances, as well as the seclusion of the husband during and for a period after childbirth.

The Kurtachi of the Solomon Islands provide a good illustration of the couvade (Blackwood, 1935: 159). During pregnancy neither the husband nor the wife is permitted to eat certain foods—a taboo that persists for a period following the child's birth. When the wife begins her labor pains,

> . . . her husband must stop working, and remain indoors, not in the hut where his wife is confined, but in that of another of his wives, or a neighbor. He must spend his time in sitting idle or dozing, and must on no account carry, or even lift, anything heavy, or touch a knife, axe, or any sharp or pointed instrument. To do the former would injure the child, the latter would cause it to die. This continues for three days. On the fourth day he may go into the hut and see his child. After this he is allowed to walk about the village. . . . He must still refrain from working. On the fifth day he goes, with his wife, and washes in the sea. . . . and he may now resume his usual activities.

Among some peoples, including the Arapesh of New Guinea (Mead, 1935) and the Copper Eskimo (Jenness, 1922), the father simulates birth, taking to his bed and going through actions suggestive of labor. Within the United States and other Western nations, some men experience what mental health professionals term the "couvade syndrome." The expectant fathers complain of morning nausea, crave certain foods, and gain weight.

In middle-class American culture, emphasis tends to fall upon the wedding ceremony rather than upon specific birth observances (Mead and Newton, 1967) An elaborate wedding emphasizes the man's assumption of economic and social responsibility for a woman and her future children. American men are also permitted to call attention to their new fatherhood by giving cigars to other men or going on a "good drunk." More recently, natural childbirth and family-centered hospital programs have undertaken to make the father an active participant in the childbirth process.

routines. They dislike the sterile steel equipment, harsh lighting, uncomfortable stirrups and table, shaving, anesthesia, and the practice of separating mother and child immediately after birth. They do not want the delivery of their babies to be a surgical procedure. And they note that infections can be spread in hospitals—sometimes by physicians and staff. Consequently, more couples are choosing to have babies at home (see the boxed insert on page 118). The medical establishment has reacted with alarm to this trend, insisting that home births pose considerable risk to both the mother and the child (Lublin, 1979; Ryan, 1982).

In response to the home-birth movement, many

THE CHILDBIRTH-AT-HOME AND MIDWIFE MOVEMENT

It is estimated that less than 20 percent of the babies born in the world today are delivered by physicians. The vast majority of births are handled by *midwives*—experienced lay practitioners who attend women during birth. Even in such technologically advanced nations as Sweden, Germany, the Netherlands, and England, professional midwives handle the majority of normal births. Indeed, as recently as 1905 midwives delivered about half of the babies born in New York City. And in the United States today, "granny" midwives deliver babies in Appalachia, Mississippi, and the Rio Grande area of Texas (Sousa, 1976).

In the past decade the rising cost of hospital care, as well as dissatisfaction among some couples with impersonal hospital procedures, has led to a renewed interest in home births attended by midwives. Paralleling this movement, some two dozen college programs have been established that allow a registered nurse with a baccalaureate degree to earn a master's degree and certification in nurse-midwifery (they graduate about 200 nurse-midwives each year). However, in contrast with the independent practice found among European midwives, the American nurse-midwife often works under the supervision of a physician (Johnson, 1979). In some hospitals and medical centers, nurse-midwives and obstetricians work closely together in a "team practice." One of the main advantages of nurse-midwife programs is that nurse-midwives are extremely generous with time, teaching, and emotional support (Hinds, 1981*a*). Nurse-midwives are also setting up their own birth centers in communities throughout the United States.

Although it is not illegal in the United States to have a baby at home, through the years most states have enacted legislation that regulates persons who may attend a birth. An increasing number of states are currently broadening their laws to permit *licensed* midwives to deliver infants in both hospital and home settings. However, couples who are interested in childbirth at home should find out which laws pertain in their particular state. The parents' legal liability in the event of either the mother's or the baby's death during a home birth is not entirely clear. There is also the more obvious danger that in a home birth the mother or the infant may develop complications that require highly skilled medical attention. Couples need to weigh this risk, with its associated tragedy, against the advantages of home delivery (Sousa, 1976).

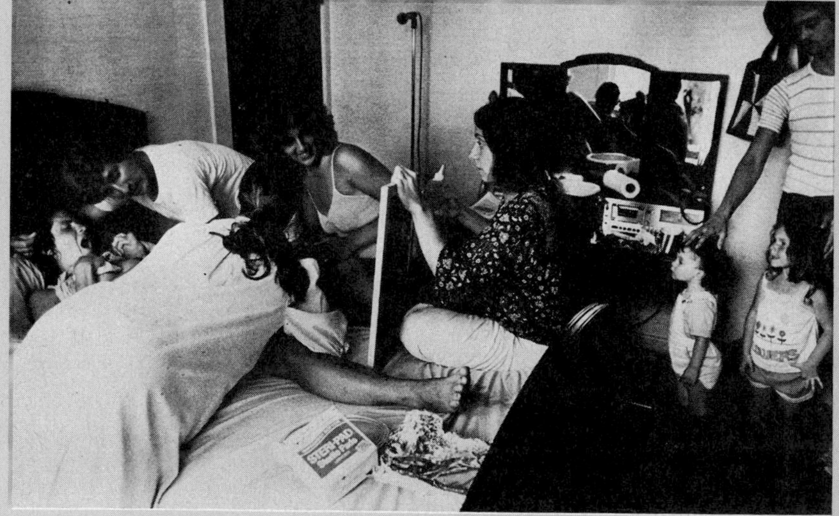

Home Birth

Troubled by the rising cost of hospital deliveries and dissatisfied with impersonal hospital environments, some American couples have chosen to have their babies at home, where they are delivered by trained midwives.

J. F. Sheckler/Picture Group

hospitals have introduced *birthing rooms.* Such rooms have a homelike atmosphere complete with wallpapered walls, window drapes, potted plants, color television, a queen-size bed, and other comforts. Medical equipment is normally out of view. The woman can give birth assisted by a nurse-midwife or obstetrician and her husband. Other relatives, friends, or even the baby's brothers and sisters may be present.

Should complications arise, the woman can be quickly moved to a regular delivery room. This arrangement allows for a homelike birth with proximity to hospital life-saving equipment. The mother and child then return home about six to twenty-four hours after an uncomplicated delivery.

Other hospitals, while retaining more traditional childbirth procedures, have introduced family-centered hospital care, in which birth is made a family experience. The father is an active member of the delivery room team. And in some hospitals children are allowed to see the new baby in the family soon after birth. The plan is usually coupled with *rooming-in,* an arrangement in which the infant spends a large portion of time in a bassinet beside the mother's bed. This practice runs counter to the long American hospital tradition of segregating infants in a common nursery.

Rooming-in offers the advantages of allowing the mother to get acquainted with her child and of integrating the father early into the child care process. Under the supervision of the nursing staff, parents gain skill in feeding, bathing, diapering, and otherwise caring for their infant. Anxieties caused by old wives' tales, misconceptions, and sheer ignorance can be put to rest. Women who desire to breast-feed their babies can initiate the process with the sympathetic help and support of the hospital staff.

The Baby's Birth Experience

Since 1975 Frederick Leboyer, a French obstetrician, has captured popular attention with his best-selling book *Birth Without Violence* (1975). Whereas Dick-Read and Lamaze focused on the mother, Leboyer focuses on the baby. Birth, says Leboyer, is an exceedingly traumatic experience. When expelled from the uterus, the infant is immediately confronted with blinding arc lights and the bustle and noise of the hospital delivery room—a terrifying "tidal wave of sensation surpassing anything we can imagine." So savage is the shock, argues Leboyer, that the infant's nervous system may be permanently damaged. Leboyer calls for a more gentle entry into the world via lowered sound and light levels in the delivery room, the immediate soothing of the infant through massaging and stroking, and a mild, sensuous bath for the newborn.

R. D. Laing, a Scottish psychoanalyst, is also dismayed by what he considers to be the brutality of medical personnel toward the newborn: "An infant has all its sense channels open and is not a lump of stuff to be turned upside down and slapped" (quoted by Anderson, 1978: 48). He calls for gentleness to the newborn. And he vigorously objects to the routine circumcision of male babies—what he calls "ritual mutilation"—a procedure often performed without even local anesthesia.

However, claims like those of Leboyer are exceedingly controversial. Canadian researchers have found that Leboyer's method offers no special clinical or behavioral advantage to the infant or mother not offered by a gentle, conventional delivery (Nelson et al., 1980). But the study found no particular risks associated with it either. However, mothers who had used the technique were more likely to believe eight months later that the childbirth experience had positively influenced their child's behavior.

Certainly, Leboyer has fostered a new and more humane view of childbirth management that compares favorably with the near-barbarism so prevalent only twenty or thirty years ago. Infants often lay agitated and screaming on examining tables or scales until they were unceremoniously subjected to silver-nitrate administration, weighed, scrubbed, wrapped, and then impersonally hustled off to nurseries. (The perceptual and cognitive capacities of the newborn will be discussed in Chapter 5.) Leboyer has highlighted the newborn's need for reassurance and human contact while affording parents a safe and satisfying emotional experience.

COMPLICATIONS OF PREGNANCY AND BIRTH

Although most pregnancies and births proceed without complications, there are exceptions. In a relatively small minority of cases, complications may arise during pregnancy or in the birth process. The purpose of good prenatal care under medical supervision is to minimize their occurrence. But if complications should develop, there is much that can be done through medical intervention to help the mother and the child.

Toxemia

Toxemia is a disorder of pregnancy characterized by high blood pressure (*hypertension*), waterlogging of tissues (*edema*), the presence of protein in the urine (*proteinuria*), and occasionally convulsions and coma.

It occurs in 5 to 10 percent of pregnant women, usually during the last three months of pregnancy. In reports of maternal mortality, toxemia ranks as the second or third leading cause of death. It also poses a problem to the fetus, because toxemia creates a chemical environment in the mother's body that interferes with the proper functioning of the placenta. In severe cases, infant mortality approaches 50 percent.

Although scientists have suggested many possible causes of toxemia, no hypothesis has gained wide medical acceptance, and most are not supported by sufficient evidence (Niswander, 1976). Some research indicates that toxemia tends to be more common among lower socioeconomic groups and unwed pregnant teenagers without adequate prenatal care. Here too the evidence is not conclusive. But it is known that women with high blood pressure, diabetes, and multiple fetuses pose a higher risk factor.

The treatment of toxemia has changed in recent years. Traditionally, many physicians administered diuretic drugs, which decrease the retention of water in body tissues by increasing the excretion of urine. But some doctors today have discontinued the practice, since diuretics have occasionally been associated with maternal death and damage to the fetus. Many physicians also traditionally placed restrictions on the sodium intake in a patient's diet, but the effectiveness of this practice has recently been seriously questioned. At the present time the most common treatment for toxemia is the administration of medication to control convulsions and enforced bed rest to reduce the woman's blood pressure.

Caesarean Sections

A common delivery procedure is the **Caesarean section,** a surgical technique by which the physician enters the uterus through an abdominal incision and removes the infant. The Caesarean section is employed when the mother's pelvis is too small to allow passage of the infant. It is also used when the baby is positioned abnormally, as in some *breech* presentations (a buttocks rather than a head positioning) and *transverse* presentations (a sideways or vertical position). (Nonetheless, fewer than 12 percent of fetuses in breech presentation were delivered by Caesarean section in 1970 whereas today the figure stands at more than 60 percent.)

Between 1970 and 1980, the number of Caesarean deliveries in the United States tripled (from 5.5 percent of all deliveries to about 18 percent). Some regard this trend with alarm. They insist that many of the operations are unnecessary. Others regard it as medical progress in bringing forth healthy babies in circumstances that might otherwise be tragic (Bottoms, Rosen, and Sokol, 1980). One explanation for the rising incidence of Caesareans is the introduction of new equipment that allows physicians to monitor the effect of birth on the child. When a monitor shows that a fetus is "in distress," Caesarean intervention can be quickly arranged. Further, the threat of malpractice suits has prompted some physicians to operate when they have the slightest doubt that a healthy baby will result from a vaginal delivery.

Repeat Caesareans account for 25 to 30 percent of the increase in Caesarean deliveries. Since early in this century, physicians have followed the dictum "Once a Caesarean, always a Caesarean." The doctrine was based on a fear that the scars from a Caesarean would rupture if subjected to the forces of labor in a subsequent delivery. However, in recent decades new surgical procedures and lower uterine incisions have minimized this risk so that many women now can have a vaginal delivery following a Caesarean (Kolata, 1980).

It should be noted, however, that a Caesarean is major surgery and entails some risks, especially to the mother. One recent study shows that major complications occur in about 6 percent of the cases. Complications include hemorrrhage, infections, blood clots, and injuries to other organs. Maternal mortality in Caesarean birth is also two to four times higher than it is for vaginal delivery.

Caesarean delivery can be a devastating experience for couples not prepared for it. Fathers may feel left out and helpless. Mothers may experience remorse, depression, and guilt. They may also be taken aback by the pain and temporary incapacitation that accompany surgery. Couples often complain that they miss not having "given birth." Some harbor hostility toward the physicians who "cheated" them out of a natural birth experience. As a response to these problems, childbirth classes now usually include units on Caesarean birth. Some hospitals allow husbands to be with their wives during a Caesarean delivery. And media materials promote the theme that "Having a Section Is Having a Baby."

Anoxia

Of all body cells, those of the brain are the most vulnerable to a lack of oxygen. They can be destroyed by insufficient oxygen. Once destroyed they are incapable of regenerating themselves (in contrast, skin cells are regenerated after a cut or laceration). Hence **anoxia**—oxygen starvation or deficiency—is a potentially serious complication of birth. When labor is long and difficult, infants commonly suffer some degree of anoxia. So do infants who are born precipitately after a short, sharp labor of less than two hours, for babies need the periods between contractions to replenish oxygen and stabilize their breathing (Yacorzynski and Tucker, 1960).

Under extreme circumstances, where infants suffer gross oxygen deprivation, severe brain damage and death may result. The extent to which lesser degrees of oxygen starvation contribute to neurological impairment, mental retardation, or behavior problems remains to be established. One group of children who experienced anoxia at birth has been studied over seven years. Judging the group in overall terms, anoxia caused the greatest impairment to the children during their first year. In this period they suffered from poor sensorimotor functioning, irritability, and poor responsiveness to visual and pain stimuli (Graham et al., 1956; Pennoyer et al., 1956).

At three years of age the anoxic children generally did not perform as well on various intelligence tests as other children did, although no differences were found on perceptual-motor tests (Graham et al., 1962). At seven years of age the anoxic youngsters no longer showed a significant deficit in intelligence, but (in contrast with the earlier period) they obtained significantly lower scores on a test of perceptual-motor functioning (Corah et al., 1965). In sum, different deficits appeared and diminished at different ages. However, these deficits were fairly minimal for most of the children.

Prematurity

A **premature infant** is commonly defined as a baby weighing less than 5½ pounds at birth or having a gestational age of less than thirty-seven weeks. Some 6 to 8 percent of all live births in the United States occur before full term. The survival rate of premature infants correlates closely with their birth weight, with better survival for the larger and more mature infants. Nonetheless, in a number of the nation's best hospitals, physicians are saving 80 to 85 percent of the infants weighing 2.2 to 3.2 pounds and, even more remarkably, 50 to 60 percent of those weighing 1.6 to 2.2 pounds (Henig, 1981; Paneth, Kiely, and Wallenstein, 1982).

Intensive-care nurseries for preterm babies are often frightening to parents who are unprepared to encounter their infant in a see-through incubator. The child may be receiving oxygen through plastic tubes inserted in the nose or windpipe. Banks of blipping lights, blinking numbers, and beeping alarms associated with electronic equipment and computerized devices monitor the baby's vital signs (Fincher, 1982). The smaller the preterm infant, the greater is the risk of lung disorders, intracranial bleeding, and intestinal complications.

A leading cause of death in premature infants is a condition called *respiratory distress syndrome* (*RDS*). Some 8,000 to 10,000 infant deaths each year are linked with RDS; another 40,000 newborns suffer from it. One difficulty is that premature infants lack a substance known as *surfactant*, a lubricant found in the amniotic fluid surrounding a fetus in the womb. It helps inflate the air sacs in the lungs after birth and prevents the lungs from collapsing or sticking together after each breath. The fetus normally does not develop surfactant until about the thirty-fifth week. Recently, investigators have found that by providing premature infants with the substance, many otherwise fatal complications can be avoided and the babies saved.

Among surviving premature infants, there is a somewhat higher incidence of abnormality (Caputo and Mandell, 1970; Keller, 1980). Low-birth-weight individuals are overrepresented in the population of mental retardates and among persons institutionalized for various disabilities. Prematurity is similarly associated with difficulties in language development, problems in various areas of academic achievement, hyperkinesis, autism, and involvement in childhood accidents. Also, low birth weight is relatively frequent in the histories of children who show deficits in physical growth, motor behavior, and neurological functioning (Francis-Williams and Davies, 1974; Lubchenco et al., 1974; Taub, Goldstein, and Caputo, 1977). It should be stressed, however, that in contemporary industrialized nations only 5 to 15 percent of low-birth-weight babies experience moderate to severe intellectual impairment (Kopp and Parmelle, 1979). Further, recent advances in the monitoring of premature babies have allowed physicians to anticipate and, in many cases, prevent or minimize some problems through therapeutic interventions. The result has been a reduction in the overall complications and mortality associated with premature birth. However, about 8 percent of infants weighing less than 3.2 pounds at birth are seriously handicapped, with problems like epilepsy, blindness, mental retardation, cerebral palsy, and heart and gastrointestinal-tract problems. Another 10 percent are moderately impaired (Henig, 1981).

The ways in which prematurity may be associated with poor development are complex (Smart and Smart, 1973; Goldstein, Caputo, and Taub, 1976; Holmes, Nagy, and Slaymaker, 1982). First, the relative immaturity of the premature infant makes it a less viable organism in coping with the stresses of birth and postnatal life and more susceptible to infections. Second, the developmental difficulties shown by the premature infant may be associated with the same prenatal disorders that caused the baby to be born early (maternal malnutrition, smoking, poverty, and maternal diabetes). Third, once delivered, the premature infant is treated differently from the full-term child. It is often kept in an incubator and deprived of normal skin contacts and other stimulation. In order to combat this adverse effect, a number of researchers suggest that premature infants be given extra human stimulation in the form of handling, cuddling, talking, singing, and rocking (Powell, 1974; Cornell and Gottfried, 1976; Gottfried et al., 1981).

Finally, although premature infants constitute less than 10 percent of all babies, they are represented among battered children at the rate of between 23 and 40 percent, depending on the study quoted. Klaus and Kennell attribute this to the greater likelihood that premature infants have experienced prolonged separation from their parents, which has impaired the parent-child bonding process (Kennell, Voos, and Klaus, 1979). Ann M. Frodi and her colleagues (1978) also suggest that the characteristics of premature infants—their high-pitched cry, their fragility and smallness, their greater irritability, their lower levels of visual alertness, and their shriveled appearance—make them less cute and responsive, even somewhat aversive beings, in the eyes of their parents.

The author of this book hastens to add (since he himself was a premature baby) that many premature infants—perhaps 50 to 75 percent—show no abnormalities or mental retardation. Winston Churchill, who was born prematurely, lived to be ninety-one and led an active, productive life. In evaluating these matters, we need to keep in mind the nature of statistical prediction and the degree of a child's prematurity (Hunt and Rhodes, 1977).

SUMMARY

1. The prenatal period normally lasts an average of 266 days. Embryologists divide it into three stages: the germinal period, the embryonic period, and the fetal period.
2. The germinal period is characterized by the growth of the zygote (the fertilized egg) and the establishment of an initial linkage between the zygote and the support system of the mother. The fertilized egg divides in a process termed "mitosis." In about six or seven days, the blastocyst begins the process of differentiation into the trophoblast and the inner cell mass. Toward the end of the second week, the embryonic portion of the inner cell mass begins to differentiate into three layers: the ectoderm, the mesoderm, and the endoderm.
3. The embryonic period lasts from the end of the second week to the end of the eighth week. It is a period characterized by rapid growth, the establishment of a placental relationship with the mother, the differentiation in early structural form of the chief organs, and the appearance of recognizable features of a human body.
4. The fetal period begins with the ninth week and ends with birth. During this period the differentiation of the major organ systems continues, and the organs themselves become competent to assume their specialized functions.
5. Environmental influences affect the developing organism from the moment of conception and continue throughout the prenatal period.
6. Many drugs and chemical agents are capable of crossing the placental barrier and affecting the embryonic and fetal systems. Current medical opinion suggests that pregnant women

should take no drugs except in situations that seriously threaten their health, and then only under the supervision of a physician.

7. Maternal infections can damage the fetus in two ways: (a) by direct infection or (b) by indirect toxic effect.
8. Nutritional deficiencies in the mother, particularly severe ones, are reflected in fetal development.
9. When pregnant women are anxious or under stress, they release various hormones into their bloodstream. These hormones can pass through the placenta and enter the bloodstream of the fetus. Women who are under prolonged stress during their pregnancies are more likely to experience complications during both pregnancy and labor. Prolonged maternal emotional stress is also associated with low birth weight, infant hyperactivity, and postnatal adjustment difficulties.
10. On the whole, women between the ages of seventeen and thirty have fewer difficulties in pregnancy and delivery, and produce fewer abnormal children, than women above or below these ages.
11. The birth process consists of three stages: labor, delivery, and afterbirth.
12. A growing number of American hospitals are introducing family-centered hospital care in which childbirth is made a family experience. Natural childbirth and rooming-in are common features of this program.
13. Frederick Leboyer has captured popular attention with his opinion that traditional childbirth practices traumatize the child. Most authorities believe, however, that the stresses ordinarily associated with birth do not exceed the infant's physical or neurological capacity.
14. In a small minority of cases, complications may arise during pregnancy or during the birth process. The purpose of good prenatal care under medical supervision is to minimize their occurrence. But if complications should develop, there is much that can be done through medical intervention to help the mother and the child. Among the possible complications are toxemia, births that require Caesarean section, anoxia, and premature birth.

KEY TERMS

afterbirth The last stage in the birth process, characterized by the expulsion of the placenta.

anoxia Oxygen starvation or deficiency; in severe cases, anoxia is associated with brain damage or death in the newborn.

Apgar Scoring System A method for appraising the normalcy of a baby's condition at birth.

birth The transition between dependent existence in the uterus and life as a separate organism; the process of being born.

blastocyst A hollow ball of cells that develops from a fertilized ovum.

Caesarian section A surgical technique by which the physician enters the uterus through an abdominal incision and removes the infant.

cephalocaudal development Development starting with the brain and head areas and then working its way down the body.

delivery A stage in the birth process that begins once the infant's head passes through the cervix (the neck of the uterus) and ends when the infant has completed its passage through the birth canal (the vagina).

embryonic period The phase in prenatal development that extends from about the end of the second week following conception to the end of the eighth week.

fetal period The phase in prenatal development that extends from the end of the eighth week until birth.

germinal period The phase in prenatal development that extends from conception to the end of the second week.

labor A stage in the birth process in which the strong muscle fibers of the uterus rhythmically contract, pushing the baby down toward the birth canal.

mitosis Within a few hours of fertilization, growth of the zygote begins by division, forming two cells identical in makeup to the first cell.

natural childbirth A variety of approaches that stress the preparation of the mother and the father for labor and delivery and their active involvement in the childbirth process.

parent-infant bonding The notion that closeness between parent and child in the first minutes of life produces a lasting effect, particularly in cementing attachment ties.

premature infant A baby weighing less than 5½ pounds at birth or having a gestational age of less than thirty-seven weeks.

prenatal period The time elapsing between conception and birth.

proximodistal development Development away from the central axis of the organism.

teratogen Any agent that contributes to birth defects.

teratology The field of study concerned with birth defects.

toxemia A disorder of pregnancy characterized by high blood pressure (hypertension), waterlogging of tissues (edema), the presence of protein in the urine (proteinuria), and occasionally convulsions and coma.

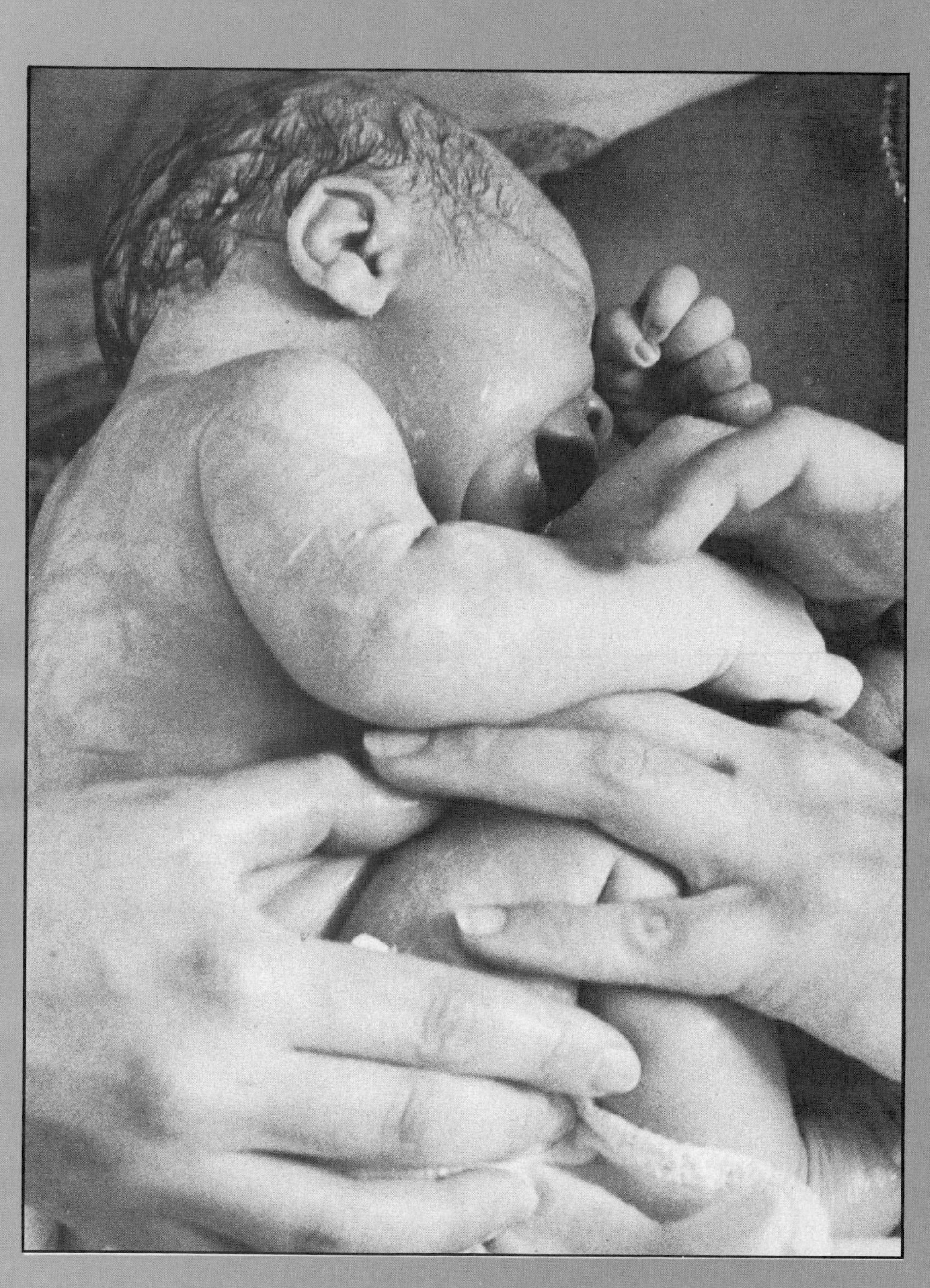

5

The Newborn

Until two decades ago, the human newborn was thought to be little more than an unresponsive vegetable who did nothing except eat, sleep, breathe, and cry. Some ninety years ago William James (1890/1950), a distinguished American philosopher and psychologist, described the world of the newborn as "one great blooming, buzzing confusion"—a world in which the infant is "assailed by eyes, ears, nose, skin, and entrails [all] at once." And around the same time, G. Stanley Hall (1891), the father of American child psychology, depicted the baby as arriving with "its monotonous and dismal cry, with its red, shriveled, parboiled skin . . ., squinting, cross-eyed, pot bellied, and bow legged." Even so keen and sensitive an observer as Jean Piaget (1952*a*: 23) dismissed the first few months of life as involving merely the exercise of "reflexes."

In light of recent research, however, psychologists are increasingly coming to view what they had previously considered the incompetent neonate as "the amazing newborn" (Acredolo and Hake, 1982). The infant arrives with all sensory systems functioning. To the watchful observer, babies communicate at least some of their perceptions and abilities. Newborns tell us what they hear, see, and feel in the same manner that any other organisms do—through systematic responses to stimulating events (Lipsitt, 1971). T. G. R.

Bower (1977: 28), an authority on infant capabilities, observes:

> I suspect that the newborn's social abilities are something parents could have told us about, had we ever bothered to ask them. Many parents have assumed that their babies are, from the beginning, social and make social responses. Nonetheless, there is a whole literature devoted to discussing how the baby comes to be socialized, how he comes to realize that he is a human being, how he comes to have special sets of responses to people that are not elicited by anything else in the environment. A great deal of this effort, although not all of it, has, I feel, been wasted, because right from the moment of birth the baby realizes he is a human being and has specific responses elicited only by other human beings.

The abilities and behavior of neonates will be the focus of this chapter. The term **neonate** refers to a newborn, and the **neonate period** refers to the newborn during the first two weeks following birth.

NEWBORN BEHAVIORS

A newborn is no beauty. At the moment when infants slip into the world, they are covered with *vernix,* the thick, white, waxy substance mentioned in Chapter 4. And some babies retain their *lanugo,* the fetus's fine, woolly facial and body hair, which disappears by the neonate's fourth month. The matting of their hair with vernix gives newborns an odd, pastelike look.

On the average, a full-term newborn is between 19 and 22 inches long and weighs 5½ to 9½ pounds. Many newborns give the appearance of a defeated prizefighter—a puffy bluish-red face, a broad, flat nose, swollen eyelids, and ears skewed at odd angles. Their heads are often misshapen and elongated, a product of *molding.* (In molding, the soft skull "bones" become temporarily distorted to accommodate passage through the birth canal.) Most infants have chins that recede and lower jaws that are underdeveloped. Bowlegs are the rule, and the feet may be cocked in a pigeon-toed manner. Of even greater interest than its appearance is the neonate's behavior. Neonate behavior can be considered in terms of three broad categories: sleeping, crying, and feeding.

Sleeping

The major "activity" of newborns is sleeping. They spend sixteen or more hours per day in sleep, packaged into seven or eight naps. Sleep and wakefulness alternate roughly in four-hour cycles—three hours in sleep and one hour awake. By six weeks, the naps become longer, with infants taking only two to four naps during the day. Beginning about this age, many sleep through most of the night.

Interest in neonate sleeping patterns has been closely linked with interest in newborn **states.** State, as viewed by Peter H. Wolff (1966), refers to a continuum of alertness ranging from regular sleep to vigorous activity. Babies' responses to the environment differ depending on their state (Ashton, 1976). In sleep, for instance, infants are insensitive to touch and most other stimuli. In contrast, infants follow moving objects with their eyes and turn toward sounds when they are alert but relatively inactive (Bower, 1974). Crying and spontaneous smiling are also state-related responses.

The noted pediatrician T. Berry Brazelton (1978) says that state is the infant's first line of defense. By means of state, infants shut out certain stimuli and thereby inhibit their responses. State is also the way infants set the stage for actively responding. Consequently, the newborn's use of various states reflects a high order of nervous system control.

Wolff (1966) identifies the following states in the neonate:

- *Regular sleep.* Infants are at full rest; little or no motor activity occurs; facial muscles are relaxed; spontaneous eye movement is absent; respirations are regular and even.
- *Irregular sleep.* Infants engage in spurts of gentle limb movement and more general stirring, squirming, and twisting; eye movement is occasional and rapid; facial grimaces (smiling, sneering, frowning, puckering, and pouting) are frequent; the rhythm of respiration is irregular and faster than in regular sleep.
- *Drowsiness.* Infants are relatively inactive; on occasion they squirm and twist their bodies; they open and close their eyes intermittently; respiratory patterns are regular, but faster than in regular sleep.

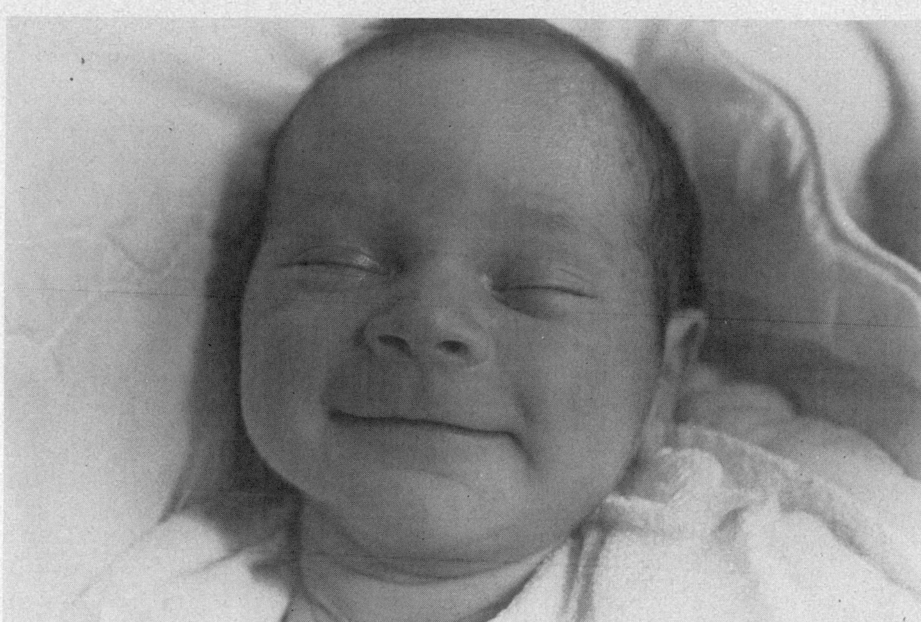

Newborn Sleeping

While sleeping, newborns exhibit spurts of stirring, squirming, and twisting with their bodies. Their faces display a variety of expressions, including smiling, sneering, frowning, and puckering.
Michael Weisbrot and Family

- *Alert inactivity.* Although infants are inactive, their eyes are open and have a bright, shining quality; respirations are regular but faster than during regular sleep.
- *Waking activity.* Infants may be silent or may moan, grunt, or whimper; spurts of diffuse motor activity are frequent; their faces may be relaxed or pinched, as when crying; their rate of respiration is irregular.
- *Crying.* Vocalizations are strong and intense; motor activity is vigorous; the babies' faces are contorted; their bodies are flushed bright red. In some infants, tears can be observed as early as twenty-four hours after birth.

In recent years, interest in neonate states has been related to interest in *REM (rapid-eye-movement)* sleep and *NREM (nonrapid-eye-movement)* sleep. Both occur in infants and adults alike (Berg and Berg, 1979). During REM sleep, eye movements are accompanied by large fluctuations in heart rate, by lowered muscular activity, and by a substantial increase in brain activity. REM sleep is associated with dreaming. Some researchers suggest that REM sleep clears the brain of neurochemicals accumulated during wakening hours and provides a "safety valve" through dreaming, so that intense daytime impulses can be discharged at night. In any event, a deprivation in REM sleep has been linked in adults to an increase in irritability, hostility, tension, and anxiety (Dement, 1960).

By recording brain activity, researchers can measure the amount of REM sleep that occurs at different ages in children and adults. Howard P. Roffwarg, Joseph N. Muzio, and William C. Dement (1966) provide evidence that REM sleep occupies almost half the sleep time of newborn infants (see Figure 5.1). It decreases rapidly to about one-quarter of the sleep time of two-year-olds. Around five years of age, the proportion drops to approximately 20 percent, which is the adult average. Roffwarg, Muzio, and Dement suggest that REM sleep in infants stimulates the development of the brain by the activity it generates. Infants spend so much time in sleep that they have little opportunity to respond to environmental events. They may require the neurological self-stimulation that REM sleep affords them.

Crying

Crying in the newborn is an unlearned, involuntary response. But at the same time it is a highly adaptive response that serves to incite the parent to caretaking activities (Murray, 1979). This is hardly surprising, since there are few sounds that humans find more disconcerting and unnerving than the infant's cry (see the boxed insert on page 132). Daniel G. Freedman

SUDDEN INFANT DEATH SYNDROME

Each year some 7,000 to 10,000 American families experience a devastating tragedy. They put their seemingly healthy baby down in the crib and return to find that the infant has died. Typically there is no warning. The disorder, termed *Sudden Infant Death Syndrome (SIDS)*, is the number-one cause of death for infants between one month and one year. It frequently results in acute agony for parents, who blame themselves and each other for permitting the baby to smother in bed. Yet suffocation from bedding is not the cause of the baby's death.

Through the years there has been an endless proliferation of theories as to what goes wrong (Mackintosh, 1982). In the broadest sense, the difficulty appears to be a respiratory problem. The babies simply stop breathing while asleep.

One theory is that death results from abnormalities in respiratory control (Naeye, 1980). According to this view, the infants suffer from *apnea*—spells in which interruptions or pauses occur in breathing during sleep. Some adults experience a similar disorder, but adults have better reflexes to survive and can go longer without suffering severe oxygen deprivation. Autopsies reveal that in about 60 percent of SIDS cases, there is evidence pointing to the underventilation of the lungs.

In some cases bacterial or viral infection may trigger sudden death. Babies who have had a cold or runny nose appear to be more susceptible to the disorder. The problem may also be maturational. Some centers of the brain may mature more rapidly than others, resulting in a temporary "misprogramming" of respiration. In addition, recent studies of SIDS victims suggest that they have unusually high levels of thyroid hormone—tri-iodothyonine, or T-3. But the significance of the finding remains to be determined. Unhappily, progress in understanding SIDS remains heartbreakingly slow.

(1974) has discovered that within hours after birth, most crying infants will quiet down when they are held and carried. Of 252 newborns that he studied, only 3 could not be quieted in this manner. Thus infants literally condition their caretakers to respond to their needs.

We can tell a good deal about the neonate from the cry. Although people in general cannot reliably dif-

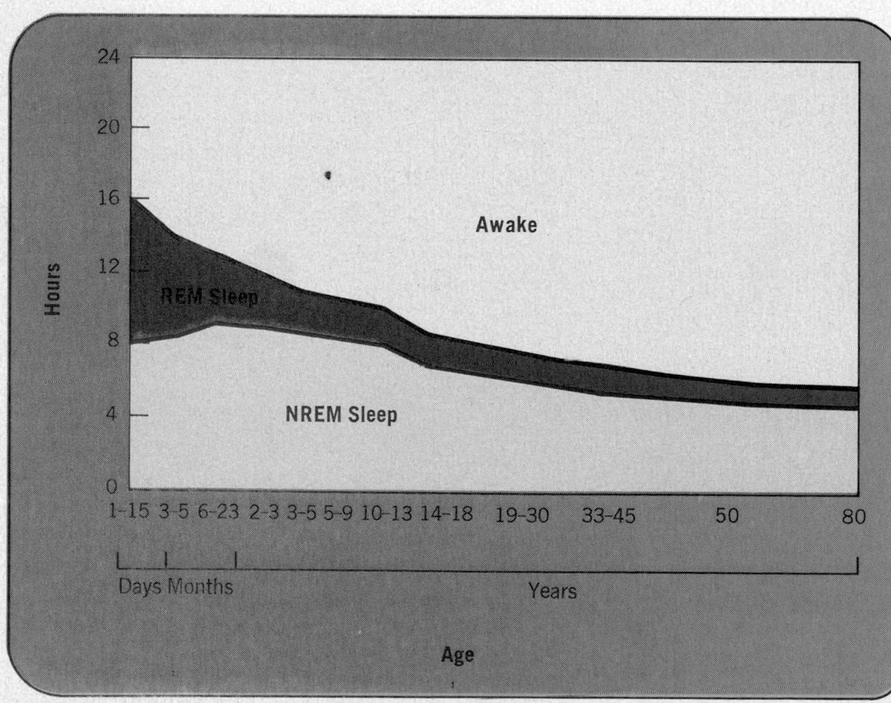

Figure 5.1 Changes with Age in Daily Amounts of Total Sleep, REM Sleep, and NREM Sleep

The graph shows a sharp decline in REM sleep in the early years until about the age of five. The amount of REM sleep falls from eight hours at birth to less than one hour in old age. In contrast, the amount of NREM sleep remains relatively undiminished for many years. The age scale employed in the graph is not proportionately true but reflects approximate values at various age intervals.

SOURCE: Adapted from H. P. Roffwarg, J. N. Muzio, and W. C. Dement, "Ontogenetic Development of the Human Sleep-Dream Cycle," *Science*, Vol. 152 (1966), pp. 604–619.

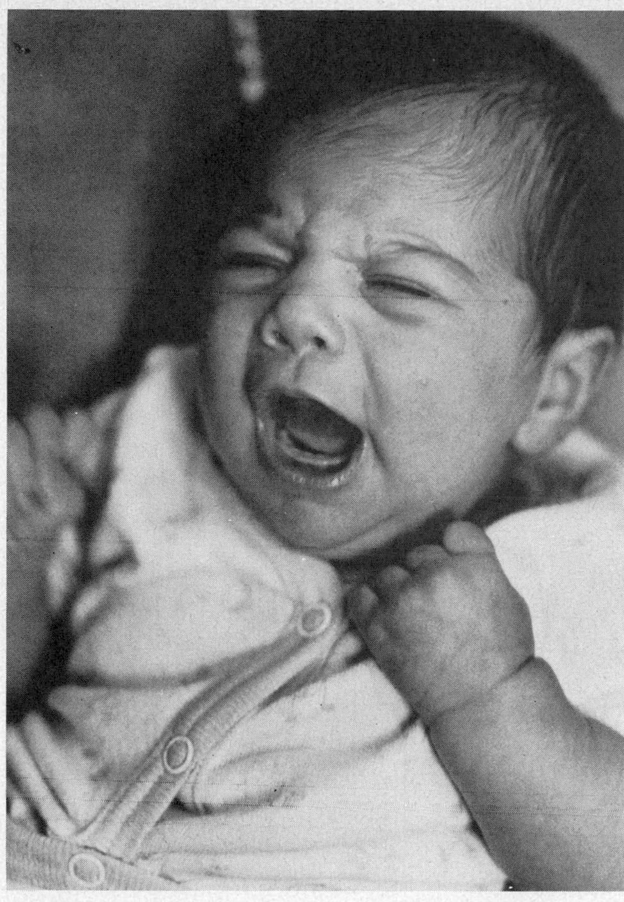

Newborn Crying

Crying is an unlearned, involuntary, but highly adaptive response that incites caretaking activities by other individuals. Most babies can be soothed by picking them up, holding them, and carrying them about.

Mark Antman/The Image Works

ferentiate types of infant crying (Zeskind, 1980), most experienced parents can and do. H. R. Schaffer (1971) identifies three distinct patterns of crying: (1) a basic pattern that begins irregularly at low intensity but gradually becomes louder and more rhythmical, (2) a "mad," or angry, cry that is also rhythmical but more energetic, and (3) a pain cry that begins with a sudden shriek, followed by several seconds of silence as the infant regains its breath, and then by episodes of energetic, gasping cries. Peter H. Wolff (1969) has found that mothers usually react with distress when they hear a pain cry, but show much less concern about cries that do not have the long, silent pauses between bursts.

The neonate's cry is also proving to be an important aid in the early detection of certain abnormalities and diseases. There are times when unusual crying provides the first indication that something may be wrong with an infant (Ostwald and Peltzman, 1974; Zeskind and Lester, 1978, 1981). Brain-damaged and Down's syndrome babies, for instance, produce a less sustained cry with less rhythmic flow in the crying than do normal infants (Fisichelli and Karelitz, 1963). Similarly, the cry of the malnourished infant has an initial longer sound, higher pitch, and lower amplitude than the cry of the well-nourished baby (Lester, 1976).

Feeding

Neonates spend a good deal of the time that they are awake feeding. Indeed, their hunger and sleep patterns are closely linked. Newborns may feed eight to fourteen times during the day: some infants prefer intervals as short as one and one-half hours; others intervals of three to four hours; and still others two- or three-hour intervals during the day and four- or five-hour intervals at night. Fortunately, infants come to require fewer daily feedings as they grow older. Most put themselves on three to five meals by the time they are twelve months old.

Self-Demand Feeding. During the 1920s and 1930s many medical authorities recommended placing infants on a regular four-hour feeding schedule. Mothers were encouraged to hold fast to a strict schedule. According to the behaviorist John B. Watson, a leading authority of the period, a child's character would be improved if its immediate needs were ignored. Today Watson's advice is rejected by most doctors. Pediatricians have come to recognize that babies differ markedly. They encourage parents to feed a baby when it is hungry. This means that the infant picks its own part of the twenty-four-hour cycle in which to feed and sleep—termed *self-demand feeding.*

Breast Feeding versus Bottle Feeding. Whatever schedule parents follow, they have to decide whether the baby will be breast-fed or bottle-fed. Before 1900 the vast majority of mothers breast-fed their babies. But in the ensuing years bottle feeding became increasingly popular, so that by 1946 only thirty-eight out of every one hundred women left the

SOOTHING THE NEONATE

Since time immemorial, harried mothers the world over have been concerned with soothing their babies. Yet the study of infant states tells us that sleep, drowsiness, alert inactivity, and crying are all normal and expected behaviors in a healthy infant. Indeed, crying is functional. During the first week of life crying helps to fill and aerate the infant's lungs. Even so, few of us can escape the psychological discomfort and frayed nerves that are associated with a wailing baby—the piercing cry, flushed red face, jerking body, quivering chin, and trembling arms and legs.

Through the centuries parents have evolved a variety of techniques that both experience and research have shown to be helpful in soothing infants. These include gentle rocking, a pacifier, a pacifier sweetened with a sugar solution, a monotonous, humming sound, and a warm bath (Birns, Blank, and Bridger, 1966; Pederson, Champagne, and Pederson, 1969; Byrne and Horowitz, 1981). Few techniques are more soothing, however, than simply picking the infant up and putting it to the shoulder, its head supported and just above shoulder level (Korner and Thoman, 1972; Thoman, Korner, and Beason-Williams, 1977). This affords contact between the adult and child. And the stimulation provided by picking the child up and moving it through space increases its visual alertness. If a pacifier is given to the infant at the same time, its visual attentiveness is further enhanced. Such stimulation serves to interrupt the crying and to shift the infant into another state. However, babies differ greatly in their soothability and in the techniques that they find to be soothing (Birns, Blank, and Bridger, 1966; Korner and Thoman, 1972).

Recently, researchers have found that they can make babies fall asleep more quickly by increasing the amount of sugar and tryptophan (an amino acid) in their evening bottles (Yogman and Zeisel, 1983). They suggest that nursing mothers may obtain the same effect if they eat candy before the infant's bedtime feeding. Tryptophan is employed in the brain to manufacture a message transmitter that is required for sleep. It is commonly found in milk.

Between 1920 and 1940 the U.S. Children's Bureau *Infant Care* pamphlets warned mothers not to "give in" to a crying baby, for to do so would create "a spoiled, fussy baby, and a household tyrant whose continual demands make a slave of the mother" (1924: 44). But a growing number of psychologists believe that this advice is ill-founded (Ainsworth and Bell, 1977; Fish and Crockenberg, 1981; Crockenberg and Smith, 1982). An infant's crying is not simply a distress signal but a powerful communicative act. How people respond to this act—whether they consistently answer or ignore the cries—teaches the child something about the environment. For instance, a study by Silvia M. Bell and Mary D. Salter Ainsworth (1972) reveals that a responsive mother provides not only the conditions that terminate crying, but also a setting that prevents the crying from occurring in the first place. Even more interesting, Bell and Ainsworth found that ignoring babies' cries actually *increases* the likelihood that they will cry more as the first year progresses. Babies who cry little and whose crying *decreases* during the year generally have mothers who respond to them when they cry. Further, infants of responsive mothers are more likely than their opposites to develop channels other than crying to communicate with their mothers.

It must also be remembered that babies possess a variety of self-soothing mechanisms. They can shift from one state to another independently of outside stimulation. As a result, crying tends to be a self-limiting state, one that is commonly replaced by sleep. Sucking is another built-in device that serves to reduce an infant's stress.

hospital with a nursing baby. This figure dropped to 21 percent in 1956. Since then breast feeding has gained in popularity, especially among middle- and upper-class parents. The National Centers for Disease Control (1984) found in a 1980 survey that 51 percent of white mothers and 25 percent of black mothers fed their babies by breast feeding. The La Leche League International (*la leche* means *milk* in Spanish), formed in 1956, has done much to revitalize interest in breast feeding. Local La Leche chapters have helped mothers by giving them practical information and assisting them with any difficulties they encounter in breast feeding.

Breast feeding offers a number of advantages (Ger-

Breast Feeding

In some areas of the world, including parts of Afghanistan, breast feeding may be prolonged until another child is born. Nursing affords both nutritional and emotional benefits to a child.

Margaret Thompson/The Picture Cube

ard, 1970; Guttmacher, 1973; Winikoff, 1978). It provides emotional and psychological rewards that are not available to women who bottle-feed their infants. Indeed, many women report that the physical act of nursing is a sensually pleasurable experience. And there are some, especially those influenced by the psychoanalytic tradition, who believe that the intimate contact afforded by breast feeding creates a sense of security and well-being in the infant that leaves a permanent favorable impact upon its later personality.

Breast feeding is also practical. The milk is always ready and at the proper temperature. And the traveling mother is free of the paraphernalia required of the nonnursing mother—the tote bag, bottles, and sterile water. Further, mother's milk is easier for an infant to digest than cow's milk. Even more important, researchers have found that mother's milk harbors an arsenal of immunological weapons that protect the infant against infections until its own defenses are built up. Simultaneously, the substances in breast milk seem to stimulate the infant's own antibody machinery and the maturation of the intestinal tract. Some studies also show a reduction in allergic problems (such as eczema) in breast-fed infants. For reasons such as these, in 1980 the Committee on Nutrition of the American Academy of Pediatrics strongly recommended breast feeding for full-term infants. The chief disadvantage of breast feeding is that it limits the physical freedom of the mother.

The advantage of bottle feeding is that it gives mothers the physical freedom that breast feeding denies them. And commercial milk preparations tend to fill babies up more, so that they can go longer between feedings. The decline of breast feeding in developing countries, however, has led to malnutrition and intestinal diseases for increasing numbers of infants (Hinds, 1982; Popkin, Bilsborrow, and Akin, 1982). Since many of the mothers live in poverty, they have only contaminated water to mix with the formula powder. Further, they frequently overdilute the expensive formula, making what should be a four-day supply last for three or more weeks.

One final word of caution. Infants of breast-feeding mothers should be regularly monitored by a pediatrician if the mother is taking medication or other drugs. In some cases these agents can be transmitted to the child in the mother's milk and constitute a health hazard (Ananth, 1978; Sovner and Orsulak, 1979; Rogan, Bagniewska, and Damstra, 1980). Also, the Committee on Nutrition of the American Academy of Pediatrics recommends that breast-fed infants be provided certain supplements, including vitamin D, iron, and fluoride (available in combined preparations).

Reflexes

The newborn infant is hardly a blank tablet (*tabula rasa*), as the English philosopher John Locke believed. On the contrary, the baby comes equipped with a number of behavioral systems ready to be activated. These are termed **reflexes.** A reflex is a relatively simple, involuntary, and unlearned response to a stimulus. In other words, it is a response that is trig-

THE BRAZELTON NEONATAL BEHAVIORAL ASSESSMENT SCALE

Over the past decade, the Brazelton Neonatal Behavioral Assessment Scale has been widely adopted as an instrument for analyzing the early behavior of the neonate. Researchers view it as a promising device for distinguishing among newborn behaviors and identifying their adaptive functions. And it has been employed to study high-risk babies.

The scale was developed by the well-known pediatrician T. Berry Brazelton (1978). He uses it to identify a baby's responses to social stimuli as the infant moves from sleep states to crying and alert states of consciousness. The scale is divided into twenty neurological items and twenty-seven behavioral items. The neurological items include a good many of the reflex behaviors, including the Moro, plantar, sucking, and rooting reflexes. The behavioral items include a newborn's responses to a light, a ball, and a rattle; its orientation to various visual and auditory stimuli; its activity and irritability levels; and its consolability. Brazelton recommends that babies be tested on the third or fourth day, when the immediate stresses of delivery have begun to wear off, and again on the ninth or tenth day, when the baby has adjusted to its home environment.

The order for administering the items is partially determined by the behavior of the baby. There is no limit placed on the number of times an item might be tried. However, the state of the infant during which a particular item is to be administered is specified. The tester seeks to secure the best performance from the child and to elicit, observe, and measure a baby's responses in the way that a caring mother or father would. The goal is to bring the newborn up from a light sleep state to alert states, then into more active states, to crying, and down to alert inactive states once again. Normally the examination takes just about a half hour.

The Brazelton scale does not yield an overall score. However, a number of researchers have attempted to combine clusters of behavior into four subscales, representing interactive, motor, state, and physiologic processes, in order to secure a unique profile for each infant (Als et al., 1979). The scale is primarily helpful in evaluating a baby's current behavior. There are only weak relationships between newborn scores and later behavior (Sameroff, 1978; Vaughn, Crichton, and Egeland, 1980).

gered automatically through built-in circuits. Reflexes are the evolutionary remains of actions seen in animals lower in the phylogenic scale (Cratty, 1970). Although they generally are no longer necessary for human survival, they are good indicators of neurological development in infants (see the boxed insert above). It is estimated that the human is born with at least twenty-seven reflexes. Let us consider some of them.

Moro and Startle Reflexes. The *Moro reflex* is elicited when infants suddenly lose support for their necks and heads. Babies throw out their arms and then bring them together, as in an embrace. Simultaneously they throw out their legs and return them to a flexed position against the body. You can obtain the Moro reflex by holding an infant with one hand under the small of the back and supporting the head with your other hand. Then suddenly lower the hand under the baby's head about an inch. The baby itself often triggers the reflex when it coughs or sneezes.

The Moro reflex is different from the *startle reflex.* The startle reflex is activated when the neonate hears a loud noise or is suddenly touched. The startle reflex resembles the Moro reflex except that the initial extension of the Moro reflex is absent—the infant flexes but does not extend the arms. Further, in the startle reflex the infant's fingers remain closed, whereas in the Moro reflex the hands curl slightly as if preparing to grasp something. In fact, if you place your finger in the baby's hand when someone provides the stimulus for the Moro reflex, you will be able to feel the infant's grip tighten on your finger.

Both the Moro and the startle reflexes may set off a cycle of crying and reflexing. Steady pressure on babies at some point on their bodies usually serves to break the cycle and calm them.

The Moro reflex appears during the ninth week after conception and disappears in six or seven months after birth. A weak Moro reflex provides an

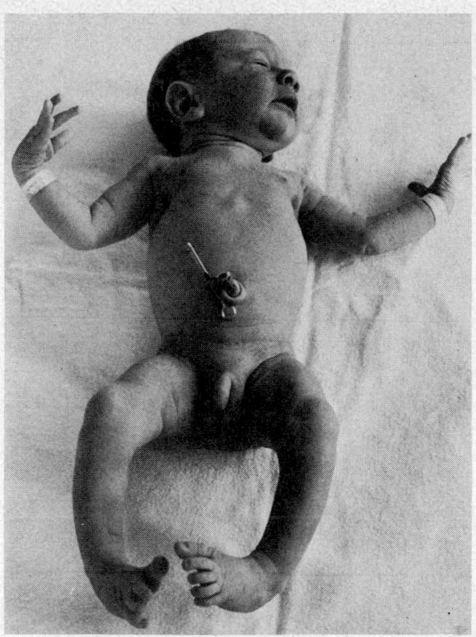

(a)

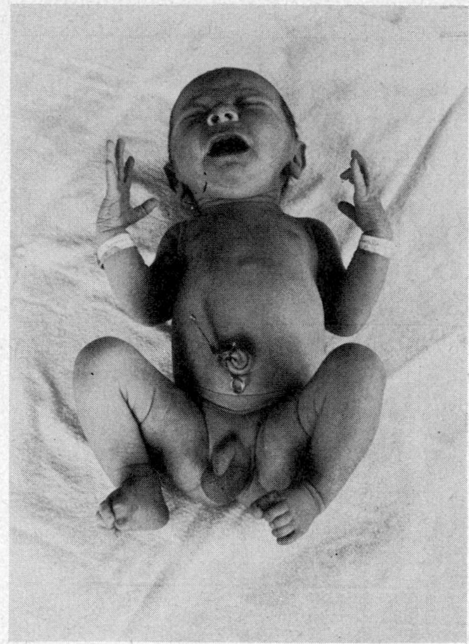

(b)

The Two Stages of the Moro Reflex

The Moro reflex occurs when a baby suddenly loses support for the head and neck. The infant extends the arms and legs (*a*) and then contracts them as if in an embrace (*b*).

Patrick Reddy

early clue that the infant's central nervous system may be malfunctioning. If the reflex is present beyond the ninth month, it may indicate mental retardation.

Rooting Reflex. When infants are gently touched near the corner of the mouth, they "root," or turn their heads toward the stroking object. Then they open their mouths and try to suck. A mother who is unfamiliar with the reflex often attempts to push the infant's head toward her breast. Since babies respond by moving toward, rather than away from, the source of stimulation—in this case the mother's hand—they give the appearance of rejecting the breast. This may inaugurate a vicious circle of frustration for both the mother and the infant: the mother repeatedly "forcing" the baby's head toward her breast and the baby persistently "rejecting" the breast.

Sucking Reflex. If the soft palates of their mouths are touched, infants begin sucking with a rapid burst of five to twenty-four sucks. They then take a brief rest. Mothers tend to jiggle the infant, breast, or bottle when the infant pauses. Feeding appears to be an exchange of turns, in which the infant's pause is answered by the mother's jiggling and the end of jiggling is answered by the next burst (Kaye and Wells, 1980). Babies put both the nipple and the areola, the dark area around the nipple, into their mouths. Sucking appears to be more than just a way to get sustenance, for infants appear to suck simply for the sake of sucking (Koepke and Barnes, 1982). Thumbs, by virtue of their convenience, seem to offer special appeal. Most children, however, outgrow thumb sucking by the age of three.

Babinski Reflex. The *Babinski reflex* is triggered by gently stroking the outer edge of the sole of the foot. This causes an extension in the infant's big toe and a fanning out of the other toes. The Babinski reflex disappears within a year. Thereafter the toes curl downward when the sole is stroked.

Palmar and Plantar Grasp Reflexes. Touching the palm of the infant's hand results in a grasping action that is often strong enough to support the infant's weight—the *palmar grasp reflex.* If pressure is applied against the ball of the foot, the toes flex, assuming a grasping position—the *plantar grasp reflex.* Some researchers believe that these two reflexes are the rudimentary remains of the grasping activity needed by primate ancestors. The palmar grasp reflex reaches its greatest strength toward the end of the first month. It is gradually replaced by voluntary grasp between the fourth and seventh months. The plantar grasp reflex disappears by the end of the first year.

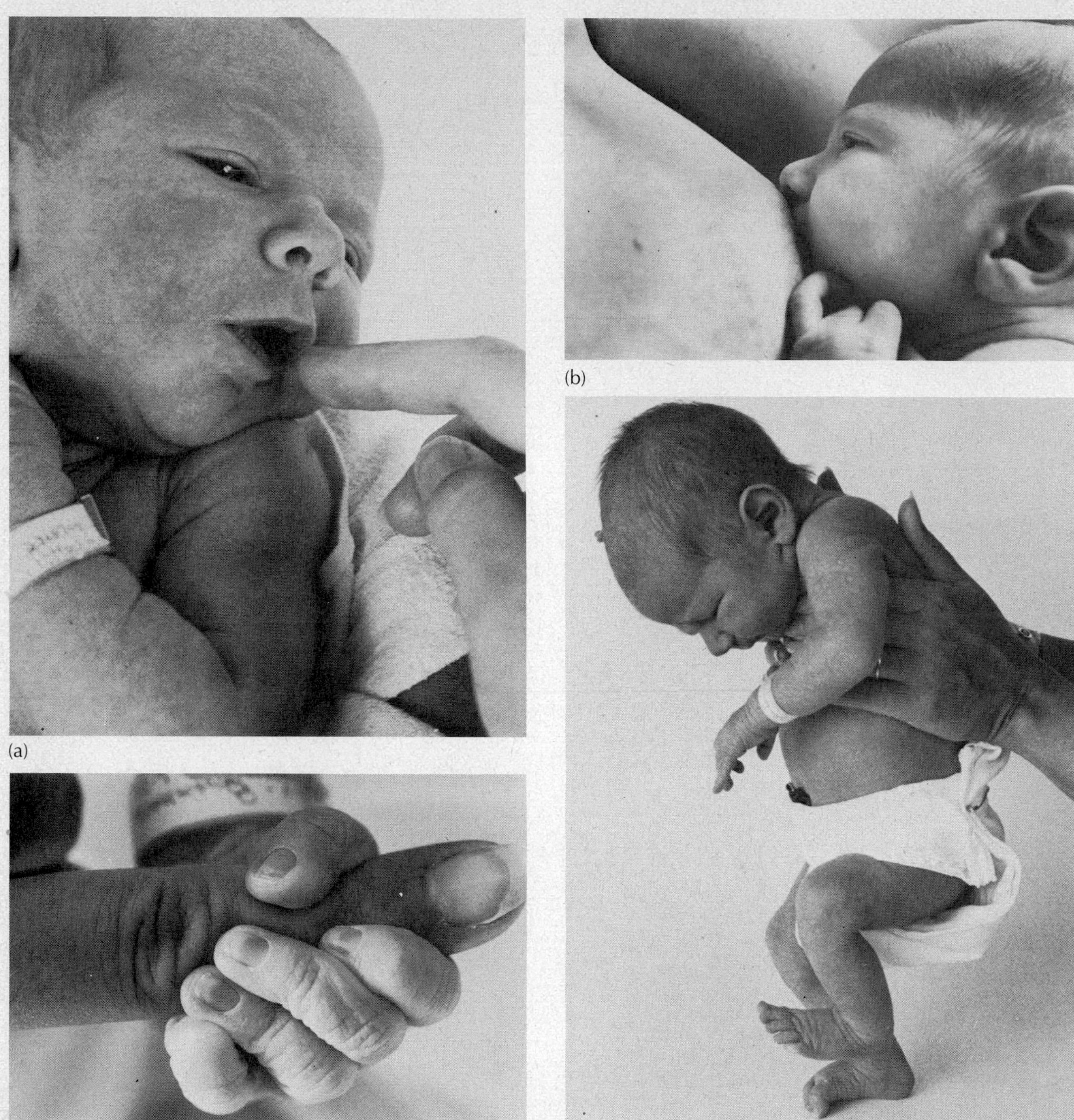

(a) (b) (c) (d)

Reflexes

Newborns are equipped with a number of behavioral systems that are ready to be activated. These systems are called reflexes. The photos depict the rooting reflex (*a*), the sucking reflex (*b*), the palmar grasp reflex (*c*), and the stepping reflex (*d*).

Patrick Reddy

Stepping Reflex. Around the end of the second week of life, 58 percent of all infants will "walk" if held in an upright position, tilted slightly to one side, and permitted to touch a level horizontal surface. This is the *stepping reflex.* The walking pattern involves a lifting and flexing of the knee but does not entail any arm swing. The neonate can be made to "climb" stairs while supported in this fashion. The reflex disappears by about the third month (Thelen and Fisher, 1982).

Swimming Reflex. If neonates are submerged in water with their stomachs down, they make rhythmic swimming movements that are capable of propelling them a short distance. This is the *swimming reflex.* The babies generally hold their breath and do not ingest water. Obviously, caution must be employed with newborns, since they are unable to keep their heads above the water level and thus may suffocate. The swimming reflex usually disappears in about five months (McGraw, 1943).

Memory: Habituation

If we repeatedly present the same stimulus to an infant, the infant will soon stop responding to it. If we then withhold the stimulus for a short period of time, the infant recovers the reflex response (Haith and Campos, 1977; Cohen and Menten, 1981). This process is termed **habituation.**

In habituation studies the infant is exposed to a stimulus—for instance, a sound, an odor, or a light—at regular but short intervals (Jeffrey and Cohen, 1971). When the baby no longer responds to the stimulus, a slightly different stimulus is introduced. If the infant then responds, it proves that the baby can distinguish the latter stimulus from the preceding one. It also proves that the infant is habituated to the initial stimulus and not simply fatigued.

Habituation represents an early *adaptive* response to the environment. If infants attended to every stimulus that came along, they would soon be exhausted. It would serve no purpose, for example, if they rooted continually whenever their cheeks accidently touched their bedding. Rather than anticipating the nipple after a few such encounters, infants simply stop this fruitless exercise. But if a new and different stimulus comes along, the babies respond to it.

A number of researchers argue that habituation gives us insight into an infant's early memory processes (Jeffrey and Cohen, 1971; Cohen and Menten, 1981). If babies respond differently to a stimulus the tenth time they experience it from the way they responded the first time, this suggests that they have "remembered" the stimulus. Using this reasoning, Y. N. Sokolov (1958/1963, 1969), a Russian psychologist, has formulated a memory theory of habituation. According to Sokolov, a model of repeated stimulus is formed in the nervous system. If a new stimulus input matches this model, the associated reflex is inhibited. If the stimulus fails to match the model, the reflex is activated as usual. Additional research is needed, however, to test Sokolov's formulation (Bernard and Ramey, 1977).

Learning

Can newborns learn? The answer to this question depends on the type of behavior involved. Most developmental psychologists agree that habituation is a very simple and elementary form of learning. Since repeated stimulation produces a lessening of response and, equally important, novel stimulation reestablishes the response, it is clear that newborns can "learn" to distinguish among stimuli.

But, we may ask, can neonates learn in the more traditional sense—can they adjust their behavior according to whether it succeeds or fails? Arnold J. Sameroff (1968) conducted a study involving neonate sucking techniques and tentatively suggests the answer is yes. It is generally recognized that two nursing methods are available to newborns. One approach—*expression*—involves pressing the nipple against the roof of the mouth with the tongue and squeezing milk out of it. A second method—*suction*—entails creating a partial vacuum by reducing the pressure inside the mouth and thus pulling the milk from the nipple. Sameroff devised an experimental nipple and nutrient delivery apparatus that permitted him to regulate the supply of milk that an infant received. He provided one group of babies with milk only when they used the expressive method (squeezing the nipple); he gave the second group milk only when they used the suction method.

Sameroff found that the infants adapted their responses according to which technique was reinforced. For instance, the group that was given milk when they used the expressive method diminished their suction responses—indeed, in many cases they abandoned the suction method during the training period. In a second experiment, Sameroff (1968) was able to induce the babies, again through reinforcement, to express milk at one of two different pressure levels. These results suggest that learning can occur among two- to five-day-old full-term infants.

Various other researchers have also demonstrated learning in newborns (DeCasper and Carstens, 1981). Einar R. Siqueland (1968) was able to influence the head-turning response in neonates through reinforcement. By presenting a group of infants with pacifier nipples when they spontaneously turned their heads, Siqueland increased their rate of head turning. Similarly, he was able to decrease head turning in another group of infants that he had reinforced for holding their heads still.

The Siqueland experiments involved the modification of head turning, an *already* existing element within the rooting-sucking-feeding reflex system. Similarly, the Sameroff experiment succeeded in conditioning an established reflex response—sucking. In both studies, then, the training procedures served to strengthen or alter organized patterns of behavior that were already built into the organism (Kessen, 1967). Most other studies that have demonstrated the existence of neonate learning have followed the same plan (Sameroff, 1971).

Arnold J. Sameroff and Patrick J. Cavanagh (1979) note that successful research results have generally been limited to such response systems as sucking and head turning that are connected with the biological survival of the infant. This leads them to question whether these behaviors can legitimately be taken to represent learning. They say that such responses are adaptations to specific stimuli for which newborns are biologically prepared. As such, they contend that the adaptations might more appropriately be judged the result of maturational processes rather than the result of learning processes (see Chapter 1).

THE SENSES

What is the world like to the newborn? It is becoming increasingly clear that infants do not perceive their environment as the "great blooming, buzzing confusion" that William James called it in 1890. The infant is hardly incompetent. Indeed, as André-Thomas observes, "the neonate is not a neophyte" (quoted by Kessen, 1963). Today, sophisticated monitoring equipment is permitting us to pinpoint what the infant sees, hears, smells, tastes, and feels. Psychologists now recognize that infants are capable of doing much more and much earlier than was believed possible even a decade ago. For instance, within three days of birth, neonates prefer the human voice, distinguish among speakers, and reveal a preference for their mothers' voices (DeCasper and Fifer, 1980).

Let us consider the processes of sensation and perception. **Sensation** refers to the reception of information by our sense organs. **Perception** has to do with the *interpretation* or *meaning* that we assign to sensation.

Vision

The Eye altering alters all.

—WILLIAM BLAKE
The Mental Traveller, 1800–1810

A full-term newborn is equipped at birth with a functional and intact visual apparatus. However, the eye contains a number of immaturities. The retina and the optic nerve, for instance, are not fully developed (Abramov et al., 1982). Nonetheless, both the central retina and the peripheral retina appear to function at birth (Lewis, Maurer, and Kay, 1978). Newborns also lack the muscular ability to keep both eyes on the same thing. Infants' eyes do not usually converge on the same point until babies are about three months old (Maurer and Maurer, 1976).

Further, neonates appear to lack visual accommodation. The muscles that control the lenses are not fully developed. As a result, the lenses are fixed in focus for about a month. Thus only objects that are about 7 to 9 inches from the neonate's eye are in focus (Haynes, White, and Held, 1965). In part this may be a blessing. It limits the stimulus input with which infants must cope. As a rule the eyes do not focus normally, adjusting to different distances, until infants reach about four months of age. Although some of the structures within the visual system are not completely formed, the eye is prepared at birth to distinguish among most aspects of its visual field (Hershenson, 1967; Reese and Lipsitt, 1970; Bronson, 1974).

Efforts have been made to measure the neonate's *visual acuity*—the ability to see objects clearly and to resolve detail. J. J. Gorman, D. G. Cogan, and S. S. Gellis (1957) estimate that a neonate has between 20/350 and 20/450 vision. This means that if newborns could see equally well at all distances, they could see at 20 feet what an adult with normal vision could see at 350 to 450 feet. (A person with normal vision can see the big E on an eye chart at a distance of 200 feet; hence if you can see *only* the big E at 20 feet, your vision is 20/200.) But Glenn O. Dayton, Jr., and his associates (1964), using more sophisticated equipment, find that 20/290 vision or better is a more accurate estimate of neonate visual acuity (indeed, nine of twenty-four neonates tested had 20/150 vision or better). However, these estimates may be conservative, since babies are not trying to do their best, as adults are when they take an eye test (Maurer and Maurer, 1976). And one study suggests that the newborn's central vision may be considerably better than the above estimates indicate (Lewis, Maurer, and Kay, 1978).

The neonate pays more attention to some things than to others (Fantz, Fagan, and Miranda, 1975; Haith, 1980). Research by Robert L. Fantz confirms that neonates are able to distinguish among various visual patterns. In one experiment, Fantz (1963) found that infants from ten hours to five days old look longer at a schematic black and white face than at a patch of newsprint; longer at newsprint than at a black and white bull's-eye; and longer at a bull's-eye than at a plain red, white, or yellow circle.

In his experiments Fantz employed an ingenious baby-testing apparatus. An infant is placed face up in a form-fitting crib. A structure above the baby's head holds two pattern boards side by side. The researcher peers through a peephole between the target patterns, noting which pattern is reflected on the surface of the infant's pupil. This allows him to record the amount of time that the infant fixates upon (attends to) each pattern. Fantz has demonstrated that neonates are more attracted to pattern than to color differences; to facelike than to other patterns; to "complex" than to "simple" figures; to oval than to plain shapes; and to curved than to straight contours (Fantz, 1966; Fantz and Miranda, 1975).

Other research reveals that neonates can follow slowly moving objects with their eyes (Greenman, 1963; Barten, Birns, and Ronch, 1971; McGurk, Turnure, and Creighton, 1977; Haith and Goodman, 1982). And Maurice Hershenson (1964) has shown that neonates can discriminate among degrees of brightness. He presented two- to four-day-old newborns with paired combinations of three uniform gray panels differing in brightness. The infants looked more at the panel of intermediate intensity than at the other two panels. Further, they looked more at the panel of bright intensity than at that of dim intensity. All this research points to an important conclusion: the world of the neonate is not an undifferentiated, chaotic mass of stimuli.

T. G. R. Bower (1971, 1974, 1977) suggests that

Baby-Testing Apparatus

The photo shows the "looking chamber" employed by Robert L. Fantz in his studies of perceptual development in children. The infant is placed on her back looking up at two panels. Contrasting visual stimuli—a face and a patch of newsprint, a red circle and a bull's-eye, a bull's-eye and newsprint—are placed on the panels. The researcher then observes the baby's eye movements to determine which of the two panels she looks at more frequently and for longer time periods.

Courtesy Dr. Robert L. Fantz

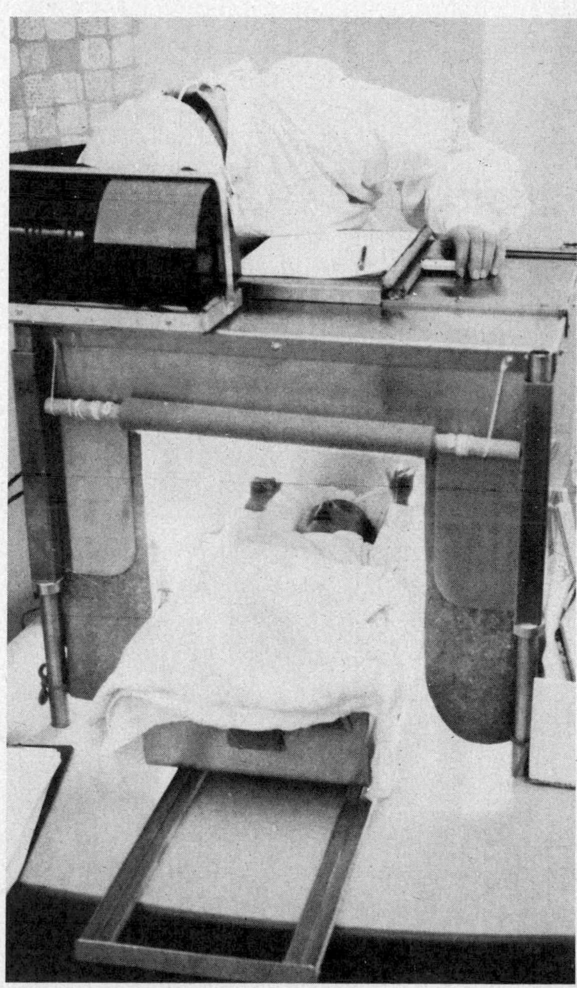

some of the infant's perceptual responses revolve around built-in abilities. In an experiment with infants between one and two weeks of age, Bower used special experimental equipment to project a *virtual image* of a solid object in front of the babies. A virtual image is an optical illusion. It looks three-dimensional in space, although it is empty air to the sense of touch. Bower found that the neonates responded with unmistakable surprise whenever their hands reached the location where the "object" seemed to be: they would emit a howl, accompanied by a change in facial expression. In contrast, none of the infants showed surprise when they reached out and touched an actual object that had been placed before them. Bower interprets this study as revealing that at least one aspect of eye-hand interaction is biologically prewired in the infant's nervous system.

Other researchers also report that some aspects of infant eye-hand coordination appear to be preprogrammed (Cruikshank, 1941; Bruner and Koslowski, 1972). Jeffery Field (1977), however, has been unable to replicate Bower's findings using a virtual image. He undertook a slightly modified version of Bower's experiment with a group of two- and five-month-old babies. The infants studied by Field did not become emotionally distressed when they reached for a visible but intangible stimulus. It is conceivable that the age difference between the infants in the two studies contributed to the conflicting results. Bower (1971, 1974, 1976) believes, for instance, that the precocious eye-hand coordination of the neonate tends to vanish and then to reappear at about five months of age (see Chapter 6).

In still another experiment, Bower (1971) found that neonates respond "defensively" to an approaching object: they widen their eyes, retract their heads, and interpose their hands between their face and the object. This and other research gives clear evidence that neonates have a number of rather sophisticated visual capacities (Lewis, 1977).

Two experimental psychologists, Andrew N. Meltzoff and M. Keith Moore (1977, 1979, 1983), also report that neonates can imitate other people's facial and manual gestures. The researchers first have an adult look at a neonate and display a passive and expressionless face. Then in random order the adult performs four actions: he purses his lips, he sticks out his tongue, he opens his mouth wide, and he opens and closes his hand. The adult pauses with a neutral expression in between each demonstration. Later, observers view each infant on videotape and pick the variation they believe the baby is imitating. When Meltzoff and Moore compared these choices with the adult's actions, they found that the babies had consistently varied their expressions and hand movements to match those of the adult.

Meltzoff and Moore do not believe that imitative behavior can be explained either by conditioning or by some sort of innate releasing mechanism. Rather, they conclude that neonates compare the sensory information from their own unseen facial and hand gestures to a mental picture they have of the adult gesture. The neonates then construct a motor expression which matches that of the adult. Hence, Meltzoff and Moore say that imitation is accomplished through an active matching process that is mediated by a picture on some inner screen. If this interpretation is correct, it represents an extraordinary cognitive capability.

Some developmental psychologists dispute the research done by Meltzoff and Moore (Anisfeld, 1979; Masters, 1979). And a number have been unable to replicate their findings experimentally (Hayes and Watson, 1981; McKenzie and Over, 1983; Koepke et al., 1983). For example, Sandra W. Jacobson (1979) finds that neonates will stick out their tongues at a pen or some other object moving toward their mouth. Since babies will open their mouth to a wide variety of stimuli, Jacobson says we cannot call it imitation. Nonetheless, other researchers like Tiffany M. Field and his associates (1982) have experimentally monitored the faces of seventy-four babies as they looked at adult models who made happy, sad, or surprised expressions and found that two-day-old newborns imitated the expressions. Unhappily, these matters remain unresolved and the debate continues.

Bower, like Meltzoff and Moore, assumes that infant perception involves some sort of internal representation of the world. But other psychologists, such as Lloyd Kaufman (1975), question whether neonates in fact experience a picture on some inner screen. They suggest that neonate perception may simply involve one dimension in a biologically preprogrammed link between an environmental stimulus and a response. The research of Jean Piaget dealing with cognitive development in infants is also inconsistent with the inner screen thesis (see Chapter 7).

Kaufman raises still another issue. Let us assume, he argues, that some future genius invents a machine that will enable us to see on a screen the infant's representation of the world. Even so, Kaufman suggests, we could not be certain that the infant makes the same sort of interpretations of the representation that adults do. These issues obviously remain unresolved. Imaginative and creative research, such as the studies undertaken by Meltzoff and Moore and by Bower, often raises a host of new questions at the same time that it provides us with an answer to one question.

Hearing

At the time of birth, the hearing apparatus of the neonate is remarkably well developed. Indeed, the human fetus can hear noises three months before birth (Birnholz and Benacerraf, 1983). However, for several hours or even days after delivery, the neonate's hearing may be somewhat impaired. Vernix and amniotic fluid frequently stop up the external ear passage, while mucus clogs the middle ear. However, these mechanical blockages disappear rapidly after birth.

Although authorities a hundred years ago believed that neonates were deaf (Preyer, 1880), we know now that they hear, and hear very well (Field et al., 1980; Acredolo and Hake, 1982). They are capable of detecting soft sounds that appear faint even to adults. Nonetheless, neonates have difficulty discriminating one tone from another (Eisenberg, 1970). It appears that they can detect only the difference between tones of 200 and 1,000 cycles per second. This is comparable to the difference between an air raid siren and a trombone (Leventhal and Lipsitt, 1964).

It has long been recognized that hearing plays an important part in the process by which children acquire language. But only recently has research revealed the startling fact that newborns are "tuned in" to the fine elements of adult speech. William S. Condon and Louis W. Sander (1974*a*, 1974*b*) have made videotapes of neonate-adult interaction and minutely analyzed them frame by frame.

At first the hands, feet, and head of an infant appear uncoordinated, clumsily flexing, twitching, and moving about in all directions. But closer examination reveals that the infant's movements are synchronized with the sound patterns of the adult's speech. Condon and Sander discovered that if an infant is squirming about when an adult begins to talk, the infant coordinates the movements of brows, eyes, limbs, elbows, hips, and mouth to start, stop, and change with the boundaries of the adult's speech segments (phonemes, syllables, or words).

For example, consider the word "come," which is made up of two sound segments: *kk* and *mm*. When an adult in the study emitted the *kk* in "come," which lasted for 0.07 second, the infant's head moved to the right very slightly, the left elbow extended slightly, the right hip rotated outward quickly, the left hip extended slightly, and the big toe of the left foot adducted (bent inward). These movements formed a "unit." When the adult concluded the word with *mm*, which lasted for 0.1 second, the left elbow increased its speed, the right hip added extension, the left hip rotated inward, the big toe stopped moving.

The infants, who were from twelve hours to two days old, were equally capable of synchronizing their movements with Chinese or English. Various tests confirmed that the correspondence between the patterns of an adult's speech and an infant's movements were not random. If infants, from birth, move in precise, shared rhythm with the speech patterns of their culture, then they participate in millions of repetitions of linguistic forms long before they employ them in communication. By the time children begin to speak, they have already laid down within themselves the form and structure of their people's language system. Thus Condon and Sander conclude that this complex, ongoing "dance" of the neonate in the presence of human speech has functional significance for later language development. The link between the infant's movements and the adult's speech further suggests to Condon and Sander that human beings possess a genetic predisposition for the acquisition and use of language.

Taste and Smell

Both taste—*gustation*—and smell—*olfaction*—are present at birth. Neonate taste preferences can be determined by measuring sucking behavior. Newborns relax and suck contentedly when provided with sweet solutions, although they reveal a preference for sucrose over glucose (Engen, Lipsitt, and Peck, 1974). They react to salty, sour, and bitter solutions by grimacing and breathing irregularly (Jensen, 1932; Crook, 1978). Charles K. Crook and Lewis P. Lipsitt (1976) found that newborns decrease their sucking speed when receiving sweet fluid, which suggests that they savor the liquid for the pleasurable taste. Hence,

Table 5.1 Neonate Responses to Strong Tastes

Response	Percentage Responding: *Less Than Twenty Hours Old (N = 75)*	Percentage Responding: *Three to Seven Days Old (N = 100)*
Sweet		
Retraction of mouth angle	81%	87%
Satisfied smile	77	73
Eager sucking and licking of upper lip	99	97
Sour		
Pursed lips	100	98
Wrinkled nose	77	73
Repeated blinking	89	70
Increased salivation	81	65
Flushing	76	64
Bitter		
"Archlike" lips with depressed mouth angles	97	96
Protruding tongue	79	81
Salivation and spitting	76	87
Expression of "anger" and dislike	79	86
Vomiting	45	52

SOURCE: Adapted from J. E. Steiner, "Facial Expressions of the Neonate Infant Indicating the Hedonics of Food-related Chemical Stimuli," in J. M. Weiffenbach (ed.), *The Genesis of Sweet Preference* (Washington, D.C.: U.S. Department of Health, Education and Welfare, 1977).

the hedonistic aspects of tasting are present at birth (Acredolo and Hake, 1982) (see Table 5.1).

Newborns respond to different odors, and the vigor of the response corresponds to the intensity and quality of the stimulant. Trygg Engen, Lewis P. Lipsitt, and Herbert Kaye (1963) tested olfaction in two-day-old infants. At regular intervals they held a cotton swab saturated with anise oil (which has a licorice smell) or asafetida (which smells like boiling onions) under an infant's nose. A polygraph recorded the babies' bodily movements, respiration, and heart rate. When they first detected an odor, infants moved their limbs, their breathing quickened, and their heart rate increased. With repeated exposure, however, habituation occurred (infants gradually came to disregard the stimulant). The olfactory thresholds decreased drastically over the first few days of life, meaning that the neonates became increasingly sensitive to nasal stimulants (Lipsitt, Engen, and Kaye, 1963). Other researchers have confirmed that neonates possess well-developed olfactory abilities, although they have found that some infants are much more sensitive to odors than others (Self, Horowitz, and Paden, 1972; Rieser, Yonas, and Wikner, 1976).

Cutaneous Senses

Heat, cold, pressure, and pain—the four major cutaneous sensations—are present in neonates (Humphrey, 1978). Kai Jensen (1932) found that a bottle of hot or cold milk (above 124°F or below 72°F) caused an irregular sucking rhythm in neonates. On the whole, however, neonates are relatively insensitive to small differences in thermal stimuli. Neonates also respond to body pressure. Touching activates many of the reflexes discussed earlier in the chapter, including the rooting, sucking, Babinski, palmar, and plantar reflexes.

We infer from neonates' responses that they experience pain sensations. So far research has not detailed just what these experiences are. A study by Lewis P. Lipsitt and N. Levy (1959) indicated that babies have an increasing sensitivity to mild electric shock during the first five days of life. Further, these researchers found a sex difference in responses to shock, with girls showing more sensitivity than boys. Observation of neonate and infant behavior also suggests that gastrointestinal upsets are a major source of discomfort. And male infants increase their crying and fussing during circumcision, providing additional evidence that neonates are sensitive to pain.

INDIVIDUAL DIFFERENCES AMONG NEWBORNS

> *Training a baby by the book is a good idea, only you need a different book for each baby.*
>
> —DAN BENNETT

According to popular wisdom, "A baby is a baby—if you've seen one, you've seen them all." Parents of large families know that this simply is not true. Infants differ—indeed, differ radically—from one another. Babies are individualists from the moment they draw breath. One baby may react to a loud noise or close physical contact in a manner opposite to that of another (Segal and Yahraes, 1978). Overall, the breadth and scope of individual differences in the behavior of babies is impressive (Rothbart, 1981).

Cuddlers and Noncuddlers

One particularly striking difference among newborns is their reaction to cuddling. H. R. Schaffer and Peggy E. Emerson (1964) studied the reactions of thirty-seven neonates to physical contact and found that the babies could be classed as *cuddlers* or *noncuddlers.* Mothers of cuddlers describe their infants in these terms: "He snuggles into you"; "She cuddles you back"; and "He'd let me cuddle him for hours." In contrast, mothers of noncuddlers give different reports of what happens when they hold their babies on their laps, press them against their shoulders, or kiss them. These mothers say, "He won't allow it—he fights to get away"; "Try and snuggle him against you and he'll kick and thrash, and if you persist he'll begin to cry"; and "She struggles, squirms, and whimpers when you try to hold her close."

Although noncuddlers object to *close* physical contact, they do not resist other forms of handling. They actively enjoy being swung, bounced, and romped with in a manner that involves contact but not restraint. They like being kissed or tickled and playing other "skin games," provided they are not held. Further, noncuddlers tolerate being held so long as they are kept in motion, as when a parent carries them about. Schaffer and Emerson found other differences between cuddlers and noncuddlers during the first two years of life. In motor development, for instance, noncuddlers are typically ahead of cuddlers; they develop the ability to sit unsupported, to stand with support, and to crawl sooner than cuddlers do.

Differences in Temperament

Alexander Thomas and his associates (Thomas et al., 1963; Thomas, Chess, and Birch, 1970) have also found, in studies of more than 200 children, that babies show a distinct individuality in temperament during the first weeks of life that is independent of their parents' handling or personality styles. These researchers term some infants *difficult babies*—they wail and cry a great deal, have violent tantrums, spit out new foods, scream and twist when their faces are washed, eat and sleep in irregular patterns, and are not easy to pacify. Other infants are characterized as *slow-to-warm-up babies*—infants who have low activity levels, adapt very slowly, tend to be withdrawn, seem somewhat negative in mood, and show wariness in new situations. And still others are termed *easy babies*—infants with generally sunny, cheerful dispositions, who adapt quickly to new routines, foods, and people. Roughly 10 percent of all infants are difficult babies, 15 percent are slow-to-warm-up babies, and 40 percent are easy babies. The remaining 35 percent show a mixture of traits that do not readily fit themselves into these categories.

Thomas and his associates emphasize that parents need to take the unique temperament of their baby into account. Children do not react in the same ways to the same developmental influences. Whereas domineering, highly authoritarian parental behavior

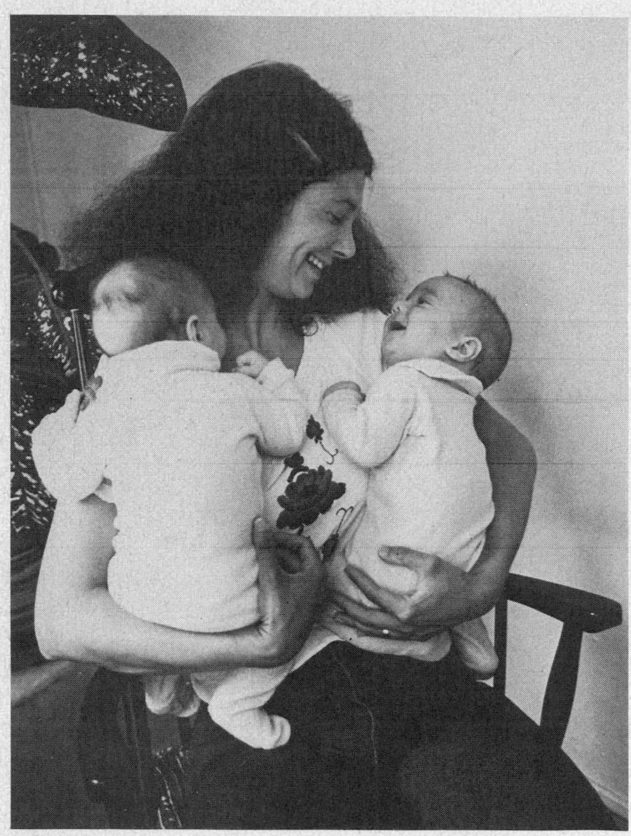

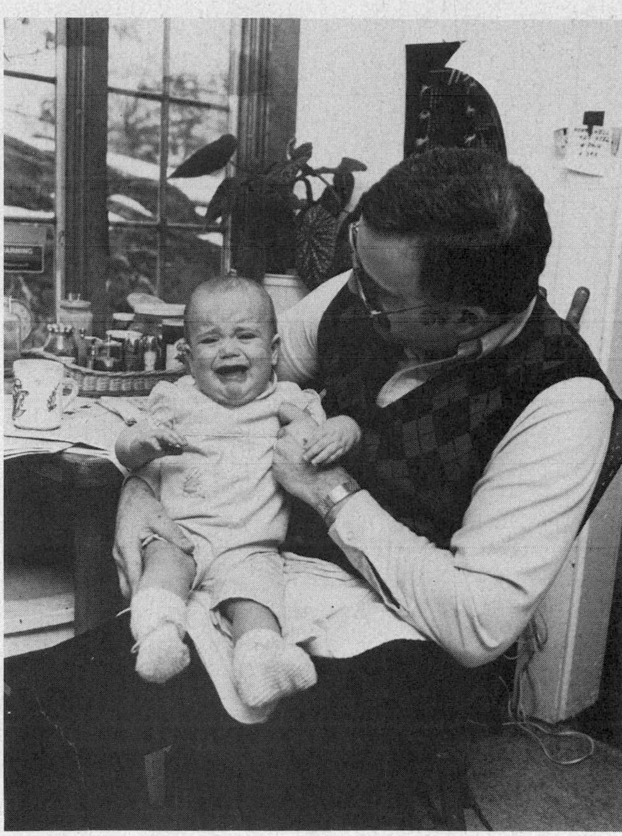

Cuddlers and Noncuddlers

The identical twin babies are cuddlers who enjoy close physical contact. In contrast, the other baby is a noncuddler who resists contact that is physically constraining. However, noncuddlers typically like being swung, bounced, and romped with, and they enjoy being kissed and tickled so long as they are not held tightly.

Left, Elizabeth Crews; *right,* Frank Siteman/Jeroboam

makes one child anxious and submissive, it leads another to be defiant and antagonistic. As a consequence, Thomas and his colleagues (1963: 85) conclude, "There can be no universally valid set of rules that will work equally well for all children everywhere."

Parents with difficult babies often feel considerable anxiety and guilt. "What are we doing wrong?" they ask. Thomas and his associates (1963: 94) have a reassuring answer for such parents:

> The knowledge that certain characteristics of their child's development are not primarily due to parental malfunctioning has proven helpful to many parents. Mothers of problem children often develop guilt feelings because they assume that they are solely responsible for their children's emotional difficulties. This feeling of guilt may be accompanied by anxiety, defensiveness, increased pressures on the children, and even hostility toward them for "exposing" the mother's inadequacy by their disturbed behavior. When parents learn that their role in shaping of their child is not an omnipotent one, guilt feelings may lessen, hostility and pressures may tend to disappear, and positive restructuring of the parent-child interaction can become possible.

All this research highlights the importance of adjusting child-rearing practices to the individual infant. A given environment does not have the identical functional consequences for all children. Much depends on the temperamental makeup of the child. In sum, both factors—environment and temperament—interact to shape the child's personality.

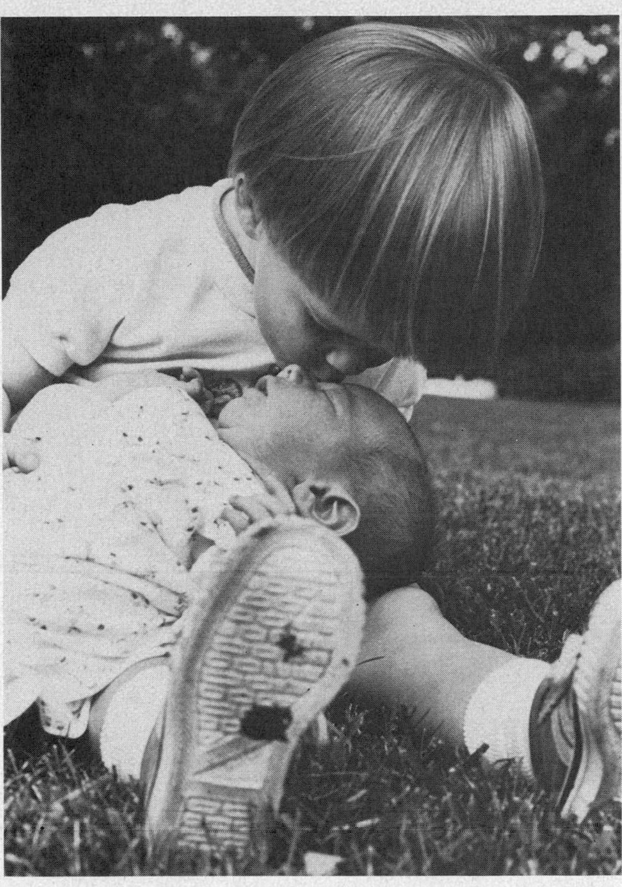

A New Brother

This infant's parents have wisely permitted his two-year-old brother to have close contact with him. This allows the older sibling to make a healthy adjustment to the new arrival and the younger child to begin to develop his own unique personality.

Patrick Reddy

Parent-Child Interaction: A Two-Way Street

Psychologists and psychiatrists have traditionally emphasized that parents have a profound influence in shaping their children's personalities. Indeed, the notion has long been popular in some educational circles that children are blank tablets on which the finger of experience writes. According to this view, children are essentially passive beings, acted on by environmental forces that condition and reinforce them in one fashion or another.

But increasingly, social and behavioral scientists have recognized that this view is misleading (Sameroff, 1975; Lamb, 1977*a*; Lytton, 1980; Martin, 1981). People began to realize that infants are much more complicated than anybody had given them credit for and have a considerable effect on everyone around them. In some respects this realization was a kind of reaction against prevailing notions that blamed the parents for everything. Clearly, children are active agents in the socialization process; they are not only influenced by, but themselves influence, their caretakers. Michael Lewis (1977) finds, for instance, that even very young infants undertake to control their mother's actions. For example, the infant and the mother may be looking at one another. Should the baby look away and upon turning back find it has lost its mother's gaze, it will start fussing and whimpering. When the mother again gazes at the infant, it stops the commotion. Lewis points out that infants quickly learn elaborate means for securing and maintaining their caretaker's attention.

As Harriet L. Rheingold (1968: 283) observes: "Of men and women he [the infant] makes fathers and mothers." Thus to a surprising degree, parents are the product of the children born to them. They themselves are molded by the very children they are trying to rear (Bell and Harper, 1977).

The characteristics of the infant—the intensity of its responses, its cuddliness, its physical attractiveness, and its temperament—elicit various types of behaviors from adults (Yarrow, Waxler, and Scott, 1971; Dion, 1974; Osofsky and Danzger, 1974; Marcus, 1975; Power, Hildebrant, and Fitzgerald, 1982). Indeed, we need not be around infants for long to become aware of the fact that different feelings are evoked in us by babies who wail no matter what we do to calm them and babies who quickly and cheerfully respond to our soothing efforts. Mary D. Salter Ainsworth and Silvia M. Bell found in their research that mothering was easier for predictable and cheery babies—the "easy babies" described by Thomas and his associates. Further, in the words of Ainsworth and Bell (1969: 60):

> Whatever role may be played by the baby's constitutional characteristics in establishing the initial pattern of mother-infant interaction, it seems quite clear that the mother's contribution to the interaction and the baby's contribution are caught up in an interacting spiral. It is because of these spiral effects—some "vicious" and some "virtuous"—that the variables are so confounded [and it is difficult to untangle them].

Arnold J. Sameroff (1975; Sameroff and Chandler,

Parent-Child Interaction

Parents do not merely socialize their children. Their children also influence them. A dynamic interchange occurs between parent and child whereby each party reciprocally shapes the behavior of the other.

Ruth Silverman/Stock, Boston

1975) finds that those infants rated as having a difficult temperament at four months of age are the children most likely to score lowest on an IQ test at thirty months. He reports that mothers of children with difficult temperaments tend to stay away from them more, to look at them less, and to interact and play with them less. In contrast the other mothers—those who stay close to their babies and play with them a good deal—have children who later tend to score higher on the intelligence test. Sameroff believes that the mothers of children with difficult temperaments become "turned off" to the infants. Consequently, they fail to provide them with the caretaking and stimulation that would lead to the children's competent performance at thirty months of age.

T. Berry Brazelton (1962) cites the case of a newborn who essentially was capable of only two states. In the one state the child would appear to be in a deep stupor, during which time he would be difficult to rouse. In the other state he was hyperactive, exceedingly sensitive to stimulation of any sort, and given to frequent and long episodes of screaming. Neurological examination failed to detect any abnormalities. From the start the mother viewed herself as "rejected" by the child. She felt overwhelmed and incapable of reaching the child in his state of withdrawal and unable to comfort him in his state of agitation. The net result was an unsatisfactory parent-child relationship. Psychiatrists working in a number of experimental settings are developing tactics for dealing with such problems. The therapy can entail adding or subtracting sensory stimuli, exercising overly tense muscles, providing affection that is absent at home, and counseling parents (Okie, 1981).

Any number of researchers have noted that difficult and unsoothable babies are overrepresented among abused children (Korner, 1979). Constant fussing, colicky fretfulness, highly irritating crying, and other exasperating behaviors seem to provoke violence in some parents. Further, some battered children continue to be abused in a succession of foster homes where no other child previously had been abused. Sadly, some children appear to convert seemingly "normal" parents into "abnormal" ones. The behavior of these children simply exceeds their parents' coping capabilities. Many such parents develop feelings of intense guilt, inadequacy, helplessness, and rage that, in individuals with low flash points, may erupt in violent outbursts. Consequently, the burden, stress, and disappointment of rearing a difficult youngster can serve to tip the balance in a precarious parent-child relationship.

Researchers have noted a variety of additional factors that may play a part in influencing parental behavior. Josephine V. Brown and her associates (1975) found in a sample of urban black mothers that the mothers rubbed, patted, touched, kissed, rocked, and talked more to male than to female newborns. Mothers of firstborn infants spend more time feeding their infants than do mothers of later-born infants (Bakeman and Brown, 1977). And both mothers' and fathers' behaviors are affected during parent-child interaction by the presence of the other (Lamb, 1976; Lytton, 1980).

All these studies suggest that the socialization process is a two-way street, a reciprocal and interactive relationship involving parent and child (Beckwith, 1972; Leifer et al., 1972; Vaughn, Crichton, and Egeland, 1982). As Joy D. Osofsky (1976: 1142) observes: "It appears that styles of mother-child interaction are established very early in the developing relationship and that both the infant and the mother contribute to the patterning."

SUMMARY

1. Sleeping, crying, and feeding are the chief behaviors of the neonate.
2. An infant's responses at any given time are related to its state. The following states have been identified in the neonate: regular sleep, irregular sleep, drowsiness, alert inactivity, waking activity, and crying.
3. Crying in the newborn is an unlearned, involuntary, and adaptive response that serves to incite the parent to caretaking activities.
4. The infant's hunger and sleep patterns are closely linked. Newborns spend much of their waking time in feeding. Both breast feeding and bottle feeding offer advantages and disadvantages.
5. The newborn is equipped at birth with a number of reflexes—behavioral systems that are readily activated. These include the Moro reflex, the startle reflex, the rooting reflex, the sucking reflex, the Babinski reflex, the palmar grasping reflex, the plantar grasping reflex, the stepping reflex, and the swimming reflex.
6. Habituation represents an early adaptive response to the environment. It is also an early form of memory.
7. Newborns show the effects of learning through conditioning.
8. A full-term newborn is equipped at birth with a functional and intact visual apparatus. The eye is prepared to respond differentially to most aspects of its visual field.
9. At the time of birth, the hearing apparatus of the neonate is remarkably well developed. And recently it has been discovered that an infant's body movements are synchronized with the sound patterns of adult speech.
10. Taste, smell, and cutaneous sensations are present in the neonate.
11. In the first days of life, infants can be distinguished in terms of their reactions to external stimuli. Some babies are cuddlers, others noncuddlers.
12. Babies show distinct individuality in temperament during the first weeks of life. This temperament is independent of their parents' handling and personality styles.

KEY TERMS

habituation An adaptive response in which an infant who is repeatedly presented with the same stimulus soon ceases to respond to the stimulus. If the stimulus is then withheld for a short period of time, the infant recovers the reflex response.

neonate A newborn.

neonate period The first two weeks following birth.

perception The process by which individuals interpret sensation.

reflex A relatively simple, involuntary, and unlearned response to a stimulus.

sensation The process by which individuals receive information through their sense organs.

state A continuum of alertness ranging from regular sleep to vigorous activity.

MALNUTRITION

Poverty breeds malnutrition. Even the wealthy United States has pockets of poverty, especially among the Appalachian, black, Spanish-speaking, and American Indian populations. Of all American age groups, children are the most likely to be living under impoverished conditions. Today one-sixth of American children are members of families whose annual income is below the officially defined poverty line. A recent study of 1,500 poor children by the Massachusetts Department of Public Health found 10 percent to be chronically malnourished (O'Discoll and Neuman, 1983).

Where protein and calorie malnutrition are severe, marasmus and kwashiorkor occur. *Marasmus* usually develops in children younger than one year of age. It is characterized by severe weight loss and irritability. *Kwashiorkor* typically occurs in children between one and three years old. Its chief characteristics are apathy, loss of hair, severe skin disorders, and a protuberant belly resulting from enlargement of the liver and water retention in the abdomen (Kaplan, 1972). Children develop kwashiorkor when their diet is deficient in protein, even if it contains enough calories.

Follow-up studies of children treated for marasmus and kwashiorkor reveal that during recovery they grow at an accelerated rate. However, they never entirely catch up with healthy children in stature or intellectual performance (Eichenwald and Fry, 1969).

Research indicates that inadequate early nutrition retards brain development. Reports on autopsied brains of children who suffered from malnutrition reveal deficits in brain weight (Brown, 1966; Parekh et al., 1970). For instance, autopsies on sixteen Chilean and Jamaican babies who died of malnutrition before they were two showed that all had fewer brain cells than normal. Three of them had less than 40 percent of the normal number (Winick, Rosso, and Waterlow, 1970). Studies also demonstrate that severely malnourished children, whether they live in rural villages or urban slums, on the whole do not perform as well on intelligence and cognitive tests as children with adequate diets (Brockman and Ricciuti, 1971; Kaplan, 1972; Jelliffe and Jelliffe, 1979; Levitsky, 1979). This cognitive gap can be narrowed if appropriate nutritional therapy is instituted, particularly if it takes place at an early age (Barnet et al., 1978; McKay et al., 1978; Barrett et al., 1982).

Malnourished children are more likely than other children to live in overcrowded homes, to enjoy fewer educational opportunities, and to suffer from illness and chronic infections. Each of these disadvantages can contribute to an intellectual and educational handicap, so that it is difficult to say which factor is the most important (Rutter, 1974). Further, malnourished infants and children are characterized by impaired attentional processes, heightened irritability, low activity levels, and reduced independence and emotional responsiveness. Consequently, the youngsters are less successful in engaging caretakers and others in interaction; the development of social competencies and positive personality characteristics is thereby inhibited (Barrett et al., 1982). The problem is aggravated if the caretakers are also malnourished. Thus malnutrition is not usually an isolated phenomenon; rather, it is part of a complex of interlocking biological and social factors that together take a severe toll in human welfare.

The Ravages of Malnutrition
This child, a Toureg in Niger, northwest Africa, exhibits the severe symptoms of malnutrition.
Agency for International Development

nization against serious childhood diseases. The other theory focuses on genetic factors associated with hybrid vigor resulting from increased interbreeding across local, regional, and national populations.

The trend toward increased size in the United States, however, seems to have ended. The leveling-off appeared several decades ago among population samples representing Americans in the highest socioeconomic classes. It now also holds for virtually every segment of the American population. Americans may have reached the limits of their genetic potential for stature (Schmeck, 1976).

Growth of Key Systems and the Brain

Not all parts of the body grow at the same rate. The nervous system, which develops more rapidly than other systems, is largely complete by four years of age (see Figure 6.2). At birth the brain is already about 25 percent of its adult weight; at six months, nearly 50 percent; at two and a half years, 75 percent; at five years, 90 percent; and at ten years, 95 percent (Tanner, 1970).

Those parts of the brain that control such basic processes as circulation, respiration, and consciousness are operative at birth. The parts that control processes less critical to immediate survival, including physical mobility and language, mature after birth. The rapid growth of the brain during the first two years of life is associated with the laying down of neural pathways and of connections among nerve cells, particularly in the *cerebral cortex* (the part of the brain responsible for learning, thinking, reading, and problem solving). In contrast, most reflexes, like sucking, rooting, and grasping, are organized at the *subcortical level* (the part of the brain that guides basic biological functioning, including sleeping, heart rate, hunger, and digestion). The rapid development of the cortex during the first twelve months provides the foundation for children's less stereotyped and more flexible behavior (Conel, 1963; Dekaban, 1970; Clifton et al., 1981) (see Figure 6.3).

Lymphoid tissue—the thymus and lymph nodes—has quite a different growth curve from tissue in the rest of the body (see Figure 6.2). At twelve years of age it is more than double the level it will reach in

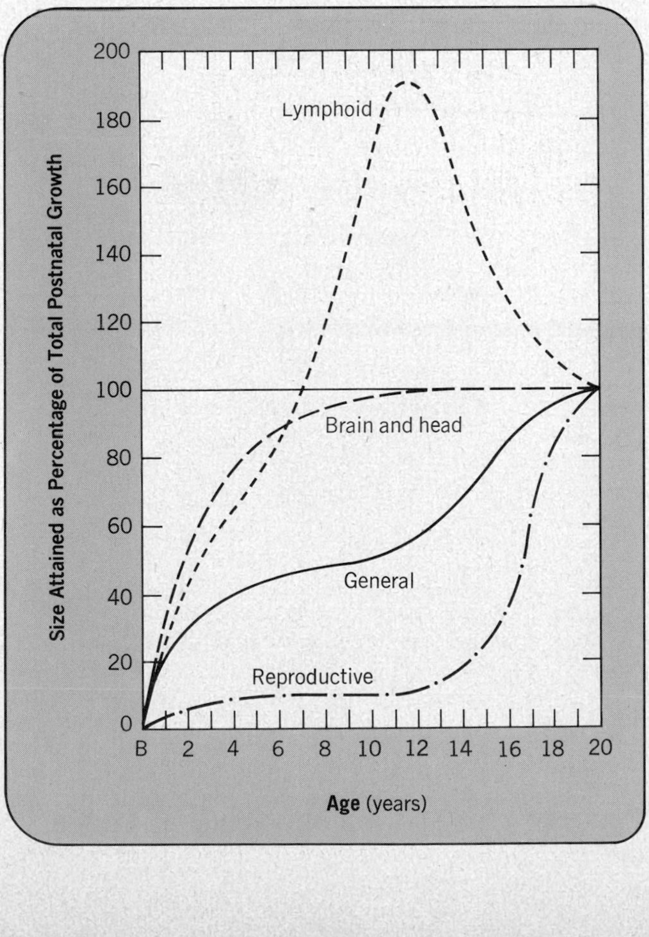

Figure 6.2 The Parts of the Body Grow at Different Rates
These curves are based on the percentage of a person's total growth attained by age twenty. Thus size at age twenty is 100 on the vertical scale. The lymphoid system includes the thymus and lymph nodes. The curve labeled "Brain and head" includes the brain, the skull, and the spinal cord. The curve labeled "General" covers the skeletal system, lungs, kidneys, and digestive organs. The reproductive system covers testes, ovaries, prostate, seminal vesicles, and Fallopian tubes.

SOURCE: Richard E. Scammon, "The Measurement of the Body in Childhood," in J. A. Harris, C. M. Jackson, D. G. Paterson, and R. E. Scammon (eds.), *The Measurement of Man* (Minneapolis: University of Minnesota Press, 1930), Figure 73, p. 193. Reprinted by permission.

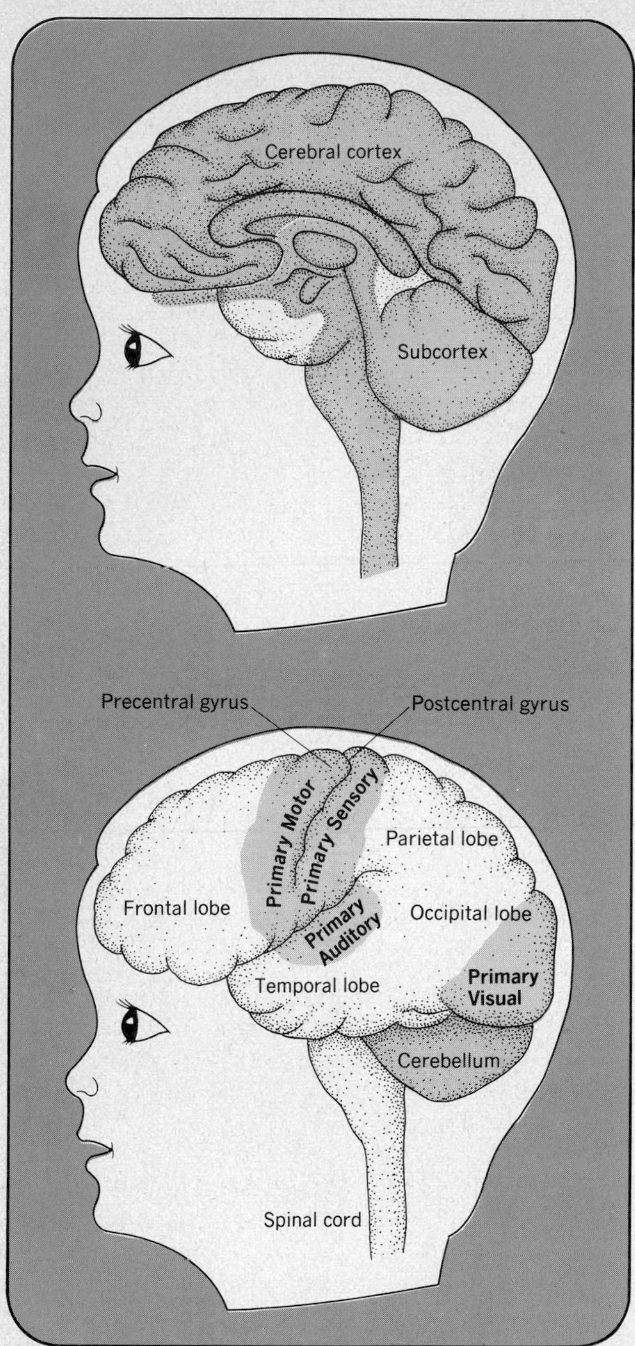

Figure 6.3 The Developing Brain

The top drawing shows a cross section of the human brain, indicating the subcortex and the cerebral cortex. The bottom drawing shows a number of the brain's major structures and their location on the cerebral cortex.

adulthood; after twelve it declines until maturity. In contrast, the reproductive system grows very slowly until adolescence, at which point it accelerates. The internal organs, including the kidneys, liver, spleen, lungs, and stomach, keep pace with the growth in the skeletal system, and these systems therefore show the same two growth spurts in infancy and adolescence.

Principles of Development

Development follows the **cephalocaudal principle,** proceeding from the head to the feet. Improvements in structure and function come first in the head region, then in the trunk, and finally in the leg region. At birth the head is disproportionately large. In adults the head makes up only about one-tenth to one-twelfth of the body, but in newborns it is about one-fourth of the body. In contrast, the arms and legs of newborns are disproportionately short. From birth to adulthood the head doubles in size, the trunk trebles, the arms and hands quadruple in length, and the legs and feet grow fivefold (Bayley, 1935, 1956) (see Figure 6.4).

Motor development likewise follows the cephalocaudal principle. Infants first learn to control the muscles of the head and neck. Then they control the arms and abdomen, and last the legs. Thus when they begin

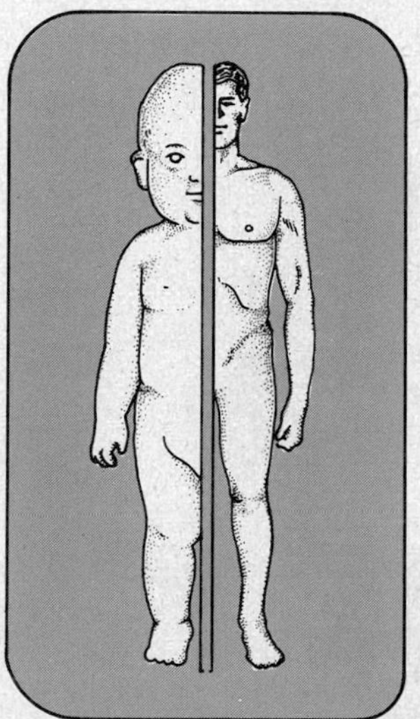

Figure 6.4 Cephalocaudal Development

The cephalocaudal principle, which says that growth progresses from head to foot, is demonstrated by the contrasting body proportions of the newborn and the adult. The head is about one-fourth of the infant's body, but only about one-twelfth of the adult's. The trunk is a much larger portion of the infant's body than the adult's, while the leg of the adult is proportionately twice as long as the newborn's.

Cephalocaudal Principle

Motor development follows the cephalocaudal principle, proceeding from the head to the feet. This eight-month-old youngster has mastered crawling on her hands and knees and now has progressed to the more sophisticated "bear crawl." She no longer uses her knees but instead propels herself with her feet. Shortly she will be standing by herself.

Elizabeth Crews

to crawl they use the upper body to propel themselves, dragging the legs passively behind. Only later do they begin to use the legs as an aid in crawling. Similarly, babies learn to hold their heads up before they acquire the ability to sit, and they learn to sit before they learn to walk.

Development follows still another pattern—the **proximodistal principle.** According to this principle, development proceeds from near to far—outward from the central axis of the body toward the extremities. Early in infancy, babies have to move head and trunk in order to orient the hands when grasping an object. Only later can they use arms and legs independently, and it is still longer before they can make refined movements with the wrists and fingers. On the whole, control over movement travels down the arm as children become able to perform increasingly precise and sophisticated manual and grasping operations. Another way of expressing the same principle is to say that in general, large-muscle control precedes fine-muscle control. Thus the child's ability to jump, climb, and run—activities involving the use of large muscles—develops ahead of the ability to draw or write—activities involving smaller muscles.

MOTOR DEVELOPMENT

Children's motor development is dependent on their overall physical growth. To crawl, walk, climb, and grasp objects with precision, they must have reached certain levels of skeletal and muscular development. As their heads become smaller relative to their bodies their balance improves (imagine how difficult it must be to move around with a head that is one-fourth of one's total size). As children's legs become stronger and longer, they can master various locomotive activities. As their shoulders widen and their arms lengthen, their manual and mechanical capacities increase. As they become able to reach out and touch people and things and navigate by themselves, their physical and social world expands. And as they get older, they can more effectively use feedback information (knowledge of results) to improve their motor performance (Barclay and Newell, 1980). Motor development occurs in accordance with maturational processes that are built into the human organism and that find expression through a child's interaction with the environment.

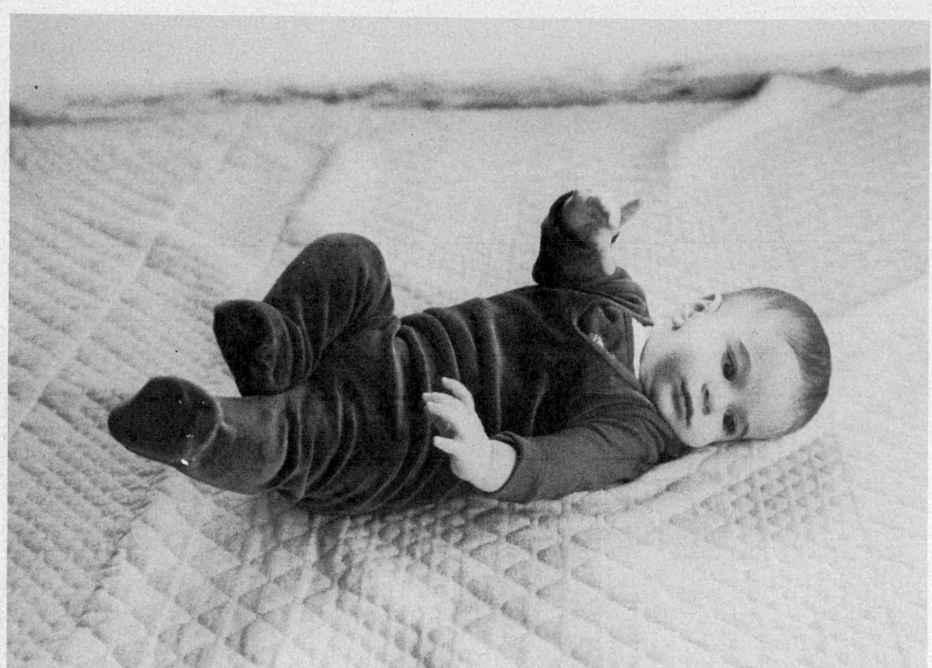

Rhythmical Behaviors
Young infants engage in bursts of rapid, repeated body movements. This youngster is kicking her feet, a behavior that typically becomes frequent during the fifth month. Shortly thereafter infants begin to crawl.
Elizabeth Crews

Rhythmical Behaviors

Probably the most interesting motor behavior displayed by young infants involves bursts of rapid, repeated movements of the limbs, torso, or head (Thelen, 1981). They kick, rock, bounce, bang, rub, thrust, and twist. Infants seem to follow the dictum, "If you can move it at all, move it rhythmically."

Such behaviors are closely related to motor development and provide the foundation for the more skilled behaviors that will come later. Hence, rhythmical patterns that involve the legs, like kicking, begin gradually, increase at about one month, peak immediately prior to a child's initiation of crawling at about six months, and then taper off. Likewise, rhythmical hand and arm movements appear before complex manual skills. Thus, bouts of rhythmic movement seem to be transitional behaviors between uncoordinated activity and complex voluntary motor control. They represent a stage in motor maturation that is more complex than that found in simple reflexes yet less variable and flexible than that found in later cortically controlled behavior.

Infants most frequently begin their kicking or rocking movements upon the appearance of a caretaker, an interruption in feeding, the presentation of a toy, or the grasping of an object. For the young infant, these incidents seem to demand, "Do something!"—greet the caretaker, express frustration, show delight, or manipulate the object. However, the immature central nervous system responds in a way that as yet is not goal directed.

Jean Piaget (1952) suggested that through rhythmical bouts of activity infants explore their environment, produce interesting effects on it, and observe the consequences of their own actions. But the behaviors also serve other functions (Thelen, 1981). Babies who receive little rocking and jiggling from their caretakers compensate by stimulating themselves through these stereotyped movements, which in turn elicit from others caretaking interventions. Even more important, these relatively simple, "prewired" behavioral components are the precursors of walking and other human motor capabilities. They are transformed to assume new functions and combined with other components to produce a more elaborate motor system.

Locomotion

The infant's ability to walk, which typically evolves between eleven and fifteen months of age, is the climax of a long series of developments. As shown in Figure 6.5, these developments progress in a sequence

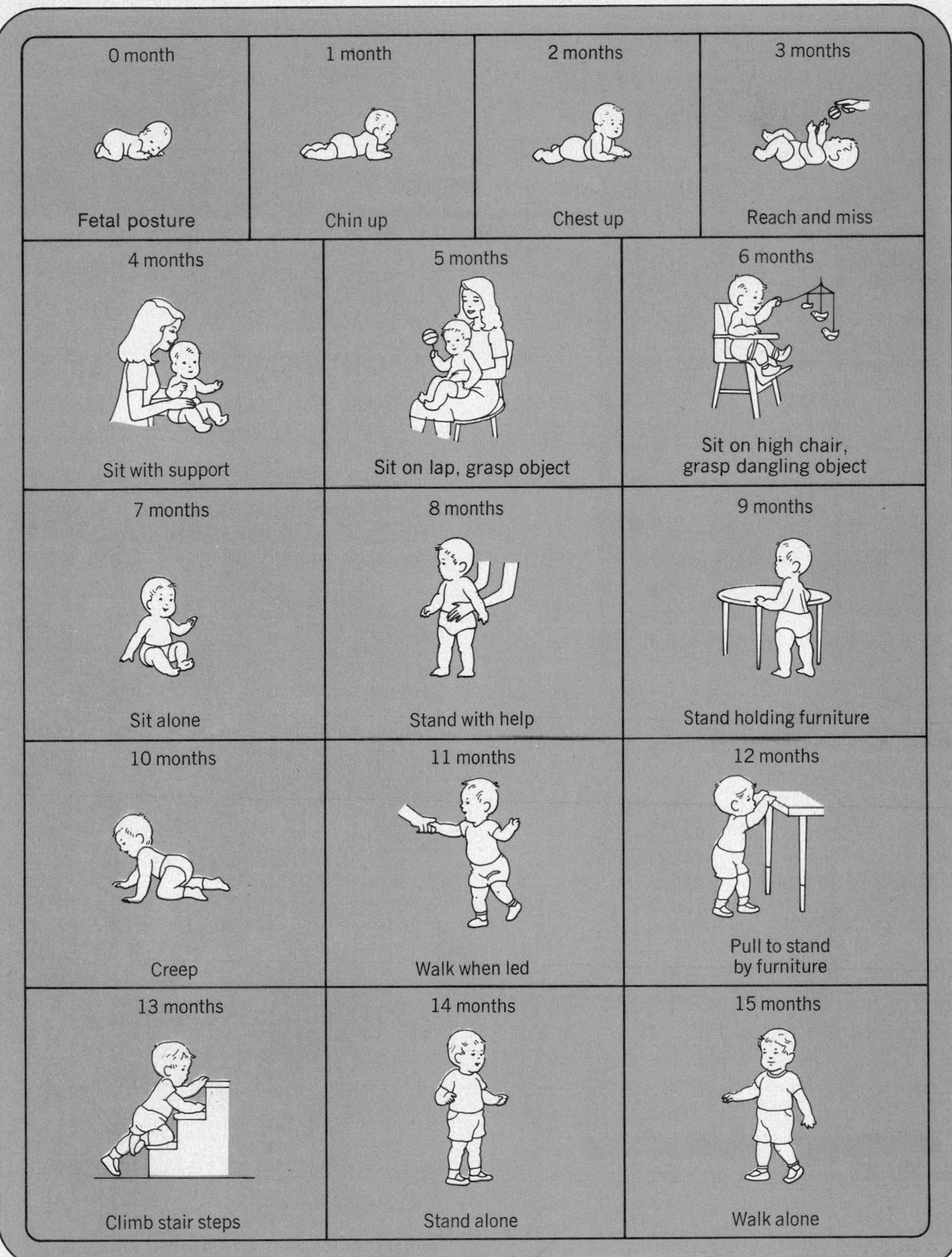

Figure 6.5 The Sequence of Motor Development

The ages at which the average infant achieves a given behavior.

SOURCE: M. M. Shirley, *The First Two Years: A Study of Twenty-Five Babies,* Vol. 2 (Minneapolis: University of Minnesota Press, 1933), Figure 1. Reprinted with permission.

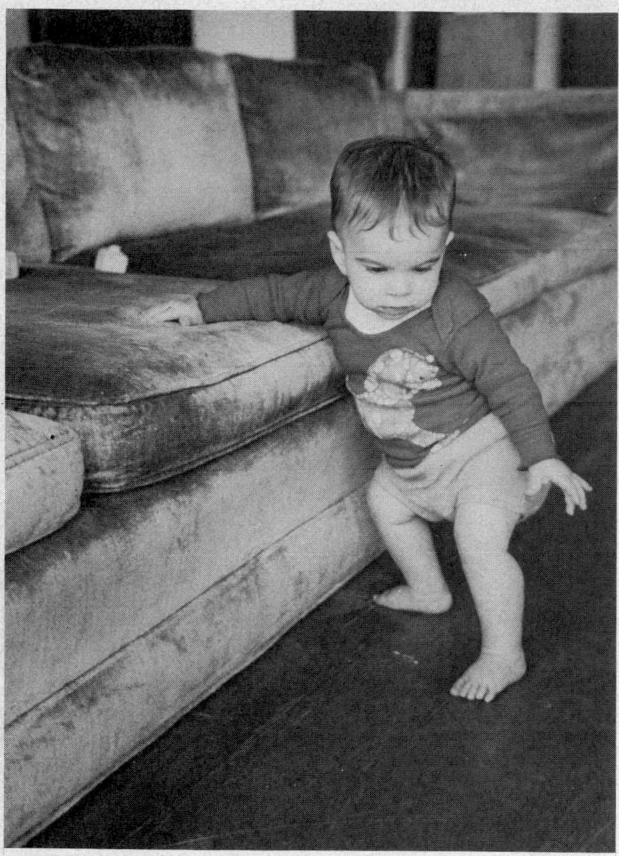

Practicing Motor Skills

By seven or eight months of age, children relentlessly cultivate new motor skills. They resemble perpetual-motion machines. Here a youngster is undaunted in his determination to master getting up and down by himself.

Elizabeth Crews

that follows the cephalocaudal principle. First, children gain the ability to lift up the head, and later the chest. Next, they achieve command of the trunk region, which enables them to sit up. Finally, they achieve mastery of their legs as they learn to stand and to walk.

For most infants the seventh month brings a surge in motor development. Usually children begin by *crawling*—moving with the abdomen in contact with the floor. They maneuver by twisting the body and pulling and tugging with the arms. Next they may progress to *creeping*—moving on hands and knees while the body is parallel with the floor. Some children also employ *hitching*—sitting and sliding along the floor by "digging in" and pushing themselves backward with the heels. In this form of locomotion they often use the arms to aid in propulsion. Indeed, an occasional infant varies the procedure by sitting and then, employing each arm as a pendulum, bouncing across the floor on its buttocks.

By seven or eight months, children resemble a perpetual-motion machine. They relentlessly tackle new tasks. At eight months they pull themselves to a standing position but usually have difficulty getting down. Often they fall over backward but, undaunted, keep practicing. The urge to master new motor skills is so powerful in infants this age that bumps, spills, falls, and other obstacles only momentarily discourage them. (For a comparison of infant locomotive development in some other cultures, see the boxed insert on pages 162–163).

Manual Dexterity

This thirteen-month-old child has grasped the relationship between keys and the opening of a door. She is attempting to gain entrance to the apartment through her own independent activity.

Patrick Reddy

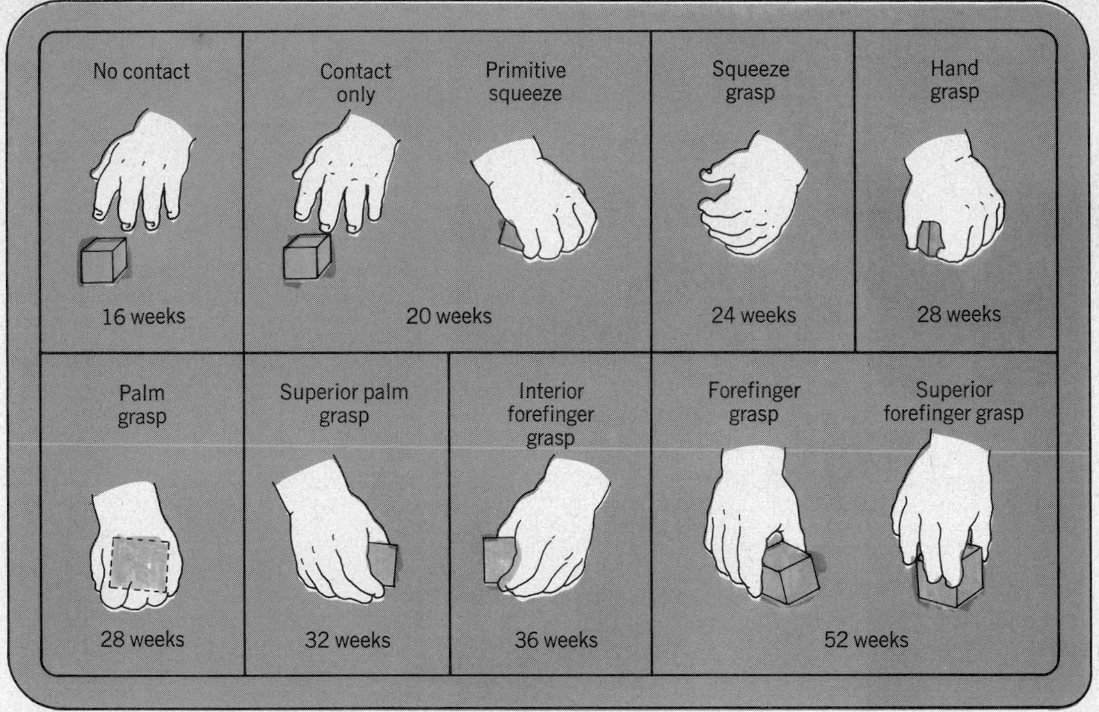

Figure 6.6 Development of Manual Skills During the First Year of Life
Children's manual dexterity progresses from a crude squeeze at twenty weeks to fingertip and forefinger grasping at age one.

SOURCE: H. M. Halverson, "An Experimental Study of Prehension in Infants by Means of Systematic Cinema Records," *Genetic Psychology Monographs*, Vol. 10 (1931), pp. 212–215. Reprinted by permission.

Manual Skills

The child's development of manual skills proceeds through a series of orderly stages in accordance with the proximodistal principle—from the center of the body toward the periphery. At two months of age, infants merely make a swiping movement toward an object with the upper body and arms. They do not attempt to grasp the object. At three months of age their reaching consists of clumsy shoulder and elbow movements. Their aim is poor, and their hands are fisted.

After about sixteen weeks, children approach an object with hands open (see Figure 6.6). At about twenty weeks they become capable of touching an object in one quick, direct motion of the hand; occasionally some of them succeed in grasping it in an awkward manner.

Infants of twenty-four weeks employ a corralling and scooping approach with the palm and fingers. At twenty-eight weeks they begin to oppose the thumb to the palm and other fingers. At thirty-six weeks they coordinate their grasp with the tips of the thumb and forefinger. Finally, at fifty-two weeks they master a more sophisticated forefinger grasp (Halverson, 1931; Ausubel and Sullivan, 1970).

Handedness

Some 5 to 10 percent of the American population is left-handed; the rest is primarily right-handed. Handedness is often mistakenly viewed as a specific trait comparable to eye color, but actually it is relative: individuals prefer their right or left hands to a greater or lesser degree (Hardyck and Petrinovich, 1977). Indeed, there are rare cases in which people are bimanual, or ambidextrous, possessing equal skill with both hands for such tasks as writing or drawing. And some people are hand-specific, preferring the left hand for some activities, such as pitching a baseball, and the right for others, such as playing tennis (Herron, 1976, 1979).

Handedness is only one manifestation of lateral

MOTOR DEVELOPMENT IN CROSS-CULTURAL PERSPECTIVE

The stages and the timing of motor development shown in Figure 6.5 are based largely on studies of infants from Western cultures. But the possibility that there are considerable differences among cultures in the timing of motor development has been raised by a number of studies of African infants. Marcelle Geber and R. F. Dean (1957*a*, 1957*b*; Geber, 1958) tested nearly 300 infants living in an urban area of Uganda. They found that these babies were clearly accelerated in motor development relative to Caucasian infants. The African precocity is greatest during the first six months of life, after which the gap between the two groups tends to decrease. It closes by the end of the second year. More recently, Constance H. Keefer and her associates (1982) found that Gusii neonates (the Gusii are a Bantu-speaking, agricultural people of southwestern Kenya) scored better on motor maturity than did a sample of white American infants.

Mary D. S. Ainsworth (1967) also made careful systematic observations of twenty-eight Ugandan children. She found that the African babies crawled about two and a half months earlier and began to creep about three and a half months earlier than average infants in Western societies. The Ugandan infants stood firmly when supported and pulled themselves to a standing position at about seven to eight months of age, whereas similar capabilities do not typically occur among Caucasian children until they reach eleven months of age. The mean age of walking was also earlier: eleven months for the Ugandan children in contrast with fourteen months for children of European ancestry.

Likewise, Janet E. Kilbride, Michael C. Robbins, and Philip L. Kilbride (1970) found in a sample of 163 rural Ugandan infants that the African babies were significantly advanced in motor development during the first year relative to white American and European infants. However, the differences between the two groups largely diminished during the second year.

Geber has advanced somewhat contradictory explanations for the apparent precocity of the Ugandan infants. At first she appeared to favor a genetic explanation (Geber and Dean, 1957*a:* 1061). Subsequently (1958) she attributed it to environmental factors that are associated with stimulating child care practices, especially the warmth and solicitude shown the neonate by adults. Ainsworth (1967) also emphasizes the part played by the close infant-mother relationship, including the intimate physical contact, the mother's constant availability, and the postural adjustments required of infants when they are carried about on the mothers' backs.

But not all researchers accept the finding that African infants are more precocious than their white European and American counterparts. In a review of the African studies and of his own research, Neil Warren (1972: 365) argues that "African infant precocity cannot be taken as an acceptably established empirical phenomenon." In particular, Warren questions the quality of the African research and the comparability of the tests performed upon the African and Caucasian infants.

In the United States, Nancy Bayley (1965*b*) found that black American infants tend to be more advanced

preference. Newborns tend to turn their heads and eyes rightward (Liederman and Kinsborne, 1980; Goodwin and Michel, 1981). Most adults choose the right foot for crushing an insect or a lighted cigarette. Similarly, most display right-eyedness in sighting a telescope and right-earedness when pressing an ear against a door to hear what is happening on the other side (Coren, Porac, and Duncan, 1981).

Handedness develops gradually, rather than appearing in an immediate all-or-none manner. Before two years of age, children generally display considerable versatility in shifting from one hand to the other. The hand used depends on the position of the person or object for which the child is reaching. By the time they are two, most children shift toward right-handedness. But between two and a half and three and a half, they again shift back toward ambidexterity, using both hands with approximately equal frequency and proficiency. It is not until they are around four years of age that most children begin to show a strong preference for use of the right hand. Two years later, when they enter the first grade, shifts from one hand to the other have become relatively infrequent (Gesell and Ames, 1947).

A disproportionate number of mathematicians, engineers, musicians, and artists are left-handed. For instance, Michelangelo, Leonardo da Vinci, Pablo Picasso, and Benjamin Franklin were southpaws. But

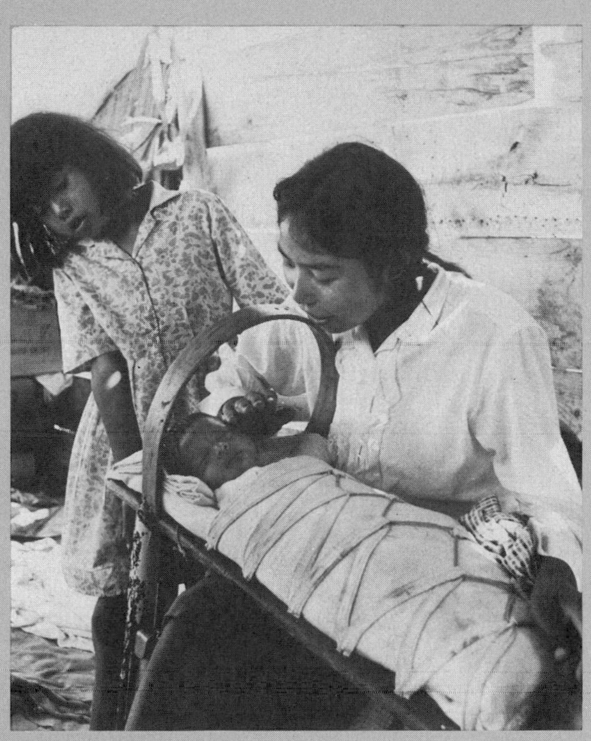

Cross-Cultural Variation

The Hopi Indians of the American Southwest bind their infants to cradleboards. Although the practice limits motor activity, the youngsters begin to walk at about the same time as children in other cultures do.

Michael Heron/Woodfin Camp & Associates

than white infants in motor development during the first twelve months. However, Judith R. Williams and Roland B. Scott (1953) have concluded on the basis of their research that accelerated motor development is not a "racial" characteristic. They have found that while infants of lower-income black parents showed acceleration, it did not occur among infants of upper-income black parents. Williams and Scott have suggested, therefore, that environmental factors are responsible for the observed group differences in motor development.

Researchers have also discovered exceptions to standard Western development patterns among the Balinese of Indonesia (Mead and MacGregor, 1951: 81):

> Where the American children go from frogging [a position resembling that of a frog] to creeping on all fours, then to standing and walking, with squatting coming after standing, the Balinese children . . . combine frogging, creeping, and all-fours simultaneously in a flexible, interchangeable state, from which they go from sitting to squatting to standing.

Other differences have also been noted between infants of Western and non-Western societies. Hopi Indian children of the Southwest, for instance, begin walking about a month or so later than Anglo children do (Dennis and Dennis, 1940). A similar pattern appears to hold for the Zinacantecos, a group of Mayan Indians living in southeastern Mexico (Brazelton, Robey, and Collier, 1969). In sum, cross-cultural research reveals that variations occur across populations in the course and timing of motor development (LeVine, 1970).

left-handers are also twelve times more likely than right-handers to have learning and reading disabilities and are twice as likely to suffer immune disorders in which the body attacks its own tissues (see the boxed insert on page 165).

A few decades ago a cerebral dominance theory was given as the explanation for handedness. The theory assumed that if the right side of the brain is dominant, the individual will be left-handed; if the left side, the individual will be right-handed. Today some authorities believe that this theory oversimplifies the facts. The division of labor between the two hemispheres is complex, with much interaction occurring between them. Consequently, the right and left hands have access to information from both hemispheres of the brain, and on many tasks the two hemispheres act in concert (Geschwind, 1979; Kalat, 1981) (see Figure 6.7). Although there is some relationship between handedness and cerebral organization, the relationship is far from precise and varies from one individual to another.

Whether handedness derives primarily from genetic factors or from learning has been the source of considerable controversy (Hardyck and Petrinovich, 1977; Corballis and Morgan, 1978; Herron, 1979). It appears most likely, however, that handedness depends on a combination of genetic and fetal factors and a child's early training.

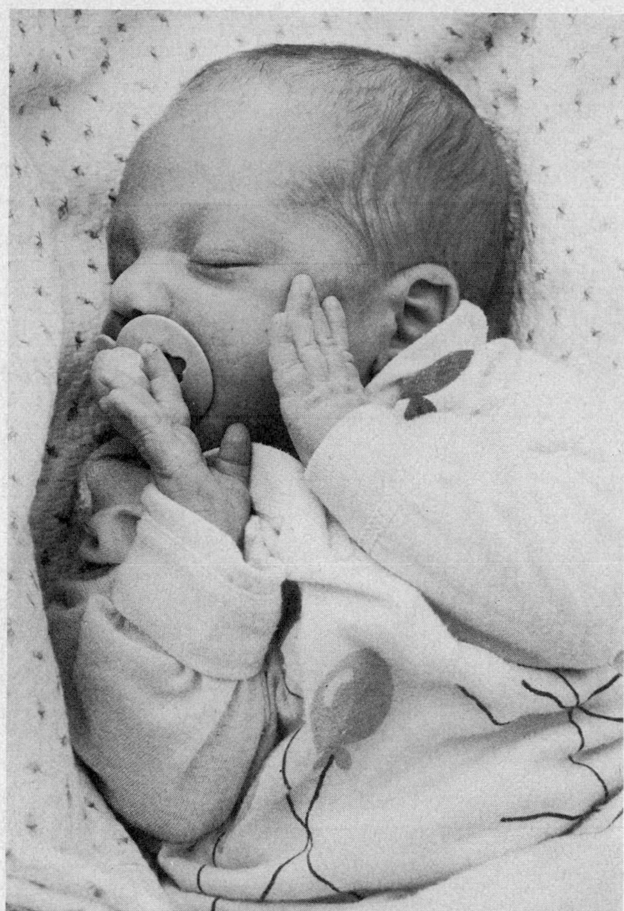

Lateral Preference

Most infants turn their heads and eyes to the right in sleeping.

Frank Siteman/The Picture Cube

PERCEPTUAL DEVELOPMENT

During the first six months of life there is a considerable discrepancy between infants' vast sensory capabilities and their relatively sluggish motor development. Their sensory apparatus yields perceptual input far beyond their capacity to use it. As a result of maturation, experience, and practice, they have already acquired the ability to extract information from the environment at a phenomenal rate. When these perceptual abilities become linked with the big spurt in motor development that begins around the seventh month, the child surges ahead in an awesome fashion. Hence ten to eleven months later, at eighteen months of age, the child is an accomplished social being (see Figure 6.8). Let us consider the nature of an infant's developing perceptual capabilities.

Visual Constancy

Perception is oriented toward *things,* not toward their sensory *features.* We can perceive features such as "blueness," "squareness," or "softness," but we generally experience them as qualities of objects. We are aware of a blue car, a square block, or a soft pillow; not of "blueness," "squareness," or "softness" as dis-

Figure 6.7 The Two Hemispheres of the Brain

This drawing of the brain viewed from above shows the complementary dominance of the cerebral hemispheres for different operations. For most individuals, language, mathematics, and analytical thinking are chiefly left hemisphere activities. Spatial, pattern, and musical recognition appear to be right hemisphere activities.

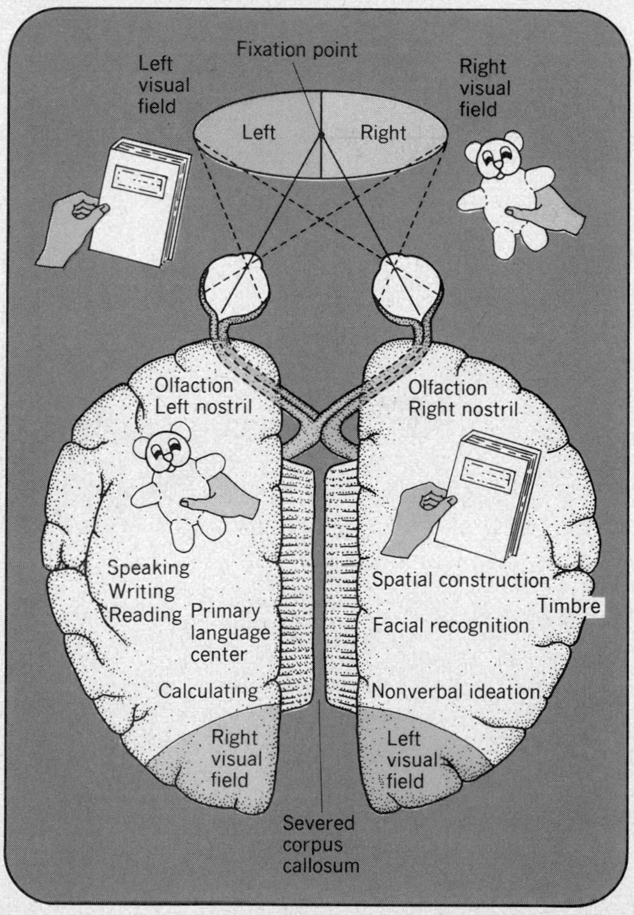

WHY LEFT-HANDERS MAY BE DIFFERENT

Neurologists are finding that left-handedness is associated with learning disabilities, autoimmune disease, and math giftedness (Marx, 1982; Kolata, 1983). About 10 percent of left-handers report some form of developmental problem like dyslexia (a reading disorder) or stuttering, compared with only 1 percent of right-handers. Further, about 11 percent of left-handers have immunity diseases like allergies and asthma, compared with 4 percent of right-handers, and 60 percent of them also have immune system disorders. Finally, 20 percent of the very best eleventh- and twelfth-grade math students (those who are the top 1 in 10,000) are left-handed; this incidence is twice that of left-handers in the population at large.

The neurologist Norman Geschwind suggests that the culprit is an excess production of, or sensitivity to, the male hormone testosterone in the fetus. It would be expected that boys (who are exposed to more testosterone than are girls in prenatal development) would be more likely than girls to be affected, and indeed almost twice as many males as females are left-handed. Boys are also more prone to learning disorders. And among students in the top category of math performance, boys outscore girls by thirteen to one.

Research reveals that testosterone affects the development of brain structures. Geschwind believes that high levels of testosterone slow growth on the left side of the brain during the prenatal period. In doing so, it may contribute to learning disabilities, for the brain's left hemisphere affects language development. Moreover, testosterone influences the immune system by reducing the size of the thymus gland, which allows the body to distinguish its own tissue from foreign agents (without these "recognizer" cells, the body attacks its own tissue).

Geschwind contends that an increase in testosterone in some pregnancies is nature's way of providing for a greater diversity of brains in the human population. Although increasing the risk of autoimmune disease, the brain organization that promotes left-handedness also leads to superior skills in math and related areas (since mathematical ability is generally believed to be primarily a left hemisphere function). Of course, if nature "overdoes" it, the result can be serious learning problems. Geschwind suggests that having children with learning problems is the price the population pays for having some of its members gifted in mathematical thought and logic.

tinct entities. We fashion and build our world in terms of things—objects that endure and that we encounter again and again.

One of the most intriguing aspects of perceptual experience is **visual constancy**—the tendency for objects to look the same to us despite fluctuations in sensory input. We perceive the colors, sizes, and shapes of objects as relatively unchanging regardless of changes in the colors, sizes, and shapes that their images project on the retina of our eye. For instance, we see the color of coal as black even though the amount of light reflected from it changes. This is called *color constancy.* Likewise, an object does not appear to shrink as we move farther away from it, even though the size of the image on our retina becomes smaller. This is *size constancy.* Finally, we see a door as a rectangle even though its shape becomes a trapezoid as the door opens, with the edge that is toward us appearing wider than the hinged edge. This is *shape constancy.*

Since the earliest days of their discipline, psychologists have been interested in how the visual constancies arise in children. A major problem, however, is that the child's inner perceptual experiences are not directly accessible to us. We must make *inferences* regarding the inner perceptual process from what a child says or does following the presentation of a perceptual stimulus. Among the indicators that investigators have used are changes in the infant's eye orientation, sucking rate, body movements, skin conductance, heart rate, and conditioned responses.

The point in time when infants acquire visual constancy is a source of much controversy. T. G. R. Bower (1966) claims to find visual constancy among infants six weeks of age. Indeed, he believes the ability rests on an innate genetic mechanism. Other researchers claim that size and shape constancies do not appear until after five to six months of age (Haith and Campos, 1977; Cohen, DeLoache, and Strauss, 1979; McKenzie, Tootell, and Day, 1980). Perhaps for the present it is best if we keep an open mind on these matters and await further research.

1. Walks alone; seldom falls
2. Sits down in small chair
3. Turns pages two or three at a time
4. Builds tower of three blocks
5. Fills cups with cubes
6. Dumps pellet from bottle
7. Imitates stroke
8. Identifies one picture
9. Hurls ball
10. On command, puts ball on chain
11. Walks into ball
12. Pulls toy

Figure 6.8 Aspects of the Behavioral Development of a Child at Eighteen Months

The skills that have been developed by a child some 540 days following birth are truly awe-inspiring.

SOURCE: H. Knobloch and B. Pasamanick, *Gesell and Amatruda's Developmental Diagnosis,* 3rd ed. (New York: Harper & Row, 1974), pp. 82–83. Reprinted by permission.

Depth Perception

Eleanor Gibson and her husband James Gibson have both had distinguished careers as psychologists. When their daughter was about two years old, the Gibsons visited the Grand Canyon in Arizona. One day the child ventured close to the rim of the canyon, and the mother became alarmed for her safety. James Gibson, an authority on perception, assured his wife that a child their daughter's age was in little danger. He told her that two-year-olds can recognize the depth of a drop-off as well as an adult can. Eleanor Gibson was not impressed by this scholarly observation and made the child move well back from the rim.

Some years later the memory of this episode led Eleanor Gibson to undertake a **visual cliff experiment** with the assistance of one of her students, Richard D. Walk (1960). In this technique an infant is placed on a center board between two glass surfaces upon which the child can crawl (see Figure 6.9). One side—the shallow side—is covered on the underside with a checkered material. The other side—the deep side—provides an illusion of a cliff by the placement of checkered material several feet below the glass. The infant's mother stands alternately at the shallow and deep sides and coaxes the infant to crawl toward her. If infants can perceive depth, they should be willing to cross the shallow side but not the cliff side, since the cliff side looks like a chasm.

Gibson and Walk tested thirty-six infants between six and a half months and fourteen months of age. Twenty-seven of the infants ventured off the center board and crawled across the shallow side toward their mothers. Only three, however, could be enticed to cross the cliff side. A number of infants actually crawled *away* from their mothers when beckoned from the deep side; others cried, presumably because they could not reach their mothers without crossing the chasm. Some patted the glass on the deep side,

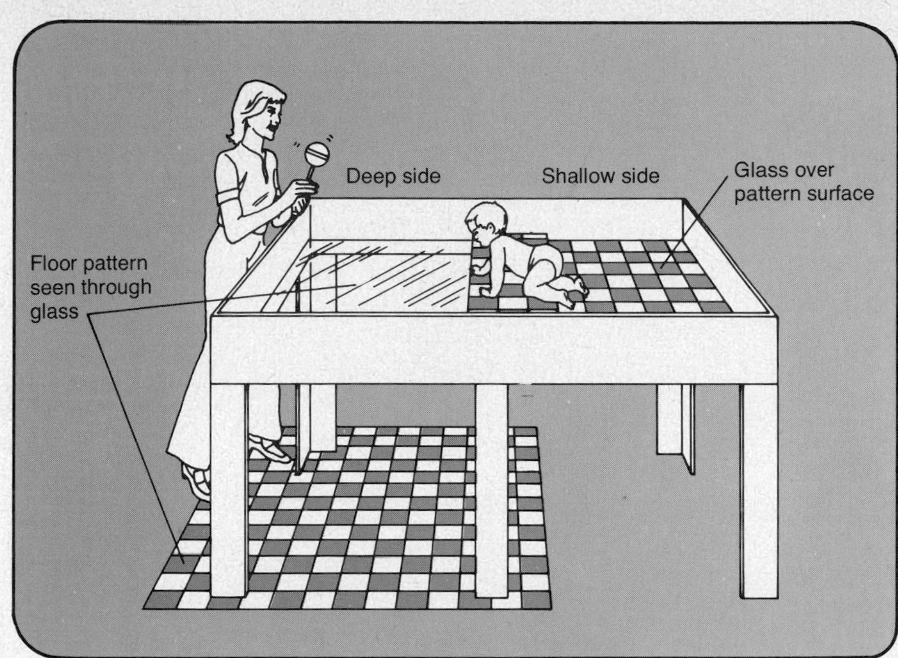

Figure 6.9 The Visual Cliff Experiment

In the visual cliff experiment, the child is placed on a center board that has a sheet of glass extending outward on either side. A checkered material is placed on one side about 40 inches below the glass, thus providing the illusion of depth. Despite its mother's coaxing and the presence of a safe glass surface, a six-month-old infant generally will not crawl across the "chasm." The infant will, however, venture across the shallow side of the apparatus to reach its mother.

SOURCE: Adapted from E. J. Gibson and R. D. Walk, "The 'Visual Cliff,' " *Scientific American*, Vol. 202 (1960), p. 65.

ascertaining that it was solid, but nonetheless backed away. Apparently they were more dependent upon the visual evidence than on the evidence provided by their sense of touch. This research suggests that the vast majority of babies can perceive a drop-off and avoid it by the time they become capable of creeping.

It seems that infants' *binocular vision*—the ability to tell the distances of various objects and to experience the world three-dimensionally—undergoes a sudden burst between three and five months of age (Fox et al., 1980; Petrig et al., 1981; Pines, 1982*a*). The fact that the ability arises quite suddenly and rapidly suggests to some psychologists that it represents a change in that portion of the brain (the visual cortex) responsible for vision. During the postnatal period, neural connections undergo substantial growth and elaboration. Apparently, these developmental changes result in the two eyes' working in concert and allowing the brain to extract reliable three-dimensional information from perceptual processes.

Perception of Form

Over the first two years of life, the way infants focus on and organize visual events changes. During the first two months, babies attend to stimuli that move and to those that contain a high degree of contrast. Even very young infants actively engage in *visual scanning*. As children get older, their scanning patterns become more exhaustive and less redundant. Consequently, the information they collect is more directly relevant to the task.

Researchers study infants' visual scanning by means of corneal photography. They train a movie camera and lights on an infant's eye and give the baby something to look at. The lights that they beam at the baby's eye are filtered so that the infant does not see them but the movie film picks up their reflections. Later the researchers develop the film, project it, and measure where the light reflections fall on the infant's eyeball. This allows them to make a fairly precise map of the parts of an object that are capturing an infant's interest and the course of the baby's scanning activity (Maurer and Maurer, 1976).

Corneal photography reveals that newborn infants, when viewing an object such as a triangle, tend to focus on a relatively limited portion of the figure. Further, if they are shown a black triangle on a white field, the infants' eyes hover on the corners of the triangle, where the contrast between black and white is strongest. Since infants do not usually scan the sides of the triangle, it is doubtful that they perceive the figure in its entirety (Salapatek and Kessen, 1966; Salapatek, 1975) (see Figure 6.10). Although infants of two to four months of age perceive the parts of a figure, they do not bring them together in a figure

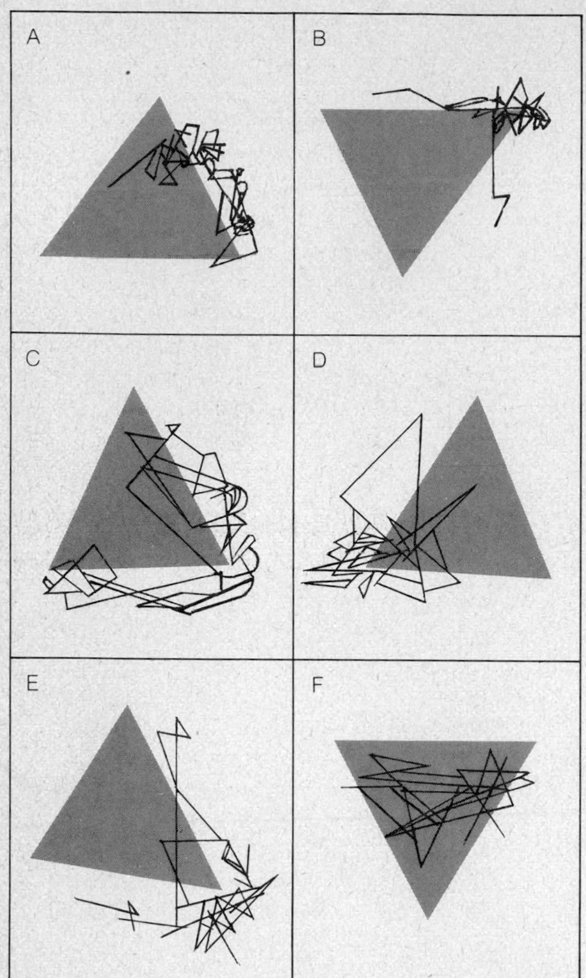

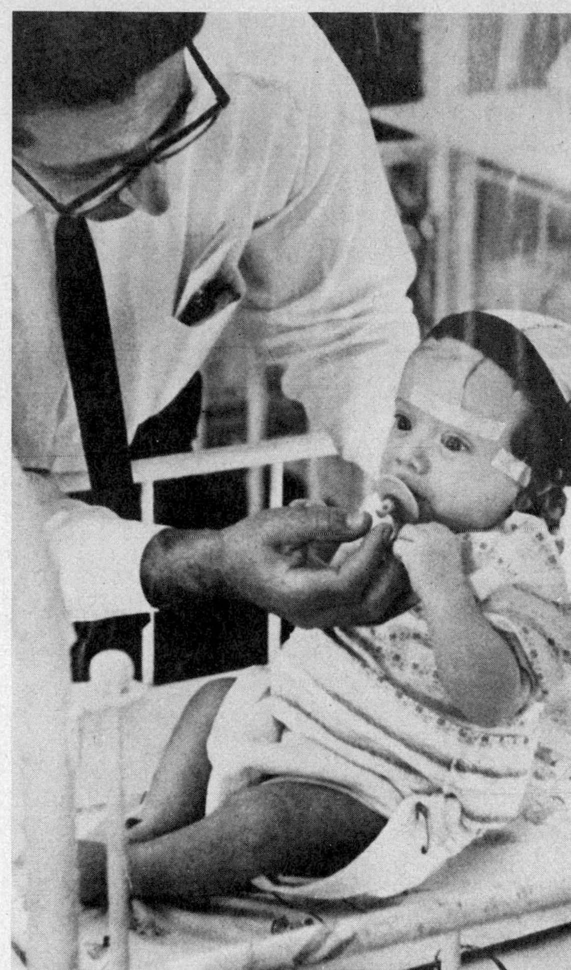

Figure 6.10 Perceptual Experiment with Newborn Infants

In this experiment, babies are shown a large black triangle on a white field. Infrared marker lights are placed behind the triangle and reflect in the infant's pupils. This procedure allows researchers to trace and photograph a newborn's eye movements. The tracings (left) reveal that infants tend to look to the corners of the triangle. Even so, the tracings from six different infants show the wide variation in patterns of scanning among babies.

SOURCE: Photograph courtesy Dr. William Kessen; data from P. H. Salapatek and W. Kessen, Visual Scanning of Triangles by the Human Newborn, *Journal of Experimental Child Psychology*, Vol. 3 (1966), pp. 155–167.

arrangement until they are about four to five months of age. If they are shown a cross inside a circle, younger infants are more likely to see it as a cross *and* a circle rather than as a cross *within* a circle. But as they mature, they increasingly respond to the whole rather than to the individual parts (Cohen, DeLoache, and Strauss, 1979; Fisher et al., 1981; Linn et al., 1982).

We are uncertain whether very young infants prefer to look at familiar or novel objects (Wetherford, 1973; Rose et al., 1982). Research does clearly reveal, however, that infants older than two or three months have a decided preference for moderately novel stimuli (Cohen and Gelber, 1975; Fantz, Fagan, and Miranda, 1975). Jerome Kagan (1970, 1972*b*), a developmental psychologist, finds that children between three and twelve months old are attracted most of all to stimuli that are sufficiently familiar to be recognized but sufficiently different to provide new information. Stimuli that are either too familiar or too novel receive little attention. Kagan believes that infants evolve a mental model, or scheme, from their accumulating experiences with a particular type of object or event. This mental representation is not a photographic image of the object or event. Instead it is a stereotyped version or caricature. For example, a child develops a conception of the human face as an oval-shaped object with a hairline, two eyes, a nose, and a mouth.

About one year of age, Kagan suggests, children take a new approach to stimuli and form a *hypothesis.* A child now interprets some unusual experience by mentally *transforming* the event into a form that is already familiar. Previously the child used a scheme to attend to or ignore a stimulus. Now the child actively uses the scheme to find meaning in very unusual stimuli. The child tries to understand why an event is odd and how it can be related to something familiar.

Kagan has experimentally shown infants oval images that resemble a human face. In some cases the features are disarranged—the mouth appears on the forehead, one eye on the cheek, another eye on the chin, and so on. At four months of age, such images are sufficiently novel that a baby usually attends to them. But by eight months of age, the discrepancy is not great enough to hold the baby's attention. However, beginning around age one and continuing through age three, children again show interest in the disarranged images.

Kagan takes these findings as confirming his thesis. Infants under one year old look at stimuli that resemble an existing scheme. Around one year of age, they are challenged by seemingly nonsensical and confusing stimuli and try to make sense out of them. Kagan says that the older children are formulating hypotheses regarding the nature of the incoming information. A scheme functions for them as a standard against which they check their hypotheses.

For a discussion of other researchers' findings regarding the infant's perception of the human face at various ages, see the boxed insert on page 171.

Exploring the Unknown
Jerome Kagan contends that at about one year of age children take a new approach to the stimuli that they find in their environment. They begin to interpret unusual experiences by mentally transforming them into a form that is already familiar to them.
Bonnie Griffith/The Picture Cube

Interconnections Among the Senses

Our sensory systems commonly operate in concert with one another. We expect to see things we hear, feel things we see, and smell things we taste. We often employ information we gain from one sensory system to "inform" our other systems (Acredolo and Hake, 1982). For instance, even newborns move both their head and their eyes in efforts to locate the source of sounds, especially when the sounds are patterned and sustained.

Scientists have two opposing theories as to how the interconnections among systems come about. Take the development of sensory and motor coordination in infants (Field, 1977). One viewpoint holds that infants only gradually achieve an integration of eye and hand activities as they interact with their environment. In the process of adapting to the larger world, infants are seen as progressively forging a closer and sharper coordination between their sensory and motor systems. This approach has been most

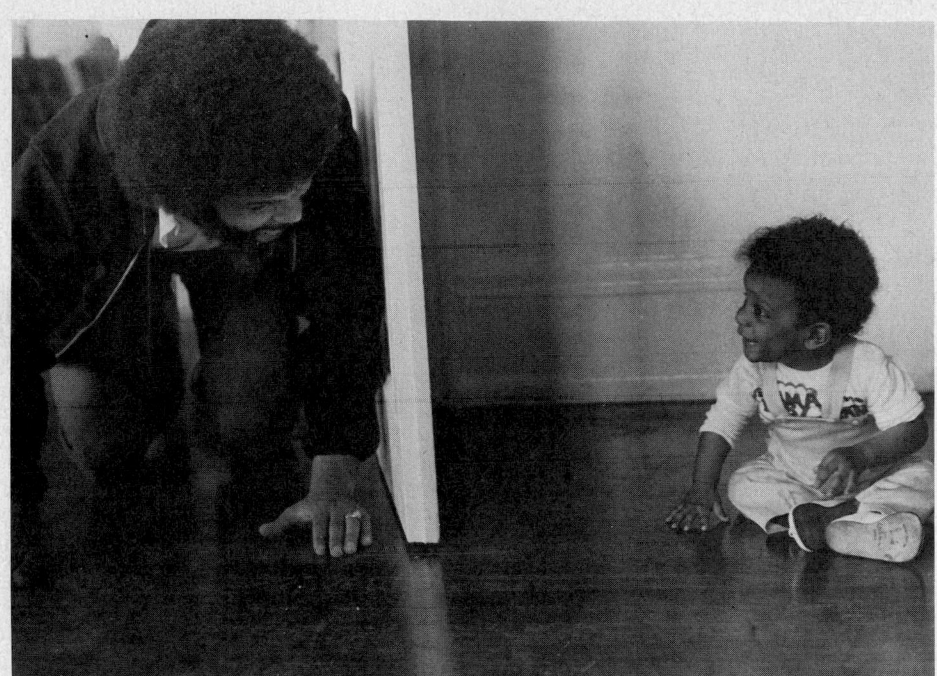

Person Permanence

This eight-month-old child is showing that he has grasped the concept of person permanence—the notion that an individual exists independently of visual display. This aspect of perception in the infant, which is extremely important in both the cognitive and social development of the child, is discussed further in Chapter 8.

Alice Kandell/Photo Researchers

clearly expressed by Jean Piaget, whose position is treated in Chapter 7. According to Piaget, infants initially lack cognitive structures for knowing the external world. Consequently, they must actively construct mental schemes that will allow them to structure their experience.

The opposing theory holds that eye-hand coordination is biologically prewired in the infant's nervous system at birth and emerges according to a maturational schedule. This interpretation is favored by T. G. R. Bower (1971, 1974, 1976). Chapter 5 described the study in which Bower found that newborn infants engage in visually initiated reaching. The neonates responded with unmistakable surprise when their hands reached toward the visual image of an object (an optical illusion) that was empty air to the sense of touch. It seems that when neonates look at an object and reach out for it, both the looking and the reaching are part of the same response by which the infants orient themselves toward the object (von Hofsten, 1982). It is as if infants prepare themselves for an encounter with an external event by pointing "feelers" toward it. Bower finds that in the average newborn this precocious eye-hand interaction vanishes, although it reappears again between four and five months of age. Hence the built-in coordinations have later to be differentiated and reestablished on a new basis.

However, if a newborn is given practice each day in reaching for and grasping objects, the infant does not show the usual decline in this ability. Without the daily exercises, babies in time merely reach toward an object without grasping it. They rely instead on their sense of touch to elicit the grasping response—for instance, when their clothes, crib, or some other object touches their hands. In any event, eye-hand coordination again emerges as a factor around the fourth or fifth month. After that, the teamwork between visual and motor skills improves as the infant grows older.

By five to six months of age, children are adept reachers. But at this age, inability to see the hand disrupts a child's behavior. This confirms that the infant is employing visual feedback to enhance reaching accuracy (Lasky, 1977; Rose, Gottfried, and Bridger, 1979).

Bower also finds that babies up to twenty weeks of age have a far greater ability to reach out and grasp a bell than do infants between twenty and forty weeks of age. However, the ability appears to be reconstructed toward the end of the first year. The coordination between auditory and motor skills then be-

THE INFANT'S CHANGING PERCEPTION OF THE HUMAN FACE

One of the infant's visual preferences is the human face. This interest is highly adaptive, since an adult face is a critical element in the infant's natural environment. Robert L. Fantz (1963) found, for instance, that infants from ten hours to five days old looked longer at a facelike stimulus than they did at newsprint, a bull's-eye, or different color disks. There is some question, however, whether the face is interesting to infants during the first ten weeks of life because it is a face or because it is a complex object (Mauer and Salapatek, 1976).

For infants under three months of age, the realism of the facial image does not appear to be crucial. They will smile just as frequently at a face with its features distorted or scrambled as they will at a realistic face (Ahrens, 1954; Hershenson, Kessen, and Munsinger, 1967; Fantz, 1970). Similarly, the outer outline or contour of the facial image seems more crucial than the realism of its features (Haaf, 1974).

Daphine Maurer and Philip Salapatek (1976) found in a study employing corneal photography that one-month-old infants tend to inspect the *external* contour of the face, usually devoting long periods of time to a particular area, such as the hairline, chin, or ear. One-month-old babies apparently can discriminate the face of their mothers from the faces of strangers, probably by differences in the hairline or chin.

At about five to seven weeks of age, a dramatic change occurs in face looking. Infants invariably inspect one or more *internal* features of the face, especially the eyes. Indeed, talking to a child increases its scanning in the eye area. It is highly likely that this activity carries special social meaning for the infant's caretakers and enhances parent-infant bonding (Haith, Bergman, and Moore, 1977).

Current research suggests that infants can detect the horizontally paired eyes in the upper part of the head by the third to fourth month. The mouth becomes differentiated by the fifth month and the broader facial configuration by the fifth or sixth month. And by the sixth to seventh month, infants come to recognize individual faces (Gibson, 1969; Caron et al., 1973). These findings are consistent with Eleanor Gibson's (1969) view that object perception in infancy begins first with the differentiation of an object's parts and later progresses to the larger structure in which the parts are embedded.

Marie E. Barrera and Daphine Maurer (1981*a*, 1981*b*) have demonstrated that three-month-olds can recognize the photographed face of the mother and discriminate it from another face. Moreover, they can recognize and discriminate faces of strangers. Apparently, infants do not require experience with pictures to be able to see them as more than a "frozen patchwork of flat colors" (Dirks and Gibson, 1977).

Research by Michael Lewis (1977: 54) reveals that infants who are six months of age show an understanding of the relationship between an individual's face and height:

> Infants are less frightened when approached by young children than by adults. To find out how they distinguished between the two—whether their cue was height or facial features—we used midgets. If the infants showed fright, we figured that the face, not height, would be their cue. If they were happy, their cue would be height. To our amazement, the babies were neither frightened nor happy when they saw the midgets. They were surprised. Their eyes opened, their eyebrows rose and their mouths formed Os, telling us that the approaching midget violated the expected features of a normal person. In other words, the face was on the wrong body.

In sum, infants have already developed rather sophisticated perceptual capabilities by the time they reach six months of age.

comes more sophisticated with the child's maturation and increasing experience. All this suggests that while natural endowment plays a critical part in early life, the "prewiring" resembles less a finished circuit board than elementary connections.

Bower's research convinces him that much behavioral and intellectual development does not occur in a strictly cumulative and incremental manner. In his view, development is frequently characterized by patterns of skill acquisition, loss, and reacquisition (Bower, 1976).

One fact stands out in any consideration of infants' sensory abilities. Infants actively search out and respond to their environment. Their natural endowment predisposes them to begin learning how the world about them operates, and as they mature, they

Eye-Hand Coordination
This ten-month-old child displays a high degree of eye-hand coordination in manipulating the sink plunger.
Patrick Reddy

refine their ability to take information from one sense and transfer it to another. All the senses, including seeing, hearing, and touch, create a system that is a whole. Information gained from multiple systems is often more important than that gained from one sense precisely because it is interactive (Lamb and Sherrod, 1981).

SUMMARY

1. Children's physical growth takes place in a generally orderly fashion, with predictable changes occurring at given age levels. Growth, however, is unevenly distributed over the first twenty years of life. One of the most striking and fundamental characteristics of growth is its "self-stabilizing" or "target-seeking" quality.
2. Not all body systems grow at the same rate: (a) The nervous system grows more rapidly than other systems. (b) At twelve years of age the lymphoid tissue is more than double the level it will reach in adulthood; after twelve it declines until maturity. (c) The reproductive system grows very slowly until adolescence, at which point its growth accelerates. (d) The skeletal and internal organ systems show two growth spurts, one in early infancy and the other at adolescence.

3. Development follows two patterns: the cephalocaudal principle and proximodistal principle.

4. The sequence of motor development proceeds in accordance with the cephalocaudal principle. Children gain mastery first over the head muscles, then the trunk muscles, and finally the leg muscles.

5. Young infants display bursts of rapid, repeated movements of the limbs, torso, and head. They seem to follow the dictum, "If you can move it at all, move it rhythmically." The behaviors are closely related to motor development and provide the foundation for later, more skilled outputs.

6. The child's development of manual skills proceeds through a series of orderly stages in accordance with the proximodistal principle—from the center of the body toward the periphery. On the whole, large-muscle control precedes fine-muscle control.

7. Right- or left-handedness develops gradually rather than appearing in an immediate all-or-none manner. It does not become well established until a child is between four and six years of age.

8. Perception is oriented toward things, not toward their sensory features. We fashion and build our world in terms of things. This fact is demonstrated by visual constancies: color constancy, size constancy, and shape constancy.

9. The visual cliff experiment reveals that children possess depth perception at a very early age.

10. Over the first two years of life, infants typically undergo a patterned sequence of changes in their method of focusing on and organizing visual events. Jerome Kagan suggests that children under one year of age have a decided preference for moderately novel stimuli. About one year of age, however, they come to employ a hypothesis for interpreting the nature of incoming information. Whereas children under one year old use a scheme, or mental model, to attend to or ignore a stimulus in terms of its degree of novelty, children over one year use the scheme to find meaning in very unusual stimuli.

11. There are two opposing theories regarding the development of sensory and motor coordination in infants. One holds that infants only gradually achieve an integration of eye and hand activities as they interact with their environment. This view has been most clearly expressed by Jean Piaget. The opposing viewpoint holds that eye-hand coordination is biologically prewired in the infant's nervous system at birth. This interpretation is favored by T. G. R. Bower.

KEY TERMS

cephalocaudal principle The rule that development proceeds from the head to the feet. Improvements in structure and function come first in the head region, then in the trunk, and finally in the leg region.

infancy The first two years of life following birth.

norms Standards for evaluating a child's developmental progress relative to the average of the child's age group.

proximodistal principle The rule that development proceeds outward, from the central axis of the body toward the extremities.

secular increase in size The fact that decade by decade over the last century, the average stature of children at any given age has been increasing in the United States, western Europe, and Japan.

visual cliff experiment A technique in which an infant is placed on a center board between two glass surfaces upon which the child can crawl. One side—the shallow side—is covered on the underside with a checkered material. The other side—the deep side—provides an illusion of a cliff by the placement of checkered material several feet below the glass. The infant's mother stands alternately at the shallow and deep sides and entices the infant to crawl toward her. The technique is used to determine depth perception in animals and in human infants.

visual constancy The tendency for objects to look the same to us despite fluctuations in sensory input.

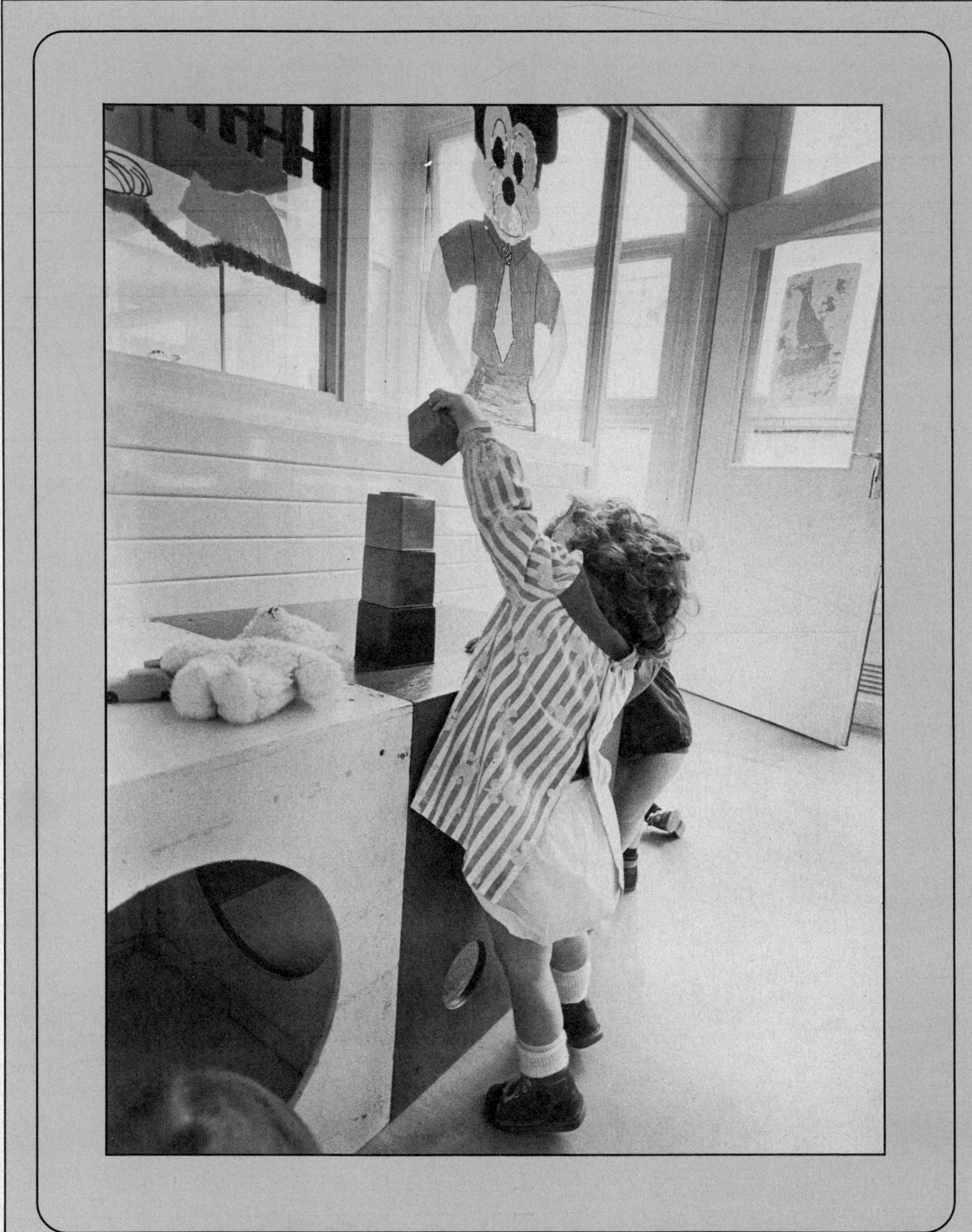

7

Infancy: Cognitive and Language Development

We do not live to think, but, on the contrary, we think in order that we may succeed in surviving.

—JOSÉ ORTEGA Y GASSET

Our cognitive and language abilities are probably our most distinctive features as human beings. Cognitive skills enable us to gain knowledge of our social and physical environment. Language enables us to communicate with one another. Without either, human social organization would be impossible. If we lacked these abilities we might still have families. The family organization is not peculiar to human beings. It also appears elsewhere in the animal kingdom. But without cognitive and language abilities, it is unlikely that our families would have the structure we recognize as typically human. We would lack rules about incest, marriage, divorce, inheritance, and adoption. We would have no political, religious, economic, or military organizations; no codes of morality; no science, theology, art, or literature. We would be virtually toolless. In sum, we would be without culture and we would not be human (White, 1949). This chapter surveys the processes by which cognition and language develop in us during the early years of childhood.

COGNITIVE DEVELOPMENT

Man is obviously made to think. It is his whole dignity and his whole merit.

—PASCAL
Pensées

As discussed in Chapter 2, *cognition* refers to the process of knowing. It encompasses such phenomena as sensation, perception, imagery, retention, recall, problem solving, reasoning, and thinking. We receive raw sensory information and transform, elaborate, store, recover, and use this information (Neisser, 1967).

Mental activity allows us to "make something" out of our perceptions. We do so by relating some happening to other events or objects in our experience. We employ information from our environment and our memories to make decisions about what we say and do. Since such decisions are based on information available to us and our ability to process the information intelligently, we view them as rational. It is this capacity that allows us to intervene in the course of events with conscious deliberation.

Psychologists are increasingly coming to view infants as very complex creatures who are capable of experiencing, thinking about, and processing enormous amounts of information. Building on the developing competencies detailed in the previous chapter, infants begin to form associations between their own behavior and events in the external world in the early months of their lives. As they do so, they progressively gain a conception of the world as an environment that possesses stable, recurrent, and reliable components and patterns. Such conceptions allow them to begin functioning as effective beings who cause events to happen in the world about them and who evoke social responses from others (Lamb and Sherrod, 1981).

Piaget: The Sensorimotor Period

Man's mind stretched to a new idea never goes back to its original dimensions.

—OLIVER WENDELL HOLMES

As discussed in Chapter 2, the Swiss developmental psychologist Jean Piaget contributed a great deal to our understanding of how children think, reason, and solve problems. Perhaps more than any other person, Piaget was responsible for the rapid growth of interest in cognitive development over the past two decades. In many respects the breadth, imagination, and originality of his work has overshadowed all other research in the field.

Piaget charted a developmental sequence of stages during which the child constructs increasingly complex notions of the world. He provided an account of how the child acts at each level and how this activity leads to the next level (covered in Chapter 2). Piaget devoted his most detailed analysis to the first two years of life, which he calls the **sensorimotor** period.

In Piaget's terminology, "sensorimotor" indicates that the major tasks of the period revolve around the coordination of motor activities with sensory inputs (perceptions). Thus babies develop the capacity to look at what they are listening to. Moreover, they learn to guide their grasping and walking by visual, auditory, or tactual cues. In sum, during the sensorimotor period the infant comes to *integrate* the motor and perceptual systems. This lays the foundation for the development of new adaptive behaviors.

A second characteristic of the sensorimotor period is that babies develop the capacity to view the external world as a permanent place. Infants fashion a notion of **object permanence:** they come to view a thing as having a reality of its own that extends beyond their immediate perception of it. As adults we take this notion for granted. However, infants do not necessarily do so during their first six to nine months.

Hence during the sensorimotor period, a baby becomes capable of searching for an object that an adult has hidden under a cloth. The child now searches for it on the basis of information about where the object went. In so doing, the infant understands that the object exists even when it cannot be seen. This developing ability provides a fixed point for constructing conceptions of space, time, and cause.

According to Piaget, a third characteristic of the sensorimotor period is the inability of infants to represent the world to themselves internally. They are limited to the immediate here and now. Since they cannot symbolically fashion mental representations of the world, they "know" the world only through their own perceptions and their own actions upon it. Thus children in the sensorimotor stage know food in that they can eat and manipulate it with their fingers. But they cannot conceive of it apart from these activities. Infants have a mental picture of food only insofar as *actual* sensory input reveals the food's existence. This

(a) (b)

(c) (d)

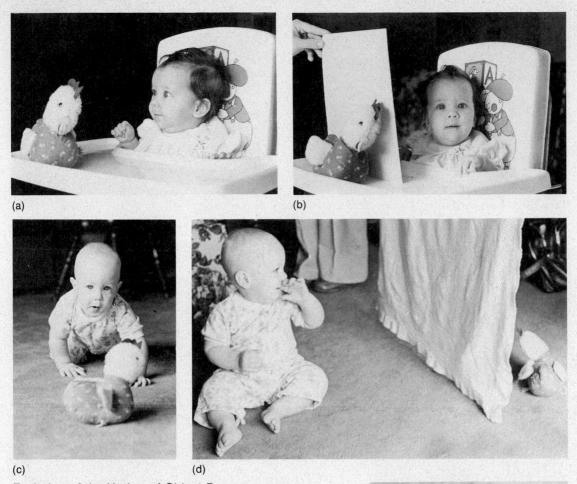

Evolution of the Notion of Object Permanence

Jean Piaget pointed out that an infant four months old does not recognize that an object has an independent existence that extends beyond the immediate perception of it. If we remove an object from the baby's vision, the four-month-old will not search for it even though the object remains within reach (photographs *a* and *b*). Between six and nine months of age, however, the child will retrieve the object. During this period children grasp the principle that an object continues to exist even though it is out of sight—the notion of object permanence (*c, d,* and *e*).

Patrick Reddy

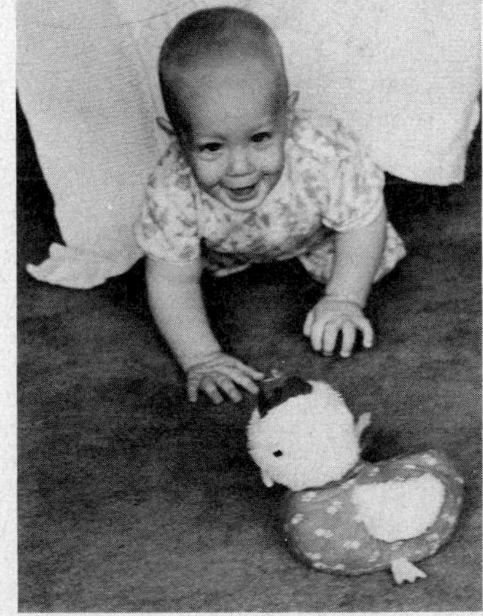

(e)

Living in the Here and Now

According to Piaget, infants in the sensorimotor period know the world only through their own perceptions and actions upon it. They thus know food only from the point of view that they eat it and play with it—but they cannot form a stable mental picture of it.

Mark Antman/The Image Works

mental picture disappears when the sensory input ceases. According to Piaget, infants are unable to form a static mental image of food "in their heads" in the absence of the actual visual display.

The sensorimotor period begins with genetically given reflexes. It ends with the appearance of language and other symbolic ways of representing the world. Piaget divided the period into six stages. Each stage represents a new level in the infant's ability to relate and adapt to the environment.

Stage 1: Reflex Acts (birth to one month). When stimulated during the first month, infants respond with biologically preprogrammed mechanisms, or *reflexes* (see Chapter 5). They suck, grasp, cry, and move the arms, head, and trunk. At first they fail to differentiate between objects; they suck on a blanket as vigorously as on a milk-producing nipple.

Reflexes provide the foundation for the baby's interaction with the environment. But the environment does not simply turn these hereditary mechanisms on and off. Even during the first month, infants come to modify and adapt their reflex responses. They learn, for instance, to recognize the nipple and to search for it. Hence, according to Piaget, the infant never simply *is*. Children are not static organisms who mechanically *re*act to the environment. Rather, children *become* something by *inter*acting with the environment.

Stage 2: Primary Circular Reactions (one to four months). In this stage infants repeat and modify behavior that they first performed by chance and found gave them satisfaction. Thumb sucking is a case in point. In the previous stage, babies sucked their thumbs only when the thumb *accidentally* came in contact with the mouth. Now infants acquire the ability to move their hands to their mouths for the express purpose of sucking their thumbs. For instance, on one occasion when his son Laurent was a month old, Piaget repeatedly removed the child's hand from his mouth and placed it at his side. Laurent consistently responded by returning his hand to his mouth. Thus hand-mouth coordination is a hallmark of this stage. Additional hallmarks are eye coordination (infants follow moving objects with their eyes) and eye-ear coordination (infants move their heads in the direction of sounds).

Because of behavior like the coordinated thumb sucking, Piaget calls this the stage of *primary circular reactions*. The responses are primary because they are centered on the infant's body, as in the case of the sucking. They are circular because they are repeated in such a fashion that they become habitual. Such activities are the child's first acquired adaptations.

Still another aspect of the infant's behavior is imitation. Piaget found that when his daughter Lucienne was nearly two months old, she would increase her vocal activity in response to sounds that he would make. At first, Lucienne's sounds bore little relation to those made by Piaget, a phenomenon he terms *vocal contagion.* When she reached three months of age, Lucienne was able to imitate his sounds, provided that she herself had just uttered the same sound. Piaget terms this phenomenon *model imitation.* Indeed, if another person—a "model"—imitates the sounds of a three-month-old child, it typically sets in motion a pattern of alternating imitation by infant and adult.

Stage 3: Secondary Circular Reactions (four to nine months). In the previous stage, infants' behavior is centered on their own bodies (*primary* reactions). In stage 3, infants expand their horizons to events and objects in the external environment (*secondary* reactions). This is illustrated by the behavior of Piaget's son at four months. Laurent had grasped a paper knife and by chance rubbed it against the wicker of the bassinet. This produced a sound that intrigued him. Laurent then attempted to produce the sound again by rubbing the knife against the wicker. The baby had recognized that his own act produced an external result. This mental connection is the foundation of learning. Once Laurent had established the connection betweeen an act and its result, he acted to repeat the result. In a primitive fashion he was intentionally manipulating and changing his environment.

Also during this stage, children begin to gain a conception of object permanence. They come to anticipate the positions through which objects pass while in motion. For example, Piaget observed that when Laurent was six months old, the infant's eyes did not follow objects that Piaget dropped in front of him. However, Laurent's eyes did search for objects that he himself dropped. If Laurent dropped a rattle, for example, his eyes searched for it even if they had not followed the beginning of the fall. Two months later, at eight months, Laurent crawled about the floor searching for objects that Piaget dropped from above him, provided that Laurent had seen the beginning of the falling movement. This revealed a more sophisticated scheme. Laurent was conferring on the object a preliminary sort of permanence. He would visually attempt to estimate where the object had fallen even though he had not seen it land.

Another skill that infants develop toward the end of stage 3 is the ability to recognize an object even when they can see only certain parts of it. If Piaget covered one of Laurent's toys with a cloth when the child was nine months old, Laurent responded as if it no longer existed. But if Piaget left visible traces of the toy, Laurent would lift the cloth to discover the rest of the toy (see Figure 7.1).

Stage 4: Coordination of Secondary Schemes (nine to twelve months). By the time children reach nine months of age, they already have a large repertoire of schemes—a variety of methods for dealing with the environment. According to Piaget, a critical feature of this stage is that children can *coordinate* a number of schemes to form new patterns. They can draw on skills that they previously used to reach a goal in one situation and apply them to solving problems in a new situation.

Piaget found that if he placed an object under a cushion, Laurent would apply a skill acquired in a previous situation (picking up an object for its own sake) to a new situation (picking up one object to search for another). In this stage, unlike stage 3, Laurent did not simply rediscover a behavior that he had accidentally found led to a goal. He displayed originality; he employed a scheme he had developed in one situation for an operation in another situation. He thus freed a learned response from its original situation. In effect, Laurent established his goal at the outset and selected his response precisely for the purpose of reaching the goal. Piaget labeled this *intentional* selection of means as the first expression of "intelligence." For Piaget, intelligence is an adaptation to the social and physical environment.

During this stage, a new dimension also appears in children's conceptions of objects. Until this time, if an object such as a toy is placed under a cover so that it vanishes from view, infants will not actively look for it. Out of sight is out of mind. When an object is no longer directly seen, it no longer exists for the young infant. Around the age of nine months, however, children begin to search for objects that disappear from their view.

In observing his daughter Jacqueline, Piaget (1954: 51) noted this new awareness of object permanence and some of its limitations:

> Jacqueline is seated on a mattress without anything to disturb or distract her (no coverlets, etc.). I take her

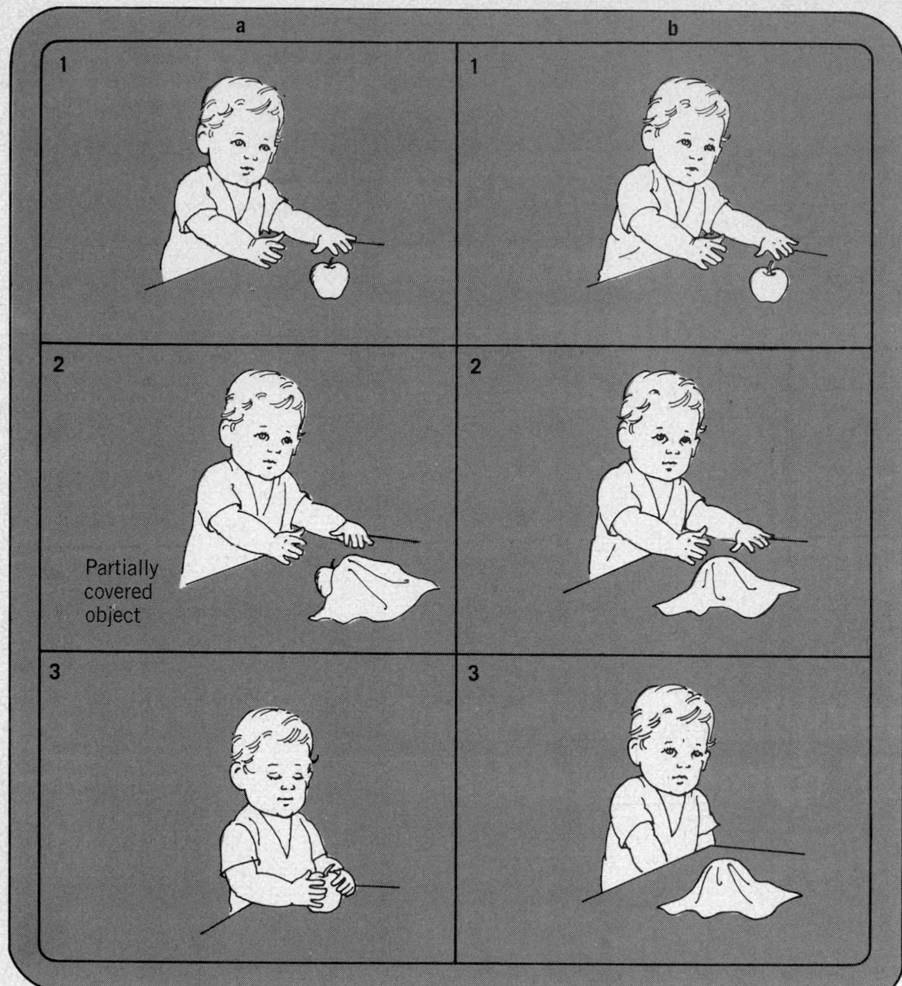

Figure 7.1 A Stage-3 Infant: Secondary Circular Reactions (Four to Nine Months)

By the end of stage 3 an infant will reach out and take a partially covered object (sequence *a*). But if the object has been completely covered by a cloth, the baby behaves as if the object no longer exists (sequence *b*).

SOURCE: T. G. R. Bower, *Development in Infancy* (New York: W. H. Freeman and Company, 1974). Reprinted by permission.

> parrot from her hands and hide it twice in succession under the mattress, on her left, in A. Both times Jacqueline looks for the object immediately and grabs it. Then I take it from her hands and move it very slowly before her eyes to the corresponding place on her right, under the mattress, in B. Jacqueline watches this movement but at the moment when the parrot disappears in B she turns to her left and looks where it was before, in A.

Thus infants in this stage (like Jacqueline at ten and a half months) are able to find an object hidden under a cover when it is hidden in one place, A. But when they see the object hidden in a second place, B, they cannot readjust their conception. They simply search once again at A.

Stage 5: Tertiary Circular Reactions (twelve to eighteen months). One of the most striking features of children's behavior as they pass their first birthday is their relentless exploration of the environment. One day Piaget observed his son Laurent playing with a small piece of bread. Laurent would continually drop the bread and pick it up again. He would even break off fragments and let them drop. Laurent seemed to be exploring the nature of falling objects. The next day Piaget saw Laurent, lying on his back, resume his experiments of the day before (1952*a*: 269):

> He grasps in succession a celluloid swan, a box, etc., stretches out his arm and lets them fall. He distinctly varies the positions of the fall. Sometimes he stretches out his arm vertically, sometimes he holds it obliquely, in front of or behind his eyes, etc. When the object falls in a new position (for example on his pillow), he lets it fall two or three times more on the same place, as though to study the spatial relation; then he modifies the situa-

Tertiary Circular Reaction

This fourteen-month-old child displays the exploratory behavior typical of stage 5 in the sensorimotor period.

Patrick Reddy

> tion. At a certain moment the swan falls near his mouth: now, he does not suck it (even though this object habitually serves this purpose), but drops it three times more while merely making the gesture of opening his mouth.

Children in this stage deliberately seek novelty. They act to produce new, unexpected, and interesting results. Piaget terms these behaviors *tertiary circular reactions.* (Remember that in stage 2, primary circular reactions, infants concentrate upon their own bodies; in stage 3, secondary circular reactions, they focus on external objects and seek to reproduce interesting events that they *accidentally* stumble upon.) During stage 5, children vigorously explore the pots and pans in cupboards, knobs on radios and television sets, objects in dresser drawers, wastepaper baskets and garbage pails, books on shelves, objects on tables, and so on.

Another hallmark of stage 5 is a further refinement in the concept of object permanence. Children will now look for an object that moves out of sight. They infer its location from the direction in which it was moving when it disappeared. For instance, if a ball rolls under a bed, they look under the bed for it. No longer do children make a stage-4 type of error—if in stage 5 a toy is hidden in place A, they search for it in place A; if hidden in place B, they search for it in place B (and not, as in the previous stage, in place A).

Stage 6: Beginning of Thought (eighteen to twenty-four months). The main feature of stage 6 is the emergence of the first traces of thinking. For Piaget, the essential characteristic of **thought** is the individual's ability to represent and act mentally on absent objects and events. In this stage, children gain "insight." They can produce an abrupt and dramatic solution to a problem with little or no trial-and-error behavior.

When Jacqueline was twenty months old, she arrived at a closed door with a blade of grass in each hand. As she reached out toward the doorknob, she realized that she could not turn it without first letting the grass go. She placed the grass on the floor, opened the door, picked up the grass, and entered the room. When she decided to leave the room, she found that in the interval someone had closed the door. As before, she put the grass down and grasped the doorknob. But Jacqueline then saw that the grass would be brushed away as she pulled the door toward her. Accordingly the child picked the grass up, put it out of range of the door's movement, and proceeded to open the door, retrieve the grass, and leave the room.

Jacqueline demonstrated insight and an awareness of causality. Her response showed a considerable advance over the trial-and-error groping of the previous stage. The quickness of her inventiveness suggests that she arrived at the solution internally through mental combinations that were independent of her immediate experiences. In brief, Jacqueline appeared to be representing the external world mentally in images or symbols.

Children also attain true object permanence during stage 6. In the previous stage they were not able to make an important kind of inference regarding the location of a vanished object: they did not consider the possibility that an object could move even though their own view of the movement was obstructed. If, for instance, you take a key in your hand, show it to a child who is in the fifth sensorimotor stage, then close your hand with the key in it, move your hand behind the pillow, place the key there, and bring your closed hand out for the child to examine, the child will eagerly search your hand. But the child will not form a hypothesis that you left the key behind the pillow while your hand was there. Children in stage 5 are unable to understand *invisible movement,* or displacement (see Figure 7.2).

In stage 6, children acquire this understanding. They will search for the key behind the pillow because they have developed the ability to represent an object by means of a mental image. They can free themselves from immediate perceptions and visualize the object "in their heads." By means of such mental representations, children can search for and find objects that they did not actually see being hidden.

Summary of the Sensorimotor Period. Piaget carefully observed the behavior of his own three children—Lucienne, Laurent, and Jacqueline—in order to discover how intelligence emerges in infancy. On the basis of his observations, he decided that there are six sensorimotor stages. The age limits associated with each stage are only approximate. They vary with individual differences in genetic endowment and social environment. But regardless of the particular age at which a behavior develops, Piaget maintained that all children pass through the same stages in the same order.

1
Object is in experimenter's hand.
2
Experimenter closes hand . . . .
3
. . . . puts hand under cloth . . . .
4
. . . . removes hand, leaving object under cloth.
5
Child looks in experimenter's hand.
6
Obviously upset child quits.

Figure 7.2. Stage 5 Switching Error: Tertiary Circular Reactions (Twelve to Eighteen Months)
The child cannot yet cope with invisible movement of objects. At stage 5 a child is unable to infer that if the object is not in the experimenter's hand, it must be under the cloth.

SOURCE: T. G. R. Bower, *Development in Infancy* (New York: W. H. Freeman and Company, 1974). Reprinted by permission.

Table 7.1 The Six Stages of the Sensorimotor Period

Stage	Approximate Age	Characteristics
1. Reflex acts	Birth to 1 month	Infants place primary reliance on reflexes, particularly sucking, in adapting to their environment.
2. Primary circular reactions	1 to 4 months	Infants stumble on a new activity and repeat it over and over again (these activities are focused primarily upon the infant's own body). Infants gain hand-mouth coordination, eye coordination, and eye-ear coordination. They engage in vocal contagion and, later in the stage, in model imitation.
3. Secondary circular reactions	4 to 9 months	Infants broaden their horizons to events and objects in their external environment. They acquire new behavior patterns as a result of acts that occur accidentally in the course of random movements. They show the beginnings of intentionality or goal orientation. They search for an object that they themselves drop. They interrupt an act and return to it. And they recognize an object even if it is partially covered.
4. The coordination of secondary schemes	9 to 12 months	Children put together skills previously used to realize a goal in one situation to solve problems in new situations. They become capable of genuinely intentional activities. They search for objects that disappear from view. And they err in searching for an object where it had previously been hidden rather than in its new location.
5. Tertiary circular reactions	12 to 18 months	Children actively seek new, unexpected, and interesting results. They engage in trial-and-error experimentation. And they can comprehend a series of object movements or displacements so long as these are visible.
6. Beginning of thought	18 to 24 months	Children show flashes of insight. They develop the potential for mental representation. And they attain true object permanence (they comprehend a series of invisible object movements or displacements).

A new stage does not displace previous behaviors. Rather, it incorporates and improves on the skills associated with previous stages. Further, the stages do not simply emerge through maturation or hereditary mechanisms. They appear only as the infant actively confronts and interacts with the environment. Through acting upon, transforming, and modifying their world, children in turn are changed and altered by their own actions. At root, then, development is adaptation. Consequently, the two-year-old is quite different in cognitive abilities from the newborn. The characteristics of the six stages of the sensorimotor period are summarized in Table 7.1. Piaget's work has stimulated other psychologists like Jonas Langer (1980) to investigate infants' interactions with objects. These objects lead infants to construct mental schemes that through time develop into adult logical operations.

T. G. R. Bower on Object Permanence

In broad terms, researchers have confirmed Piaget's observations regarding the course of children's development over the first two years of life (Gratch, 1975). But a number of psychologists have challenged the *interpretations* that Piaget made of these observations. T. G. R. Bower (1975) has been one of Piaget's most prominent and vigorous critics. Bower does not question the accuracy of Piaget's report that children under eight months of age fail to retrieve an object that they see being covered by a cloth. But Bower does challenge Piaget's conclusion that very young children lack a conception of object permanence.

Bower argues that infants come into the world biologically preprogrammed with relatively accurate conceptions of objects and object permanence. Such competence resides *within* children. Development consists of children's learning to *use* this knowledge within practical contexts. Bower maintains that what Piaget traced was not the development of object permanence but children's developing skill in deploying knowledge *about* object permanence.

In support of his position Bower cites his own research, which reveals that within the first two months of life children possess an awareness of size and shape constancy (see Chapter 6). He also refers to two other experiments involving very young infants that he undertook with J. G. Wishart. In the first experiment (Bower and Wishart, 1972), the researchers showed each baby a toy. Before the infants could begin to reach for the toy, however, the room was plunged into total darkness. Consequently, the babies could see neither the toy nor their own hands. Bower and Wishart observed each infant's behavior in the dark on an infrared television system. In spite of the darkness, all the babies in the experiment reached out and took the toy with no difficulty. But when a researcher in full view of the infants covered the toy with a cloth (the standard Piagetian experiment), none of the babies made any attempt to retrieve the toy. Thus in both experimental conditions the toy was out of sight, yet only in the case of the covering experiment did "out of sight" pose difficulties for the infants.

In another experiment Bower (1975) showed a toy to infants who were about five months old. When the toy was allowed to dangle freely in the air, the children reached for it. But when the toy was placed *on top of* another object, such as a table, the infants stopped trying to grasp the toy. Instead they pulled away from it and acted as if it no longer existed. Even though the toy was in full view on top of another object, the toy ceased to exist for the children in the same way that an object covered by a cloth did.

Bower concludes from these experiments that Piaget put the wrong interpretation on the difficulty young infants have with some object-permanence tasks (such as retrieving a toy that they have seen covered). According to Piaget, young infants are the slaves of their immediate stimulus input. They cannot mentally represent objects that have gone out of sight. But as Bower (1975: 45) views the problem, the difficulty children experience in such situations comes from a different source. The children's confusion arises from the way they perceive objects in three-dimensional space:

> The infant's most primitive definition of an object goes as follows: An object is a bounded volume of space in a place or on a path of movement. By a bounded volume of space I mean a volume with a top and bottom, a back and front, and a right bound and a left bound. If any of these bounds are missing, the infant does not treat the presented element as an object. . . . An infant who will reach for an object that is dangling in free space will not reach for an object placed upon, under, or against another object. This behavior indicates most clearly that the object no longer exists as an individual unique entity once it has lost one of its boundaries; rather the object becomes part of the object it is placed upon, so that both lose their identity, becoming a single object for the young infant.

In sum, according to Bower, infants do not realize that two objects can be in the same place if one is put

Concept of Inside-Outside

T. G. R. Bower disputes Piaget's explanation of why young infants have difficulty with the notion of object permanence. Bower says that once children grasp the notion that one object goes under or inside another, they are able to comprehend that two objects can be in the same place at the same time.

James R. Holland/Stock, Boston

on top of the other. Until they can comprehend that two objects can be in the same place at the same time, the object-permanence presentation (covering a toy with a cloth) is a totally mysterious event. In Bower's view, it is not the fact of disappearance that perplexes the child; rather, the child is confused by the nature of the transformation because one object goes *under* or *inside* another. Hence the disappearance of an object in a suddenly darkened room presents no problem for infants. Bower argues that the typical Piagetian procedures used to assess infants' knowledge of object permanence are not in fact tests of the knowledge of object permanence. Instead, the procedures test children's knowledge that an object has not changed when it is placed under or inside another object.

The issues that Bower raises regarding the infant's conceptions of object permanence remain unresolved (Gratch, 1975, 1982; Moore, Borton, and Darby, 1978). Just as Bower finds fault with one or another of Piaget's experiments or experimental procedures, so some psychologists find fault with Bower's research (McCall and Cool, 1976; Haith and Campos, 1977). The chief difficulty is that children's cognitions are not directly available for scientific observation. A further complication is that during the first eighteen months or so of life, children lack language skills. As a consequence of these problems, the inner states of infants can only be *inferred* from their observable behaviors. And this, of course, opens the door to a great many controversies.

Jerome S. Bruner on Modes of Cognitive Representation

One of the first American psychologists to appreciate the importance of Piaget's work was Jerome S. Bruner. Bruner is a distinguished psychologist in his own right who has served as president of the American Psychological Association. Many of Bruner's papers show a strong Piagetian influence, especially in the way he treats the stages of cognitive development.

Through the years, however, Bruner and Piaget developed differences of opinion about the roots and nature of intellectual growth. Most particularly, the two men fell out over Bruner's view that "the foundations of any subject may be taught to anybody at any age in some form" (1970: 53). Piaget, in contrast, held to a rigorous stage approach, in which knowledge of certain subjects can be gained *only* when all the components of that knowledge are present and properly developed.

One of Bruner's primary contributions to our understanding of cognitive development concerns the changes that occur in children's *favored* modes for representing the world as they grow older (Bruner, Olver, and Greenfield, 1966). At first, during the time that Piaget called the sensorimotor period, the representative process is *enactive;* children represent the world through their motor acts. In the preschool and kindergarten years, *ikonic* representation prevails: children use mental images or pictures that are closely linked to perception. In the middle school years, the emphasis shifts to *symbolic* representation: children use arbitrary and socially standardized representations of things. Doing so enables them to manipulate internally symbols that are characteristic of abstract and logical thought.

Thus, according to Bruner, we "know" something in three ways: through doing it (enactive); through a picture or image of it (ikonic); and through some symbolic means such as language (symbolic). Take, for instance, our "knowing" a knot. We can know it by the actual physical operations entailed in tying it; we can have a mental image of a knot as an object on the order of a pretzel (or a mental "motion picture" of the knot being formed); and we can represent a knot linguistically by combining four alphabetical letters, *k-n-o-t* (or by linking together utterances in sentences to describe the process of tying string). Through these three means, human beings increase their ability to achieve and use knowledge.

LANGUAGE AND THOUGHT

Language is the armory of the human mind, and at once contains the trophies of its past and the weapons of its future conquests.

—SAMUEL TAYLOR COLERIDGE

Human beings are set apart from other animals by their possession of a highly developed system of language communication (see Figure 7.3). This system allows them to acquire and transmit the knowledge and ideas provided by the culture in which they live. To be sure, a number of scientists claim that skills characteristic of the use of language have been developed in a dozen or so chimpanzees. But while the

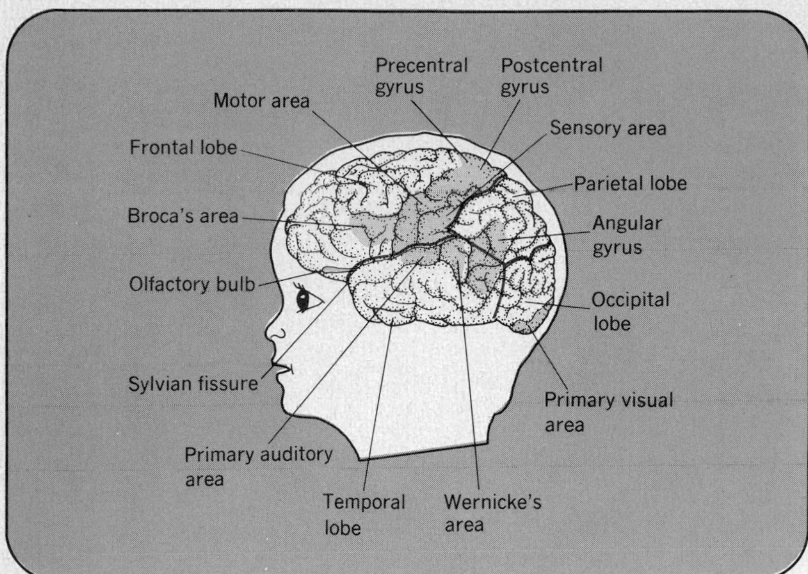

Figure 7.3 Areas of the Brain Associated with Speech
The drawing shows the left hemisphere of the cortex, where for most individuals speech is located in Broca's and Wernicke's areas.

skills exhibited by the chimps are clearly related to human skills, they are hardly equivalent to our intricate and subtle language capacity. And the methods by which chimps must be trained are quite different from the spontaneous ways in which children learn a language (Limber, 1977). **Language** is a structured system of sound patterns (words and sentences) that have socially standardized meanings. Language provides a set of symbols that rather thoroughly catalog the objects, events, and processes in the human environment (De Vito, 1970). Specifically, language is made up of three components: *phonology,* the joining together of units of sound to form words; *semantics,* a system of meanings associated with words; and *syntax,* rules for joining together words to form phrases and sentences.

Language and cognition have a number of characteristics in common. Like language, cognition has three principal elements: a system of categories used to organize perceptual input (comparable to phonology); rules for assigning meaning to information by recognizing objects or events and placing them within appropriate categories (similar to semantics); and mechanisms for ascertaining the interrelations among various categories (akin to syntax). Indeed, some psycholinguists like Noam Chomsky (1975) consider the study of language to be a "branch of cognitive psychology" and claim that a theory of language is necessarily a theory of mind.

The Functional Importance of Language

Language is by its very nature a communal thing; that is, it expresses never the exact thing but a compromise—that which is common to you, me and everybody.

—THOMAS ERNEST HULME

Language makes two vital contributions to the human condition. First, it enables us to communicate with one another (*inter*individual communication). Second, it facilitates thinking (*intra*individual communication). The first contribution, called **communication,** is the process by which people transmit information, ideas, attitudes, and emotions to one another ("tune themselves together"). This feature of language allows human beings to coordinate complex group activities. They fit their developing lines of activity to the developing actions of others on the basis of the "messages" they provide one another. Thus, language provides the foundation for family, economic, political, religious, and educational institutions—indeed, for society itself.

Language has enabled human beings alone of all animals to transcend biological evolution. Evolutionary processes took millions of years to fashion amphibians—creatures that can live on land or in water. In contrast, a second set of amphibians—astronauts who can live in the earth's atmosphere or in the space outside it—have "evolved" in a comparatively short period of time (Brown and Herrnstein, 1975).

The difference is that biological evolution works only through genes, whereas cultural evolution takes place through the linguistic transmission of information. Each generation of human beings does not need to go through the entire inventive process associated with science, technology, agriculture, art, and law again. Culture permits each new generation to spring from the shoulders of the preceding one. Thus human anatomy did not alter so that it could survive in space. Rather, human beings increased their knowledge to the point where they could employ it to complement and supplement their anatomy. In this manner they made themselves spaceworthy.

The second contribution of language is that it facilitates thought and other cognitive processes. Language enables us to encode our experiences by assigning names to them. As such, it provides us with concepts by which we dissect the world around us and categorize informational input. Thus language helps us to partition the environment into manageable units and into areas that are relevant to our concerns.

Moreover, the association between a verbal symbol and experience makes it possible for us to use the symbol in the absence of experience. As a result we are able to refer to the parts of our experience that are not immediately present. Thus language allows us to deal with past experiences and to anticipate future experiences. As such, it enlarges the scope of our environment and experience (Kerckhoff, 1972).

It is this second function, the relation of language to thought, that has been the subject of intense debate. According to one view, language is merely the container of thought. The contrary view holds that language is the determinant of thought. Let us examine each of these positions more closely.

Acquiring Language

According to Piaget, children initially form mental images of objects and later map words onto their preexisting concepts.

Robert Eckert/Stock, Boston

Language as the Container of Thought

Language is the dress of thought.

—SAMUEL JOHNSON

Those who hold that language is the container of thought say that thought takes place *independently* of language. They believe that words are not necessary for thought but only for conveying it to others. For instance, some types of thought are primarily nonverbal visual images and "feelings." Probably you are most aware of language as a vehicle for conveying thought when someone asks you to describe something—your mother, the view from your room, the main street in your hometown. You seek to translate a mental picture into words. But often you find that the task of verbally transmitting a visual image is complex and difficult.

Piaget (1952*a*, 1962) took the view that structured language presupposes the prior development of other kinds of mental representation. On the basis of his studies, Piaget concluded that language has only a limited role in young children's mental activity. According to Piaget, children form mental images of objects (water, food, a ball) and events (drinking, sucking, holding), and these images are based on mental reproduction or imitation, not on word labels. Thus the children's task in acquiring words is to map language onto their preexisting concepts.

William Zachry (1978), on the basis of his study of children between twelve and twenty-four months of age, comes to a conclusion somewhat similar to Piaget's. He finds that solid progress in mental representation is necessary for sentence production. Zachry suggests, like Piaget, that in stage 6 (the beginning of thought) children gain the ability to represent motor schemes (certain generalized activities) internally as images. Thus the various actions associated with bottles would come to be represented by such visual images as holding a bottle, sucking a bottle, pouring from a bottle, and so on. Later the child comes to represent the motor scheme—the activities associated with "bottle"—by the auditory sound—the word "bottle." This auditory image ("bottle") enters the child's implicit "dictionary." It becomes a semantic "marker" that represents the qualities associated with a bottle—holdable, suckable, pourable, and so on. In this manner, Zachry says, words come to function as semantic markers for internal representations.

A number of other psychologists share the view that representation precedes language. However, they believe that infants possess, either through biological preprogramming or through early learning, a variety of conceptual categories by which they group certain perceptions. For example, psychologists Marc H. Bornstein, William Kessen, and Sally Weiskopf (1976) showed that four-month-old infants partition the color spectrum into four basic hues—blue, green, yellow, and red.

In their research, Bornstein and his associates made use of the fact that babies look less and less at a visual stimulus that is repeatedly presented to them—a phenomenon termed *habituation* (see Chapter 5). Once an infant became habituated to a stimulus, the researchers introduced a new stimulus. If the infant responded to the new stimulus, it meant that the baby was capable of distinguishing the new stimulus from the preceding one.

The visual stimuli employed in the study were different colors (hues). The range of light wavelengths that is visible to adults—the *color spectrum*—extends from 400 to 700 millimicrons. The blues and violets correspond to short wavelengths (near 400 millimicrons), the reds to long wavelengths (near 700 millimicrons).

The researchers found that the infants responded to differences in wavelength as though they perceived *categories* of hue—blue, green, yellow, and red. For example, they responded differently to two wavelengths selected from adjacent adult hue categories, such as "blue" at 480 millimicrons and "green" at 510 millimicrons. (In other words, when the infants were habituated to blue, they were then shown green, and they again became interested in the stimulus presentation.) However, the infants did not respond differently to two wavelengths selected from the same adult hue category although separated by a similar physical distance (30 millimicrons), such as "blue" at 450 and "blue" at 480 millimicrons. (In other words, they remained bored with the stimulus presentations.)

The researchers concluded from their evidence that the mental representations of infants are organized into blue, green, yellow, and red—rather than as exact wavelength codes (Bornstein, 1976; Bornstein and Marks, 1982). Only later do the children come to apply verbal labels (words) to these categories. All this it taken by Bornstein, Kessen, and Weiskopf as indicating that color organization *precedes* and is not a product of the categories (the verbal labels "blue," "green," "yellow," and "red") provided by language and culture. Hence, children's knowledge of language is seen as dependent on a prior mastery of concepts about the world to which words will refer (Bruner, 1979).

Language as a Determinant of Thought

The second viewpoint is that language develops parallel with or even prior to thought. Consequently, language is said to shape thought. This theory is set forth in the writings of sociologists who are termed symbolic interactionists and follow in the tradition of Charles Horton Cooley (1902, 1909) and George Herbert Mead (1934). It is also endorsed by anthropologists sympathetic to the approach of Edward Sapir (1949) and Benjamin L. Whorf (1956), and by contemporary Russian developmental psychologists whose work bears the imprint of L. S. Vygotsky (1962).

The Role of Concepts. This theory emphasizes the role that concepts play in allowing human beings to partition stimuli into manageable units and into areas that are relevant to their concerns. Through **conceptualization**—grouping perceptions into classes or categories on the basis of certain similarities—children and adults alike can identify and classify informational input. They can "tune out" certain stimuli and "tune in" others. Consequently, they are able to view the same object as being the same despite changes in stimulus display (despite the fact that the object varies from perspective to perspective and from moment to moment). And people are able to treat two different but similar objects as equivalent—as being the same kind of thing. Since categories allow human beings to make the mental leap from the specific to the general, they provide the basis for more advanced cognitive thinking.

Concepts also perform a second service. They make it possible for individuals to go beyond the immediate information provided them. People can mentally manipulate concepts and imaginatively link them together to fashion new adaptations. This attribute of concepts allows human beings to make additional inferences about the unobserved properties of objects and events (Bruner, Goodnow, and Austin, 1956).

Human beings have an advantage over other animals in that they can use *words* in the conceptualization process. Some social and behavioral scientists claim that the activity of "naming" or "verbally labeling" (1) facilitates thought by producing linguistic symbols for integrating ideas, (2) expedites memory storage and retrieval via a linguistic code, and (3) influences perception by sensitizing people to some stimuli and desensitizing them to others.

Critics contend, however, that it is easy to oversimplify and overstate the relationship between language and various cognitive processes. Eric H. Lenneberg (1967) and Katherine Nelson (1972) note that children's first words are often names of preexisting cognitive categories. And as pointed out in the previous section, Bornstein and his associates established that color organization in infants *precedes* learned categories provided by language. This suggests that language is not the sole source for the internal representation on which thought depends. Nor is language the sole source for the representation of information in memory (Kimball and Dale, 1972; Perlmutter and Myers, 1975, 1976). And as the following section discusses in evaluating the linguistic relativity thesis, language has at best only a minor impact upon perception.

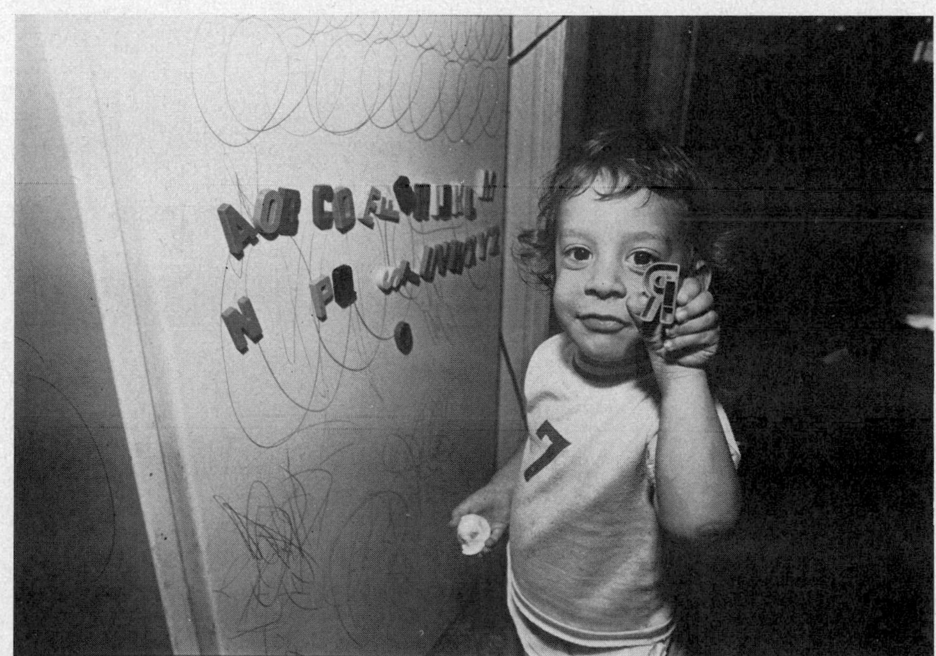

Naming

Naming—verbally labeling—facilitates the process by which human beings put a "handle" on their world of experience and render it meaningful. Thus language expedites much mental activity and functioning.

Michael Weisbrot and Family

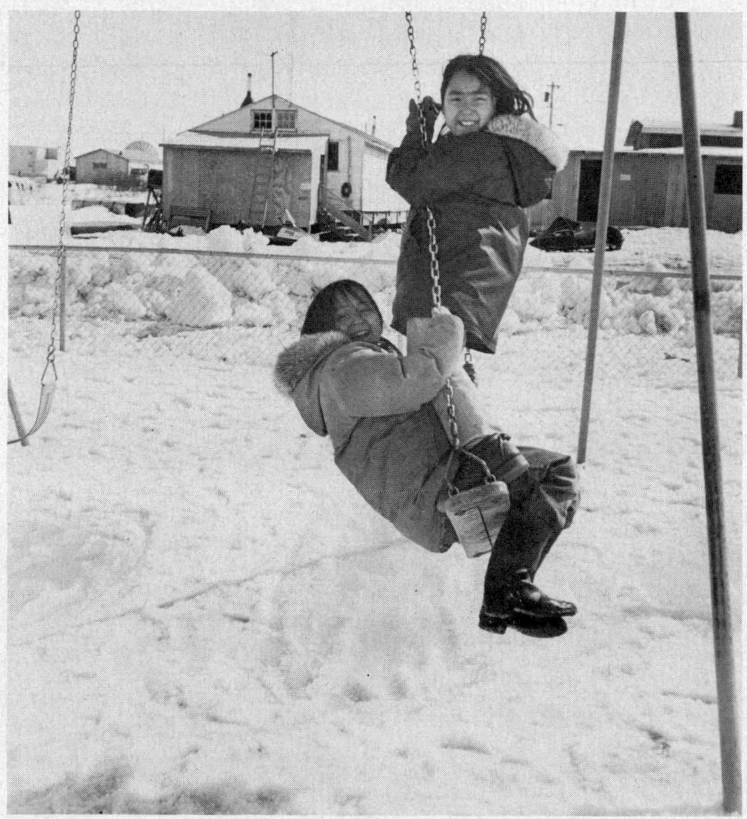

Linguistic Relativity Hypothesis

The linguistic relativity hypothesis holds that people who speak different languages experience different social realities. Hence the Hanunoo of the Philippines and the Eskimos are said to organize and react to the world differently because of the different linguistic systems in their minds. But most social behavioral scientists dispute this view. Rather than determining thought, language is believed merely to facilitate or hinder certain kinds of thinking.

Top, Pat Goudvis/Picture Group; *bottom,* Sharon Fox/The Picture Cube

The Linguistic Relativity Thesis. A popular hypothesis about the relation of language to thought is the **linguistic relativity thesis** put forth by Edward Sapir (1949) and Benjamin L. Whorf (1956). According to this view, languages "slice up" the world of experience differently. The Arabs, for example, have some 6,000 different ways of naming camels. The Hanunoo, a people of the Philippine Islands, have a name for each of 92 varieties of rice. Eskimos have five different words for "snow." The linguistic relativity thesis states that such differences in language portray different social realities. People who speak different languages inhabit different sensory worlds, since they selectively screen sensory data in terms of the way they are programmed by their language. They admit some things while filtering out other things. Consequently, experience that is perceived through one set of linguistically patterned sensory screens is different from experience perceived through another (Hall, 1966).

Few psychologists challenge the premise of the linguistic relativity thesis that the words people employ reflect their chief cultural concerns—camels, rice, snow, or whatever. For the most part, however, psychologists argue that regardless of their culture, people can make the same distinctions made by Arabs with regard to camels, the Hanunoo with respect to rice, and the Eskimos with regard to snow. They may not have a word to name each distinction, but they perceive it. Language is viewed as simply helping or hindering certain types of thinking, rather than determining thought. While it is possible to have the same thoughts in all languages, certain thoughts are easier to frame in some languages than in others. (For example, it is easier to use one word to refer to "small brown grains of rice with dark brown spots," as the Hanunoo can, than with the nine words required in English.)

The linguistic relativity thesis and the language as a container of thought thesis stand in sharp contrast. The one argues that speech shapes thought; the other that thought shapes speech. Yet many linguists and psychologists believe that the two views are not mutually exclusive—that language and thought *interact* in such a fashion that each reciprocally influences and shapes the other. The problem in some respects parallels the learning and nativist controversy surrounding the acquisition of language, a matter to which we now turn our attention.

THEORIES OF LANGUAGE ACQUISITION

But I gotta use words when I talk to you. But here's what I was going to say.

—T. S. ELIOT
Sweeney Agonistes

How are we to explain the development of speech in children? Is language acquired through learning processes? Or is the human organism biologically "preprogrammed" or "prewired" for language usage? As with a good many other issues in human development, environmentalists and nativists (hereditarians) vigorously and heatedly disagree on these matters (see Chapter 3).

Learning Theory

A number of psychologists have studied the language environment in which infants and children are reared (Wexler and Culicover, 1981; Molfese et al., 1982). They follow in the tradition of B. F. Skinner (see Chapter 3). In his book *Verbal Behavior* (1957), Skinner argued that language is acquired in the same manner as any other behavior, namely, through such learning processes as reinforcement.

Caretaker Speech. Much recent research has focused on **caretaker speech.** In caretaker speech, mothers and fathers systematically modify the language that they employ with adults when addressing infants and young people. Caretaker speech differs from everyday speech in its simplified vocabulary; higher pitch; exaggerated intonation; short, simple sentences; and high proportion of questions and imperatives. Speech with the first two characteristics is termed *baby talk.* Baby talk has been documented in numerous languages, from Gilyak and Comanche (languages of small, isolated, preliterate Old World and New World communities) to Arabic and Marathi (languages spoken by people with literary traditions). Further, adults phonologically simplify vocabulary for children—"wa-wa" for "water," "choo-choo" for "train," "tummy" for "stomach," and so on. Baby talk also serves the psychological function of marking speech as affectionate (Moskowitz, 1978).

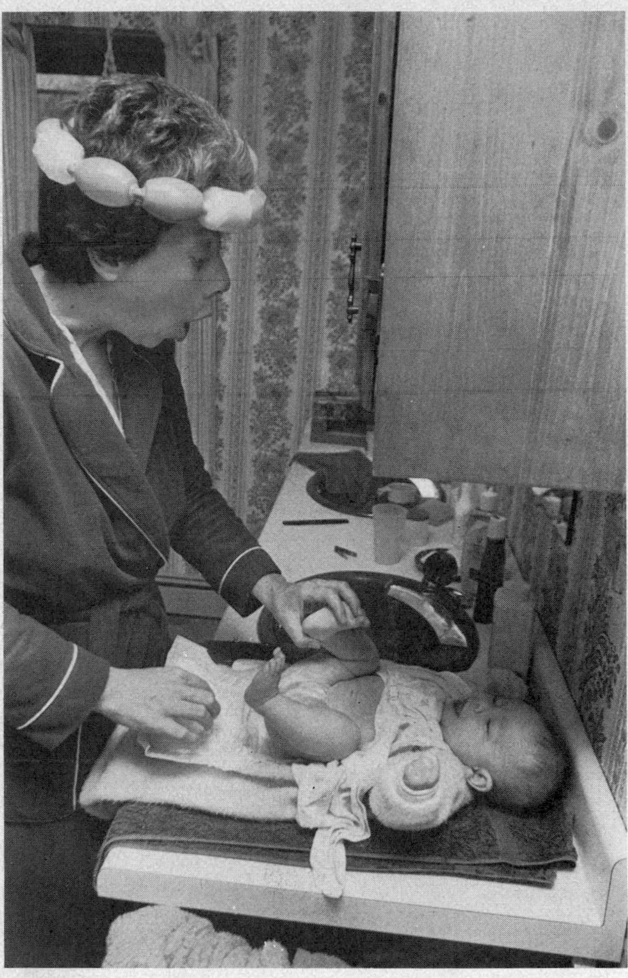

Motherese
Caretakers typically speak to infants in a simplified, redundant, and highly grammatical sort of language.
George Bellerose/Stock, Boston

Motherese. When infants are still in their babbling phase, adults often address long, complex sentences to them. But when infants begin responding to adults' speech, especially when they start uttering meaningful, identifiable words (around twelve to fourteen months), caretakers invariably speak what is termed **motherese**—a simplified, redundant, and highly grammatical sort of language. It seems that parents are less concerned with providing mini–language lessons for their children than with trying to communicate with them.

Importance of Social Interaction. *Interaction* between parents and infants plays a critical part in language acquisition. Parents adjust their use of motherese in response to cues from the child. The type of interaction depends on the child's linguistic level, cognitive capabilities, and interests. For instance, the child may introduce the topic, with the parent following the child's lead by commenting on it (Molfese, Molfese, and Carrell, 1982). Many of the features of motherese result from the process of carrying on conversations with immature conversational partners (Snow, 1977). Parents tend to restrict their utterances to the present tense, to concrete nouns, and to comments on what the child is doing or experiencing (for example, statements as to what objects are called, what color they are, and where they are located).

The interactional nature of caretaker speech actually begins with birth (Rheingold and Adams, 1980). Hospital staff, both men and women, speak to the newborns in their care. The speech focuses primarily on the baby's behavior and characteristics and on an adult's own caretaking activities. Moreover, the caretakers speak as though the infants understand them. Their words reveal that they view the newborns as persons with feelings, wants, wishes, and preferences. Similarly, a burp, yawn, cough, or sneeze typically elicits a comment to the child from the caretaker (Snow, 1977). Often the utterances are in the form of questions to which the caretakers answer as they imagine the children might respond. Indeed, caretakers impute intention and meaning to infants' earliest behavior, making the babies appear more adept than they in fact are. By building on these imputations, children's language acquisition is facilitated, much in the manner of self-fulfilling prophecies. Findings such as these, and the research of William S. Condon and Louis W. Sander discussed in Chapter 7, suggest that language learning begins with the first utterance heard.

Innateness Theory

Rather than stressing the part that learning plays in language acquisition, some psychologists—like Noam Chomsky (1957, 1965, 1968, 1980), David McNeill (1970), and Eric H. Lenneberg (1967, 1969)—focus on the biological endowments that human beings bring to the environmental context. Such psychologists, called *nativists,* view human beings as having evolved in ways that make some kinds of behavior like language acquisition easier and more natural

DEAF CHILDREN INVENT THEIR OWN SIGN LANGUAGE

Oral language is a part of most infants' environment. This is not the case, however, for deaf children. Nonetheless, deaf infants manage to create a sign language of their own. Susan Goldin-Meadow and Heidi Feldman (1977) studied six deaf children, ranging in age from seventeen to forty-nine months. The children's parents had normal hearing. Despite their children's deafness, the parents wanted the children to depend on oral communication. Consequently, they did not expose the children to a manual sign language.

The researchers observed the children in their homes at periodic intervals. At the time they were studied, the children had learned only a few spoken words. In contrast, each child had individually developed a languagelike system of communication that included properties found in the language of hearing children. First, the children would indicate the object to be acted on, next the action itself, and finally the recipient of the action (should there be one). For instance, one child pointed at a shoe and then pointed at a table to request that the shoe (the object) be put (the act) on the table (the recipient). On another occasion the child pointed at a jar (the object) and then produced a twisting motion (the act) to comment on how his mother had opened the jar. Interestingly, even when the children were playing alone, they employed signs to "talk" to themselves, as hearing children would.

Once the researchers had determined that the children had acquired a sign language, the question that confronted them was, Who had first elaborated the signs, the children or their parents? The researchers concluded that most of each child's communication system was original and *not* invented by the parents. Some of the children used complex combinations of words before their parents did. Moreover, although the parents produced as many different characterizing signs as the children, only about a quarter of the signs were common to both parties.

Goldin-Meadow and Feldman (1977: 403) were especially impressed by the deaf children's achievements, in view of the ability of Lucy, Washoe, and other chimpanzees to employ sign language, which has aroused considerable interest:

> While chimpanzees seem to learn from manual language training, they have never been shown to spontaneously develop a language-like communication system without such training—even when the chimp is lovingly raised at a human mother's knee. On the other hand, even under difficult circumstances, the human child reveals a natural inclination to develop a structured communication system.

Additional research by Goldin-Meadow with deaf children has confirmed that children have a strong bias to communicate in languagelike ways (Goldin-Meadow and Mylander, 1983).

than others. According to this perspective, human beings are "prewired" by their brain circuitry for language use. The potential for the behavior has been "built into" human beings by genes and only needs to be elicited by an appropriate environmental setting. Nativists point out that, although the languages of the world appear on the surface to be extremely diverse, they share certain underlying similarities. Philip S. Dale (1976: 3) observes:

> In analyzing a new language a linguist knows that certain aspects of speech-sound production are likely to be important (where the tongue is, whether or not the passage to the nasal cavity is open, and so on); that there will be subjects and predicates; that it will be possible to ask questions, give commands, deny statements, and more. Similarly, the child may already "know" about certain universal aspects of language; this knowledge may be innate or at least present by the time the child approaches the task of language acquisition. Indeed, the assumption of such prior knowledge may offer an explanation for the presence of language universals in adult languages.

Even deaf children manifest a natural inclination to develop a structured means of communication (see the boxed insert above).

Critique of Learning Theory. In many respects the nativist position has been shaped, sharpened, and clarified as its proponents have done battle against learning theory. Let us consider a number of the major inadequacies that the nativists find in the position of Skinner and other learning theorists.

First, nativists point out that children acquire language with little difficulty. Even very young children do so, despite the fact that they must master an incredibly complex and abstract set of rules for transforming strings of sounds into meanings. By way of illustration, consider how formidable a foreign language such as Japanese or Arabic seems to you. The Soviet scholar Kornei Ivanovich Chukovsky observes:

> It is frightening to think what an enormous number of grammatical forms are poured over the poor head of the young child. . . . If an adult had to master so many grammatical rules within so short a time, his head would surely burst. (Quoted by Slobin, 1972: 82)

Second, nativists note that the child's problem is further complicated by the garbled nature of much adult speech. Nativists argue that from a grammatical point of view the speech children hear about them is "noisy slop." Further, the words we utter in speaking are more like one giant word than neat packages of words. Usually we do not pause between words. Reflect for a moment on how a conversation carried on in an unfamiliar language sounds to you. Indeed, linguists have experimentally shown that even in our own language we often cannot make out a word correctly if it is taken out of context. From recorded conversations, linguists splice out individual words, play them back to people, and ask the people to identify the words. Listeners can generally understand only about half the words, although the same words were perfectly intelligible to them in the original conversation (Cole, 1979).

Third, nativists observe that children's speech is not a mechanical playback of adult speech. Eric H. Lenneberg and others (1967) note that children combine words in unique ways and also make up words. Expressions such as "I buyed," "foots," "gooder," "Jimmy hurt hisself," and the like reveal that children do not imitate adult speech in a strict fashion. Rather, according to nativists, children are *fitting* their speech to underlying language systems with which they are born.

Chomsky's Theory of Language Development. Noam Chomsky (1957, 1965, 1968, 1975), a linguist at the Massachusetts Institute of Technology, has provided a nativist theory of language development that has had a major impact on education and psychology over the past twenty-five years. Supporters and critics alike acknowledge that Chomsky's theoretical formulations have provided many new directions in the study of linguistics.

Central to Chomsky's position is the observation that mature speakers of a language can understand and produce an *infinite* set of sentences, even sentences they have never before heard or uttered and so could not have learned. Accordingly he argues that human beings possess an *inborn language-generating mechanism,* which he terms the **language acquisition device (LAD).** As viewed by Chomsky, the basic structure of language is biologically channeled. The human brain is wired to simplify the chaos of the auditory world by sorting through incoming frequencies and shunting speech sounds into forty or so intelligible *phonemes* (the smallest units of language). In the process of language acquisition, children merely need to learn the peculiarities of their society's language, not the basic structure of language. Although Chomsky's theory has attracted a good deal of attention as well as controversy, it is difficult to test by established scientific procedures and hence remains neither verified nor disproved.

In support of his view, Chomsky cites data on linguistic universals. He points out that while the world's languages differ in their surface characteristics, which he calls *surface structure,* they have basic similarities in their composition, which he terms *deep structure.* The most universal features of deep structure include grammatical relations between subject (noun) and predicate (verb) and the possibility of posing questions, giving commands, and expressing negatives.

Chomsky says that sentences may have the same surface structure but different deep structures. Consider the sentence "They are eating apples":

1. (They) [(are eating)(apples)].
2. (They) [(are)(eating apples)].

Sentence 1 means that some people are eating apples. Sentence 2 means that the apples are for eating rather than for cooking. The surface structure of the sentence is the actual sound or word sequence. The deep structure refers to the intent of the sentence (the thought behind it).

By the same token, two sentences can have different surface structures but identical deep structures:

1. Hank pushed the bike.
2. The bike was pushed by Hank.

Chomsky suggests that through preverbal, intuitive rules—which he terms *transformational grammar*—individuals turn deep structure into surface structure, and vice versa. Such transformational grammar (rewrite rules) is biologically built into the functioning of the human organism. Chomsky does *not* claim that a child is genetically endowed with a specific language (English, French, or Chinese). He simply maintains that children possess an inborn capacity for generating productive rules (grammar).

It is important to note, however, that Chomsky's theory deals only with syntax (rules for joining words together to form phrases and sentences). Critics point out that he does not provide a model for understanding crucial aspects of meaning or semantics (Grice, 1968; Searle, 1969).

A Resolution of Divergent Theories?

The strongest aspect of learning theory is the weakest aspect of innateness theory, and vice versa. Comparing the theories to a river, environmentalists and nativists both trace the river to its source, but each group stays on its own bank. Their parallel routes condemn them never to meet.

The observation that Heinz Werner and Bernard Kaplan (1963: v) made nearly two decades ago still holds today:

> There are multiple approaches to the problems of language . . . each of which probes into these problems with its own presuppositions, its specific concerns, its own techniques and modes of analysis. . . . Each approach yields some information on the complex and many-sided problems and none can claim reasonably to be the only avenue of truth.

Language acquisition cannot be understood by examining learning or genetic factors in isolation from one another. Rather, complex and dynamic *interactions* take place between biochemical processes, maturational factors, learning strategies, and the social environment (Blount, 1975; Nelson, 1977; Hoff-Ginsberg and Shatz, 1982). No aspect by itself can produce a language-using human. Instead of asking which factor is most important, we need to study the ongoing process by which the factors dynamically come together. We must understand both learning and genetic components in order to understand either.

Although he is commonly identified with the nativist school, Eric H. Lenneberg (1969: 641) suggests one approach for viewing the continual interchange that goes on between the organism and the environment:

> Maturation may be characterized as a sequence of states. At each state, the growing organism is capable of accepting some specific input; this it breaks down and resynthesizes in such a way that it makes itself develop into a new state. This new state makes the organism sensitive to new and different types of input, whose acceptance transforms it to yet a further state, which opens the way to still different input, and so on.

In conclusion, infants are biologically adapted to acquire a linguistic tradition. They possess a genetically determined plan that leads them toward language usage. Their attentional and perceptual apparatus seems biologically pretuned to make phonetic distinctions. But simply because human beings possess a biological predisposition for the development of language does not mean that environmental factors play no part in language acquisition. Indeed, language is acquired only in a social context. Further, human beings have fashioned learning systems and practices, including baby talk and motherese, that facilitate the acquisition of a complex linguistic code.

LANGUAGE DEVELOPMENT

How do children learn to talk? This question has fascinated people for centuries. The Greek historian Herodotus (1964: 102–103) reports on the research of Psammetichus, ruler of Egypt in the seventh century B.C.—the first attempt at a controlled psychological experiment in recorded history. The king's research was based on the notion that vocabulary is transmitted genetically and that children's babbling sounds are words from the world's first language:

> Psammetichus . . . took at random, from an ordinary family, two newly born infants and gave them to a shepherd to be brought up amongst his flocks, under strict orders that no one should utter a word in their presence. They were to be kept by themselves in a lonely cottage, and the shepherd was to bring in goats from time to time, to see that the babies had enough milk to drink, and to look after them in any other way that was necessary. All these arrangements were made by Psammetichus because he wished to find out what word the children would first utter . . . The plan succeeded; two years later the shepherd, who during that time had done everything he had been told to do, happened one day to open the door of the cottage . . . [and both children ran up to him and] pronounced the word "becos."

When the king learned that the children had said "becos," he undertook to discover the language to which the word belonged. From the information produced by his inquiries, he concluded that "becos" was the Phrygian word for "bread." As a consequence the Egyptians reluctantly yielded their claim to being the most ancient people and admitted that the Phrygians surpassed them in antiquity.

Communication Processes

Systematic research on how children acquire language did not begin until the late nineteenth century. And during the past two decades Chomsky's formulations have dominated the field. As noted in the previous section, Chomsky deals primarily with syntax. More recently, any number of researchers and theorists have argued that Chomsky's emphasis on syntax has served to narrow and even distort the study of language development in children. Becoming competent in a language is not simply a matter of employing a system of rules for linking sounds and meaning. It also entails the ability to use such a system for communication. Hence, some psychologists, such as Ernst L. Moerk (1977) and Eve V. Clark (1978), call for a study of the totality of children's communicative processes.

The essence of language is the ability to transmit messages. Yet language is only one channel or form of message transmission. We also communicate by *body language* (also termed *kinesics*)—the nonverbal communication of meaning through physical movements and gestures. For instance, we wink an eye to demonstrate intimacy; we lift an eyebrow in disbelief; we tap our fingers to show impatience; we rub our noses or scratch our heads in puzzlement. Likewise, a number of investigators find that babies employ a gaze as a communicative device (Gratch, 1979). The same holds true for pointing behavior. Apparently one-quarter of infants engage in pointing by nine months, and two-thirds by fourteen months of age. The pointing gesture (usually combined with an intense gaze) is a nonverbal precursor of language development. Mothers commonly employ pointing when talking to their youngsters. Children use the gesture to mark out features of a book or to call attention to an activity. Mothers typically look at the object and verbally acknowledge the gesture. They supply the infants with the names and properties of the object and with descriptions of their own and the infants' behavior (Leung and Rheingold, 1981). Although pointing begins to emerge at about nine months of age, children do not commonly synchronize their gestures with verbal labeling until they are about fourteen months of age (Murphy, 1978).

Another form of communication is *paralanguage*—the stress, pitch, and volume of vocalizations by which we communicate expressive meaning. Paralanguage has to do with *how* something is said, not *what* is said. Tone of voice, pacing of speech, and extralinguistic sounds (such as sighs) are examples of paralanguage. By the late babbling period, infants already control the intonation, or pitch modulation, of their utterances (Moskowitz, 1978).

Most of the research on language development has focused on *language production,* the ability of children to string together sounds so as to communicate a message in a meaningful fashion. Until recently, little research dealt with *language reception,* the quality of receiving or taking in messages. Yet children's recep-

Gesturing

As is quite typical of one-year-old youngsters, this child uses pointing as a gesture to call attention to an aspect of her environment.

Elizabeth Crews

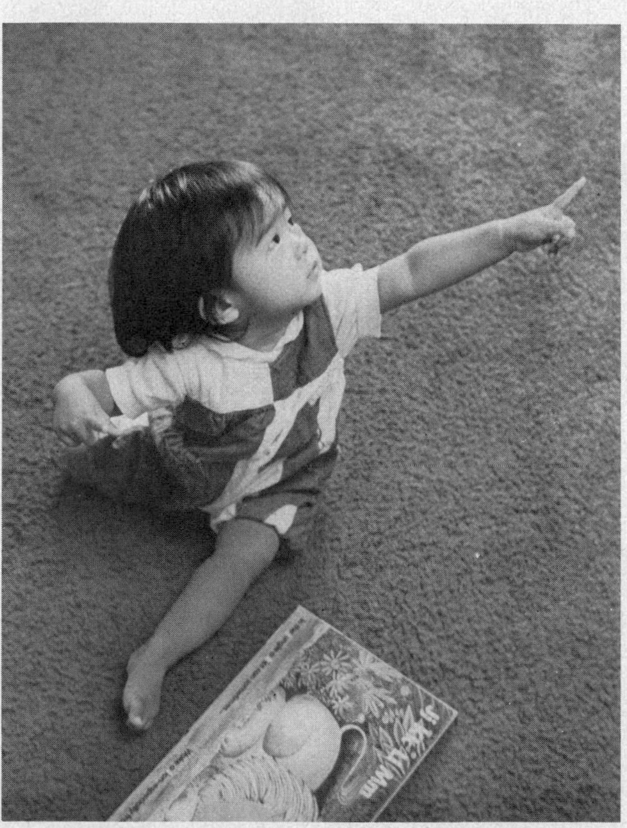

tive capacities tend to outdistance their productive capabilities. For instance, even very young babies are able to make subtle linguistic discriminations—as between the sounds *p* and *b* (Eimas et al., 1975).

Older children similarly make finer distinctions in comprehension than they reveal in their own language productions (Gruendel, 1977; Nelson et al., 1978; Oviatt, 1980). Consider the now somewhat classic conversation that linguist Roger Brown had with a young child (Moskowitz, 1978): The child made reference to "fis" and Brown repeated "fis." The child was dissatisfied with Brown's pronunciation of the word. After a number of exchanges between Brown and the child, Brown tried "fish," and the child, finally satisfied, replied, "Yes, fis." Although the child was as yet unable to pronounce the distinction between *s* and *sh,* he knew that such a sound difference did exist.

The Sequence of Language Development

Until a couple of decades or so ago, linguists assumed that children merely spoke an imperfect version of adult language, one that reflected their handicaps of limited attention, limited memory span, and other cognitive deficits. However, it is now generally accepted that children speak their own language—a language with characteristic patterns that develops through a series of stages (Dale, 1976).

Children reveal tremendous individual variation in the rate and form of language development (Nelson, 1981; Whitehurst, 1982). Indeed, some children may not begin to talk until well into their third year, whereas others are producing long sentences at this point. Such variations do not appear to have implications for adult language skill, provided that a child is otherwise normal. Table 7.2 summarizes the typical milestones in language development of the "average" child.

Early Vocalizations. Crying is the most noticeable sound uttered by the newborn. As discussed in Chapter 5, variations on the basic rhythm include the "mad" and "pain" cries. Although it serves as the infant's primary means of communication, crying cannot be considered true language. Young infants also produce a number of other sounds, including yawns, sighs, coughs, sneezes, and belches. Between the sixth and eighth week, infants diversify their vocalizations and employ new noises when playing alone, including "Bronx cheers," gurgling, and tongue games (Wolff, 1969).

Cooing and Babbling. Infants begin making cooing sounds around their third month and babbling sounds by the sixth month (see Table 7.2). In *cooing,* babies make squealing-gurgling noises, which they sustain for about fifteen to twenty seconds. In *babbling,* they produce sequences of alternating vowels and consonants that resemble one-syllable utterances, for example, "da-da-da" (Lenneberg, 1967). Babies appear to engage in cooing and babbling for their own sake. Indeed, infants seem to play with sounds. They enjoy the process and explore their own capabilities. Among the most frequently babbled sounds are nasals such as *n* and *m,* glides such as *y* and *w,* and single-stop consonants such as *d, t,* or *b,* followed by a vowel formed with the tongue near its "home" position, such as the *eh* sound in "bet." Consonants such as *l, r, f,* and *v* and consonant clusters such as *st* are rare. Babbling appears to mark a discontinuity in linguistic development, with the chunks of sound clearly divided into small segments or syllables.

Deaf infants also go through the cooing and babbling phase, even though they have never heard any spoken sounds. They babble in much the same fashion as normal infants do, despite the fact that they cannot hear themselves (Lenneberg, 1967). This suggests that a hereditary mechanism underlies the early cooing and babbling process. However, deaf babies later show a somewhat more limited range of babbling sounds than normal children do. Further, unless congenitally deaf children are given special training, their language development is severely retarded. These observations suggest that although vocal behavior emerges through maturating mechanisms, it flourishes only in the presence of adequate environmental stimulation. And deaf babies, of course, are incapable of "talking back," the process of vocal contagion and model imitation noted by Piaget.

On the other hand, children do not seem to learn language simply by hearing it spoken. A boy with normal hearing but with deaf parents who communicated by the American Sign Language was daily exposed to television so that he might learn English. Because the child suffered from asthma, he was confined to his home. Consequently, he interacted only with people at home who, as family members or visitors, communicated in sign language. By the time

Table 7.2 Milestones in Language Development

Age	Characteristic Sounds
1 month	Cries; makes small throaty noises.
2 months	Begins producing vowellike cooing noises, but the sounds are unlike those of adults.
3 months	Cries less, coos, gurgles at the back of the throat, squeals, and occasionally chuckles.
4 months	Cooing becomes pitch-modulated; vowellike sounds begin to be interspersed with consonantal sounds; smiles and coos when talked to.
6 months	Vowel sounds are interspersed with more consonantal sounds (*f, v, th, s, sh, z, sz,* and *n* are common), which produce babbling (one-syllable utterances); displays pleasure with squeals, gurgles, and giggles, and displeasure with growls and grunts.
8 months	Displays adult intonation in babbling; often uses two-syllable utterances such as "mama" or "baba"; imitates sounds.
10 months	Understands some words and associated gestures (may say "no" and shake head); may pronounce "dada" or "mama" and use holophrases (words with many different meanings).
12 months	Employs more holophrases, such as "baby," "bye-bye," and "hi"; may imitate sounds of objects, such as "bow-bow"; has greater control over intonation patterns; gives signs of understanding some words and simple commands (such as "Show me your nose").
18 months	Possesses a repertoire of 3 to 50 words; may begin using two-word utterances; still babbles, but employs several syllables with intricate intonation pattern.
24 months	Has repertoire of more than 50 words; uses two-word utterances more frequently; displays increasing interest in verbal communication.
30 months	Rapid acceleration in learning new words; speech consists of two or three words and even five words; sentences have characteristic child grammar and rarely are verbatim imitations of adult speech; intelligibility of the speech is poor, although children differ in this regard.
36 months	Has a vocabulary of some 1,000 words; about 80 percent of speech is intelligible, even to strangers; grammatical complexity is roughly comparable to colloquial adult language.
48 months	Language well established; deviations from adult speech are more in style than in grammar.

SOURCE: Adapted from F. Caplan, *The First Twelve Months of Life* (New York: Grosset & Dunlap, 1973); and E. H. Lenneberg, *Biological Foundations of Language* (New York: John Wiley & Sons, 1973), pp. 128–130.

he reached three years of age, he was fluent in sign language but he neither understood nor spoke English. This suggests that in order to learn a language, children must be able to interact with people in that language (Moskowitz, 1978; Hoff-Ginsberg and Shatz, 1982).

Holophrastic Speech. Most developmental psychologists agree that children speak their first word at about ten to thirteen months of age. However, the precise time that a child arrives at this milestone is often difficult to determine. The child's first word is so eagerly anticipated by many parents that they read meaning into the infant's babbling—for instance, they note "mama" and "dada" but ignore "tete" and "roro." Hence one observer may credit a child with a "first word" where another observer would not.

Children's first truly linguistic utterances are termed **holophrases.** Holophrases are single words that convey different meanings depending on the context in which they are used. G. de Laguna (1927: 90–91) first noted the characteristics of holophrases more than fifty years ago:

> It is precisely because the words of the child are so indefinite in meaning, that they can serve such a variety of uses. . . . A child's word does not . . . designate an object *or* a property *or* an act; rather it signifies loosely and vaguely the object together with its interesting properties and the acts with which it is commonly associated in the life of the child. . . . Just because the terms of the child's

language are themselves so indefinite, it is left *to the particular setting and context to determine the specific meaning for each occasion.* In order to understand what the baby is saying you must see what the baby is doing.

The utterance "mama," a not uncommon word in the early repertoire of English-language youngsters, provides a good illustration of a holophrase. In one situation it may communicate "I want a cookie"; in another, "Let me out of the playpen"; and in another, "Don't take my toy away from me." A holophrase is most often a noun, an adjective, or a self-invented word. Only gradually do the factual and emotional components of the infant's early words become clearer and more precise in their discriminatory power.

Katherine Nelson and her associates (1978) found that children typically pass through three phases in their early learning of language. At about ten to thirteen months of age they become capable of matching a number of words used by adults to already existing concepts, or mental images, such as the concept "bottle" discussed earlier in the chapter. One study reveals that the average child of thirteen months *understands* about fifty words. In contrast, the *production* of fifty words does not occur until six months later (Benedict, 1976).

In the second phase, usually occurring between eleven and fifteen months of age, children themselves begin to produce (utter) a small number of words. These words are closely bonded to a particular context or action.

In the third phase—from sixteen to twenty months—children produce a good many words, but they tend to extend or overgeneralize a word beyond its core sense. For instance, one child, Hildegard, first applied the word "tick-tock" to her father's watch, but then broadened the meaning of the word, first to include all clocks, then all watches, then a gas meter, then a firehose wound on a spool, and then a bathroom scale with a round dial (Moskowitz, 1978). In general, children overextend meanings on the basis of similarities of movement, texture, size, and shape.

Overgeneralization apparently derives from discrepancies between comprehension and production. For example, one child, Rachel, overextended "car" in her own verbal productions to include a wide range of vehicles. But she could pick out a motorcycle, a bicycle, a truck, a plane, and a helicopter in response to their correct names. Once her vocabulary expanded—once she acquired the productive labels for these concepts—the various vehicles began to emerge from the "car" cluster (Rescorla, 1976).

Children first tend to acquire words that relate to their own actions or to events in which they are participants (Bloom, 1973; Edmonds, 1976; Greenfield and Smith, 1976). Nelson (1973) noted that children begin by naming objects whose most salient property is change—the objects do things like roll (ball), run (dog, cat, horse), growl (tiger), continually move (clock), go on and off (light), and drive away (car, truck). The most obvious omissions in children's

Learning Words

Children's first words tend to relate to their own actions or to events that are important to them. Words relating to eating are quite common.

Paul Fortin/Picture Group

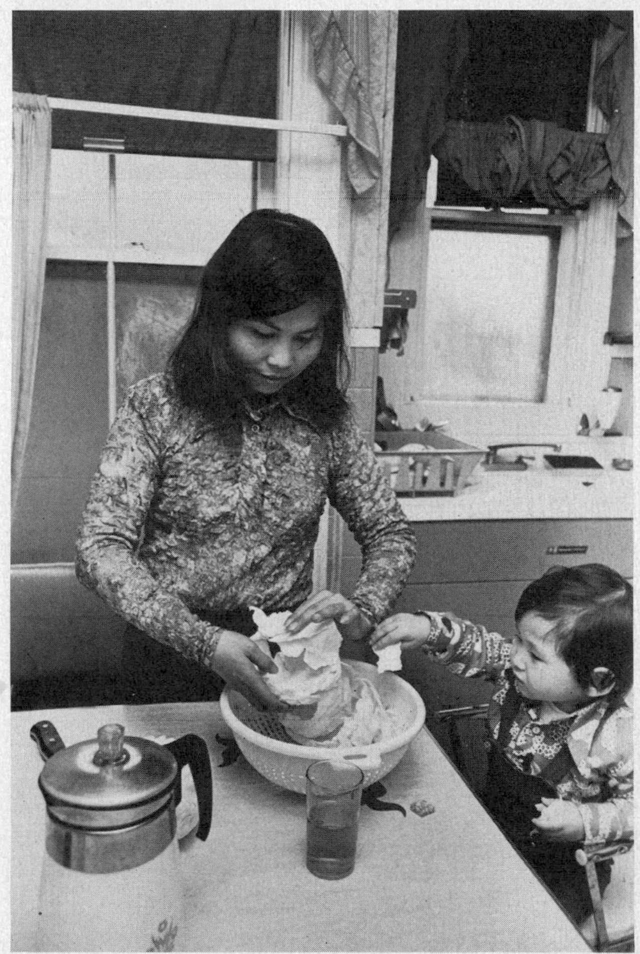

early vocabularies are immobile objects (sofas, tables, chests, sidewalks, trees, grass).

Children also typically produce a holophrase when they are engaged in activities to which the holophrase is related. Marilyn H. Edmonds (1976: 188) observed that her subjects

> . . . named the objects they were acting on, saying "ball" as they struggled to remove a ball from a shoe; they named where they placed objects, saying "bed" as they put their dolls to bed; they named their own actions, saying "fall" when they fell; they asserted possession, saying "mine" as they recovered objects appropriated by siblings; they denied the actions of their toys, yelling "no" when a toy cow fell over; and so forth.

Very often a child's single-word utterances are so closely linked with action that the action and speech appear fused. In a Piagetian sense, a word becomes "assimilated" to an existing sensorimotor scheme—the word is fitted or incorporated into the child's existing behavioral or conceptual organization (see Chapter 2). It is as if the child *has* to produce the word in concert with the action. Edmonds (1976: 188) cites the case of a child at one year and nine months of age who said "car" forty-one times during thirty minutes as he played with a toy car.

Two-Word Sentences. When they are about eighteen to twenty-two months old, most children begin to use two-word sentences. Examples include "Allgone sticky," said after washing hands; "More page," a request to an adult to continue reading aloud; and "Allgone outside," said after a door is closed behind the child ("allgone" is treated as one word, since "all" and "gone" do not appear separately in children's speech). Most of the two-word sentences are not acceptable adult English sentences. And in most cases they are not imitations of parental speech; typical constructions are "More wet," "No down," "Not fix," "Mama dress," "Allgone lettuce," and "Other fix" (Braine, 1963). Two-word sentences represent attempts by children to express themselves in their own way through their own unique linguistic system.

As in the case of holophrases, it is often necessary to interpret children's two-word sentences in terms of the context. Lois Bloom (1970), for instance, observed that one of her young subjects, Kathryn, employed the utterance "Mommy sock" in two different contexts with two different meanings. "Mommy sock" could mean that Mommy was in the act of putting a sock on Kathryn, or it could mean that Kathryn had just found a sock that belonged to Mommy.

Children's actual utterances are simpler than the linguistic structures that underlie them (Brown, 1973). Dan I. Slobin (1972: 73) observes that even with a two-word horizon, children can convey a host of meanings:

> Identification: "See doggie."
> Location: "Book there."
> Repetition: "More milk."
> Nonexistence: "Allgone thing."
> Negation: "Not wolf."
> Possession: "My candy."
> Attribution: "Big car."
> Agent-action: "Mama walk."
> Agent-object: "Mama book" (meaning "Mama read book").
> Action-location: "Sit chair."
> Action-direct object: "Hit you."
> Action-indirect object: "Give papa."
> Action-instrument: "Cut knife."
> Question: "Where ball?"

Children also use intonation to distinguish meanings, as when a child says "*Baby* chair" to indicate possession and "Baby *chair*" to indicate location.

Three-Word Sentences. When children begin to use three words in one phrase, the third word frequently fills in the part that was implied in the two-word statement (Slobin, 1972). "Want that" becomes "Jerry want that" or "Mommy milk" becomes "Mommy drink milk."

Psycholinguist Roger Brown (1973) characterizes the language of two-year-old children as *telegraphic speech.* Brown observes that words in a telegram cost money, so that we have good reason to be brief. Take the message, "My car has broken down and I have lost my wallet; send money to me at the American Express in Paris." We would word the telegram, "Car broken down; wallet lost; send money American Express Paris." In this manner we would omit eleven words: "my," "has," "and," "I," "have," "my," "to," "me," "at," "the," "in." The omitted words are pronouns, prepositions, articles, conjunctions, and auxiliary verbs. We retain the nouns and verbs (Brown, 1973: 74–75):

> The adult user of English when he writes a telegram operates under a constraint on length and the child when he first begins to make sentences also operates under some kind of constraint that limits length. The curious fact is that the sentences the child makes are like adult

). Language also facilitates
idual communication).

have been two opposing
circles regarding the rela-
anguage and thought. The
ought takes place indepen-
and that language is merely
ready established thought.
anguage shapes thought by
epts or categories into which
y sort their perceptual stim-

and nativists disagree
determinants of language.
argue that language is
nsist that human beings pos-
nguage-generating mecha-

ave concluded that the ac-
ge cannot be understood by
earning or genetic factors in
another. Complex interac-
between biochemical pro-
al factors, learning strategies,
ironment.

guage is the ability to trans-
language is only one form of
sion. We also communicate
ge—the nonverbal commu-
ing through physical move-
es. Another form of commu-
guage—the stress, pitch, and
zations by which we com-
ve meaning.

heir own language, one that
cteristic patterns. Speech de-
series of stages: early vocali-
y crying), cooing and bab-
astic speech, two-word
ree-word sentences.

with relatively accurate conceptions both of
objects and of object permanence.

5. Human beings are set apart from other animals by their highly developed system of language communication. Language enables people to communicate with one another (interindivid-

caretaker speech A systematically modified version of the language used with adults with which parents address infants and young children. Caretaker speech differs from everyday speech in its simplified vocabulary; higher pitch; exaggerated intonation; short, simple sentences; and high proportion of questions and imperatives.

communication The process by which people transmit information, ideas, attitudes, and emotions to one another.

conceptualization The grouping of perceptions into classes or categories based upon certain similarities.

holophrase Children's first truly linguistic utterance; a single word that conveys different meanings depending on the context in which it is used.

language A structured system of sound patterns (words and sentences) that have socially standardized meanings.

language acquisition device (LAD) An inborn language-generating mechanism that, according to Noam Chomsky, all human beings possess. Chomsky believes that the brains of children are prewired with the basic structure of language. As they encounter the words and sentences of their society's particular language, they reinvent the rules of grammar and become able to speak.

linguistic relativity thesis The theory that we adopt the view of the world that is fashioned and portrayed by our language. Thus since our languages differ, our world views differ.

motherese A simplified, redundant, and highly grammatical form of language employed by parents in communicating with their infants.

object permanence The notion that an object continues to exist when it is outside the perceptual field.

sensorimotor A concept in Piaget's terminology that refers to the adaptive integration of the motor and perceptual systems over the first two years of life.

thought The ability of an individual to represent and act mentally on absent objects and events.

8

Infancy: Psychosocial Development

In the orphanage, children become sad and many of them die of sadness.

—From the Diary of a Spanish Bishop, 1760

Above all else, people are *social* beings. As Harriet L. Rheingold (1969*b*: 781), a developmental psychologist, puts it, "The human infant is born into a social environment; he can remain alive only in a social environment; and from birth he takes his place in that environment." Humanness, then, is a social product.

This fact is starkly reflected in two separate cases involving children who were reared under conditions of extreme isolation. The cases of Anna and Isabelle are similar in a number of respects. Ashamed of their illegitimate birth, the children's mothers had kept them hidden in secluded rooms over a period of years. Anna and Isabelle received only enough care to keep them alive. When they were discovered by local authorities, both were extremely retarded, showing few if any human capabilities or responses. In Anna's case (Davis, 1949: 204–205):

> . . . [the child] could not talk, walk, or do anything that showed intelligence. She was in an extremely emaciated and undernourished condition . . . completely apathetic, lying in a limp, supine position and remaining immobile, expressionless, and indifferent to everything.

Anna was placed in an institution for retarded children, where she died of hemorrhagic jaundice at ten years of age.

In contrast with Anna, Isabelle received special training from members of the staff at Ohio State University. Within a week after training was begun she attempted her first vocalization. Isabelle rapidly progressed through the stages of social and cultural learning that are considered typical of American children. She finished the sixth grade at age fourteen and was judged by her teachers to be a competent and well-adjusted student. Isabelle is reported to have completed high school, married, and had her own normal family.

A report on the two cases by sociologist Kingsley Davis (1949: 207–208) concluded:

> Isolation up to the age of six, with failure to acquire any form of speech and hence missing the whole world of cultural meaning, does not preclude the subsequent acquisition of these. . . . Most of the human behavior we regard as somehow given in the species does not occur apart from training and example by others. Most of the mental traits we think of as constituting the human mind are not present unless put there by communicative contact with others.

More recently, interest has focused on Genie, a girl who was found in 1970 at the age of thirteen after having experienced a childhood of severe and unusual deprivation and abuse (Curtiss, 1977; Pines, 1981). From the age of twenty months, she had been locked in a small room by her father and rarely saw anyone. Her vocalizations and noises were punished by beatings. Under these conditions, it is not surprising that Genie did not develop language.

From the time of Genie's discovery, a program was undertaken to rehabilitate and educate her. Over the course of eight years Genie made considerable progress in the comprehension and production of language. Yet her speech was still far from normal, resembling a somewhat garbled telegram. For instance, it lacked proforms ("what," "which," "this," and the like), movement rules (she produced no passive sentences, such as "John was hit by the ball"), and auxiliary structure (for instance, she consistently omitted "have" and "will" in such sentences as "Tom will go home"). After living for a few years with a foster family, Genie was able to approach strangers and initiate physical contact, and she seemed to expect kindness, not hostility, from adults. Nonetheless, some of her behavior remained strange— a not surprising outcome given the deprivation of her formative years. In 1978, Genie's mother became her legal guardian and removed her from the special program in which she had been participating. Likewise, all research on Genie's language and intellectual development was halted.

For a discussion of other kinds of child abuse and neglect, see the boxed insert on pages 208–209.

THE DEVELOPMENT OF EMOTION AND SOCIAL BONDS

> *We are molded and remolded by those who have loved us; and though the love may pass, we are nevertheless their work, for good or ill.*
>
> —FRANÇOIS MAURIAC

The importance of children's early years in shaping their psychological and social being has been emphasized by many child psychologists. Erik Erikson (1963), a neo-Freudian psychoanalyst (see Chapter 2), maintains that the essential task of infancy is the development of a basic trust in others. He believes that during infancy children learn whether the world is a good and satisfying place or a source of discomfort, frustration, and misery. If the child's basic needs are met with genuine and sensitive care, the child develops a "basic trust" in people and evolves a foundation for self-trust (a sense of being "all right" and a complete self). In Erikson's view, a baby's first social achievement is the willingness to let its mother move out of sight without undue anxiety or rage, because "she has become an inner certainty as well as an outer predictability" (1963: 247).

Many psychologists, especially those influenced by the Freudian psychoanalytic tradition, hold that children's early relationships serve as prototypes for their later relationships with people. Viewed from this perspective, the flavor, maturity, and stability of a person's relationships derive from his or her early ties. When a child fails to develop ties to one or a few significant persons, or when these ties are disrupted, the child is thought to be impaired in developing close personal relationships in adulthood (Bowlby, 1969; B. L. White, 1973, 1975; Rutter, 1974).

As pointed out in Chapter 2, many developmental psychologists dispute the view that the first several years of a child's life are all-important. They stress instead that development occurs across the entire life

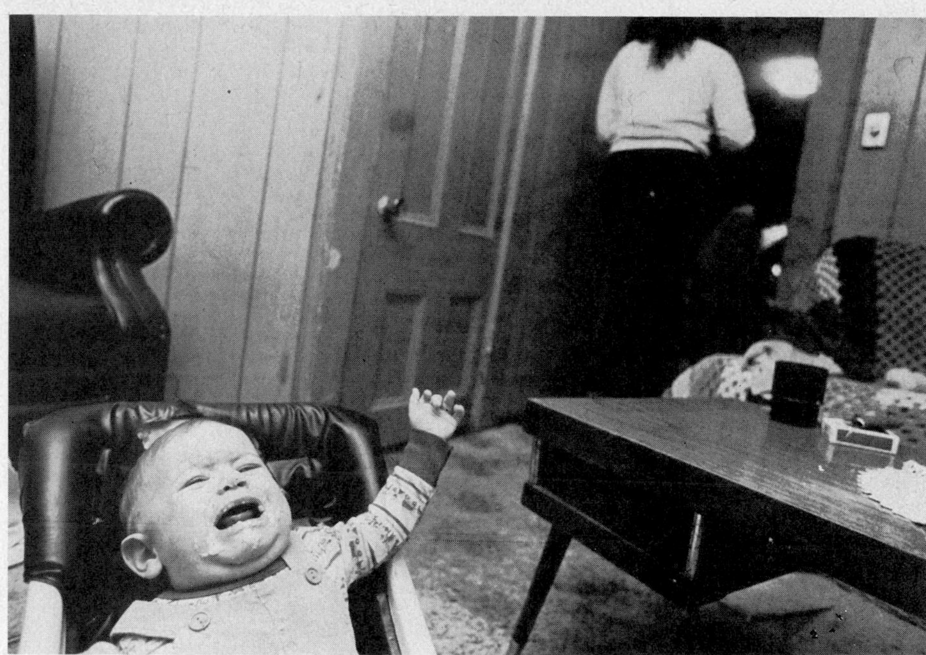

Learning Basic Trust

According to Erik Erikson, an infant's first social achievement is coming to terms with the fact that his mother periodically moves out of sight. As the child develops confidence that she will return, he is less likely to cry and rage when she departs.

Polly Brown/The Picture Cube

span. Hence no one period is more critical than another. These psychologists do not deny that development is influenced by early experiences. But they portray human beings as considerably more resilient than Freud and his followers imagined them to be. Let us begin our examination of these matters by considering the nature of emotion and then move on to a consideration of the process by which infants establish social and emotional ties with other human beings.

The Role of Emotion

It is terribly amusing how many different climates of feeling one can go through in a day.

—ANNE MORROW LINDBERGH
Bring Me a Unicorn

Emotions play a critical part in our daily existence. Indeed, if we lacked the ability to experience love, joy, grief, and rage, we would find it difficult to recognize ourselves as human. Emotions set the tone for much of our lives.

Psychologists have characterized emotion in different ways. Some have viewed it as a reflection of physiological changes that occur in our bodies, including rapid heartbeat and breathing, muscle tension, perspiration, and a "sinking feeling" in the stomach. Others have portrayed it as the subjective feelings that we experience—the "label" we assign to a state of arousal. Still others have depicted it in terms of the expressive behavior that we display, including crying, moaning, laughing, smiling, and frowning. Yet emotion is not one thing, but many, and it is best characterized as a combination of all these components. Thus we may view **emotion** as the physiological changes, subjective experiences, and expressive behaviors that are involved in such feelings as love, joy, grief, and rage.

Charles Darwin was intrigued by the expression of emotions and proposed an evolutionary theory for them. In *The Expression of Emotions in Man and Animals,* published in 1872, Darwin contended that many of the ways in which we express emotions are inherited patterns that have survival value. He observed, for instance, that dogs, tigers, monkeys, and human beings all bare their teeth in the same way during rage. In so doing, they communicate to other members of their own species and to other species important messages regarding their inner dispositions.

The Nature of Attachment

Attachment is an affectional bond that one individual forms for another and that endures across time and space (Ainsworth and Bell, 1970). It is expressed

CHILD ABUSE AND NEGLECT

If you must beat a child, use a string.

Talmud: Baba Bathra

Officials of the National Center on Child Abuse and Neglect (a federal agency) estimate that more than 1 million American children suffer neglect or physical abuse each year. *Neglect* is defined as the absence of adequate social, emotional, and physical care. *Abuse* is defined as nonaccidental physical attack on or injury to children by individuals caring for them. Physicians term severe injuries associated with physical abuse the **battered child syndrome**—abrasions, lacerations, burns, fractures, concussions, hemorrhages, and bruises caused by a caretaker's hitting, yanking, shaking, kicking, choking, burning, or throwing a child.

Research sponsored by the National Institute of Mental Health suggests that the estimates made by the National Center on Child Abuse and Neglect may be too low. From interviews with 2,143 married couples representing a demographic cross section of American families, sociologists at three Eastern universities estimate that parents kick, punch, or bite as many as 1.7 million children a year, beat up 460,000 to 750,000 more, and attack 46,000 others with knives or guns. Further, they estimate that 2.3 million children wield a knife or gun against a brother or sister (*New York Times*, March 20, 1977; Gelles and Straus, 1979).

Some authorities consider much too narrow definitions that limit the term "child abuse and neglect" to the infliction of actual physical harm. These authorities would include such categories as emotional abuse, emotional neglect, and sexual abuse (Kinard, 1979). *Emotional abuse* represents injury to a child's psychological self. If often takes the form of parental hostility, rejection, verbal criticism, and harassment. *Emotional neglect* involves the failure of a caretaker to provide the love and involvement necessary for a child's psychological growth and development. *Sexual abuse* is any act of a sexual nature performed by a parent or caretaker without a child's consent and understanding. (Sexual abuse will be considered in Chapter 10.)

The psychologist Byron Egeland is engaged in a longitudinal study of children who are at risk because of poor quality of care (Brody, 1983*g*). He and his associates find that the psychological unavailability of caretakers affects a child's development as seriously as does physical abuse and neglect. Emotionally unresponsive mothers tend to ignore their youngsters when the children are unhappy, uncomfortable, or hurt, and they do not share their children's pleasures. Consequently, the children find that they cannot look to their mothers for security and comfort. Both physically abused and emotionally deprived children have low self-esteem, poor self-control, and negative feelings about the world. However, whereas physically abused youngsters tend to show high levels of rage, frustration, and aggression, those reared by emotionally unavailable mothers tend to be withdrawn and dependent and to exhibit more severe mental and behavioral damage as they become older.

It is difficult to generalize about parents who abuse children. It is now clear that multiple factors are usually involved. Further, the relative importance of the various factors differs for different individuals, times, and social environments (Bybee, 1979; Herrenkohl and Herrenkohl, 1981; Martin and Walters, 1982). Nonetheless, a number of social factors are related to abuse and violence (Gelles, 1980). Research suggests that child abuse is more prevalent among economically disadvantaged families (Garbarino and Crouter, 1978; Gelles and Straus, 1979). However, this finding does not mean that domestic violence is confined to lower–socioeconomic-status households; it is found across the class spectrum. Child abuse is also related to social stress in families (Conger, Burgess, and Barrett, 1979). For instance, job loss is associated with an increasing incidence of child maltreatment (Steinberg, Catalano, and Dooley, 1981). And families that are socially isolated and outside neighborhood support networks are more likely to abuse children than are families with rich social ties (Garbarino and Sherman, 1980).

Psychiatrists Brandt F. Steele and Carl B. Pollock (1968) made intensive studies of sixty families in which significant child abuse had occurred. The parents came from *all* segments of the population: from all socioeconomic strata, all levels of intelligence and education, and most religious and ethnic groups. Steele and Pollock found a number of elements common to many child abusers. On the whole these parents demanded a great deal from their infants, far more than the babies could understand or respond to (1968: 110):

> Henry J., in speaking of his sixteen-month-old son, Johnny, said, "He knows what I mean and understands it when I say 'come here.' If he doesn't come immediately, I go and give him a gentle tug on the ear to remind him of what he's supposed to do." In the hospital it was found that Johnny's ear was lacerated and partially torn away from his head.

The parents also felt insecure and unsure of being loved, and looked to the child as a source of reassurance, comfort, and affection (1968: 110):

> Kathy made this poignant statement: "I have never felt really loved all my life. When the baby was born, I thought he would love me; but when he cried all the time, it meant he didn't love me, so I hit him." Kenny, age three weeks, was hospitalized with bilateral subdural hematomas [multiple bruises].

Steele and Pollock found that child abusers, without exception, had been raised in the same authoritarian style that they were recreating with their own children. Other researchers have confirmed that abusive parents are themselves likely to have been abused when they were children (Steinmetz, 1977). Indeed, evidence suggests that the pattern is unwittingly transmitted from parent to child, generation after generation. Moreover, the greater the frequency of violence, the greater the chance that the victim will grow up to be a violent parent (Straus, Gelles, and Steinmetz, 1980).

Probably no more than 10 percent of abusing parents show severe psychotic tendencies or other signs of serious psychiatric disorders. In this small percentage of cases it may be advisable to remove the child from the home. Psychiatrists estimate that the other 90 percent of abusing parents are treatable if they receive competent counseling (Helfer and Kempe, 1977).

Abusing parents usually do not abuse all their children—one is commonly selected to be the victim. Some children appear to be more "at risk for abuse" than other children. They include children who were premature infants, were born out of wedlock, possess congenital anomalies or other handicaps, or were "difficult" babies. Overall, a child whom an abuse-prone parent views as being "strange" or "different" is more at risk than are other children in the family (Soeffing, 1975; Brenton, 1977).

Maltreated children show a variety of symptoms (Kempe and Kempe, 1978). Infants may not thrive, and they may lag in motor, social, and language development. Preschoolers may display a lack of basic trust, "frozen watchfulness," and anxious and compliant behavior among adults. School-aged children may internalize the feeling that they are responsible for family problems and perform poorly on academic tasks. And adolescents may show masked depression, rebelliousness, anger, truancy, and antisocial behavior.

Since teachers are the only adults outside the family whom many children see with any consistency, they are often in a position to detect signs of child abuse or neglect and to begin to remedy the situation by reporting it to the proper authorities. In fact, most states require teachers to report cases of child abuse, and the law provides them with legal immunity for erroneous reports made in good faith. The American Humane Association has published a list of the signs teachers should look for as possible tip-offs of child abuse or neglect. They include the following:

- Does the child have bruises, welts, or contusions?
- Does the child complain of beatings or maltreatment?
- Does the child frequently arrive early to school and stay late? (The child may be seeking an escape from home.)
- Is the child frequently absent or late?
- Is the child aggressive, disruptive, destructive, shy, withdrawn, passive, or overly compliant?
- Is the child inadequately dressed for the weather, unkempt, dirty, undernourished, tired, in need of medical attention, or frequently injured?

Over the past decade, the problem of child abuse and neglect has emerged as one of the most pressing issues of our time. Nonetheless, considerable ambivalence still exists on the subject. At the same time that we condemn abuse and neglect, we condone the physical punishment of children at home and at school (Bybee, 1979). Indeed, in the 1977 case of *Ingraham* v. *Wright*, the U.S. Supreme Court held that physical punishment in school is neither cruel nor unusual punishment.

in behaviors that promote proximity and contact. Among infants these include approaching, following, clinging, and signaling (smiling, crying, and calling). Through these activities a child demonstrates that specific people are important, satisfying, and rewarding. Some writers call this constellation of socially oriented reactions *dependency* (Maccoby and Masters, 1970; Gewirtz, 1972), and lay people refer to it simply as "love."

The security of the infant-parent attachment is related to a child's social and emotional development. Thus, securely attached infants are more confident, enthusiastic, persistent, cooperative, and in general more effective beings by the time they reach two years of age than are infants who are insecurely attached to their primary caretaker (Matas, Arend, and Sroufe, 1978; Ainsworth et al., 1979; Pastor, 1981; Thompson and Lamb, 1983).

The quality of an infant's attachment derives from the ongoing interaction that the child has with caretakers. Infants with caretakers who are responsive to their cues tend to develop secure attachments. Hence the quality of the attachment depends largely on the stresses and family circumstances experienced by the caretakers. For instance, mothers who receive help and support from their husbands, relatives, and friends are typically less harried, feel less overwhelmed, and have fewer demands on their time than do mothers who do not. Consequently, they have more opportunities to care for and enjoy their babies.

Infants also contribute to the evolving quality of the relationship with their caretakers (see Chapter 5). Easy babies are considerably more likely than are difficult babies to develop secure attachments to their caretakers. Even when they have less responsive mothers, easy babies seem to be less affected than are difficult babies by their mothers' behavior by virtue of their easy temperaments. Further, easy babies are less likely to demand as much of their caretakers as do difficult babies (Crockenberg, 1981).

More recently, Paul Ekman (1972, 1980) has proposed that there are certain constants across cultures regarding the connection between specific emotions and specific facial expressions. He and his colleagues have shown subjects from widely different cultures photographs of faces that individuals from Western societies would judge to display six basic emotions: happiness, sadness, anger, surprise, disgust, and fear. Ekman finds that subjects in the United States, Brazil, Argentina, Chile, and Japan use the same emotion words to describe the same faces. He takes this as evidence demonstrating that the central nervous system of human beings is genetically prewired for the facial expression of emotion.

Not too long ago it was believed that newborns lack differentiated emotions except for unfocused ex-

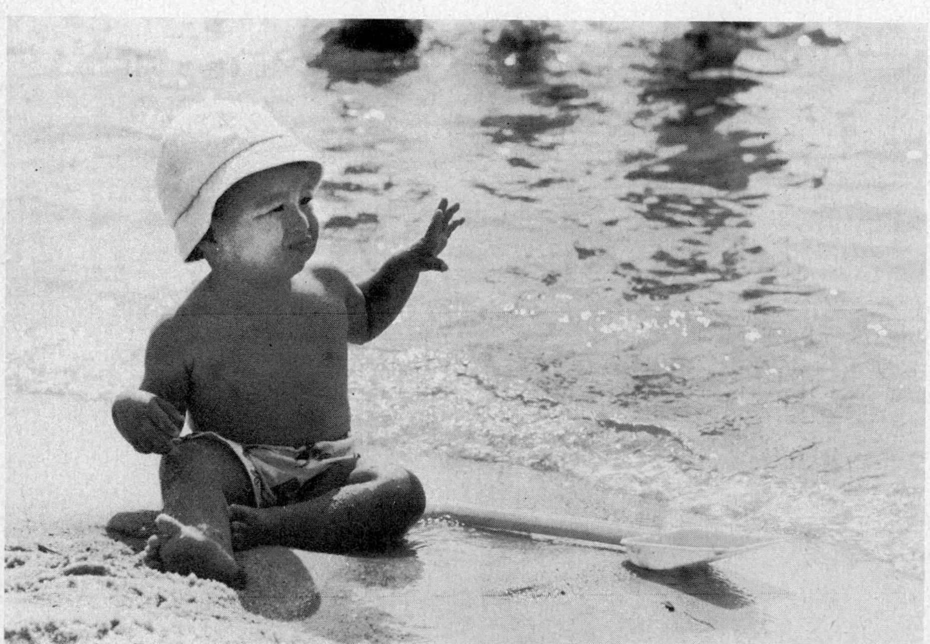

Emotional Development

Like adults, infants experience a full range of emotional states. Not too long ago it was assumed that babies lack differentiated emotions except for unfocused expressions of excitement.

Gabor Demjen/Stock, Boston

pressions of excitement, as when they wiggle, thrash about, and cry. For instance, a half century ago Katherine B. Bridges (1932) proposed that children's emotions develop in a treelike pattern, from a state of general excitement toward specific emotional states such as fear, joy, and anger. Yet as our discussion in Chapter 5 suggested, it is easy to underestimate the capabilities of newborns. More recently, the psychologist Carroll Izard (1977) has suggested that a variety of distinctive emotional expressions—surprise, happiness, disgust, distress, and interest—are present at birth. Depending on the circumstances, babies display interest, joy, surprise, sadness, fear, anger, and disgust in their early months (Izard, 1980). The most difficult emotions to distinguish in infants—as in adults—are anger, disgust, and contempt. Children's emotions play a critical part in their bonding or attachment to others, a matter to which we now turn our attention.

By virtue of the multitude of factors affecting the members of a family, there ensues between a baby and its caretakers a dynamic relationship that requires an ongoing negotiation and renegotiation of expectations and behavior. At times these transactions result in changes in the quality of the attachment (Crockenberg, 1981; Thompson et al., 1982). Further, where infants have an insecure relationship with one parent, the "effects" of the insecure relationship can often be mitigated by a secure relationship with the other parent or another caretaker (Main and Weston, 1981).

The Course of Attachment

H. Rudolph Schaffer and Peggy E. Emerson (1964) studied the development of attachment in sixty Scottish infants over their first eighteen months of life. At four-week intervals during the first year, the researchers interviewed each infant's mother concerning her child's responses to a variety of separation situations (for instance, being left alone in a room, being left in a baby carriage outside a shop, being put down after having been held in an adult's arms, and so on). Monthly observations were also made of the child's reaction on being approached by the interviewer (a stranger) at various distances. Another follow-up session was held when the infants were eighteen months old.

Schaffer and Emerson identified three stages in the development of infant social responsiveness. During their first two months of life (the first stage), infants are aroused by *all* parts of their environment. They seek arousal equally from human and nonhuman aspects. The second stage is one of *indiscriminate attachment*. During this stage, which occurs around the third

The Mother-Child Relationship
Some psychologists, particularly those influenced by the psychoanalytic tradition, believe that a child's early relationship with the mother serves as a prototype for later relationships with other people. They say the mother is the infant's primary object of attachment.
Patrick Reddy

month, infants become responsive to human beings as a general class of stimuli. They protest the withdrawal of any person's attention, whether the person is familiar or strange. When they are about seven months old, babies enter the third stage, that of *specific attachment*. They begin displaying a preference for a particular person and over the next three to four months make progressively more effort to be near this attachment object.

One way children show specific attachment is through *separation distress*—the tendency of children to cry, become upset, and stop their usual activities following the departure of a primary caretaker. Children are less likely to display separation distress when they crawl or walk away from a caretaker than when the caretaker leaves them. Separation distress typically appears in North American children at about eight months of age, rises to a peak at thirteen to fifteen months, and decreases thereafter.

Children differ greatly in the age at which specific attachment occurs. Among the sixty babies in the Schaffer and Emerson study, one showed specific attachment at twenty-two weeks, while two did not display it until after their first birthdays. Cross-cultural differences also play a part in this development. Mary D. Salter Ainsworth (1967) found that infants in Uganda show specific attachment at about six months of age—a month or so earlier than the Scottish infants studied by Schaffer and Emerson. Similarly, Barry M. Lester and his associates (1974) found that separation protest occurred earlier among infants in Guatemala than among those in the United States.

Both Ainsworth and Lester attribute the precocity of the Ugandan and Guatemalan infants to cultural factors. Ugandan infants spend most of their time in close physical contact with their mothers (they are carried about on the mother's back). Accordingly, separation is a rare occurrence. In the United States infants are placed in their own rooms shortly after birth. Such separation is virtually unknown in Guatemala, where most rural families live in a one-room rancho. As a consequence, separation seems to be a more noticeable event to Guatemalan children, and they respond to it earlier than children reared in the United States.

Schaffer (1971) suggests that the onset of separation protest is directly related to a child's level of object permanence. Social attachment depends on the ability of infants to differentiate between their mother and strangers and on their ability to recognize that their mother continues to exist even when she is not visible. (In terms of Piaget's framework, outlined in Chapter 7, these abilities do not appear until the fourth sensorimotor stage.) Indeed, Silvia M. Bell (1970) finds that in some instances the concept of **person permanence**—the notion that an individual exists independently of immediate visibility—may appear in a child before the concept of object permanence. Studies by other researchers also confirm that protests over parental departures are related to a child's level of cognitive development (Spelke et al., 1973; Kagan, Kearsley, and Zelazo, 1978).

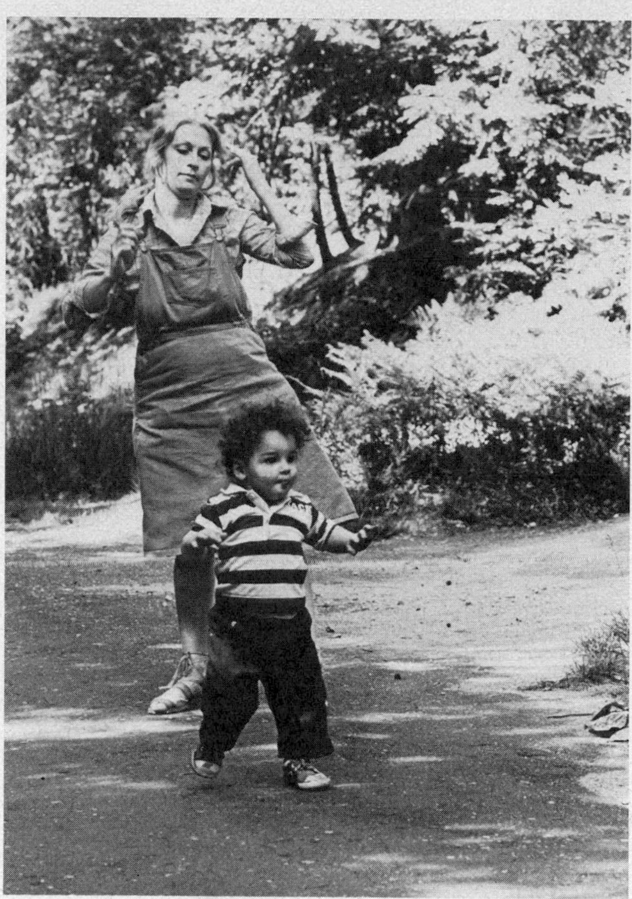

Separation Distress

Children are less likely to experience separation distress when they crawl or walk away from a caretaker than when the caretaker leaves them.

Bob Kalman/The Image Works

In their study of Scottish infants, Schaffer and Emerson found that the mother was most commonly the first object of specific attachment (in 65 percent of the cases). However, there were some instances in which the first attachment was to the father or a grandparent (5 percent). And in 30 percent of the cases, initial attachments occurred simultaneously to the mother and another person. Further, the number of a child's attachments increased rapidly. By eighteen months only 13 percent displayed attachment to only one person, and almost one-third of the babies had five or more attachment persons. Indeed, Marsha Weinraub, Jeanne Brooks, and Michael Lewis (1977) believe that the concept of attachment as presently formulated is too narrow. Since infants have ongoing relationships with their fathers, grandparents, and siblings, these psychologists suggest that the focus of theory and research should fall on the *social network*—an encompassing web of ties to significant others. In this regard Michael E. Lamb (1976) finds that American infants eight months of age show no preference for one parent over the other on his measures related to attachment.

Theories of Attachment

Attachments play an important part in an infant's social development. What are the origins or determinants of these socially oriented responses? Two different answers have been advanced, one based on an ethological and the other on a learning perspective.

Attachment According to Ethologists. As pointed out in Chapter 2, John Bowlby (1969), a British psychoanalyst influenced by the ethological tradition, suggests that a process akin to *imprinting* accounts for attachment responses in human infants. In Bowlby's view, attachment behaviors have biological underpinnings that can be best understood in a Darwinian evolutionary perspective. For the human species to survive despite an extended period of infant immaturity and vulnerability, both mothers and infants were endowed with innate tendencies to be close to each other. This reciprocal bonding functioned to protect the infant from predators when humans lived in small nomadic groups.

According to Bowlby, human infants are biologically preadapted with a number of behavioral systems ready to be activated by appropriate "elicitors" or "releasers" within the environment. Thus close physical contact—especially holding, caressing, and rocking—serves to soothe and quiet a distressed, fussing infant. A human face "triggers" an infant's smile. An infant's crying literally compels attention from a caretaker. And smiles and coos accomplish much the same end. Sucking, clinging, calling, approaching, and following are other kinds of behavior that promote both contact and proximity. Hence, viewed from the evolutionary perspective, a child is genetically programmed to a social world and "in this sense is social from the beginning" (Ainsworth, Bell, and Stayton, 1974: 997). And parents, in turn, are said to be genetically predisposed to respond with behaviors that complement the infant's behaviors (Ainsworth et al., 1979). The baby's small size, distinctive body proportions, and infantile head shape apparently elicit parental caregiving (Alley, 1983).

Critics argue, however, that analogies drawn between imprinting among domestic birds or animals

The Smile as a Bonding Mechanism

A human face "triggers" an infant's smile, which in turn invites cuddling behaviors. As viewed by ethologists, a baby is genetically "equipped" with smiling as an "elictor" of caretaking behavior.

Irene Kane/Jeroboam

and attachment responses in humans only serve to confuse rather than clarify matters. The notion of critical periods (some writers prefer a milder concept, "sensitive periods") implies a rigidity in human development. Life experiences are said to have an impact on certain aspects of personality only during a limited span of time. And the notion of irreversibility implies that the effects of infantile experiences always predominate over the effects of experiences later in life. Both of these notions are controversial (Rajecki, Lamb, and Obmascher, 1978) and raise issues that will be considered later when this chapter examines the effects of social and sensory deprivation. (Also see Chapter 2.)

Attachment According to Learning Theorists. Whereas Bowlby believes that inborn mechanisms account for attachment behaviors, learning theorists attribute attachment to socialization processes. According to psychologists like Robert R. Sears (1963, 1972), Jacob L. Gewirtz (1972), and Sidney W. Bijou and Donald M. Baer (1965), the mother is initially a *neutral* stimulus for her child. She comes to take on rewarding properties, however, as she feeds, warms, dries, and snuggles her baby and otherwise reduces the infant's pain and discomfort. Since the mother is associated with the satisfaction of the infant's needs, she acquires *secondary reinforcing* properties—her mere physical presence (her talking, smiling, and gestures of affection) becomes valued in its own right. Thus according to learning theorists, the child comes to acquire a need for the presence of the mother. In brief, attachment develops.

Learning theorists stress that the attachment process is a two-way street. The mother also finds gratification in her ability to terminate the child's piercing cries and with it to allay her own discomfort that is associated with the nerve-wracking sound. Further, infants reward their caretakers with smiles and coos. Thus, as viewed by learning theorists, the socialization process is reciprocal and derives from a mutually satisfying and reinforcing relationship.

Smiling

Both ethologists and learning theorists stress the important part that infant smiling plays in the attachment process. Harriet L. Rheingold (1969*a*: 784) captures its social significance:

> As aversive as the cry is to hear, just so rewarding is the smile to behold. It has a gentling and relaxing effect on the beholder that causes him to smile in turn. Its effect upon the caretaker cannot be exaggerated. Parents universally report that with the smile the baby now becomes "human." With the smile, too, he begins to count as a person, to take his place as an individual in the family group, and to acquire a personality in their eyes. Furthermore, mothers spontaneously confide that the smile of the baby makes his care worthwhile. In short, the infant learns to use the coin of the social realm. As he grows older and becomes more competent and more discriminating, the smile of recognition appears; reserved for the caretaker, it is a gleeful response, accompanied by vocalizations and embraces.

Developmental psychologists commonly identify three phases of smiling through which infants pass during their first year of life (Wolff, 1963; Gewirtz, 1965). At first babies engage in *spontaneous,* or *reflexive, smiling*. The smiling is involuntary and unlearned. It does not occur as a response to any clearly identifiable social stimulus. Indeed, it most typically appears during sleep and drowsiness (Wolff, 1963; Emde and Koenig, 1969). Such smiles are fleeting and incomplete, resembling a grimace. They also lack the crinkling effect at the corners of the eyes which characterizes later smiling. An old wives' tale attributes this early form of smiling to "gas." However, there is no systematic evidence in support of the claim.

The second phase, that of *nonselective social smiling,* begins between two and eight weeks of age. Mouth movements broaden, the infant's eyes crinkle, and the baby typically smiles when it is alert and bright-eyed. The stimulus that most often produces a smile is a human face or voice (especially a high-pitched one). It is not unusual for infants to stop crying or sucking for a moment and to respond with a full-fledged smile when they hear the sound of a human voice.

At five or six months of age, babies enter the stage of *selective social smiling*. Indeed, even earlier—by the end of an infant's third month—general social smiling begins to diminish and the child increasingly comes to smile only for caretakers (Ambrose, 1961).

Smiling occurs in newborn babies and those less than a month of age in the absence of external stimulation and learning experiences. Blind infants, for instance, begin to smile at much the same time and in much the same fashion as sighted babies do (Freedman, 1974). This lends support to the argument of ethologists that infants are genetically equipped and preadapted to give smiling responses.

Research also suggests, however, that environmental reinforcers become progressively more important after the first month (Lewis, 1969). And research by Jacob L. Gewirtz (1965) reveals that infants reared in institutional settings are slower than home-reared infants to develop strong smiling responses. Further, institutionally raised children show a rapid drop in their smiling reactions. Gewirtz attributes these differences between home- and institutionally raised children to differences in the amount of adult reinforcement of smiling behavior. In other experiments, Barbara C. Etzel and Gewirtz (1967) found that reinforcing infant smiles with nods, talk, and smiles—and discouraging crying, frowning, and fussing with expressionless faces—makes for "smiley" babies.

Stranger Wariness and Stranger Anxiety

Not only do infants become more discriminating about the persons they smile at, but many also show an increasing wariness of strangers (Sroufe, 1977). Various investigators have observed that **stranger anxiety** appears in some infants during the second six months of life. Generally it begins around the eighth month and becomes more prevalent by the tenth (Schaffer and Emerson, 1964; Morgan and Ricciuti, 1969; Waters, Matas, and Sroufe, 1975). Further, Gordon W. Bronson (1972) finds that some infants at three and four months of age stare fixedly at a strange person, and occasionally this prolonged inspection leads to crying.

A decade ago psychologists generally took it for granted that "fear of the stranger" was a developmental milestone that occurred in normal children. However, Harriet L. Rheingold and Carol O. Eckerman (1973) have since shown that even infants ten to twelve months old do not invariably fear unfamiliar people. Indeed, a more common reaction is one of acceptance and friendly overtures. Further, mothers show significantly more "wary" behaviors than their infants do. Clearly, subtle negative behaviors on the approach of an unfamiliar person are not a response unique to infants. Hence an infant's wariness toward strangers may simply reflect the fact that it is becoming an increasingly sophisticated participant in human interaction (Kaltenbach, Weinraub, and Fullard, 1980).

Developmental psychologists are finding that the setting in which children encounter a stranger plays an important part in their response (Corter, 1973; Greenberg, Hillman, and Grice, 1973; Brookhart and Hock, 1976; Skarin, 1977). It appears that infants are both attracted to and wary of novel objects. The situation does much to determine which reaction will be activated (Eckerman and Whatley, 1975; Waters, Matas, and Sroufe, 1975; Ross and Goldman, 1977).

Studies have shown that a number of factors influence the responses that infants between six and twelve months of age make to unfamiliar persons. First, they show the greatest amount of stranger anxiety when their mothers are not present and the least amount when their mothers hold them (Morgan and Ricciuti, 1969; Greenberg, Hillman, and Grice, 1973). Second, they show fear when an unfamiliar adult comes near them and attempts to pick them up or take them from their mothers' arms (Morgan and Ricciuti, 1969; Bronson, 1972). Friendly responses are more likely if infants are given ample time to "warm up" to a friendly stranger (Rheingold and Eckerman, 1973; Trause, 1977; Bretherton, Stolberg, and Kreye, 1981). Third, infants are more likely to seek out strangers and maintain contact with them in the absence of their mothers if they are in unfamiliar surroundings. Apparently, the stranger is the most comforting object available in an alien environment (Brookhart and Hock, 1976). And fourth, infants are more likely to react positively to a child than to an adult stranger (Greenberg, Hillman, and Grice, 1973).

Research suggests that the mother's presence is also important for most babies if they are to explore new and strange surroundings (Rheingold, 1969*a*; Ainsworth and Bell, 1970). Children typically use the mother as "a secure base" from which they can venture forth. The presence of the mother encourages a child to investigate new toys or an adjoining room. In contrast, her absence has the opposite effect and serves to curtail the child's exploratory behavior.

THE SIGNIFICANCE OF EARLY SOCIAL EXPERIENCE

During the 1930s and 1940s, studies by Margaret A. Ribble (1943), René Spitz (1945, 1946), and William

Goldfarb (1945) did much to draw both scientific and humanitarian attention to the problems of homeless and neglected children. This work popularized the concept of **maternal deprivation**—the view that the absence of normal mothering can result in psychological damage and physical deterioration in children. In the intervening decades, clinical and behavioral scientists have come to recognize that "maternal deprivation" is actually a catchall term. It encompasses many conditions, including insufficient sensory stimulation, the failure to form attachment bonds, the disruption of attachment bonds, unstable or rejecting mothering, inadequate intellectual stimulation, and even malnutrition (Rutter, 1974, 1979; Yarrow, Rubenstein, and Pedersen, 1975). Since the term "maternal deprivation" has become so highly charged and a synonym for all that is destructive in child care, most researchers prefer to avoid it and use terms that refer to specific conditions, such as *social deprivation* and *sensory deprivation.*

Institutionalized Children

It long has been recognized that children raised in orphanages, foundling homes, and other institutional settings generally do not flourish compared with children reared by their parents in home surroundings. Records of the Dublin Foundling Home reveal, for instance, that between 1775 and 1800 only 45 of the 10,272 children admitted survived (Kessen, 1965). Even during the twentieth century one of the major foundling homes in Germany had a mortality rate higher than 70 percent for infants under one year of age (Spitz, 1945). And in 1915 James H. M. Knox, Jr., of the Johns Hopkins Hospital noted that in spite of adequate physical care, 90 percent of the infants in Baltimore orphanages and foundling homes died within a year of admission (Gardner, 1972).

The first large-scale study of infants raised in an institutional setting was undertaken by René Spitz (1945, 1946), an Austrian psychoanalytic physician. He compared infants who had been reared in a foundling home during the first year of life with infants reared in a prison nursery. In the foundling home, the overworked nursing personnel provided the babies with good physical care but little or no individual contact and attention. By contrast, babies in the prison nursery spent most of their time with their mothers, receiving individual care and love.

Spitz found that the infants raised by their own mothers made considerably better progress by all standards of development. The foundling home infants showed severe mental and motor retardation. Despite impeccable hygiene, they were especially susceptible to infection and illness (37 percent died in the two-year period). Spitz interpreted his results as demonstrating that the impairment of the mother-child relationship during the first year of life inflicts permanent damage on an infant.

William Goldfarb (1945, 1947, 1949) came to a somewhat similar conclusion. He compared the development of two groups of children when they were between ten and fourteen years of age. One group had lived for a little more than three years in a foundling home before being placed in foster homes. The other group had been reared wholly in foster homes (except for a short period early in their lives). Goldfarb found that compared with the children who had been reared in foster homes, the children who had spent their early years in the foundling institution were socially immature, apprehensive, less able to inhibit deviant behavior, deficient in intellectual and language development, and insatiable in their need for affection (although they were unable to form genuine social bonds). Goldfarb blamed these intellectual and emotional scars on the absence of adequate mothering during the children's first three years.

A third study, by Wayne Dennis (1973), also emphasizes the retarding effects of institutional life on infants. However, Dennis concluded that the source of the difficulty was not the absence of a mother-child tie but the absence of adequate cognitive experiences. For a period in the 1950s and again in the 1960s, Dennis studied children at the Crèche, a foundling home in Beirut, Lebanon. Because of a staff shortage at the home, infants were taken from their cribs only to be bathed or changed. Two- and three-year-old children spent most of their time in cribs and playpens. They had little or no opportunity to walk or creep about on the floor. It is not surprising, therefore, that infants under one year of age could not sit alone, crawl, or creep and that children two years of age could not walk.

Intelligence tests were administered to the children at the Crèche when they were two years old. The children had an average IQ score of 53 (a score that classed them as mentally deficient). However, foundlings who were adopted *within* the first two years of life improved rapidly in their capabilities. By the age of four, these children had attained an IQ of approx-

Institutionalized Children
Children in institutionalized environments, such as this resettlement camp in Nicaragua, often lack the individual attention and care, as well as the adequate cognitive experiences, so essential for healthy development.
Marcelo Montecino/Picture Group

imately 100. Although the test scores of those adopted *after* they were two years old increased beyond the mean score of 53 that they had registered at adoption, they retained the absolute deficiency in mental age they had shown at that time. (For instance, those adopted at age six were already three years retarded, so that at age fifteen they had an average mental age of only twelve.) Thus Dennis concluded that after two years of age, the effects of deprivation caused by inadequate cognitive experience are irreversible.

The Spitz, Goldfarb, and Dennis studies have been widely criticized for faulty design and interpretation (Casler, 1961; Biehler, 1976). Samuel R. Pinneau (1955) points out that much of the serious decline observed in the foundling home children studied by Spitz had occurred even before they had been separated from their mothers. And in all three studies, some of the institutionalized children had been adopted or placed in foster homes during the first year. This raises the question of whether the children who went unadopted or unplaced were in some way less desirable and hence unrepresentative. Such children had been twice screened and twice rejected: first, their parents would not or could not establish a home for them; and, second, for one reason or another, potential foster parents had selected other children instead of them (Jersild, Telford, and Sawrey, 1975).

The results of the Spitz and Goldfarb studies were published in the 1940s. Since then, researchers have demonstrated that physical contact and sensory stimulation serve to improve the sensorimotor functioning of children in institutionalized settings (Rheingold, 1961; Skeels, 1966; White, 1969; Saltz, 1973). Indeed, even a small amount of extra handling highlights the value of "enrichment," at least over the short term. And, as pointed out in Chapter 2, children show greater resilience than child psychologists believed was the case only a few decades ago. But it is important to note that, as in most other matters, children differ. Some show greater vulnerability to deprivation experiences than others do (Schaffer, 1966; Rutter, 1974; Langmeier and Matějček, 1974). Overall, the research on institutionalized infants has given encouragement to the trends toward earlier adoption and the use of foster homes rather than institutions.

Sensory Stimulation and Deprivation

Both human and animal studies have confirmed the general premise that under some circumstances extreme deprivation in early life can retard development and distort personality. Through the years, however, controversy has raged over the question of whether these disabilities are caused by lack of sensory stimulation or by lack of "mother love." A number of psychologists, the most prominent of whom is Lawrence Casler (1961, 1967), have challenged the belief that a warm, affectionate relationship with the mother is essential or even important for healthy development. These psychologists argue that the crucial factors are the degree of sensory stimulation and the range of experiences provided for the child. Others, especially psychologists influenced by the Freudian psychoanalytic tradition, insist instead that the lack of intimate interpersonal relationships is responsible for the impairment observed in institutionalized children (Ainsworth, 1962).

In many respects, however, this is a pseudocontroversy. The underlying feelings of warmth or aversion that mothers have toward their children are communicated largely through their behavior—for instance, whether or not they talk to their infants, touch and caress them, hold them, carry them about, and otherwise provide them with sensory stimulation. But the controversy has been beneficial in that it has called attention to the great variety of environmental factors that influence a child's development (Rutter, 1979).

In particular, the controversy has stimulated research, including a valuable study by Leon Yarrow, Judith L. Rubenstein, and Frank A. Pedersen (1975). These investigators closely observed forty-one five-month-old babies in their home settings. They found that sweeping descriptions of environments as "depriving" or "stimulating" are oversimplified. According to their report, visual and auditory stimulation of the infants promoted social responsiveness but had no effect on development in other areas. In contrast, kinesthetic stimulation (rocking, jiggling, and carrying the child about the home) was related to goal-directedness (for instance, the persistence shown by the baby in reaching for an object or attempting to manipulate it). Further, Yarrow, Rubenstein, and Pedersen found that there was little relationship between social and inanimate stimulation. Whereas human stimulation affected a child's social responsiveness and language development, inanimate stimulation (provided by toys, mobiles, and other objects) affected exploratory behavior. In sum, the issue of environmental influences is considerably more complex than advocates of either sensory stimulation or mother love suggest.

Still another dimension may be involved in cases of extreme deprivation—the hormonal. Researchers at Duke University found that normal cell growth may depend on regular doses of fondling and touching (Kuhn, Bulter, and Schamberg, 1978). In the course of studying the ability of infant rats to metabolize polyamines (chemicals involved in cell growth), the investigators initially encountered confusing and frustrating results. At first they thought the problem lay in their inadequate control of the pups' nutrition or temperature. Then they stumbled on the real source of the difficulty. Less than an hour after a pup is removed from its mother's care, its pituitary gland starts secreting less growth hormone. When the pup

Importance of Sensory Stimulation

Children benefit from a rich sensory environment at all ages. Even young infants require stimulating settings for maximum cognitive development.

Gabor Demjen/Stock, Boston

is returned to its mother and receives licking and touching from her (nursing is not necessary), the polyamines return to normal levels. Unfortunately, we do not know whether comparable processes operate in human infants.

Freudian Child-Rearing Variables

As discussed in Chapter 2, Sigmund Freud and the psychoanalytic school have stressed the part that early experience plays in fashioning the adult personality. Central to Freud's thinking was the idea that adult neurosis has its roots in childhood conflicts associated with the meeting of instinctual needs (sucking, expelling urine and feces, and masturbation). Over the past sixty years Freudian thinking has had an important influence on child-rearing practices in the United States. Many pediatricians, clinical psychologists, and family counselors have accepted major tenets of Freudian theory, especially as popularized by Dr. Benjamin Spock. (Spock's all-time best-selling *Baby and Child Care* first appeared in 1946 and has since gone through multiple paperback revisions and editions.)

According to the Freudians, the systems of infant care that produce emotionally healthy personalities include breast feeding, a prolonged period of nursing, gradual weaning, a self-demand nursing schedule, delayed and patient bowel and bladder training, and freedom from punishment. Research, however, has offered little or no support for these premises. In an extensive study of child-rearing practices, William H. Sewell and Paul H. Mussen (1952) found no tie between the type of feeding schoolchildren had received as infants and their oral symptoms such as nail biting, thumb sucking, and stuttering. Likewise, a longitudinal study carried out by M. I. Heinstein (1963) revealed no significant differences in the later behavior of bottle-fed and breast-fed babies.

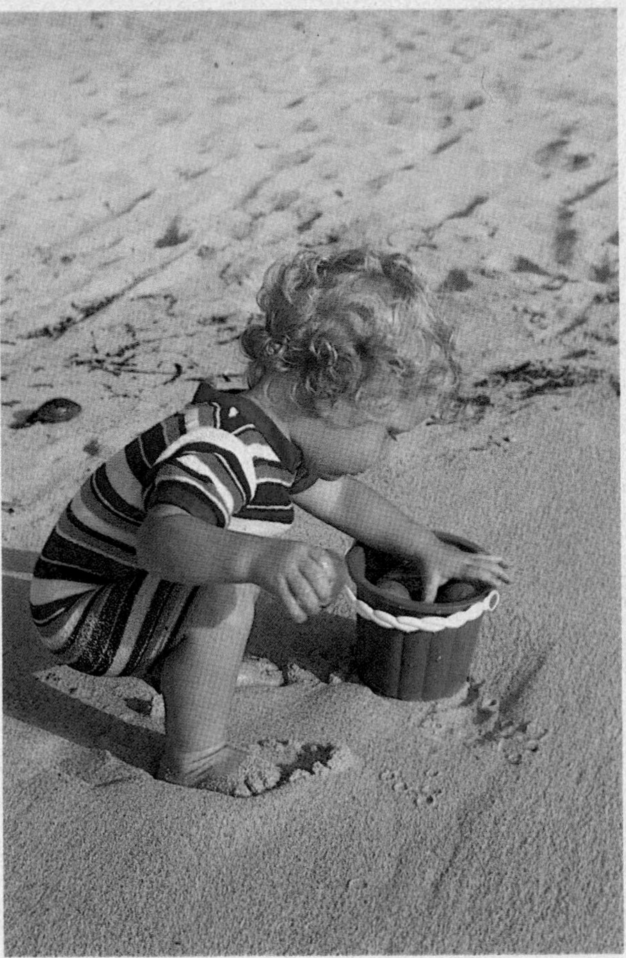

Freudian Child-Rearing Variables
Freud believed that adult neurosis has its roots in childhood conflicts. Research has shown, however, that children are not as psychologically fragile and vulnerable as Freud believed and that emotionally healthy personalities do not depend on Freudian child-rearing practices.
Elizabeth V. Gemmette

THE IMPACT OF POVERTY

There was an old woman who lived in a shoe,
She had so many children she didn't know what
to do,
She gave them some broth without any bread;
She whipped them all soundly and sent them to bed.

Mother Goose rhyme, 1784

Now, they'll come back at me, oh, do they, with first one question and then another, until I don't know what to say, and I tell them to stop. Sometimes I have to hit them, yes sir, I'll admit it. They'll be asking about why, why, why, and I don't have the answers and I'm tired out, and I figure sooner or later they'll have to stop asking and just be glad they're alive.

A migrant worker father, interviewed by Robert Coles in *Uprooted Children* (New York: Harper & Row, 1970), p. 30.

Research has also demonstrated that other variables emphasized in psychoanalytic literature, including those associated with bladder and bowel training, are not related to later personality characteristics (Sewell, 1952; Behrens, 1954; Schaffer and Emerson, 1964). It is now generally conceded that such practices in themselves have few demonstrable effects on later development. Children are not the psychologically fragile and vulnerable beings depicted by the Freudians (Skolnick, 1978). They are considerably more resilient and less easily damaged by traumatic events and emotional stress than was once thought to be true (see Chapters 2 and 10). Nor can parents expect to inoculate their children with love against future misfortune, misery, and psychopathology. And contrary to Freudian expectation, many people who had nurturant and devoted parents during their early years feel unloved as young adults (Kagan, 1979).

The Role of the Father

When men abandon the upbringing of their children to their wives, a loss is suffered by everyone, but perhaps most of all by themselves. For what they lose is the possibility of growth in themselves for being human, which the stimulation of bringing up one's children gives.

—ASHLEY MONTAGU

In keeping with the strong influence that the psychoanalytic tradition has had on American life, researchers have focused almost exclusively on the mother-child tie (see the boxed insert on page 221, for example). At the same time, the role of the father has been largely ignored. Over the past decade, however, all this has changed. We have seen something

The Father as a Caretaker

Western society has long assumed that child care and rearing is "women's work." The women's liberation movement has helped break this tradition, and in so doing it has contributed to the benefit and enrichment of both father and child.

Cary Wolinsky/Stock, Boston

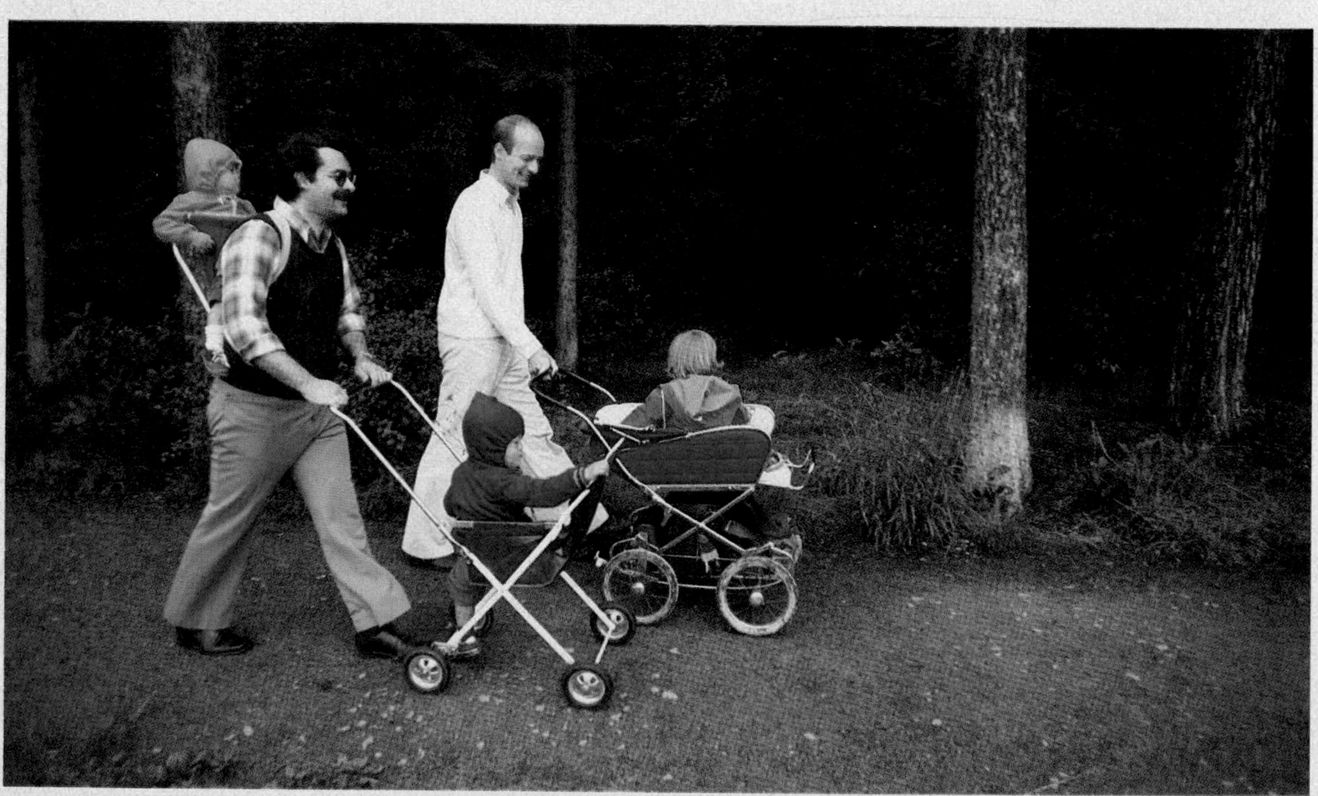

EFFECTIVE MOTHERING

It is the duty of society to evolve adults fit for children to live with.

LILLIEN J. MARTIN

Since 1965 Burton L. White and his colleagues have been studying the development of overall competence in children (White and Watts, 1973). The goal of the research, christened the Harvard Preschool Project, has been to find ways to optimize human development. This work has convinced White that the mother's relationship with her child, especially during the second year of life, is the most powerful formative factor in the child's development.

The Harvard researchers intensively studied the mother-child interactions of thirty-one children with different competence ratings. White (1973: 242) concluded that a number of child-rearing practices appear to foster competence:

> [The effective mothers] talk a great deal to their children. . . . They make them feel as though whatever they are doing is usually interesting. They provide access to many objects and diverse situations. They lead the child to believe that he can expect help and encouragement most, but *not all* the time. They demonstrate and explain things to the child, but mostly on the child's instigation rather than their own. . . . They are secure enough to say "no" to the child from time to time without seeming to fear that the child will not love them. They are imaginative, so that they make interesting associations and suggestions to the child when opportunities present themselves. They very skillfully and naturally strengthen the child's intrinsic motivation to learn. They also give him a sense of task orientation, a notion that it is desirable to do things well and completely. They make the child feel secure.

One finding of considerable interest was that the most effective mothers did not devote the bulk of their day to child rearing. They were busy women and in some cases held part-time jobs. Instead of giving the children all of their time, these effective mothers tried to create an environment compatible with the burgeoning curiosity of their toddlers. They recognized that an infant and a spotless, meticulously kept home are incompatible. Their children had access to small, manipulable, visually detailed objects (toys, plastic refrigerator containers, empty milk cartons, old shoes, magazines, and the like) and to materials that help to develop motor skills (scooters, tricycles, and so forth). Also, the effective mothers did not necessarily drop what they were doing to respond to their toddlers' requests. If they were busy they said so, giving the child a small but realistic taste of things to come in the larger world. Overall, children whose mothers expected them to learn very little developed more slowly than children whose mothers expected them to begin learning early in life.

of a revolution in the thinking of child developmentalists about the importance of fathers in the development of young children (Parke, 1979; Pedersen, 1980, Lamb, 1981; Biller, 1982). Moreover, being a father often makes a major contribution to a man's self-concept, personality functioning, and overall satisfaction with life (Levinson et al., 1978).

The historic neglect of the father's role in child rearing has been linked with the notion that women are somehow more inclined toward child care and parenting than men are. It has been speculated that biological predeterminers contribute to a more nurturant, "maternal" disposition in women and a more instrumental, "paternal" disposition in men (Erikson, 1964*b*; Harlow, 1971; Rossi, 1977). Others suggest that the differences between men and women are products of the distinct, socially defined roles assumed by mothers and fathers (Parsons, 1955).

Evidence supporting the view that child care is more compatible with the "natural" inclinations of one sex rather than the other is at best very limited (Berman, 1980). If anything, the physiological responses that human beings display to infant coos, cries, and other signals seems to be *species specific* (genetically preprogrammed within human organisms) and not sex specific (Frodi and Lamb, 1978). But it is also true that our culture prepares females for parenting to a far greater extent than it does males. Simultaneously, women in the Western world have traditionally been expected to be the ones to assume primary responsibility for child care. Nonetheless, societies throughout the world show considerable variation in their definitions of the parenting roles. For instance, in a survey of 141 societies, fathers in 45 societies (32 percent) maintained a "regular, close" or "frequent, close" proximity with the infant. At the other extreme, in 33 societies (23 percent), fathers exhibited no or rare instances of close proximity (Crano and Aronoff, 1978).

Increasingly, researchers are concluding that men have at least the potential to be as good caretakers of children as women are. Ross D. Parke and his colleagues (Parke and Sawin, 1977; Parke, 1979) have observed the behavior of both middle-class and lower-class parents of newborns on hospital maternity wards. Fathers are just as responsive as mothers to their infants' vocalizations and movements. Fathers touch, look at, talk to, rock, and kiss their babies in much the same fashion as mothers do. However, in response to their infants' vocalizations, fathers are more likely than mothers to increase their vocalization rate; mothers, in contrast, are more likely to react with touching. And fathers, when alone with their infants, are as protective, giving, and stimulating as mothers. In fact, fathers are more likely than mothers to hold their babies and to look at them. Mothers exceed fathers in only one kind of stimulation—they smile at their babies more.

Parke and his associates have measured the amount of milk that is left over in a baby's bottle after feeding time. Babies drink virtually the same amount of milk when fathers do the feeding as when mothers do. Further, fathers are equally competent in correctly reading subtle changes in infants' behavior and reacting to them. Fathers respond to such distress signs as sneezing, coughing, or spitting up just as quickly as mothers do. At these times, fathers (like mothers) momentarily cease feeding, look more closely to check for any problems, and talk to the baby. However, fathers tend to leave child care to their wives when both parents are present.

All of this is not to say that mothers and fathers are interchangeable. Each makes his or her own unique contribution to the care and development of children. Research suggests that the mother-child and father-child relationships may well be qualitatively different and may have a different influence on a child's development (Lynn, 1974; Lamb, 1975, 1977*a*, 1981; Biller, 1982). Michael E. Lamb (1977*a*) finds, for instance, that mothers most often hold babies to perform caretaking functions, while fathers most often hold babies to play with them. Indeed, according to some studies, fathers spend four to five times as much time playing with their infants as in caring for them—diapering them, feeding them, washing them, and the like. And Henry B. Biller (1974, 1976) notes that whereas mothers are more likely to inhibit their children's exploration of the environment, fathers encourage curiosity and challenge their children to attempt new cognitive and motor activities.

Researchers similarly find that American mothers play more verbal games with their babies. The games are characterized by "turn-taking" dialogues composed of rapidly alternating bursts of words or cooing and brief pauses. Mothers also play more conventional games, such as peekaboo. In contrast, fathers play more physical games with their children. They tend to touch their infants in rhythmic tapping patterns. And they also play more rough-and-tumble games, such as tossing the baby in the air (Yogman et al., 1977; Parke, 1979; Russell, 1982). It should not be concluded that either type of parental stimulation is superior to the other. They are simply different. Each parent affords the child somewhat different kinds of experiences. However, many of these gender differences in play styles are not found among Swedish fathers and mothers (Lamb et al., 1982).

Fathers are important in still another respect. Studies show that a mother performs better in the parenting role when the father provides her with emotional support and encouragement (Pedersen, 1980; Belsky, 1981). The man who gives warmth, love, and ego gratification to his wife helps her feel good about herself, and she is then more likely to pass on these feelings to their child. And the father who shares household responsibilities and infant caretaking tasks permits the mother to have more time for playful and other noncaretaking activities. Finally, the father's attitudes and behaviors toward his child affect the mother's attitudes toward the child (Parke, 1979).

Research seems to indicate that boys are more affected by the absence of a father than girls are (Biller, 1982; Levy-Shiff, 1982). In comparison with other boys, boys from fatherless homes exhibit less well-internalized standards of moral judgment. They tend to evaluate the seriousness of misbehavior according to the probability of detection or punishment rather than in terms of interpersonal relations and social responsibility (Hoffman, 1971).

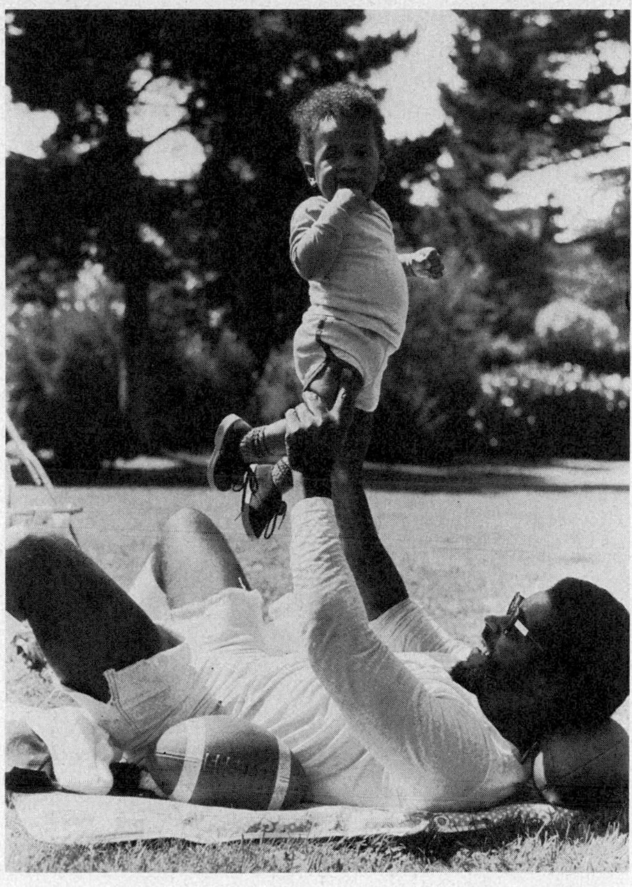

Paternal Play

Research has shown that while American mothers tend to play more conventional games with their children, fathers play more physical ones. Each kind of play exposes the child to a different experience.

Suzanne Arms/Jeroboam

Research data also reveal that the absence of a positive father-son relationship impairs a boy's overall academic achievement and his IQ test performance (Carlsmith, 1964; Biller, 1971; Epstein and Radin, 1975). The extent of the impairment is greater the younger the child when he lost his father and the longer the father has been absent (Carlsmith, 1964; Blanchard and Biller, 1971). Moreover, one of the most consistently reported effects of the father's absence on a boy is a deterioration in school performance (Lamb, 1981). And the mother's remarriage, especially if it occurs early in the child's life, appears to be associated with an improvement in intellectual performance (Lessing, Zagorin, and Nelson, 1970; Santrock, 1972).

It should be noted, however, that the presence of the father is no guarantee of adequate fathering. The quality of the father-child relationship seems to be more important than the father's mere physical tenancy (Lamb, 1981). Perhaps in the final analysis the matter is not so much one of fathering or mothering as one of parenting.

The important complementary role of the father points up the need for modern societies to give wider thought and support to paternity leaves (Parke and Sawin, 1977). In the past decade, Sweden has launched a major effort to involve fathers more actively in the rearing of their children. It has extended to fathers most of the child-care benefits—such as time off at nearly full pay—that it extends to mothers. According to Sweden's Ministry for Social Affairs, about 10 to 12 percent of eligible fathers now take paternity leave. Another aspect of the program allows parents of preschoolers to work shortened weeks at little loss in pay. Parents are also given time off to care for sick children.

Multiple Mothering

In the United States the preferred arrangement for raising children is the nuclear family, which consists of two parents and their children. The view that mothering should be provided by one figure has been celebrated and extolled by most professionals as the key to good mental health (Bowlby, 1969). Yet this is a culture-bound perspective, for children throughout the world are successfully reared in situations of **multiple mothering**—an arrangement in which responsibility for a child's care is dispersed among several people.

In some cases one major mother figure shares mothering with a variety of mother surrogates, including aunts, grandmothers, older cousins, nonkin neighbors, or co-wives. Consider, for example, the diffused nurturance given a child among the Ifaluk of Micronesia (Spiro, 1947: 89–97):

> For the Westerner, the amount of handling the infant receives is almost fantastic. The infant, particularly after it can crawl, is never allowed to remain in the arms of one person. In the course of a half hour conversation, the baby might change hands ten times, being passed from one person to another. . . . The adults, as well as the older children, love to fondle the babies and to play with them, with the result that the infant does not stay with one person very long. . . . Should an infant cry, it is immediately picked up in an adult's arms, cuddled,

> consoled or fed. . . . There is little distinction between one's own relatives and "strangers." . . . If he needs something anyone will try to satisfy his need. Every house is open to him and he never has to learn that some houses are different from others.

Another fascinating approach to child care is found in the Israeli agricultural settlements that have a collective form of social and economic life (termed *kibbutzim*). From early infancy, children are reared in a nursery with other children by two or three professional caretakers. Their own mothers visit them regularly and are primarily responsible for meeting their children's affectional needs. The burden of discipline and punishment falls primarily upon the professional caretakers (Devereux et al., 1974). Despite this arrangement of "concomitant mothering," systematic observation, testing, and clinical assessment have demonstrated that kibbutz children are within the normal range in intelligence, motor development, mental health, and social adjustment (Kohen-Raz, 1968; Moyles and Wolins, 1971; Maccoby and Feldman, 1972; Regev, Beit-Hallahmi, and Sharabany, 1980).

Child Day-Care Centers

More than half of American mothers of preschool children are in the work force (compared with 14 percent in 1950 and 29 percent in 1970). This trend, and the increase in single-parent families, has given considerable impetus to the child day-care movement in the United States. Many of the centers are operated by churches (Austin, 1982). Still, licensed day-care facilities are currently available for fewer than one out of six of the children with working mothers. According to 1982 figures of the Census Bureau, of 5.1 million women with jobs and children under five years of age, 15 percent sent their children to group care centers, 40 percent took them to someone else's home, 31 percent arranged for care in their home, and 14 percent arranged for children to be watched by fathers (Schreiner, 1983).

Sharply divergent views exist among Americans regarding the desirability of day care. For that matter, experts in child development are themselves in disagreement. Some worry that day care may do serious emotional and psychological damage to children—damage that may not show up until the teen or adult years. Others say that while good quality day care does not help children, it does not hurt them either. And still others applaud day care as liberating for the mother and enriching for the child. In any event, modern societies are increasingly confronting this question: how are we to manage the successful care and rearing of future generations of children when parents spend a substantial portion of time at work away from home?

One of those who is deeply concerned about the possible harmful effects of day care is Selma Fraiberg, a child psychoanalyst in the department of psychiatry at the University of Michigan Medical School. In her book, *Every Child's Birthright* (1977), Fraiberg points out that a child must share the attention of a day-care worker with other youngsters. Add to this vacations and job turnover, and a child ends up with no one special person to be close to. Even under the best of circumstances, day-care workers are not equally fond of all children. Indeed, Fraiberg and other child psychologists note that problem children are rarely the favorites of overburdened workers, yet these are usually the children who need love the most.

Fraiberg believes that children require continuity, stability, and predictability of care. She says that they need loving persons who are with them day after day. Like other followers of the psychoanalytic tradition, Fraiberg insists that a child's emotional breadth and depth and capacity to love are derived from the experience of love in the early years. Only the rare nonfamily member can give to a child the magnitude of love and understanding, and the permanence of attachment that are essential. Fraiberg suggests that federal and state policy should encourage women with young children to stay home instead of working and that government should find other public-sponsored ways to supplement the incomes of these families.

Jerome Kagan, the noted Harvard developmental psychologist, used to take a position quite similar to that of Fraiberg. But more recently he has reversed his opposition to day care on the basis of research he undertook with Richard B. Kearsley and Philip R. Zelazo (1978). Kagan and his associates set up a day-care facility for thirty-three children from middle- and working-class homes in the South End of Boston. The children entered the center at around four months of age and left it at twenty-nine months. The caretakers were carefully selected on the basis of their nurturing qualities, and the center afforded a ratio of one worker for each three or four children.

High-Quality Day Care

We would like to know considerably more than we currently do regarding the long-term effects of day care upon children, parents, and society. However, most authorities agree that parents can rest assured that high-quality day care is an acceptable alternative to home care.

Patrick Reddy

Like other investigators of day care, Kagan and his associates compared the infants placed in day-care facilities with home-reared children of the same age, social class, and ethnic background. The researchers found that the day-care children were not much different—intellectually, emotionally, or socially—from their home-raised counterparts. And the day-care children were neither more nor less attached to their mothers than the other children. However, the home-raised youngsters were somewhat more socially advanced at twenty-nine months of age than the day-care children.

Jay Belsky and Laurence D. Steinberg (1978) have made a careful survey of the day-care research conducted over the past decade. They approached this work with great caution, noting in particular that most of the studies on day care have been undertaken in university-based or university-connected centers. Such centers have high staff-child ratios and well-designed programs directed at fostering the children's cognitive, emotional, and social development. Yet most of the day care currently available to North American parents is not of this type and quality (Vaughn et al., 1980). Indeed, the vast majority of American parents cannot afford to buy quality day care at full market prices. The problem is aggravated by the decline in federal subsidies for child care. Hence parents must often settle for whatever child care they can find.

There is an additional problem associated with low-quality day-care facilities. They commonly function as networks for spreading a variety of diseases, particularly hepatitis A, diarrhea, dysentery, and other intestinal illnesses. Although day-care centers often serve more meals than a restaurant on a given day, their workers typically have little training in handling food and display tolerance toward lapses in sanitary routines. And since children enter and leave many of the centers in an erratic pattern, there is considerable opportunity for the mixing of infected and susceptible children.

Belsky and Steinberg note that most researchers have concluded that the day-care experience neither improves nor impairs most children's intellectual development. For economically disadvantaged children, however, the day-care experience can lessen the decline in IQ scores that typically takes place among children from "high-risk" environments. Further, high-quality day care is not disruptive of children's emotional bonds with their mothers. Finally, day care increases the degree to which children interact, both positively and negatively, with peers.

Some evidence suggests that children enrolled in day care for extended periods of time show increased aggression toward peers and adults and decreased cooperation with adults. But this may be a culture-bound outcome. Studies of peer group socialization in Israel, the USSR, and a number of other contemporary societies reveal quite different outcomes. In brief, the American peer group may simply predispose children toward greater aggressiveness, impulsiveness, and egocentrism.

We would like solid answers to questions regarding

the effects of day care on children. But Belsky and Steinberg (1978: 946) conclude their review of the literature with this observation:

> To even say that the jury is still out on day care would be in our view both premature and naively optimistic. The fact of the matter is, quite frankly, that the majority of evidence has yet to be presented, much less subpoenaed.

They point out in addition that we know shockingly little about the impact of day care on parents, the family, and social institutions in general.

For now, perhaps the safest conclusion we can make is this: most research suggests that high-quality day care is an acceptable alternative child care arrangement (Etaugh, 1980). Children display remarkable resilience. Infants around the world are raised under a great variety of conditions; the day-care arrangement is just one of them. The effects of day care depend to some extent on the amount of time a child spends at a center and on the quality of parent-child interaction during the time that the family is together. It should also be stressed that home care, in and of itself, does not guarantee secure attachments or healthy social and emotional development.

SUMMARY

1. Humanness is a social product that arises as children interact with the significant people in their environment. Erik Erikson stresses the importance of an infant's early years in fashioning a basic trust in others, an essential foundation for successful social functioning.
2. Infants pass through three stages in the development of social responsiveness. During their first two months of life they are aroused by all parts of their environment. In the second stage, occurring around the third month, they become responsive to humans as a general class of stimuli. At about seven months of age, children enter the third stage, that of specific attachment.
3. Ethologists claim that attachment in humans occurs through a process akin to the imprinting that is encountered among some bird and animal species. Whereas ethologists look to inborn mechanisms to account for attachment behaviors, learning theorists place the entire burden on the socialization process. According to learning theorists, the mother acquires secondary reinforcing properties through satisfying the infant's primary needs.
4. Children pass through three phases in smiling during their first year of life: spontaneous, or reflexive, smiling; nonselective social smiling; and selective social smiling.
5. A good many children display stranger anxiety during the second six months of life. However, infants are both attracted to and wary of novel objects; hence the situation does much to determine which reaction will be activated.
6. Children reared in institutional settings generally do not develop well compared with children reared in home surroundings. The impairment experienced by many institutionalized children derives from conditions of social and sensory deprivation.
7. Social stimulation and sensory stimulation each make a distinct contribution to the child's development. Global characterizations of environments as "depriving" or "stimulating" are oversimplified. Various aspects of an environment have different consequences for the socialization of children.
8. Freudians stress the view that the development of emotionally healthy personalities is associated with breast feeding, a prolonged period of nursing, gradual weaning, a self-demand nursing schedule, delayed and patient bowel and bladder training, and freedom from punishment. However, research has provided little or no support for these psychoanalytic assumptions.
9. The mother-child and father-child relationships are qualitatively different and apparently have a different impact on a child's development.
10. Infants around the world are raised under a great variety of conditions. Among them are multiple mothering and child day care. Children display remarkable resilience. Research suggests that multiple mothering and high-quality day care are acceptable child care arrangements.

KEY TERMS

attachment An affectional bond that one individual forms for another and that endures across time and space.

battered child syndrome A variety of severe injuries associated with the physical abuse of a child by a caretaker: abrasions, lacerations, burns, fractures, concussions, hemorrhages, and bruises caused by a caretaker's hitting, yanking, shaking, kicking, choking, burning, or throwing a child around.

emotion The physiological changes, subjective experiences, and expressive behaviors that are involved in such feelings as love, joy, grief, and rage.

maternal deprivation The absence of normal mothering resulting in psychological damage and physical deterioration in children. Since the term "maternal deprivation" has become so highly charged and a synonym for all that is destructive in child care, most authorities prefer to avoid it and use terms that refer to specific conditions, such as "social deprivation" and "sensory deprivation."

multiple mothering An arrangement in which responsibility for a child's care is dispersed among several people. In some cases, one major mother figure shares mothering with a variety of mother surrogates.

person permanence The notion that an individual exists independently of immediate visibility.

stranger anxiety Increasing wariness of strangers shown by infants beginning around the eighth month and becoming most prevalent around the tenth month.

Part Four

Early Childhood: Two to Six

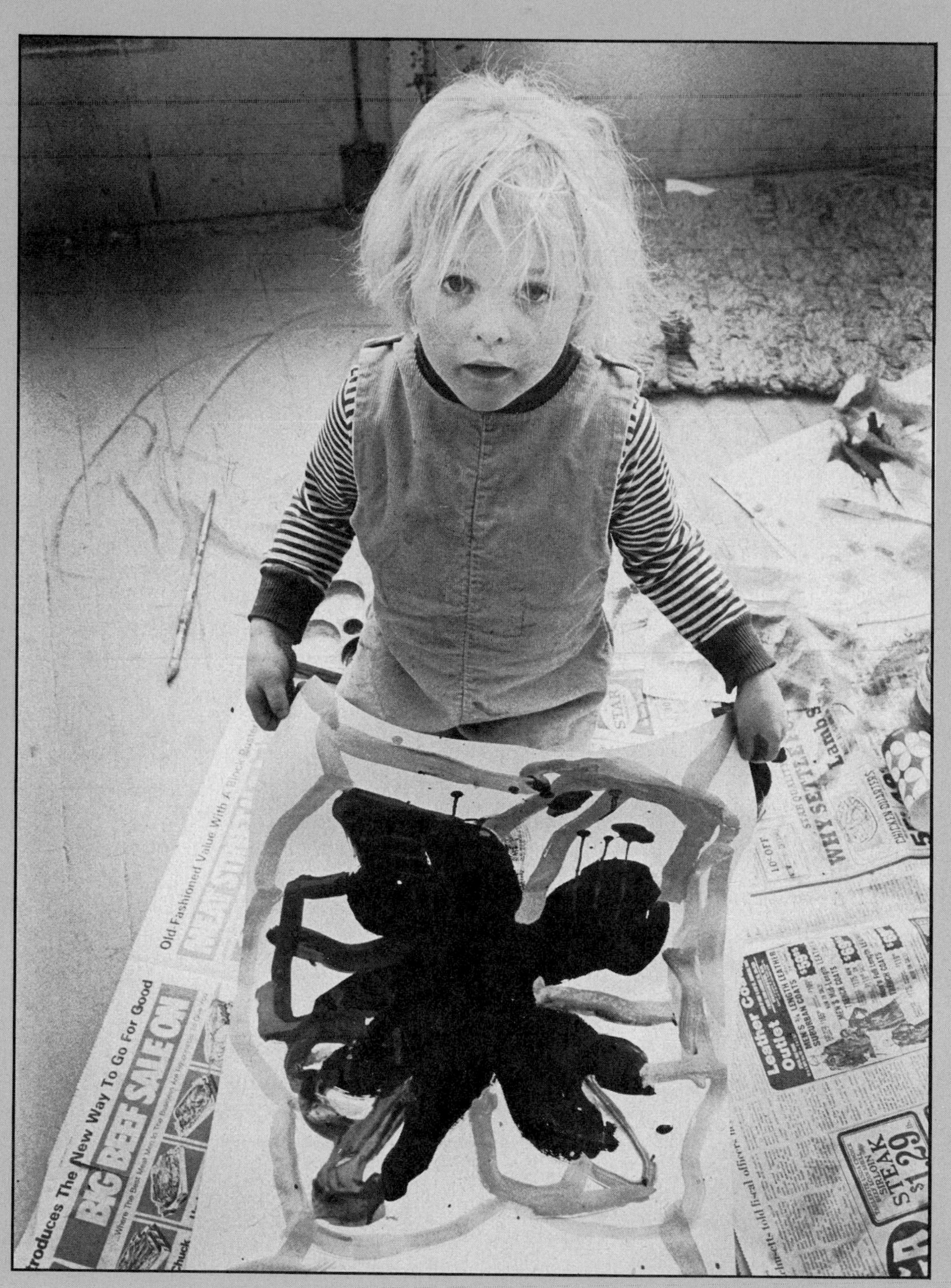

troduces The New Way To Go For Good
BIG BEEF SALE ON
Old Fashioned Value With A Block Butcher
WHY SEATTLE
Lambs
Leather Co
Outlet
SIRLOIN
STEAK
$1.29

9

Early Childhood: Expanding Competencies

COGNITIVE DEVELOPMENT
- Intelligence
- Intelligence and the Nature-Nurture Controversy
- The Early Development of Intelligence
- Causality

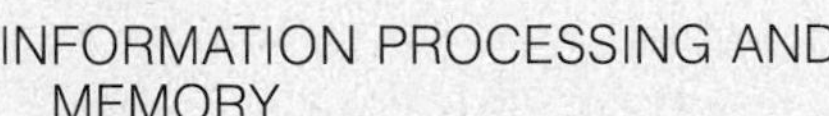

INFORMATION PROCESSING AND MEMORY
- Early Memory
- Information Processing
- Metacognition and Metamemory
- Categorizing as a Memory Strategy
- Rehearsing as a Memory Strategy

COGNITIVE FOUNDATIONS FOR SOCIAL INTERACTION
- Roles
- The Self

GENDER IDENTIFICATION
- Hormonal Influences on Gender Behaviors
- Social Influences on Gender Behaviors
- Theories Regarding the Acquisition of Gender Identities
- Mothers, Fathers, and Sex Typing

THE DEVELOPMENT OF EMOTION

Passing hence from infancy, I came to boyhood, or rather it came to me, displacing infancy.
Nor did that depart—(for whither went it?)—and yet it was no more.

—*Confessions of St. Augustine*

During the period between age two and age six, children enlarge their repertoire of behaviors. They refine their previously learned skills and evolve new ones for relating to other people and to the larger world. By doing so they become progressively integrated into the broader context of group life. And in this way the child's needs and capacities are fused with the ideas and sentiments of the culture. It is a process of psychic amalgamation, in which a child becomes human and society perpetuates itself from one generation to the next (Davis, 1949).

Simultaneously, children progressively develop as social beings in their own right. Erik Erikson (see Chapter 2) suggests that children acquire a sense of autonomy or independence as they struggle with their own conflicting needs and rebel against parental controls. These upheavals find expression in the "terrible twos," when toddlers display negativism and temper tantrums. Children come to see themselves as individuals who are separate from their parents, although still dependent on them.

During this age period, children become physically

Developing a Sense of Autonomy

In developing a sense of their own independence, children at times engage in negativism and temper tantrums. The behavior allows them to define themselves as separate individuals—distinct, bounded, and coherent beings.

Michael Weisbrot and Family

better coordinated. Walking, climbing, reaching, grasping, and releasing are no longer simply activities in their own right but rather the means for new endeavors. Their developing skills give children new ways to explore the world and to accomplish new things.

In turn, the expansion of their social and physical worlds confronts children with new developmental requirements. According to Erikson, children between three and five years old need to acquire a sense of initiative. They actively seek new opportunities for affecting the environment and in doing so achieve a sense of their own effectiveness in the world. Early childhood thus lays the cognitive and social foundations for the more complex life of the school years (see Table 9.1).

COGNITIVE DEVELOPMENT

In the preschool period, mental development is characterized by the rapid expansion of cognitive abilities. Children become more adept at obtaining information, ordering it, and using it. Gradually, these abilities evolve into the attribute called *intelligence.* Whereas sensorimotor processes largely dominate development during infancy, a significant transition occurs after eighteen months toward the more abstract processes of reasoning, inference, and problem solving. By the time children are seven years old, they have developed a diversified set of cognitive skills that are functionally related to the elements of adult intelligence.

Intelligence

Most of us share a common conception of **intelligence** as referring to a person's general problem-solving ability. As psychologist Dalbir Bindra (1976: 1) observes: "Actions of man and other creatures are said to be intelligent when they are more purposive than haphazard, more intentional than accidental, and more foresightful and innovative than impulsive and stereotyped." In our daily lives we regularly employ the notion of intelligence in sizing up people as "bright" or "dull."

Although most of us have a fairly good idea of what we mean by intelligence, psychologists find it difficult to formulate a precise definition. Indeed, they disagree strongly on the matter. The problem is that we never observe intelligence but only intelligent *behavior.* From what a person says or does, we *infer* an underlying quality or trait that we call intelligence.

Table 9.1 Motor and Skills Development Among Preschoolers

Age Two	Age Three	Age Four	Age Five
Capable of running	Can stand on one foot	Capable of doing stunts on a tricycle	Capable of skipping
Kicks a large ball	Can hop on both feet	Can descend a ladder, alternating feet	Can hop on one foot for 10 feet
Can jump 12 inches	Can ride a tricycle	Capable of galloping	Capable of copying squares
Navigates stairs alone	Can propel a wagon with one foot	Can cut on a line with a scissors	Can copy letters and numbers
Can construct tower of six to eight blocks	Can copy a circle	Can make crude letters	Can throw a ball well
Can turn pages of a book singly	Can draw a straight line	Can catch a ball with elbows in front of the body	Can fasten buttons that are visible to the eye
Capable of putting on simple clothing	Capable of pouring from a pitcher	Can dress oneself	Can catch a ball with elbows at the sides
Can hold a glass with one hand	Capable of catching a ball with arms extended		

Some psychologists compare intelligence to electricity, which physicists find equally difficult to define. Ledford J. Bischof (1976: 137) says that intelligence, like electricity, "is measurable, and its effect, but not its properties, can be only imprecisely described."

Intelligence as a Composite of Abilities. One recurrent issue dividing psychologists is whether intelligence is a single general intellectual capacity or a composite of many special, independent abilities. Alfred Binet (1857–1911), the French psychologist who devised the first widely used intelligence test in 1905, viewed intelligence as a general capacity for comprehension and reasoning. Although his test used many different types of items, Binet assumed that he was measuring a general ability that found expression in the performance of many kinds of tasks.

In England Charles Spearman (1863–1945) quickly rose to eminence in psychological circles by advancing a somewhat different view. After serving in the Burmese Campaign of 1885 and the Boer War, Spearman resigned his commission in the British Army and entered academic life at the age of forty. Spearman (1904, 1927) concluded that there is a general intellectual ability, labeled the "g" (for "general") factor, that is employed for abstract reasoning and problem solving. He viewed the "g" factor as a basic intellectual power that pervades all of a person's mental activity. However, since an individual's performance across various tasks is not perfectly consistent, Spearman identified special factors (the "s" factors) that are peculiar to given tasks—for instance, arithmetic or spatial relations. This approach is known as the **two-factor theory of intelligence.**

In the 1930s and 1940s Louis L. Thurstone (1887–1955) refined and elaborated Spearman's procedures for factor analysis. Thurstone had left his job as an electrical engineer in Thomas Edison's laboratory in East Orange, New Jersey, to work on psychological measurement. He rejected the notion of general intelligence and focused instead on what he viewed as seven primary abilities: verbal comprehension, word fluency, numerical ability, space visualization, associative memory, perceptual speed, and reasoning (1938, 1947). More recently, J. P. Guilford (1967) has carried the tradition further by identifying 120 factors of intellect. Not all psychologists are happy, however, with such minute distinctions. Many prefer to speak of "general ability"—a mixture of abilities that can be more or less arbitrarily measured by a general-purpose intelligence test.

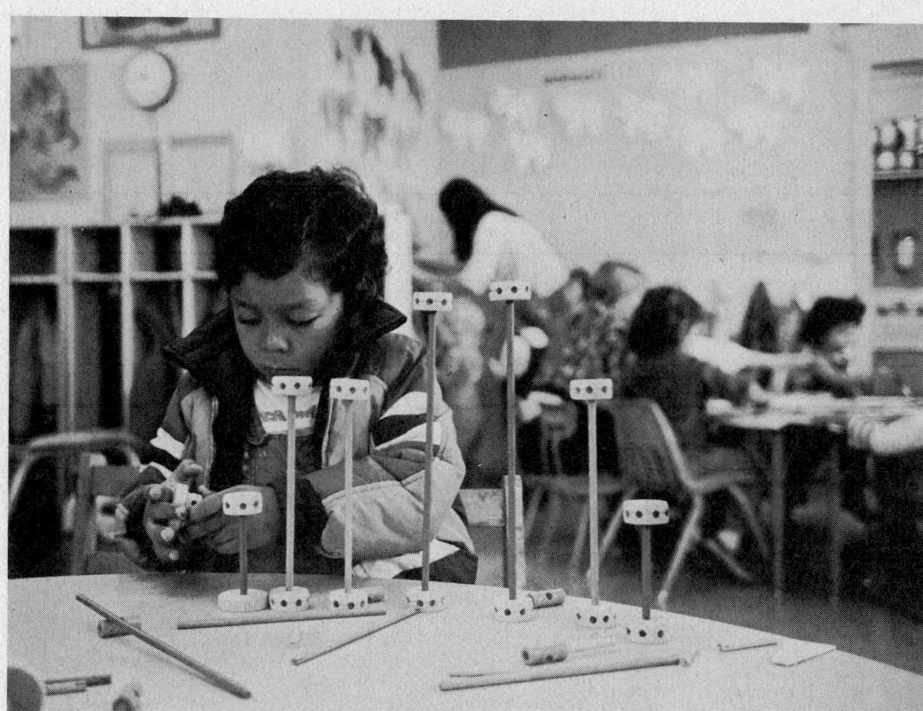

Cognitive Development

Children rapidly develop their mental abilities in the preschool years. Even by two years of age they have made significant strides toward more abstract processes of reasoning, inference, and problem solving.

Elizabeth Crews

Intelligence as Process. Quite different from an "abilities" approach to intelligence are those perspectives that view intelligence as a *process*. These psychologists are less concerned with the "stuff" that allows people to think intelligently and more concerned with the operations involved in thinking. For instance, as discussed in Chapter 2, Jean Piaget concerned himself with the stages of development during which given modes of thought appear. He focused on the continual and dynamic interplay between children and their environment through which they come to know the world and to modify their understanding of it. Since Piaget did not view intelligence in set or fixed terms, he had little interest in the static assessment of individual differences in ability.

Intelligence as Information Processing. More recently, a number of psychologists have proposed a cognitive information-processing view of intelligence (Sternberg, 1979, 1981, 1982; Hunt, 1983). Cognitive psychologists believe that mental behavior should be explained by identifying the processes involved in problem solving rather than focusing on abstract descriptions of the outcome of thinking. For instance, Robert J. Sternberg has investigated the step-by-step mental operations that people employ in tackling an intellectual task. Sternberg finds that individuals differ in the effectiveness with which they carry out various operations such as encoding the items comprising a problem, inferring relationships among its parts, and devising appropriate responses to it. Hence, according to Sternberg, intelligence has to do with *strategies* for approaching problem-solving tasks, a matter we examine more carefully in Chapter 15. Interest in information-processing models has been stimulated by recent developments in computer technology (see the boxed insert on page 235).

Intelligence and the Nature-Nurture Controversy

Psychologists differ in the relative importance that they attribute to heredity and environment in fashioning an individual's intelligence. As discussed in Chapter 3, some investigators of the nature-nurture issue have asked the "which" question, others the "how much" question, and still others the "how" question. And since they ask different questions, they come up with different answers.

The Hereditarian Position. Arthur R. Jensen, an educational psychologist at the University of Cal-

INFORMATION PROCESSING AND COMPUTERS

Very often when we think of computers, we envision some sort of electronic marvel that possesses mystical powers. Yet in reality computers depend ultimately on the imagination of the people who design both their hardware and software. *Hardware,* sometimes compared with the human brain and nervous system, consists of the machinery and electrical circuitry that comprise a computer system. *Software,* analogous to human learning, memory, and thought, is made up of programs that provide step-by-step instructions for performing certain operations. The objective of using computers is to convert raw data into information that can be used for problem solving and decision making.

Computers are more than fast adding machines. They are general-purpose processors of information that is conveyed by symbols. Computers have been programmed to play backgammon and chess, diagnose medical problems, navigate spaceships to distant planets, solve complex mathematical problems, design chemical compounds, and draw analogies among Shakespearean plays.

Computer scientists like Herbert A. Simon (1981), a leading expert on artificial intelligence, use the word "thinking" to refer to some of the tasks that computers can perform. They claim that computers are also capable of creativity. Simon and his associates at Carnegie-Mellon University have developed a computer program they call BACON. If they supply BACON the data used by Johann Kepler in 1609, BACON "discovers" Kepler's law relating to planetary motion. If supplied the data used by Georg Ohm in relating resistance with current and voltage in an electric wire, BACON comes up with Ohm's Law. The program employs many of the *heuristics* (shortcuts and rules of thumb) used by human beings in their problem-solving activities. By means of humanlike strategies for attacking problems, BACON arrives at sudden "insight" regarding the solution to a problem.

However, it is easy to overestimate the capacities of contemporary computers. They possess no independent intelligence and they cannot perform any tasks that a human being has not predetermined. In this respect, the computer's IQ is zero! Although information processing by computers has increased our understanding of a complex human behavior, electronic models do not as yet provide a perfect or even near-perfect analogy to human thinking processes. Nor do computers grow and learn, exhibit emotion, or operate from complex motives (Neisser, 1983). Above all, computers lack a sense of self-awareness, the human experience of "I."

In fact, Marvin Minsky, one of the chief architects of the field of artificial intelligence, contends that computers will not be able to learn how to "think" until they can be programmed to have emotions (Huyghe, 1983). He believes that the distinction between emotions and thought is a false one and that an emotional component is needed to "think" well. Thus children can learn which of several chairs would be safe or unsafe to sit in, but a computer cannot make that kind of assessment. The computer lacks fear, yet fear is necessary if one is to "know" what things should be avoided because they will inflict injury or "ruin" a computer system.

ifornia (Berkeley), has been a leading representative of the viewpoint that favors heredity. In 1969, he argued in the prestigious *Harvard Educational Review* that hereditary factors have a major influence on "racial" differences in intelligence, touching off an impassioned and bitter exchange in academic circles. In the intervening years, Jensen (1973*a*, 1973*b*, 1977, 1980) has not appreciably altered his views. His position on IQ and race is especially controversial (see the boxed insert on pages 236–237).

Like others who phrase the nature-nurture question primarily in terms of "how much," Jensen has sought his answer in family resemblance studies (see Chapter 3) based on intelligence tests. Psychologists have devised tests of intelligence, employing a single number termed the *intelligence quotient,* or *IQ,* to describe various intellectual abilities. Table 9.2 summarizes current data from family resemblance studies. Note that the data in the table make reference to the correlation coefficient. A **correlation coefficient** is a numerical expression of the degree of relationship between two variables or conditions. It tells the extent to which two groups of measures tend to covary, or go together.

A correlation coefficient can range from −1.00 to +1.00. If it is +1.00, there is a *perfect positive relationship* between two variables—meaning that as one of the variables increases, the other also increases. If

IQ AND RACE

Since the turn of the century, psychologists have been testing members of various racial and ethnic groups and have found differences in their average IQ scores (Vander Zanden, 1983). Some psychologists have cited these differences as evidence of different innate intellectual capacities among the groups. For instance, Arthur R. Jensen (1969, 1973*b*) has argued that hereditary factors are "strongly implicated" in the average 15-point difference that he finds in IQ performance between blacks and whites.

Jensen distinguishes between two levels of intelligence. The first level entails the ability to recall material in essentially the same form as it was first presented. Jensen calls this skill *associative learning ability.* In associative learning we memorize lists of numbers, learn to spell, and master tasks through repetition. The second level of intelligence (higher-order thinking) involves problem solving and abstract reasoning and is termed by Jensen *conceptual learning ability.* In conceptual learning we mentally manipulate, elaborate, and transform incoming information. Jensen interprets data from IQ tests as showing that blacks are skillful at associative learning tasks (recalling numbers and counting groups of dots) but are genetically deficient in abilities associated with conceptual learning (solving puzzles, analogies, and ratio problems).

Many psychologists have challenged these interpretations of racial differences in IQ test performance. The first major counterattack came in the 1920s, when educators took a second look at the intelligence test

Institutional Racism
Institutional racism has historically served to impose more burdens and give less benefits to blacks than to whites. Whites control the gates that regulate the flow of people into positions and offices of power, status, and privilege. And white gatekeepers have systematically barred blacks from these positions.
Patrick Reddy

it is −1.00, there is a *perfect negative relationship* between two variables—meaning that as one of the variables increases, the other decreases. If the correlation coefficient is .00, there is no relationship between the variables.

More specifically, if there is no relationship between the IQ scores of pairs of individuals, the correlation coefficient would be .00. This means that knowing the IQ score of one twin would tell us nothing about the IQ score of the other twin. If the correlation coefficient is +1.00, the correspondence in IQ scores between pairs of individuals would be perfect. This means that knowing the IQ score of one twin would tell us the IQ score of the other twin. But we seldom find a correlation coefficient of .00 or +1.00. Usually the figure falls somewhere in between. What we need to remember is this: the nearer the correlation coefficient is to +1.00, the closer the overall correspondence of the IQ scores of one twin is to those of the other twin in the pairs being studied. It should be stressed that correlation coefficients do not in themselves imply any causal link between variables.

The data in Table 9.2 reveal that the median IQ correlation coefficient of separated identical twins in three studies is +.72. Data are also shown from twenty-nine studies of fraternal twins of the same sex who were reared together. The median IQ correlation coefficient of the fraternal twins is +.62. In sum, the identical twins reared in *different* homes are much more alike in IQ than the fraternal twins reared *to-*

scores of a sample of World War I recruits. The results revealed that blacks from the South, where economic and educational handicaps were greatest, scored lower than Northern blacks. Even more important, blacks from some Northern states had higher average scores than those of whites from some Southern states. Evidently the superior environmental opportunities enjoyed by Northern blacks accounted for their superior test performance.

Some psychologists challenge an underlying assumption of those who emphasize heredity: the assumption that intelligence and IQ test performance can be equated. A number of psychologists contend that IQ tests are biased in favor of white middle-class Americans. John Garcia (1972) observes that Lewis M. Terman, in fashioning the Stanford-Binet test, restricted his choice of items to those found in the school curriculum. Furthermore, rather than taking items from machine shop, music class, art class, and other areas, he narrowed the range to reading, writing, and arithmetic. Garcia charges that the Stanford-Binet and related tests measure "scholastic-performance" intelligence and not "general" intelligence. Thus the tests make "a narrow, biased collection of items the 'real measure' of all persons."

Most of us recognize the cultural bias inherent in administering a Stanford-Binet type of test to a tribe of Amazon Indians. The cultural distance between the suburb and the ghetto of an American city is small compared with the distance between either one and the Amazon jungle. Nonetheless, the cultural distance between suburb and ghetto is not zero (Loehlin, Lindzey, and Spuhler, 1975; Scarr and Barker, 1981).

Leon J. Kamin (1974) charges that IQ tests have been used by America's elites to justify privilege and to define inequality, injustice, and racism as natural, proper, and moral. If intelligence is largely inherited, then little can be done to improve people's abilities through education. And if people's abilities cannot be improved, then differences in power and rewards, being largely inherited, are here to stay. Hence existing social arrangements and stratification systems are defined as unchangeable and fair.

Carrying the argument even further, some environmentalists suggest that if IQ tests do not measure intelligence, but merely the mastery of white middle-class values and language skills, then the tests serve as a device to ensure the continued advantage of existing elites. Although most occupational positions are theoretically open to all Americans on the basis of merit, the use of IQ tests for educational and job placement serves to guarantee that the sons and daughters of the elite—having acquired the "proper" credentials as measured by IQ tests—are thus able to secure the best positions.

Clearly these matters are not simply academic squabbles; they have profound consequences for the life of our society. It is important for all of us to become familiar with the various arguments and the evidence, and to take a stand on the issues that are involved.

gether (Jensen, 1972). Also note in Table 9.2 that as the biological kinship between two people increases (gets closer), the correlation between their IQ scores increases. On the basis of this and other evidence, Jensen concludes that from 60 to 80 percent of the variation in IQ scores in the general population is attributable to genetic differences and the remainder to environmental differences.

The Environmentalist Rebuttal. A number of scientists dispute the claim by Jensen and like-minded psychologists that differences in intelligence are primarily a function of heredity. Some disagree with the formulation of the nature-nurture question in terms of "how much" and insist that the question should be *how* heredity and environment interact to produce intelligence. And others like Leon J. Kamin (1974: 1) go so far as to assert: "There exist no data which should lead a prudent man to accept the hypothesis that IQ test scores are in any degree heritable." Psychologists of Kamin's view, commonly termed *environmentalists,* argue that mental abilities are learned. They believe that intellect is increased or decreased according to the degree of enrichment or impoverishment provided by a person's social and cultural environment (Feuerstein, 1979, 1980).

Kamin (1974, 1975, 1977, 1981) has vigorously challenged the adoption and identical-twin research that the advocates of heredity use to support their conclusions. He insists that it is improper to speak of

Table 9.2 Correlation Coefficients of IQ Scores Compared with the Degree of Family Relationship

Correlations Between	Number of Studies	Median Correlation Coefficients
Unrelated Persons		
Foster parent and child	6	+.19
Children reared together	6	+.34
Collaterals		
Cousins	4	+.15
Half siblings	2	+.31
Siblings reared apart	2	+.24
Siblings reared together	69	+.47
Dizygotic twins, different sex	18	+.57
Dizygotic twins, same sex	29	+.62
Monozygotic twins, reared apart	3	+.72
Monozygotic twins, reared together	34	+.86
Direct Line		
Parent and child, different sex	12	+.39
Parent and child, same sex	14	+.40

SOURCE: Adapted from Thomas J. Bouchard, Jr., and Matthew McGue, "Familial Studies of Intelligence: A Review," *Science*, Vol. 212 (1981), pp. 1055–1059.

individuals as being reared in differing environments simply because they were brought up in different homes. In some cases identical twins labeled as being "reared apart" were hardly separated at all: they were raised by relatives, or they lived next door to one another, or they went to the same school. Similarly, environmentalists charge that studies of adopted children are biased by the fact that adoption agencies traditionally attempt to place children in a social environment that is religiously, ethnically, and racially similar to the one into which they were born.

Environmentalists cite evidence of their own to bolster their argument that differences in intelligence are primarily a function of social conditions. Benjamin S. Bloom (1969), a psychologist, found that Israeli children of European Jewish parents have a mean IQ of 105. In contrast, Israeli children of Middle Eastern Jews have an IQ of only 85. This is not the case, however, for children residing on collective farms (*kibbutzim*), where they spend twenty-two hours of the day in a nursery. Under the intensive learning experiences provided in the nurseries, both European and Middle Eastern Jewish children have an average IQ of 115—a 10-point improvement for the one group and a 30-point improvement for the other. Environmentalists insist that such evidence shows how flexible IQ can be and how it can be altered under different social conditions.

Contemporary Scientific Consensus. Most social and behavioral scientists believe that any extreme view in the nature-nurture controversy is unjustified at the present time. Estimates based on twin and adoption studies suggest that hereditary differences account for 45 to 80 percent of the variation found in the intelligence test performance of a population. Christopher Jencks (1972), a sociologist, has employed path analysis—a relatively new statistical technique—to partition the amount of variance within a group into an estimate of 45 percent for heredity, 35 percent for environment, and 20 percent for gene-environment covariance.

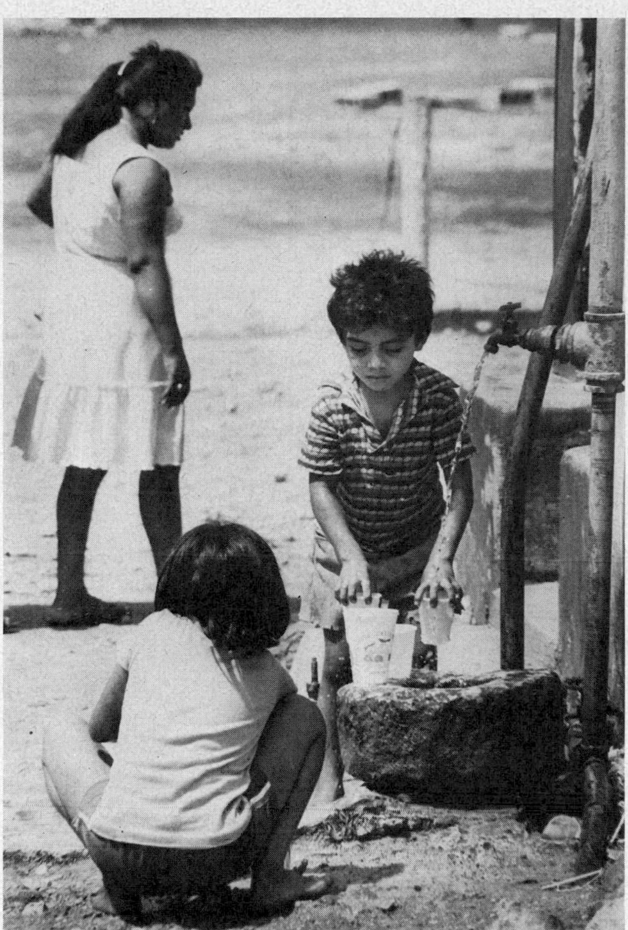

Cultural Bias in Intelligence Testing

A "noncultural" or "culture-free" intelligence test is an impossibility. Membership in a particular culture influences what an individual is likely to learn or fail to learn. It would be ridiculous, for example, to give these children in Mexico the Stanford-Binet intelligence test, designed by and for English-speaking Americans.

Patrick Reddy

Jencks has introduced the third element of gene-environment covariance because he feels that dividing IQ into hereditary and environmental components oversimplifies the matter. For example, consider the following circumstances (Loehlin, Lindzey, and Spuhler, 1975: 77–78):

> Suppose that intelligent parents tend to provide their children with genes conducive to the development of high intelligence, but also tend to provide them with environments favorable to the development of this trait, such as good schools, intellectual stimulation at home, and so forth. We may need to divide the observed variance among individuals in a population into a component that is associated with genetic endowment, when intellectual stimulation is held constant, a component that is associated with environmental stimulation, with genetic potential constant, and a third component associated with the covariance of heredity and environment, that is, with how the first two components vary relative to each other.

If, as in this example, genes and environment reinforce each other, the added component of variance cannot logically be assigned to either nature or nurture. Rather, it is a result of the association of their separate effects. In a careful appraisal of evidence in the nature-nurture controversy, John C. Loehlin, Gardner Lindzey, and J. N. Spuhler (1975) introduced a number of changes in Jencks's analysis that modified his estimates of 45 percent for heredity, 35 percent for environment, and 20 percent for gene-environment covariance to 60 percent, 25 percent, and 15 percent, respectively.

The Early Development of Intelligence

Jean Piaget, the Swiss developmental psychologist, pioneered the study of the development of intelligence in infants and children. He called the years between two and seven the **preoperational period.** The principal achievement of that period is the developing capacity of children to represent the external world *internally* through the use of symbols. *Symbols* are things that stand for something else. They free children from the rigid boundaries of the here and now. Using symbols, they can represent not only present events but past and future ones.

At first, the symbols a child uses are dependent on action and physical similarity for their development and expression. However, during the preoperational period symbols become more and more remote from the child's immediate action and from any physical resemblance to the object. Thus symbols become increasingly internalized images, thereby forming the foundations for representational thought (Ungerer et al., 1981). Language acquisition facilitates children's ability to employ and manipulate symbols. However, preoperational thought retains much of the inflexibility of sensorimotor thought, although it surpasses sensorimotor thought in quality.

Difficulties in Solving Conservation Problems. Piaget observed that although children make major strides in cognitive development during the

Enriched Environment
Children benefit intellectually from enriched and stimulating environments. But warm, supportive human contact is equally important. Children are emotionall beings who are something more than computerized machines awaiting "programming."
Jean-Claude Lejeune

preoperational period, their reasoning and thinking processes have a number of limitations. These limitations can be seen in the difficulties preschool children have when they try to solve conservation problems. **Conservation** refers to the concept that the quantity or amount of something stays the same regardless of changes in its shape or position.

A preoperational child cannot understand that when water is poured out of a full glass into a wider glass, which it fills only halfway, the amount of water remains unchanged. Instead, the child sees that the new glass is half empty and concludes that there is less water than before.

Similarly, if we show a child under six two parallel rows of eight evenly spaced pennies and ask which row has more pennies, the child always correctly answers that both rows have the same number. But if, in full view of the child, we move the pennies in one of the rows farther apart and again ask which row has more pennies, the child will reply that the longer row has more. The child fails to recognize that the number of pennies does not change simply because we made a change in another dimension, the length of the row (see Figure 9.1).

Piaget said that the difficulties preschoolers have in solving conservation problems derive from the characteristics of preoperational thought. These characteristics inhibit logical thought by posing obstacles that are associated with centering, transformations, reversibility, and egocentrism.

Centering. Preoperational children concentrate on one feature of a situation and neglect other aspects, a process termed **centering.** When water is poured out of a full glass into a wider glass, preschool children focus on only one attribute. They fix their attention on either the height or the width of the water in the glass while ignoring the other dimension. In order to solve the conservation problem correctly, they must *decenter*—that is, they must attend simultaneously to both height and width.

Likewise, in the case of the pennies, children need to recognize that a change in length is compensated for by a change in the other dimension, density. Thus there is no change in quantity. Here too, the ability to decenter—to explore more than one aspect of the stimulus—is beyond preoperational children.

States and Transformations. Another characteristic of preoperational thinking is that children pay attention to *states* rather than *transformations* (see Figure 9.2). In observing water being poured from one glass into another, preschool children focus on the original state and the final state. The intervening process is lost to them. They do not pay attention to the gradual shift in the height or width of the water in the glasses as the experimenter pours the liquid. Preoperational thought fixes on static states. It fails to link successive states into a coherent sequence of events.

The inability of preschool children to follow trans-

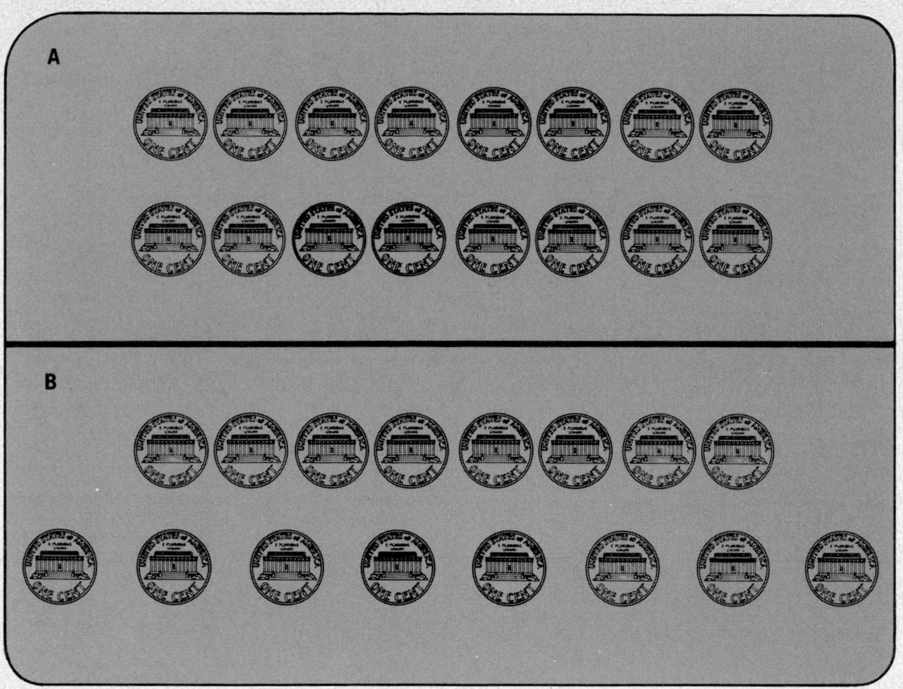

Figure 9.1 Conservation Experiment with Pennies

Children are first shown two rows of pennies arranged as in *A*. The experimenter asks if both rows contain the same number of pennies. Then with the children watching, the experimenter spreads out the pennies in the bottom row, as in *B*. Children are once again asked if both rows contain the same number of pennies. Preoperational children will respond that they do not.

formations interferes with logical thinking. Only by appreciating the continuous and sequential nature of various operations can we be certain that the quantities remain the same. Since preoperational children fail to see the relationship between events, their comparisons between original and final events are incomplete. Thus they cannot solve conservation problems.

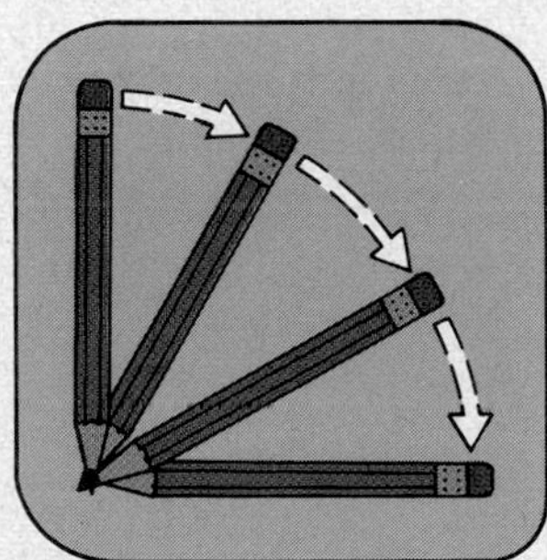

Figure 9.2 An Experiment in Preoperational Thinking

Hold a pencil in an upright position, then slowly lower it to a horizontal position while a child under seven watches it. Immediately afterward the child will not be able to draw the sequence of events or arrange in order a series of prepared drawings reconstructing the movement of the pencil. Children in Piaget's preoperational period (ages two to seven) pay attention only to initial and final states, not to transformations. They cannot identify the successive movements required for the pencil to shift from the upright to the prone position.

Nonreversibility. According to Piaget, the most important characteristic of preoperational thought is the child's failure to recognize that operations are **reversible**—that they can be turned back to an earlier state. In other words, we can always go back to the starting point in a series of operations. After we pour water from a narrow into a wider container, we can demonstrate that the amount of water remains the same by pouring it back into the narrow container. But preoperational children do not understand that the operation can be reversed. Once they have carried out an entire operation, they cannot *mentally* regain the original state. Awareness of reversibility is a requirement of logical thought.

Egocentrism. Still another element that interferes with the preschool child's understanding of reality is **egocentrism**—lack of awareness that there are viewpoints other than one's own. According to Piaget, preoperational children are so absorbed in their own impressions that they fail to recognize that their thoughts and feelings may be different from those of other people. Children simply assume that everyone thinks the same thoughts they do at the same time they do.

In a classic study of egocentrism, Piaget and Bärbel Inhelder (1956) showed children a three-dimensional model of a mountain landscape. Each child was given a set of photographs taken from different positions around the model. The child was asked to select the picture that best represented what a doll "saw" when a researcher placed a doll at a given point on the landscape. Piaget and Inhelder discovered that before seven years of age, most children assume that the doll sees what they see, regardless of the doll's location. This finding was taken by Piaget and Inhelder to be evidence of egocentric thinking in preoperational children.

More recent research suggests, however, that while egocentricity is characteristic of preoperational thinking, preschool children are also capable of recognizing other people's viewpoints (Flavell, 1974; Marvin, Greenberg, and Mossler, 1976; Liben, 1978). In fact, a number of investigators have found that Piaget and Inhelder's mountain test is too novel, difficult, and complex for young children. It requires a variety of cognitive skills and abilities that are not necessarily related to egocentrism (Borke, 1975; Walker and Gollin, 1977). Therefore the test may mask children's true competence.

Researchers are increasingly uncovering many *sociocentric* (people-oriented) responses in young children. Indeed, some have questioned the characterization of children as egocentric. Consider the following evidence:

- *Talking and communicating.* Catherine Garvey and Robert Hogan (1973) found that during the greater part of the time that children three to five years of age spend in nursery school, they interact with others, largely by talking. Further, most of their speech is mutually responsive and adapted to the speech or nonverbal behavior of a partner (Spilton and Less, 1977). In another study Michael P. Maratsos (1973) found that nursery school children are far more verbally explicit when communicating with a blindfolded person than with a person who can see.
- *Sharing.* Harriet L. Rheingold, Dale F. Hay, and Meredith J. West (1976) have shown that children in their second year of life share with others what they see and find interesting. In laboratory settings, for instance, children commonly share by showing objects to other people, giving them

Sociocentric Behavior
Developmental psychologists are discovering that young children are considerably less egocentric and more sociocentric than early studies indicated.
Patrick Reddy

objects, and engaging others as partners in playing with the objects. Children share not only with their parents but also with unfamiliar persons, both male and female.

Rheingold and her associates also found considerable evidence for sharing behavior in field observations. Children usually pointed at objects—a window display, an airplane, an automobile, or a picture on a cereal box—in order to call another person's attention to them. Indeed, the researchers observed pointing behavior in children even before their first birthday. They report seeing pointing in an infant at 10.1 months of age, holding up a toy at 11.2 months, and giving at 11.3 months. Rheingold and her colleagues (1976: 1157) concluded:

> In showing an object to another person, the children demonstrate not only that they know that other people can see what they see but also that others will look at what they point to or hold up. We can surmise that they also know that what they see may be remarkable in some way and therefore worthy of another's attention. . . . That children so young share contradicts the egocentricity so often ascribed to them and reveals them instead as already able contributors to social life.

Hence, by the time children are about one year of age, they seem to have acquired the ability not only to take the visual perspective of others but also to begin sharing with them their own perspective of the world (Leung and Rheingold, 1981).

- *Altruism.* Researchers have found evidence of altruistic and prosocial behavior even in very young children (Zahn-Waxler, Radke-Yarrow, and Brady-Smith, 1977; Buckley, Siegel, and Ness, 1979). Not untypical are the following examples. A two-year-old boy accidentally hits a small girl on the head. He looks aghast. "I hurt your hair. Please don't cry." Another child, a girl of eighteen months, sees her grandmother lying down to rest. She goes over to her own crib, takes her own blanket, and covers her grandmother with it (Pines, 1979*b*). Chapter 11 will consider prosocial behavior at greater length.

In conclusion, newly developing lines of research reveal that we have been hampered in our efforts to understand children by adult-centered concepts and by our preoccupation with the adult-child relationship—in other words, by *adult* egocentrism (Belle, 1978).

Causality

Piaget's procedures tended to underestimate many of the cognitive capabilities of preschool children (Gelman and Gallistel, 1978). As a result, he concluded that children younger than seven or eight fail to grasp cause-and-effect relationships. When he would ask younger children why the sun and the moon move, they would respond that heavenly bodies "follow us about because they are curious" or "in order to look at us." Or if Piaget showed four-year-olds a bicycle and asked them what makes the wheels turn, they might reply, "The street makes the bicycle go." Such fanciful explanations for events led Piaget to emphasize the shortcomings associated with young children's intellectual operations.

But contemporary developmental psychologists investigating the thinking of young children are finding that they do understand a good many things, including causality. **Causality** involves our attribution of a cause-and-effect relationship to two paired events that recur in succession. It is based on the expectation that when one event occurs, another event, one that ordinarily follows the first, will again follow it.

Young children's grasp of causality is being demonstrated in a variety of experiments (Pines, 1983). One such experiment involves a toy rabbit named Fred and a series of upright wooden blocks that topple over like dominos. When the last domino falls over, it trips a small but visible lever that sends Fred flying from a platform. Three- and four-year-olds can correctly predict about 75 percent of the time that as the blocks fall over, they will trigger Fred's release regardless of whether the rod pushing over the first domino is long or short and regardless of whether or not one of the blocks is hidden from view.

Young children are also capable of distinguishing between animate and inanimate objects. They do so by considering the cause of an object's movement. Living things move because of self-generating forces within them whereas nonliving things move only when activated by external forces. Thus children talk a good deal about the inability of a doll to propel itself, apparently a fact that is quite significant to them. The difficulty that young children may have in determining what makes the sun or moon move is perhaps one reason they responded as they did to Piaget's inquiry.

The versatility of young children in grasping causality has led some psychologists to conclude that human beings are biologically prewired to understand the existence of cause-and-effect relationships (Pines, 1983). Children appear to operate on an implicit theory of causality. Clearly the ability to appreciate that a cause must always precede an effect would have enormous survival value in the course of evolution. Hence, as in the case of language, children may be preordained to distinguish between cause and effect.

INFORMATION PROCESSING AND MEMORY

> *Memory is a net; one finds it full of fish when he takes it from the brook; but a dozen miles of water have run through it without sticking.*
>
> —OLIVER WENDELL HOLMES
> *The Autocrat of the Breakfast Table*

Memory is a critical cognitive ability. Indeed, all learning implies memory. In its broadest sense, **memory** refers to the retention of what has been experienced. Without memory we would react to every event as if we had never before experienced it. Further, we would be incapable of thinking and reasoning—of any sort of intelligent behavior—if we could not use remembered facts. Hence memory is critical to information processing.

Early Memory

During infancy and childhood, we learn a prodigious amount about the world (Ungerer, Brody, and Zelazo, 1978; Gottfried and Rose, 1980; M. W. Sullivan, 1982). Yet by adulthood our memories of our early experiences have faded, a phenomenon termed *childhood amnesia.* We remember as adults only fleeting scenes and isolated moments prior to the time we reached seven or eight years of age. Although some individuals have no recollections prior to eight or nine years of age, many of us can recall some things that took place between our third and fourth birthdays. Most commonly, first memories involve visual imagery and most of the imagery is in color. In many cases, we visualize ourselves in these memories from afar, as we would look at an actor on a stage (Nelson, 1982).

Just why early memories should wane remains an enigma (Goleman, 1981). Sigmund Freud theorized that we repress or alter childhood memories because of their disturbing sexual and aggressive content. Others, particularly Piagetians and cognitive developmentalists, claim that adults have trouble recalling the events of childhood because they no longer think as children do (for instance, adults typically employ as aids to memory words and abstract concepts that do not mesh with the mental habits they employed as young children). Still others say that the brain and nervous system are not entirely formed in the young and do not allow for the development of adequate memory stores and effective retrieval strategies. Nonetheless, our understanding of childhood amnesia continues to be elusive, with theorizing remaining at the speculative level.

Information Processing

Memory includes recall, recognition, and the facilitation of relearning. In *recall,* we remember what we learned earlier, such as the definition of a scientific concept or the lines of a play. In *recognition,* we experience a feeling of familiarity when we again perceive something that we have previously encountered. In the *facilitation of relearning,* we find that we can learn material that is already familiar to us more readily than we can learn totally unfamiliar material.

On the whole, children's recognition memory is superior to their recall memory. In recognition, the information is already available, and children can simply check their perceptions of an occurrence against their memory. Recall, in contrast, requires them to retrieve all the information from their own memory. Children ten years of age who are shown sixty pictures and asked to remember them can *recognize* about 90 percent of the pictures the next day, but they can *recall* only about 30 percent of them (Kagan et al., 1973).

Memory permits us to store information for different periods of time. Some psychologists distinguish between sensory information storage, short-term memory, and long-term memory (see Figure 9.3). In **sensory information storage,** information from the senses is preserved in the sensory register just long enough to permit the stimuli to be scanned for processing (generally less than two seconds). It provides

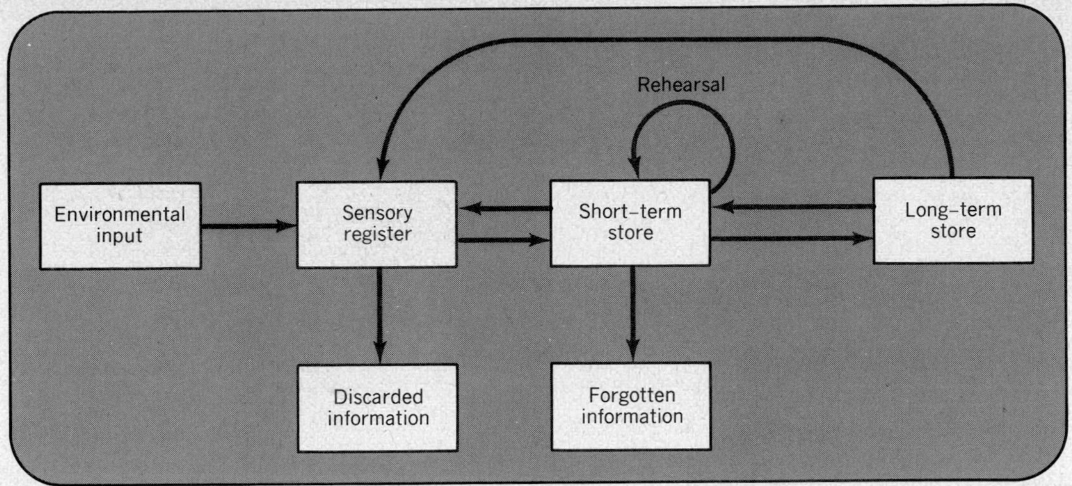

Figure 9.3 Simplified Flow Chart of the Three-Store Model of Memory
Information flow is represented by three memory stores: the sensory register, the short-term store, and the long-term store. Inputs from the environment enter the sensory register, where they are selectively passed on to short-term storage. Information in the short-term store may be forgotten or copied by the long-term store. In some cases, individuals mentally rehearse information in order to keep it in active awareness in short-term storage. Complicated feedback operations take place among the three storage components.

a relatively complete, literal copy of the physical stimulation. For instance, if you tap your finger against your cheek, you note an immediate sensation, which quickly fades away.

Short-term memory refers to the retention of information for a very brief period, usually not more than thirty seconds. For example, you may look up a number in the telephone directory and remember it just long enough to dial it, whereupon you promptly forget it.

Long-term memory is the retention of information over an extended period of time. A memory may be retained because it arose from a very intense single experience or because it is repeatedly rehearsed. Through yearly repetition and constant media reminders, you come to remember that Memorial Day is in late May, Labor Day in early September.

Metacognition and Metamemory

As children develop, they become increasingly active agents in the remembering process (Speer and Flavell, 1979; Chechile et al., 1981). The development of memory occurs in two ways: through alterations in the biological structuring of the brain (its "hardware") and through changes in types of information processing (the "software" of acquisition and retrieving). Researchers have observed striking changes as a function of age, both in children's performance on memory tasks and in their use of memory strategies. As they grow older, children acquire a complex set of skills that enables them to control just what they will learn and retain. In short, they come to "know how to know," so that they can engage in deliberate remembering (Craik and Lockhart, 1972; Brown, 1975, 1982).

Human beings require more than the factual and strategic information that comprises a knowledge base. They must also have access to this knowledge base and apply strategies appropriate to task demands. This flexibility in calibrating solutions to specific problems is the hallmark of intelligence. It reaches its zenith in the conscious control that adults bring to bear over a broad range of their mental functioning (Brown, 1982). Individuals' awareness and understanding of their mental processes is termed **metacognition.** Their awareness and understanding of their memory processes is termed **metamemory.**

Research reveals that even three-year-olds engage in intentional memory behavior. They appear to understand that when they are told to remember something, they are expected to store and later retrieve it. Indeed, even two-year-olds can hide, misplace, search for, and find objects on their own (Wellman, 1977). By the time children enter kindergarten, they have developed considerable knowledge of the memory process. They are aware that forgetting occurs (that items get lost in memory), that spending more time in study helps them retain information, that it is more difficult to remember many items than a few, that distraction and interference make tasks harder, and that they can employ records, cues, and other people to help them recall things (Kreutzer, Leonard, and Flavell, 1975; Wellman, 1977; Fabricius and Wellman, 1983). They also understand such terms as "remember," "forget," and "learn."

Categorizing as a Memory Strategy

One strategy that facilitates remembering is to group information into meaningful categories. Sheila Rossi and M. C. Wittrock (1971) found that a developmental progression occurs in the categories children use to organize words for recall. In this experiment children ranging from two to five years old were read a list of twelve words ("sun," "hand," "men," "fun," "leg," "work," "hat," "apple," "dogs," "fat," "peach," "bark"). Each child was asked to recall as many words as possible. The responses were scored in pairs in terms of the order in which a child recalled them: rhyming ("sun-fun," "hat-fat"); syntactical ("men-work," "dogs-bark"); clustering ("apple-peach," "hand-leg"); or serial ordering (recalling two words serially from the list). Rossi and Wittrock found that rhyming responses peak at two years of age, followed by syntactical responses at three, clustering responses at four, and serial ordering responses at five. In many respects the progression is consistent with Piaget's theory, which depicts development as proceeding from concrete to abstract functioning and from perceptual to conceptual responding.

Other research also confirms that changes occur in children's spontaneous use of categories during the developmental span from age two to adolescence. While children as young as two benefit from the presence of categories in recall tasks, older children benefit even more. Not only does recall increase with age, but in comparison with older children, children of four to six show less categorical grouping of items in recall tasks, fewer subordinate categories in tasks requesting that similar items be grouped together, and lower consistency in the assignment of items to selected categories (Nelson and Earl, 1973; Jablonski, 1974; Paris, 1978; Wellman, Collins, and Glieberman, 1981).

Rehearsing as a Memory Strategy

Another strategy that facilitates memory is *rehearsing,* a process in which we repeat information to ourselves. Many individuals who are adept at remembering people's names cultivate the talent by mentally rehearsing a new name several times to themselves when they are introduced to a person. Researchers have demonstrated that children as young as three are capable of various rehearsal strategies. For instance, if three-year-olds are instructed to remember where an object is hidden, they often prepare for future memory retrieval by extended looking at, touching, or pointing to the hiding place (Wellman, Ritter, and Flavell, 1975).

As children grow, their rehearsal mechanisms become more active and effective (Cuvo, 1975; Ornstein, Naus, and Liberty, 1975; Naus, Ornstein, and Kreshtool, 1977). Some researchers believe that the process is facilitated through language, as children become increasingly skillful at verbally labeling stimuli. According to these investigators, the organizing and rehearsing process inherent in naming is a powerful aid to memory (Loughlin and Daehler, 1973; Rosinski, Pellegrino, and Siegel, 1977).

COGNITIVE FOUNDATIONS FOR SOCIAL INTERACTION

The cognitive skills acquired during the preschool years have profound implications for children's ability to function as members of society. In order to enter sustained social interaction with others, we must impute meaning to the people around us. All of us, children and adults alike, confront the social world in terms of categories of people—we classify them as adults, doctors, teachers, storekeepers, and so on. Society does not merely consist of so many isolated individuals. It is composed of individuals who are

Rehearsing and Memory

Caretakers often help children develop retention and recall by repeating certain operations with them. Here the nursery-school teacher says a number, and the child places a chestnut on the appropriate card.

Patrick Reddy

classed as similar because they play similar roles. And just as we impute meaning to others, we must also attribute meaning to ourselves. We have to develop a sense of ourselves as distinct, bounded, identifiable units. In sum, we acquire conceptions of roles and self.

Roles

All the world's a stage,
And all the men and women merely players.
They have their exits and their entrances,
And one man in his time plays many parts.

—WILLIAM SHAKESPEARE
As You Like It, Act II, Scene 7

In order to function effectively within social settings, children must develop the mental capacity to "locate" or "place" individuals in a wide variety of social categories: brother, neighbor, dentist, store clerk, playmate, and so on. Social psychologists call such categories **roles.** Roles specify who does what, when, and where. Roles define the expectations that group members hold regarding an individual's behavior in a given setting. As such, roles are key ingredients in group life. Without roles society would be an impossibility.

Roles impinge on us as sets of social norms that define our *obligations* and *expectations.* Obligations are the actions that *others* can legitimately insist that we perform. Expectations are the actions that *we* can legitimately insist that others perform (Goffman, 1961). Every role is tied to one or more other roles and is *reciprocal* to these other roles. Without children there would be no fathers; without wives, no husbands; without patients, no doctors; without teachers, no students. And vice versa: without fathers there would be no children; without husbands, no wives; without doctors, no patients; without students, no teachers.

In sum, roles provide social guidelines that define for us our obligations and our expectations. Roles link us within a social network through the web created by their interconnections. Hence we are joined in social life through role relationships, the expectations of the one end being the obligations of the other. For example, the obligations of the father role—to provide economic support for his offspring, to furnish moral direction, to communicate a sense of warmth and acceptance—are the expectations of the child role. The expectations of the father role—to be obeyed, to be respected, to be shown affection—are the obligations of the child role. Children must grasp such expectations and obligations in order to function effectively within a group setting.

Both Piaget and the sociologist George Herbert Mead (1934) pointed out that children must overcome an egocentric perspective if they are to participate in mature social interaction. For children to play their role properly, they must know something about other roles. This requirement derives from the reciprocal character of roles discussed above. Hence in human interaction we *construct* our acts point by point by *fitting* them to those of the other person. We start or stop, abandon or postpone, implement or transform given lines of action on the basis of the feedback we receive from others (Turner, 1962; Blumer, 1969).

During the early preschool years children can recognize that people are independent agents who initiate action, and they begin to understand the nature of social roles (Watson and Fischer, 1980). Some categories for classing people apparently emerge quite early. For instance, six-month-old infants are able to distinguish between an adult and a baby, suggesting that infants use age as one dimension to categorize the social world (Lewis and Brooks-Gunn, 1979). By eighteen months, most middle-class children can pretend that they are carrying out some action (for instance, pretending to drink from an empty cup). This ability testifies that they view themselves as agents producing behavior. By the time they reach two years of age, they can make a doll do something, as if it were acting on its own, thus demonstrating an elementary ability for representing other people as independent agents. Most three-year-olds can make a doll carry out several role-related activities, revealing knowledge of a social role (for example, they can pretend to be a doctor and examine a doll). Four-year-olds can typically act out a role, relating one social role to a reciprocal role (for instance, they can pretend that a patient doll is sick and that a doctor doll examines it, in the course of which both dolls make appropriate responses). During the late preschool years children become capable of combining roles in more complicated ways (for example, being a doctor and a father at the same time). Hence, most six-year-olds can pretend to carry out several roles simultaneously.

As children gain the ability to "take the role of the other" they become better able to take into account the behavior of another person in fashioning their own behavior. To do so, they must develop a concept of the *self.*

The Self

> *Man can be defined as the animal that can say "I," that can be aware of himself as a separate entity.*
>
> —ERICH FROMM

Among the cognitive achievements of the child's early years is a growing self-awareness—the human sense of "I." At any one time, we are confronted with a greater quantity and variety of stimulation than we can attend to and process. Accordingly, we must select what we will notice, learn, infer, or recall. Selection does not occur in a random manner but depends on our use of internal cognitive structures—mental "scripts" or "frames"—for processing information. Of particular importance to us is the cognitive structure that we employ for selecting and processing information about ourselves. This structure is the **self**—the system of concepts we use in defining ourselves. It is the awareness we have of ourselves as separate entities who are able to think and initiate action. In sum, the self provides us with the capacity to observe, respond to, and direct our own behavior. The sense of self distinguishes each of us as a unique individual—different from others in society. It gives us a feeling of placement in the social and physical world and of continuity across time. And it provides the cognitive basis for our identities.

Sociologists who follow in the tradition of George Herbert Mead view the self as crucial to role playing. The self enables us to imagine ourselves in other people's positions and see what they expect of us in a given role. In imagination, we put ourselves in their shoes—mentally exchange roles—to grasp the requirements for sustained interaction. In so doing, we "get outside ourselves" and view ourselves as objects.

Michael Lewis and Jeanne Brooks-Gunn (1979) studied children's emerging sense of self in a novel way. They observed children's reactions to their reflections in a mirror. Their sample involved young

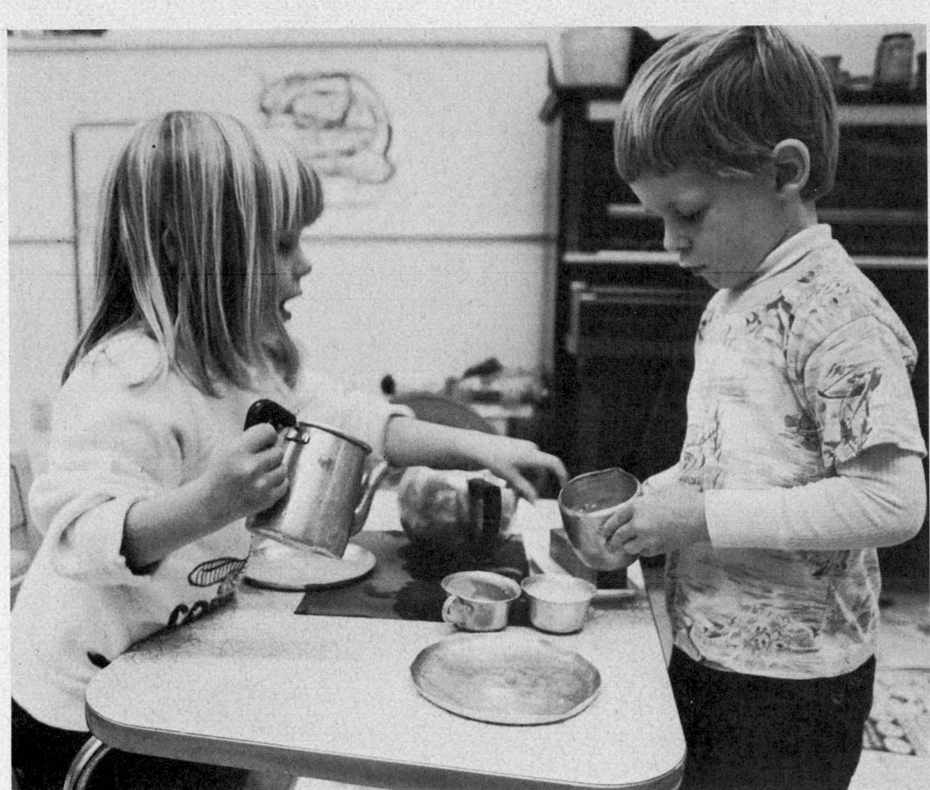

Roles and the Self

In order to play our own role successfully, we must know the requirements both of our role and of the other person's role. According to George Herbert Mead, in the course of translating the requirements of our role into action, we imagine ourselves in the role of the other person. This process of the self enables us to take into account the behavior of the other person when we fashion our own reciprocal behavior.

Patrick Reddy

children aged nine, twelve, fifteen, eighteen, twenty-one, and twenty-four months. The children were placed individually in front of a mirror, and their actions were recorded on videotape. Then each child's mother took her child away from the mirror, wiped the child's nose and in doing so placed red paint on it, and brought the child back to the mirror. The videotapes of the children's behavior at this point showed a clear developmental pattern. Few children under twelve months of age responded to the paint. But 25 percent of those between fifteen and eighteen months, and 88 percent of those at twenty-four months, responded by touching their noses. Such a reaction suggests that they had a sense of self-awareness in that they knew what their own faces looked like.

Lewis and Brooks-Gunn also found that infants as young as from nine to twelve months of age are capable of making some distinction between pictures of themselves and pictures of others. However, the evidence for this discrimination becomes stronger at about fifteen months when they become particularly attuned to physical features associated with their sex and their age (it seems that they discern that females have differently shaped faces and different hairstyles from males and that babies have faces and heads that are shaped differently from those of adults). Of particular interest is children's use of *self-referents*—their own proper names and personal pronouns. Such self-referents emerge between the ages of eighteen and thirty months (Lewis and Brooks-Gunn, 1979).

Lewis and Brooks-Gunn suggest that there are four major advances in infants' self-knowledge during the first two years of life. At first, from birth to three months, infants are especially fascinated by human faces (see Chapter 6). The second advance takes place between three and eight months of age when infants come to recognize themselves in mirrors and experimental TV screens through contingency cues (when the image of the body moves along with the self, one recognizes the self in that image). The third advance in self-knowledge occurs between eight and twelve months of age as infants come to construct the self in Piagetian terms as a permanent object with enduring qualities. Finally, the fourth advance occupies the second year. During this phase children gain knowledge of particular physical attributes that distinguish them from other children and adults. They also gain a sense of "mine" with respect to toys and territory (Levine, 1983). The development of a child's sense of "self" as separate and distinct from others is a central issue of toddlerhood.

During the preschool years, young children conceive of the self strictly in physical terms—body parts (the head), material attributes ("I have blue eyes"), and bodily activities ("I walk to the park") (Broughton, 1978; Keller, Ford, and Meacham, 1978; Selman, 1980). They view the self and the mind as simply parts of the body (Damon and Hart, 1982). For the most part, children locate the self in the head, although they may also cite other body parts like the chest or the whole body. And they often say that animals, plants, and dead people also have selves and minds.

Between six and eight years of age, children begin to distinguish between the mind and the body. The emerging distinction between the mental and the physical allows children to appreciate the subjective nature of the self. They begin to recognize that a person is unique not only because each of us looks different from other people but because each of us has different feelings and thoughts. Hence, children come to define the self in internal rather than external terms and to grasp the difference between psychological and physical attributes. During adolescence, the distinction between mind and body and the qualities of the self become more finely articulated (see Chapter 13).

GENDER IDENTIFICATION

One of the early attributes of self is gender. A major developmental task for the child during the first six years of life is to acquire a gender identification. All societies appear to have seized on the anatomical differences between men and women to assign **gender roles**—sets of cultural expectations that define the ways in which the members of each sex should behave.

Societies throughout the world display considerable differences in the types of activities assigned to men and women (Murdock, 1935). Sometimes the division of labor is not at all like our own. In some societies, for instance, women do most of the manual labor; in others, such as that of the inhabitants of the Marquesas Islands, cooking, housekeeping, and baby tending are male occupations.

Most people evolve gender identities that are reasonably consistent with the gender role standards of their society. **Gender identities** are the conceptions that people have of themselves as being male or female. Over the past twenty-five years, a good deal of research has explored the process by which children come to conceive of themselves in masculine or feminine terms and to adopt the behaviors that are considered culturally appropriate for them as males or females. It has also activated debate regarding the psychology of sex differences, a topic considered in the boxed insert on pages 252–253.

Hormonal Influences on Gender Behaviors

What are little boys made of?
What are little boys made of?
Frogs and snails,
And puppy dogs' tails,
That's what little boys are made of.

What are little girls made of?
What are little girls made of?
Sugar and spice
And all that's nice,
That's what little girls are made of.

—J. O. HALLIWELL
Nursery Rhymes of England, 1844

Some research suggest that biological differences between men and women contribute to the development of behavioral differences (Hines, 1982). This research, primarily conducted with lower animals, reveals various linkages between hormonal conditions, brain functions, and behavior (Money and Ehrhardt, 1972; Hines, 1982). Endocrine glands secrete hormones—special chemical messengers—that are carried by the bloodstream to every part of the body. Among the most important are *testosterone,* the major male sex hormone, and *progesterone* and *estrogen,* the two principal female sex hormones. Each sex has some male and some female hormones. Differences between the sexes, and also within the two sex groups, result from differences in the *ratio* in which these hormones are present in the individual.

Researchers at the Oregon Regional Primate Research Center have experimented with the prenatal altering of hormone ratios in rhesus monkeys by injecting female rhesus monkey fetuses with male hormones. After birth, these masculinized females exhibit genital alterations and behaviors typical of male monkeys. They engage in much of the rough-and-tumble play, the threatening gesturing, and the sexual mounting characteristic of male monkeys. Indeed, sometimes a masculinized female works her way up to the dominant position in her troop by sheer aggressiveness (Phoenix, Goy, and Resko, 1969).

Over the past twenty years experimental studies with rats, guinea pigs, and monkeys have revealed that their brains contain sensitive tissues that have a bisexual potential. During the prenatal period, these tissues become "imprinted" and subsequently serve to stimulate either masculine or feminine mating behavior at puberty. Testosterone suppresses the "female" pattern, so that "male" neural tissues become organized in programming later male sexual responses. If the ratio of testosterone is minimal, the sensitive brain areas differentiate as "female." It is as if some inner behavioral dial is set at "male" or "female" during prenatal life (Scarf, 1972*a*; Gerall, 1973; MacLusky and Naftolin, 1981).

John Money, a psychologist at Johns Hopkins Medical Center, suggests that a somewhat similar bipotential for maleness or femaleness exists prenatally in human beings (Money and Ehrhardt, 1972). He believes that the parts of the brain involved in sexuality are prenatally primed to make people more or less sensitive to certain kinds of environmental experiences. Money's research reveals that if the existing hormone balance is altered prenatally, it will result in altering postnatal behavior patterns. For example, if a female human fetus is given male hormones at a critical period during its development, the child who is born will tend to be more aggressive and more receptive to a variety of stimuli that are considered masculine in our culture than the average female. This is most apparent in cases of girls suffering from *adrenogenital syndrome* (Ehrhardt and Meyer-Bahlburg, 1981). The condition is caused by a genetic defect in which the adrenal glands produce an excess of male hormones during the prenatal period. Somewhat similar effects are produced among females whose mothers were administered male hormones to prevent miscarriage during pregnancy.

In one group of twenty-five girls with adrenogenital syndrome who were studied by Money and his associates, twenty claimed to be "tomboys." Compared with a matched group of other girls, the girls with the adrenogenital syndrome showed considerably less interest in dolls and infant care. The tomboys preferred to be outdoors playing athletic games. Many of them had a high level of physical energy and liked playing with boys more than girls. They tended to prefer toy cars, trucks, and guns and showed little interest in cosmetics, perfume, jewelry, or hairstyles. While all

Girls as Tomboys
Some parents worry when their daughters display behavior that they interpret as "masculine." Of interest, only a third of the heterosexual women in a study conducted under the auspices of the Kinsey Institute described themselves as "highly feminine" in their childhood.
Rick Smolan/Stock, Boston

THE PSYCHOLOGY OF SEX DIFFERENCES

Intense debate currently surrounds questions about the psychological nature of men and women. Traditionally the concepts "male" and "female" have been employed as opposites—as symbols of profound differences. Eleanor E. Maccoby and Carol N. Jacklin (1974) set out to assess the current state of scientific knowledge on male-female differences. They spent three years reviewing and interpreting over 2,000 books and articles on sex differences in behavior, motivation, and intelligence. They conclude that the following notions are *myths*:

- Girls are more sociable, empathic, and socially oriented than boys.
- Girls are more suggestible and susceptible to outside influences than boys.
- Girls have less self-esteem than boys.
- Girls excel at rote learning and simple repetitive tasks, while boys are superior at tasks requiring creative thinking.
- Boys are superior to girls in analyzing.
- Boys are more affected by environment, girls by heredity.
- Girls lack the drive and achievement motivation characteristic of boys.

Maccoby and Jacklin, however, did find four fairly "well-established" sex differences between boys and girls:

- Beginning around age eleven, girls exhibit greater verbal ability than boys.
- Boys are superior to girls on visual-spatial tasks in adolescence and adulthood, although not during childhood.
- At about twelve or thirteen years of age, boys move ahead of girls in mathematical ability.
- Boys are more aggressive than girls.

Not unexpectedly, the Maccoby-Jacklin findings have produced considerable controversy. Other psychologists launched new surveys of the literature regarding gender differences and have come to quite different conclusions. For example, Julia Sherman (1978) and Janet Shibley Hyde (1981) reexamined the evidence for the three cognitive gender differences that Maccoby and Jacklin considered to be "well-established" (verbal ability, visual-spatial ability, and mathematical ability). They concluded that the magnitude of the differences is at best quite small. And another reviewer, David B. Boles (1980), could find no support

the control-group girls were certain that they wanted to be mothers when they grew up, one-third of the girls with adrenogenital syndrome said that they would prefer not to have children. They also lagged behind their agemates in beginning their dating life and venturing into the beginnings of love play. But despite these signs of tomboyishness, they showed no indications of lesbianism in their erotic interests. Hence, although possibly influencing gender-related behavior, the introduction of excess male hormones during the prenatal period does not appear to affect gender identity.

David M. Quadagno and his associates (1977) suggest an alternative, nonhormonal hypothesis to that offered by Money. They believe that much of the modification of gender behavior in these girls was due to their having been reared differently by their parents. Further, the girls may have been unsure of their role as mothers due to certain biological problems (for instance, a number of the girls experienced a delay in the onset of menstruation). Even so, much of the animal literature supports the conclusion that prenatal endocrine factors play a part in influencing later behaviors. It seems unlikely that human beings are immune to such influences. A number of researchers suggest that hormonal factors again assume a major role at puberty, "pushing" individuals in the direction of male or female sex identities and behaviors (Imperato-McGinley et al., 1981).

Perhaps the safest conclusion we can draw at the present time is that hormones "flavor" a person for one kind of gender behavior or another. But even though hormones may predispose a person toward given kinds of behavior, they do not dictate that the behavior be learned. Rather, hormones make it easier for an individual to learn certain gender-related be-for the hypothesis that differences in spatial ability among adults are mediated by male hormones acting on the brain or by a sex-linked gene. Hence some psychologists conclude that if all we know about a child is the child's sex, we know next to nothing about the child's cognitive abilities (Plomin and Foch, 1981).

Maccoby and Jacklin also believe it highly likely that there is a biological component underlying gender differences in aggression. They base this conclusion on the following data:

- Subhuman primates show a male-female difference in aggression that resembles the difference between men and women.
- The overall greater aggressiveness of men is cross-culturally universal.
- Levels of aggression are responsive to alterations in the quantity and ratio of sex hormones.
- "There is no good evidence that adults reinforce boys' aggression more than girls' aggression; in fact, the contrary may be true."

But here too some psychologists take issue with Maccoby and Jacklin. For example, Todd Tieger (1980) has conducted his own survey of the literature and argues that gender differences in aggression become observable in children's spontaneous behavior only after five years of age. Further, during these early years, environmental conditions foster the differential learning of aggression by the two sexes. Whereas adults encourage boys to exhibit aggression, girls are pressured to inhibit it. However, in commenting on Tieger's review, Maccoby and Jacklin (1980) see little reason to alter their earlier conclusions. Nonetheless, they do point out that aggressiveness is not so much a characteristic of individuals as it is behavior that characterizes people in certain kinds of situations.

Although the psychology of sex differences remains a highly controversial area, one fact nevertheless stands out. The average behavioral differences between men and women allow considerable room for individual variations in the sexes. Not all men are more aggressive or better at math than all women, and not all women show greater language abilities than all men. Average differences between males and females appear to be trivial compared with individual differences within sexual groups. The only firm differences relate to primary sexual attributes and functions: women menstruate, gestate, and lactate; men ejaculate. In sum, it appears that there is little that is psychologically either male or female, although it often seems so.

haviors. And these behaviors are constantly being shaped and modified by the environment.

Some researchers have also looked to physical differences in the structure of the brain among male and female animals as a possible source of behavioral differences. For instance, a number of investigators report that male and female rats differ in the tissue of several brain regions (for example, in the density of synaptic connections among nerve cells of the hypothalamus) (MacLusky and Naftolin, 1981; Hines, 1982).

Researchers have likewise scrutinized the human brain for sex differences. The human brain is composed of two hemispheres, each of which is specialized for certain kinds of tasks. For example, the left hemisphere typically excels at verbal processing and the right hemisphere at spatial processing (see Chapter 6). Some evidence suggests that patterns of cognitive specialization of the hemispheres are stronger, on the average, in males than in females (Hines, 1982). These differences in the lateralization of function may be related to sex differences in the shape and size of the human *corpus callosum* (the thick band or cable of nerves that carry messages back and forth between the two hemispheres) (De LaCoste-Utamsing and Holloway, 1982). It should be emphasized, however, that we do not know whether sex differences in the structuring of particular regions of the brain are the source of differences in gender identity, behavior, sexual orientation, or cognitive processes.

Social Influences on Gender Behaviors

The fact that hormonal factors sometimes contribute to behavioral differences between men and women does not mean that environmental influences are unimportant. The major role played by environment is highlighted by **hermaphrodites**—individuals having the reproductive organs of both sexes. As a consequence of prenatal detours at critical junctures, individuals may develop both male and female internal reproductive organs; or they may possess external reproductive organs that are ambiguous, so that they appear to be one sex at birth only to find at puberty that they are the other.

John Money has conducted research with hermaphrodites that reveals the crucial part that social definitions play in influencing a child's gender identity. One of his most dramatic case histories is that of the identical-twin boy whose penis was accidentally cauterized during circumcision. When the child was seventeen months old, his parents decided in consultation with medical authorities that he should be reared as a girl. Surgical reconstruction was undertaken to make him a female. Since then, the child has successfully developed a female gender identification. Although the child was the dominant twin in infancy, by the time the twins were four years old there was little doubt about which twin was the girl and which the boy. At five the girl preferred dresses to pants; enjoyed wearing hair ribbons, bracelets, and frilly blouses; experimented happily with styles for her long hair; headed her Christmas list with dolls and a doll carriage; and, unlike her brother, was neat and dainty (Money and Tucker, 1975).

In another case, an individual who appeared "male" at birth learned at puberty, when breasts began to develop, that he possessed female sex organs. He demanded and received medical assistance, which enabled him to marry and, except for his inability to impregnate a woman, live an impeccably male life.

On the basis of his research with hermaphrodites, Money (Money and Tucker, 1975: 86–89) concludes that the most powerful factors in the shaping of gender identity are environmental:

> The chances are that society had nothing to do with the turnings you took in the prenatal sex development road, but the minute you were born, society took over. When the drama of your birth reached its climax, you were promptly greeted with the glad ritual cry, "It's a boy!" or "It's a girl!" depending on whether or not those in attendance observed a penis in your crotch. . . . The label "boy" or "girl," however, has tremendous force as a self-fulfilling prophecy, for it throws the full weight of society to one side or the other as the newborn heads for the gender identity fork [in the road], and the most decisive sex turning point of all. . . . [At birth you were limited to] something that was ready to become your gender identity. You were wired but not programmed for gender in the same sense that you were wired but not programmed for language.

Clearly, anatomy in itself does not provide us with our gender identity. Because of being labeled a boy or a girl, a higly stylized treatment of the child is inaugurated that is repeated countless times each day. Boys receive more toy vehicles, sports equipment, machines, toy animals, and military toys; girls receive more dolls, doll houses, and domestic toys. Boys' rooms are more often decorated with animal motifs; girls' rooms with floral motifs accompanied by lace, fringes, and ruffles (Rheingold and Cook, 1975). Behind many parents' concerns about the type of toys their children play with are unexpressed fears about homosexuality. Yet there is absolutely no evidence that children's toy preferences have anything to do with their later sexual preferences (Collins, 1984*b*).

Theories Regarding the Acquisition of Gender Identities

Social scientists have proposed a number of theories regarding the processes by which children psychologically become males or females. Among these are the psychoanalytic, cognitive learning, and cognitive-developmental approaches.

Psychoanalytic Theory. According to Sigmund Freud, children are psychologically bisexual at birth. They develop their gender identities as they resolve their conflicting feelings of love and jealousy in relation to their parents (see Chapter 2). A boy develops a strong love attraction for his mother but fears that his father will punish him by cutting off his penis. The usual outcome of this Oedipal situation is for a boy to repress his erotic desire for his mother and identify defensively with the potential aggressor, his father. As a consequence of coming to feel identified with their fathers, boys later erotically seek out females.

Meanwhile, Freud said, girls fall in love with their fathers. A girl blames her mother for her lack of a penis. But she soon comes to realize that she cannot replace her mother in her father's affections. So most girls resolve their Electra conflicts by identifying with their mothers, and later by finding suitable men to love.

Cognitive Learning Theory. Cognitive learning theorists take the view that children are essentially neutral at birth and that the biological differences between boys and girls are insufficient to account for later differences in gender identities. They stress the part that selective reinforcement and imitation play in the process of acquiring a gender identity (see Chapter 2). Viewed from this perspective, children reared in normal family settings are rewarded for modeling the behavior of the same-sex parent. And

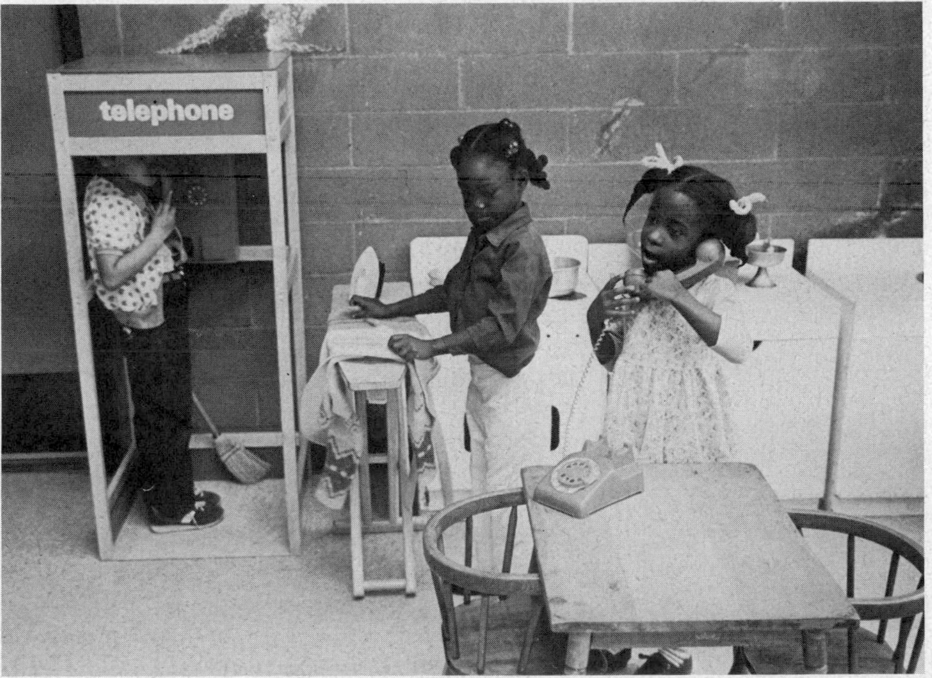

Acquiring Gender Identities

The members of society typically take considerable pains to socialize their children in the roles they deem appropriate for men and women. Children "pick up" the gender expectations that permeate their environment, and adults also intervene to cue children when they engage in behavior thought to be either appropriate or inappropriate for their gender.

Top, Michael Weisbrot and Family; *bottom*, Elizabeth Crews

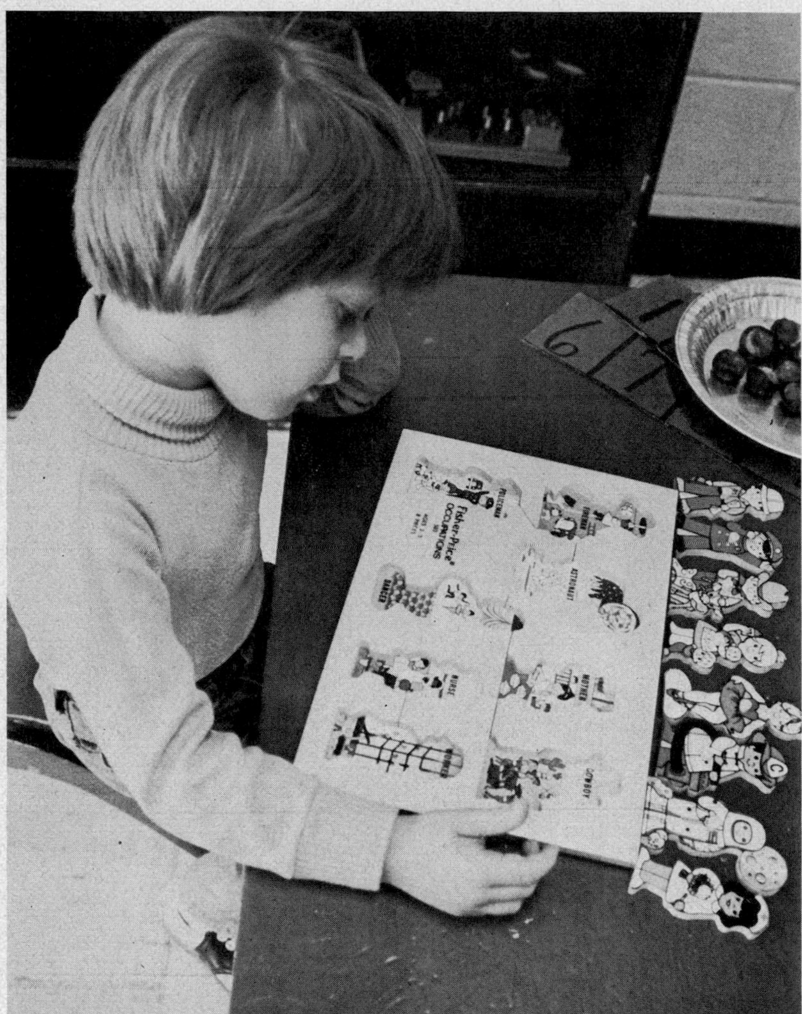

Sexist Toys

Children are taught their culture's definitions of appropriate male and female behaviors in a great variety of ways. Notice the gender typing of the occupations on the play board. Lawrence Kohlberg suggests that children use these stereotyped images in selecting and cultivating behaviors that are consistent with their gender concepts.

Patrick Reddy

the larger society later reinforces this type of imitation through systematic rewards and punishments. Boys and girls are actively rewarded and praised, both by adults and by their peers, for what society perceives to be sex-appropriate behavior, and they are ridiculed and punished for behavior inappropriate to their sex. Walter Mischel (1970) claims that children attend to, learn from, and imitate same-sex models more than opposite-sex models largely because they think of same-sex models as more like themselves.

Albert Bandura (1971*a*, 1973) gives an additional dimension to cognitive learning theory. He points out that in addition to imitating the behavior of adults, children engage in observational learning (see Chapter 2). According to Bandura, children mentally encode a model's behavior as they watch it but they will not imitate behavior they have observed unless they believe that it will have a positive outcome for them. He says that children discern which behaviors are appropriate for each sex by watching the behavior of many male and female models. They notice which kinds of behavior are performed by which sex in which kinds of situations. In turn, they employ these abstractions of sex-appropriate behavior as "models" for their own imitative actions. But not everything learned is performed. Thus, although boys may know how to wear a dress and apply makeup, few boys actually choose to perform these behaviors. Rather, they are most likely to perform those behaviors that they have coded as appropriate to their own gender. Consequently, the responses children select from their behavioral repertoires depend chiefly on the consequences they anticipate will follow from the behaviors (Perry and Bussey, 1979).

Cognitive-Developmental Theory. Still another approach, which is identified with Lawrence Kohlberg (Kohlberg, 1966; Kohlberg and Ullian, 1974), focuses on the part that cognitive development plays in children's acquisition of gender identities. This theory claims that children first learn to label themselves as males or females and then attempt to acquire and master the behaviors that fit their gender category. This process is called *self-socialization.* According to Kohlberg, children form a stereotyped conception of maleness and femaleness—an oversimplified, exaggerated, cartoonlike image. Then they use this stereotyped image in organizing their environment. They select and cultivate behaviors that are consistent with their gender concepts.

Kohlberg distinguishes between his approach and cognitive learning theory in these terms. According to the cognitive learning model, the following sequence occurs: "I want rewards; I am rewarded for doing boy things; therefore I want to be a boy." In contrast, Kohlberg (1966: 89) believes that the sequence goes like this: "I am a boy; therefore I want to do boy things; therefore the opportunity to do boy things (and to gain approval for doing them) is rewarding."

Genital anatomy plays a relatively minor part in young children's thinking about sex differences. Instead children notice and stereotype a relatively limited set of highly visible traits—hairstyle, clothes, stature, and occupation. Children use the stereotyped schemes or models of gender that they evolve to structure their experiences and to make inferences and interpretations regarding gender behaviors (Martin and Halverson, 1981). These schemes or models begin developing rather early in life. Thus Michael Lewis finds that by twelve months of age boys are more likely to look at pictures of boys when they are given a choice of pictures whereas girls are more likely to look at pictures of girls (Collins, 1984*b*). Likewise, when given a choice of toys, boys more often play with "boy" toys and girls more often play with "girl" toys. On the basis of her research, Marsha Weinraub concludes that by the time they are three years of age, 80 percent of American children are aware of gender differences (Collins, 1984*b*). By the age of twenty-six months, most children can reliably indicate what sex they are, and what sex others are. And by thirty-six months, most youngsters categorize tasks like driving a truck or delivering mail as "masculine" and cooking, cleaning, and sewing as "feminine" tasks.

Evaluation of Theories. It is easy to become caught up in the bickering between differing theorists and to overlook the extent to which their theories converge. All three theories that we have considered stress the importance of children's knowledge about gender stereotypes as powerful determinants of sex-typed behavior. And all three emphasize that behavioral differences between the sexes are at least in part perpetuated by the fact that children are more inclined to imitate the behavior of same-sex models than they are to imitate the behavior of opposite-sex models.

Further, as pointed out by Janet Shibley Hyde and B. G. Rosenberg (1976: 48–50), it is not difficult to find merit in all three theories:

> No theory is completely wrong. Each contributes something to our understanding. Freudian theory was important historically in emphasizing the notion of psychosexual development, highlighting the notion that individual sex identity and behavior have their roots in previous experiences. . . . Social [cognitive] learning theory is important in its emphasis on the social and cultural components of sex-role development—the importance of society in shaping sex-typed behaviors. . . . Social learning investigators have . . . contributed some very impressive laboratory demonstrations of the power of reinforcements in shaping children's behavior, in particular sex-typed behaviors. Social learning theory also highlights the importance of imitation in the acquisition of sex roles. . . . Finally, cognitive-developmental theory emphasizes that sex-role learning is a part of the rational learning process of childhood. . . . Children actively seek to acquire sex roles.

Thus, rather than counterposing the three theories in an either-or fashion, some social scientists prefer to see them as supplementing and complementing one another.

Mothers, Fathers, and Sex Typing

Parents have clear stereotypes regarding the behaviors they expect to be associated with male infants and female infants. Daughters are more often described by both their mothers and their fathers as "little," "beautiful," "pretty," and "cute" than sons are. Further, there are marked and relatively consistent dif-

Sex Typing

Evidence suggests that fathers are more concerned than mothers are about their children's development of culturally appropriate sex roles. Traditionally, it has been thought that boys learn to be masculine by identifying with their fathers. However, it now seems that a boy's masculinity may not be related to the masculinity of his father, and that the absence of a father in the home does not necessarily result in inadequate masculinity in a boy.

Paula Bronstein/Picture Group

ferences in paternal and maternal reactions to female and male infants (Parke, 1979). Fathers are more likely than mothers to view their sons as "firm," "large-featured," well-coordinated," "alert," "strong," and "hard." And they are more likely than mothers to describe their daughters as "soft," "fine-featured," "awkward," "inattentive," "weak," and "delicate" (Rubin, Provenzano, and Luria, 1974).

Evidence suggests that in American society it is the father who plays the critical role in encouraging "femininity" in females and "masculinity" in males in traditional terms (Block, 1974; Lynn, 1974, 1976; Johnson, 1975; Langlois and Downs, 1980). Fathers tend to be more concerned than mothers over their children's development of culturally appropriate sex roles (Lynn, 1974, 1976). And fathers treat their sons differently from their daughters. For instance, at twelve months of age, boys are punished more by their fathers than girls are. Further, whereas fathers give trucks and dolls with equal frequency to their daughters, most fathers withhold dolls from their sons (Snow, Jacklin, and Maccoby, 1983).

Both fathers and mothers are more eager to push their sons toward masculinity than their daughters toward femininity. David B. Lynn (1976: 406) observes:

> For many [parents], the issue is less a positive concern that the boy may be masculine than a negative concern that he not be feminine. Being a "sissy" means doing anything that little girls do. To a large extent masculinity is defined through negative admonishments: "Don't cry," "Don't dress up in your sister's clothes," "Don't play with dolls."

Parents generally express more negative reactions when boys make choices culturally defined as feminine than when girls make choices commonly defined as masculine.

Over the past forty years the following theory has dominated psychological inquiry and thinking regarding masculinity: boys learn to be masculine by identifying with their own fathers. Mentally healthy men have a good, firm sense of themselves as masculine beings. However, since fathers are frequently absent from many American homes during the formative years, large numbers of males grow into manhood lacking a secure sense of their masculinity. Male difficulties are compounded because so many teachers in the early grades are women. The results are very often homosexuality, exaggerated and overcompensating masculine behaviors, negative attitudes toward women, and poor psychological functioning.

These entrenched tenets are now being subjected to scrutiny and challenge. The psychologist Joseph H. Pleck (1981) has recently examined the evidence in support of traditional assumptions regarding masculinity and found the evidence wanting. He concludes that a boy's masculinity is not necessarily related to the masculinity of his father, a father's absence does not produce inadequate masculinity, and homosexuals do not invariably lack a sense of masculinity. In fact, Pleck believes that the old assumptions have damaging consequences for both men and women. They reinforce conventional expectations of what it means to be a man, feed feelings of inadequacy if these expectations are not achieved, and inhibit the expression of many emotions.

Other psychologists have also challenged traditional formulations regarding sex-typed behavior (Bem, 1975; Russell, 1978; Spence and Helmreich, 1978). They claim that individuals differ in their gender role attitudes and behaviors. As a consequence, some people successfully integrate aspects of both the traditional masculine and the traditional feminine gender roles within their own gender role concepts. **Androgyny** is the term commonly used to refer to the capacity of men and women to be both masculine and feminine in their attitudes and behavior—both tough and tender, dominant and submissive, active and passive (DeFrain, 1979).

THE DEVELOPMENT OF EMOTION

Cognitive factors also play an important part in influencing our experience of emotion. Chapter 8 examined the development of emotion and the establishment of social bonds among infants. As children grow older, they become able to identify and attach labels like "anger," "fear," "sadness," and "happiness" to their inner states (Russell and Ridgeway, 1983). They also come to realize that the emotions they experience internally need not be translated into overt action (for instance, rage need not become aggression) (Saarni, 1979).

During the preschool years, fear plays an unusually important part in the lives of young children. Psychologists define **fear** as an unpleasant emotion aroused by impending danger, pain, or misfortune. Some psychologists use the terms "fear" and "anxiety" interchangeably. Others define fear as a response to tangible stimuli (for instance, snakes, fast-moving vehicles, or high places) and anxiety as a diffuse, unfocused emotional state. In actual practice, however, it is often difficult to distinguish between fear and anxiety. Psychologists also distinguish between fear and phobia. Whereas fear may be viewed as a normal reaction to threatening stimuli, **phobia** is an excessive, persistent, and unadaptive fear response (usually to benign or ill-defined stimuli).

Between two and six years of age, children's fear of certain tangible and immediate situations decreases (Jersild and Holmes, 1935*a*; 1935*b*; Formanek, 1983). For instance, they become less afraid of noises, strange objects and persons, falling, high places, and sudden movements accompanied by changes in light (shadows and flashes). But they become more afraid of imaginary creatures, the dark, and being alone or abandoned. Between six and nine years of age, children often fear preternatural figures, such as ghosts, Dracula, and monsters. And as children move into the elementary-school years, fears regarding their personal safety (fears of kidnapping, accidents, and storms) tend to decline, while social fears associated with school (worries about grades and teachers) increase. Two-thirds of American elementary-school children are afraid that "somebody bad" might get into their homes, and one-fourth are afraid that when they go outside, somebody might hurt them. Nowadays children seem more afraid than they were in the past of nuclear war, lung cancer, pollution, and muggings (Brozan, 1983*b*).

Children's fears are not completely irrational. For example, most of the children who say that they are afraid to go outside also say that in the past, someone (child or adult) outside the home hurt them or made them afraid. Another finding is that some children are afraid of their parents; one in ten children name their fathers as the person they are most afraid of (Flaste, 1977). In some circumstances, children have legitimate concern that a parent may abuse them or a divorced parent kidnap them. It is important to note, however, that children show marked differences in their susceptibility to fear and in the sources of their fears.

While fear can sometimes get out of hand and take on incapacitating and destructive qualities, it does serve an essential "self-preservation" function (see the boxed insert on page 260). If we did not have a healthy fear of fierce animals, fire, and speeding automobiles, few of us would be alive today. Selma H. Fraiberg (1959: 11), a clinical psychologist, observes:

> [The child] learns to *anticipate* "danger" and prepare for it. And he prepares for "danger" by means of *anxiety!* . . . From this we immediately recognize that anxiety is not a pathological condition in itself but a necessary and normal physiological and mental preparation for danger.

HELPING CHILDREN COPE WITH THEIR FEARS

Early and provident fear is the mother of safety.

—EDMUND BURKE

Fear is an inescapable and necessary human emotion. It fosters caution and prudence and increases our energy in times of danger. But fear can also outlast its usefulness or become misplaced, so that it interferes with healthy adaptations to life. Instead of aiding us to mobilize our resources, fear may immobilize them.

Many fears that children develop cannot be avoided, nor should they be. Rather, a child can be encouraged to develop constructive mechanisms for coping with fear. Here are some techniques that psychologists have found useful for helping children deal with fear (Jersild and Holmes, 1935*b*; Jersild, Telford, and Sawrey, 1975; Formanek, 1983):

- Create an accepting situation in which children feel at ease in sharing their fears with you. Help them to appreciate that adults, including yourself, also have fears.
- Encourage a child to acquire skills that will provide specific aid in dealing with the feared situation or object. Children are usually eager to shed their fears, and they are most successful when they themselves develop the competence to do so. Children who are afraid of the dark can be provided with the means to "control darkness": a night-light with a readily accessible switch can be placed next to their beds.
- Lead children by degrees into active contact with and participation in situations that they fear (an approach termed *desensitization*). This technique has been successfully employed in the reduction of fears associated with snakes, spiders, heights, airplanes, and hospitals.
- Give children opportunities to encounter a feared stimulus in normal environmental circumstances and to deal with it on their own terms. That is, they should be permitted to inspect, ignore, approach, or avoid the stimulus as they see fit. And pair the feared stimulus with pleasant activities.
- Allow the child to observe the fearless actions of other children and adults when they encounter the same stimulus that the child fears. In one study, a group of nursery school children who were afraid of dogs watched another child their own age happily playing with a dog. After eight sessions in which they saw the child romp with the dog, two-thirds of the children were willing to play with the experimental dog, and with an unfamiliar dog as well (Bandura, Grusec, and Menlove, 1967).

In contrast, the following techniques are relatively ineffective and may complicate the child's difficulties:

- Coercing the child into contact with the feared situation by physical force, scolding, or ridicule ("Don't be such a baby!" or "Come on, pet the nice doggie. He won't hurt you!")
- Making fun of the child's fear
- Shaming the child before others because of the fear
- Ignoring the child's fear
- Goading children into trying things they are not ready for, such as riding a roller coaster or diving off a diving board

In sum, although caretakers cannot protect children from all fear (and it would be undesirable if they could), they can help children deal with their fears in a constructive manner.

SUMMARY

1. Intelligence refers to a person's general problem-solving abilities. Psychologists have applied differing models to the study of intelligence. Some psychologists view intelligence as a composite of many special, independent abilities. Others depict it as a process deriving from the interplay between children and their environment. Still others portray intelligence as an information-processing activity.
2. Psychologists differ in the relative importance that they attribute to heredity and environment in fashioning an individual's intelligence.

However, most social and behavioral scientists believe that any extreme view regarding the nature-nurture controversy is unjustified at the present time.

3. Jean Piaget calls the years between two and seven the "preoperational period." The principal achievement of the preoperational period is the developing capacity of children to represent the external world internally through the use of symbols.
4. During the preoperational period children have difficulty solving conservation problems. Logical thought is inhibited by obstacles associated with centering, transformations, reversibility, and egocentrism.
5. Memory is an integral component of cognition. Without memory, we could hardly think or reason.
6. Memory includes recall, recognition, and the facilitation of relearning.
7. As children develop, they become increasingly active agents in the remembering process. Among the strategies that facilitate remembering are grouping information into meaningful categories and rehearsing information.
8. In order to function as effective members of society, children need to develop the capacity mentally to "locate" or "place" individuals in their appropriate social categories. Sociologists call these categories "roles."
9. Through the cognitive structure termed the "self," we are able to take the viewpoint of other people and imagine what they anticipate and expect of us in a given role. It allows us imaginatively to exchange roles in order to grasp the requirements for sustained social interaction. A sense of self does not develop all at once, in an all-or-none fashion; it evolves through early, middle, and later childhood and in fact changes throughout life.
10. Research by John Money suggests that a bipotential for maleness or femaleness exists before birth. According to Money, prenatal hormones influence the subsequent course of a child's attraction to "masculine" or "feminine" behaviors.
11. On the basis of his research with hermaphrodites, Money concludes that the most powerful factors in the shaping of gender identity are environmental. Individuals are wired but not programmed for gender identity.
12. Psychoanalytic theory stresses the part that Oedipal conflicts play in shaping children's gender identities. Cognitive learning theory emphasizes the part played by selective reinforcement and imitation. Cognitive-developmental theory claims that children first come to categorize themselves as male or female and then attempt to acquire and master those behaviors that fit their gender category.
13. Evidence suggests that in American society it is the father who plays the critical part in encouraging "femininity" in females and "masculinity" in males.
14. Between two and six years of age, children's fear of certain tangible and immediate situations decreases, while their fear of imaginary creatures, the dark, and being alone or abandoned increases.

KEY TERMS

androgyny The capacity of men and women to be both masculine and feminine in their attitudes and behavior.

causality The attribution of a cause-and-effect relationship to two paired events that recur in succession.

centering Concentration on one feature of a situation while neglecting other aspects. The process is characteristic of preoperational children.

conservation The concept that the quantity or amount of something stays the same regardless of changes in its shape or position.

correlation coefficient A numerical expression of the degree of relationship between two variables or conditions.

egocentrism Lack of awareness that there are viewpoints other than one's own.

fear An unpleasant emotion aroused by impending danger, pain, or misfortune.

gender identity The conception that people have of themselves as being female or male.

gender role A set of cultural expectations that define the ways in which the members of each sex should behave.

hermaphrodite An individual having the reproductive organs of both sexes. As a consequence of prenatal detours at critical junctures, individuals may develop both male and female internal reproductive organs; or they may possess external reproductive organs that are ambiguous, so that they appear to be one sex at birth only to find at puberty that they are the other.

intelligence A person's problem-solving ability.

long-term memory The retention of information over an extended period of time, through repeated rehearsal or because of a very intense single experience.

memory The retention of what has been experienced or learned.

metacognition Individuals' awareness and understanding of their mental processes.

metamemory Individuals' awareness and understanding of their memory processes.

phobia An excessive, persistent, and unadaptive fear response (usually to benign or ill-defined stimuli).

preoperational period According to Piaget, a stage in cognitive development that occurs between two and seven years of age. The principal achievement of the period is the developing capacity of children to represent the external world internally through the use of symbols. Its primary limitation is the inability of children to solve conservation problems.

reversible Operations capable of being turned back in opposite order to an earlier state. Children in the preoperational period fail to recognize that operations are reversible.

role A definition that specifies who does what, and when and where they do it; an expectation that group members hold regarding people's behavior in given settings.

self The system of concepts we use in defining ourselves; an awareness of oneself as a separate entity who is able to think and initiate action.

sensory information storage The preservation of information from the senses just long enough to permit the stimuli to be scanned for processing (generally less than two seconds).

short-term memory The retention of information for a very brief period, usually not more than thirty seconds.

two-factor theory of intelligence An approach that views intelligence as made up of two components: (1) a general, or "g," factor that is employed for abstract reasoning and problem solving, and (2) special, or "s," factors that are peculiar to given tasks.

10

Early Childhood: Integration into the Human Group

What we desire our children to become, we must endeavour to be before them.

—ANDREW COMBE
Physiological and Moral Management of Infancy

Children are newcomers to the human group, strangers in an alien land. Genes do not convey *culture*—the socially standardized lifeways of a people. Clyde Kluckhohn (1960: 21–22), a distinguished anthropologist, provides an illustration of this point:

> Some years ago I met in New York City a young man who did not speak a word of English and was obviously bewildered by American ways. By "blood" he was as American as you or I, for his parents had gone from Indiana to China as missionaries. Orphaned in infancy, he was reared by a Chinese family in a remote village. All who met him found him more Chinese than American. The facts of his blue eyes and light hair were less impressive than a Chinese style of gait, Chinese arm and hand movements, Chinese facial expression, and Chinese modes of thought. The biological heritage was American, but the cultural training had been Chinese. He returned to China.

The process of transmitting culture, of transforming children into bona fide, functioning members of society, is called **socialization.** Through socialization children acquire the knowledge, skills, and dispositions that enable them to participate effectively in group life. Since infants enter a society that is already an ongoing concern, they need to be fitted to their people's unique social environment. They must come to guide their behavior by the established standards—the accepted dos and don'ts—of their society.

The magnitude of a child's accomplishment over a relatively short period of time is truly astonishing. By their fourth birthday most American children have mastered the complicated and abstract structure of the English language. And they can carry on complex social interactions in accordance with American cultural patterns.

The enormity of this achievement strikes us when as adults we find ourselves in a society with a different culture from our own. Edmund Carpenter (1965: 55), an anthropologist, describes his feelings when he first began living among the Aivilik, an Eskimo people:

> For months after I first arrived among the Aivilik, I felt empty, clumsy. I never knew what to do, even where to sit or stand. I was awkward in a busy world, as helpless as a child, yet a grown man. I felt like a mental defective.

Only as Carpenter slowly and patiently learned the cultural ways of the Aivilik and became accepted by them did he feel comfortable in the new setting.

By the time a child reaches the age of two, the socialization process has already begun. Developmental psychologists David P. Ausubel and Edmund V. Sullivan (1970: 260) observe:

> At this time parents become less deferential and attentive. They comfort the child less and demand more conformity to their own desires and to cultural norms. During this period [in most societies] the child is frequently weaned, is expected to acquire sphincter control, approved habits of eating and cleanliness, and do more things for himself. Parents are less disposed to gratify his demands for immediate gratification, expect more frustration tolerance and responsible behavior, and may even require performance of some household chores. They also become less tolerant toward displays of childish aggression.

Hence it is within the family setting that the child is first introduced to the requirements of group life.

PARENTING

> *A young branch takes on all the bends that one gives it.*
>
> —*Chinese Proverb*

It is generally agreed that parenting is one of the most difficult tasks any adult faces. Moreover, most parents are well intentioned and desire to succeed at parenting. Since the task is a difficult one that encompasses many years and consumes much energy, parents have looked to experts in child psychology to provide them with guidelines for rearing mentally and physically healthy youngsters. But when parents turn to "authorities," they encounter immense frustration. They confront an endless array of child-rearing books, misinformation, gimmickry, and outright quackery.

Let us consider parenting and attempt to make sense of some of these matters.

The Search for Key Child-Rearing Practices

> *Parents wonder why the streams are bitter, when they themselves have poisoned the fountain.*
>
> —JOHN LOCKE

For many years, psychologists assumed that socialization effects flow essentially in one direction, namely, from parent to child (see Chapter 5). Consequently, they dedicated themselves to the task of uncovering the part that different parenting practices have in shaping a child's personality and behavior. Three dimensions emerged from this research:

- The warmth or hostility of the parent-child relationship (acceptance-rejection)
- The control or autonomy of the disciplinary approach (restrictiveness-permissiveness)
- The consistency or inconsistency that parents show in using discipline

The Warmth-Hostility Dimension. Many psychologists have insisted that one of the most significant aspects of the home environment is the warmth of the relationship between parent and child (Symonds, 1939; Sears, Maccoby, and Levin, 1957; Becker, 1964; McClelland et al., 1978). Parents show warmth toward their children through affectionate, accepting, approving, understanding, and child-centered behaviors. When disciplining their children, parents who are warm tend to employ frequent explanations, use words of encouragement and praise, and only infrequently resort to physical punishment. Hostility, in contrast, is shown through cold, rejecting, disapproving, self-centered, and highly punitive behaviors (Becker, 1964).

Wesley C. Becker (1964), in a review of the research on parenting, found that love-oriented techniques tend to promote children's acceptance of self-responsibility and to foster self-control through inner mechanisms of guilt. In contrast, parental hostility interferes with conscience development and breeds aggressiveness and resistance to authority.

The Control-Autonomy Dimension. Psychologists have emphasized that a second dimension also assumes critical importance in shaping the home environment: the restrictions that parents place on a child's behavior in such areas as sex play, modesty, table manners, toilet training, neatness, orderliness, care of household furniture, noise, obedience, and aggression toward others (Sears, Maccoby, and Levin, 1957; Becker, 1964). On the whole, psychologists have suggested that highly restrictive parenting fosters dependency and interferes with independence training (Maccoby and Masters, 1970). However, as Becker (1964: 197) observes in his review of the research literature, psychologists have had difficulty coming up with a "perfect" all-purpose set of parental guidelines:

> The consensus of the research suggests that both restrictiveness and permissiveness entail certain risks. Restrictiveness, while fostering well-controlled, socialized behavior, tends also to lead to fearful, dependent, and submissive behaviors, a dulling of intellectual striving and inhibited hostility. Permissiveness on the other hand, while fostering outgoing, sociable, assertive behaviors and intellectual striving, tends also to lead to less persistence and increased aggressiveness.

Combinations of Parenting Approaches. Rather than examine the warmth-hostility and control-autonomy dimensions in isolation from one another, a number of psychologists (Schaefer, 1959; Becker, 1964) have explored their four combinations: warmth-control, warmth-autonomy, hostility-control, and hostility-autonomy. Figure 10.1 utilizes these descriptive categories to show various parent-child relations and their assumed consequences.

Warm but restrictive parenting is believed to lead to politeness, neatness, obedience, and conformity. It also is thought to be associated with immaturity, dependency, low creativity, blind acceptance of authority, and social withdrawal and ineptness (Levy, 1943; Becker, 1964). Eleanor E. Maccoby (1961) found that twelve-year-old boys who had been reared in warm

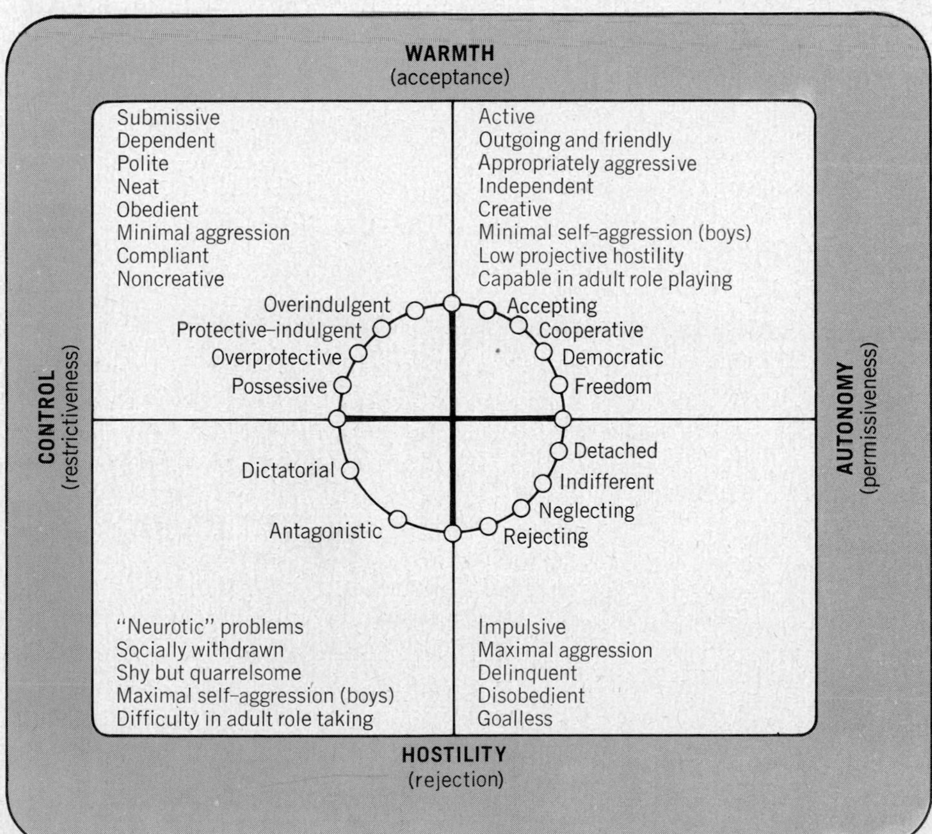

Figure 10.1 Relationships Between Parents' and Children's Behavior

This figure represents the four combinations of the warmth-hostility and control-autonomy dimensions of parenting: warmth-control, warmth-autonomy, hostility-control, and hostility-autonomy. The terms around the circle (in black) are types of parental behavior. Listed in each box (in color) are children's personality traits that are associated with each of the four combinations of parenting. Of course, even at best, these are only general tendencies and not hard-and-fast results.

SOURCE: Adapted from E. S. Schaefer, "A Circumplex Model for Maternal Behavior," *Journal of Abnormal and Social Psychology*, Vol. 59 (1959), p. 232; and W. C. Becker, "Consequences of Different Kinds of Parental Discipline," in M. L. Hoffman and L. W. Hoffman (eds.), *Review of Child Development Research* (New York: Russell Sage Foundation, 1964), pp. 169–208.

and restrictive homes were strict rule enforcers with their peers. Compared with other children, these boys also displayed less overt aggression, less misbehavior, and greater motivation toward schoolwork.

Psychologists report that children whose homes combine warmth with democratic procedures tend to develop into socially competent, resourceful, friendly, active, and appropriately aggressive individuals (Kagan and Moss, 1962; Becker, 1964; Lavoie and Looft, 1973). Where parents also encourage self-confidence, independence, and mastery in social and academic situations, the children are likely to show self-reliant, creative, goal-oriented, and responsible behavior. Where parents fail to foster independence, permissiveness often produces self-indulgent children with little impulse control and low academic standards.

Hostile (rejecting) and restrictive parenting is believed to interfere with children's developing self-identities and a sense of personal adequacy and competence. Children come to see the world as dominated by powerful, malignant forces over which they have no control. The combination of hostility and restrictiveness is said to foster resentment and inner rage. Some of the anger is turned against the self or experienced as internalized turmoil and conflict. This can result in "neurotic problems," self-punishing and suicidal tendencies, and inadequacy in adult role playing (Becker, 1964).

Parenting that combines hostility with permissiveness is thought to be associated with delinquent and aggressive behavior in children. Rejection breeds resentment and hostility, which, when combined with inadequate parental control, can be translated into aggressive and antisocial actions. When such parents do employ discipline, it is usually physical, capricious, and severe. It often reflects parental rage and rejection and hence fails as a constructive instrument for developing appropriate standards of conduct (Becker, 1964).

Consistency in Discipline. Consistency in discipline is the third dimension of parenting that many psychologists have stressed is central to a child's home environment. Effective discipline is consistent and unambiguous. It builds a high degree of predictability into the child's environment. While it is often difficult to punish children on a consistent, regular basis, re-

Discipline

Parents take different approaches to discipline, and research suggests that these different approaches have different consequences in shaping children's personalities and behavior.

Patrick Reddy

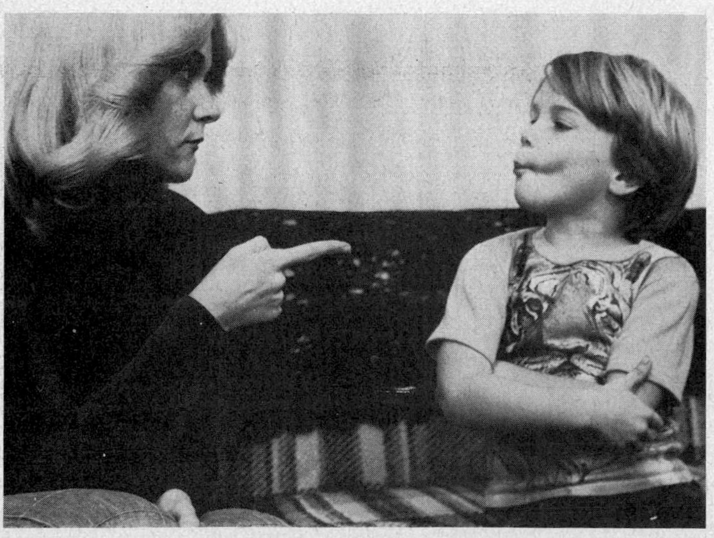

search by Ross D. Parke and Jan L. Deur reveals that erratic punishment generally fails to inhibit the punished behavior (Deur and Parke, 1970; Parke and Deur, 1972). (The boxed insert on pages 270–271 discusses punishment as a teaching mechanism.) In the case of aggression, it has been found that the most aggressive children are those whose parents are permissive toward aggression on some occasions but severely punish it on others (Sears, Maccoby, and Levin, 1957). Research suggests that parents who use punishment inconsistently actually create in their children a resistance to future attempts to extinguish the undesirable behavior (Deur and Parke, 1970; Parke, 1974).

Inconsistency can occur when the same parent responds differently at different times to the same behavior. It can also occur when one parent ignores or encourages a behavior that the other parent punishes. On the basis of his observation of family interaction patterns in the homes of 136 middle-class preschool boys, Hugh Lytton (1979) found that mothers typically initiate more actions designed to control their children's behavior than fathers do. However, the boys were less inclined to obey their mothers than they were their fathers. But when their fathers were present, they were more likely to be responsive to their mothers' commands and prohibitions. By the same token, the father's presence spurred the mother's behavior. She was more likely to reinforce the child's compliance, especially by positive, friendly acts. Lytton says it seemed as if she "knew" what was "expected" of her as a mother. However, she did not always carry it out to the same extent when she was alone with the child.

Parenting Styles

Diana Baumrind (1966, 1971*a*), a developmental psychologist, provides another scheme for examining and analyzing patterns of parental authority. She distinguishes among *authoritarian, authoritative, permissive,* and *harmonious* techniques of control:

- **Authoritarian parenting.** The authoritarian parent attempts to shape, control, and evaluate a child's behavior in accordance with traditional and absolute values and standards of conduct. Obedience is stressed, verbal give-and-take discouraged, and punitive, forceful discipline preferred.
- **Authoritative parenting.** The authoritative parent provides firm direction for a child's overall activities but gives the child considerable freedom within reasonable limits. Parental control is not rigid, punitive, intrusive, or unnecessarily restrictive. The parent provides reasons for given policies and engages in verbal give-and-take with the child, meanwhile responding to the child's wishes and needs.
- **Permissive parenting.** Permissive parents seek to provide a nonpunitive, accepting, and affirmative environment in which the children regulate their own behavior as much as possible. Children are consulted about family policies and decisions. Parents make few demands on children for household responsibility or orderly behavior.
- **Harmonious parenting.** Harmonious parents seldom exercise direct control over their children. They attempt to cultivate an egalitarian relationship, one in which the child is not placed at a power disadvantage. They typically emphasize humane values as opposed to the predominantly materialistic and achievement values they view as operating within mainstream society.

In a number of studies of white middle-class nursery-school children, Baumrind (1971*a*) found that different types of parenting tend to be related to quite different behaviors in children. Authoritative parenting was often associated with self-reliant, self-controlled, explorative, and contented children. In contrast, the offspring of authoritarian parents tended to be discontented, withdrawn, and distrustful. (And as pointed out in the boxed insert on page 273, in some cases authoritarian parenting may be associated with child abuse and incest.) The least self-reliant, explorative, and self-controlled children were those with permissive parents.

The harmonious parents identified by Baumrind were only a small group. Of the eight children studied, six were girls and two were boys. The girls were extraordinarily competent, independent, friendly, achievement-oriented, and intelligent. The boys, in contrast, were cooperative but notably submissive, aimless, dependent, and not achievement-oriented. Although the sample was too small to be the basis for definitive conclusions, Baumrind tentatively suggests that these outcomes of harmonious parenting may be sex-related.

PUNISHMENT

Punishment is widely applied in our society as a technique to control people's behavior. We spank children, fire employees, fail students, and put lawbreakers in jail.

Negative Aspects of Punishment

A disadvantage of punishment as a method of behavior control is its essential negativity; it aims only to eliminate or reduce an undesired behavior, not to establish or develop a desired behavior. That is, it teaches individuals what *not* to do, but it fails to teach them what *to* do. Moreover, children may concentrate on attempting to avoid the punishing agent, which can be a serious hindrance to learning because it deprives the child of the opportunity to acquire the socially desired behaviors.

People tend to associate the term "punishment" exclusively with punishment that inflicts physical hurt. But this is only one type of punitive action, and it is generally considered by experts to be the most undesirable (Parke, 1977; Walters and Grusec, 1977). In its extreme forms, physical punishment is more accurately labeled physical abuse.

Verbal violence—yelling, threatening, criticizing, ridiculing, scolding, and so on—is the most common form of punishment in the home. Violence, whether verbal or physical, sets a poor example. A parent or teacher who yells at or slaps a child is unwittingly supplying a model for aggression.

Another common form of punishment involves the withdrawal of rewards or privileges. Examples are the withholding of an allowance, the curtailment of television viewing, and the banishment of a favorite toy.

Effectiveness of Punishment

A variety of factors influence the effectiveness of punishment:

- *Level of intensity.* Research with animals reveals that a very intense level of punishment is more effective than a very mild level of punishment (Solomon, 1964). Studies investigating the effects of various levels of punishing noise on children tend to substantiate the finding that the maximum effect is derived from high-intensity punishment (Parke, 1974). However, the overall negative effects of severe punishment seem to indicate that it is counterproductive, as well as being inhumane. Moreover, in some learning situations, such as those involving subtle discriminations, children benefit more from low-intensity punishment. It seems that high-intensity punishment creates a level of anxiety too high to allow adaptive learning to take place (Parke, 1977).
- *Timing.* The timing of a punishing stimulus influences its effectiveness. With young children, punishment has its greatest impact if it is applied immediately after the transgression begins, rather than after the transgression has continued for a time. For instance, children who are immediately reprimanded for playing with a forbidden toy are more likely not to play with the toy again than children who are permitted to hold it or play with it for a while before being reprimanded (Aronfreed and Reber, 1965). With older children, especially those aged ten or more, delayed punishment is

Baumrind believes that authoritative parenting gives children a comfortable, supported feeling while they explore the environment and gain interpersonal competence. Such children do not experience the anxiety and fear associated with strict, repressive parenting or the indecision and uncertainty associated with unstructured, permissive parenting.

On the basis of her research, Baumrind (1972) found a number of parental practices and attitudes that seem to facilitate the development of socially responsible and independent behavior in children:

- It helps when the parents themselves are socially responsible and self-assertive people who serve as daily models of these behaviors.
- Parents should employ firm enforcement policies geared to reward socially responsible and independent behavior and to punish deviant behavior. This technique uses the reinforcement principles of conditioning (see Chapter 2). It is even more effective when parental demands are accompanied by explanations and when punish-

effective so long as the misbehavior is verbally restated at the time of punishment so the child understands the nature of his or her wrongdoing (Verna, 1977).

- *Consistency.* To be most effective, the punishing stimulus should be delivered on *every* occasion that the individual engages in the undesired behavior. A person should not be permitted to avoid the punishment except by avoiding the deviant behavior (Johnston, 1972). As the text points out, inconsistent punishment makes a behavior exceedingly resistant to change.

- *Providing alternatives.* Punishment of a behavior is likely to be more effective if a socially acceptable method for obtaining a comparable kind of gratification is made available to the child (Johnston, 1972). In addition to punishing a child for opening the oven door, the adult should provide the child with another door that can be opened and freely explored—for instance, a cupboard containing pots and pans or toys.

- *Relationship with punisher.* Punishment delivered by an adult who has a close and affectionate relationship with the child is more effective than that administered by a person whose relationship is distant and impersonal (Parke, 1967; Aronfreed, 1968). Punishment may achieve effectiveness partly because the child views it as symbolizing the loss of approval and affection. The child may be motivated to eliminate certain behaviors in order to reinstate the affectional relationship (Parke, 1974).

- *Use of reason.* Punishment is more effective if the person is told the reasons for the prohibition and the punishment. Ross D. Parke (1974) has found in his experiments that children show greater subsequent inhibition of a behavior if they are told in the course of punishment that a toy is "fragile and may break" than if they are punished without an explanation. Moreover, he finds that an explanation in the absence of punishment is more effective than punishment in the absence of an explanation. Still, the most potent method is the combination of punishment and explanation.

- *Setting an example.* Punishment by parents who "practice what they preach" tends to be more effective than punishment by parents who do not (Mischel and Liebert, 1966).

Punishment in its various forms is an inescapable aspect of life and an important mechanism of socialization. As James M. Johnston (1972: 1051) observes:

> Throughout our daily activities we are constantly barraged by a variety of stimuli which have punishing effects, whether it be someone's frown or bumping into a chair we did not see. In other words, unconditioned and conditioned punishing stimuli as consequences to behavior delivered by our social and physical environment are as much a natural part of our lives as are positively reinforcing consequences. This being the case, behavioral science should undertake to understand and to control the results of [the use of punishment].

In so doing, human beings may be able to apply punishment more constructively while minimizing its use in an inhumane manner or for inhumane purposes.

ment is accompanied by reasons that are consistent with principles the parents themselves live by.

- Parents who are nonrejecting serve as more attractive models and reinforcing agents than rejecting parents do.

- Parents should emphasize and encourage individuality, self-expression, initiative, divergent thinking, and socially appropriate aggressiveness. These values are translated into daily realities as parents make demands upon their children and assign them responsibility.

- Parents should provide their children with a complex and stimulating environment that offers challenge and excitement. At the same time, children should experience their environment as affording security and opportunities for rest and relaxation.

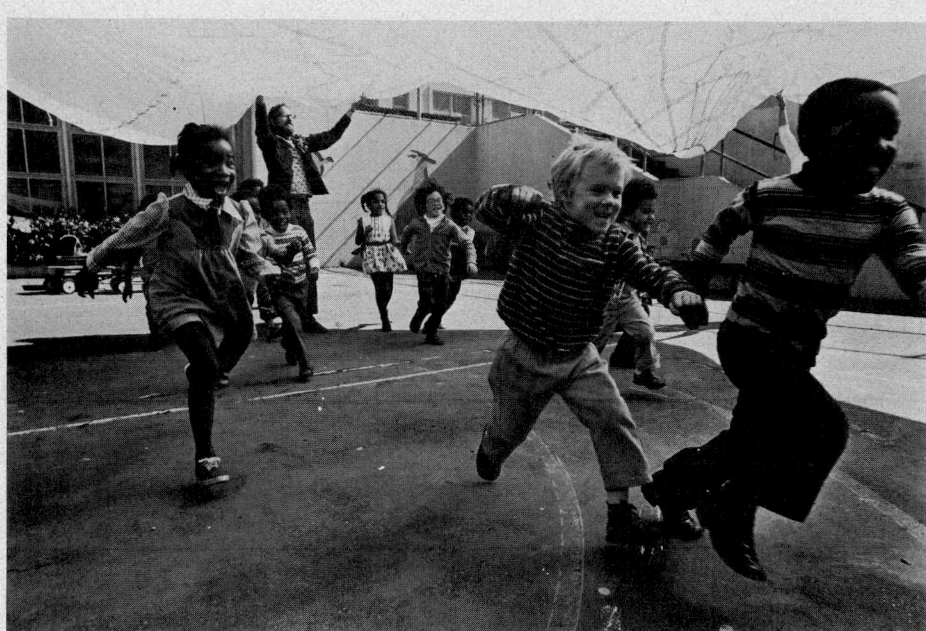

Styles of Child Rearing

In seeking out day care centers and nursery schools for their children, middle-class parents often look for an arrangement that is compatible with their own child-rearing philosophy. For instance, parents who favor permissive parenting tend to prefer a non-punitive, accepting caretaking environment.

Peeter Vilms/Jeroboam

The Parent-Child Relationship

As discussed in Chapter 5, for many years psychologists and psychiatrists stressed the parents' role in shaping children's personalities and behavior. They paid little attention to the children's role as active agents in their own socialization and in influencing the behavior of their caretakers. All this has changed over the past decade, resulting in a more balanced perspective (Lytton, 1980; Walters and Walters, 1980). Indeed, the entire panorama of childhood experience has been expanded to encompass the study of the broad web of relationships in which children find themselves. In addition to parents, this network may include siblings, grandparents, stepparents, playmates, teachers, and others.

The parenting dimensions and styles that we have considered thus far in the chapter have had as their focus global patterns and practices. But they are much too abstract and gross to capture the subtleties of parent-child interaction. In everyday life parents reveal a great variety of parenting behaviors, depending on the situation. For instance, they can be warm or cold, restrictive or permissive, and consistent or inconsistent, depending on the setting and circumstances (Grusec and Kuczynski, 1981; Clarke-Stewart and Hevey, 1981; Passman and Blackwelder, 1981). Further, as discussed in Chapter 5, psychologists find that a child's characteristics influence the treatment he or she receives from adults. These characteristics include such variables as age (Kagan and Moss, 1962), sex (Maccoby and Jacklin, 1974; Martin, 1981), and temperament (Bell, 1968).

The interactive character of the parent-child relationship assumes paramount importance in the socialization process. The child's response to being disciplined modifies the parent's behavior and the parent's choice of future disciplinary measures (Parke, 1977). Certain situational contexts also influence an adult's evaluation of a child's behavior, and this in turn affects the nature and severity of the disciplinary practices the adult chooses. And finally, the way the child *perceives* the actions of the parent may be more decisive than the parent's actions in themselves (Levenson, 1973). Thus children are not interchangeable, responding in identical fashion to the same type of caretaker input.

A recent follow-up on a classic study helps us in clarifying some of these matters. In the 1950s, three Harvard psychologists had carried out one of the most enterprising studies of child rearing ever undertaken in the United States. Robert Sears, Eleanor Maccoby, and Harry Levin (1957) had attempted to identify those parenting techniques that make a difference in personality development. They had interviewed 379 mothers of kindergartners in the Boston area and

INCEST

Most of us find the idea that parents may be sexually attracted to their children so offensive that we prefer not to think about it. Indeed, only in the past decade or so have professionals come to view incest as a major mental health problem. Approximately one-third of all reported cases of child molestation are committed by strangers. Another third involve acquaintances known to the child (a neighbor, a friend of the family, or a community figure). Finally, one-third are committed by primary relatives. It is estimated that for every ten female victims of incest there is one male victim (Hinds, 1981*b*). Mother-son incest is rare.

Incest usually occurs in large families. The perpetrator is commonly the father, an uncle, or another male authority figure in the household. In cases of father-daughter incest, the fathers tend to be "family tyrants" who use physical force and intimidation to dominate their families (Finkelhor, 1979; Herman and Hirschman, 1981). However, the daughter chosen as the object of the father's sexual attention may be exempted from physical attack and may tolerate the father's sexual advances so as to preserve her privileged position. Sexual contact usually begins when the child is between five and twelve years old, and it typically consists at first of fondling and masturbation. The behavior continues over time and may eventually proceed to intercourse.

Sexually abused children are usually afraid to tell others about their experiences. However, they may show a variety of behavioral problems or bodily complaints (particularly urinary problems or pelvic pain). On occasion the child may exhibit sexual knowledge and preoccupations that are precocious for her age. Not uncommonly teenage runaways and prostitutes are the victims of incest. Adolescent pregnancy, drug abuse, and suicidal behavior are often associated with the experience. And the women tend to show lifetime patterns of psychological shame and stigmatization.

Mothers in incestuous families are usually passive, have a poor self-image, and are overly dependent on their husbands. They frequently suffer from mental illness, physical disability, or repeated pregnancy. Under these circumstances, much of the housework and child care falls on the oldest daughter, who is the one most likely to be sexually victimized by the father. Although incest commonly involves the oldest daughter, the behavior is often repeated with younger daughters, one after another. Moreover, a father's incestuous behavior places his daughters at greater risk of sexual abuse by other male relatives and family intimates.

Incest victims and their families can find help by consulting a women's center, a rape crisis center, or the child protective services in a community. Sexual abuse should always be reported to the appropriate authorities. Adults should never dismiss a child's complaint of sexual abuse because false complaints are quite rare. Measures need to be taken that strengthen the role of the mother in the family and the relationship between the mother and daughter. All parties—the child, the offender, the mother, and other family victims—should receive professional treatment (Herman and Hirschman, 1981).

rated each mother on about 150 different child-rearing practices. Some twenty-five years later, a number of Harvard psychologists led by David C. McClelland (1978) contacted many of these children—then thirty-one years old, most of them married and with children of their own.

McClelland and his associates interviewed the individuals and administered psychological tests to them. They concluded that not much of what people think and do as adults is determined by the specific techniques of child rearing their parents used during their first five years. Practices associated with breast feeding, toilet training, and spanking are not all that important. It is how parents *feel* about their children that *does* make a difference. It mattered whether a mother liked her child and enjoyed playing with the child or whether she considered the child a nuisance, with many disagreeable characteristics. Further, children of affectionate fathers were more likely as adults to show tolerance and understanding than were the offspring of other fathers. The Harvard researchers (McClelland et al., 1978: 53) conclude:

> How can parents do right by their children? If they are interested in promoting moral and social maturity in later life, the answer is simple: they should love them, enjoy them, want them around. They should not use their power to maintain a home that is only designed for the

How Parents Feel About Their Children Makes a Difference

Increasingly psychologists are coming to the conclusion that how parents feel about their children makes a greater difference than the specific child-rearing techniques they employ. Parenting is not a matter of magical formulas but one of enjoying children and loving them.

Peter Menzel/Stock, Boston

self-expression and pleasure of adults. They should not regard their children as disturbances to be controlled at all costs.

Clearly, parenting is not a matter of employing a surefire set of recipes or formulas. Parents differ and children differ. Parents who employ identical "good" child-rearing techniques have children who grow up to be exceedingly different (Martin, 1981). Further, situations differ, so that what may work in one setting may boomerang in another. As highlighted by the Harvard research, the essence of parenting has to do with the parent-child *relationship*. In interaction with one another, parents and children evolve ongoing accommodations that reflect one another's needs and desires. Parent-child relationships differ so much, both within the same family and among families, that in many respects each parent-child relationship is unique (Elkind, 1974).

If we can distill a message from the work of contemporary developmental psychologists regarding parenting it would be this. Enjoy your children and love them. There is no mysterious, secret method you must master. It is the child that matters, not the technique. Be skeptical of the exaggerated claims of the popularizers and commercializers of this or that fad. Trust yourself. On the whole, most parents do very well.

The developmental psychologist Michael Lewis places these matters in sound perspective:

> To my mind, the critical thing a scientist can do is to show parents the process by which they can understand their own children—to show how we work, rather than to behave as experts dispensing information. You can assess your children as a scientist does. . . . Connect your own facts about your children, and act on them. Do what parents have always done—inquire of peers who have children, and of older people who have been through it. (Quoted by Collins, 1981*a*: 17)

Finally, it is worth noting that even the experts do not put all their faith in books. They too find, "You have to be yourself—be genuine. You can't raise your children by someone else's rules and principles" (Fedak, 1981). And most experts say that if they ran into difficulty, they would not hesitate to consult another expert about their children. Parents should not think that they must handle their problems all by themselves.

Single-Parent Families and Children of Divorce

It is estimated that nearly half of all children born in the 1980s will live in a single-parent home for at least part of their childhood. Between 1970 and 1981, the number of single-parent families in the United States rose from 3.3 million to 6.6 million. About 70 percent of them originated through divorce or separation. Another 10 percent resulted from the death of a spouse and still another 20 percent through the birth of a child to an unmarried woman. Most one-parent families are headed by women, although some 800,000 one-parent families are headed by fathers. In many cases (perhaps 50 percent), the parent marries or remarries within five years, creating a parent-stepparent pattern.

Until recently many psychologists and sociologists viewed the single-parent family as a lamentable, defective, and even pathological arrangement in need of fixing. Many professionals referred to it as "broken," "disorganized," or "disintegrated" (for exam-

Single-Parent Families

Although the single-parent family has traditionally enjoyed a bad reputation, it is increasingly coming to be recognized as a viable family form. Most children are resilient and can flourish in a wide variety of family arrangements so long as they are loved and their basic needs are met.

Meri Houtchens-Kitchens/The Picture Cube

ple, see Cavan, 1964). But over the past fifteen years, they have increasingly come to recognize that the single-parent home is a different but viable family form (Brandwein, Brown, and Fox, 1974; Marotz-Baden et al., 1979; Bilgé and Kaufman, 1983). Nonetheless, the nation's schools in large measure continue to stigmatize the children and their situations as abnormal, both in school practices and in the attitudes of school personnel (Collins, 1981*c*).

Although it is true that many single-parent families have serious financial problems, this is hardly evidence of pathology. In 1981 government figures revealed that the poverty rate for families headed by single women was 34.6 percent compared with 11.2 percent for all families and 10.3 percent for families headed by men. One major difference between husband-wife families and one-parent families is that many of the former have two incomes and the latter have at most one income. Additionally, women's employment tends to pay less well and is more sporadic than that of men. Only half of divorced mothers receive any money whatever from their children's fathers, and this is seldom much. Among never-married mothers, only 6 percent get any financial help from their children's fathers (Jencks, 1982).

In the United States the major cause of single-parent families is divorce. In 1982, divorces in the United States reached a high of 1.2 million, and more than half the couples who divorced had children. An estimated 1 million children each year are added to the category of single-parent families. Additionally, about 100,000 children a year are kidnapped by one of their divorced parents.

The most frequent family arrangement in the period immediately following a divorce is one in which children are living with their mothers and having only intermittent contact with their fathers. E. Mavis Hetherington, Martha Cox, and Roger Cox (1976, 1977) made a two-year longitudinal study in which they matched a preschool child in a divorced family with a child in an intact family, on the basis of age, sex, birth-order position, and the age and education of the parents. In all, forty-eight divorced couples were paired with forty-eight intact families.

Hetherington, Cox, and Cox (1977: 42) found that the first year after the divorce was the most stressful—for both parents:

> The divorced mother complained most often of feeling helpless, physically unattractive, and of having lost the identity associated with her husband's status. Fathers complained of not knowing who they were, of being rootless, of having no structure or home in their lives. The separation induced profound feelings of loss, previously unrecognized dependency needs, guilt, anxiety, and depression in both parents.
>
> Divorce was a blow to both parents' feelings of competence for the first year. They thought they had failed as parents and spouses and doubted their ability to adjust well in any future marriages. They felt that they did not handle themselves well in social situations, and that they were incompetent in sexual relations.

Many of the stresses that parents experience following divorce and the accompanying changes in their life-styles are reflected in their relationships with their children (Wallerstein and Kelly, 1980). Hetherington and her associates (1976: 424) found that the interaction patterns between the divorced parents and their children differed significantly from those encountered in the intact families:

> Divorced parents make fewer maturity demands of their children, communicate less well with their children, tend to be less affectionate with their children and show marked inconsistency in discipline and lack of control over their children in comparison to parents in intact families. Poor parenting seems most marked, particularly for divorced mothers, one year after divorce, which seems to be a peak of stress in parent-child relations. [Many of the mothers referred to their relationship with their child one year after divorce as involving "declared war" and a "struggle for survival."] Two years following the divorce, mothers are demanding more . . . [independent and] mature behavior of their children, communicate better and use more explanation and reasoning, are more nurturant and consistent and are better able to control their children than they were the year before. A similar pattern is occurring for divorced fathers in maturity demands, communication and consistency, but they are becoming less nurturant and more detached from their children. . . . Divorced fathers were ignoring their children more and showing less affection [while their extremely permissive and "every day is Christmas" behavior declined].

Hence many single-parent families had a difficult period of readjustment following the divorce, but the situation generally improved during the second year.

Hetherington found that much depends on the ability of the custodial mother to control her children. Homes in which the mother loses control are associated with drops in children's IQ scores, poorer school grades, and a decrease in children's problem-solving skills. Children whose mothers maintain good control show no drop in school performance. Hetherington also found that when single-parent mothers lose control of their sons, a "coercive cycle" typically appears. The sons tend to become more abusive, demanding, and unaffectionate. The mother responds with depression, low self-esteem, and less control, and her parenting becomes worse (Albin, 1979).

Children often respond to their parents' divorce by pervasive feelings of sadness, strong wishes for reconciliation, and worries about having to take care of themselves. Many of them must also deal with deep anger toward one or both parents, feelings of rejection, and guilt for having caused the breakup (Wallerstein and Kelly, 1980). Hence it is not surprising that the quality of the child's relationship with *both* parents is the best predictor of his or her postdivorce adjustment. Children who maintain stable, loving relationships with both parents appear to experience fewer emotional scars (they exhibit less stress and less aggressive behavior and their school performance and peer relations are better) than do children lacking such relationships (Clingempeel and Reppucci, 1982).

The importance for the child of maintaining a postdivorce relationship with both parents has led to the concept of joint legal custody (Luepnitz, 1982). Under this arrangement both parents share equally in the making of significant child-rearing decisions and both parents mutually share in regular child care responsibilities. The child lives with each parent a substantial amount of time (for example, the child may spend part of the week or month in one parent's house and part in the other's). Joint custody also eliminates the "winner-loser" character of custodial disposition and much of the sadness, sense of loss, and loneliness that the noncustodial parent frequently feels.

But joint custody is not an answer for all children. Critics point out that parents who cannot agree during marriage cannot be expected to reach agreement on rules, discipline, and styles of parenting after marriage. And they say that alternating between homes interferes with a child's need to sense continuity in his or her life (Goldstein, Ereud, and Solnit, 1973). Further, the geographically mobile nature of contemporary society and the likelihood of parental remarriage render a good many joint-custody arrangements vulnerable to collapse (Benedek and Benedek, 1979).

Despite the problems that many parents and children have during the first year or two following divorce, most authorities believe that divorce is not necessarily disastrous for children. With respect to school achievement, social adjustment, and delinquent behavior, the differences are small or nonexistent between children from one- and two-parent homes of comparable social status (Burchinal, 1964; Kohn, 1977). Some research suggests that children and adolescents from single-parent homes show less delinquent behavior, less psychosomatic illness, better adjustment to their parents, and better self-concepts than those from unhappy intact homes (Nye, 1957; Raschke and Raschke, 1979; Cooper, Holman, and Braithwaite, 1983). Even so, neither an unhappy marriage nor a divorce is especially congenial for children. Each alternative poses its own sets of stresses (Wallerstein and Kelly, 1980).

Many authorities argue that the behavior problems of some children who have divorced parents derive not directly from the disruption of family bonds but from the difficulties in interpersonal relations with which the disruption is associated (Rutter, 1974). They point to the part that parental conflict, tension, and discord play in feeding negative self-conceptions and identities and in jeopardizing a child's sense of well-being and security (Despert, 1953). Psychiatrists and clinical psychologists note that in many cases, divorce actually serves to reduce the amount of friction and unhappiness that a child experiences; consequently divorce leads to better behavioral adjustments (Hetherington, 1979). Indeed, most divorced mothers believe that their children are living better lives in a divorced family than in a family agonized by marital conflict (Goode, 1956). Overall, research strongly suggests that it is the *quality* of children's relationships with their parents that matters much more than the fact of divorce (Rutter, 1974; Emery, 1982).

PEER RELATIONSHIPS

Man is a knot, a web, a mesh into which relationships are tied.

—ANTOINE DE SAINT-EXUPÉRY

From the beginning, children enter a world of people, an encompassing social network. With time, specific relationships change in form, intensity, and function, but the social network itself stretches across the life span. Yet social and behavioral scientists mostly ignored the rich tapestry of children's social networks until the past decade or so. They regarded social intimacy as centering on one relationship, that of the infant and mother. Thus they treated the ties that young children have with other family members and with age-mates as if they did not exist or had no importance. However, a growing body of research that points to the significance of other relationships in the development of interpersonal competencies is becoming available. This section will discuss children's peer relationships and friendships. **Peers** are individuals who are approximately the same age.

Peer Relationships and Friendships

Friendship is a single soul dwelling in two bodies.

—ARISTOTLE

From birth to death we find ourselves immersed in countless relationships. Few are as important to us as those we have with our peers and friends (Tesch, 1983). Thus, not surprisingly, research reveals that peer relationships and friendships are in their own right a meaningful experience in the lives of young children (Gottman, 1983). Carol O. Eckerman, Judith L. Whatley, and Stuart L. Kutz (1975) studied sixty normal, home-reared children under two years of age. Each child was paired with an age-mate in a laboratory setting. Although interactions were infrequent, children from ten to twelve months old occasionally smiled and "vocalized" to each other, offered and accepted toys, imitated each other, and struggled over or fussed about toys. At each age interval between ten and twenty-four months, children paid increasingly more attention to toys and peers and less attention to their mothers. Further, the children increasingly integrated their activities with toys and peers, so that by two years of age social play predominated.

In another study, Judith Rubenstein and Carollee Howes (1976) observed a number of eighteen-month-old children who regularly played together in a one-to-one situation in their homes. A greater amount of positive social interaction took place among these long-acquainted peers than among the unacquainted children studied by Eckerman, Whatley, and Kutz. During a peer's visit, the acquainted children would spend over 50 percent of their time socially interacting with each other. Other research also shows that acquainted peers have more positive interaction with each other, and engage in less conflict, than unacquainted peers do (Mueller and Lucas, 1975; Becker, 1976; Doyle, Connolly, and Rivest, 1980).

Children as young as three years of age form friendships with other children that are surprisingly similar to those of adults (Rubin, 1980). And just as different relationships meet different needs for adults, so do they for young children. Some relationships are reminiscent of strong adult attachments; others of relationships between adult mentors and protégés; and still others of the camaraderie of adult co-workers. Although young children may lack the reflective understanding that many adults bring to their relation-

Peer Relationships

Even at an early age, children live in a complex network of social relationships. Among the most important are the relationships they form with other children.

Patrick Reddy

ships, they nonetheless often invest their friendships with an intense emotional quality (Selman, 1980). Moreover, some young children bring a considerable measure of social competence to their relationships and a high level of mutuality and give-and-take (Masters and Furman, 1981; Berndt, 1981*a*, 1981*b*; Krantz, 1982).

A variety of studies reveal that with increasing age, peer relationships are more likely to be formed and more likely to be successful. Four-year-olds, for instance, spend about two-thirds of the time when they are in contact with other people associating with adults and one-third of the time with peers. Eleven-year-olds, in contrast, spend about an equal amount of time with adults and with peers (Wright, 1967).

A number of factors contribute to this shift in interactive patterns. First, as children grow older their communicative skills improve, facilitating effective interaction (Mueller et al., 1976; Gottman, 1983). Second, children's increasing cognitive competencies enable them to attune themselves more effectively to the roles of others (Selman, 1980; Furman and Bierman, 1983). Third, nursery- and elementary-school attendance offers increasing opportunities for peer interaction. And fourth, increasing motor competencies expand the child's ability to participate in many joint activities.

Interestingly, children of preschool age assort themselves into same-sex play groups (Serbin, Tonick, and Sternglanz, 1977; Jacklin and Maccoby, 1978). Moreover, preschool girls tend to interact in small groups, especially two-person groups, whereas boys more often play in larger groups (Eder and Hallinan, 1978; Lever, 1978). One reason for this is that boys tend to select games that require a larger number of participants than those selected by girls. (But these differences in the play activities of boys and girls are often fostered by parental and teacher socialization practices.) Another reason is that girls engage in more intimate behavior than boys do, and two-person groups are conducive to intimate behavior. Girls are more likely than boys to disclose intimate information to a friend and to hold hands and display other signs of affection.

Sibling Relationships

Big sisters are the crab grass in the lawn of life.

—CHARLES M. SCHULZ
Peanuts

Some of the most important relationships that children have with other children are those that they have with their brothers and sisters. A child's position in the family (*birth order*) and the number and sex of his or her siblings are thought to have major consequences for the child's development and socialization. These factors structure the child's social environment, providing a network of key relationships and roles. An only child, an oldest child, a middle child, and a youngest child all seem to experience a somewhat different world because of the different social webs that encompass their lives. Moreover, sibling interactions often continue across the life span. The "pioneering function" of older brothers and sisters may persist lifelong, providing role models in coping with bereavement, retirement, or widowhood (Sobel, 1980). And many individuals rely on a living sibling for help and companionship in old age. Indeed, by virtue of today's frequent divorces and remarriages, some children form stronger bonds with their siblings than they do with their parents or stepparents (Cicirelli, 1980).

Through the years, research has been focused on first-born children, for they appear to be fortune's favorites (Cicirelli, 1978). First-borns are overrepresented in college populations (Altus, 1965), at the higher-IQ levels (Zajonc, 1976), among National Merit and Rhodes Scholars, in *Who's Who in America* and *American Men and Women of Science,* among individuals on *Time*'s cover, among American presidents (52 percent), among men and women in Congress, and in the astronaut corps (twenty-one of the first twenty-three United States astronauts who flew on space missions were either only children or first-born sons). However, these birth-order advantages do not hold in a good many families and for individuals from lower socioeconomic backgrounds (Glass et al., 1974; Ernst and Angst, 1983). Further, some research suggests that middle-borns tend to have lower self-esteem than do first-borns and last-borns, perhaps a

Sibling Relationships
Some research suggests that first-born children appear to be fortune's favorites. One explanation is that the first-born plays a parent-surrogate role in dealing with later-born siblings. Such a role seems to facilitate the development of verbal and cognitive skills.
Elizabeth Hamlin/Stock, Boston

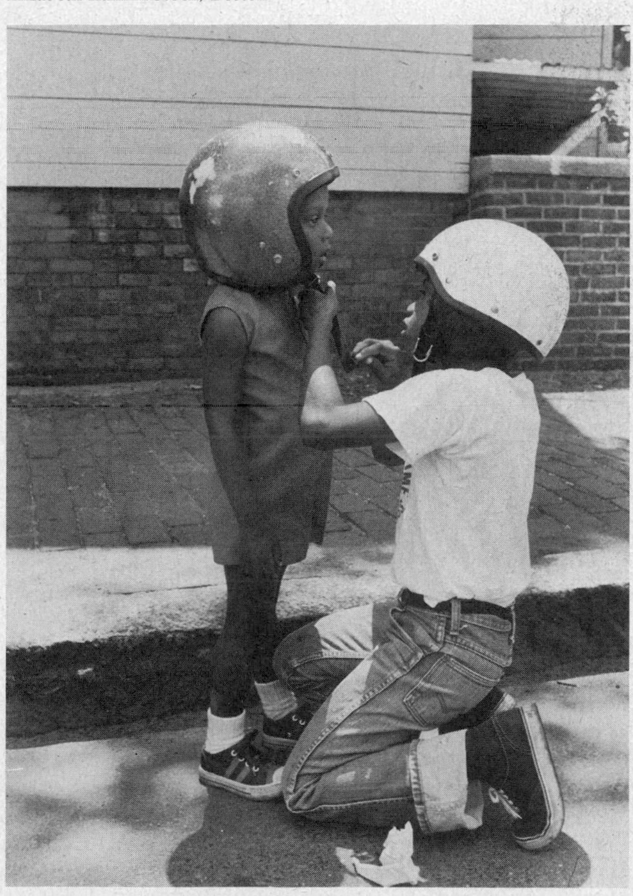

function of their less well-defined position within the family (Kidwell, 1981, 1982). And some, but not all, researchers find that later-borns possess better social skills than do first-borns (Miller and Maruyama, 1976; Snow, Jacklin, and Maccoby, 1981).

Fewer effects related to birth order are found in the United States than in most other societies. A cross-cultural study of thirty-nine societies reveals that first-borns are more likely than later-borns to receive elaborate birth ceremonies, to have authority over siblings, and to receive respect from siblings. In comparison with other sons, first-born sons generally have more control of property, more power in the society, and higher social positions (Rosenblatt and Skoogberg, 1974). Moreover, older siblings act as caretakers for their younger siblings in a good many cultures (Dunn, 1983).

A number of explanations have been advanced to account for differences between first-born and later-born children. First, research reveals that parents attach greater importance to their first child (Sears, Maccoby, and Levin, 1957; Clausen, 1966). There are more social, affectionate, and caretaking interactions between parents and their first-borns (Jacobs and Moss, 1976; Cohen and Beckwith, 1977). Thus first-borns have more exposure to adult models and to adult expectations and pressures.

A second explanation of the differences between first- and later-born children focuses on the interaction that takes place among siblings. The first-born is seen as playing a parent-surrogate or teacher role in dealing with later-born siblings (Brody et al., 1982). Such a "helper" role appears to be instrumental in the development of verbal and cognitive skills (Cicirelli, 1973; Dunn, 1983). Further, the psychologist Robert B. Zajonc (1975, 1983) hypothesizes that the oldest sibling experiences a richer intellectual environment than younger siblings do. He says that each additional child "waters down" the intellectual climate by increasing the incidence of interactions with childish minds as opposed to adult minds. But not all researchers find a relationship between sibling spacing and intellectual development (Brackbill and Nichols, 1982; Galbraith, 1982).

A third explanation, which was first advanced by Alfred Adler, stresses the part that sibling power and status rivalry play in a child's personality formation (Ansbacher and Ansbacher, 1956). Adler viewed the "dethroning" of the first-born as a crucial event in the development of the first child. With the birth of a brother or sister, the first-born suddenly loses his or her monopoly on parental attention (Kendrick and Dunn, 1980). This loss, Adler said, arouses a strong lifelong need for recognition, attention, and approval that the child, and later the adult, seeks to acquire through high achievement. An equally critical factor in the development of the later-born child is the competitive race for achievement with older and more accomplished siblings. In many cases, the rancor disappears when individuals get older and learn to manage their own careers and married lives (Sobel, 1980).

The sex of a child's sibling may also be of significance. It appears that individuals with an older, opposite-sex sibling are especially likely to have rewarding interactions with strangers of the opposite sex (Ickes and Turner, 1983). And Helen Koch (1956) found that the sex of a sibling has consequences for a person's gender role performance. She showed that children imitate their older siblings' behavior and that as a result boys who have a slightly older sister tend to develop a less masculine role than do first-born boys or boys with older brothers. Likewise, girls with older brothers are more disposed toward "tomboy" behavior than girls with older sisters.

However, more recent research by Gerald S. Leventhal (1970) reveals that men with older sisters often display more masculine behavior as traditionally defined in the United States than men with older brothers do. In a family of two male children, the younger boy may adopt behavior patterns opposite to those of his older brother to avoid unfavorable comparison with his more accomplished brother. Another study, made by Karen Vroegh (1971), shows that neither the sex of all a child's siblings nor the sex of a child's older siblings has any consistent effect on gender role identity. Hence the effect of the sex of one sibling upon the gender role identity of another remains unresolved. Very likely the relationship is considerably more complex than that suggested by Koch's earlier research. This conclusion is supported by other recent studies (Grotevant, 1978; Scarr and Grajek, 1982). The relationships between young siblings are particularly affected by the children's relationships with their parents (Dunn, 1983).

In sum, birth order, family size, and the sex of a child's siblings do not stand up well as indicators of how well an individual child will fare in life. Many unique genetic and environmental factors intervene in individual families, producing wide differences among families and among their members.

Peer Reinforcement and Modeling

Children play an important part as reinforcing agents and behavioral models for one another—a fact that adults at times overlook. Much learning takes place as a result of children's interaction with other children. Here is a typical example (Lewis et al., 1975: 27):

> Two four-year-olds are busily engaged in playing with "Playdoh." The room echoes with their glee as they roll out long "snakes." Each child is trying to roll a longer snake than the other. The one-year-old sibling of one of the children, hearing the joyful cries, waddles into the room. She reaches for the Playdoh being used by her sibling. The older child hands the one-year-old some Playdoh, and the child tries to roll her own snake. Unable to carry out the task and frustrated, the one-year-old becomes fussy, at which point the older sibling gives the child a knife. The four-year-old then shows the sibling how to cut the snakes the other children have made.

Indeed, the old one-room school functioned, and functioned well, with the teacher teaching the older children and the older children teaching the younger boys and girls.

One way that children influence one another is through actions that encourage or discourage given behaviors. Robert G. Wahler (1967) demonstrated the importance of such reinforcement processes by enlisting five children in a nursery school as his experimenter confederates. These children were instructed to ignore certain classmates when they showed a specific behavior and to pay positive attention to them when they showed another behavior. The result was that the classmates performed the ignored activity less often, and the rewarded activity more often, than they had done before. Then Wahler's child confederates resumed their usual patterns of peer interaction, and the behavior of their classmates returned to what it had been before the experiment. In general, it appears that spontaneous peer reinforcement increases with age, occurring more frequently among four-year-olds than among three-year-olds (Charlesworth and Hartup, 1967).

Seeing other children behave in certain ways can also affect a child's behavior. A study of Robert D. O'Connor (1969) reveals that severely withdrawn nursery-school children engage in considerably more peer interaction after they watch a twenty-minute sound film that portrays other children playing together happily. And as noted in the boxed insert "Helping Children Cope with Their Fears" in Chapter 9, modeling has proved to be an important tool for aiding children to overcome various fears.

Play

> *It is a happy talent to know how to play.*
>
> —RALPH WALDO EMERSON

Americans tend to view play as an irrational, trivial, and ephemeral activity, one that is not especially important (Sutton-Smith, 1971). To the extent that the United States has inherited the Puritan work ethic—where busyness is equated with virtue, and idleness with evil—play has been regarded as a suspect activity (Weber, 1930). Yet play makes an important contribution to personal and social development over a person's entire life span. Historians and anthropologists find that play can be traced back through antiquity to the earliest peoples. **Play** may be defined as voluntary activities that are not performed for any sake beyond themselves. They are activities that people commonly view as being outside the serious business of life.

There are many forms of play, including pretend play, exploration play, games, social play, and rough-and-tumble play. In recent years, pretend play has captivated the interest of many psychologists (Fein, 1981; Pederson, Rook-Green, and Elder, 1981). They have viewed make-believe or fantasy behavior as an avenue for exploring the "inner person" of the child and as an indicator of underlying cognitive changes. Thus, during the first two years children's play shifts from the simple, undifferentiated manipulation of objects to an exploration of the objects' unique properties and to make-believe play involving ever more complex and cognitively demanding behaviors (Belsky and Most, 1981; McCune-Nicolich, 1981). As will be discussed in Chapter 11, pretend play is associated with the development of children's role-taking capabilities.

In a classic study, Mildred B. Parten (1932) observed the play of children in nursery-school settings. She identified six types of play, based on the nature and extent of the children's social involvement:

- *Unoccupied play.* Children spend their time watching others, idly glancing about, or engaging in aimless activities (standing around, getting on and off a chair, tugging on their clothing, and so on).

(a)

(b)

(c)

(d)

Play

A number of play patterns can be observed among nursery-school children. These photos show (*a*) unoccupied play, (*b*) solitary play, (*c*) associative play, and (*d*) cooperative play.
Patrick Reddy

- *Solitary play.* Children play with toys by themselves and make no effort to get close to or speak with other children.
- *Onlooker behavior.* Children watch other children at play, occasionally talking to them or asking them questions. However, they do not themselves join the play.
- *Parallel play.* Children play independently beside other children but not with them. Although they play close together and with similar toys, they do not interact.

- *Associative play.* Children interact with one another, borrowing or lending play material, following one another with carts, cars, or trains, and attempting to influence each other's behavior. Each child does as he or she sees fit; no division of labor or integration of activity takes place.
- *Cooperative play.* Children integrate their play activities. In this kind of play, the members usually take on different role responsibilities, and they often think of themselves as belonging to a group from which other children are excluded.

Once Parten had developed her descriptive categories, she made use of the time-sampling technique (see Chapter 1) to classify children's activities. She discovered that social participation among preschoolers tends to increase with age. Parallel play predominated among two-year-olds and remained an important type of behavior throughout the preschool period. Associative play came to the foreground among three-year-olds, slightly exceeding parallel play in overall frequency. Cooperative play likewise increased among three- and four-year-olds (Parten and Newhall, 1943).

More recent studies suggest, however, that there is considerable variation among preschool children in the relative frequency of the various types of play (Barnes, 1971). For instance, one study finds that the incidence of parallel play is greater among lower-class than among middle-class children. The incidence of associative and cooperative play is greater among middle-class children (Rubin, Maioni, and Hornung, 1976). This study also reports that girls engage in more parallel play than boys, while boys engage in more associative and cooperative play than girls. Other research shows that while some children go through successive stages of predominantly solitary, then parallel, and then group play, many others do not (Smith, 1978). In fact, some children alternate between periods of predominantly group play and periods of predominantly solitary play.

Edward Mueller and his associates (Mueller and Lucas, 1975; Mueller and Brenner, 1977) find that toddlers within playgroup settings often progress in developmental fashion from object-centered contacts to sophisticated interchanges. Object-centered contacts arise when two or more children simultaneously become interested in the same plaything. At first they engage in an "act-watch" rhythm—they take turns playing with an object that can be manipulated by only one child at a time. Little conscious sharing occurs at the beginning of the process. But as the process continues, children become aware of the responses of other children. They then try to determine what other reactions they can produce in their peers. Once two or more children discover and pay attention to one another's potential for making responses, a fully social peer relationship becomes possible. In similar fashion, parallel play frequently functions as a prelude to group play (Bakeman and Brownlee, 1980).

Psychologists believe that play makes a number of major contributions to children's development (see Herron and Sutton-Smith, 1971; Weisler and McCall, 1976):

- *Children's exploratory and play behavior is a vehicle of cognitive stimulation* (Piaget, 1952*a*). Through play, children make motor and sensory discoveries concerning sizes and shapes, up and down, hard and soft, smooth and rough, and so on. They handle, manipulate, identify, order, pattern, match, and measure. In building up and tearing down, children learn about the properties of things and gain conceptions of weight, height, volume, and texture (Caplan and Caplan, 1973; McCall, 1974; Fenson et al., 1976).
- *Play prepares children for life, but on their own terms.* Children at play can experience themselves as active agents in their environment, not merely as reacting ones. In the family and at school, children are usually called on to perform according to set patterns. But in the world of play, they can be the decision makers. Through play, children can trim the world down to manageable size and manipulate it to suit their whims (Caplan and Caplan, 1973).
- *Play provides opportunities for rehearsing adult roles,* a process called *anticipatory socialization* (Merton, 1968). Children can play house, store, school, or clinic and try on the roles of spouses, merchants, teachers, and medical personnel. Games are particularly effective vehicles by which young children learn to take turns and relate their activities to those of a partner (Mead, 1934; Ross, 1982).
- *Play helps children build their own individual sense of identity.* It allows them to get outside themselves and view themselves from other perspectives. In so doing they come to shape and mold their self-images and self-conceptions.

Fantasy Play

Fantasy play allows children to come to terms with their fears regarding witches, ghosts, dogs, and villains. Through imaginary episodes, they can confront these creatures and find that they can cope with them. For handicapped children, such as those shown here, play takes on special significance.

Meri Houtchens-Kitchens/The Picture Cube

- *Play allows for both reality and fantasy.* It is a pliable medium that enables children to come to terms with their fears—of villains, witches, ghosts, lions, dogs, robbers, and so on. Through imaginary episodes, children can harmlessly confront these creatures and perhaps even triumph over them.

By virtue of these functions, play makes a vital contribution in the development of children.

Peer Aggression

Much human aggression takes place in the context of group activity. **Aggression** is behavior that is socially defined as injurious or destructive. Even young children display aggression. Moreover, they are exposed to aggression and violence at an early age, especially by the mass media (see the boxed insert on pages 286–287). Across time, children come to express aggression somewhat differently. With increasing age, their aggressive behavior becomes less diffuse and more directed (Feshbach, 1970). The proportion of aggressive acts of an undirected, temper-tantrum type decreases gradually during the first three years of life, then shows a sharp decline after the age of four. In contrast, the relative frequency of retaliatory responses increases with age, especially after children reach their third birthdays. Verbal aggression also increases between two and four years of age.

Children have a considerable influence on one another in the expression of aggressive behavior. Gerry R. Patterson, Richard A. Littman, and William Bricker (1967) have described how the process frequently operates in nursery-school settings. They recorded the aggressive interactions that occurred among thirty-six nursery-school children over a twenty-six-week period. They found that when an aggressive response (for instance, a kick or a punch) was followed by crying, withdrawing, or acquiescing, the attacker was likely to aggress against the victim again. These reactions functioned as positive reinforcers for the aggressor. When aggressive behavior was followed by punishment (for instance, retaliatory responses, efforts to recover the seized item, or teacher intervention), aggressors were more likely to pick a different victim for their future aggression or to alter their interactions with the original victim. Hence the feedback provided for aggressors influences their subsequent behavior.

The researchers also found that while some children entered nursery school with a repertoire of aggressive behaviors, others were passive and unassertive at first. But after the relatively unaggressive children learned to counteraggress and thus end other

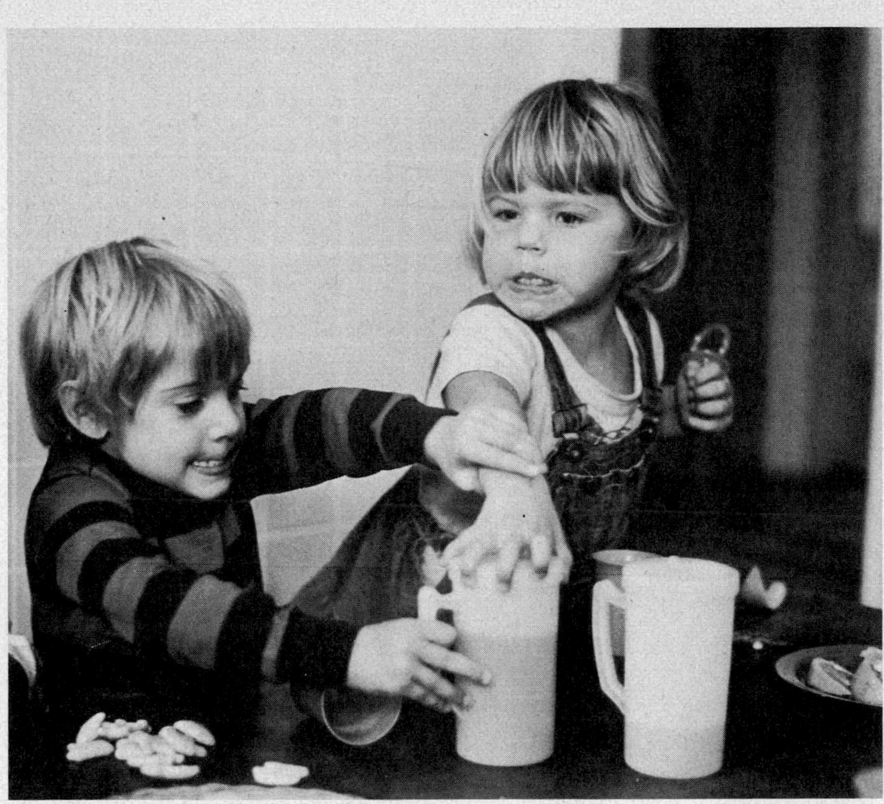

Peer Aggression

Many aggressive children attribute hostile intentions to their peers even under benign circumstances. Consequently, they are more likely than other children to respond with aggression in interpersonal settings.

Cynthia R. Benjamins/Picture Group

children's aggressive acts, they themselves began to aggress against new victims. In sum, this and other research highlights the part that learning plays in the acquisition of aggressive behavior.

Even so, some children appear more prone to engage in aggressive behavior than do others. In some cases, aggressiveness derives from a developmental lag in children's acquisition of role-taking skills (Selman, 1980). But this is not the entire story. Many aggressive boys also tend to attribute hostile intentions to their peers even under benign circumstances. Consequently, they inappropriately respond with aggression (Dodge and Frame, 1982).

Similarly, Dan Olweus (1978, 1979, 1980) finds in his studies of Swedish boys that "bullies" react aggressively in many different situations, possess weak inhibitions against aggressive tendencies, and have positive attitudes toward violence. They tend to be fearless, confident, tough youngsters with positive self-images. In contrast, "whipping boys"—youngsters who are teased, ridiculed, hit, and pushed about—tend to be anxious, insecure, and isolated children, physically weaker and more athletically inept than other boys, and somewhat low in self-esteem. These latter youngsters seem to "attract" aggression and become its recurrent victims.

Situational factors, especially competition, may also precipitate aggression (Vander Zanden, 1984). Research has shown that the keener the competition for valued but scarce resources, the more aggressively children behave (Rocha and Rogers, 1976; Santrock et al., 1976). Indeed, where children can maximize their payoff by aggressively defeating their opponent, aggressive responses are reinforced. Moreover, competitive situations frequently arouse feelings of rivalry that extend beyond merely winning the competition; children then go out of their way to hurt their opponents (Rocha and Rogers, 1976).

Nursery Schools

Much of what was said in Chapter 8 about child day-care centers also holds for nursery schools. Like child day-care programs, the nursery-school experience has been seen by a number of educators, child psychol-

TELEVISION AND VIOLENCE

Authorities are expressing increasing concern over the effects of media violence on the behavior of the nation's youth (Eron, 1982). A report prepared by the National Institute of Mental Health concludes that there is "overwhelming" scientific evidence that "excessive" violence on television leads directly to aggression and violent behavior among children and teenagers (Pearl, 1982). Terming television a "beguiling" instrument that has become "a major socializing agent of American children," the report finds that "television violence is as strongly correlated with aggressive behavior as any other behavioral variable that has been measured."

According to the A. C. Nielsen Company, a firm that specializes in assessing the popularity of television programs, the television set stays on an average of fifty-three hours a week in homes with preschool children. This figure compares with forty-three hours a week in the average United States household. Many of the programs directed toward child audiences are saturated with mayhem, violence, and aggression.

The Bugs Bunny-Roadrunner cartoons are typical of Saturday morning programs, averaging 50 violent acts per hour (Zimmerman, 1983). In one sequence a mean gray coyote barrels down a highway chasing the roadrunner (a birdlike creature). The coyote crashes into a tree. Shortly afterward he falls off a cliff and a two-ton boulder lands on top of him. A slab of highway pavement then flips over and buries the coyote. Next a piano wired with dynamite blows up in his face and

Sesame Street
The Sesame Street programs on public educational television are designed to help children learn basic arithmetic and reading skills and to foster the development of socially valued, caring, and cooperative activities.
Patrick Reddy

ogists, and political leaders as a possible solution to many of the massive social problems of illiteracy, underachievement, poverty, and racism that confront Western nations. Hopes such as these led in 1965 to the inception of the Head Start Program as an offshoot of the War on Poverty. The program was designed to provide children from low-income families with early intervention education in nursery-school settings. It was believed that appropriate services from outside the family could compensate for the disadvantages these youngsters experienced during their early years.

Early evaluations of Head Start, particularly a 1969 report by the Westinghouse Learning Corporation, led to the view that early childhood programs provide negligible benefits. With few exceptions, the report claimed, the gains in IQ that children exhibited while in the program were not maintained when the program was discontinued. In recent years, however, longer-term data have become available that reveal, contrary to the earlier conclusions, that children in such programs do indeed get a head start (Lazar and Darlington, 1982). Children who had participated in the preschool programs in the 1960s have performed equal to or better than have their peers in regular school and have had fewer grade retentions and special class placements. The project has also provided hundreds of thousands of young children with essential health care services.

Although the improvement in children's IQ scores typically dissipates within several years, the children the coyote flies through the air, landing with a mouthful of piano keys.

A variety of studies reveal that viewing media violence fosters aggressive behavior in a number of ways (Bandura et al., 1961, 1963; Liebert and Baron, 1972; Eron, 1982; Eron et al., 1983). First, it provides opportunities for children to learn new aggressive skills. Second, watching violent behavior weakens children's inhibitions against behaving in the same way. And third, it affords occasions for *vicarious conditioning,* in which children acquire aggressive behaviors by imaginatively participating in the violent experiences of another person. Research also demonstrates that media violence increases children's toleration of aggression in real life (Drabman and Thomas, 1974).

In a study by Lynette K. Friedrich and Aletha H. Stein (1973), children attending a nine-week nursery-school session were shown three types of television programs each day between the fourth and seventh weeks of the term. One group of children watched aggressive *Batman* and *Superman* cartoons. A second group watched the *Mister Rogers' Neighborhood* program, in which socially valued and cooperative activities are highlighted. And a third group watched informational films that contained little or no aggressive or prosocial material. Careful records were kept throughout the nine-week period to assess each child's behavior before, during, and after the child had been exposed to the programs.

Friedrich and Stein found that children who witnessed the aggressive films showed a decline both in their ability to tolerate mild frustrations and in their willingness to accept responsibility. Even more important, children who had shown high levels of aggression before the study became even more aggressive after exposure to the *Batman* and *Superman* cartoons. On the other hand, the aggressive cartoons had no effect on the behavior of children who were initially low in aggression. Other studies have also found that children who are already predisposed to be aggressive are more likely to imitate aggressive models than other children are (Bailyn, 1959; Schramm, Lyle, and Parker, 1961).

Children who watched the *Mister Rogers' Neighborhood* programs were encouraged to be cooperative and supportive of other people—to show sympathy, affection, friendship, altruism, and self-control. In the concluding weeks of the school session, these children became increasingly persistent in completing their tasks, conscientious in obeying rules, and tolerant of frustrating circumstances. As for prosocial interpersonal behavior, it remained largely unchanged among children from families of higher socioeconomic class, but it increased among children from families of low socioeconomic class. In sum, an accumulating body of literature suggests that television provides entertainment for children but functions as an important socializer as well (Leifer, Gordon, and Graves, 1974; Friedrich and Stein, 1975; Pearl, 1982).

ultimately achieve a higher academic level than do those children lacking preschool instruction. Children who have been in compensatory-education classes score significantly higher on mathematics achievement tests and have a better self-image than do their peers in control groups. The programs have also produced dramatic "sleeper effects" on children later in adolescence and young adulthood. Youth who were in a Head Start program engage in less antisocial and delinquent behavior and are more likely to finish high school and get jobs or go to college than are their peers who were not in a program.

Another significant impact of Head Start has been its effects on parents. The program has given parents access to community resources and has provided support for the entire family. It has contributed to an improvement in parenting abilities and in later parent participation in school programs.

In sum, the payoff of Head Start programs has been not only in education but in dollars, for in the long run its participants are less likely to need remedial programs as children and social support systems like welfare as adults. Apparently, children with preschooling learn how to extract a better education from the school system. Moreover, a program's effectiveness is increased by involving the parents, bringing them into partnership with the educational enterprise. Of course not any nursery school will do. It must be a quality program (see boxed insert on page 289).

Nursery School

Nursery school can offer children experiences that involve both learning and play.

Patrick Reddy

SUMMARY

1. Since infants enter a society that is already an ongoing concern, they need to be fitted to their society's cultural ways, a process termed "socialization."
2. Love-oriented parenting techniques tend to promote a child's conscience formation and self-responsibility. In contrast, parents who show hostility and rejection tend to interfere with conscience development and to breed aggressiveness and resistance to authority.
3. Restrictive parenting tends to be associated with well-controlled as well as fearful, dependent, and submissive behaviors. Permissiveness, while fostering outgoing, sociable, assertive behaviors and intellectual striving, also tends to decrease persistence and increase aggressiveness.
4. Effective discipline is consistent and unambiguous. The most aggressive children are those whose parents are permissive toward aggression on some occasions but severely punish it on other occasions.
5. The interactive character of the parent-child relationship assumes paramount importance in the socialization process. In interaction with one another, parents and children evolve on-

SELECTING A NURSERY SCHOOL

There are many different types of preschools and programs. Some, such as Montessori schools and schools following the techniques of psychologists Carl Bereiter and Siegfried Engelmann, emphasize the teaching of a variety of cognitive skills with an academic content. Traditional nursery schools, in contrast, typically seek to expand a child's social environment, provide stimulating material for physical and cognitive development, and foster a sense of individual self-worth. Below are listed a number of tips that parents may wish to employ in picking a school for their youngster:

- Inquire of neighbors about their experiences with various preschools.
- Visit a school at least twice—once alone and once with your youngster.
- Meet the teachers and aides who will be caring for your child.
- Determine whether the staff is professionally trained, particularly whether the director has a degree in early childhood education.
- Determine the goals of the program; for instance, whether it stresses academics or social development.
- Determine the approach that the school and the individual teachers take toward discipline.
- Pay close attention to the sorts of interaction that go on between teachers and children and among the children themselves.
- Appraise the physical facilities; for instance, does the school have adequate space for play, accessible toilets and wash basins, ample facilities for children when the weather is inclement, and inviting playthings?
- Select a school that offers a program that is consistent with your family's values.
- Select a school that is compatible with the family budget because one that is too expensive may contribute to family stress.
- Select a school whose location fits the parents' daily patterns of living and does not entail excessive transportation.

Selecting a Nursery School
Parents would be well advised to visit several nursery schools, both alone and with their child, before choosing one. Both the parents and the children should feel comfortable with the arrangement that is selected.
Michael Weisbrot and Family

going accommodations that reflect one another's needs and desires. Parent-child relationships differ so much, both within the same family and among families, that in many respects each parent-child relation is unique.

6. Divorce is a stressful experience for both children and their parents. The interaction patterns between divorced parents and their children differ from those encountered in intact families. Children often respond to their parents'

divorce by pervasive feelings of sadness, strong wishes for reconciliation, and worries about having to take care of themselves.

7. Peer relationships are in their own right a meaningful experience in the lives of young children. Such relationships become more likely to be formed and more successful with increasing age.
8. First-born children seem to be fortune's favorites. Three explanations have been advanced to account for differences between first- and later-borns. (a) First-borns have greater exposure to adult models and to adult expectations and pressures. (b) They function as intermediaries between parents and later-borns, a role that appears to foster the development of verbal and cognitive skills. (c) The "dethroning" of the first-born by later siblings arouses a strong lifelong need for recognition, attention, and approval.
9. Children are important to one another as reinforcing agents and behavioral models.
10. Play makes a number of major contributions to children's development. It functions as a vehicle of cognitive stimulation, allows children to handle the world on their own terms, provides for anticipatory socialization, fosters an individual sense of identity, and enables children to come to terms with their fears.
12. With increasing age, children's aggression becomes less diffuse, more directed, more retaliatory, and more verbal.
13. Children who have participated in quality Head Start programs indeed do get a head start. They achieve a higher academic level than do those children lacking preschool instruction. The programs have also had positive "sleeper effects" on children later in adolescence and young adulthood.

KEY TERMS

aggression Behavior that is socially defined as injurious or destructive.

authoritarian parenting Child-rearing practices that are aimed at shaping a child's behavior in accordance with traditional and absolute values and standards of conduct. Obedience is stressed, verbal give-and-take discouraged, and punitive, forceful discipline preferred.

authoritative parenting Child-rearing practices that provide firm direction for a child's overall activities but give the child considerable freedom within reasonable limits.

harmonious parenting Child-rearing practices in which almost no control is exercised over a child, although the parents appear to have control in that their children seem to sense intuitively what their parents want and try to do it.

peers Individuals who are approximately the same age.

permissive parenting Child-rearing practices in which the parent seeks to provide a nonpunitive, accepting, and affirmative environment in which the children regulate their own behavior as much as possible.

play Voluntary activities that are not performed for any sake beyond themselves; activities that people commonly view as being outside the serious business of life.

socialization The process of transforming children into bona fide, functioning members of society. Socialization is the channel through which children acquire the knowledge, skills, and dispositions that enable them to participate effectively in group life.

Part Five

Later Childhood: Seven to Twelve

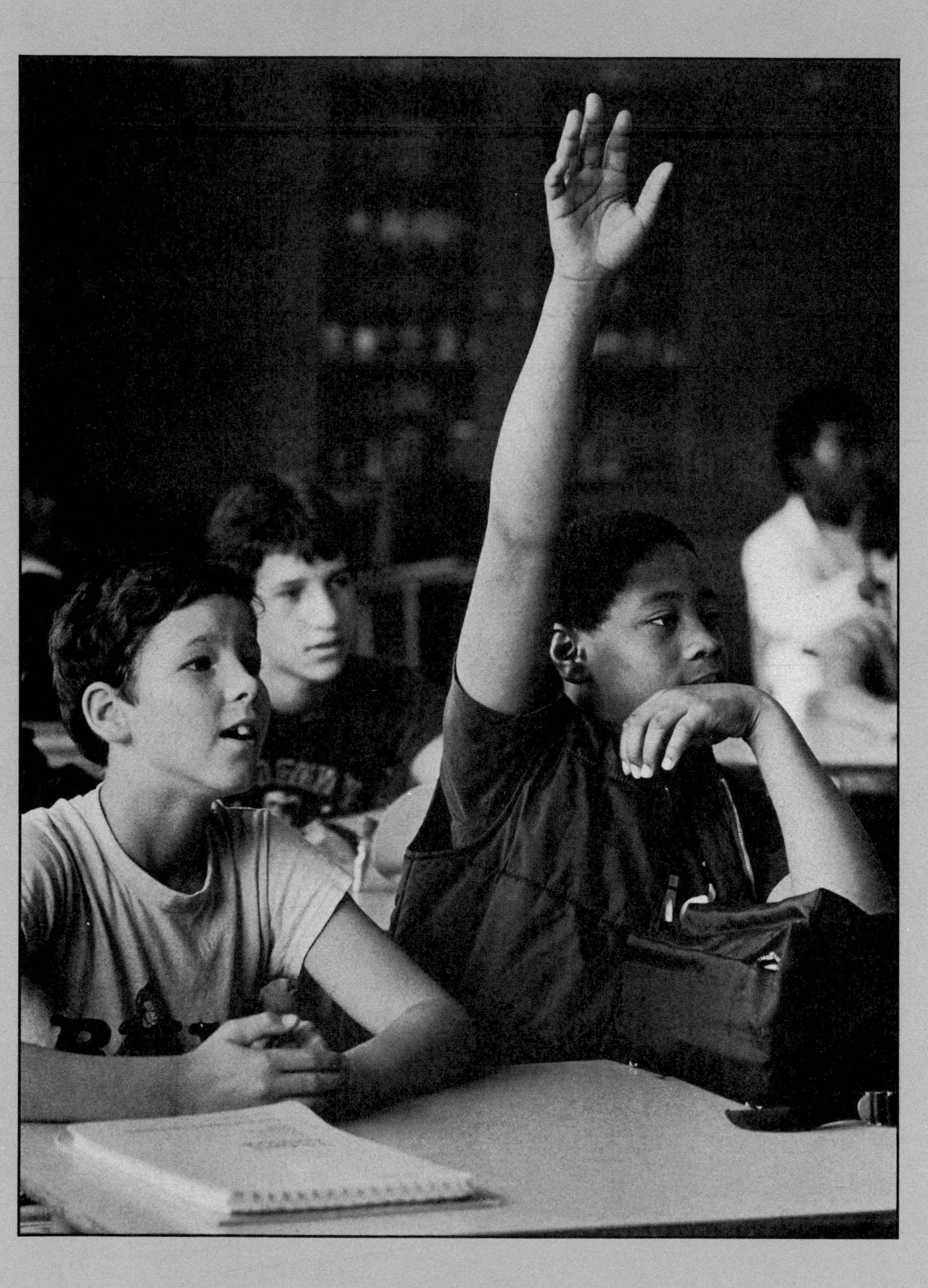

11

Later Childhood: Advances in Cognitive and Moral Development

COGNITIVE SOPHISTICATION
Period of Concrete Operations
Cognitive Style
Person Perception

MORAL DEVELOPMENT
Psychoanalytic Theory
Cognitive Learning Theory
Cognitive-Developmental Theory
Moral Behavior: Consistency or Inconsistency?
Correlates of Moral Conduct

PROSOCIAL BEHAVIOR

We went home and when somebody said, "Where were you?" we said, "Out," and when somebody said, "What were you doing until this hour of night?" we said, as always, "Nothing."

But about this doing nothing: we swung on swings. We went for walks. We lay on our backs in backyards and chewed grass . . . and when we were done, he [my best friend] walked me home to my house, and when we got there I walked him back to his house, and then he ———

We watched things: we watched people build houses, we watched men fix cars, we watched each other patch bicycle tires with rubber bands . . . our fathers playing cards, our mothers making jam, our sisters skipping rope, curling their hair. . . .

We strung beads on strings . . . we tied each other up with string, and belts and clothesline.

We sat in boxes; we sat under porches; we sat on roofs; we sat on limbs of trees.

We stood on boards over excavations; we stood on tops of piles of leaves; we stood under rain dripping from the eaves; we stood up to our ears in snow.

We looked at things like knives . . . and grasshoppers and clouds and dogs and people.

We skipped and hopped and jumped. Not going anywhere—just skipping and hopping and jumping and galloping.

We sang and whistled and hummed and screamed. What I mean, Jack, we did a lot of nothing.

—ROBERT PAUL SMITH, DESCRIBING HIS ELEMENTARY-SCHOOL YEARS
*Where Did You Go? Out. What Did You Do? Nothing.**

In this passage the writer Robert Paul Smith portrays the marked development that occurs during the elementary-school years in children's ability to receive, create, and use knowledge about their physical and social worlds. Erik Erikson (see Chapter 2) singles out the elementary-school years as one of his psychosocial stages. He calls this period the stage of *industry versus inferiority.* During these years, Erikson says, children confront the challenge of developing healthy self-conceptions. They must master the social and learning skills that are essential for the school setting and that lay the foundations for coping with the tasks of adulthood. If children fail to acquire these skills, they may develop feelings of inferiority. From peers, parents, and teachers they receive continual feedback regarding their adequacy. This feedback shapes their self-images and self-esteem.

COGNITIVE SOPHISTICATION

An important feature of the elementary-school years is an advance in children's ability to learn about themselves and their environment. During this period they come to rely increasingly on the mental manipulation of concepts in adapting to their world. They become more adept at processing information in that their reasoning abilities become progressively more rational and logical.

Underlying the improvement in children's intellectual capabilities is a growing awareness and understanding of their own mental processes, what psychologists term *metacognition* (see Chapter 9). In many respects, Jean Piaget's stages constitute sets of so-called **executive strategies** (Case, 1978), which are analogous to the tasks performed by a corporate executive. Executives select, sequence, evaluate, revise, and monitor the effectiveness of problem-solving plans and behavior within their corporations. Applied to human mental functioning, executive strategies refer to the ability to integrate and orchestrate lower-level cognitive skills. At higher stages, the strategies are more complex and more powerful than at lower stages. Psychomotor skills provide a good illustration of these processes (see the boxed insert on page 295).

* Reprinted by permission of W. W. Norton & Company, Inc.

Period of Concrete Operations

Piaget calls middle childhood the **period of concrete operations.** He refers to it as "concrete" because children are bound by immediate physical reality and cannot transcend the here and now. Consequently, during this period children still have difficulty dealing with remote, future, or hypothetical matters.

Despite the limitations of concrete operational thought, this period witnesses major advances in children's cognitive capabilities. Its hallmark is that various classifying and ordering activities begin to occur internally as mental activities. For example, in the preoperational period before six or seven years of age, children arrange sticks by size in their proper sequence by physically comparing each pair in succession. But in the period of concrete operations, children "mentally" survey the sticks, then quickly place them in order, usually without any actual measurement. Since the activities of preoperational children are dominated by actual perceptions, the task takes them several minutes to complete. Children in the period of concrete operations finish the same project in a matter of seconds since their actions are directed by internal cognitive processes.

Conservation Tasks. As concrete operational thought evolves, a liberation occurs in children's thought processes. This unfreezing of the rigidity of preoperational thought allows them to solve conservation problems. **Conservation** requires the recognition that the quantity or amount of something stays the same despite changes in shape or position. It implies that children are mentally capable of compensating in their minds for various external changes in objects. As such, concrete operational thought entails a reorganization of cognitive structure—a progressive amalgamation of experience and mental activity.

Elementary-school children come to recognize that pouring liquid from a short, wide container into a

PSYCHOMOTOR SKILLS

Psychomotor skills involve "mind-guided" muscular movements and their coordination. They are voluntary as opposed to involuntary or reflex activities. These skills entail learned capabilities that find expression in rapid, accurate, forceful, or smooth movements of the body. For example, in driving a car, we link a variety of complex perceptual and cognitive operations to motor behavior in order to apply the brakes, accelerate, and steer left or right. Likewise, children employ psychomotor skills in the course of their activities, including using a pencil, writing on a blackboard, painting pictures, employing measuring instruments, and playing.

Psychomotor behavior has a number of characteristics (Sage, 1971). First, it necessitates an organized sequence of movements (for instance, in the jump shot in basketball, both knee-bending and elbow flexion precede elbow extension, and wrist flexion takes place with the release of the ball). Second, the behavior requires synchronization (for example, in a tennis serve the movements of the legs, shoulders, arms, and wrist must be brought into play in a synchronized operation). And third, the behavior must be goal-directed (for example, fullbacks are taught to fold their hands close to their stomachs and charge into the line after receiving a fake handoff from the quarterback so as to mislead opponents).

Paul M. Fitts and Michael I. Posner (1967) identify three main phases in the learning of motor skills:

1. *Early or cognitive phase.* At first the learner seeks to "understand" the task. Accordingly, it is helpful if the instructor identifies the separate parts of the skill, demonstrates each, then gives the learner an opportunity to practice each part (for instance, it is customary to teach beginning swimmers the kick, arm and hand movements, head positioning, and breathing techniques as separate skills). During this phase, learners typically depend on a good many cues that later they can dispense with (for example, the inexperienced automobile driver tends to look for the control pedals, and beginning typists often watch their fingers on the keys).
2. *Associative or intermediate phase.* As learning progresses, learners are able to integrate the new patterns and eliminate inappropriate responses. The individual skills become progressively fitted into a sequential order, so that each aspect of the movement becomes the signal for the next.
3. *Final or autonomous phase.* In the final phase people no longer need to "think about what to do next." The activity requires little conscious attention or cognitive regulation. In fact, at this stage conscious introspection tends to impair smooth performance.

Much motor learning takes place through feedback. Feedback provides information about the performance or about the consequences of the performance. As such it affords the kind of input that allows individuals to make adjustments in their responses. Feedback also has reinforcing properties, which derive from the rewarding effect of correct performance and the punishing effect of incorrect performance. And finally, feedback provides motivation and increases the interest level (Ammons, 1956; Sage, 1971).

Psychomotor Activities and Skills
The school environment demands complex and coordinated movements from children.
Patrick Reddy

from non–pottery-making families (Ashton, 1975). And Patricia M. Greenfield (1966) found in her studies involving Wolof children in Senegal, West Africa, that it made a difference whether the experimenter or the children themselves poured the water in the classic Piagetian experiment involving wide and narrow containers. Two-thirds of a group of children under eight years old who themselves transferred the water achieved the concept of conservation. In contrast, only one-fourth of a group who had watched the experimenter pour the water then realized that the amount of water was the same. The children attributed "magical action" to the experimenter that they did not attribute to their own performance. It seems clear that cultural factors need to be taken into account in considering children's performance on cognitive tests.

Cognitive Style

Piaget has shown us that children pass through somewhat similar stages in intellectual functioning between birth and adulthood. But researchers have demonstrated that people differ in their *ways* of processing information. In dealing with various aspects of our environment, each of us employs a particular **cognitive style.** This may be defined as the stable preferences that each of us exhibits in organizing and categorizing our perceptions.

One way that people differ in cognitive style is in their approach to problem solving. Some respond to a problem very rapidly without worrying about accuracy. Others of equal intelligence take considerably more time. The former group is termed *impulsive,* the latter *reflective* (Kagan, 1966). Presumably reflective people, unlike impulsive ones, pause to consider alternative solutions before suggesting an answer to a problem.

Research has revealed that reflective children tend to perform better than impulsive children on reading tasks (Kagan, 1965), recognition memory tests (Siegel, Kirasic, and Kilburg, 1973), tasks involving reasoning (Kagan, Pearson, and Welch, 1966), and creative projects (Fuqua, Bartsch, and Phye, 1975). In contrast, impulsive children excel at intellectual tasks requiring broad analysis (Zelniker and Jeffrey, 1976). Further, whereas reflective children favor a direct and assertive approach on a reasoning task entailing social conflict, impulsive children prefer a more passive and yielding approach (Peters and Bernfeld, 1983).

Another dimension of cognitive style is *field independence* versus *field dependence* (Witkin and Goodenough, 1981). In colloquial terms, some people tend to be "splitters" while others are "lumpers." This characteristic shows up in tests requiring people to find simple figures that are camouflaged by more complex figures. The skill involved is the ability to isolate some characteristic of a scene from a deceiving background. To some extent, individuals move from field dependence toward field independence during development. But even so, at each age, individual differences remain.

Field-independent people tend to analyze the elements of a scene; they focus on items as being separate from their backgrounds. In contrast, field-dependent people tend to categorize a scene as a whole and to overlook the individual items that compose it. Overall, researchers find that field-independent people are more likely to have an impersonal orientation toward others, whereas field-dependent individuals tend toward a more interpersonal orientation. Not surprisingly, people often describe field-independent individuals as cold, manipulating, and distant, whereas they characterize field-dependent individuals as warm, considerate, and accommodating. It also appears that field-independent college students tend to be attracted to mathematics, the natural sciences, engineering, and subjects that require a high level of analytical reasoning. Field-dependent students tend to major in the humanities, the social sciences, education, and fields that involve a global and often service-oriented perspective.

Educators are increasingly coming to recognize the importance of differences in cognitive style among students. They used to ask which method (or methods) was best—lecture, recitation, or discussion; a highly structured classroom or a more informal classroom; programmed instruction or a live teacher. And the answer was that for the mythical *average* student it makes little difference which alternative is employed. But when the data were examined student by student, it was found that some of them improve, others remain unaffected, and still others regress under certain teaching conditions. The process of averaging the pluses, the minuses, and the no-changes masks the fact that different strategies work with different students (Cross, 1976; Cronbach and Snow, 1977). Hence considerably more attention needs to be given to breaking lock-step practices in education and making allowance for individual differences.

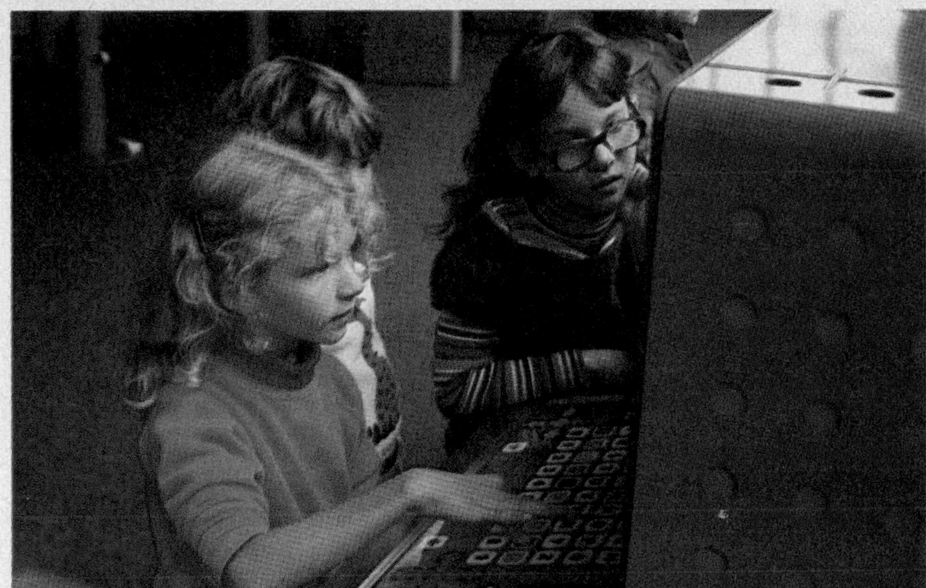

Cognitive Style
Children differ in the way they approach problem-solving tasks. Some respond very rapidly, giving minimum consideration to accuracy. Others are more deliberate and reflective, taking more time to arrive at an answer.
Joseph Nettis/Photo Researchers

Person Perception

The elementary-school years are a time of rapid growth in children's knowledge of the social world and of the requirements for social interaction. Consider what is involved when we enter the wider world of people (Lee, 1975; Vander Zanden, 1984). We need to assess certain key statuses of the people we encounter, such as their age and sex. We must also consider the behavior in which they are involved (walking, eating, reading), their emotional state (happy, sad, angry), their roles (teacher, clerk, parent), and the social context (church, home, restaurant).

Accordingly, when we enter a social setting we mentally attempt to "place" or "locate" people within the broad network of possible social relationships. By scrutinizing them for a variety of clues—certain telltale "signs" or "marks"—we place them in social categories. For instance, if they wear wedding rings we infer that they are married; if they wear business clothes during working hours, that they are employed in white-collar jobs; if they are in a wheelchair, that they are handicapped; and so on. Only in this manner can we decide what to expect of given people and what they expect of us. In sum, we activate *stereotypes*—certain exaggerated cultural understandings—that guide us in identifying the mutual set of expectations that will govern the social exchange.

Research by W. J. Livesley and D. B. Bromley (1973), based on a sample of 320 English children between seven and sixteen years of age, has traced developmental trends in children's perceptions of people. The study reveals that the number of dimensions along which children conceptualize other people grows throughout childhood. The greatest increase in children's ability to distinguish people's characteristics occurs between seven and eight years of age. Thereafter the rate of change is generally much slower. Indeed, the differences between children who are seven years old and those who are eight are often greater than the differences between eight-year-olds and fifteen-year-olds. This leads Livesley and Bromley (1973: 147) to conclude that "the eighth year is a critical period in the developmental psychology of person perception."

Children under eight years of age describe people largely in terms of external, readily observable attributes. Their conception of people tends to be inclusive. It embraces not only personality but also an individual's family, possessions, and physical characteristics. At this age, children categorize people in a simple, absolute, moralistic manner and employ vague, global descriptive terms such as "good," "bad," "horrible," and "nice." Consider this account by a seven-year-old girl of a woman she likes (1973: 214):

> She is very nice because she gives my friends and me toffee. She lives by the main road. She has fair hair and she wears glasses. She is forty-seven years old. She has

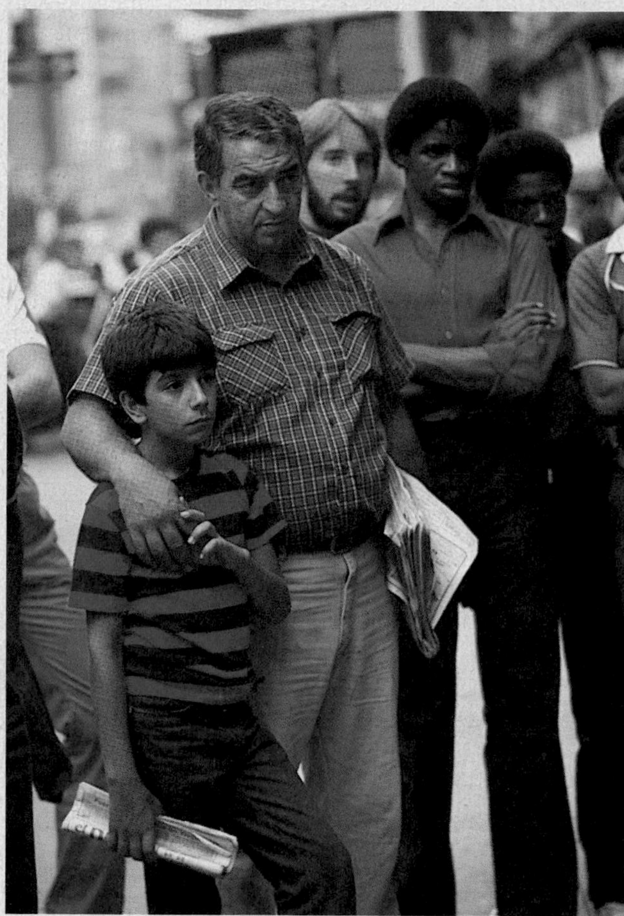

Person Perception
As children get older, their social worlds expand. The number of dimensions they employ for conceptualizing people grow, and they gain an appreciation for the complexity of the role networks that characterize social relationships.
Day Williams/Photo Researchers

> an anniversary today. She has been married since she was twenty-one years old. She sometimes gives us flowers. She has a very nice garden and house. We only go in the weekend and have a talk with her.

When they are about eight years old, children show rapid growth in their vocabularies for appraising people. Their phrases become more specific and precise. After this age children increasingly come to recognize certain regularities or unchanging qualities in the inner dispositions and overt behaviors of individuals. Here is a description of a boy by a nine-year-old girl (1973: 130):

> David Calder is a boy I know. He goes to this school but he is not in our class. His behavior is very bad, and he is always saying cheeky [impudent] things to people. He fights people of any age and he likes getting into trouble for it. He is always being told off by his teachers and other people.

Around the same age children also become aware that people display what seem to be incompatible qualities: for instance, sometimes they are "bad" and other times "good"; sometimes they are "mean" and other times "nice." As they move into their teens, children become capable of integrating one quality with another. A fourteen-year-old girl describes her girl friend in these terms (1973: 222): "Sometimes she gets a bit cross but that doesn't last long and soon she is her normal self."

In summary, Livesley and Bromley find the following developmental changes in the ways in which children see and describe people:

- Children use an increasing number of descriptive adjectives and categories.
- They display greater flexibility and precision in the use of these categories.
- They exhibit greater coherence, integration, and complexity in the ideas they form about people.
- They become more adept at recognizing and describing the subtle qualities that people reveal in their behavior.
- They show greater insight into people and are increasingly capable of analyzing and interpreting their behavior.
- They display more care in formulating statements about people in order to provide accurate and convincing descriptions of them.

Hence a rapid development occurs during middle childhood in children's abilities to make "psychological" inferences about other people—their thoughts, feelings, personality attributes, and general behavioral dispositions (Barenboim, 1977, 1981).

MORAL DEVELOPMENT

Morals are an acquirement—like music, like a foreign language, like piety, poker, paralysis—no man is born with them.

—MARK TWAIN

As human beings we live our lives in groups. Because we are interdependent, one person's activities can affect the welfare of others. Consequently, if we are to live with one another—if society is to be possible—we must share certain conceptions of what is right and what is wrong. Each of us must pursue our interests, be it for food, shelter, clothing, sex, power, or fame, within the context of a moral order governed by rules. Morality has to do with how we go about distributing the benefits and burdens of a cooperative group existence.

A functioning society also requires that its standards of morality be passed on to children—that moral development take place in its young. **Moral development** refers to the process by which children adopt principles that lead them to evaluate given behaviors as "right" and others as "wrong" and to govern their own actions in terms of these principles.

Historically, there have been three major philosophical doctrines regarding the moral development of children (Hoffman, 1970). One is the doctrine of "original sin," favored by such theologians as Saint Augustine (A.D. 354–430). According to this view, children are naturally sinful beings. As such they require redemption through the deliberate and punitive intervention of adults. Another view, put forward by John Locke (1632–1704), maintains that the child is morally neutral—a *tabula rasa*—and that training and experience determine whether the child becomes righteous or sinful. The third doctrine, represented by the writings of Jean Jacques Rousseau (1712–1778), holds that children are characterized by "innate purity" and that immoral behavior results from the corrupting influence of adults.

Each of these views finds expression in the three major contemporary psychological approaches to moral development. The first approach appears in modified form in the work of Sigmund Freud. The second is represented in cognitive learning theory, which treats moral development as a function of conditioning and modeling experiences. And the third approach is reflected to some degree in the cognitive-developmental theory of moral behavior as formulated by Jean Piaget and Lawrence Kohlberg.

Psychoanalytic Theory

Psychoanalytic theory (see Chapter 2) was the first fully psychological model of moral development. According to Freud, moral development is rooted in the emergence of the *superego*, a concept roughly equivalent to that of "conscience." Freud said that children possess various inborn drives—basic sexual and aggressive instincts—that are called the *id*. Parents frustrate these drives in order to socialize children in accordance with the standards of the wider society. This generates hostility in the children toward their parents. But since children fear the loss of parental

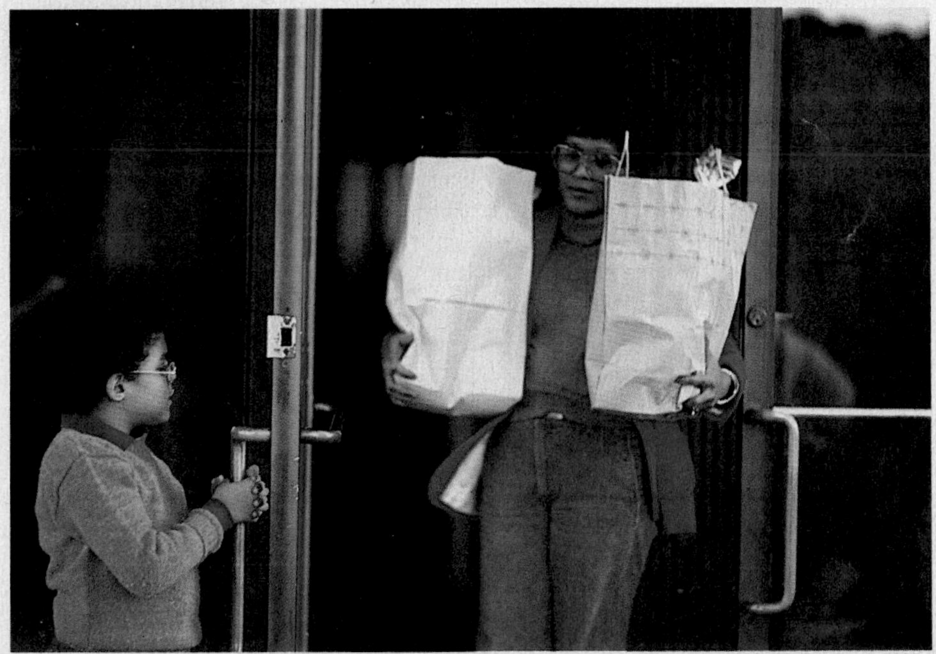

Internalizing Adult Prohibitions

According to psychoanalytic theory, in the course of moral development children come to transform external punishment into self-punishment. They behave morally in order to avoid guilt and anxiety. In this sense, children are said to *internalize* adult standards.

Richard Hutchings/Photo Researchers

love and anticipate parental retaliation, they repress their hostility and incorporate—in Freudian terms, **internalize**—the parental prohibitions.

The process of taking on, or internalizing, parental standards leads children to behave morally in order to avoid self-punishment, anxiety, and guilt. It is as if children become their own parents through the mechanism of the superego; external punishment is transformed into self-punishment and external control into self-control. Thus, by adopting their parents' evaluations of their own behavior, children incorporate within themselves the moral standards of the wider society.

Freud (1930) said that civilization requires people to restrain their instinctual impulses toward aggressive behaviors. Guilt feelings are the mechanism by which this is achieved. Aggressive impulses are turned *inward* on oneself. Freud (1930: 134) concluded that "the price we pay for our advance in civilization is a loss of happiness through the heightening of the sense of guilt." And in Freud's view, excessive guilt is the foundation of many mental disorders.

All the details of orthodox psychoanalytic theory are no longer accepted by most behavioral and social scientists. But the assumption that socialization occurs at least in part because children *identify* with their

Cognitive Learning Theory

According to cognitive learning theory, individuals learn behavior in social contexts. Morality is seen not as a unitary trait but as behavior that the group defines as socially acceptable. Since individuals are members of multiple groups with somewhat different standards, a person's behavior varies across different settings and is evaluated somewhat differently in each of the settings.

Richard Hutchings/Photo Researchers

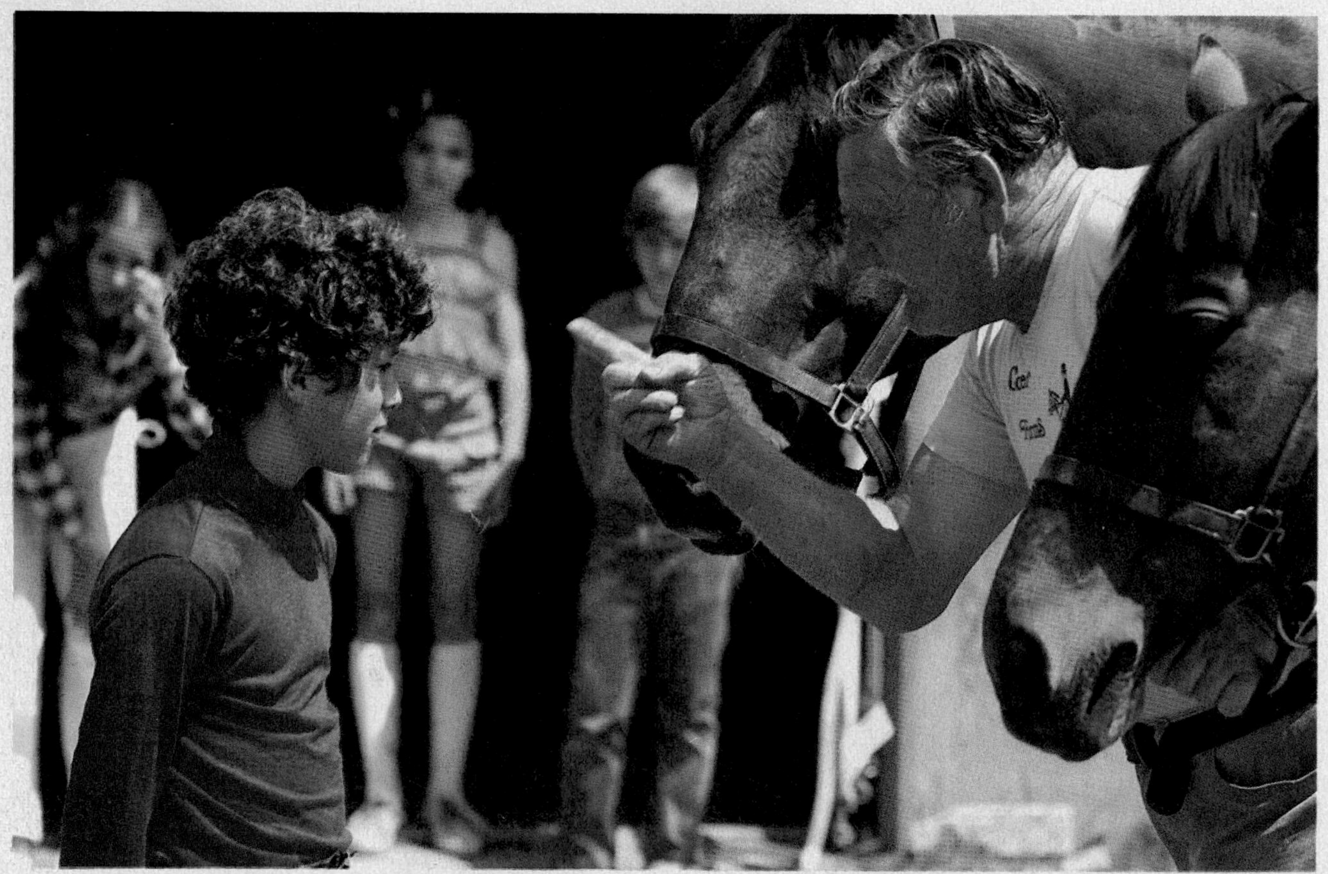

parents remains a major tenet of much contemporary research and therapy.

Cognitive Learning Theory

To make your children capable of honesty is the beginning of education.

—JOHN RUSKIN
Time and Tide, 1867

In discussing cognitive learning theory, Chapter 2 emphasized the important part that imitation plays in the socialization process. According to psychologists like Albert Bandura and Walter Mischel, children acquire moral standards in much the same way that they learn any other behavior. In contrast to the psychoanalytic position, social learning theorists deny that moral behavior comes from some single agency like the superego. In addition, they deny that moral behavior represents some unitary trait such as honesty. Rather, they insist that social behavior is variable and dependent on situational contexts. Most actions lead to positive consequences in some situations and not in others. Consequently, individuals develop highly discriminating and specific response patterns that fail to generalize across all life circumstances (Mischel and Mischel, 1976).

Studies carried out by cognitive learning theorists have generally been concerned with the effect that models have on other people's resistance to temptation (Bandura, Ross, and Ross, 1961, 1963). In such research, children typically observe a model who either yields or does not yield to temptation. Chapter 1 described an experiment of this sort by Richard H. Walters, Marion Leat, and Louis Mezei (1963). One group of boys individually watched a movie in which a child was punished by his mother for playing with some forbidden toys. A second group saw another version of the movie in which the child was rewarded for the same behavior. And a third group, a control group, did not see any movie. The experimenter took each boy to another room and told him not to play with the toys in the room. The experimenter then left the room.

The study revealed that boys who had observed the model being rewarded for disobeying his mother themselves disobeyed the experimenter more quickly and more often than the boys in the other two groups. The boys who had observed the model being punished showed the greatest reluctance of any of the groups to disobey the experimenter. In short, observing the behavior of another person does seem to have a modeling effect on children's obedience or disobedience to social regulations. Of interest, other research reveals that dishonest or deviant models often have a considerably greater impact on children than do honest or nondeviating models (Stein, 1967; Ross, 1971; Rosenkoetter, 1973; Grusec et al., 1979).

Cognitive-Developmental Theory

Cognitive learning theorists view moral development as a cumulative process that builds on itself gradually and continuously, without any abrupt changes. In sharp contrast to this idea, cognitive-developmental theorists like Jean Piaget and Lawrence Kohlberg conceive of moral development as taking place in stages. They see the course of moral development as divided into steps, with clear-cut changes between them. Consequently, a child's morality in a particular stage differs substantially from that of earlier and later stages.

Jean Piaget. The scientific study of moral development was launched half a century ago by Jean Piaget. In his classic study, *The Moral Judgment of the Child* (1932), Piaget said that there is an orderly and logical pattern in the development of children's moral judgments. This development is based on the sequential changes associated with children's intellectual growth, especially the stages that are characterized by the emergence of logical thought.

In keeping with his interactionist perspective (see Chapter 2), Piaget believed that moral development occurs as children act upon, transform, and modify the world they live in. As they do, they in turn are transformed and modified by the consequences of their actions. Hence Piaget portrayed children as *active* participants in their own moral development. In this respect Piaget differed from the cognitive learning theorists. As depicted in cognitive learning theory, the environment acts on children and modifies them; children are *passive* recipients of environmental forces. Cognitive learning theorists picture children as learning *from* their environment rather than, as Piaget would have insisted, in dynamic interaction *with* their environment.

Games and Moral Conduct

In games young people learn the importance of rules for ordering human affairs. Piaget believed that autonomous morality arises out of the reciprocal interaction that takes place among peers.

Patrick Reddy

Piaget provided a two-stage theory of moral development. The first stage, that of **heteronomous morality,** arises from the unequal interaction between children and adults. During the preschool and early elementary-school years, children are immersed in an authoritian environment in which they occupy a position decidedly inferior to that of adults. Piaget said that in this context children develop a conception of moral rules as absolute, unchanging, and rigid. (Hence the stage is also termed one of *moral realism* and a *morality of constraint.*)

As children approach and enter adolescence, a new stage emerges in moral development—the stage of **autonomous morality.** Whereas heteronomous morality evolves from the unequal relationships between children and adults, autonomous morality arises from the interaction among status *equals*—relationships among peers. Such relationships, when coupled with general intellectual growth and a weakening in the constraints of adult authority, create a morality characterized by rationality, flexibility, and social consciousness. Through their peer associations, young people acquire a sense of justice—a concern for the rights of others, for equality, and for reciprocity in human relations. Piaget described autonomous morality as egalitarian and democratic, a morality based on mutual respect and cooperation. (Hence the stage is also termed the *morality of cooperation.*)

Piaget identified four dimensions that distinguish between the heteronomous and autonomous stages

(Lickona, 1976). These dimensions are defined in terms of the immature, or heteronomous, stage:

- *Moral absolutism.* Young children assume that at all times and in all places the identical rules prevail (the "My daddy says . . ." ploy to solve disputes). They view rules as having an existence of their own, as being real in their own right. Accordingly, they take rules as "givens," unquestionable and sacred.
- *The conception of rules as unchangeable.* Children believe that rules are rigid and unalterable.
- *The belief in immanent justice.* Children assume that misfortune is inflicted on wrongdoers by God or nature. For instance, a child who steals an object and later falls down and skins her knee will think, "That happened because I stole."
- *The evaluation of responsibility in terms of its consequences.* Children appraise an act on the basis of its outcome rather than on the intent of the actor.

Piaget suggested that these limitations of heteronomous morality are linked to the shortcomings of preoperational and concrete operational thought. Thus the development of children's moral judgments parallels their cognitive development. Piaget identified two factors that underlie the limitations in young children's moral judgment. First, during the preoperational period children are *egocentric;* they are unable to "decenter" their viewpoint and perceive the world from the perspective of other people (see Chapter 9). Second, young children's *intellectual realism* leads them to confuse external reality with their own experiences and thought processes. They view themselves as the center of the universe. But as the rigidity of preoperational thought unfreezes in concrete operational thought, and as concrete operational thought in turn gives way to logical and rational thought during the period of formal operations, children's view of morality becomes more flexible, qualified, and socially oriented.

Lawrence Kohlberg. Lawrence Kohlberg (1963, 1969, 1976, 1978; Kohlberg and Gilligan, 1971), a psychologist at Harvard, has undertaken to refine, extend, and revise Piaget's basic theory of the development of moral values. Like Piaget, Kohlberg focuses on the development of moral *judgments* in children rather than on their actions. He is interested in the child as a "moral philosopher."

Like Piaget, Kohlberg has gathered his data by asking subjects questions about hypothetical stories. One of these stories (1963: 18–19) has become famous as a classic ethical dilemma:

> In Europe, a woman was near death from a special kind of cancer. There was one drug that the doctors thought might save her. It was a form of radium that a druggist in the same town had recently discovered. The drug was expensive to make, but the druggist was charging ten times what the drug cost him to make. He paid $200 for the radium and charged $2,000 for a small dose of the drug. The sick woman's husband, Heinz, went to everyone he knew to borrow the money, but he could only get together about $1,000, which is half of what it cost. He told the druggist that his wife was dying, and asked him to sell it cheaper or let him pay later. But the druggist said, "No, I discovered the drug and I'm going to make money from it." Heinz got desperate and broke into the man's store to steal the drug for his wife. Should the husband have done that?

On the basis of responses to this type of dilemma, Kohlberg has identified six stages in the development of moral judgment. He groups these stages into three major levels: the *preconventional level* (stages 1 and 2); the *conventional level* (stages 3 and 4); and the *postconventional level* (stages 5 and 6). These levels and stages are summarized in Table 11.1, together with typical responses to the story of Heinz. Study the table carefully for a complete overview of Kohlberg's theory. Note that the stages are not based on whether the moral decision about Heinz is pro or con, but on what reasoning is used to reach the decision.

Each of Kohlberg's levels reflects a different type of relationship between the *self* and *society's rules and expectations.* The preconventional level is characteristic of most children under nine years of age, some adolescents, and many criminal offenders. At this level, rules and expectations are *external* to the self. The conventional level is typical of most adolescents and adults. At this level, the self has *internalized* the rules and expectations of the wider society. The postconventional level is attained by less than 25 percent of all Americans. At this level, individuals *differentiate* between themselves and the rules and expectations of others, preferring instead to define their values in terms of rationally considered, self-chosen principles.

According to Kohlberg, people in all cultures employ the same basic moral concepts, including justice, equality, love, respect, and authority. Further, all individuals, regardless of culture, go through the same stages of reasoning with respect to these concepts,

On the basis of their research, however, Marian Radke-Yarrow and Carolyn Zahn-Waxler (Radke-Yarrow and Zahn-Waxler, 1976; Zahn-Waxler, Radke-Yarrow, and King, 1979) say that parental love is not enough to perpetuate and encourage altruistic behavior in children. Rather, it is necessary that parents have the ability to convey a certain intensity about their own concern for other living things. If a cat is hit by a car, it matters in the development of a child's prosocial behavior whether the parent appears to care about the cat—speaks about the cat's suffering, attempts to do something to alleviate it—or appears callous and unconcerned. Or, should the child hurt someone else, it is important to describe to the child how that person feels. Yet Radke-Yarrow and Zahn-Waxler admit there is a fine line between encouraging altruism and fostering guilt; parents, they say, should not inject too much intensity into such situations lest their children become overanxious.

Many investigators have demonstrated that a child's sharing and helping behavior can be increased when adults (1) model the behavior before the child, and (2) reinforce the behavior when the child displays it (Bryan and Walbek, 1970; Grusec and Skubiski, 1970; Gelfand et al., 1975; Rushton, 1976; Staub, 1978). Mary B. Harris (1970) found, for instance, that fourth- and fifth-grade children would share with an adult model if the model has shared with them, donate their winnings from a game to a charity if they had observed the model doing so, or retain their winnings if the model had done so. In another study, Harris (1971) found that children distributed their winnings among several charities in a manner similar to that which they had witnessed in the behavior of a model.

Not surprisingly, research reveals that adults' actions speak louder than their words. Lecturing influences children's verbal comments but has practically no effect on their overt behavior. Indeed, research by Elizabeth Midlarsky, James H. Bryan, and Philip Brickman (1973: 323) suggests that adult hypocrisy may boomerang. The study involved a sample of seventy-two sixth-grade girls. Each of the girls played a game with an adult model in which both received winnings from a "rigged" pinball machine. After the model had completed her games, she told the child:

> Now it is your turn. But before you begin, let me remind you about the poor children [a canister for poor children stood nearby]. Please think about them as you are playing and about how very much they would love to receive the prizes that these chips can buy. It would make them very happy to get toys and candy—because it is so easy for a needy child to feel forgotten. Let us let them know that we remember them.

This research revealed that when the adult modeled selfish behavior (kept her winnings) but preached altruism and praised the child when the child dropped a chip into the canister, the child was less likely to be charitable on subsequent occasions than when the hypocritical adult had not praised the child. In brief, by approving charitable behavior, a selfish-acting, generous-sounding model actually serves to discourage it.

David Rosenhan (1972) found that young people who were involved in the civil rights movement of the 1960s were more likely to be fully committed—to leave their homes, schools, and jobs so that they could participate full-time—if their parents had also been prosocial activists in an earlier era (such as in the Spanish Civil War, World War II, or religious education). In contrast, partially committed young people—those who were motivated by transient feelings of group camaraderie and short-term personal rewards rather than by altruistic motives—tended to come from families in which altruism was limited to preaching and where the ideals were often violated in practice. These young people, angered by the discrepancy between parental postures and actions, had undergone a "crisis of hypocrisy" during childhood. The result was an inability to make enduring commitments to prosocial causes later on.

SUMMARY

1. An important feature of the elementary-school years is a marked growth in children's cognitive sophistication. During this time, which Piaget calls the *period of concrete operations,* children achieve mastery of conservation problems. They become capable of decentering, attending to transformations, and recognizing the reversibility of operations.
2. Considerable controversy exists as to whether the development of conservation can be accelerated through training procedures. There is also some question about whether the acquisition of conservation skills in the period of concrete operations occurs in the invariant se-

quence—horizontal décalage—postulated by Piaget.

3. Although all children tend to pass through the same sequence of cognitive stages outlined by Piaget, they differ in cognitive style. Some children are impulsive and respond to problems very rapidly with minimum consideration for accuracy; others are reflective and take considerably more time in responding. Children differ in still another dimension of cognitive style, that of field independence and field dependence.

4. The greatest increase in children's ability to distinguish people's characteristics occurs between seven and eight years of age. Thereafter the rate of change is generally much slower.

5. There are three major psychological approaches to moral development: the psychoanalytic, cognitive learning, and cognitive-developmental theories.

6. The psychoanalytic view conceives of the child as a bundle of sexual and aggressive drives that need to be subordinated by adults to societal objectives. As a consequence of internalizing parental standards, children behave morally so as to avoid self-punishment, anxiety, and guilt.

7. Cognitive learning theory views moral development as a cumulative process that builds in a gradual and continuous process. Children acquire moral standards primarily through imitating the observable values and behavior of others.

8. Cognitive-developmental theorists such as Jean Piaget and Lawrence Kohlberg conceive of moral development as taking place in stages. The course of moral development is seen as divided into stepped levels, with clear-cut changes distinguishing one phase from the next.

9. Research reveals that morality tends to be specific to situations. Most children will cheat, lie, or steal in certain situations and not in others. Little support exists for the notion of a unitary conscience or superego. Some individuals tend to be more consistently honest than others, some more consistently dishonest. But inconsistency is the more dominant tendency.

10. Intelligence, age, and sex differences play a small part in moral conduct. Group codes and motivational factors have a much larger role.

11. Moral development represents more than simply learning prohibitions against misbehavior. Like honesty, prosocial behavior tends to have a strong situational component, although some individuals have a more general prosocial orientation than do others. Not surprisingly, research reveals that adults' actions speak louder than their words and that adult hypocrisy may boomerang.

KEY TERMS

altruism Behavior that is carried out to benefit another without expectation of an external reward.

autonomous morality The second stage in Jean Piaget's two-stage theory of moral development. Moral judgments derive from an egalitarian and democratic perspective that is based upon mutual respect and cooperation.

class inclusion The ability acquired by children during the period of concrete operations to group elementary classes into a superordinate class and to reverse the process by reducing the broader class into its subordinate components. Class inclusion involves the recognition of the subordinate-superordinate, or part-whole, relationship.

cognitive style The stable preferences that individuals exhibit in organizing and categorizing their perceptions.

conservation The concept that the quantity or amount of something stays the same regardless of any changes in its shape or position.

executive strategy A method for selecting, sequencing, evaluating, revising, and monitoring a problem-solving plan and behavior.

heteronomous morality The first stage in Jean Piaget's two-stage theory of moral development. Judgments are rigid and absolute and derive from moral rules laid down by persons in authority, such as parents.

internalize The concept from Freudian psychoanalytic theory that children incorporate within their personalities the prohibitions of their parents. Since children fear the loss of parental love and anticipate parental retaliation if they express open hostility and defiance toward their parents, the children repress their hostility and take on their parents' moral standards.

moral development The process by which children adopt principles that lead them to evaluate given behaviors as "right" and others as "wrong" and to govern their own actions in terms of these principles.

period of concrete operations One of Piaget's four stages in the development of cognition, or intelligence. The stage marks the beginning of rational activity in children, one in which various classifying and ordering activities begin to occur internally as mental activities.

prosocial behavior (altruism) Ways of responding to others that include sympathetic, cooperative, helpful, rescuing, comforting, and giving acts.

psychomotor skill A mind-guided muscular movement and its coordination.

seriation The ability acquired by children during the period of concrete operations to order objects in a series according to some abstract dimension, such as size, weight, or brightness.

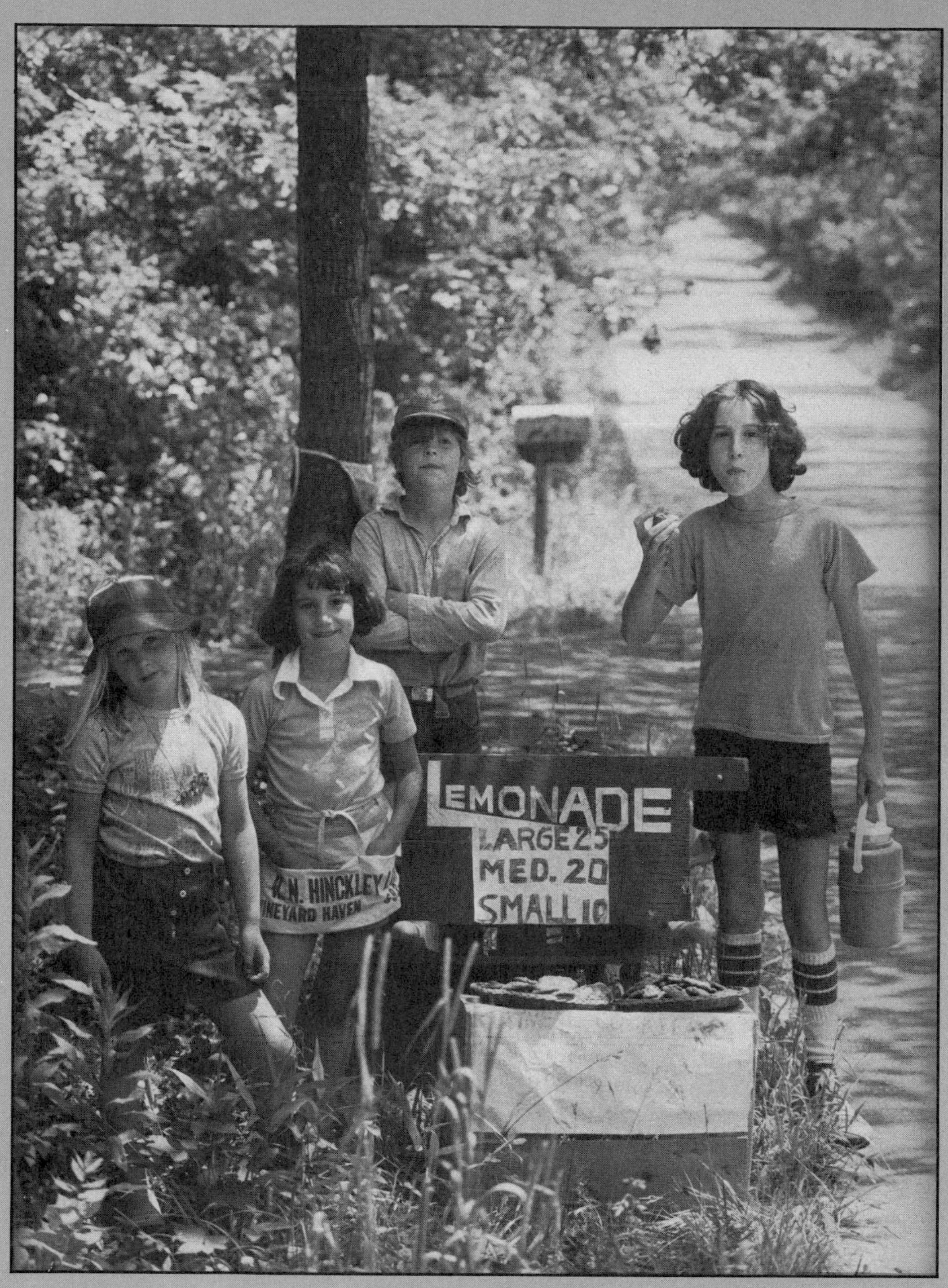
LEMONADE
LARGE 25
MED. 20
SMALL 10
HINCKLEY
HAVEN

orientation to a heterosexual orientation to social behavior.

3. Specify the relationship between the following terms: "group," "values," and "sociometry."

4. Compare the effects of the following factors on social desirability and perceived attractiveness: (a) physical attractiveness and body build, (b) desirability of first names, (c) behavioral characteristics (e.g., hyperactivity), and (d) social maturity.

5. Discuss the meaning, origins, and factors associated with the development of self-esteem in children.

6. Explain how the following phenomena are measured in children: (a) conformity and its influencing factors, (b) social awareness and prejudice and their influencing factors.

7. Categorize the developmental functions that schools serve, and on the basis of the research presented in the text, evaluate the effectiveness of schools in fulfilling these functions (e.g., whether mainstreaming works for the learning-disabled). (Box)

8. Describe the relationship between social class, self-fulfilling prophecies, and school performance.

Chapter **12**

Later Childhood: The Broadening Social Environment

LEARNING OBJECTIVES

When you have mastered the material in this chapter, you should be able to:

1. Appreciate the significant functions of children's peer relationships and peer groups.

1. Peer relationships. -

provide an arena in which children can exercise independence & from adult controls. * children experience with relationships in which they are on equal footing with others. * peer group is only social institution in which the position of children is not marginal. * peer groups are agencies for the transmission of informal knowledge, superstition folklore jokes fads etc.

2. children hang out with the same sex in sex cleavage. changes in heterosexual relationship.

3.

10. reality riddles based on conceptual trick, within the context of reality.

ambiguity riddles: ambiguity ride in the answer or question

absurdity riddles some blatant impossibility is postulated in the question or offered as a solution in the answer -

12

Later Childhood: The Broadening Social Environment

Life is with people.

—*Jewish Proverb*

School is the child's first big step into the larger society. Some American children enter the world of school when they are enrolled in a day-care program, others when they attend nursery school, still others when they enter elementary school. When they attend school on a regular basis, children are outside their homes and their immediate neighborhoods for several hours a day. In this new setting teachers become a major source of potential influence. In school children also encounter peers of approximately the same age and grade level who will pass with them through a series of classrooms. Thus school is a radical departure from a child's previous way of life. The environment it affords has a major influence on the development of a child's personality, intellectual capabilities, interpersonal skills, and social behavior.

THE WORLD OF PEER RELATIONSHIPS

As children in elementary school develop and refine their cognitive and social skills, they become increasingly self-directed. Consequently they choose a large portion of their own social contacts. Many of these are with peers with whom they form "chum" relationships (McGuire and Weisz, 1982). From six to fourteen years of age, children's conceptions of friendship show an increasing emphasis on reciprocity, intimacy, and mutual understanding (Sullivan, 1953; Youniss, 1980). The information that they consider important to know about a friend also undergoes developmental change (Selman, 1980). Preschoolers cite nonintimate information that enables friends to get together, such as their living near one another. During middle childhood, children begin focusing on a friend's preferences, such as his or her favorite games, activities, and people. As they enter adolescence, young people become increasingly concerned with a friend's internal feelings and personality traits. Hence there is a progressive shift from concern with the observable and external qualities of a friend to concern with a friend's internal psychological world. Clearly, peer relationships assume a vital role in children's development.

Developmental Functions of Peer Groups

There are many different kinds of peer relationships and groups: a friendship, a school or neighborhood clique, a scout troop, a basketball or baseball team, a gang, and so on. Children may simultaneously be involved in a number of peer relationships. These relationships provide a world of children, in contrast to a world of adults.

Sometimes peer groups are in open conflict with adults, as in the case of delinquent gangs. A gang's behavior is oriented toward evading and flouting the rules and regulations of school and the larger adult-dominated society. Nondelinquent children also find themselves in conflict with parental expectations, as when they argue, "The other kids can stay out till twelve o'clock; why can't I?" At the other extreme, the expectations of some peer groups may fully accord with those of adults. This is usually true of scout organizations and religious youth groups.

Peer groups serve a variety of functions. First, they provide an arena in which children can exercise independence from adult controls. Because of the support they receive from their peer group, children can gain the courage and confidence that is needed for weakening their emotional bonds to their parents. By creating peer standards for behavior and then appealing to these standards, the peer culture operates as a pressure group. The peer group becomes an important agency for extracting concessions for its members on such matters as bedtime hours, dress codes, choices of social activities, and amounts of spending money. It affirms children's right to a considerable measure of self-determination (Ausubel and Sullivan, 1970; Siman, 1977). Hence the peer group furnishes an impetus for young people to seek greater freedom and provides them with support for behavior they would never dare attempt on their own.

Second, peer groups give children experience with relationships in which they are on an equal footing with others. In the adult world, in contrast, children occupy the position of subordinates, with adults directing, guiding, and controlling their activities. Group living calls for relationships characterized by sociability, self-assertion, competition, cooperation, and mutual understanding among equals. By interacting with peers, children learn the functional and reciprocal basis for social rules and regulations. They practice "getting along with others" and subordinating their own interests to group goals. As discussed in Chapter 11, Jean Piaget views these relationships among status equals as the foundation for the stage in moral development that he terms autonomous morality.

Third, the peer group is the only social institution in which the position of children is not marginal. In it children can acquire status and realize an identity in which their own activities and concerns are supreme. Further, the "we" feeling—the solidarity associated with group membership—furnishes security, companionship, acceptance, and a general sense of well-being. And it helps children avoid boredom and loneliness during the unstructured hours when school is not in session.

Fourth, peer groups are agencies for the transmission of informal knowledge, superstitions, folklore, fads, jokes, riddles (see the boxed insert on page 324), games, and secret modes of gratification. In the United States, for instance, only a portion of sexual information is learned through parents or schools. Peer groups transmit the larger part of this information (and misinformation). Even when sex education is not limited to the peer group, some types of sexual behavior (such as "necking") require private experimentation, since instruction would be awkward and

Peer Relationships

In their relationships with peers, children acquire interpersonal skills essential for the management of adult life. Peer groups provide children with experiences in equalitarian relationships. In contrast, children are subordinates when dealing with adults.

Bill Owens/Jeroboam

embarrassing. Upstairs, behind the garage, and in other out-of-the-way places children acquire and develop many skills essential for the management of adult life.

Obviously, peers are as necessary to children's development as adults are. The complexity of social life requires that children be involved in networks both of adults and of peers.

Same-Sex Groupings

A striking feature of peer relationships during the elementary-school years is **sex cleavage**—the tendency for boys to associate with boys and girls with girls. For many individuals, same-sex friendships are closer and more intense in late childhood and early adolescence than at any other phase of the life span (Douvan and Adelson, 1966). Although the social distance between the sexes appears as early as two or three years of age, it does not become conspicuous until the formal school years. Research reveals, for instance, that when first-grade children are given photographs of everyone in their class and asked to point out their best friend, 95 percent select a child of the same sex as themselves. Moreover, when they are asked to point out their four best friends, 82 percent likewise choose children of the same sex (Haskett, 1971).

Although first-grade children overwhelmingly name members of their own sex as best friends, both boys and girls can be observed playing together on school playgrounds during recess. By the third grade, however, children have divided themselves into two sexual camps. This separation tends to reach its peak around the fifth grade. Much of the interaction between groups of boys and girls at the fifth-grade level takes the form of bantering, teasing, chasing, name calling, and displays of open hostility. This "them-against-us" view of the opposite sex serves to emphasize the differences between the sexes. As such, it may function as a protective phase in life during which children can fashion a coherent sex-based identity (Kerckhoff, 1972).

The prevalence of this childhood sex cleavage provided Sigmund Freud with his concept of *latency* (see Chapter 2). In Freud's view, once children no longer look on the parent of the opposite sex as a love object (thereby resolving their Oedipal or Electra conflict), they reject all members of that sex until they reach adolescence. Hence according to Freud, the elemen-

CHILDREN'S HUMOR: RIDDLES AND DITTIES

Children's humor shifts across childhood (Tamashiro, 1979). During the late preschool and early school years, bodily noises—hiccups, burps, and passing gas—commonly draw laughter. Children also laugh at bodily and facial contortions, physical clowning, slapstick humor, and accidents resulting from clumsiness. Between six and eight years of age, children's humor tends to change from inventive, rambling, and absurd narration to the appreciation and sharing of jokes (Whitt and Prentice, 1977). The earlier type of humor resembles a riddle but lacks the riddle's logical resolution. For instance: "Why is a hippo so fat? Because he has too many babies!" Children of eight and older prefer jokes in which some logical, even if incongruous, linkage exists between the two parts of the riddle. For example: "What kind of dog tells the best time? A watch dog!"

Daniel Yalisove (1978) finds that riddles based on conceptual tricks are most popular among younger children; riddles based on language ambiguity among intermediate ages; and riddles based on absurdity among high-school students. Riddles usually have two elements—a misleading element, which makes the answer difficult to guess, and a resolution element, which makes the answer logical.

In *reality riddles,* popular among children in the first three years of elementary school, the joke is based on a conceptual trick that remains within the context of reality. For example: "How many balls of string would it take to reach the moon? One, but it would have to be a big one!" A person would normally assume regular-sized balls of string to be involved, of which a great number would be required. But since the size is not specified, one big ball of string would suffice.

In *ambiguity riddles,* popular among children in the middle school years, some sort of ambiguity resides either in the question or in the answer. For instance: "Why do birds fly south? Because it's too far to walk!" The question the riddle seems to be asking is, "Why is it that birds fly south?" But the question that is answered is, "Why do birds use flying as their means for going south?"

Finally, in *absurdity riddles,* some blatant impossibility is postulated in the question or offered as a solution in the answer. For example, in the following riddle a blatant impossibility is postulated in the question, which, if mentally negated, allows the riddle to be answered logically: "How can you fit six elephants into a VW? Three in the front and three in the back!" Whereas in the second stage the child focuses only on the reasonableness of the answer, in the third stage the child becomes aware that language can be used to refer to the hypothetical and that the hypothetical can be logical. This mode of thought is related to Piaget's stage of formal operational thought (see Chapter 13).

Moron jokes, puns, knock-knock jokes, and ditties are also popular among elementary-school children. As in the following ditties, the humor contains considerable ridicule, sarcasm, and "put-downs":

You liar, you liar,
Your pants are on fire
Your nose is as long
As a telephone wire.

When you get old
And think you're sweet,
Take off your shoes
And smell your feet.

Brad! Brad!
Don't be blue.
Frankenstein
Was ugly too.

Children's humor tends to parallel the issues that they are confronting in their personal and social development (Tamashiro, 1979). Bodily functions serve as the focus of early humor when children are attempting to gain control of these processes. Hostile, manipulative humor emerges as children undertake to clarify the psychological boundaries associated with their evolving sense of selfhood. And riddles and jokes that children memorize and retell ritualize their linkage to the peer group and their conformity to its standards.

tary-school years are a kind of developmental plateau, one in which sexual impulses are repressed.

But more recent research casts doubts on Freud's notion that sexual interests are minimal during the elementary-school years. Carlfred B. Broderick and George P. Rowe (1968) studied a sample of 1,029 Pennsylvania school children between ten and twelve years of age. They found that preadolescents exhibit

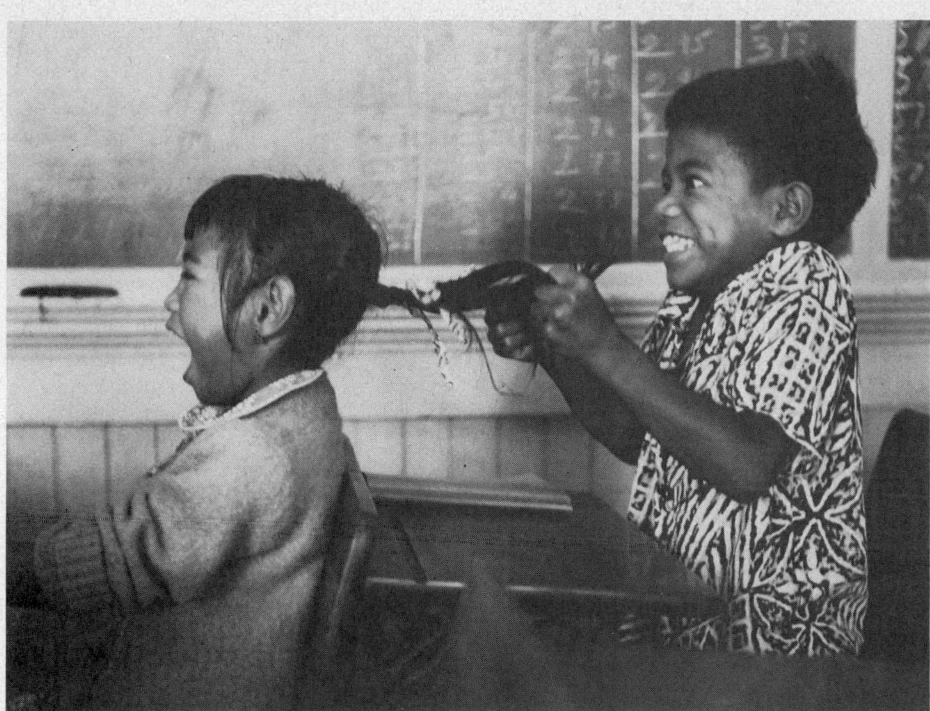

Boy-Girl Interaction
A good deal of the interaction between boys and girls at the fifth-grade level takes the form of bantering, teasing, chasing, name calling, and even open hostility—a "them-against-us" view of the opposite sex.
David Strickler/The Picture Cube

the developing roots of adult heterosexual interests and activities (see Figure 12.1). In their sample, 84 percent of the girls and 62 percent of the boys indicated that they expect to get married; 71 percent of the girls responded that they had a boyfriend and 56 percent of the boys that they had a girlfriend; and 51 percent of the girls and 47 percent of the boys admitted to having been in love.

Broderick and Rowe suggest that children typically pass through a series of stages in the course of heterosexual social development. First, preschool children acquire an awareness of marriage as involving a relationship between a man and a woman who are attracted to each other. Second, and somewhat later, children come to view marriage as an attractive and desirable prospect in their own imagined future. Third, children single out some member of the opposite sex as being especially attractive to them and then place this person in the special category of "boyfriend" or "girlfriend" (1968: 100):

> At this [preadolescent] age the boyfriend-girlfriend relationship was quite likely to be nonreciprocal and . . . commonly the object of the affection was unaware of his or her status. Despite the largely imaginary nature of these relationships, however, the children who feel these attachments apparently take them quite seriously. The majority described themselves as having been "in love."

Having been "in love" appears to lay the foundation for the fourth stage, an appreciation of the desirability of engaging in an activity with a member of the opposite sex, such as going to see a movie together. And fifth, appreciating the possibility of companionship with a member of the opposite sex leads to the next major step, actually going out on a date. In sum, the Broderick and Rowe research reveals that even though same-sex friendships predominate among ten- and eleven-year-old children, the children show a steady and progressive development of cross-sex interests as they advance toward puberty. Whether these patterns in heterosexual social development are peculiar to children reared in the United States, or whether they can be generalized to children reared in other cultural settings, remains to be determined.

Social Acceptance and Rejection

Peer relationships often take on enduring and stable characteristics. These are the properties of a **group,** which can be defined as two or more people who

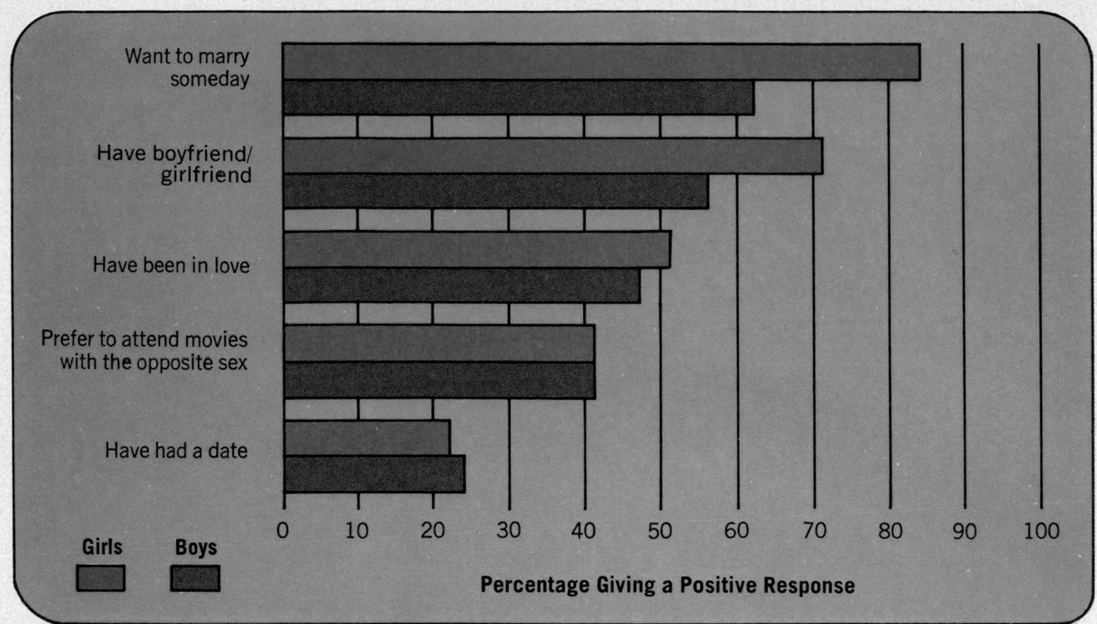

Figure 12.1 Beginnings of Adult Heterosexual Interests in Preadolescents
The figure charts the percentage of girls and boys who responded positively to items on a questionnaire measuring their social heterosexual development. In all, there were 1,029 subjects in the sample (530 boys and 499 girls), consisting of all ten- to twelve-year-olds in the fifth, sixth, and seventh grades of ten central Pennsylvania schools.

SOURCE: Adapted from Carlfred B. Broderick and George P. Rowe, "A Scale of Preadolescent Heterosexual Development," *Journal of Marriage and the Family,* Vol. 30 (1968), p. 99, Table 2.

share a feeling of unity and are bound together in relatively stable patterns of social interaction. Group members commonly have a psychological sense of oneness—an assumption that their own inner experiences and emotional reactions are shared by the other members. This gives individuals the feeling that they are not merely *in* the group but *of* the group.

A group's awareness of unity is expressed in many ways. One of the most important is through shared **values,** which are the criteria that people use in deciding the relative merit and desirability of things (themselves, other people, objects, events, ideas, acts, and feelings). Values play a critical part in influencing people's social interaction. They function as the standards—the social "yardsticks"—that people use to appraise one another. In short, in fashioning accepting or rejecting relationships, people size up one another according to various group standards of excellence.

Peer groups are no exception. Elementary-school children arrange themselves in ranked hierarchies with respect to a variety of qualities. Even first-graders have notions of one another's relative popularity or status. (Boys, for instance, regularly rate one another in terms of such attributes as "toughness.") Consequently, children differ in the extent to which their peers desire to be associated with them.

One common measure used for assessing patterns of attraction, rejection, or indifference is **sociometry.** The technique involves a questionnaire or interview in which people are asked to name the three (or sometimes five) individuals in the group whom they would most like to sit next to (eat with, have as a close friend, go on a picnic with, live next to, have on their own team, or whatever). Researchers also use sociometry to establish patterns of rejection, discrimination, antagonism, or whatever by asking people to name the individuals whom they would least like to interact with in a given context. The data derived from a sociometric study can be presented in a *sociogram,* which depicts the patterns of choice existing among members of a group at a given time (see Figure 12.2).

Physical Attractiveness and Body Build. Researchers have found a good many qualities that

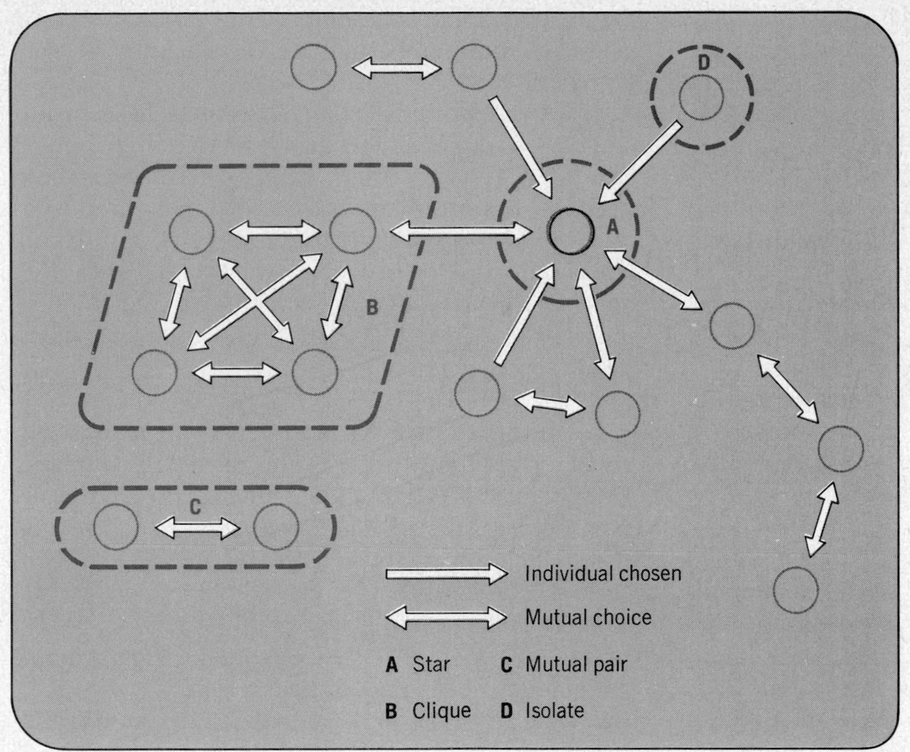

Figure 12.2 A Sociogram

Sociometry is a technique used for identifying the social relations in a group. Each individual is asked to name three (or sometimes five) group members with whom he or she would like to participate in a particular activity. It is a simple method, inexpensive and easy to administer. The data gathered can be graphically depicted in a sociogram like this one, which portrays the network of relationships and identifies popular individuals (stars), cliques, friendship pairs, and social isolates.

make children appealing or unappealing in the eyes of their peers. Among the most important are physical attractiveness and body build. Studies using many different methods have reported a significant relationship between physical attractiveness and popularity (Byrne, Ervin, and Lamberth, 1970; Lerner and Lerner, 1977; Langlois and Stephan, 1977). Furthermore, attractive strangers are typically rated as more socially desirable than are unattractive strangers (Adams and Crane, 1980). The marked agreement that

Standards of Excellence: Physical Attractiveness

Among the most important traits influencing peer relationships and popularity are those associated with physical attractiveness and body build. Children who meet their culture's standards enjoy a decided advantage over youngsters who do not.

Donald Dietz/Stock, Boston

is found among the members of a society on what constitutes "good-looking" suggests that beauty is not in the eye of the beholder. Rather, physical attractiveness is culturally defined and is differently defined by different cultures (Cavior and Dokecki, 1973; Langlois and Downs, 1979).

Children begin to acquire these cultural definitions at about six years of age; by the age of eight, their criteria are the same as older people's. Before age six, children's conceptions of physical attractiveness tend to be highly individualistic (Cavior and Lombardi, 1973). Then as children shift from the thought processes characteristic of the preoperational period to those of the period of concrete operations, they come to judge physical attractiveness in much the same manner as adults.

Stereotypes and appraisals of body configurations are also learned relatively early in life (Staffieri, 1967; Kirkpatrick and Sanders, 1978). "Lean and muscular," "tall and skinny," and "short and fat" are all bodily evaluations that influence the impressions people form of one another. Evidence suggests that negative attitudes toward fatness are already well developed among kindergarten children (Staffieri, 1967). Among boys, a favorable stereotype of the *mesomorph* (the person with an athletic, muscular, and broad-shouldered build) is evident at age six. However, their desire to look like a mesomorph does not appear until age seven and is not clearly established until age eight (Staffieri, 1967).

Children tend to stereotype mesomorphs as strong, popular, happy, helpful, healthy, honest, brave, and smart. In contrast, their stereotypes of *endomorphs* (people with rotund and soft body builds) tend to be unfavorable: dishonest, lazy, lying, sloppy, mean, ugly, and stupid. *Ectomorphs* (thin people with poor muscular development) tend to be viewed as quiet, worrisome, sneaky, anxious, and weak (Staffieri, 1967, 1972).

Desirability of First Name. The social desirability of a child's first name is also related to popularity (McDavid and Harari, 1966). Americans tend to view men named Michael and James as liked, active, and masculine individuals, and women named Wendy as feminine. In contrast, the masculinity of Percival and Horace, and the femininity of Alfreda, are regarded as dubious (Marcus, 1976). Favorable or unfavorable connotations become attached to personal names, so that children who have unpopular or unattractive names are often handicapped in their social interactions with peers.

We should not assume, however, that unusual first names necessarily have a negative impact on their

Desirability of First Name

Names like "Lisa" have favorable connotations and play a part in defining the acceptability of a person.

Joel Gordon

possessors. Among the upper classes, having an unusual first name does not seem to be a barrier to success; in fact, it may even help (Garwood, 1976).

Children also often assign one another nicknames—"Dumbo," "Einstein," "Bear," "Big Foot," and so on. Nicknaming is a powerful tool for advertising the norms of acceptable behavior while publicizing the norms of improper and disagreeable behavior. By limiting the privilege of using the most intimate names to a small, select group, members of the inner circle can effect social solidarity and separateness (Harré, 1980).

Behavioral Characteristics. A variety of behavioral characteristics appear related to children's acceptance by their peers. Popular children tend to be described by their associates as active, outgoing, alert, self-assured, helpful, good-natured, peppy, cheerful, and friendly. They are children who, while interested in others, do not too obviously or aggressively seek attention; they are active but not hyperactive; and they are confident but not boastful (Hartup, 1970; Dodge, 1983). Children who successfully gain entry into ongoing interaction apparently possess the ability to read the social situation and adapt their behavior to it on an ongoing basis (Putallaz, 1983). They take "a process view" in which they recognize that relationships take time and that they may have to work themselves into a group slowly (Asher, 1983).

Several clusters of traits likewise tend to characterize children who are unpopular with their peers (Ausubel and Sullivan, 1970; Dodge, 1983). First, there are those who are social isolates because they are physically listless, lethargic, and apathetic. Second, there are the children who are so psychologically introverted—timid, overdependent on adults, and withdrawn—that they do not have much contact with their peers. And third, there are the children who are overbearing, aggressive, and egocentric—those who are described by their peers and teachers as noisy, attention-seeking, demanding, rebellious, and arrogant. Such children have often been labeled "hyperactive" and placed on amphetamines in order to "control" their behavior (see the boxed insert on page 330). Unpopular children require help by parents and teachers—at times by professionals—because evidence suggests that they continue to have the same problems even when placed in totally new situations with unfamiliar peers (Coie and Kupersmidt, 1983). Through interventions, it is hoped that they can acquire more effective social skills (Asher, 1983).

Social Maturity. Children's social maturity increases rapidly during the early school years. A. Jackson Stenner and William G. Katzenmeyer (1976) found that in one school system 50 percent of the first-graders said they would rather play with younger children. This figure dropped to one-third among third-graders. Moreover, whereas one out of three first-graders said they would rather play alone, less than one in five third-graders expressed this preference. And while being with other children bothered one out of three first-graders, only one out of five third-graders reported this difficulty. In fact, some children go through school with few or no friends. For example, Norman E. Gronlund (1959) found that about 6 percent of third- through sixth-grade children in one school system were not selected by any classmate on a sociometric questionnaire.

Self-Esteem

A man cannot be comfortable without his own approval.

—MARK TWAIN
What Is a Man? 1906

In interacting with peers and adults, the child is provided with clues to their appraisals of his or her desirability, worth, and status. Through the accepting and rejecting behaviors of others, children continually receive answers to the questions, "Who am I?" "What kind of person am I?" and "How valued am I?" Central to much theory and research in social psychology is the notion that people discover themselves in the behavior of others toward them (Vander Zanden, 1984). The writings of social psychologists like Charles Horton Cooley (1902, 1909) and George Herbert Mead (1934), and of neo-Freudian psychiatrists like Harry Stack Sullivan (1947, 1953), are based on the view that our self-conceptions emerge from social interaction with others and that our self-conceptions in turn influence and guide our behavior.

According to this social psychological tradition, individuals' self-appraisals tend to be "reflected appraisals." If children are accepted, approved, and respected for what they are, they will most likely acquire attitudes of self-esteem and self-acceptance. But if the significant people in their lives belittle, blame, and

AMPHETAMINE TREATMENT OF HYPERACTIVE CHILDREN

The average child is an almost nonexistent myth. To be normal one must be peculiar in some way or other.

—HEYWOOD BROUN
Sitting in the World

The incidence and treatment of "hyperactivity" in children has become a matter of concern and controversy among parents, educators, social scientists, and physicians. The use of drugs, primarily amphetamines, in the management of "problem" children is on the increase. Current estimates place the number of American school children who are receiving amphetamines for the control of "attention deficit disorder" or "ADD" (the designation employed by the American Psychiatric Association) at between 500,000 and 1.5 million.

Hyperactivity is a descriptive term that entails a judgment about a child's behavior. Since it involves a collection of vague and global symptoms, medical experts tend to disagree on its nature and the means for diagnosing it. Children who tend to be labeled as having attention deficit disorder are those who have short attention spans, exhibit sleep problems, throw temper tantrums, and have difficulty learning, sitting still, or responding to discipline.

Experts have advanced a variety of theories to explain the source of attention deficit disorder, including genetic defects, poor parenting, food additives, allergies, lead poisoning, fluorescent lights, insufficient oxygenation, and too much television. Experts also disagree on the precise mechanisms by which amphetamines produce their calming effect on hyperactive children, since they have an opposite, stimulating effect on adults.

In many cases parents and teachers report a significant improvement in symptoms, classroom behavior, and academic performance as a result of administering amphetamines (commonly Ritalin) to hyperactive children (Whalen et al., 1981). Some researchers believe that the medication somehow allows the hyperactive child to attend to critical aspects of the learning situation and to filter out distractions (Ellis et al., 1974; Swanson and Kinsbourne, 1976). However, not all children respond to drug therapy. Moreover, as with any medication, adverse side effects occasionally occur—insomnia, gastrointestinal distress, dizziness, weight loss, and retardation of growth.

Many professionals and members of the public fear that the widespread enthusiasm for administering amphetamines to "hyperactive" children has led to abuses and to the acceptance of drug therapy for children who may not benefit from it. It becomes frighteningly easy for parents and teachers to control behavioral "problems" and "difficulties" under the guise of giving children "medicine." The drugs then become "conformity pills" for rebellious youngsters. Some physicians have prescribed medication on the basis of teachers' and parents' reports that a child is doing poorly in school, without giving the child a thorough medical evaluation. While some children benefit from amphetamine treatment, the trend toward its indiscriminate use is cause for concern.

reject them, they are likely to evolve unfavorable self-attitudes. On the whole, social psychological research has supported the overall postulate that we hold the keys to one another's self-conceptions and identities (Vander Zanden, 1984).

But the fact is not simply that children can *discover* themselves only in the actions of others toward them. The sociologist J. Milton Yinger (1965: 149) observes:

> More than that, the self is *formed* out of the actions of others, which become part of the individual as a result of his having identified with these others and responded to himself in their terms. Retrospectively, one can ask "Who am I?" *But in practice, the answer has come before the question.* The answer has come from all the definitions of one's roles, values, and goals that others begin to furnish at the moment of birth. "You are a boy; you are my son; you are French"; "You are a good boy and fully part of this group" (with rewards confirming the words); or "You are a bad boy" (with significant others driving the point home by the sanctions they administer).

It should be stressed that children are not simply passive beings who mirror other people's attitudes

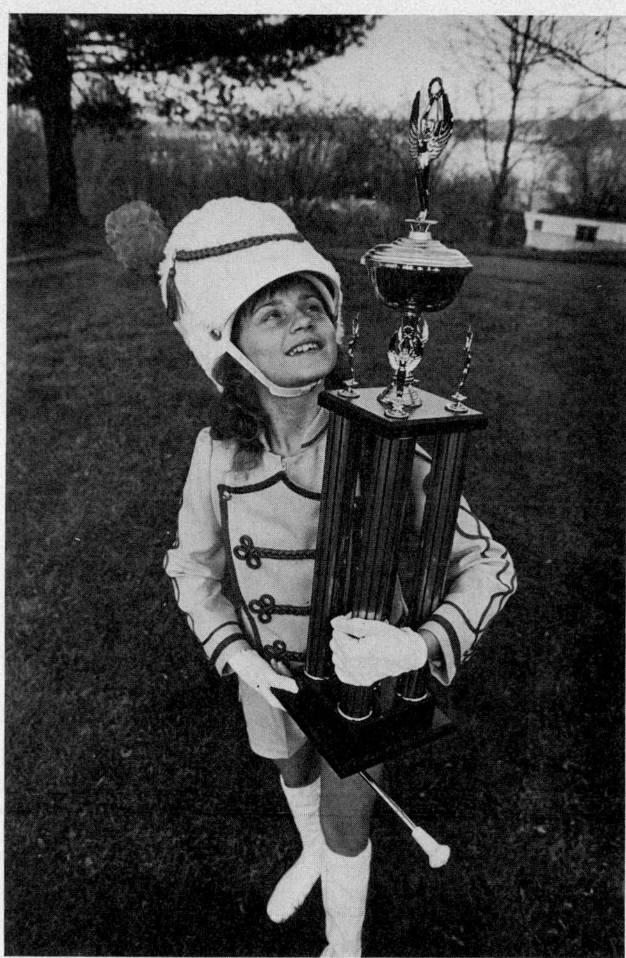

Self-Appraisals as Reflected Appraisals

How we come to perceive ourselves is powerfully influenced by other people's definitions of us. And how they respond to us plays a part in how we respond to ourselves. If children are respected and approved for what they are, their self-esteem and self-acceptance will most likely be greater.

Alan Carey/The Image Works

toward them. They *actively* shape their self-conceptions as they go about their daily activities and test their power and competence in a great many situations. Through their interactions with others and through the effects they produce on their material environment, they derive a sense of their energy, skill, and industry (Franks and Marolla, 1976).

Stanley Coopersmith (1967) has studied the kinds of parental attitudes and practices that are associated with the development of high levels of self-esteem in a sample consisting of eighty-five preadolescent boys. He found that three conditions were correlated with high self-esteem in children. First, the parents themselves had high levels of self-esteem and were very accepting toward their children (1967: 178–179):

> The mothers of children with high self-esteem are more loving and have closer relationships with their children than do mothers of children with less self-esteem. . . . The child apparently perceives and appreciates the attention and approval expressed by his mother and tends to view her as favoring and supportive. He also appears to interpret her interest and concern as an indication of his significance; basking in these signs of his personal importance, he comes to regard himself favorably. This is success in its most personal expression—the concern, attention, and time of significant others.

Second, Coopersmith (1967: 238) found that children with high self-esteem tended to have parents who enforced clearly defined *limits:*

> Imposition of limits serves to define . . . the point at which deviation from . . . [group norms] is likely to evoke positive action; enforcement of limits gives the child a sense that norms are real and significant, contributes to self-definition, and increases the likelihood that the child will believe that a sense of reality is attainable.

Consequently, such children are more likely to be independent and creative than those reared under open and permissive conditions.

Third, although parents of children with high self-esteem did set and enforce limits for their children's behavior, they showed *respect* for the children's rights and opinions. Thus, within "benign limits," the children were given considerable latitude. The parents supported their children's right to have their own points of view and to participate in family decision making.

These findings from the Coopersmith study suggest that competent, firm, accepting, and warm parenting tends to be associated with the development of high self-esteem. By providing well-defined limits, the parents structure their children's world so that the children have effective standards by which to gauge the appropriateness of their behavior. And by accepting their children, the parents convey a warm, approving reflection that allows the children to fashion positive self-conceptions. On the whole, other researchers have confirmed Coopersmith's finding that warm and accepting parenting tends to be associated with children who have high self-esteem (Sears, 1970; Loeb, Horst, and Horton, 1980).

Conformity to the Peer Group

Trumpet in a herd of elephants; crow in the company of cocks; bleat in a flock of goats.

—*Malay Proverb*

Peer influences operate in many ways. One of the most important is through the pressure that peer groups put on their members to conform to various standards of conduct. Although peer groups constrain the behavior of their members, they also facilitate interaction. They define shared goals and clarify acceptable means for pursuing these goals. Social and behavioral scientists have employed two primary procedures in the laboratory for investigating social conformity.

The first procedure, developed by the social psychologist Muzafer Sherif (1936), involves the use of an optical illusion: the so-called *autokinetic effect*. If a small, fixed spot of light is briefly exposed in a darkened room, it appears to move in an erratic manner. Individuals—both children and adults—differ in their estimates of how far the spot "moves." Sherif found that when tested alone, each individual evolves a standard or norm by which he or she gauges the light's "movement."

Sherif brought together in peer groups individuals who had developed standards very *different* from one another in their solitary sessions. He exposed them collectively to the light and asked them to report aloud on their appraisal of its movement. Under these experimental conditions, the group members quickly converged toward a common estimate of the light's movement. Moreover, when they were later brought back again for individual sessions, the group-evolved norms persisted. And the majority of subjects reported not only that their judgments were made before the others spoke, but also that they were *not* influenced by the others.

A second procedure for studying group factors in conformity was developed by the social psychologist Solomon E. Asch (1952). In this research design, seven to nine people are seated side by side. Unlike the Sherif procedure, in which a vague, *ambiguous* stimulus is employed, individuals in the Asch type of experiment are presented with an *unambiguous* situation. Two sets of cards with lines drawn on them are placed in the front of the room, and subjects are asked to match the lines in length (see Figure 12.3). Each subject gives his or her response aloud.

The catch is that except for one person, the so-called "critical" subject, all the members of the peer group are confederates of the experimenter. They have previously been briefed to provide unanimous incorrect answers on certain trials. Asch has found that although the correct answer is obvious, nearly one-third of all judgments by adult "critical" subjects contain errors identical with or in the direction of the rigged errors of the majority. Moreover, 74 percent of the adult subjects conform on at least one of the trials.

Studies reveal that children display different conformity responses to the two types of experiments. Where the highly *ambiguous* autokinetic effect is employed, conformity tends to *increase* with age over the elementary-school years (Hamm and Hoving, 1969). But where the task is *unambiguous*, as in the Asch type of experiment, conformity *declines* with age (Berenda, 1950; Hoving, Hamm, and Galvin, 1969; Allen and Newtson, 1972; Cohen, Bornstein, and Sherman, 1973). For example, in her classic Asch-type experiments conducted over three decades ago, Ruth W. Berenda (1950) found that although 93 percent of younger children (aged seven to ten) can provide correct responses when alone under anonymous conditions, only 43 percent actually do so under the pressure of the peer group. On the other hand, while 94 percent of older children (aged ten to thirteen) can provide the correct responses when alone under anonymous conditions, a higher proportion—54 percent—actually does so in the group setting.

Berenda also varied the Asch type of experiment by employing a two-person situation—a child and the child's teacher. When the teacher, functioning as Berenda's confederate, gave incorrect answers, only 14 percent of the younger children yielded to her influence. Even fewer of the older children—5 percent—gave the teacher's incorrect answers. This suggests that the influence of the teacher was significantly weaker than the influence of the children's peers.

The research of Berenda points to the conclusion that no simple statement concerning peer conformity is valid. Much depends upon the age of the children, the kind of peers they are with, the nature and clarity of the task, and the structure of the social situation.

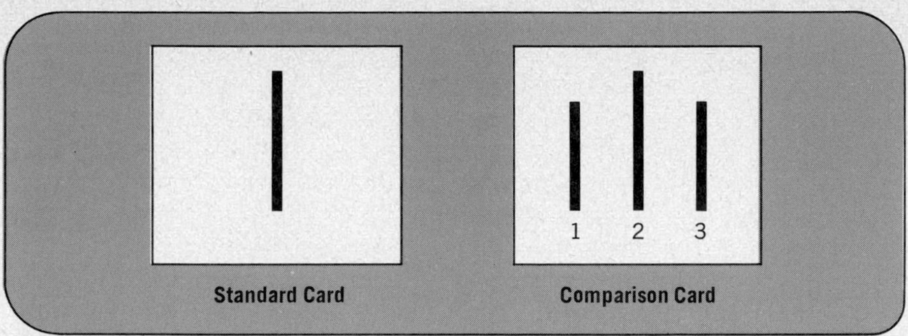

Figure 12.3 Cards in Asch-type Conformity Experiments

Two sets of cards like these are placed at the front of the room, and subjects are asked to match the lines in length. One card has a single black line (the standard). The other card has three lines, one of which is the same length as the standard while the other two are obviously either longer or shorter. When answers are written anonymously, control subjects match the lines with almost complete accuracy. But under experimental conditions where there is pressure toward group conformity, many "naïve" subjects, who are asked to match the lines publicly after confederates of the experimenter intentionally give incorrect answers, also give the incorrect answers.

Racial Awareness and Prejudice

I have a dream that my four little children will one day live in a nation where they will not be judged by the color of their skin but by the content of their character.

—MARTIN LUTHER KING, JR.
Speech, June 15, 1963

A key aspect of children's peer experiences involves relations with members of different racial and ethnic groups. A considerable body of research indicates that children as young as three can correctly identify racial differences between blacks and whites. By the age of five, the vast majority of children can make such identifications accurately (Goodman, 1952; Porter, 1971; Williams and Morland, 1976; Katz, 1976). Children's perceptions and concepts about racial differences follow a developmental sequence similar to that of their perceptions and concepts about other stimuli (Clark et al., 1980).

Phyllis A. Katz and her associates (1975) find that during the preschool period, white children attend less to differences among blacks than they do among whites. For instance, the presence of eyeglasses or a smile on black faces is a less important distinguishing feature than the same cue is for white faces. During middle childhood, white children explore racial cues more and attend more closely to the vast individual differences that are to be found among both black and white people. However, as the children enter adolescence, they once more pay less attention to individual differences among blacks, suggesting that they have come to perceive and think about blacks in more stereotyped terms.

John E. Williams and his associates have also investigated racial awareness and attitudes in children (Williams and Stabler, 1973; Williams, Best, and Boswell, 1975; Williams, Boswell, and Best, 1975; Williams and Morland, 1976). Their research points to the tendency of many preschool children to view the color white, perceived in a *nonracial* context, more positively than the color black. In one experiment, preschoolers were shown items such as a rubber snake, a coin, plastic vomit, a lollipop, a spider, a dirty Kleenex tissue, a cigarette butt, and bubble gum. Each child was asked to evaluate each object positively or negatively by pointing to a painted smiling face or a frowning face.

The children were then shown two boxes that had been nailed shut. One box was white and the other was black, but both contained identical objects. The experimenter asked each child which box held an object "just like" the plastic vomit, "just like" the

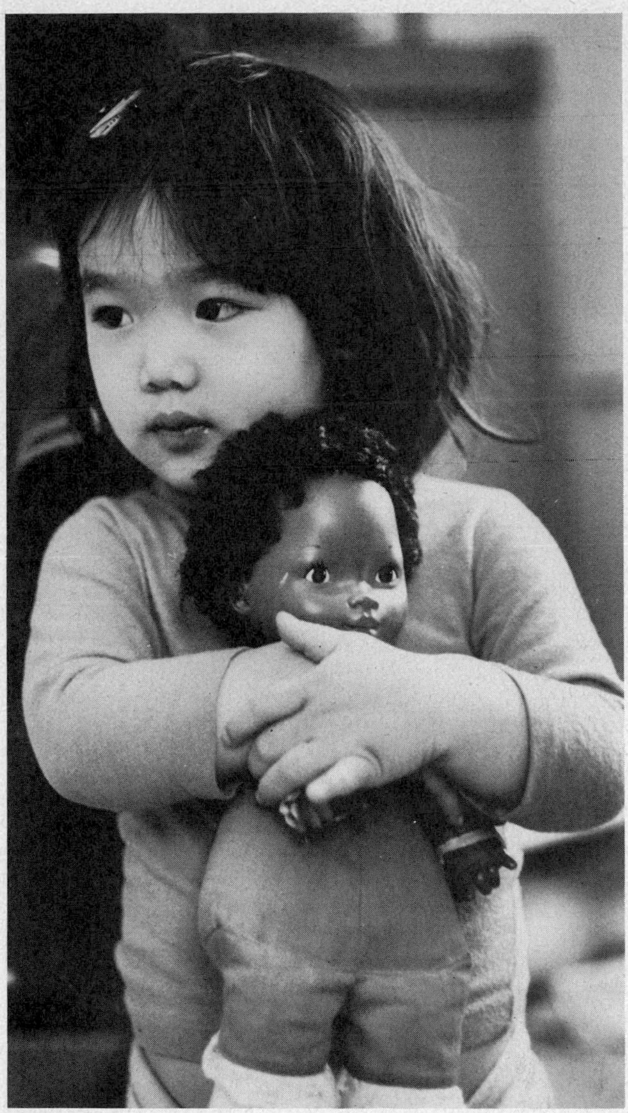

Racial Awareness

The vast majority of children in our society can accurately identify a person's racial membership by the time they reach five years of age.

Patrick Reddy

coin, and so on. The children were encouraged to shake the boxes to help them guess which one contained duplicates of the objects they had previously observed. When the children were asked to choose, they usually guessed that the good objects were in the white box and the bad objects in the black box. Black and white children responded similarly, although the blacks were less consistent in associating white with good and black with bad.

Williams speculates that these preferences reflect children's early experiences with light and darkness. Human beings, he argues, require reasonably high levels of illumination to interact effectively with their environment. Hence they find the disorientation associated with darkness to be intrinsically aversive. This preference for light over darkness may then generalize to the colors white and black. In turn, the preference may be reinforced by various cultural and linguistic connotations associated with the words "white" (purity, virginity, virtue, beneficence, and God) and "black" (filthiness, sin, baseness, evil, and the devil).

Williams argues that the tradition of calling racial groups "white" and "black" serves to link the goodness and badness of the color names to the respective racial groups. Hence, once developed, the color bias provides the foundation for racial preference. It should be stressed, however, that Williams finds that a white preference among blacks is "not a particularly powerful phenomenon" (Williams and Morland, 1979: 31). And some psychologists question whether it exists at all (Banks, McQuater, and Ross, 1979). Further, much of the research by Williams and his associates was undertaken before the full impact of the Black Power movement (with its strong emphasis on black standards of beauty and black cultural heritage) was felt in black communities. Indeed, some evidence suggests that the generalization takes place in the opposite direction, from racial bias to color bias rather than the reverse (Lessing, 1977). Finally, some question exists as to whether skin color is the principal determinant of racial prejudice (Dent, 1978; Sorce, 1979). Hair and eye characteristics may play an equal or even more important role.

Prejudice studies give us little information about the specific interracial behavior that children should exhibit. Indeed, it is doubtful that children, especially younger grade-school children, show coherent, consistent **prejudice**—a system of negative conceptions, feelings, and action orientations regarding the members of a particular religious, racial, or nationality group. It is one thing to demonstrate that prejudice *can* develop in young children; it is quite another to say that prejudice is *characteristic* of young children (Westie, 1964; Katz, Sohn, and Zalk, 1975). At times what adults perceive to be prejudice in children is instead a preference for other children who share similar subcultural practices and values and hence who provide a more comfortable "relational fit" (Steinberg and Hall, 1981).

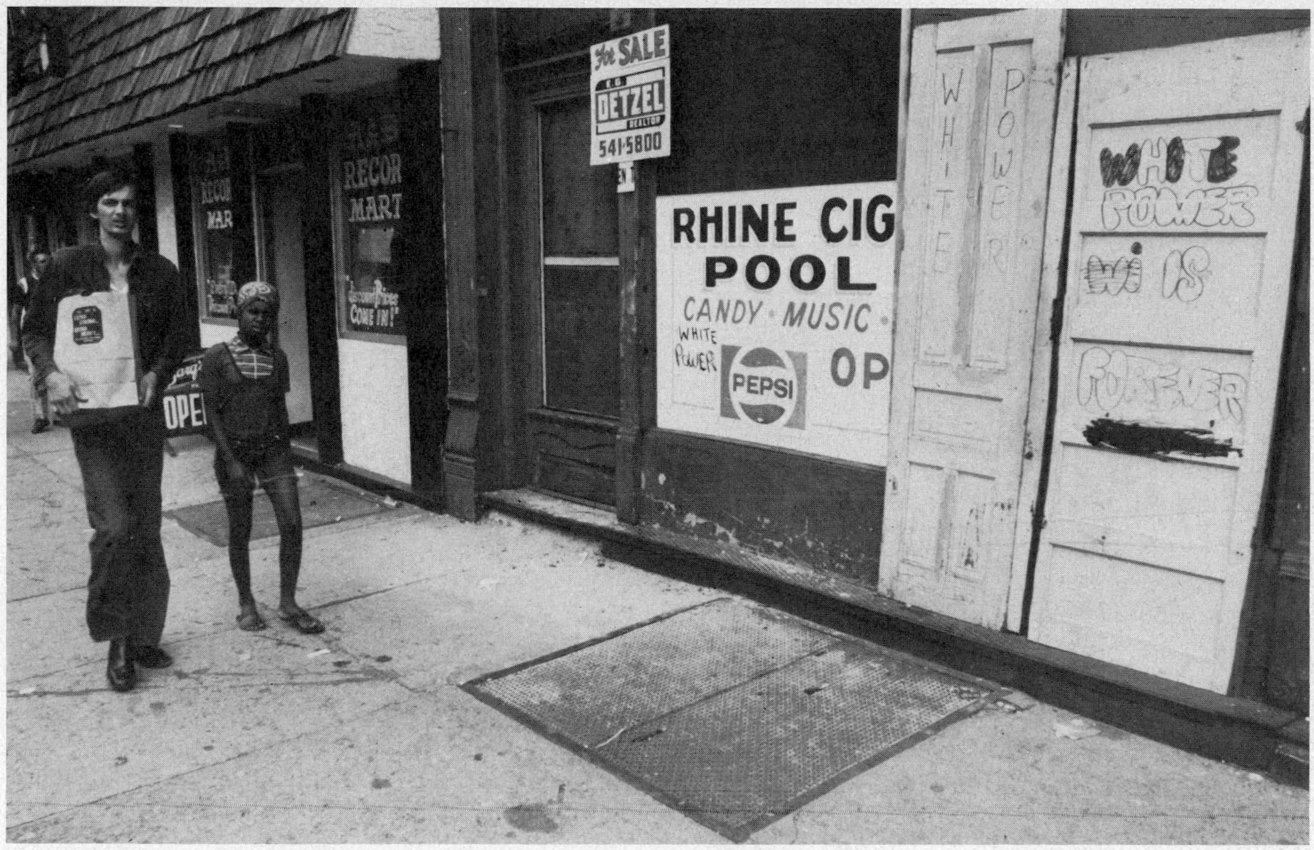

Racism in the Larger Society
Children are immersed in a social world that conveys racist communications on many different levels. Notice the racist graffiti on the wall at right.
Patrick Reddy

Much research shows that how people act in an interracial group situation bears little or no relation to how they feel or what they think (Wicker, 1969; Vander Zanden, 1983, 1984). The *social setting* in which individuals find themselves does much to determine their specific responses. Thus in the United States today, a public show of blatantly racist and discriminatory behavior is commonly defined as counter to the nation's democratic ideals and as being "in poor taste." Yet simultaneously, many whites define an interracial neighborhood as unacceptable and "flee" from it to a virtually all-white suburb. Gordon W. Allport (1962: 121) a distinguished social psychologist, pointed out twenty years ago what research has since consistently confirmed: "Segregationists act like integrationists where social prescription requires; integrationists behave like segregationists when it is socially appropriate to do so."

THE WORLD OF SCHOOL

I tell you we don't educate our children in school; we stultify them and then send them out into the world half-baked. And why? Because we keep them utterly ignorant of real life. The common experience is something they never see or hear. All they know is pirates trooping up the beaches in chains, tyrants scribbling edicts, oracles condemning three virgins to be slaughtered to stop some plague. Action or language, it's all the same; great sticky honeyballs of phrases, every sentence looking as though it has been plopped and rolled in poppyseed and sesame.

—GAIUS PETRONIUS
Roman satirist, first century A.D.

The nature and mission of schools have been a source of dispute through the ages. Contemporary Americans are no more in agreement about their schools than the citizens of Rome were 2,000 years ago. Controversy rages—about the content of school curriculums, about teaching approaches (highly structured or informal), about busing to realize better racial mixes, about the amount and sources of school financing, about special programs for exceptional and disadvantaged youngsters, about the applications of academic freedom.

Developmental Functions of Schools

> *What the best and wisest parent wants for his own child, that must the community want for all its children.*
>
> —JOHN DEWEY

We commonly think of **schools** as agencies that provide formal, conscious, and systematic training. It appears that schools came into existence several thousand years ago to prepare a select few to govern the many and to occupy certain professions. Over the past century or so, public schools have become the vehicle by which the entire population has been taught the basic skills of reading, writing, and arithmetic that an industrial-urban society requires.

Elementary schools serve many functions. First, they teach specific cognitive skills, primarily the three Rs. But they also inculcate, as they did in the past, more general skills, such as paying attention, sitting quietly, and participating in classroom activities (Murphy, Murphy, and Newcomb, 1937: 652):

> [Children] are expected to conform to a group pattern imposed by an adult who is in charge of too many children to be constantly aware of each child as an individual. Flash cards are flashed at the group all at once. Stories are told and everybody must listen whether he will or not. Drawing paper and crayons are meted out whether you happen to feel like drawing at that moment or not. One child who found this shift quite beyond endurance remarked after his first day in school, "It's awful; all you do is mind all day long." And another day he added, "It really is awful. All you do is sit and sit and sit."

As political economists Samuel Bowles and Herbert Gintis (1976) point out, the authoritarian structure of the school mirrors the bureaucratic hierarchy of the workplace. Hence schooling functions to prepare students for future work conditions. Even the school grading system of A, B, C, D, and E has its parallel in the system of wage and salary scales as a device for motivating individuals.

Second, schools have come to share with the family the responsibility for transmitting a society's dominant cultural goals and values. The schools perform

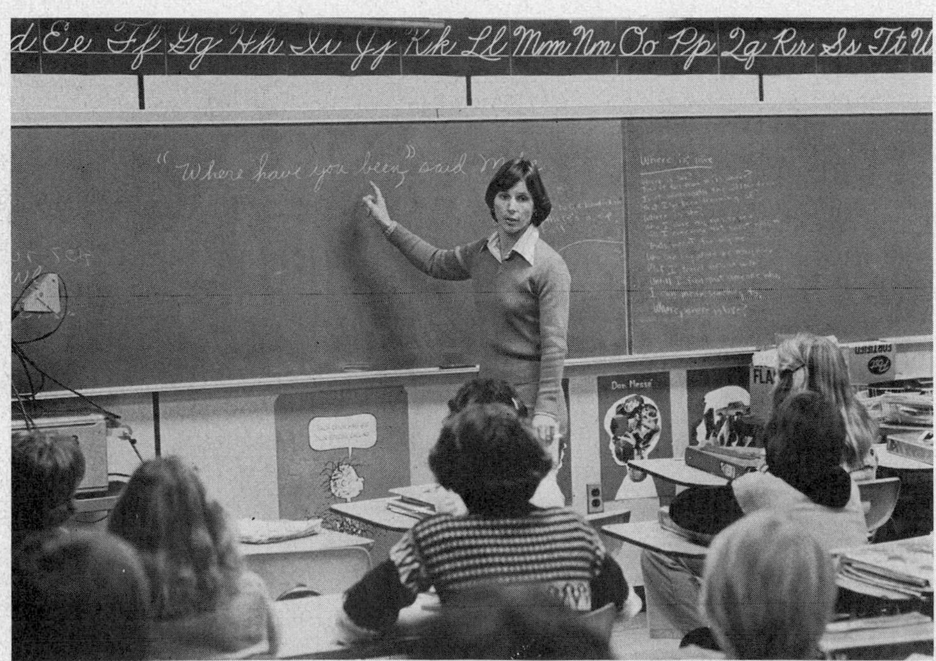

Schools Mirror the Larger Society

The values and social arrangements of the larger society find expression in a nation's schools. Indeed, the schools are designed to transmit the cultural values and goals that characterize the society, such as the correct use of language.

Elizabeth Hamlin/Stock, Boston

a similar function in other societies. Like the United States, China and the Soviet Union stress patriotism, national history, obedience, diligence, personal cleanliness, physical fitness, the correct use of language, and so on in their schools. With respect to basic social norms, values, and beliefs, all education indoctrinates.

Third, to one degree or another schools function as a "sorting and sifting agency" that selects young people for upward social mobility. In the United States, for instance, the continual expansion of technical, managerial, and professional jobs has allowed able and industrious students to ascend the social ladder through careers open to the "talents." Schools, especially colleges and universities, seek to transmit various technical competencies and to encourage the development of leadership and decision-making skills. Hence in many cases, education operates as a critical intervening variable in the transmission of status from one generation to the next. In this sense schools are "mobility escalators" (Blau and Duncan, 1967; Heyns, 1974; Persell, 1977).

Fourth, schools attempt to overcome gross deficits or difficulties in individual children that interfere with their adequate social functioning and participation (see the boxed insert on page 338). Often this is done in consultation with parents as well as with school psychologists and guidance personnel.

In addition, schools meet a variety of needs not directly educational. They serve a custodial function, providing a baby-sitting service that keeps children out from under the feet of adults and from under the wheels of automobiles. They function as a dating and marriage market. And compulsory education, coupled with child labor laws, serves to keep younger children out of the labor market and hence out of competition with adults for jobs in the society.

The Effectiveness of Schools

> *The principal goal of education is to create men [and women] who are capable of doing new things, not simply of repeating what other generations have done—men [and women] who are creative, inventive and discoverers.*
>
> —JEAN PIAGET

On the whole, educators and the general American public alike believe that schools affect their students' intellectual and social development and that "good" schools have a more favorable influence than "poor" schools. Hence the Coleman Report of 1966 startled the nation by its conclusion that schools contribute relatively little to the academic and social development of their pupils. The study—named after its principal author, James S. Coleman, a prominent sociologist—was funded by Congress and involved tests and surveys of 645,000 pupils and 60,000 teachers in 4,000 public schools. The report (1966:325) concluded that:

> . . . schools bring little influence to bear on a child's achievement that is independent of his background and general social context [the family and community from which the child comes]; and that this very lack of an independent effect means that the inequalities imposed on children by their home, neighborhood, and peer environment are carried along to become the inequalities with which they confront adult life at the end of school.

Some teacher characteristics—race, verbal scores, and attitudes toward integration—were related to the achievement of some categories of students (primarily minority-group children). But such characteristics as experience, academic degree, student-teacher ratio, and the availability of counselors were not. And virtually no achievement effect was accounted for by variations in physical facilities, teaching aids, libraries, or science labs. In other words, the children who went to excellent, well-equipped public schools with low teacher-pupil ratios did no better on the intelligence tests than children who went to poor schools with poorly trained teachers, dilapidated buildings, and crowded classrooms, once the researchers had corrected for the initial differences in intelligence and social background of the children attending the two types of schools. The view that the schools are relatively ineffective in influencing cognitive achievement received new support with the publication in 1972 of *Inequality,* a book by sociologist Christopher Jencks and his associates at Harvard's Center for Educational Policy Research.

Needless to say, these conclusions run counter to the disposition of many Americans to believe that the schools routinely *do* have powerful effects on the children attending them. It is difficult for many of us to believe that children who individually have logged 7,000 hours in the classroom by the time they enter junior high school and who collectively have 1,000 interpersonal contacts with their teachers each day (Jackson, 1968) are not somehow affected by these experiences.

LEARNING DISABILITIES

Educators have come to employ the term **learning disabilities** as an umbrella concept to refer to children and adolescents who encounter difficulty with school-related material despite the fact that they appear to have normal intelligence and lack a demonstrable physical, emotional, or social handicap. In practice the notion implies that a discrepancy exists between a student's estimated ability and his or her academic performance. Unlike those diagnosed as mentally retarded, the population of youngsters categorized as learning disabled is relatively unrestricted. In fact, as part of their efforts to secure adequate funding, school officials often reclassify pupils as learning disabled to fit a program that will provide financial assistance.

A variety of youngsters are designated as learning disabled. There are some whose eyes see correctly but whose brains improperly receive or process the informational input. For instance, they may get letters mixed up, reading "saw" for "was" or "dog" for "god." Others have difficulty selecting the specific stimulus that is relevant to the task at hand from among a mass of sensory information. Still others may hear but fail to remember what they have heard by virtue of an auditory-memory problem. For instance, they may turn to the wrong page in the book or attempt the wrong assignment when they rely on oral instructions. However, whatever the source may be, learning disabled youngsters have problems in reading (*dyslexia*), in writing (*dysgraphia*), or in mathematics (*dyscalcula*).

The placement of children in a category like "learning disabled" is a serious matter. It can blight their lives by stigmatizing them, reducing their opportunities, lowering their self-esteem, and alienating them from others. On the other hand, it can open doors to services and experiences that can facilitate learning, a sense of self-worth, and social integration. Hence teachers and the public must be aware of the possible harmful effects of labeling so that the labels are not used for obscure, covert, or hurtful purposes.

Over the past decade or so there has been an appreciable change in the policy and philosophy of educators toward the mildly and moderately handicapped. It has resulted in a shift away from segregated or separate classrooms toward **mainstreaming**—the integration of students with special needs within the regular programs of the school. The movement has received an impetus from federal legislation that has required that handicapped youngsters be educated in the "least restrictive environment" that is possible. While considerable hope has been placed in mainstreaming, educators and psychologists warn that the mere physical presence of children with special needs in regular classrooms does not guarantee academic or social success. It works only where school officials, teachers, parents, and students are committed to making it work through designing, implementing, and supporting appropriate restructuring of the educational enterprise (Madden and Slavin, 1983).

As might be expected, the Coleman and Jencks studies aroused considerable controversy in educational and scientific circles. Critics challenged the representatives of the samples on which the conclusions were based, the reliability of the data, the validity of the measures, the ways the researchers aggregated their data, the choice of statistics, and the ways the investigators interpreted the statistics (Bowles, 1968; Mosteller and Moynihan, 1972; Luecke and McGinn, 1975).

A reanalysis of some of the Coleman data suggests that the racial and social class composition of schools bears an important relationship at least to verbal achievement, especially for black youth (Wilson, 1967). Further, cross-cultural research reveals that school facilities and teacher characteristics have a greater impact on achievement in less industrially developed countries (Heyneman, 1976; Stevenson et al., 1978). And in other Western nations, although the home is more important than the school to a child's overall achievement, school factors do appear to make a substantial difference (Farnen et al., 1974; Harnqvist, 1975).

It should also be stressed that large-scale sociological studies such as those undertaken by Coleman and Jencks provide us with data about the mythical "statistical average" student. But as pointed out in the previous chapter, the process of averaging the pluses, the minuses, and the no changes masks the fact that different school strategies work with some students and not with other students. Moreover, research demonstrates that good teachers do make a difference.

Do Good Schools Make a Difference?

Considerable controversy has raged in academic circles regarding research findings that suggest a school's physical facilities, including libraries and labs, contribute little to the academic achievement of students. According to one view, the schools bring little influence to bear on children's achievement that is independent of their family and community background.

Jean-Claude Lejeune

Using a complicated and innovative methodology, Eigil Pedersen, Thérèse A. Faucher, and William W. Eaton (1978) were able to show a positive relationship between one first-grade teacher and the adult success of children from a disadvantaged urban neighborhood. Two-thirds of "Miss A's" pupils achieved the highest adult status; less than half of the former pupils of other first-grade teachers did. None of her pupils were in the lowest category, although more than a third of other teachers' students were.

"Miss A" enjoyed a reputation as an excellent teacher. She gave extra time to slow learners and invariably stayed after hours to help children. The researchers concluded that "Miss A," by helping to shape the academic self-concept and achievement of a pupil, laid an early foundation that yielded cumulative benefits in later life. Although not all schools may be effective, capable teachers apparently can make a difference.

It is now recognized in educational circles that the Coleman and Jencks studies, by aggregating and averaging their data, also masked differences among schools. Increasingly, researchers are finding that effective schools differ from ineffective ones in important ways (Brookover et al, 1979; Clark, Lotto, and McCarthy, 1980; Rutter, 1983). Perhaps the most important element is the "ethos" or "climate" of the school. Successful schools foster expectations that order will prevail and that learning is a serious matter. Within effective schools, teachers devote considerable care to their lesson plans, spend a high proportion of time on instruction as opposed to classroom management, assign and check homework, encourage their students to use the library, and have high expectations for student achievement. Further, a sense of social order pervades successful schools. Much of the success enjoyed by private and Catholic schools has derived from their ability to provide students with an ordered environment and with strong academic demands (Coleman et al., 1982*a*). Academic achievement is just as high in the public sector when the policies and resulting behavior are like those in the private sector (Coleman et al., 1982*b*).

School Performance and Social Class

We must open the doors of opportunity. But we must also equip our people to walk through those doors.

—LYNDON B. JOHNSON
Address, December 10, 1964

Study after study has shown a close relationship between school performance and socioeconomic status (Boocock, 1972; Matras, 1975). This relationship is evident regardless of the measure employed (occupation of principal breadwinner, family income, or parents' education). Studies have shown that the

"BIG GUY'S SCHOOL"

This is the story of "Big Guy's School." As I noted in the preface, my wife died when our sons were quite young. As the years rolled by, more out of need than premeditation, the boys and I evolved a warm, caring partnership in the management of our household. As each boy gained the ability to do a task for himself, he assumed that task. And we would divide up and share household responsibilities on an ongoing basis, taking up the slack for one another as conditions dictated. Although our governing principles were never made explicit, I believe in hindsight they are captured by the notions "One for all, and all for one" and "From each according to his ability, to each according to his need." Somehow when the name "Daddy" began to seem too "little boyish," I became known as "Big Guy." I think it reflected the nature of our relationship in which I was the older partner and the boys were the younger partners.

"Big Guy's School" came about 1972. Brad was then seven years old and in second grade. Nels was six and in first grade. It was late spring and Nels was unable to read or do simple arithmetic. In a class of twenty-four students, he found himself with two other classmates in the "slow-learner" ("dummy") group. I had become quite concerned. He seemed to be falling farther and farther behind his classmates and his teacher had lost hope for him. I had him "checked out" at Ohio State University, but the "experts" could find nothing "wrong."

I had had a similar problem when I was a youngster. My mother, a former teacher, undertook to provide me with the basics in the evening when I returned home from school. I recall she would place word-cards about the house, with the card "LAMP" taped to a lamp, the card "TABLE" placed on a table, and so on. And she would flash addition, subtraction, multiplication, and division cards for me.

I thought I had better institute a similar program for Nels. I enlisted Brad's help, and we set about teaching Nels his basic skills. Brad was especially helpful. He spent a half hour each evening with Nels, teaching him to read in the same manner that he had been taught to read in first and second grade. We continued the program through the summer. By fall, Nels found himself placed in the "fast-learner" group in second grade.

That same fall I attended a conference with Brad's third-grade teacher. She told me, "We no longer teach children the multiplication tables. If you want Brad to know them, you will have to teach them to him yourself." So I set about teaching Brad and Nels their multiplication tables. By then, however, I had lost confidence in the school system's ability to educate my sons. (Incidentally, we live in an upper–middle-class school district with a "good" reputation.) Although the boys continued to attend the public school, we again set up "Big Guy's School."

For whatever reasons, we had evolved the habit of eating our dinner at 5:00 in the evening. By 5:45 we had eaten and taken care of our kitchen chores. For an hour and a half, until 7:15, the boys would study math or write themes. We had visited local libraries looking for the "right" set of math books. Then I had sent off for the books and the teacher answer manuals. Each boy was on his own. He would study the text, do the problems, and then check his answers with me.

We handled the themes a little differently. The boys would put their themes through at least five drafts. Each boy would go over the other boy's theme, critically appraise it, and make suggestions. Then I would go over the draft and attempt to impart good organization and writing skills. Further, for a half hour before bedtime, each boy would read a library book of his own choosing (as Brad got older, he preferred to read the *New York Times*).

During the summer months, "Big Guy's School" ran from 8:00 to 11:00 A.M., with a twenty-minute "recess." The time schedules worked out well for play time, since on school days most neighborhood children finished dinner about 7:15 P.M. and in summer they did not begin appearing at our door until about 11:00 A.M. (our home and yard functioned as the neighborhood playground).

When Brad entered fourth grade, I introduced him to algebra. By then I was no longer particularly concerned with the boys grasping the three Rs. I saw "Big Guy's School" as a vehicle for dealing with other concerns. Brad seemed to have a low tolerance for frustration and would throw temper tantrums. By giving him algebra, I hoped to help him confront frustration under controlled circumstances and to work out with him techniques for coping with stress. Over the next several years we found that Brad was best served when he could identify for himself when he was building up tension and "nip it in the bud." This consisted of getting

Christmas, 1976
Nels, Brad, and "Big Guy."
Patrick Reddy

away from the situation for a short period of time. Most commonly he would go for a walk or shoot baskets in the backyard. At first we tried talking about the source of his frustration—a ventilating of his feelings. But we found that such discussions only deepened his inner turbulence; he simply would rehearse and recycle his distress. However, if he could shift his cognitions, he found that his internal turmoil dissipated within thirty minutes.

In the course of "Big Guy's School" we focused primarily on problem-solving strategies and attack skills rather than on the particulars of content. In fact, I did very little teaching, since the greater part of the time the boys were involved with their own work. I was handy to offer insights. I periodically called for the termination of "Big Guy's School" but the boys would insist that it be continued. I think it was their desire for mastery and achievement (what Abraham Maslow termed "self-actualization") that made them want to go on with it.

When Brad completed ninth grade, it was clear to us that he was simply "spinning his wheels" and that he should move on to college. On his initiative, he was specially tested and admitted to Ohio State University at age fifteen. He graduated three years later with a perfect 4 grade-point average, majoring in accounting and computer science, and secured a job with one of the Big Eight accounting firms. Later in the year, he improved his situation by taking a computer position with another firm. At age nineteen, he received a National Science Foundation fellowship and began his Ph.D. program in computer science at Cornell.

Nels also entered Ohio State University at age fifteen and will graduate at eighteen, majoring in electrical engineering and computer science. Here is a young man who has maintained a 3.7 grade-point average and who only ten years earlier was the "dummy" of his first-grade class. I am certain that Nels would have become a high-school dropout had I not taken his schooling in hand (as I also would have become had my mother not provided me with the basics). His teacher had given up on him, he was becoming demoralized, and he had lost confidence in his ability to master reading and math. I wonder how many other youngsters like Nels are currently being failed by our educational system.

higher the social class of children's families, (1) the greater will be the number of the formal grades the children will complete, the academic honors and awards they will receive, and the elective offices they will hold; (2) the greater will be their participation in extracurricular activities; (3) the higher will be their scores on various academic achievement tests; and (4) the lower will be their rates of failure, truancy, suspensions, and premature dropping out of school. Among the hypotheses that have been advanced to explain these facts are the middle-class bias of schools, subcultural differences, and educational self-fulfilling prophecies.

Middle-Class Bias. Boyd McCandless (1970: 295) has observed that "schools succeed relatively well with upper- and middle-class youngsters. After all, schools are built for them, staffed by middle-class people, and modeled after middle-class people." Even when teachers are originally from a different social class, they still view their role as one of encouraging the development of a middle-class outlook on such matters as thrift, cleanliness, punctuality, respect for property and established authority, sexual morality, ambition, and neatness.

In some cases, middle-class teachers, without necessarily being aware of their prejudice, find lower-class youngsters unacceptable—indeed, different and depressing. Their students tend to respond by taking the attitude "If you don't like me, I won't cooperate with you." The net result is that the children fail to acquire basic reading, writing, and math skills.

Subcultural Differences. Children of different social classes are thought to bring somewhat different experiences and attitudes into the school situation. Middle-class parents generally make it clear to their children that they are *expected* to apply themselves to school tasks. And their children commonly enter school already exposed to and possessing a variety of skills that lower-class children often lack—for example, conceptions regarding books, crayons, pencils, drawing paper, numerals, and the alphabet. Robert J. Havighurst, a distinguished educator who conducted a survey of Chicago schools, observes:

> These [ghetto] children come to school pitifully unready for the usual school experiences, even at the kindergarten level. Teachers remark that some don't even know their own names and have never held a pencil. Their speech is so different from that of the teachers and the primer that they almost have a new language to learn. They have had little practice in discriminating sounds, colors or shapes, part of the everyday experiences of the middle-class preschool child, whose family supplies educational toys and endless explanations. (Quoted by Star, 1965: 59)

Perhaps even more important, middle-class children are much more likely than lower-class youngsters to possess the conviction that they can affect their environments and their futures (Friend and Neale, 1972; Stephens and Delys, 1973). Finally, as pointed out by Havighurst, minority-group children who speak Spanish or Black English are likely to find themselves handicapped in schools where Standard English is employed (Seitz, 1975; Gay and Tweney, 1975).

Educational Self-Fulfilling Prophecies. Another explanation advanced for social class differences in the performance of school children is that lower-class and minority-group youngsters are the victims of educational self-fulfilling prophecies. Kenneth B. Clark (1965: 131), a renowned black psychologist, charges:

> [Ghetto] children, by and large, do not learn because they are not being taught effectively and they are not being taught because those who are charged with the responsibility of teaching them do not believe that they can learn, do not expect that they can learn, and do not act toward them in ways which help them to learn.

Clark's view that teacher expectations affect teacher behavior in such a way as to shape student performance is one that has been widely accepted among social psychologists. However, the research findings on educational self-fulfilling prophecies have been confusing and contradictory (Rosenthal and Jacobson, 1968; Fleming and Anttonen, 1971; Rosenthal, 1973; Harvey and Slatin, 1975). Nonetheless, there seems to be little doubt that white teachers tend to expect less of black children than they do of white children.

Effects of School Desegregation

> *The problem of the Twentieth Century is the problem of the color-line.*
>
> —W. E. B. DU BOIS
> *The Souls of Black Folk, 1903*

In 1954 the United States Supreme Court ruled in a number of school cases that separate schools for black and white children were inherently unequal and hence that mandatory school segregation was unconstitutional. Three decades later, a fifth of the nation's black students will attend schools that are almost all black in enrollment and more than half still attend schools in which the majority of students are black. The greatest difficulty in achieving desegregation is that black children typically outnumber white children in big cities and that each race is concentrated in different areas of the city. Today blacks, Hispanics, and Asians outnumber whites in thirty-three of the fifty biggest central-city school districts.

At the time of the Supreme Court's ruling, many educators and social scientists believed that a number of positive social gains would flow from school desegregation. First, the Coleman Report (1966) seemed to show that the academic performance of black students improved as the proportion of white students in a school increased. It was assumed that this change resulted from black students' acquiring the achievement-related values held by middle-class whites (Stephan, 1978). Second, it was thought that close and daily association of black and white schoolchildren would in itself lead to greater interracial understanding and harmony. And third, it was expected that equal educational facilities and institutional arrangements would improve black self-esteem.

Nancy St. John (1975), a sociologist, has reviewed the findings of more than 120 studies on the effects of school racial composition on both black and white pupils. In her highly regarded appraisal, St. John concludes that the findings are contradictory and that, taken as a whole, the evidence is inconclusive. Nonetheless, one major finding does stand out. Desegregation has rarely *lowered* academic achievement for either black or white pupils. Many other social scientists agree that academic achievement, as measured by conventional standardized tests, is usually not adversely affected by desegregation (Hawley, 1979; Reinhold, 1979). Overall, the effects of desegregation on black children's achievement are not uniform. This is because other factors, such as socioeconomic status, family background, degree of racial tension in the community, and interracial acceptance in the schools, also play a part.

St. John concludes from studies on racial prejudice that desegregation has at times promoted interracial friendships and reduced prejudice, but at other times it has encouraged conflict, cleavage, and stereotyping. Other research also suggests that the extent of racial clustering in desegregated schools varies markedly, but nonetheless it seems to occur everywhere (Schofield, 1978). Clustering occurs least in majority white classrooms and most in racially balanced classrooms. In majority white classrooms, black students choose a considerable number of white friends. In racially

Racial Clustering in Desegregated Schools

Racial clustering occurs in many desegregated settings. Schools tend to mirror the racial patterns that prevail in the larger community.

Alan Carey/The Image Works

balanced classrooms, however, it appears that there are a sufficient number of students from each racial group to permit the formation of racially segregated cliques (Hallinan, 1982).

On the question of black children's self-esteem, many studies have shown that the levels of self-esteem among black children are higher than among white youngsters or at least that there are no differences between the two racial groups (Vander Zanden, 1983). However, black children in predominantly white schools often have had lower self-esteem than blacks in segregated schools. Rarely has any researcher found that black self-esteem has been increased in desegregated schools (Sage, 1978; Simmons et al., 1978).

In part, the failure to bring about many of the hoped-for benefits of desegregation is not surprising. Schools tend to mirror the racist order of the larger society. Further, it is unreasonable to expect the schools to undo what the larger society continually reestablishes.

There is much more to successful "integration" than merely mixing children from different racial backgrounds. We need to abandon the simplistic question "Does desegregation work?" and study the *conditions* for effective desegregation. We need to find out how students in desegregated situations can be most benefited. The factors that must be considered include the size of the school district, voluntary and mandatory conditions of desegregation, busing, ethnic compositions, varying ratios of white and minority-group students, the social origins and attitudes of teachers, the socioeconomic backgrounds of students, and community traditions. Further, we need to recognize that the effects of the drastic school reorganization brought about by desegregation are realized over many years and with wide variation on a school-by-school basis.

SUMMARY

1. Peer groups provide children with situations in which they are independent of adult controls, give them experience in egalitarian relationships, furnish them with status in a realm where their own interests reign supreme, and transmit informal knowledge.
2. Sex cleavage reaches its peak at about the fifth-grade level. Although same-sex friendships predominate during the elementary-school years, children show a steady and progressive development of cross-sex interests as they advance toward puberty.
3. Elementary-school children arrange themselves in hierarchies with regard to various standards, including physical attractiveness, body build, first names, and behavioral characteristics.
4. Children's self-conceptions tend to emerge from the feedback that others provide regarding their desirability, worth, and status. But children are not simply passive beings who mirror other people's attitudes toward them. Through their interactions with others and through the effects they produce on their material environment, they derive a sense of their energy, skill, and industry.
5. Over the elementary-school years, conformity tends to increase with age in situations in which children are confronted with highly ambiguous tasks. But where the tasks are unambiguous, conformity tends to decline with age.
6. Children develop racial awareness between three and five years of age. However, it is doubtful whether children, especially younger school children, show coherent, consistent prejudice.
7. Schools teach specific cognitive skills (the three Rs), general skills associated with effective participation in classroom settings, and the society's dominant cultural goals and values. They also function as a "mobility escalator" for able students to rise in status, and they attempt to overcome gross deficits in individual children that interfere with the children's effective social participation.
8. Although not all schools are effective, capable teachers can make a difference. Further, effective schools differ from ineffective ones in important ways. Perhaps the most important element is the climate of the school. Successful schools foster expectations that order will prevail and that learning is a serious matter.
9. Overall, the higher the social class of children's families, the higher their academic achieve-

ment is likely to be. A number of hypotheses have been advanced to explain this fact, including the middle-class bias of schools, subcultural differences, as well as educational self-fulfilling prophecies.

10. Desegregation has rarely lowered academic achievement for either black or white pupils. However, it has failed to eliminate the gap that is usually found between the achievement levels of black and white children.

KEY TERMS

group Two or more people who share a feeling of unity and are bound together in relatively stable patterns of social interaction.

learning disability An umbrella concept referring to difficulty with school-related material despite the appearance of normal intelligence and lack of a demonstrable physical, emotional, or social handicap.

mainstreaming The integration of students with special needs within the regular programs of the school.

prejudice A system of negative conceptions, feelings, and action orientations regarding the members of a particular religious, racial, or nationality group.

school An agency that provides formal, conscious, and systematic training.

sex cleavage The tendency for elementary-school boys to associate with boys and elementary-school girls with girls.

sociometry An objective method for assessing patterns of attraction, rejection, or indifference among group members. Individuals are asked to name three (or sometimes five) individuals in the group with whom they would most like (or least like) to interact in a given context.

value A criterion that people use in deciding the relative merit and desirability of things (themselves, other people, objects, events, ideas, acts, and feelings).

Part Six

Adolescence

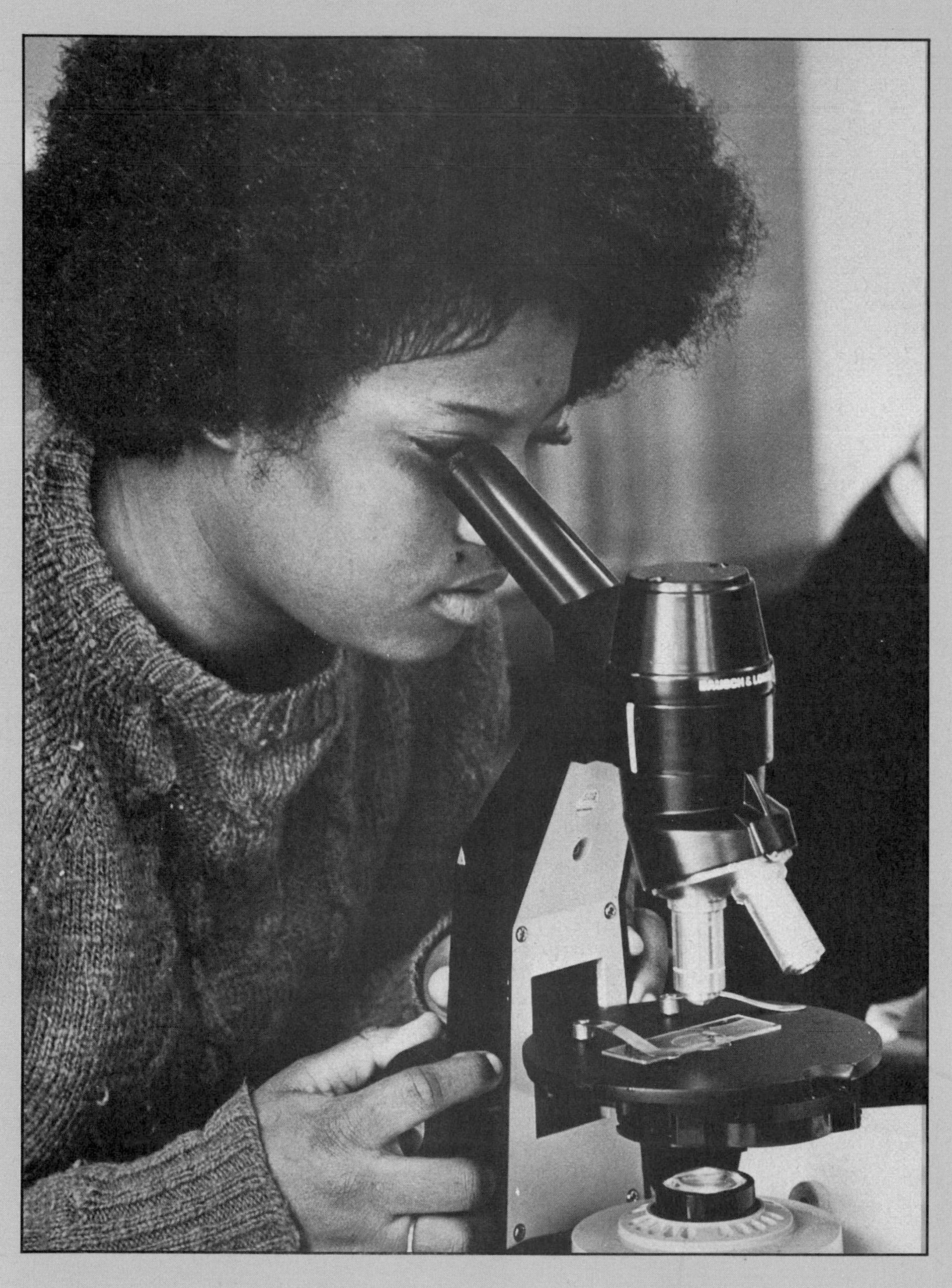

leration

out fourteen or fifteen, it
vas a miserable thing and that
erson around. Hardly any-
f I liked a certain girl it
ks to get up enough nerve to
uld come down with a bad
e supposed to meet. Or if
he liked me, I wouldn't believe
eball team, which cheered me
out a lot, and that was hu-
half the time I didn't do my
ally I felt guilty about that.
t I felt guilty about getting up
staying up late at night, and
l doing a lot of things.

—JAMES LINCOLN COLLIER

urrents within American life glo-
between childhood and adult-
ers have called this "the cult of
is frequently depicted as a care-
attractiveness, vitality, robust fun,
nd activity. However, many ado-
iter James Lincoln Collier, quoted
xtremely difficult period. And although many adult Americans glorify youth, they hold contrasting images of adolescents. Sometimes

they regard young people as "the enemy within," given to juvenile delinquency, political extremism, drug addiction, premarital pregnancies, and "disrespect" for authority. At other times, they stereotype adolescents as being less hypocritical, dishonest, materialistic, and cynical than their elders (Conger, 1977).

It is easy to become so locked into our own cultural perspective that we overlook the considerable diversity that societies throughout the world show in their approach to adolescence. Indeed, in much of the world adolescence is not a socially distinct period in the human life span. Although young people everywhere undergo puberty, children often assume many adult responsibilities by age thirteen and even younger. Consequently adolescence may be largely glossed over.

In the United States, adolescence appears to be an "invention" of the past hundred years (Demos and Demos, 1969; Bakan, 1972; Kett, 1977; Thornburg, 1983). As the nation changed from a rural to an urban society, the role of children shifted. They no longer had a significant economic function in the family once the workplace became separated from the home. In time, mandatory school attendance, child labor laws, and special legal procedures for "juveniles" served to establish adolescence as a well-defined social reality.

PUBERTY

During adolescence, young people undergo changes in growth and development that are truly revolutionary. After a lifetime of inferiority, they suddenly catch up with adults in physical size and strength. And accompanying these changes is the rapid development of the reproductive organs that signals sexual maturity. The term **puberty** is applied to this period of the life cycle when sexual and reproductive maturation becomes evident. Puberty is not a single event, or set of events, but a crucial phase in a long and complex process of maturation that begins prenatally (Petersen and Taylor, 1980). However, unlike infants and young children, older children experience the dramatic changes of puberty through a developed sense of consciousness and self-awareness. Hence they not only respond to the biological changes; their psychological states also have a bearing on those changes. For instance, under conditions of severe stress, the menstrual cycle may be interrupted or even cease (Boxer, Tobin-Richards, and Petersen, 1983).

The dramatic changes that occur in children at puberty are regulated, integrated, and orchestrated by the central nervous system and endocrine glands. The *pituitary gland*, a pea-sized structure located at the base of the brain, plays a particularly important role. It is called the "master gland" because it secretes hormones into the bloodstream that in turn stimulate other glands to produce their particular kind of hormone. At puberty, the pituitary gland steps up the production of the growth hormones and triggers the manufacture of the two gonadotrophic hormones (*gonadotrophins*): the *follicle-stimulating hormone (FSH)* and the *luteinizing hormone* (*LH*). In females, FSH and LH stimulate the ovaries to manufacture and secrete the feminizing hormones, estrogen and progesterone (see Chapter 3). In males, LH is termed the *interstitial-cell-stimulating hormone* (*ICSH*), since it stimulates the interstitial cells of the testes to manufacture and secrete the masculinizing sex hormone, testosterone. Hence puberty is a time when a system that was established prenatally becomes activated. Although puberty has a biological foundation, its social and psychological significance is a major determinant of how it is experienced by adolescents.

The Adolescent Growth Spurt

During the early adolescent years most children experience the **adolescent growth spurt**, a rapid increase in height and weight. Usually this spurt occurs in girls two years earlier than in boys (see Figure 13.1). The average age at which the peak is reached varies somewhat depending on the people being studied. Among British and North American children it comes at about age twelve in girls and age fourteen in boys. For a year or more, the child's rate of growth approximately doubles. Consequently children often grow at a rate they last experienced when they were two years old (Tanner, 1970, 1972, 1973). The spurt usually lasts about two years, and during this time girls gain about 6 to 7 inches and boys about 8 to 9 inches in height. By age seventeen in girls and age eighteen in boys, the majority of young people have reached 98 percent of their final height.

James M. Tanner (1972:5), an authority on adolescent growth, writes that practically all skeletal and muscular dimensions of the body take part in the spurt, although not to an equal degree:

> Most of the spurt in height is due to acceleration of trunk length rather than length of legs. There is a fairly regular

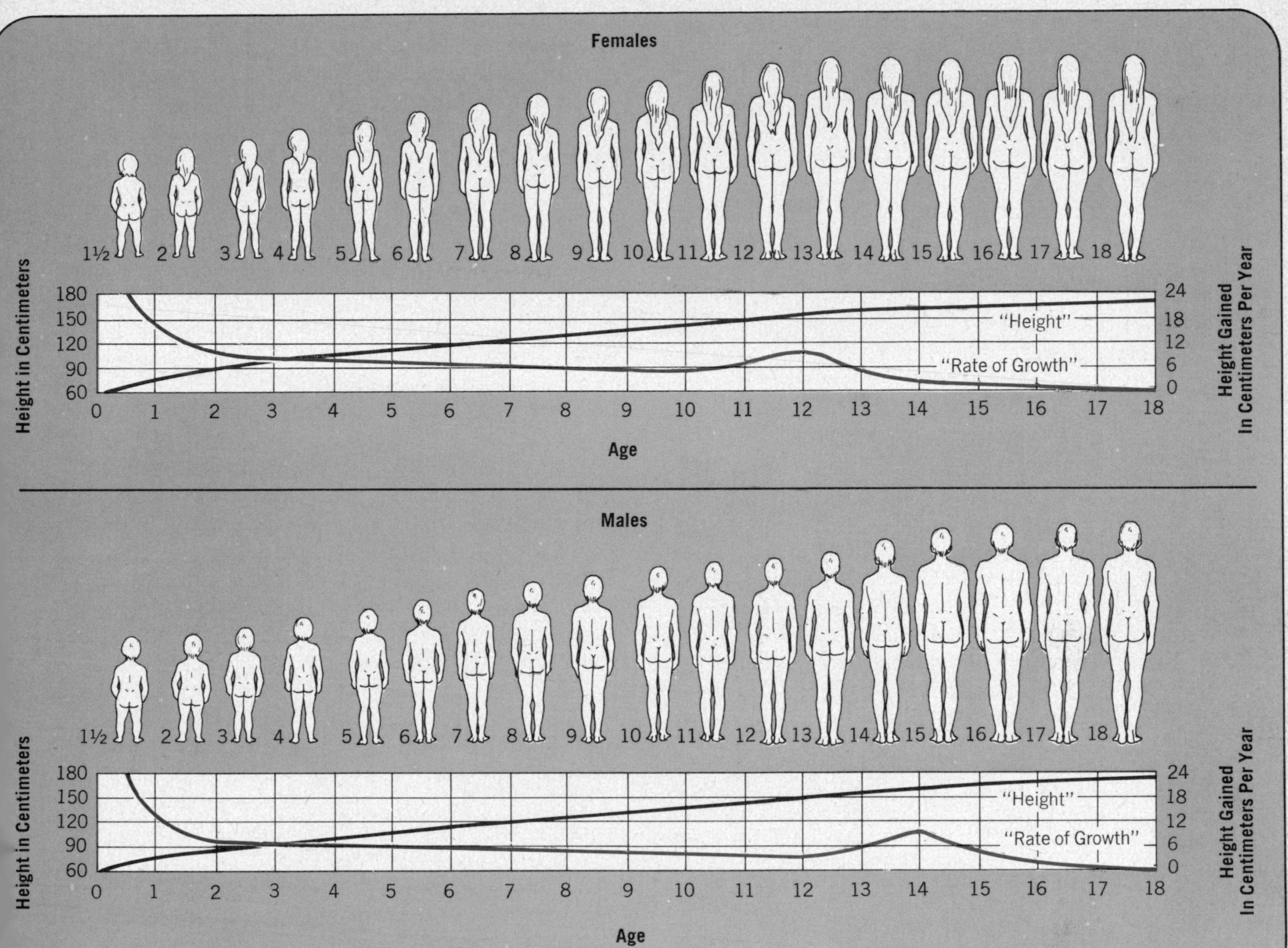

Figure 13.1 Growth from Infancy to Maturity

The figure depicts for each sex the changes in body form and the increases in height that occur between infancy and adulthood. In each case the height curve (black) is an average for children in North America and western Europe. Superimposed on the height curve is the curve for the *rate* of growth (color). This curve shows the increments of height that are gained from one age to the next. Note the sharp peak in the rate of growth that is associated with the adolescent growth spurt. As the graph illustrates, this peak is achieved two years earlier in girls than in boys.

SOURCE: J. M. Tanner, "Growing Up," *Scientific American*, Vol. 229 (September 1973), pp. 36–37.

order in which the dimensions accelerate; leg length as a rule reaches its peak first, followed by the body breadths, with shoulder width last. Thus a boy stops growing out of his trousers (at least in length) a year before he stops growing out of his jackets. The earliest structures to reach their adult status are the head, hands, and feet. At adolescence, children, particularly girls, sometimes complain of having large hands and feet. They can be reassured that by the time they are fully grown their hands and feet will be a little smaller in proportion

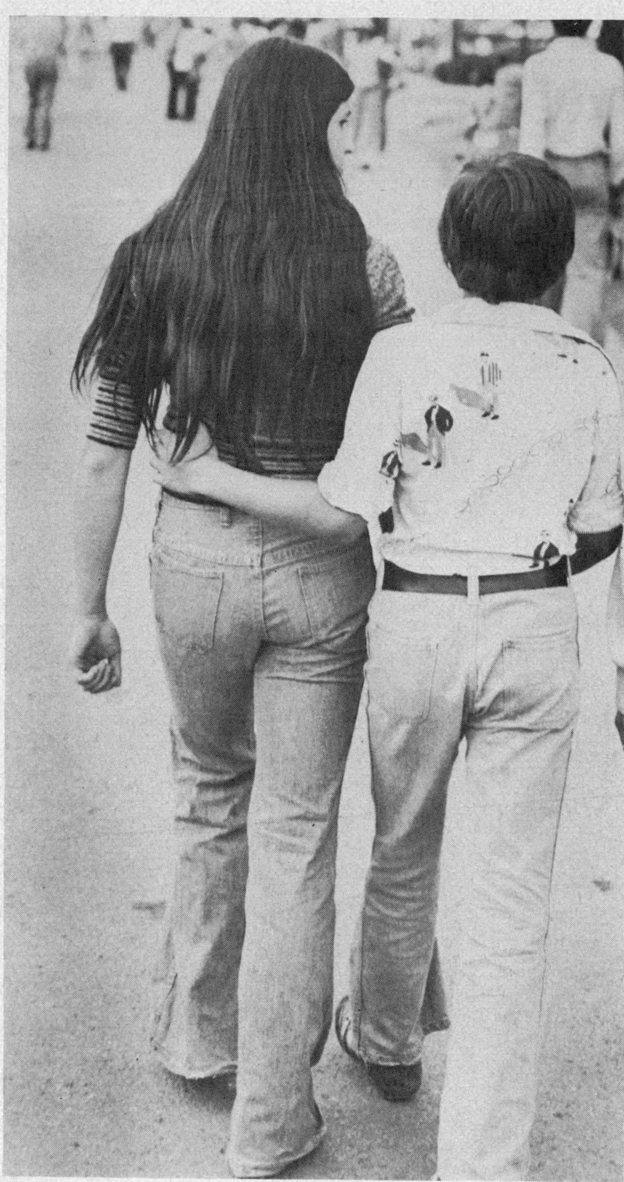

Adolescent Growth Spurt
The rapid increase in height and weight that accompanies early adolescence tends to occur two years earlier in girls than in boys.
Patrick Reddy

to their arms and legs, and considerably smaller in proportion to their trunk.

Asynchrony is a term used to describe this dissimilarity in the growth rates of different parts of the body. As a result of asynchrony, many teenagers have a long-legged or coltish appearance. Asynchrony often results in clumsiness and misjudgments of distance. This may lead to various minor accidents, such as tripping on or knocking over furniture. It can produce an exaggerated sense of self-consciousness and awkwardness in adolescents.

The marked growth of muscle tissue during adolescence contributes to differences between and within the sexes in strength and motor performance (Chumlea, 1982). A muscle's strength—its force when it is contracted—is proportional to its cross-sectional area. Men typically have larger muscles than do women, which accounts for the greater strength of most males. Girls' performance on motor tasks involving speed, agility, and balance peaks at about fourteen years of age. However, the performance of boys on similar tasks improves throughout adolescence.

At puberty, the head shows a small acceleration in growth after remaining almost the same size for six to seven years. The heart grows more rapidly, almost doubling in weight. The abdominal viscera also increase in size. However, the lymphoid tissues (thymus, lymph nodes, and intestinal lymph masses) shrink. Most children steadily put on subcutaneous fat between eight years of age and puberty, but the rate drops off when the adolescent growth spurt begins. Indeed, boys actually tend to lose fat at this time; girls simply experience a slowdown in fat accumulation (Tanner, 1969; Chumlea, 1982).

Maturation Among Girls

In addition to the adolescent growth spurt, puberty is characterized by the development of the reproductive system. The complete transition to reproductive maturity takes place over several years and is accompanied by extensive physical changes (see Figure 13.2). As in the case of the adolescent growth spurt, girls begin their sexual development earlier than boys.

When puberty begins in girls, the breasts increase in size as a result of the proliferation of glandular cells and the formation of fatty and connective tissue. The pigmented area around the nipple (the areola) becomes elevated, and the nipples begin to project forward. This usually starts at about ten years of age and is called the *bud stage* of breast development. (In some girls, perhaps one-half, the appearance of unpigmented pubic down—soft hair in the pubic region—precedes the bud stage.) Also early in puberty, hormonal action begins to produce an increase in fatty and supportive tissue in the buttocks and hip region.

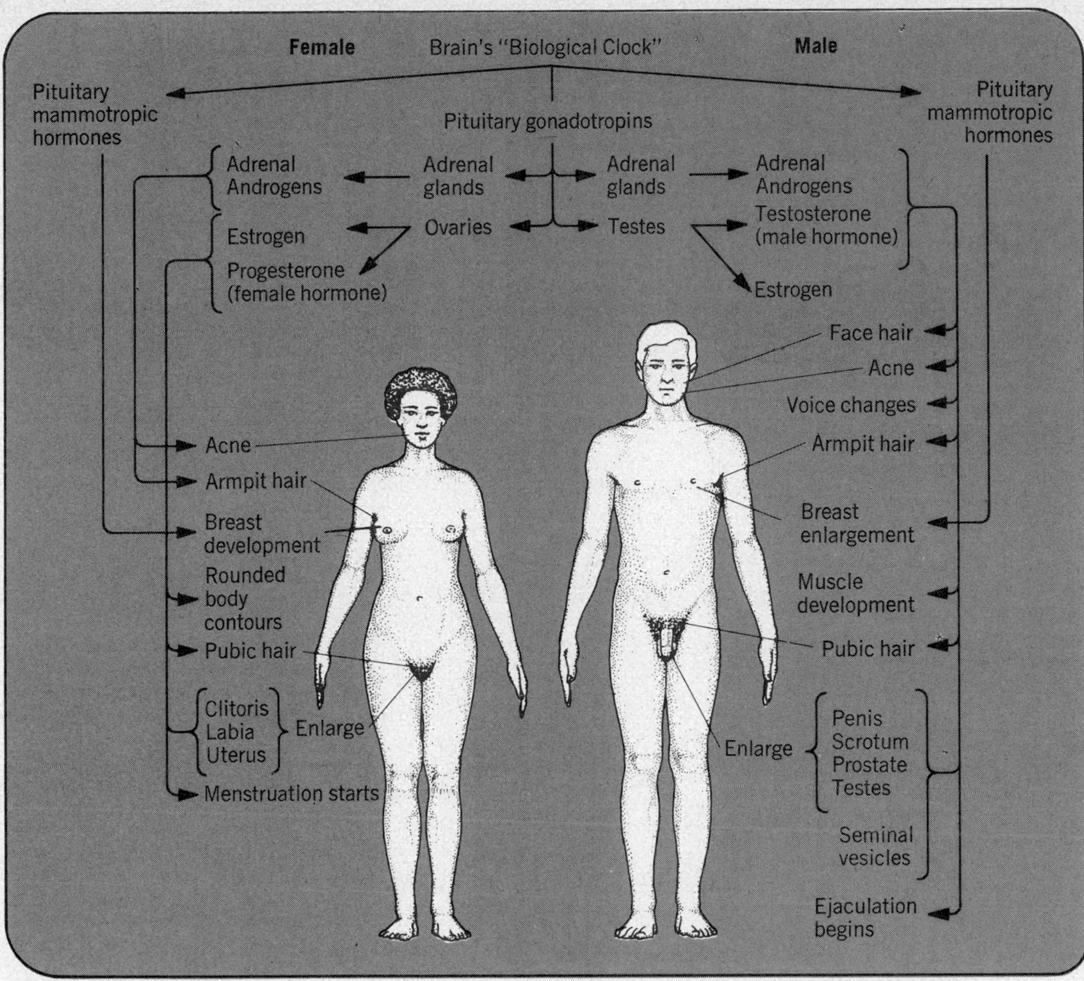

Figure 13.2 Effects of Sex Hormones on Development at Puberty

At puberty the production of the pituitary gonadotrophins (the follicle-stimulating hormone and the luteinizing hormone) stimulates the manufacture and secretion of the sex-hormones. The release of these hormones affects a wide range of body tissues and functions.

SOURCE: From *Human Sexualities* by John H. Gragnon. Copyright © 1977 by Scott, Foresman and Company. Reprinted by permission.

Another visible change in puberty is the growth of axillary (underarm) hair (Chumlea, 1982).

Menarche. The uterus and vagina mature simultaneously with the development of the breasts. However, **menarche**—the first menstrual period—occurs relatively late in puberty, usually following the peak of the growth spurt (Faust, 1977; Tanner, 1973). Early menstrual periods tend to be irregular. Further, *ovulation* (the release of a mature ovum) usually does not take place for twelve to eighteen months after the first menstruation; hence the girl remains sterile during this time (Boxer, Tobin-Richards, and Petersen, 1983).

The Earlier Onset of Menarche. For over one hundred years the average age of menarche in industrialized nations has shown a steady downward trend. This development has paralleled the decade-by-decade increase in the average stature of children in the Western world (see Chapter 6). However, at least half of what has often passed as an increase in children's size is merely the result of their growing up at an earlier age. Hence most of the trend toward greater

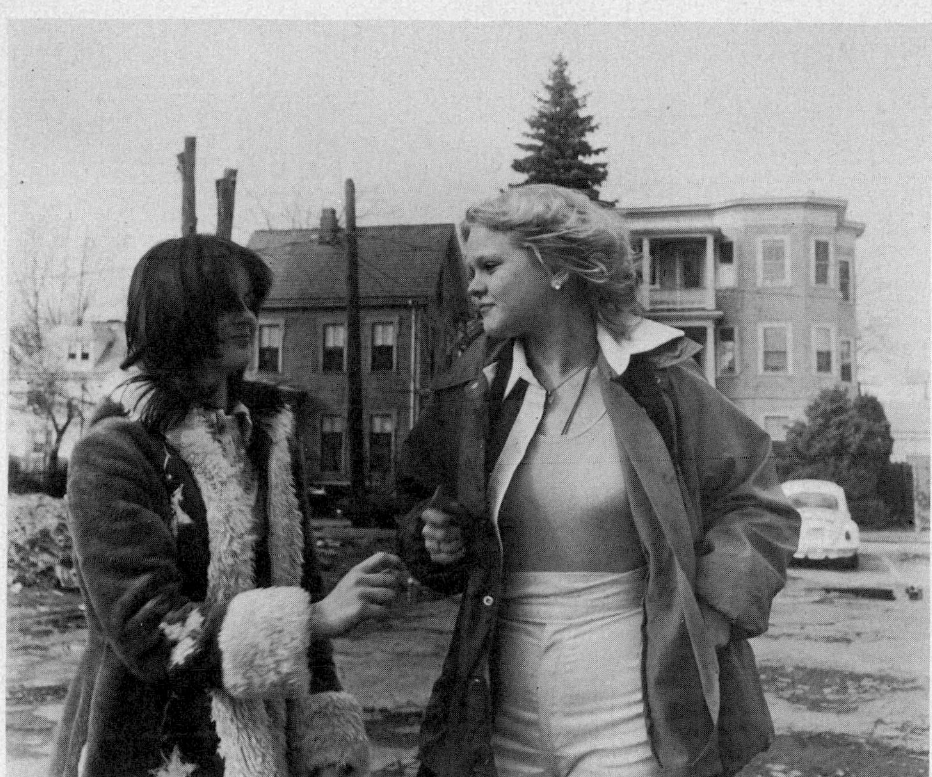

Maturation Among Young Women

The complex transition to reproductive maturity occurs over several years. As in the case of the adolescent growth spurt, women begin their sexual development earlier than men do.

Judy Herzl/The Picture Cube

size in children seems to be due to more rapid maturation; only a minor part reflects a large ultimate size (Tanner, 1972).

The earlier onset of menarche appears to be caused largely by nutritional improvement. James M. Tanner (1972) points out that among well-nourished Western populations, the onset of menarche occurs at about 12 to 13 years of age. In contrast, the latest recorded menarcheal ages are found among peoples with scarce food resources—in the highlands of New Guinea the average age of onset is 17, among the marginally nourished Bush people of the Kahahari 16.5, and in the Bantu poverty areas of South Africa 15.5 (Tanner, 1972; Howell, 1979). Well-nourished girls of the African upper classes, however, have a median menarcheal age of 13.4.

Among European women, the average age for menarche was between 14 and 15 years in 1840, whereas today it is between 12 and 13 (Bullough, 1981). A similar trend has occurred in the United States, where the average age has fallen by about a year and a half since 1905. But among middle-class girls, at least, the trend toward a decline in age at menarche seems to have ended; over the past thirty years it has stabilized at about 12.8 years of age. Although girls show considerable variation in age at their first menstrual period, early menarche tends to be associated with a stout physique and late menarche with a thin one (Zacharias, Rand, and Wurtman, 1976; Faust, 1977). Menarche is also delayed by strenuous physical exercise, occurring at about 15 years of age among dancers and athletes in affluent countries (Wyshak and Frisch, 1982).

Rose E. Frisch (1978) advances the hypothesis that menarche requires a critical level of fat stored in the body. She reasons that pregnancy and lactation impose a great caloric drain. Consequently, if fat reserves are inadequate to meet this demand, a woman's body responds by limiting its reproductive ability. The improvement in children's nutrition has apparently contributed to an earlier onset of menarche because they reach the critical fat/lean ratio, or "metabolic level," sooner.

The Significance of Menarche. Menarche is a pivotal event in an adolescent girl's experience (Koff, Rierdan, and Silverstone, 1978; Greif and Ulman, 1982). Most girls are both happy and frightened by their first menstruation (Petersen, 1983). It is a symbol of a girl's developing sexual maturity and portends her full-fledged status as a woman. As such, menarche plays an important part in shaping a girl's image of her body and her sense of identity as a woman. Postmenarcheal girls report that they experience themselves as more womanly and that they give greater thought to their reproductive role.

In the above respects, menarche has positive connotations. But simultaneously, it is also portrayed within many Western nations as a hygienic crisis (Ruble and Brooks-Gunn, 1982). Menstruation is often associated with a variety of negative events, including physical discomfort, moodiness, and disruption of activities. And the adolescent girl is often led to believe that menstruation is somehow unclean and embarrassing, even shameful. Unhappily, such negative expectations of menstruation may prove to be self-fulfilling prophecies (Brooks-Gunn and Ruble, 1982). Thus preparedness for menarche is important. Indeed, the better prepared a woman feels she was as a girl, the more positive she rates the experience of menarche and the less likely she is to encounter menstrual distress as an adult (Petersen, 1983).

Maturation Among Boys

The first sign of puberty in males begins about twelve years of age with an acceleration in the growth of the testes and scrotum, followed by the appearance of fine, straight hair at the base of the penis. Between thirteen and sixteen years of age, pubic hair multiplies, the testes and scrotum continue growing, the penis lengthens and thickens, and the voice begins to change as the larynx enlarges and the vocal folds double in length (resulting at times in the embarrassing cracking of the adolescent boy's voice). By about fourteen years of age, the prostate gland is producing fluid that can be ejaculated during orgasm. However, mature sperm are not present in the ejaculatory fluid until about a year later, although there is a wide variation among individuals. Also at about fourteen

Maturation Among Young Men
Puberty begins at about twelve years of age among males although individual boys show great variation in its onset. Girls usually enter puberty earlier than boys do.
Janice Fullman/The Picture Cube

to fifteen years of age, boys begin to have "wet dreams," or involuntary emissions of seminal fluid during sleep.

Axillary and facial hair generally make their first appearance about two years after the beginning of pubic hair growth. The relationship is sufficiently variable, however, so that in some cases axillary hair appears first. The growth of facial hair begins with an increase in the length and pigmentation of the hair at the corners of the upper lip. This spreads to complete the mustache. Next, hair appears on the sides of the face in front of the ears and just below the lower lip, and finally it sprouts on the chin and lower cheeks (Tanner, 1969, 1973). Facial hair is downy at first but becomes coarser by late adolescence.

Whereas girls develop fat deposits in the breasts and the hip region, boys acquire additional weight in the form of increased muscle mass. Further, whereas the female pelvis undergoes enlargement at puberty, the most striking expansion in males takes place in the shoulders and rib cage (Chumlea, 1982).

Generally men do not develop a hairy chest until late adolescence or the early twenties. The loss of head hair, causing indentation of the male hairline on each side of the upper forehead, is another post-pubertal development.

The Impact of Early or Late Maturation

Children show enormous variation in growth and sexual maturation. As Figure 13.3 demonstrates, some children do not begin their growth spurt and the development of secondary sexual characteristics until other children have virtually completed these stages (Tanner, 1970, 1973). A study of 781 girls in a middle-class Boston suburb revealed that the age at menarche ranged from 9.1 to 17.7 (Zacharias, Hand, and Wurtman, 1976). Thus it is impossible to appreciate the facts of physical growth and development without taking account of individual differences.

Young people in the United States move in chronological lockstep through elementary and secondary school. Consequently, fairly standardized criteria are applied to children of the same age with respect to their physical, social, and intellectual development. But because children mature at varying rates, they differ in their ability to meet these standards. Individual differences become most apparent at adolescence. Whether adolescents mature early or late has important consequences for them in their relationships with both adults and peers.

Because of different rates of maturation, some adolescents have an advantage in the "ideals" associated with height, strength, physical attractiveness, and athletic prowess. Hence some young people receive more favorable feedback regarding their overall worth and desirability. This in turn influences self-image and behavior. For example, the value placed on manly appearance and athletic excellence means that early-maturing boys often enjoy the admiration of their peers. In contrast, late-maturing boys often receive negative feedback from their peers and hence may be more susceptible to feelings of inadequacy and insecurity.

Investigators at the University of California at Berkeley studied the physical and psychological characteristics of a large group of individuals over an extended period of time. On the basis of this work, Mary Cover Jones and Nancy Bayley (1950:146) reached the following conclusion regarding adolescent boys:

> Those who were physically accelerated are usually accepted and treated by adults and other children as more mature. They appear to have relatively little need to strive for status. From their ranks came the outstanding student-body leaders in senior high school. In contrast, the physically retarded boys exhibit many forms of relatively immature behaviors: this may be in part because others tend to treat them as the little boys they appear to be. Furthermore, a fair proportion of these boys give evidence of needing to counteract their physical disadvantage in some way—usually by greater activity in striving for attention, although in some cases by withdrawing.

The late-maturing boys in the Berkeley study also tended to exhibit feelings of inadequacy, negative self-concept, and feelings of rejection. These feelings were coupled with a rebellious quest for autonomy and freedom from restraint (Mussen and Jones, 1957). Results of a study of college students by Donald Weatherley (1964) largely confirm the findings of Jones and Bayley. Late-maturing boys of college age were less likely than their earlier-maturing peers to have resolved the conflicts attending the transition from childhood to adulthood. They were more inclined to seek attention and affection from others and readier to defy authority and assert unconventional behavior. More recent research also supports the finding that later maturation for boys is associated with a less positive self- and body-image (Boxer, Tobin-Richards, and Petersen, 1983; Tobin-Richards, Boxer, and Petersen, 1983). For boys, being "late" is apparently a psychological disadvantage.

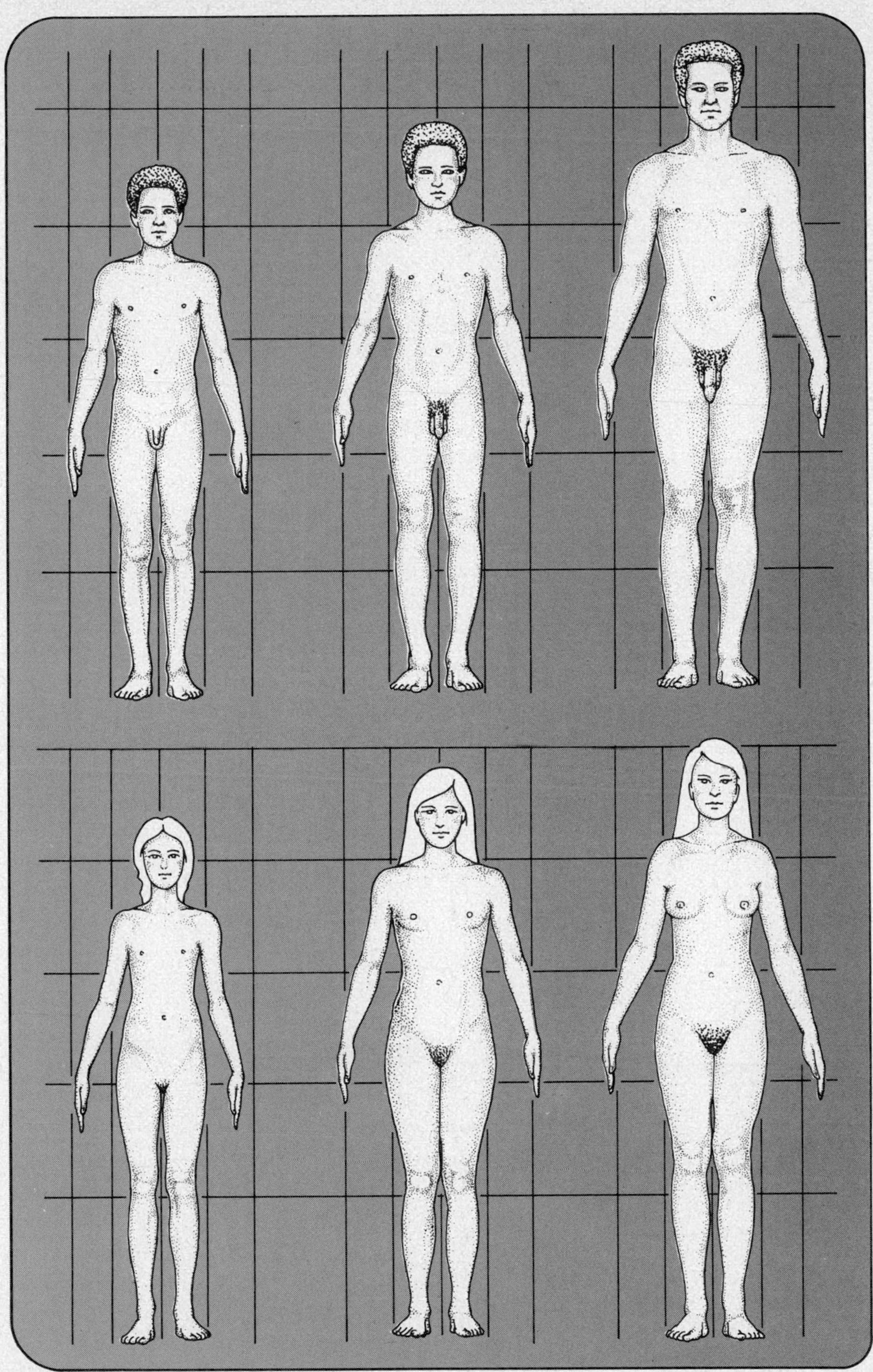

Figure 13.3 Variations in Adolescent Growth

All the girls in the lower row are the same chronological age: 12.75 years. All the boys in the upper row are also the same chronological age: 14.75 years. Some persons of the same sex have completed their growth and sexual maturation when the others are just beginning the process.

SOURCE: J. M. Tanner, "Growing Up," *Scientific American,* Vol. 229 (September 1973), p. 38.

A follow-up study of the early- and late-maturing males in the Berkeley sample was conducted when the men were thirty-three years old. Their behavior patterns were surprisingly similar to the descriptions recorded of them in adolescence (Jones, 1957). The early maturers were more poised, relaxed, cooperative, sociable, and conforming. Late maturers tended to be more eager, talkative, self-assertive, rebellious, and touchy.

In contrast, research on girls has produced diverse

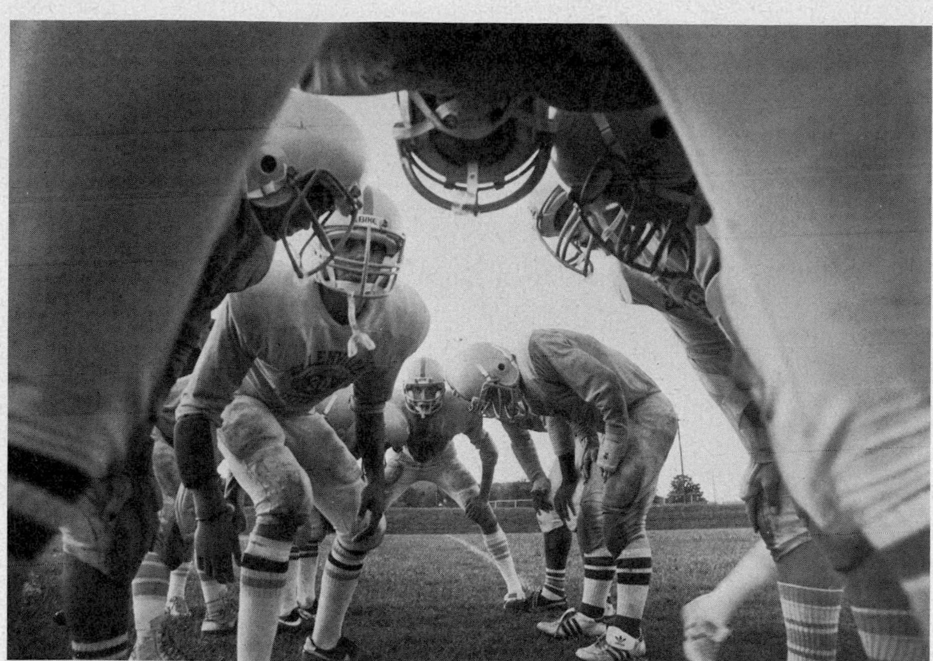

Some Youth Are Favored by Early Maturation

Since athletic excellence is usually prized among American adolescents, those boys who mature early are at a decided advantage in winning the admiration of their peers.

Dan Chidester/The Image Works

and contradictory results. Some findings show that late-maturing girls exhibit greater sociability, leadership, poise, cheerfulness, and expressiveness than early-maturing girls (Jones, 1949). Other research indicates that, as with boys, late physical maturation has adverse effects on the personality adjustment of girls (Weatherley, 1964). And still other research suggests that for girls being "on time" is associated with a more positive set of self-perceptions than being "off time"—either early or late (Tobin-Richards, Boxer, and Petersen, 1983).

These conflicting findings suggest that the situation for girls is more complicated than that for boys. Research by Margaret S. Faust (1960: 185) reveals that among sixth-grade girls, early maturation tends to be a handicap. But when the late-maturing girls enter middle or junior high school, the picture shifts and they are at a disadvantage:

> The findings of the present research point out the complex nature of variables which interact in producing a girl's reputation during adolescence. . . . The discontinuity between rate of change in evaluations of prestige and rate of physical changes during adolescence means that, for girls, accelerated development is not a sustained asset throughout the adolescent period, as it is for boys. Accelerated development for girls is somewhat detrimental to prestige status before the junior high school years, while it places a girl in a very favorable social position throughout the junior high school years.

Mary Cover Jones and Paul H. Mussen (1958) point to still another factor. Early-maturing girls are more likely to be stout and to develop a stocky physique. In contrast, late-maturing girls are more likely to be thin and to acquire a slim, slight build that is more in keeping with the feminine ideal of many Western nations. Thus over the long run (in contrast to the short run), late maturation in girls may be associated with factors other than maturation itself that function as assets in social adjustment.

Self-Image

The image that adolescents have of themselves is particularly susceptible to peer influences. Any difference from the peer group in growth and development tends to be a difficult experience for the adolescent. This is especially true when it places the individual at a physical disadvantage or in a position of unfavorable contrast to peers. Adolescents are quick to reject or ridicule age-mates who deviate in some way from the physical norm. Indeed, few words have the capacity to cause as much pleasure—and as much pain—to adolescents as does the word "popularity." Consequently, many teenagers are preoccupied with their physical acceptability and adequacy (Lerner et al., 1980; Eisert and Kahle, 1982).

Adolescent girls often feel troubled about the size

and shape of their breasts. And they express considerable concern about their facial features, including their skin and hair (Tobin-Richards, Boxer, and Petersen, 1983). Teenage boys tend to worry about the size of their bodies, and, in particular, the relative size of their penises. Boys are particularly anxious to develop athletic-related strengths and abilities. Concern and self-consciousness over their complexions are common among adolescents. The acne, blackheads, and pimples that frequently accompany puberty are a common source of anxiety and tension. Besides skin problems, teenagers frequently express concern about irregular teeth, orthodontic braces, glasses, and the shape of their faces and noses.

A large proportion of adolescents want to change their weight; they feel that they are either "too thin" or "too heavy." Indeed, medical authorities classify at least 10 percent of North American elementary-school children as obese and 30 to 35 percent of adolescents as overweight. About one-fourth of all boys show a large increase in fatty tissue during early adolescence; another 20 percent show a moderate increase (Stolz and Stolz, 1951). During the adolescent growth spurt, however, the rate of fat accumulation declines in both boys and girls. Whatever the source of obesity, the overweight adolescent is at a personal and social disadvantage. In fact, a stigma is associated with obesity in the United States (see the boxed insert on page 360).

THE DEVELOPMENT OF IDENTITIES AND SELF-CONCEPTS

According to the neo-Freudian psychoanalyst Erik Erikson, the main task of adolescence is to build and confirm a reasonably stable **identity.** In the simplest terms, identity is composed of the answers an individual gives to the questions Who am I? and Who am I to be? Identity is a person's sense of placement within the world—the meaning that one attaches to oneself in the broader context of life.

In their everyday lives, people interact with one another not so much on the basis of what they actually are as of what conceptions they have of themselves and of others. Accordingly, their identity leaves its signature on everything they do. Identities are not fixed, formed once and for all time. They undergo continual shaping and reshaping over the course of the human life span.

Erikson: The Crisis of Youth

Don't laugh at a youth for his affectations; he is only trying on one face after another to find a face of his own.

—LOGAN PEARSALL SMITH
Afterthoughts, 1931

Erik Erikson's work has focused attention on the struggle of adolescents to develop and clarify their identity. As described in Chapter 2, Erikson divides the developmental sequence into eight psychosocial stages. Each stage poses a somewhat different issue—presents a necessary turning point or crucial period, when development must move in either a positive or negative direction. The focus of each psychosocial stage is upon a major task in ego-development or self-development.

Erikson's fifth stage, which covers the period of adolescence, consists of the search for identity. He suggests (1968*b*: 165) that an optimal feeling of identity is experienced as a sense of well-being: "Its most obvious concomitants are a feeling of being at home in one's body, a sense of 'knowing where one is going,' and an inner assuredness of anticipated recognition from those who count."

Erikson observes that the adolescent, like a trapeze artist, must release his or her safe hold on childhood and reach in midair for a firm grasp on adulthood. The search for identity becomes particularly acute because the individual is undergoing rapid physical change while simultaneously confronting many imminent adult tasks and decisions. The adolescent must often make an occupational choice, or at least decide whether or not to continue formal schooling. Other aspects of the environment also provide testing grounds for the self-concept: broadening peer relationships, heterosexual contacts and roles, moral and ideological commitments, and emancipation from adult authority.

Adolescents must synthesize a variety of new roles in order to come to terms with themselves and their environment. Erikson suggests that some societies, such as our own, allow a *moratorium,* or period of delay, during which adolescents can experiment with or "try on" various roles, ideologies, and commitments. It is a stage between childhood and adulthood when the individual can explore various dimensions

OBESITY

Few of our characteristics are more readily apparent than our physical appearance. And our appearance has a major impact on our self-esteem. This seems to be especially true during adolescence. Developmental psychologists such as Erik Erikson stress that adolescents are consumed with such questions as What am I like? How good am I? and What will I become? Although being liked and accepted is important at any age, they may be particularly crucial during adolescence. Personal appearance plays a central part in one's relations with others. Consequently, social expectations of and reactions to body build are a preoccupation among many adolescents (Hendry and Gillies, 1978).

Obesity presents a special problem for adolescent and adult alike. Our understanding of obesity has undergone change in recent years (Brody, 1979*b*; Bennett and Gurin, 1982). The major assumption long underlying the treatment of obesity was that overweight results from excess food consumption due to faulty eating habits. Yet several decades of research have shown that, on the whole, the obese eat no more than the lean. The proposition that obese people eat abnormally large amounts of food simply does not hold in many cases. Further, studies of eating behavior—the number, timing, and composition of meals and snacks, the rate at which bites are taken, and the size of bites—reveal no consistent differences between the obese and the lean. And an accumulating body of research clearly indicates that overeating alone is not sufficient to cause most people to become or to remain obese.

These findings have led researchers to a closer examination of energy expenditure. Yet studies of activity levels in the obese have produced highly variable results. There are about an equal number of studies that show no differences in activity levels between the obese and the lean and studies that demonstrate lower activity levels in the obese. And among those researchers who do find differences between the two groups, some claim that obese people are less active because of their excess weight, rather than the other way around.

Various psychiatrists used to argue that obesity is a response to psychological disorders. But this premise has found little support among researchers. While being fat in our society may be associated with self-disdain and rejection by others—and with feelings of being deprived, left out, and lonely—these problems appear to be more the consequences of obesity than the causes of it.

Some researchers also question hereditary explanations of obesity. Any number of medical authorities say that obesity is constitutionally determined in only a small fraction of cases. Even studies of adopted children and identical twins reared together and apart result in conflicting findings.

One recent theory of obesity that has attracted considerable interest holds that fat babies and fat children are more likely to become overweight adults because they develop a permanent excess of fat cells. This provides them with a lifelong storehouse of fat cells capable of being filled. When such individuals later become adults, the existing fat cells enlarge but are not thought to increase in number.

Another popular theory postulates the existence of a metabolic regulator or "set-point" (Nisbett, 1972; Bennett and Gurin, 1982). According to this view, a control system is built into each of us—a kind of fat thermostat that dictates how much fat we should carry. Some of us have a high setting and tend to be obese; others of us have a low setting and tend to be lean. Consequently, the attempt by obese people to lose weight is in most cases bound to fail because it constitutes an attempt to overpower the body's internal controls. Likewise, the skinny person who seeks to gain weight by overeating is fighting a losing battle.

The confused state of our knowledge regarding obesity has led some obese people to challenge prevailing social stereotypes and prejudices. Like the physically handicapped, the obese wear their "problem" for all to see at all times. Yet unlike the physically handicapped, obese people are held responsible for their condition. They are the object of much concern, criticism, and overt discrimination. Negative attitudes seem to intensify during adolescence, particularly among females. But increasingly, obese people are "fighting back." They call for a revamping of prevailing cultural stereotypes that proclaim "large is ugly," and they insist that their needs and feelings be given at least as much consideration as are those of other people.

of life without yet having to choose any. Adolescents may start or stop, abandon or postpone, implement or transform given courses of action.

As a result of "trying on" various roles and facing the complications of arriving at a stable sense of self, many adolescents are left with a blurred self-image.

Developing and Clarifying Identity
According to Erik Erikson, adolescence presents young people with the developmental task of synthesizing a variety of new roles and crystallizing their self-conceptions. As he views the process, a certain amount of role confusion, turmoil, and uncertainty is inevitable.
Patrick Reddy

Erikson calls this difficulty **role confusion,** a state characterized by bewilderment about who one is, where one belongs, and where one is going. Erikson believes that a certain amount of role confusion is an almost inevitable, indeed even desirable, experience of adolescence. To "find" oneself too soon, he argues, is to run the risk of inadequately exploring alternative roles and foreclosing many of life's potentialities.

Since the identities of adolescents are diffuse, uncrystallized, and fluctuating, Erikson says, adolescents are often at sea with themselves and others. He believes (1968*b*: 132) that this ambiguity and lack of stable anchorage lead many adolescents to overcommit themselves to cliques, allegiances, loves, and social causes:

> To keep themselves together they temporarily overidentify with the heroes of cliques and crowds to the point of an apparently complete loss of individuality. Yet in this stage not even "falling in love" is entirely, or even primarily, a sexual matter. To a considerable extent adolescent love is an attempt to arrive at a definition of one's identity by projecting one's diffused self-image on another and by seeing it thus reflected and gradually clarified. This is why so much of young love is conversation. On the other hand, clarification can also be sought by destructive means. Young people can become remarkably clannish, intolerant, and cruel in their exclusion of others who are "different," in skin color or cultural background, in tastes and gifts, and often in entirely petty aspects of dress and gesture arbitrarily selected as the signs of an in-grouper or out-grouper.

According to Erikson, this explains the appeal that various extremist and totalitarian movements have for some adolescents.

In Erikson's view every adolescent confronts a major danger: that he or she will fail to arrive at a consistent, coherent, and integrated identity. Consequently adolescents may experience what Erikson terms **identity diffusion**—a lack of ability to commit oneself, even in late adolescence, to an occupational or ideological position and to assume a recognizable station in life. Another danger is that adolescents will fashion a **negative identity**—a debased self-image and social role (Erikson, 1964*a*: 97). Still another course taken by some adolescents is formation of a **deviant identity**—a life-style that is at odds with, or at least not supported by, the values and expectations of society. Some psychologists and psychiatrists deem identity crises to be precipitating factors in two eating disorders, anorexia and bulimia nervosa (Bruch, 1982) (see the boxed insert on pages 362–363).

Portrayal of "Storm and Stress"

Erikson's view of adolescence is in keeping with a long psychological tradition that has portrayed adolescence as a difficult period. The notion that adolescence is a distinct and turbulent developmental period received impetus in 1904 with the publication of G. Stanley Hall's monumental work, *Adolescence.* Hall, one of the major figures of early American psychology, depicted adolescence as a stage of "storm and stress." According to Hall, adolescence is character-

ANOREXIA AND BULIMIA NERVOSA

Anorexia nervosa is a disorder in which the individual willfully suppresses appetite, resulting in self-starvation. Once considered to be quite rare, the incidence of anorexia nervosa has increased dramatically over the past twenty years (Bemis, 1978). It occurs primarily in adolescent or young adult females of the middle and upper-middle classes. The victims have a fierce desire to succeed in their project of self-starvation; have a morbid terror of having any fat on their bodies; and deny that they are thin or ill, insisting that they have never felt better even when they are so weak they can barely walk. Simultaneously, these people may long for food and even have secret binges of eating (often interrupted by self-induced vomiting).

One explanation for the recent epidemic in cases of anorexia nervosa is the emphasis that Western societies place on slimness. In some cases the refusal to eat is preceded by "normal" dieting, which may be prompted by casual comments that the young woman is "filling out" or "getting plump." Further, the victim's overestimation of her body size seems to increase with the severity of the illness. According to this interpretation, the disorder entails self-induced starvation by women who desperately want to be beautiful but end up being grotesquely unattractive.

Another explanation of the disorder is that it is an attempt to avoid adulthood and adult responsibilities. The anorexic young woman invariably diets away her secondary sexual characteristics: her breasts diminish; her periods cease entirely (interestingly, menstruation ceases *prior* to pronounced weight reduction and hence cannot be attributed to starvation); and her body comes to resemble that of a prepubescent child. According to this view, such women are seeking a return to the remembered comfort and safety of childhood (Kaye, 1979).

Approximately two-thirds of anorexic victims recover or improve, with one-third remaining chronically ill or dying of the disorder. Most authorities now recognize that anorexia nervosa usually has multiple causes and that it requires a combination of various treatment strategies adjusted to the individual needs of the patient (Bemis, 1978; Schwartz and Thompson, 1981).

A number of psychiatrists have suggested that a subgroup of male athletes—"obligatory runners"—resemble anorexic women (Yates, Leehey, and Shisslak, 1983). These men devote their lives to running and are obsessed with the distance they run, their diets, their equipment, and their daily routines while ignoring illness and injury. Both anorexics and obligatory runners lead strict lives that assiduously avoid pleasure. Both groups are concerned about their health, feel uncomfortable with anger, are self-effacing and hard working,

ized by inevitable turmoil, maladjustment, tension, rebellion, dependency conflicts, and exaggerated peer-group conformity. This view was subsequently taken up and popularized by Anna Freud (1936) and other psychoanalysts. Indeed, Anna Freud (1958: 275) went so far as to assert: "The upholding of a steady equilibrium during the adolescent process is itself abnormal." Viewed from this perspective, the adolescent undergoes so many rapid changes that a restructuring of identity or self-concept is required if these changes are to be properly integrated into the individual's personality.

Any number of sociologists and anthropologists have suggested that few people make the transition from childhood to adulthood more difficult than Western nations do (Dragastin and Elder, 1975; Sebald, 1977; Elkind, 1979). At adolescence, boys and girls are expected to stop being children, yet they are not expected to be men and women. The definitions provided for them are quite inconsistent. They are told that they are no longer children, but they are still treated like dependents, economically supported by their parents, and frequently viewed by society as untrustworthy and irresponsible individuals. According to this view, conflicting expectations generate an identity crisis among American and European youth.

Many non-Western societies make the period of adolescence considerably easier, or at least more definitive. They ease the shift in status by providing **puberty rites**—initiation ceremonies that socially symbolize the transition from childhood to adulthood (Brown, 1969; Herdt, 1981, 1982). Adolescents are subjected to various thoroughly distasteful, painful, and humiliating experiences during such ceremonies,

Anorexia Nervosa

Anorexia nervosa is a disorder that has surfaced in recent years as a major health problem. Its victims, primarily women, starve themselves and deny that they are ill or emaciated. Anorexia nervosa disrupts the chemistry of the body and can culminate in death.

Neal Boenzi/The New York Times

and tend to be high achievers from affluent families. And like anorexics, obligatory runners are exceedingly concerned about their weight and feel compelled to maintain a lean body mass.

A stepsister disorder of anorexia nervosa is *bulimia nervosa* (also termed the *binge-purge syndrome*). Bulimia nervosa is a disorder characterized by repeated episodes of binging, particularly on high-calorie foods like candy bars and ice cream. The binge is followed by an attempt to get rid of the food through self-induced vomiting, taking laxatives, or fasting.

Like anorexics, bulimics have an obsessive fear of becoming fat. However, bulimics are typically within normal weight range and have healthy, outgoing appearances, whereas anorexics are skeletally thin. Although young women are the primary victims of the binge-purge syndrome, young men in contact sports, especially wrestling, may likewise engage in similar behavior to squeeze into a lower weight class. The disorder can produce such long-term side effects as ulcers, hernias, dental problems (stomach acid destroys the teeth), and electrolyte imbalance (resulting in heart attacks). Like anorexia nervosa, bulimia nervosa calls for treatment. Some researchers believe that a hereditary form of depression may underlie some forms of both disorders, and indeed some patients respond to antidepressant medication.

but they are then pronounced grown up. Boys may be terrorized, ritualistically painted, and circumcised; girls may be secluded at menarche. But the tasks and tests are clearly defined, and young people know that if they accomplish the goals set for them, they will acquire adult status.

The Dahomeans of West Africa are a people who have puberty rites (Murdock, 1934: 579):

> A boy shortly before his twentieth year is circumcised in company with a group of youths of his own age. The specialist who performs the latter operation keeps the youths in his own house until they have recovered, when he shaves their heads and sends them home. . . . When a girl reaches puberty she is isolated from the opposite sex for five or seven days and receives visits and presents from her female relatives and friends. When she emerges from her chamber, her father gives her a white mantle and a new mat and sends her to the market on a ceremonial errand.

Hence many societies of the world recognize puberty through special initiation ceremonies. By doing so, they are believed to provide an institutional means of easing the transition of their youth to adulthood. Even so, Western societies do provide a number of less obvious rites of passage. There is the Jewish Bar Mitzvah and Bat Mitzvah and the Christian confirmation. Securing a driver's license at age sixteen or seventeen and voting at age eighteen also function in their own fashion as rites of passage. And graduation from high school and college—each affording a formal diploma and pomp—are special kinds of initiation ceremonies. But all of these are rather mild versions of what youth must go through in many non-Western societies.

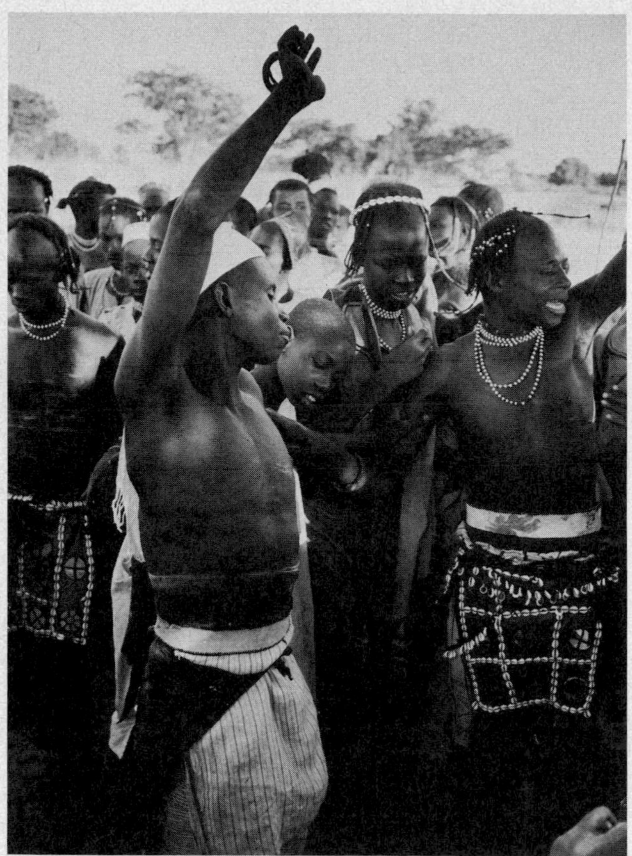

Puberty Rite

The nomadic Fulani people of Nigeria are seen here celebrating a puberty rite, which symbolizes the transition from childhood to adulthood. As part of this initiation ceremony, boys (at left) are struck across the abdomen with a 6-foot stick while they stand silent and still.

Peter Buckley/Photo Researchers

The Self-Concept and Self-Esteem of Adolescents

In recent years researchers have increasingly come to the conclusion that adolescence in the United States is *not* the period of "storm and stress" that earlier psychologists and sociologists held it to be (Bachman, O'Malley, and Johnston, 1978; Adelson, 1979; Prawat, Jones, and Hampton, 1979; Blyth and Traeger, 1983). They do not deny that young people of Western nations undergo changes in self-image and self-concept during adolescence (Waterman, Geary, and Waterman, 1974; Montemayor and Eisen, 1977; Waterman, 1982) but suggest that the changes are not necessarily "stormy." Indeed, the overall self-esteem of most individuals *increases* with age across the adolescent years (Bachman, O'Malley, and Johnston, 1978; McCarthy and Hoge, 1982; O'Malley and Bachman, 1983). Of course, there are exceptions. Changes in social environment, including changing schools, in some cases interfere with those forces that otherwise bolster a child's self-esteem. Thus the transition into a middle or junior high school can have a disturbing effect under certain circumstances, particularly for girls (Simmons, Rosenberg, and Rosenberg, 1973; Simmons et al., 1979).

The psychologist Albert Bandura (1964) believes that the stereotyped storm-and-stress portrait of adolescence most closely fits the behavior of "the deviant 10 percent of the adolescent population that appears repeatedly in psychiatric clinics, juvenile probation departments, and in the newspaper headlines." Bandura argues that the "stormy-decade myth" is due more to cultural expectations and the representations of teenagers in movies, literature, and the media than to actual fact.

Daniel Offer (1969; Offer, Ostrov, and Howard, 1981) likewise finds little evidence of "turmoil" or "chaos" in his longtudinal study of a sample of sixty-one middle-class adolescent boys. Most were happy, responsible, and well-adjusted boys who respected their parents. Adolescent "disturbance" tended to be limited mostly to "bickering" with their parents. Like Bandura, Offer concludes that the portrayal of adolescence as a turbulent period comes from the work of such investigators as Erik Erikson who have spent their professional careers primarily studying disturbed adolescents. He concludes (Offer and Offer, 1975: 197): "Our data lead us to hypothesize that adolescence, as a stage in life, is not a uniquely stressful period."

Offer's conclusion finds support in a longitudinal study involving students in grades five through twelve undertaken by Jerome B. Dusek and John F. Flaherty (1981). The self-concepts of the adolescents developed in a continuous and stable way. Rather than experiencing dramatic change and turbulence, the adolescents gradually fashioned their self-concepts on the basis of their social circumstances and evolving cognitive competencies and skills. These findings are hardly surprising given the fact that the changes associated with adolescence typically extend over a period of time and allow adolescents ample opportunity to adjust to them. But when the changes occur si-

HELPING ADOLESCENTS BUILD POSITIVE SELF-CONCEPTS

Many psychologists and psychiatrists believe that we can have no stronger ally in life than a healthy and positive self-concept. In large measure our attitudes toward ourselves evolve in much the same fashion as do our other attitudes—through social interaction with other people who are meaningful to us. Accordingly, parents, teachers, and other adults can contribute to the building of positive self-concepts among children and adolescents. Here are a number of suggestions gleaned from the literature:

- Listen to what young people have to say. Make them feel that their ideas are important and worthy.
- Show young people respect and consideration. Let them know that you value each of them as a unique human being.
- Ask young people for advice and make use of it.
- Pay more attention to what young people do right than what they do wrong. Do not overcorrect with verbal comments or critical responses.
- Provide young people with tasks that are interesting and challenging yet within their range of ability so they can succeed and derive a sense of achievement.
- Be patient with young people and slow to judge them.
- Afford young people opportunities to make decisions within their competence, but do not overload them with complex and excessive options.
- Make young people aware of their successes and the satisfaction that they afford through comments such as "You really did well with that."
- Employ praise and encouragement often, especially for youth who are more introverted and lack self-assurance.
- Be alert to your own body language and check to make certain it carries the same message you express in words. A smile, a grin, a friendly hug, or even a casual swat on the seat can express warmth and acceptance.
- Help young people to recognize the buildup of tension and to develop their own acceptable defusing device.
- Select a few basic skills, rules, and responsibilities to work on. Let the rest go lest you overwhelm.
- Maintain your sense of humor. A lighthearted approach will often work. But do not ridicule.
- Avoid such descriptions as "She's lazy" or "He could do it if he really wanted." A more accurate statement would be, "She (he) would do it if only she (he) could."

multaneously, the probability of disturbance is more likely (Coleman, 1978). The boxed insert above provides a number of suggestions to adults for helping adolescents build positive self-concepts.

According to a longitudinal study of 2,213 young men conducted by the Institute for Social Research at the University of Michigan (Bachman, O'Malley, and Johnston, 1978), adolescence may also be overrated as a time of major attitudinal change. Aspirations, self-concepts, and political attitudes (including those on racial issues) generally are well established by age sixteen. Though differences in these areas show up between individuals who achieve success in education (and later on the job) and those who do not, these differences are already largely established by the tenth grade. In other words, young people who enter high school with high aspirations and positive self-concepts are likely to retain these advantages at least five years beyond high school. Hence students in graduate and professional schools typically have high self-esteem that mirrors the positive self-images they possessed five years earlier. Similarly, the poor self-images of school dropouts are already established before these adolescents withdraw from school. Thus differences are quite stable across time.

Perhaps the most reasonable conclusion to be drawn from cross-cultural studies and from the variations encountered in our own society is that puberty and adolescence have different meanings for different people. There is not one adolescent experience but many experiences; hence there are multiple roads to adulthood. Because of the diversity found among cultures, and even among individuals within the same culture, it is hardly surprising that the beliefs, feelings,

Self-Concepts of Adolescents

A mounting body of research suggests that the self-concepts of most adolescents develop in a continuous and stable way. Dramatic change and turbulence are not inherent to the process by which young people make the transition from childhood to adulthood. Rather, adolescents gradually build their self-concepts on the basis of social circumstances and evolving competencies.

Jane Scherk/Jeroboam

and perceptions associated with puberty are not neatly preprogrammed in some rigidly fashioned mold.

COGNITIVE AND MORAL DEVELOPMENT

During adolescence, young people gradually acquire several substantial new intellectual capacities. They begin to reflect about themselves; their parents, teachers, and peers; and the world they live in. They develop an increasing ability to think about hypothetical and future situations and events. In our society, they also must evolve a set of standards regarding family, religion, school, drugs, and sexuality.

Period of Formal Operations

Thinking is not a heaven-born thing. . . . It is a gift men and women make for themselves. It is earned, and it is earned by effort. There is no effort, to my mind, that is comparable in its qualities, that is so taxing to the individual, as to think, to analyze fundamentally.

—SUPREME COURT JUSTICE LOUIS D. BRANDEIS

Jean Piaget called adolescence the **period of formal operations,** the final and highest stage in the development of intelligence from infancy to adulthood. This mode of thought has two major attributes. First, adolescents gain the ability to think about their own thinking—to deal efficiently with the complex problems involved in reasoning. Second, they acquire the ability to imagine many possibilities inherent in a situation—to generate mentally all possible outcomes of an event and thus to place less reliance upon real objects and events. In sum, adolescents gain the capacity to think in *logical* and *abstract* terms.

Formal operational thought so closely parallels scientific thinking that it is termed by some "scientific reasoning." It allows people to mentally restructure information and ideas so that they can make sense out of a new set of data. Through logical operations, individuals can transfer the strategic attack skills they employ in a familiar problem area to an unfamiliar area and thus derive new answers and solutions. In so doing they generate a higher level of analytical capability in discerning relationships among various classes of events.

Formal operational thought is quite different from the concrete operational thought of the previous period (see Chapter 11). Piaget said that children in the period of concrete operations cannot transcend the immediate. They are limited to solving tangible problems of the present and have difficulty dealing with remote, future, or hypothetical matters. For instance, a twelve-year-old will accept and think about the following problem: "All three-legged snakes are purple; I am hiding a three-legged snake; guess its color" (Kagan, 1972*a*: 92). In contrast, seven-year-old children are confused by the initial premise because it violates their notion of what is real. Consequently they refuse to cooperate.

Likewise, if adolescents are presented with the problem: "There are three schools, Roosevelt, Kennedy, and Lincoln schools, and three girls, Mary, Sue, and Jane, who go to different schools. Mary goes to the Roosevelt school, Jane to the Kennedy school. Where does Sue go?" they quickly respond "Lincoln." The seven-year-old may excitedly answer, "Sue goes to Roosevelt school, because my sister has a friend called Sue and that's the school she goes to" (Kagan, 1972*a*: 93).

Similarly, Bärbel Inhelder and Piaget (1958: 252) found that below twelve years of age most children cannot solve this verbal problem:

> Edith is lighter than Suzanne.
> Edith is darker than Lily.
> Which is the darkest of the three?

Children under twelve often conclude that both Edith and Suzanne are light-complexioned and that Edith and Lily are dark-complexioned. Accordingly, they say that Lily is the darkest, Suzanne is the lightest, and Edith falls in between. In contrast, children in the stage of formal operations can correctly reason that Suzanne is darker than Edith, that Edith is darker than Lily, and therefore that Suzanne is the darkest girl.

In one of their experiments, Inhelder and Piaget gave children five flasks of colorless liquid and asked them to produce a yellow liquid (see Figure 13.4). They described the experiment as follows (1958: 109):

> The child is given four similar flasks containing colorless, odorless liquids which are perceptually identical. We number them: (1) diluted sulphuric acid; (2) water; (3) oxygenated water; (4) thiosulphate; we add a bottle (with a dropper) which we will call *g*; it contains potassium iodide. It is known that oxygenated water oxidizes potassium iodide in an acid medium. Thus mixture (1 + 3 + *g*) will yield a yellow color. The water (2) is neutral, so that adding it will not change the color, whereas the thiosulphate (4) will bleach the mixture [cancel out the yellow]. The experimenter presents to the subject two glasses, one containing 1 + 3, the other containing 2. In front of the subject, he pours several drops of *g* in each of the two glasses and notes the different reactions. Then the subject is asked simply to reproduce the color yellow, using flasks 1, 2, 3, 4, and *g* as he wishes.

Children under twelve typically approach the problem by taking one flask (*g*—the flask with the potassium iodide) and adding liquid from it separately to each of the other flasks (1, 2, 3, and 4). When this procedure fails to produce the desired outcome, they tend to fall into a hit-or-miss pattern. They begin pouring liquid from one flask into another in a relatively aimless manner, hoping to stumble on the right combination by chance. Should they find a correct combination, they stop their search, failing to appreciate that another combination is also possible (the two combinations that produce yellow liquid are *g* + 1 + 3 and *g* + 1 + 2 + 3).

Young people in the stage of formal operations handle the problem differently. They undertake to test *all* possible combinations in a systematic fashion. They, too, typically begin by adding the liquid from one flask (*g*) separately to the other flasks. But in contrast to younger children, they then proceed to combine the flasks three at a time and finally four at a time, arriving at the fifteen possible outcomes. Thus formal operational thought closely parallels the kind of rea-

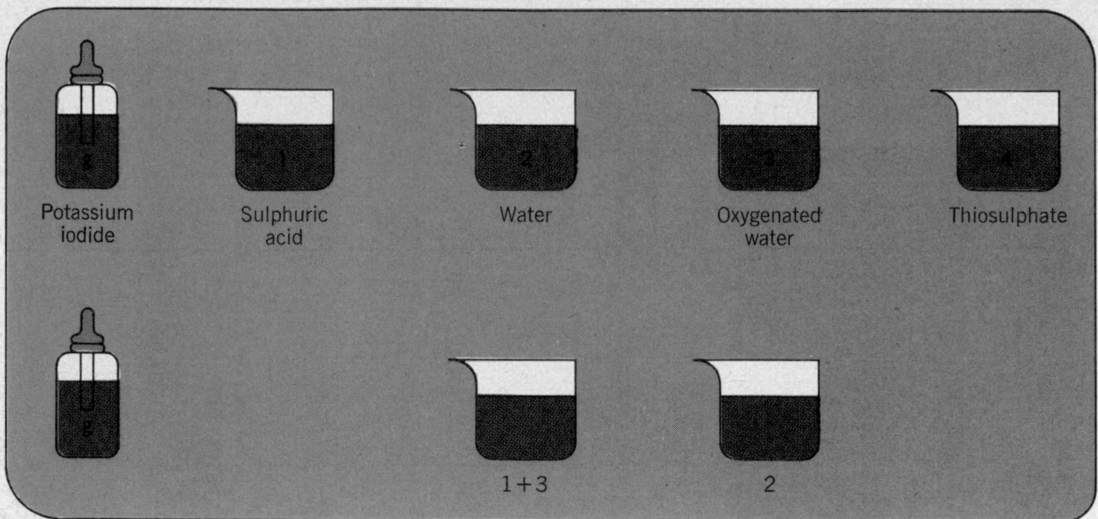

Figure 13.4 Piaget's Yellow Liquid Experiment

A flask with a dropper in it, labeled *g*, contains potassium iodide. Four beakers contain colorless, odorless liquids, each of which is labeled with a number: 1 (sulphuric acid), 2 (water), 3 (oxygenated water), and 4 (thiosulphate). Two other beakers are presented to the subject. One contains 1 + 3 (sulphuric acid and oxygenated water); the other contains 2 (water). As the subject watches, the experimenter adds liquid from *g* (potassium iodide) to each of the two beakers by means of the dropper. The liquid in the beaker containing 1 + 3 becomes yellow. The subject is then instructed to reproduce the yellow color, using flask *g* and the beakers 1, 2, 3, and 4 as he or she wishes. The following combinations are logically possible in the experiment:

(1) $g + 1$	(6) $g + 1 + 3$	(11) $g + 1 + 2 + 3$
(2) $g + 2$	(7) $g + 1 + 4$	(12) $g + 1 + 2 + 4$
(3) $g + 3$	(8) $g + 2 + 3$	(13) $g + 1 + 3 + 4$
(4) $g + 4$	(9) $g + 2 + 4$	(14) $g + 2 + 3 + 4$
(5) $g + 1 + 2$	(10) $g + 3 + 4$	(15) $g + 1 + 2 + 3 + 4$

Combinations 6 and 11 produce the yellow liquid.

SOURCE: Adapted from Barbel Inhelder and Jean Piaget, *The Growth of Logical Thinking* (New York: Basic Books, 1958), p. 108.

soning employed in the solution of scientific problems.

Piaget suggested that the transition from concrete operational to formal operational thought takes place as children become increasingly proficient in organizing and structuring input from their environment with concrete operational methods (see Chapter 11). In so doing, they come to recognize the inadequacies of concrete operational methods for solving problems in the real world—the gaps, uncertainties, and contradictions inherent in concrete operational processes. For instance, when in the course of the flask experiment children in the stage of concrete operations are required to take more than two variables into account in a systematic manner, they flounder. They lack an analytical system appropriate to such situations. Accordingly, when they are confronted with new problems—those not amenable to solution by concrete operational methods—they must search for new methods of attack. Thus children are themselves intellectually transformed in the process of coping with and adjusting to their environments. In this fashion they gain the unique feature of adolescent thought: the ability to generate all possible combinations within a system (Flavell, 1963; Elkind, 1968*a*).

John H. Flavell and Joachin F. Wohlwill (1969), David Moshman (1977), and others have attempted to specify the phases that occur in the gradual transition between a particular developmental stage (for instance, concrete operations) and the stage that succeeds it (for instance, formal operations). They distinguish between *competence*—the underlying possession of some operation such as that involved in the flask experiment—and *performance*—the ability to *apply* the operation to a particular task. These developmental psychologists identify four phases in the formation of a new cognitive structure (Moshman, 1977: 95–96):

> In the first, the operation in question has not yet begun to develop and the individual fails at any task requiring it. In the second phase, the operation is developing at the competence level and the probability of success on any particular task, though always greater than zero, depends on the performance factors involved in that task. In phase 3, the operation is fully developed at the competence level, but performance factors may still hinder its application to certain tasks. [In phase 4] performance factors no longer hinder successful application of the operation.

These phases are not stages in their own right but merely transformational patterns in the consolidation of a particular operation or skill.

Not all adolescents, or for that matter all adults, attain full formal operational thought. Therefore they fail to acquire its associated abilities for logical and abstract thinking. This is true, for instance, of people who score below average on standard intelligence tests (Jackson, 1965; Yudin, 1966; Neimark, 1974). Indeed, as judged by Piaget's strict testing standards, less than 50 percent of American adults reach the stage of formal operations (Martorano, 1977; Roberge and Flexer, 1979). Some evidence suggests that secondary schools may provide students with experiences in mathematics and science that expedite the development of formal operational thought. And some psychologists speculate that these experiences may be necessary to its development (Sharp, Cole, and Lave, 1979; Hobbs and Robinson, 1982).

Further, cross-cultural studies fail to demonstrate the full development of formal operations in all societies (Ashton, 1975; Douglas and Wong, 1977). For example, rural villagers in Turkey never seem to reach the formal operational stage, yet urbanized educated Turks do reach it (Kohlberg and Gilligan, 1971). Overall, a growing body of research suggests that full formal operational thinking may not be the rule in adolescence (Dulit, 1972; Elkind, 1975).

Despite this research, Piaget (1972: 10) continued to maintain that all "normal" individuals reach the stage of formal operational thought by age twenty:

> However, they reach this stage in different areas according to their aptitudes and their professional specializations (advanced studies or different types of apprenticeship for the various trades): the way in which these formal structures are used, however, is not necessarily the same in all cases.

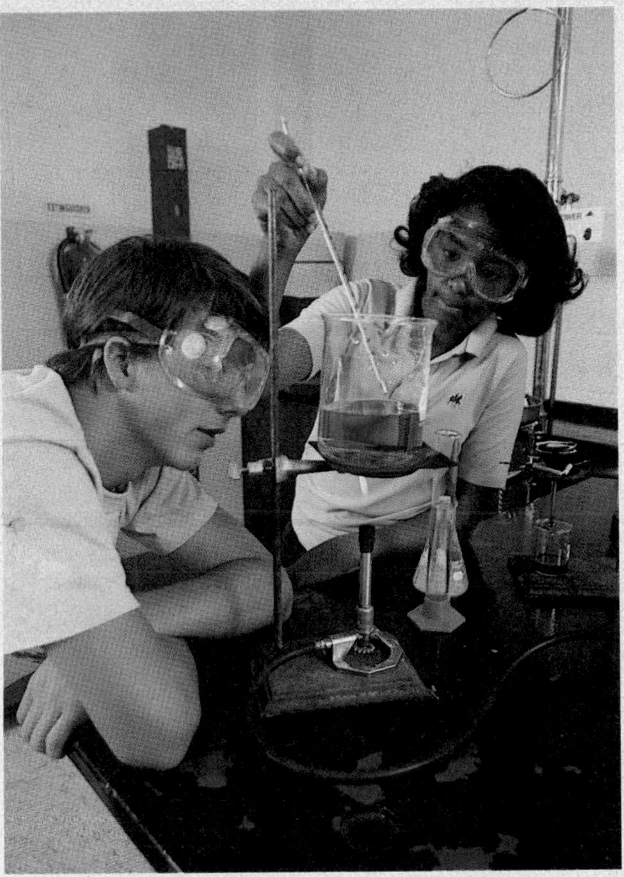

Formal Operational Thought

Formal operational thought enables individuals to generate a higher level of analytical capability, allowing them to discern new relationships among various classes of events. It closely parallels the reasoning encountered in scientific thinking.

Charles Gupton/Stock, Boston

Some investigators find themselves substantially in agreement with Piaget. They say that adolescent competence is better than would be inferred from the generally poor test performance shown even among mature adults. These researchers claim that much of the earlier work on formal operations overestimated the age of the stage's onset and underestimated the frequency of its occurrence (Danner and Day, 1977; Stone and Day, 1978). There are also those who speculate that there exists a higher or postformal operational stage characterized by even more powerful and complex thought processes than exist in formal operational thought—a type of cognition found in high-level and abstract mathematical and scientific thinking (Commons, Richards, and Kuhn, 1982; Kramer, 1983).

Adolescent Egocentricity

Every one believes in his youth that the world really began with him, and that all merely exists for his sake.

—GOETHE
December 6, 1829

Piaget (1967) said that adolescence produces its own characteristic form of egocentrism, a view expanded by the psychologist David Elkind (1967, 1968*b*). As adolescents gain the ability to conceptualize their own thought, they also achieve the capacity to conceptualize the thought of others. But adolescents do not always make a clear distinction between the two.

In turning their new powers of thought introspectively upon themselves, adolescents simultaneously assume that their thoughts and actions are equally interesting to others. They conclude that other people are as admiring or critical of them as they are themselves. They tend to view the world as a stage on which they are the principal actors and all the world is the audience. According to Elkind (1968*a*: 153), this accounts for the fact that teenagers tend to be extremely self-conscious:

> The [preoperational] child is egocentric in the sense that he is unable to take another person's point of view. The adolescent, on the other hand, takes the other person's point of view to an extreme degree.

As a result adolescents tend to view themselves as somehow unique and even heroic—as destined for unusual fame and fortune. Elkind dubs this romantic imagery the *personal fable*.

Elkind (1967: 103) observes:

> A good deal of adolescent boorishness, loudness, and faddish dress is probably provoked, partially in any case, by a failure to differentiate between what the young person believes to be attractive and what others admire. It is for this reason that the young person frequently fails to understand why adults disapprove of the way he dresses and behaves. The same sort of egocentrism is often seen in behavior directed toward the opposite sex. The boy who stands in front of the mirror for 2 hours combing his hair is probably imagining the swooning reactions he will produce in the girls. Likewise, the girl applying her makeup is more likely than not imagining the admiring glances that will come her way. When these young people actually meet, each is more concerned with being the observed than with being the observer.

Elkind (1968*b*: 153) suggests that adolescent egocentrism helps explain the importance of the peer group to the teenager:

> The adolescent is so concerned with the reactions of others toward him, particularly his peers, that he is willing to do many things which are opposed to all of his

Adolescent Egocentricity
Adolescents tend to be self-conscious and preoccupied with the impression that they are projecting of themselves. Grooming is exceedingly important to them, since teenagers commonly take the other person's point of view to an extreme degree and believe that others are constantly admiring or criticizing them.
Larry Nicholson/Photo Researchers

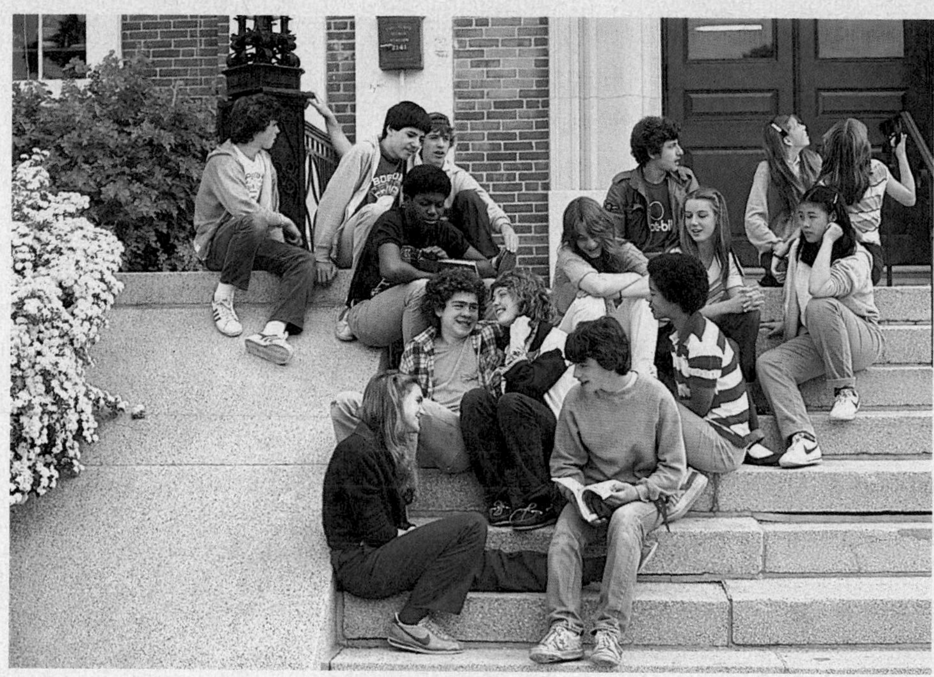

Importance of the Peer Group According to psychologist David Elkind, adolescent egocentricity may help to explain the importance of the peer group to the teenager. Because the teenager is so concerned with others' reactions, he or she may blindly conform to others' behaviors.

Peter Vandermark/Stock, Boston

previous training and to his own best interests. At the same time, this egocentric impression that he is always on stage may help to account for the many and varied adolescent attention-getting maneuvers.

By fifteen to sixteen years of age, this extreme egocentrism gradually declines, as the adolescent comes to realize that other people are primarily concerned with themselves and their own problems.

Other psychologists, such as Robert Selman (1980), also find that young adolescents become aware of their own self-awareness. They recognize that they can consciously monitor their own mental experience and control and manipulate their thought processes. However, only later in adolescence do they come to realize that some mental experiences that influence their actions are not accessible to conscious inspection. In brief, they become capable of distinguishing between conscious and nonconscious levels of experience. Hence, although they retain a conception of themselves as self-aware beings, they realize that their ability to control their own thoughts and emotions has limits. In so doing they gain a more sophisticated notion of their mental self and what constitutes self-awareness (Broughton, 1978; Damon and Hart, 1982).

The Adolescent as a Moral Philosopher

> *The fundamental idea of good is thus, that it consists in preserving life, in favoring it, in wanting to bring it to its highest value, and evil consists in destroying life, doing it injury, hindering its development.*
>
> —ALBERT SCHWEITZER
> *June 13, 1953*

At no other period in life are people as likely to be as concerned with moral values and principles as they are during adolescence. A recurrent theme of American literature from *Huckleberry Finn* to *Catcher in the Rye* has been the innocent child who is brought at adolescence to a new awareness of adult reality, and who concludes that the adult world is hypocritical, corrupt, and decadent (Kohlberg and Gilligan, 1971). Adolescent idealism, coupled with adolescent egocentricity, frequently breeds "egocentric reformers." These are adolescents who assume that it is their solemn duty to reform their parents and the world in keeping with their own highly personalized standards (Hurlock, 1968).

As discussed in Chapter 11, Kohlberg and his col-

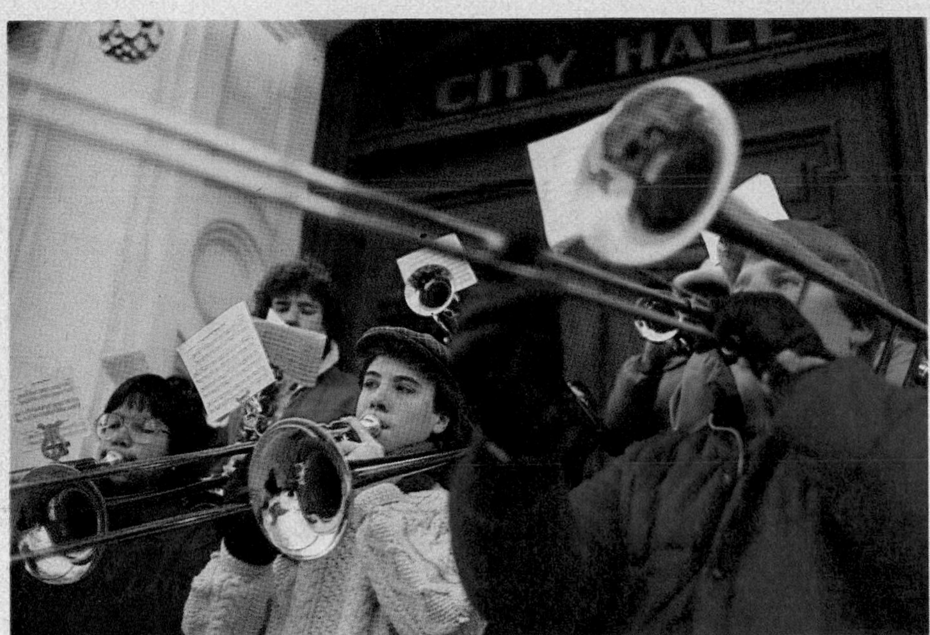

Conventional Morality

People in Kohlberg's stage of conventional morality view the rules and expectations of their family, group, or nation as valuable in their own right. These teenagers playing Christmas songs are probably in that stage.

Ellis Herwig/The Picture Cube

leagues have found that in the course of moral development people tend to pass through an orderly sequence of six stages. These six stages of moral thought are divided into three major levels: the *preconventional,* the *conventional,* and the *postconventional.* Preconventional children are responsive to cultural labels of good and bad out of consideration for the kinds of consequences of their behavior—punishment, reward, or the exchange of favors. Persons at the conventional level view the rules and expectations of their family, group, or nation as valuable in their own right. Such people hold rather simplistic, absolutist conceptions of what is right and true. Individuals who pass to the postconventional level (and most people do not) come to define morality in terms of self-chosen principles that they view as having universal ethical validity and application (see Figure 13.5).

The impetus for moral development results from increasing cognitive sophistication of the sort described by Piaget. Consequently, postconventional morality becomes possible only with the onset of adolescence and the development of formal operational thought—the ability to think in logical and abstract terms. Thus postconventional morality depends primarily on changes in the structure of thought, rather than on an increase in the individual's knowledge of cultural values. In other words, Kohlberg's stages tell us *how* an individual thinks, not *what* he or she thinks about given matters.

Kohlberg and his colleagues (Kramer, 1968) have come across some cases in which young people seemingly "retrogress" in moral development, especially after entering college. From a mixture of conventional (stage 4) and social contract (stage 5) thought at the end of high school, they appear to return to a stage 2 orientation, one distinguished by an extreme relativistic and instrumental outlook. (Refer to Table 11.1, which summarizes the characteristics of these and other stages.) Such individuals often deny the existence of any universal or divinely inspired set of moral values or principles. Accordingly they argue that it cannot be said that one outlook is morally superior to another. One "retrogressor" observes (Kohlberg and Gilligan, 1971: 1074):

> I don't think anybody should be swayed by the dictates of society. It's probably very much up to the individual all the time and there's no general principle except when the views of society seem to conflict with your views and your opportunities at the moment and it seems that the views of society don't really have any basis as being right and in that case, most people, I think, would tend to say forget it and I'll do what I want.

However, retrogressors generally return to a stage 5 morality by age twenty-five.

Elliot Turiel (1969, 1974, 1978) comes to a somewhat different conclusion about the moral relativism expressed by some young people during late adolescence and early adulthood. While Turiel also finds

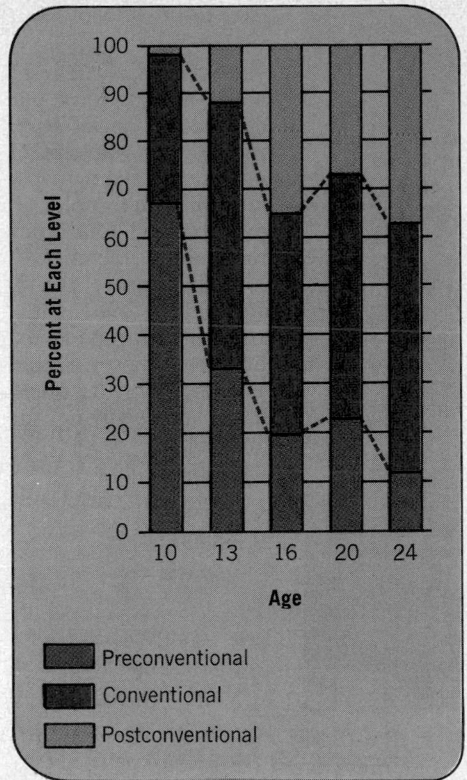

Figure 13.5 Age and Level of Moral Development

The subjects in this study were urban middle-class male Americans. All percentages are approximate and are extrapolated from charts in the references cited below. The sizes of the samples studied are not stated in the originals.

SOURCES: Lawrence Kohlberg and Carol Gilligan, "The Adolescent as a Philosopher: The Discovery of the Self in a Postconventional World," *Daedalus*, Vol. 100 (1971), pp. 1051–1086; Lawrence Kohlberg, "Continuities in Childhood and Adult Moral Development Revisited," in L. Kohlberg (ed.), *Collected Papers on Moral Development and Moral Education*. Mimeographed.

that some of his subjects deny the validity of moral judgments, he notes that they simultaneously make moral statements regarding war, civil rights, and other issues.

Turiel takes this as clear evidence that these young people do not genuinely regress to a stage 2 type of morality. Rather, freed from their previously unquestioned, simplistic, and absolutist conventional thinking, they begin to consider an infinite number of possible alternatives. One set of beliefs appears no more inherently truthful to them than another. Yet they do not "opt out," since they view themselves as holding moral beliefs on particular issues.

Turiel concludes that the retrogressors are passing through a transitional phase between stage 4 and stage 5 morality. As they shift from one moral stage to another, the moral structure or outlook that characterized their thinking in the earlier period breaks apart or is otherwise "de-formed," since it needs to be integrated into a new moral structure or outlook. The process is one of rejecting the logic of an existing stage and fashioning a new stage. In sum, Turiel views changes in moral reasoning as the result of disequilibrium and the need to construct a new equilibrium.

Development of Political Thinking

If I do not acquire ideals when young, when will I? Not when I am old.

—MAIMONIDES
(A Twelfth-Century Jewish Scholar)

The development of political thinking, like the development of moral values and judgments, depends to a considerable extent on an individual's level of cognitive development (Abraham, 1983). The psychologist Joseph Adelson (1972, 1975, 1980) and his colleagues have interviewed large numbers of adolescents between eleven and eighteen years of age. Their aim has been to discover how adolescents of different ages and circumstances think about political matters and organize their political philosophies.

Adelson (1972: 107) presents adolescents with the following premise:

> Imagine that a thousand people venture to an island in the Pacific to form a new society; once there they must compose a political order, devise a legal system, and in general confront the myriad problems of government.

Each subject is then asked a large number of hypothetical questions dealing with justice, crime, the citizen's rights and obligations, the functions of government, and so on.

Adelson (1975: 64–65) summarizes his findings as follows:

> The earliest lesson we learned in our work, and the one we have relearned since, is that neither sex, nor race, nor level of intelligence, nor social class, nor national origin is as potent a factor in determining the course of political thought in adolescence as is the youngster's sheer maturation. From the end of grade school to the end of high school, we witness some truly extraordinary changes in how the child organizes his thinking about society and government.

Adelson finds that the most important change in

and self-expression ("do your own thing") orientation (Langman, 1971). Research has demonstrated the continuing impact of the 1960s on the "involved generation's" political attitudes and life-styles (Bengtson and Starr, 1975; Nassi and Abramowitz, 1979). Even so, individuals' political attitudes and other orientations do not necessarily crystallize in the preadult years, or even in early adulthood, but remain potentially open to change throughout life (Holsti and Rosenau, 1980; Jennings and Niemi, 1981).

Since 1970, young people in the United States have shifted away from the more radical political mood of the 1960s. But although radical political activism is gone, the new life-styles have remained. In some respects young people have pressed forward in their search for a cultural revolution while taking a step backward from political revolution. Compared with college classes in the 1960s, contemporary students desire more sexual freedom and privacy and put more emphasis on careers (Yankelovich, 1974*b*; Hoge, 1976; Hyatt, 1979).

Although some sociologists like Mannheim have sought explanations for generational differences in the differing historical circumstances to which differing cohorts of youth are exposed, others have advanced another explanation (Johnson, 1984). They find that adolescents tend to reject the conventional wisdom of their instructors when they perceive it as constituting a monolithic orthodoxy. It matters little whether the orthodoxy is radical or conservative, idealistic or materialistic. According to this view, a principal reason that contemporary college students have turned to self-advancement is that they are reacting against the left-wing idealism of their professors, many of whom participated in the social movements of the 1960s and early 1970s. Thus whereas youth of the 1930s responded to the Great Depression by moving to the political left and embracing idealism, contemporary youth reacted to the recession of the early 1980s by moving to the political right and embracing materialism. Each generation, then, rejected the dominant orthodoxy of the previous generation. Yet, as will be noted in the next chapter, it is easy to overemphasize the differences between generations.

SUMMARY

1. During adolescence young people experience a very rapid increase in height and weight, which is referred to as the *adolescent growth spurt.* The spurt typically occurs in girls two years earlier than in boys.
2. Adolescence is also characterized by the development of the reproductive system. The complete transition to reproductive maturity takes place over several years and is accompanied by extensive physical changes.
3. Children of the same chronological age show enormous variations in growth and sexual maturation. Whether they mature early or late has important consequences for them in their relationships with both adults and peers. Because of different rates of maturation, some adolescents have an advantage in height, strength, physical attractiveness, and athletic prowess.
4. Any difference from the peer group in growth and development tends to be a difficult experience for the adolescent. This is especially true when it places the individual at a physical disadvantage or in a position of unfavorable contrast to peers.
5. According to Erik Erikson, the main task of adolescence is to build and confirm a reasonably stable identity. He says that the adolescent, like a trapeze artist, must release his or her safe hold on childhood and reach in midair for a firm grasp on adulthood.
6. Some developmental psychologists believe that human development is less continuous and more erratic than Erikson believes. They maintain that much behavior appears to be a function of random events and situational demands rather than a complex of solidified personality dimensions carried over from earlier periods.
7. Erikson's view of adolescence is in keeping with a long psychological tradition that has portrayed it as a difficult and turbulent period. According to this perspective, adolescence is characterized by inevitable turmoil, maladjustment, tensions, rebellion, dependency conflicts, and exaggerated peer-group conformity.
8. In recent years researchers have increasingly come to the conclusion that adolescence in the United States is not the period of "storm and stress" that earlier psychologists and sociologists held it to be. Many young people of Western nations undergo changes in self-image and

self-concept during adolescence. But these changes need not be a source of turmoil.

9. Jean Piaget called adolescence the period of formal operations. Its hallmarks are logical and abstract reasoning. Neither all adolescents nor all adults, however, attain the stage or acquire its associated abilities for logical and abstract thought.
10. Adolescence produces its own form of egocentrism. In turning their new powers of thought introspectively upon themselves, adolescents assume that their thoughts and actions are equally interesting to others.
11. At no other period of life are individuals as likely to be concerned with moral values and principles as they are during adolescence. Some, but not all, adolescents attain Kohlberg's postconventional level of morality. In the process, a number of young people go through a transitional phase of moral relativism.
12. During adolescence, young people undergo major changes in the way they organize their thinking about society and government. Maturation appears to be the most potent source of these changes. As children move through adolescence their political thinking becomes more abstract, less static, and less authoritarian.
13. As a consequence of the unique events and circumstances of the era in which they enter adolescence, each generation tends to fashion a somewhat unique style of thought and life. At particular junctures in history, an emerging youth cohort may develop an unusually sharp consciousness of itself as a distinct group with a distinctive ideology.

KEY TERMS

adolescent growth spurt A period that begins at about age twelve in girls and fourteen in boys when they undergo a very rapid increase in height and weight.

asynchrony A dissimilarity in the growth rates of different body parts.

deviant identity A life-style that is at odds with, or at least not supported by, the values and expectations of the larger society.

generation A historically conscious group of individuals who come of age at a certain point in time and experience in common certain decisive economic, social, political, or military events.

identity The answers given by an individual to the questions Who am I? and Who am I to be? Identity is a person's sense of placement within the world—the meaning that one attaches to oneself in the broader context of life.

identity diffusion A lack of ability to commit oneself, even in late adolescence, to an occupational or ideological position and to assume a recognizable station in life.

ideology A set of shared definitions that offer interpretations and solutions to what is felt to be an unsatisfactory social condition.

menarche The first menstrual period.

negative identity A debased self-image and social role.

period of formal operations In Piaget's theory, the fourth and highest state in the development of cognition or intelligence from infancy to adulthood. During this period individuals gain the ability to think about their own thinking and to imagine many possibilities inherent in a situation.

puberty The period of the life cycle during which sexual and reproductive maturation takes place.

puberty rites An initiation ceremony that socially symbolizes the transition from childhood to adulthood.

role confusion A state characterized by bewilderment about who one is, where one belongs, and where one is going.

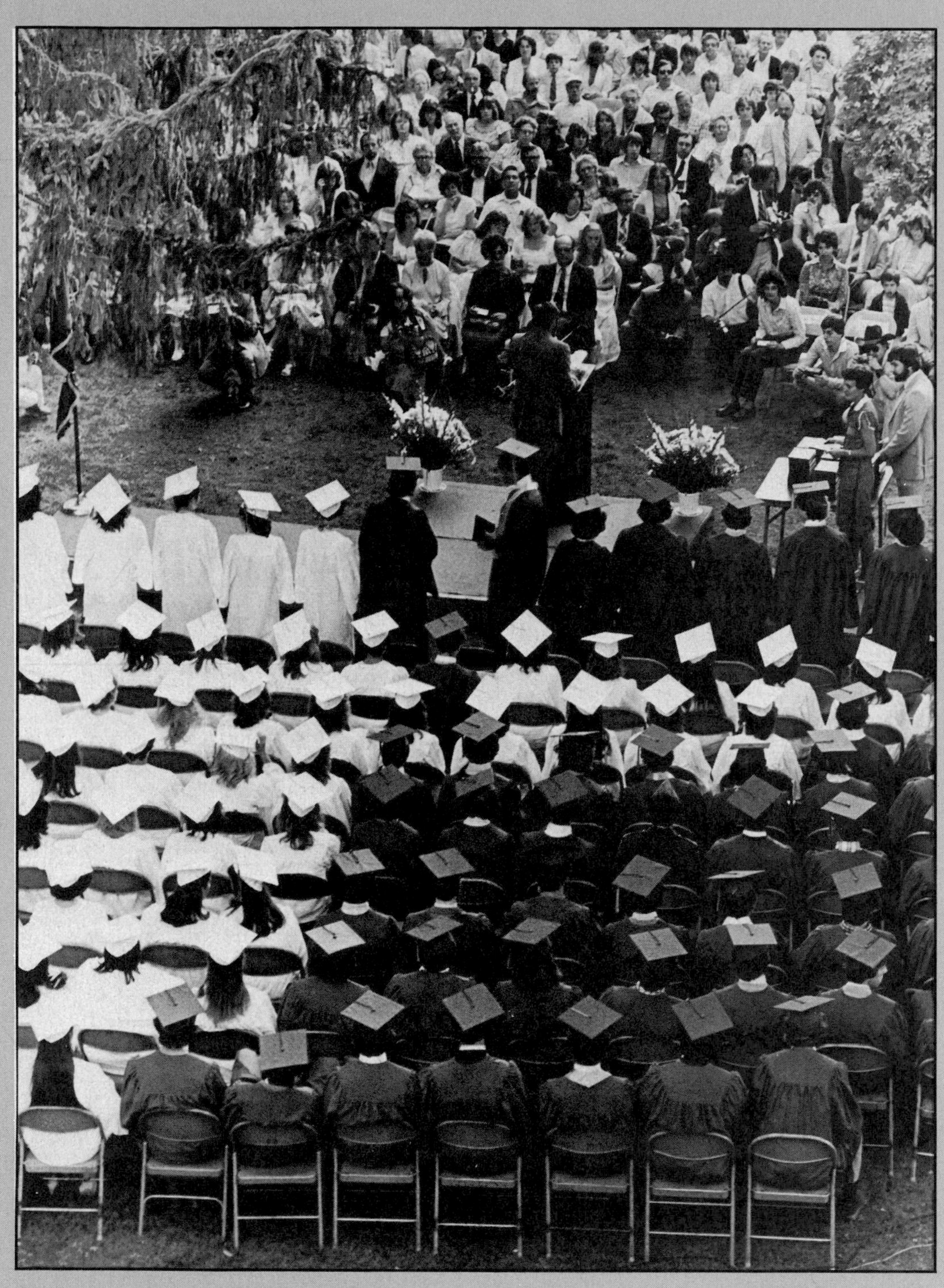

14

Adolescence: Threshold of Adulthood

In the United States the social boundaries of adolescence are rather ill defined. By tradition, the shift from elementary to junior high school signaled entry into adolescence. But with the advent of the middle school the transition became blurred. Nor is it entirely clear when a person leaves adolescence. Roughly speaking, adolescence is regarded as having ended when the individual assumes one or more adult roles, such as marriage, parenthood, full-time employment, or financial independence.

Many Western industrialized nations have put off entrance into adulthood for economic, educational, and other reasons. Today college postpones full adult status for many socially and economically advantaged young people. Unemployment and underemployment produce a somewhat similar effect among less advantaged groups. At the same time, children are reaching puberty earlier than children did a century ago (see Chapters 6 and 13). Thus physically mature people are told that they must wait ten and in some cases twenty years before they can assume the full rights and obligations of adulthood. Many young people are thereby placed in a kind of social no-man's-land.

The extension of adolescence and youth has posed two related problems for society and for young people (Elder, 1975). Society has the problem of providing the young with a bridge to adult roles through ap-

ceived less social recognition, and tended to come from lower-socioeconomic-class families.

Burlingame concludes that the youth culture can function as a useful growth medium, promoting independence and maturity. But for young people who are characterized by less academic achievement, social contact, or economic means, he says that excessive adherence to the youth culture may hinder personal growth. Their total commitment to it may supply them with a social anchorage and identification that makes up for their feelings of inner doubt and inadequacy. Yet as a result of overconformity to the youth culture, a disadvantaged adolescent may fail to evolve a solidly grounded, independent identity.

Caution in Applying the Concept of Youth Culture. Although many young people share certain standardized ways of thinking, feeling, and acting that differentiate them from other age groups, these differences should not be overestimated or exaggerated. Some psychologists and sociologists believe that the term "culture" in the expression "youth culture" clouds our understanding of adolescence. It implies that there is a larger gap or break between generations that in fact exists. Indeed, rather than being impressed by the differences between young people and adults in values and attitudes, some researchers have been struck by the similarities they find between the two groups (Elkin and Westley, 1955; Hill and Aldous, 1969).

Among these researchers are Daniel Offer and Judith Baskin Offer (1975:187–188, 190), who made a longitudinal study of a sample of sixty-one middle-class adolescent boys over ten years:

> We have not seen convincing data from our work or that of others to indicate the existence of a different system of [social] norms governing adolescent life. . . . Continuity of values can be seen both between individual parents and their sons and between the parent generation and the adolescent and young adult generation. Peer group values do have an influence on behavior, but most often the influence can be negated by the stronger inculcated parental values. This conflict, however, seems to be minimal as peer group values themselves are likely to be extensions of parental values. Youth peer groups are not homogeneous; rather, there are differences between them outweighing observable similarities. In most instances, the teenager or young adult will feel more comfortable within the peer grouping that adopts values similar to his own. Further, the values of the peer group as a whole are reflective of the culture as a whole.

Clearly, we must be careful in applying the concept of youth culture to young people lest we imply that an all-encompassing, monolithic membership group exists for all adolescents. To do so would be to overlook the considerable differences among them in socioeconomic class, race, ethnicity, age, and rural or urban background (Sebald, 1977). Further, every high school tends to have several "crowds" (see the boxed insert on pages 384–385), which are often mutually exclusive and even antagonistic to one another (Kerckhoff, 1972). Such distinctions as "brains," "hoodies," "freaks," "jocks," "goodies," "swingers," "burn-outs," and so on are commonly encountered in the nation's high schools. In sum, our search for similarities among young people should not lead us to overlook the differences that also exist among them.

Adolescents and Their Families

> *When I was sixteen, I thought my father was a damn fool. When I became twenty-one, I was amazed to find how much he had learned in five years.*
>
> —MARK TWAIN

As we noted earlier in the chapter, the media have made a good deal out of generational differences between young people and their parents. However, the notion of the generation gap vastly oversimplifies the relationship between young people and adults. It implies that attachment to one group precludes attachment to the other. Further, it assumes that the discontinuity between generations is total and pervades every area of an individual's life. Neither of these premises is supported by research (Kandel, 1974, 1978; Troll and Bengtson, 1982).

A recent youth poll sponsored by the National Association of Secondary School Principals (Cromer, 1984) found that three-fourths of the nation's young people (grades 7-12) reported having no serious family problems and feeling free to discuss their concerns with a parent. Ten years earlier, only half of the youth had felt that way and more than 40 percent had said they would be happier living away from home. In 1983, 80 percent of the students agreed with their parents on the topics of drugs, education, and work, and 60 percent agreed on the topic of sex. Said Janis Cromer, an educational analyst who authored the report, "If there was a generation gap in the 60's, it narrowed to a crack in the 1970's and it's a hairline fracture in the 1980's."

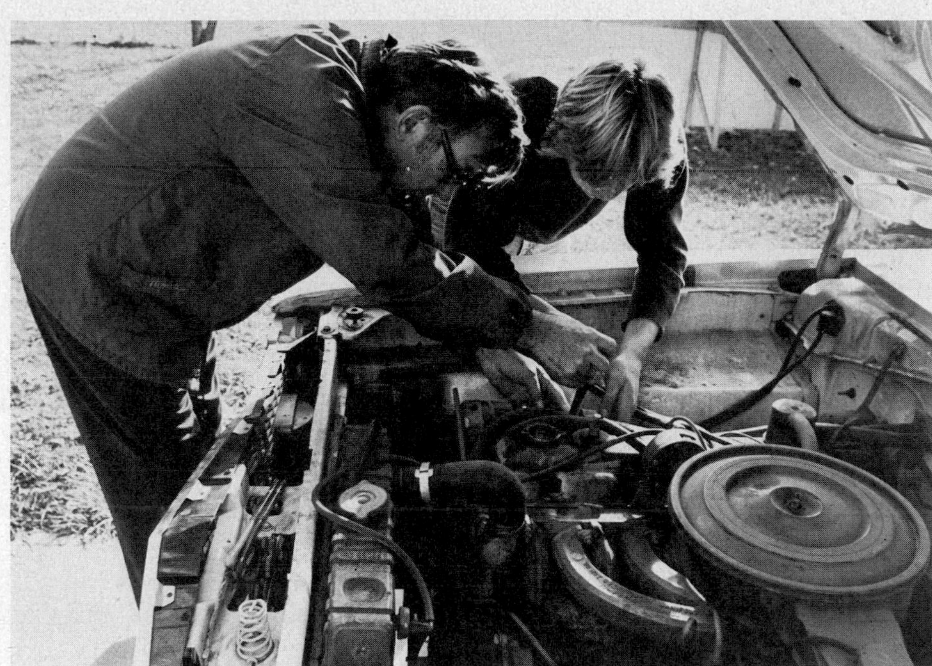

Generation Gap?
Many of the values and interests of teenagers are learned from and shared with their parents.
Patrick Reddy

Influence in Different Realms of Behavior. Both the family and the peer group are anchors in the lives of most teenagers. However, the relative influence of the two groups varies with the issue involved. No behavior comes under the exclusive dominance of a particular generation, either peers or parents. When the issues involve immediate gratifications, such as marijuana use, smoking, drinking, and academic cheating, or peripheral matters, such as musical tastes, personal adornment, and entertainment idols, the peer group tends to have greater influence than when the issues involve future life goals, fundamental behavioral codes, and core values (Kandel, 1974; Davies and Kandel, 1981; Krosnick and Judd, 1982). Even the college activists of the 1960s and early 1970s were not rebelling against parental values so much as carrying these values to their logical conclusion in political expression (Bengtson, 1970; Braungart, 1975; Braungart and Braungart, 1979).

In many respects there is little in adolescent beliefs and values that fundamentally differs from the beliefs and values of the adult world. A great many of the values and interests of adolescents seem to be derived from and shared by a majority of their parents. Indeed, a substantial proportion of young people see no reason to differentiate between the value system of their parents and that of their friends (Troll and Bengtson, 1982). Thus there is little foundation for the "hydraulic" view, which holds that the greater the influence of the one group, the less the influence of the other.

Further, it is easy to overestimate the socializing influence that occurs among peer-group members. Much of the similarity found in the attitudes and behaviors of friends is the result of people purposely selecting as friends individuals who are already compatible with them. Not surprisingly, therefore, adolescents who share similar political orientations, values, and levels of educational aspiration are more likely to associate with one another and then to influence one another as a result of continued association (Kandel, 1978; Cohen, 1983).

Afford Different Kinds of Experience. Parents and peers provide adolescents with different kinds of experience (Montemayor, 1982). Time with parents centers around household activities like eating, shopping, performing chores, and viewing television. Peer time is spent "hanging out," playing games, joking, and conversing. The intimacy of peer relationships increases dramatically between middle childhood and adolescence (Berndt, 1982). Overall, parent-child and peer relations fulfill fundamentally different functions for young people (Hunter and Youniss, 1982).

Teenagers report that they look to interaction with

THE STRUCTURE OF ADOLESCENT PEER GROUPS

Dexter C. Dunphy (1963), a social psychologist, has spent many hours at street corners, hangouts, homes, and beach parties observing and interviewing teenagers. His careful and painstaking field study reveals that peer relationships tend to fall into three categories: the "crowd," the "clique," and individual friendships.

Dunphy found that a crowd consisted of fifteen to thirty members. A clique, in contrast, was a smaller group ranging from three to nine members. Several cliques would coalesce to form a crowd. As a consequence, an individual could be a clique member without being a crowd member. But the reverse was not possible—an individual could not be a crowd member without being a member of a clique.

Cliques and crowds performed quite different functions. The main activity of cliques was visiting and talking. The crowd, in contrast, was the center of larger and more organized social activities, such as parties and dances, which provided for interaction between the sexes.

Although adolescents generally claimed that their groups lacked leaders, in point of fact one person was implicitly recognized as the leader. Indeed, cliques were commonly referred to by the name of one person, for instance, "John Palmer's group." Generally the clique leader was the member who dated most often, who was most likely to be going steady, and who had achieved a heterosexual role earlier than had other group members.

Dunphy found that adolescent group development often passed through a series of five stages:

- *Stage 1: The precrowd stage.* As was characteristic of friendship patterns during the preadolescent period, adolescent cliques were composed of individuals of the same sex.
- *Stage 2: The beginning of the crowd.* Cliques of the same sex began participating with cliques of the opposite sex in heterosexual interaction. Such mingling was made less hazardous through a safety-in-numbers approach.
- *Stage 3: The crowd in structural transition.* High-status members of same-sex cliques initiated heterosexual individual-to-individual interaction. These contacts resulted in the first dating experiences, which marked the advent of the heterosexual clique. However, adolescents who belonged to these emergent heterosexual cliques retained membership in their same-sex cliques, so that they were members of two intersecting groups.
- *Stage 4: The fully developed crowd.* The transformation of group structure was completed as lower-status members of the same-sex cliques became involved in heterosexual cliques. Consequently, the same-sex cliques were reconstructed as groups consisting of both sexes.

friends to produce "good times" (Larson, 1983). They characterize these positive times as containing an element of "rowdiness": they act "crazy," "out of control," "loud," and even "obnoxious"—deviant behavior that they describe as "fun." Such activities provide a spirited, contagious mood, a group state in which they feel free to do virtually anything. In contrast, interactions within the family typically afford less opportunity for this kind of fluid, convivial interchange. Family interaction more closely parallels the goals of socialization dictated by the larger community. The functional constraints provided by the family and the excitement by friends both have their part to play in development. The boxed insert on pages 386–387 examines adolescent decision making.

Girls tend to find that their peer relationships with members of either sex afford them strong, rewarding friendships (Wright and Keple, 1981). And they typically view their mothers as offering them more interpersonal rewards than their fathers do (except in those cases where they frequently argue with their mothers). Boys report few differences in the interpersonal rewards that they receive from their parents and peers. Even so, boys tend to regard their relationships with female friends as more rewarding to them than those with male friends.

Shift in the Family Power Equation. Between childhood and adolescence, sons tend to acquire power at the expense of their mothers, while the father-son relationship remains relatively unchanged (Steinberg, 1981). During early adolescence, males

Adolescent Peer Groups

In the process of "hanging-out" with one another, adolescents form clique relationships. Oftentimes cliques of the same sex begin participating with cliques of the opposite sex in heterosexual interaction.

Alan Carey/The Image Works

- *Stage 5: Beginning of crowd disintegration.* In late adolescence the crowd began to disintegrate, as cliques were formed that consisted of couples who were engaged or going together.

In this manner the structural transformation of adolescent peer groups served to facilitate the transition of their members from childhood groups to the wider adult society.

become more assertive in their dealings with their parents, particularly with their mothers. Only during the later stages of puberty does the conflict subside. This largely results from the mother's having backed off. Hence an important shift seems to occur in the two-parent family's interaction patterns. Prior to a son's puberty, parents have about equal influence over family decisions, and the son occupies a subordinate position. But by late puberty, the adolescent enjoys a position in the influence hierarchy above that of the mother and below that of the father.

In sum, for the most part the majority of young people and their parents do not find the generation gap to be the problem that the mass media and various social critics and clinical observers would have us think it to be (Troll and Bengtson, 1982).

DATING, LOVE, AND SEXUALITY

One of the most difficult adjustments, and perhaps the most critical, that adolescents must make revolves about their developing sexuality. Approaching biological maturity as well as social pressures require that adolescents come to terms with their awakening sexual impulses. Consequently, sexual attraction and sexual considerations become dominant forces in their lives. Indeed, first sexual intercourse is a developmental milestone of major personal and social significance (Jessor et al., 1983). It is often viewed as a declaration of independence from parents, an affirmation of sexual identity, and a statement of capacity

ADOLESCENT DECISION MAKING

Life dictates that we all engage in decision making, and adolescence affords no moratorium on this rule. Most of the decisions that adolescents must make revolve about their daily routines, including choice of clothing, school activities, household chores, and peer relationships. For the most part, teenagers do not have to make decisions concerning career selection, marriage, or politics on a regular day-to-day basis. Yet it is many of

Adolescent Decision Making
As they enter adolescence, youth are required to make a growing number of decisions concerning the direction that their lives will take. When they leave home to take jobs or enter college, they find that they have to assume a good deal more responsibility for themselves and for the consequences of their decisions.
Peter Southwick/Stock, Boston

for interpersonal intimacy (Jessor and Jessor, 1975).

Youth vary a good deal in the age at which they first experience intercourse. Young people who remain virgins longer than their peers are more likely to value academic achievement, enjoy close ties with their parents, report stricter moral standards, and exhibit more conventional behavior with respect to alcohol and drug use. However, virgins are decidedly not "maladjusted," socially marginal, or otherwise unsuccessful. They report no less satisfaction and no more stress than do nonvirgins, and they typically achieve greater educational success than nonvirgins (Jessor et al., 1983).

Dating

In the United States, dating has been the principal vehicle for fostering and developing heterosexual relations. Over the past fifteen years, however, dating has undergone rapid change. Traditionally, dating began with a young man inviting a young woman for an evening's public entertainment at his expense. The first invitation was often given during a nervous conversation on the telephone several days or even weeks in advance. Ideally, the man would call for the woman at the appointed hour in a car and return her by car.

these latter decisions that most trouble adolescents. They worry that the decisions they do make may be irrevocable, failing to appreciate that much decision making across the life span entails continuous rethinking and the changing of one's mind (McCandless and Coop, 1979). Moreover, a rather substantial number of decisions are profoundly affected by situational factors and random events. For instance, students may have to abandon or postpone their plans for attending college by virtue of a turndown in the economy, illness, accidents, or pregnancy.

Decision making is a difficult skill to learn and it takes time to master. Not surprisingly, adolescents experience considerable ambivalence regarding planning and decisions. Although they commonly desire increasing amounts of freedom to make decisions and to be independent, they are often reluctant to abandon the security of their families. Further, they often lack the experience, perspective, and information needed to make wise decisions. Even so, adolescents must confront the issues of freedom and control as part of the price they pay for living in modern societies that afford so many options and alternatives (Schvaneveldt and Adams, 1983).

Researchers have concerned themselves with the effect that parental decision-making patterns have on adolescents. The General Mills (1981) study of American families found that of the sampled teenagers, 85 percent reported that their mothers made the daily decisions having to do with meals, family activities, and household chores. With respect to child rearing, 55 percent thought that their mothers made most of the decisions, whereas 29 percent said that both parents were involved. Boys saw their fathers as more likely to make the decisions related to finance, whereas girls thought their mothers were more likely to make them.

In Chapter 10 we discussed various parenting styles. Glen H. Elder (1963, 1968) has assessed authoritarian families, in which parents allow youth little expression; democratic families, in which parents invite the adolescent to participate in family decision-making processes; and permissive families, in which the adolescent is relatively free of parental constraints in arriving at his or her own decisions. His research suggests that adolescents reared by democratic parents reveal the greatest autonomy. Other investigators also conclude that adolescents do not fare as well when their parents are either excessively controlling or excessively permissive (Baumrind, 1968; Bowerman and Bahr, 1973).

The development of adult-level competency in decision making is not a straight-line, upward process. It is a stop-and-go, up-and-down journey interspersed with plateaus and spurts of rapid change. Further, skill in decision making neither begins nor ends with adolescence. And psychological and social forces associated with age, sex, social class, religion, temperament, and family life-style all play a part. Parents and teachers can help adolescents acquire an openness to experiences and ideas that will help them maximize their refinement of the necessary techniques (Schvaneveldt and Adams, 1983).

Although the traditional pattern has not been entirely replaced, new patterns of dating were swept in on the wave of the various youth movements of the late 1960s and early 1970s. The term "dating" itself has become in many ways too stiff and formal to describe the "just hanging out" and "getting together" that take place among contemporary youth (Knox, 1980). A more relaxed style has come to govern the interaction between the sexes, including informal get-togethers, group activities like "keggers," and spur-of-the-moment mutual decisions to go out for a pizza. Even so, by the 1980s there was some indication of a return to dating, but the term had been broadened to encompass both formal and casual arrangements. In some cases, the two separate streams had come to coexist, the one reminiscent of the 1950s and the other characterized by a spirit of comradeship and more continuous interaction (Scanzoni and Scanzoni, 1981).

In whatever form dating occurs, it serves a variety of functions. It allows members of the opposite sex to meet and explore mutual compatibility. This occurs within a framework that permits either partner to end the relationship without losing face. It allows occasions for sexual exploration and discovery within mutually acceptable limits. It provides companionship—

a friend for informal pair activities and sympathetic problem sharing. And it is a means of status grading and achievement in which individuals who are seen with persons rated as "highly desirable" may raise their status and prestige within the peer group (Skipper and Nass, 1966).

Love

> *Americans, who make more of marrying for love than any other people, also break up more of their marriages . . . but the figure reflects not so much failure of love as the determination of people not to live without it.*
>
> —MORTON HUNT
> *The National History of Love, 1967*

In the United States, everyone is expected to fall in love eventually. Pulp literature, women's magazines, "brides only" and traditional "male" publications, movies, television, and popular music reverberate with themes of romantic ecstasy. In sharp contrast to the American arrangement, consider these words of the elders of an African tribe (Gluckman, 1955: 76). They were complaining to the 1883 Commission on Native Law and Custom about the problems of "runaway" marriages and illegitimacy: "It is all this thing called love. We do not understand it at all. This thing called love has been introduced." The elders viewed romantic love as a disruptive force. In their culture, marriage did not necessarily involve a feeling of attraction for the spouse-to-be; marriage was not the free choice of the couple marrying; and considerations other than love played the most important part in mate selection.

In sum, different societies view romantic love quite differently. At one extreme are societies that consider a strong love attraction as a laughable or tragic aberration. At the other are societies that define marriage without love as shameful. American society tends to insist on love; traditional Japan and China to regard it as irrelevant; ancient Greece in the period after Alexander, and ancient Rome during the Roman Empire, fell somewhere in the middle (Goode, 1959).

All of us are familiar with the concept of romantic love, yet social scientists have found it exceedingly difficult to define. If letters to "Dear Abby" and "Ann Landers" are any indication, it appears that a good many Americans—especially teenagers—are also uncertain about what love is supposed to feel like and how they can recognize the experience within themselves. Some social psychologists conclude that romantic love is simply an agitated state of physiological arousal that individuals come to *define* as love (Berscheid and Walster, 1974; Rubin, 1977). The stimuli producing the agitated state may be sexual arousal, gratitude, anxiety, guilt, loneliness, anger, confusion, or fear. What makes these diffuse physiological reactions love, they say, is that individuals *label* them as love.

Some researchers reject the notion that love and other states of physiological arousal are interchangeable except for the label we give them. For instance, Michael R. Liebowitz (1983) says that love has a unique chemical basis, perhaps associated with phenylthylamine (a compound related to the amphetamines). In romantic attraction, certain brain centers are believed to release vast amounts of the substance, setting in motion a chain of neurochemical events that resemble an amphetamine high. Liebowitz claims that love and romance are among the most powerful activators of the brain's pleasure centers. And they may also contribute to a special transcendent feeling—a sense of being beyond time, space, and one's own body—that Liebowitz says parallels descriptions of psychedelic experiences. Intense romantic attractions may trigger neurochemical reactions that produce effects much like those produced by such psychedelic drugs as LSD, mescaline, and psilocybin. Just how we come to experience such changes in brain chemistry as feelings of love remains for Liebowitz an unanswered question.

Romantic love generally refers to an awe-struck state of deep involvement with another person. The social psychologist Zick Rubin (1973) has found that persons who report that they love their boyfriends or girlfriends express a number of sentiments. From a seventy-item questionnaire given to University of Michigan students, Rubin identified three components as making up romantic love: (1) *attachment* (for example, "If I could never be with __________, I would feel miserable"), (2) *caring* (for example, "I would do almost anything for __________"), and (3) *intimacy* (for example, "I feel that I can confide in __________ about almost anything"). Rubin's work demonstrates that love, like any other attitude, can be measured.

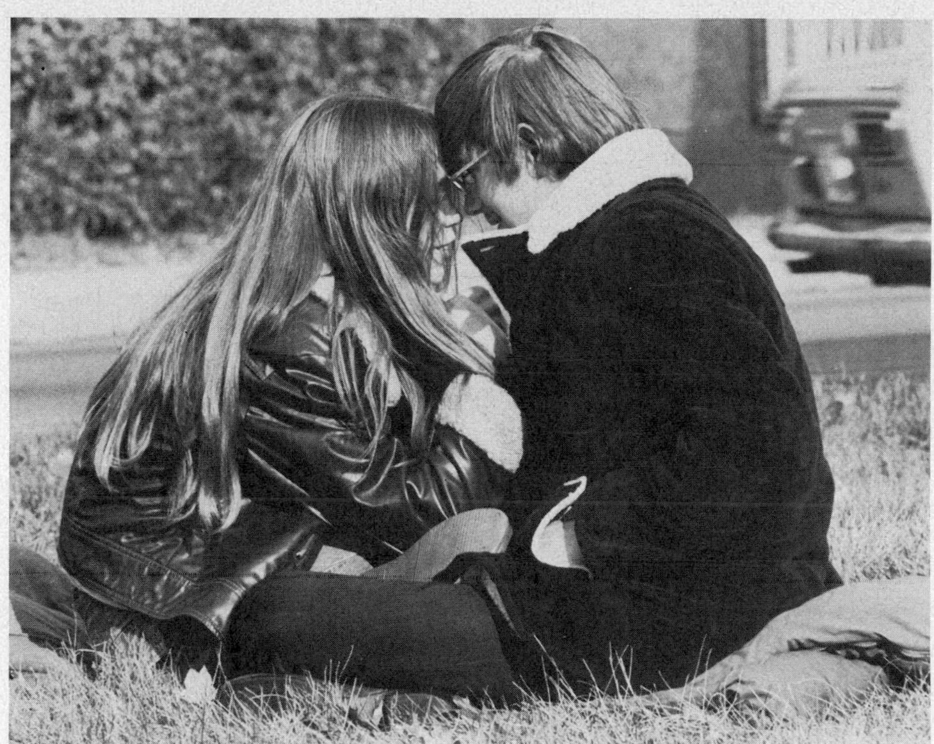

Romantic Love

Social scientists commonly view romantic love as an awe-struck state of deep involvement with another person. Central to the concept of romantic love is a state of diffuse physiological arousal.

Patrick Reddy

Sexual Attitudes and Behavior

Although we commonly equate adolescent sexuality with heterosexual intercourse, sexual expression takes a good many different forms. Further, sexuality begins early in life and merely takes on more adult forms during adolescence.

Development of Sexual Behavior. Observations of male and female infants suggest that at least some of them are capable of sexual arousal and orgasm. Although we do not know what their subjective experiences are, their behavior so closely resembles that of sexually aroused adults that authorities have little doubt that the behavior is sexual in nature. Sexual arousal is easier to detect in boys than in girls because it finds visible expression in penile erections. However, even though erections may be observed among male newborns, it appears to be reflexive in origin. Just when and how this reflexive response becomes "eroticized" is as yet poorly understood (Katchadourian and Lunde, 1977; Rosen and Hall, 1984).

Both male and female infants show interest in exploring their own bodies, initially in a random and indiscriminate fashion. Even at four months of age babies respond to genital stimulation in a manner that suggests that they are experiencing erotic pleasure. When children reach two and three years of age, they will investigate their playmates' genitals and, if permitted, those of adults as well. But by this time, strong social prohibitions come into effect, and children are socialized to restrain these behaviors.

Masturbation, erotic self-stimulation, is common among children. In many cases, children experience their first orgasm through self-stimulation. It may occur through the fondling of the penis or the manual stimulation of the clitoris or by rubbing against a bedcover, mattress, toy, or other object. Boys often learn about masturbation from other boys, whereas girls learn to masturbate primarily through accidental discovery (Kinsey et al., 1948, 1953).

A good many children also engage in some form of sex play with other children prior to adolescence. The activity is usually sporadic and typically does not culminate in orgasm. On the basis of his research in the 1940s and early 1950s, Alfred C. Kinsey and his associates (1948, 1953) found that the peak age for sex play among girls was nine, when about 7 percent engaged in heterosexual play and 9 percent in homosexual play. The peak age for boys was twelve, when 23 percent participated in heterosexual play and 30 percent in homosexual play. But Kinsey believed that his reported figures were too low and that about a fifth of all girls and the vast majority of all boys had engaged in sex play with other children before reaching puberty.

Genital exhibition, demonstration of masturbation, group masturbation, and related activities apparently are not uncommon among group-oriented preteen boys (Katchadourian and Lunde, 1977). Prepubescent homosexual play generally stops at puberty. However, even though homosexual behavior during prepuberty does not necessarily lead to adult homosexuality, adult homosexuals typically report that their homosexual orientation had already been established before they reached puberty (see Chapter 16). Usually the transition from homosexual experiences to predominantly heterosexual relationships occurs easily because many teenage boys do not regard their sexual contact with other boys as "homosexual" in the adult sense (Rosen and Hall, 1984).

Adolescent Sexual Expression. Adolescent sexuality finds expression in a number of ways, including masturbation, nocturnal orgasm, heterosexual petting, heterosexual intercourse, and homosexual activity. Teenage masturbatory behavior is often accompanied by erotic fantasy. One study of thirteen- to nineteen-year-olds found that 57 percent of the males and 46 percent of the females reported that they fantasized on most occasions while masturbating; about 20 percent of the males and 10 percent of the females rarely or never fantasized when masturbating (Sorensen, 1973). Many myths have attributed harmful effects to masturbation. However, the physiological harmlessness of the practice has now been so thoroughly documented by medical authorities that there is no need to labor the issue. But individuals may experience a good deal of guilt about the practice for a variety of social, religious, or moral reasons.

Adolescent boys commonly begin experiencing *nocturnal orgasms,* or "wet dreams," between ages thirteen and fifteen. Erotic dreams that are accompanied by orgasm and ejaculation occur most commonly among men in their teens and twenties and less frequently later in life. Women also have erotic dreams that culminate in orgasm, but apparently they are less frequent among women than among men.

Petting refers to erotic caressing that may or may not lead to orgasm. If it eventuates in sexual intercourse, petting is more accurately termed "foreplay." Although usually applied to heterosexual encounters, homosexual relations may entail similar techniques. There are few current statistics on the incidence of petting among teenagers because the practice is exceedingly prevalent and both public and scientific interest have moved beyond the issue (Katchadourian and Lunde, 1977).

Research on homosexual behavior among adolescents is relatively limited and will be discussed in Chapter 16. In contrast, heterosexual intercourse has been the focus of considerable research, a matter to which we now turn our attention.

Adolescent Heterosexual Behavior. In the past twenty years there have been substantial changes in American attitudes toward teenage sexual activity. Greater openness and permissiveness prevail today with regard to premarital sex, homosexuality, extramarital sex, and a variety of specific sexual acts. And television, movies, and magazines bombard young people and adults alike with sexual stimuli on an unprecedented scale.

Yet it is easy to overemphasize the changes that have occurred (Diepold and Young, 1979). Sociologist Ira L. Reiss (1972: 167) notes:

> One of our most prevalent myths is that in past centuries the typical form of courtship was that of two virgins meeting, falling in love, and doing little with each other sexually. They then married, learned about sex together in the marital bed, and remained faithful to each other until death separated them. I am certain that some couples did have exactly that type of experience. . . . But the key point is that I am sure it was never the common pattern for the majority of Americans. . . . We know . . . that in Massachusetts at a well-known church in the last part of the eighteenth century one in every three women who married confessed fornication to her minister. The major reason for making such a confession would be that the woman was pregnant and if she did not make that confession at her marriage, the baby could not be baptized.

Evidence also suggests that this century has witnessed *two* periods of very rapid change regarding sexual attitudes and behavior. The first period occurred around the time of World War I; the second, during the Vietnam War years.

Before 1915, approximately 75 percent of all first-time brides were virgins; by 1920 the figure had dropped to around 50 percent (Terman, 1938; Burgess and Wallin, 1953; Kinsey et al., 1953). This decrease in virginity among women could be accounted for largely in terms of the increase in the proportion of women having premarital relations with their future husbands. During the same period the proportion of men in middle-class samples who were virgins at marriage declined from about 51 percent to around 33 percent (Terman, 1938; Burgess and Wallin, 1953). However, these figures understate the incidence of male premarital sexual experience because they are derived from samples of middle-class men. Men from lower- and working-class backgrounds appear to have had a considerably higher rate of premarital experience. One study placed the figure for men with only a grade-school education at 98 percent, for those with a high-school education at 85 percent, and for those with some college education at 68 percent (Kinsey et al., 1953).

Research suggests that in the United States during the period 1920 to 1965, little overall change occurred in actual premarital sexual *behavior.* The proportion of women who had premarital sexual relations stabilized at about 50 percent and that of men at around 85 percent (Reiss, 1972, 1976). However, in the post–World War II period, *attitudes* did change, becoming more permissive (Reiss, 1976; Clayton, 1979).

Dramatic changes in sexual behavior showed up again after 1965. A growing proportion of teenagers are sexually active and are beginning their sexual activity at earlier ages. National surveys show that 49.8 percent of single female teenagers experienced intercourse in 1979 compared with 43.4 percent in 1976 and 30.4 percent in 1971. Much of the increase is attributable to white women, 46.6 percent of whom said that they had had premarital intercourse, up from 38.3 percent in 1976 and 26.4 percent in 1971. Of black women, 66.2 percent were sexually active in 1979 compared to 66.4 percent in 1976 and 53.7 percent in 1971. The average age of the first sexual experience is sixteen. By the time they reach age nineteen, only a third of adolescent females have not had intercourse (Lincoln, 1981; Zelnick, Kanter, and Ford, 1981). In contrast, less than 20 percent of women in their mother's generation had engaged in sexual intercourse while in their teens (Kinsey et al., 1953). Even so, teenage sexual activity tends to be sporadic. The 1979 survey reported that about half of the sexually experienced teenagers had not had intercourse in the month prior to the survey.

The shift in sexual attitudes and behavior has also been pronounced among college students (Bell and Coughey, 1980; Clayton and Bokemeier, 1980). The change largely reflects a narrowing of the gap between the sexual activity of males and females, rather than a marked increase in that of males. For instance, at the University of Georgia, the percentage of the men having premarital intercourse rose from 65.1 percent in 1965 to 77.4 percent in 1980; during this same period, the percentage of the women doing so rose from 28.7 percent to 63.5 percent (Robinson and Jedlicka, 1982). In most college communities, an equalitarian premarital sexual standard appears to be replacing the traditional double standard. Further, the decision among college women to have sexual intercourse appears to be less dependent on engagement to marry and more dependent on their feelings of affection for and emotional involvement with a male.

Much of the recent change in the sexual behavior of young people is a result of the growing power of the young to run their own lives without interference by parents, schools, churches, and the law. Findings show that higher rates of sexual permissiveness tend to be associated with lack of church attendance, identification with peers rather than parents, personal values and political orientations that favor social change, and the frequent use of marijuana, illicit drugs, or alcohol (Vener and Stewart, 1974; Reiss, 1976).

Emergent Codes of Sexual Morality

Recent changes in patterns of sexual behavior among many young people do not amount to a breakdown in morality, as is sometimes charged. Rather, they mean that young people have modified the codes of moral behavior. If anything, the young appear to be more concerned today with the moral aspects of sexual behavior than previous generations were.

Many young people have come to judge the acceptability of sexual behavior in terms of a couple's emotional involvement. Sexual intercourse is defined as morally permissible so long as the couple are engaged or feel love or strong affection for each other (Reiss, 1976). Any sexual behavior, even "petting," is unacceptable if affection is absent.

Clearly, most young Americans do not regard the new morality as license for promiscuous thrill seeking (Zelnick and Kantner, 1972; McKenry, Walters, and Johnson, 1979). They appear to seek a sense of identity through an affectionate and emotionally involved form of physical intimacy. And in keeping with this

New Code of Sexual Morality

Increasingly, young people in the United States have come to judge the acceptability of any sexual behavior by a standard based on a couple's emotional involvement with each other.

Patrick Reddy

focus, the new morality includes a desire for greater openness and honesty about sex. Although there seems to have been a movement since 1975 toward the older attitudes that prevailed before the so-called sexual revolution, there remains a tendency to hold both men and women to the *same* standards for behavior. Thus there is a greater tendency among college students today than in 1975 to judge sexual intercourse with a great many partners as immoral regardless of the person's sex (Robinson and Jedlicka, 1982).

Although it may seem that young people are in rebellion against adult values, in truth the newer morality is an attempt to realize many traditional American values: equalitarianism, honesty, openness, autonomy, free choice, love, happiness, and individual well-being. It has been fostered by many of the same social sources that produced the equalitarian movements for black and women's rights. Today, many people of college age believe that they have as much right to choose their sexual life-style as their political or religious life-style or their marriage partners (Reiss, 1976). Indeed, the differences between generations may not be as great as they seem. On the whole, adults are also becoming more permissive in their sexual norms, with single adults in particular speaking up in favor of premarital intercourse (Hunt, 1974; Yankelovich, 1981).

Contraception and Pregnancy

In the United States, three out of ten teenage girls who have premarital sexual experience become pregnant. Although teenagers constitute only 18 percent of sexually active women considered capable of becoming pregnant, they account for 31 percent of the abortions and 46 percent of out-of-wedlock births. Of teenage pregnancies, 17 percent are conceived after marriage, 22 percent result in out-of-wedlock births, 38 percent are terminated by abortion, and the remainder are miscarried (Lincoln, 1981).

The level and consistency of contraceptive use increased among teenagers during the 1970s. In 1979, seven in ten teenagers said they had taken precautions at the last instance of intercourse, compared with five in ten in 1971 and six in ten in 1976 (Zelnick, Kantner, and Ford, 1981). Some 27 percent of the sexually active teenagers reported in 1979 that they had never used a birth-control method. In most cases teenagers who employ contraception wait until they have been sexually active about nine months before beginning its use.

General nervousness about the pill contributed to its decline as the first choice among contraceptive methods. Between 1976 and 1979, teenage contraceptive users who said pills were their most recent birth-control method fell from 53 percent to 51 percent among blacks and from 46 to 38 percent among whites. The use of condoms remained steady. However, teenagers relying on withdrawal (generally con-

Teenage Pregnancy
With the fading of the stigma long attached to illegitimacy, increasing numbers of teenage mothers now keep their babies. This young woman has received emotional support in her pregnancy from her boyfriend.
Richard Bermack/Jeroboam

sidered to be the least reliable technique) increased from 7 to 8 percent among blacks and from 17 to 21 percent among whites.

With the fading of the stigma long attached to illegitimacy, about nine out of ten unwed teenage mothers now keep their babies. Eighty percent of those who first become pregnant by age seventeen never complete high school. Moreover, the younger an adolescent is when her first child is born, the more likely she is to wind up in poverty and on welfare. Some teenagers attempt to cope by marrying before the baby is born. However, teen marriages are from two to three times more likely to break up than marriages occurring after age twenty; 60 percent of brides aged seventeen years or less divorce within six years (20 percent divorce within the first year). Inept parenting, child neglect, and child abuse are also comparatively more common among teenage parents.

VOCATIONAL CHOICE

We cannot always build the future for our youth, but we can build our youth for the future.

—FRANKLIN D. ROOSEVELT
Speech of September 20, 1940

A critical developmental task confronting adolescents is that of making a vocational decision. In the United States, as in other Western societies, the jobs that people hold have significant implications for their lives (see the boxed insert on page 394 for a cross-cultural perspective). Position in the labor force influences their general life-style, important aspects of their self-concept, their children's life-chances, and most of the relationships they have with others in the community (Blau and Duncan, 1967; Sewell, 1981). Further, jobs tie individuals into the wider social system and give them a sense of purpose in life.

The Occupational Entry Process

Adolescents are faced with the fact that a lot depends on their ability to find and keep a job. It has immediate consequences for their emancipation from their parents, for their acceptance and status ranking among their peers, and for the standard of living and life-style they can assume. Yet adolescents usually have only vague ideas about what they are able to do successfully, what they would enjoy doing, what requirements are attached to given jobs, what the current job market is like, and what it will probably be like in the future (DeFleur and Menke, 1975).

A 1980 Gallup Youth Survey asked a national cross section of young people aged thirteen to eighteen about their career preferences. The top career choices of boys, in order of preference, were skilled worker (carpenter, plumber, electrician), auto-diesel mechanic, doctor, professional athlete, engineer, busi-

INTRODUCING CHILDREN TO WORK ROLES

Plateau Tonga, Northern Zimbabwe

Girls from the time they can toddle are gradually introduced to the tasks of the housewife, and very soon after this to the work in the fields as well as the gathering of relish and firewood. This happens as a small girl follows around after her mother or the older woman in whose care she is. . . . Small boys may help with some of the work of the household, especially in planting season when it is their job to lead the oxen before the plough. About the age of six to seven they are introduced into the ranks of the herdboys, where they remain until roughly the age of fourteen to fifteen. . . . All children receive some training in the care of infants and toddlers. Most small girls and some small boys spend a period as nursemaids to smaller children, which gives them a notable skill in handling infants and an apparent pleasure in doing so which lasts into later life. (Colson, 1958: 262–264)

Muria, India

But directly a child is old enough to play, he is regarded as old enough to work. The early stage of "eating while playing and playing while eating" is soon over and the little girls and boys have to take their share of the work of the house. Tiny girls may often be seen staggering about with the youngest baby in their arms or helping their mothers to cowdung the house. Sometimes you may see a line of boys and girls following their elders back from the jungle, each with a tiny basket of fruit or a minute bundle of leaves on their heads. During this period the children are very dependent on their parents and go everywhere with them. A boy takes his little axe and follows his father to the jungle. A girl takes a pot and goes with her mother to the well. (Elwin, 1947: 76)

Reindeer Chuckchee, Siberia

The reindeer-breeding Chuckchee send boys of ten, and girls hardly much older than that, to help in tending the herd. I remember having met one summer-time two such young reindeer-breeders, a boy and a girl. They were from ten to twelve years old. They were walking through the bushes quite alone, staff in hand, and wallet [knapsack] on back. They had to walk some ten miles before they could reach their herd. It was strange to see these young children wandering in the bush without any protection and shelter. (Bogoras, 1909: 553)

Copper Eskimo, Canada

A girl receives a little elementary education in cooking and sewing and in dressing meat. She is encouraged to make dolls and to mend her own clothing, her mother teaching her how to cut out the skins. Both boys and girls learn to stalk game by accompanying their elders on hunting excursions; their fathers make bows and arrows for them suited to their strength. One of their favourite pastimes is to carry out, in miniature, some of the duties they will have to perform when they grow up. Thus little girls often have tiny lamps in the corners of their huts over which they will cook some meat to share with their playmates. . . .

The children naturally have many pastimes that imitate the actions of their elders. . . . Both boys and girls play at building snow houses. In summer, with only pebbles to work with, they simply lay out the grand plans, but in winter they borrow their parents' snow-knives and make complete houses on a miniature scale. (Jenness, 1922: 170, 219)

nessperson, lawyer, musician or artist, architect, and computer operator. Those of girls, in order of preference, were doctor, secretary, nurse, artist, teacher, beautician, lawyer, businessperson, accountant, and computer operator. Interestingly, these career preferences continued to reflect, at least to some extent, traditional sex-segregated career patterns.

The Effects of Part-time Employment

In 1940, less than 5 percent of American high-school students had a part-time job. Currently, about 50 percent of all high-school juniors and seniors and about 30 percent of all ninth- and tenth-graders work at some time during the school year (Cole, 1980). Over the past decade or so many policy advisers have argued that for adolescents work is a good complement to school (Carnegie Commission, 1980; National Commission on Youth, 1980). A job is thought to teach adolescents responsibility, to instill in them an appreciation for hard work, to bring them into closer contact with adults from whom they can learn, and to keep them out of trouble.

Yet an emerging body of research suggests that ad-

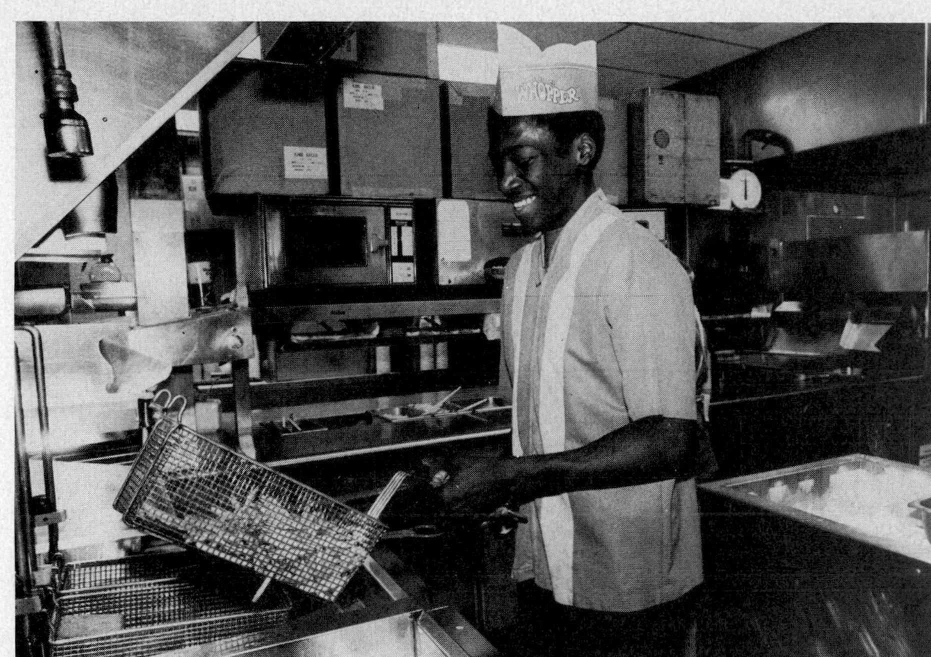

Part-Time Employment for Teenagers

The jobs that are open to teenagers typically involve repetitive operations that require few skills. Although it is commonly assumed that youth gain on-the-job training, they actually derive very little that is technically useful to them. But they do gain a "work orientation" and practical knowledge of how the business world operates.

Rick Friedman/The Picture Cube

olescents may not get as much out of work as some proponents of youth job programs have hoped (Cole, 1980; Greenberger and Steinberg, 1981; Steinberg et al., 1982). Though working is associated with greater personal responsibility, requiring relatively high levels of punctuality, dependability, and self-reliance on the job, there is little evidence to support the notion that working enhances adolescents' concern for others or promotes overall social responsibility.

It is commonly assumed that work provides youth with on-the-job training of a technically useful kind. Yet it actually provides very little. In practice, younger teenagers are confined to doing such odd jobs as mowing lawns, shoveling snow, delivering newspapers, and baby-sitting, while older teenagers clerk in stores, wash dishes, and wait on tables at local cafés. Usually the jobs involve repetitive operations that require little training or skills learned in other settings. However, young people do gain a "work orientation"—practical knowledge of how the business world operates, how to find and hold a job, and how to manage their time and money. And adolescents are exposed to a variety of new situations in which they must learn to deal with a good many different kinds of people. Not surprisingly, even when young people are dissatisfied with their jobs, they like the independence and power they get from earning their own money.

Holding a job is also associated with higher rates of cigarette and marijuana use. Further, a surprising number of adolescent job holders admit to cheating their employers or stealing from them. And adolescents who work feel less involved in school than their nonworking classmates do, are absent more often, and do not enjoy school as much. About 27 percent report a decline in grades after beginning work, whereas 16 percent say their grades had improved. Working reduces family closeness among girls but increases it among boys. And while increasing the educational expectations of girls, working lowers those of boys.

Adolescent Encounters with Racism and Sexism

Some youth encounter special difficulties in entering the job market, especially women and those from racial and ethnic minorities. These young people find that structural features of the social system serve to limit their job prospects (Vander Zanden, 1983). **Gatekeepers**—individuals who admit others to scarce positions and offices of power, privilege, and status in a society—have traditionally been white and male. Gatekeepers are found in schools and colleges, in employment agencies, and in the hiring offices of business and government.

Even when gatekeepers are well meaning—dedicated to objective, nonprejudiced hiring and sympathetic to the American democratic creed—minorities and women frequently find themselves victimized. Since talent and skill are relative matters, subtle and "taken-for-granted" considerations come into operation. Representatives of various minorities and women's groups note that the standards of excellence—the evaluative yardsticks employed for determining who is "bright," "industrious," "resourceful," and "proficient"—are those of the white and male community. Further, and equally important, the *judges* who make the decisions as to which individuals meet the standards of excellence tend to be white and male.

Racism. For many American adolescents, a steady, decent-paying job is a distant hope. High rates of unemployment have traditionally been the lot of many young people, especially blacks in the big-city ghettos. Government figures reveal that in 1984 the unemployment rate for white teenagers exceeded 16 percent. The rate of unemployment for black teenagers, however, was more than 43 percent.

Since the Labor Department's measures of joblessness do not include those who have given up looking for work and those who have part-time jobs but want full-time ones, the actual level of teenage unemployment was higher. It is estimated, for instance, that during the 1970s black teenage unemployment periodically exceeded 65 percent. White racism appeared to be a factor contributing to the high black unemployment level, since the unemployment rate of white high-school *dropouts* was about equal that of black high-school *graduates*.

The employment difficulties of young workers are expected to get worse rather than better in the years ahead. In 1975 there were 39 million workers in the "prime" age bracket, twenty-five to forty. In 1990 there are expected to be 60.5 million workers in the prime category. This bunching of the work force is a result of the baby boom that came after World War II. Consequently, young workers will have to jostle and elbow to find room in an increasingly dense labor market.

Sexism. The earliest experiences of adolescents in the labor force mirror the sex differences of the adult work world (Greenberger and Steinberg, 1983). Boys are more likely than girls to be employed as manual laborers, newspaper deliverers, and recreation aides, whereas girls are more likely than boys to work as clerical workers, retail sales clerks, child care workers, health aides, and education aides. Sex segregation also occurs within industries. Hence, among food service workers, boys more often work with things (they cook food, bus tables, and wash dishes) whereas girls more often work with people (they fill orders and serve as waitresses and hostesses). And among hucksters, boys are overrepresented in jobs that require

Minority Youth Often Experience Special Difficulty Getting Jobs

For many American youth, a steady, decent-paying job is a distant hope. Ghetto youth and youth in communities characterized by high unemployment find their lot particularly difficult. This unemployed teenager lives in Flint, Michigan, a community hard hit by the demise of its industries.

Michael Hayman/Stock, Boston

selling "on the street," whereas girls predominate in "telephone sales."

A young person's gender is also associated with the number of hours worked. Boys typically work more hours than girls do. Further, boys tend to earn higher hourly wages than girls do. For instance, when the minimum wage was $3.10, the average wages of sophomore boys and girls were $3.02 and $2.24, respectively; for seniors, $3.42 and $3.13. These differences are maintained over the early job histories of men and women. In sum, from the time that young people go to work outside the home, they enter a labor force where sex segregation prevails, where men work longer hours than do women, and where the work of males is more highly remunerated than that of females. One consequence of these early employment patterns is the reinforcement and perpetuation of occupational sexism.

SOME SPECIAL ISSUES

To me it seems that youth is, like spring, an overpraised season . . . more remarkable, as a general rule, for biting east winds, than genial breezes.

—SAMUEL BUTLER

Although adolescence is often heralded in the United States as the "beautiful age," many adolescents have great difficulty with it. Even if adolescents do not perceive themselves as having "problems"—as in the past, many do not in the case of their marijuana usage—adult society nonetheless defines various teenage behaviors as "deviant." Since adults control the channels of power, including legislative agencies, the courts, the police, and the mass media, they are in a better position than adolescents to make their definitions and values the predominant ones in human affairs.

Drug Abuse

Nowadays everyone talks about drugs, but the word itself is imprecise. If we consider a drug to be a chemical, then everything that we ingest is technically a drug. To avoid this difficulty, a *drug* is usually arbitrarily defined as a chemical that produces some extraordinary effect beyond the life-sustaining functions associated with food and drink. For instance, a drug may heal, put to sleep, relax, elate, inebriate, produce a mystical experience, or whatever (Sebald, 1977).

Our society assigns different statuses to different types of drugs. Through the Federal Drug Administration, the Bureau of Narcotics, and other agencies, the government takes formal positions on whether a given drug is "good" or "bad," and if "bad," how bad. Sociologists note that some drugs enjoy official approval. This is the case with caffeine, a mild stimulant that finds institutional approval through the coffee break and coffee shop. Likewise the consumption of alcohol, a central nervous system depressant, has become so prevalent in recreational and business settings that nonusers of the drug are often regarded as somewhat peculiar. And at least until a few years ago, the same held true for the use of nicotine (smoking), a drug usually categorized as a stimulant (though the smoking ritual itself is experienced by many people as relaxing).

Whether they are culturally sanctioned or not, drugs can be abused. **Drug abuse** refers to the excessive or compulsive use of chemical agents to an extent that interferes with people's health, their social or vocational functioning, or the functioning of the rest of society. Among adolescents, as among their elders, alcohol is the most frequently abused drug in the United States. A recent poll of students at ninety-three colleges found that 86.4 percent of the men and 79.4 percent of the women drink. Nearly 21 percent of the undergraduates considered themselves to be heavy drinkers, consuming six or more drinks at a sitting at least once a week. Nearly a third admitted to driving while intoxicated, and a fifth said they had missed class because of excessive drinking (Ingalls, 1983). A 1983 survey of high-school seniors by the University of Michigan's Institute for Social Research (1984) found that 5.5 percent said they drank daily (down from 6.9 percent in 1979, the peak year).

Another drug frequently used by adolescents is marijuana. The effects of marijuana differ from user to user. Most commonly, it produces a relatively mild and light-headed form of inebriation. Some users also report an increase in the intensity of sense impressions; for instance, colors may appear brighter and music may sound richer and more resonant. In 1982 the National Academy of Sciences (1982) summarized the available scientific evidence about the health effects of marijuana. Although it found no conclusive

Drug Abuse

Marijuana use among teenagers rose steadily throughout the 1970s but fell back during the 1980s. Coping with drugs in their environment is one of the developmental tasks adolescents must now reckon with.

Anestis Diakopolous/Stock, Boston

evidence that the drug has long-term, permanent effects, it nonetheless said that marijuana's short-term effects justify "serious national concern." It concluded that marijuana temporarily impairs motor coordination; hampers short-term memory, oral communication, and learning; and may trigger temporary confusion and delirium. Thus daily use can be expected to harm the adolescent user's academic performance. Chronic use may lead to impaired lung function, decreased sperm counts, interference with ovulation, and diminished immune response and possibly lung cancer.

In 1967 only 5 percent of young people in the United States had used marijuana. Its use rose over the next decade so that by 1978 one in nine high-school seniors said they were daily users. By 1983, however, the figure had dropped to one in eighteen. The decline in marijuana use among high-school students resulted from growing personal concerns about its health consequences and mounting peer disapproval. The use of hallucinogens also dropped. However, cocaine use at least once a month has apparently stabilized at about 5 percent. Coping with the presence of drugs in their social environment may now be a developmental task that adolescents must reckon with just as they must reckon with separation from parents, career development, and sexuality (Collins, 1983*a*).

A variety of factors have contributed to the illicit use of drugs by young people. One overriding circumstance has been the very important part that the recreational use of illegal drugs has played in many adolescent peer groups over the past fifteen years. Generally speaking, adolescents who use illegal drugs move in peer groups in which drugs are not only approved but also have an important part in day-to-day interactions (Kandel, 1974; Thomas, Petersen, and Zingraff, 1975; Kandel and Adler, 1982; Brook, Whiteman, and Gordon, 1983).

Another factor in the use of illegal drugs by young people is that they view their parents as users of psychoactive agents—such as tranquilizers, barbiturates, and stimulants (Smart and Fejer, 1972; Kandel, 1974). The contribution that parental drug behavior makes to children's illegal use of drugs is certainly not intended by the parents; more than 80 percent of adolescents report that their family has a rule against illicit drugs. Nonetheless, children in the United States are reared in a pill-oriented, happiness-seeking society. Many see their parents using psychoactive drugs, and as a consequence they begin taking mood-changing drugs themselves. In this context, drug use by adolescents is a juvenile manifestation of adult behavior. It is more accurate to view drug abuse not simply as a teenage problem but as a societywide problem (Collins, 1983*a*).

Teenage Suicide

To die—to sleep—
No more; and by a sleep to say we end
The heartache, and the thousand natural shocks
That flesh is heir to. 'Tis a consummation
Devoutly to be wish'd. To die—to sleep.

—WILLIAM SHAKESPEARE
Hamlet, Act III, Scene 1

The suicide rate among young people has tripled over the past twenty-five years (an increase that is real and not the result of better reporting of the problem). Consequently, suicide ranks today as the second or third leading cause of death among adolescents in virtually every industrialized nation of the world. And the actual incidence of suicide is believed to be even higher than what is recorded in official government statistics. Since a stigma is often attached to suicide in Western countries, medical personnel frequently report a suicidal death as an accident or as a death from natural causes. In 1983 an estimated 400,000 teenagers in the United States attempted suicide, and 5,000 to 10,000 were successful (Brody, 1984*b*).

There are considerably more suicide *attempts* among young women than young men (and this ratio holds true for other age groups as well). But *completed* suicides are higher among men than women, since men are likely to use active methods—shooting or hanging—while women typically use passive methods—taking poisons or drugs (Farberow and Shneidman, 1961; Stengel, 1964; Conger, 1977). It should be emphasized that individuals differ in the seriousness of their suicidal attempts. Erwin Stengel (1964: 71), a psychiatrist, notes:

> It is generally believed that most if not all people who commit suicidal acts are clearly determined to die. The study of attempted suicides does not bear this out. Many suicidal attempts and quite a few suicides are carried out in the mood "I don't care whether I live or die," rather than with a clear and unambiguous determination to end life. A person who denies, after what seems an obvious suicidal attempt, that he *really* wanted to kill himself, may be telling the truth. Most people, in committing a suicidal act, are just as muddled as they are whenever they do anything of importance under emotional stress. Carefully planned suicidal acts are as rare as carefully planned acts of homicide. Many are carried out on sudden impulse, although suicidal thoughts were usually present before.

In some cases, psychological depression underlies suicide and suicidal attempts. Depression is usually characterized by prolonged feelings of gloom, despair, and futility, profound pessimism, and a tendency toward excessive guilt and self-reproach. Other common symptoms include fatigue, insomnia, poor concentration, irritability, anxiety, reduced sexual

Crisis Intervention: The Hotline
Many communities have set up suicide hotlines that provide an instant, economical, and effective way to deal with emergency situations. In addition to providing emotional support and sympathy, hotline volunteers give information on the community services that are available to deal with a caller's problems.
Paul Fortin/Stock, Boston

SUICIDE WARNING SIGNALS AMONG ADOLESCENTS

Teachers and other school personnel are often in a unique position to notice behavior changes that may indicate that an adolescent is at high risk for suicide. Such changes include the following:

- A dramatic decline in the quality of school work.
- Social behavior changes, including excessive use of drugs or alcohol.
- Changes in daily behavior and living patterns, including extreme fatigue, boredom, decreased appetite, preoccupation, or inability to concentrate.
- Open signs of mental illness, including hallucinations or delusions.
- Giving away prized possessions.
- Any type of serious sleep disturbance—nightmares, difficulty in falling asleep, or early morning awakening.
- A preoccupation with thoughts and signs of death, which may be expressed in such statements as, "Oh, I don't care. I won't be around anyway to find out what happens!"; "I would like to sleep forever and never wake up!"; "Sometimes I would just like to take a gun and blow off my head . . . but I'm only joking!"; or "How many aspirin does it take to kill yourself?"

We should trust in our own judgment and our own subjective feelings in assessing a potentially suicidal person. If we believe that someone is in danger of suicide, we should act on our belief. We would be well advised not to let others mislead us into ignoring suicidal signals.

The troubled adolescent should be put in touch with an appropriate agency or specialist. One program that has come into existence in recent years is the *crisis hotline.* Hotlines are staffed by volunteers who have been screened and trained to respond in an appropriate fashion. Their job is to listen, to buy time, and to refer callers to counselors.

interest, and overall loss of interest and boredom. At times depression appears in the guise of other disorders—for instance, vague pains, headaches, or recurrent nausea. The U.S. Office of Education has named depression as a major cause of students' dropping out of college.

Medical authorities do not agree on what causes depression. Some trace their patients' feelings of helplessness and despair to emotionally difficult life circumstances and stresses (Seligman, 1973). Others believe that both depression and suicide are rooted in a malfunction of the chemistry of the brain, particularly in the levels of serotonin (Brown et al., 1982; Stanley, Viriglio, and Gershon, 1982). Still others attribute depression to some combination of biochemical factors and psychological feelings of worthlessness (Beck, 1967, 1976). Increasing evidence suggests that all three views may be correct. It appears that depression is not a single illness but an illness of various kinds, just as there are different kinds of pneumonia (Scarf, 1977). Although the symptoms may be similar, the causes of depression may differ among different individuals.

After studying the life histories of fifty adolescents who attempted suicide, Jerry Jacobs (1971) concluded that they typically became increasingly cut off from sympathetic, warm, and secure contacts and ties with others. In the course of this progressive isolation, they tended to pass through the following phases (1971: 64):

1. A long-standing history of problems (from childhood to the onset of adolescence).
2. A period of "escalation of problems" (since the onset of adolescence and in excess of those "normally" associated with adolescence).
3. The progressive failure of available adaptive techniques for coping with old and increasing new problems which leads the adolescent to a progressive social isolation from meaningful social relationships.
4. The final phase, characterized by the chain reaction dissolution of any remaining meaningful social relationships in the weeks and days preceding the suicide attempt.

See the boxed insert above for a discussion of suicide warning signals among adolescents.

Researchers at the University of Nebraska Medical Center and Creighton University School of Medicine have compared fifty consecutive self-poisoning victims aged six through eighteen with fifty other children of similar age and circumstances. They found that 88 percent of the poisoning victims (compared with 12 percent of the controls) had a history of such difficulties as behavior problems, delinquency, dropping out of school, and being a loner. Many of the victims, but few of the controls, had experienced hostility, indifference, and rejection by their parents (Brody, 1979*a*). In another study, a number of Canadian researchers have found that youth who attempt suicide are more likely than a matched group of controls to come from homes with a higher incidence of alcohol and drug abuse, suicide, paternal unemployment, economic stress, and an absence of the biological parents (Garfinkel, Froese, and Hood, 1982). New research is also focusing on "suicide clusters" in which young people apparently follow the example of peers in their school who take their own lives (Head, 1984).

Treatment of adolescents with suicidal tendencies usually involves psychotherapy. The therapist seeks to help the teenager come to terms with his or her problems and acquire more effective techniques for coping with life and stressful circumstances. The therapist also attempts to foster self-understanding, a sense of inner strength, self-confidence, and a positive self-image. In more severe cases, the patient may also be placed on antidepressant medication. (Among the more commonly prescribed antidepressants are Elavil and Tofranil.)

Juvenile Delinquency

Youthful "deviance" has been a common problem reported by societies throughout human history (see the boxed insert on page 402). In the United States today, vandalism and violence have emerged as major problems among adolescents in many school districts. Acts of violence and property destruction in schools increased through the 1960s and into the early 1970s but have since leveled off.

When the National Institute of Education (1977) undertook to determine the dimensions of the problems in the nation's schools, it came up with the following estimates:

- Some 1.3 percent of secondary-school students report that they are attacked at school in a typical month. Twice as many junior-high-school students report attacks as senior-high students (2.1 percent compared with 1 percent). About two-fifths of the reported attacks result in some injury. However, only 4 percent involve injuries serious enough to require medical attention.
- In a typical month, 12 percent of the teachers in secondary schools report that something worth more than $1 has been stolen from them.
- About 0.5 percent of secondary-school teachers are physically attacked at school in a month. Nearly one-fifth of these attacks require medical attention.

Vandalism in the Schools
The cost of repairing damage to the nation's schools caused by vandals comes to more than $600 million a year. This is about as much as the schools spend on textbooks.
Patrick Reddy

YOUTHFUL "DEVIANCE" IN ANCIENT TIMES

Our earth is degenerate. . . . Children no longer obey their parents.

—A carving on a stone by an Egyptian priest 6,000 years ago

Our youths now love luxury. They have bad manners, contempt for authority, [and] disrespect for older people. Children nowadays are tyrants. They no longer rise when their elders enter the room. They contradict their parents, chatter before company, gobble their food, and tyrannize their teachers.

—Socrates not long before his death in 399 B.C.

The young are in character prone to desire and ready to carry any desire they may have formed into action. Of bodily desires it is the sexual to which they are most disposed to give way, and in regard to sexual desire they exercise no self-restraint. They are changeful too, and fickle in their desires, which are as transitory as they are vehement; for their wishes are keen without being permanent, like a sick man's fits of hunger and thirst.

They are passionate, irascible, and apt to be carried away by their impulses. They are the slaves, too, of their passion, as their ambition prevents their ever brooking a slight and renders them indignant at the mere idea of enduring an injury.

—Aristotle, 384–322 B.C.

Our young men have grown slothful. Their talents are left idle, and there is not a single honorable occupation for which they will toil day and night. Slumber and languor, and an interest in evil which is worse than slumber and languor, have entered into men's hearts. They sing and dance and grow effeminate, and curl their hair, and learn womanish tricks of speech; they are languid as women, and deck themselves out with unbecoming ornaments. Without strength, without energy, they add nothing during life to the gifts with which they are born, and then they complain of their lot.

—Seneca in the first century A.D.

- A school's risk of experiencing some vandalism in a month is greater than one in four. The average cost of an act of vandalism is $81. In addition, one in ten schools is broken into, at an average cost per burglary of $183. Schools are about five times more likely than commercial establishments to be burglarized.
- For property offenses, the risks to schools do not differ much throughout metropolitan areas. However, the per capita cost of school crime is higher in the suburbs than in the cities.
- The risk of being a victim of either attack or robbery in secondary school declines steadily as grade level increases. Seventh-graders are the most likely to be attacked or robbed, twelfth-graders the least likely.

In recent years, youth eighteen years of age and under have accounted for about 20 percent of all violent crime arrests in the United States, 44 percent of all serious property arrests, and 39 percent of all overall serious crime arrests. Chronic youthful offenders commit many more crimes than chronic adult offenders do—an average of thirty-six per year for juveniles and twelve a year for adults. However, many juvenile delinquents later become law-abiding citizens. It seems they change, not out of fear of being arrested, but because they realize that what was fun as a teenager is no longer appropriate behavior for an adult (Shannon, 1982). Overall, the rate of juvenile crime in the United States, while remaining high, has not risen since the mid-1970s (Chambers, 1981).

High-School Dropouts

Estimates place the dropout rate among high-school students in the United States at about 23 percent. However, the proportion is higher among the poor and minorities (35 percent for blacks and 45 percent for Hispanics). And in some big-city school systems like Chicago and St. Louis, 52 percent of the young people do not graduate from high school. Many later regret leaving school (National Center for Education Statistics, 1983).

Because of the technological orientation and requirements of contemporary society, young people who do not complete high school or who fail to acquire basic reading, writing, and mathematical skills find themselves at a serious disadvantage in the job market. Whereas in 1950 34 percent of all jobs were open to workers without a high-school diploma, by 1970 only 9 percent were open, and today the rate is even lower. Consequently, there are fewer jobs for high-school dropouts. Many dropouts spend their time visiting and loafing, and some engage in a wide range of problem behaviors, including the use of marijuana and hard drugs, drinking, smoking, physical aggression, and theft (Biddle, Bank, and Anderson, 1981). Those who fail to move into stable employment by age twenty find it increasingly difficult to make the transition to an adult life of gainful employment (Osterman, 1980).

School difficulties, both educational and social, are prominent in the history of most dropouts. Lucius Cervantes (1965) has made a comparative study of high-school graduates and dropouts. He found that dropouts tended to share a number of characteristics: many had failed at least one grade; by seventh grade they were two years behind their classmates in reading and arithmetic; their attendance record was poor; often they were "underachievers"; they had changed schools frequently; many had behavior problems or were troubled emotionally; and they tended to resent authority. Overall, research reveals that academic difficulties become cumulative, showing a gradual rise over the elementary-school years and reaching a high point in the ninth and tenth grades (Fitzsimmons et al., 1969). Some 24 percent of high-school dropouts leave school in their sophomore year; 47 percent in their junior year; and 29 percent in their senior year (National Center for Education Statistics, 1983).

Not surprisingly, students who have difficulties with academic work and who view their assignments as incomprehensible and not germane typically find school frustrating and disheartening. Moreover, many adolescents fail to see any "payoff" associated with school attendance and continued effort. Many young people, especially those in the nation's big-city ghettos, regard the school experience as irrelevant to their personal, social, and vocational needs.

For the most part, school authorities, police officials, and the public have argued that young people should be retained in school at least until they complete high school. The idea is that school will keep adolescents out of mischief while simultaneously providing them with the skills necessary for gainful employment.

Research over the past two decades, however, is questioning this line of reasoning (Elliott, 1966; Kelly, 1971; Bachman, O'Malley, and Johnston, 1978). While it is indisputable that high-school dropouts have a higher delinquency rate and poorer self-image than students who stay in school, their having dropped out does not appear to aggravate these difficulties. Indeed, these adolescents' scores on self-esteem tests improve somewhat after they drop out (Bachman, O'Malley, and Johnston, 1978). And sociologist Delbert S. Elliott (1966) found that dropouts committed fewer offenses *after* leaving school than in a comparable period before they dropped out. Elliott suggests that the boy or girl who drops out is no longer involved in unequal competition at school and escapes the frustration of continual failure. In sum, dropping out of school is more likely to reflect an adolescent's problems than to be a cause of them.

SUMMARY

1. Western industrial nations have prolonged the transition from childhood to adulthood and segregated the young from the rest of society and its activities. This has given rise to a kind of institutionalized adolescence or youth culture.

2. The most obvious features of the youth culture revolve about various peer-group trademarks: preferred recordings, dance steps, and entertainment idols; approved personal adornment; and distinctive jargon and slang. It is also embodied in conceptions of qualities and performances that are thought to reveal an individual's masculinity or femininity.

3. The notion of the generation gap oversimplifies the relationship between youth and adults. Both the family and the peer group are anchors in the lives of most teenagers.

4. One of the most difficult adjustments, and perhaps the most critical, that adolescents must make revolves about their developing sexuality. In the United States, dating has been the principal vehicle for fostering and developing heterosexual relations. Over the past fifteen years dating has undergone rapid change.

5. In the United States, notions concerning romantic love play an important part in our spouse selection and in our conceptions of

married life. However, societies throughout the world view romantic love quite differently.

6. In the twentieth century there have been two periods of very rapid change in sexual attitudes and behavior. The first period occurred around the time of World War I; the second, during the Vietnam War years.
7. Recent changes in patterns of sexual behavior among many young people do not amount to a breakdown in morality. Rather, they mean that the young have modified the codes of moral behavior. Many adolescents have come to judge the acceptability of sexual behavior in terms of the degree of a couple's emotional involvement.
8. A critical developmental task confronting adolescents is that of deciding on a vocation. Yet adolescents usually have only vague ideas about the working world. And those who do work typically get less out of the experience than proponents of youth job programs have hoped.
9. Many young people have great difficulty with adolescence. Among the problems some of them face are those associated with drug abuse, suicide, delinquency, disinterest in and dropping out of school, and high levels of unemployment.

KEY TERMS

consciousness of oneness A sympathetic identification in which group members come to feel that their inner experiences and emotional reactions are similar.

drug abuse The excessive or compulsive use of chemical agents to an extent that interferes with people's health, their social or vocational functioning, or the functioning of the rest of society.

gatekeeper An individual who admits others to scarce positions and offices of power, privilege, and status in a society.

generation gap The existence of mutual antagonism, misunderstanding, and separation between young people and adults.

youth culture More or less standardized ways of thinking, feeling, and acting that are characteristic of a large body of young people.

Part Seven

Early Adulthood

15

Early Adulthood: Perspectives and Development

When we truly comprehend and enter into the rhythm of life, we shall be able to bring together the daring of youth with the discipline of age in a way that does justice to both.

—J. S. BIXLER
Two Blessings of Joseph

The term "adulthood" generally lacks the concreteness of "infancy," "childhood," and "adolescence." Even in the scientific literature it has functioned as a kind of catchall category for everything that happens to individuals after they "grow up." Sigmund Freud, for instance, viewed adult life as merely a ripple on the surface of an already set personality structure; Jean Piaget assumed that no additional cognitive changes occur after adolescence; and Lawrence Kohlberg sees moral development as reaching a lifetime plateau after early adulthood.

Following the lead of psychologists like Erik Erikson (1963, 1968*a*), Charlotte Bühler (Bühler and Massarik, 1968), Carl G. Jung (1933), Sidney L. Pressey (Pressey and Kuhlen, 1957), and others, the scientific community is coming to recognize that adulthood is not a single monolithic stage—an undifferentiated phase of life between adolescence and old age. Scientists increasingly see the individual as undergoing change across the entire life span. The notion that adulthood is a state of *being*—a sort of mopping-up operation—is being replaced by a view of adulthood as a process of *becoming* (Baltes and Willis, 1977; Lerner and Busch-Rossnagel, 1981; Eichorn et al., 1982). Thus adulthood is coming to be seen not as a plodding passage across a plateau but as an adventure that involves negotiating ups and downs and changing direction to surmount obstacles.

DEVELOPMENTAL PERSPECTIVES

In the United States, the beginning of adulthood is most often defined as the point at which a person leaves school, takes a full-time job, or gets married. However, becoming an adult is a rather different matter for different segments of the society. And adulthood itself has different meanings for different age groups within the population. Since adulthood is not one experience but many experiences, people's conceptions of adulthood frequently differ.

Demographic Aspects of Adulthood

People's feelings, attitudes, and beliefs about adulthood are influenced by the relative proportion of individuals who are adults. In the United States, major population changes are under way that will have important social consequences. By 1990, the typical American will be 32.5 years of age (2.5 years more than the current median age). This is because of the large number of Americans born in the post–World War II period. The baby-boom generation represents a huge "age lump" passing through the population—a sort of demographic tidal wave. This age cohort was responsible for the 70 percent jump in the number of school-age children between 1950 and 1970.

At the present time, the "baby-boomers" have brought about a rapid expansion in the nation's labor force. In the early 1970s there were about 52 million Americans between twenty and thirty-nine years of age (25.8 percent of the population). By 1980, the number had risen to 72.4 million (32 percent of the population) (see Table 15.1). Some experts believe this maturing of the labor force will bring greater productivity because of the greater work experience of the average employee. But a surplus of well-educated individuals will also mean keen competition for an array of managerial and professional positions.

As the crest of the postwar baby boom advances, the number of teenagers will drop. This will trigger a good many side effects. It is likely to lessen current problems of juvenile crime and youth unemployment. But it will also make it more difficult for the military

Youth-Centered Society

The large numbers of Americans who comprise the "baby-boom generation" are having a profound impact upon American political preferences, housing patterns, and marketing tastes.

Bohdon Hrynewych/Southern Light

Table 15.1 Population Trends Within the United States

Age Range	Total Number	Percentage of Population
People under age 20		
1960	69.0 million	38.5
1970	77.0 million	37.9
1980	72.4 million	31.8
People 20 to 39 years (young adults)		
1960	46.1 million	25.7
1970	52.4 million	25.8
1980	72.4 million	32.0
People 40 to 64 years (the middle-aged)		
1960	47.7 million	26.6
1970	53.8 million	26.5
1980	56.2 million	24.8
People 65 years and over (the elderly)		
1960	16.6 million	9.2
1970	19.9 million	9.8
1980	25.5 million	11.3

SOURCE: Census Bureau.

services to sign up youthful recruits. Further, the contemporary emphasis on youth and youthful tastes and fashions may gradually give way to an emphasis on adult singles and young married couples.

Conceptions of Age Periods

For the most part, people in the United States perceive adults of all ages in a favorable fashion. Nevertheless, older adults are viewed less favorably and as less desirable to be around than younger adults. Such attitudes are influenced by a variety of factors. Adults who have had more formal education and more experience with a range of older adults have more positive attitudes toward older people than is true of the population generally. Adults who encounter burdens or conflicts associated with the elderly have more negative attitudes toward them (Knox, 1977).

College students, for instance, tend to evaluate older people more negatively than they do younger people. They see young people as more adaptable, more capable of pursuing goals, and more active than older people (Rosencranz and McNevin, 1969; O'Connell and Rotter, 1979). They also rate older employees more negatively than younger employees on the physical, cognitive, and emotional dimensions associated with managerial ability (Rosen and Jerdee, 1976*b*). At the same time, they see older employees as providing an organization with greater stability than do younger employees (Rosen and Jerdee, 1976*a*).

People also evaluate different stages of the life cycle differently depending on their current age (Chiriboga, 1978). The teen years are looked on more favorably by high-school seniors than by others, the twenties by newlyweds, the thirties by middle-aged parents, and the forties by men and women entering retirement. Younger people tend to view all the later years, commencing with the sixties, as equally bad; but older people distinguish between the young-old and the old-old, portraying the young-old period as a time of continued satisfaction. However, older people make fewer distinctions between the different stages of life in general.

Overall, people of all ages choose either adolescence or old age as the "worst age" (although adolescents are the least likely to view adolescence negatively). And except for the elderly, people tend to place the "best age" in the future. In contrast, the five- or ten-year period just passed tends to have somewhat low ratings. The single exception is preretirement men, among whom the past five years were among the top-ranked periods.

Americans also have some difficulty specifying the

Age Perceptions
Surveys reveal that the vast majority of adult Americans perceive themselves as being younger than they actually are. Consequently, they often do not feel inhibited when engaging in behaviors that run counter to age-related stereotypes.
Jim Ritscher/Stock, Boston

age at which an average man or woman becomes old. Much depends on the person's health, activity level, and related circumstances. Further, the boundaries between adjacent age stages are somewhat permeable. Americans have little difficulty characterizing a person as a young or an elderly adult. But the boundaries between adjacent age categories are vague. For instance, regarding the transition period between middle age and elderliness, the placing of an individual is only weakly connected to the chronological age of the person being judged (Kogan, 1979).

A person's gender likewise makes a difference. Women are viewed as aging more quickly than men do. But this tendency to assign women to older categories than comparably aged men becomes less pronounced when categorizing the elderly. And women are less inclined than men to employ a "double standard of aging" (Kogan, 1979; O'Connell and Rotter, 1979).

According to a nationwide survey of adult Americans, two-thirds perceive themselves as being younger than they actually are, though those under thirty years of age often perceive themselves as being older than they actually are (Nemy, 1982). Once individuals reach middle age, however, they think of themselves as from five to fifteen years younger. Indeed, people frequently say that they feel between thirty and thirty-five years old, regardless of their actual age. The thirties seem to have eternal appeal.

Overall, men say they feel about six years younger and women seven years younger than in fact they are. The peak period for feeling younger is the decade between forty and forty-nine years of age. The feeling then trails off during the fifties, tapering off more rapidly for women than for men. Like those under thirty, those over sixty perceive themselves as being older than they are, but to a lesser degree. These findings have proven of interest to those concerned with marketing products. They help to explain the failure of "special food for seniors" and the even more dismal failure of a shampoo aimed at "hair over forty."

Age Norms and the Social Clock

We commonly associate adulthood with **aging**—biological and social change across the life span. **Biological aging** refers to changes in the structure and functioning of the human organism through time. **Social aging** refers to changes in an individual's assumption and relinquishment of roles through time. People pass through a socially regulated cycle from birth to death just as surely as they pass through the biological cycle (Neugarten, 1969). Thus the life course of individuals is punctuated by transition points—the relinquishment of familiar roles and the assumption of new ones (Foner and Kertzer, 1978; Hogan, 1981).

Age, as reckoned by society, is a set of behavioral expectations associated with given points in the life span. Much social behavior is prescribed for us in terms of dos and don'ts. Conformity with these expectations generally has favorable results; violation, unpleasant ones. Such dos and don'ts are termed **social norms**—standards of behavior that members of a group share and to which they are expected to conform. Social norms are enforced by positive and negative sanctions.

Social norms define what is appropriate for people to be and to do at various ages—what are termed **age norms.** Sociologists Bernice L. Neugarten, Joan W. Moore, and John C. Lowe (1965: 711) say:

> There exists what might be called a prescriptive timetable for the ordering of major life events: a time in the life span when men and women are expected to marry, a time to raise children, a time to retire.

A societal "Big Ben" (the age norms) tends to define the "best age" for a man or woman to marry, to finish school, to settle on a career, to hold a top job, to become a grandparent, and to be ready to retire. Individuals tend to set their personal "watches" (their internalized age norms) by society's Big Ben (Kimmel, 1980).

Age norms are most obvious when they are embodied in *formal* rules or explicit policies about a role. Examples are compulsory school attendance laws, the minimum voting age in election laws, the age at which youth may purchase alcoholic beverages, and the age at which individuals become eligible for Social Security benefits.

Age Grading and Social Clocks
Most individuals have an inner timetable by which they tend to pace major family and occupational events.
Patrick Reddy

Age norms may also represent *informal* expectations about the kinds of roles appropriate for people of various ages. At times such expectations are only vague notions about who is "too old," "too young," or "the right age" for certain activities (Riley, Johnson, and Foner, 1972). The appeal "Act your age!" pervades a great many aspects of life. Variations on this theme are often heard in such remarks as, "She's too young to wear that style of clothing" and "That's a strange thing for a man of his age to say" (Neugarten, Moore, and Lowe, 1965).

Age grading at the social level, the arranging of people in social layers that are based on periods in the life cycle, creates what Neugarten (1968*a*) calls the **social clock—**a set of internalized concepts that regulate our progression through the age-related milestones of the adult years. The social clock sets the standards that individuals use in assessing their conformity to age-appropriate expectations. In her research Neugarten has found that adult men and women readily tell an interviewer what they believe to be the best age to marry, to have children, to become grandparents, to be settled in one's career, to have reached the top, and to retire. Likewise, people describe what personality characteristics ought to be salient in particular age periods; for example, they think it appropriate to be impulsive in adolescence, but not in middle age. And they readily report whether they themselves are "early," "late," or "on time" with regard to family and occupational events. Such an internal sense of social timing can act as a "prod" to speed up accomplishment of a goal or as a "brake" to slow down passage through age-related roles.

Any period of transition or crisis in life can initiate a life-review process and an assessment of where one stands with respect to age-related milestones (Bourque and Back, 1977). Exposure to death has the power to do this at all ages, even when one is not of an age when one's own death is imminent. Serious illness—one's own or that of another—may also have such an impact.

Although the members of a society tend to share similar expectations about their life cycle, some variations do occur. Social class is one important factor. The lower the social class, the more rapid the pacing of the social clock tends to be. The higher the social class, the later the individual generally leaves school, acquires his or her first job, gets married, begins parenthood, secures his or her top job, and begins grandparenthood (Neugarten, 1968*a*).

Age-Grade Systems

In a number of African societies, age norms are embodied in an age-grade system (Foner and Kertzer, 1978). Members of each age grade are alike in chronological age or life stage and have certain roles that are age-specific. For instance, the Latuka of Sudan distinguish among five age grades: children, youths, rulers of the village, retired elders, and the very old. In such societies, the individuals of each age grade are viewed as a corporate body and move as a unit from one age grade to another. For example, among the African Tiriki, uninitiated boys may not engage in sexual intercourse, they must eat with other children and with women, and they are permitted to play in the women's section of the hut. After initiation, they may engage in sexual intercourse, are expected to eat with other men, and are forbidden to enter the women's section of the hut.

Further, age grades differ in the access they afford their members to highly rewarded economic and political roles. In Western societies, in contrast, people's chronological age is but a partial clue to their social locations. Class and ethnic factors cut across lines of age stratification and provide additional sources of identity.

On the surface, societies with age-grade systems seem to provide an orderly method for role allocation and reallocation. But in practice the transition process is often less than orderly. Conflicts frequently arise between age grades, essentially a version of the time-honored struggle between the "ins" and the "outs." The desire of people to gain access to or hold on to various privileges and rewards fuels social discord and individual grievances. The rules governing transition may not be clear. Even when they seem to be unambiguous, the rules are always open to different interpretations and to "bending" in one or another group's favor. The continuing debate in the United States over Social Security funding and benefits reflects this type of tugging between the young and the elderly.

All societies are faced with the fact that aging is inevitable and continuous. Hence they all must make provision for the perpetual flow of one cohort after another by fitting each age group into an appropriate array of social roles. Societies with age-grade systems attempt to achieve the transition by establishing points in the life course for entering roles and leaving them. Another solution, more closely approximated in Western societies, is to allow "natural" forces to operate: younger people assume adult roles when they are ready to do so, while older people give up roles when they are ready to do so or when they become ill or die.

In the United States no collective rituals mark the passage from one age grade to another. High-school and college graduation ceremonies are an exception, but even here not all individuals in a cohort graduate from either high school or college. And there is some flexibility in the operation of the age system, in that gifted children skip grades in elementary school and bright youths are allowed to enter college after only two or three years of high school. At the older age levels, too, flexibility often operates—within some companies and some occupations—with regard to retirement (for instance, one can retire from the military after twenty years of service). Nevertheless, age norms serve as a counterpart of the age-grade system in broadly defining what is appropriate for people to be and to do at various ages.

Life Events

People locate themselves across the life span in terms of social timetables. They also do so in terms of **life events**—turning points at which individuals change direction in the course of their lives. Some life events are related to social clocks, including entering school, graduating from school, and starting to work. But others may take place under circumstances that are largely independent of age, including losing a limb in an automobile accident, being raped, winning a lottery, undergoing a "born again" conversion, or living at the time Pearl Harbor was attacked. We often employ major life events as reference points or time markers in our lives, speaking of "the time I left home for school," "the day I had my heart attack," and "when I started going with Chris." Such life events define transitions.

Life events may be examined in a great many ways (Hultsch and Plemmons, 1979; Brim, 1980). For in-

Life Events
Leaving home for college is a major life event that individuals often employ as a "bench mark" in their lives.
Jean-Claude Lejeune

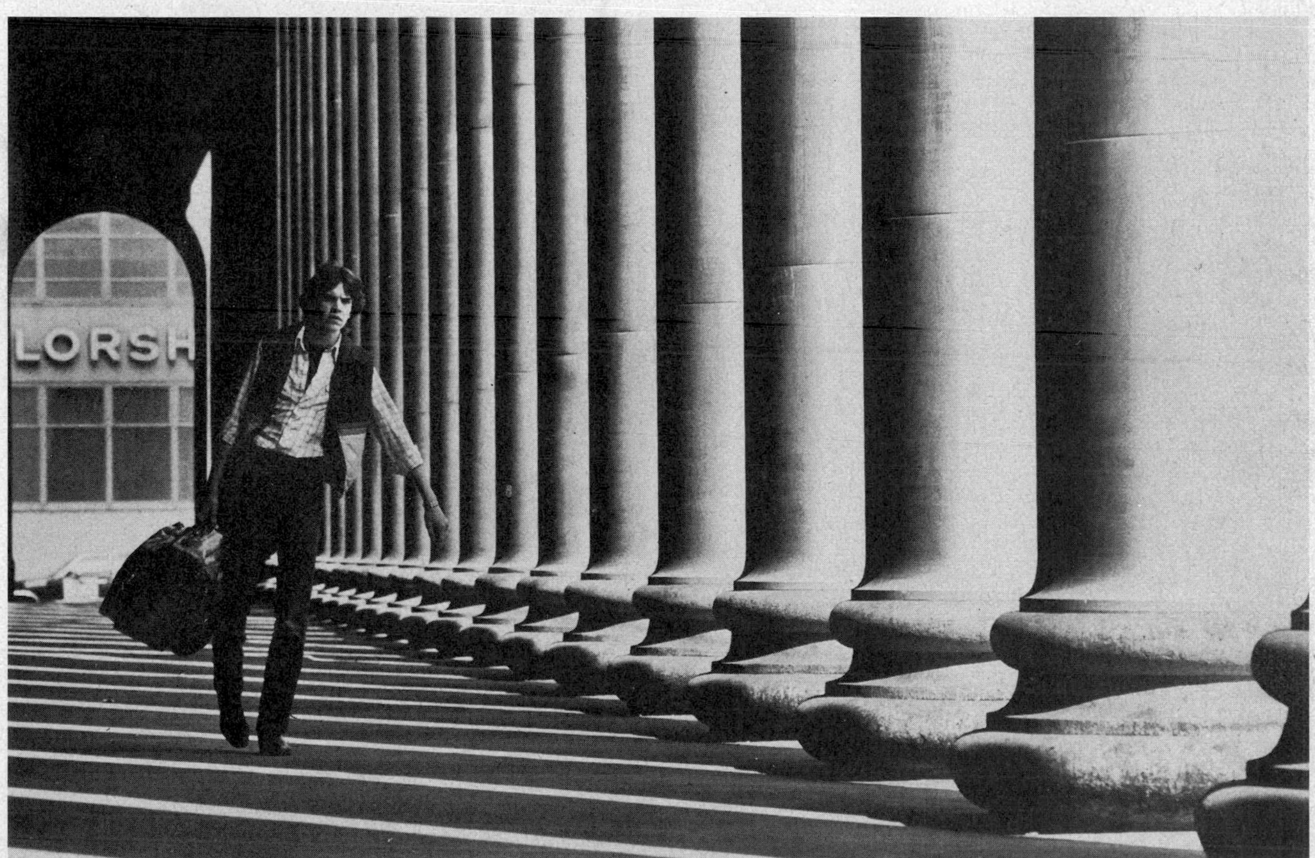

stance, some are associated with internal growth or aging factors like puberty or old age. Others, including wars, national economic crises, and revolutions, are the consequences of living in society. And still others derive from events in the physical world such as fires, storms, tidal waves, earthquakes, or avalanches. And there are those events that have a strong inner or psychological component, including a profound religious experience, the realization that one has reached the zenith of one's career, or the decision to leave one's spouse. Any of these events we may view as good or bad, a gain or a loss, controllable or uncontrollable, and stressful or unstressful.

Often in thinking about a life event, we ask ourselves three questions: "Will it happen to me?"; "If so, when will it occur?"; and "If it happens, will others also experience it or will I be the only one?" The first question has to do with the probability of an event's taking place, for instance, getting married or experiencing a serious football injury. If we believe that the probability of an event's occurring is low, we are unlikely to attend to or anticipate it in advance (for instance, most of us are more likely to give thought to and prepare for marriage than we are for a serious football injury). The second question has to do with an event's correlation with chronological age, for example, the death of one's spouse or the suffering of a heart attack. Age relatedness matters because it influences whether or not we are caught unexpectedly by the event. The third question has to do with the social distribution of an event, whether everyone will experience it or just one or a few persons. This question is important because it will largely determine whether people will organize social support systems to assist us in buffering the change.

THE SEARCH FOR PERIODS IN ADULT DEVELOPMENT

Any number of psychologists have undertaken the search for what they view as the regular, sequential periods and transitions in the life cycle (see Chapter 2). Like childhood, they conceive of adult development as a succession of stages. They depict adulthood as a sort of stairway made up of a series of discrete steplike levels. One of the most popular versions of the stage approach is contained in Gail Sheehy's best-selling book, *Passages* (1976). She views each stage as posing problems that must be resolved before the individual can successfully advance to the next stage. By passing from one stage to the next—*passages*—each person acquires new strengths and evolves an *authentic identity.* Such an identity has many of the qualities that Abraham Maslow associates with the self-actualized person (see Chapter 2).

Other psychologists have taken exception to the stage approach. Some believe that an individual's identity is fairly well established during the formative years and does not fundamentally change much in adulthood. According to this view, people may change jobs, addresses, even faces, but the personality persists, much in the manner of adult height and weight, with only minor changes. Let us examine these matters more carefully.

Erikson: Psychosocial Stages

One of the most influential stage approaches has been that pioneered by Erik Erikson. It will be recalled from our discussion in Chapter 2 that Erikson identified eight life-span stages, three of which apply to adulthood: early adulthood, which involves intimacy versus isolation; middle adulthood, which involves generativity versus stagnation; and old age, which involves integrity versus despair.

The principal developmental task confronting young adults in the stage of intimacy versus isolation is one of reaching out and making contact with other people. They must cultivate the ability to enter and establish close and intimate relationships with others. Should they fail to accomplish this task, they confront the danger of leading shallow lives devoid of meaningful bonds.

In middle adulthood the task of generativity requires individuals to reach out beyond their own immediate concerns and assist younger people to realize their potentials. During this stage they assume responsibility for the generation that is to follow them. Should they instead become preoccupied with themselves, they confront stagnation and emptiness.

As individuals approach their later years, Erikson contends, they must finally come to terms with themselves and with the meaning of their lives. They take stock of themselves, looking back and reminiscing about what they have accomplished through the years. In doing so, they can experience a positive sense of achievement or a negative feeling of despair regarding their worth.

Singles

Census data reveal that single status among l
and women under thirty-five years of age ha
increased in recent years. This has resulte
from the tendency of young people to postp
riage. For example, half the women and tv
of the men twenty to twenty-four years old
married in 1980, up from 36 percent of the
and 55 percent of the men in 1970. There
been a marked increase in the proportion of
uals between twenty-five and forty years of
are divorced.

More than two-thirds of adult singles l
someone else: a friend, relative, or "spouse
lent." By 1990, fully 45 percent of all housel
expected to be headed by a man or woman
a spouse. Twenty-nine percent will be hea
woman and 16 percent by a man. Also, man
live alone. In 1980, one of every five house
the United States consisted of one person li
tirely alone. The figure is expected to reacl
four by 1990. Although many single individu
alone are elderly widows, the biggest incre
tween 1970 and 1980 came among young m
to a lesser extent, young women. The figu
than tripled for men under age thirty-four an
tripled for women in the same age catego

Phases in Ad
Until relativel
to their repro
aside from th
Patrick Reddy

cycle. But w
for pay at so
side the hor
role in the s
all, there ha
marital statu
and roles a
pause and th
that are com
ters 17 and 1

Family ar
the phases L
opment do n
thing, work

Intimacy Versus Isolation

According to Erik Erikson, the major developmental task confronting young adults has to do with developing the capacity to reach out and establish close and intimate relationships with others.

Gabor Demjen/Stock, Boston

Erikson says that each stage of life confronts individuals with a unique crisis with which they must grapple. When successfully mastered, the crisis serves as a turning point that allows each person to reach a higher level of development and potential. Should the individual fail to come to terms with the critical developmental task of a stage, the rest of his or her development is impaired. The person has difficulty coming to terms with reality and finding happiness in life.

The psychiatrist George E. Vaillant and his associates (Vaillant and Milofsky, 1980) found support for Erikson's formulations when they followed up a group of 392 white lower-class youth and 94 highly educated men who were first studied in the 1940s. They concluded, as Erikson contends, that the post-childhood stages of an individual's life cycle must be passed through sequentially. Failure to master one of Erikson's stages typically precluded mastery of later stages. However, the age at which the men mastered a given stage varied enormously. In fact, one man in six was still struggling in his forties with adolescent-type issues. When the researchers examined subsequent employment patterns, those men who typically showed the greatest childhood maturity were five times more likely to have ended up being well paid for their adult work than those men showing the least maturity. Further, the most emotionally mature boys were sixteen times less likely to have experienced significant unemployment by the time they had reached their mid-forties.

Levinson: Phases in Adult Male Development

Whoever, in middle age, attempts to realize the wishes and hopes of his early youth, invariably deceives himself. Each ten years of a man's life has its own fortunes, its own hopes, its own desires.

—GOETHE
Elective Affinities, 1809

A number of Yale researchers, led by psychologist Daniel J. Levinson (1974, 1976, 1978), have also approached adulthood from a stage perspective. They have constructed a descriptive framework for defining phases in the life-span development of adult males.

we invest ourselves in and commit ours
other person. Many of our needs can only
in this fashion. Through association with
are meaningful to us, we realize a sense
love, acceptance, companionship, an
worth.

Social interactions that rest on expres
termed **primary relationships.** We vie
lationships—with friends, family, and love
in themselves, valuable in their own righ
lationships tend to be personal, intimate
sive.

An **instrumental tie** is a social link th
when we cooperate with another person
a limited goal. At times this may mean w
our enemies, as in the old political sayi
makes strange bedfellows." More commo
means that we find ourselves integrated
networks of diverse people—for instance,
of labor extending from the farmers who
to the grocers who sell bread.

Social interactions that rest on instrume
called **secondary relationships.** We vi
lationships as means to ends rather than
their own right. Examples are our relati
the cashier at the supermarket, the clerk i
trar's office, or a gas station attendant.
relationships are everyday touch-and-go
which individuals need have little or no
of one another.

Plural Spouses

Although marriage is apparently found in all societies, only about a fifth of the 238 societies in the sample of George Peter Murdock were strictly monogamous. As in the case of this Bakhtiari chief in Iran, polygyny—a one-husband-and-plural-wives arrangement—is a common pattern.

Tony Howarth/Daily Telegraph Magazine/Woodfin Camp & Associates

women; it has often meant simply that younger brothers have sexual access to the wife of an older brother. Thus where a father is unable to afford wives for each of his sons, he may secure a wife for only his oldest son. W. H. R. Rivers (1906: 515) gives this account of polyandrous practices among the Todas, a non-Hindu tribe of India:

> The Todas have a completely organized and definite system of polyandry. When a woman marries a man, it is understood that she becomes the wife of his brothers at the same time. When a boy is married to a girl, not only are his brothers usually regarded as also the husbands of the girl, but any brother born later will similarly be regarded as sharing his older brother's right. . . . The brothers live together, and my informants seemed to regard it as a ridiculous idea that there should even be disputes or jealousies of the kind that might be expected in such a household. . . . Instead of adultery being regarded as immoral . . . according to the Toda idea, immorality attaches rather to the man who grudges his wife to another.

Anthropologists disagree on whether group marriage genuinely exists in any society as a normatively encouraged life-style. There is some evidence that it may take place among the Marquesans of the South Pacific, the Chukchee of Siberia, the Kaingang of Brazil, and the Todas of India. On occasion, as among the Todas, polyandry slides into group marriage when a number of brothers share more than one wife.

As in the past, monogamy remains the dominant life-style in the United States. Of Americans aged thirty-five or older, over 90 percent have been married at least once. But about four in ten marriages end in divorce. If current divorce rates continue, about 32 percent of the couples married in 1952 will divorce. The figure stands at 45 percent for those married in 1967. And population experts predict that fully half of all recently married couples could eventually divorce (Weed, 1982). In most cases—four out of five—divorced people remarry (an estimated 44 percent of all current marriages are remarriages). In turn, about 45 percent of those who divorce and remarry divorce a second time. Hence, rather than having recourse to polygyny, polyandry, or group marriage, many Americans have maintained a monogamous arrangement through *serial monogamy*—a pattern of marriage, divorce, and remarriage.

In sum, Americans have not given up on marriage. Public opinion surveys show that Americans depend very heavily on their marriages for their psychological well-being (Glenn and Weaver, 1981). Indeed, history reveals marriage to be a very resilient institutional arrangement. Not surprisingly, marriage is the most prevalent American life-style (see Table 16.2). Increasingly numbers of Americans have simply come to define marriage as something that can be ended and reentered. Hence many Americans no longer view it as a permanent institution. Moreover, marriages differ. Marriage encompasses a wide range of interaction patterns, each of which entails a somewhat different life-style. We will return to this topic in Chapter 18.

THE FAMILY LIFE CYCLE AND PARENTHOOD

Over the course of their lives, most Americans find themselves members of two family groups. First, a

Table 16.2 Marital Status of Americans

	1980	Percent
Males, 15 and Over	83,839,270	100.0
Single	25,074,755	29.9
Married	50,518,621	60.3
Separated	1,588,846	1.9
Widowed	2,125,493	2.5
Divorced	4,531,555	5.4
Females, 15 and Over	91,414,347	100.0
Single	21,037,493	23.0
Married	50,138,720	54.8
Separated	2,404,936	2.6
Widowed	11,231,965	12.3
Divorced	6,601,233	7.2

SOURCE: Census Bureau.

person belongs to a nuclear family that typically consists of oneself and one's father, mother, and siblings. This group is termed the *family of orientation.* Second, since over 90 percent of Americans marry at least once, the vast majority of the population are members of a nuclear family consisting of oneself and one's spouse and often children. This group is termed the *family of procreation.*

Various psychologists and sociologists have sought to find a framework for describing the changes that occur across a person's life span that are related to these shifts in family patterns. One tool that they have devised is the concept of the **family life cycle**—the sequential changes and realignments that occur in the structure and relationships of family life between the time of marriage and the death of one or both spouses (Deutscher, 1964; Rapoport, Rapoport, and Strelitz, 1976; Nock, 1979). The family life cycle model views families, like individuals, as undergoing development that is characterized by identifiable phases or stages.

Stages in the Family Life Cycle

In the United States, families have traditionally had a fairly predictable natural history. Major changes in expectations and requirements are imposed upon a husband and wife as their children are born and grow up. The sociologist Reuben Hill (1964) describes the major milestones in a nine-stage cycle:

1. Establishment—newly married, childless
2. New parents—until first infant three years old
3. Preschool family—oldest child three to six years old, possibly younger siblings
4. School-age family—oldest child six to twelve years old, possibly younger siblings
5. Family with adolescent—oldest child thirteen to nineteen years old, possibly younger siblings
6. Family with young adult—oldest child twenty years or more, until first child leaves home

Family Life Cycle

The family life cycle approach depicts the sequential changes and realignments that occur in the structure and relationships of the family between the time of marriage and the death of one or both spouses.

Patrick Reddy

7. Family as launching center—from departure of first child to departure of last child
8. Postparental family—after children have left home, until father retires
9. Aging family—after retirement of father

As viewed by Hill and other sociologists, the family begins with the simple husband-wife pair and becomes increasingly complex as members are added, creating new roles and multiplying the number of interpersonal relations. The family then stabilizes for a brief period, after which it begins shrinking as each of the adult children is launched. Finally it returns once again to the husband-wife pair and then terminates with the death of a spouse.

Each modification in the role content of one family member has implications for all other members, since they are bound together in a network of complementary roles—a set of mutually contingent relationships. Consequently, each stage in the family life cycle requires new adaptations and adjustments. Of particular importance are the events surrounding parenthood. Accordingly, let us examine more closely the significance of parenthood for young adults.

Pregnancy

Within the life cycle of a couple, particularly a woman, the first pregnancy is an event of unparalleled importance (Grossman, Eichler, and Winickoff, 1980; Valentine, 1982; Gloger-Tippelt, 1983). It signals that a couple is entering into the family cycle, bringing about new role requirements. As such the first pregnancy functions as a major marker or transition and confronts a couple with new developmental tasks (Duvall, 1977).

Pregnancy requires a woman to marshal her resources and adjust to a good many changes. Unfortunately, in many cases a woman's earliest experiences of pregnancy may be somewhat negative; she may encounter morning sickness, vomiting, and fatigue (see Chapter 4). Pregnancy may also compel a woman to reflect on her long-term life plans, particularly as they relate to marriage and a career. And pregnancy may cause her to reconsider her sense of identity. Her partner faces many of these same concerns. He may have to reappraise his conception of age, responsibility, and autonomy. Similarly, pregnancy frequently contributes to changes in the couple's sexual behavior. Since few events equal pregnancy in suddenness or significance, many couples experience the initial phase of pregnancy as somewhat disruptive (Gloger-Tippelt, 1983).

On the broader social level, relatives, friends, and acquaintances commonly offer judgments on numerous matters, including whether or not the woman stands in a proper social relationship with the father-to-be. An employed woman may have to confront changed relationships in the work setting as her employer and colleagues reappraise their ties with her. If she should withdraw from the paid work force in preparation for childbirth, the mother-to-be may find that her domestic situation also alters: the more egalitarian values and role patterns of dual-career couples tend to give way to the stereotyped role patterns found in traditional nuclear families.

Researchers have identified four major developmental tasks confronting a pregnant woman. First, she must come to accept her pregnancy. She must define herself as a parent-to-be and incorporate into her life frame an impending sense of parenthood. This process requires developing an emotional attachment to her unborn child. Women typically become progressively preoccupied with the fetus and, especially around the time that they begin to detect clear movements of the child in the uterus, ascribe personal characteristics to it.

Second, as a woman's pregnancy progresses, she must come to differentiate herself from the fetus and establish a distinct sense of self. She may accomplish this task by reflecting on a name for the infant and imagining what the baby will look like and how it will behave. This process is expedited when her increasing size brings about alterations in her clothing and she assumes a "pregnancy identity."

Third, a pregnant woman typically reflects on and reevaluates her relationship with her own mother (Fischer, 1981). This process often entails the woman's reconciliation with her mother and the working through of numerous feelings, memories, and identifications.

Fourth, a woman must come to terms with the issue of dependency. Her pregnancy and impending motherhood often arouse anxiety concerning her loss of certain freedoms and her reliance on others for some measure of support, maintenance, and help. Such concerns are frequently centered on her relationship with her husband or partner.

The accomplishment of these developmental tasks is often expedited by childbirth-training classes (Doering, Entwisle, and Quinlan, 1980). Such classes teach

Pregnancy
Pregnancy functions as a major marker or transition in the life of a woman. It confronts her with new developmental tasks, including coming to terms with her pregnancy, taking better physical care of herself, and redefining her relationships with other people who are important to her.
J. Howard/Stock, Boston

women what to expect during pregnancy and labor. They have an opportunity to verbalize their concerns. And the knowledge and techniques they gain from the classes afford them a measure of "active control" and self-help. Finally, when husbands or partners also participate in the training classes, mothers-to-be find additional social support and assistance. Both preparation in pregnancy and a husband's presence are positively associated with the quality of a woman's birth experience (Norr et al., 1977). Indeed, much that happens before birth influences what transpires between parent and child after birth (Heinicke et al., 1983).

Transition to Parenthood

Psychologists and sociologists who view the family as an integrated system of roles and statuses have often depicted the onset of parenthood as a "crisis" because it involves a shift from a two-person to a three-person system (LeMasters, 1957; Dyer, 1963). The three-person system is thought to be inherently more stressful than the two-person system. The sociologist Alice S. Rossi (1968: 35) also finds other reasons why the transition to parenthood may pose a crisis:

> The birth of a child is not followed by any gradual taking on of responsibility, as in the case of a professional work role. It is as if the woman shifted from a graduate student to a full professor with little intervening apprenticeship experience of slowly increasing responsibility. The new mother starts out immediately on twenty-four-hour duty, with responsibility for a fragile and mysterious infant totally dependent on her care.

But many researchers have questioned these conclusions (Hobbs, 1965, 1968; Hobbs and Cole, 1976). Their research suggests that relatively few couples view the onset of parenthood as especially stressful. They point out that any role change is likely to involve transitional difficulties and that it seems an exaggeration to term the experience a crisis (Lamb, 1978; McLaughlin and Micklin, 1983). Indeed, many couples find that there are many rewards associated with having a baby (Russell, 1974).

No one disputes the fact that parenthood brings changes, and major changes at that. This is also the finding of a 1975 study, conducted by the University of Michigan Institute for Social Research, that employed a national sample of husbands and wives (Campbell et al., 1976). One of the most significant changes found by the Michigan researchers was the marked separation that occurs in the roles of husband and wife. The woman is likely to give up employment outside the home, and the man becomes less likely to help with household tasks. The couple typically shift toward a more traditional pattern of family living. And there is an increased likelihood that the

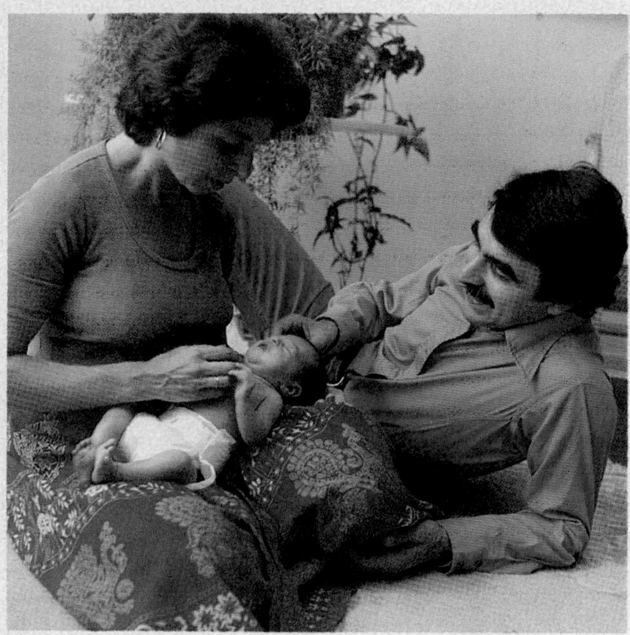

Parenthood Brings Changes

When people assume new roles—and parenthood is a new role—they acquire new rights and duties. As such, they are called upon to change their behavior in significant ways. Contemporary parents appear to have less romantic and more realistic conceptions of what parenthood entails than earlier generations of Americans did.

Freda Leinwand/Monkmeyer

husband and wife will evolve separate friendships.

Overall, according to the Michigan study, most men and women feel that children bring a couple closer together and symbolize the bond between them. Many say that children give them a common goal and compel them to pull together for their children's welfare. Despite the fact that children may diminish the time the partners have for each other, they believe that children affect their marriages positively.

Of interest, it is the couples in the early stage of parenting who report the most satisfaction from children, even though they are also the ones who register the most severe complaints. Among the disadvantages they cite are that children give the parents less time to spend together as a couple, that children curtail one's freedom, that disagreements arise over child-rearing ideas and practices, and that the wife becomes so absorbed in mothering that she often shortchanges her role as wife. But parents also see parenthood as a growing experience. Many new parents mentioned that they had become "more responsible," that they felt themselves "needed," and that they found greater "meaning in life." When asked what they liked most about having children, they often simply said that "kids are fun."

Other research suggests that wives' sense of how well they are adjusting to their marriage decreases significantly after the birth of their first child (Waldron and Routh, 1981; Belsky, Spanier, and Rovine, 1983). And some researchers find evidence of a "baby honeymoon," with parents' personal and marital stress more evident when babies are eight months old than when they are one month old (Miller and Sollie, 1980). (However, parents may initially experience a short period termed the *postpartum blues*, which is discussed in the boxed insert on page 457.)

Overall, contemporary parents seem to have a less romantic and more realistic view of the probable effects of children on their lives than did earlier generations of parents. This recognition seems to prepare them for coping with the changes that parenthood brings. They have to juggle a whole new set of questions about their work roles, demands on their time, communication patterns, privacy, and the companionship aspects of their relationship. But on the whole they report enormous satisfaction in parenthood.

Employed Mothers

If a woman's adult efforts are concentrated exclusively on her children, she is more likely to stifle than broaden her children's perspective and preparation for adult life.

—ALICE S. ROSSI
The Woman in America

One aspect of motherhood that appears particularly stressful is the balancing of motherhood and career. One young mother observes (Miller and Sollie, 1980: 463):

> Like many new mothers I am faced with hard decisions about the future of my career since my baby was born. I am full of doubts, and I'm uncertain how to maintain my career and raise my child satisfactorily.

When mothers do interrupt their careers, they often note that they experience an intellectual and social void in their lives.

Over the past several decades, more and more mothers with young children have found employment outside the home. In 1982 over half of all children under eighteen had working mothers—fully 32

Employed Mothers

One arrangement that working mothers have found to be helpful is the corporate nursery. As their time permits, mothers can visit their children to play with them or feed them.

David Woo/Stock, Boston

million children. The mothers of more than 45 percent of preschoolers and about 60 percent of school-age children are in the labor force (see Figure 16.1).

In its original formulation, the family life cycle approach made no reference at all to the mother's participation in the paid labor force. But today the career woman and the mother are increasingly one and the same person. Newer versions of the scheme have recognized this fact, especially during the early stages when women leave paid employment upon the birth of the first child and later resume a labor-market career (Waite, 1980). (See the discussion of the phases in adult female development in Chapter 15.)

Serious concern is frequently voiced about the future of America's children as more and more mothers enter the work force. Many people fear that the working mother represents a loss to children in terms of supervision, love, and cognitive enrichment. Much of the earlier research of maternal employment and juvenile delinquency was based on this assumption: mothers were working, children were unsupervised, and thus they became delinquents. But the matter is not that simple. In a classic study of lower-class boys, Sheldon and Eleanor Glueck (1957) found that sons of regularly employed mothers were no more likely to be delinquent than sons of nonemployed mothers. However, inadequate supervision does appear to be associated with delinquency, whatever the mother's employment status (Hoffman, 1974).

Flora F. Cherry and Ethel L. Eaton (1977) studied 200 lower-income families in order to determine possible harmful outcomes due to maternal employment during a child's first three years of life. When the children were seven and eight years old, they were all compared with respect to physical growth and weight, IQ, and reading, arithmetic, and spelling achievement. Cherry and Eaton found that those whose mothers had worked were no different in physical and cognitive development from those whose mothers had not worked. Most researchers have arrived at essentially the same conclusion (Schubert, Bardley-Hohnson, and Nuttal, 1980; Farel, 1981; Schachter, 1981).

Increasingly, psychologists and sociologists are no longer asking whether it is good or bad that mothers work outside the home. Instead, they are finding that the central question is whether or not the mother, regardless of employment, is satisfied in her situation (Hoffman and Nye, 1974; Stuckey et al., 1982; Sweeney, 1982). They conclude that the working mother who obtains personal satisfaction from employment, who does not feel excessive guilt, and who has adequate household arrangements is likely to perform as well as or better than the nonworking mother. Mothers who are *not* working and would like to, and working mothers whose lives are beset by harassment and strain, are the ones whose children are most likely to show maladjustment and behavioral problems. Hence

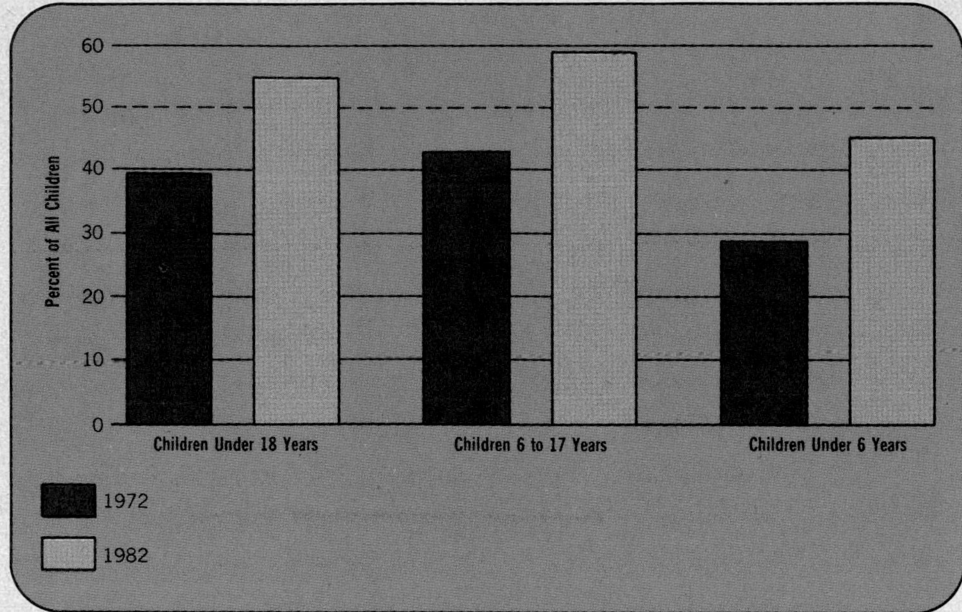

Figure 16.1 Children with Employed Mothers, 1972 and 1982

The proportion of mothers in the labor force has increased dramatically over the past decade.

SOURCE: *Women at Work: A Chartbook*, Bulletin 2168 (Washington, D. C.: U.S. Department of Labor, Bureau of Labor Statistics).

much depends on the family's socioeconomic circumstances, the father's role, the attitudes of other family members, and the availability of support systems ranging from child care facilities to helpful friends and relatives.

The working mother also provides a somewhat different role model for her children from that of the nonworking mother. Consequently, maternal employment tends to be associated with less traditional sex role concepts, more approval of working mothers, and a higher evaluation of female competence (Gold and Andres, 1978*a*, 1978*b*). Evidence from Brazil points to somewhat similar outcomes (Pasquali and Callegari, 1978).

Among dual-earner couples with children, it is not uncommon for the parents to work different shifts. Although this arrangement reduces the time in the evening or night that both parents can be with the children, it maximizes the time that at least one parent can be present. A 1980 Census sample of dual-earner couples with children found that in one-third of the cases at least one spouse worked a schedule other than a regular day shift. In about one-tenth of the households, the spouses worked entirely different shifts with no overlap in their hours (Presser and Cain, 1983). This finding should encourage an exploration of the family and social implications of this child care arrangement.

Single-Parent Mothers

Over the past twenty years, single-parent families have increased seven times more rapidly than have traditional two-parent, or nuclear, families. As noted in Chapter 10, it is estimated that nearly half of all children born in the 1980s will live in a single-parent home for at least part of their childhood. The vast majority of children in single-parent homes are reared by their mothers; less than 9 percent are brought up by fathers.

Single-parent homes are produced by divorce, desertion, marital separation, death, or unmarried parenthood. Now that many states have begun permitting unmarried persons to adopt children, a small number also result from adoption. In single-parent families the responsibilities fall upon one adult rather than two, a fact frequently mentioned by single parents. One divorced mother says (Brown et al., 1976: 123):

> There's nobody to stand with you (but he didn't before). You have to come up with all the answers. There's just no one between you and the children. It's scary at times. There are good things, like a lot less interference. You have more freedom, but also more responsibility.

Another mother says (Brown et al., 1976: 123):

> The hard part is having to make important decisions alone—not having anyone to share these with, having

POSTPARTUM BLUES

About two or three days after delivery, some new mothers experience what is commonly termed the *postpartum blues.* The symptoms include irritability, waves of sadness, frequent crying spells, difficulty in sleeping, diminished appetite, and feelings of helplessness and hopelessness. Generally the episode is mild and lasts only a short time—several days to two weeks. Similar symptoms often appear in women who adopt a child, and some new fathers also report that they feel "down in the dumps." One study reported that 89 percent of new mothers experienced some symptoms that have been traditionally associated with the postpartum blues and 62 percent of the fathers had similar symptoms (Collins, 1981*b*).

Various explanations have been advanced for the postpartum blues. Some authorities believe that hormonal changes associated with childbirth and metabolic readjustment to a nonpregnant state can influence a woman's psychological state. Following childbirth, marked changes occur in the levels of various hormones. There is a dramatic decline in the female sex hormones, and changes may also occur in thyroid and adrenal hormones. All these changes can contribute to depressive reactions.

Other explanations of a more psychological nature emphasize the adjustments required of a woman in her new role as a mother. Many women experience a loss of independence—a sense of being tied down and trapped by the new infant. Other women may feel guilty about the anger they develop when their infants cry and cannot be comforted. And some women also feel overwhelmed by the responsibility of caring for, rearing, and shaping the behavior of another human being.

Psychoanalytic theorists say that the precipitating factor in postpartum blues is the unconscious conflict a woman experiences when she assumes the mothering role. The conflict is derived from a woman's ambivalent identification with her own mother. According to this view, deep-seated, repressed childhood feelings of attraction (love) and repulsion (aggressive and destructive impulses) toward her mother are activated when a woman becomes a mother in her own right. Since she identifies with her mother as a woman, the new mother develops a love-hate conflict with respect to herself. The result is psychological depression.

In a small number of cases, the birth of a child may act as a catalyst that triggers severe mental illness among women who are predisposed to schizophrenic or manic-depressive psychoses. Psychiatrists generally make no distinction between a psychosis that appears during the postpartum period and a psychotic episode at other periods of life, except for the fact that the precipitating event is the birth of a child. In more devastating forms of mental illness, a woman may attempt suicide and require hospitalization.

> the feeling of sole responsibility. There's the constancy of the burden—no one else to take over. A married woman doesn't feel so "on her own."

Single parents must allocate their time to cover both their own and their children's physical, social, and psychological needs. The matter is complicated by the fact that schools and workplaces have inflexible hours, and these hours do not coincide. One divorced mother describes her day in the following way (Brown et al., 1976: 123):

> Everything is a tradeoff, a continuing conflict. There is no one else to do anything—shopping, dentists, chores, everything has to be done in evenings and weekends. I need the job, so I can't tell the boss to go to hell and take time off.

In sum, single-parent mothers frequently suffer from a lack of free time, spiraling child care costs, loneliness, and the unrelenting pressures of attempting to fill the needs posed by both home and work.

Being a single parent calls for a somewhat different kind of parenting. Many single parents report that they establish a closer tie with their children since another adult is not present. Frequently, single parents find themselves making "the speech," as one mother termed it, explaining (McCoy, 1982: 21):

> I sat down with my three children and said: "Look. Things are going to have to be different. We're all in this together and we're going to have to be partners. I'm earning a living for us now. I'm doing it all. I need your help, if this household is going to work."

Women heading single-parent families typically experience greater stress than women in two-parent families (McLanahan, 1983). Lower incomes and a lower level of social support lead to chronic strain. Disruptions due to substantial income changes, residential relocations, and household-composition changes are also more likely. Not surprisingly, female heads report much lower self-esteem, a lower sense of effectiveness, and less optimism about the future than their counterparts in two-parent settings. However, recently divorced, separated, and widowed women are more likely to experience major life-event disruptions than women who have been single for three or more years.

Not uncommonly, single-parent mothers find themselves in difficult economic circumstances. Nearly one-half live below the poverty level, and many are dependent on government agencies for assistance. The National Advisory Council on Economic Opportunity describes this "feminization of poverty" as "the most compelling social fact" of the past decade (Mann, 1983). Lack of job training, loss of skill during the childbearing years, and discriminatory hiring and promotion patterns often mean that single mothers work for low wages.

In addition, a social stigma often attaches to the single mother as a result of her unwed or divorced status, and she is further discriminated against as a female head of household. In her dealings with people in the world about her, she must contend with being stereotyped as financially irresponsible, sexually "fair game," and psychologically "disabled." In many respects a single father is in a better position than a single mother, since he is frequently viewed as a heroic figure who is doing something extraordinary (Brown et al., 1976).

According to the Census Bureau, only 47 percent of 4 million women who are supposed to receive child-support payments are collecting the full amount (Sanders, 1983). In America, divorce often removes all a man's fathering functions save for one, the monetary obligation. And as men start seeing their children less, they often start paying less. Should they remarry, as most divorced men do, they also have the financial obligations associated with their new families. In the United States, child support accounts for about 13 percent of the average income of fathers. In 1981 the average child-support payment was $2,180 for white women, $1,640 for black women, and $2,070 for Hispanic women.

Many families headed by women survive these hardships with few ill effects. Some even blossom as a result of the spirit of cooperation that is required to make the households work. But a disturbing number of children and parents are saddled with problems. Some studies show that juvenile-delinquency rates are twice as high for children from single-parent households as they are for children from two-parent households. Lack of parental supervision and chronic social and psychological strains are often complicated by the problems associated with poverty (Mann, 1983).

In about 50 percent of all single-parent families, the parent marries or remarries within five years. This results in a "blended" or "reconstituted" family, which can produce complicated kinship networks (see Chapter 18). Where both partners have been previously married, each has to deal with the former spouse of the current partner as well as with his or her own former spouse. Then there are stepparent-stepchildren relationships—one's own children's reactions to the current spouse, one's own reactions to the current spouse's children, and the children's reactions to one another.

Single-Parent Fathers

What was portrayed in the hit movie *Kramer vs. Kramer* is becoming a way of life for increasing numbers of American men: rearing children alone. Because of prenatal medical attention and advances in medical technology, there has been a decline in the number of men who become single parents as a result of their wives' death. But overall the number of single fathers has grown, as more men are awarded custody of children in divorce proceedings and as a growing number of women abandon their families in search of new life-styles and working opportunities. Indeed, fifteen years ago a father was awarded custody of his children only if he could demonstrate in court that the mother was "unfit" for parenthood.

As Joseph W. Maxwell (1976: 387) points out, fatherhood in the United States is defined by a set of precise role expectations:

> Fatherhood may be an enigma to the social scientists who theorize about it or attempt to understand it as a social role. It seems, however, to wear a plain face for those who practice it. There is nothing ambiguous or uncertain about what it means to be a father in middle-class America, if one can believe what fathers say about themselves. Like an isolated beacon light, fatherhood seems to pulsate with a singular purpose—to provide for the family. . . . A father in America today is likely to view

Single-Parent Fathers

Not too long ago parenting was equated with "mothering." But changes in American life, including the growing number of single-parent fathers, has made child care and parenting increasingly a non–gender-denominated role.

Peter Menzel/Stock, Boston

> himself as the center pole in the family tent, the base on which the family rests, the one who—more than any other—is obligated to see that its needs are supplied and its physical security maintained.

Although the expectations attached to the father role in a two-parent family are fairly explicit, this is not true for a father in the single-parent family. The vast majority of single fathers previously performed their parental responsibilities in partnership with their children's mothers. But in single fatherhood there is no role clarity about what they are to do and how they are to do it (Mendes, 1976). As one single father exclaims: "I'm a male mother in a society in which only women are supposed to mother!"

A number of studies have shown that even though single fathers are confronted with some unique adjustment requirements, most of them are successful in raising their children (Gasser and Taylor, 1976; Mendes, 1976; Orthner, Brown, and Ferguson, 1976). Juggling work and child care commonly poses difficulties for single fathers, especially those with preschool youngsters. One widower with small children notes (Thornton, 1982: 620):

> You have to worry about the kids all the time. You get accustomed to doing everything alone—refereeing battles or playing Solomon over the telephone. You have to make sure that keys are always available. Schools and doctors have to have your phone number at work. You must keep easy-to-prepare food at the house in case you can't get home in time to fix meals. You cancel your social plans quite often, too.

Many fathers try at first to have someone come into their homes and care for the children while they are at work. The vast majority, however, soon find this to be an unsatisfactory arrangement. Fathers generally report that their children are inadequately supervised and cared for by hired baby-sitters. Further, the arrangement tends to be unstable, with a high turnover rate among the caretakers. Consequently, fathers tend to gravitate toward nurseries and child care centers, where they feel that the staff has a professional commitment to children (Mendes, 1976).

Once the children begin attending elementary school, fathers usually allow them to stay alone after school. Simultaneously, a good many fathers try to structure after-school activities on some weekdays by having their children join scout organizations or athletic teams or take gymnastic, music, or dancing lessons. At times fathers undertake to supervise their children's activities by telephone.

Instead of hiring domestic help, most single fathers themselves assume the responsibility for cleaning, cooking, shopping, and generally managing the household. It appears, however, that they are more inclined than two-parent families to assign their children various household chores and to integrate the children into the management of the home. Some fathers eliminate the irksome problem of ironing by purchasing nothing but wash-and-wear clothing.

Generally, single fathers seem better prepared for the physical aspects of parenting—shopping, cooking, cleaning, taking the child to the doctor, and the like—than for dealing with their children's emotional needs. Men who adeptly juggle work schedules to stay home and nurse a sick child report that they fall apart in the face of a healthy temper tantrum. They view their children's strong displays of emotion as "irrational," especially when they cannot trace those emotions to some specific event in the children's lives. In sum, a good many single fathers admit that they have had to learn to deal with their children's emotional needs and to develop their own nurturing skills (Dullea, 1978).

Single fathers with younger children are more inclined to declare their love for their children openly and to hug and kiss them than fathers of adolescents are. Helen A. Mendes (1976) found in her interviews with thirty-two single fathers that only two of them believed that their children did not love them; three others had sought psychotherapeutic help in achieving a better understanding of their children and themselves. One single-parent father observes (Thornton, 1982: 61): "It is more personally rewarding than many things I have done. There is a close relationship with the children, and my life is so much richer."

Single fathers with daughters often report that they are concerned and even troubled about their daughters' sexuality. Many, especially men over forty, find it difficult to discuss sexual matters with their daughters; they believe that this is a task for women. Single fathers also tend to express more anxiety over the sexual behavior of their daughters than of their sons. And many are concerned about the absence of adult female role models within the home. Overall, however, single fathers feel that they are successful in rearing their daughters.

Perhaps the biggest difficulty that fathers have in making the transition to single parenthood is losing their wife's companionship. Their greatest stress is associated with becoming single rather than becoming a single parent (Smith and Smith, 1981). Consequently, dating is often an important part of the man's life-style. When studying a sample of twenty single fathers in the Greensboro, North Carolina, area, Dennis K. Orthner and his associates (1976) found that most of the fathers considered themselves to be "dating around" rather than seeing one woman exclusively. The men appeared to be in no hurry to marry again. Indeed, half were uncertain if they wanted to remarry and were committed to remaining single for the present.

Orthner and his associates (1976: 436) concluded their report with this observation:

> If there is one most impressive conclusion we can make from our interviews with single-parent fathers, it is this: these fathers feel quite capable and successful in their ability to be the primary parent of their children. The confidence they express and the satisfaction they seem to derive in their fatherhood is very difficult to deny. We had anticipated a significant problem with role strain and adjustment to being the primary parent but we found little evidence that this is a major handicap. All of the fathers experienced some problems but these were not unlike the difficulties experienced in most families. The sense of pride in being able to cope with the challenge of parenthood and seeing their children mature under their guidance is a major compensating force.

Overall, single-parent fathers, like single-parent mothers, find that one of their greatest difficulties is balancing the demands of work and parenthood. Let us examine the role that work plays in the lives of adults more closely.

WORK

> *Originality and the feeling of one's own dignity are achieved only through work and struggle.*
>
> —FYODOR DOSTOEVSKY
> *Diary of a Writer, 1873*

The central portion of the adult life span of both men and women is spent at work. However, men are spending less of their lives working than they did during the 1950s and 1960s. In contrast, time spent by women in the paid labor force has increased steadily since the turn of the century. Women currently spend about ten fewer years in the work force than men do, compared with twenty-six years in 1900 (see Figure 16.2). The work experience of Americans has also undergone a significant change over the past 150 years. Although more than 70 percent of the labor force worked on the farm in 1820, by 1910 only 31 percent were engaged in agriculture. Today employment in the service industries is approaching 70 percent, the same number that were involved in farming a century and a half ago (Ginzberg, 1982) (see Table 16.3).

For many young people the transition to adult occupational roles is postponed by college, which, as psychologist Jerome Bruner (1974: 195) observes,

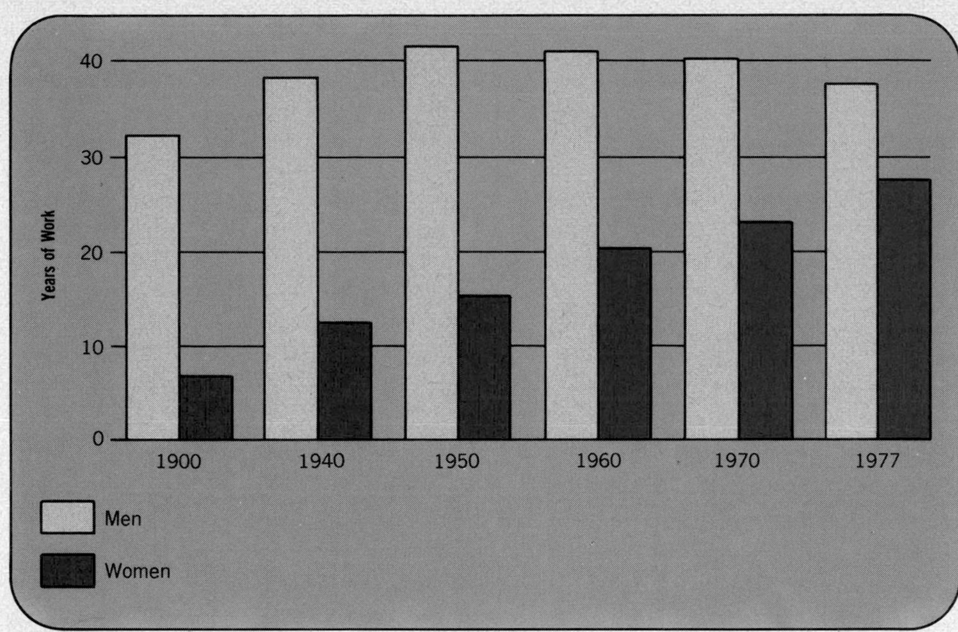

Figure 16.2 The Work Life Expectancy at Birth of Men and Women

Although in recent decades men have been spending less of their lives working than they did in the 1950s and 1960s, women have been steadily increasing the amount of time they spend in the paid labor force.

SOURCE: Bulletin 2157 (Washington, D.C.: U.S. Department of Labor, Bureau of Labor Statistics, 1982).

can have important personal and social consequences:

> The decision to delay vocational or job decisions until comparatively late in the life cycle inevitably makes fuzzy one's definition of oneself as an adult. At the very moment the young man or woman is seeking authenticity, the only legitimate role that is open to him is that of student. Youth culture becomes more deeply entrenched, more prolonged, more ideologically in opposition, more "adult" in the sense of being a timeless status.

Many youth view a college education as a bargaining chip for use in the job market. In recent years, however, the number of students enrolling in college right after graduating from high school has been dropping. In 1970, the percentage of college freshmen who went directly from high school to college was 65 percent. Today the figure stands at 54 percent, with about 21 percent waiting one to three years before enrolling in college; another 25 percent wait four years or more. Further, since 1970, part-time enrollments have grown from 32 to 42 percent of the total, and the proportion of female students has jumped from 41 to 52 percent.

Table 16.3 Percent of Labor Force

	Agriculture	Blue-Collar/ Manufacturing	White-Collar/ Service Workers
1910	31%	38%	31%
1920	27	40	33
1930	21	40	39
1940	17	40	43
1950	12	41	47
1960	6	41	54
1970	3	37	60
1980	3	30	67

SOURCE: Census and Bureau of Labor Statistics data.

The Significance of Work

People work for a great many reasons. "Self-interest" in its broadest sense, including the interests of one's family and friends, is an underlying motivation of work in all societies. However, self-interest is not simply the accumulation of wealth. For instance, among the Maori, a Polynesian people of the Pacific, a desire for approval, a sense of duty, a wish to conform to custom, a feeling of emulation, and a pleasure in craftsmanship also contribute to economic activity (Hsu, 1943).

Even in the United States, few activities seriously compete with work in providing basic life satisfaction. In a study conducted thirty years ago (Morse and Weiss, 1955), and since replicated several times (Kaplan and Tausky, 1972), a representative sample of American men were asked whether they would continue working if they inherited enough money to live comfortably. About 80 percent said they would. The reasons are not difficult to discover. Public opinion surveys reveal that work, in addition to its economic functions, structures time, provides a context in which to relate to other people, offers an escape from boredom, and sustains a sense of worth (Yankelovich, 1974*a;* de Boer, 1978).

As sociologist Harry Levinson (1964: 20) observes, work has quite a few social meanings:

> When a man works he has a contributing place in society. He earns the right to be the partner of other men. . . . The fact that someone will pay for his work is an indication that what he does is needed by others, and therefore that he himself is a necessary part of the social fabric. He matters—as a man. . . .
>
> A man's work . . . is a major social device for his identification as an adult. Much of who he is, to himself and others, is interwoven with how he earns his livelihood.

Much the same assessment can be made regarding the meaning that work has for women. Although paid work is becoming an economic necessity for an increasing number of women, one of the central themes of the women's movement has been the symbolic meaning of a paid job. For many contemporary women, exclusive commitment to the unpaid work of homemaker and mother implies being cut off from the full possibilities of self-fulfillment. A paid job is seen as a badge of membership in the larger society. It has increasingly come to be defined as the "price of admission" to independence and as a symbol of self-worth (Yankelovich, 1978, 1981).

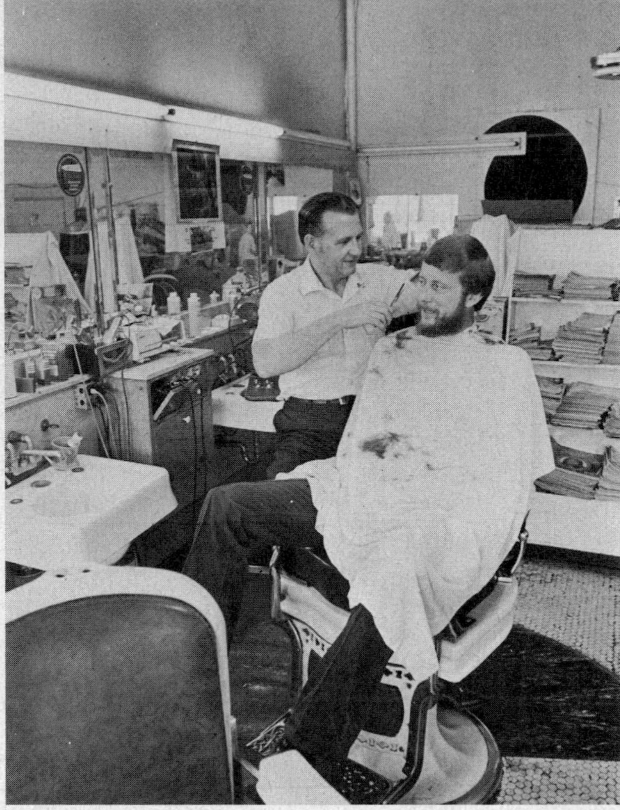

The Significance of Work
Work is a social link integrating individuals into a network of human relationships. Through their work people fulfull many needs in addition to the need for money.
Patrick Reddy

The willingness and capacity of adults to work may have its roots in childhood (Vaillant and Vaillant, 1981). Among 456 white men from working-class families who were tested and interviewed at periodic intervals over a thirty-five-year-period, those who had been industrious as youngsters turned out to be the most well-adjusted adults. They also had the most successful work lives and the warmest and most satisfying personal relationships. Industriousness proved more predictive of mental health in adulthood than having a strong family background. Indeed, in some cases boys who showed early industriousness went on to reap its promise despite having very weak home environments as children.

In the United States it is a blunt and ruthlessly

public fact that to do nothing is to be nothing and to do little is to be little. Work is commonly viewed as the measure of the individual. To be out of work is to be out of the day-to-day operations of society. Thus to be unemployed, especially in the case of a man, is to be a social outcast whose very membership in American society is suspended. Since work means so much to us, it is hardly surprising that the large majority of the poor—the hard-core unemployed—do not want to remain idle and to accept welfare (Kaplan and Tausky, 1972). The poor, like other Americans, are imbued with the dominant values and myths embodied in the American dream (Goodwin, 1972).

Anthropologist Elliot Liebow (1967: 57–58, 63), in a study of black "streetcorner men" living in a Washington, D.C., ghetto, found that the inability to gain steady, remunerative, and meaningful employment undermines an individual's sense of self-respect and self-worth:

> *For his part, the streetcorner man puts no lower value on the job than does the larger society around him.* . . . In a real sense, every pay day, he counts in dollars and cents the value placed on the job by society at large. . . . Neither the streetcorner man who performs these jobs nor the society which requires him to perform them assesses the job as one "worth doing and worth doing well." Both employee and employer are contemptuous of the job. The employee shows his contempt by his reluctance to accept it or keep it, the employer by paying less than is required to support a family. Nor does the low-wage job offer prestige, respect, interesting work, opportunity for learning or advancement, or any other compensation . . . his job fails him. The job and the man are even. The job fails the man and the man fails the job.

Liebow concluded that much of the behavior of the streetcorner man is directed toward attempting to achieve the goals and values of the larger society, and when he fails to do so, he tries to conceal this failure as best he can from himself and others.

Status Attainment: The Socioeconomic Life Cycle

Sociologists Peter Blau and Otis Dudley Duncan (1967) have developed a technique for studying the course of an individual's occupational status attainment over the life cycle. Termed the **socioeconomic life cycle,** it entails a sequence of stages that begins with birth into a family with a specific social status and proceeds through childhood, socialization, schooling, job seeking, occupational achievement, marriage, and the formation and functioning of a new family unit. The outcomes of each stage are seen as affecting *subsequent* stages in the cycle. Blau and Duncan based their formulations on data collected by the Census Bureau in 1962 from a single cross-sectional sample of the American adult male population. In order to capture the specific contributions of each stage, the researchers analyzed the data by means of a statistical procedure called **path analysis** (1972: 163):

> We think of the individual's life cycle as a sequence in time that can be described, however partially and crudely, by a set of classificatory or quantitative measurements taken at successive stages. . . . Given this scheme, the questions we are continually raising in one form or another are: how and to what degree do the circumstances of birth condition [determine] subsequent status? And how does status attained . . . at one stage of the life cycle affect the prospects for a subsequent stage?

Blau and Duncan concluded that the social status of a man's parents typically has little *direct* impact on his occupational attainment. Instead, the primary influence of parental status is *indirect,* through its effect on a man's level of schooling. (One of the virtues of path analysis is its ability to sort out direct from indirect effects.) Overall, education (years of schooling completed) was the factor that had the greatest impact on a man's occupational attainment, both early and late.

Another factor that had a sizable effect was the level on the occupational status ladder at which a man started his career. The lower he began, the higher he had to rise, and the less likely he was to reach the top positions. In this regard sociologists George L. Maddox and James Wiley (1976: 25) point out:

> Serial dependence is produced by making the entry into roles conditional on performance in temporally prior roles. Failure, deviance, mediocre or exceptional achievement—each affects the probabilities of entry into subsequent roles, especially if these events are formally recorded. Every society has some way of "remembering" socially relevant aspects of an individual's biography, and that information is used to structure his current opportunities. In modern societies, individual role histories are efficiently assembled by records-keeping departments of impersonal bureaucracies.

Whereas Blau and Duncan employed cross-sectional data collected at one point in time, a group of

University of Wisconsin sociologists working with William E. Sewell analyzed longitudinal status data for individuals over a ten-year period (Sewell, 1981). The Wisconsin findings are based on a survey of all the state's high-school seniors in 1957 and a follow-up study of one-third of the subjects from 1964 through 1967.

Sewell and his associates concluded that educational and occupational attainments are the outcome of two related processes: those by which status aspirations are formed and those by which the aspirations become translated into an actual position in the status hierarchy. The Wisconsin results reveal that practically the entire effect of a family's socioeconomic status on a child's educational and occupational attainments is the result of the personal influences it exerts upon the child's status aspirations during adolescence. Other early factors that play a part in the formation of an adolescent's status aspirations are parental and teacher encouragement to attend college and the college plans of the adolescent's best friend.

But once these factors are controlled (statistically taken into account and allowed for), the effects of parental social status become insignificant and have no other direct influence on status attainment. Instead, as Blau and Duncan also found, it is level of schooling that has the principal influence on an individual's subsequent occupational attainment.

Overall, these sociological studies suggest that the main importance of parental status lies in its influence on the adolescent's aspirations. These aspirations then contribute to the individual's educational attainment, which in turn influences the person's first occupational placement and through it, later occupational attainment. Portrayed in this manner, occupational attainment is a function of a large number of intervening or mediating links in a chain extending from birth across the life span.

Studies by sociologist Christopher Jencks (1979; Jencks, Crouse, and Mueser, 1983) largely confirm these findings. The portrait drawn by Jencks is that of a class-ridden society, in which being born into the "right" family assumes considerable importance. According to Jencks, by seventh grade a man's academic test scores shape his own expectations and those of others toward him (none of Jencks's surveys include women, a serious drawback). Of particular importance in "getting ahead in America" is educational attainment; but what counts most is finishing college and getting credentials, rather than what one learns while in college.

Like other sociologists, Jencks finds that the factors making for success are interrelated: if a man comes from the right family background, he is more likely to finish college, to have high academic test scores, and to have the personality characteristics associated

Head Start for the Middle Class

Middle-class children generally complete more years of school and achieve more positive feedback from the academic environment than working- and lower-class children do. Many middle-class students come from homes where academic achievement is valued and where materials that facilitate academic success are at hand. In a very real sense, such children have a head start in the race for society's higher-paying and higher-status positions.

Patrick Reddy

with success. But Jencks also recognizes that much depends on a variety of intangible factors, which in an earlier study (1972: 227) he labeled "luck"—countless unpredictable accidents such as:

> . . . chance acquaintances who steer you to one line of work rather than another, the range of jobs that happen to be available in a particular community when you are job hunting, . . . whether bad weather destroys your strawberry crop, [and] whether the new super highway has an exit near your restaurant.

SUMMARY

1. Love and work provide the central themes of adult life. Both place us in a complex web of relationships with others. Relationships derive from two types of bonds: expressive ties and instrumental ties. Relationships that rest on expressive ties are termed primary relationships; those that rest on instrumental ties are termed secondary relationships.
2. Individuals in modern complex societies generally enjoy some options in selecting and changing their life-styles. A striking aspect of American society over the past two decades has been the rapid expansion in life-styles. Greater latitude is permitted individuals in tailoring a life-style that is less constrained by standards of what a "respectable" person should be like.
3. Census data reveal that single status among both men and women under thirty-five years of age has sharply increased in recent years. This has resulted in part from the tendency of young people to postpone marriage. More than two-thirds of adult singles live with someone else: a friend, a relative, or a "spouse-equivalent."
4. The number of couples who are not married but live together has increased substantially over the past decade, and those who follow this life-style do so more openly than they used to. The backgrounds of cohabiting and noncohabiting college students are surprisingly similar. Cohabitation is not restricted to the younger generation. It is becoming increasingly prevalent among the middle-aged and elderly who are divorced or widowed.
5. The term "commune" is an umbrella word that covers a great many types of living styles and philosophies. Communes are fragile human undertakings, and the vast majority last for less than a year. They have become heirs to many of the same problems that confront traditional families.
6. Homosexuals are a varied group. The current state of scientific knowledge does not allow us to arrive at firm conclusions regarding the causes or sources of homosexuality, though there is no shortage of theories.
7. Marriage is a life-style found in all societies. It remains the dominant life-style in the United States. Since about four in ten marriages ends in divorce, many Americans have managed to maintain a monogamous arrangement through serial monogamy.
8. Families, like individuals, undergo development. In the United States most families have traditionally had a fairly predictable natural history. Major changes in expectations and requirements are imposed on a husband and wife as their children are born and grow up.
9. Within the life cycle of a couple, particularly a woman, the first pregnancy is an event of unparalleled importance. It signals that a couple are entering the family cycle, bringing about new role requirements. As such the first pregnancy functions as a major marker or transition and confronts a couple with new developmental tasks.
10. Psychologists and sociologists who view the family as an integrated system of roles and statuses have often depicted the onset of parenthood as a "crisis" because it involves a shift from a two-person to a three-person system. But many researchers have questioned this conclusion. Their research suggests that relatively few couples view the onset of parenthood as especially stressful.
11. One aspect of motherhood that appears particularly stressful is the balancing of motherhood and career. Many people fear that the working mother represents a loss to children in terms of supervision, love, and cognitive enrichment. But researchers are finding that the working mother who obtains personal satisfaction from employment, who does not feel excessive guilt,

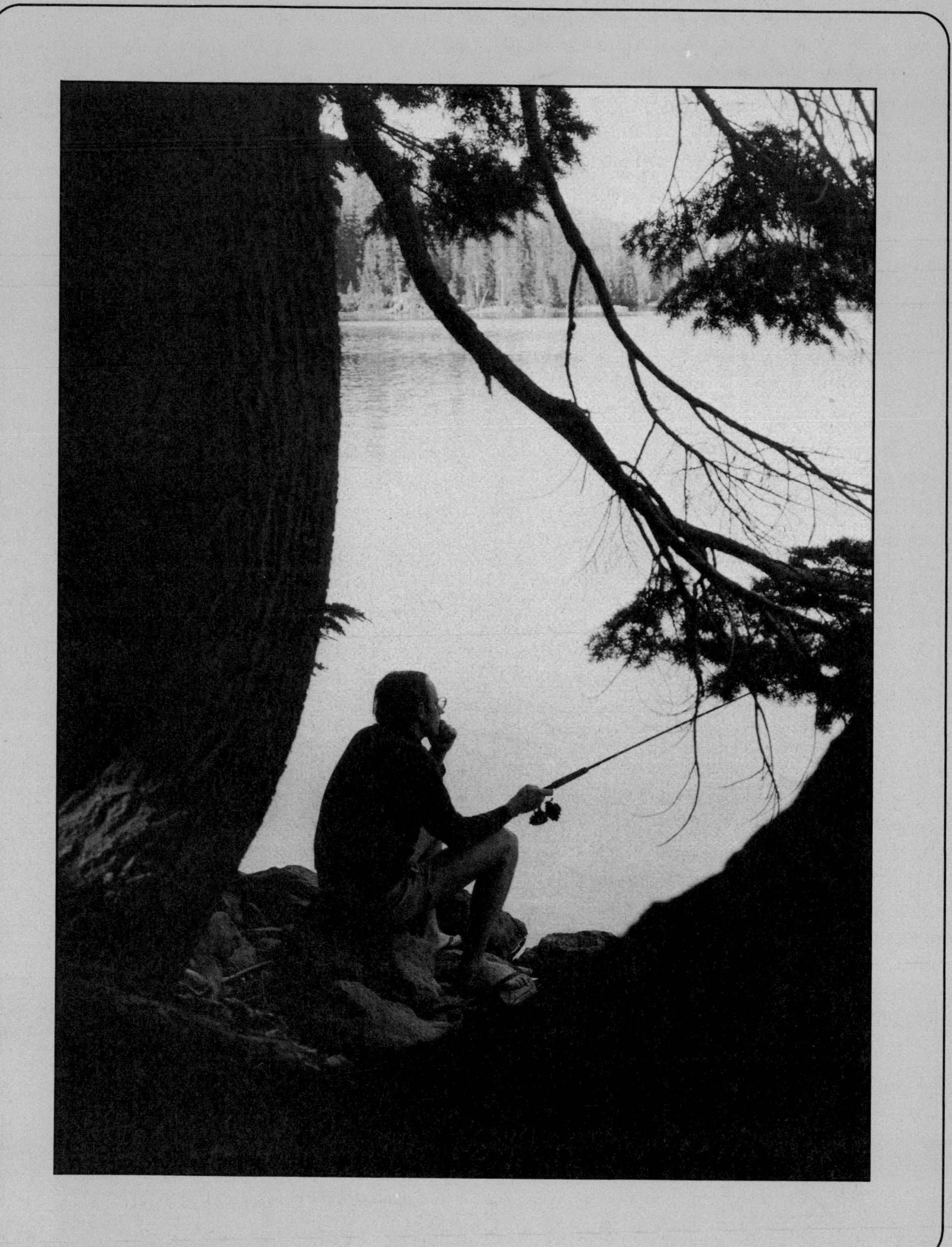

17

Middle Adulthood: Continuity and Change

Middle-aged Americans—those roughly between forty-five and sixty-four years old—are often deemed to be the power brokers, the decision-makers, and the establishment in our society. No longer young—but not particularly old—they comprise about a fifth of the population. There are some 44 million of them, 47.6 percent men and 52.4 percent women. Nearly nine of ten live in families. They were born shortly before or during the Great Depression of the 1930s and lived out their youth during World War II and the Korean War. They entered the job market and made their way in the labor force during the economic Golden Years of the 1950s and early 1960s. Now they are experiencing the physical changes of middle life and, for many, the psychological pressures associated with the shift from the "smokestack" industrial age to the age of computers. But, significantly, having learned to cope with the many contingencies of childhood, adolescence, and young adulthood, middle-aged individuals have a substantial repertoire of strategies for dealing with life (Maloney, 1982).

PHYSICAL CHANGES AND HEALTH

In the fashion of aging machines, a human body that has been functioning for a number of decades tends to work less efficiently than it did when it was "new." At age fifty or sixty, the kidneys, lungs, heart, and other organs are less efficient than they were at twenty. Yet across middle adulthood the physical changes that occur are for the most part not precipitous. They are so gradual as to present, not a steep slope, but a long plateau (Troll, 1975). It is estimated that after adolescence most integrated body functions decline at the rate of about 1 percent a year. But even in later adulthood at age seventy-five, the heart's efficiency is about 70 percent of what it was at thirty years of age, the lungs' efficiency is 60 percent, the liver's efficiency is 90 percent, and the kidneys' efficiency is about 60 percent.

Overall, middle-aged individuals report that they are not noticeably different from what they were in their early thirties. They mention that their hair has grayed, they have more wrinkles, they are paunchier, they have "lost a step," they tire more easily, and they rebound less quickly. Even so, except for those in poor health, they find that on the whole they carry on in much the manner that they did in their younger years. The best preventive of disabling loss of strength and vitality is an active life and exercise.

Vision and Hearing

During middle adulthood the eye loses its ability to "zoom" in the manner that it did in youth. Accordingly, most people in their forties find that they need glasses, especially to see near objects (Fozard and Popkin, 1978; Sekuler, Hutman, and Owsley, 1980). (If this problem is not corrected, people find they can read printed material only by holding it farther and farther away from their eyes, until eventually they cannot see to read even at arm's length.) Adaptation to darkness and recovery from glare also take longer, making night driving somewhat more taxing.

A number of disorders that affect sight become more common with age. In *glaucoma,* pressure builds up inside the eye because the normal drainage of fluid does not occur properly. The disorder has no symptoms in the early stages and can be detected only by an eye examination. If the disease is detected early, it can be treated, but failure to receive treatment eventually leads to blindness. Another condition, the *cataract,* typically occurs much later in life but in some instances appears among individuals in their late fifties and early sixties. The most common cause is the deterioration and clouding of the lens, contributing to a progressive loss of vision. The condition can usually be remedied by surgical removal of the affected lens. The resulting vision impairment can then be corrected by eyeglasses, a contact lens, or a plastic lens placed in the eye at the time of the operation.

Job-Related Hazards to Health
Since people spend a good deal of their lives in work-related activities, environmental factors in the workplace have a substantial impact on their health. For instance, workers in jobs with high noise levels are more likely to develop hearing loss than workers in other occupations are.
Ulrike Welsch/Picture Group

Changes in hearing usually begin about age thirty. Typically, the ability to hear high-pitched notes declines, but the magnitude of the change varies appreciably among individuals. At age fifty, about one in every three men and one in every four women have difficulty understanding a whisper. However, only about 5 percent of the population at fifty can be deemed to have substantial hearing problems (at age seventy-five, some 27 percent have hearing difficulties). People who have jobs associated with high noise levels—miners, truck drivers, air-hammer operators, and so on—are particularly at risk. Also, some individuals in their sixties report that they "take in" information more slowly than they did earlier in life.

Menopause

One of the more notable changes that takes place among women in middle age is **menopause**—the end of menstrual activity. It is one of the most readily identifiable signs of the climacteric. The **climacteric** is characterized by changes in the ovaries and in the various biological processes associated with these changes. Probably the most significant change is the profound drop in the production of the female hormones (particularly estrogen) by the ovaries. The average age at which there is a complete cessation of menses is around forty-seven to fifty-two years in Western countries. In less than 4 percent of all cases, menopause occurs before age forty; and in less than 2 percent, after age fifty-five—but only rarely does it occur later than age fifty-eight (Wharton, 1967; Bongaarts, 1982). Younger women also undergo an early menopause should they have their ovaries surgically removed.

The stoppage of menstruation typically takes two to four years to be completed, with an intermittent missing of periods and the extension of the intervals between periods. Symptoms that have been commonly attributed to menopause include hot flashes (feelings of extreme heat), hot flushes (the flushing of the skin), episodes of profuse sweating, fatigue, dizziness, headaches, insomnia, nervousness, and depression. Estimates of the proportion of women who experience menopausal symptoms vary widely; some estimates are as low as 24 percent while others as high as 90 percent (Crawford and Hooper, 1973; Goodman, Stewart, and Gilbert, 1977; Brozan, 1983*a*).

During the 1960s estrogen-replacement therapy (ERT) became one of the hottest fads in the medical management of menopause, especially in the treatment of hot flashes. By 1975 some 27 million estrogen prescriptions were being written annually. However, about this time evidence was uncovered connecting ERT with increased risks of cancer of the uterus. As a result, there was a marked drop in its use. More recently, scientists have found that small doses of the hormone progesterone can reduce the rate of precancerous changes in women being administered estrogen as postmenopausal therapy (Whitehead, Townsend, and Pryse-Davies, 1981). This finding is particularly good news for women who require estrogen supplements because they suffer from *osteoporosis* and require estrogen supplements. In osteoporosis, the bone tissue thins as a result of a diminished supply of estrogen, rendering women

Coming to Terms with Middle Age

In a society that stresses youthfulness and physical attractiveness, the transition to middle life may pose difficulties for some individuals. This is especially true for those people whose definition of self resides in youthful vigor and "good looks."

Joel Gordon

Aging found that the sexual activity of healthy participants declined progressively with age from a mean of forty-three events per year in men sixty to sixty-four years to twenty-one events in men seventy-five to seventy-nine. Overall, the general level of sexual activity of the individuals when they were between twenty and thirty-nine years of age correlated highly with the frequency of their sexual activity in later life (Tsitouras, Martin, and Harman, 1982). Hence, if men have maintained elevated levels of sexual activity from their earlier years, and if acute or chronic ill health does not intervene, they are able to continue some form of active sexual expression into advanced age. However, if aging males are not stimulated over long periods of time, their responsiveness may be permanently lost (Masters and Johnson, 1966).

Masters and Johnson likewise find no reason why menopause or advancing age should interfere with the sexual capacity, performance, or drive of women. Basically, older women respond as they did when they were younger, and they continue to be capable of sexual activity and orgasm. Older women tend to lubricate more slowly than they did earlier in life, and the walls of the vagina become thinner. This means that the tissues can be easily irritated and torn with forceful sexual activity. Male gentleness and the use of artificial vaginal lubricants can do much to minimize this difficulty. Like aging men, older women also typically have fewer orgasmic contractions (younger women average between five and ten contractions whereas older women average between three and five contractions).

According to the Kinsey (1953) research and the National Fertility Study (Westoff, 1974), married couples in their teens have intercourse nearly three times a week, on the average. The frequency drops to about twice a week at age thirty, one and a half times a week at age forty, once a week by age fifty, and once about every twelve days by age sixty. However, these average figures conceal considerable variation among couples.

The incidence of sexual problems among adults has only recently been the subject of scientific investigation. The University of Pittsburgh's Department of Psychiatry studied one hundred middle-class couples who described themselves as happily married. Almost half of the women and one-third of the men reported problems with sex (the average age of the women was thirty-five; that of the men, thirty-seven). Nonetheless, 90 percent said that they would marry the same person if they had their lives to live over.

Difficulty in becoming aroused was the most frequently reported factor in a woman's sexual dissatisfaction (nearly half of the women had this difficulty and 46 percent had difficulty reaching an orgasm). Many of these women said that they could not relax during sex and complained of too little foreplay and too little tenderness after intercourse. The most fre-

Strong Marital Ties

A happy marriage can be a key factor in a person's physical and mental health. Although all couples have some problems in their marriages, 90 percent of those in one study said that they would marry the same person if they had their lives to live over.

Alan Carey/The Image Works

quent problem mentioned by the men was premature ejaculation (36 percent); 16 percent had difficulty getting or maintaining an erection.

The American male is often stereotyped in the popular media as preoccupied with sex. Yet, a 1979 Louis Harris and Associates survey of men between the ages of eighteen and forty-nine revealed that slightly less than half (49 percent) described sex as being "very important" for their own personal happiness. And from a list of factors commonly linked to adult happiness, 17 percent of the men reported that sex is among the least important. When the men were asked to select the three values in life most important to them personally, the following were the most frequently cited: family life, 56 percent; health, 35 percent; peace of mind, 32 percent; love, 25 percent; money, 25 percent; friends, 20 percent; work, 19 percent; religion, 16 percent; respect from others, 10 percent; education, 9 percent; sex, 8 percent.

It also appears that American men are becoming more aware of their own sensitivity and humanness (Shanor, 1978). Within the privacy of their own minds, they are increasingly coming to recognize—and even approve—the presence of such feelings as tenderness, dependence, weakness, and pain. But a good many of them, especially older men, are not yet able to talk freely about these traditionally "unmasculine" emotions.

If men are becoming more aware of their own sensitivity and humanness, women are becoming more aware of their own sexuality (Hite, 1976). A growing number of women are tired of the traditional pattern of sexual relations, which focused on male erection, male penetration, and male orgasm. Women are increasingly admitting to themselves what they like sexually and are asking their partners for it. (Interestingly, one survey [Hite, 1976] suggests that 95 percent of women—even those who think themselves "frigid"—are capable of reaching orgasm when they masturbate.) In large measure, this shift in attitudes has been associated with the women's movement.

Health

As people grow older, the incidence of a number of health problems becomes greater. One such problem, cardiovascular (heart and blood vessel) disease, accounts for over half of all deaths in the United States. Most of these deaths are due to coronary artery disease and hypertension (high blood pressure), which are caused by *atherosclerosis,* a thickening of the internal lining of the blood vessels that is thought to be associated with fatty substances (including cholesterol) in the blood. Approximately one-third of the deaths of people between the ages of thirty-five and sixty-four years result from heart disease. The American Heart Association reports that heart disease afflicts nearly 43 million Americans, including 37 million with high blood pressure. Roughly 1 million die of heart disorders or strokes each year. Of the 1.5 million people who suffer heart attacks, nearly two-thirds survive and must be treated with drugs or surgery.

Some individuals are more at risk for heart disease than others are. More young men than young women suffer from cardiovascular disease, although the risk for women increases after menopause (women over sixty are nearly as susceptible to the disorder as are men). Death from the disorder in the thirty-five to forty-five age group is five times more common among smokers than among nonsmokers. Male diabetics are twice as susceptible as other men, and female diabetics are five times as susceptible as other women. People who are overweight and who have sedentary jobs are also more at risk for heart disease (see Chapter 15). And, as discussed in the boxed insert on page 476, "Type A" patterns of behavior have been implicated in cardiovascular disorders.

Over the past thirty years, cardiovascular mortality has decreased more than 30 percent, with over 60 percent of the decrease occurring in the past decade (Levy and Moskowitz, 1982). Among individuals aged twenty-five to forty-four, heart disease has declined from first to third place as a cause of death, but for people forty-five and over, it remains the leading cause. The decline in overall cardiovascular mortality has meant that both men and women have gained more than two years in life expectancy over the last decade.

Many factors are associated with the decline in death from cardiovascular disease. More people are smoking less, eating more sensibly, and jogging more. Medical services have also improved. And new drugs that control high blood pressure and cardiac arrest have revolutionized the treatment of cardiovascular disease. When patients do not respond to drugs, *coronary-bypass surgery* may be employed (surgeons take veins, usually from the leg, and create detours around blocked arteries). A new, cheaper, and simpler technique is called *coronary angioplasty*—a thin tube tipped

Table 17.3 Five-Year Survival Rates for Cancer

Type of Cancer	Diagnosed in	
	*1960–63**	*1973–80*
Lining of uterus	73%	87%
Testis	63	82
Melanoma of skin	60	79
Breast	63	73
Bladder	53	72
Hodgkin's disease	40	70
Uterine cervix	58	67
Prostate	50	67
Colon	43	50
Kidney	37	50
Rectum	38	48
Non-Hodgkin's lymphoma	31	46
Ovary	32	37
Leukemia	14	32
Brain	18	22
Stomach	11	15
Lung	8	12
Esophagus	4	4
Pancreas	1	3
*Among children**—		
Hodgkin's disease	52%	84%
Wilms's tumor	57	75
Acute lymphocytic leukemia	4	58
Brain and central nervous system	35	53
Neuroblastoma	25	47
Bone	20	46
Non-Hodgkin's lymphoma	18	46
Acute granulocytic leukemia	3	22

* Estimates for whites only. Data for all races combined were not available.

SOURCE: National Cancer Institute, December 1983.

cells develops into a *malignant* tumor, which keeps growing and invades neighboring tissues. Noncancerous tumors are termed *benign.* Although benign tumors may enlarge, the cells do not multiply and spread uncontrollably. In malignant tumors, the cells *metastasize,* or spread, and form secondary growths in other parts of the body.

Although a diagnosis of cancer is cause for considerable concern, it should not be regarded as an automatic death sentence. The latest data on cancer hardly justify such a fatalistic outlook (see Table 17.3). Cancer therapy has made remarkable strides in recent decades. Surgery remains the most common method of treating cancers that form solid tumors, such as breast, colon, and rectal cancers. Radiation is also a common treatment. It takes advantage of the fact that many types of cancer cells are more sensitive than normal cells are to the destructive effects of radiation. Finally, more than sixty drugs have been found effective against cancer. Drug therapy—known as *chemotherapy*—may be employed as the primary therapy or as an adjunct to surgery and radiation. Unfortunately, radiation and chemotherapies commonly produce side effects, including nausea, vomiting, diarrhea, temporary hair loss, increased susceptibility to infection, fatigue, and depression.

Much can be done to prevent cancer. Many medical scientists believe that up to 80 percent of all cancers result in part from contamination of the environment by chemicals called *carcinogens.* Exactly how these substances cause cells to become malignant is as yet poorly understood. Among substances that have been identified as carcinogens are asbestos, coal tar pitch, benzene, vinyl chloride, and nuclear radiation. The American Cancer Society estimates that 75,000 lives a year could be saved in the United States by getting 15 million of the nation's 33 million smokers to stop.

PERSONALITY ACROSS THE ADULT YEARS

We must always change, renew, rejuvenate ourselves; otherwise we harden.

—JOHANN WOLFGANG VON GOETHE

Traditionally, developmental psychologists have focused their attention on changes that occur during infancy, childhood, and adolescence. But in recent years a life-span perspective of development has emerged that views adulthood as a period of continuing change. Individuals must constantly adapt to new life situations and make a variety of role transitions. This involves the performance of new tasks, the relinquishing of others, and the redefinition of basic assumptions, attitudes, and behaviors. And in the process of this ongoing adaptation, people are required to reorient and reorganize their personalities.

Psychosocial Tasks of Middle Adulthood

As pointed out in Chapter 2 and again in Chapter 15, Erik Erikson (1963) deems the central task of middle age to concern the issue of generativity versus stagnation. He stresses that humans are both learning and instructing beings. Whereas personality development in the earlier phases of the life cycle centers on learning, in later phases instruction is the focal point. Erikson's notion of *generativity* captures this concern. It entails the expansion of one's own being to encompass a commitment to younger people, assisting them in making their way in life. Rather than indulge oneself, the developing person brings his or her special talents and gifts to bear on the "ultimate concerns" of advancing the overall interests of humankind. To do otherwise is to become self-centered and to turn inward, resulting in a type of psychological invalidism.

The psychologist Robert C. Peck (1968) follows in Erikson's footsteps. However, he takes a closer look at middle life and suggests that it is useful to identify more precisely the tasks confronting individuals during it. The four aspects he defines include valuing wisdom versus valuing physical powers, socializing versus sexualizing in human relationships, cathectic flexibility versus cathectic impoverishment, and mental flexibility versus mental rigidity.

Valuing Wisdom vs. Valuing Physical Powers. As individuals pass into middle age, they experience a decline in their physical strength. Even more importantly, in a culture that emphasizes looking youthful, people lose much of their edge in physical attractiveness. But they also enjoy new advantages. The sheer experience of longer living brings with it an increase in accumulated knowledge and greater judgmental powers. Rather than relying primarily on their "hands" and physical capabilities, they must now come to employ their "heads" with greater frequency in coping with life.

Socializing vs. Sexualizing in Human Relationships. Allied to middle-life physical decline, although in some ways separate from it, is the sexual climacteric. In their interpersonal lives, individuals must now cultivate greater understanding and compassion. They must come to value others as personalities in their own right rather than chiefly as sex objects.

Cathectic Flexibility vs. Cathectic Impoverishment. This task concerns the ability to become emotionally flexible. In doing so, people find the capacity to shift emotional investments from one person to another and from one activity to another. At this

Generativity Versus Stagnation
Erik Erikson contends that the chief developmental task of middle age has to do with people's ability to turn outward, help younger individuals, and take an interest in broad human concerns and issues.
Jean-Claude Lejeune/Stock, Boston

time of life many middle-aged individuals confront the death of their parents and the departure of their children from the home. Hence they must widen their circle of acquaintances to embrace new people in the community. And they must try on and cultivate new roles to replace those that they are relinquishing.

Mental Flexibility vs. Mental Rigidity. As they grow older, people too often become "set in their ways." And they become "close-minded," unreceptive to new ideas. Since many of them have reached their peak in status and power, they are tempted to forgo the search for novel solutions to problems. But what worked in the past may not work in the future. Hence they must strive for mental flexibility and, on an ongoing basis, cultivate new perspectives as provisional guidelines to tackling problems.

Psychological Conceptions of Personality

Although personality development has long been a major interest of many psychologists, they have not been able to arrive at a mutually accepted definition of personality. Underlying most of their approaches, however, is the notion that each individual has a relatively unique and enduring set of psychological tendencies and reveals them in the course of interacting with the environment (Bischof, 1970; Maddi, 1972).

Trait Models of Personality. Until recently, it was widely believed that personality patterns are established during childhood and adolescence and then remain relatively stable over the rest of the life span. This view largely derived from Sigmund Freud's psychoanalytic theory. As described in Chapter 2, Freud traced the roots of behavior to personality components formed in infancy and childhood—needs, defenses, identifications, and so on. He deemed any changes that occur in adulthood as simply variations on established themes, for he believed that an individual's character structure is relatively fixed by late childhood.

Likewise, clinical psychologists and personality theorists have typically assumed that an individual gradually forms certain characteristics that become progressively resistant to change with the passage of time. These patterns are usually regarded as reflections of inner traits, cognitive structures, dispositions, habits, or needs. Indeed, almost all forms of personality assessment are based on the assumption that the individual has stable traits (stylistic consistencies in behavior) that the investigator is attempting to describe (Hogan, DeSota, and Solano, 1977).

Similarly, whenever a person's life is reviewed, whether in an autobiography, a biography, a psychohistory, or a clinical report, an implicit assumption is usually made: not only is the subject's life uniquely different from that of other people, but it has a certain coherence. Indeed, a biography would be unimaginable if the events in the subject's life course were portrayed in a purely haphazard, unordered fashion (Csikszentmihalyi and Beattie, 1979). Likewise, sociologist Kurt Back (1976; Bourque and Back, 1977) suggests that everyone looks on his or her own life as a unit. People consider themselves consistent, and they anticipate and adapt to many events without appreciably changing their picture of their whole lives. Hence, according to Back, individuals see the self as essentially stable but as assuming somewhat different guises in response to changing life circumstances.

Situational Models of Personality. The trait approach to personality views a person's behavior in terms of recurring patterns. In contrast, proponents of situational models view a person's behavior as the outcome of the characteristics of the situation in which the person is momentarily located. The cognitive learning theorist Walter Mischel (1968, 1969, 1977) provides a forthright statement of the situational position.

Mischel says that behavioral consistency is in the eye of the beholder and hence is more illusory than real. Indeed, he wonders if it makes sense to speak of "personality" at all. Mischel concludes that we are motivated to believe that the world around us is orderly and patterned because only in this manner can we take aspects of our daily lives for granted and view them as predictable. Consequently, we perceive our own behavior and that of other people as having continuity. Even so, Mischel admits that a fair degree of consistency exists in people's performance on certain intellectual and cognitive tasks. However, he notes that correlations between personality test scores and behavior seem to reach a maximum of about .30, not a particularly high figure (see Chapter 9). People's behavior across situations is highly consistent only when the situations in which the behavior is tested are quite similar. When circumstances vary, little similarity is apparent.

Interactionist Models of Personality. In recent years psychologists have come to recognize the inadequacies of both the trait and situational models. Instead, they have come to favor an interactionist approach to personality. Pointing out that the question "Which is more important, the trait or the situation?" is meaningless, they claim that behavior is always a joint product of the person and the situation (see Chapter 3). Moreover, people seek out congenial environments—selecting settings, activities, and associates that provide a comfortable context—and thereby reinforce their preexisting bents. And through their actions, individuals create as well as select environments. By fashioning their own circumstances, they produce some measure of stability in their behavior (Epstein, 1979; Bandura, 1982).

Psychologists have employed a variety of approaches for specifying the form of interaction that transpires between a person and a situation. One approach is to distinguish between those people for whom a given trait can be used to predict behavior across situations and those people for whom that trait cannot be used. For example, individuals who report that their behavior is consistent across situations with respect to friendliness and conscientiousness do indeed exhibit these traits in their behavior. In contrast, individuals who report that their behavior is inconsistent across situations with respect to these qualities reveal little consistency in their behavior with regard to them (Bem and Allen, 1974). Moreover, people vary in their consistency on different traits (Underwood and Moore, 1981). Hence, if we are asked to characterize a friend, we typically do not run through a rigid set of traits that we use to inventory all people. Instead, we select a small number of traits that strike us as particularly pertinent and discard as irrelevant the ten thousand or so other traits. Usually the traits that we select are those that we find hold for the person across a variety of situations.

Personality Continuity and Discontinuity

Psychologists have long been interested in the degree to which our personalities remain the same across the life span. Yet the evidence that they have produced is contradictory (Epstein, 1979, 1980). Some studies suggest that personality remains largely the same; others that it changes over time. Such conflicting results suggest that personality is complex and multifaceted, not one but many things. As a consequence, some components may show considerable stability and others considerable change. On the whole, the greatest consistency appears in various intellectual and cognitive dimensions, such as IQ, cognitive style, and self-concept. The least consistency is found in the realm of interpersonal behavior and attitudes (Kelly, 1955; Mischel, 1969).

Psychologist E. Lowell Kelly (1955) has investigated personality constancy and change from a longitudinal perspective. As part of a marriage study, Kelly administered a battery of psychological tests to nearly 300 engaged college students between 1935 and 1938. In 1954 he was able to locate and readminister the tests to 86 percent of the people in the

Personality Continuity and Discontinuity

Personality is complex and multifaceted. Some of the components show considerable stability over time, while others change markedly.

Patrick Reddy

initial sample. Of the thirty-eight personality variables that Kelly measured, twenty showed no significant change over the two decades. In the case of the other eighteen variables, change had occurred, but for the most part it was not substantial. Values and vocational interests tended to be most stable; self-ratings were moderately consistent; attitudes (toward marriage, religion, entertaining, gardening, and the like) were least consistent. Kelly (1955: 681) concluded:

> Our findings indicate that significant changes in the human personality may continue to occur during the years of adulthood. Such changes, while neither so large nor sudden as to threaten the continuity of the self percept or impair one's day-to-day interpersonal relations, are potentially of sufficient magnitude to offer a basis of fact for those who dare to hope for continued psychological growth during the adult years.

Diana S. Woodruff and James E. Birren (1972), like Kelly, were able to follow up on a sample of college students who had completed a self-descriptive personality inventory (the California Test of Personality) in 1944. In 1969, twenty-five years later, longitudinal comparisons revealed that the men and women described themselves in virtually the same terms they had used in 1944. In addition to describing themselves, the follow-up subjects were asked to answer the California Personality Test as they thought they had answered it in 1944 (Woodruff and Birren, 1972: 257):

> In the retrospection condition, adults projected a relatively negative picture of themselves as adolescents. In retrospect they thought that their adolescent level of adjustment was much lower than it actually had been. Adults seemed to subjectively experience a discontinuity between their adolescent and adult personality which did not exist objectively.

Researchers have also followed up on the sample of Berkeley and Oakland youth who were first studied in the 1930s when they were in their early teens (see Chapter 1). The individuals were again assessed when they were in their late teens, mid-thirties, and mid-forties (Block, 1980). On the vast majority of the ninety personality scales, researchers found statistically significant correlations between the earliest and later scores. Even so, despite strong evidence of continuity, individuals differed in the consistency they exhibited in their personalities over time.

The picture gained from the research undertaken by psychologists at the Gerontology Research Center in Baltimore is not too different. Paul T. Costa, Jr., and Robert R. McCrae (1980) find considerable continuity in a person's personality across the adult years. They have tracked individuals' scores over time on standardized self-report personality scales. On such personality dimensions as warmth, impulsiveness, gregariousness, assertiveness, anxiety, and disposition to depression, high correlations exist in the ordering of persons from one decade to another. An assertive nineteen-year-old is typically an assertive forty-year-old and later an assertive eighty-year-old. Likewise, "neurotics" are likely to be "complainers" throughout life (they may complain about their love life in early adulthood while decrying their poor health in late adulthood). Although people may "mellow" with age or become less impulsive by the time they are in their sixties, the relation of individuals to one another regarding a given trait remains much the same (when tested, most persons drop the same few standard points).

In sum, for many facets of our personality there is strong evidence of continuity across the adult years (Costa, McCrae, and Arenberg, 1980; Moss and Susman, 1980). This element of stability makes us adaptive; we know what we are like and hence can make more intelligent choices regarding our living arrangements, careers, spouses, and friends. If our personality continually changed in an erratic fashion, mapping our future and making wise decisions would be severely impaired.

Dynamic Properties of Growth

Although our personality possesses an underlying coherence across time, we are dynamic organisms capable of growth (Brim and Kagan, 1980). We are active, vigorous beings, not simple carriers of stable motives and traits. Because the world in which we live is constantly changing, we must continually undertake to cope with and master our environment. Likewise, as we move through different phases in life, we undergo physical alterations in our bodies that are often mirrored in our circumstances and roles (see the boxed insert on pages 484–485). Consequently, the human experience reflects a tension between continuity and change.

This conclusion emerges from the studies undertaken in Kansas City by Bernice L. Neugarten and her associates (1964). In particular, the research sheds light on personality change over the life span. The first set of studies was based on cross-sectional data from more than 700 men and women aged forty to seventy from all socioeconomic class levels. The second set of data came from a group of nearly 300 people aged fifty to ninety who were interviewed at regular intervals over a six-year period. Analyzing this research, Neugarten (1964: 189–190) identified a number of fairly consistent age-related differences in personality:

> Forty-year-olds seem to see the environment as one that rewards boldness and risk-taking and to see themselves possessing energy congruent with the opportunities presented in the outer world. Sixty-year-olds seem to see the environment as complex and dangerous, no longer to be reformed in line with one's wishes, and to see the self as conforming and accommodating to outer-world demands. This change . . . [involves] movement from active to passive mastery. . . . Older men seem to be more receptive than younger men of their affiliative, nurturant, and sensual promptings; older women, more receptive than younger women of their aggressive and egocentric impulses. Men appear to cope with the environment in increasingly abstract and cognitive terms; women, in increasingly affective and expressive terms. . . . Older people seem to move toward more eccentric, self-preoccupied positions and to attend increasingly to the control and the satisfaction of personal needs.

Researchers associated with the Baltimore Longitudinal Study (Douglas and Arenberg, 1978) also found age-related differences and changes that occurred across time. Participants were male volunteers who ranged in age from seventeen to ninety-eight years, were in relatively good health, and were employed in (or retired from) professional or managerial positions. A seven-year follow-up revealed that the pace of activity of men in their twenties had increased, while that of those over fifty had declined. Likewise, the "masculinity" scores of the men in the survey (as measured by highly "masculine" interests and restraint in displaying emotion) had declined. Over the period of the study, a decline also occurred among men of all ages in scores associated with thoughtfulness (introspective and meditative behavior), personal relations (trustfulness, tolerance, and cooperativeness), and friendliness (agreeable and nonbelligerent tendencies). But these latter changes appeared to reflect cultural changes associated with the times, rather than maturational factors.

It is not surprising that various investigators have uncovered major discontinuities in some facets of personality across the life span. As Neugarten (1968*b*, 1969) notes, the psychological realities confronting the individual shift with time. Middle age, for instance, often brings with it responsibilities for aging

The Sandwich Generation

Middle age often brings with it responsibilities for one's own children and one's aging parents. The tasks fall disproportionally upon women, who in the American "gender division of labor" are the individuals assigned primary responsibility for family care-taking functions.

Michael Serino/The Picture Cube

SOCIALIZATION OVER THE LIFE SPAN

People move through a variety of social roles in accordance with different stages in the life cycle. Through socialization they acquire the knowledge, skills, and tendencies to action that prepare them for the roles they are expected to fill. Socialization is a never-ending process (Bush and Simmons, 1981). A "senior citizen" is socialized into a golden-age village; a bride and groom into marriage; an upwardly mobile person into a new social class; a religious convert into a new religion; a new patient into a hospital ward; an engineering student into his or her profession; and a new member into the League of Women Voters.

Role socialization frequently involves three distinct phases (Mortimer and Simmons, 1978). First, anticipatory socialization commonly takes place prior to the assumption of the new role. For example, children play "house" and "try on" the roles of spouse and parent in preparation for adult family roles. More formally, individuals try out roles in apprenticeship programs, probationary programs, and rehabilitative settings. The process of anticipatory socialization often mitigates some of the stress that might otherwise be associated with major role transitions. Second, socialization continues once the new role is occupied. For instance, moving from the single to the married state requires the learning of many new interpersonal skills, since much of the marital role is hidden from children. Similarly, much job preparation is necessarily inadequate, while changing times require the continuous acquisition of new skills. And third, role socialization often involves not only adjusting to new role expectations and relationships but "disengaging" from old ones. Rituals such as graduation, marriage, and other "rites of passage" may ease some role transitions. Such rituals signal to other people that our status has changed while prompting us to alter our self-definitions.

At times, difficulties inhere in the role transition process. As anthropologist Ruth Benedict (1938) has pointed out, cultural discontinuities often exist, so that successive roles do not build on one another and may even conflict with earlier training. For instance, the child is socialized to be nonresponsible, submissive, and sexually inactive, whereas the adult is expected to be responsible, dominant, and sexually active (Mortimer and Simmons, 1978). Irving Rosow (1974) notes a discontinuity in the reverse direction toward the end of the life cycle, in that the experiences of middle age do not train people to occupy themselves during retirement.

Sociologist Orville G. Brim (1966) mentions other factors that create discontinuity in modern complex and changing societies. The geographical and social

parents and for one's own minor children. With these obligations comes the awareness of oneself as the bridge between the generations—the so-called "sandwich generation" (Lang and Brody, 1983). As a perceptive woman observed in Neugarten's study (1968*b*: 98):

> It is as if there are two mirrors before me, each held at a partial angle. I see part of myself in my mother who is growing old, and part of her in me. In the other mirror, I see part of myself in my daughter. I have had some dramatic insights, just from looking in those mirrors. . . . It is a set of revelations that I suppose can only come when you are in the middle of three generations.

In a sense, individuals in their forties and fifties are catching up with their own parents; therefore, they may experience increased identification with them and a greater awareness of their own approaching senescence (Stein et al., 1978). Some of the issues of middle age are related to increased stocktaking, in which individuals come to restructure their time perspective in terms of time-left-to-live rather than time-since-birth.

Old age confronts the individual with still other issues (Neugarten, 1969: 122):

> Some are issues that relate to renunciation—adaptation to losses of work, friends, spouse, the yielding up of a sense of competency and authority . . . reconciliation with members of one's family, one's achievements, and one's failures . . . the resolution of grief over the death of others, but also over the approaching death of self . . . the need to maintain a sense of integrity in terms of what one has been, rather than what one is . . . the concern with "legacy" . . . how to leave traces of oneself . . . the psychology of survivorship.

Thus as Neugarten points out, one's concerns and preoccupations alter and shift across the life cycle.

mobility characteristic of achievement-oriented societies combine to make people's career patterns somewhat unpredictable. Different subcultures and countercultures compound the effects of mobility by the novel role demands they place on individuals. Much childhood learning is made obsolete by rapid change: technological advances in various occupations, shifts in sexual folkways, new opportunities for women and minority-group members, and so on.

Brim (1966) points out that the content of socialization changes as individuals progress through the life cycle. He identifies a number of these changes. First, society tends to focus on the overt behavior of adults, whereas with children the focus is on values and motives. Such major institutions as the family are organized to direct the values and motives of children.

Second, adult socialization requires a synthesis of elements from already learned responses, with perhaps the addition of some new elements to fill out the required acts. The child, in contrast, must learn an entirely new range of responses, and socialization is primarily directed toward such elementary matters as toilet training, language competency, and so on.

Third, adult socialization tends to focus more on realism than on idealism. Children are taught ideal behaviors, but as they mature, they learn that there is a distinction between the real and the ideal. For example, they are taught to be honest and not to lie. But later they learn that cheating on one's income tax and telling "little white lies" are quite acceptable behaviors.

Fourth, later socialization places greater emphasis on mediating conflicting demands than early socialization does. As people move through the life cycle, they are forced to develop ways to deal with conflicting role expectations. At times, for instance, the requirements of the parental role conflict with those of the spouse role; or the employer's demands for job performance may conflict with the demands of one's family. As individuals mature, they learn various mechanisms for handling role conflict. For example, they develop techniques for avoiding the situation, withdrawing acceptably from a conflict, acting one way in one context and a different way in another, giving precedence to the demands of one role over another role, and so on.

And fifth, change in the content of socialization occurs along the dimension of generality-specificity. Individuals come to know whether given role requirements apply to many social situations or to just a few. For instance, one's sex role applies to multiple settings, whereas one's role as a member of a bowling team does not. In all these ways the content of socialization changes as individuals move through the life cycle.

Continuity and Discontinuity in Gender Characteristics

In the long years liker must they grow;
The man be more of woman, she of man.

—ALFRED, LORD TENNYSON
The Princess

As mentioned earlier, some research has suggested that men and women move in *opposite* directions across the life span with respect to assertiveness and aggressiveness, so that patterns of a later-life "unisex" tend to emerge (Zube, 1982). David Gutmann (1969) pursued this possibility by comparing the male subjects in Neugarten's Kansas City study with men in a number of other cultures: the subsistence, village-dwelling lowland and highland Maya of Mexico; the migratory Navajo herdsmen of the high desert plateau of northeastern Arizona; and the village-dwelling Galilean Druze herdsmen and farmers of Israel. Gutmann found that the younger men (aged thirty-five to fifty-four) in all four cultures relied on and relished their own internal energy and creative capabilities. They tended to be competitive, aggressive, and independent. On the other hand, the older men (aged fifty-five and over) tended to be more passive and self-centered. They relied on supplicative and accommodative techniques for influencing others. Gutmann concluded that this change from active to passive mastery seems to be more age- than culture-related. Other researchers similarly report that on the whole older men are more reflective, sensual, and mellow than are younger men (Zube, 1982).

Gutmann (1977) has continued to study personality and aging in a wide range of cultures. In subsequent research he reports that his earlier finding has been confirmed—that around age fifty-five, men begin to use passive instead of active techniques in dealing with the demands of their environment. Women, however, appear to move in the opposite direction, from passive to active mastery. They tend to become more forceful, domineering, managerial, and independent. He concludes (1977: 312):

> In effect, "masculine" and "feminine" qualities are distributed not only by sex but by life period. Men are not forever "masculine"; rather, they can be defined as the sex that shows "masculine" traits before the so-called "feminine" pattern. The reverse is true for women.

Gutmann suggests a tentative explanation for these sex differences. He believes that the requirements of parenthood place different demands on the sexes in early adulthood. If women are to succeed in their roles as the primary caretakers of children (given traditional patterns in the division of labor), they need to cultivate the tender, affiliative elements in their personalities while suppressing the aggressive components. By the same token, if men are to succeed in their traditional role as economic providers, they need to highlight and free the aggressive aspects of their personalities and constrain the more tender, affiliative aspects. But as their children grow up, both parents can afford to express the full potential of their personalities. Men can recapture the "femininity" that was previously repressed in the interests of economic competition, ambition, and accomplishment; women can recapture the "masculinity" that was repressed in order to provide emotional security for their offspring.

Age-Related Differences in Personality?
David Gutmann finds that men aged fifty-five and over tend to move from active to passive techniques in dealing with the demands of their environment. In contrast, women seem to move in the opposite direction—from passivity to active mastery.
Patrick Reddy

Gutmann's approach to gender behaviors—a functional, role-based theory—is admittedly controversial. S. Shirley Feldman and Sharon C. Nash (1979) find some support for the theory among a sample of white, upper-middle-class, married Americans. As predicted by Gutmann, grandparents showed heightened interest in babies. Indeed, grandfathers showed greater responsiveness to babies than did men at any other point in the life cycle. But contrary to Gutmann's expectations, the men's masculinity scores did not significantly change in the later stages of life. Although the men gave evidence of a higher incidence of typically "feminine" traits in their later years, they did not do so at the expense of their well-established masculinity. Likewise, women showed an increase in their masculinity scores without a decline in their femininity.

It should be stressed that in recent years many psychologists have moved away from the traditional assumption that masculinity and femininity are inversely related characteristics of personality and behavior, the former appropriate to men and the latter to women. *Androgyny*—the incorporation of both male-typed and female-typed characteristics within a single personality—provides an alternative perspective. As was pointed out in Chapter 9, individuals differ in their gender role attitudes and behaviors along a continuum of gender roles. Androgynous individuals do not restrict their behavior to that embodied in cultural stereotypes of masculinity and femininity. The findings of Gutmann and other researchers seem to suggest that in later life people tend toward androgyny. Androgynous responses are thought to be associated with increased flexibility and adaptability and hence with successful aging (Sinnott, 1977, 1982).

Other research suggests that the conceptions individuals have of their own and other people's gender roles fluctuate in accordance with specific life situations. Social definitions "call forth" certain types of attitudes and behaviors. Accordingly, sexist social arrangements can be expected to elicit highly sex-typed behaviors while more equalitarian arrangements will result in a higher incidence of androgynous behaviors (Abrahams, Feldman, and Nash, 1978).

ADAPTATION ACROSS THE ADULT YEARS

Perhaps no theme has been more recurrent throughout this text than that life is a process of unending adaptation. Not only do we age in our biological structure and functioning, but the life course from birth to death is punctuated by transition points in which we relinquish familiar roles and assume new ones. To complicate matters further, the world itself alters because of wars, economic crises, shifts in governments and governmental policies, shortages of natural resources, epidemics, and the like. Consequently, the stage on which we enact our roles is in constant flux. The other actors, the script (culture), and the audience likewise change over time. All of this requires that we continuously assess and reassess our behavior as we cope with life's new fortunes and evolve new patterns of adjustment. These dynamic qualities are captured by dialectical psychology, the subject of the boxed insert on pages 488–489.

Maturity and Self-Concept

Most personality theorists emphasize the importance to individuals of maturity as they move through life. **Maturity** is the capacity of individuals to undergo continual change in order to adapt successfully and cope flexibly with the demands and responsibilities of life. Maturity is not some sort of plateau or final state, but a lifetime process of becoming. It is a never-ending search for a meaningful and comfortable fit between ourselves and the world—a struggle to "get it all together." Gordon W. Allport (1961: 307) identifies six criteria that psychologists commonly employ for assessing individual personalities:

> The mature personality will (1) have a widely extended sense of self; (2) be able to relate himself warmly to others in both intimate and nonintimate contacts; (3) possess a fundamental emotional security and accept himself; (4) perceive, think, and act with zest in accordance with outer reality; (5) be capable of self-objectification, of insight and humor; (6) live in harmony with a unifying philosophy of life.

Underlying many of these elements of the mature personality is a positive self-concept. **Self-concept** is the view we have of ourselves through time as "the real me" or "I myself as I really am." The self-concept in part derives from our social interaction because it is based on the feedback that other people provide us. But it also derives from the effectiveness we impute to ourselves as we confront and adapt to life's circumstances and events.

Self-concept is more independent and stable than are **self-images**—mental pictures we have of ourselves that are relatively temporary and subject to change as we move from one social situation to another. For the most part, a succession of self-images serves to *edit* rather than supplant the self-concept (Turner, 1968).

Self-concept has considerable impact on behavior. Consider the "born losers"—people whose lives are stalked by failure and misfortune. Frequently they appear to be on the verge of success, only to find that adversity mysteriously snatches triumph from their grasp. Psychiatrists and clinical psychologists have many clients of this sort, individuals who seem bent on making themselves miserable by setting up situations in which they will eventually fail. It would appear that born losers acquire a conception of themselves as "failures" and then undertake to be "true to self" by failing. They bring about failure in order to maintain a consistent conception of themselves and the world (Aronson and Carlsmith, 1962).

Taking a group of female college students as subjects, Jeanne Marecek and David R. Mettee (1972) explored the relationship between low self-esteem and success. They used the self-esteem subscales of the California Psychological Inventory, a personality test, to distinguish between women who had low self-esteem and women who had high self-esteem. They also found out which women in both groups were certain and convinced of their self-appraisals and which ones were uncertain and unconvinced. (That is, the researchers determined the validity of the women's self-esteem appraisals.) The subjects were

DIALECTICAL PSYCHOLOGY

By acting on the external world and changing it, he [the individual] at the same time changes his own nature.

—KARL MARX
Das Kapital

Over the past years the psychologist Klaus F. Riegel (1925–1977), among others, pioneered a dialectical approach to human development. **Dialectical psychology,** as it has come to be called, seeks to understand the changing individual in the changing world. Among those who have contributed to this tradition are Georg Hegel, Karl Marx, and Friedrich Engels (Lawler, 1975). Dialectical psychology focuses on "becoming"—the notion of constant change.

Viewed from the dialectical perspective, human life is characterized by contradictions and conflict. All change is said to be the product of a constant conflict between opposites, arising from the contradiction inherent in all things and all processes. Development proceeds through the resolution of existing contradictions and the eventual emergence of new contradictions. The outcome of the clash between opposing forces in a person's life is not a compromise (an averaging out of the differences among them) but an entirely new product, one born of struggle. Individuals make their own history—they evolve or develop—as they confront and master the requirements of life. Thus people forge their own personalities as they actively and relentlessly pursue their various ends.

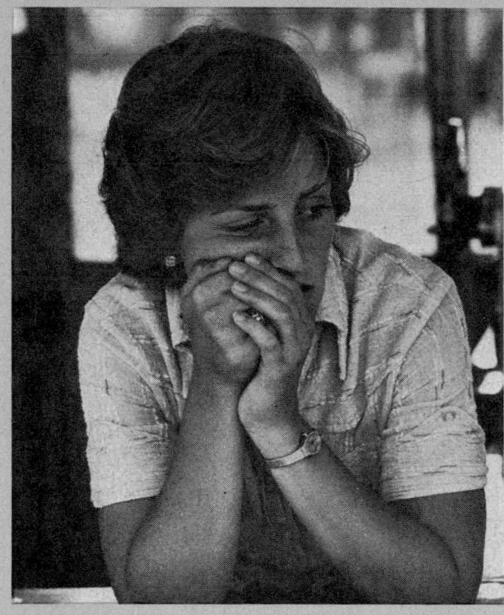

Crisis
Life is characterized by contradictions and conflict. In mastering its requirements we forge our personalities.
Patrick Reddy

Riegel (1975*a*, 1975*b*, 1976) thinks of human development as moving simultaneously along at least four dimensions: (1) inner-biological, (2) individual-psychological, (3) cultural-sociological, and (4) outer-physical. Development occurs when these dimensions get out of balance. For instance, an inner-biological crisis may arise from an incapacitating illness. Because of it the individual may be unable to meet the requirements of the individual-psychological dimension, such as the requirements of the child-parent or husband-wife relationship. Or a crisis in the cultural-sociological dimension (as represented in various social groups such as families, social classes, business organizations, communities, or nations) may arise as the result of change in the outer-physical dimension by virtue of an earthquake, flood, or some climatic change.

next given a task in which they earned points by matching geometric figures on a display board. At the halfway point (after ten of the twenty trials), the subjects were casually informed that they were doing quite well. But half were told that their success was entirely a matter of luck, while the other half were told that their achievement came from skill. Then the subjects completed the trials.

Following the break, Marecek and Mettee found that (1) all high-self-esteem groups showed improvement in the trials, (2) low-self-esteem subjects who had been uncertain of their low self-appraisal improved as much as the high-esteem subjects did, (3) low-self-esteem subjects who had been certain of their low self-appraisal and who had been told that their first-half success was due to *luck* improved more than any other group, and (4) low-self-esteem subjects who had been certain of their low self-appraisal

Since changes along the various dimensions are not always synchronized, conflict develops between them and produces a crisis. A **crisis** is a highly demanding situation in which individuals must adjust their behavior to new circumstances (Lieberman, 1975: 139):

> Crises are events that elicit in the person subjective experiences of control and loss. Generally, most of those events considered crises are of two major types: events associated with *loss,* a subjective experience associated with a break in previous attachments to persons, places, or things; and situations that *disrupt the customary modes of behavior* of the people concerned, which alter both their circumstances and their plans and impose a need for strenuous psychological work. They present the individual with the opportunity and obligation to abandon many assumptions and to replace them with others, thereby constituting a challenge.

The loss of a job, marriage, the birth of a child, departure of children, divorce, serious illness, death of a parent, moving, and retirement are events across the adult life span that require major adjustment.

Thus, as viewed from the perspective of dialectical psychology, crises are not necessarily negative happenings. Rather, by forcing constructive confrontations, they are the vehicles through which contradiction gives impetus to change within individuals and society (Riegel, 1975*b*: 51):

> The changing events within individuals interact with and influence the changing events in the outer world of which they are a part. Conversely, the changing events in the outer world are influencing the changing events within the individual.

Development, then, lies neither in the individual alone nor in the social group alone but in the *dynamic interactions* of both. Individuals are involved in a reciprocal relationship with the world. Consequently, by acting to change the world, they change it in ways that in turn ultimately act back upon themselves and bring about new changes in themselves.

Dialectical psychologists believe, for instance, that Piaget's conceptions of cognitive development do not go far enough (Riegel, 1976: 696–697):

> A dialectical interpretation of human development, in contrast to Piaget's theory of cognitive development, does not emphasize the plateaus at which equilibrium or balance is achieved. Development is rather seen as consisting in continuing changes along several dimensions of progressions at the same time. Critical changes occur whenever two sequences are in conflict, that is, when coordination fails and synchrony breaks down. These contradictory conditions are the basis for developmental progressions. Stable plateaus of balance, stability, and equilibrium occur when a developmental or historical task is completed. *But developmental and historical tasks are never completed.* At the very moment when completion seems to be achieved, new questions and doubts arise in the individual and in society. The organism, the individual, society, and even outer nature are never at rest. . . . There is no preestablished harmony. [Italics added]

In sum, whereas Piaget views development as reaching periodic levels of balance and harmony, dialectical psychologists believe that a developmental plateau lasts only a short time. They say that new discrepancies continually arise that produce new contradictions and conflict—and with them, change. Dialectical psychology highlights the disharmonious aspects of development. It draws our attention to the part that conflict and crisis play in compelling change.

and who had been told that their first-half success was due to their *own skill* failed to show any improvement.

These results demonstrate that not all people with low self-esteem undertake to avoid success; rather, it is only those who harbor a chronic and consistently low self-concept who avoid success. Even they are capable of achieving a successful outcome *provided* they believe that their success is *not self-produced.* But when individuals with chronic low self-esteem believe that success is the product of their own efforts, they experience inner pressure to behave in a self-consistent manner and hence they fail. Such individuals find themselves locked into patterns of self-imposed failure. This is one way the self-concept plays a key role in fashioning behavior.

Mounting evidence suggests that sad people and happy people are each biased in their basic percep-

Maturity
Maturity is a lifelong process of finding a meaningful and comfortable fit between ourselves and the world.
Patrick Reddy

tions of themselves and the world (Carver and Ganellen, 1983; Kanfer and Zeiss, 1983). Each brings to the world a somewhat different cognitive template or filter through which they view their experiences. And the way they structure their experiences determines their mood and behavior. Hence, if we see things as negative, we are likely to feel and act depressed. If we see things as positive, we are likely to feel and act happy. For instance, depressed people are more likely to recall tasks that they fail on, whereas nondepressed people are more likely to recall tasks that they succeed on (Beck, 1976). Such perceptions tend to reinforce and even intensify people's feelings about their self-worth and their adequacy in the larger world.

Life Satisfaction

Most people, including most researchers and professional therapists, seem to agree that life satisfaction is a major component in any overall conception of "adjustment" and "mental health" (Sells, 1969). Research reveals, however, that the objective conditions of people's lives are not closely related to their evaluations of their happiness. Analyzing national surveys, the psychologist Angus Campbell (1976) and his associates have found that during the period 1957 to 1972, the "Golden Age of American prosperity" when most economic and social indicators were moving rapidly upward in the United States, the proportion of the population who described themselves as "very happy" steadily declined. And this decline was limited almost entirely to the more affluent part of the population under the age of fifty. Likewise, although the Southern states have historically ranked at the bottom of most socioeconomic measures, Southerners consistently evaluated the quality of their lives more positively than people living in other regions (Liu, 1973).

Surveys of Americans reveal that an individual's race and self-evaluation of his or her health are the best predictors of life satisfaction: whites report their lives to be more satisfactory than blacks do, and people who describe themselves as being in excellent health score appreciably higher than do those who say they are in poor health (Clemente and Sauer, 1976). While health emerges in a variety of studies as an especially important variable in life satisfaction (Sears, 1977; Flanagan, 1978; Quinn, 1983), neither education nor income proves to be a reliable predictor of satisfaction.

Angus Campbell (1976) and his associates studied a random sample of 2,164 American adults in order to appraise how people subjectively feel about the quality of their lives and how these feelings change across the life cycle. Overall, men and women evaluated their lives quite similarly. The investigators did not find, as some might expect, that more women are unhappy and dissatisfied than men. Indeed, single women of all ages were happier and more satisfied with their lives than were single men, thus putting to rest the stereotype of the carefree bachelor and the blighted spinster.

Fewer than 10 percent of all the Americans surveyed described their lives in negative terms—as being boring, miserable, lonely, empty, useless. In contrast, the vast majority viewed their lives as worthwhile, full, hopeful, and interesting.

However, differences did show up among the various social categories in the population. Married people generally reported higher levels of satisfaction and positive feelings about their lives than unmarried ones (the single, divorced, and widowed). But it is not entirely clear whether marriage contributes to happiness or whether happy people are more likely to marry.

Perhaps unexpectedly, Campbell and his associates found that feelings about the emotional quality of one's life are not necessarily related to feelings of pressure or stress. The lowest amounts of stress were reported by widowed men and women, who also tended to feel depressed about life. In contrast, married couples with small children reported the greatest amount of stress, yet they were happier than single people.

Of all Americans, married couples in their twenties were the happiest, especially young wives. Young married men were also happy, though not as happy as their wives. Wives generally reported less stress following marriage than before, while husbands reported more stress after marriage. Further, the child-free marriage, which used to be pitied or disparaged, has increasingly come to be viewed as a fulfilling life-style. Childless husbands over thirty reported a somewhat higher level of satisfaction with life than did other men at that age level. Childless wives over thirty did not describe their lives in terms quite as rosy as did their husbands, but they were as satisfied as women of the same age who had children.

Divorced women, especially those with children, appeared to be the most dissatisfied of all Americans. They felt the greatest pressure and stress of any group and described the emotional quality of their lives in gloomy terms. Whereas only 8 percent of divorced men said that they worried about having a nervous breakdown, one-fourth of divorced women expressed this fear. Divorced men were not particularly happy, but they reported much less pressure than divorced women, who generally had to work (71 percent) and care for children (84 percent) without the assistance of a partner. In sum, the research by Campbell and his associates suggests that if we are to understand how people feel about their lives, it is highly important to distinguish among various social categories within the population.

Duke University researchers (Palmore and Kivett, 1977) have also studied changes in life satisfaction. However, rather than using the cross-sectional approach adopted by Campbell and his associates, the Duke researchers undertook a four-year longitudinal study of 378 people between forty-six and seventy

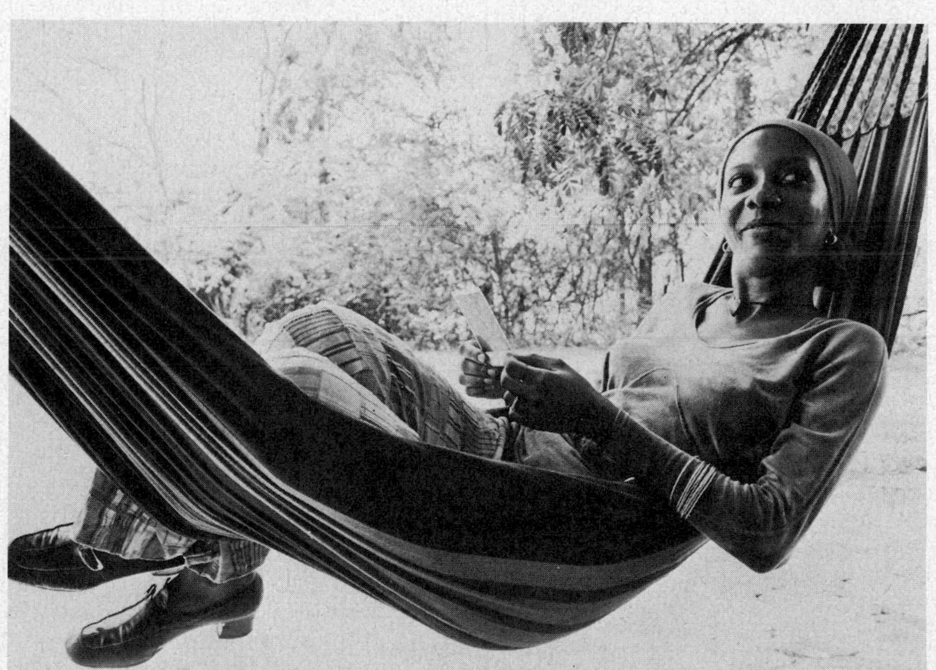

Life Satisfaction

Psychologists find that sad people and happy people each bring to the world a somewhat different cognitive template through which they view their experiences. How they structure their experiences in turn influences how they appraise their satisfaction with life.

Frank Siteman/Jeroboam

years old. The measures of life satisfaction were based on the individuals' own expectations and values. The results revealed that no significant changes occurred in average life satisfaction for most of the subjects over the four-year period. The best single predictor of a person's life satisfaction at the end of the four-year period was his or her life satisfaction level at the beginning of the period. The only other factor that appeared to be significantly related to life satisfaction was self-rated health.

As part of a larger longitudinal study—the Oakland Growth Study, begun in 1932 with a sample of schoolchildren—forty-six men and forty-five women were asked when they were thirty-eight years old to estimate the average satisfaction of each year of their past (Runyan, 1979). They were also asked to identify the events and experiences that determined their ratings. In the first decade following high school, men said that high points were associated with family life (a new marriage and/or children—48 percent), occupational success (20 percent), and a new job or environment (18 percent). Women most frequently attributed high points to family life (a new marriage and/or children—80 percent) and a new job or environment—9 percent).

In the second decade after high school, men attributed high points to occupational success (39 percent), general enjoyment (18 percent), and family life (a new marriage and/or children—16 percent). The reasons most often cited by women were family life (a new marriage and/or children—41 percent) and general enjoyment (14 percent). During this same period, men most frequently attributed their low points to occupational stress (41 percent), physical or emotional health problems (23 percent), and problems in marriage or child rearing (15 percent); women, to the death or absence of loved ones (40 percent) and physical or emotional health problems (25 percent).

SUMMARY

1. In the fashion of aging machines, a human body that has been functioning for a number of decades tends to work less efficiently than it did when it was "new." At age fifty or sixty, the kidneys, lungs, heart, and other organs are less efficient than they were at twenty. Even so, middle-aged individuals typically report that they are not noticeably different from what they were in their early thirties.
2. During middle adulthood the eye loses its ability to "zoom" in a manner that it did in youth. Accordingly, most people in their forties find that they need glasses, especially to see near objects. Changes in hearing usually begin about age thirty. Typically a falloff takes place in the ability to hear high-pitched notes.
3. The average age at which women complete menopause is around forty-seven to fifty-two. There are still many "old wives' tales" that contribute to the anxiety some women feel about menopause. Very often, however, the most upsetting thing about menopause is its anticipation.
4. Some men experience a mid-life crisis. To explain it, psychologists and sociologists look mostly for changes in a man's life circumstances that produce a crisis in his self-concept.
5. Sexual effectiveness need not disappear as humans age. Healthy men and women often function sexually into their eighties. Although time takes its toll, it need not eliminate sexual desire or bar its fulfillment.
6. As people grow older, they are more likely to suffer from a number of health problems. Cardiovascular disease and cancer are two of these. Over the past thirty years, medical science has made great strides in combating these illnesses. However, prevention remains the number-one priority.
7. Underlying most psychological approaches to personality is the notion that each individual has a relatively unique and enduring set of psychological tendencies and reveals them in the course of interacting with the environment. Trait models view personality as recurring patterns in the behavior of individuals. Situational models see a person's behavior as the outcome of the characteristics of the situation in which the person is momentarily located. Interactionist models see personality as a joint product of the person and the situation.
8. Research has provided contradictory data regarding personality continuity over the life

span. On the whole, the greatest consistency appears in various intellectual and cognitive dimensions, such as IQ, cognitive style, and self-concept. The least consistency is found in the realm of interpersonal behavior and interpersonal attitudes.

9. Some research suggests that men and women move in opposite directions across the life span with respect to assertiveness and aggressiveness, so that patterns of a later-life "unisex" tend to emerge. David Gutmann finds support for this hypothesis in his study of personality and aging in a wide range of cultures. However, in recent years many psychologists have moved away from the traditional assumption that masculinity and femininity are inversely related characteristics of personality and behavior, the former appropriate to men and the latter to women. Androgyny—the incorporation of both male-typed and female-typed characteristics within a single personality—provides an alternative perspective.

10. Maturity is not some sort of plateau or end state, but a lifelong process of becoming. Underlying many of the elements of a mature personality is a positive self-concept. Self-concept plays a key part in fashioning behavior.

11. Life satisfaction is a major component in any overall conception of adjustment and mental health. Differences in life satisfaction show up among the various social categories in the population. For instance, married people generally report higher levels of satisfaction and positive feelings about their lives than unmarried ones.

KEY TERMS

climacteric The gradual degeneration of the ovaries and the various biological processes associated with it.

crisis A highly demanding situation in which individuals must adjust their behavior to new sets of circumstances.

dialectical psychology A theoretical approach that seeks to understand the changing individual in a changing world. It stresses the contradictions and conflicts that characterize human life and hence give to it the quality of ceaseless flux and change.

maturity The capacity of individuals to undergo continual change in order to adapt successfully and cope flexibly with the demands and responsibilities of life.

menopause The cessation in women of menstrual activity, one of the most readily identifiable signs of the climacteric. In popular usage, menopause refers to a wide array of biological and psychological symptoms that are commonly associated with the climacteric and the ending of a woman's reproductive ability.

self-concept The view we have of ourselves through time as "the real me" or "I myself as I really am."

self-image The mental picture we have of ourselves that is relatively temporary and subject to change as we move from one social situation to another.

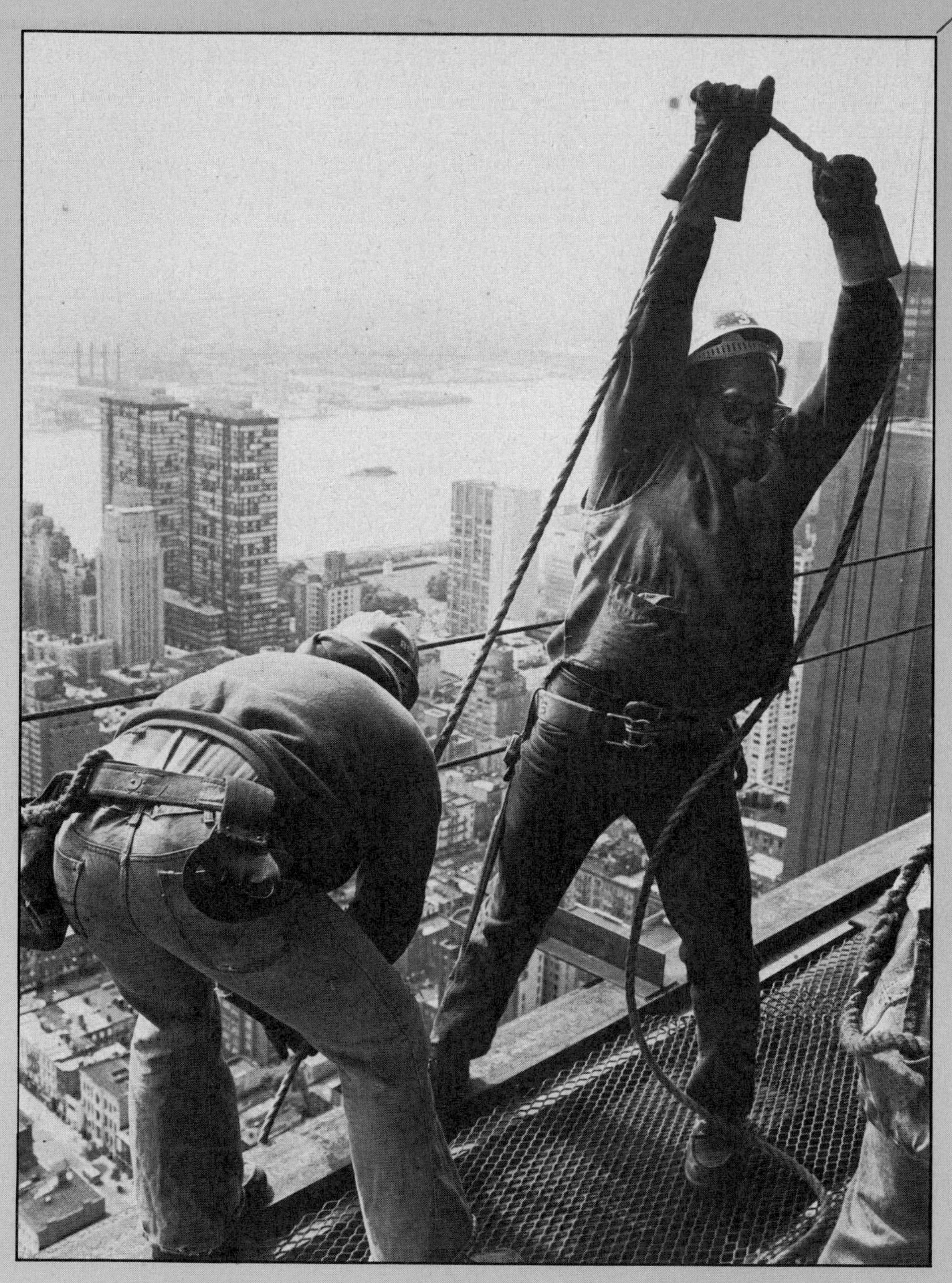

18

Middle Adulthood: Love and Work

As in other phases of life, in middle adulthood change and adaptation are central features. Human development over the life span remains a process of becoming something different while staying in some respects the same. Some of the changing aspects of middle age are associated with the family life cycle (see Chapter 16). Parents enter the "empty nest" period of life. But simultaneously many of them find that they have to assume increasing responsibility for their own elderly parents. Changes also take place in the workplace. Job obsolescence because of technology and international competition confront many blue-collar workers. And those in white-collar and professional positions may be reaching the upper limits of ladder-type careers and realize that they now must settle for lateral occupational shifts. In this chapter, we will consider the changing psychosocial context of middle adulthood.

THE PSYCHOSOCIAL DOMAIN

Within our social relationships we meet most of our psychological needs and realize various social satisfactions. From them we derive companionship, a sense of worth, acceptance, and a general feeling of their divorce, they sometimes went through a good many partners to demonstrate to themselves that they were still loveable and attractive (almost a third of the Dayton divorced had had eleven or more sexual partners, compared to 15 percent of the never-married and 6 percent of the married). Two-thirds of the never-married claimed to have had only three or fewer partners during their sexual history, hardly confirming the fantasy stereotype of the "swinging single." Overall, it seems that many divorced people have some difficulty reconnecting with the opposite sex. For example, men may experience impotence because they are apprehensive about again committing themselves to a relationship (Brody, 1983*f*).

When a couple who are in their forties or fifties divorce, the woman usually anticipates the breakup much sooner than the man does (Hagestad and Smyer, 1983). Wives typically recognize that their marriage is not working ten years or more before the actual divorce. In contrast, men usually come to realize that their marriage is crumbling fewer than three years before the divorce. It thus seems that women monitor their marriages more closely than men do. Consequently, more women than men report that the worst part of the divorce is the period before the divorce decree. Women start the process of mourning earlier and make earlier attempts to get their lives back in order, such as securing a job. Generally, women receive more support from their children than men do, at times leading to bitterness among fathers (Jacobs, 1983: 1297):

> Case 3. Mr. C, a forty-five-year-old divorcing father of a twelve-year-old boy and a fourteen-year-old girl, came to [psychiatric] treatment anxious and depressed, complaining that his wife was turning his children against him. . . . Mr. C reported that his children's complaints were very similar to his wife's accusations that she was not getting enough money and that he was not providing enough economic security. He would respond to his children by saying, "This is none of your business. How dare you take her side? Stay out of it." He reported that simultaneously he had fantasies of fleeing to the Caribbean and living as a beachcomber for the rest of his life.

Divorce has changed considerably over the past fifteen years. In 1970 California became the first state to abandon the "fault" concept of divorce, and by 1984 only South Dakota did not have a "no-fault" measure. Most states previously required long separations to demonstrate that a divorce was warranted. And judges were called on to determine which partner caused the rift and to specify a reason such as "mental cruelty" or "adultery." Under "no-fault" arrangements, grounds for divorce usually include mutual consent, incompatibility, living apart for a specified period, or irretrievable breakdown of the marriage. Most states now have guidelines to promote a fair distribution of the couple's wealth at the time of divorce. And the drive for equal custody rights for fathers has led to the decline of the old presumption that favored mothers in divorce cases.

Remarriage

Most divorced people eventually remarry. About five of every six divorced men and three of every four divorced women marry again. But the remarriage rate may be dropping (Glick, 1984). Men are more likely to remarry than women are for a number of reasons. For one thing, men typically marry younger women, and thus they have a larger pool of potential partners from which to choose. Moreover, they are more likely to marry someone who was not previously married. And they often marry women with less education than themselves. For all these reasons, the likelihood that a woman will remarry declines with age and with increasing levels of education.

A survey of 1,100 middle-aged singles in the East, mostly upper-middle-income people, highlights some of these findings (Brooks, 1983). Marvin Berkowitz, an associate professor of market research at Fairfield University, observed:

> Most men say they want a woman at least five to ten years younger while most women say their ideal mate is their own age. By chasing younger women, men through the ages have rejuvenated themselves. Women rarely have this option. Rejection isn't comfortable for anyone. But if the woman isn't aggressive or hasn't retained fabulous looks or hasn't a marvelous personality, she can expect a few blows to her self-esteem. Men tend to think they are attractive no matter how they look, how they dress or how old they are. (Quoted by Brooks, 1983: 23)

Whereas 40 percent of the men indicated they would be content with a woman with a high-school education, only 11 percent of the women said they would find acceptable a mate who had not gone to college. The women also were looking for someone who could be a good provider and could give them additional social status. Only 25 percent of the men and about 30 percent of the women said that religion was an important consideration for them. Sixty percent of the singles indicated that they were not satisfied with their "intimate relationships."

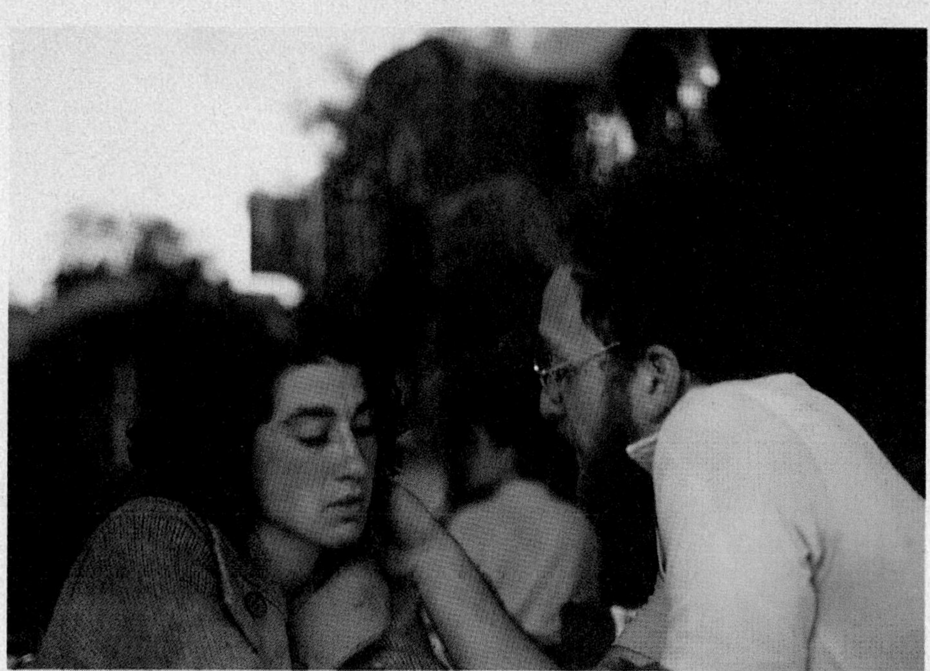

Breaking Up
Women are typically attuned to the fact that a marriage is crumbling earlier than men are. Overall, wives tend to monitor their marriages more closely than husbands do.
Ann Chwatsky/Leo deWys

Should divorced individuals remarry, they are more likely to divorce again than individuals in first marriages are. Current projections are that 61 percent of men and 54 percent of women in their thirties who remarry will experience a second divorce. Further, in recent years there has been an upward trend in second divorces, indicating that those who divorce once may have fewer of the personality traits or social skills to make a marriage work. And having undergone a divorce, they may feel less threatened by the experience.

Some research suggests that remarriage itself does not necessarily contribute to the newly remarried person's sense of well-being (Spanier and Furstenberg, 1982). But where individuals report the quality of the new marriage to be good, it does contribute to a renewed feeling of well-being. Apparently men have a harder time living alone than women do (Brody, 1983*f*). If men do not remarry, their rates of car accidents, drug abuse, alcoholism, and emotional problems tend to rise, especially five to six years after their divorce.

Stepfamilies

Remarriage often results in stepfamilies. Half of remarried persons are parents. For better or worse, their new partners become stepparents. At the present time, some 10 to 15 percent of all households in the United States are stepfamilies. By 1990, the number of stepfamilies and single-parent households will outnumber the number of traditional families.

Stepparents are probably the most overlooked group of parents in the United States. Professionals have by and large studied intact, original families or single-parent families. And for their part, a good number of stepparents feel stigmatized. Images of wicked stepmothers, cruel stepbrothers and stepsisters, and victimized stepchildren, found in such tales as *Cinderella, Snow White,* and *Hansel and Gretel,* still abound. Nor do present-day depictions of blended families like television's Brady Bunch help matters because they are so simple-minded as to becloud the realities of stepfamily life.

Yet the number of stepfamilies is growing too rapidly to be ignored any longer. Paul Bohannan (Bohannan and Erickson, 1978), an anthropologist, studied 1,764 families in the San Diego area, selected from a variety of backgrounds and living conditions. He found that stepchildren fare no better or worse than children living with both natural parents when it comes to how happy they are at home and how successful they are socially and academically at school. Further, stepchildren appear to get along as well with their stepfathers as other children do with their natural fathers.

Remarriage

Most divorced people eventually remarry, although recent research shows that the remarriage rate may be dropping. Here a bride's son poses with his mother and new stepfather at their wedding.

Mike L. Wannemacher/Taurus Photos

Most stepparents are stepfathers. Although growing numbers of fathers are winning child custody cases, most children still live primarily with their mothers. Overall, research suggests that relationships between children and stepparents are better in mother-stepfather families than in father-stepmother families (Bowerman and Irish, 1962; Benson, 1968; Duberman, 1973). In fact, John Santrock and his associates (1982) found that boys six to eleven years of age who lived in stepfather families showed more maturity and confidence in a variety of situations than boys in single-parent or intact families. However, girls from stepfather families tended to be more anxious. It seems that boys benefit from the introduction of a man into a single-parent household, whereas girls may find that their mothers do not give them as much attention as they once did.

Despite the fact that stepchildren on the whole seem to do as well with their stepfathers as other children do with their natural fathers, Bohannan found that stepfathers see themselves as less adequate than do biological fathers. He speculates that in some cases stepfathers feel they have failed their own offspring of a previous marriage (with whom they no longer live) and project that concern onto their new parent-child relationships. They are also more likely to reflect on their roles and responsibilities, and consequently to be more self-conscious and self-critical. In contrast, natural fathers are more likely to take their fatherhood for granted.

It is generally agreed that stepparents need to tread cautiously. One stepfather puts it this way: "It has to be approached the same way that porcupines make love—very carefully." A stepfather, after all, is moving into an already functioning in-group. The mother and children share a common history. He has a quite different personal history. Accordingly, the new family has two subgroups: husband and wife compose one group, mother and children the other.

Children typically approach a parent's remarriage with apprehension rather than joy. It shatters their fantasy that the mother and father will get together again someday. And the new spouse may seem to threaten the special bond that often forms between a child and a single parent. Moreover, after having dealt with divorce or separation and single parenthood, they are again confronted with new upheaval and adjustment. Matters are complicated because people often expect instant love in the new arrangement. Many women assume, "I love my new husband, so I will love his children and they will love me, and we all will find happiness overnight." Such notions invite disappointment because relationships take time to develop (Nelson and Nelson, 1982).

The process of creating a new stepfamily is stressful, and it is not always possible to avoid conflict. Complicated scenarios like the following arise that would not occur in traditional families (Fishman, 1983: 365):

> My ex-husband has money and he bought our son Ricky a car. That's great! But when my stepson David needs transportation, he is not permitted to borrow Ricky's car because my ex is adamant about not wanting to support

Stepfamilies

A growing number of American households are composed of stepfamilies. Since half of all remarried persons are parents, their new partners become stepparents. In this family, two children are the man's and two are the woman's. Research by Paul Bohannan suggests that stepchildren fare no better and no worse than children living with both natural parents.

Ann Chwatsky/Leo deWys

> someone else's child. Ricky would love to share the car with his stepbrother, but he can't risk angering his father. Besides, David is sensitive about being the "poor" brother and would not drive it anyway. It just burned us up [her and her current husband]. So we scraped together some money we could ill afford and bought an old junker for David. Of course, we fixed it up so it runs safely, and now we've put that problem behind us.

Most stepparents attempt to recreate an intact-family setting because it is the only model they have. However, they cannot do so because of the complicating relationships that a stepfamily entails. The more complex the social system of the remarriage (for instance, stepsiblings, stepgrandparents, and in-laws from a previous marriage), the greater the likelihood of difficulties. One woman in a stepfamily with seven children tells of this experience (Collins, 1983*b*: 21):

> Our first-grader had a hard time explaining to his teacher whether he had two sisters or four, since two of them weren't living in our home. The teacher said, "Justin seems unusually confused about his family situation," and we told her, "He's absolutely right to be confused. That's how it *is*."

Consequently, each stepfamily presents its own set of problems and requires its own unique solutions (Fishman and Hamel, 1981).

Five matters of everyday living are common sources of friction for stepfamilies (Bohannan and Erickson, 1978; Visher and Visher, 1979):

- *Food.* Differences in food preferences are quite salient, especially to the stepchildren.
- *Division of labor.* To resolve the problem of who is going to do which chores, many families find it necessary to put up charts on the wall allocating duties. This practice seems to work.
- *Personal territory.* Changes in living arrangements pose problems of "turf." The stepparent finds that areas of the house are already designated for particular uses, and intrusions are deeply resented. This matter is more easily handled by moving to a new house.
- *Financial matters.* Since the stepfather often is making child-support payments to another household, there may be financial strains when that money is needed to support the present family. Where monies come from and for whom and how funds should be used are matters that must be dealt with.
- *Discipline.* Perhaps the touchiest point of all is discipline. Children used to one pattern of discipline have to make adjustments to another. Most professionals agree that the parenting styles of both adults must yield to change and compromise so that the children are presented with a

> united front. Children must not have the opportunity to pit one parent against the other. In the case of natural families, parenting techniques can evolve gradually as the parents and their children move through the family life cycle. But in blended families, there is no time for such evolution. Whatever is decided must be fast and firm, and such decisions are best worked out prior to taking the marriage vows (Einstein, 1979).

With stepfamilies there is yet another dimension—the absent natural parent, whose existence can pose loyalty problems for the children. They wonder, "If I love my stepfather (stepmother), will I betray my 'real' Dad (Mom)?" In most cases children are happier when they can maintain an easy relationship with the absent parent. Not uncommonly, however, ex-husbands resent having lost control of raising their children and fail to maintain strong relationships or make child-support payments.

On the basis of the research currently available, it seems fair to conclude that children may turn out well or poorly in either a stepfamily or a natural family. Clearly, the stepfamily is required to adjust to many types of challenges not encountered by most natural families. Yet the opportunities for personal growth and satisfaction are considerable. As Aristotle once observed, "Those who educate children well are more to be honored than those who produce them."

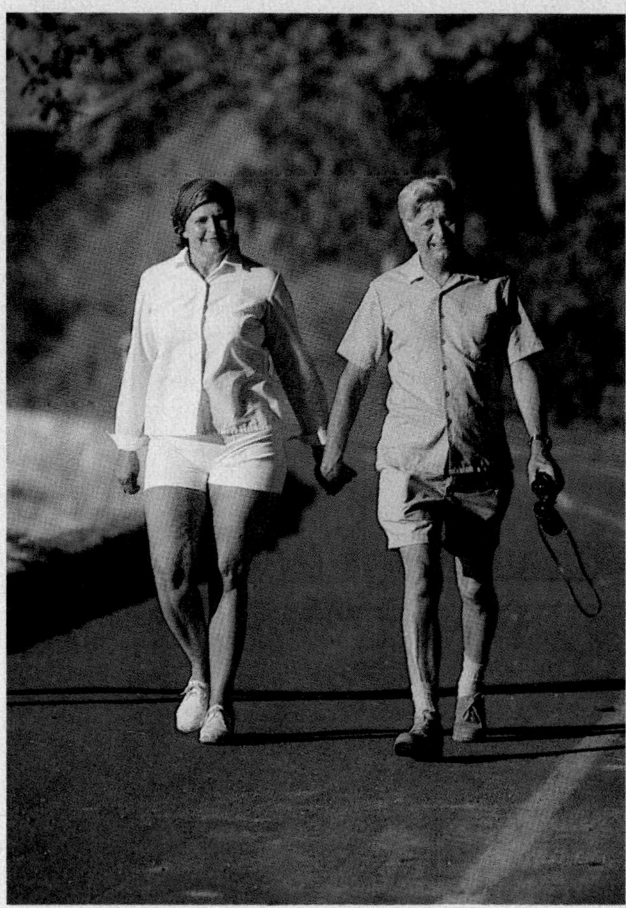

The Empty Nest

Although the media and popular stereotypes depict the empty nest phase of adult life as a difficult and stressful one, this image is not confirmed by surveys of the American public. In fact, evidence suggests that parents in the empty nest phase experience greater overall happiness than do parents with children who are still home.

Dan Cabe/Photo Researchers

The Empty Nest: Post-Parental Life

The term **empty nest** is applied to that period of life when children have grown up and left home. Although both men and women experience the transition, it has been viewed as especially stressful for women. Women lose a major component of the feminine role, that of mother—a central ingredient in many women's lives and identities. Clinical psychologists and psychiatrists have emphasized the emotional difficulties that women face when their children leave home, dubbing the problems the **empty nest syndrome.** Full-page advertisements in the *American Journal of Psychiatry* and the *Journal of the American Medical Association* herald the need and value of antidepressant medications in combating the syndrome. Likewise, the horrors of the empty nest have been a journalistic staple for years, with editors portraying the middle-aged woman as sitting alone at home, unneeded, unwanted, neglected, and miserable.

The description undoubtedly does fit some individuals. Difficulty is often most apparent among couples who have used their children's presence to disguise the emptiness of their own relationship. Similarly, a parent who has found his or her meaning in life primarily in the children often experiences a profound sense of loss when the children are no longer around. One mother who had been completely wrapped up in a selfless nurturing of her four children told the author a few months after the last child had left home for college, "I feel such a hole in my life, such a void. It is like I'm a rock inside. Just a vast, solid emptiness. Really, I have nothing to look forward to. It is all downhill from here on!"

Overall, however, the findings of research do not support the view that most couples experience difficulty with the empty nest period (Harkins, 1978). Based on a representative sample of 2,164 Americans, Angus Campbell (1975: 39) observes:

> Couples settled back in the "empty nest" reported feelings of companionship and mutual understanding even higher than they felt as newlyweds. Raising a family seems to be one of those tasks, like losing weight or waxing the car, that is less fun to be doing than to have done.

Similarly, the sociologist Norval Glenn (1975), analyzing data from six national surveys, found that middle-aged wives whose children had left home experienced greater general happiness and enjoyment of life, as well as greater marital happiness, than middle-aged wives with children still living at home did. For men, the differences were less, but fathers whose children were no longer at home were also somewhat happier than were fathers with children still at home.

Couples often report that they view the empty nest period "as a time of new freedom" (Deutscher, 1964). One forty-two-year-old woman whose two children were off at college and who had returned to Ohio State University to secure her degree in accounting told the author:

> Sure, I experienced a throb or two when Ida [her youngest child] left home. But, you know, I had expected it to be a lot worse. I really like the freedom I have now. I can do the things I want to do when I want to do them and I don't have to worry about getting home to make dinner or to do household chores. I'm now back in school, and I love it.

A neighbor voiced to the author a concern that is often heard today among middle-class parents:

> Jennie and I finally have got the kids off. And it feels great. We have more time for traveling, entertaining, and hobbies. What scares the h—— out of me, though, is that they'll land back on our doorstep. Bee is having trouble in her marriage and I just pray she doesn't expect to come back home. Jean is in her last year at college and hasn't gotten a job yet. I told her not to major in English but you know kids! Hank, though—thank God for Hank. He's off, married, got two kids, and is already an office manager at Arthur Andersen [a Big Eight accounting firm].

Often both parents and children can adjust to the empty nest on a gradual basis. Children may live at home for a period after securing their first job. Or they may go off to college and return home for vacations. One forty-five-year-old mother voiced this observation recently to the author while both were waiting in a check-out line at a supermarket:

> Pete [her only son] left home last year for college. But we still get to see him. He was home for Thanksgiving and in three weeks he'll be back again for Christmas break. I used to worry what would happen to me when he went off to college. But I started preparing myself in his junior year about the time he was taking the SAT tests. I got a part-time job and took a closer look at my life and where I was going. And during the summer break between his junior and senior years in high school I encouraged Pete to go off with his friend on a five-week trip. It gave Pete and me a chance to try out what it would be like.

In sum, most parents seem to accommodate themselves to the empty nest period quite well.

Care for Elderly Parents

Psychologists term middle-aged adults the **sandwich generation.** The middle generation find themselves with responsibilities for their own teenage children on the one side and for their elderly parents on the other. At the very time that they are launching their own children and looking forward to more time for themselves, middle-aged individuals often encounter new demands from their parents. In some cases, a couple at mid-life find that they no sooner reach the empty nest stage of the family life cycle than the nest is refilled either with an elderly parent or a grown son or daughter who returns home after a divorce or the loss of a job (see Chapter 16).

At times aging parents require increased time, emotional energy, and financial aid from their adult children. Some 40 percent of individuals between the ages of fifty-five and fifty-nine have at least one living parent, as do 20 percent of those sixty to sixty-four (Brody et al., 1983). Despite the profound changes in the roles of family members, it is the grown children who still bear the primary responsibility for their aged parents. The sense of obligation is strong even when the emotional ties between the parent and child were previously weak (Cicirelli, 1981; Neugarten, 1982*b*). In 80 percent of the cases, any care an elderly person will require will be provided by their families. This

RELIGION

Religion has to do with how people deal with the ultimate problems of life. It focuses on aspects of experience that transcend the mundane events of everyday existence and center on some kind of "beyond" or "otherness." Religion is one of the principal means by which human beings come to terms with the ultimate questions of the meaning and purpose of life. As such, religion provides interpretations for the most complex problems such as suffering, death, injustice, evil, and uncertainty.

Polls show that about 94 percent of Americans believe in God, compared with 76 percent in Britain, 72 percent in France and West Germany, 46 percent in Italy, and 35 percent in Scandinavia (Gallup Report, 1982). Some 55 percent of Americans say that religion is "very important" in their lives, and 81 percent consider themselves to be religious. Of interest, 58 percent of American adults claim to have experienced ESP, 27 percent say that they have talked with one or more dead friends, and 6 percent indicate that they have undergone profound mystical encounters very much like that experienced by Saint Paul on the road to Damascus (Hadden and Swann, 1981).

Religion helps people to deal with the "breaking points" of life. Humanity is confronted with more or less recurrent crises and haunting perplexities—the holocausts of nature, flood, epidemic, drought, famine, war, accident, sickness, vast and sudden social change, personal defeat and humiliation, conflict and dissension, injustice, the nature and meaning of life, the mystery of death, and the enigma of the hereafter. At "breaking points" beyond ordinary, daily experience, religion provides "answers" and offers the prospect of hope. For such reasons, evangelistic messages on radio and television have a large audience. The programs typically appeal to the poor and less educated segments of society, individuals who often have a good many problems and feel a sense of helplessness in dealing with them. Television evangelism attracts an audience of over 20 million viewers. Two-thirds to three-quarters of them are fifty years of age or over, roughly two-thirds of whom are women (Hadden and Swann, 1981).

Religion also plays an important role in consecrating important life events. Birth, maturity, marriage, and death—universal aspects of the human life cycle—are celebrated and explained by most religions. The beliefs and rituals surrounding these events additionally afford support for basic societal values. Festivities, marriage and funeral ceremonies, church services, and public gatherings symbolize the reality of the group and people's relation to the larger community.

assistance may be supplemented by help with income and health care costs through Social Security, Medicare, and Medicaid programs. Despite the fact that the vast majority of adult children provide help to their parents, Americans continue to echo the myth that "nowadays adult children do not take as much care of their parents as they did in past generations."

Responsibility for the elderly falls most commonly on daughters and daughters-in-law. These women have traditionally been regarded as the guardians of aging parents—the "kin keepers" of our society (Lang and Brody, 1983). Sons tend to transfer parent-care responsibilities to their wives. Yet 61 percent of middle-aged women also work. Not surprisingly, "women in the middle" are subjected to role-overload stresses similar to those experienced by younger women in relation to work, child care, and other household responsibilities. Their difficulties are often compounded by their own age-related circumstances, such as lower energy levels, the onset of chronic ailments, and family losses (Brody et al., 1983). (These facts in part explain the appeal that religion has for many middle-aged and elderly women; see the boxed insert above.) One sixty-year-old woman, whose ninety-year-old father shares her home along with her husband and thirty-year-old daughter, who moved back home to save money, says (Langway, 1982: 61):

> At a time of my life I should have less to do, I have greater demands put on me. I have my own getting older to cope with. Sometimes I get angry, not at him [her father], but at what age brings with it. Whenever he gets ill, I panic: now what? Still I couldn't live with myself if I resorted to a nursing home.

Although being employed substantially reduces the hours of assistance that sons provide their elderly parents, it does not have a significant impact on that provided by daughters (Stoller, 1983). Despite the changing roles of women, when it comes to the elderly, the old maxim still seems to hold: "A son's a son till he takes a wife, but a daughter's a daughter for the rest of her life." Thus adult daughters and daughters-in-law often face complex time-allocation pressures. They must juggle competing role demands of employed worker, homemaker, wife, mother, grandmother, and caregiving daughter.

The motivations, expectations, and aspirations of the middle-aged and the elderly differ to some extent because of their different life periods and cohort memberships (see Chapter 13). At times, these differences may be a source of intergenerational strain. However, resentment and hostility are usually less where the financial independence of the generations enables them to maintain separate residences. Both the elderly and their adult offspring seem to prefer intimacy "at a distance" and opt for residing independently so long as is possible. Consequently, the elderly parents who need to call on children for assistance are apt to be frail, greatly disabled, gravely ill, or failing mentally. When middle-aged adults express reluctance to take on primary care for an ailing parent, it does not necessarily reflect "hardheartedness." Rather, the reluctance is often born of the realization that the situation may be more emotionally stressful than the offspring can handle. The person recognizes that his or her own marriage or emotional health may be endangered by taking on caretaking responsibilities. Simultaneously, this realization may produce strong feelings of guilt (Hess and Waring, 1978).

Evidence suggests that adult children are more likely to provide helping behavior to a parent when they feel a greater sense of filial responsibility and when they live near each other (Cicirelli, 1983). It is reinforced by a feeling of attachment, the type of affectional or emotional bond that arises between children and their parents (see Chapter 8). Indeed, 83 percent of women perceive their relationships with their mothers as either quite or extremely close (Adams, 1968). Many women experience the mother-daughter relationship as a source of considerable psychological gratification and support (Baruch and Barnett, 1983; Walker and Thompson, 1983).

THE WORKPLACE

Today new currents are at play in the workplace. These currents involve new technologies, new industries, new markets, job migration, and population shifts. Old jobs in manufacturing, mining, and on the farm are disappearing. The smokestack belt extending through the Midwest from Pennsylvania to eastern Iowa has been particularly hard hit by these developments. Some have applied the label "The Second Industrial Revolution" to the vast changes being brought about by computers and other electronic innovations. In some respects old terms like "blue-collar," "white-collar," and "service economy" no longer define the realities of the workplace with precision.

Job Satisfaction

Without work all life goes rotten. But when work is soulless, life stifles and dies.

—ALBERT CAMUS

In the above quotation, Albert Camus captures the importance of work in giving meaning and satisfaction to our lives. Yet work that is not fulfilling can erode and undermine much of our humanness. Some psychologists and sociologists have employed the concept of alienation for describing many of our troubles and have sought solutions to these problems in programs designed to decrease alienation. As commonly used, **alienation** implies a pervasive sense of powerlessness, meaninglessness, normlessness, isolation, and self-estrangement (Seeman, 1959; Kanungo, 1979). At times alienation may find expression in "job burnout" (see the boxed insert on page 513).

Many of the major ideas regarding alienation have come from the writings of Karl Marx and Erich Fromm. Marx (1844/1960: 500) believed that in capitalist societies individuals lose control of their labor and become commodities, objects used by others:

> Labor . . . is external to the worker, i.e., it does not belong to his essential being; . . . in his work, therefore, he does not affirm himself but denies himself. . . . His labor is . . . merely a *means* to satisfy needs external to it. . . . It belongs to another; it is the loss of self.

Erich Fromm (1947: 69–70, 72) likewise argues that individuals become alienated from work when they can no longer experience themselves as creators of their own acts:

> The principle of evaluation is the same on both the personality and the commodity market: on the one, personalities are offered for sale; on the other commodities. . . . We find that only in exceptional cases is success predominantly the result of skill and of certain other

Alienation in Work

Often the structuring of work in contemporary societies does not allow the individual independent mastery, discretion, initiative, and direction. A person becomes an appendage of a machine, governed by the technological requirements of production.
Patrick Reddy

> human qualities like honesty, decency, and integrity. . . . Success depends largely on how well a person sells himself on the market, how well he gets his personality across, how nice a "package" he is; whether he is "cheerful," "sound," "aggressive," "reliable," "ambitious." . . . Since modern man experiences himself both as the seller and as the commodity to be sold on the market, his self-esteem depends on conditions beyond his control. If he is "successful," he is valuable; if he is not, he is worthless.

The Survey Research Center at the University of Michigan asked a cross section of Americans about their work. The pollsters found that 46.7 percent of the workers were "very satisfied" with their jobs. Although 60 percent said they would prefer a different job, a similar proportion (61.8 percent) indicated they would "strongly recommend" their job to a friend. Thirty-six percent of the workers said they had skills they could not use on the job, while 32 percent felt they were overeducated for the job (*U.S. News § World Report,* September 3, 1979: 38).

However, individuals show considerable differences in their reactions to various work requirements. What one person finds a challenge another may view as an unendurable pressure. Even assessments of monotony

JOB BURNOUT

Work that once was fulfilling and satisfying may over time become unfulfilling and unsatisfying. Psychologists term this condition **job burnout.** Its symptoms include a sense of boredom, apathy, reduced efficiency, fatigue, frustration, and even despondency (Brody, 1982). The psychologist Christina Maslach says that burnout typically occurs in three phases (Bishop, 1980). First, the individual experiences emotional exhaustion, a feeling of being drained, used up, and having nothing more to give. Second, the person becomes increasingly cynical, callous, and insensitive toward the people encountered in the work setting. Finally, the individual concludes that his or her career has been unsuccessful and that all job effort is fruitless.

Victims of burnout are often highly efficient, competent, and energetic people. They tend to be idealistic and dedicated individuals with unrealistically high expectations of making the world a better place in which to live (Farber, 1983). For instance, nurses seem particularly vulnerable to burnout, a fact that may account for the shortage of nurses. Nursing commonly attracts committed and compassionate individuals who later may find themselves unprepared for the frustrations of their jobs, the constant pressures, the erratic hours, and the constraints on rewarding interactions with patients. Others who are especially prone to burnout are divorce and criminal lawyers, police officers, teachers, and staffers in mental hospitals and hospices. At times the realities confronting workers in the helping professions crush their humanism and render them severely disillusioned. Still other victims are ambitious people who are blocked in climbing the corporate ladder and people who are driven by relentless creative impulses.

A case in point is Gail R., a thirty-eight-year-old social worker for a mental health center (Bishop, 1980: 32). Ten years earlier she had returned to college to earn a master's degree in psychology:

> Since then, things have soured. Federal funds for her clinic have been reduced. She's swamped with cases, mostly black and Hispanic families, who call her at home. She says she tries to help, but they won't listen. She has no chance to get a supervisory job, but she can't quit because her divorce five years ago left her with two children to support.
>
> Her supervisor doesn't care, she says, because he's much more interested in interagency politics. Gail's childhood asthma has resumed, as have her allergies. And she alternately starves and gorges herself, just as she did as a fat teenager.

Self-insight and self-awareness are probably the best defenses against burnout. But people living on the treadmill of work are unlikely to stop long enough to analyze their circumstances. An important step in avoiding burnout is to develop nonwork interests and supports for self-esteem. And individuals must learn to say "no," to set realistic standards for their performance, and to savor the small blessings of life. Cultivating family and friendship ties can also make a big difference. Some individuals find it helpful to set aside a "decompression period" at least once a week in which they afford themselves an opportunity to relax and leisurely pursue their hobbies and personal interests. But if one feels incapable of remedying the situation by oneself, professional assistance should be sought (Freudenberger and Richelson, 1981; Farber, 1983).

vary widely. Indeed, almost any job will seem boring to some people (Stagner, 1975).

Overall, studies reveal that job satisfaction is associated with the opportunity to exercise discretion, accept challenges, and make decisions (Kohn and Schooler, 1973, 1982; Kalleberg, 1977; Gruenberg, 1980). In terms of psychological effects, the problem that confronts most people in occupational life today is not so much that they are employees rather than employers, but that they cannot gain a sense of self-actualization in their work. People appear to thrive on occupational challenges. Hence the most potent factors in job satisfaction are those that relate to workers' self-respect, their chance to perform well, their opportunities for achievement and growth, and the chance to contribute something personal and quite unique.

Jobs that permit occupational self-direction—initiative, thought, and independent judgment in work—foster people's intellectual flexibility. For example, individuals with such jobs become more open in approaching and weighing evidence on current social and economic issues. The effects of occupational self-direction also generalize to other nonwork settings.

Individuals who enjoy opportunities for self-direction in their work are more likely to become more self-confident, less authoritarian, less conformist in their ideas, and less fatalistic in their nonwork lives than other individuals are. In turn, these traits lead, in time, to more responsible jobs that allow even greater latitude for occupational self-direction. In sum, the job affects the person and the person affects the job in a reciprocal relationship across adult life (Kohn and Schooler, 1982).

Research on work satisfaction has consistently shown that older people are more satisfied with their jobs than younger people (Wright and Hamilton, 1978; Janson and Martin, 1982; Kalleberg and Loscocco, 1983). Two major hypotheses have been advanced as explanations for this tendency. According to one interpretation, the "now" generation of workers subscribes to a set of leisure-oriented values that are different from those of the past. The pollster Daniel Yankelovich (1978: 46) says:

> A new breed of Americans, born out of the social movements of the 60s and grown into a majority in the 70s, holds a set of values and beliefs so markedly different from the traditional outlook that they promise to transform the character of work in America in the 80s. . . . Today, millions who do hold paid jobs find the present incentive system so unappealing that they are no longer motivated to work hard.

In most discussions, proponents of this view cite as key features of the "new values" a willingness to question authority, a weakening of materialist standards, and a demand that work be fulfilling and enriching. These values, it is claimed, contradict those of an industrial order founded on deference to authority and responsiveness to such traditional rewards as income and promotion.

Data from various public opinion surveys suggest that between 1955 and 1980 some measure of slippage occurred from one generation to the next in the satisfaction that individuals derive from their work (Glenn and Weaver, 1982). Even so, a 1980 Gallup Survey showed that 88 percent of all working Americans feel that it is personally important to them to work hard and to do their best on the job. And a 1982 Gallup Survey revealed that 84 percent of Americans take a great deal of pride in their work (only 36 percent of Europeans and 37 percent of Japanese had this response). Although polls show that Americans *believe* that people currently take less pride in their work than they did a decade ago, it seems premature to conclude that the American work ethic has fallen by the wayside (Wright and Hamilton, 1978; Yankelovich, 1982). Even so, it may be in danger. A 1983 survey of American workers found that only 22 percent of them said there is a direct relationship between how hard they work and how much they

Work Satisfaction of Americans

Research suggests that older people are more satisfied with their jobs than younger people are. Although some slippage has occurred from one generation to the next in the satisfaction individuals derive from their work, some of the age differences between older and younger people are related to life-cycle effects.

Sarah Putnam/The Picture Cube

are paid (Serrin, 1983*b*). Only 23 percent indicated that they were performing to full capacity, and 44 percent admitted that they did not put any more effort into their work than was required.

A second interpretation of age differences in job satisfaction looks to life-cycle effects (Quinn, Staines, and McCullogh, 1974; Wright and Hamilton, 1978). Proponents of this hypothesis say that older workers are more satisfied with their jobs because on the whole they have better jobs than younger workers do. In the usual career pattern, a person begins at or near the bottom and, where possible, moves up. Young people typically begin their careers when they have relatively few pressing responsibilities. Usually they are unmarried or without children or both. They require little more than a start—a job that is "good enough" for the immediate present, supplies sufficient money to meet short-term needs, and affords some opportunity for advancement. There are many jobs that, although not providing much meaning or enrichment and requiring little skill, are good enough—satisfactory, if not satisfying. But as the needs of workers change (as they marry, have children, and grow old), they also accumulate the experience, skills, and seniority that allow them to find positions that are progressively more satisfying.

Using data gathered by the University of Michigan's Survey Research Center (based on national surveys of the economically active United States labor force), sociologists find age differences in the rewards that workers look for from their jobs and in certain of their work values (Wright and Hamilton, 1978; Kalleberg and Loscocco, 1983). For instance, younger workers attach considerably greater importance to their promotion and advancement chances than older workers. But they attach less importance than older workers to job security, fringe benefits, and convenient hours. These differing concerns can be explained by life-cycle effects. What is typically required at the beginning of a career is not so much a secure job and the certainty of retirement provisions, but a chance to move up. In sum, today's younger workers hold many of the same values as did their elders at a comparable point in the latter's career cycle.

Mid-Life Career Change

Most of us start off our careers with the assumption that we will spend our lives in one line of work. This perspective is most characteristic of professionals like physicians, lawyers, accountants, engineers, and college professors. Such individuals spend their late adolescence and early adulthood acquiring special skills and credentials. They—and their family, friends, and associates, as well—assume that they will spend their remaining years successfully pursuing a career that constitutes a lifetime commitment. Their work is expected to produce a considerable sense of fulfillment, and with few exceptions, unfold in an orderly progression of steps from an entry position to eventual retirement. Each step—for instance, assistant professor, associate professor, and professor for academics, and staff, senior, manager, and partner for accountants—is thought to bring new levels of satisfaction and well-being.

But according to the psychologist Seymour B. Sarason (1977), this view is excessively optimistic and for many people quite unrealistic. He tracked the careers of some 2,300 individuals listed in *Who's Who.* Roughly 40 percent of them had experienced a career shift. And nearly 10 percent of the shifts represented a substantial movement from one area to another, such as from medicine to business or vice versa.

Both men and women switch careers for a variety of reasons. Some find that their career has not provided the fulfillment that they had expected or that it no longer challenges them. One professor who left academic life at age forty-three for a career in marketing told the author:

> I just got fed up with teaching. It no longer turned me on. I would wake up in the morning and dread the day ahead. When driving over to the university I would develop waves of nausea. I began thinking to myself, "This is no way to spend the rest of my life." I had always been interested in marketing and I had done consulting for a number of years before I left the university. It took me about five years before I got the business really rolling but now I'm doing pretty well. I like being my own boss and I like making money—big money. I never could do that as a prof.

Others leave one career for another because they feel bored, because they would like to give a new direction to their lives, or because they have been having difficulty with their supervisor or employer. At mid-life, many people take stock of themselves and reassess where they are going and what they are doing with their lives (see Chapter 15). Some look to formal education to provide them with new skills. Others may build on contacts, interests, skills, or hobbies that they have acquired. They reach a point at which they find themselves disenchanted with their existing work situation and decide that, rather than remain alienated in a one-career trap, they had better strike out in a new direction (Clopton, 1973; Levinson et al., 1978). So they change their career—a "repotting" so to speak—to stimulate interests they can pursue into their seventies.

The Impact of Unemployment

Most people find unemployment a painful experience. Unemployment may result from the inability to find a first job, layoffs, recession, dismissal because of poor job performance, or even leaving a job voluntarily. Based on data for the 1970s, M. Harvey Brenner of Johns Hopkins University has calculated that a rise of one percentage point in the national rate of unemployment, when sustained over a six-year period, is associated with a 4.1 percent increase in suicide, a 5.7 percent increase in homicide, and a 4.3 percent increase in first-time male admissions to state mental institutions (Nelson, 1983*b*).

George Clem, a thirty-one-year-old unemployed manufacturing worker in Jackson, Michigan, observes (Nelson, 1983*b*: 8):

> I've lost everything I ever had—it's all gone. I've lost my job. I've lost my home. I thought I had my future assured, but now I know I have no future.

A woman in the same community says:

> Emotionally, you begin to feel worthless. Rationally, you know you're not worthless but the rational and the emotional don't always meet.

Studies of workers reveal that their reactions to unemployment typically pass through several stages (Kaufman, 1982). Initially they undergo a sequence of shock, relief, and relaxation. In many cases they have anticipated that they were about to lose their jobs. Hence, when the dismissal comes, they may feel a sense of relief that at last the suspense has ended. On the whole they remain confident and hopeful that they will find a new job when they are ready. During this time they maintain normal relationships with their family and friends. The first stage lasts for about a month or two.

The second stage centers on a concerted effort to find a new job. If workers have been upset or angry about losing their jobs, the feeling tends to evaporate as they marshal their resources and concentrate their energy on finding a new job. This stage may last for up to four months. But if another job is not found during this time, individuals move into the third stage, which lasts about six weeks. Their self-esteem begins to crumble, and they experience high levels of self-doubt and anxiety.

The fourth stage finds unemployed workers drifting into a state of resignation and withdrawal. They be-

Picking up Unemployment Checks

As unemployment stretches out over time, it typically takes a toll on a person's self-conception and his or her relationship with family members and friends.

Arthur Grace/Stock, Boston

come exceedingly discouraged and convinced that they are not going to find work. They either stop looking for work or search for it only half-heartedly and intermittently. Some come through the stage and look back on it as a "cleansing" experience. They may make a conscious decision to change careers or to settle for some other line of work. And they may look for other sources of self-esteem, including their family, friends, and hobbies.

However, individuals who undergo long-term unemployment often find that their family life deteriorates. Unemployment benefits end and most Americans lose their health insurance when they lose their jobs. Financial pressures mount. People are unable to keep up their mortgage payments, or they fall behind in the rent. They see their cars and furniture repossessed. It is little wonder that they feel that they are losing control of their lives. Child abuse, violence, family quarreling, alcoholism, and other evidences of maladjustment mount. The divorce rate soars among the long-term unemployed. Many men feel emasculated when confronted by an involuntary change of roles in the family, and they lash out with destructive reactions.

When the husband is unemployed and the wife becomes the principal breadwinner, the stress may become intense. One unemployed assembly-line worker admits that he is ashamed to be financially dependent on his wife (Hymowitz, 1982: 1): "You better believe I feel badly about her being out there on her feet all those hours. It's supposed to be the other way around. I don't like taking her money." Some days, he says, he feels "so disgusted" that he drinks until he is "in pretty high spirits." He adds, "I can't continue to stay around here like this."

Part-Time Jobs

Increasing numbers of Americans are working part time because of choice or because full-time jobs are not available. In 1982, 18.3 million people, nearly a fifth of the nation's employed workers, were employed part time. From 1970 to 1982, while the number of those employed rose 26.5 percent, to 99.5 million from 78.3 million, the number of part-time employees rose 57.9 percent, to 18.3 million from 11.5 million. Many homemakers and parents with small children welcome the opportunities afforded by part-time work. But part-time workers who want full-time work find themselves frustrated and dissatisfied. According to the Bureau of Labor Statistics, there are more than twice as many people working part time because they want to than those who work part time because they cannot find a full-time job (Serrin, 1983*a*).

Some employers are turning to part-time workers to save on labor costs. In many cases part-time employees do not receive sick pay, vacations, and health, hospital, or life insurance, benefits that employers find now represent an increasing part of their costs. Likewise, with some employees working part time, employers gain flexibility in scheduling their work force. For instance, fast-food chains use part-time workers, primarily students and women who are homemakers, during peak business hours. Another benefit accruing to employers of part-time workers is that a temporary, transient work force is difficult for unions to organize.

Generally, few managerial or professional people are employed on a part-time basis. Employers tend to deem them insufficiently involved or interested in their firms if they only work limited hours. An exception is college teaching. A 1981 survey conducted by the American Association of University Professors found that part-time instructors make up 24 percent of the faculty at four-year liberal arts colleges and 20 percent of the faculty at major universities. About 51 percent of the instructors at two-year community colleges are part-time teachers (Serrin, 1983*a*). Often colleges and universities use part-time instructors because they can pay them less than they do full-time professors, give them fewer or no benefits, and need not assure them job security.

Sex Roles: Persistence and Change

> *Among all the achievements of the past century, . . . it may be doubted whether any is so profoundly significant and in the long run so beneficial as the emancipation of women.*
>
> —DAG HAMMARSKJÖLD

In the past, most women provided unpaid child-rearing and domestic services. Although most men in our society have always belonged to the wage sector of the economy, until very recently the vast majority of women were left out of the wage economy altogether. Since household labor and child care take place outside of trade and the marketplace, they have not been considered "real work"—a reflection of a sexist value system. In a society where money determines worth, women's domestic labor has been belittled because it does not yield a monetary return.

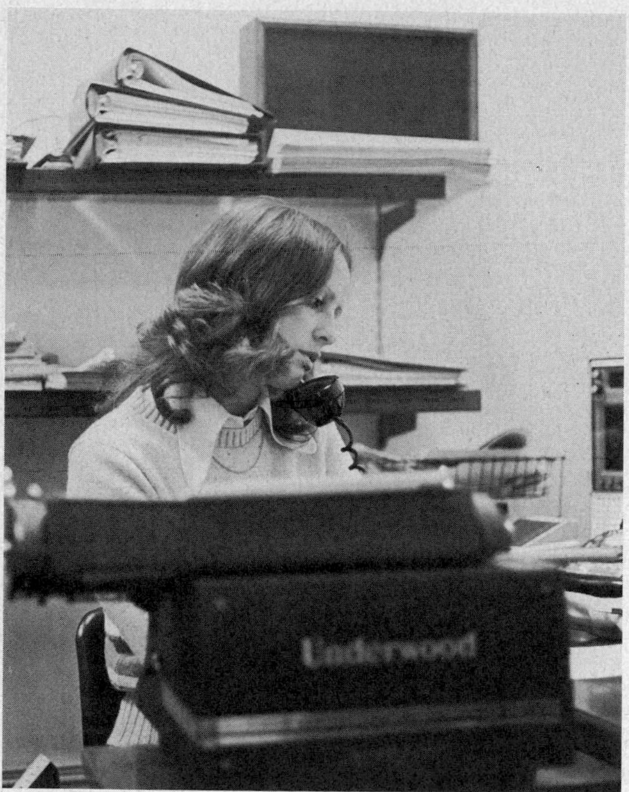

Secretarial Roles

Women predominantly work at low-paying jobs in patriarchal office settings. Not only do they do much of the menial labor, but they are also expected to supply "office decoration" through their physical attractiveness.
Patrick Reddy

But the past two decades have brought considerable economic and social change in the status of women. More than half of all American women over sixteen, and more than half of all women with school-age children (a figure that is projected to reach 75 percent by 1990), are either holding jobs outside the home or looking for such jobs.

The expansion of the female work force can be traced to many factors: the increasing availability of new contraceptive methods and legal abortions; a growing preference for smaller families; economic pressures that have made two family paychecks increasingly attractive; a rising divorce rate, which has contributed to a substantial rise in the number of households headed by women; an increasing number of female college graduates who desire careers; expansion of the service-oriented economy, which has been accompanied by an increased demand for white-collar workers; changing attitudes toward careers for women outside the home; and legislation that has broken down discriminatory barriers and increased employment opportunities for women.

Despite these changes, many of the current figures on the employment of women in American industry bear a striking resemblance to those of previous decades. Although the proportion of women in the labor force has greatly increased, there has been little substantial change in the sex labeling or sex segregation of occupations since 1900 (Scott, 1982). Much of the increase in female employment has been achieved through the displacement of men by women in some low-paying categories and through the rapid expansion of the "pink-collar" occupations. In the United States, women fill more than 90 percent of all secretarial, bookkeeping, and receptionist positions (see Table 18.1). Moreover, many jobs in the service industries involve an extension of the work that women do as homemakers—teaching children, nursing the sick, and preparing food.

Women also earn less than men do (a woman working full time in 1983 earned 62 cents for each dollar earned by her male counterpart). Underlying this gap is the occupational segregation discussed

Table 18.1 Sexism in the Labor Force, 1982

Occupation	% Women	% Men	Median Income
Secretaries	99.2		$12,636
Receptionists	97.5		10,764
Typists	96.6		11,804
Registered nurses	95.6		18,980
Sewers, stitchers	95.5		8,632
Keypunch operators	94.5		12,480
Bank tellers	92.0		10,348
Telephone operators	91.9		13,988
RR switch operators		100	22,828
Firefighters		99.5	20,438
Plumbers, pipefitters		99.2	21,944
Auto mechanics		99.1	15,964
Carpet installers		98.8	15,392
Surveyors		98.5	17,472
Truck drivers		97.9	17,160
Garbage collectors		97.3	12,116

SOURCE: Bureau of Labor Statistics, 1984.

Table 18.2 Men and Women: Same Job, Different Pay

Occupation	Weekly Earnings, Men	Weekly Earnings, Women	Earnings Ratio: % Women to Men
Lawyer	$653	$492	75.3
Engineer	592	479	80.9
Health administrator	587	394	67.1
Social scientist	580	420	72.4
Bank financial officer and manager	574	336	58.5
Computer systems analyst	568	428	75.3
Elementary-, secondary-school administrator	566	338	59.7
Physician	564	412	73.0
Life and physical scientist	553	378	68.3
Public-relations specialist	550	341	62.0
Operations and systems analyst	547	417	76.2
Personnel and labor-relations worker	530	354	66.7
College and university teacher	528	415	78.5
Designer	526	302	57.4
Public administrator	501	392	78.2
Computer programmer	478	382	79.9
Accountant	468	325	69.4
Vocational and educational counselor	459	348	75.8
Editor and reporter	451	325	72.0
Advertising agent, sales worker	449	286	63.6
Real-estate agent	435	292	66.8
Insurance agent, underwriter	419	284	67.7
Wholesale, retail buyer	412	271	65.7
Elementary-school teacher	411	339	82.4
Secondary-school teacher	411	357	86.8

SOURCE: Bureau of Labor Statistics, Current Population Survey, 1982.

above. Earnings in traditional "female" jobs and professions are considerably lower than those in comparable male-dominated occupations (McLaughlin, 1978; Wolf and Fligstein, 1979). Sociologists David L. Featherman and Robert M. Hauser (1978) calculate that discrimination accounts for 84 percent of the earnings gap between men and women. The earnings of contemporary women still seem to be determined by the Old Testament rule, as stated in Leviticus 27:3–4: "A male between 20 and 60 years old shall be valued at 50 silver shekels. . . . If it is a female, she shall be valued at 30 shekels" (see Table 18.2).

One of the most significant trends of the 1980s has been the movement of women into fields that traditionally have been closed to them. Three of every ten law degrees now go to women, and nearly one in every four new physicians is a woman. In 1972, women in companies with one hundred or more employees held only one of eight management positions. Today they occupy one in five (Byrne, 1982).

Yet it is easy to overestimate the magnitude of the gains that women have made. For instance, there appears to be an invisible ceiling for women in senior management positions at the $75,000 to $100,000 salary level. Only one of the 500 largest corporations in the United States is headed by a woman chief executive. She is Katharine Graham of the Washington Post Company, and she readily admits that she got the job because her family owns a controlling share of the corporation. Nor do executive recruiters and corporate officials expect the situation to improve for women in the foreseeable future. For example, in 1984, women had only four of the 154 spots in the Harvard Business School's Advancement Management Program, a prestigious thirteen-week program to which corporations send executives they are grooming for top positions. The numbers were not much better at comparable conclaves held at Stanford and at Dartmouth's Tuck School (Fraker, 1984).

Various explanations are advanced for the failure of women to reach senior-level management positions. Ann Carol Brown, a consultant to a number of the nation's largest corporations, says that the biggest hurdle is the matter of male comfort, since competence does not seem to be an issue:

> Men I talk to would like to see more women in senior management. But they don't recognize the subtle barriers that stand in the way. At senior management levels, competence is assumed. What you're looking for is someone who fits, someone who gets along, someone you trust. Now that's subtle stuff. How does a group of men feel that a woman is going to fit? I think it's very hard. (Quoted by Fraker, 1984: 40)

A common concern of women, especially in law, accounting, and investment banking, is that men receive the best assignments. Consequently, women have fewer opportunities to shine and to win advancement. Further, women do not receive the same types of constructive feedback and criticism that men receive from their male colleagues and superiors. Male supervisors often fail to confront female workers because they believe women "can't handle it" (they think the women will break down and cry).

It is also difficult for women to rise in an organization without depending on the sponsorship and protection of a male superior. Yet the danger confronting women in this type of situation is that the man may attempt to exploit the friendship and trust to initiate a sexual affair. However, a sexual affair with a mentor typically hurts a woman's career, causing her to lose credibility within the organization and to be resented by her peers (Klemesrud, 1981). To combat these patterns, women across America have been organizing female-career networks to broaden their business contacts, facilitate their promotions, and provide themselves with emotional support.

The economist Lester C. Thurow (1981) points out that women also encounter a substantial disadvantage should they have children. The years between ages twenty-five and thirty-five constitute the decade in the life span that is especially critical in the development of a career. During this period lawyers and accountants become partners in the top firms, business managers make it onto the "fast track," college professors secure tenure at good universities, and blue-collar workers find positions that generate high earnings and seniority. But it is also the decade when women are most likely to leave the labor force to have children. When they do, the present system for achieving promotions and acquiring critical skills extracts an enormous lifetime price. Even when new mothers return to work within a few months, men often assume that they are no longer free to take on time-consuming tasks and the women are passed over for promotion (Fraker, 1984).

In sum, the career patterns of women are quite different from those of men. And, given our contemporary family and work arrangements, the economic advancement of women is complicated by the social organization of child care. All this gives a decidedly different cast to the life cycle of women.

Dual-Career Couples

Some 27.7 million American households—67 percent of all married families—have two breadwinners. The figure continues to grow as more women take jobs outside the home. The stress associated with our society's transition from the one-income to the two-career household has fallen primarily on women (Gappa, O'Barr, and St. John-Parsons, 1980; Schwartz, 1981). Most household responsibilities continue to be shouldered by women. One survey shows that in addition to their full-time jobs, wives spend thirty-one hours a week on average for housework and child care; husbands, twenty-three hours (Shenon, 1983). No matter how equal men and women are in their careers, or how deeply they believe in sexual equality, couples typically revert to traditional gender roles (Gappa, O'Barr, and St. John-Parsons, 1980). When women are expected to assume an unequal portion of the household division of labor, they may be less effective on the job than they otherwise would be and they may not realize their true career potential or advancement. Or they may fall victim to the superwoman syndrome, attempting to excel both on the job and in the home.

If a spouse has to give up something in a dual-career arrangement, it is almost always the wife who makes the sacrifice. For instance, if a husband is offered a better position elsewhere in the country, the wife typically makes the move regardless of the effect that the transfer has on her career. Only rarely does the reverse pattern occur. In sum, the burden of meshing the differing career cycles of the husband and wife typically falls on the wife.

In two-career families, the man tends to have a larger voice in major household decisions than the woman does. Most families entail junior-senior relationships, with the wife usually secondary in most respects (Gappa, O'Barr, and St. John-Parsons, 1980). For example, the husband commonly decides where the family should live. Further, some wives fear that should they assume responsibility for their own finances, their husbands will feel that their masculinity is threatened. But should they relinquish control of their income to the husband, they often feel some measure of resentment and bitterness. Consequently, many couples maintain separate accounts or pool only a portion of their salaries. One thirty-eight-year-old teacher who earns one-third her banker husband's salary finds that keeping completely separate accounts "makes me feel more equal than I am. I see where my money goes. I see clothes on the kids and music lessons" (Moore, 1981: 94).

For middle-aged men, accommodating a wife's new career can often be a confusing and bruising experience. They are of a generation that typically viewed marriage as a one-provider, one-homemaker effort. When their wives undertake a career outside the home, they may feel isolated and conclude that their wives value their careers more highly than they do their marriages. For those who manage to overcome their doubts and fears, their wives' new careers often add new dimensions of excitement and vibrancy to their relationships. Further, family income also swells. Says one man whose wife embarked on an airline career at age forty-six, "I felt deflated. She could get along without me. But in a way it was a relief. After all, I had been the only one bringing in the outside world" (Bralove, 1981: 1).

Scheduling time together presents a frequent source of tension for dual-career couples (Moore, 1984). It seems to become a highly charged emotional issue because scheduling often masks problems of commitment, lack of intimacy, and divergent goals. Arguments about work schedules typically have more to do with "how much does he/she care" than with the amount of time the couple actually spend together. Guilt about working so hard and long or anger for having to wait around for the spouse can poison mates' feelings for each other. Hence, couples need to identify their problems and find ways to structure time for being together.

Another source of tension has to do with income differences. As of 1982, the wife had a higher income than the husband or was the sole wage earner in 12.1 percent of the husband-wife households in America. Under these circumstances, couples run a higher risk of mutual psychological and physical abuse, marital conflict, and sexual difficulty. It seems that patterns of sexist thinking lead many of the husbands to experience a loss in self-esteem. But even if the risks run high in these marriages, they are not insuperable (Rubenstein, 1982). Couples can come to terms with old expectations and new realities and learn what works best for them. Women are growing more confident of their knowledge and their right to a voice in money matters, while men are learning to share family responsibility and power. The dynamics of decision making in the family are currently undergoing change in the United States. In the process, dual-career couples are evolving new patterns and traditions for family life (Moore, 1981).

SUMMARY

1. Individuals seem to maintain a relatively stable pattern in their social behavior throughout much of their adult lives. But making and keeping new friends in later years often becomes more difficult because the pool of likely candidates diminishes. Women are more likely to enjoy intimate friendships than men are.
2. Most adult Americans have a profound wish to be part of a couple. Despite recent changes, American couples remain quite conventional. Women still do most of the household chores. Men, both straight and homosexual, place a considerable premium on power and dominance. All couples benefit when one or both members serve as the "caretaker" of the relationship.
3. Traditionally, Western society has strongly disapproved of extramarital sexual relations. Husbands are more likely than are wives to engage in and repeat extramarital liaisons.
4. Although divorce is becoming more common, it is hardly a routine experience. In many cases, divorce exacts a greater emotional and physical toll than almost any other life stress, including the death of a spouse. Compared with married, never-married, and widowed adults, the di-

vorced have higher rates of psychological difficulties, accidental death, and death from cardiovascular disease, cancer, pneumonia, and cirrhosis of the liver. The trauma of divorce tends to be greatest for women who are older, married longer, have two or more children, whose husband initiated the divorce, and who still have positive feelings for their husbands or want to punish them.

5. Most divorced people eventually remarry. About five of every six divorced men and about three of every four divorced women marry again. Men typically marry younger women, and thus they have a larger pool of potential partners from which to choose.
6. Half of remarried persons are parents, and for better or worse, their new partners become stepparents. A good number of stepparents feel stigmatized. Most stepparents are stepfathers. Boys particularly seem to benefit when their mothers remarry.
7. Middle-aged adults constitute a sandwich generation. They find themselves with responsibilities for their own teenage children on the one side and for their elderly parents on the other side. In 80 percent of the cases, any care an elderly person will require will be provided by their families. The responsibility for the elderly falls most commonly on daughters and daughters-in-law.
8. Job satisfaction is associated with the opportunity to exercise discretion, accept challenges, and make decisions. People appear to thrive on occupational challenges.
9. The past two decades have brought considerable economic and social change in the status of women. Despite such changes, however, many of the current figures on the employment of women in American industry bear a striking resemblance to those of previous decades.
10. The stress associated with our society's transition from the one-income to the two-career household has fallen primarily on women. Most household responsibilities continue to be shouldered by women. If a spouse has to give up something in a dual-career arrangement, it is almost always the wife who makes the sacrifice.

KEY TERMS

alienation A pervasive sense of powerlessness, meaninglessness, normlessness, isolation, and self-estrangement.

displaced homemaker A woman who dedicates her life to managing a home and raising children and then finds herself widowed or divorced.

empty nest That period in life when children have grown up and left home.

empty nest syndrome The emotional difficulties that individuals, particularly women, face when their children leave home.

job burnout When work that once was fulfilling and satisfying becomes over time unfulfilling and unsatisfying.

religion The manner in which people deal with the ultimate problems of life.

sandwich generation Middle-aged adults who find themselves with responsibilities for their own teenage children on the one side and for their elderly parents on the other.

Part Nine

Later Adulthood

19

Later Adulthood: Physical and Cognitive Development

Each of us stands alone at the heart of the Earth
Pierced through by a ray of sunlight:
And suddenly it's evening.

—SALVATORE QUASIMODO

Many of us have a half-conscious and irrational fear that one day we will find ourselves old. It is as if we will suddenly fall off a cliff—as if what we will become in old age has little to do with what we are now (Neugarten, 1971). But at no point in life do people stop being themselves and suddenly turn into "old people." Aging does not destroy the continuity of what we have been, what we are, and what we will be.

The older the elderly become, especially as they reach quite advanced age, the more likely they are to be unfavorably stereotyped. At times they are depicted as "cute" old people, and thus assumed to be like clever children. At other times they are portrayed as "funny" creatures who behave inappropriately and chatter endlessly about the past. And at still other times they are seen as troublesome, cranky, touchy, and sickly beings. In some respects, the very old have become this nation's lepers. Hence, along with racism and sexism, some critics charge our society with **ageism**—the systematic stereotyping of and discrimination against people because they are old (Butler, 1975, 1978; Comfort, 1976).

AGING: MYTH AND REALITY

Ignorance, superstition, and prejudice have surrounded aging for generations. Although myths of one sort or another have clouded the issue, scientific evidence can help to dispel some of the mystery and confusion. The field of study that deals with aging and the special problems of the elderly is termed **gerontology. Geriatrics** is that branch of medicine that is concerned with the diseases, debilities, and care of elderly persons.

The Elderly: Who Are They?

> *A grandmother becomes palsied. Her grown child gives her a wooden bowl that trembling hands cannot break. The old woman dies, and the bowl is discarded. But the granddaughter retrieves it; the bowl, she knows, will be needed again.*
>
> —*A Yiddish Folk Anecdote*

The time at which old age begins is ill-defined. It varies according to period, place, and social rank. In preindustrial societies, life expectancy tends to be relatively short and the onset of old age early (Amoss and Harrell, 1981). It was reported, for instance, that the Arawak of Guyana (South America) seldom lived more than fifty years and that between the thirtieth and fortieth years in the case of men, and even earlier in the case of women, "the body, except the stomach, shrinks, and fat disappears, [and] the skin hangs in hideous folds" (Im Thurn, 1883). Life expectancy for the Andaman Islanders of the Bay of Bengal rarely exceeded sixty years (Portman, 1895), and the Arunta women of Australia were regarded as fortunate to reach fifty (Spencer and Gillen, 1927). The Creek of North America were considered lucky if they lived to see gray hair on the heads of their children (Adair, 1775).

In contrast, there are several regions of the world in which some of the inhabitants are reported to live to be 140 or 150 years old. One of these is Vilcabamba in southern Ecuador. Baptismal records, which date back several centuries, have been cited to show that some villagers now living were born before the American Civil War. However, researchers have recently discounted these claims (Mazess and Forman, 1979). They find that individuals begin exaggerating their age at about 70 years (for instance, one man who had said he was 122 in 1971 claimed to be 134 when again interviewed in 1974). Further, since many living and deceased villagers have identical names, baptismal records are an unreliable indicator of a person's birth date. Careful investigation has shown that the average age of the reputed centenarians in Vilcabamba is 86 years, with a range of from 75 to 96 years. Likewise, any number of scientists are skeptical of reports that mountain villagers in the Soviet Caucasus enjoy exceedingly long life spans (Sullivan, 1982). Because older people are so revered there, they are given to overstating their ages. A 1979 Soviet census found 548 residents of Abkhazia, out of a population of 520,000, who claimed to be 100 years of age or older. When the cases were investigated, the number of centenarians was pared to 241—in proportion, a figure nonetheless five times higher than that of the United States. In 1983 there were some 32,000 people residing in the United States who were 100 years of age or older.

Americans born in 1982 could expect to live to an average age of 74.5 years (men to 70.7; women to 78.2). Table 19.1 shows the life expectancies at birth found in major nations of the world. As to when in life old age begins, probably the simplest and safest rule is to consider individuals "old" whenever they become so regarded and treated by their contemporaries (Simmons, 1960).

The number and proportion of elderly people in the United States is growing (see Figure 19.1). In 1860 one person in thirty-seven was sixty-five or older. In 1960 the ratio was one in twelve; at the present time it is one in nine. An even more substantial rise will

Table 19.1 Life Expectancies at Birth Around the World (1975–1980)

Country	Male	Female
Japan	72.7	77.9
Sweden	72.3	77.4
Canada	70.1	77.0
Soviet Union	65.0	74.3
China	62.1	65.9
India	52.0	51.0
Ethiopia	37.5	40.6

SOURCE: United Nations data.

Long Life Spans in the Soviet Caucasus

Although centenarians in the Soviet Caucasus are proportionately more numerous than centenarians in the United States are, the figures are overstated because older people in Abkhazia are given to exaggerating their age. For instance, the man in the center of the photo claims to be 139 years old.

Novosti/Sovfoto

occur between 2010 and 2030, when the post–World War II baby-boom generation passes sixty-five. At that time the proportion will be nearly one in five. Those eighty-five and over are projected to be the fastest-growing part of the population, jumping to more than 5 percent of the total population in 2050 from slightly more than 1 percent in 1984. Among some of the likely effects of these population changes are (1) increased societal and governmental attention to the aged, especially regarding problems of health and income; (2) an increased dependency ratio in the nation—today 75 percent of the adult population is in the labor force compared to a projected figure of less than 60 percent in 2020; (3) increased demand by the aged for various resources: Social Security, welfare, medical facilities and services, recreational centers, and so on; and (4) the emergence of older people as a political force and social movement (Bengston et al., 1977). Since some 25 percent of total federal expenditures is going to the elderly—a figure expected to rise to 40 percent over the next several decades—there is a growing concern over the so-called "graying of the budget." Although it long has been accepted that there is no politics of age in the United States, uneasiness that age divisiveness may appear is increasing (Neugarten, 1982*b*).

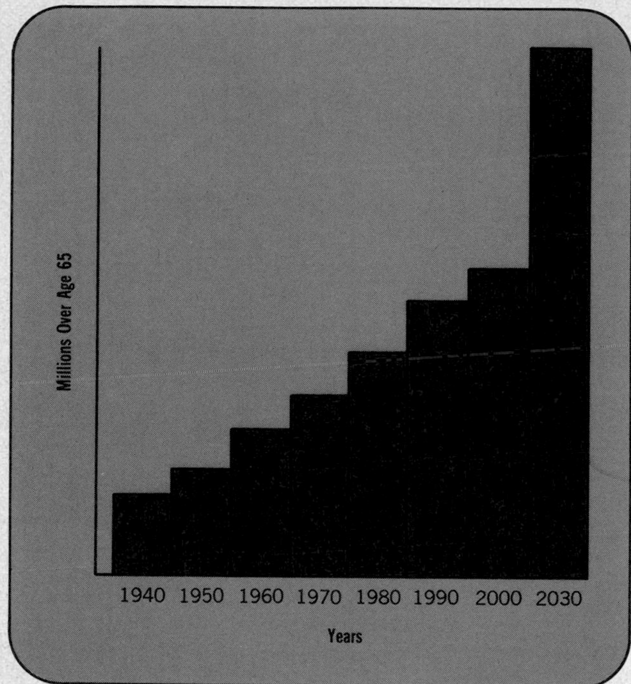

Figure 19.1 Americans Age Sixty-Five and Over
From 6.8 percent of the population in 1940, older Americans may grow to 13.1 percent of the population by the year 2000 and to 21.1 percent by 2030.
SOURCE: U.S. Department of Commerce, 1983.

Women Live Longer Than Men

The gap between the life expectancy rates of men and women has been increasing since 1920. White females born in 1982 can expect to live 78.7 years and black females 73.8 years. In contrast, white males born in 1982 have a life expectancy of 71.4 years and black males a life expectancy of 64.8 years. Because of the greater longevity of women, there are currently in the United States three women for every two men over the age of sixty-five. And in the over-eighty-five bracket, the 1980 Census counted 1,558,293 women and 681,428 men, a margin of more than 2 to 1. Although at birth there are about 105 males for every 100 females, the male death rate is consistently higher, so that by the age of twenty-seven, females start outnumbering men.

Genetic differences may play a part in granting women greater longevity than that enjoyed by men (Epstein, 1983). Women seem to be more durable organisms because of an inherent sex-linked resistance to some types of life-threatening disease. It appears that a woman's hormones give her a more efficient immune system. The different effects of the female hormone estrogen and the male hormone testosterone point to estrogen as a means of protection against cardiovascular disease. As pointed out, premenopausal women have a substantially lower risk of heart disease than men of comparable ages do.

Life-style differences also contribute to gender dif-

Senior Power
As the proportion and numbers of the elderly have increased, older people have begun to realize that they share a variety of concerns and problems. They have also become aware of their potential political power and the advantages of concerted social action.
Patrick Reddy

Women Outlive Men

By virtue of the gap between life expectancy rates of men and women, there are more older women than there are older men. Both genetic and life-style factors appear to be implicated in producing the disparity.

Joel Gordon

ferences in life expectancies. A major factor is the higher incidence of smoking among men (Holden, 1983). A retrospective study of the smoking habits of 4,394 people who died in Erie County, Pennsylvania, between 1972 and 1974 revealed that men who never smoked and were not killed by violence lived as long as women. But the study appears to overstate the impact of smoking. Another study examined 17,000 Seventh Day Adventists (nonsmoking vegetarians) and found that women outlived men by three years. Most medical experts believe that smoking accounts for about half of the difference in longevity between men and women. Hence the rising incidence of smoking among teenaged girls may mean that women will lose some of their statistical advantage.

Myths

It is not old age that is at fault but our attitude toward it.

—CICERO *(106–43 B.C.)*

The facts of aging are befogged by a great many myths that have little to do with the actual process of growing old:

- *Myth:* Much of the elderly population lives in hospitals, nursing homes, homes for the aged, and other such institutions.
  Fact: Only 12 persons out of 1,000 in the sixty-five to seventy-four age group live in nursing homes. The figure rises to 59 for the seventy-five

to eighty-four range, and to 237 above age eighty-five. Overall, only one in five Americans over sixty-five will ever be relegated to a nursing home.

- *Myth:* Many of the elderly are incapacitated and spend much of their time in bed because of illness.
  Fact: In the United States about 3 percent of the elderly who live at home are bedridden and about 7 percent are housebound (Shanas et al., 1968; Shanas, 1982). An additional 5 percent are seriously incapacitated, and another 11 to 16 percent are restricted in mobility. By contrast, one-half to three-fifths function without any limitation (even 37 percent of those eighty-five and over report no incapacitating limitation on their activity). Further, people over sixty-five years of age experience 14.5 days of bed disability per year compared to 6.9 days for individuals of all ages. And whereas 34.8 out of every 100 persons of all ages are injured each year, only 21.4 of the elderly experience injuries (Turner, 1982).
- *Myth:* Most people over sixty-five find themselves in serious financial straits.
  Fact: America's elderly, long assumed to be among the nation's poorest, have higher incomes than most people do (see Table 19.2). The 1980 Census revealed that people sixty-five and older on average had $6,299 in after-tax income per capita. This figure was $335 more than the national average and more than that for any group except individuals in their peak earning years over age fifty. The reason is that the elderly pay the smallest share of their income to taxes. How-

Table 19.2 Age Groups: Taxes and Income, 1980

Age of Head of Household	After-Tax Income Per Family Member	Taxes as Share of Income
15–24 years	$5,152	18.6%
25–29 years	5,631	22.0
30–34 years	5,329	23.6
35–39 years	5,248	24.9
40–44 years	5,465	25.1
45–49 years	6,082	25.4
50–54 years	6,648	25.6
55–59 years	7,572	25.9
60–64 years	7,426	23.0
65 and older	6,299	13.0
All households	5,964	22.7

SOURCE: Census Bureau, August 17, 1983.

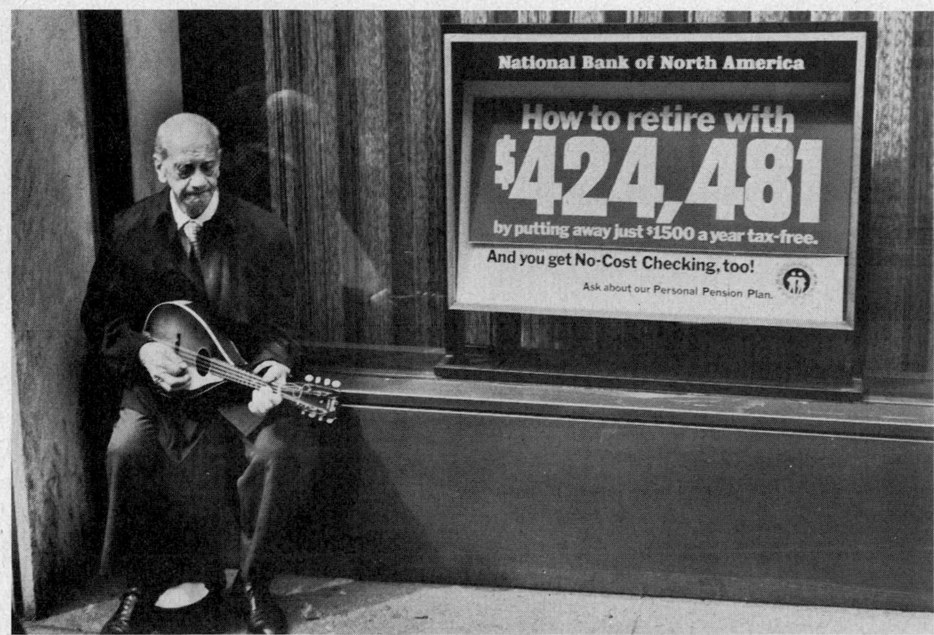

Financial Circumstances of the Elderly

Although overall America's elderly have higher after-tax incomes than do most people, the figures disguise the fact that some 25 percent of Americans over age sixty-five live below or just over the government's designated poverty line.

Mark Antman/The Image Works

ever, these figures disguise the fact that some 25 percent of Americans over age sixty-five remain below or just over the government's designated poverty line.

Although 68 percent of the public assume that money is a major difficulty for people over sixty-five, only 17 percent of the elderly report that "not having enough money to live on" is a serious problem. Significantly, a higher proportion of people aged eighteen to sixty-four—18 percent—report this difficulty (Harris, 1981; Neugarten, 1982*b*).

Today, 92 percent of Americans over sixty-five receive Social Security benefits (compared with 60 percent in 1965). Social Security provides 38 percent of the total income of older Americans. It is followed by earnings from employment, 23 percent; income from assets, 19 percent; money from private pensions, 7 percent; government pensions, 7 percent; local public assistance, 2 percent; and other sources, 4 percent (Gottschalk, 1983).

About 6 percent of the elderly can be classified as poor when *all* government benefits (including food stamps) are taken into account, down from 33 percent who were officially poor thirty years ago. Worst off are blacks and single or widowed women over age seventy. One seventy-two-year old black widow living in a Washington, D.C., housing project says, "Social Security payments are so low that they don't even want you to have enough money to eat or buy medicine." She notes that the costs of electricity, food, rent, and prescription drugs have climbed more rapidly than her benefit payments (Gottschalk, 1983: 1).

- *Myth:* People's lives and interests change radically in later life.
  Fact: A study among undergraduates at the University of Wisconsin, Madison, revealed that the favorite activities of these young people are such things as horseback riding, sailing, and basketball. But when asked to list the leisure activities they most often actually pursued, the students listed napping, walking, eating, and conversation, in that order. A similar survey among Madison-area elderly showed that their most common leisure activities were napping, walking, eating, and conversation—the same ordering of activities indicated by the college students (Harper, 1978).
- *Myth:* Most elderly people are "prisoners of fear" who are "under house arrest" by virtue of their fear of crime.

Most Elderly People Are Resilient and Very Much Alive
Most elderly Americans are much better off than popular stereotypes and mythology suggest.
Peter Menzel/Stock, Boston

Fact: Although 74 percent of the public view fear of crime as a major concern of people over sixty-five, only 25 percent of the elderly agree (Harris, 1981). Meanwhile, crimes against the person, such as rape, robbery, and assault, occur at a rate of 30 per 1,000 to the elderly, but four times as often, at a rate of 130 per 1,000, to the population as a whole. And the burglary rate for elderly households is 50 per 1,000 compared with 89 per 1,000 for all households (Russell, 1980).

Additional myths will be considered in the course of this chapter. While the problems cited above are often folklore so far as the majority of the elderly are concerned, they are realities for some segments of the older population, especially for those who are poor and black. But by and large there is a great gap between the actual experiences of most older people and the problems attributed to them by others. Most of the elderly are resilient and very much alive and not a hopeless, inert mass teetering on the edge of senility and death. Generalizations that depict the elderly as an economically and socially deprived group may actually do them a disservice by tagging them with unfavorable societal definitions and reflected appraisals. And such stereotypes allow younger people to separate themselves comfortably from older ones and to relegate the elderly to inferior status.

Health

Although 47 percent of the general public attribute "poor health" to the elderly, only 21 percent of those sixty-five and over consider poor health to be a serious problem for them (Harris, 1981). Indeed, the incidence of self-reported acute illnesses (upper respiratory infections, injuries, digestive disorders, and the like) is lower among the elderly than among other segments of the population. However, the incidence of chronic diseases (heart conditions, arthritis, diabetes, varicose veins, and so on) rises steadily with advancing years. Under age fifteen there are about four chronic diseases to every ten children, while at age sixty-five there are about forty chronic diseases to every ten adults (many of the adults have multiple disorders). This is a tenfold increase in the incidence of chronic diseases. Despite the higher incidence of chronic health problems among the elderly, most older individuals do not consider themselves to be seriously handicapped in pursuing their ordinary activities. Fully 60 percent of people over age sixty-five who are not in institutions rate their health as good to excellent compared to 74 percent of the total population (Robey, 1982).

Most of the conditions that create chronic disease increase with advanced age. The fact that larger numbers of Americans are living to be eighty-five or over means that the nation has a growing population of people with chronic disease and disability (Schneider and Brody, 1983). Since women live on average eight years longer than men do, women spend a larger percentage of their lives with more chronic infirmities and disabilities. Whereas men between sixty-five and sixty-nine spend an average of 71 percent of their remaining years in good health, their female counterparts can expect to live only 54 percent of the rest of their lives in good health. For those over eighty-five, men can expect to enjoy functional health for 51 percent of their remaining years and women for 36 percent (Katz, 1983).

The Baltimore Longitudinal Study, which began in 1958, has contributed much to our understanding of the health of older Americans (Knudson, 1980; Filka, 1982). It consists of a group of 950 volunteers ranging in age from the early twenties through the late eighties. Every two years the individuals undergo two and a half days of exhaustive physical tests. The study's findings that many people over sixty-five tend to be "overweight" has caused researchers to reexamine traditional weight tables that equate healthy with thin. Further, since 60 percent of those over age sixty have high blood-sugar levels in glucose-tolerance tests, medical authorities are questioning many diagnoses of diabetes in older people. It appears that a slowing down in insulin production may be a normal occurrence. As a result of this research, the American Diabetes Association and the World Health Organization have narrowed the statistical range used to diagnose the disease. Observes Dr. Reubin Andres, one of the researchers with the project, "Think of it, several million people 'cured' by the stroke of a pen."

Good nutrition is one factor contributing to health in old age that can be controlled (Yearick, Wang, and Pisias, 1980). Although energy requirements decrease with advancing age, elderly people do not require fewer nutrients than younger adults. However, older people tend to decrease their intake of essential nutrients and calories. Calcium, vitamin A, and thiamin are the nutrients most likely to be deficient, particularly in women.

Elderly women may require calcium supplements to forestall broken hips and fractured wrists in later life (Horsman et al., 1983). From 150,000 to 200,000 women fracture their hips every year in the United States because of **osteoporosis**—a condition associated with a slow insidious loss of calcium, producing porous bones. Calcium supplements seem to slow or stop bone loss, but by themselves they do not increase bone mass. However, in some cases an increase in bone mass can occur when fluoride is taken in conjunction with the calcium supplements. The therapy should be supervised by a physician since overdoses of fluoride can be highly toxic. Similarly, estrogen therapy may be useful in treating the condition. But estrogen therapy has little or no effect if not started in the decade following menopause. While there is no absolute cure for osteoporosis, if treatment is begun early enough, its progress can be slowed and later fractures prevented.

Brief blackouts are also a major hazard among the elderly that can result in broken hips, bleeding inside the skull, and other injuries. Medical researchers find that many elderly people have a 20-point drop in their blood pressure when they stand up. Eating also lowers the blood pressure in the elderly for an hour after meals. When the two factors coincide, an elderly person may experience a fainting spell (Lipsitz, 1983).

Some of the health problems experienced by older Americans are the product of side effects associated with medication. Currently there are more than 7,000 prescription drugs and over 100,000 over-the-counter medications available in the United States. Elderly persons do not absorb drugs as readily from the intestinal tract, their livers are less efficient in metabolizing medications, and their kidneys are 50 percent less efficient that those of a younger person in excreting chemicals. Hence a person over age sixty is two to seven times more likely to suffer adverse side effects than a younger patient.

Although older people need higher doses of some medications, they need lower doses of others. For instance, the aging brain and nervous system are unusually sensitive to antianxiety drugs like Valium and Librium, so that confusion and lethargy can result from taking these medications. Sedatives such as phenobarbital often have a paradoxical effect on the elderly, inducing excitement and agitation rather than sleep.

These facts are quite dismaying when we realize that people over sixty-five take more than 25 percent of all prescription drugs. Indeed, the average *healthy* elderly person takes at least eleven different prescription medicines in the course of a year. When taken in combination with one another, the medications can produce severe secondary reactions (Gilman, 1984). At times problems arise because the elderly have dif-

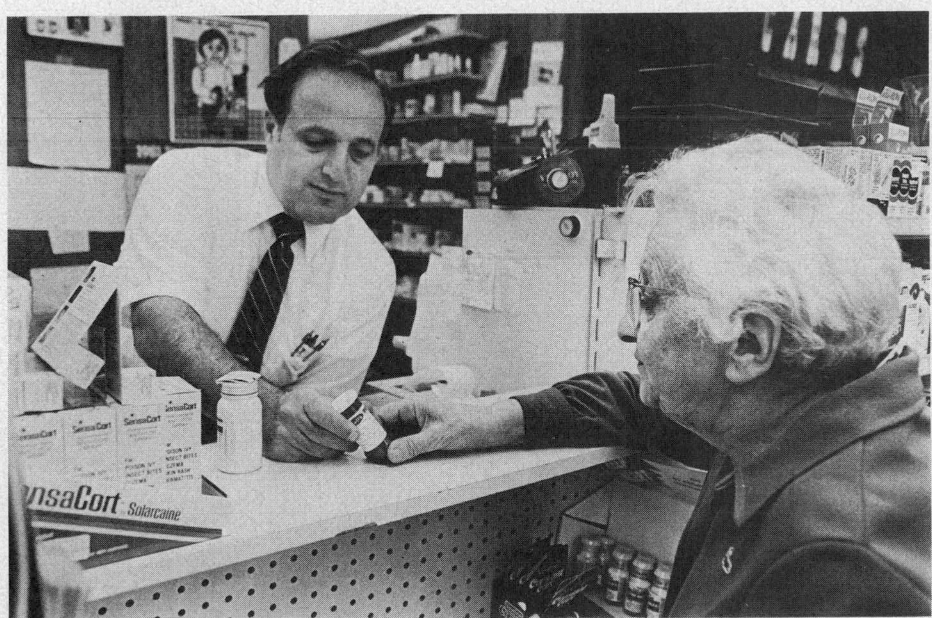

Overmedication

Some of the health problems experienced by older Americans result from the side effects of their medications. When some medications are taken in combination with one another, they can produce severe reactions. Indeed, some authorities believe that elderly Americans are overmedicated.

Bryce Flynn/Picture Group

ferent doctors treating them for different conditions. Hence each doctor may prescribe several potent medications, unaware of the other medications that have been prescribed.

BIOLOGICAL AGING

To me old age is always fifteen years older than I am.

—BERNARD BARUCH

Biological aging refers to changes that occur in the structure and functioning of the human organism through time. It is sometimes termed **senescence.** Aging is a continuous process that begins at conception and ceases at death. As human beings advance from infancy through young adulthood, biological change typically enables them to make a more efficient and effective adaptation to the environment. Beyond this period, however, biological change generally leads to impairment in the ability to adapt to the environment, and ultimately it jeopardizes survival. Improvements in the conditions of life and advances in medicine, however, have allowed more people to reach old age.

Sensory Ability

Some sensory abilities decline with age. Hearing, vision, taste, and smell afford less information about the environment than they did earlier in life.

Abigail Heyman/Magnum

Physical Changes

Some of the most obvious changes associated with aging are related to an individual's physical characteristics. The hair grows thinner, turns gray, and becomes somewhat coarser. The skin changes texture, loses its elasticity and moistness, and gathers spot pigmentation. Some of the subcutaneous fat and muscle bulk built up during earlier adulthood begins to decrease; this, coupled with the loss of the elasticity of the skin, produces skin folds and wrinkling. A slight loss in stature accompanies these changes because of alterations in the discs between the spinal vertebrae. The spine also bows, producing a stooping posture.

Collagen, a substance that constitutes a very high percentage of the total protein in the body, appears to be implicated in the aging process. It is a basic structural component of connective tissue. Loose connective tissue resembles packing material. It supports and holds in place blood vessels, nerves, and internal organs while simultaneously permitting them some freedom of movement. It also holds muscle cells together and binds skin to underlying tissue. Over time collagen fibers become thicker and less elastic. In early life, these changes are fundamental to development. But once set in motion, the process apparently is not halted, contributing to a loss of elasticity in the skin, hardening of the arteries, and stiffening of the joints. Thus over time collagen speeds the destruction of the organism that it helped to build.

Some sensory abilities also decline with age. As discussed in earlier chapters, visual efficiency decreases after age forty. Some visual loss in later life may also be associated with a loss in both the quantity and quality of the neurons in the brain's visual cortex (Devaney and Johnson, 1980). Studies also reveal a marked loss of hearing among older people, especially in the higher frequencies (Marsh and Thompson, 1973; Corso, 1976; Warren, Wagener, and Herman, 1978). Long-term exposure to noise in urban and industrial environments appears to be a contributing

B. F. SKINNER'S STRATEGIES FOR MANAGING OLD AGE

Old age is honored only on condition that it defends itself, maintains its rights, is subservient to no one, and to its last breath rules over its own domain.

—CICERO
De Senectute

At seventy-eight years of age, the noted behaviorist psychologist B. F. Skinner (see Chapter 2) told the 1982 convention of the American Psychological Association how he had been coping with some of the problems of old age. He pointed out that many of the harmful effects of aging can be compensated for. Glasses can help poor vision, and hearing aids can correct poor hearing. The volume can be turned up on radios and television sets. Foods can be highly flavored, and pornography can be employed to extend sexuality into old age.

Forgetting, he said, is a major problem. But here too remedies exist. He encouraged the elderly to jot down their ideas right away when the ideas occur to them—even if it is in the middle of the night. He had other recommendations. Keep a pencil and notebook or a tape recorder handy. Or leave reminders for yourself. For instance, if the morning weather report forecasts rain, hang your umbrella on the doorknob or put it through the handle of your briefcase so you will not forget it.

He advised "prompters" to help you recall names. If you plan to attend a class reunion, look over the alumni register for the names of those who are likely to be there, attempt to visualize them, and mentally rehearse their names. But if you still forget a name when you need it, do not be flustered. Becoming flustered will only make it harder to remember the next time. Learn to pass off the failure with a joke or a graceful apology.

Skinner acknowledged that he now finds it harder to "think big thoughts." And he finds that he can no longer move easily from one part of a paragraph to another or from one part of a chapter to another. But again he proposes remedies. Use outlines—spatial arrangements of the materials of a paragraph, a chapter, or a book. Numbering points is also helpful. Even so, Skinner (1983: 242) said:

> One of the most disheartening experiences of old age is discovering that a point you have just made—so significant, so beautifully expressed—was made by you in something you published a long time ago.

He emphasized that the elderly can have creative ideas. To offset the loss of youthful skills and energy, it may be necessary to acquire new ways of thinking or to move into a new field of activity. According to Skinner (1983: 242), a problem that the elderly often encounter is a lack of motivation:

> Our culture does not generously reinforce the behavior of old people. . . . Old people are not particularly important to younger people.

Accordingly, older people must improve their own environments to provide new stimulations.

He warns that the older generation should not be too hasty in turning things over to another generation. To do so is to lose their position in the world and destroy important social reinforcers (1983: 242–243):

> Parents who turn their fortunes over to their children and then complain of neglect are the classical example, and aging scholars often do something of the same as they bring their work to an end in the expectation that they will be satisfied with well-deserved kudos. They find themselves out of date as the world moves forward.

factor. Hearing loss can often be partially remedied by a properly prescribed hearing aid. The apparatus contains a tiny microphone that collects sounds and turns them into electrical signals, an amplifier that increases the strength of the signals, and an earphone that transforms the signals into louder sounds. (The boxed insert above discusses a number of B. F. Skinner's strategies for managing old age.)

Older people frequently report impairment in their ability to enjoy food (Cowart, 1981). This is related to a decline in the taste buds per papilla (the small nipplelike protuberances on the surface of the tongue). While young adults average 245 taste buds per papilla, persons seventy to eighty-five years old average only 88 (Shock, 1962). As for olfactory (smell) sensitivity among the elderly, the evidence is contradictory. Some researchers find that olfactory sensitivity decreases with age (McCartney, 1968; Schiffman, 1977; Schiffman and Pasternak, 1979). Others find it has no relation to age (Rovee, Cohen, and Shlapack, 1975). Touch sensitivity also decreases, but older people differ widely in this regard (Thornbury and Mistretta, 1981).

Sensitivity to temperature changes decreases among the elderly. Young adults can detect a temperature drop of only 1 degree Fahrenheit in the surrounding air. Elderly individuals may fail to notice a drop of up to 9 degrees Fahrenheit. Consequently, older people tend to be susceptible to **hypothermia**—a condition in which body temperature falls more than 4 degrees Fahrenheit and persists for a number of hours. It can be life-threatening, especially because the aging body becomes less able to maintain an even temperature in winter weather. Early symptoms of hypothermia include drowsiness and mental confusion. A loss of consciousness follows.

Aging is likewise accompanied by various physiological changes. One of the most obvious is a decline in the individual's capacity for physical work and exercise. According to the physiologist Nathan W. Shock (1962), the maximum oxygen intake declines 60 percent and the maximum ventilatory volume declines 57 percent during exercise between thirty and seventy years of age. Since oxygen is needed to combine with nutrients for the release of chemical building blocks and energy, the older person generally has

Muscle Tone in Elderly People

The nerve fibers that connect directly with the muscles show little decline with age. The speed of nerve impluses among the elderly is only 10 to 15 percent less than that among young people.

Alice Grossman/The Picture Cube

less staying power and lower reserves. Further, the heart pumps only about 65 percent as much blood at age seventy-five as at age thirty. (The brain receives 80 percent as much blood, but the kidneys only 42 percent as much.) However, the nerve fibers that connect directly with the muscles show little decline with age—the speed of nerve impulses along single fibers in elderly people is only 10 to 15 percent less than in young people. Even so, psychomotor performance is slower and less consistent in the elderly (Spirduso, 1980; Perone and Baron, 1982; Quilter, Giambra, and Benson, 1983).

Sleep patterns also change across the life span (see Chapter 5). For instance, the sleep of healthy men and women between the ages of fifty and sixty years is characterized by more frequent and prolonged awakenings and shorter sleep stages than is that of people between twenty and thirty years. Older men display greater age-related sleep changes than older women do (Webb, 1982). Overall, elderly individuals distribute their sleep somewhat differently across the twenty-four-hour cycle. It is quite normal for them to take several catnaps of fifteen to sixty minutes several times during the daytime hours.

Biological Theories of Aging

Many theories seek to explain the biological processes of aging, but so far none has been widely accepted by researchers (Shock, 1977). Indeed, the process of aging may be too complex for any one-factor explanation. Here are a number of the more prominent theories:

- *Genetic preprogramming.* Some scientists think that deterioration and death are "written" into the fertilized egg by the hereditary language of genes much as gray hair and menopause are "written" in. About twenty-five years ago, scientists discovered that normal human cells growing in tissue culture are not immortal but eventually degenerate and die after many generations of reproduction. This led some scientists to speculate that certain types of cells have built-in "time-clocks" that count off the amount of life already lived (a biochemical mechanism within the cells counts the number of divisions or replications and allows only so many more). Consequently, once the propagation of the species is ensured and an additional eighteen or so years provided for the rearing of offspring, nature is ready for the organism to die and make way for newcomers. In brief, the genes "selfishly" produce disposable bodies because this is the most economical way of perpetuating the genes themselves (Comfort, 1976; Rosenfeld, 1976; Hayflick, 1980).
- *Mean time to failure.* Engineers contend that every machine has a built-in obsolescence and that its lifetime is limited by the wear and tear on the parts. In the same way, aging is viewed as a product of the gradual deterioration of the various organs needed for life (Hayflick, 1980).
- *Accumulation of copying errors.* According to this theory, human life eventually ends because body cells develop errors in copying. The prints taken from prints are thought to deteriorate in accuracy with the number of recopying events (Busse, 1969; Comfort, 1976).
- *Error in DNA.* Another line of evidence suggests that alterations (mutations) occur in the DNA molecules of the cells—that is, errors creep into the chemical blueprint—that impair cell function and division (Busse, 1969; Comfort, 1976).
- *Auto-immune mechanisms.* Some scientists believe that aging has a marked impact on the capabilities of the immunity system. They are convinced that the body's natural defenses against infection begin to attack normal cells because the information is blurring or because the normal cells are changing in ways that make them appear "foreign" (Walford, 1969; Comfort, 1976; Schmeck, 1982).
- *Accumulation of metabolic wastes.* It has been suggested that organisms age because their cells are slowly poisoned or hampered in functioning by waste products of metabolism. Such waste products accumulate, leading to progressive organic malfunctioning (Carpenter, 1965; Chown, 1972). For instance, researchers have found significant changes with age in the amounts and kinds of metals in certain organs, including the lens of the eye.
- *Stochastic processes.* "Stochastic" implies that the probability of a random happening increases with the number of events. Radiation, for instance, may alter a chromosome through a random "hit," which either kills a cell or produces a mutation in it (Busse, 1969; Comfort, 1970).

The chances for such an event obviously increase the longer one lives.

- *Longevity assurance theory.* The theories outlined above focus on cell-destroying mechanisms. In sharp contrast to these approaches, George Sacher offers what he terms a "positive" theory of aging because he portrays evolution as having prolonged life among some species. Thus, instead of asking why organisms age and die, he asks why they live as long as they do. Sacher observes that the life spans of mammals vary enormously, from about two years for some shrews to more than sixty years for great whales, elephants, and human beings. He says that in long-living species natural selection has favored genes that repair cells while weeding out genes that impair cell functioning. Individuals who are the bearers of cell-repair genes are more likely to survive and thus pass on their favorable genes to their offspring. In support of this explanation, Sacher notes that when researchers exposed cells from seven species to ultraviolet light, the amount of DNA repair that occurred was in direct proportion to the lifetime of the species. Because animals with large brains produce small litters, evolution has favored them with longevity genes that lengthen the life span and make up for the losses in reproductive potential (Lewin, 1981).

Many of the explanations of biological aging overlap. Further, the processes that they depict may coincide to produce similar outcomes. Although the effects of aging are often confounded with the effects of disease, aging is not the same thing as disease (Weg, 1973). However, some scientists view aging itself as a pathological condition and hence merely a special kind of disease (Rosenfeld, 1976).

COGNITIVE FUNCTIONING

> *There is a wicked inclination in most people to suppose an old man decayed in his intellect. If a young or middle-aged man, when leaving a company, does not recollect where he laid his hat, it is nothing; but if the same inattention is discovered in an old man, people will shrug their shoulders and say "His memory is going."*
>
> —SAMUEL JOHNSON

For decades, both popular opinion and psychological literature portrayed intellectual functioning as declining in advanced adulthood and old age (though the poet Henry Wadsworth Longfellow, for one, made an eloquent plea for recognition of the creative potential of the elderly; see the boxed insert on page 539). Such conclusions have been the subject of considerable controversy. During the 1970s, developmental psychologists like Paul B. Baltes and K. Warner Schaie (Baltes and Schaie, 1974, 1976; Schaie, 1978) declared that it is a myth to assume that intellectual decline is inevitable, that it affects all of an individual's cognitive abilities, or that it is universal. Their research suggested much more plasticity in adult development than had traditionally been supposed.

John L. Horn and Gary Donaldson (1976, 1977), who are also psychologists, challenged the position

Plasticity in Human Development
Research reveals that there is considerably more plasticity in human development than had been assumed. Many of the declines in intellectual and cognitive functioning begin later in life, are smaller in magnitude, and involve fewer functions than scientists used to think.
Patrick Reddy

LONGFELLOW ON OLD AGE

But why, you ask me, should this tale be told
Of men grown old, or who are growing old?
Ah, Nothing is too late
Till the tired heart shall cease to palpitate;
Cato learned Greek at eighty; Sophocles
Wrote his grand *Oedipus*, and Simonides
Bore off the prize of verse from his compeers,
When each had numbered more than four score years,
And Theophrastus, at four score and ten,
Had just begun his *Characters of Men*.
Chaucer, at Woodstock with the nightingales,
At sixty wrote the *Canterbury Tales;*
Goethe at Weimar, toiling to the last,
Completed *Faust* when eighty years were past.
These are indeed exceptions; but they show
How far the gulf-stream of our youth may flow
Into the arctic regions of our lives
When little else than life itself survives.
Shall we then sit us idly down and say
The night hath come; it is no longer day?
The night hath not yet come; we are not quite
Cut off from labor by the failing light;
Some work remains for us to do and dare;
Even the oldest tree some fruit may bear;
And as the evening twilight fades away
The sky is filled with stars, invisible by day.

—Henry Wadsworth Longfellow
Morituri Salutamus, 1875

of Baltes and Schaie. They claim that it is oversimplified and dangerously overoptimistic to deny that intellectual decline takes place, because it discourages research that may discover the causes of intellectual decline and find ways to lessen it. On the basis of their survey of the literature, they concluded (1976: 707):

> The results from cross-sectional and longitudinal analyses . . . suggest that the longer one lives through adulthood, the more likely it is that some important aspects of his intellectual performance will become inferior (relative to what once was and relative to what is found in younger individuals comparable to oneself).

Psychologist Jack Botwinick (1977: 580) also surveyed the research on the controversy, and he concluded in his *Handbook of the Psychology of Aging:*

> . . . the "no decline" side of the controversy . . . catches the imagination and seems to please. Nevertheless, after reviewing the available literature, both recent and old, the conclusion here is that decline in intellectual ability is clearly part of the aging picture. The more recent literature, however, is bringing attention to what has been underemphasized in the older literature . . . [namely] these declines may start later in life than heretofore thought and they may be smaller in magnitude; they may also include fewer functions.

Botwinick's statement is a reasonable appraisal of the currently available evidence. On the basis of his ongoing research on adult intellectual development, Schaie (one of the original proponents of the "no decline" position) has also recently concluded that a decline in adult intelligence becomes clearly evident after age sixty (Schaie and Hertzog, 1983). He finds that small declines may even begin to occur by fifty-three years of age. But overall, there is less decline for individuals enjoying favorable life styles. Thus, although some aspects of intellectual functioning may diminish, the decline is often relatively inconsequential, and the decrease was greatly exaggerated in the past (Goleman, 1984). Let us take a closer look at some of these matters.

The Varied Course of Different Abilities

As discussed in Chapter 9, intelligence is not a unitary concept in the same sense that a chemical compound is a single entity. People do not have intelligence as such but rather intelligences. Thus it should not come as a surprise that different abilities may follow quite different courses as a person grows older (Denney and Palmer, 1981). Although the data on age changes in intelligence are not definitive, tests that measure *verbal* abilities tend to show little or no decline after the age of sixty or sixty-five, while those that measure *performance* do seem to show a decline (Doppelt and Wallace, 1955; Blum, Fosshage, and Jarvik, 1972; Eisdorfer and Wilkie, 1973). Very late in life, however, a general decline tends to occur in both verbal and performance scores (Blum, Fosshage, and Jarvik, 1972; Eisdorfer and Wilkie, 1973). Verbal scores usually come from tests in which people are asked to do something verbally, such as define a series of words, solve arithmetic story problems, or determine similarities between two objects. Performance scores are commonly based on people's ability to do something physically, such as assemble a puzzle or fill in symbols to correspond to numbers.

Some psychologists distinguish between **fluid intelligence**—the ability to make original adaptations in novel situations—and **crystallized intelligence**—the ability to reuse earlier adaptations on later occasions (Cattell, 1943, 1971). Fluid intelligence (Horn, 1976) is generally tested by measuring an individual's facility in reasoning, often by means of figures and nonword materials (letter series, matrices, mazes, block designs, and picture arrangements). Crystallized intelligence is commonly measured by testing an individual's awareness of concepts and terms in vocabulary and general information tests (science, mathematics, social studies, English literature, and many other areas).

Presumably, fluid intelligence is "culture-free" and based on the physiological structure of the organism, while crystallized intelligence is acquired in the course of social experience. It is the scores on tests of crystallized intelligence, rather than those on tests of fluid intelligence, that are most influenced by formal education. Often, crystallized intelligence shows an increase with age (or, at least, does not decline), while fluid intelligence shows a drop with age in later life (Horn and Cattell, 1967; Horn and Donaldson, 1977; Hayslip and Sterns, 1979).

One of the major studies dealing with developmental changes in intelligence over the life span was launched in 1956 by K. Warner Schaie (Baltes and Schaie, 1974; Schaie and Labouvie-Vief, 1974). Nearly 500 people, ranging in age from twenty-one to seventy, completed a number of intelligence tests. Seven years later Schaie and his associates retested approximately 61 percent of the subjects in the original sample.

The research of Schaie and his associates revealed that intelligence increases with age along two dimensions: (1) *crystallized intelligence,* which as just pointed out entails the sorts of skills, such as verbal comprehension, numerical skills, and inductive reasoning, that a person acquires through education and the mass media, and (2) *visualization,* meaning the processing and organizing of pictorial material. No strong age-related changes were associated with *cognitive flexibility*—the ability to shift verbal thinking, as, for example, in dealing with synonyms and antonyms. Performance declined, however, with respect to *visual-motor flexibility*—coordinating visual and motor tasks when moving from familiar to unfamiliar material.

From a review of the research, these seem to be the most reasonable conclusions: a decline in intellectual ability tends to occur with aging, particularly in very late life. Some aspects of intelligence, mainly those that are measured by tests of performance and fluid ability, appear to be more affected by aging than others. But older people can learn to compensate. They can still learn what they need to, although it may take a little longer. Other aspects of intelligence, notably crystallized ability, may increase, at least until rather advanced age. There are also considerable differences among people, some faring poorly and others quite well. One of the major factors in maintaining or improving mental capabilities is using them. Too often the expectation of decline becomes a self-fulfilling prophecy. Those who expect to do well in old age seem to remain involved in the world about them and thus do not become ineffective before their time.

Overestimating the Effects of Aging

What happens in psychological aging is complex and only poorly understood. It is becoming clear, however, that psychologists have taken too negative a view of the impact that aging has upon intellectual functioning. One reason is that researchers have relied too heavily on cross-sectional studies. As described in Chapter 1, cross-sectional studies employ the snapshot approach; they test individuals of *different* ages and compare their performance. Longitudinal studies, in contrast, are more like case histories; they retest the *same* individuals over a period of years.

Psychologists such as Baltes and Schaie (1974, 1976) have pointed out that cross-sectional studies of adult aging do not allow for *generational* differences in performance on intelligence tests. Because of increasing educational opportunities and other social changes, successive generations of Americans perform at progressively higher levels. Hence the measured intelligence (IQ) of the population is increasing. When individuals who were fifty years old in 1963 are compared with those who were fifty in 1956, the former make higher scores. But since the people who were fifty years old in 1963 were forty-three in 1956,

Cognitive Functioning Among the Elderly
Although some aspects of intellectual functioning diminish after age sixty, the decline is often of little consequence and greatly exaggerated.
Betty Barry/The Picture Cube

a cross-sectional study undertaken in 1956 would falsely suggest that they were "brighter" than those who were fifty in 1956. This result would lead to the false conclusion that intelligence declines with age. Thus cross-sectional studies tend to confuse generational differences with differences in chronological age.

Other factors have also contributed to an overestimation of the decline in intellectual functioning that occurs with aging. Research suggests that a marked intellectual decline, called the **death-drop,** occurs just a short time before a person dies (Riegel and Riegel, 1972; Siegler, McCarty, and Logue, 1982). Since relatively more people in an older age group can be expected to die within any given span of time, the average scores of older age groups are depressed relatively more as a result of the death-drop effect than the average scores for younger age groups.

Whereas the cross-sectional method tends to magnify or overestimate the decline in intelligence with age, the longitudinal method tends to minimize or underestimate it. One reason is that some people drop out of the study over time. Generally it is the more able, healthy, and intelligent subjects who remain available. Those who perform poorly on intelligence tests tend to be less available for longitudinal retesting. Consequently the researchers are left with an increasingly biased sample as the subjects are retested at each later time period (Botwinick, 1977; Siegler and Botwinick, 1979).

Memory and Aging

Memory is one aspect of cognitive functioning that often is affected by aging (Craik, 1977; Burke and Light, 1981). But as the psychologist Jack Botwinick (1967, 1978) points out, it is incorrect to conclude that a progressive loss of memory *necessarily* accompanies advancing age. Instead, some memory loss is found in an increasing proportion of older people with each advance in chronological age. This means that a part of the elderly population retains a sound memory regardless of age. Further, not all aspects of memory appear to be equally affected by aging; for instance, age-related decreases are more severe for recall tasks than for recognition tasks (Craik, 1977; Inman and Parkinson, 1983) (see Chapter 9).

Phases in Information Processing. When information is remembered, three things occur: (1) **encoding,** the process by which information is put into the memory system; (2) **storage,** the process by which information is retained in memory until it is needed; and (3) **retrieval,** the process by which information is regathered from memory when it is required. These components are assumed to operate sequentially. Incoming signals are transformed into a "state" where they can be stored, termed a **trace.** A trace is a set of information; it is the residue of an event that remains in memory after the event has vanished. When encoded, the trace is said to be placed in storage. Finally, depending on environmental requirements, the individual actively searches for the stored material.

Information processing has been likened to a filing system (Vander Zanden and Pace, 1984). Suppose you are a secretary and have the task of filing a company's correspondence. You have a letter from a customer criticizing a major product of your firm. Under what category are you going to file the letter? If the contents of the letter involve a defect in a product, will you decide to create a new category—"product defects"—or will you file the letter under the customer's name? The procedure you employ for categorizing the letter must be used consistently for categorizing all other correspondence you receive. You cannot file this letter under "product defects" and the next letter like it under the customer's name.

Encoding involves perceiving information, abstracting from it one or more characteristics needed for classification, and creating corresponding memory traces for it. As in the case of the filing system, the way in which you encode information has an enormous impact on your ability to retrieve it. If you "file" an item of experience haphazardly, you will have difficulty recalling it. But encoding is not simply a passive process whereby you mechanically register environmental events on some sort of trace. Rather, in information processing you tend to abstract general ideas from material. Hence you are likely to have a good retention of the meaning or gist of prose material but poor memory for the specific words.

Memory Failure. Memory failure may occur at any phase in information processing. For instance, difficulty may occur in the encoding phase. Returning to the example of the office filing system, you may receive a letter from a customer. You may accidentally place the letter with trash and discard it. In this case, the letter is never encoded because it is not placed in the filing cabinet. It is unavailable since it was never stored. This difficulty is more likely to be experienced by older than by younger people. Older individuals are not as effective as younger ones are in carrying out the elaborate encoding of information that is essential to long-term retention. For instance, the elderly tend to organize new knowledge less well and less completely than they did when they were younger (Rabbitt and Vyas, 1980; Murphy et al., 1981; Hess and Higgins, 1983). Thus, overall, older adults process information less effectively than younger adults (Cohen and Faulkner, 1983; Petros, Zehr, and Chabot, 1983).

Memory failure may also stem from storage problems. For instance, when filing you may place the letter in the filing cabinet but by mistake put it in the wrong folder. The letter is available but it is not accessible because it was improperly stored. Apparently, the elderly encounter this problem more frequently than younger adults. But other factors are also involved. Some psychologists have suggested a **decay theory**—forgetting is due to deterioration in the memory traces in the brain (Broadbent, 1963; Posner, 1967). The process is believed to resemble the gradual fading of a photograph over time or the progressive obliteration of the inscription on a tombstone. Others have advanced an **interference theory**—retrieval of a cue becomes less effective as more and newer items come to a classed or categorized in terms of it (Tulving and Pearlstone, 1966). For example, as you file more and more letters in the cabinet, there are more items competing for attention. Thus your ability to find a letter is impaired by all the other folders and letters.

Faulty retrieval of knowledge is a third major cause of memory loss. Older persons may suffer breakdown in the mechanisms and strategies by which stored information is recalled (Shaps and Nilsson, 1980; Burke and Light, 1981; Rabinowitz, 1984). Fergus I. M. Craik (1977) suggests that the elderly may experience a higher incidence of *cue overload*—a state of being overwhelmed or engulfed by excessive stimuli. Accordingly they may fail to process retrieval information effectively. (For instance, they may not sharpen the retrieval cue sufficiently until it comes to specify adequately the desired event in memory. Analogously, you may file the letter under the customer's name but later lack the proper cue to activate the category under which you filed it.) Some researchers suggest that the elderly may be subject to greater inertia or failure of a "selector mechanism" to differentiate between appropriate and inappropriate sets of responses (Kausler and Klein, 1978; Hoyer, Rebok, and Sved, 1979). Also, retrieval time becomes longer with advancing age (Anders and Fozard, 1972).

Overall, older adults have more difficulty with memory than younger adults. This fact has practical implications. Older people are more likely to be plagued by doubts as to whether or not they carried out particular activities—"Did I mail that letter this morning?"; "Did I close the window earlier this evening?" (Kausler and Hakami, 1983). And they are more likely to have difficulty remembering where they placed an item or where buildings are geographically located (Pezdek, 1983).

Learning and Aging

Psychologists are finding that the distinctions they once made between learning and memory are becoming blurred (Ellis and Hunt, 1977). Learning parallels the encoding process whereby individuals put into memory material that is presented to them. Indeed, the psychologist Endel Tulving (1968) says that learning constitutes an improvement in retention. Hence, he contends, the study of learning is the study of memory.

Clearly, all processes of memory have consequences for learning. If people do not learn (encode) well, they have little to recall. And conversely, if their memory is poor, they show few signs of having learned much (Botwinick, 1967, 1978). It is hardly surprising, therefore, that psychologists should find that younger adults do better than older adults on various learning tasks (Arenberg and Robertson-Tchabo, 1977). This fact has given rise to the old adage "You can't teach an old dog new tricks." But this adage is clearly false. Both older dogs and human beings can and do learn. They would be incapable of adapting to their environment and coping with new circumstances if they did not.

Research suggests that both younger and older individuals benefit when they are given more time to inspect a task (Arenberg and Robertson-Tchabo, 1977; Labouvie-Vief and Schell, 1982). Allowing people ample time gives them more opportunity to rehearse a response and establish a linkage between events. It increases the probability that information will be encoded in a fashion that facilitates later search and recall. Older adults benefit even more than younger ones when more time is made available for them to learn something.

Older people often give the impression that they have learned less than younger people have because they tend to be more reluctant to venture a response. At times the elderly do not provide learned responses, especially at a rapid pace, although they can be induced to do so under appropriate incentive conditions. And when tested in a laboratory setting, older adults seem to be less motivated to learn arbitrary materials that appear to be irrelevant and useless to them. Complicating matters, today's young adults are better educated than their older counterparts. Further, another hidden bias is that many elderly individuals take medications that can diminish mental function. All these factors suggest that we should exercise caution when appraising the learning potential of the elderly lest we prematurely conclude that they are incapable of learning new things.

Senility and Alzheimer's Disease

My wife refused to believe I was her husband. Every day we went through the same routine: I would tell her we had been married for thirty years, that we had four children. She listened, but she still thought she lived in her hometown with her parents. Every night when I got into bed she'd say, "Who are you?"

—HUSBAND OF AN ALZHEIMER'S PATIENT

Until recently, many physicians and members of the lay public accepted the view that senility is the penalty people pay for living longer than the biblical three score and ten years. *Senility* is typically characterized by progressive mental deterioration, memory loss, and disorientation regarding time and place. Irritability and other personality changes usually accompany the intellectual decline.

In persons over sixty-five, about 20 to 25 percent of all senility results from **multiinfarcts** (better known as "little strokes"), each of which destroys a small area of brain tissue. Another 50 percent is due to **Alzheimer's disease**—a progressive, degenerative disorder that involves deterioration of brain cells. Autopsies of victims show microscopic changes in brain structure, especially in the cerebral cortex. Some of the nerve cells look like infinitesimal bits of braided yarn. Apparently the clumps of degenerating nerve cells disrupt the passage of electrochemical signals across the brain and nervous system.

Alzheimer's disease affects between 1.5 and 2.5 million Americans. An estimated 5 percent of the elderly experience the disorder. The National Institutes of Health estimate that 60 percent of nursing-home patients over age sixty-five suffer from the disease. It is also the fourth leading cause of death in the United States.

Unfortunately, as yet there is no cure for Alzheimer's disease. The disorder has a devastating impact not only on its victims but on their relatives as well. Family members find their loved one progressively regressing, eventually unable to perform the simplest tasks. (See the boxed insert on page 544 for a discussion of a number of ways that can prove helpful in caring for Alzheimer victims.) One woman, Marion Roach (1983: 22), tells of her experiences with her fifty-four-year-old mother who suffers from the disease:

> In the autumn of 1979, my mother killed the cats. We had seven; one morning, she grabbed four, took them to

CARING FOR A FAMILY MEMBER WITH ALZHEIMER'S DISEASE

Alzheimer's disease has been described as "a funeral that has no end." It not only takes a heavy toll on the victim but on the victim's family as well. Caring for a person with the disease is an exceedingly taxing and frustrating experience. To do so requires considerable stamina, fortitude, patience, and love. Below are listed a number of guidelines offered by experts (Brody, 1983*d*, 1983*e*):

- Provide the patient with an uncluttered and well-organized environment and with consistent routines. In the early stages of the disease employ memory aids including labels and word pictures on appliances and doors, especially in the bathroom.
- Provide the patient with clothing that has elasticized waistbands instead of buttons and zippers and slip-on shoes instead of shoes with laces.
- Remove knickknacks that can be easily knocked over and furniture that might be tripped over.
- Install grab bars where needed in the bathroom, strong railings on staircases, and night-lights in poorly lit but frequently traveled areas.
- Have the patient wear an identification bracelet with his or her name, address, and phone number and the words "memory impaired" inscribed on it.
- Provide instructions in a soft, calm voice, using short sentences and simple words.
- Allow the patient to perform tasks within his or her capabilities, such as watering the plants or folding the laundry. Keep the tasks simple and focused on one step at a time.
- Find satisfaction in what one can with the patient but do not hold excessive expectations.
- Recognize that family members of Alzheimer patients often feel despair, resentment, guilt, and sadness.
- Avoid angry outbursts, but acknowledge to oneself the right to feel anger toward the patient.
- Do not assume that the patient does irritating things because he or she is vindictive or mean.
- Learn as much as you can about the disease.

the vet and had them put to sleep. She said she didn't want to feed them anymore. . . . Day by day, she became more disoriented. She would seem surprised at her surroundings, as if she had just appeared there. She stopped cooking, and had difficulty remembering the simplest things. . . . Until she recently began to take sedation, she would hallucinate that the television or the toaster was in flames. She repeats the same few questions and stories over and over again, unable to remember that she has just done so a few moments before.

Another woman, Jean Freeman, reports that her husband, a victim of Alzheimer's disease, is like a child again. He follows her about the house babbling and needs to be bathed and dressed. But whereas a child learns and progresses, her husband regresses. After thirty-four years of marriage, she is disturbed that her husband "doesn't remember anything that was part of our life. It's like he is gone, but still here" (Fedak, 1982: C–1).

The disease typically proceeds through a number of phases (Schneck, Reisberg, and Ferris, 1982). At first, in the "forgetfullness phase," individuals forget where things are placed and have difficulty recalling events of the recent past. Later, in the "confusional phase," difficulties in cognitive functioning worsen and can no longer be overlooked. Finally, in the "dementia phase," individuals become severely disoriented. They are likely to confuse a spouse or a close friend with another person. Behavior problems surface: victims may wander off, roam the house at night, engage in bizarre actions, hallucinate, and exhibit "rage reactions" of verbal and even physical abuse. In time, they become incontinent and unable to feed or otherwise care for themselves. Victims show a marked decrease in life expectancy in comparison with age-matched men and women. Patients usually die of infections, often from pneumonia.

One hypothesis relates Alzheimer's disease to a puzzling infectious agent known as a "slow virus." Such brain disorders as kuru and Creutzfeldt-Jakob disease are caused by slow viruses and are accompanied by distinctive brain lesions or plaques that bear a close resemblance to those that characterize Alzheimer's disease. Kuru, a disease occurring in New Guinea and once believed to be of hereditary origin, is a slow-acting virus infection transmitted from person to person by ritual cannibalism. Creutzfeldt-Jakob disease may simply be a form of pre–senile dementia that strikes at an earlier age than Alzheimer's disease (in laboratory experiments, young chimpanzees injected with extracts from the brains of Alzheimer's disease patients develop unmistakable signs of Creutzfeldt-Jakob disease). Researchers find that the brains of patients suffering from "slow virus" diseases have a huge deficit in a key enzyme, choline acetyltransferase (a substance used in the manufacture of material employed by the brain to transmit nerve signals from cell to cell).

Another hypothesis implicates increased levels of aluminum in the brain as the source of Alzheimer's disease (Schneck, Reisberg, and Ferris, 1982). Still another postulates the existence of a defect in the immune system of Alzheimer's victims. And finally, since Down's syndrome patients who survive to adulthood eventually succumb to Alzheimer's lesions, some researchers speculate that chromosomal factors may underlie the disorder.

Senility is one of the most serious conditions that a physician can diagnose in a patient. The prognosis is grim, and the effectiveness of current treatments is uncertain. Consequently, it is incumbent upon professionals who treat the elderly to do a full battery of tests to make certain a treatable cause for a patient's symptoms has not been overlooked. Often, underlying physical diseases that may make an elderly person *seem* senile go unnoticed and untreated. Such individuals are simply dumped into the wastebasket category of "senile" by families and physicians who have accepted the conventional wisdom that senility is an inevitable part of the aging process (Henig, 1978). Among common problems often mistakenly diagnosed as senility are tumors; vitamin deficiencies (especially B_{12} or folic acid); anemia; depression; such metabolic disorders as hyperthyroidism and chronic liver or kidney failure; and toxic reactions to prescription or over-the-counter drugs (including tranquilizers, anticoagulants, and heart and high-blood-pressure medications). Many of these conditions can be reversed if they are identified and treated early in the course of the illness.

SUMMARY

1. At no point in life do people stop being themselves and suddenly turn into "old people," with all the stereotypes and myths that the term implies. Aging does not destroy the continuity between what we have been, what we are, and what we will be.
2. The gap between the life expectancy rates of men and women has been increasing since 1920. On the average women live eight years longer than men. Women seem to be more durable organisms because of an inherent sex-linked resistance to some types of life-threatening disease. Life-style differences also contribute to gender differences in life expectancies. A major factor is the higher incidence of smoking among men.
3. The facts of aging are befogged by a great many myths that have little to do with the actual process of growing old. Included among these myths are those that portray a large proportion of the elderly as institutionalized, incapacitated, in serious financial straits, and living in fear of crime.
4. Despite the higher incidence of chronic health problems among the elderly, most older individuals do not consider themselves to be seriously handicapped in pursuing their ordinary activities. Most of the conditions that create chronic disease increase with advanced age. Some of the health problems experienced by older Americans are the product of side effects associated with medication.
5. Some of the most obvious changes associated with aging are related to an individual's physical characteristics. The hair grows thinner, the skin changes texture, some of the bulk built up during earlier adulthood begins to decrease, and some individuals experience a slight loss in stature. The sensory abilities also decline with age. Aging is likewise accompanied by various physiological changes. One of the most obvious is a decline in the individual's capacity for physical work and exercise. Sleep patterns also change.
6. Many theories seek to explain the biological process of aging by focusing on cell-destroying

mechanisms. Many of the mechanisms overlap. Although the effects of aging are often confounded with the effects of disease, aging is not the same thing as disease.

7. A decline in adult intelligence becomes clearly evident after age sixty. Small declines may even begin to occur by fifty-three years of age. However, different abilities follow quite different courses as a person grows older. Those aspects of intelligence that are measured by tests of performance and fluid ability appear to be more affected by aging than others.
8. Psychologists have traditionally taken too negative a view of the impact that aging has on intellectual functioning. One reason is that researchers have relied too heavily upon cross-sectional studies.
9. Memory is one aspect of cognitive functioning that in many cases is affected by aging. But it is incorrect to assume that a progressive loss of memory *necessarily* acccompanies advancing age. Memory loss among the elderly has many causes, some of them related to the acquisition of new knowledge, others to the retention of knowledge, and still others to the retrieval of knowledge.
10. Senility is typically characterized by progressive mental deterioration, memory loss, and disorientation regarding time and place. In persons over sixty-five, about 20 to 25 percent of all senility results from multiinfarcts. Another 50 percent is due to Alzheimer's disease—a progressive, degenerative disorder that involves deterioration of brain cells. The disorder has a devastating impact not only on its victims but on their relatives as well.

KEY TERMS

ageism The systematic stereotyping of and discrimination against people because they are old.

Alzheimer's disease A progressive, degenerative disorder that involves deterioration of brain cells.

collagen A substance that constitutes a very high percentage of the total protein of the body and that appears to be implicated in the aging process. It is a basic component of connective tissue.

crystallized intelligence The ability to reuse earlier adaptations on later occasions.

death-drop A marked drop in intelligence that may occur just a short time before a person dies.

decay theory The view that forgetting is due to deterioration in the memory traces in the brain.

encoding The process by which information is put into the memory system.

fluid intelligence The ability to make original adaptations in novel situations.

geriatrics The branch of medicine that is concerned with the diseases, debilities, and care of elderly persons.

gerontology The field of study that deals with aging and the special problems of the elderly.

hypothermia A condition in which body temperature falls more than 4 degrees Fahrenheit and persists for a number of hours. It can be life-threatening.

interference theory The view that retrieval of a cue becomes less effective as more and newer items come to be classed or categorized in terms of it.

multiinfarct A "little stroke," or the rupture of blood vessels in the brain.

osteoporosis A condition associated with excessive loss of bone mass, making the bones susceptible to fracture.

retrieval The process by which information is regathered from memory when it is needed.

senescence Changes that occur in the structure and functioning of the organism through time.

storage The process by which information is retained in memory until it is needed.

trace A set of information; it is the residue of an event that remains in memory after the event has vanished.

ise of Social Security and Medicare; that is, they "retire." However, as their numbers and political resources grow, the elderly may mount social movements in the years ahead to extract from society a more favorable distribution for themselves of benefits and privileges (Dowd, 1980).

Social exchange theorists claim that their conceptions are supported by the inverse relationship they find between modernization and the status of the aged (Cowgill and Holmes, 1972; Cowgill, 1974; Bengston et al., 1985). They assume that the position of the aged in preindustrial, traditional societies is high because the aged tend to accumulate knowledge and control through their years of experience. Social exchange theorists believe that industrialization, on the other hand, undermines the importance of traditional knowledge and control.

However, exceptions can be found to the social exchange theorists' assumption that the aged are assigned low status in modern industrial societies. Japan is one exception, for the Japanese values of filial piety and ancestor worship have mediated the impact of economic factors on the treatment of the elderly (Palmore, 1975). While social exchange theory is helpful in drawing attention to elements of exchange that influence the position of the elderly in a society, the theory falls short of providing a complete explanation.

PSYCHOSOCIAL ASPECTS OF AGING

Unless we are old already, the next "old people" will be us.

—ALEX COMFORT
A Good Old Age, 1976

The social world of later adulthood differs in some respects from that of early and middle adulthood. Changes in physical vigor and health and in cognitive functioning have social consequences. And shifts in work and marital roles profoundly affect the lives of elderly people through the behavioral expectations and activities that they allow. Hence the "social life space" of aging adults provides the context in which elderly men and women, like their younger counterparts, define reality, formulate their self-images, and generate their interaction with other individuals.

Retirement

The proportion of males aged sixty-five and over who were gainfully employed dropped from 68 percent in 1890, to 48 percent in 1947, to only 17 percent today. Perhaps of equal social significance, employed men aged fifty-five to sixty-four declined from 89 percent in 1947 to 69 percent currently, a drop of 20 percentage points. Two-thirds of all Americans retiring on Social Security currently leave their jobs before they are sixty-five, and in companies with high early-retirement pensions, the retirement age drops below sixty. In government, nearly two out of three civil servants retire before age sixty-two. If they retire at age sixty or sixty-two, many of today's workers can expect to have twenty to twenty-five years of life remaining. Hence retirement appears to be a factor of mounting significance in the lives of American men. And it is taking on added significance in the lives of women, as more and more women enter the labor force (about 8 percent of women over sixty-five hold jobs or are seeking work, down from 9.5 percent in 1971).

Involuntary Retirement. In 1978, Congress passed legislation banning compulsory retirement for most workers before age seventy. Many Americans view the practice of compelling workers to retire as a curtailment of basic rights. Prior to this legislation, about half of the nation's employers had policies requiring employees to step down at sixty-five. However, high unemployment in many industries, coupled with the prospect of an extended layoff or a difficult search for a new job, has led many older workers to opt for early retirement. But this option is not always available to workers in their fifties, who therefore frequently bear the brunt of plant closings. They find themselves unemployed. A recent House Aging Committee report notes that when older workers start looking for work (Lublin, 1983: 1, 12):

> . . . most if not all of the comparable jobs in the community have already been taken by the younger workers who were laid off earlier in the process. The result is often permanent unemployment for these older workers.

Raymond Arnista, a fifty-seven-year-old laid-off machinist, bitterly observes: "Just because we're at a certain age, we shouldn't be totally discarded as not useful anymore."

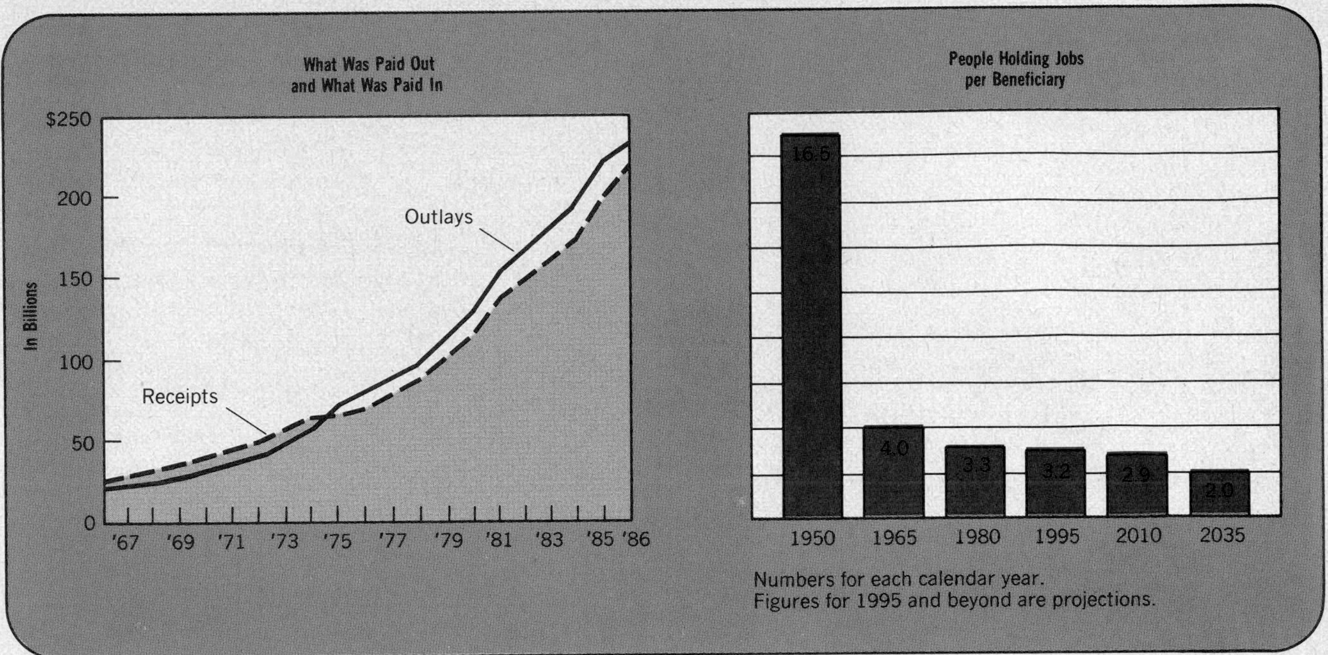

Figure 20.1 Mounting Costs of Social Security

Although Social Security taxes have been rising steadily, the gap between expenditures and receipts is widening. And matters are complicated by the fact that there will be fewer people holding jobs per beneficiary.

SOURCE: Social Security Administration, 1983.

Inflationary Factors. Although there has so far been no evidence of a reversal in the trend toward earlier retirement, long-term inflationary pressures may slow the tendency. Many individuals fear that fixed-income pensions will erode and hence feel safer remaining on a regular payroll. However, some income protection now exists for older people. Savings accounts are effectively indexed to the inflation rate (through bank certificates and money-market mutual funds), and Social Security payments rise with the cost of living.

Rising Costs of Retirement Programs. Early retirement has been welcomed by many people. But as growing numbers of the middle-aged leave the labor force, the economic costs mount (see Figure 20.1). Social Security remains in long-term trouble. Corporations are attempting to ease away from fixed lifetime-payment retirement plans. And government spending has been soaring on various income-support programs, including Medicaid, pensions, and veterans' benefits.

The Negative View of Retirement. Traditionally, retirement has been portrayed as having profoundly negative consequences for the individual. In Western societies people are depicted as integrated into the larger society by their work roles. Work is seen as an important aspect of self-concept and as providing people with many personal satisfactions, meaningful peer relationships, and opportunities for creativity—in sum, the foundation for enduring life satisfactions. The loss of these satisfactions through retirement is therefore seen as being inherently demoralizing and the precursor of major problems in older age (Cumming and Henry, 1961; Miller, 1965; Back, 1969). Further, time, which is scarce for working people, becomes suddenly excessive and acquires a negative value. Hence much of postretirement life is believed to be aimless, and giving structure to the long, shapeless day is seen as the retired person's most urgent challenge (Butler, 1975).

The Positive View of Retirement. In recent years the negative view of retirement has been challenged (Glamser, 1976; George and Maddox, 1977). There is reason to believe, for instance, that attitudes toward work and retirement have been changing in the United States (Maddox, 1966; Simpson, Back, and McKinney, 1966; Back, 1969). Indeed, even thirty years ago Robert Dubin (1956) found that for three out of four male industrial workers, work was *not* a central life interest. Further, only one worker in ten saw his important primary social relationships as located in the workplace. Moreover, recent research suggests that it is money that is most missed in retirement, and that when people are assured an adequate income, they will retire early (Atchley, 1971; Shanas, 1972; Beck, 1982). One longitudinal survey of 5,000 men found that most men who retire for reasons other than poor health are "very happy" in retirement and would, if they had to do it over again, retire at the same age. Only about 13 percent of whites and 17 percent of blacks said they would choose to retire later if they could choose again (Parnes, 1981). Other studies have similarly found that when individuals are healthy and their incomes are adequate, they typically express satisfaction with retirement (Streib and Schneider, 1971; Atchley, 1976).

Social scientists are increasingly coming to recognize that preretirement life-style and planning play an important part in retirement satisaction (Kimmel, Price, and Walker, 1978; McPherson and Guppy, 1979). Positive anticipation of retirement, and concrete and realistic planning for this stage in life, are related to adjustment in retirement. On the whole, voluntary retirees are more likely to have positive attitudes and higher satisfaction in retirement than nonvoluntary retirees. However, other factors, not always controllable, also influence retirement satisfaction. For instance, those with better health and higher socioeconomic status seem to make a better adjustment to retirement. The boxed insert on page 562 discusses phases in retirement.

Marital Relations

Americans generally believe that marriages that do not terminate in divorce begin with passionate love and evolve into cooler but closer companionship. However, researchers portray a somewhat different picture. Both marital satisfaction and adjustment begin declining quite early in marriage. The speed and intensity of this decline varies from one study to another. In the middle and later stages of the family life cycle, the evidence is less clear (Spanier, Lewis, and Cole, 1975). Some invesitgators find a continual decline (Blood and Wolfe, 1960; Paris and Luckey, 1966). Usually, however, they report a U-shaped curve, with a decline in satisfaction during the early

Satisfaction with Marriage

Most elderly couples report greater happiness and satisfaction with marriage than at any time since the newlywed phase. Many say their marriage improved during late adulthood. The couple shown here are celebrating their fiftieth wedding anniversary.

Robert V. Eckert, Jr./ EKM-Nepenthe

years, a leveling off during the middle years, and an increase in satisfaction during the later years (Burr, 1970; Rollins and Feldman, 1970; Glenn, 1975).

While the quality of marriage varies from couple to couple, most elderly husbands and wives report greater happiness and satisfaction with marriage during their later years that at any other time except for the newlywed phase. Many say that companionship, respect, and the sharing of common interests improve during later adulthood (Stinnett, Carter, and Montgomery, 1972; Powers and Bultena, 1976). One study found that about 90 percent of older couples felt that their relationships were harmonious "most of the time." Less than 10 percent indicated that they had negative feelings about their marriages more than once or twice a month (Rollins and Feldman, 1970).

A number of factors appear to contribute to the improvement of marriage in the later years. For one thing, children are launched. Parenthood requires a heavy commitment and is often the source of role overload and strain (Rollins and Cannon, 1974). Children also interfere with the amount of communication that takes place between spouses and with the time that they have available for companionable activities (Miller, 1976; Thornton, 1977). And children often create new sources of conflict while intensifying existing sources (Urdy, 1971). Furthermore, in later life problems with such issues as in-laws, money, and sex have often been resolved or the stresses associated with them dissipated. And as pointed out in Chapter 17, older adults tend to be more androgynous in their roles than younger adults are.

However, retirement may create new strains for a couple. One retiree points out (Brody, 1981: 13):

> A husband and wife may each have a dream of what retirement would be, but those dreams don't necessarily mesh. They've got to sit down and talk—outline their activities, restructure their time and define their territories. I discovered that my wife was very afraid that after I retired she'd have to wait on me hand and foot and would lose all her freedom.

Some women report that they feel "smothered" having their husbands about the house so much of the time. Men may attempt to increase their involvement in household tasks and be seen by their wives as intruders. Even so, some wives welcome the participation of their husbands, as it leads to a decrease in their own responsibilities. Further, the loss of privacy and independence is often offset by opportunities for nurture and companionship. And wives mention the "time available to do what you want" and the greater flexibility afforded in life schedules as advantages of retirement. Yet perhaps the most important factors influencing a wife's satisfaction with her husband's retirement are her own and her husband's

Importance of Friendship
Older people typically report that their friends afford them greater companionship and satisfaction than they derive from their relationships with their adult children.
Cary Wolinsky/Stock, Boston

good health and adequate finances (Keating and Cole, 1980; Hill and Dorfman, 1982).

Kin and Friendship Ties

The notion that most aged people are lonely and isolated from their families and other meaningful social ties is false. A Harris poll (1981) shows that although 65 percent of the public assume that most of the elderly are frequently lonely, only 13 percent of people sixty-five and over view loneliness as a serious problem for them. Further, about four of every five of the elderly have living children. Of this group, reputable surveys show that 85 percent live within an hour's travel of at least one child, 55 percent see their children every day or so, and another 26 percent see them about every week. Moreover, the elderly are often involved in exchanges of mutual aid with their grown children as both providers and receivers. Many times the elderly parent helps the adult child by performing child care and other home-related roles while the adult child helps the parent with heavy housework, shopping, bureaucratic mediation, and transportation. (See the boxed insert on pages 564–565) on home care for the elderly.) In sum, the elderly are not so isolated from kin and friendship networks as is commonly believed (Arling, 1976; Powers and Bultena, 1976; Petrowsky, 1976; Shanas, 1980; Quinn, 1983).

A majority of elderly men—75 percent—live with their spouses. But because there are far more widows than there are widowers, only 37 percent of elderly women still reside with their husbands. Thirty percent of noninstitutionalized individuals sixty-five and over live alone, 16 percent of the men and 40 percent of the women (Russell, 1980). Only 15 percent of the elderly lived with their children in 1980, down from 30 percent in 1950.

The elderly value their privacy and independence (Cicirelli, 1981). Those with adult children prefer to live near but not with them, what psychologists term "intimate distance." And contrary to the popular view that grandmothers are delighted to baby-sit for their grandchildren, many older women resent the frequent imposition that their adult children make on their time and energy.

Overall, friends are more important and satisfying to older people in terms of companionship than relationships with their offspring are (Beckman, 1981). In fact, some research suggests that greater loneliness exists among the single elderly who live with relatives than among those who live alone. Hence an elderly widow who lives with her daughter's family may be quite lonely if she has little contact with associates her own age. Children no longer seem to provide a form of old-age happiness insurance. Public opinion surveys reveal that having children contributes little or nothing to "global happiness" among the elderly (Glenn and McLanahan, 1981; Lee and Ellithorpe, 1982). And there is little evidence that individuals derive important psychological rewards or a sense of emotional well-being from the later stages of parenthood (Keith, 1983).

Family Networks
The elderly are not as isolated from kin and family networks as is sometimes believed. Grandmothers, for instance, often act as baby-sitters, parental surrogates, and helpers in time of family emergency.
John E. Fogle/The Picture Cube

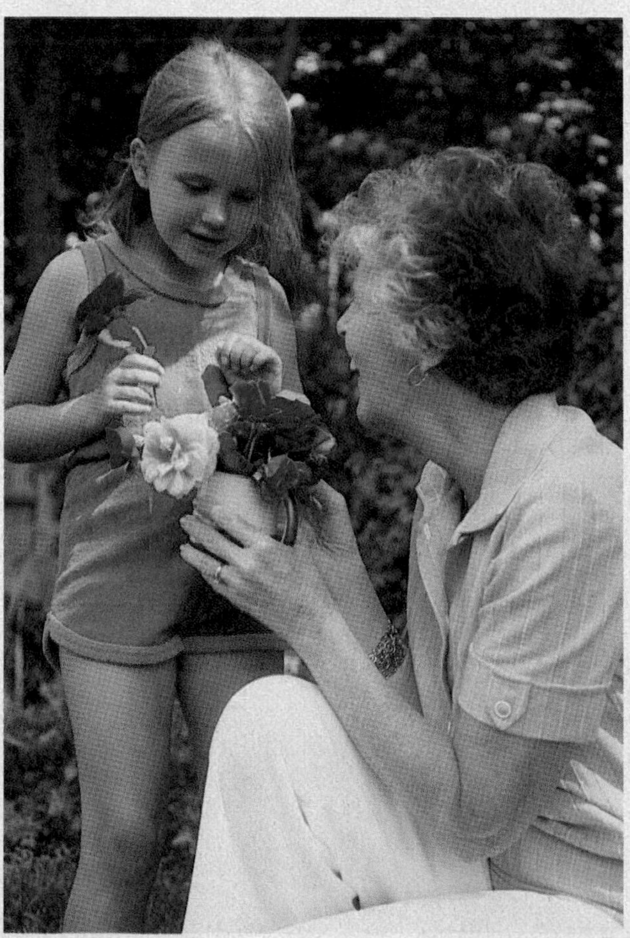

As in other aspects of human affairs, individuals differ enormously in what they view as adequate or inadequate contact with other people. Indeed, research reveals that lifelong isolates tend to have average or better morale in old age, and to be no more prone to mental illness, than anyone else (Lowenthal, 1964). Further, it is not a certain absolute degree of isolation that produces feelings of loneliness in old age but rather the fact of *becoming* socially more isolated than one had previously been (Gubrium, 1974).

Loneliness is not simply a matter of being alone (Busse and Pfeiffer, 1969: 188):

> Solitude need not be experienced as loneliness, while loneliness can be felt in the presence of other people. For instance, persons residing in nursing homes often complain of loneliness, even though they are surrounded by people and, at a superficial level, are interacting with them. Loneliness is the awareness of an absence of meaningful integration with other individuals or groups of individuals, a consciousness of being excluded from the system of opportunities and rewards in which other people participate.

In sum, the quality of a relationship is more important than is the mere frequency of contact.

Overall, it appears that the maintenance of even one meaningful, stable relationship is more closely associated with good mental health and high morale among the elderly than is a high level of social interaction. A confidant serves as a buffer against gradual losses in interaction and against the losses associated with widowhood and retirement (Lowenthal and Haven, 1968).

Grandparents

Child psychologists emphasize that both children and their grandparents are better off when they spend a good deal of time in each other's company (Kornhaber and Woodward, 1981). But for many American youngsters, grandparents are becoming a vanishing breed. Many grandparents do not have the time to spend with their grandchildren because both grandparents—the grandmother as well as the grandfather—are increasingly employed. One fifty-four-year-old married and employed grandmother observes (Robertson, 1977: 172):

> I really wasn't too happy at first because I felt I was much too young for that [being a grandmother]. But, now as I look back, my grandchildren have enriched our lives. . . . I'm glad to be young and healthy enough to do things with them when I can; I don't have much time though. . . . I work and we have so many things to do ourselves and so do the kids these days . . . they don't have time for us either.

Geographical mobility is also separating grandparents and grandchildren. Not only are the younger generation moving, but the older generation are moving away from their home communities to Sun Belt cities and villages when they retire. And divorces and remarriages also affect grandparents, complicating their relationships with their grandchildren. Finally, the three-generation family living in one household is less common in America than it once was.

Despite changing family patterns, 94 percent of older people with children are grandparents; 46 percent are great-grandparents. Thus almost half of all persons sixty-five and over in the United States who have living children are members of four-generation families. The likelihood of being a great-grandparent increases with age, so that among individuals eighty and over, almost three-fourths are great-grandparents. In fact, one-fourth of those aged sixty-six are already great-grandparents (Shanas, 1978).

Traditionally, the media have portrayed grandmothers as jolly, white-haired, bespectacled older women who lavish goodies and attention on their grandchildren. But grandmothers are also depicted as meddlesome intruders in family life who must be politely tolerated. And grandfathers are often seen as "male grandmothers." In fact, when college students are asked to list their images of the roles of grandfather and grandmother, they make few distinctions between them (Hess and Markson, 1980).

Despite popular portrayals of what grandparents are like, research suggests that considerable variation exists in the way grandparents approach their role. A study undertaken by Bernice Neugarten and Karol Weinstein (1964) found a number of distinct styles of grandparenting—formal, fun-seeking, the surrogate parent, and the distant figure. About a third of the grandparents followed the formal style, a somewhat stereotyped, "proper" role playing according to conventional norms. The grandparents showed interest in their grandchildren but were careful not to offer child-rearing advice or to intrude on the parenting role. A quarter of the grandparents were characterized by the fun-seeker style. They focused on playfulness and mutual satisfaction with grandchildren in leisure-time activities. In the surrogate-parent style, making and an overall deterioration of thought processes.

3. Most older people do not experience sudden and dramatic transformations in personality or self-concept. Moreover, for every older person who feels that life is now worse than he or she thought it would be, there are three who say life is currently better than they had expected.
4. Sociologists have advanced many theories that describe changes in the elderly in terms of changes in their social environment. These theories include disengagement theory, activity theory, role exit theory, and social exchange theory.
5. Traditionally, the scientific literature has portrayed retirement as having profoundly negative consequences for individuals. But more recently this view has been challenged. Attitudes toward work and retirement have been changing in the United States. Research suggests it is money that is most missed in retirement; when people are assured an adequate income, they will retire early.
6. While the quality of marriage varies from couple to couple, most elderly husbands and wives report greater happiness and satisfaction with their marriage during their later years than at any other time except for the newlywed phase. Many say that companionship, respect, and the sharing of common interests improves during later adulthood.
7. The notion that most aged people are lonely and isolated from their families and other meaningful social ties is false. Yet overall, friends are more important and satisfying to older people in terms of companionship than relationships with their offspring are.
8. Child psychologists emphasize that both children and their grandparents are better off when they spend a good deal of time in each other's company. But for many American youngsters, grandparents are becoming a vanishing breed. One survey shows that only 5 percent of the grandchildren said they had close, regular contact with at least one grandparent.
9. In the United States, 5 percent of all people who are sixty-five and older live in nursing homes. Inadequate staffing and care are major problems for the elderly in institutional settings.
10. Once in a nursing home, the elderly typically become physically, emotionally, and economically dependent on the facility for the rest of their lives. Staff practices all too often foster and promote patient dependency. It is important that the elderly not be deprived of the opportunity to make decisions and choices for themselves.

KEY TERMS

activity theory of aging The view that except for inevitable changes in biology and in health, older people are the same as middle-aged people, with essentially the same psychological and social needs. According to activity theory, successful aging requires sustained social interaction with others.

disengagement theory of aging The notion that aging is a progressive process of physical, psychological, and social withdrawal from the wider world. The theory assumes that aging involves a mutual withdrawal that results in decreased interaction between the elderly and other members of the society.

role exit theory of aging The view that retirement and widowhood terminate the participation of the elderly in the principal institutional structures of society—the job and the family. The loss of these roles is regarded as devastating to the self-identity of older people.

social exchange theory of aging The idea that people in their interactions are engaged in a sort of mental bookkeeping that involves a ledger of rewards, costs, and profits. As applied to the elderly, the theory suggests that they find themselves in a situation of increasing vulnerability because of deterioration in their bargaining position.

of counseling, antidepressive medications, and high-dose morphine preparations. Most hospice programs are centered about care of the dying person at home.

8. Bereavement and grief have a considerably greater impact than is evident in the immediate short-term period following the death of a loved one. The survivor experiences a heightened vulnerability to physical and mental illness, even to death. In adult bereavement, the individual typically passes through a number of phases. The first phase is characterized by shock, numbness, denial, and disbelief. The second phase entails pining, yearning, and depression. The third phase involves emancipation from the loved one and an adjustment to the new circumstances. The fourth phase is characterized by identity reconstruction.
9. Women sixty-five and over are much more likely to be widowed than married. The difficulty women have in adjusting to widowhood tends to vary with the degree to which their social relationships revolved about or were integrated with those of their husbands.

KEY TERMS

autopsy An operation performed on a body after death to determine the cause of death.

bereavement A state in which a person has been deprived of a relative or friend by death.

euthanasia Mercy killing; putting to death painlessly an individual suffering from an incurable and painful disease.

grief Keen mental anguish and sorrow over the death of a loved one.

hospice A program or mode of care that seeks to make dying less painful and emotionally traumatic for both patient and loved one.

life review A process in which the elderly take stock of their lives, reflecting and reminiscing about them.

mourning The socially established manner of displaying signs of sorrow over a person's death (for instance, wailing, wearing black, hanging flags at half-mast, and the like).

thanatology The study of death.

Bibliography

Abel, E. L. 1980. Fetal alcohol syndrome: Behavioral teratology. *Psychological Bulletin,* 87:29–50.

Abraham, K. G. 1983. Political thinking in the elementary years: An empirical study. *Elementary School Journal,* 84:221–231.

Abrahams, B., Feldman, S. S., and Nash, S. C. 1978. Sex role self-concept and sex role attitudes: Enduring personality characteristics or adaptations to changing life situations? *Developmental Psychology,* 14:393–400.

Abramov, I., Gordon, J., Hendrickson, A., Hainline, L., Dobson, V., and LaBossiere, E. 1982. The retina of the newborn human infant. *Science,* 217:265–267.

Abrams, P., and McCulloch, A. 1976. *Communes, Sociology, and Society.* New York: Cambridge University Press.

Abramson, L. Y., Seligman, M. E. P., and Teasdale, J. D. 1978. Learned helplessness in humans: Critique and reformulation. *Journal of Abnormal Psychology,* 87:49–74.

Acredolo, L. P., and Hake, J. K. 1982. Infant perception. In Wolman, B. B. (ed.), *Handbook of Developmental Psychology.* Englewood Cliffs, N.J.: Prentice-Hall.

Adair, J. 1775. *The History of the American Indians.* London: E. D. Dilly.

Adams, B. 1968. *Kinship in an Urban Setting.* Chicago: Markham Publishing.

Adams, G. R., and Crane, P. 1980. An assessment of parents' and teachers' expectations of preschool children's social preference for attractive and unattractive children and adults. *Child Development,* 51:224–231.

Adams, V. 1979. Studies relate physical causes to delinquency. *New York Times* (June 26):C1, C3.

Adelson, J. 1972. The political imagination of the young adolescent. In Kagan, J., and Coles, R. (eds.), *Twelve to Sixteen.* New York: Norton.

———. 1975. The development of ideology in adolescence. In Dragastin, S. E., and Elder, G. H., Jr. (eds.), *Adolescence in the Life Cycle: Psychological Change and Social Context.* New York: Wiley.

———. 1979. Adolescence and the generation gap. *Psychology Today,* 12 (February):33–37.

———. 1980. Children and other political naifs. *Psychology Today,* 14 (November):56–70.

Agrest, S. 1982. "This is mine and I'm the boss." *Newsweek* (November 1):59.

Ahrens, R. 1954. Beitrag zur entwicklung des physiognomieund mimikerkennens. *Zeitschrift für Experimentelle und Angewandte Psychologie,* 2:412–454, 599–633.

Ainsworth, M. D. S. 1962. The effects of maternal deprivation: A review of findings and controversy in the context of research strategy. In *Deprivation of Maternal Care: A Reassessment of Its Effects.* Geneva: World Health Organization.

———. 1967. *Infancy in Uganda: Infant Care and the Growth of Attachment.* Baltimore: Johns Hopkins University Press.

———, and Bell, S. M. 1969. Some contemporary patterns of mother-infant interaction in the feeding situation. In Ambrose, A. (ed.), *Stimulation in Early Infancy.* London: Academic Press.

———, and ———. 1970. Attachment, exploration, and separation: Illustrated by the behavior of one-year-olds in a strange situation. *Child Development,* 41:49–67.

———, and ———. 1977. Infant crying and maternal responsiveness: A rejoinder to Gewirtz and Boyd. *Child Development,* 48:1208–1216.

———, ———, and Stayton, D. J. 1974. Infant-mother attachment and social development. In Richards, M. P. M. (ed.), *The Integration of a Child into a Social World.* Cambridge: Cambridge University Press.

———, Blehar, M. C., Waters, E., and Wall, S. 1979. *Patterns of Attachment: A Psychological Study of the Strange Situation.* New York: Halsted.

Albin, R. 1979. Children and divorce. *APA Monitor,* 10:4.

Aleksandrowicz, M. K., and Aleksandrowicz, D. R. 1974. Obstetrical pain-relieving drugs as predictors of infant behavior variability. *Child Development,* 45:935–945.

Allen, V. L., and Newtson, D. 1972. Development of conformity and independence. *Journal of Personality and Social Psychology,* 22:18–30.

Alley, T. R. 1983. Growth-produced changes in body shape and size as determinants of perceived age and adult caretaking. *Child Development,* 54:241–248.

Allport, G. W. 1961. *Pattern and growth in personality.* New York: Holt, Rinehart and Winston.

———. 1962. Prejudice: Is it societal or personal? *Journal of Social Issues,* 18:120–134.

Als, H., Tronick, E., Lester, B. M., and Brazelton, T. B. 1979. Specific neonatal measures: The Brazelton Neonatal Behavioral Assessment Scale. In Osofsky, J. D. (ed.), *Handbook of Infant Development.* New York: Wiley.

Altman, L. K. 1979. Study of dying disputes idea that doctors prolong life at any cost. *New York Times* (June 3):50.

———. 1983. Decline in autopsies raises concern. *New York Times* (September 13):21.

Altmann, J. 1973. Observational study of behavior: Sampling methods. *Behaviour,* 49:228–267.

Altus, W. D. 1965. Birth order and academic primogeniture. *Journal of Personality and Social Psychology,* 2:872–876.

Ambrose, J. A. 1961. The development of smiling response in early infancy. In Foss, B. M. (ed.), *Determinants of Infant Behavior.* Vol. 1. New York: Wiley.

Ambrus, C. M., Ambrus, J. L., Horvath, C., Pederson, H., Sharma, S., Kant, C., Mirand, E., Guthrie, R., and Paul, T. 1978. Phenylalanine depletion for the management of phenylketonuria: Use of enzyme reactors with immobilized enzymes. *Science,* 201 (September 1):837–839.

American Psychiatric Association. 1980. *Diagnostic and Statistical Manual of Mental Disorders,* 3rd ed. Washington, D.C.: American Psychiatric Association.

American Psychological Association. 1982. *Ethical Principles in the Conduct of Research with Human Participants.* Washington, D.C.: American Psychological Association.

Ammons, R. B. 1956. Effects of knowledge of performance: A survey and tentative theoretical formulation. *Journal of General Psychology,* 54:279–299.

Amoss, P. T., and Harrell, S. (eds.). 1981. *Other Ways of Growing Old: Anthropological Perspectives.* Stanford: Stanford University Press.

Ananth, J. 1978. Side effects in the neonate from psychotropic agents excreted through breast-feeding. *American Journal of Psychiatry,* 135:801–805.

Anastasi, A. 1958. Heredity, environment, and the question "how?" *Psychological Review,* 65:197–208.

Anders, T. R., and Fozard, J. L. 1972. Effects of age upon retrieval from short-term memory. *Developmental Psychology,* 6:214–217.

Anderson, S. H. 1978. A plea for gentleness to the newborn. *New York Times* (January 15):48.

Anisfeld, M. 1979. Interpreting "imitative" responses in early infancy. *Science,* 205:214–215.

Ansbacher, H. L., and Ansbacher, R. R. 1956. *The Individual Psychology of Alfred Adler.* New York: Basic Books.

Apgar, V. 1953. Proposal for a new method of evaluation of the newborn infant. *Anesthesia and Analgesia,* 32:260–267.

Apple, D. 1956. The social structure of grand-parenthood. *American Anthropologist,* 58:656–663.

Arenberg, D., and Robertson-Tchabo, E. A. 1977. Learning and aging. In Birren, J. E., and Schaie, K. W. (eds.), *Handbook of the Psychology of Aging.* New York: Van Nostrand Reinhold.

Arey, L. B. 1974. *Developmental Anatomy,* 7th ed., rev. Philadelphia: Saunders.

Ariès, P. 1962. *Centuries of Childhood.* Trans. by R. Baldick. New York: Random House.

———. 1978. *Western Attitudes Toward Death: From the Middle Ages to the Present.* Baltimore: Johns Hopkins University Press.

———. 1981. *The Hour of Our Death.* New York: Knopf.

Arling, G. 1976. The elderly widow and her family, neighbors and friends. *Journal of Marriage and the Family,* 38:757–768.

Aronfreed, J. 1968. *Conduct and Conscience.* New York: Academic Press.

———, and Reber, A. 1965. Internalized behavior suppression and the timing of social punishment. *Journal of Personality and Social Psychology,* 1:3–16.

Aronson, E., and Carlsmith, J. M. 1962. Performance expectancy as a determinant of actual performance. *Journal of Abnormal and Social Psychology,* 65:178–182.

Asch, S. E. 1952. *Social Psychology.* Englewood Cliffs, N.J.: Prentice-Hall.

Asher, S. R. 1983. Social competence and peer status: Recent advances and future directions. *Child Development,* 54:1427–1434.

Ashton, P. T. 1975. Cross-cultural Piagetian research: An experimental perspective. *Harvard Educational Review,* 45:475–506.

Ashton, R. 1976. Infant state and stimulation. *Developmental Psychology,* 12:569–570.

Atchley, R. C. 1971. Retirement and work orientation. *The Gerontologist,* 2:29–32.

———. 1975. The life course, age-grading, and age-linked demands for decision making. In Datan, N., and Ginsberg, L. (eds.), *Life Span Developmental Psychology: Normative Life Crises.* New York: Academic Press.

———. 1976. *The Sociology of Retirement.* Cambridge, Mass.: Schenkman.

Austin, C. 1982. Churches are main suppliers of day care, a study reports. *New York Times* (November 6):8.

Ausubel, D. P., and Sullivan, E. V. 1970. *Theory and Problems of Child Development,* 2nd ed. New York: Grune & Stratton.

Babchuk, N., Peters, G. R., Hoyt, D. R., and Kaiser, M. A. 1979. The voluntary associations of the aged. *Journal of Gerontology,* 34:579–587.

Bachman, J. G., O'Malley, P., and Johnston, J. 1978. *Youth in Transition.* Vol. 6: *Adolescence to Adulthood—Change and Stability in the Lives of Young Men.* Ann Arbor: Institute for Social Research, University of Michigan.

Back, K. W. 1969. The ambiguity of retirement. In Busse, E. W., and Pfeiffer, E. (eds.), *Behavior and Adaptation in Late Life.* Boston: Little, Brown.

———. 1976. Personal characteristics and social behavior theory and method. In Binstock, R. H., and Thomas, E. (eds.), *Handbook of Aging and the Social Sciences.* New York: Van Nostrand.

Bailyn, L. 1959. Mass media and children. *Psychological Monographs,* 73:1–48.

Bakan, D. 1972. Adolescence in America: From idea to social fact. In Kagan, J., and Coles, R. (eds.), *Twelve to Sixteen: Early Adolescence.* New York: Norton.

Bakeman, R., and Brown, J. V. 1977. Behavioral dialogues: An approach to the assessment of mother-infant interaction. *Child Development,* 48: 195–203.

———, and Brownlee, J. R. 1980. The strategic use of parallel play: A sequential analysis. *Child Development,* 51:873–878.

Balkwell, C. 1981. Transition to widowhood: A review of the literature. *Family Relations,* 30:117–127.

Baltes, P. B. 1968. Longitudinal and cross-sectional sequences in the study of age and generation effects. *Human Development,* 11:145–171.

———, and Schaie, K. W. 1974. The myth of the twilight years. *Psychology Today,* 7 (March):35–38f.

———, and ———. 1976. On the plasticity of intelligence in adulthood and old age. *American Psychologist,* 31:720–725.

———, and Willis, S. L. 1977. Toward psychological theories of aging and development. In Birren, J. E., and Schaie, K. W. (eds.), *Handbook on the Psychology of Aging.* New York: Van Nostrand.

Bandura, A. 1964. The stormy decade: Fact or fiction? *Psychology in the Schools,* 1:224–231.

———. 1971*a*. *Psychological Modeling: Conflicting Theories.* Chicago: Aldine-Atherton.

———. 1971*b*. *Social Learning Theory.* Morristown, N.J.: General Learning Corporation.

———. 1973. *Aggression: A Social Learning Analysis.* Englewood Cliffs, N.J.: Prentice-Hall.

———. 1977. *Social Learning Theory.* Englewood Cliffs, N.J.: Prentice-Hall.

———. 1982. The psychology of chance encounters and life paths. *American Psychologist,* 37:747–755.

———, Grusec, J. E., and Menlove, F. L. 1967. Vicarious extinction of avoidance behavior. *Journal of Personality and Social Psychology,* 5:16–23.

———, Ross, D., and Ross, S. 1961. Transmission of aggression through imitation of aggressive models. *Journal of Abnormal and Social Psychology,* 63:575–582.

———, ———, and ———. 1963. Imitation of film-mediated aggressive models. *Journal of Abnormal and Social Psychology,* 66:3–11.

Banks, W. C., McQuater, G. V., and Ross, J. A. 1979. On the importance of white preference and the comparative difference of blacks and others: Reply to Williams and Morland. *Psychological Bulletin,* 86:33–36.

Barclay, C. R., and Newell, K. M. 1980. Children's processing of information in motor skill acquisition. *Journal of Experimental Child Psychology,* 30:98–108.

Barenboim, C. 1977. Developmental changes in the interpersonal cognitive system from middle childhood to adolescence. *Child Development,* 48:1467–1474.

———. 1981. The development of person perception in childhood and adolescence: From behavioral comparisons to psychological constructs to psychological comparisons. *Child Development,* 52:129–144.

Barkas, J. L. 1980. *Single in America.* New York: Atheneum.

Barker, R. G. 1963. The stream of behavior as an empirical problem. In Barker, R. G. (ed.), *The Stream of Behavior.* New York: Appleton-Century-Crofts.

Barnes, K. E. 1971. Preschool play norms: A replication. *Developmental Psychology,* 5:99–103

Barnet, A. B., Weiss, I. P., Sotillo, M. V., Ohlrich, E. S., Shkurovich, M., and Cravioto, J. 1978. Abnormal auditory evoked potentials in early infancy malnutrition. *Science,* 201 (August 4): 450–451.

Barnett, R. C., and Baruch, G. K. 1983. *Lifeprints: New Patterns of Love and Work for Today's Women.* New York: New American Library.

Barrera, M. E., and Maurer, D. 1981*a*. Discrimination of strangers by the three-month-old. *Child Development,* 52:558–563.

———, and ———. 1981*b*. Recognition of mother's photographed face by the three-month-old infant. *Child Development,* 52:714–716.

Barrett, D. E., Radke-Yarrow, M., and Klein, R. E. 1982. Chronic malnutrition and child behavior. *Developmental Psychology,* 18:541–556.

Barten, S., Birns, B., and Ronch, J. 1971. Individual differences in the visual pursuit behavior of neonates. *Child Development,* 42:313–319.

Barton, E. M., Baltes, M. M., and Orzech, M. J. 1980. Etiology of dependence in older nursing home residents during morning care: The role of staff behavior. *Journal of Personality and Social Psychology,* 38:423–431.

Baruch, G., and Barnett, R. C. 1983. Adult daughters' relationships with their mothers. *Journal of Marriage and the Family,* 45:601–606.

Baumrind, D. 1966. Effects of authoritative parental control on child behavior. *Child Development,* 37:887–907.

———. 1967. Child care practices anteceding three patterns of preschool behavior. *Genetic Psychology Monographs,* 75:43–88.

———. 1968. Authoritarian versus authoritative parental control. *Adolescence,* 3:255–272.

———. 1971*a*. Current patterns of parental authority. *Developmental Psychology Monographs,* 4:1–103.

———. 1971*b*. Harmonious parents and their preschool children. *Developmental Psychology,* 4:99–102.

———. 1972. Socialization and instrumental competence in young children. In Hartup, W. W. (ed.), *The Young Child.* Vol. 2. Washington, D.C.: National Association for the Education of Young Children.

Bayley, N. 1935. The development of motor abilities during the first three years. *Monographs of the Society for Research in Child Development,* 1.

———. 1956. Individual patterns of development. *Child Development,* 27: 45–74.

———. 1965*a*. Research in child development: A longitudinal perspective. *Merrill-Palmer Quarterly,* 11:184–190.

———. 1965*b*. Comparisons of mental and motor test scores for ages 1–15 months by sex, birth order, race, geographical locations, and education of parents. *Child Development,* 36:379–411.

Beaconsfield, P., Birdwood, G., and Beaconsfield, R. 1980. The placenta. *Scientific American,* 243 (August):95–102.

Beadle, G., and Beadle, M. 1966. *The Language of Life.* Garden City, N.Y.: Doubleday.

Beck, A. T. 1967. *Depression: Clinical, Experimental, and Theoretical Aspects.* New York: Harper & Row.

———. 1976. *Cognitive Therapy and the Emotional Disorders.* New York: International Universities Press.

Beck, S. H. 1982. Adjustment to and satisfaction with retirement. *Journal of Gerontology,* 37:616–624.

Becker, M. T. 1976. A learning analysis of the development of peer-oriented behavior in nine-month-old infants. Paper presented at the 56th Annual Meeting of the Western Psychological Association, Los Angeles, April 1976.

Becker, W. C. 1964. Consequences of different kinds of parental discipline. In Hoffman, M. L., and Hoffman, L. W. (eds.), *Review of Child Development Research.* New York: Russell Sage Foundation.

Beckman, L. J. 1981. Effects of social interaction and children's relative inputs on older women's psychological well-being. *Journal of Personality and Social Psychology,* 41:1075–1086.

Beckwith, L. 1972. Relationships between infants' social behavior and their mothers' behavior. *Child Development,* 43:397–411.

Behrens, M. L. 1954. Child rearing and the character structure of the mother. *Child Development,* 20:225–238.

Bell, A. P., and Weinberg, M. S. 1978. *Homosexualities: A Study of Diversity Among Men and Women.* New York: Simon & Schuster.

———, ———, and Hammersmith, S. K. 1981. *Sexual Preference: Its Develop-*

ment in Men and Women. Bloomington: Indiana University Press.

Bell, R. Q. 1953. Convergence: An accelerated longitudinal approach. *Child Development,* 24:145–152.

———. 1954. An experimental test of the accelerated longitudinal approach. *Child Development,* 25:281–286.

———. 1968. A reinterpretation of effects in studies of socialization. *Psychological Review,* 75:81–95.

———, and Harper, L. V. 1977. *Child Effects on Adults*. Hillsdale, N.J.: Lawrence Erlbaum Associates.

Bell, R. R., and Coughey, K. 1980. Premarital sexual experience among college females, 1958, 1968, 1978. *Family Relations,* 29:353–357.

———, Turner, S., and Rosen, L. 1975. A multivariate analysis of female extramarital coitus. *Journal of Marriage and the Family,* 37:375–384.

Bell, S. M. 1970. The development of the concept of object as related to infant-mother attachment. *Child Development,* 41:291–311.

———, and Ainsworth, M. D. S. 1972. Infant crying and maternal responsiveness. *Child Development,* 43:1171–1190.

Belle, D. E. 1978. Book reviews. *Harvard Educational Review,* 48:290–295.

Belsky, J. 1981. Early human experience. A family perspective. *Developmental Psychology,* 17:3–23.

———, and Most, R. K. 1981. From exploration to play: A cross-sectional study of infant free play behavior. *Developmental Psychology,* 17:630–639.

———, Spanier, G. B., and Rovine, M. 1983. Stability and change in marriage across the transition to parenthood. *Journal of Marriage and the Family,* 45:567–577.

———, and Steinberg, L. D. 1978. The effects of day care: A critical review. *Child Development,* 49:929–949.

Bem, D., and Allen, A. 1974. On predicting some of the people some of the time: The search for cross-situational consistencies in behavior. *Psychological Review,* 81:506–520.

Bem, S. L. 1975. Sex role adaptability: One consequence of psychological androgyny. *Journal of Personality and Social Psychology,* 31:634–643.

Bemis, K. M. 1978. Current approaches to the etiology and treatment of anorexia nervosa. *Psychological Bulletin,* 85:593–617.

Benedek, E. P., and Benedek, R. S. 1979. Joint custody: Solution or illusion? *American Journal of Psychiatry,* 136: 1540–1544.

Benedict, H. 1976. Language comprehension in 10 sixteen-month-old infants. Unpublished doctoral dissertation, Yale University.

Benedict, R. 1938. Continuities and discontinuities in cultural conditioning. *Psychiatry,* 1:161–167.

Bengston, V. L. 1970. The generation gap: A review and typology of social-psychological perspectives. *Youth and Society,* 2:7–32.

———, Cuellar, J. B., and Ragan, P. K. 1977. Stratum contrasts and similarities in attitudes toward death. *Journal of Gerontology,* 32:76–88.

———, Dowd, J. J., Smith, D. H., and Inkeles, A. 1975. Modernization, modernity, and perceptions of aging: A cross-cultural study. *Journal of Gerontology,* 30:688–695.

———, and Starr, J. M. 1975. Contrast and consensus: A generational analysis of youth in the 1970s. In Havighurst, R. J., and Dreyer, P. H. (eds.), *Youth: The Seventy-fourth Yearbook of the National Society for the Study of Education*. Chicago: University of Chicago Press.

Bennett, W., and Gurin, J. 1982. *The Dieter's Dilemma*. New York: Basic Books.

Benson, L. 1968. *Fatherhood: A Sociological Perspective*. New York: Random House.

Berenda, R. W. 1950. *The Influence of the Group on the Judgments of Children*. New York: King's Crown Press.

Berg, W. K., and Berg, K. M. 1979. Psychophysiological development in infancy: State, sensory function, and attention. In Osofsky, J. D. (ed.), *Handbook of Infant Development*. New York: Wiley.

Berkowitz, B. 1965. Changes in intellect with age: IV. Changes in achievement and survival in older people. *Journal of Genetic Psychology,* 107:3–14.

Berman, P. W. 1980. Are women more responsive than men to the young? A review of developmental and situational variables. *Psychological Bulletin,* 88:668–695.

Bermant, G., and Davidson, J. M. 1974. *Biological Bases of Sexual Behavior*. New York: Harper & Row.

Bernard, J. A., and Ramey, C. T. 1977. Visual regard of familiar and unfamiliar persons in the first six months of infancy. *Merrill-Palmer Quarterly,* 23:121–127.

Berndt, T. J. 1981*a*. Age changes and changes over time in prosocial intentions and behavior between friends. *Developmental Psychology,* 17:408–416.

———. 1981*b*. Effects of friendship on prosocial intentions and behavior. *Child Development,* 52:636–643.

———. 1982. The features and effects of friendship in early adolescence. *Child Development,* 53:1447–1460.

Berscheid, E., Dion, K., Walster, E., and Walster, G. W. 1971. Physical attractiveness and dating choice: A test of the matching hypothesis. *Journal of Experimental Social Psychology,* 7:173–189.

———, and Walster, E. 1974. A little bit about love. In Huston, E. L. (ed.), *Foundations of Interpersonal Attraction*. New York: Academic Press.

Biddle, B. J., Bank, B. J., and Anderson, D. S. 1981. The structure of idleness. *Sociology of Education,* 54:106–119.

Bieber, I. 1962. *Homosexuality: A Psychoanalytic Study of Male Homosexuals*. New York: Basic Books.

Biehler, R. F. 1976. *Child Development: An Introduction*. Boston: Houghton Mifflin.

Bijou, S. W., and Baer, D. M. 1965. A social learning model of attachment. Socialization—the development of behavior to social stimuli. In *Child Development II*. New York: Appleton-Century-Crofts.

Bilgé, B., and Kaufman, G. 1983. Children of divorce and one-parent families: Cross-cultural perspectives. *Family Relations,* 32:59–71.

Biller, H. B. 1971. *Father, Child, and Sex Roles*. Lexington, Mass.: Heath Lexington Books.

———. 1974. The father-infant relationship: Some naturalistic observations. Unpublished manuscript, University of Rhode Island.

———. 1976. The father and personality development: Paternal deprivation and sex-role development. In Lamb, M. E. (ed.), *The Role of the Father in Child Development*. New York: Wiley.

———. 1982. Fatherhood: Implications for child and adult development. In Wolman, B. B. (ed.), *Handbook of Developmental Psychology*. Englewood Cliffs, N.J.: Prentice-Hall.

Bindra, D. 1976. *A Theory of Intelligent Behavior*. New York: McGraw-Hill.

Birnholz, J. C., and Benacerraf, B. R. 1983. The development of human fetal hearing. *Science,* 222:516–518.

Birns, G., Blank, M., and Bridger, W. H. 1966. The effectiveness of various soothing techniques on human neonates. *Psychosomatic Medicine,* 28: 316–322.

Bischof, L. J. 1970. *Interpreting Personality Theories,* 2nd ed. New York: Harper & Row.

———. 1976. *Adult Psychology,* 2nd ed. New York: Harper & Row.

Bishop, J. E. 1980. The personal and business costs of "job burnout." *Wall Street Journal* (November 11):25, 32.

———. 1983. New gene probes may permit early predictions of disease. *Wall Street Journal* (December 23):11.

Blackwood, B. M. 1935. *Both Sides of Buka Passage.* New York: Oxford University Press.

Blanchard, R. W., and Biller, H. B. 1971. Father availability and academic performance among third-grade boys. *Developmental Psychology,* 4:301–305.

Blasi, A. 1980. Bridging moral cognition and moral action: A critical review of the literature. *Psychological Bulletin,* 88:1–45.

Blau, P. M. 1964. *Exchange and Power in Social Life.* New York: Wiley.

———, and Duncan, O. D. 1967. *The American Occupational Structure.* New York: Wiley.

———, and ———. 1972. *The American Occupational Structure,* 2nd ed. New York: Wiley.

Blau, Z. S. 1973. *Old Age in a Changing Society.* New York: New Viewpoints.

Block, J. 1980. From infancy to adulthood: A clarification. *Child Development,* 51:622–623.

———. 1981*a*. The many faces of continuity. *Contemporary Psychology,* 26:748–750.

———. 1981*b*. Some enduring and consequential structures in personality. In Rabin, A. I. (ed.), *Further Explorations in Personality.* New York: Wiley.

Block, J. H. 1974. Conceptions of sex role: Some cross-cultural and longitudinal perspectives. In Winch, R. F., and Spanier, B. B. (eds.), *Selected Studies in Marriage and the Family,* 4th ed. New York: Holt, Rinehart and Winston.

Blood, R. O., Jr., and Wolfe, D. M. 1960. *Husbands and Wives.* New York: The Free Press.

Bloom, B. L., Asher, S. J., and White, S. W. 1978. Marital disruption as a stressor: A review and analysis. *Psychological Bulletin,* 85:867–894.

Bloom, B. S. 1969. Letter to the editor. *Harvard Educational Review,* 39:419–421.

Bloom, L. 1970. *Language Development: Form and Function in Emerging Grammar.* Cambridge, Mass.: MIT Press.

———. 1973. *One Word at a Time.* The Hague: Mouton.

Bloomgarden, Z. T. 1977. The end of the line. *New York Times* (January 18):31.

Blount, B. G. 1975. Studies in child language. *American Anthropologist,* 77:580–600.

Blum, J. E., Fosshage, J. L., and Jarvik, L. F. 1972. Intellectual changes and sex differences in octogenarians: A twenty-year longitudinal study of aging. *Developmental Psychology,* 7:178–187.

Blumer, H. 1969. *Symbolic Interactionism: Perspective and Method.* Englewood Cliffs, N.J.: Prentice-Hall.

Blumstein, P., and Schwartz, P. 1983. *American Couples.* New York: William Morrow.

Blyth, D. A., and Traeger, C. M. 1983. The self-concept and self-esteem of early adolescents. *Theory Into Practice,* 22:91–97.

Boffey, P. M. 1984. Study reports prove cholesterol can cut heart diseases' risk. *New York Times* (January 13):1, 11.

Bogoras, W. 1909. The Chukchee. *Memoirs of the American Museum of Natural History,* 11:553.

Bohannan, P., and Erickson, R. 1978. Stepping in. *Psychology Today,* 11 (January):53+.

Boles, D. B. 1980. X-linkage of spatial ability: A critical review. *Child Development,* 51:625–635.

Bongaarts, J. 1982. Malnutrition and fertility. *Science,* 215:1273–1274.

Boocock, S. S. 1972. *An Introduction to the Sociology of Learning.* Boston: Houghton Mifflin.

Boonsong, S. 1968. The development of conservation of mass, weight, and volume in Thai children. Unpublished master's thesis, College of Education, Bangkok, Thailand.

Borke, H. 1975. Piaget's mountains revisited: Change in the egocentric landscape. *Developmental Psychology,* 11:240–243.

Bornstein, M. H. 1976. Infants' recognition memory for hue. *Developmental Psychology,* 12:185–191.

———, Kessen, W., and Weiskopf, S. 1976. Color vision and hue categorization in young human infants. *Journal of Experimental Psychology: Human Perception and Performance,* 2:115–129.

———, and Marks, L. E. 1982. Color revisionism. *Psychology Today,* 16 (January):64–73.

Bottoms, S. F., Rosen, M. G., and Sokol, R. J. 1980. The increase in the Cesarean birth rate. *New England Journal of Medicine,* 302:559–563.

Botvin, G. J., and Murray, F. B. 1975. The efficacy of peer modeling and social conflict in the acquisition of conservation. *Child Development,* 46:796–799.

Botwinick, J. 1967. *Cognitive Processes in Maturity and Old Age.* New York: Springer.

———. 1977. Intellectual abilities. In Birren, J. E., and Schaie, K. W. (eds.), *Handbook of the Psychology of Aging.* New York: Van Nostrand.

———. 1978. *Aging and Behavior: A Comprehensive Integration of Research Findings,* 2nd ed. New York: Spinger.

———, West, R., and Storandt, M. 1978. Predicting death from behavioral test performance. *Journal of Gerontology,* 33:755–762.

Bourque, L. B., and Back, K. W. 1977. Life graphs and life events. *Journal of Gerontology,* 32:669–674.

Bouton, K. 1982. Fighting male infertility. *New York Times Magazine* (June 13):84+.

Bower, T. G. R. 1955. The visual world of infants. *Scientific American,* 215 (December):80–92.

———. 1971. The object in the world of the infant. *Scientific American,* 225 (October):30–38.

———. 1974. *Development in Infancy.* San Francisco: Freeman.

———. 1975. Infant perception of the third dimension and object concept development. In Cohen, L. B., and Salapatek, P. (eds.), *Infant Perception: From Sensation to Cognition.* Vol. 2. New York: Academic Press.

———. 1976. Repetitive processes in child development. *Scientific American,* 235 (November):38–47.

———. 1977. *A Primer of Infant Development.* San Francisco: Freeman.

———, and Wishart, J. G. 1972. The effects of motor skill on object permanence. *Cognition,* 1:165–172.

Bowerman, C., and Irish, D. 1962. Some relationships of stepchildren to their parents. *Journal of Marriage and the Family,* 36:498–514.

Bowerman, C. E., and Bahr, S. J. 1973. Conjugal power and adolescent identification with parents. *Sociometry,* 36:366–377.

Bowes, W. A., Jr., Brackbill, Y., Conway, E., and Steinschneider, A. 1970. The effects of obstetrical medication on fetus and infant. *Monographs of the Society for Research in Child Development,* 35 (Whole No. 137).

Bowlby, J. 1969. *Attachment.* New York: Basic Books.

Bowles, S. 1968. Toward equality of educational opportunity? *Harvard Educational Review,* 38:89–99.

———, and Gintis, H. 1976. *Schooling in Capitalist America: Educational Reform and the Contradictions of Economic Life.* New York: Basic Books.

Boxer, A. M., Tobin-Richards, M., and Petersen, A. C. 1983. Puberty: Physical change and its significance in early adolescence. *Theory Into Practice,* 22:85–90.

Brackbill, Y. 1979. Obstetrical medication and infant behavior. In Osofsky, J. D. (ed.), *Handbook of Infant Development.* New York: Wiley.

———, and Nichols, P. L. 1982. A test of the confluence model of intellectual development. *Developmental Psychology,* 18:192–198.

Braine, M. D. S. 1963. The ontogeny of English phrase structure: The first phase. *Language,* 39:1–14.

Brainerd, C. J. 1978. The stage question in cognitive-developmental theory. *Behavioral and Brain Sciences,* 1:173–213.

———. 1979. Concept learning and development. In Klausmeir, H. J. (ed.), *Cognitive Development from an Information Processing and a Piagetian View: Results of a Longitudinal Study.* Cambridge, Mass.: Ballinger.

Bralove, M. 1981. For middle-aged man, a wife's new career upsets old balances. *Wall Street Journal* (November 9):1, 24.

Brandwein, R. A., Brown, C. A., and Fox, E. M. 1974. Women and children last: The social situation of divorced mothers and their families. *Journal of Marriage and the Family,* 36:498–514.

Braungart, R. G. 1975. Youth and social movements. In Dragastin, S. E., and Elder, G. H., Jr. (eds.), *Adolescence in the Life Cycle: Psychological Change and Social Context.* New York: Wiley.

———, and Braungart, M. M. 1979. Reference group, social judgment, and student politics. *Adolescence,* 14:135–157.

Brazelton, T. B. 1962. Observations of the neonate. *Journal of Child Psychiatry,* 1:38–58.

———. 1978. Introduction. In Sameroff, A. J. (ed.), Organization and stability of newborn behavior: A commentary on the Brazelton Neonatal Behavior Assessment Scale. *Monographs of the Society for Research in Child Development,* 43 (177):1–13.

———, Robey, J. S., and Collier, G. A. 1969. Infant development in the Zinacanteco Indians of Southern Mexico. *Pediatrics,* 44:274–293.

Brenton, M. 1977. What can be done about child abuse? *Today's Education,* 66:51–53.

Bretherton, I., Stolberg, U., and Kreye, M. 1981. Engaging strangers in proximal interaction: Infants' social initiative. *Developmental Psychology,* 17:746–755.

Bridges, K. B. 1932. Emotional development in early infancy. *Child Development,* 3:324–341.

Brim, O. G., Jr. 1966. Socialization through the life cycle. In Brim, O. G., Jr., and Wheeler, S. (eds.), *Socialization after Childhood.* New York: Wiley.

———. 1976. Male mid-life crisis: A comparative analysis. In Hess, B. (ed.), *Growing Old in America.* New Brunswick, N.J.: Transaction, Inc.

———. 1980. Types of life events. *Journal of Social Issues,* 36:148–157.

———, and Kagan, J. (eds.). 1980. *Constancy and Change in Human Development.* Cambridge, Mass.: Harvard University Press.

Broadbent, D. E. 1963. Flow of information within the organism. *Journal of Verbal Learning and Verbal Behavior,* 2:34–39.

Brockman, L. M., and Ricciuti, H. N. 1971. Severe protein-calorie malnutrition and cognitive development in infancy and early childhood. *Developmental Psychology,* 4:312–319.

Broderick, C. B., and Rowe, G. P. 1968. A scale of preadolescent heterosexual development. *Journal of Marriage and the Family,* 30:97–101.

Brodie, H. K. 1974. Plasma testosterone levels in heterosexual and homosexual men. *American Journal of Psychiatry,* 131:82–83.

Brody, E. M., Johnsen, P. T., Fulcomer, M. C., and Lang, A. M. 1983. Women's changing roles and help to elderly parents. *Journal of Gerontology,* 38:597–607.

Brody, G. H., Stoneman, Z., and MacKinnon, C. E. 1982. Role asymmetries in interactions among school-aged children, their younger siblings, and their friends. *Child Development,* 53:1364–1370.

Brody, J. E. 1976. Genetic defects sought in fetus. *New York Times* (May 12):16.

———. 1979*a*. Personal health. *New York Times* (May 16):C12.

———. 1979*b*. Researchers challenge old theories on obesity. *New York Times* (February 10):C1–2.

———. 1981. Planning to prevent retirement "shock." *New York Times* (May 27):13.

———. 1982. Examining the causes, symptoms and treatment of burnout. *New York Times* (October 6):19.

———. 1983*a*. "Bonding" at birth: A major theory being questioned. *New York Times* (March 29):15, 18.

———. 1983*b*. Heart attacks: Turmoil beneath the calm. *New York Times* (June 21):17, 19.

———. 1983*c*. Autopsies can give help and comfort. *New York Times* (September 14):16.

———. 1983*d*. A disease afflicting the mind. *New York Times* (November 23):16.

———. 1983*e*. Guidance in the care of patients with Alzheimer's disease. *New York Times* (November 30):17.

———. 1983*f*. Divorce's stress extracts long-term health toll. *New York Times* (December 13):17+.

———. 1983*g*. Emotional deprivation seen as devastating form of child abuse. *New York Times* (December 20):21–22.

———. 1984*a*. The growing militancy of the nation's nonsmokers. *New York Times* (January 15):6E.

———. 1984*b*. Seeking to prevent teenage suicide. *New York Times* (March 7):15, 17.

Broman, S. H., Nichols, P. L., and Kennedy, W. A. 1975. *Preschool IQ: Prenatal and Early Developmental Correlates.* Hillsdale, N.J.: Lawrence Erlbaum Associates.

Bronfenbrenner, U. 1970. *Two Worlds of Childhood.* New York: Free Press.

———. 1977. Toward an experimental ecology of human development. *American Psychologist,* 32:513–531.

Bronson, G. 1977*a*. Long exposure to waste anesthetic gas is peril to workers, U.S. safety unit says. *Wall Street Journal* (March 1):10.

———. 1977*b*. Mean sperm counts in American men may have dropped. *Wall Street Journal* (October 12):16.

Bronson, G. W. 1972. Infants' reactions to unfamiliar persons and novel objects. *Monographs of the Society for Research in Child Development,* 37 (3).

———. 1974. The postnatal growth of visual capacity. *Child Development,* 45:873–890.

Brook, J. S., Whiteman, M., and Gordon, A. S. 1983. Stages of drug use in adolescence: Personality, peer, and family correlates. *Developmental Psychology,* 19:269–277.

Brookhart, J., and Hock, E. 1976. The effects of experimental context and experiential background on infants' behavior toward their mothers and a stranger. *Child Development,* 47:333–340.

Brookover, W., Beady, C., Flood, P., Schweitzer, J., and Wisenbaker, J. 1979. *School Social Systems and Student Achievement: Schools Can Make a Difference.* New York: Praeger.

Brooks, A. 1981. When married children come home to live. *New York Times* (January 19):28.

———. 1983. Older singles found to value tradition. *New York Times* (June 5):23.

Brooks-Gunn, J., and Ruble, D. N. 1982. The development of menstrual-related beliefs and behaviors during early adolescence. *Child Development,* 53:1567–1577.

Broughton, J. 1978. Development of concepts of self, mind, reality, and knowledge. *New Directions for Child Development,* 1:75–100.

Brown, A. L. 1975. The development of memory: Knowing, knowing about knowing, and knowing how to know. In Reese, H. W. (ed.), *Advances in Child Development,* Vol. 10. New York: Academic Press.

———. 1982. Learning and development: The problems of compatibility, access and induction. *Human Development,* 25:89–115.

Brown, C. A., Feldberg, R., Fox, E. M., and Kohen, J. 1976. Divorce: Chance of a new lifetime. *Journal of Social Issues,* 32:119–133.

Brown, G. L., Ebert, M. H., and Goyer, P. F. 1982. Aggression, suicide, and serotonin: Relationships to CSF amine metabolites. *American Journal of Psychiatry,* 139:741–746.

Brown, J. K. 1969. Female initiation rites: A review of the current literature. In Rogers, D. (ed.), *Issues in Adolescent Psychology.* New York: Appleton-Century-Crofts.

Brown, J. V., Bakeman, R., Snyder, P. A., Fredrickson, W. T., Morgan, S. T., and Hepler, R. 1975. Interactions of black inner city mothers with their newborn infants. *Child Development,* 46:677–686.

Brown, R. 1973. *A First Language.* Cambridge, Mass.: Harvard University Press.

———, and Herrnstein, R. J. 1975. *Psychology.* Boston: Little, Brown.

Brown, R. E. 1966. Organ weight in malnutrition with special reference to brain weight. *Developmental Medicine and Child Neurology,* 8:512–522.

Brozan, N. 1982. Infertility: Couples' reactions. *New York Times* (July 26):20.

———. 1983*a*. Hot flashes are topic for research and group therapy. *New York Times* (January 12):13.

———. 1983*b*. New look at fears of children. *New York Times* (May 2):20.

Bruch, H. 1982. Anorexia nervosa: Therapy and theory. *American Journal of Psychiatry,* 139:1531–1538.

Bruck, C. 1979. Menopause. *Human Behavior,* 8 (April):38–46.

Bruner, J. S. 1970. A conversation with Jerome Bruner. *Psychology Today,* 4 (December):51–74.

———. 1974. The uses of immaturity. In *Annual Editions: Readings in Human Development.* Guilford, Conn.: Dushkin Publishing Group.

———. 1979. Learning how to do things with words. In Aaronson, D., and Rieber, R. W. (eds.), *Psycholinguistic Research: Implications and Applications.* Hillsdale, N.J.: Erlbaum.

———, Goodnow, J. J., and Austin, G. A. 1956. *A Study of Thinking.* New York: Wiley.

———, and Koslowski, B. 1972. Visually preadapted constituents of manipulatory action. *Perception,* 1:3–14.

———, Olver, R. R., and Greenfield, P. M. 1966. *Studies in Cognitive Growth.* New York: Wiley.

Bryan, J. H., and Walbek, N. H. 1970. Preaching and practicing generosity: Children's actions and reactions. *Child Development,* 41:329–353.

Bryant, B. K., and Crockenberg, S. B. 1980. Correlates and dimensions of prosocial behavior: A study of female siblings with their mothers. *Child Development,* 51:529–544.

Buckley, N., Siegel, L. S., and Ness, S. 1979. Egocentrism, empathy, and altruistic behavior in young children. *Developmental Psychology,* 15:329–330.

Bühler, C., Keith-Spiegel, P., and Thomas, K. 1973. Developmental psychology. In Wolman, B. B. (ed.), *Handbook of General Psychology.* Englewood Cliffs, N.J.: Prentice-Hall.

———, and Massarik, F. 1968. *The Course of Human Life: A Study of Goals in the Humanistic Perspective.* New York: Springer.

Bullough, V. L. 1981. Age at menarche: A misunderstanding. *Science,* 213: 365–366.

Bultena, G. 1976. Sex differences in intimate friendships of old age. *Journal of Marriage and the Family,* 38:739–747.

Bunney, W. E., Jr. 1978. Drug therapy and psychobiological research advances in the psychoses in the past decade. *American Journal of Psychiatry,* 135 (Supplement):8–13.

Burchinal, L. G. 1964. Characteristics of adolescents from unbroken, broken, and reconstituted families. *Journal of Marriage and the Family,* 26:44–51.

Burgess, E., and Wallin, P. 1953. *Engagement and Marriage.* Philadelphia: Lippincott.

Burke, B. S., Beal, V. A., Kirkwood, S. B., and Stuart, H. C. 1943. Nutrition studies during pregnancy. *American Journal of Obstetrics and Gynecology,* 46:38–52.

Burke, D. M., and Light, L. L. 1981. Memory and aging: The role of retrieval processes. *Psychological Bulletin,* 90:513–546.

Burlingame, W. V. 1970. The youth culture. In Evans, E. D. (ed.), *Adolescents: Readings in Behavior and Development.* Hinsdale, Ill.: Dryden Press.

Burnham, D. 1976. Rise in birth defects laid to job hazards. *New York Times* (March 14):1f.

Burr, W. R. 1970. Satisfaction with various aspects of marriage over the life cycle: A random middle-class sample. *Journal of Marriage and the Family,* 26:29–37.

Burton, R. V. 1976. Honesty and dishonesty. In Lickona, T. (ed.), *Moral Development and Behavior: Theory, Research, and Social Issues.* New York: Holt, Rinehart and Winston.

Bush, D. M., and Simmons, R. G. 1981. Socialization processes over the life course. In Rosenberg, M., and Turner, R. H. (eds.), *Social Psychology: Sociological Perspectives.* New York: Basic Books.

Busse, E. W. 1969. Theories of aging. In Busse, E. W., and Pfeiffer, E. (eds.), *Behavior and Adaptation in Late Life.* Boston: Little, Brown.

———, and Pfeiffer, E. 1969. Functional psychiatric disorders in old age. In Busse, E. W., and Pfeiffer, E. (eds.), *Behavior and Adaptation in Late Life.* Boston: Little, Brown.

Butler, R. N. 1963. The life review: An interpretation of reminiscence in the aged. *Psychiatry,* 26:65–76.

———. 1971. The life review. *Psychology Today,* 5 (December):49–51f.

———. 1975. *Why Survive?* New York: Harper & Row.

———. 1978. Thoughts on aging. *American Journal of Psychiatry,* 135:14–16.

Bybee, R. W. 1979. Violence toward youth: A new perspective. *Journal of Social Issues,* 35:1–14.

Byrne, D., Ervin, C. H., and Lamberth, J. 1970. Continuity between the experimental study of attraction and real-life computer dating. *Journal of Personality and Social Psychology,* 16:157–165.

Byrne, H. S. 1982. Firms are adding female directors more slowly than during the 1970s. *Wall Street Journal* (April 7):27.

Byrne, J. M., and Horowitz, F. D. 1981. Rocking as a soothing intervention: The influence of direction and type of movement. *Infant Behavior and Development,* 4:207–218.

Cain, B. S. 1982. Plight of the gray divorcee. *New York Times Magazine* (December 19):89–93.

Caldwell, B. M. 1969. A new "approach" to behavioral ecology. In Hill, J. P. (ed.), *Minnesota Symposia on Child Psychology.* Vol. 2. Minneapolis: University of Minnesota Press.

Cameron, P. 1970. The generation gap: Beliefs about sexuality and self-reported sexuality. *Developmental Psychology,* 3:272.

Campbell, A. 1975. The American way of mating: Marriage si, children only maybe. *Psychology Today,* 8 (May): 37–43.

———. 1976. Subjective measures of

well-being. *American Psychologist,* 31:117–124.

———, Converse, P. E., and Rodgers, W. L. 1976. *The Quality of American Life: Perceptions, Evaluations, and Satisfactions.* New York: Russell Sage Foundation.

Campion, E. W., Bang, A., and May, M. I. 1983. Why acute-care hospitals must undertake long-term care. *New England Journal of Medicine,* 308:71–75.

Caplan, F., and Caplan, T. 1973. *The Power of Play.* Garden City, N.Y.: Anchor Books.

Caporael, L. R. 1981. The paralanguage of caregiving: Baby talk to the institutionalized aged. *Journal of Personality and Social Psychology,* 40:876–884.

Caputo, D. V., and Mandell, W. 1970. Consequences of low birth weight. *Developmental Psychology,* 3:363–383.

Carey, J. 1983. Weight gained later in life is more risky for the heart. *USA Today* (December 16):9D.

Cargan, L. 1981. Singles: An examination of two stereotypes. *Family Relations,* 30:377–385.

Carlsmith, L. 1964. Effect of early father-absence on scholastic aptitude. *Harvard Educational Review,* 34:3–21.

Carnegie Commission. 1980. *Giving Youth a Better Chance.* San Francisco: Jossey-Bass.

Caron, A. J., Caron, R. F., Caldwell, R. C., and Weiss, S. J. 1973. Infant perception of the structural properties of the face. *Developmental Psychology,* 9:385–399.

Carpenter, D. G. 1965. Diffusion theory of aging. *Journal of Gerontology,* 20:191–195.

Carpenter, E. 1965. Comments. *Current Anthropology,* 6:55.

Carver, C. S., and Ganellen, R. J. 1983. Depression and components of self-punitiveness. *Journal of Abnormal Psychology,* 92:330–337.

Case, R. 1978. Intellectual development from birth to adulthood: A neo-Piagetian interpretation. In Siegler, R. (ed.), *Young Children's Thinking: What Develops?* Hillsdale, N.J.: Erlbaum.

Casler, L. R. 1961. Maternal deprivation: A critical review of the literature. *Monographs of the Society for Research in Child Development,* 26 (No. 2).

———. 1967. Perceptual deprivation in institutional settings. In Newton, G., and Levine, S. (eds.), *Early Experience and Behavior.* New York: Springer.

Cattell, R. B. 1943. The measurement of adult intelligence. *Psychological Bulletin,* 40:153–193.

———. 1971. *Abilities: Their Structure, Growth, and Action.* Boston: Houghton Mifflin.

Cavan, R. S. 1964. Structural variations and mobility. In Christense, H. T. (ed.), *Handbook of Marriage and the Family.* Chicago: Rand McNally.

Cavior, N., and Dokecki, P. R. 1973. Physical attractiveness, perceived attitude similarity, and academic achievement as contributors to interpersonal attraction among adolescents. *Developmental Psychology,* 9:44–54.

———, and Lombardi, D. A. 1973. Developmental aspects of judgment of physical attractiveness in children. *Developmental Psychology,* 8:67–71.

Census Bureau. 1983. *America in Transition: An Aging Society.* P–23, No. 128. Washington, D.C.: Government Printing Office.

Cervantes, L. 1965. *The Dropout: Causes and Cures.* Ann Arbor: University of Michigan Press.

Chambers, M. 1981. How the police target young offenders. *New York Times Magazine* (September 20):116–124.

Charlesworth, R., and Hartup, W. W. 1967. Positive social reinforcement in the nursery school peer group. *Child Development,* 38:993–1002.

Chechile, R. A., Richman, C. L., Topinka, C., and Ehrensbeck, K. 1981. A developmental study of the storage and retrieval of information. *Child Development,* 52:251–259.

Chedd, G. 1981. Who shall be born? *Science 81,* 2 (January):32–41.

Cherry, F. F., and Eaton, E. L. 1977. Physical and cognitive development in children of low-income mothers working in the child's early years. *Child Development,* 48:158–166.

Chiriboga, D. A. 1978. Evaluated time: A life course perspective. *Journal of Gerontology,* 33:388–393.

Chomsky, N. 1957. *Syntactic Structures.* The Hague: Mouton.

———. 1965. *Aspects of a Theory of Syntax.* Cambridge, Mass.: MIT Press.

———. 1968. *Language and Mind.* New York: Harcourt Brace Jovanovich.

———. 1975. *Reflections on Language.* New York: Pantheon.

———. 1980. *Rules and Representations.* New York: Columbia University Press.

Chown, S. M. (ed.). 1972. *Human Ageing.* Baltimore: Penguin.

Chumlea, W. C. 1982. Physical growth in adolescence. In Wolman, B. B. (ed.), *Handbook of Developmental Psychology.* Englewood Cliffs, N.J.: Prentice-Hall.

Cicirelli, V. G. 1973. Effects of sibling structure and interaction on children's categorization style. *Developmental Psychology,* 9:132–139.

———. 1978. The relationship of sibling structure to intellectual abilities and achievement. *Review of Educational Research,* 48:365–379.

———. 1980. A comparison of college women's feelings toward their siblings and parents. *Journal of Marriage and the Family,* 42:111–118.

———. 1981. *Helping Elderly Parents: The Role of Adult Children.* Boston: Auburn House.

———. 1983. Adult children's attachment and helping behavior to elderly parents: A path model. *Journal of Marriage and the Family,* 45:815–825.

Clark, D. L., Lotto, L. S., and McCarthy, M. M. 1980. Factors associated with success in urban elementary schools. *Phi Delta Kappan,* 61:467–470.

Clark, E. V. 1978. Strategies for communicating. *Child Development,* 49:953–959.

Clark, K. B. 1965. *Dark Ghetto.* New York: Harper & Row.

Clarke, A. C. 1952. An examination of the operation of residential propinquity as a factor in mate selection. *American Sociological Review,* 17:17–22.

Clarke, A. M., and Clarke, A. D. B. 1976. Overview and implications. In Clarke, A. M., and Clarke, A. D. B. (eds.), *Early Experience: Myth and Evidence.* London: Open Books.

Clarke-Stewart, K. A., and Hevey, C. M. 1981. Longitudinal relations in repeated observations of mother-child interaction from 1 to 2½ years. *Developmental Psychology,* 17:127–145.

Clausen, J. A. 1966. Family structure, socialization and personality. In Hoffman, L. W., and Hoffman, M. L. (eds.), *Review of Child Development Research.* Vol. 2. New York: Russell Sage Foundation.

———. 1973. The life course of individuals. In Riley, M. W., Johnson, M., and Foner, S. (eds.), *Aging and Society.* Vol. 3. New York: Russell Sage Foundation.

Clayton, R. R. 1979. *The Family, Marriage, and Social Change,* 2nd ed. Lexington, Mass.: D. C. Heath.

———, and Bokemeier, J. L. 1980. Premarital sex in the seventies. *Journal of Marriage and the Family,* 42:759–775.

Clemente, F., and Sauer, W. J. 1976. Life satisfaction in the United States. *Social Forces,* 54:621–631.

Cleveland, W. P., and Gianturco, D. T. 1976. Remarriage probability after widowhood: A retrospective method. *Journal of Gerontology,* 31: 99–103.

Clifton, R. K., Morrongiello, B. A., Kulig, J. W., and Dowd, J. M. 1981. Newborns' orientations toward sound: Possible implications for cortical development. *Child Development,* 52: 833–838.

Clingempeel, W. G., and Reppucci, N. D. 1982. Joint custody after divorce: Major issues and goals for research. *Psychological Bulletin,* 91:102–127.

Clopton, W. 1973. Personality and career change. *Industrial Gerontology,* 17:9–17.

Cohen, G., and Faulkner, D. 1983. Age differences in performance on two information-processing tasks. *Journal of Gerontology,* 38:447–454.

Cohen, J. 1983. Peer influence on college aspirations with initial aspirations controlled. *American Sociological Review,* 48:728–734.

Cohen, L. B., DeLoache, J. S., and Strauss, M. S. 1979. Infant visual perception. In Osofsky, J. D. (ed.), *Handbook of Infant Development.* New York: Wiley.

———, and Gelber, E. R. 1975. Infant visual memory. In Cohen, L. B., and Salapetek, P. (eds.), *Infant Perception: From Sensation to Cognition.* Vol. 1. New York: Academic Press.

———, and Menten, T. G. 1981. The rise and fall of infant habituation. *Infant Behavior and Development,* 4:269–280.

Cohen, R., Bornstein, R., and Sherman, R. C. 1973. Conformity behavior of children as a function of group makeup and task ambiguity. *Developmental Psychology,* 9:124–131.

Cohen, S. E., and Beckwith, L. 1977. Caregiving behaviors and early cognitive development as related to ordinal position in preterm infants. *Child Development,* 48:152–157.

Cohen, Y. A. 1968. Macroethnology: Large-scale comparative studies. In Clifton, J. A. (ed.), *Introduction to Cultural Anthropology.* Boston: Houghton Mifflin.

Coie, J. D., and Kupersmidt, J. B. 1983. A behavioral analysis of emerging social status in boys' groups. *Child Development,* 54:1400–1416.

Colby, A., Kohlberg, L., Gibbs, J., and Lieberman, M. 1983. A longitudinal study of moral judgment. *Monographs of the Society for Research in Child Development,* 48 (200).

Cole, C. L. 1977. Cohabitation in social context. In Libby, R. W., and Whitehurst, R. N. (eds.), *Marriage and Alternatives.* Glenview, Ill.: Scott, Foresman.

Cole, R. A. 1979. Navigating the slippery stream of speech. *Psychology Today,* 12 (April):77–87.

Cole, S. 1980. Send our children to work? *Psychology Today,* 14 (July): 44–68.

Coleman, J. 1978. Current contradictions in adolescent theory. *Journal of Youth and Adolescence,* 7:1–11.

———, Hoffer, T., and Kilgore, S. 1982*a*. *High School Achievement: Public, Catholic and Other Private Schools Compared.* New York: Basic Books.

———, ———, and ———. 1982*b*. Cognitive outcomes in public and private schools. *Sociology of Education,* 55: 65–76.

Coleman, J. S. 1966. *Equality of Educational Opportunity.* Washington, D.C.: U.S. Government Printing Office.

Coleman, L. M., and Antonucci, T. C. 1983. Impact of work on women at midlife. *Developmental Psychology,* 19:290–294.

Collins, G. 1981*a*. The childhood "industry": Conflicting advice. *New York Times* (March 16):17.

———. 1981*b*. Fathers get postpartum blues, too. *New York Times* (April 6):19.

———. 1981*c*. Schools stereotype children with one parent. *New York Times* (February 2):16.

———. 1983*a*. U.S. social tolerance of drugs found on rise. *New York Times* (March 27):1, 9.

———. 1983*b*. Stepfamilies share their joys and woes. *New York Times* (October 24):21.

———. 1984*a*. Care for far-off elderly: Sources of help. *New York Times* (January 5):15, 17.

———. 1984*b*. New studies on 'girl toys' and 'boy toys.' *New York Times* (February 13):17.

Collins, J. A., Wrixon, W., Janes, L. B., and Wilson, E. H. 1983. Treatment-independent pregnancy among infertile couples. *New England Journal of Medicine,* 309:1201–1209.

Colombo, J. 1982. The critical period concept: Research, methodology, and theoretical issues. *Psychological Bulletin,* 91:260–275.

Colson, E. 1958. *Marriage and the Family among the Plateau Tonga of Northern Rhodesia.* Manchester: Manchester University Press.

Comfort, A. 1970. Biological theories of aging. *Human Development,* 13:127–139.

———. 1976. *A Good Age.* New York: Crown.

Commons, M. L., Richards, F. A., and Kuhn, D. 1982. Systematic and metasystematic reasoning: A case for levels of reasoning beyond Piaget's stage of formal operations. *Child Development,* 53:1058–1069.

Condon, W. S., and Sander, L. W. 1974*a*. Neonate movement is synchronized with adult speech: Interactional participation and language acquisition. *Science,* 183:99–101.

———, and ———. 1984*b*. Synchrony demonstrated between movements of the neonate and adult speech. *Child Development,* 45:456–462.

Conel, J. L. 1963. *The Cortex of the Newborn.* Vol. 1. Cambridge, Mass.: Harvard University Press.

Conger, J. J. 1977. *Adolescence and Youth,* 2nd ed. New York: Harper & Row.

Conger, R. D., Burgess, R. L., and Barrett, C. 1979. Child abuse related to life change and perceptions of illness: Some preliminary findings. *Family Coordinator,* 28:73–78.

Conner, K. A., Powers, E. A., and Bultena, G. L. 1979. Social interaction and life satisfaction: An empirical assessment of late-life patterns. *Journal of Gerontology,* 34:116–121.

Cooke, R. A. 1982. The ethics and regulation of research involving children. In Wolman, B. B. (ed.), *Handbook of Developmental Psychology.* Englewood Cliffs, N.J.: Prentice-Hall.

Cooley, C. H. 1902. *Human Nature and the Social Order.* New York: Scribner.

———. 1909. *Social Organization.* New York: Scribner.

Cooper, J. E., Holman, J., and Braithwaite, V. A. 1983. Self-esteem and family cohesion: The child's perspective and adjustment. *Journal of Marriage and the Family,* 45:153–159.

Coopersmith, S. 1967. *Antecedents of Self-Esteem.* San Francisco: Freeman.

Corah, N. L., Anthony, E. J., Painter, P., Stern, J. A., and Thurston, D. L. 1965. Effects of perinatal anoxia after seven years. *Psychological Monographs,* 79(3, Whole No. 596).

Corballis, M. C., and Morgan, M. J. 1978. On the biological basis of human laterality. *Behavioral and Brain Science,* 2:261–336.

Coren, S., Porac, C., and Duncan, P. 1981. Lateral preference behaviors in preschool children and young adults. *Child Development,* 52:443–450.

Cornell, E. H., and Gottfried, A. W. 1976. Intervention with premature human infants. *Child Development* 47:32–39.

Cornfield, N. 1983. The success of urban communes. *Journal of Marriage and the Family,* 45:115–126.

Corso, J. F. 1976. Auditory perception and communication. In Birren, J. E., and Schaie, K. W. (eds.), *Handbook of the Psychology of Aging.* New York: Van Nostrand.

———. 1977. Auditory perception and communication. In Birren, J. E., and

Schaie, K. W. (eds.), *Handbook of the Psychology of Aging*. New York: Van Nostrand.

Corter, C. M. 1973. A comparison of the mother's and a stranger's control over the behavior of infants. *Child Development*, 44:705–713.

Costa, P. T., Jr., and McCrae, R. R. 1980. Still stable after all these years: Personality as a key to some issues in adulthood and old age. In Baltes, P. B., and Brim, O. G., Jr. (eds), *Life-Span Development and Behavior*. Vol. 3. New York: Academic Press.

———, ———, and Arenberg, D. 1980. Enduring dispositions in adult males. *Journal of Personality and Social Psychology*, 38:793–800.

———, ———, and Norris, A. H. 1981. Personal adjustment to aging: Longitudinal prediction from neuroticism and extraversion. *Journal of Gerontology*, 36:78–85.

Cowart, B. J. 1981. Development of taste perception in humans: Sensitivity and preference throughout the life span. *Psychological Bulletin*, 90:43–73.

Cowgill, D. O. 1974. Aging and modernization: A revision of the theory. In Gubrium, J. F. (ed.), *Late Life*. Springfield, Ill.: Charles C. Thomas.

———, and Holmes, L. D. (eds.). 1972. *Aging and Modernization*. New York: Appleton-Century-Crofts.

Craik, F. I. M. 1977. Age differences in human memory. In Birren, J. E., and Schaie, K. W. (eds.), *Handbook of the Psychology of Aging*. New York: Van Nostrand.

———, and Lockhart, R. S. 1972. Levels of processing: A framework for memory research. *Journal of Verbal Learning and Verbal Behavior*, 11: 671–684.

Crano, W. D., and Aronoff, J. 1978. A cross-cultural study of expressive and instrumental role complementarity in the family. *American Sociological Review*, 43:463–471.

Cratty, B. J. 1970. *Perceptual and Motor Development in Infants and Children*. New York: Macmillan.

Crawford, M. P., and Hooper, D. 1973. Menopause, ageing, and family. *Social Science and Medicine*, 7:469–482.

Crockenberg, S. B. 1981. Infant irritability, mother responsiveness, and social support influences on the security of infant-mother attachment. *Child Development*, 52:857–865.

———, and Smith, P. 1982. Antecedents of mother-infant interaction and infant irritability in the first three months of life. *Infant Behavior and Development*, 5:105–119.

Cromer, J. 1984. *The Mood of American Youth*. Washington, D.C.: National Association of Secondary School Principals.

Cronbach, L. J., and Snow, R. E. 1977. *Aptitudes and Instructional Methods: A Handbook for Research on Interactions*. New York: Irvington.

Crook, C. K. 1978. Taste perception in the newborn infant. *Infant Behavior and Development*, 1:52–69.

———, and Lipsitt, L. P. 1976. Neonatal nutritive sucking: Effects of taste stimulation upon sucking rhythm and heart rate. *Child Development*, 47:518–522.

Cross, K. P. 1976. *Accent on Learning*. San Francisco: Jossey-Bass.

Cruikshank, R. M. 1941. The development of visual size constancy in early infancy. *Journal of Genetic Psychology*, 58:327–351.

Csikszentmihalyi, M., and Beattie, O. A. 1979. Life themes: A theoretical and empirical exploration of their origins and effects. *Journal of Humanistic Psychology*, 19:45–63.

Cuber, J. F., and Harroff, P. B. 1965. *The Significant Americans*. New York: Appleton-Century-Crofts.

Cumming, E., and Henry, W. E. 1961. *Growing Old*. New York: Basic Books.

Cummings, J. 1983. Plea by patient for starvation barred by court. *New York Times* (December 17):8.

Curtiss, S. 1977. *Genie: A Psycholinguistic Study of a Modern Day "Wild Child."* New York: Academic Press.

Cutler, S. J. 1977. Aging and voluntary association participation. *Journal of Gerontology*, 32:470–479.

Cuvo, A. J. 1975. Developmental differences in rehearsal and free recall. *Journal of Experimental Child Psychology*, 19:265–278.

Dale, P. S. 1976. *Language Development: Structure and Functions*, 2nd ed. New York: Holt, Rinehart and Winston.

Damon, W. 1977. *The Social World of the Child*. San Francisco: Jossey-Bass.

———, and Hart, D. 1982. The development of self-understanding from infancy through adolescence. *Child Development*, 53:841–864.

Danner, F. W., and Day, M. C. 1977. Eliciting formal operations. *Child Development*, 48:1600–1606.

Dasen, P. R. (ed.). 1977. *Piagetian Psychology: Cross-Cultural Contributions*. New York: Gardner Press.

Davids, A., Holden, R. H., and Gray, G. B. 1963. Maternal anxiety during pregnancy and adequacy of mother and child adjustments 8 months following childbirth. *Child Development*, 34:993–1002.

Davies, M., and Kandel, D. B. 1981. Parental and peer influences on adolescents' educational plans: Some further evidence. *American Journal of Sociology*, 87:363–387.

Davis, K. 1949. *Human Society*. New York: Macmillan.

Davison, M. L., King, P. M., Kitchener, K. S., and Parker, C. A. 1980. The stage sequence concept in cognitive and social development. *Developmental Psychology*, 16:121–131.

Dayton, G. O., Jr., Jones, M. H., Aiu, P., Rawson, R. A., Steele, B., and Rose, M. 1964. Developmental study of coordinated eye movements in the human infant. 1. Visual acuity in the newborn human: A study based on induced opticokinetic nystagmus recorded by electrooculography. *Archives of Ophthalmology*, 71:865–870.

de Boer, C. 1978. The polls: Attitudes toward work. *Public Opinion Quarterly*, 42:414–423.

DeCasper, A. J., and Carstens, A. A. 1981. Contingencies of stimulation: Effects on learning and emotion in neonates. *Infant Behavior and Development*, 4:19–35.

———, and Fifer, W. P. 1980. Of human bonding: Newborns prefer their mothers' voices. *Science*, 208:1174–1176.

DeCherney, A. H., and Berkowitz, G. S. 1982. Female fecundity and age. *New England Journal of Medicine*, 306:424–426.

DeFleur, L. B., and Menke, B. A. 1975. Learning about the labor force: Occupational knowledge among high school males. *Sociology of Education*, 48:324–345.

DeFrain, J. 1979. Androgynous parents tell who they are and what they need. *Family Coordinator*, 28:237–243.

Dekaban, A. 1970. *Neurology of Early Childhood*. Baltimore: Williams & Wilkins.

De Lacoste-Utamsing, C., and Holloway, R. L. 1982. Sexual dimorphism in the human corpus callosum. *Science*, 216:1431–1432.

deLemos, M. M. 1969. The development of conservation in Aboriginal children. *International Journal of Psychology*, 4:255–269.

deMause, L. 1974. The evolution of childhood. In deMause, L. (ed.), *The History of Childhood*. New York: Harper & Row.

Dembroski, T. M. 1981. The type A coronary-prone behavior pattern: A review. *Circulation*, 63:1199–1215.

Dement, W. C. 1960. The effect of dream deprivation. *Science*, 131:1705–1707.

Demos, J., and Demos, V. 1969. Adolescence in historical perspective. *Journal of Marriage and the Family*, 31:632–638.

Denney, N. W., and Palmer, A. M. 1981.

Adult age differences on traditional and practical problem-solving measures. *Journal of Gerontology,* 36:323-328.

Dennis, W. 1973. *Children of the Crèche.* New York: Appleton-Century-Crofts.

———, and Dennis, M. G. 1940. The effect of cradling practices upon the onset of walking in Hopi children. *Journal of Genetic Psychology,* 56:77–86.

Dent, E. M. 1978. The salience of pro-white/antiblack bias. *Child Development,* 49:1280–1283.

Depue, R. A., and Monroe, S. M. 1978. Learned helplessness in the perspective of the depressive disorders: Conceptual and definitional issues. *Journal of Abnormal Psychology,* 87:3–20.

Despert, J. L. 1953. *Children of Divorce.* Garden City, N.Y.: Doubleday.

Deur, J. L., and Parke, R. D. 1970. Effects of inconsistent punishment on aggression in children. *Developmental Psychology,* 2:403–411.

Deutscher, I. 1964. The quality of post-parental life: Definitions of the situation. *Journal of Marriage and the Family,* 26:52–59.

Devaney, K. O., and Johnson, H. A. 1980. Neuron loss in the aging visual cortex of man. *Journal of Gerontology,* 35:836–841.

Devereux, E. C., Shouval, R., Bronfenbrenner, U., Rodgers, R. R., Kav-Venaki, S., Kiely, E., and Karson, E. 1974. Socialization practices of parents, teachers, and peers in Israel: The kibbutz versus the city. *Child Development,* 45:269–281.

DeVito, J. A. 1970. *The Psychology of Speech and Language.* New York: Random House.

De Vries, R. G. 1981. Birth and death: Social construction at the poles of existence. *Social Forces,* 59:1074–1093.

Dick-Read, G. 1944. *Childbirth without Fear: The Principles and Practice of Natural Childbirth.* New York: Harper & Row.

Diener, C. I., and Dweck, C. S. 1980. An analysis of learned helplessness: II. The processing of success. *Journal of Personality and Social Psychology,* 39:940–952.

Diepold, J., Jr., and Young, R. D. 1979. Empirical studies of adolescent sexual behavior: A critical review. *Adolescence.* 14:45–64.

Dion, K. 1974. Children's physical attractiveness and sex as determinants of adult punitiveness. *Developmental Psychology,* 10:772–778.

———, Berscheid, E., and Walster, E. 1972. What is beautiful is good. *Journal of Personality and Social Psychology,* 24:285–290.

Dirks, J., and Gibson, E. 1977. Infants' perception of similarity between live people and their photographs. *Child Development,* 48:124–130.

Dobzhansky, T. 1962. *Mankind Evolving.* New Haven: Yale University Press.

Dodge, K. A. 1983. Behavioral antecedents of peer social status. *Child Development,* 54:1386–1399.

———, and Frame, C. L. 1982. Social cognitive biases and deficits in aggressive boys. *Child Development,* 53:620–635.

Doering, S. G., Entwisle, D. R., and Quinlan, D. 1980. Modeling the quality of women's birth experience. *Journal of Health and Social Behavior,* 21:12–21.

Dohrenwend, B. S., and Dohrenwend, B. P. (eds.). 1974. *Stressful Life Events: Their Nature and Effects.* New York: Wiley.

Doppelt, J. E., and Wallace, W. L. 1955. Standardization of the Wechsler Adult Intelligence Scale for older persons. *Journal of Abnormal and Social Psychology,* 51:312–330.

Douglas, J. D., and Wong, A. C. 1977. Formal operations: Age and sex differences in Chinese and American children. *Child Development,* 48:689–692.

Douglas, J. W. B., Ross, J. M., and Simpson, H. R. 1968. *All Our Future.* London: Peter Davies.

Douglas, K., and Arenberg, D. 1978. Age changes, cohort differences, and cultural changes on the Guilford-Zimmerman Temperament Survey. *Journal of Gerontology,* 33:737–747.

Douvan, E., and Adelson, J. 1966. *The Adolescent Experience.* New York: Wiley.

Dowd, J. J. 1975. Aging as exchange: A preface to theory. *Journal of Gerontology,* 30:584–594.

———. 1980. Exchange rates and old people. *Journal of Gerontology,* 35:596–602.

———. 1984. Beneficence and the aged. *Journal of Gerontology,* 39:102–108.

Doyle, A., Connolly, J., and Rivest, Louis-Paul. 1980. The effect of playmate familiarity on social interactions of young children. *Child Development,* 51:217–223.

Drabman, R. S., and Thomas, M. H. 1974. Does media violence increase children's toleration of real-life aggression? *Developmental Psychology,* 10:418–421.

Dragastin, S. E., and Elder, G. H., Jr. 1975. *Adolescence in the Life Cycle.* New York: Wiley.

Driver, H. E. 1973. Cross-cultural studies. In Honigmann, J. J. (ed.), *Handbook of Social and Cultural Anthropology.* Chicago: Rand McNally.

Duberman, L. 1973. Step kin relationships. *Journal of Marriage and the Family,* 35:283–292.

Dubin, R. 1956. Industrial workers' worlds. *Social Problems,* 3:131–142.

Dulit, E. 1972. Adolescent thinking à la Piaget: The formal stage. *Journal of Youth and Adolescence,* 1:281–301.

Dullea, G. 1978. Divorced fathers: Who are happiest? *New York Times* (February 4):20.

Dunn, J. 1983. Sibling relationships in early childhood. *Child Development,* 54:787–811.

Dunphy, D. C. 1963. The social structure of urban adolescent peer groups. *Sociometry,* 26:230–246.

Dusek, J. B., and Flaherty, J. F. 1981. The development of the self-concept during the adolescent years. *Monographs of the Society for Research in Child Development,* 46 (191).

Duvall, E. M. 1977. *Family Development,* 5th ed. Philadelphia: Lippincott.

Dweck, C. S. 1975. The role of expectations and attributions in the alleviation of learned helplessness. *Journal of Personality and Social Psychology,* 31:674–685.

Dyer, E. D. 1963. Parenthood as crisis: A re-study. *Marriage and Family Living,* 25:196–201.

Eckerman, C. O., and Whatley, J. L. 1975. Infants' reactions to unfamiliar adults varying in novelty. *Developmental Psychology,* 11:562–566.

———, ———, and Kutz, S. L. 1975. Growth of social play with peers during the second year of life. *Developmental Psychology,* 11:42–49.

Eder, D., and Hallinan, M. T. 1978. Sex differences in children's friendships. *American Sociological Review,* 43:237–250.

Edmonds, M. H. 1976. New directions theories of language acquisition. *Harvard Educational Review,* 46:175–198.

Edwards, J. N., and Klemmack, D. L. 1973. Correlates of life satisfaction: A re-examination. *Journal of Gerontology,* 28:497–502.

Egan, K. 1980. On Piaget and education. *Harvard Educational Review,* 50:263–269.

Ehrhardt, A. A., and Meyer-Bahlburg, H. F. L. 1981. Effects of prenatal sex hormones on gender-related behavior. *Science,* 211:1312–1318.

Eichenwald, H. F., and Fry, P. C. 1969. Nutrition and learning. *Science,* 163:644–648.

Eichorn, D. H., Clausen, J. A., Haan, N., Honzik, M. P., and Mussen, P. H. (eds.), 1982. *Present and Past in Middle Life.* New York: Academic Press.

Eimas, P. D. 1975. Speech perception in infancy. In Cohen, L. B., and Salapatek, P. (eds.), *Infant Perception.* Vol. 2. New York: Academic Press.

Einstein, E. 1979. Stepfamily lives. *Human Behavior,* 8 (April):63–68.

Eisdorfer, C., and Wilkie, F. 1973. Intellectual changes with advancing age. In Jarvik, L. F., Eisdorfer, C., and Blum, J. E. (eds.), *Intellectual Functioning in Adults.* New York: Springer.

Eisenberg, N. 1982. *The Development of Prosocial Behavior.* New York: Academic Press.

———, Lennon, R., and Roth, K. 1983. Prosocial development: A longitudinal study. *Developmental Psychology,* 19:846–855.

Eisenberg, R. B. 1970. The development of hearing in man: An assessment of current status. *American Speech and Hearing Association,* 12:119–123.

Eisenstadt, S. N. 1956. *From Generation to Generation.* New York: Free Press.

———. 1963. Archetypal patterns of youth. In Erikson, E. H. (ed.), *The Challenge of Youth.* Garden City, N.Y.: Doubleday.

Eisert, D. C., and Kahle, L. R. 1982. Self-evaluation and social comparison of physical and role change during adolescence: A longitudinal analysis. *Child Development,* 53:98–104.

Ekman, P. 1972. Universals in cultural differences in facial expressions of emotion. In Cole, J. K. (ed.), *Nebraska Symposium on Motivation.* Vol. 19. Lincoln: University of Nebraska Press.

———. 1980. *The Face of Man: Expressions of Universal Emotions in a New Guinea Village.* New York: Garland STPM Press.

Elder, G. H. 1963. Parental power legitimation and its effect on the adolescent. *Sociometry,* 26:50–65.

———. 1968. Democratic parent-youth relations in cross-cultural perspective. *Social Science Quarterly,* 49:216–228.

———. 1975. Adolescence in the life cycle: An introduction. In Dragastin, S. E., and Elder, G. H., Jr. (eds.), *Adolescence in the Life Cycle.* New York: Wiley.

Elias, M. 1983. Do aggressive Type A kids risk heart attack as adults? *USA Today* (December 23):1.

Elkin, F., and Westley, W. A. 1955. The myth of adolescent peer culture. *American Sociological Review,* 20:680–684.

Elkind, D. 1961. Children's discovery of the conservation of mass, weight, and volume: Piaget replication study II. *Journal of Genetic Psychology,* 98:219–227.

———. 1967. Egocentrism in adolescence. *Child Development,* 38:1025–1034.

———. 1968*a*. Cognitive development in adolescence. In Adams, J. F. (ed.), *Understanding Adolescence.* Boston: Allyn & Bacon.

———. 1968*b*. Giant in the nursery—Jean Piaget. *New York Times Magazine* (May 26):25ff.

———. 1970. Erik Erikson's eight ages of man. *New York Times Magazine* (April 5):25ff.

———. 1974. *A Sympathetic Understanding of the Child from Birth to Sixteen.* Boston: Allyn & Bacon.

———. 1975. Recent research on cognitive development in adolescence. In Dragastin, S. E., and Elder, G. H., Jr. (eds.), *Adolescence in the Life Cycle.* New York: Wiley.

———. 1979. Growing up faster. *Psychology Today,* 12 (February):38–45.

Elliott, D. S. 1966. Delinquency, school attendance, and dropout. *Social Problems,* 13:307–314.

Ellis, H. C., and Hunt, R. R. 1977. Memory: The processing of information. In Marx, M. H., and Bunch, M. E. (eds.), *Fundamentals and Applications of Learning.* New York: Macmillan.

Ellis, M. J., Witt, P. A., Reynolds, R., and Sprague, R. L. 1974. Methylphenidate and the activity of hyperactives in the informal setting. *Child Development,* 45:217–220.

Elwell, F., and Maltbie-Crannell, A. D. 1981. The impact of role loss upon coping resources and life satisfaction of the elderly. *Journal of Gerontology,* 36:223–232.

Elwin, V. 1947. *The Muria and Their Ghotul.* Bombay: Oxford University Press.

Emde, R. N., and Koenig, K. L. 1969. Neonatal smiling and rapid eye movement states. *Journal of the American Academy of Child Psychiatry,* 8:57–67.

Emery, R. E. 1982. Interparental conflict and the children of discord and divorce. *Psychological Bulletin,* 92:310–330.

Emler, N., Renwick, S., and Malone, B. 1983. The relationship between moral reasoning and political orientation. *Journal of Personality and Social Psychology,* 45:1073–1080.

Engen, T., Lipsitt, L. P., and Kaye, H. 1963. Olfactory responses and adaptation in the human neonate. *Journal of Physiology and Psychology,* 56:73–77.

———, ———, and Peck, M. B. 1974. Ability of newborn infants to discriminate sapid substances. *Developmental Psychology,* 10:741–744.

Epstein, A. S., and Radin, N. 1975. Motivational components related to father behavior and cognitive functioning in preschoolers. *Child Development,* 46:831–839.

Epstein, S. 1979. The stability of behavior: I. On predicting most of the people much of the time. *Journal of Personality and Social Psychology,* 37: 1097–1126.

———. 1980. The stability of behavior: II. Implications for psychological research. *American Psychologist,* 35: 790–806.

Epstein, S. H. 1983. Why do women live longer than men? *Science 83,* 4 (October):30–31.

Erikson, E. 1980. On the generational cycle. *International Journal of Psychoanalysis,* 61:213–223.

Erikson, E. H. 1959. Identity and the life cycle. *Monograph, Psychological Issues.* Vol. 1. New York: International Universities Press.

———. 1963. *Childhood and Society.* New York: Norton.

———. 1964*a*. *Insight and Responsibility.* New York: Norton.

———. 1964*b*. Inner and outer space: Reflections on womanhood. *Daedalus,* 93:582–606.

———. 1968*a*. Life cycle. In Sills, D. L. (ed.), *International Encyclopedia of the Social Sciences.* Vol. 9. New York: Free Press and Macmillan.

———. 1968*b*. *Identity: Youth and Crisis.* New York: Norton.

Ernst, C., and Angst, A. 1983. *Birth Order.* New York: Springer-Verlag.

Eron, L. D. 1982. Parent-child interaction, television violence, and aggression of children. *American Psychologist,* 37:197–211.

———, Huesmann, L. R., Brice, P., Fischer, P., and Mermelstein, R. 1983. Age trends in the development of aggression, sex typing, and related television habits. *Developmental Psychology,* 19:71–77.

Etaugh, C. 1980. Effects of nonmaternal care on children. *American Psychologist,* 35:309–319.

Etzel, B. C., and Gewirtz, J. L. 1967. Experimental modification of caretaker-maintained high-rate operant crying in a 6- and a 20-week-old infant *(Infans tyranno-tearus):* Extinction of crying with reinforcement of eye contact and smiling. *Journal of Experimental Child Psychology,* 5:303–317.

Evans, D. R., Newcombe, R. G., and Campbell, H. 1979. Maternal smoking habits and congenital malformations: A population study. *British Medical Journal,* 2:171–173.

Evans, R. B. 1972. Physical and biochemical characteristics of homosexual men. *Journal of Consulting and Clinical Psychology,* 39:140–147.

Fabricius, W. V., and Wellman, H. M. 1983. Children's understanding of retrieval cue utilization. *Developmental Psychology,* 19:15–21.

Fantz, R. L. 1963. Pattern vision in newborn infants. *Science,* 140:296–297.

———. 1966. Pattern discrimination and selective attention as determinants of perceptual development from birth. In Kidd, A. H., and Rivoire, J. F. (eds.), *Perceptual Development in Children.* New York: International Universities Press.

———. 1970. Visual perception and experience in infancy: Issues and approaches. In Lindsly, B., and Young, F. (eds.), *Early Experience and Visual Information Processing In Perceptual and Reading Disorders.* Washington, D.C.: National Academy of Sciences.

———, Fagan, J. F., and Miranda, S. B. 1975. Early visual selectivity. In Cohen, L. B., and Salapatek, P. (eds.), *Infant Perception: From Sensation to Cognition.* Vol. 1. New York: Academic Press.

———, and Miranda, S. B. 1975. Newborn infant attention to form of contour. *Child Development,* 46:224–228.

Farber, B. A. (ed.). 1983. *Stress and Burnout in the Human Service Professions.* Elmsford, N.Y.: Pergamon Press.

Farber, S. L. 1981. *Identical Twins Reared Apart.* New York: Basic Books.

Farberow, N. L., and Shneidman, S. E. 1961. *The Cry for Help.* New York: McGraw-Hill.

Farel, A. M. 1980. Effects of preferred maternal roles, maternal employment, and sociodemographic status on school adjustment and competence. *Child Development,* 51:1179–1186.

Farnen, R. F., Marklund, S., Oppenheim, A. W., and Torney, J. V. 1974. *International Studies in Evaluation VI: Civic Education in 10 Countries.* Stockholm: Almqvist and Wiksell.

Farrell, M. P., and Rosenberg, S. D. 1981. *Men at Midlife.* Boston: Auburn House.

Faust, M. S. 1960. Developmental maturity as a determinant in prestige of adolescent girls. *Child Development,* 31:173–186.

———. 1977. Somatic development of adolescent girls. *Monographs of the Society for Research in Child Development,* 42 (No. 1).

Featherman, D. L., and Hauser, R. M. 1978. Sexual inequalities and socioeconomic achievement in the U.S., 1962–1973. *American Sociological Review,* 41:462–483.

Fedak, L. 1981. Child rearing the "expert" way. *Columbus* (Ohio) *Dispatch* (April 10):C1.

———. 1982. Trapped in a diminishing world. *Columbus Dispatch* (February 17):C1.

Fein, G. 1981. Pretend play in childhood: An integrative review. *Child Development,* 52:1095–1118.

Feldman, S. S., and Nash, S. C. 1979. Sex differences in responsiveness to babies among mature adults. *Developmental Psychology,* 15:430–436.

Fenson, L., Kagan, J., Kearsley, R. B., and Zelazo, P. R. 1976. The developmental progression of manipulative play in the first two years. *Child Development,* 47:232–236.

Fenwick, R., and Barresi, C. M. 1981. Health consequences of marital-status change among the elderly: A comparison of cross-sectional and longitudinal analyses. *Journal of Health and Social Behavior,* 22:106–116.

Ferreira, A. J. 1969. *Prenatal Environment.* Springfield, Ill.: Charles C Thomas.

Feshbach, S. 1970. Aggression. In Mussen, P. H. (ed.), *Carmichael's Manual of Child Psychology,* 3rd ed. Vol. 2. New York: Wiley.

Festinger, L., Schachter, S., and Back, K. 1950. *Social Pressures in Informal Groups.* New York: Harper & Row.

Feuerstein, R. 1979. *The Dynamic Assessment of Retarded Performers.* Baltimore, Md.: University Park Press.

———. 1980. *Instrumental Enrichment.* Baltimore, Md.: University Park Press.

Fialka, J. J. 1982. Long-term federal study on aging debunks some old medical ideas. *Wall Street Journal* (March 30):29.

Field, D. 1981. Can preschool children really learn to conserve? *Child Development,* 52:326–334.

Field, J. 1977. Coordination of vision and prehension in young infants. *Child Development,* 48:97–103.

———, Muir, D., Pilon, R., Sinclair, M., and Dodwell, P. 1980. Infants' orientation to lateral sounds from birth to three months. *Child Development,* 51:295–298.

Field, T. M., Woodson, R., Greenberg, R., and Cohen, D. 1982. Discrimination and imitation of facial expressions by neonates. *Child Development,* 218: 179–181.

Fields, C. M. 1981. Minors found able to decide on taking part in research. *The Chronicle of Higher Education* (September 9):7.

Fincher, J. 1982. Before their time. *Science 82,* 3 (July):68–78.

Findlay, S. 1983. Study finds family link to heart ills. *USA Today* (December 6):1.

Finkelhor, D. 1979. *Sexually Victimized Children.* New York: Free Press.

Fischer, L. R. 1981. Transitions in the mother-daughter relationship. *Journal of Marriage and the Family,* 43:613–622.

Fish, M., and Crockenberg, S. 1981. Correlates and antecedents of nine-month infant behavior and mother-infant interaction. *Infant Behavior and Development,* 4:69–81.

Fisher, C. B., Ferdinandsen, K., and Bornstein, M. H. 1981. The role of symmetry in infant form discrimination. *Child Development,* 52:457–462.

Fishman, B. 1983. The economic behavior of stepfamilies. *Family Relations,* 32:359–366.

———, and Hamel, B. 1981. From nuclear to stepfamily ideology. *Alternative Lifestyles,* 4:181–204.

Fisichelli, V., and Karelitz, S. 1963. The cry latencies of normal infants and those with brain damage. *Journal of Pediatrics,* 62:724–734.

Fitts, P. M., and Posner, M. I. 1967. *Human Performance.* Belmont, Calif.: Wadsworth.

Fitzsimmons, S. J., Cheever, J., Leonard, E., and Macunovich, D. 1969. School failures: Now and tomorrow. *Developmental Psychology,* 1:134–146.

Flanagan, J. C. 1978. A research approach to improving our quality of life. *American Psychologist,* 33:138–147.

Flaste, R. 1977. Survey finds that most children are happy at home but fear world. *New York Times* (March 2):A12.

Flavell, J. H. 1963. *The Developmental Psychology of Jean Piaget.* Princeton, N.J.: Van Nostrand.

———. 1974. The development of inferences about others. In Mischel, T. (ed.), *Understanding Other Persons.* Oxford: Blackwell.

———. 1978. Developmental stage: Explanans or explanandum? *Behavioral and Brain Sciences,* 1:187.

———. 1982. On cognitive development. *Child Development,* 53:1–10.

———, and Wohlwill, J. F. 1969. Formal and functional aspects of cognitive development. In Elkind, D., and Flavell, J. H. (eds.), *Studies in Cognitive Development: Essays in Honor of Jean Piaget.* New York: Oxford University Press.

Fleming, E. S., and Anttonen, R. G. 1971. Teacher expectancy as related to the academic and personal growth of primary-age children. *Monographs of the Society for Research in Child Development,* 36 (5).

Fletcher, J. C., and Evans, M. I. 1983. Maternal bonding in early fetal ultrasound examinations. *New England Journal of Medicine,* 308:392–393.

Folkman, S., and Lazarus, R. S. 1980. An analysis of coping in a middle-aged community sample. *Journal of Health and Social Behavior,* 21:219–239.

Foner, A., and Kertzer, D. 1978. Transitions over the life course: Lessons from age-set societies. *American Journal of Sociology,* 83:1081–1104.

Foote, C. 1978. Minding the new physics. *Human Behavior,* 7 (October):28–31.

Ford, D. A. 1983. Wife battery and criminal justice: A study of victim decision making. *Family Relations,* 32:463–476.

Formanek, R. 1983. How children's fears are changing. *U.S. News & World Report* (August 22):43–44.

Fortes, M. 1949. *The Web of Kinship Among the Tallensi.* Fair Lawn, N.J.: Oxford University Press.

Fox, R., Aslin, R. N., Shea, S. L., and Dumais, S. T. 1980. Stereopsis in human infants. *Science,* 207:323–324.

Fozard, J. L. 1977. Visual perception and communication. In Birren, J. E., and Schaie, K. W. (eds.), *Handbook of the Psychology of Aging.* New York: Van Nostrand.

———, and Popkin, S. J. 1978. Optimizing adult development. *American Psychologist,* 33:975–989.

Fraiberg, S. H. 1959. *The Magic Years.* New York: Scribner.

———. 1977. *Every Child's Birthright.* New York: Basic Books.

Fraker, S. 1984. Why women aren't getting to the top. *Fortune* (April 16):40–45.

Francis-Williams, J., and Davies, P. A. 1974. Very low birth-weight and later intelligence. *Developmental Medicine and Child Neurology,* 16:709–728.

Frankel, M. S. 1978. Social, legal, and political responses to ethical issues in the use of children as experimental subjects. *Journal of Social Issues,* 34:101–113.

Franks, D. R., and Marolla, J. 1976. Efficacious action and social approval as interacting dimensions of self-esteem: A tentative formulation through construct validation. *Sociometry,* 39:324–341.

Freedman, D. G. 1974. *Human Infancy: An Evolutionary Perspective.* New York: Halsted Press.

Freud, A. 1936. *The Ego and the Mechanisms of Defense.* New York: International Universities Press.

———. 1958. Adolescence. *Psychoanalytic Study of the Child,* 16:225–278.

Freud, S. 1930/1961. *Civilization and Its Discontents.* London: Hogarth.

———. 1952. *An Autobiographical Study.* New York: Norton.

Freudenberger, H. J., and Richelson, G. 1981. *Burn-Out.* New York: Bantam.

Freudenheim, M. 1983. Hospices for the dying show dramatic growth. *New York Times* (December 24):8.

Friedman, M., and Rosenman, R. 1974. *Type A Behavior and Your Heart.* New York: Knopf.

Friedrich, L. K., and Stein, A. H. 1973. Aggressive and prosocial television programs and the natural behavior of preschool children. *Monographs of the Society for Research in Child Development,* 38 (No. 151).

———, and ———. 1975. Prosocial television and young children: The effects of verbal labeling and role playing on learning and behavior. *Child Development,* 46:27–38.

Friend, R. M., and Neale, J. M. 1972. Children's perceptions of success and failure. *Developmental Psychology,* 7:124–128.

Frisch, R. E. 1978. Menarche and fatness. *Science,* 200 (June 30):1509–1513.

Frodi, A., and Lamb, M. 1978. Sex differences in responsiveness to infants: A developmental study of psychophysiological and behavioral responses. *Child Development,* 49:1182–1188.

———, ———, Leavitt, L. A., Donovan, W. L., Neff, C., and Sherry, D. 1978. Fathers' and mothers' responses to the faces and cries of normal and premature infants. *Developmental Psychology,* 14:490–498.

Fromm, E. 1947. *Man for Himself.* New York: Holt, Rinehart and Winston.

Fuqua, R. W., Bartsch, T. W., and Phye, G. D. 1975. An investigation of the relationship between cognitive tempo and creativity in preschool-age children. *Child Development,* 46:779–782.

Furman, W., and Bierman, K. L. 1983. Developmental changes in young children's conceptions of friendship. *Child Development,* 54:549–556.

Galbraith, R. C. 1982. Sibling spacing and intellectual development: A closer look at the confluence models. *Developmental Psychology,* 18:151–173.

Gallup Report. 1982. *Religion in America.* Report Nos. 201–202 (June–July). Princeton, N.J.

Gallup Youth Survey. 1980. Computers hit career list. *Columbus* (Ohio) *Dispatch* (March 12):A13.

Gappa, J. M., O'Barr, J. F., and St. John-Parsons, D. 1980. The dual-career couple and academe: Can both prosper? *Anthropology Newsletter,* 21: 16+.

Garbarino, J., and Crouter, A. 1978. Defining the community context for parent-child relations: The correlates of child maltreatment. *Child Development,* 49:604–616.

———, and Sherman, D. 1980. High-risk neighborhoods and high-risk families: The human ecology of child maltreatment. *Child Development,* 51:188–198.

Garcia, J. 1972. IQ: The conspiracy. *Psychology Today,* 6 (September):40–43ff.

Gardner, H. 1976. The grasp of consciousness. *New York Times Book Review* (August 1):1–2.

———. 1978. *The Children of Prosperity.* New York: St. Martin's.

———. 1979. Getting acquainted with Jean Piaget. *New York Times* (January 3):C1, C9.

Gardner, L. 1972. Deprivation dwarfism. *Scientific American,* 227 (July):76–82.

Garfinkel, B. D., Froese, A., and Hood, J. 1982. Suicide attempts in children and adolescents. *American Journal of Psychiatry,* 139:1257–1261.

Garibaldi, R. A., Brodine, S., and Matsumiya, S. 1981. Infections among patients in nursing homes. *New England Journal of Medicine,* 305:731–735.

Garvey, C., and Hogan, R. 1973. Social speech and social interaction: Egocentrism revisited. *Child Development,* 44:562-568.

Garwood, S. G. 1976. First-name stereotypes as a factor in self-concept and school achievement. *Journal of Educational Psychology,* 68:482–487.

Gasser, R. D., and Taylor, C. M. 1976. Role adjustment of single parent fathers with dependent children. *Family Coordinator,* 25:397–401.

Gaudia, G. 1972. Race, social class, and age of achievement of conservation on Piaget's tasks. *Developmental Psychology,* 6:158–165.

Gay, J., and Tweney, R. D. 1975. Comprehension and production of standard and black English by lower-class black children. *Developmental Psychology,* 12:262–268.

Geber, M. 1958. The psycho-motor development of African children in the first year, and the influence of maternal behavior. *Journal of Social Psychology,* 47:185–195.

———, and Dean, R. F. 1957*a.* Gesell tests on African children. *Pediatrics,* 20:1055–1065.

———, and ———. 1957*b.* The state of

development of newborn African children. *Lancet,* 1:1216–1219.

Gelfand, D. M., Hartmann, D. P., Cromer, C. C., Smith, C. L., and Page, B. C. 1975. The effects of instructional prompts and praise on children's donation rates. *Child Development,* 46:980–983.

Gelles, R. J. 1979. *Family Violence.* Beverly Hills: Sage Publications.

———. 1980. Violence in the family: A review of research in the seventies. *Journal of Marriage and the Family,* 42:873–885.

———, and Straus, M. A. 1979. Violence in the American family. *Journal of Social Issues,* 35:15–39.

Gelman, D. 1983. A great emptiness. *Newsweek* (November 7): 120–126.

Gelman, R. 1969. Conservation acquisition: A problem of learning to attend to relevant attributes. *Journal of Experimental Child Psychology,* 7:167–187.

———, and Gallistel, C. R. 1978. *The Child's Understanding of Number.* Cambridge, Mass.: Harvard University Press.

General Mills. 1981. *Families: Strengths and Strains at Work.* Minneapolis: Louis Harris and Associates.

George, L. K., and Maddox, G. L. 1977. Subjective adaptation to loss of the work role: A longitudinal study. *Journal of Gerontology,* 32:456–462.

Gerall, A. A. 1973. Influence of perinatal androgen on reproductive capacity. In Zubin, J., and Money, J. (eds.), *Contemporary Sexual Behavior: Critical Issues in the 1970s.* Baltimore: Johns Hopkins University Press.

Gerard, A. 1970. *Please Breast-Feed Your Baby.* New York: New American Library.

Geschwind, N. 1979. Specializations of the human brain. *Scientific American,* 241 (September):180–199.

Gesell, A. 1928. *Infancy and Human Growth.* New York: Macmillan.

———, and Ames, L. B. 1947. The development of handedness. *Journal of Genetic Psychology,* 70:155–175.

Gewirtz, J. L. 1965. The course of infant smiling in four child-rearing environments in Israel. In Foss, B. M. (ed.), *Determinants of Infant Behavior.* Vol. 3. New York: Wiley.

———. 1972. *Attachment and Dependency.* Washington, D.C.: Winston.

Gibson, E. J. 1969. *Principles of Perceptual Learning and Development.* New York: Appleton-Century-Crofts.

———, and Walk, R. D. 1960. The "visual cliff." *Scientific American,* 202 (April):64–71.

Gilligan, C. 1982. Why should a woman be more like a man? *Psychology Today,* 16 (June):68–77.

Gilligan, C. F. 1963. Responses to temptation: An analysis of motives. Unpublished doctoral dissertation, Harvard University.

Gilman, A. D. 1984. Grandma junkies. *Health* (January): 52–55.

Ginsburg, H., and Opper, S. 1969. *Piaget's Theory of Intellectual Development.* Englewood Cliffs, N.J.: Prentice-Hall.

Ginzberg, E. 1982. The mechanization of work. *Scientific American,* 247 (September):67–75.

Glamser, F. D. 1976. Determinants of a positive attitude toward retirement. *Journal of Gerontology,* 31:104–107.

Glaser, B. G., and Strauss, A. L. 1965. Temporal aspects of dying as a nonscheduled status passage. *American Journal of Sociology,* 71:48–59.

Glass, D. C., Neulinger, J., and Brim, O. G., Jr. 1974. Birth order, verbal intelligence, and educational aspiration. *Child Development,* 45:807–811.

Glenn, N. D. 1975. Psychological well-being in the post-parental stage: Some evidence from national surveys. *Journal of Marriage and the Family,* 37:105–110.

———. 1981. Age, birth cohorts, and drinking: An illustration of the hazards of inferring effects from cohort data. *Journal of Gerontology,* 36:362–369.

———, and McLanahan, S. 1981. The effects of offspring on the psychological well-being of older adults. *Journal of Marriage and the Family,* 43:409–421.

———, and Weaver, C. N. 1981. The contribution of marital happiness to global happiness. *Journal of Marriage and the Family,* 43:161–168.

———, and ———. 1982. Enjoyment of work by full-time workers in the U.S., 1955 and 1980. *Public Opinion Quarterly,* 46:459–470.

Glick, P. C. 1984. How American families are changing. *American Demographics,* 6 (January):21–25.

Gloger-Tippelt, G. 1983. A process model of the pregnancy course. *Human Development,* 26:134–148.

Gluckman, M. 1955. *Custom and Conflict in Africa.* Oxford: Blackwell.

Glueck, S., and Glueck, E. 1957. Working mothers and delinquency. *Mental Hygiene,* 41:327–352.

Godbey, G. 1979. Theory of the leisure mass. *Public Opinion,* 2 (August/September):47–48.

Goetz, T. E., and Dweck, C. S. 1980. Learned helplessness in social situations. *Journal of Personality and Social Psychology,* 39:246–255.

Goffman, E. 1961. *Encounters.* Indianapolis: Bobbs-Merrill.

———. 1963. *Stigma.* Englewood Cliffs, N.J.: Prentice-Hall.

Gold, D., and Andres, D. 1978*a.* Comparisons of adolescent children with employed and nonemployed mothers. *Merrill-Palmer Quarterly,* 24:243–254.

———, and ———. 1978*b.* Developmental comparisons between ten-year-old children with employed and nonemployed mothers. *Child Development,* 49:75–84.

Goldberg, H. 1976. *The Hazards of Being Male: Surviving the Myth of Masculine Privilege.* New York: Nash.

Goldfarb, W. 1945. Psychological privation in infancy and subsequent adjustment. *American Journal of Orthopsychiatry,* 15:247–255.

———. 1947. Variations in adolescent adjustment of institutionally reared children. *American Journal of Orthopsychiatry,* 17:449–457.

———. 1949. Rorschach test differences between family-reared, institution-reared, and schizophrenic children. *American Journal of Orthopsychiatry,* 19:624–633.

Goldin-Meadow, S., and Feldman, H. 1977. The development of language-like communication without a language model. *Science,* 197:401–403.

———, and Mylander, C. 1983. Gestural communication in deaf children: Noneffect of parental input on language development. *Science,* 221: 372–373.

Goldstein, J., Freud, A., and Solnit, A. J. 1973. *Beyond the Best Interests of the Child.* New York: Macmillan.

Goldstein, K. M., Caputo, D. V., and Taub, H. B. 1976. The effects of prenatal and perinatal complications on development at one year of age. *Child Development,* 47:613–621.

Goleman, D. 1981. Forgetfulness of things past. *Psychology Today,* 15 (October):17–20.

———. 1984. The aging mind proves capable of lifetime growth. *New York Times* (February 21):17, 20.

Goode, W. J. 1956. *Women in Divorce.* New York: Free Press.

———. 1959. The theoretical importance of love. *American Sociological Review,* 24:38–47.

Goodman, M. E. 1952. *Race Awareness in Young Children.* Reading, Mass.: Addison-Wesley.

Goodman, M. J., Stewart, C. J., and Gilbert, F., Jr. 1977. Patterns of menopause: A study of certain medical and physiological variables among Caucasian and Japanese women living in Hawaii. *Journal of Gerontology,* 32:291–298.

Goodstein, R. K., and Page, A. W. 1981. Battered wife syndrome: Overview of dynamics and treatment. *American Journal of Psychiatry,* 138:1036–1044.

Goodwin, L. 1972. *Do the Poor Want to Work?* Washington, D.C.: The Brookings Institution.

Goodwin, R. S., and Michel, G. F. 1981. Head orientation position during birth and in infant neonatal period, and hand preference at nineteen weeks. *Child Development,* 52:819–826.

Gorman, J. J., Cogan, D. G., and Gellis, S. S. 1957. Apparatus for grading the visual acuity of infants on the basis of opticokinetic nystagmus. *Pediatrics,* 19:1088–1092.

Gottfried, A. W., and Rose, S. A. 1980. Tactile recognition memory in infants. *Child Development,* 51:69–74.

———, Wallace-Lande, P., Sherman-Brown, S., King, J., and Coen, C. 1981. Physical and social environment of newborn infants in special care units. *Science,* 214 (November 6):673–675.

Gottman, J. M. 1983. How children become friends. *Monographs of the Society for Research in Child Development,* 48 (201).

Gottschalk, E. C., Jr. 1983. The aging made gains in the 1970s, outpacing rest of the population. *Wall Street Journal* (February 17):1, 16.

Gough, E. K. 1960. Is the family universal? The Nayar case. In Bell, N. W., and Vogel, E. F. (eds.), *A Modern Introduction to the Family.* New York: Free Press.

Gould, R. L. 1962. The phases of adult life: A study in developmental psychology. *American Journal of Psychiatry,* 129:33–43.

———. 1978. *Transformations.* New York: Simon & Schuster.

Graham, F. K., Ernhart, C. B., Thurston, D., and Craft, M. 1962. Development three years after perinatal anoxia and other potentially damaging newborn experiences. *Psychological Monographs,* 76(3, Whole No. 522).

———, Matarazzo, R. C., and Caldwell, B. M. 1956. Behavioral differences between normal and traumatized newborns: II. Standardization, reliability, and validity. *Psychological Monographs,* 70 (21, Whole No. 428).

Graney, M. J. 1975. Happiness and social participation in aging. *Journal of Gerontology,* 30:701–706.

Gratch, G. 1975. Recent studies based on Piaget's view of object concept development. In Cohen, L. B., and Salapatek, P. (eds.), *Infant Perception: From Sensation to Cognition.* Vol. 2. New York: Academic Press.

———. 1979. The development of thought and language in infancy. In Osofsky, J. D. (ed.), *Handbook of Infant Development.* New York: Wiley.

———. 1982. Responses to hidden persons and things by 5-, 9-, and 16-month-old infants in a visual tracking situation. *Developmental Psychology,* 18:232–237.

Green, R. 1974. *Sexual Identity: Conflict in Children and Adults.* New York: Basic Books.

Greenberg, D. J., Hillman, D., and Grice, D. 1973. Infant and stranger variables related to stranger anxiety in the first year of life. *Developmental Psychology,* 9:207–212.

Greenberg, J. 1981*a.* Unstable emotions of children tied to poor diet. *New York Times* (August 18):15, 17.

———. 1981*b.* Study finds widowers die more quickly than widows. *New York Times* (July 3):1, 7.

Greenberg, R. P., and Fisher, S. 1978. Testing Dr. Freud. *Human Behavior* (September):28–33.

Greenberger, E., and Steinberg, L. 1981. The workplace as a context for the socialization of youth. *Journal of Youth and Adolescence,* 10:185–210.

———, and ———. 1983. Sex differences in early labor force experience: Harbinger of things to come. *Social Forces,* 62:467–486.

Greenblatt, M. 1978. The grieving spouse. *American Journal of Psychiatry,* 135:43–47.

Greenfield, P. M. 1966. On culture and conservation. In Bruner, J., Olver, R. R., and Greenfield, P. M. (eds.), *Studies in Cognitive Growth.* New York: Wiley.

———, and Bruner, J. S. 1971. Work with the Wolof. *Psychology Today,* 2 (July):40–43ff.

———, and Smith, J. H. 1976. *The Structure of Communication in Early Language Development.* New York: Academic Press.

Greenman, G. W. 1963. Visual behavior of newborn infants. In Solnit, A. J., and Provence, S. A. (eds.), *Modern Perspectives in Child Development.* New York: International Universities Press.

Greif, E. B., and Ulman, K. J. 1982. The psychological impact of menarche on early adolescent females: A review of the literature. *Child Development,* 53:1413–1430.

Greyson, B., and Stevenson, I. 1980. The phenomenology of near-death experiences. *American Journal of Psychiatry,* 137:1193–1196.

Grice, H. P. 1968. Utterer's meaning, sentence-meaning, and word-meaning. *Foundations of Language,* 4:1–18.

Gronlund, N. E. 1959. *Sociometry in the Classroom.* New York: Harper & Row.

Gross, A. 1977. Marriage counseling for unwed couples. *New York Times Magazine* (April 24):52ff.

Grossman, F. K., Eichler, L. S., and Winickoff, S. S. 1980. *Pregnancy, Birth and Parenthood.* San Francisco: Jossey-Bass.

Grossmann, K., Thane, K., and Grossmann, K. E. 1981. Maternal tactual contact of the newborn after various postpartum conditions of mother-infant contact. *Developmental Psychology,* 17:158–169.

Grotevant, H. D. 1978. Sibling constellations and sex typing of interests in adolescence. *Child Development,* 49:540–542.

———, Scarr, S., and Weinberg, R. A. 1977*a.* Intellectual development in family constellations with adopted and natural children: A test of the Zajonc and Markus model. *Child Development,* 48:1699–1703.

———, ———, and ———. 1977*b.* Patterns of interest similarity in adoptive and biological families. *Journal of Personality and Social Psychology,* 35:667–676.

———, ———, and ———. 1978. *Psychology Today,* 11 (March):88–90.

Grove, W. M. 1982. Psychometric detection of schizotypy. *Psychological Bulletin,* 92:27–38.

Gruenberg, B. 1980. The happy worker: An analysis of educational and occupational differences in determinants of job satisfaction. *American Journal of Sociology,* 86:247–271.

Gruendel, J. M. 1977. Referential extension in early language development. *Child Development,* 48:1567–1576.

Grusec, J. E., and Kuczynski, L. 1981. Direction of effect in socialization: A comparison of the parent's versus the child's behavior as determinants of disciplinary techniques. *Developmental Psychology,* 16:1–9.

———, ———, Rushton, J. P., and Simutis, Z. M. 1979. Learning resistance to temptation through observation. *Developmental Psychology,* 15:233–240.

———, and Skubiski, S. L. 1970. Model nurturance, demand characteristics of the modeling experiment, and altruism. *Journal of Personality and Social Psychology,* 14:352–359.

Gubrium, J. F. 1974. Marital desolation and the evaluation of everyday life in old age. *Journal of Marriage and the Family,* 36:107–113.

Guilford, J. P. 1967. *The Nature of Human Intelligence.* New York: McGraw-Hill.

Guillemin, R. 1982. Growth hormone-releasing factor from a human pancreatic tumor that caused acromegaly. *Science,* 218:585–587.

Gutmann, D. 1969. The country of old men: Cross-cultural studies in the psychology of later life. Occasional Papers in Gerontology No. 5. Ann Arbor: Institute of Gerontology, University of Michigan-Wayne State.

———. 1977. The cross-cultural perspective. In Birren, J. E., and Schaie, K. W. (eds.), *Handbook of the Psychology of Aging.* New York: Van Nostrand.

Guttmacher, A. F. 1973. *Pregnancy, Birth and Family Planning.* New York: New American Library.

Haaf, R. 1974. Complexity and facial resemblance as determinants of response to facelike stimuli by 5- and 10-week-old infants. *Journal of Experimental Child Psychology,* 18:480–487.

Hadden, J. K., and Swann, C. E. 1981. *Prime Time Preachers: The Rising Power of Televangelism.* Reading, Mass.: Addison-Wesley.

Hagestad, G., and Smyer, M. 1983. Divorce at middle-age. In Weissman, S., Cohen, R., and Cohler, B. (eds.), *Dissolving Personal Relationships.* New York: Academic Press.

Haith, M. H., and Campos, J. J. 1977. Human infancy. In Rosenzweig, M. R., and Porter, L. W. (eds.), *Annual Review of Psychology.* Vol. 28. Palo Alto, Calif.: Annual Reviews Inc.

Haith, M. M. 1980. *Rules That Babies Look By: The Organization of Newborn Visual Activity.* Hillsdale, N.J.: Erlbaum.

———, Bergman, T., and Moore, M. J. 1977. Eye contact and face scanning in early infancy. *Science,* 198:853–854.

———, and Goodman, G. S. 1982. Eye-movement control in newborns in darkness and in unstructured light. *Child Development,* 53:974–977.

Hall, E. T. 1966. *The Hidden Dimension,* Garden City, N.Y.: Doubleday.

Hall, G. S. 1891. *Notes on the Study of Infants.* The Pedagogical Seminary, 1:127–138.

———. 1904. *Adolescence.* Vols. 1 and 2. New York: Appleton-Century-Crofts.

Hallinan, M. T. 1982. Classroom racial composition and children's friendships. *Social Forces,* 61:56–72.

Halverson, H. M. 1931. An experimental study of prehension in infants by means of systematic cinema records. *Genetic Psychology Monographs,* 10:107–286.

Hamachek, D. E. 1977. Humanistic psychology: Theoretical-philosophical framework and implications for teaching. In Treffinger, D. J., Davis, J. K., and Ripple, R. E. (eds.), *Handbook on Teaching Educational Psychology.* New York: Academic Press.

Hamm, N. H., and Hoving, K. L. 1969. Conformity of children in an ambiguous perceptual situation. *Child Development,* 40:773–783.

Hardyck, C., and Petrinovich, L. F. 1977. Left-handedness. *Psychological Bulletin,* 84:385–404.

Harkins, E. B. 1978. Effects of empty nest transition on self-report of psychological and physical well-being. *Journal of Marriage and the Family,* 40:549–556.

Harkness, S., Edwards, C. P., and Super, C. M. 1981. Social roles and moral reasoning: A case study in a rural African community. *Developmental Psychology,* 17:595–603.

Harlow, H. F. 1971. *Learning to Love.* San Francisco: Albion.

Harnqvist, K. 1975. The international study of educational achievement. In Kerlinger, K. N. (ed.), *Review of Research in Education.* Itasca, Ill.: Peacock.

Harper, P. A., and Wiener, G. 1965. Sequelae of low birthweight. *Annual Review of Medicine,* 16:405–420.

Harper, T. 1978. It's not true about people 65 or over. *Green Bay* (Wis.) *Press-Gazette* (November 15):D1.

Harré, R. 1980. What's in a nickname? *Psychology Today,* 13 (January):78–84.

Harris, L. 1981. *Aging in the Eighties: America in Transition.* Washington, D.C.: National Council on Aging.

Harris, Louis, and Associates. 1979. The Playboy report on American men. *Playboy,* 26 (March):91+.

Harris, M. B. 1970. Reciprocity and generosity: Some determinants of sharing in children. *Child Development,* 41:313–326.

———. 1971. Models, norms, and sharing. *Psychological Reports,* 29:147–153.

Harry, J., and Lovely, R. 1979. Gay marriages and communities of sexual orientation. *Alternative Lifestyles,* 2: 177–200.

Hartshorne, H., and May, M. A. 1928. *Studies in the Nature of Character.* Vol. 1: *Studies in Deceit.* New York: Macmillan.

———, ———, and Maller, J. B. 1929. *Studies in the Nature of Character.* Vol. 2: *Studies in Self-Control.* New York: Macmillan.

———, ———, and Shuttleworth, F. K. 1930. *Studies in the Nature of Character.* Vol. 3: *Studies in the Organization of Character.* New York: Macmillan.

Hartup, W. W. 1970. Peer interaction and social organization. In Mussen, P. H. (ed.), *Carmichael's Manual of Child Psychology,* 3rd ed. Vol. 2. New York: Wiley.

Harvey, C. D., and Bahr, H. M. 1974. Widowhood, morale, and affiliation. *Journal of Marriage and the Family,* 36:97–106.

Harvey, D. G., and Slatin, G. T. 1975. The relationship between child's SES and teacher expectations: A test of middle-class bias hypothesis. *Social Forces.* 54:140–159.

Haskett, G. J. 1971. Modification of peer preferences of first-grade children. *Developmental Psychology,* 4:429–433.

Havighurst, R. J. 1973. Social roles, work, leisure, and education. In Eisdorfer, C., and Lawton, M. P. (eds.), *The Psychology of Adult Development and Aging.* Washington, D.C.: American Psychology Association.

———, Neugarten, B. L., and Tobin, S. S. 1968. Disengagement and patterns of aging. In Neugarten, B. L. (ed.), *Middle Age and Aging.* Chicago: University of Chicago Press.

Hawley, W. D. 1979. Getting the facts straight about the effects of school desegregation. *Educational Leadership,* 36:314–321.

Hayes, L. A., and Watson, J. S. 1981. Neonatal imitation: Fact or artifact? *Developmental Psychology,* 17:655–660.

Hayflick, L. 1980. The cell biology of aging. *Scientific American,* 242 (January):58–65.

Haynes, H., White, B. L., and Held, R. 1965. Visual accommodation in human infants. *Science,* 148:528–530.

Hayslip, B., and Sterns, H. L. 1979. Age differences in relationships between crystallized and fluid intelligences and problem solving. *Journal of Gerontology,* 34:404–414.

Head, J. 1984. Death cluster areas studied. *USA Today* (March 16):3A.

Heinicke, C. M., Diskin, S. D., Ramsey-Klee, D. M., and Given, K. 1983. Pre-birth parent characteristics and family development in the first year of life. *Child Development,* 54:194–208.

Heinonen, O. P., Slone, D., Monson, R. R., Hook, E. B., and Shapiro, S. 1977. Cardiovascular birth defects and antenatal exposure to female sex hormones. *New England Journal of Medicine,* 296:67–70.

———, ———, and Shapiro, S. 1977. *Birth Defects and Drugs in Pregnancy.* Littleton, Mass.: Publishing Sciences Group.

Heinstein, M. I. 1963. Behavioral correlations of breast-bottle regimens under varying parent-child relationships. *Monographs of the Society for Research in Child Development,* 28 (4).

Helfer, R. E., and Kempe, C. H. 1977. *The Battered Child.* Chicago: University of Chicago Press.

Hendry, L. B., and Gillies, P. 1978. Body type, body esteem, school, and leisure: A study of overweight, average, and underweight adolescents. *Journal of Youth and Adolescence,* 7:181–195.

Henig, R. M. 1978. Exposing the myth of senility. *New York Times Magazine* (December 3):158+.

———. 1981. The child savers. *New York Times Magazine* (March 22):34–44.

———. 1982. Saving babies before birth. *New York Times Magazine* (February 28):18–48.

Henze, L. F., and Hudson, J. W. 1974. Personal and family characteristics of cohabiting college students. *Journal of Marriage and the Family,* 36:722–726.

Herdt, G. H. 1981. *Guardian of the Flutes: Idioms of Masculinity.* New York: McGraw-Hill.

——— (ed). 1982. *Rituals of Manhood.* Berkeley: University of California Press.

Herman, J., and Hirschman, L. 1981. Families at risk for father-daughter incest. *American Journal of Psychiatry,* 138:967–970.

Herodotus. 1964. *The Histories.* Trans. by Aubrey de Selincourt. London: Penguin.

Herrenkohl, R. C., and Herrenkohl, E. C. 1981. Some antecedents and developmental consequences of child maltreatment. *New Directions for Child Development,* 11:57–76.

Herron, J. 1976. Southpaws: How different are they? *Psychology Today,* 9 (March):50–56.

———. 1979. *Neuropsychology of Left-Handedness.* New York: Academic Press.

Herron, R. E., and Sutton-Smith, B. 1971. *Child's Play.* New York: Wiley.

Hershenson, M. 1975. Visual discrimination in the human newborn. *Journal of Comparative and Physiological Psychology,* 58:270–278.

———. 1967. Development of the perception of form. *Psychological Bulletin,* 67:326–336.

———, Kessen, W., and Munsinger, H. 1967. Ocular orientation in the human newborn infant: A close look at some positive and negative results. In Wathen-Dunn, W. (ed.), *Models for the Perception of Speech and Visual Form.* Cambridge, Mass.: MIT Press.

Hess, B. B. 1979. Sex roles, friendship, and the life course. *Research on Aging,* 1:494–515.

———, and Markson, E. W. 1980. *Aging and Old Age: An Introduction to Social Gerontology.* New York: Macmillan.

———, and Waring, J. M. 1978. Parent and child in later life: Rethinking the relationship. In Lerner, R. M., and Spanier, G. B. (eds.), *Child Influences on Marital and Family Interaction.* New York: Academic Press.

Hess, T. M., and Higgins, J. N. 1983. Context utilization in young and old adults. *Journal of Gerontology,* 38:65–71.

Hetherington, E. M. 1979. Divorce. *American Psychologist,* 34:851–858.

———, Cox, M., and Cox, R. 1976. Divorced fathers. *Family Coordinator,* 25:417–427.

———, ———, and ———. 1977. Divorced fathers. *Psychology Today,* 10 (April):42–46.

Heyneman, S. P. 1976. Influences on academic achievement: A comparison of results from Uganda and more industrialized societies. *Sociology of Education,* 49:200–211.

Heyns, B. 1974. Social selection and stratification within schools. *American Journal of Sociology,* 79:1434–1451.

Hilberman, E. 1980. Overview: The "wife-beater's wife" reconsidered. *American Journal of Psychiatry,* 137:1336–1347.

Hill, E. A., and Dorfman, L. T. 1982. Reaction of housewives to the retirement of their husbands. *Family Relations,* 31:195–200.

Hill, J. P., and Kochendorfer, R. A. 1969. Knowledge of peer success and risk of detection as determinants of cheating. *Developmental Psychology,* 1:231–238.

Hill, R. 1964. Methodological issues in family development research. *Family Process,* 3:186–206.

———, and Aldous, J., Jr. 1969. Socialization for marriage and parenthood. In Goslin, D. (ed.), *Handbook of Socialization Theory and Research.* Chicago: Rand McNally.

Himmelberger, D. V., Brown, B. W., Jr., and Cohen, E. N. 1978. Cigarette smoking during pregnancy and the occurrence of spontaneous abortion and congenital abnormality. *American Journal of Epidemiology,* 108:470–479.

Hinds, M. D. 1981*a.* Midfwife births gaining wider acceptance. *New York Times* (January 24):18.

———. 1981*b.* The child victim of incest. *New York Times* (June 15):22.

———. 1982. Countries acting on baby formula. *New York Times* (May 2):10.

Hines, M. 1982. Prenatal gonadal hormones and sex differences in human behavior. *Psychological Bulletin,* 92:56–80.

Hinkle, L. E., Jr. 1974. The effect of exposure to culture change, social change, and changes in interpersonal relationships on health. In Dohrenwend, B. S., and Dohrenwend, B. P. (eds.), *Stressful Life Events: Their Nature and Effects.* New York: Wiley.

Hiroto, D. S. 1974. Locus of control and learned helplessness. *Journal of Experimental Psychology,* 102:187–193.

Hite, S. 1976. *The Hite Report.* New York: Macmillan.

Hobbs, D. F., Jr. 1965. Parenthood as crisis: A third study. *Journal of Marriage and the Family,* 27:367–382.

———. 1968. Transition to parenthood: A replication and an extension. *Journal of Marriage and the Family,* 30:413–417.

———, and Cole, S. P. 1976. Transition to parenthood: A decade replication. *Journal of Marriage and the Family,* 38:723–731.

Hobbs, N., and Robinson, S. 1982. Adolescent development and public policy. *American Psychologist,* 37:212–223.

Hochschild, A. R. 1975. Disengagement theory: A critique and proposal. *American Sociological Review,* 40:553–569.

Hoff-Ginsberg, E., and Shatz, M. 1982. Linguistic input and the child's acquisition of language. *Psychological Bulletin,* 92:3–26.

Hoffman, L. W. 1974. Effects of maternal employment on the child—A review of the research. *Developmental Psychology,* 10:204–228.

———, and Nye, F. I. 1974. *Working Mothers.* San Francisco: Jossey-Bass.

Hoffman, M. L. 1970. Moral development. In Mussen, P. H. (ed.), *Carmichael's Manual of Child Psychology,* 3rd ed. Vol. 2. New York: Wiley.

———. 1971. Father absence and conscience development. *Developmental Psychology,* 4:400–406.

Hogan, D. P. 1981. *Transitions and Social Change: The Early Lives of American Men.* New York: Academic Press.

Hogan, R., DeSota, C. B., and Solano, C. 1977. Traits, tests, and personality research. *American Psychologist,* 32:255–264.

Hoge, D. R. 1976. Changes in college students' value patterns in the 1950's, 1960's, and 1970's. *Sociology of Education,* 49:155–163.

Holden, C. 1980*a.* Identical twins reared apart. *Science,* 207 (March 21):1323–1328.

———. 1980*b.* Twins reunited. *Science 80,* 1 (November):55–59.

———. 1983. Can smoking explain ultimate gender gap? *Science,* 221: 1034.

Holmes, D. L., Nagy, J. N., and Slaymaker, F. 1982. Early influences of prematurity, illness, and prolonged hospitalization on infant behavior. *Developmental Psychology,* 18:744–750.

Holmes, T. H., and Masuda, M. 1972. Psychosomatic syndrome. *Psychology Today,* 5 (April):71ff.

———, and ———. 1974. Life change and illness susceptibility. In Dohrenwend, B. S., and Dohrenwend, B. P. (eds.), *Stressful Life Events: Their Nature and Effects.* New York: Wiley.

Holstein, C. B. 1976. Irreversible, stepwise sequence in the development of moral judgment: A longitudinal study of males and females. *Child Development,* 47:51–61.

Holsti, O. R., and Rosenau, J. N. 1980. Does where you stand depend on when you were born? The impact of generation on post-Vietnam foreign policy beliefs. *Public Opinion Quarterly,* 44:1–22.

Homans, G. C. 1974. *Social Behavior: Its Elementary Forms,* Rev. ed. New York: Harcourt Brace Jovanovich.

Hooker, E. 1969. *Final Report of the Task Force on Homosexuality.* Bethesda, Md.: National Institute of Mental Health.

Horn, J. L. 1976. Human abilities: A review of research and theory in the early 1970s. *Annual Review of Psychology,* 27:437–485.

———, and Cattell, R. B. 1967. Age differences in fluid and crystallized intelligence. *Acta Psychologica,* 26:107–129.

———, and Donaldson, G. 1976. On the myth of intellectual decline in adulthood. *American Psychologist,* 31:701–719.

———, and ———. 1977. Faith is not enough. *American Psychologist,* 32: 369–373.

Horowitz, F. D., Ashton, J., Culp, R., Gaddis, E., Levin, S., and Reichmann, B. 1977. The effects of obstetrical medication on the behavior of Israeli newborn infants and some comparisons with Uruguayan and American infants. *Child Development,* 48:1607–1623.

Horsman, A., Jones, M., Francis, R., and Nordin, C. 1983. The effect of estrogen dose on postmenopausal bone loss. *New England Journal of Medicine,* 309:1405–1407.

Householder, J., Hatcher, R., Burns, W., and Chasnoff, I. 1982. Infants born to narcotic-addicted mothers. *Psychological Bulletin,* 92:453–468.

Hoving, K. L., Hamm, N., and Galvin, P. 1969. Social influence as a function of stimulus ambiguity at three age levels. *Developmental Psychology,* 1: 631–636.

Howell, N. 1979. *The Demography of the Dobe! Kung.* New York: Academic Press.

Hoyer, W. J., Rebok, G. W., and Sved, S. M. 1979. Effects of varying irrelevant information on adult age differences in problem solving. *Journal of Gerontology,* 34:553–560.

Hsu, F. L. K. 1943. Incentives to work in primitive communities. *American Sociological Review,* 8:638–642.

Hudgens, R. W. 1974. Personal catastrophe and depression. In Dohrenwend, B. S., and Dohrenwend, B. P. (eds.), *Stressful Life Events: Their Nature and Effects.* New York: Wiley.

Hultsch, D. F., and Plemmons, J. K. 1979. Life events and life span development. In Baltes, P. B., and Brim, O. G., Jr. (eds.), *Life-Span Development and Behavior.* Vol. 2. New York: Academic Press.

Humphrey, T. 1978. Function of the nervous system during prenatal life. In Stave, U. (ed.), *Perinatal Physiology.* Hillsdale, N.J.: Erlbaum.

Humphreys, L. 1970. *Tearoom Trade: Impersonal Sex in Public Places.* Chicago: Aldine.

Hunt, E. 1983. On the nature of intelligence. *Science,* 219:141–146.

Hunt, J. McV. 1969. Has compensatory education failed? Has it been attempted? *Harvard Educational Review,* 39:278–300.

Hunt, J. V., and Rhodes, L. 1977. Mental development of preterm infants during the first year. *Child Development,* 48:204–210.

Hunt, M. 1974. *Sexual Behavior in the 1970's.* Chicago: Playboy Press.

Hunter, F. T., and Youniss, J. 1982. Changes in functions of three relations during adolescence. *Developmental Psychology,* 18:806–811.

Huntington, R., and Metcalf, P. 1979. *Celebrations of Death.* New York: Cambridge University Press.

Hurlock, E. B. 1968. The adolescent reformer. *Adolescence,* 3:273–306.

Huyghe, P. 1983. Of two minds. *Psychology Today,* 17 (December):26–35.

Hyatt, J. C. 1979. Youth survey shows attitudes becoming more conservative. *Wall Street Journal* (August 6):16.

Hyde, D. M. 1959. An investigation of Piaget's theories of the development of number. Unpublished doctoral dissertation, University of London.

Hyde, J. S. 1981. How large are cognitive gender differences? *American Psychologist,* 36:892–901.

———, and Rosenberg, B. G. 1976. *Half the Human Experience.* Lexington, Mass.: D. C. Heath.

Hymowitz, C. 1982. Wives of jobless men support some families—but at heavy cost. *Wall Street Journal* (December 8):1, 14.

Ickes, W., and Turner, M. 1983. On the social advantages of having an older, opposite-sex sibling. *Journal of Personality and Social Psychology,* 45: 210–222.

Imperato-McGinley, J., Peterson, R. E., Gautier, T., and Sturla, E. 1981. The impact of androgens on the evolution of male gender identity. In Kogan, S. J., and Hafez, E. S. E. (eds.), *Pediatric Andrology.* The Hague: Martinus Nijhoff.

Im Thurn, E. F. 1883. *Among the Indians of Guiana.* London: Kegan Paul, Trench & Trubner.

Ingalls, Z. 1983. Although drinking is widespread, student abuse of alcohol is not rising, new study finds. *The Chronicle of Higher Education* (January 19):9.

Inhelder, B., and Piaget, J. 1958. *The Growth of Logical Thinking from Childhood to Adolescence.* New York: Basic Books.

Inman, V. W., and Parkinson, S. R. 1983. Differences in Brown-Peterson recall as a function of age and retention interval. *Journal of Gerontology,* 38:58–64.

Izard, C. E. 1977. *Human Emotions.* New York: Plenum.

———. 1980. The young infant's ability to produce discrete emotion expression. *Developmental Psychology,* 16: 132–140.

Jablonski, E. M. 1974. Free recall in children. *Psychological Bulletin,* 81:522–539.

Jacklin, C. N., and Maccoby, E. E. 1978. Social behavior at thirty-three months in same-sex and mixed-sex dyads. *Child Development,* 49:557–569.

Jackson, D. L., and Youngner, S. 1979. Patient autonomy and "death with dignity." *New England Journal of Medicine,* 301:404–408.

Jackson, P. W. 1968. *Life in Classrooms.* New York: Holt, Rinehart and Winston.

Jackson, S. 1965. The growth of logical thinking in normal and subnormal children. *British Journal of Educational Psychology,* 35:255–258.

Jacobs, B. S., and Moss, H. A. 1976. Birth order and sex of sibling as determinants of mother-infant interaction. *Child Development,* 47:315–322.

Jacobs, J. 1971. *Adolescent Suicide.* New York: Wiley.

Jacobs, J. W. 1983. Treatment of divorcing fathers. *American Journal of Psychiatry,* 140:1294–1299.

Jacobson, S. W. 1979. Matching behavior in the young infant. *Child Development,* 50:425–430.

Jacques, J. M., and Chason, K. J. 1979. Cohabitation: Its impact on marital success. *Family Coordinator,* 28:35–39.

James, W. 1890. *The Principles of Psychology.* Vol. 1. New York: Dover, 1950.

Janson, P., and Martin, J. K. 1982. Job satisfaction and age: A test of two views. *Social Forces,* 60:1089–1102.

Jeffers, F. C., and Verwoerdt, A. 1969. How the old face death. In Busse, E. W., and Pfeiffer, E. (eds.), *Behavior and Adaptation in Late Life.* Boston: Little, Brown.

Jeffrey, W. E., and Cohen, L. B. 1971. Habituation in the human infant. In Reese, H. (ed.), *Advances in Child Development and Behavior.* Vol. 6. New York: Academic Press.

Jelliffe, D. B., and Jelliffe, F. F. P. 1979. *Nutrition and Growth.* Vol. 2. New York: Plenum.

Jencks, C. 1972. *Inequality: A Reassessment of the Effect of Family and Schooling in America.* New York: Basic Books.

———. 1979. *Who Gets Ahead? The Determinants of Economic Success in America.* New York: Basic Books.

———. 1982. Divorced mothers, unite! *Psychology Today,* 16 (November): 73–75.

———, Crouse, J., and Mueser, P. 1983. The Wisconsin model of status attainment: A national replication with improved measures of ability and aspiration. *Sociology of Education,* 56:3–19.

Jenness, D. 1922. The life of the Copper Eskimos. *Report of the Canadian Arctic Expedition, 1913–1918.* Vol. 12.

Jennings, M. K., and Niemi, R. G. 1981. *Generations and Politics: A Panel Study of Young Adults and Their Parents.* Princeton, N.J.: Princeton University Press.

Jensen, A. R. 1969. How much can we boost IQ and scholastic achievement? *Harvard Educational Review,* 39:1–123.

———. 1972. The heritability of intelligence. *Saturday Evening Post* (Summer):149.

———. 1973*a*. Race, intelligence and genetics: The differences are real. *Psychology Today,* 7 (December):80–86.

———. 1973*b*. *Educability and Group Differences.* New York: Harper & Row.

———. 1977. Did Sir Cyril Burt fake his research on heritability of intelligence? Part II. *Phi Delta Kappan,* 56:471, 492.

———. 1980. *Bias in Mental Testing.* New York: Free Press.

Jensen, I. W., and Gutek, B. A. 1982. Attributions and assignment of responsibility in sexual harassment. *Journal of Social Issues,* 38:121–136.

Jensen, K. 1932. Differential reactions to taste and temperature stimuli in newborn infants. *Genetic Psychological Monographs,* 12:363–479.

Jensen, T. S., Genefke, I. K., Hyldebrandt, N., and others. 1982. Cerebral atrophy in young torture victims. *New England Journal of Medicine,* 307: 1341.

Jersild, A. T., and Holmes, F. B. 1935*a*. Children's fears. *Child Development Monographs,* No. 20.

———, and ———. 1935*b*. Methods of overcoming children's fears. *Journal of Psychology,* 1:75–104.

———, Telford, C. W., and Sawrey, J. M. 1975. *Child Psychology,* 7th ed. Englewood Cliffs, N.J.: Prentice-Hall.

Jessor, R., Costa, F., Jessor, L., and Donovan, J. E. 1983. Time of first intercourse: A prospective study. *Journal of Personality and Social Psychology,* 44:608–626.

Jessor, S., and Jessor, R. 1975. Transition from virginity to nonvirginity among youth: A social-psychological study over time. *Developmental Psychology,* 11:473–484.

Johnson, M. M. 1975. Fathers, mothers, and sex typing. *Sociological Inquiry,* 45:15–26.

Johnson, P. 1984. The loss of ideals of youth. *New York Times Magazine* (March 25):90–98.

Johnson, S. 1979. Midwives: Acceptance is growing nationwide. *New York Times* (June 19):C5.

Johnston, J. M. 1972. Punishment of human behavior. *American Psychologist,* 27:1033–1054.

Johnston, L. 1979. Artist ends her life after ritual citing "self-termination" right. *New York Times* (June 17):1, 10.

Jones, H. E. 1949. Adolescence in our socicty. *The Family in a Democratic Society: Anniversary Papers of the Community Service Society of New York.* New York: Columbia University Press.

Jones, M. C. 1957. The later careers of boys who were early- or late-maturing. *Child Development,* 28:113–128.

———, and Bayley, N. 1950. Physical maturing among boys as related to behavior. *Journal of Educational Psychology,* 41:129–148.

———, and Mussen, P. H. 1958. Self-conceptions, motivations and interpersonal attitudes of early- and late-maturing girls. *Child Development,* 29:491–501.

Joseph, N. 1981. Campus couples and violence. *New York Times* (June 23):22.

Jung, C. G. 1933. *Modern Man in Search of a Soul.* New York: Harcourt, Brace, & World.

Kagan, J. 1965. Reflection-impulsivity and reading ability in primary grade children. *Child Development,* 36:609–628.

———. 1966. Reflection-impulsivity: The generality and dynamics of conceptual tempo. *Journal of Abnormal Psychology,* 71:17–24.

———. 1970. The determinants of attention in the infant. *American Scientist,* 58:298–306.

———. 1972*a*. A conception of early adolescence. In Kagan, J., and Coles, R. (eds.), *Twelve to Sixteen: Early Adolescence.* New York: Norton.

———. 1972*b*. Do infants think? *Scientific American,* 226 (March):74–82.

———. 1973. Do the first two years matter? *Saturday Review of Education,* 1 (3):41–43.

———. 1979. Overview: Perspectives on human infancy. In Osofsky, J. D. (ed.), *Handbook of Infant Development.* New York: Wiley.

———, Kearsley, R. B., and Zelazo, P. R. 1978. *Infancy: Its Place in Human Development.* Cambridge, Mass.: Harvard University Press.

———, and Klein, R. E. 1973. Cross-cultural perspectives on early development. *American Psychologist,* 28:947–961.

———, ———, Haith, M. M., and Morrison, F. J. 1973. Memory and meaning in two cultures. *Child Development,* 44:221–223.

———, and Moss, H. A. 1962. *Birth to Maturity.* New York: Wiley.

———, Pearson, L., and Welch, L. 1966. Conceptual impulsivity and inductive reasoning. *Child Development,* 37:583–594.

Kahn, R. L., and Antonucci, T. C. 1980. Convoys over the life course. In Baltes, P. B., and Brim, O. G., Jr. (eds.), *Life-Span Development and Behavior.* New York: Academic Press.

Kalat, J. W. 1981. *Biological Psychology.* Belmont, Calif.: Wadsworth.

Kalish, H. I. 1981. *From Behavioral Science to Behavior Modification.* New York: McGraw-Hill.

Kalleberg, A. L. 1977. Work values and job rewards: A theory of job satisfaction. *American Sociological Review,* 42:124–143.

———, and Loscocco, K. A. 1983. Aging, values, and rewards: Explaining age differences in job satisfaction. *American Sociological Review,* 48:78–90.

Kallmann, F. J. 1952. Twin sibships and the study of male homosexuality. *American Journal of Human Genetics,* 4:136–146.

———. 1953. *Heredity in Health and Mental Disorder.* New York: Norton.

Kaltenbach, K., Weinraub, M., and Fullard, W. 1980. Infant wariness toward strangers reconsidered: Infants' and mothers' reactions to unfamiliar persons. *Child Development,* 51:1197–1202.

Kalter, H., and Warkany, J. 1983*a*. Congenital malformations. I. *New England Journal of Medicine,* 308:424–431.

———, and ———. 1983*b*. Congenital malformations. II. *New England Journal of Medicine,* 308:491–497.

Kamin, L. J. 1974. *The Science and Politics of IQ.* Hillsdale, N.J.: Lawrence Erlbaum Associates.

———. 1975. Is IQ heritable? *Contemporary Psychology,* 20:545–547.

———. 1977. Burt's IQ data. *Science,* 195:246–248.

———. 1981. Commentary. In Scarr, S. (ed.), *IQ: Race, Social Class, and Individual Differences.* Hillsdale, N.J.: Erlbaum.

Kandel, D. B. 1974. Inter- and intragenerational influences on adolescent marijuana use. *Journal of Social Issues,* 30:107–135.

———. 1978. Homophily, selection, and socialization in adolescent friendships. *American Journal of Sociology,* 84:427–436.

———, and Adler, I. 1982. Socialization into marijuana use among French adolescents: A cross-cultural comparison with the United States. *Journal of Health and Social Behavior,* 23:295–309.

Kane, R. L., and Kane, R. A. 1978. Care of the aged: Old problems in need of new solutions. *Science,* 200 (May 26):913–919.

Kanfer, R., and Zeiss, A. M. 1983. Depression, interpersonal standard setting, and judgments of self-efficacy. *Journal of Abnormal Psychology,* 92:319–329.

Kanter, R. M. 1972. *Commitment and Community: Communes and Utopias in Sociological Perspective.* Cambridge, Mass.: Harvard University Press.

———. 1973. *Communes: Creating and Managing the Collective Life.* New York: Harper & Row.

———. 1974. Communes in cities. *Working Papers,* 2 (Summer):36–44.

Kanungo, R. N. 1979. The concepts of alienation and involvement revisited. *Psychological Bulletin,* 86:119–138.

Kaplan, B. J. 1972. Malnutrition and mental deficiency. *Psychological Bulletin,* 78:321–334.

Kaplan, H. R., and Tausky, C. 1972. Work and the welfare Cadillac. *Social Problems,* 19:469–483.

Kart, C. S., and Beckham, B. L. 1976. Black-white differentials in the institutionalization of the elderly: A temporal analysis. *Social Forces,* 54:901–910.

Kastenbaum, R. 1975. Is death a life crisis? On the confrontation with death in theory and practice. In Datan, N., and Ginsberg, L. H. (eds.), *Life-Span Developmental Psychology: Normative Life Crisis.* New York: Academic Press.

———. 1977. Temptations from the ever after. *Human Behavior,* 6 (September):28–33.

———. 1979. "Healthy dying": A paradoxical quest continues. *Journal of Social Issues,* 35:185–206.

———, and Costa, P. T., Jr. 1977. Psychological perspectives on death. In Rosenzweig, M. R., and Porter, L. W. (eds.), *Annual Review of Psychology.* Vol. 28. Palo Alto, Calif.: Annual Reviews, Inc.

Kasun, J. R. 1978. A reply to zero population growth. *Society,* 15 (May–June):9+.

Katchadourian, H. A., and Lunde, D. T. 1977. *Fundamentals of Human Sexuality.* 2nd ed. New York: Holt, Rinehart and Winston.

Katz, P. A. 1976. The acquisition of racial attitudes in children. In Katz, P. A. (ed.), *Towards the Elimination of Racism.* New York: Pergamon.

———, Sohn, M., and Zalk, S. R. 1975. Perceptual concomitants of racial attitudes in urban grade-school children. *Developmental Psychology,* 11:135–144.

Katz, S. 1983. Active life expectancy. *New England Journal of Medicine,* 309:1218–1223.

Kaufman, H. G. 1982. *Professionals in Search of Work: Coping with the Stress of Job Loss and Underemployment.* New York: Wiley.

Kaufman, L. 1975. Review of T. G. R. Bower, *Development in Infancy. Contemporary Psychology,* 20:866–868.

Kausler, D. H., and Hakami, M. K. 1983. Memory for activities: Adult age differences and intentionality. *Developmental Psychology,* 19:889–894.

———, and Klein, D. M. 1978. Age differences in processing relevant versus irrelevant stimuli in multiple-item recognition learning. *Journal of Gerontology,* 33:87–93.

Kaye, E. 1979. On starving oneself to death. *Family Health* (September):38–43.

Kaye, K., and Wells, A. J. 1980. Mothers' jiggling and the burst-pause pattern in neonatal feeding. *Infant Behavior and Development,* 3:29–46.

———. 1975. Implicators of cognitive development for moral reasoning. In DePalma, D. J., and Foley, J. M. (eds.), *Moral Development: Current Theory and Research.* Hillsdale, N.J.: Lawrence Erlbaum Associates.

Keating, N. C., and Cole, P. 1980. What do I do with him 24 hours a day? Changes in the housewife role after retirement. *Gerontologist,* 20:84–89.

Keefer, C. H., Tronick, E., Dixon, S., and Brazelton, T. B. 1982. Special differences in motor performance between Gusii and American newborns and a modification of the neonatal behavioral assessment scale. *Child Development,* 53:754–759.

Keith, P. M. 1983. A comparison of the resources of parents and childless men and women in very old age. *Family Relations,* 32:403–409.

Keller, A., Ford, L. H., Jr., and Meacham, J. A. 1978. Dimensions of self-concept in preschool children. *Developmental Psychology,* 14:483–489.

Keller, C. 1980. Epidemiologic characteristics of preterm births. In Friedman, S. L., and Sigman, M. (eds.), *Preterm Birth and Psychological Development.* New York: Academic Press.

Kelly, D. H. 1971. Social failure, academic self-evaluation, and school avoidance and deviant behavior. *Youth and Society,* 2:489–503.

Kelly, E. L. 1955. Consistency of the adult personality. *American Psychologist,* 10:659–681.

Kelly, G. A. 1955. *The Psychology of Personal Constructs.* New York: Norton.

Kempe, R. S., and Kempe, C. H. 1978. *Child Abuse.* Cambridge, Mass.: Harvard University Press.

Kendler, K. S. 1983. Overview: A current perspective on twin studies of schizophrenia. *American Journal of Psychiatry,* 140:1413–1425.

Kendrick, C., and Dunn, J. 1980. Caring for a second baby: Effects on interaction between mother and firstborn. *Developmental Psychology,* 16:303–311.

Keniston, K. 1970. Youth: A "new" stage in life. *American Scholar* (Autumn):586–595.

Kennell, J. H., Voos, D. K., and Klaus, M. H. 1979. Parent-infant bonding. In Osofsky, J. D. (ed.), *Handbook of Infant Development.* New York: Wiley.

Kenny, T. 1984. 73% polled back right to die. *USA Today* (January 3):3A.

Kerckhoff, A. C. 1972. *Socialization and Social Class,* Englewood Cliffs, N.J.: Prentice-Hall.

Kessen, W. 1963. Research in the psychological development of infants: An overview. *Merrill-Palmer Quarterly,* 9:83–94.

———. 1965. *The Child.* New York: Wiley.

———. 1967. Sucking and looking. Two organized congenital patterns of behavior in the human newborn. In Stevenson, H. W., Hess, E. H., and Rheingold, H. L. (eds.), *Early Behavior.* New York: Wiley.

Kett, J. F. 1977. *Rites of Passage: Adolescence in America, 1970 to the Present.* New York: Basic Books.

Kety, S. S. 1983. Mental illness in the biological and adoptive relatives of schizophrenic adoptees: Findings relevant to genetic and environmental factors in etiology. *American Journal of Psychiatry,* 140:720–727.

———, Rosenthal, D., and Wender, P. H. 1978. The biologic and adoptive families of adopted individuals who became schizophrenic: Prevalence of mental illness and other characteristics. In Wynne, L. C., Cromwell, R. L., and Matthysse, S. (eds.), *The Nature of Schizophrenia.* New York: Wiley.

Kidwell, J. S. 1981. Number of siblings, sibling spacing, sex, and birth order: Their effects on perceived parent-adolescent relationship. *Journal of Marriage and the Family,* 43:315–332.

———. 1982. The neglected birth order: Middleborns. *Journal of Marriage and the Family,* 44:225–235.

Kiester, E., Jr. 1976. Six generations of one family—linked together by a deadly gene. *Today's Health* (March):32+.

Kilbride, J. E., Robbins, M. C., and Kilbride, P. L. 1970. The comparative motor development of Baganda, American white, and American black infants. *American Anthropologist,* 72:1422–1428.

Kimball, M. M., and Dale, P. S. 1972. The relationship between color naming and color recognition abilities of preschoolers. *Child Development,* 43:972–980.

Kimmel, D. C. 1980. *Adulthood and Aging: An Interdisciplinary, Developmental View,* 2nd ed. New York: Wiley.

———, Price, K. F., and Walker, J. W. 1978. Retirement choice and retirement satisfaction. *Journal of Gerontology,* 33:575–585.

Kinard, E. M. 1979. The psychological consequences of abuse for the child. *Journal of Social Issues,* 35:82–100.

Kingsley, R., and Hall, V. 1967. Training of conservation through the use of learning sets. *Child Development,* 38:1111–1126.

Kinsey, A. C., Pomeroy, W. B., and Martin, C. E. 1948. *Sexual Behavior in the Human Male.* Philadelphia: Saunders.

———, ———, ———, and Gebhard, P. H. 1953. *Sexual Behavior in the Human Female.* Philadephia: Saunders.

Kirkpatrick, S. W., and Sanders, D. M. 1978. Body image stereotypes: A developmental comparison. *Journal of Genetic Psychology,* 132:87–95.

Klaus, M. H., and Kennell, J. H. 1976. *Maternal-Infant Bonding: The Impact of Early Separation or Loss on Family Development.* St. Louis: Mosby.

Klein, J. 1980. *Woody Guthrie.* New York: Knopf.

Klemesrud, J. 1981. Voice of authority still male. *New York Times* (February 2):16.

Kluckhohn, C. 1960. *Mirror for Man.* Greenwich, Conn.: Fawcett.

Knox, A. B. 1977. *Adult Development and Learning.* San Francisco: Jossey-Bass.

Knox, D. 1980. Trends in marriage and the family—the 1980's. *Family Relations,* 29:145–150.

Knudson, M. 1980. Baltimore study shows age not calendar matters. *Columbus Dispatch* (July 14):B3.

Kobasa, S. C., Maddi, S. R., and Kahn, S. 1982. Hardiness and health: A prospective study. *Journal of Personality and Social Psychology,* 42:168–177.

Koch, H. L. 1956. Sissiness and tomboyishness in relation to sibling characteristics. *Journal of Genetic Psychology,* 88:231–244.

Koepke, J. E., and Barnes, P. 1982. Amount of sucking when a sucking object is readily available to human newborns. *Child Development,* 53: 978–983.

———, Hamm, M., Legerstee, M., and Russell, M. 1983. Neonatal imitation: Two failures to replicate. *Infant Behavior and Development,* 6:113–116.

Koff, E., Rierdan, J., and Silverstone, E. 1978. Changes in representation of body image as a function of menarcheal status. *Developmental Psychology,* 14:635–642.

Kogan, N. 1979. A study of age categorization. *Journal of Gerontology,* 34:358–367.

Kohen-Raz, R. 1968. Mental and motor development of kibbutz, institutionalized, and home-reared infants in Israel. *Child Development,* 39:489–504.

Kohlberg, L. 1963. The development of children's orientations toward a moral order. I: Sequence in the development of human thought. *Vita Humana,* 6:11–33.

———. 1966. A cognitive-developmental analysis of children's sex-role concepts and attitudes. In Maccoby, E. E. (ed.), *The Development of Sex Differences.* Stanford, Calif.: Stanford University Press.

———. 1969. Stage and sequence: The cognitive-developmental approach to socialization. In Goslin, D. A. (ed.), *Handbook of Socialization Theory and Research.* Chicago: Rand McNally.

———. 1973. Continuities in childhood and adult moral development revisited. In Baltes, P. B., and Schaie, K. W. (eds.), *Life-Span Developmental Psychology: Personality and Socialization.* New York: Academic Press.

———. 1976. Moral stages and moralization. In Lickona, T. (ed.), *Moral Development and Behavior: Theory, Research, and Social Issues.* New York: Holt, Rinehart and Winston.

———. 1978. Revisions in the theory and practice of moral development. *New Directions for Child Development,* 2:83–87.

———. 1980. High school democracy and educating for a just society. In Mosher, R. L. (ed.), *Moral Education.* New York: Praeger.

———. 1981. *The Philosophy of Moral Development.* New York: Harper & Row.

———, and Gilligan, C. F. 1971. The adolescent as philosopher: The discovery of the self in a postconventional world. *Daedalus,* 100:1051–1086.

———, and Ullian, D. Z. 1974. Stages in the development of psychosexual concepts and attitudes. In Friedman, R. C., Richart, R. N., and Vande Wiele, R. L. (eds.), *Sex Differences in Behavior.* New York: Wiley.

Kohn, M., and Schooler, C. 1973. Occupational experience and psychological functioning: An assessment of reciprocal effects. *American Sociological Review,* 38:97–118.

Kohn, M. L. 1977. *Class and Conformity: A Study in Values,* 2nd ed. Chicago: University of Chicago Press.

———, and Schooler, C. 1982. Job conditions and personality: A longitudinal assessment of their reciprocal effects. *American Journal of Sociology,* 87:1257–1286.

Kolata, G. 1983. Math genius may have hormonal basis. *Science,* 222:1312.

Kolata, G. B. 1975. Behavioral development: Effects of environment. *Science,* 189:207–209.

———. 1977. Infertility: Promising new treatments. *Science,* 202:200–203.

———. 1979. Scientists attack report that obstetrical medications endanger children. *Science,* 204:391–392.

———. 1980. NIH panel urges fewer Cesarean births. *Science,* 210:176–177.

Kolodny, R. C., Jacobs, L. S., Masters,

W. H., Toro, G., and Daughaday, W. H. 1972. Plasma gonadotrophins and prolactin in male homosexuals. *Lancet,* 2:18–20.

Kopp, C. B., and Parmelee, A. H. 1979. Prenatal and perinatal influences on infant behavior. In Osofsky, J. D. (ed.), *Handbook of Infant Development.* New York: Wiley.

Korner, A. F. 1979. Conceptual issues in infancy research. In Osofsky, J. D. (ed.), *Handbook of Infant Development.* New York: Wiley.

———, and Thoman, E. B. 1972. The relative efficacy of contact and vestibular-proprioceptive stimulation in soothing neonates. *Child Development,* 43:443–453.

Kornhaber, A., and Woodward, K. L. 1981. *Grandparents/Grandchild: The Vital Connection.* New York: Anchor Press.

Kramer, D. A. 1983. Post-formal operations? A need for further conceptualization. *Human Development,* 26:91–105.

Kramer, R. B. 1968. Changes in moral judgment response pattern during late adolescence and young adulthood: Retrogression in a developmental sequence. Unpublished doctoral dissertation. Chicago: University of Chicago.

Krantz, M. 1982. Sociometric awareness, social participation, and perceived popularity in preschool children. *Child Development,* 53:376–379.

Kreutzer, M. A., Leonard, C., and Flavell, J. H. 1975. An interview study of children's knowledge about memory. *Monographs of the Society for Research in Child Development,* 40 (Serial No. 159).

Krogman, W. M. 1972. *Child Growth.* Ann Arbor: University of Michigan Press.

Krosnick, J. A., and Judd, C. M. 1982. Transitions in social influence at adolescence: Who induces cigarette smoking? *Developmental Psychology,* 18:359–368.

Kübler-Ross, E. 1969. *On Death and Dying.* New York: Macmillan.

———. 1981. *Living with Death and Dying.* New York: Macmillan.

Kuhn, C. M., Butler, S. R., and Schamberg, S. M. 1978. Selective depression of serum growth hormone during maternal deprivation in rat pups. *Science,* 201:1034–1036.

Kuhn, D. 1974. Inducing development experimentally: Comments on a research paradigm. *Developmental Psychology,* 10:590–600.

Labouvie, E. W. 1982. Issues in life-span development. In Wolman, B. B. (ed.), *Handbook of Developmental Psychology.* Englewood Cliffs, N.J.: Prentice-Hall.

Labouvie-Vief, G., and Schell, D. A. 1982. Learning and memory in later life. In Wolman, B. B. (ed.), *Handbook of Developmental Psychology.* Englewood Cliffs, N.J.: Prentice-Hall.

Lamaze, F. 1958. *Painless Childbirth: Psychoprophylactic Method.* London: Burke.

Lamb, M. 1982. Second thoughts on first touch. *Psychology Today,* 16 (April): 9–11.

Lamb, M. E. 1975. Fathers: Forgotten contributors to child development. *Human Development,* 18:245–266.

———. 1976. The role of the father: An overview. In Lamb, M. E. (ed.), *The Role of the Father in Child Development.* New York: Wiley.

———. 1977*a*. Father-infant and mother-infant interaction in the first year of life. *Child Development,* 48:167–181.

———. 1977*b*. A re-examination of the infant social world. *Human Development,* 20:65–85.

———. 1978. Influence of the child on marital quality and family interaction during the prenatal, perinatal, and infancy periods. In Lerner, R. M., and Spanier, G. B. (eds.), *Child Influences on Marital and Family Interaction: A Life-Span Perspective.* New York: Academic Press.

——— (ed.). 1981. *The Role of the Father in Child Development.* New York: Wiley.

———, Frodi, A. M., Hwang, C., Frodi, M., and Steinberg, J. 1982. Mother- and father-infant interaction involving play and holding in traditional and nontraditional Swedish families. *Developmental Psychology,* 18:215–221.

———, and Sherrod, L. R. 1981. *Infant Social Cognition: Empirical and Theoretical Considerations.* Hillsdale, N.J.: Erlbaum.

Lambert, W. W. 1960. Interpersonal behavior. In Mussen, P. H. (ed.), *Handbook of Research Methods in Child Development.* New York: Wiley.

Lang, A. M. and Brody, E. M. 1983. Characteristics of middle-aged daughters and help to their elderly mothers. *Journal of Marriage and the Family,* 45:193–202.

Lang, O. 1946. *Chinese Family and Society.* New Haven: Yale University Press.

Langer, E. J., and Rodin, J. 1976. The effects of choice and enhanced personal responsibility for the aged: A field experiment in an institutional setting. *Journal of Personality and Social Psychology,* 34:191–198.

Langer, J. 1980. *The Origins of Logic: Six to Twelve Months.* New York: Academic Press.

Langlois, J. H., and Downs, A. C. 1979. Peer relations as a function of physical attractiveness: The eye of the beholder or behavioral reality? *Child Development,* 50:409–418.

———, and ———. 1980. Mothers, fathers, and peers as socialization agents of sex-typed play behaviors in young children. *Child Development,* 51:1237–1247.

———, and Stephan, C. 1977. The effects of physical attractiveness and ethnicity on children's behavioral attributions and peer preferences. *Child Development,* 48:1694–1698.

Langman, L. 1971. Dionysus—Child of tomorrow. *Youth and Society,* 3:84–87.

Langmeier, J., and Matějček, Z. 1974. *Psychological Deprivation in Childhood.* New York: Halsted Press.

Langway, L. 1980. Flying back to the nest. *Newsweek* (April 7):86.

———. 1982. Growing old, feeling young. *Newsweek* (November 1):56–65.

———. 1983. Bringing up superbaby. *Newsweek* (March 28):62–68.

Larson, R. 1978. Thirty years of research on the subjective well-being of older Americans. *Journal of Gerontology,* 33:109–125.

Larson, R. W. 1983. Adolescents' daily experience with family and friends: Contrasting opportunity systems. *Journal of Marriage and the Family,* 45:739–750.

Lasky, R. E. 1977. The effect of visual feedback of the hand on the reaching and retrieval behavior of young infants. *Child Development,* 48:112–117.

———, Klein, R. E., Yarbrough, C., Engle, P. L., Lechtig, A., and Martorell, R. 1981. The relationship between physical growth and infant behavioral development in rural Guatemala. *Child Development,* 52:219–226.

Latané, B. 1970. Field studies of altruistic compliance. *Respresentative Research in Social Psychology,* 1:49–61.

———, and Darley, J. M. 1968. Group inhibition of bystander intervention in emergencies. *Journal of Personality and Social Psychology,* 10:215–221.

———, and ———. 1970. *The Unresponsive Bystander.* New York: Appleton-Century-Crofts.

Laufer, R. S., and Bengtson, V. L. 1974. Generations, aging, and social stratification: On the development of generational units. *Journal of Social Issues,* 30:181–205.

Lavoie, J. C., and Looft, W. R. 1973. Parental antecedents of resistance-to-temptation behavior in adolescent males. *Merrill-Palmer Quarterly,* 19:107–116.

Lawler, J. 1975. Dialectical philosophy and developmental psychology: Hegel and Piaget on contradiction. *Human Development,* 18:1–17.

Lazar, I., and Darlington, R. 1982. Lasting effects of early education: A report from the Consortium for Longitudinal Studies. *Monographs of the Society for Research in Child Development,* 47 (No. 195).

Lazarus, R. S. 1966. *Psychological Stress and the Coping Process.* New York: McGraw-Hill.

Leboyer, F. 1975. *Birth Without Violence.* New York: Knopf.

Lee, G. R., and Ellithorpe, E. 1982. Intergenerational exchange and subjective well-being among the elderly. *Journal of Marriage and the Family,* 44:217–224.

Lee, L. C. 1975. Toward a cognitive theory of interpersonal development: Importance of peers. In Lewis, M., and Rosenblum, L. A. (eds.), *Friendship and Peer Relations.* New York: Wiley.

Lefcourt, H. 1973. The function of the illusion of control and freedom. *American Psychologist,* 28:417–425.

Leifer, A. D., Gordon, N. J., and Graves, S. B. 1974. Children's television more than mere entertainment. *Harvard Educational Review,* 44:213–245.

———, Leiderman, P. H., Barnett, C. R., and Williams, J. A. 1972. Effects of mother-infant separation on maternal attachment behavior. *Child Development,* 43:1203–1218.

LeMasters, E. E. 1957. Parenthood as crisis. *Marriage and Family Living,* 19:352–355.

Lenneberg, E. H. 1967. *Biological Foundations of Language.* New York: Wiley.

———. 1969. On explaining language. *Science,* 164:635–643.

Lennon, M. C. 1982. The psychological consequences of menopause: The importance of timing of a life stage event. *Journal of Health and Social Behavior,* 23:353–366.

Lerner, R. M. 1976. *Concepts and Theories of Human Development.* Reading, Mass.: Addison-Wesley.

———. 1978. Nature, nurture, and dynamic interactionism. *Human Development,* 21:1–20.

———, and Busch-Rossnagel, N. A. 1981. *Individuals as Producers of Their Development.* New York: Academic Press.

———, Iwawaki, S., Chihara, T., and Sorell, G. T. 1980. Self-concept, self-esteem, and body attitudes among Japanese male and female adolescents. *Child Development,* 51:847–855.

———, and Lerner, J. V. 1977. Effects of age, sex, and physical attractiveness on child-peer relations, academic performance, and elementary school adjustment. *Developmental Psychology,* 13:585–590.

———, and Spanier, G. B. (eds.). 1978*a*. *Child Influences on Marital and Family Interaction: A Life-Span Perspective.* New York: Academic Press.

———, and ———. 1978*b*. A dynamic interactionist view of child and family development. In Lerner, R. M., and Spanier, G. B. (eds.), *Child Influences on Marital and Family Interaction: A Life-Span Perspective.* New York: Academic Press.

Lessing, E. E. 1977. Racial prejudice: Doing what comes naturally? *Contemporary Psychology,* 22:680–682.

———, Zagorin, S. W., and Nelson, D. 1970. WISC subtest and IQ score correlates of father absence. *Journal of Genetic Psychology,* 117:181–195.

Lester, B. M. 1976. Spectrum analysis of the cry sounds of well-nourished and malnourished infants. *Child Development,* 46:237–241.

———, Als, H., and Brazelton, T. B. 1982. Regional obstetric anesthesia and newborn behavior: A reanalysis toward synergistic effects. *Child Development,* 53:687–692.

———, Kotelchuck, M., Spelke, E., Sellers, M. J., and Klein, R. E. 1974. Separation protest in Guatemalan infants: Cross-cultural and cognitive findings. *Developmental Psychology,* 10:79–85.

Leung, E. H. L., and Rheingold, H. L. 1981. Development of pointing as a social gesture. *Developmental Psychology,* 17:215–220.

Levenson, H. 1973. Perceived parental antecedents of internal, powerful others, and chance locus of control orientations. *Developmental Psychology,* 9:260–265.

Leventhal, A. S., and Lipsitt, L. P. 1964. Adaptation, pitch discrimination, and sound localization in the neonate. *Child Development,* 35:759–767.

Leventhal, G. S. 1970. Influence of brothers and sisters on sex-role behavior. *Journal of Personality and Social Psychology,* 16:452–465.

Lever, J. 1978. Sex differences in the complexity of children's play and games. *American Sociological Review,* 43:471–483.

Levine, L. E. 1983. Mine: Self-definition in 2-year-old boys. *Developmental Psychology,* 19:544–549.

LeVine, R. A. 1970. Cross-cultural study in child psychology. In Mussen, P. H. (ed.), *Carmichael's Manual of Child Psychology,* 3rd ed. New York: Wiley.

Levinson, D. J., Darrow, C. M., Klein, E. B., Levinson, M. H., and McKee, B. 1974. The psychosocial development of men in early adulthood and the midlife transition. In Ricks, D. F., Thomas, A., and Roff, M. (eds.), *Life History Research in Psychopathology.* Vol. 3. Minneapolis: University of Minnesota Press.

———, ———, ———, ———, and ———. 1976. Periods in the adult development of men: Ages 18 to 45. *The Counseling Psychologist,* 6:21–25.

———, ———, ———, ———, and ———. 1978. *The Seasons of a Man's Life.* New York: Knopf.

Levinson, H. 1964. Money aside, why spend life working? *National Observer* (March 9):20.

Levitas, G. 1976. Second start. *New York Times Magazine* (June 6):42ff.

Levitsky, D. A. 1979. *Malnutrition, Environment, and Behavior.* Ithaca, N.Y.: Cornell University Press.

Levy, D. M. 1943. *Maternal Overprotection.* New York: Columbia University Press.

Levy, R. I., and Moskowitz, J. 1982. Cardiovascular research: Decades of progress, a decade of promise. *Science,* 217:121–129.

Levy-Shiff, R. 1982. The effects of father absence on young children in mother-headed families. *Child Development,* 53:1400–1405.

Lewin, R. 1981. Is longevity a positive selection? *Science,* 211:373.

Lewis, M. 1969. Infants' responses to facial stimuli during the first year of life. *Developmental Psychology,* 1:75–86.

———. 1977. The busy, purposeful world of a baby. *Psychology Today,* 10 (February):53–56.

———, and Brooks-Gunn, J. 1979. *Social Cognition and the Acquisition of Self.* New York: Plenum.

———, and Starr, M. D. 1979. Developmental continuity. In Osofsky, J. D. (ed.), *Handbook of Infant Development.* New York: Wiley.

———, Young, G., Brooks, J., and Michalson, L. 1975. The beginning of friendship. In Lewis, M., and Rosenblum, L. A. (eds.), *Friendship and Peer Relations.* New York: Wiley.

Lewis, T. L., Maurer, D., and Kay, D. 1978. Newborns' central vision: Whole or hole? *Journal of Experimental Child Psychology,* 26:193–203.

Liang, J., Dvorkin, L., Kahana, E., and Mazian, F. 1980. Social integration and morale: A re-examination. *Journal of Gerontology,* 35:746–757.

Libby, R. W. 1977. Creative singlehood as

a sexual life-style: Beyond marriage as a rite of passage. In Libby, R. W., and Whitehurst, R. N. (eds.), *Marriage and Alternatives.* Glenview, Ill.: Scott, Foresman.

Liben, L. S. 1978. Perspective-taking skills in young children: Seeing the world through rose-colored glasses. *Developmental Psychology,* 14:87–92.

Lickona, T. 1976. Research on Piaget's theory of moral development. In Lickona, T. (ed.), *Moral Development and Behavior: Theory, Research, and Social Issues.* New York: Holt, Rinehart and Winston.

Lidz, T., Blatt, S., and Cook, B. 1981. Critique of the Danish-American studies of the adopted-away offspring of schizophrenic parents. *American Journal of Psychiatry,* 138:1063–1068.

Lieberman, M. A. 1965. Psychological correlates of impending death: Some preliminary observations. *Journal of Gerontology,* 20:182–190.

———. 1975. Adaptive processes in late life. In Datan, N., and Ginsberg, L. H. (eds.), *Life-Span Developmental Psychology: Normative Life Crisis.* New York: Academic Press.

———, and Coplan, A. S. 1970. Distance from death as a variable in the study of aging. *Developmental Psychology,* 2:71–84.

Liebert, R. M., and Baron, R. A. 1972. Some immediate effects of television violence on children's behavior. *Developmental Psychology,* 6:469–475.

———, Poulos, R. W., and Marmor, G. S. 1977. *Developmental Psychology,* 2nd ed. Englewood Cliffs, N.J.: Prentice-Hall.

Liebow, E. 1967. *Tally's Corner: A Study of Negro Streetcorner Men.* Boston: Little, Brown.

Liebowitz, M. R. 1983. *The Chemistry of Love.* Boston: Little, Brown.

Liederman, J., and Kinsbourne, M. 1980. The mechanism of neonatal rightward turning bias: A sensory or motor asymmetry? *Infant Behavior and Development,* 3:223–238.

Limber, J. 1977. Language in child and chimp? *American Psychologist,* 32:280–295.

Lincoln, R. 1981. *Teenage Pregnancy: The Problem That Hasn't Gone Away.* New York: Alan Guttmacher Institute.

Lindsey, R. 1984. A new generation finds it hard to leave the nest. *New York Times* (January 25):10.

Linn, S., Reznick, J. S., Kagan, J., and Hans, S. 1982. Salience of visual patterns in the human infant. *Developmental Psychology,* 18:651–657.

Linton, R. 1936. *The Study of Man.* New York: Appleton-Century-Crofts.

Lipinski, A. M. 1982. Nuclear war: The topic boggles a child's mind. *Columbus Dispatch* (July 16):C1.

Lipman, A. 1961. Role conceptions and morale of couples in retirement. *Journal of Gerontology,* 16:267–271.

Lipsitt, L. P. 1971. Babies: They're a lot smarter than they look. *Psychology Today,* 5 (December):70–72ff.

———, Engen, T., and Kaye, H. 1963. Developmental changes in the olfactory threshold of the neonate. *Child Development,* 34:371–376.

———, and Levy, N. 1959. Electrotactual threshold in the neonate. *Child Development,* 30:547–554.

Lipsitz, L. A. 1983. Postprandial reduction in blood pressure in the elderly. *New England Journal of Medicine,* 309:81–83.

Liu, B. C. 1973. *The Quality of Life in the United States.* Kansas City, Mo.: Midwest Research Institute.

Livesley, W. J., and Bromley, D. B. 1973. *Person Perception in Childhood and Adolescence.* New York: Wiley.

Loeb, R. C., Horst, L., and Horton, P. J. 1980. Family interaction patterns associated with self-esteem in preadolescent girls and boys. *Merrill-Palmer Quarterly,* 26:205–217.

Loehlin, J. C., Lindzey, G., and Spuhler, J. N. 1975. *Race Differences in Intelligence.* San Francisco: Freeman.

Lofland, L. 1978. *The Craft of Dying.* Beverly Hills: Sage.

Longino, C. F., Jr., and Kart, C. S. 1982. Explicating activity theory: A formal replication. *Journal of Gerontology,* 37:713–722.

Lopata, H. Z. 1973. *Widowhood in an American City.* Cambridge, Mass.: Schenkman.

———. 1981. Widowhood and husband satisfaction. *Journal of Marriage and the Family,* 43:439–450.

Loraine, J. A., Ismail, A. A. A., Adamopolous, D. A., and Dove, G. A. 1970. Endocrine function in male and female homosexuals. *British Medical Journal,* 4:406–409.

Lorenz, K. Z. 1935. Imprinting. In Birney, R. C., and Teevan, R. C. (eds.), *Instinct.* London: Van Nostrand, 1961.

Loughlin, K. A., and Daehler, M. W. 1973. The effects of distraction and added perceptual cues on the delayed reaction of very young children. *Child Development,* 44:384–388.

Lowenthal, M. F. 1964. Social isolation and mental illness in old age. *American Sociological Review,* 29:54–70.

———, and Haven, C. 1968. Interaction and adaptation: Intimacy as a critical variable. *American Sociological Review,* 33:20–30.

———, and Robinson, B. 1976. Social networks and isolation. In Binstock, R., and Shanas, E. (eds.), *Handbook of Aging and the Social Sciences.* New York: Van Nostrand.

———, Thurner, M., and Chiriboga, D. 1975. *Four Stages of Life.* San Francisco: Jossey-Bass.

Lowing, P. A., Mirsky, A. F., and Pereira, R. 1983. The inheritance of schizophrenia spectrum disorders: A reanalysis of the Danish Adoptee Study data. *American Journal of Psychiatry,* 140:1167–1171.

Lubchenco, L. O., Bard, H., Goldman, A. L., Coyer, W. E., McIntyre, C., and Smith, D. M. 1974. Newborn intensive care and long-term prognosis. *Developmental Medicine and Child Neurology,* 16:421–431.

Lublin, J. S. 1979. The birthing room. *Wall Street Journal* (February 15): 1+.

———. 1981. Resisting advances. *Wall Street Journal* (April 24):1, 21.

———. 1983. Older jobless workers seeking a new position find years hurt them. *Wall Street Journal* (August 28):1, 12.

Luecke, D. E., and McGinn, N. F. 1975. Regression analyses and education production functions: Can they be trusted? *Harvard Educational Review,* 43:325–350.

Luepnitz, D. A. 1982. *Child Custody: A Study of Families After Divorce.* Lexington, Mass.: Lexington Books.

Lynn, D. B. 1974. *The Father: His Role in Child Development.* Monterey, Calif.: Brooks/Cole.

———. 1976. Fathers and sex-role development. *Family Coordinator,* 25: 403–409.

Lyons, N. P. 1983. Two perspectives: On self, relationships, and morality. *Harvard Educational Review,* 53:125–145.

Lyons, R. D. 1983*a*. Health officials report herpes surge in newborns. *New York Times* (December 9):8.

———. 1983*b*. Sex in America: Conservative attitudes prevail. *New York Times* (October 4):17, 19.

Lytton, H. 1971. Observation studies of parent-child interaction: A methodological review. *Child Development,* 42:651–684.

———. 1979. Disciplinary encounters between young boys and their mothers and fathers: Is there a contingency system? *Developmental Psychology,* 15:256–268.

———. 1980. *Parent-Child Interaction: The Socialization Process Observed in Twin and Single Families.* New York: Plenum Press.

McCall, R. B. 1974. Exploratory manipulation and play in the human infant. *Monographs of the Society for Research in Child Development,* 39 (2).

———, and Cool, S. J. 1976. Perceptual development. *Science,* 193:478–479.

McCandless, B. R. 1970. *Adolescents: Behavior and Development.* New York: Holt, Rinehart and Winston.

———, and Coop, R. H. 1979. *Adolescents: Behavior and Development.* New York: Holt, Rinehart and Winston.

McCarthy, J. D., and Hoge, D. R. 1982. Analysis of age effects in longitudinal studies of adolescent self-esteem. *Developmental Psychology,* 18:372–379.

McCartney, W. 1968. *Olfaction and Odours.* New York: Springer-Verlag.

McClelland, D. C., Constantian, C. A., Regalado, D., and Stone, C. 1978. Making it to maturity. *Psychology Today,* 12 (June):42+.

Maccoby, E. E. 1961. The taking of adult roles in middle childhood. *Journal of Abnormal and Social Psychology,* 63: 493–503.

———, and Feldman, S. S. 1972. Mother-attachment and stranger-reactions in the third year of life. *Monographs of the Society for Research in Child Development,* 37 (No. 1).

———, and Jacklin, C. N. 1974. *The Psychology of Sex Differences.* Stanford, Calif.: Stanford University Press.

———, and ———. 1980. Sex differences in aggression: A rejoinder and reprise. *Child Development,* 51:964–980.

———, and Maccoby, N. 1954. The interview: A tool of social science. In Lindzey, G. (ed.), *Handbook of Social Psychology.* Reading, Mass.: Addison-Wesley.

———, and Masters, J. C. 1970. Attachment and dependency. In Mussen, P. H. (ed.), *Carmichael's Manual of Child Psychology,* 3rd ed. New York: Wiley.

McCoy, E. 1982. Children of single parents. *New York Times* (May 6):19, 21.

McCrea, F. B. 1983. The politics of menopause: The "discovery" of a deficiency disease. *Social Problems,* 31:111–123.

McCune-Nicolich, L. 1981. Toward symbolic functioning: Structure of early pretend games and potential parallels with language. *Child Development,* 52:785–797.

McDavid, J. W., and Harari, H. 1966. Stereotyping of names and popularity in grade school children. *Child Development,* 37:453–459.

McDonald, R. L. 1968. The role of emotional factors in obstetric complications: A review. *Psychosomatic Medicine,* 30:222–237.

Macfarlane, J. W. 1963. From infancy to adulthood. *Childhood Education,* 39:336–342.

———. 1964. Perspectives on personality consistency and change from the guidance study. *Vita Humana,* 7:115–126.

———. 1971. The Berkeley studies: Problems and merits of longitudinal approach. In Jones, M. C., Bayley, N., Macfarlane, J. W., and Honzik, M. P. (eds.), *The Course of Human Development.* Waltham, Mass.: Xerox College Publishing.

McGraw, M. B. 1943. *The Neuromuscular Maturation of the Human Infant.* New York: Columbia University Press.

McGuire, K. D., and Weisz, J. R. 1982. Social cognition and behavior corelates of preadolescent chumship. *Child Development,* 53:1478–1484.

McGurk, H., Turnure, C., and Creighton, S. J. 1977. Auditory-visual coordination in neonates. *Child Development,* 48:138–143.

McKay, J., Sinisterra, L., McKay, A., Gomez, H., and Lloreda, P. 1978. Improving cognitive ability in chronically deprived children. *Science,* 200 (April 21):270–278.

McKenry, P. C., Walters, L. H., and Johnson, C. 1979. Adolescent pregnancy: A review of the literature. *Family Coordinator,* 28:17–28.

McKenzie, B., and Over, R. 1983. Young infants fail to imitate facial and manual gestures. *Infant Behavior and Development,* 6:85–96.

McKenzie, B. E., Tootell, H. E., and Day, R. H. 1980. Development of visual size constancy during the first year of human infancy. *Developmental Psychology,* 16:163–174.

Mackintosh, E. 1982. Mysteries. *Science 82,* 3 (October):108.

Macklin, E. D. 1974. Going very steady. *Psychology Today,* 8 (November):53–59.

———. 1978. Nonmarital heterosexual cohabitation. *Marriage and Family Review,* 1:2–10.

McLanahan, S. S. 1983. Family structure and stress: A longitudinal comparison of two-parent and female-headed families. *Journal of Marriage and the Family,* 45:347–357.

McLaughlin, S. D. 1978. Occupational sex identification and the assessment of male and female earnings inequality. *American Sociological Review,* 43:909–921.

———, and Micklin, M. 1983. The timing of the first birth and changes in personal efficacy. *Journal of Marriage and the Family,* 45:47–55.

MacLusky, N. J., and Naftolin, F. 1981. Sexual differentiation of the central nervous system. *Science,* 211:1294–1303.

McMorrow, F. 1974. *Midolescence: The Dangerous Years.* New York: Quadrangle.

McNeill, D. 1970. *The Acquisition of Language.* New York: Harper & Row.

McPherson, B., and Guppy, N. 1979. Preretirement life-style and the degree of planning for retirement. *Journal of Gerontology,* 34:254–263.

Madden, N. A., and Slavin, R. F. 1983. Mainstreaming students with mild handicaps: Academic and social outcomes. *Review of Educational Research,* 53:519–569.

Maddi, S. R. 1972. *Personality Theories: A Comparative Analysis,* rev. ed. Homewood, Ill.: Dorsey Press.

Maddox, G. L. 1963. Activity and morale: A longitudinal study of selected elderly subjects. *Social Forces,* 42: 195–204.

———. 1966. Retirement as a social event in the United States. In McKinney, J. C., and De Vyver, F. T. (eds.), *Aging and Social Policy.* New York: Appleton-Century-Crofts.

———. 1969. Disengagement theory: A critical evaluation. *The Gerontologist,* 4:80–83.

———, and Douglass, E. B. 1974. Aging and individual differences: A longitudinal analysis of social, psychological, and physiological indicators. *Journal of Gerontology,* 29:555–563.

———, and Wiley, J. 1976. Scope, concepts and methods in the study of aging. In Binstock, R. H., and Shanas, E. (eds.), *Handbook of Aging and the Social Sciences.* New York: Van Nostrand.

Main, M., and Weston, D. R. 1981. The quality of the toddler's relationship to mother and to father: Related to conflict behavior and the readiness to establish new relationships. *Child Development,* 52:932–940.

Malinak, D. P., Hoyt, M. F., and Patterson, V. 1979. Adults' reactions to the death of a parent: A preliminary study. *American Journal of Psychiatry,* 136:1152–1156.

Malinowski, B. 1964. Parenthood—The basis of social structure. In Coser, R. (ed.), *The Family: Its Structure and Functions.* New York: St. Martin's.

Maloney, L. D. 1982. Middle age. *U.S. News & World Report* (October 25):67–68.

———. 1983. A new understanding of death. *U.S. News & World Report* (July 11):62–65.

Mann, J. 1983. One-parent family: The troubles and the joys. *Newsweek* (November 28):57–62.

Mannheim, K. 1952. The problem of generations. In Mannheim, K., *Essays on the Sociology of Knowledge.* London: Routledge and Kegan Paul.

Maracek, J., and Mettee, D. R. 1972.

Avoidance of continued success as a function of self-esteem, level of esteem certainty, and responsibility for success. *Journal of Personality and Social Psychology,* 22:98–107.

Maratsos, M. P. 1973. Nonegocentric communication abilities in preschool children. *Child Development,* 44:697–700.

Marcus, M. G. 1976. The power of a name. *Psychology Today,* 10 (October):75–76f.

Marcus, R. F. 1975. The child as elicitor of parental sanctions for independent and dependent behavior: A simulation of parent-child interaction. *Developmental Psychology,* 11:443–452.

Markides, K. S., and Martin, H. W. 1979. A causal model of life satisfaction among the elderly. *Journal of Gerontology,* 34:86–93.

Markson, E. W., and Hand, J. 1970. Referral for death: Low status of the aged and referral for psychiatric hospitalization. *Aging and Human Development,* 1:261–272.

Markus, H. 1977. Self-schemata and processing information about the self. *Journal of Personality and Social Psychology,* 35:63–78.

Marotz-Baden, R., Adams, G. R., Bueche, N., Munro, B., and Munro, G. 1979. Family form or family process? Reconsidering the deficit family model approach. *Family Coordinator,* 28:5–14.

Marsh, G. R., and Thompson, L. W. 1973. Effects of age on the contingent negative variation in a pitch discrimination task. *Journal of Gerontology,* 28:56–62.

Marsh, R. M. 1967. *Comparative Sociology.* New York: Harcourt, Brace & World.

Martin, C. L., and Halverson, C. F., Jr. 1981. A schematic processing model of sex typing and stereotyping in children. *Child Development,* 52:1119–1134.

Martin, D. 1976. *Battered Wives.* San Francisco: Glide.

Martin, J. A. 1981. A longitudinal study of the consequences of early mother-infant interaction. *Monographs of the Society for Research in Child Development,* 46 (190).

Martin, M. J., and Walters, J. 1982. Familial correlates of selected types of child abuse and neglect. *Journal of Marriage and the Family,* 44:267–276.

Martorano, S. C. 1977. A developmental analysis of performance on Piaget's formal operations tasks. *Developmental Psychology,* 13:666–672.

Marvin, R. S., Greenberg, M. T., and Mossler, D. G. 1976. The early development of conceptual perspective taking: Distinguishing among multiple perspectives. *Child Development,* 47:511–514.

Marx, J. L. 1982. Autoimmunity in left-handers. *Science,* 217:141–144.

Marx, K. 1844. Estranged labour—Economic and philosophic manuscripts of 1844. In Mills, C. W. (ed.), *Images of Man.* New York: George Braziller, 1960.

Maslow, A. H. 1955. Deficiency motivation and growth motivation. In Jones, M. R. (ed.), *Nebraska Symposium on Motivation.* Lincoln: University of Nebraska Press.

———. 1967. Self-actualization and beyond. In Bugental, J. F. T. (ed.), *Challenges of Humanistic Psychology.* New York: McGraw-Hill.

———. 1968. *Toward a Psychology of Being,* 2nd ed. New York: Van Nostrand.

———. 1970. *Motivation and Personality,* 2nd ed. New York: Harper & Row.

Masters, J. C. 1979. Interpreting "imitative" responses in early infancy. *Science,* 205:215.

———, and Furman, W. 1981. Popularity, individual friendship selection, and specific peer interaction among children. *Developmental Psychology,* 17:344–350.

Masters, W. H., and Johnson, V. E. 1966. *Human Sexual Response.* Boston: Little, Brown.

Matas, L., Arend, R. A., and Sroufe, L. A. 1978. Continuity of adaptation in the second year: The relationship between quality of attachment and later competence. *Child Development,* 49:547–556.

Matras, J. 1975. *Social Inequality, Stratification, and Mobility.* Englewood Cliffs, N.J.: Prentice-Hall.

Matthews, K. A. 1982. Psychological perspectives on the Type A behavior pattern. *Psychological Bulletin,* 91:293–323.

Maurer, D. M., and Maurer, C. E. 1976. Newborn babies see better than you think. *Psychology Today,* 10 (October): 85–88.

———, and Salapatek, P. 1976. Developmental changes in the scanning of faces by young infants. *Child Development,* 47:523–527.

Maxwell, J. W. 1976. The keeping fathers of America. *Family Coordinator,* 25:387–392.

Mazess, R. B., and Forman, S. H. 1979. Longevity and age exaggeration in Vilcabamba, Ecuador. *Journal of Gerontology,* 34:94–98.

Mazor, M. D. 1979. Barren couples. *Psychology Today,* 12:101 +.

Mead, G. H. 1934. *Mind, Self, and Other.* Chicago: University of Chicago Press.

Mead, M. 1935. *Sex and Temperament in Three Primitive Societies.* New York: Morrow.

———. 1949. *Male and Female.* New York: Morrow.

———, and MacGregor, F. C. 1951. *Growth and Culture: A Photographic Study of Balinese Childhood.* New York: Putnam.

———, and Newton, N. 1967. Fatherhood. In Richardson, S. A., and Guttmacher, A. F. (eds.), *Childbearing—Its Social and Psychological Aspects.* Baltimore: Williams and Wilkins.

Medawar, P. B. 1977. Unnatural science. *New York Review of Books,* 24 (February 3):13–18.

Melko, M., and Cargan, L. 1981. The singles boom and bust. *American Demographics,* 3:30–31.

Meltzoff, A. N., and Moore, M. K. 1977. Imitation of facial and manual gestures by human neonates. *Science,* 198:75–78.

———, and ———. 1979. Interpreting "imitative" responses in early infancy. *Science,* 205:217–219.

———, and ———. 1983. Methodological issues in studies of imitation: Comments on McKenzie & Over and Koepke et al. *Infant Behavior and Development,* 6:103–108.

Mendes, H. A. 1976. Single fathers. *Family Coordinator,* 25:439–444.

Meredith, H. V. 1973. Somatological development. In Wolman, B. B. (ed.), *Handbook of General Psychology.* Englewood Cliffs, N.J.: Prentice-Hall.

Merton, R. K. 1968. *Social Theory and Social Structure,* enlarged ed. New York: Free Press.

Meyers, C. E. 1966. New trends in child study. *Child Study,* 28 (No. 3).

Midlarsky, E., Bryan, J. H., and Brickman, P. 1973. Aversive approval: Interactive effects of modeling and reinforcement on altruistic behavior. *Child Development,* 44:321–328.

Mileski, M., and Black, D. 1972. The social organization of homosexuality. *Urban Life and Culture,* 1:187–199.

Milgram, S. 1974. *Obedience to Authority.* New York: Harper & Row.

Miller, B. C. 1976. A multivariate developmental model of marital satisfaction. *Journal of Marriage and the Family,* 38:643–657.

———, and Sollie, D. L. 1980. Normal stresses during the transition to parenthood. *Family Relations,* 29:459–465.

Miller, E. 1981. Elevated maternal hemoglobin A in early pregnancy and major congenital anomalies in infants of diabetic mothers. *New England Journal of Medicine,* 304:1331–1334.

Miller, N., and Maruyama, G. 1976. Ordinal position and peer popularity.

Journal of Personality and Social Psychology, 33:123–131.

Miller, S. J. 1965. The social dilemma of the aging leisure participant. In Rose, A. M., and Peterson, W. A. (eds.), *Older People and Their Social World.* Philadelphia: F. A. Davis.

Milne, L. 1924. *The Home of an Eastern Clan.* Oxford: Clarendon Press.

Mindel, C. H., and Vaughan, C. E. 1978. A multidimensional approach to religiosity and disengagement. *Journal of Gerontology,* 33:103–108.

Mischel, W. 1968. *Personality and Assessment.* New York: Wiley.

———. 1969. Continuity and change in personality. *American Psychologist,* 24:1012–1018.

———. 1970. Sex-typing and socialization. In Mussen, P. H. (ed.), *Carmichael's Manual of Child Psychology,* 3rd ed. Vol. 2. New York: Wiley.

———. 1971. *Introduction to Personality.* New York: Holt, Rinehart and Winston.

———. 1973. Toward a cognitive social learning reconceptualization of personality. *Psychological Review,* 80:252–283.

———. 1977. On the future of personality measurement. *American Psychologist,* 32:246–254.

———, and Liebert, R. M. 1966. Effects of discrepancies between deserved and imposed reward criteria on their acquisition and transmission. *Journal of Personality and Social Psychology,* 3:45–53.

———, and Mischel, H. N. 1976. A cognitive social learning approach to morality and self-regulation. In Lickona, T. (ed.), *Moral Development and Behavior: Theory, Research, and Social Issues.* New York: Holt, Rinehart and Winston.

Moerk, E. L. 1977. *Pragmatic and Semantic Aspects of Early Language Development.* Baltimore: University Park Press.

Mogul, K. M. 1979. Women in midlife: Decisions, rewards, and conflicts related to work and careers. *American Journal of Psychiatry,* 136:1139–1143.

Molfese, D. L., Molfese, V. J., and Carrell, P. L. 1982. Early language development. In Wolman, B. B. (ed.), *Handbook of Developmental Psychology.* Englewood Cliffs, N.J.: Prentice-Hall.

Money, J., and Ehrhardt, A. 1972. *Man and Woman; Boy and Girl.* Baltimore: Johns Hopkins University Press.

———, and Tucker, P. 1975. *Sexual Signatures: On Being a Man or a Woman.* Boston: Little, Brown.

Montada, L., and Filipp, S. H. 1976. Implications of life-span developmental psychology for childhood education. In Reese, H. W. (ed.), *Advances in Child Development and Behavior.* Vol. 2. New York: Academic Press.

Montagu, A. 1964. *Life Before Birth.* New York: New American Library.

———. 1981. *Growing Young.* New York: McGraw-Hill.

Montemayor, R. 1982. The relationship between parent-adolescent conflict and the amount of time adolescents spend alone and with parents and peers. *Child Development,* 53:1512–1519.

———, and Eisen, M. 1977. The development of self-conceptions from childhood to adolescence. *Developmental Psychology,* 13:314–319.

Moore, D. 1981. The perils of a two-income family. *New York Times Magazine* (September 27):91–96.

———. 1983. America's neglected elderly. *New York Times Magazine* (January 30):30–35.

———. 1984. It's either me or your job! *Working Woman* (April):108–111.

Moore, M. K., Borton, R., and Darby, B. L. 1978. Visual tracking in young infants: Evidence for object identity or object permanence? *Journal of Experimental Child Psychology,* 25:183–198.

Morgan, G. A., and Ricciuti, H. N. 1969. Infants' responses to strangers during the first year. In Foss, B. M. (ed.), *Determinants of Infant Behavior.* Vol. 4. New York: Wiley.

Morgan, W. G. 1973. Situational specificity in altruistic behavior. *Representative Research in Social Psychology,* 4:56–66.

Morganthau, T. 1983. Gay America in Transition. *Newsweek* (August 8):30–40.

Morin, S. F., and Garfinkle, E. M. 1978. Male homophobia. *Journal of Social Issues,* 34:29–47.

Morrice, G. 1979. Life-or-death issue faces public. *Columbus Dispatch* (June 16):B3.

Morse, N. C., and Weiss, R. S. 1955. The function and meaning of work and the job. *American Sociological Review,* 20:191–198.

Mortimer, J. T., and Simmons, R. G. 1978. Adult socialization. *Annual Review of Sociology,* 4:421–454.

Moshman, D. 1977. Consolidation and stage formation in the emergence of formal operations. *Developmental Psychology,* 13:95–100.

Moskowitz, B. A. 1978. The acquisition of language. *Scientific American,* 239 (November):92–108.

Moss, H. A., and Susman, E. J. 1980. Constancy and change in personality development. In Brim, O. G., Jr., and Kagan, J. (eds.), *Constancy and Change in Human Development.* Cambridge, Mass.: Harvard University Press.

Mosteller, F., and Moynihan, D. P. 1972. *On Equality of Educational Opportunity.* New York: Vintage.

Moustakas, C. E., Sigel, I. E., and Schalock, M. D. 1956. An objective method for the measurement and analysis of child-adult interaction. *Child Development,* 27:109–134.

Moyles, E. W., and Wolins, M. 1971. Group care and intellectual development. *Developmental Psychology,* 4:370–380.

———, Bleier, M., Krakow, J., Hegedus, K., and Cournoyer, P. 1976. The development of peer verbal interaction among two-year-old boys. *Child Development,* 48:284–287.

———, and Brenner, J. 1977. The origins of social skills and interaction among playgroup toddlers. *Child Development,* 48:854–861.

———, and Lucas, T. 1975. A developmental analysis of peer interaction among toddlers. In Lewis, M., and Rosenblum, L. A. (eds.), *Friendship and Peer Relations.* New York: Wiley.

Mueller, R. F. 1983. Evaluation of a protocol for post-mortem examination of stillbirths. *New England Journal of Medicine,* 309:586–590.

Muller, P. F., Campbell, H. E., Graham, W. E., Brittain, H., Fitzgerald, J. A., Hogan, N. A., Muller, V. H., and Ritterhouse, A. H. 1971. Perinatal factors and their relationship to mental retardation and other parameters of development. *American Journal of Obstetrics and Gynecology,* 109:1205–1210.

Munroe, R. L., and Munroe, R. W. 1975. *Cross-Cultural Human Development.* Monterey, Calif.: Brooks/Cole.

Murdock, G. P. 1934. *Our Primitive Contemporaries.* New York: Macmillan.

———. 1935. Comparative data on the division of labor by sex. *Social Forces,* 15:551–553.

———. 1949. *Social Structure.* New York: Macmillan.

———. 1957. Anthropology as a comparative science. *Behavioral Science,* 2:249–254.

———, Ford, C. S., Hudson, A. E., Kennedy, R., Simmons, L. W., and Whiting, J. W. M. 1971. *Outline of Cultural Materials.* New Haven: Human Relations Area Files.

Murphy, C. M. 1978. Pointing in the context of a shared activity. *Child Development,* 49:371–380.

Murphy, G., Murphy, L. B., and Newcomb, T. 1937. *Experimental Social Psychology.* New York: Harper & Row.

Murphy, L. B. 1937. *Social Behavior and Child Personality.* New York: Columbia University Press.

Murphy, M. D., Sanders, R. E., Gabrie-sheski, A. S., and Schmitt, F. A. 1981. Metamemory in the aged. *Journal of Gerontology,* 36:185–193.

Murray, A. D. 1979. Infant crying as an elicitor of parental behavior: An examination of two models. *Psychological Bulletin,* 86:191–215.

———, Dolby, R. M., Nation, R. L., and Thomas, D. B. 1981. Effects of epidural anesthesia on newborns and their mothers. *Child Development,* 52:71–82.

Murstein, B. I. 1972. Physical attractiveness and marital choice. *Journal of Personality and Social Psychology,* 22:8–12.

Muson, H. 1979. Moral thinking: Can it be taught? *Psychology Today,* 12 (February): 48+.

Mussen, P. H., Harris, S., Rutherford, R., and Keasey, C. B. 1970. Honesty and altruism among preadolescents. *Developmental Psychology,* 3:169–194.

———, Honzik, M. P., and Eichorn, D. H. 1982. Early adult antecedents of life satisfaction at age 70. *Journal of Gerontology,* 37:316–322.

———, and Jones, M. C. 1957. Self-conceptions, motivations, and interpersonal attitudes of late- and early-maturing boys. *Child Development,* 28:243–256.

Mynatt, C., and Sherman, S. J. 1975. Responsibility attribution in groups and individuals: A direct test of the diffusion of responsibility hypothesis. *Journal of Personality and Social Psychology,* 32:1111–1118.

Nadel, S. F. 1951. *The Foundations of Social Anthropology.* New York: Free Press.

Naeye, R. L. 1980. Sudden infant death. *Scientific American,* 242 (April):56–62.

Nahemow, L., and Lawton, M. P. 1975. Similarity and propinquity in friendship formation. *Journal of Personality and Social Psychology,* 32:205–213.

Nassi, A. J., and Abramowitz, S. I. 1979. Transition or transformation? Personal and political development of former Berkeley Free Speech Movement activists. *Journal of Youth and Adolescence,* 8:21–35.

National Academy of Sciences. 1982. *Marijuana and Health.* Washington, D.C.: National Academy Press.

National Center for Education Statistics. 1983. *High School and Beyond.* Washington, D.C.: Government Printing Office.

National Centers for Disease Control. 1984. Press release, March 22—on breast feeding.

National Commission on Youth. 1980. *The Transition of Youth to Adulthood: A Bridge Too Long.* Boulder, Col.: Westview Press.

National Institute of Education. 1977. *Violent Schools—Safe Schools.* Washington, D.C.: Government Printing Office.

National Institute of Mental Health. 1980. *Special Report: Schizophrenia 1980.* Washington, D.C.: Government Printing Office.

Naus, M. J., Ornstein, P. A., and Kreshtool, K. 1977. Developmental differences in recall and recognition: The relationship between rehearsal and memory as test expectation changes. *Journal of Experimental Child Psychology,* 23:252–265.

Neale, J. M., and Oltmanns, T. F. 1980. *Schizophrenia.* New York: Wiley.

Neimark, E. D. 1974. Intellectual development during adolescence. In Horowitz, F. (ed.), *Review of Research in Child Development.* Vol. 5. New York: Academic Press.

Neisser, U. 1967. *Cognitive Psychology.* New York: Appleton-Century-Crofts.

———. 1983. A conversation. *Psychology Today,* 17 (May):54–62.

Nelson, B. 1982. Early memory: Why is it so elusive? *New York Times* (December 7):17.

———. 1983*a*. Age link is found for mental woes. *New York Times* (October 23):24.

———. 1983*b*. Despair among jobless is on rise, studies find. *New York Times* (April 2):8.

Nelson, K. 1972. The relation of form recognition to concept development. *Child Development,* 43:67–74.

———. 1973. Structure and strategy in learning to talk. *Monographs of the Society for Research in Child Development,* 38 (No. 149).

———. 1981. Individual differences in language development: Implications for language development. *Developmental Psychology,* 17:170–187.

———, Rescorla, L., Gruendel, J., and Benedict, H. 1978. Early lexicons: What do they mean? *Child Development,* 49:960–968.

Nelson, K. E. 1977. Facilitating children's syntax acquisition. *Developmental Psychology,* 13:101–107.

———, and Earl, N. 1973. Information search by preschool children: Induced use of categories and category hierarchies. *Child Development,* 44: 682–685.

Nelson, M., and Nelson, G. K. 1982. Problems of equity in the reconstituted family: A social exchange analysis. *Family Relations,* 31:223–231.

Nelson, N. M., Enkin, M. W., Saigal, S., Bennett, K. J., Milner, R., and Sackett, D. L. 1980. A randomized clinical trial of the Leboyer approach to childbirth. *New England Journal of Medicine,* 302:655–660.

Nemy, E. 1982. Most feel their age is unreal. *New York Times* (November 10):19.

Neugarten, B. L. 1964. *Personality in Middle and Late Life.* New York: Atherton Press.

———. 1968*a*. Adult personality: Toward a psychology of the life cycle. In Vinacke, E. (ed.), *Readings in General Psychology.* New York: American Book.

———. 1968*b*. The awareness of middle age. In Neugarten, B. L. (ed.), *Middle Age and Aging.* Chicago: University of Chicago Press.

———. 1969. Continuities and discontinuities of psychological issues into adult life. *Human Development,* 12:121–130.

———. 1971. Grow old along with me! The best is yet to be. *Psychology Today,* 6 (December):45–48ff.

———. 1977. Personality and aging. In Birren, J. E., and Schaie, K. W. (eds.), *Handbook of the Psychology of Aging.* New York: Van Nostrand.

———. 1979. Time, age, and the life cycle. *American Journal of Psychiatry,* 136:887–894.

———. 1982*a*. The aging society. *National Forum,* 42:3.

———. 1982*b*. Age or need? *National Forum,* 42:25–27.

———, and Hagestad, G. O. 1976. Age and the life course. In Binstock, R. H., and Shanas, E. (eds.), *Handbook of Aging and the Social Sciences.* New York: Van Nostrand.

———, Havighurst, R. J., and Tobin, S. S. 1968. Personality and patterns of aging. In Neugarten, B. L. (ed.), *Middle Age and Aging.* Chicago: University of Chicago Press.

———, Moore, J. W., and Lowe, J. C. 1965. Age norms, age constraints, and adult socialization. *American Journal of Sociology,* 70:710–717.

———, and Weinstein, K. 1964. The changing American grandparent. *Journal of Marriage and the Family,* 26:199–204.

———, Wood, V., Kraines, R. J., and Loomis, B. 1963. Women's attitudes toward the menopause. *Vita Humana,* 6:140–151.

Newcomb, M. D., and Bentler, P. M. 1980. Cohabitation before marriage. *Alternative Lifestyles,* 3:65–85.

Newcomb, P. R. 1979. Cohabitation in

America: An assessment of consequences. *Journal of Marriage and the Family,* 41:597–603.

Newmark, S. R., Rose, L. I., Todd, R., Birk, L., and Naftolin, F. 1979. Gonadotropin, estradiol, and testosterone profiles in homosexual men. *American Journal of Psychiatry,* 136: 767–771.

New York Times. 1977. Violence is occurring in the best of families. (March 20):6E.

New York Times. 1982. New views on marriage. (December 23):14.

Nietzke, A. 1977. The miracle of Kübler-Ross. *Human Behavior,* 6 (September):18–27.

Nisan, M., and Kohlberg, L. 1982. Universality and variation in moral judgment: A longitudinal and cross-sectional study in Turkey. *Child Development,* 53:865–876.

Nisbett, R. E. 1972. Hunger, obesity, and the ventromedial hypothalamus. *Psychological Review,* 79:433–453.

Niswander, K. R. 1976. *Obstetrics.* Boston: Little, Brown.

Nock, S. L. 1979. The family life cycle: Empirical or conceptual tool? *Journal of Marriage and the Family,* 41: 15–26.

Nora, J. J., and Nora, A. H. 1973. Birth defects and oral contraceptives. *Lancet,* 1:941–942.

———, and ———. 1975. A syndrome of multiple congenital anomalies associated with teratogenic exposure. *Archives of Environmental Health,* 30:17–21.

———, ———, Sommerville, R. J., Hill, R. M., and McNamara, D. G. 1967. Maternal exposure to potential teratogens. *Journal of the American Medical Association,* 202:1065–1069.

Norr, K. L., Block, C. R., Charles, A., Meyering, S., and Meyers, E. 1977. Explaining pain and enjoyment in childbirth. *Journal of Health and Social Behavior,* 18:260–275.

Nye, F. I. 1957. Child adjustment in broken and in unhappy unbroken homes. *Marriage and Family Living,* 19:356–361.

Nyiti, R. M. 1976. The development of conservation in the Meru children of Tanzania. *Child Development,* 47: 1122–1129.

Nylan, W. L. 1976. *The Heredity Factor: Genes, Chromosomes, and You.* New York: Grosset & Dunlap.

O'Connell, A. N., and Rotter, N. G. 1979. The influence of stimulus age and sex on person perception. *Journal of Gerontology,* 34:220–228.

O'Connor, R. D. 1969. Modification of social withdrawal through symbolic modeling. *Journal of Applied Behavior Analysis,* 2:15–22.

O'Discoll, P., and Neuman, J. 1983. Federal hunger report due. *USA Today* (December 12):1, 2.

Offer, D. 1969. *The Psychological World of the Teen-Ager: A Study of Normal Adolescent Boys.* New York: Basic Books.

———, and Offer, J. B. 1975. *From Teenage to Young Manhood.* New York: Basic Books.

———, Ostrov, E., and Howard, K. I. 1981. *The Adolescent: A Psychological Self-Portrait.* New York: Basic Books.

Okie, S. 1981. Parents inspire infant woes. *Columbus* (Ohio) *Dispatch* (January 11):E1.

Olweus, D. 1978. *Aggression in the Schools: Bullies and Whipping Boys.* Washington, D.C.: Hemisphere.

———. 1979. Stability of aggressive reaction patterns in males: A review. *Psychological Bulletin,* 86:852–875.

———. 1980. Familial and temperamental determinants of aggressive behavior in adolescent boys: A causal analysis. *Developmental Psychology,* 16:644–660.

O'Malley, P. M., and Bachman, J. G. 1983. Self-esteem: Change and stability between ages 13 and 23. *Developmental Psychology,* 19:257–268.

Oppenheimer, J. R. 1955. Analogy in science. *American Psychologist,* 11:126–135.

O'Reilly, J. 1983. Wife beating: The silent crime. *Time* (September 5):23–26.

Ornstein, P. A., Naus, M. J., and Liberty, C. 1975. Rehearsal and organizational processes in children's memory. *Child Development,* 46:818–830.

Orthner, D. K., Brown, T., and Ferguson, D. 1976. Single-parent fatherhood: An emerging family life style. *Family Coordinator,* 25:429–437.

Osis, K., and Haraldsson, E. 1977. *At the Hour of Death.* New York: Avon.

Osofsky, J. D. 1976. Neonatal characteristics and mother-infant interaction in two observational situations. *Child Development,* 47:1138–1147.

———, and Danzger, B. 1974. Relationships between neonatal characteristics and mother-infant interactions. *Developmental Psychology,* 10:124–130.

Osterman, P. 1980. *Getting Started: The Youth Labor Market.* Cambridge, Mass.: MIT Press.

Ostwald, P. F., and Peltzman, P. 1974. The cry of the human infant. *Scientific American,* 230 (March):84–90.

Overmier, J. B., and Seligman, M. E. P. 1967. Effects of inescapable shock upon subsequent escape and avoidance learning. *Journal of Comparative and Physiological Psychology,* 63:28–33.

Oviatt, S. L. 1980. The emerging ability to comprehend language: An experimental approach. *Child Development,* 51:97–106.

Oyama, S. 1979. The concept of the sensitive period in developmental studies. *Merrill-Palmer Quarterly,* 25:83–103.

Paige, K. E., and Paige, J. M. 1973. The politics of birth practices: A strategic analysis. *American Sociological Review,* 38:663–676.

Palmore, E. 1975. *The Honorable Elders.* Durham, N.C.: Duke University Press.

———. 1976. Review of Irving Roscow, *Socialization to Old Age. Social Forces,* 55:215–216.

———. 1978. When can age, period, and cohort be separated? *Social Forces,* 57:282–295.

———, and Cleveland, W. 1976. Aging, terminal decline, and terminal drop. *Journal of Gerontology,* 31:76–81.

———, and Kivett, V. 1977. Change in life satisfaction: A longitudinal study of persons aged 46–70. *Journal of Gerontology,* 32:311–316.

Paneth, N., Kiely, J. L., and Wallenstein, S. 1982. Newborn intensive care and neonatal mortality in low-birth-weight infants. *New England Journal of Medicine,* 307:149–155.

Parekh, V. C., Pherwani, A., Udani, P. M., and Mukherjie, S. 1970. Brain weight and head circumference in fetus, infant and children of different nutritional and socio-economic groups. *Indian Pediatrics,* 7:347–358.

Paris, B. L., and Luckey, E. B. 1966. A longitudinal study of marital satisfaction. *Sociology and Social Research,* 50:212–223.

Paris, S. G. 1978. Memory organization during children's repeated recall. *Developmental Psychology,* 14:99–106.

Parke, R. D. 1967. Nurturance, nurturance withdrawal, and resistance to deviation. *Child Development,* 38: 1101–1110.

———. 1974. Rules, roles, and resistance to deviation: Recent advances in punishment, discipline, and self-control. In Pick, A. D. (ed.), *Minnesota Symposia on Child Psychology.* Vol. 8. Minneapolis: University of Minnesota Press.

———. 1977. Punishment in children: Effects, side effects, and alternative strategies. In Hom, H. L., Jr., and Robinson, P. A. (eds.), *Psychological Processes in Early Education.* New York: Academic Press.

———. 1979. Perspectives on father-infant interaction. In Osofsky, J. D. (ed.), *Handbook of Infant Development.* New York: Wiley.

———, and Deur, J. L. 1972. Schedule of punishment and inhibition of aggression in children. *Developmental Psychology,* 7:266–269.

———, and Sawin, D. B. 1977. Fathering: It's a major role. *Psychology Today,* 11:109–112.

Parnes, H. S. 1981. *Work and Retirement—A Longitudinal Study of Men.* Cambridge, Mass.: MIT Press.

Parsons, T. 1955. Family structure and the socialization of the child. In Parsons, T., and Bales, R. (eds.), *Family, Socialization and Interaction Process.* New York: Free Press.

Parten, M. B. 1932. Social participation among pre-school children. *Journal of Abnormal and Social Psychology,* 27:243–269.

———, and Newhall, S. M. 1943. Social behavior of preschool children. In Barker, R. G., Kounin, J. S., and Wright, H. F. (eds.), *Child Behavior and Development.* New York: McGraw-Hill.

Pasamanick, B., and Knobloch, H. 1966. Retrospective studies on the epidemiology of reproductive causality: Old and new. *Merrill-Palmer Quarterly,* 12:7–26.

Pasquali, L., and Callegari, A. I. 1978. Working mothers and daughters' sex-role identification in Brazil. *Child Development,* 49:902–905.

Passman, R. H., and Blackwelder, D. E. 1981. Rewarding and punishing by mothers: The influence of progressive changes in the quality of their sons' apparent behavior. *Developmental Psychology,* 17:614–619.

Pastor, D. L. 1981. The quality of mother-infant attachment and its relationship to toddlers' initial sociability with peers. *Developmental Psychology,* 17:326–335.

Patterson, G. R., Littman, R. A., and Bricker, W. 1967. Assertive behavior in children: A step toward a theory of aggression. *Monographs of the Society for Research in Child Development,* 32 (5).

Pearl, D. 1982. *Television and Behavior: 10 Years of Scientific Research.* Washington, D.C.: Government Printing Office.

Peck, R. C. 1968. Psychological developments in the second half of life. In Neugarten, B. L. (ed.), *Middle Age and Aging.* Chicago: University of Chicago Press.

Pedersen, E., Faucher, T. A., and Eaton, W. W. 1978. A new perspective on the effects of first-grade teachers on children's subsequent adult status. *Harvard Educational Review,* 48:1–31.

Pedersen, F. A. (ed.). 1980. *The Father-Infant Relationship: Observational Studies in the Family Setting.* New York: Praeger.

Pedersen, J. 1977. *The Pregnant Diabetic and Her Newborn: Problems and Management,* 2nd ed. Baltimore: Williams & Wilkins.

Pederson, D. R., Champagne, L., and Pederson, L. 1969. Relative soothing effects of vertical and horizontal rocking. Paper presented at the meeting of the Society for Research in Child Development, Santa Monica, California, March 1969.

———, Rock-Green, A., and Elder, J. L. 1981. The role of action in the development of pretend play in young children. *Developmental Psychology,* 17:756–759.

Pennington, B. F., Bender, B., Puck, M., Salbenblatt, J., and Robinson, A. 1982. Learning disabilities in children with sex chromosome anomalies. *Child Development,* 53:1182–1192.

Pennoyer, M. M., Graham, F. K., Hartmann, A. F., Sr., Jones, B., McCoy, E. L., Swarm, P. A., Meyer, R. J., and Endres, R. K. 1956. The relationship of paranatal experience to oxygen saturation in newborn infants. *Journal of Pediatrics,* 49:685–698.

Pentella, C. 1983. More students say good night at the front door. *On Campus* (January):16.

Perlmutter, M., and Myers, N. A. 1975. Young children's coding and storage of visual and verbal material. *Child Development,* 46:215–219.

———, and ———. 1976. Recognition memory in preschool children. *Developmental Psychology,* 12:271–272.

Perone, M., and Baron, A. 1982. Age-related effects of pacing on acquisition and performance of response sequences: An operant analysis. *Journal of Gerontology,* 37:443–449.

Perry, D. G., and Bussey, K. 1979. The social learning theory of sex differences: Imitation is alive and well. *Journal of Personality and Social Psychology,* 37:1699–1712.

Persell, C. H. 1977. *Education and Inequality.* New York: Free Press.

Peterman, D. J., Ridley, C. A., and Anderson, S. M. 1974. A comparison of cohabiting and noncohabiting college students. *Journal of Marriage and the Family,* 36:344–354.

Peters, R. D., and Bernfeld, G. A. 1983. Reflection-impulsivity and social reasoning. *Developmental Psychology,* 19:78–81.

Petersen, A. C. 1983. Menarche: Meaning of measures and measures of meaning. In Golub, S. (ed.), *Menarche: The Transition from Girl to Woman.* Lexington, Mass.: Heath.

———, and Taylor, B. 1980. The biological approach to adolescence. In Adelson, J. (ed.), *Handbook of Adolescent Psychology.* New York: Wiley.

Peterson, W. F., Morese, K. N., and Kaltreider, D. F. 1965. Smoking and prematurity: A preliminary report based on study of 7740 Caucasians. *Obstetrics and Gynecology,* 26:775–779.

Petrig, B., Julesz, B., Kropfl, W., Baumgartner, G., and Anliker, M. 1981. Development of stereopsis and cortical binocularity in human infants: Electrophysiological evidence. *Science,* 213:1402–1404.

Petros, T. V., Zehr, H. D., and Chabot, R. J. 1983. Adult age differences in accessing and retrieving information from long-term memory. *Journal of Gerontology,* 38:589–592.

Petrowsky, M. 1976. Marital status, sex, and the social networks of the elderly. *Journal of Marriage and the Family,* 38:749–756.

Pezdek, K. 1983. Memory for items and their spatial locations by young and elderly adults. *Developmental Psychology,* 19:895–900.

Phoenix, C. H., Goy, R. W., and Resko, J. A. 1969. Psychosexual differentiation as a function of androgenic stimulation. In Diamond, M. (ed.), *Reproduction and Sexual Behavior.* Bloomington: Indiana University Press.

Piaget, J. 1932. *The Moral Judgment of the Child.* Trans. by M. Gabain. London: Kegan Paul, Trench, Trubner and Company.

———. 1952*a*. *The Origins of Intelligence in Children.* Trans. by M. Cook. New York: International Universities Press.

———. 1952*b*. *The Child's Conception of Number.* New York: Humanities Press.

———. 1954. *The Construction of Reality in the Child.* New York: Basic Books.

———. 1962. *Play, Dreams and Imitation in Childhood.* New York: Norton.

———. 1967. *Six Psychological Studies.* New York: Random House.

———. 1970. Conversations. *Psychology Today,* 3 (May):25–32.

———. 1972. Intellectual evolution from adolescence to adulthood. *Human Development,* 15:1–12.

———, and Inhelder, B. 1956. *The Child's Conception of Space.* London: Routledge and Kegan Paul.

Pines, M. 1971. A child's mind is shaped

before age 2. *Life* (December 17):63–71ff.

———. 1979*a*. Superkids. *Psychology Today,* 12 (January):53–63.

———. 1979*b*. Good Samaritans at age two? *Psychology Today,* 13 (June):66–77.

———. 1980. Psychological hardiness. *Psychology Today,* 14 (December):34–44+.

———. 1981. The civilizing of Genie. *Psychology Today,* 15 (September):28–34.

———. 1982*a*. Baby, you're incredible. *Psychology Today,* 16 (February):48–53.

———. 1982*b*. Behavior and heredity: Links for specific traits are growing stronger. *New York Times* (June 29):19, 22.

———. 1983. Can a rock walk? *Psychology Today,* 17 (November):46–54.

Pinneau, S. F. 1955. The infantile disorders of hospitalism and anaclitic depression. *Psychological Bulletin,* 52:429–452.

Platt, B. S., and Stewart, R. J. C. 1971. Reversible and irreversible effects of protein-calorie deficiency on the central nervous system of animals and man. *World Review of Nutrition and Dietetics,* 13:43–85.

Pleck, J. H. 1981. *The Myth of Masculinity.* Cambridge, Mass.: MIT Press.

Plomin, R., DeFries, J. C., and McClearn, G. E. 1980. *Behavioral Genetics: A Primer.* San Francisco: Freeman.

———, and Foch, T. T. 1981. Sex differences and individual differences. *Child Development,* 52:383–385.

Plumb, J. H. 1972. *Children.* London: Penguin.

Popkin, B. M., Bilsborrow, R. E., and Akin, J. S. 1982. Breast-feeding patterns in low-income countries. *Science,* 218:1088–1093.

Porter, J. 1971. *Black Child, White Child: The Development of Racial Attitudes.* Cambridge, Mass.: Harvard University Press.

Portman, M. V. 1895. Notes on the Andamanese. *Anthropological Institute of Great Britain and Ireland,* 25:361–371.

Posner, M. I. 1967. Short-term memory systems in human memory. *Acta Psychologica,* 27:267–284.

Postman, N. 1982. *The Disappearance of Childhood.* New York: Delacorte Press.

Potkin, S. G., Cannon, H. E., Murphy, D. L., and Wyatt, R. J. 1978. Are paranoid schizophrenics biologically different from other schizophrenics? *New England Journal of Medicine,* 298:61–66.

Powell, L. F. 1974. The effect of extra stimulation and maternal involvement on the development of low-birth-weight infants and on maternal behavior. *Child Development,* 45:106–113.

Power, T. G., Hildebrandt, K. A., and Fitzgerald, H. E. 1982. Adults' responses to infants varying in facial expression and perceived attractiveness. *Infant Behavior and Development,* 5:33–44.

Powers, E. A., and Bultena, G. L. 1976. Sex differences in intimate friendships of old age. *Journal of Marriage and the Family,* 38:739–747.

Prawat, R. S., Jones, H., and Hampton, J. 1979. Longitudinal study of attitude development in pre-, early, and later adolescent samples. *Journal of Educational Psychology,* 71:363–369.

Presser, H. B., and Cain, V. S. 1983. Shift work among dual-earner couples with children. *Science,* 219:876–879.

Pressey, S. L., and Kuhlen, R. G. 1957. *Psychological Development through the Life-Span.* New York: Harper & Row.

Preyer, W. 1880. Psychogenesis. *Dt. Rundschau,* 23:198–221.

Priest, R. F., and Sawyer, J. 1973. Proximity and peership: Bases of balance in interpersonal attraction. *American Journal of Sociology,* 72:633–649.

Prince, J. R. 1968. The effect of Western education on science conceptualization in New Guinea. *British Journal of Educational Psychology,* 38:64–74.

Putallaz, M. 1983. Predicting children's sociometric status from their behavior. *Child Development,* 54:1417–1426.

Quadagno, D. M., Briscoe, R., and Quadagno, J. S. 1977. Effect of perinatal gonadal hormones on selected nonsexual behavior patterns: A critical assessment of the nonhuman and human literature. *Psychological Bulletin,* 84:62–80.

Quilter, R. E., Giambra, L. M., and Benson, P. E. 1983. Longitudinal age changes in vigilance over an eighteen year interval. *Journal of Gerontology,* 38:51–54.

Quinn, R. P., Staines, G. L., and McCullough, M. R. 1974. *Job Satisfaction: Is There a Trend?* Manpower Research Monograph No. 30. U.S. Department of Labor. Washington, D.C.: Government Printing Office.

Quinn, W. H. 1983. Personal and family adjustment in later life. *Journal of Marriage and the Family,* 45:57–73.

Rabbitt, P., and Vyas, S. M. 1980. Selective anticipation for events in old age. *Journal of Gerontology,* 35:913–919.

Rabinowitz, J. C. 1984. Aging and recognition failure. *Journal of Gerontology,* 39:65–71.

Rabkin, J. G., and Struening, E. L. 1976. Life events, stress, and illness. *Science,* 194 (December 3):1013–1020.

Radcliffe-Brown, A. R. 1940. On joking relationships. *Africa,* 13:195–210.

Radke-Yarrow, M., and Zahn-Waxler, C. 1976. Dimensions and correlates of prosocial behavior in young children. *Child Development,* 47:118–125.

Rahe, R. H. 1968. Life-change measurements as a predictor of illness. *Proceedings of the Royal Society of Medicine,* 61:1124–1126.

Rajecki, D. W., Lamb, M. E., and Obmascher, P. 1978. Toward a general theory of infantile attachment: A comparative review of aspects of the social bond. *Behavioral and Brain Sciences,* 3:417–464.

Rapoport, R., Rapoport, R. N., and Strelitz, Z. 1976. *Fathers, Mothers and Society: Towards New Alliances.* New York: Basic Books.

Raschke, H. J., and Raschke, V. J. 1979. Family conflict and children's self-concepts: A comparison of intact and single-parent families. *Journal of Marriage and the Family,* 41:367–374.

Rasmussen, O. V., and Lunde, I. 1980. Evaluation of investigations of 200 torture victims. *Danish Medical Bulletin,* 27:241–243.

Rebenkoff, M. 1979. Study shows teen years are easiest for childbirth. *New York Times* (April 24):C5.

Reese, H. W., and Lipsitt, L. P. 1970. *Experimental Child Psychology.* New York: Academic Press.

———, and Overton, W. F. 1970. Models of development and theories of development. In Goulet, L. R., and Baltes, P. B. (eds.), *Life-Span Developmental Psychology: Research and Theory.* New York: Academic Press.

Regev, E., Beit-Hallahmi, B., and Sharabany, R. 1980. Affective expression in kibbutz-communal, kibbutz-familial, and city-raised children in Israel. *Child Development,* 51:232–237.

Reich, W. 1981. Psycho-ideology. *New York Times* (January 11):25.

Reimanis, G., and Green, R. F. 1971. Imminence of death and intellectual decrement in the aging. *Developmental Psychology,* 5:270–272.

Reinhold, R. 1979. Have blacks done better? *New York Times* (July 8):2E.

———. 1981. U.S. panel proposes uniform law saying life ends at brain's death. *New York Times* (July 10):1, 6.

Reiss, I. L. 1972. Premarital sexuality: Past, present and future. In Reiss, I. L. (ed.), *Readings on the Family Sys-*

tem. New York: Holt, Rinehart and Winston.

———. 1976. *Family Systems in America*, 2nd ed. Hinsdale, Ill.: Dryden Press.

Relman, A. S. 1982. *Marijuana and Health*. Washington, D.C.: National Academy Press.

Rensberger, B. 1981. Tinkering with life. *Science 81*, 2 (November):45–49.

Rescorla, L., 1976. Concept formation in word learning. Unpublished doctoral dissertation, Yale University.

Rescorla, R. A. 1967. Pavlovian conditioning and its proper control procedures. *Psychological Review*, 74:71–80.

Restak, R. 1975. Genetic counseling for defective parents: The danger of knowing too much. *Psychology Today*, 9 (September):21–23ff.

Rheingold, H. L. 1961. The effect of environmental stimulation upon social and exploratory behavior in the human infant. In Foss, B. M. (ed.), *Determinants of Infant Behavior*. Vol. 1. New York: Wiley.

———. 1968. Infancy. In Sills, D. (ed.), *International Encyclopedia of the Social Sciences*. New York: Macmillan.

———. 1969*a*. The effect of a strange environment on the behavior of infants. In Foss, B. M. (ed.), *Determinants of Infant Behavior*. Vol. 4. New York: Wiley.

———. 1969*b*. The social and socializing infant. In Goslin, D. A. (ed.), *Handbook of Socialization Theory and Research*. Chicago: Rand McNally.

———. 1982. Little children's participation in the work of adults, a nascent prosocial behavior. *Child Development*, 53:114–125.

———, and Adams, J. L. 1980. The significance of speech to newborns. *Developmental Psychology*, 16:397–403.

———, and Cook, K. V. 1975. The contents of boys' and girls' rooms as an index of parents' behavior. *Child Development*, 46:459–463.

———, and Eckerman, C. O. 1973. Fear of the stranger: A critical examination. In Reese, H. W. (ed.), *Advances in Child Development and Behavior*. Vol. 8. New York: Academic Press.

———, Hay, D. F., and West, M. J. 1976. Sharing in the second year of life. *Child Development*, 47:1148–1158.

Ribble, M. A. 1943. *The Rights of Infants: Early Psychological Needs and Their Satisfaction*. New York: Columbia University Press.

Riegel, K. F. 1973. Dialectic operations: The final period of cognitive development. *Human Development*, 16: 346–370.

———. 1975*a*. Adult life crises: A dialectic interpretation of development. In Datan, N., and Ginsberg, L. H. (eds.), *Life-Span Developmental Psychology: Normative Life Crisis*. New York: Academic Press.

———. 1975*b*. Toward a dialectical theory of development. *Human Development*, 18:50–64.

———. 1976. The dialectics of human development. *American Psychologist*, 31:689–700.

———, and Riegel, R. M. 1972. Development, drop, and death. *Developmental Psychology*, 6:306–319.

Rieser, J., Yonas, A., and Wikner, K. 1976. Radial localization of odors by human newborns. *Child Development*, 47:856–859.

Riley, M. W. 1978. Aging, social change, and the power of ideas. *Daedalus*, 107:39–52.

———, and Foner, A. 1968. *Aging and Society: An Inventory of Research Findings*. New York: Russell Sage Foundation.

———, Johnson, M., and Foner, A. 1972. *Aging and Society: A Sociology of Age Stratification*. Vol. 3. New York: Russell Sage Foundation.

Risman, B. J., Hill, C. T., Rubin, Z., and Peplau, L. A. 1981. Living together in college: Implications for courtship. *Journal of Marriage and the Family*, 43:77–83.

Rivers, W. H. R. 1906. *The Todas*. New York: Macmillan.

Roach, M. 1983. Another name for madness. *New York Times Magazine* (January 16):22–31.

Roazen, P. 1976. *Erik H. Erikson: The Power and Limits of a Vision*. New York: Free Press.

Roberge, J. J., and Flexer, B. K. 1979. Further examinations of formal operational reasoning abilities. *Child Development*, 50:478–484.

Robertson, J. F. 1977. Grandmotherhood: A study of role conceptions. *Journal of Marriage and the Family*, 39:165–174.

Robey, B. 1982. Older Americans. *American Demographics*, 4 (June):40–41.

Robinson, B. E., Skeen, P., Hobson, C. F., and Herrman, M. 1982. Gay men's and women's perceptions of early family life and their relationships with parents. *Family Relations*, 31:79–83.

Robinson, I. E., and Jedlicka, D. 1982. Change in sexual attitudes and behavior of college students from 1965 to 1980: A research note. *Journal of Marriage and the Family*, 44:237–240.

Rocha, R. E., and Rogers, R. W. 1976. Ares and Babbitt in the classroom: Effects of competition and reward on children's aggression. *Journal of Personality and Social Psychology*, 33: 588–593.

Roche, A. F. 1979. Secular trends in human growth, maturation, and development. *Monographs of the Society for Research in Child Development*, 44 (Nos. 3–4).

Rodin, J., and Langer, E. J. 1977. Long-term effects of a control-relevant intervention with the institutionalized aged. *Journal of Personality and Social Psychology*, 35:897–902.

Roffwarg, H. P., Muzio, J. N., and Dement, W. C. 1966. Ontogenetic development of the human sleep-dream cycle. *Science*, 152:604–619.

Rogan, W. J., Bagniewska, A., and Damstra, T. 1980. Pollutants in breast milk. *New England Journal of Medicine*, 302:1450–1453.

Rogers, C. R. 1970. *On Becoming a Person: A Therapist's View of Psychotherapy*. Boston: Houghton Mifflin—Sentry edition.

———. 1977. Beyond education's watershed. *Educational Leadership*, 34:623–631.

Rollins, B. C., and Cannon, K. L. 1974. Marital satisfaction over the family life cycle: A reevaluation. *Journal of Marriage and the Family*, 36:271–282.

———, and Feldman, H. 1970. Marital satisfaction over the family life cycle. *Journal of Marriage and the Family*, 32:20–28.

Rose, R. J. 1982. Separated twins: Data and their limits. *Science*, 215 (February 19):959–960.

Rose, R. M., Bourne, P. G., Poe, R. O., Mougey, E. H., Collins, D. R., and Mason, J. W. 1969. Androgen responses to stress. II. Excretion of testosterone, epitestosterone, androsterone, and etiocholanolone during basic combat training and under threat of attack. *Psychosomatic Medicine*, 31:418–436.

Rose, S. A., Gottfried, A. W., and Bridger, W. H. 1979. Effects of haptic cues on visual recognition memory in full-term and preterm infants. *Infant Behavior and Development*, 2:55–67.

———, ———, Melloy-Carminar, P., and Bridger, W. H. 1982. Familiarity and novelty preferences in infant recognition memory. *Developmental Psychology*, 18:704–713.

Rosen, B., and Jerdee, T. H. 1976*a*. The nature of job-related age stereotypes. *Journal of Applied Psychology*, 61: 180–183.

———, and ———. 1976*b*. The influence of age stereotypes on managerial decisions. *Journal of Applied Psychology*, 61:428–432.

Rosen, R., and Hall, E. 1984. *Sexuality*. New York: Random House.

Rosenberg, R. N. 1981. Biochemical genetics of neurologic disease. *New Eng-*

land Journal of Medicine, 305:1181–1193.

Rosenblatt, P. C., and Skoogberg, E. H. 1974. Birth order in cross-cultural perspective. *Developmental Psychology,* 10:48–54.

Rosencranz, H. A., and McNevin, T. E. 1969. A factor analysis of attitudes toward the aged. *Gerontologist,* 9:55–59.

Rosenfeld, A. 1976. *Prolongevity.* New York: Knopf.

Rosenhan, D. 1972. Prosocial behavior in children. In Hartup, W. W. (ed.), *The Young Child.* Vol. 2. Washington, D.C.: National Association for the Education of Young Children.

———, Moore, B. S., and Underwood, B. 1976. The social psychology of moral behavior. In Lickona, T. (ed.), *Moral Development and Behavior.* New York: Holt, Rinehart and Winston.

Rosenkoetter, L. I. 1973. Resistance to temptation: Inhibitory and disinhibitory effects of models. *Developmental Psychology,* 8:80–84.

Rosenthal, R. 1973. The Pygmalion effect lives. *Psychology Today,* 7 (September):56–63.

———, and Jacobson, L. 1968. *Pygmalion in the Classroom.* New York: Holt, Rinehart and Winston.

Rosenthal, T. L., and Zimmerman, B. J. 1978. *Social Learning and Cognition.* New York: Academic Press.

Rosenzweig, M. R., and Bennett, E. L. 1978. Experiential influences on brain anatomy and brain chemistry in rodents. In Gottlieb, G. (ed.), *Early Influences.* New York: Academic Press.

Rosett, H. L., and Sander, L. W. 1979. Effects of maternal drinking on neonatal morphology and state regulation. In Osofsky, J. D. (ed.), *Handbook of Infant Development.* New York: Wiley.

Rosinski, R. R., Pellegrino, J. W., and Siegel, A. W. 1977. Developmental changes in the semantic processing of pictures and words. *Journal of Experimental Child Psychology,* 23:282–291.

Rosow, I. 1974. *Socialization to Old Age.* Berkeley: University of California Press.

Ross, H. S. 1982. Establishment of social games among toddlers. *Developmental Psychology,* 18:509–518.

———, and Goldman, B. D. 1977. Infants' sociability toward strangers. *Child Development,* 48:638–642.

Ross, S. A. 1971. A test of the generality of the effects of deviant preschool models. *Developmental Psychology,* 4:262–267.

Rossi, A. S. 1968. Transition to parenthood. *Journal of Marriage and the Family,* 30:26–39.

———. 1977. A biosocial perspective on parenting. *Daedalus,* 106:1–31.

Rossi, S., and Wittrock, M. C. 1971. Developmental shifts in verbal recall between mental ages two and five. *Child Development,* 42:333–338.

Roszak, T. 1972. The making of a counter culture. In Manning, P. K., and Truzzi, M. (eds.), *Youth and Sociology.* Englewood Cliffs, N.J.: Prentice-Hall.

Rothbart, M. K. 1981. Measurement of temperament in infancy. *Child Development,* 52:569–578.

Rovee, C. K., Cohen, R. Y., and Shlapack, W. 1975. Life-span stability in olfactory sensitivity. *Developmental Psychology,* 11:311–318.

Rubenstein, C. 1982. Real men don't earn less than their wives. *Psychology Today,* 16 (November):36–41.

Rubenstein, J., and Howes, C. 1976. The effects of peers on toddler interaction with mothers and toys. *Child Development,* 47:597–605.

Rubin, J. Z., Provenzano, F. J., and Luria, Z. 1974. The eye of the beholder: Parents' views on sex of newborns. *American Journal of Orthopsychiatry,* 43:720–731.

Rubin, K. H., Maioni, T. L., and Hornung, M. 1976. Free play behaviors in middle- and lower-class preschoolers: Parten and Piaget revisited. *Child Development,* 47:414–419.

Rubin, L. B. 1980. Women of a certain age. *Society,* 17 (March/April):68–76.

Rubin, R. T., Reinisch, J. M., and Haskett, R. F. 1981. Postnatal gonadal steroid effects on human behavior. *Science,* 211 (March 20):1318–1324.

Rubin, Z. 1973. *Liking and Loving: An Invitation to Social Psychology.* New York: Holt, Rinehart and Winston.

———. 1977. The love research. *Human Behavior,* 6 (February):56–59.

———. 1980. *Children's Friendships.* Cambridge, Mass.: Harvard University Press.

———. 1981. Does personality really change after 20? *Psychology Today,* 15 (May):18–27.

Ruble, D. N., and Brooks-Gunn, J. 1982. The experience of menarche. *Child Development,* 53:1557–1566.

Ruch, L. O. 1977. A multidimensional analysis of the concept of life change. *Journal of Health and Social Behavior,* 18:71–83.

Rugh, R., and Shettles, L. B. 1971. *From Conception to Birth: The Drama of Life's Beginnings.* New York: Harper & Row.

Runyan, W. M. 1979. Perceived determinants of highs and lows in life satisfaction. *Developmental Psychology,* 15:331–333.

———. 1980. A stage-state analysis of the life course. *Journal of Personality and Social Psychology,* 38:951–962.

Rushton, J. P. 1976. Socialization and the altruistic behavior of children. *Psychological Bulletin,* 83:898–913.

Russell, C. 1980. The elderly: Myths and facts. *American Demographics,* 2:30–31.

Russell, C. S. 1974. Transition to parenthood: Problems and gratifications. *Journal of Marriage and the Family,* 36:294–302.

Russell, G. 1978. The father role and its relation to masculinity, femininity, and androgyny. *Child Development,* 49:1174–1181.

———. 1982. Shared-caregiving families: An Australian study. In Lamb, M. E. (ed.), *Nontraditional Families: Parenting and Child Development.* Hillsdale, N.J.: Erlbaum.

Russell, J. A., and Ridgeway, D. 1983. Dimensions underlying children's emotion concepts. *Developmental Psychology,* 19:795–804.

Rutter, M. 1974. *The Qualities of Mothering.* New York: Jason Aronson.

———. 1979. Maternal deprivation, 1972–1978: New findings, new concepts, new approaches. *Child Development,* 50:283–305.

———. 1983. School effects on pupil progress: Research findings and policy implications. *Child Development,* 54:1–29.

Ryan, K. J. 1982. Hospital or home births. *The Harvard Medical School Health Letter,* 8 (November):3–4.

Ryder, N. 1965. The cohort as a concept in the study of social change. *American Sociological Review,* 30:843–861.

Saarni, C. 1979. Children's understanding of display rules for expressive behavior. *Developmental Psychology,* 15:424–429.

Sage, G. H. 1971. *Introduction to Motor Behavior.* Reading, Mass.: Addison-Wesley.

Sage, W. 1978. Social scientists have some answers about the busing controversy. What are they? To find out you pay your money and take your choice. *Human Behavior,* 7:18–23.

St. John, N. 1975. *School Desegregation: Outcomes for Children.* New York: Wiley.

Salapatek, P. 1975. Pattern perception in early infancy. In Cohen, L. B., and Salapatek, P. (eds.), *Infant Perception: From Sensation to Cognition.* New York: Academic Press.

———, and Kessen, W. 1966. Visual

scanning of triangles by the human newborn. *Journal of Experimental Child Psychology,* 3:155–167.

Saltz, R. 1973. Effects of part-time "mothering" on IQ and SQ of young institutionalized children. *Child Development,* 44:166–170.

Sameroff, A. J. 1968. The components of sucking in the human newborn. *Journal of Experimental Child Psychology,* 6:607–623.

———. 1971. Can conditioned responses be established in the newborn infant: 1971? *Developmental Psychology,* 5:1–12.

———. 1975. Transactional models in early social relations. *Human Development,* 18:65–79.

——— (ed.). 1978. Organization and stability of newborn behavior: A commentary on the Brazelton Neonatal Behavior Assessment Scale. *Monographs of the Society for Research in Child Development,* 43 (177).

———, and Cavanagh, P. J. 1979. Learning in infancy: A developmental perspective. In Osofsky, J. D. (ed.), *Handbook of Infant Development.* New York: Wiley.

———, and Chandler, M. J. 1975. Reproductive risk and the continuum of caretaking causality. In Horowitz, F. D. (ed.), *Review of Child Development Research.* Vol. 4. Chicago: University of Chicago Press.

Sanders, R. 1983. *Child Support and Alimony: 1981.* Washington, D.C.: Government Printing Office.

Sanders, W. B. 1974. *The Sociologist as Detective.* New York: Praeger.

Santrock, J. W. 1972. Relation of type and onset of father absence to cognitive development. *Child Development,* 43:455–469.

———, Smith, P. C., and Bourbeau, P. E. 1976. Effects of social comparison on aggression and regression in groups of young children. *Child Development,* 47:831–837.

———, Warshak, R., Lindbergh, C., and Meadows, L. 1982. Children's and parents' observed social behavior in stepfather families. *Child Development,* 53:472–480.

Sapir, E. 1949. *Selected Writings in Language, Culture, and Personality.* Berkeley: University of California Press.

Sarason, S. B. 1977. *Work, Aging, and Social Change: Professionals and the One Life-One Career Imperative.* New York: Basic Books.

Sassen, G. 1980. Success anxiety in women: A constructivist interpretation of its source and significance. *Harvard Educational Review,* 50:13–24.

Scanzoni, L., and Scanzoni, J. 1981. *Men, Women, and Change,* 2nd ed. New York: McGraw-Hill.

Scarf, M. 1972*a*. He and she: The sex hormones and behavior. *New York Times Magazine* (May 7):30ff.

———. 1972*b*. Husbands in crisis. *McCall's,* 99:76–77ff.

———. 1977. From joy to depression. *New York Times Magazine* (April 24):31–36.

———. 1980. *Unfinished Business: Pressure Points in the Lives of Women.* Garden City, N.Y.: Doubleday.

Scarr, S., and Barker, W. 1981. The effects of family background: A study of cognitive differences among black and white twins. In Scarr, S. (ed.), *IQ: Race, Social Class and Individual Differences.* Hillsdale, N.J.: Erlbaum.

———, and Grajek, S. 1982. Similarities and differences among siblings. In Lamb, M. E., and Sutton-Smith, B. (eds.), *Sibling Relationships.* Hillsdale, N.J.: Erlbaum.

Schachter, F. F. 1981. Toddlers with employed mothers. *Child Development,* 52:958–964.

Schaefer, E. S. 1959. A circumplex model for maternal behavior. *Journal of Abnormal and Social Psychology,* 59:226–235.

Schaffer, H. R. 1966. Activity level as a constitutional determinant of infantile reaction to deprivation. *Child Development,* 37:595–602.

———. 1971. *The Growth of Sociability.* Baltimore: Penguin.

———, and Emerson, P. E. 1964. The development of social attachments in infancy. *Monographs of the Society for Research in Child Development,* 29 (3).

———, and ———. 1964. Patterns of response to physical contact in early human development. *Journal of Child Psychology and Psychiatry,* 5:1–13.

Schaie, K. W. 1965. A genderal model for the study of development problems. *Psychological Bulletin,* 64:92–107.

———. 1967. Age changes and age differences. *The Gerontologist,* 7:128–132.

———. 1978. External validity in the assessment of intellectual development in adulthood. *Journal of Gerontology,* 33:695–701.

———, and Hertzog, C. 1982. Longitudinal methods. Wolman, B. B. (ed.), *Handbook of Developmental Psychology.* Englewood Cliffs, N.J.: Prentice-Hall.

———, and ———. 1983. Fourteen-year cohort-sequential analyses of adult intellectual development. *Developmental Psychology,* 19:531–543.

———, and Labouvie-Vief, G. 1974. Generational versus ontogenetic components of change in adult cognitive behavior: A fourteen-year cross-sequential study. *Developmental Psychology,* 10:305–320.

Schiffman, S. 1977. Food recognition by the elderly. *Journal of Gerontology,* 32:586–592.

———, and Pasternak, M. 1979. Decreased discrimination of food odors in the elderly. *Journal of Gerontology,* 34:73–79.

Schmeck, H. M., Jr. 1976. Trend in growth of children lags. *New York Times* (June 10):13C.

———. 1982. Mysterious thymus gland may hold the key to aging. *New York Times* (January 26):17, 18.

———. 1983*a*. Alcoholism tests back disease idea. *New York Times* (September 2):A10.

———. 1983*b*. U.S. panel calls for patients' right to end life. *New York Times* (March 22):1, 18.

Schneck, M. K., Reisberg, B., and Ferris, S. H. 1982. An overview of current concepts of Alzheimer's disease. *American Journal of Psychiatry,* 139: 165–173.

Schneider, E. L., and Brody, J. A. 1983. Aging, natural death, and the compression of morbidity: Another view. *New England Journal of Medicine,* 309:854–855.

Schofield, J. W. 1978. School desegregation and intergroup relations. In Dar Tal, D., and Saxe, L. (eds.), *The Social Psychology of Education.* New York: Halsted Press.

Schofield, M. 1965. *Sociological Aspects of Homosexuality: A Comparative Study of Three Types of Homosexuals.* Boston: Little, Brown.

Schramm, W. T., Lyle, J., and Parker, E. B. 1961. *Television in the Lives of Our Children.* Stanford, Calif.: Stanford University Press.

Schreiner, T. 1983. Working mothers. *USA Today* (December 9):1.

Schubert, J. B., Bardley-Hohnson, S., and Nuttal, J. 1980. Mother-infant communication and maternal employment. *Child Development,* 51: 246–249.

Schulz, R., and Hanusa, B. H. 1980. Experimental social gerontology: A social psychological perspective. *Journal of Social Issues,* 36:30–46.

Schvaneveldt, J. D., and Adams, G. R. 1983. Adolescents and the decision-making process. *Theory into Practice,* 22:98–104.

Schwartz, D. M., and Thompson, M. G. 1982. Do anorectics get well? *American Journal of Psychiatry,* 138:319–323.

Schwartz, F. N. 1981. Reducing stress in

two-career families—Expert's advice. *U.S. News & World Report* (November 2):89–90.
Schwartz, G., and Merten, D. 1967. The language of adolescence: An anthropological approach to the youth culture. *American Journal of Sociology,* 72:453–468.
Scott, J. W. 1982. The mechanization of women's work. *Scientific American,* 247:167–187.
Scriver, C. R., and Clow, C. L. 1980*a.* Phenylketonuria: Epitome of human biochemical genetics: I. *New England Journal of Medicine,* 303:1336–1342.
———, and ———. 1980*b.* Phenylketonuria: Epitome of human biochemical genetics: II. *New England Journal of Medicine,* 303:1394–1400.
Searle, J. 1969. *Speech Acts.* Cambridge: Cambridge University Press.
Sears, F. W., Zemansky, M. W., and Young, H. D. 1982. *University Physics,* 6th ed. Reading, Mass.: Addison-Wesley.
Sears, R. R. 1963. Dependency motivation. In Jones, M. (ed.), *Nebraska Symposium on Motivation.* Lincoln: University of Nebraska Press.
———. 1970. Relation of early socialization experiences to self-concepts and gender role in middle childhood. *Child Development,* 41:267–289.
———. 1972. Attachment, dependency, and frustration. In Gewirtz, J. L. (ed.), *Attachment and Dependency.* Washington, D.C.: Winston.
———. 1977. Sources of life satisfactions of the Terman gifted men. *American Psychologist,* 32:119–128.
———, Maccoby, E. E., and Levin, H. 1957. *Patterns of Child Rearing.* New York: Harper & Row.
———, Rau, L., and Alpert, R. 1965. *Identification and Child Rearing.* Stanford, Calif.: Stanford University Press.
Sebald, H. 1977. *Adolescence: A Social Psychological Analysis,* 2nd ed. Englewood Cliffs, N.J.: Prentice-Hall.
Seeman, M. 1959. On the meaning of alienation. *American Sociological Review,* 24:783–791.
Segal, J., and Yahraes, H. 1978. Bringing up mother. *Psychology Today,* 12 (November):90–96.
Segal, M. W. 1974. Alphabet and attraction: An unobtrusive measure of the effect of propinquity in a field setting. *Journal of Personality and Social Psychology,* 30:654–657.
Seitz, V. 1975. Integrated versus segregated school attendance and immediate recall for standard and nonstandard English. *Developmental Psychology,* 11:217–223.
Sekuler, R., Hutman, L. P., and Owsley, C. J. 1980. Human aging and spatial vision. *Science,* 209:1255–1256.
Self, P. A., Horowitz, F. D., and Paden, L. Y. 1972. Olfaction in newborn infants. *Developmental Psychology,* 7:349–363.
Seligman, M. E. P. 1973. Fall into helplessness. *Psychology Today,* 7 (June):43–48.
———. 1975. *Helplessness.* San Francisco: Freeman.
———. 1978. Comment and integration. *Journal of Abnormal Psychology,* 87:165–179.
———, and Maier, S. F. 1967. Failure to escape traumatic shock. *Journal of Experimental Psychology,* 74:1–9.
Sells, S. 1969. *The Definition and Measurement of Mental Health.* Public Health Service publication number 1873. Washington, D.C.: Government Printing Office.
Selltiz, C., Wrightsman, L. S., and Cook, S. W. 1976. *Research Methods in Social Relations,* 3rd ed. New York: Holt, Rinehart and Winston.
Selman, R. L. 1980. *The Growth of Interpersonal Understanding: Developmental and Clinical Analyses.* New York: Academic Press.
Selye, H. 1956. *The Stress of Life.* New York: McGraw-Hill.
Serbin, L. A., Tonick, I. J., and Sternglanz, S. H. 1977. Shaping cooperative cross-sex play. *Child Development,* 48:924–929.
Serrin, W. 1983*a.* Up to a fifth of U.S. workers now rely on part-time jobs. *New York Times* (August 14):1, 14.
———. 1983*b.* Study says work ethic is alive but neglected. *New York Times* (September 5):8.
Sewell, W. H. 1952. Infant training and the personality of the child. *American Journal of Sociology,* 59:150–159.
———. 1981. Notes on educational, occupational, and economic achievement in American society. *Phi Delta Kappan,* 62:322–325.
———, and Mussen, P. H. 1952. The effects of feeding, weaning, and scheduling procedures on childhood adjustment and the formation of oral symptoms. *Child Development,* 23:185–191.
Shanas, E. 1972. Adjustment of retirement: Substitution or accommodation? In Carp, F. (ed.), *Retirement.* New York: Behavioral Publications.
———. 1978. A national survey of the aged. *Final Report to the Administration of the Aging.* Washington, D.C.: U.S. Department of Health, Education, and Welfare.
———. 1980. Other people and their families: The new pioneers. *Journal of Marriage and the Family,* 42:9–15.
———. 1982. The family relations of old people. *National Forum,* 42:9–11.
———, Townsend, P., Wedderburn, D., Fries, H., Milhøj, P., and Stehouwer, J. 1968. *Old People in Three Industrial Societies.* New York: Atherton.
Shannon, L. 1982. *Assessing the Relationship of Adult Criminal Careers to Juvenile Careers.* Washington, D.C.: Government Printing Office.
Shanor, K. 1978. *The Shanor Study: The Sexual Sensitivity of the American Male.* New York: Dial Press.
Shanteau, J., and Nagy, G. F. 1979. Probability of acceptance in dating choice. *Journal of Personality and Social Psychology,* 37:522–533.
Shaps, L. P., and Nilsson, L. 1980. Encoding and retrieval operations in relation to age. *Developmental Psychology,* 16:636–643.
Sharp, D., Cole, M., and Lave, C. 1979. Education and cognitive development: The evidence from experimental research. *Monographs of the Society for Research in Child Development,* 44 (178).
Shaw, M. E., and Costanzo, P. R. 1982. *Theories of Social Psychology,* 2nd ed. New York: McGraw-Hill.
Sheehy, G. 1976. *Passages.* New York: Dutton.
Sheleff, L. 1981. *Generations Apart: Adult Hostility to Youth.* New York: McGraw-Hill.
Shelton, J., and Hill, J. P. 1959. Effects on cheating of achievement anxiety and knowledge of peer performance. *Developmental Psychology,* 1:449–455.
Shenon, P. 1983. What's new with dual-career couples. *New York Times* (March 6):F29.
Sherif, M. 1936. *The Psychology of Social Norms.* New York: Harper & Row.
Sherman, J. 1978. *Sex-Related Cognitive Differences.* Springfield, Ill.: Charles C. Thomas.
Shields, J. 1976. Genetics in schizophrenia. In Kemali, D., Bartholini, G., and Richter, D. (eds.), *Schizophrenia Today.* New York: Pergamon.
Shock, N. W. 1962. The physiology of aging. *Scientific American,* 206 (January):100–110.
———. 1977. Biological theories of aging. In Birren, J. E., and Schaie, K. W. (eds.), *Handbook of the Psychology of Aging.* New York: Van Nostrand.
Siegel, A. W., Kirasic, J. C., and Kilburg, R. R. 1973. Recognition memory in reflective and impulsive preschool children. *Child Development,* 44:651–656.
Siegel, R. K. 1981. Accounting for "afterlife" experiences. *Psychology Today,* 15 (January):65–75.

Siegler, I. C., and Botwinick, J. 1979. A long-term longitudinal study of intellectual ability of older adults. The matter of selective subject attrition. *Journal of Gerontology,* 34:242–245.

———, McCarty, S. M., Logue, P. E. 1982. Wechsler memory scale scores, selective attrition, and distance from death. *Journal of Gerontology,* 37:176–181.

Silverman, P. 1983. Coping with grief—It can't be rushed. *U.S. News & World Report* (November 14):65–68.

Siman, M. L. 1977. Application of a new model of peer group influence to naturally existing adolescent friendship groups. *Child Development,* 48:270–274.

Simmons, L. W. 1945. *The Role of the Aged in Primitive Society.* New Haven, Conn.: Yale University Press.

———. 1960. Aging in preindustrial societies. In Tibbitts, C. (ed.), *Handbook of Social Gerontology.* Chicago: University of Chicago Press.

Simmons, R. G., Blyth, D. A., Van Cleave, E. F., and Bush, D. M. 1979. Entry into early adolescence: The impact of school structure, puberty, and early dating on self-esteem. *American Sociological Review,* 44:948–967.

———, Brown, L., Bush, D. M., and Blyth, D. A. 1978. Self-esteem and achievement of black and white adolescents. *Social Problems,* 26:86–96.

———, Rosenberg, F., and Rosenberg, M. 1973. Disturbance in the self-image at adolescence. *American Sociological Review,* 38:553–568.

Simon, H. A. 1981. The social impact of computers. In Forester, T. (ed.), *The Microelectronics Revolution.* Cambridge, Mass.: MIT Press.

Simpson, E. L. 1974. Moral development research: A case study of scientific cultural bias. *Human Development,* 17:81–106.

———. 1976. A holistic approach to moral development and behavior. In Lickona, T. (ed.), *Moral Development and Behavior: Theory, Research, and Social Issues.* New York: Holt, Rinehart and Winston.

Simpson, I., Back, K. W., and McKinney, J. C. 1966. Work and retirement. In Simpson, I. H., and McKinney, J. C. (eds.), *Social Aspects of Aging.* Durham, N.C.: Duke University Press.

Singer, M. I. 1970. Comparisons of indicators of homosexuality on the MMPI. *Journal of Consulting and Clinical Psychology,* 34:15–18.

Singh, B. K., Walton, B. L., and Williams, J. S. 1976. Extramarital sexual permissiveness: Conditions and contingencies. *Journal of Marriage and the Family,* 38:701–702.

Sinnott, J. D. 1977. Sex-role inconstancy, biology, and successful aging: A dialectical model. *The Gerontologist,* 17:459–463.

———. 1982. Correlates of sex roles of older adults. *Journal of Gerontology,* 37:587–594.

Siqueland, E. R. 1968. Reinforcement patterns and extinction in human newborns. *Journal of Experimental Child Psychology,* 6:431–442.

Skarin, K. 1977. Cognitive and contextual determinants of stranger fear in six- and eleven-month-old infants. *Child Development,* 48:537–544.

Skeels, H. M. 1966. Adult status of children with contrasting early life experiences. *Monographs of the Society for Research in Child Development,* 31 (3).

Skinner, B. F. 1957. *Verbal Behavior.* New York: Appleton-Century-Crofts.

———. 1983. Intellectual self-management in old age. *American Psychologist,* 38:239–244.

Skipper, J. K., and Nass, G. 1966. Dating behavior: A framework for analysis and an illustration. *Journal of Marriage and the Family,* 28:412–420.

Skolnick, A. 1978. The myth of the vulnerable child. *Psychology Today,* 11 (February):56–65.

Slobin, D. I. 1972. They learn the same way all around the world. *Psychology Today,* 6 (July):71–82.

Smart, M. S., and Smart, R. C. 1973. *Infants: Development and Relationships.* New York: Macmillan.

Smart, R., and Fejer, D. 1972. Drug use among adolescents and their parents: Closing the generation gap in mood modification. *Journal of Abnormal Psychology,* 79:153–160.

Smedslund, J. 1961. The acquisition of conservation of substance and weight in children. *Scandinavian Journal of Psychology,* 2:71–84ff.

Smith, E. L. III, Bennett, M. J., Harwerth, R. S., and Crawford, M. L. J. 1978. Binocularity in kittens reared with optically induced squint. *Science,* 204 (May 25):875–877.

Smith, P. K. 1978. A longitudinal study of social participation in preschool children: Solitary and parallel play reexamined. *Developmental Psychology,* 14:517–523.

Smith, R. M., and Smith, C. W. 1981. Child rearing and single-parent fathers. *Family Relations,* 30:411–417.

Snow, C. E. 1977. The development of conversation between mothers and babies. *Journal of Child Language,* 4:1–22.

Snow, M. E., Jacklin, C. N., and Maccoby, E. E. 1981. Birth-order differences in peer sociability at thirty-three months. *Child Development,* 52:589–595.

———, ———, and ———. 1983. Sex-of-child differences in father-child interaction at one year of age. *Child Development,* 54:227–232.

Snyder, S. H. 1981. Dopamine receptors, neuroleptics, and schizophrenia. *American Journal of Psychiatry,* 138:460–464.

Sobel, D. 1980. Siblings: Studies find rivalry, dependency revive in adulthood. *New York Times* (October 28):C1.

Society for Research in Child Development. 1972. *Ethical Standards for Research with Children.* Chicago.

Soeffing, M. 1975. Abused children are exceptional children. *Exceptional Children,* 42:126–133.

Sokolov, Y. N. 1958/1963. *Perception and the Conditioned Reflex.* Trans. by S. W. Waydenfeld. New York: Macmillan.

———. 1969. The modeling properties of the nervous system. In Coles, M., and Maltzman, I. (eds.), *A Handbook of Contemporary Soviet Psychology.* New York: Basic Books.

Solnit, A. J., and Provence, S. 1979. Vulnerability and risk in early childhood. In Osofsky, J. D. (ed.), *Handbook of Infant Development.* New York: Wiley.

Solomon, R. L. 1964. Punishment. *American Psychologist,* 19:239–253.

Sontag, L. W. 1944. Differences in modifiability of fetal behavior and physiology. *Psychosomatic Medicine,* 6:151–154.

———. 1966. Implications of fetal behavior and environment for adult personalities. *Annals of the New York Academy of Science,* 134:782–786.

———, Reynolds, E. L., and Torbet, V. 1944. Status of infant at birth as related to basal metabolism of mothers in pregnancy. *American Journal of Obstetrics and Gynecology,* 48:208–214.

Sorce, J. F. 1979. The role of physiognomy in the development of racial awareness. *Journal of Genetic Psychology,* 134:33–41.

Sorensen, R. C. 1973. *Adolescent Sexuality in Contemporary America.* New York: World Publishing.

Sosa, R., Kennell, J., and Klaus, M. 1980. The effect of a supportive companion on perinatal problems, length of labor, and mother-infant interaction. *New England Journal of Medicine,* 303:597–600.

Sousa, M. 1976. *Childbirth at Home.* Englewood Cliffs, N.J.: Prentice-Hall.

Sovner, R., and Orsulak, P. J. 1979. Excretion of imipramine and desipramine in human breast milk. *Ameri-*

can Journal of Psychiatry, 136:451–453.

Spanier, G. B. 1982. Living together in the eighties. *American Demographics,* 4:17–23.

———, and Furstenberg, F. F., Jr. 1982. Remarriage after divorce: A longitudinal analysis of well-being. *Journal of Marriage and the Family,* 44:709–720.

———, Lewis, R. A., and Cole, C. L. 1975. Marital adjustment over the family life cycle: The issue of curvilinearity. *Journal of Marriage and the Family,* 37:263–275.

Spearman, C. 1904. "General intelligence" objectively determined and measured. *American Journal of Psychology,* 15:201–293.

———. 1927. *The Abilities of Man.* New York: Macmillan.

Speer, J. R., and Flavell, J. H. 1979. Young children's knowledge of the relative difficulty of recognition and recall memory tasks. *Developmental Psychology,* 15:214–217.

Spelke, E., Zelazo, P., Kagan, J., and Kotelchuck, M. 1973. Father interaction and separation protest. *Developmental Psychology,* 9:83–90.

Spence, J. T., and Helmreich, R. L. 1978. *Masculinity and Femininity: Their Psychological Dimensions, Correlates, and Antecedents.* Austin: University of Texas Press.

Spencer, B., and Gillen, F. J. 1927. *The Arunta.* Vol. 1. London: Macmillan.

Spezzano, C. 1981. Prenatal psychology: Pregnant with questions. *Psychology Today,* 15 (May):49–57.

Spielberg, S. P. 1982. Pharmacogenetics and the fetus. *New England Journal of Medicine,* 307:115–116.

Spilton, D., and Lee, L. C. 1977. Some determinants of effective communication in four-year-olds. *Child Development,* 48:968–977.

Spirduso, W. W. 1980. Physical fitness, aging, and psychomotor speed: A review. *Journal of Gerontology,* 35:850–865.

Spiro, M. E. 1947. Ifaluk: A South Sea culture. Unpublished manuscripts: Coordinated Investigation of Micronesian Anthropology, Pacific Science Board, National Research Council, Washington, D.C.

———. 1954. Is the family universal? *American Anthropologist,* 56:839–846.

Spitz, R. A. 1945. Hospitalism: An inquiry into the genesis of psychiatric conditions in early childhood. *Psychoanalytic Study of the Child,* 1:53–74.

———. 1946. Hospitalism: A follow-up report. *Psychoanalytic Study of the Child,* 2:113–117.

Sroufe, L. A. 1977. Wariness of strangers and the study of infant development. *Child Development,* 48:731–746.

Staffieri, J. R. 1967. A study of social stereotype of body image in children. *Journal of Personality and Social Psychology,* 7:101–104.

———. 1972. Body build and behavioral expectancies in young females. *Developmental Psychology,* 6:125–127.

Stagner, R. 1975. Boredom on the assembly line: Age and personality variables. *Industrial Gerontology,* 2:23–44.

Stanley, M., Virgilio, J., and Gershon, S. 1982. Tritiated imipramine binding sites are decreased in the frontal cortex of suicides. *Science,* 216:1337–1339.

Stannard, C. I. 1973. Old folks and dirty work: The social conditions for patient abuse in a nursing home. *Social Problems,* 20:329–342.

Stannard, D. E. 1980. *Shrinking History: On Freud and the Failure of Psychohistory.* New York: Oxford University Press.

Star, J. 1965. Chicago's troubled schools. *Look* (May 4):59.

Staub, E. 1970. A child in distress: The influences of age and number of witnesses on children's attempts to help. *Journal of Personality and Social Psychology,* 14:130–140.

———. 1971*a.* Helping a person in distress: The influence of implicit and explicit "rules" of conduct on children and adults. *Journal of Personality and Social Psychology,* 17:137–144.

———. 1971*b.* The use of role playing and induction in children's learning of helping and sharing behavior. *Child Development,* 42:805–816.

———. 1974. Helping a distressed person: Social, personality, and stimulus determinants. In Berkowitz, L. (ed.), *Advances in Experimental Social Psychology.* Vol. 7. New York: Academic Press.

———. 1975. To rear a prosocial child: Reasoning, learning by doing, and learning by teaching others. In DePalma, D. J., and Foley, J. M. (eds.), *Moral Development: Current Theory and Research.* Hillsdale, N.J.: Lawrence Erlbaum Associates.

———. 1978. *Positive Social Behavior and Morality: Social and Personal Influences.* Vol. 1. New York: Academic Press.

———, and Sherk, L. 1970. Need for approval, children's sharing behavior, and reciprocity in sharing. *Child Development,* 41:243–253.

Stechler, G., and Halton, A. 1982. Prenatal influences on human development. In Wolman, B. B. (ed.), *Handbook of Developmental Psychology.* Englewood Cliffs, N.J.: Prentice-Hall.

Steele, B. G., and Pollock, C. B. 1968. A psychiatric study of parents who abuse infants and small children. In Helfer, R. E., and Kempe, C. H. (eds.), *The Battered Child.* Chicago: University of Chicago Press.

Stein, A. H. 1967. Imitation of resistance to temptation. *Child Development,* 38:157–169.

Stein, S. P., Holzman, S., Karasu, T. B., and Charles, E. S. 1978. Mid-adult development and psychopathology. *American Journal of Psychiatry,* 135:676–681.

Stein, Z., Susser, M., Saenger, G., and Marolla, F. 1972. *Science,* 178:708–713.

Steinberg, J. A., and Hall, V. C. 1981. Effects of social behavior on interracial acceptance. *Journal of Educational Psychology,* 73:51–56.

Steinberg, L. D. 1981. Transformations in family relations at puberty. *Developmental Psychology,* 17:833–840.

———, Catalano, R., and Dooley, D. 1981. Economic antecedents of child abuse and neglect. *Child Development,* 52:975–985.

———, Greenberger, E., Garduque, L., Ruggiero, M., and Vaux, A. 1982. Effects of working on adolescent development. *Developmental Psychology,* 18:385–395.

Steinmetz, S. K. 1977. *The Cycle of Violence.* New York: Praeger.

Stengel, E. 1964. *Suicide and Attempted Suicide.* Baltimore: Penguin.

Stenner, A. J., and Katzenmeyer, W. G. 1976. Self-concept development in young children. *Phi Delta Kappan,* 58:356–357.

Stephan, W. G. 1978. School desegregation: An evaluation of predictions made in *Brown* v. *Board of Education. Psychological Bulletin,* 85:217–238.

Stephens, M. W., and Delys, P. 1973. External control expectancies among disadvantaged children at preschool age. *Child Development,* 44:670–674.

Sternberg, D. E., Van Kammen, D. P., Learner, P., and Bunney, W. E. 1982. Schizophrenia: Dopamine B-hydroxylase activity and treatment response. *Science,* 216:1423–1425.

Sternberg, R. J. 1979. The nature of mental abilities. *American Psychologist,* 34:214–230.

———. 1981. Testing and cognitive psychology. *American Psychologist,* 36:1181–1189.

———. 1982. Who's intelligent? *Psychology Today,* 16 (April):30–39.

———, and Downing, C. J. 1982. The development of higher-order reasoning in adolescence. *Child Development,* 53:209–221.

Steuer, J., LaRue, A., Blum, J. E., and Jarvik, L. F. 1981. "Critical loss" in the eighth and ninth decades. *Journal of Gerontology,* 36:211–213.

Stevenson, H. W., Parker, T., Wilkinson, A., Bonnevaux, B., and Gonzalez, M. 1978. Schooling, environment, and cognitive development: A cross-cultural study. *Monographs of the Society for Research in Child Development,* 43 (No. 3).

Stevenson, J. S. 1979. Options often denied to aging parents. *Columbus* (Ohio) *Dispatch* (September 5):B3.

Stinnett, N., Carter, L. M., and Montgomery, J. E. 1972. Older persons' perceptions of their marriages. *Journal of Marriage and the Family,* 34:665–670.

Stoller, E. P. 1983. Parental caregiving by adult children. *Journal of Marriage and the Family,* 45:851–858.

Stolz, H. R., and Stolz, L. M. 1951. *Somatic Development of Adolescent Boys.* New York: Macmillan.

Stone, C. A., and Day, M. C. 1978. Levels of availability of a formal operational strategy. *Child Development,* 49: 1054–1065.

Storms, M. D. 1980. Theories of sexual orientation. *Journal of Personality and Social Psychology,* 38:783–792.

Stott, D. H. 1973. Follow-up study from birth of the effects of prenatal stresses. *Developmental Medicine and Child Neurology,* 15:770–787.

———, and Latchford, S. A. 1976. Prenatal antecedents of child health, development and behavior: An epidemiological report of incidence and association. *Journal of the American Academy of Child Psychiatry,* 15:161–191.

Straus, M. A., Gelles, R. J., and Steinmetz, S. K. 1980. *Behind Closed Doors: Violence in the American Family.* Garden City, N.Y.: Doubleday.

Streib, G. F., and Schneider, C. J. 1971. *Retirement in American Society.* Ithaca, N.Y.: Cornell University Press.

Streissguth, A. P., Landesman-Dwyer, S., Martin, J. C., and Smith, D. W. 1980. Teratogenic effects of alcohol in human and laboratory animals. *Science,* 209 (July 18): 353–361.

Stroebe, M. S., and Stroebe, W. 1983. Who suffers more? Sex differences in health risks of the widowed. *Psychological Bulletin,* 93:279–301.

Strube, M. J., and Barbour, L. S. 1983. The decision to leave an abusive relationship: Economic dependence and psychological commitment. *Journal of Marriage and the Family,* 45:785–793.

Stuart, M. J., Gross, S. J., Elrad, H., and Graeber, J. E. 1982. Effects of acetylsalicyclic-acid ingestion on maternal and neonatal hemostasis. *New England Journal of Medicine,* 307: 909–912.

Stuckey, M. F., McGhee, P. E., and Bell, N. J. 1982. Parent-child interaction: The influence of maternal employment. *Developmental Psychology,* 18: 635–644.

Sullivan, H. S. 1947. *Conceptions of Modern Psychiatry.* Washington, D.C: William A. White Psychiatric Foundation.

———. 1953. *The Interpersonal Theory of Psychiatry.* New York: Norton.

Sullivan, M. W. 1982. Reactivation: Priming forgotten memories in human infants. *Child Development,* 53:516–523.

Sullivan, W. 1982. Clues to longevity in the Soviet Union. *New York Times* (November 30):17.

Sutton-Smith, B. 1971. Child's play. *Psychology Today,* 5 (December):67–87.

Svejda, M. J., Campos, J. J., Emde, R. N. 1980. Mother-infant "bonding": Failure to generalize. *Child Development,* 51:775–779.

Swanson, J. M., and Kinsbourne, M. 1976. Stimulant-related state-dependent learning in hyperactive children. *Science,* 192:1354–1357.

Sweeney, J. 1982. All moms spend about same time with kids. *Columbus Dispatch* (October 21):Il.

Swenson, W. M. 1961. Attitudes toward death in an aged population. *Journal of Gerontology,* 16:49–52.

Symonds, P. M. 1939. *The Psychology of Parent-Child Relationships.* New York: Appleton-Century-Crofts.

Tamashiro, R. T. 1979. Children's humor: A developmental view. *The Elementary School Journal,* 80:69–75.

Tanner, J. M. 1969. Growth and endocrinology of the adolescent. In Gardner, L. I. (ed.), *Endocrine and Genetic Diseases of Childhood.* Philadelphia: Saunders.

———. 1970. Physical growth. In Mussen, P. H. (ed.), *Carmichael's Manual of Child Psychology,* 3rd ed. New York: Wiley.

———. 1972. Sequence, tempo, and individual variation in growth and development of boys and girls aged twelve to sixteen. In Kagan, J., and Coles, R. (eds.), *Twelve to Sixteen: Early Adolescence.* New York: Norton.

———. 1973. Growing up. *Scientific American,* 229 (September):34–43.

———, and Taylor, G. R. 1971. *Growth,* rev. ed. New York: Time-Life Books.

Taub, H. B., Goldstein, K. M., and Caputo, D. V. 1977. Indices of neonatal prematurity as discriminators of development in middle childhood. *Child Development,* 48:797–805.

Templin, M. C. 1958. *Certain Language Skills in Children.* Institute of Child Welfare Monograph Series, No. 26. Minneapolis: University of Minnesota Press.

Terman, L. M. 1938. *Psychological Factors in Marital Happiness.* New York: McGraw-Hill.

Tesch, S. A. 1983. Review of friendship development across the life span. *Human Development,* 26:266–276.

Thelen, E. 1981. Rhythmical behavior in infancy: An ethological perspective. *Developmental Psychology,* 17:237–257.

———, and Fisher, D. M. 1982. Newborn stepping: An explanation for a "disappearing" reflex. *Developmental Psychology,* 18:760–775.

Thibaut, J. W., and Kelley, H. H. 1959. *The Social Psychology of Groups.* New York: Wiley.

Thoman, E. B., Forner, A. F., and Beason-Williams, L. 1977. Modification of responsiveness to maternal vocalization in the neonate. *Child Development,* 48:563–569.

Thomas, A., and Chess, S. 1984. Genesis and evolution of behavioral disorders: From infancy to early adult life. *American Journal of Psychiatry,* 141:1–9.

———, ———, and Birch, H. G. 1970. The origin of personality. *Scientific American,* 223 (August):102–109.

———, ———, ———, Hertzig, M. E., and Korn, S. 1963. *Behavioral Individuality in Early Childhood.* New York: New York University Press.

Thomas, C. W., Petersen, D. M., and Zingraff, M. T. 1975. Student drug use. A re-examination of the "hang-loose ethic" hypothesis. *Journal of Health and Social Behavior,* 16:63–73.

Thompson, R. A., and Lamb, M. E. 1983. Security of attachment and stranger sociability in infancy. *Developmental Psychology,* 19:184–191.

———, ———, and Estes, D. 1982. Stability of infant-mother attachment and its relationship to changing life circumstances to an unselected middle-class sample. *Child Development,* 53:144–148.

Thornburg, H. D. 1983. Is early adolescence really a stage of development? *Theory into Practice,* 22:79–84.

Thornbury, J. M., and Mistretta, C. M. 1981. Tactile sensitivity as a function of age. *Journal of Gerontology,* 36:34–39.

Thornton, A. 1977. Children and marital stability. *Journal of Marriage and the Family,* 39:531–540.

Thornton, J. 1982. When fathers raise children alone. *U.S. News & World Report* (April 12):61–62.

Thurow, L. C. 1981. Why women are paid less than men. *New York Times* (March 8):E5.

Thurstone, L. L. 1938. *Primary Mental Abilities.* Chicago: University of Chicago Press.

———. 1947. *Multiple Factor Analysis: A Development and Expansion of "The Vectors of the Mind."* Chicago: University of Chicago Press.

Tieger, T. 1980. On the biological basis of sex differences in aggression. *Child Development,* 51:943–963.

Tobin-Richards, M., Boxer, A. M., and Petersen, A. C. 1983. The psychological significance of pubertal change: Sex differences in perceptions of self during early adolescence. In Brooks-Gunn, J., and Petersen, A. C. (eds.), *Girls at Puberty.* New York: Plenum.

Tognoli, J. 1980. Male friendship and intimacy across the life span. *Family Relations,* 29:273–279.

Tourney, G., and Hatfield, L. M. 1973. Androgen metabolism in schizophrenics, homosexuals, and normal controls. *Biological Psychiatry,* 6:23–36.

Trause, M. A. 1977. Stranger responses: Effects of familiarity, stranger's approach, and sex of infant. *Child Development,* 48:1657–1661.

Troll, L. E. 1975. *Early and Middle Adulthood.* Monterey, Calif.: Brooks/Cole.

———, and Bengtson, V. L. 1982. Intergenerational relations throughout the life span. In Wolman, B. B. (ed.), *Handbook of Developmental Psychology.* Englewood Cliffs, N.J.: Prentice-Hall.

Truninger, E. 1971. Marital violence: The legal solutions. *The Hastings Law Journal,* 23:259–276.

Tsitouras, P. D., Martin, C. E., and Harman, S. M. 1982. Relationship of serum testosterone to sexual activity in healthy elderly men. *Journal of Gerontology,* 37:288–293.

Tulving, E. 1968. Theoretical issues in free recall. In Dixon, T. R., and Horton, D. L. (eds.), *Verbal Behavior and General Behavior Theory.* Englewood Cliffs, N.J.: Prentice-Hall.

———, and Pearlstone, Z. 1966. Availability versus accessibility of information in memory for words. *Journal of Verbal Learning and Verbal Behavior,* 5:381–391.

Turiel, E. 1969. Developmental process in the child's moral thinking. In Mussen, P. H., Langer, J., and Covington, M. (eds.), *Trends and Issues in Developmental Psychology.* New York: Holt, Rinehart and Winston.

———. 1974. Conflict and transition in adolescent moral development. *Child Development,* 45:14–29.

———. 1978. Conflict and transition in adolescent moral development, II: The resolution of disequilibrium through structural reorganization. *Child Development,* 48:634–637.

Turner, B. F. 1982. Sex-related differences in aging. In Wolman, B. B. (ed.), *Handbook of Developmental Psychology.* Englewood Cliffs, N.J.: Prentice-Hall.

Turner, R. H. 1962. Role-taking: Process versus conformity. In Rose, A. M. (ed.), *Human Behavior and Social Processes.* Boston: Houghton Mifflin.

———. 1968. The self-conception in social interaction. In Gordon, C., and Gergen, K. J. (eds.), *The Self in Social Interaction.* New York: Wiley.

University of Michigan, Institute for Social Research. 1984. News release (February 6).

U.S. Children's Bureau. 1924. *Infant Care.* Care of Children Series No. 2. Bureau Publication No. 8 (revised).

Underwood, B., and Moore, B. S. 1981. Sources of behavioral consistency. *Journal of Personality and Social Psychology,* 40:780–785.

Ungerer, J. A., Brody, L. R., and Zelazo, P. R. 1978. Long-term memory for speech in 2- to 4-week-old infants. *Infant Behavior and Development,* 1:177–186.

———, Zelazo, P. R., Kearsley, R. B., and O'Leary, K. 1981. Developmental changes in the representation of objects in symbolic play from 18 to 34 months of age. *Child Development,* 52:186–195.

Urdy, J. R. 1971. *The Social Context of Marriage.* Philadelphia: Lippincott.

U.S. News & World Report. 1978. America's adults: In search of what? (August 21):56–59.

———. 1979. New breed of workers. (September 3):35–38.

———. 1982. When the "empty nest" fills up again. (October 25):70–72.

Vachon, M. L. S. 1976. Grief and bereavement following the death of a spouse. *Canadian Psychiatric Association Journal,* 21:35–44.

Vaillant, G. E., and Milofsky, E. 1980. Natural history of male psychological health. IX: Empirical evidence for Erikson's model of the life cycle. *American Journal of Psychiatry,* 37: 1348–1359.

———, and Vaillant, C. O. 1981. Natural history of male psychological health. X: Work as a predictor of positive mental health. *American Journal of Psychiatry,* 138:1433–1440.

Valentine, D. P. 1982. The experience of pregnancy: A developmental process. *Family Relations,* 31:243–248.

Vander Zanden, J. W. 1983. *American Minority Relations,* 4th ed. New York: Ronald Press.

———. 1984. *Social Psychology,* 3rd ed. New York: Random House.

———, and Pace, A. 1984. *Educational Psychology,* 2nd ed. New York: Random House.

Vaughn, B. E., Crichton, L., and Egeland, B. 1982. Individual differences in qualities of caregiving during the first six months of life. *Infant Behavior and Development,* 5:77–95.

———, Taraldson, B., Crichton, L., and Egeland, B. 1980. Relationships between neonatal behavioral organization and infant behavior during the first year of life. *Infant Behavior and Development,* 3:47–66.

Vecsey, G. 1983. Survey discloses a nation of fans. *New York Times* (March 16):25.

Vener, A. M., and Stewart, C. S. 1974. Adolescent sexual behavior in middle America revisited: 1970–1973. *Journal of Marriage and the Family,* 36:728–735.

Vermeulen, A., Rubens, R., and Verdonck, L. 1976. Testosterone secretion and metabolism in male senescence. *Journal of Clinical Endocrinology and Metabolism,* 34:730–735.

Verna, G. B. 1977. The effects of four-hour delay of punishment under two conditions of verbal instruction. *Child Development,* 48:621–624.

Visher, E. B., and Visher, J. S. 1979. *Stepfamilies.* New York: Brunner/Mazel.

von Glaserfeld, E., and Kelley, M. F. 1982. On the concepts of period, phase, stage, and level. *Human Development,* 25:152–160.

von Hofsten, C. 1982. Eye-hand coordination in the newborn. *Developmental Psychology,* 18:450–461.

Vroegh, K. 1971. The relationship of birth order and sex of siblings to gender role identity. *Developmental Psychology,* 4:407–411.

Vygotsky, L. S. 1962. *Thought and Language.* Cambridge, Mass.: MIT Press.

Wack, J., and Rodin, J. 1978. Nursing homes for the aged: The human consequences of legislation-shaped environments. *Journal of Social Issues,* 34:6–21.

Wahler, R. G. 1967. Child-care interactions in free field settings: Some experimental analyses. *Journal of Experimental Child Psychology,* 5:278–293.

Waite, L. J. 1980. Working wives and the family life cycle. *American Journal of Sociology,* 86:272–294.

Waldholz, M. 1983. New programs seek to care for the aging in their own homes. *Wall Street Journal* (March 8): 1, 22.

Waldron, H., and Routh, D. K. 1981. The effect of the first child on the marital relationship. *Journal of Marriage and the Family,* 43:785–788.

Walford, R. L. 1969. *The Immunologic Theory of Aging.* Baltimore: Williams and Wilkins.

Walker, A. J., and Thompson, L. 1983. Intimacy and intergenerational aid and contact among mothers and daughters. *Journal of Marriage and the Family,* 45:841–849.

Walker, L. D., and Gollin, E. S. 1977. Perspective role-taking in young children. *Journal of Experimental Child Psychology,* 24:343–357.

Walker, L. J. 1982. The sequentiality of Kohlberg's stages of moral development. *Child Development,* 53:1330–1336.

Wallerstein, J. S., and Kelly, J. B. 1980. *Surviving the Breakup: How Children Actually Cope with Divorce.* New York: Basic Books.

Walster, E., and Walster, G. W. 1970. The matching hypothesis. Unpublished manuscript, University of Wisconsin.

Walters, G. C., and Grusec, J. E. 1977. *Punishment.* San Francisco: Freeman.

Walters, J., and Walters, L. H. 1980. Parent-child relationships: A review, 1970–1979. *Journal of Marriage and the Family,* 42:807–822.

Walters, R. H., Leat, M., and Mezei, L. 1963. Inhibition and disinhibition of responses through empathetic learning. *Canadian Journal of Psychology,* 17:235–243.

Ward, R. A. 1979. The meaning of voluntary association participation to older people. *Journal of Gerontology,* 34:438–445.

Warren, L. R., Wagener, J. W., and Herman, G. E. 1978. Binaural analysis in the aging auditory system. *Journal of Gerontology,* 33:731–736.

Warren, N. 1972. African infant precocity. *Psychological Bulletin,* 78:353–367.

Waterman, A. S. 1982. Identity development from adolescence to adulthood: An extension of theory and a review of research. *Developmental Psychology,* 18:341–358.

———, Geary, P. S., and Waterman, C. K. 1974. Longitudinal study of changes in ego identity status from the freshman to the senior year at college. *Developmental Psychology,* 10:387–392.

Waters, E., Matas, L., and Sroufe, L. A. 1975. Infants' reactions to an approaching stranger: Description, validation, and functional significance of wariness. *Child Development,* 46:348–356.

Watson, M. W., and Fischer, K. W. 1980. Development of social roles in elicited and spontaneous behavior during the preschool years. *Developmental Psychology,* 16:483–494.

Watson, R. E. L. 1983. Premarital cohabitation vs. traditional courtship: Their effects on subsequent marital adjustment. *Family Relations,* 32: 139–147.

Weatherley, D. 1964. Self-perceived rate of physical maturation and personality in late adolescence. *Child Development,* 35:1197–1210.

Webb, W. B. 1982. Sleep in older persons: Sleep structures of 50- to 60-year-old men and women. *Journal of Gerontology,* 37:581–586.

Weber, M. 1930. *The Protestant Ethic and the Spirit of Capitalism.* Trans. by T. Parsons. New York: Scribner.

Weed, J. A. 1982. Divorce: Americans' style. *American Demographics,* 4:13–17.

Weg, R. B. 1973. The changing physiology of aging. *The American Journal of Occupational Therapy,* 27:213–217.

Weinraub, M., Brooks, J., and Lewis, M. 1977. The social network: A reconsideration of the concept of attachment. *Human Development,* 20:31–47.

Weisberg, D. K. 1977. The Cinderella children. *Psychology Today,* 10 (April):84+.

Weisfeld, G. E. 1982. The nature-nurture issue and the integrating concept of function. In Wolman, B. B. (ed.), *Handbook of Developmental Psychology.* Englewood Cliffs, N.J.: Prentice-Hall.

Weisler, A., and McCall, R. B. 1976. Exploration and play. *American Psychologist,* 31:492–508.

Weisner, T. S., and Martin, J. C. 1979. Learning environments for infants: Communes and conventionally married families in California. *Alternative Lifestyles,* 2:201–242.

Weiss, R. S. 1976. The emotional impact of marital separation. *Journal of Social Issues,* 32:135–145.

Welford, A. T. 1977. Motor performance. In Birren, J. E., and Schaie, K. W. (eds.), *Handbook of the Psychology of Aging.* New York: Van Nostrand.

Wellman, H. M. 1977. The early development of intentional memory behavior. *Human Development,* 20:86–101.

———, Collins, J., and Glieberman, J. 1981. Understanding the combination of memory variables: Developing conceptions of memory limitations. *Child Development,* 52:1313–1317.

———, Ritter, K., and Flavell, J. H. 1975. Deliberate memory behavior in the delayed reactions of very young children. *Developmental Psychology,* 11:780–787.

Wender, P. H. 1979. Nurture and psychopathology: Evidence from adoption studies. In Barrett, J. E., Rose, R. M., and Klerman, G. L. (eds.), *Stress and Mental Disorder.* New York: Raven Press.

———, and Klein, D. F. 1981. The promise of biological psychiatry. *Psychology Today,* 15 (February):25–41.

Werner, E. E., and Smith, R. S. 1982. *Vulnerable but Invincible: A Longitudinal Study of Resilient Children and Youth.* New York: McGraw-Hill.

Werner, H., and Kaplan, B. 1963. *Symbol Formation.* New York: Wiley.

West, D. J. 1960. *Homosexuality.* Baltimore: Penguin.

Westie, F. R. 1964. Race and ethnic relations. In Faris, R. E. L. (ed.), *Handbook of Modern Sociology.* Chicago: Rand McNally.

Westoff, C. F. 1974. Coital frequency and contraception. *Family Planning Perspectives,* 6:136–141.

Wetherford, M. J. 1973. Developmental changes in infant visual preferences for novelty and familiarity. *Child Development,* 44:416–424.

Wexler, K., and Culicover, P. W. 1981. *Formal Principles of Language Acquisition.* Cambridge, Mass.: MIT Press.

Whalen, C. K., Henker, B., and Dotemoto, S. 1981. Teacher response to the Methylphenidate (Titalin) versus placebo status of hyperactive boys in the classroom. *Child Development,* 52:1005–1014.

Wharton, L. 1967. *The Ovarian Hormones.* Springfield, Ill.: Charles C Thomas.

White, B. L. 1969. Child development research: An edifice without a foundation. *Merrill-Palmer Quarterly,* 15:49–79.

———. 1973. Discussions and conclusions. In White, B. L., and Watts, J. C. (eds.), *Experience and Environment.* Englewood Cliffs, N.J.: Prentice-Hall.

———. 1975. *The First Three Years of Life.* Englewood Cliffs, N.J.: Prentice-Hall.

———, and Watts, J. C. (eds.). 1973. *Experience and Environment.* Englewood Cliffs, N.J.: Prentice-Hall.

White, L. A. 1949. *The Science of Culture: A Study of Man and Civilization.* New York: Farrar, Straus.

White, S. H. 1975. Commentary. In Miller, L. B., and Dyer, J. L., Four preschool programs: Their dimensions and effects. *Monographs of the Society for Research in Child Development,* 40 (5–6):168–170.

Whitehead, M. I., Townsend, P. T., and Pryse-Davies, J. 1981. Effects of estrogens and progestins on the biochemistry and morphology of the postmenopausal endometrium. *New England Journal of Medicine,* 305: 1599–1605.

White House Conference on Children. 1970. *Profiles of Children.* Washington, D.C.: U.S. Government Printing Office.

Whitehurst, G. J. 1982. Language development. In Wolman, B. B. (ed.), *Handbook of Developmental Psychology.* Englewood Cliffs, N.J.: Prentice-Hall.

Whitt, J. K., and Prentice, N. M. 1977. Cognitive processes in the development of children's enjoyment and comprehension of joking riddles. *Developmental Psychology,* 13:129–136.

Whorf, B. L. 1956. *Language, Thought, and Reality.* Cambridge, Mass.: MIT Press.

Wicker, A. W. 1969. Attitudes versus actions: The relationship of verbal and overt behavioral responses to attitude objects. *Journal of Social Issues,* 25:41–78.

Wiener, G. 1968. Scholastic achievement at age 12–13 of prematurely born infants. *Journal of Special Education,* 2:237–250.

———, Rider, R. V., Oppel, W. C., Fischer, L. K., and Harper, P. A. 1965. Correlates of low birth weight: Psychological status at six to seven years of age. *Pediatrics,* 35:434–444.

Willems, E. P., and Alexander, J. L. 1982. The naturalistic perspective in research. In Wolman, B. B. (ed.), *Handbook of Developmental Psychology.* Englewood Cliffs, N.J.: Prentice-Hall.

Williams, J. E., Best, D. L., and Boswell, D. A. 1975. The measurement of children's racial attitudes in the early school years. *Child Development,* 46:494–500.

———, Boswell, D. A., and Best, D. L. 1975. Evaluative responses of preschool children to the colors white and black. *Child Development,* 46: 501–508.

———, and Morland, J. K. 1976. *Race, Color, and the Young Child.* Chapel Hill: University of North Carolina Press.

———, and ———. 1979. Comment on Banks's "White preference in blacks": A paradigm in search of a phenomenon. *Psychological Bulletin,* 86:28–32.

———, and Stabler, J. R. 1973. If white means good then black . . . *Psychology Today,* 7 (July):51–54.

Williams, J. R., and Scott, R. B. 1953. Growth and development of Negro infants: IV. Motor development and its relationship to child-rearing practices in two groups of Negro infants. *Child Development,* 24:103–121.

Wilson, A. B. 1967. Educational consequences of segregation in a California community. In *Racial Isolation in the Public Schools.* Vol. 2. Washington, D.C.: Government Printing Office.

Winch, R. F. 1958. *Mate Selection: A Study of Complementary Needs.* New York: Harper & Row.

Winick, M., Brasel, J., and Valasco, E. G. 1973. Effects of prenatal nutrition upon pregnancy risk. *Clinical Obstetrics and Gynecology,* 16:184–198.

———, Rosso, P., and Waterlow, J. 1970. Cellular growth of cerebrum, cerebellum, and brain stem in normal and marascic children. *Experimental Neurology,* 26:393–400.

Winikoff, B. 1978. Nutrition, population, and health: Some implications for policy. *Science,* 200:895–907.

Winn, M. 1983. *Children Without Childhood.* New York: Pantheon Books.

Witkin, H. A., and Goodenough, D. R. 1981. *Cognitive Styles: Essence and Origins.* New York: International Universities Press.

Wohlwill, J. F. 1973. The concept of experience: S or R? *Human Development,* 16:90–107.

———, and Lowe, R. C. 1962. An experimental analysis of the development of the conservation of number. *Child Development,* 33:153–167.

Wolf, W. C., and Fligstein, N. D. 1979. Sex and authority in the workplace: The causes of sexual inequality. *American Sociological Review,* 44:235–252.

Wolff, P. H. 1963. Observations on the early development of smiling. In Foss, B. M. (ed.), *Determinants of Infant Behavior.* Vol. 2. New York: Wiley.

———. 1966. The causes, controls, and organization of behavior in the neonate. *Psychological Issues,* 5 (Whole No. 17).

———. 1969. The natural history of crying and other vocalizations in early infancy. In Foss, B. M. (ed.), *Determinants of Infant Behavior.* Vol. 4. London: Methuen.

Wolpe, J. 1973. *The Practice of Behavior Therapy,* 2nd. ed. New York: Pergamon Press.

———. 1981. Behavior therapy versus psychoanalysis. *American Psychologist,* 36:159–164.

Woodruff, D. S., and Birren, J. E. 1972. Age changes and cohort differences in personality. *Developmental Psychology,* 6:252–259.

Wright, H. 1960. Observational child study. In Mussen, P. H. (ed.), *Handbook of Research Methods in Child Development.* New York: Wiley.

———. 1967. *Recording and Analyzing Child Behavior.* New York: Harper & Row.

———, and Barker, R. 1950. *Methods in Psychological Ecology.* Lawrence: Department of Psychology, University of Kansas.

Wright, J. D., and Hamilton, R. F. 1978. Work satisfaction and age: Some evidence of the "job change" hypothesis. *Social Forces,* 56:1140–1158.

Wright, P. H., and Keple, T. W. 1981. Friends and parents of a sample of high school juniors: An exploratory study of relationship intensity and interpersonal rewards. *Journal of Marriage and the Family,* 43:550–570.

Wuthnow, R., Christiano, K., and Kuzlowski, J. 1980. Religion and bereavement: A conceptual framework. *Journal for the Scientific Study of Religion,* 18:408–422.

Wyatt, R. J., Potkin, S. G., and Murphy, D. L. 1979. Platelet MAO activity in schizophrenia: A review of the data. *American Journal of Psychiatry,* 136:377–385.

Wyshak, G., and Frisch, R. E. 1982. Evidence for a secular trend in age of menarche. *New England Journal of Medicine,* 306:1033–1035.

Yacorzynski, J. K., and Tucker, B. E. 1960. What price intelligence? *American Psychologist,* 15:201–203.

Yalisove, D. 1978. The effect of riddle structure on children's comprehension of riddles. *Developmental Psychology,* 14:173–180.

Yalom, N., Green, R., and Fisk, N. 1973. Prenatal exposure to female hormones: Effect on psychosexual development in boys. *Archives of General Psychiatry,* 28:554–561.

Yang, R. K., Zweig, A. R., Douthitt, T. C., and Federman, E. J. 1976. Successive relationships between maternal attitudes during pregnancy, analgesic medication during labor and delivery, and newborn behavior. *Developmental Psychology,* 12:8–14.

Yankelovich, D. 1974*a*. The meaning of work. In Rosow, J. M. (ed.), *The Worker and the Job.* Englewood Cliffs, N.J.: Prentice Hall.

———. 1974*b*. *The New Morality: A Profile of American Youth in the 70's.* New York: McGraw-Hill.

———. 1978. The new psychological contracts at work. *Psychology Today,* 11 (May):46–50.

———. 1981. New rules in American life. *Psychology Today,* 15 (April):35–91.

———. 1982. The work ethic is underemployed. *Psychology Today,* 16 (May):5–8.

Yarrow, L., Rubenstein, J. L., and Pedersen, F. A. 1975. *Infant and Environment.* New York: Wiley.

———, McQuiston, S., MacTurk, R. H., and others. 1983. Assessment of mastery motivation during the first year of life: Contemporaneous and cross-age relationships. *Developmental Psychology,* 19:159–171.

Yarrow, M. R., Scott, P. M., and Waxler, C. Z. 1973. Learning concern for others. *Developmental Psychology,* 8:240–260.

———, Waxler, C. Z., and Scott, P. M. 1971. Child effects on adult behavior. *Developmental Psychology,* 5:300–311.

Yates, A., Leehey, K., and Shisslak, C. M. 1983. Running—an analogue of anorexia? *New England Journal of Medicine,* 308:251–255.

Yearick, E. S., Wang, M. L., and Pisias, S. 1980. Nutritional status of the elderly. *Journal of Gerontology,* 35:663–671.

Yinger, J. M. 1965. *Toward a Field Theory of Behavior.* New York: McGraw-Hill.

Yllo, K., and Straus, M. A. 1981. Interpersonal violence among married and cohabiting couples. *Family Relations,* 30:339–347.

Yogman, M. J., Dixon, S., Tronick, E., Als, H., and Brazelton, T. B. 1977. The goals and structure of face-to-face interaction between infants and fathers. Paper presented at the biennial meeting of the Society for Research in Child Development, New Orleans, March 1977.

Yogman, M. W., and Zeisel, S. H. 1983. Diet and sleep patterns in newborn infants. *New England Journal of Medicine,* 309:1147–1149.

Youniss, J. 1980. *Parents and Peers in Social Development.* Chicago: University of Chicago Press.

Yudin, L. W. 1966. Formal thought in adolescence as a function of intelligence. *Child Development,* 37:697–708.

Yudkin, M. 1984. When kids think the unthinkable. *Psychology Today,* 18 (April):18–25.

Zablocki, B. 1980. *Alienation and Charisma: A Study of Contemporary American Communes.* New York: Free Press.

Zacharias, L., Rand, W. M., and Wurtman, R. J. 1976. A prospective study of sexual development and growth in American girls: The statistics of menarche. *Obstetrical and Gynecological Survey,* 31:325–337.

Zachry, W. 1978. Ordinality and interdependence of representation and language development in infancy. *Child Development,* 49:681–687.

Zahn-Waxler, C., Radke-Yarrow, M., and Brady-Smith, J. 1977. Perspective-taking and prosocial behavior. *Developmental Psychology,* 13:87–88.

———, ———, and King, R. A. 1979. Child rearing and children's prosocial initiations toward victims of distress. *Child Development,* 50:319–330.

Zajonc, R. B. 1975. Dumber by the dozen. *Psychology Today,* 8 (January):37–43.

———. 1976. Family configuration and intelligence. *Science,* 192:227–236.

———. 1983. Validating the confluence model. *Psychological Bulletin,* 93:457–480.

Zamenhof, S., and Van Marthens, E. 1978. Nutritional influences on prenatal brain development. In Gottlieb, G. (ed.), *Early Influences.* New York: Academic Press.

Zelnick, M., and Kantner, J. F. 1972. Sexuality, contraception and pregnancy among young unwed females in the United States. In *Demographic and Social Aspects of Population Growth.* Vol. 1. Washington, D.C.: Government Printing Office.

———, ———, and Ford, K. 1981. *Sex and Pregnancy in Adolescence.* Beverly Hills, Calif.: Sage.

Zelniker, T., and Jeffrey, W. E. 1976. Reflective and impulsive children: Strategies of information processing underlying differences in problem solving. *Monographs of the Society for Research in Child Development,* 41 (168).

Zeskind, P. S. 1980. Adult responses to cries of low and high risk infants. *Infant Behavior and Development,* 3:167–177.

———, and Lester, B. M. 1978. Acoustic features and auditory perceptions of cries of newborns with prenatal and perinatal complications. *Child Development,* 49:580–589.

———, and ———. 1981. Analysis of cry features in newborns with differential fetal growth. *Child Development,* 52:207–212.

———, and Ramey, C. T. 1981. Preventing intellectual and interactional sequelae of fetal malnutrition: A longitudinal, transactional, and synergistic approach to development. *Child Development,* 52:213–218.

Zimmerman, B. J. 1978. A social learning explanation for age-related changes in children's conceptual behavior. *Contemporary Educational Psychology,* 3:11–19.

———, and Rosenthal, T. L. 1974. Conserving and retaining equalities and inequalities through observation and correction. *Developmental Psychology,* 10:260–268.

Zimmerman, D. 1983. Where are you Captain Kangaroo? *USA Today* (December 22):1D.

Zisook, S., Devaul, R. A., and Click, M. A., Jr. 1982. Measuring symptoms of grief and bereavement. *American Journal of Psychiatry,* 139:1590–1593.

Zube, M. 1982. Changing behavior and outlook of aging men and women: Implications for marriage in the middle and later years. *Family Relations,* 31:147–156.

Zubin, J., and Spring, B. 1977. Vulnerability—A new view of schizophrenia. *Journal of Abnormal Psychology,* 86:103–126.

Key Term Index

(After each term, the text pages on which it is defined are given.)

Name Index

Subject Index

About the Author

James W. Vander Zanden is a professor in the College of Social and Behavioral Sciences at the Ohio State University and previously taught at Duke University. His Ph.D. is from the University of North Carolina. Professor Vander Zanden's published works include more than twenty professional articles and seven books, including *Understanding Psychology,* Fourth Edition (with Sandra Scarr), *Educational Psychology,* Second Edition (with Ann Pace), and *Social Psychology,* Third Edition, which are published by Random House.